Securities Regulation

Securities Regulation

SEVENTH EDITION

Marc I. Steinberg
RADFORD PROFESSOR OF LAW
SOUTHERN METHODIST UNIVERSITY

CAROLINA ACADEMIC PRESS
Durham, North Carolina

ISBN 978-1-53100-143-8
eISBN 978-1-53100-145-2
LCCN 2017943787

Carolina Academic Press, LLC
700 Kent Street
Durham, North Carolina 27701
Telephone (919) 489-7486
Fax (919) 493-5668
www.cap-press.com

Printed in the United States of America

Contents

Table of Principal Cases

Acknowledgments — First Edition

I owe many thanks to several individuals for helping to make this project a reality. Foremost, I thank Professor Alan Bromberg, an outstanding academician and individual, who generously supported my proposal when it was in a very formative stage. I also extend my gratitude to Richard Adin, Esq., who expertly served as the Matthew Bender editor for this project. In addition, I particularly thank Professor Mark Sargent for his insightful comments which were of tremendous assistance.

The University of Maryland School of Law deserves my special thanks. I express my deep appreciation to Dean Michael Kelly, one of this country's great law school deans, for his continual strong support. My research assistants, many of whom now are practicing attorneys, performed admirably to ease my task in completing this project. I thank Jennifer Crabb, Esq., Robin Goldman, Esq., Jeff Hines, Esq., Joan Karasinski, Esq., Dawn Lettman, Esq., and Greg Neville, Esq. for their invaluable assistance. I also thank Peter Brennan, Esq., Elizabeth Jacobs, Esq., and Bruce Mendelsohn, Esq. for their help.

I also benefitted from receiving excellent typing and other technological assistance. I especially thank Ms. Lu Ann Marshall for her expert typing of the great bulk of the manuscript. My thanks also to Mrs. Ann Garrett, Mrs. Laura Mrozek, Mrs. Helen Ramia, and Mrs. Frieda Whitney for their help. Also, I thank Dean Linda McDonnell for her assistance throughout this project.

I dedicate this book to certain individuals who have been generous to me in their encouragement, support and guidance. In particular, I dedicate this book: To my parents, Gerald and Phyllis Steinberg, my sister and brother-in-law, Nancy and Bob Gossman, my grandmothers, Anne Marblestone and Belle Steinberg, and my cousin, David Steinberg, for their love and constant support; to Judge Stanley N. Barnes and Judge Anthony J. Celebrezze who provided me with the opportunity to serve as one of their law clerks; to Senator Robert P. Griffin who offered me perhaps the most exciting job a young lawyer could have, being legislative counsel to a U.S. Senator; to Judge Stanley Sporkin, who was kind enough to hire me as an enforcement attorney at the Securities and Exchange Commission; to Ralph C. Ferrara, Esq., former SEC General Counsel, with whom I had the pleasure of working at the SEC; to Dean Jerome Barron who offered me my first full-time teaching job; to Dean Michael Kelly who helps make my being at the Maryland Law School a pleasure; to Deans Murray Schwartz, William Warren and Susan Westerberg Prager and the faculty of the UCLA Law School for their support throughout the years; to Professors Ted Fiflis, Bill

Reynolds, Stan Siegel, Lew Solomon, and Greg Young for their wise counsel; and to some very good friends, Howard Bartnick, Peter Brennan, Sam Gruenbaum, Fred Jacobs, Jeff and Judy Karr, John Koneck, Cliff Losh, Barry Quinn, Ben Rosenberg, Jerry Rosen and Liz Hardy, Jim Singer, Richard Starr, Richard Wasserstrom, and Lloyd and Kris Zemmol, for being good friends.

Acknowledgments — Second Edition

I wish to thank the SMU School of Law and its Dean, Paul Rogers, for supporting this project. My gratitude is also extended to Ms. Kathleen Vaughan for her expert assistance as well as to my former research assistants Elizabeth Farrell, Esq. and Daryl Lansdale, Esq. for their help. I also thank Ralph Janvey, Esq. for his input.

It is fitting that I dedicate this Second Edition to one of the individuals for whom the First Edition was dedicated — Judge Stanley N. Barnes (of the U.S. Court of Appeals for the Ninth Circuit) who passed away in 1990. I had the privilege of clerking for Judge Barnes. He was a great man and I am lucky that our paths crossed. Judge Barnes perhaps was the most successful person I've ever known — a fine judge (trial and appellate), an Assistant Attorney General of the United States, a superb trial attorney, a member of the National Collegiate Football Hall of Fame (he was an All-American on the "Cal Wonder Team"), National President of his fraternity, Sigma Chi, an avid traveler with an impressive anthropological mask collection, an active bridge player and stamp collector, a giver of his time to worthwhile causes, including the Los Angeles Orthopaedic Hospital for Children, and a dedicated family man. Judge Barnes taught me that a person can be very successful at his or her career while actively pursuing other objectives and joys. To all this, Judge Barnes would probably say: "My good friend Earl Warren said, 'compliments to me is like water running down a duck's back but the duck likes it.'"

Acknowledgments—Third Edition

I thank the SMU School of Law for supporting this project. The Law School graciously provided me with Summer Research Grants in connection with this Third Edition.

As with the Second Edition, I extend my appreciation to Ms. Kathleen Vaughan for her expert assistance. I also thank my colleagues and good friends on the SMU Law Faculty who have been instrumental in enabling me to enjoy my relationship with this fine school. In particular, I wish to dedicate this book to a few of my very special friends in Dallas who I am lucky to have in my life: Laurie Beth Dodic, Roy Anderson, Alan Bromberg, Tim Davis, Robert Feiger, Chris Hanna, Linda and Jim Hobbs, Ralph Janvey, George Martinez, Joe Norton, Doug Ramsey, Henry Rosen, Wayne Secore and Bob Wise.

Acknowledgments—Fourth Edition

It has been nearly twenty years since the First Edition of this textbook was published. Much has happened in securities regulation, in the world, and in my life—Thank God, mostly for the better.

I thank Dean John B. Attanasio and the SMU Dedman School of Law. The strong support I receive from this superb law school is truly appreciated by me. I wish to extend my gratitude for the summer research grant awarded for this project. I also extend my appreciation to Ms. Jan Spann for her excellent secretarial assistance.

I dedicate the Fourth Edition to my terrific dad, Gerry Steinberg, in honor of his 90th birthday on March 3, 2004. I am blessed to have such a wonderful, kind and supportive father. Dad, this is dedicated to you with all my love.

Acknowledgments — Fifth Edition

I thank the SMU Dedman School of Law for supporting this project. The Law School graciously provided me with a Summer Research Grant in connection with this Fifth Edition. My gratitude is expressed to Dean John B. Attanasio and my administrative assistant Ms. Jan Spann. The strong support I receive from this superb law school is truly appreciated by me.

I also thank my good friend Ralph Janvey, a superb securities law practitioner and adjunct professor at the Law School, for his assistance.

I dedicate this Fifth Edition to my terrific Uncle, Irving Steinberg, in honor of his 90th birthday on May 6, 2008. Uncle Irv, the younger brother of my Dad Gerry Steinberg, honorably served our country as a Major during World War II, being awarded a Bronze Star at the Battle of the Bulge. He and my Dad were "best friends" and business partners for nearly fifty years. Dedicating this Fifth Edition to you, Uncle Irv, is a way for me to say thanks for being a wonderful uncle to our family and personally to me.

Acknowledgments — Sixth Edition

I thank the SMU Dedman School of Law for supporting this project. The Law School graciously provided me with a Summer Research Grant (the Michael C. and Jacqueline M. Barrett Endowed Faculty Research Fund) in connection with this Sixth Edition. My gratitude is expressed to Dean John B. Attanasio and my administrative assistant Ms. Jan Spann. The strong support I receive from this superb law school is truly appreciated by me.

I dedicate this Sixth Edition to my cousin David Steinberg. Not having a brother, David comes as close to a brother as I have. He is a wonderful and loyal friend as well as a man of integrity. In addition, David is a superb attorney, has keen judgment, and a good sense of humor. Dedicating this Sixth Edition to you, David, is a way for me to say thanks for being my terrific "younger brother."

Acknowledgments — Seventh Edition

Since the publication of the First Edition of this textbook in 1986 (when I was a "youngster"), much has changed in the field of securities regulation. This edition, like its predecessors, reflects important developments since the publication of the Sixth Edition in 2013.

With respect to this Seventh Edition, I wish to thank: Dean Jennifer Collins for her strong support of my scholarship; Director of the SMU Law Library, Mr. Greg Ivy, for his superb assistance; my administrative assistant, Ms. Carolyn Yates, for her excellent technological support; and my research assistants — Ms. Katherine Grosskopf, Mr. Matthew Hortenstine, and Mr. Logan Weissler — for their diligent proofing of the manuscript for the Seventh Edition. The wonderful support that I receive from this superb law school truly is appreciated by me.

I dedicate the Seventh Edition to my terrific Uncle — Mr. Fred Marblestone — in honor of his 90th birthday. Uncle Fred, the younger brother of my Mother, has been a supportive and loving Uncle through the years. This is a way for me to say thank you Uncle Fred for being so wonderful to our family and personally to me.

Preface

The developments in securities regulation during the past several years have been multi-faceted. A text for a course on this subject should therefore not only present the basic theories and principles but also should (1) present the material in a manner that reflects the current trends and developments, (2) encompass timely additional material, including law review commentary and SEC releases, and (3) make the material as interesting as possible, given that the class will be comprised of upper-level students who are anxious for creative and practical "lawyering." With these thoughts in focus, the text is organized and directed toward a number of different perspectives. For example:

(1) The Securities and Exchange Commission, through rulemaking, has integrated the Securities Act of 1933 with the Securities Exchange Act of 1934. From the standpoint of applicable disclosure obligations, both in the primary and secondary markets, the integration concept has a tremendous impact. Moreover, grave liability concerns are raised in this context.

(2) The Supreme Court and the lower federal courts have been extremely active in the securities law area. Supreme Court decisions during this era generally reflect a trend towards restricting the scope of the securities laws. The lower federal courts, however, have not necessarily followed the High Court's restrictive approach.

(3) The Private Securities Litigation Reform Act, enacted by Congress in 1995, reflects a trend towards facilitating capital formation and the conducting of business, with private litigation viewed frequently as an undue impediment. The JOBS Act enacted in 2012 similarly reflects a strong federal policy seeking to enhance capital raising by smaller enterprises.

(4) The SEC continues to facilitate capital formation through its rulemaking process in both the private and public offering settings.

(5) The Sarbanes-Oxley Act of 2002 federalizes key aspects of corporate governance and sets forth new obligations for corporate insiders as well as professionals, including accountants and legal counsel. The Dodd-Frank Act of 2010 likewise federalizes aspects of corporate governance.

(6) There is the role of counsel as adviser and planner which is the principal function of the securities lawyer. In connection therewith, the attorney and his/her client may have conflict of interest dilemmas, disclosure duties, and the apprehension of SEC enforcement action. This apprehension is magnified in view of the Sarbanes-Oxley and Dodd-Frank Acts.

(7) During the past several years, there have surfaced a number of intriguing issues, some of which directly impact on traditional securities regulation. For example, we have seen the Supreme Court restricting the scope of primary liability and a renewed interest in state securities regulation.

The coverage of the text is designed for both the basic securities regulation course and advanced seminars. The text covers the traditional issues as well as the developing areas. Subjects that receive extensive treatment include: definition of a security, exemptions from registration, the JOBS Act, the registration process, Sarbanes-Oxley, Dodd-Frank, the policy debate underlying disclosure, resales (including SEC Rule 144), due diligence (including the integrated disclosure framework), disclosure obligations in a myriad of contexts, international securities developments including global offerings, remedies and liabilities under both federal and state securities law, broker-dealer regulation, corporate control transactions, attorney professional responsibility, SEC enforcement, and "Blue Sky" regulation.

The objective of the text is to treat the above subjects in a comprehensive, understandable, yet intellectually challenging manner, seeking to combine both the theoretical and practical in this complex subject area. While the case method is employed, it is by no means exclusive. In addition to case law, the text includes other relevant material such as SEC releases and scholarly commentary. Moreover, the problem method is extensively used. This method is particularly suitable for a "practical" course where upper level students are seeking to do some "lawyering." Thus, it is hoped that the text will stimulate intellectual discussion, and, at the same time, provide students who await either a sophisticated securities or, alternatively, a general business practice with much needed practical analyses and skills.

Securities Regulation

Chapter 1

An Introduction to Securities Regulation

§ 1.01 Overview

Enacted in the aftermath of "The Great Crash," the Securities Act of 1933 (hereinafter the "Securities Act" or "1933 Act") and the Securities Exchange Act of 1934 (hereinafter the "Exchange Act" or "1934 Act") have become the principal governors of federal securities law regulation. Basically, the 1933 Act deals with the initial distribution of securities while the 1934 Act primarily concerns trading and regulation in the secondary markets. Both Acts also prohibit manipulative and deceptive practices. Undoubtedly, the central focus of the federal securities laws is that of disclosure, thereby providing shareholders and the marketplace with sufficient information to make relevant decisions and to be apprised of significant developments. Congress thus sought to promote investor protection and the maintenance of fair and orderly markets. Generally, Congress in enacting these Acts, declined to adopt a merit approach.[1] Rather, irrespective of the value or fairness of a transaction or other corporate action, the investor may decide for him or herself after receiving disclosure of pertinent information.

It would be a mistake, however, to assume that disclosure does not affect substantive conduct. As Justice Brandeis wisely stated: "Publicity is justly commended as a remedy for social and industrial diseases. Sunlight is said to be the best of disinfectants."[2] Or, as more contemporaneously phrased in this context, "[t]oday the disclosure requirements of the securities laws are used, in a variety of ways, for the explicit purpose of influencing a wide range of corporate primary behavior."[3]

It bears mentioning that the Exchange Act addresses a number of other matters, including oversight of brokers, dealers, and the stock exchanges, as well as proxy and tender offer regulation. In addition, the Exchange Act directs the Securities and Exchange Commission ("SEC" or "Commission") to facilitate the functioning of a national market system.

---

1. *See* M. Parrish, Securities Regulation and the New Deal 42–72 (1970) (explaining Congress' rejection of blue sky merit model).

2. L. Brandeis, Other People's Money, 92 (1914).

3. R. Stevenson, Corporations and Information — Secrecy, Access & Disclosure 81–82 (1980). *See* M. Steinberg, Corporate Internal Affairs — A Corporate and Securities Law Perspective 28–29 (1983); Weiss, *Disclosure and Corporate Accountability*, 34 Bus. Law. 575 (1979).

In 2002, in the wake of major financial debacles, such as Enron, WorldCom, Tyco, Adelphia and Global Crossings, Congress enacted the Sarbanes-Oxley Act. Going beyond disclosure, this Act federalizes state corporation law in significant respects. For example, the composition and functions of audit committees are statutorily prescribed. Chief executive officers and chief financial officers must "certify" the accuracy of disclosures in periodic reports filed by subject companies with the SEC. In order to help ensure the accuracy of these certifications, reasonably effective internal controls must be implemented. Moreover, accounting firms auditing publicly held companies now are subject to far greater regulation and oversight.

Continuing the trend of the Sarbanes-Oxley Act of 2002, the Dodd-Frank Act of 2010 likewise impacts aspects of corporate governance that traditionally have been within the purview of state corporate law. Key provisions of the Dodd-Frank Act affecting corporate governance are covered in this text.

Returning to a deregulatory posture, the Jumpstart Our Business Startups Act (JOBS Act) was enacted in 2012. This Act seeks to facilitate the raising of capital by ostensibly small businesses and startup enterprises, largely by relaxing specified securities law requirements. The JOBS Act is covered in this text.

In addition to the foregoing legislation, Congress has enacted other securities legislation, including: the Public Utility Holding Company Act of 1935, the Trust Indenture Act of 1939, the Investment Company Act of 1940, the Investment Advisers Act of 1940, and the Securities Investor Protection Act of 1970.

Also, the individual states have passed their own securities statutes, called "blue sky" laws. This term came into being due to the original purpose of the "blue sky" laws, which was to prevent "speculative schemes which have no more basis than so many feet of blue sky." *Hall v. Geiger-Jones Co.*, 242 U.S. 539, 550 (1917). Or, as phrased by one commentator, it was believed by some state legislators in the early part of the twentieth century that "if securities legislation was not passed, financial pirates would sell citizens everything in [the] state but the blue sky."[4] Today, depending on the particular state, blue sky statutes provide for significant investor protection and substantive regulation.[5]

The Securities and Exchange Commission (hereinafter the "SEC" or the "Commission") is the agency that administers and enforces the federal securities laws. Not surprisingly, the Commission over the years has had both its ardent supporters and outspoken critics, including during the 2008 financial crisis.[6] Nonetheless, as

---

4. M. PARISH, SECURITIES REGULATION AND THE NEW DEAL 3 (1970). For an article questioning the frequency of fraud as the justification for these statutes, see Macey & Miller, *Origin of the Blue Sky Laws*, 70 TEX. L. REV. 347 (1991).

5. The "blue sky" laws are addressed in a number of chapters in the text.

6. *See* R. KARMEL, REGULATION BY PROSECUTION — THE SECURITIES AND EXCHANGE COMMISSION VERSUS CORPORATE AMERICA (1982); H. KRIPKE, THE SEC AND CORPORATE DISCLOSURE: REGULATION IN SEARCH OF A PURPOSE (1979); J. SELIGMAN, THE TRANSFORMATION OF WALL STREET — A HISTORY OF THE SECURITIES AND EXCHANGE COMMISSION AND MODERN CORPORATE

described in the NEW YORK TIMES on the fiftieth anniversary of the stock market crash of 1929, "the agency created in 1934 to enforce [the securities] laws, the Securities and Exchange Commission, is still widely regarded as the nation's finest independent regulatory agency."[7] It is clear, however, that the recent financial debacles have adversely impacted the SEC's reputation. As a NEW YORK TIMES article stated, the Commission "is plagued by problems that go deeper than its leadership difficulties and have undermined its ability to police companies and markets."[8]

Turning to state securities regulation, the first such statute was enacted in Kansas a century ago. Today, all the states have enacted some form of "blue sky" law designed to apply to securities activities within their individual borders. In general, these statutes seek to regulate such activities by one or more of the following routes: "(1) to prohibit fraud in the offer and sale of securities; (2) to require and regulate licensing of investment advisors, broker-dealers, and their agents; (3) to require the registration of securities, and (4) to determine that the securities meet certain standards that are often referred to as 'merit' or 'fair, just, and equitable' standards."[9]

The concept of self-regulation also plays a critical role in the U.S. securities markets. Generally, a self-regulatory organization (SRO) is a non-government organization that regulates the conduct, operations, and practices of its members. SROs adopt and implement measures to promote investor protection and the integrity of the securities markets. They also have disciplinary authority to impose sanctions upon members who engage in improper conduct. SROs are subject to oversight by the SEC, which is the ultimate authority over the U.S. securities markets and industry.

Key SROs in the United States are the stock exchanges and the Financial Industry Regulatory Authority (FINRA). FINRA is the principal independent regulator for securities firms conducting business in this country. In terms of numbers, FINRA oversees approximately 4,000 brokerage firms and 643,000 registered securities representatives. As the focus of its mission, FINRA "register[s] and educate[s] all brokers, examine[s] securities firms, write[es] [and enforces] the rules they must

---

FINANCE (1982), M. STEINBERG, CORPORATE INTERNAL AFFAIRS — A CORPORATE AND SECURITIES LAW PERSPECTIVE (1983); Symposium, *The SEC at 75*, 78 U. CIN. L. REV. No. 3 (2009); Goshen & Parchomovsky, *The Essential Role of Securities Regulation*, 55 DUKE L.J. 711 (2006); Ratner, *The SEC: Portrait of the Agency as a Thirty-Seven Year Old*, 45 ST. JOHN'S L. REV. 583 (1971); Macey, *Administrative Agency Obsolescence and Interest Group Formation: A Case Study of the SEC at Sixty*, 15 CARDOZO L. REV. 909 (1994); Wolfson, *A Critique of the Securities and Exchange Commission*, 30 EMORY L.J. 119 (1981).

7. Miller, *S.E.C.: Watchdog 1929 Lacked*, N.Y. TIMES, Oct. 31, 1979, at D.1.

8. Labaton, *S.E.C. Facing Deeper Trouble*, N.Y. TIMES, Dec. 1, 2002, at D1.

9. Walker & Hadaway, *Merit Standards Revisited*, 7 J. CORP. L. 651, 653 (1982). *See generally* J. LONG, M. KAUFMAN AND J. WUNDERLICH, BLUE SKY LAW (2016); L. LOSS, COMMENTARY ON THE UNIFORM SECURITIES ACT (1976); Macey & Miller, *Origin of the Blue Sky Laws*, 70 TEX. L. REV. 347 (1991).

follow, . . . monitor[s] trading in the U.S. stock markets and administer[s] the largest securities-related dispute resolution forum in the world."[10]

The following excerpt provides a succinct overview of the "work of the SEC."

§ 1.02 A Look at the SEC

The "Work" of the SEC
(Available at http:www.sec.gov/about/whatwedo.shtml)

The mission of the U.S. Securities and Exchange Commission is to protect investors, maintain fair, orderly, and efficient markets, and facilitate capital formation.

. . . .

The laws and rules that govern the securities industry in the United States derive from a simple and straightforward concept: all investors, whether large institutions or private individuals, should have access to certain basic facts about an investment prior to buying it, and so long as they hold it. To achieve this, the SEC requires public companies to disclose meaningful financial and other information to the public. This provides a common pool of knowledge for all investors to use to judge for themselves whether to buy, sell, or hold a particular security. Only through the steady flow of timely, comprehensive, and accurate information can people make sound investment decisions.

The result of this information flow is a far more active, efficient, and transparent capital market that facilitates the capital formation so important to our nation's economy. To insure that this objective is always being met, the SEC continually works with all major market participants, including especially the investors in our securities markets, to listen to their concerns and to learn from their experience.

The SEC oversees the key participants in the securities world, including securities exchanges, securities brokers and dealers, investment advisors, and mutual funds. Here the SEC is concerned primarily with promoting the disclosure of important market-related information, maintaining fair dealing, and protecting against fraud.

Crucial to the SEC's effectiveness in each of these areas is its enforcement authority. Each year the SEC brings hundreds of civil enforcement actions against individuals and companies for violation of the securities laws. Typical infractions include insider trading, accounting fraud, and providing false or misleading information about securities and the companies that issue them.

. . . .

Though it is the primary overseer and regulator of the U.S. securities markets, the SEC works closely with many other institutions, including Congress, other federal departments and agencies, the self-regulatory organizations (e.g. the stock exchanges),

---

10. About the Financial Industry Regulatory Authority, at www.finra.org/AboutFINRA.

state securities regulators, and various private sector organizations. In particular, the Chairman of the SEC, together with the Chairman of the Federal Reserve, the Secretary of the Treasury, and the Chairman of the Commodity Futures Trading Commission, serves as a member of the President's Working Group on Financial Markets.

This article is an overview of the SEC's history, responsibilities, activities, organization, and operation.

Creation of the SEC

The SEC's foundation was laid in an era that was ripe for reform. Before the Great Crash of 1929, there was little support for federal regulation of the securities markets. This was particularly true during the post-World War I surge of securities activity. Proposals that the federal government require financial disclosure and prevent the fraudulent sale of stock were never seriously pursued.

Tempted by promises of "rags to riches" transformations and easy credit, most investors gave little thought to the systemic risk that arose from widespread abuse of margin financing and unreliable information about the securities in which they were investing. During the 1920s, approximately 20 million large and small shareholders took advantage of post-war prosperity and set out to make their fortunes in the stock market. It is estimated that of the $50 billion in new securities offered during this period, half became worthless.

When the stock market crashed in October 1929, public confidence in the markets plummeted. Investors large and small, as well as the banks who had loaned to these investors, lost great sums of money in the ensuing Great Depression. There was a consensus that for the economy to recover, the public's faith in the capital markets needed to be restored. Congress held hearings to identify the problems and search for solutions.

Based on the findings in these hearings, Congress — during the peak year of the Depression — passed the Securities Act of 1933. This law, together with the Securities Exchange Act of 1934, which created the SEC, was designed to restore investor confidence in our capital markets by providing investors and the markets with more reliable information and clear rules of honest dealing. . . .

Monitoring the securities industry requires a highly coordinated effort. Congress established the Securities and Exchange Commission [SEC] in 1934 to enforce the newly-passed securities laws, to promote stability in the markets and, most importantly, to protect investors. President Franklin Delano Roosevelt appointed Joseph P. Kennedy, President John F. Kennedy's father, to serve as the first Chairman of the SEC.

Organization of the SEC

The SEC consists of five presidentially-appointed Commissioners, with staggered five-year terms. One of them is designated by the President as Chairman of the Commission — the agency's chief executive. By law, no more than three of the Commissioners may belong to the same political party, ensuring non-partisanship.

The agency's functional responsibilities are organized into five Divisions and 16 Offices, each of which is headquartered in Washington, DC. The Commission's approximately 3,500 staff are located in Washington and in 11 Regional Offices throughout the country.

It is the responsibility of the Commission to:

- interpret federal securities laws;
- issue new rules and amend existing rules;
- oversee the inspection of securities firms, brokers, investment advisers, and ratings agencies;
- oversee private regulatory organizations in the securities, accounting, and auditing fields; and
- coordinate U.S. securities regulation with federal, state, and foreign authorities.

The Commission convenes regularly at meetings that are open to the public and the news media unless the discussion pertains to confidential subjects, such as whether to begin an enforcement investigation.

Divisions

Division of Corporation Finance

The Division of Corporation Finance assists the Commission in executing its responsibility to oversee corporate disclosure of important information to the investing public. Corporations are required to comply with regulations pertaining to disclosure that must be made when stock is initially sold and then on a continuing and periodic basis. The Division's staff routinely reviews the disclosure documents filed by companies. The staff also provides companies with assistance interpreting the Commission's rules and recommends to the Commission new rules for adoption.

The Division of Corporation Finance reviews documents that publicly-held companies are required to file with the Commission. The documents include:

- registration statements for newly-offered securities;
- annual and quarterly filings (Forms 10-K and 10-Q);
- proxy materials sent to shareholders before an annual shareholder meeting;
- annual reports to shareholders;
- documents concerning tender offers (a tender offer is an offer [made by a bidder to shareholders of a target corporation] to buy a large number of shares of [such target] corporation, [normally] at a premium above the current market price); and
- filings related to mergers and acquisitions.

These documents disclose information about the companies' financial condition and business practices to help investors make informed investment decisions. Through the Division's review process, the staff checks to see if publicly-held companies are meeting their disclosure requirements and seeks to improve the quality of the disclosure. To meet the SEC's requirements for disclosure, a company issuing securities or whose securities are publicly traded must make available [specified] information, whether it is positive or negative, that [is significant] to an investor's decision to buy, sell, or hold the security.

. . . .

Division of Trading and Markets

The Division of Trading and Markets assists the Commission in executing its responsibility for maintaining fair, orderly, and efficient markets. The staff of the Division provide day-to-day oversight of the major securities market participants: the securities exchanges; securities firms; self-regulatory organizations (SROs) including the Financial Industry Regulatory Authority (FINRA), the Municipal Securities Rulemaking Board (MSRB); clearing agencies that help facilitate trade settlement; transfer agents (parties that maintain records of securities owners); securities information processors; and credit rating agencies.

The Division also oversees the Securities Investor Protection Corporation (SIPC), which is a private, non-profit corporation that insures the securities and cash in the customer accounts of member brokerage firms against the failure of those firms. Importantly, SIPC insurance does not cover investor losses arising from market declines or fraud.

The Division's additional responsibilities include:

- carrying out the Commission's financial integrity program for broker-dealers;
- reviewing (and in some cases approving, under authority delegated from the Commission) proposed new rules and proposed changes to existing rules filed by the SROs;
- assisting the Commission in establishing rules and issuing interpretations on matters affecting the operation of the securities markets; and
- surveilling the markets.

Division of Investment Management

The Division of Investment Management assists the Commission in executing its responsibility for investor protection and for promoting capital formation through oversight and regulation of America's $26 trillion investment management industry. This important part of the U.S. capital markets includes mutual funds and the professional fund managers who advise them; analysts who research individual assets and asset classes; and investment advisers to individual customers. Because of the high concentration of individual investors in the mutual funds, exchange-traded funds, and other investments that fall within the Division's purview, the Division of Investment Management is focused on ensuring that disclosures about these investments are useful to retail customers, and that the regulatory costs which consumers must bear are not excessive.

The Division's additional responsibilities include:

- assisting the Commission in interpreting laws and regulations for the public and SEC inspection . . . ;

- responding to no-action requests and requests for exemptive relief;

- reviewing investment company and investment adviser filings;

- assisting the Commission in enforcement matters involving investment companies and advisers; and

- advising the Commission on adapting SEC rules to new circumstances.

Division of Enforcement

First and foremost, the SEC is a law enforcement agency. The Division of Enforcement assists the Commission in executing its law enforcement function by recommending the commencement of investigations of securities law violations, by recommending that the Commission bring civil actions in federal court or before an administrative law judge, and by prosecuting these cases on behalf of the Commission. As an adjunct to the SEC's civil enforcement authority, the Division works closely with law enforcement agencies in the U.S. and around the world to bring criminal cases when appropriate.

The Division obtains evidence of possible violations of the securities laws from many sources, including market surveillance activities, investor tips and complaints, other Divisions and Offices of the SEC, the self-regulatory organizations and other securities industry sources, and media reports.

All SEC investigations are conducted privately. Facts are developed to the fullest extent possible through informal inquiry, interviewing witnesses, examining brokerage records, reviewing trading data, and other methods. With a formal order of investigation, the Division's staff may compel witnesses by subpoena to testify and produce books, records, and other relevant documents. Following an investigation, SEC staff present their findings to the Commission for its review. The Commission can authorize the staff to file a case in federal court or bring an administrative action. In many cases, the Commission and the party charged decide to settle a matter without trial.

Common violations that may lead to SEC investigations include:

- misrepresentation or omission of important information about securities;

- manipulating the market prices of securities;

- stealing customers' funds or securities;

- violating broker-dealers' responsibility to treat customers fairly;

- insider trading (violating a trust relationship by trading on material, non-public information about a security); and

- selling unregistered securities.

Whether the Commission decides to bring a case in federal court or within the SEC before an administrative law judge may depend upon the type of sanction or relief that is being sought. For example, the Commission may bar someone from the brokerage industry in an administrative proceeding. . . . Often, when the misconduct warrants it, the Commission will bring both proceedings.

- *Civil action*: The Commission files a complaint with a U.S. District Court and asks the court for a sanction or remedy. Often the Commission asks for a court order, called an injunction, that prohibits any further acts or practices that violate the law or Commission rules. An injunction can also require audits, accounting for frauds, or special supervisory arrangements. In addition, the SEC can seek civil monetary penalties, or the return of illegal profits (called disgorgement). The court may also bar or suspend an individual from serving as a corporate officer or director [of a publicly-traded company]. A person who violates the court's order may be found in contempt and be subject to additional fines or imprisonment.

- *Administrative action*: The Commission can seek a variety of sanctions through the administrative proceeding process. Administrative proceedings differ from civil court actions in that they are heard by an administrative law judge (ALJ), who is independent of the Commission. The administrative law judge presides over a hearing and considers the evidence presented by the Division staff, as well as any evidence submitted by the subject of the proceeding. Following the hearing, the ALJ issues an initial decision that includes findings of fact and legal conclusions. The initial decision may also contain sanction[s]. Both the Division staff and the defendant may appeal all or any portion of the initial decision to the Commission. The Commission may affirm the decision of the ALJ, reverse the decision, or remand it for additional hearings. Administrative sanctions include cease and desist orders, suspension or revocation of broker-dealer and investment advisor registrations, censures, bars from association with the securities industry, civil monetary penalties, and disgorgement.

Division of Risk, Strategy, and Financial Innovation

The Division of Risk, Strategy, and Financial Innovation was established in 2009 to help further identify developing risks and trends in the financial markets.

This new Division is providing the Commission with sophisticated analysis that integrates economic, financial, and legal disciplines. The Division's responsibilities cover three broad areas: risk and economic analysis; strategic research; and financial innovation.

The emergence of derivatives, hedge funds, new technology, and other factors have transformed both capital markets and corporate governance. The Division of Risk, Strategy, and Financial Innovation is working to advise the Commission through an interdisciplinary approach that is informed by law and modern finance and economics, as well as developments in real world products and practices on Wall Street and Main Street.

Among the functions being performed by the Division are: (1) strategic and long-term analysis; (2) identifying new developments and trends in financial markets and systemic risk; (3) making recommendations as to how these new developments and trends affect the Commission's regulatory activities; (4) conducting research and analysis in furtherance and support of the functions of the Commission and its divisions and offices; and (5) providing training on new developments and trends and other matters.

Offices

Office of the General Counsel

The General Counsel is appointed by the Chairman as the chief legal officer of the Commission, with overall responsibility for the establishment of agency policy on legal matters. The General Counsel serves as the chief legal advisor to the Chairman regarding all legal matters and services performed within, or involving, the agency, and provides legal advice to the Commissioners, the Divisions, the Offices, and other SEC components as appropriate.

The General Counsel represents the SEC in civil, private, or appellate proceedings as appropriate, including appeals from the decisions of the federal district courts or the Commission in enforcement matters, and appeals from the denial of requests under the Freedom of Information Act. Through its amicus curiae program, the General Counsel often intervenes in private appellate litigation involving novel or important interpretations of the securities laws, and the Office is responsible for coordinating with the Department of Justice in the preparation of briefs on behalf of the United States involving matters in which the SEC has an interest.

The General Counsel is also responsible for determining the adherence by attorneys in the SEC to appropriate professional standards, as well as for providing advice on standards of conduct to Commissioners and staff, as appropriate. It is responsible for the final drafting of all proposed legislation that the Chairman or the Commission choose to submit for consideration to the Congress or the states, and for coordinating the SEC staff positions on such legislation.

Office of the Chief Accountant

The Chief Accountant is appointed by the Chairman to be the principal adviser to the Commission on accounting and auditing matters. The Office of the Chief Accountant assists the Commission in executing its responsibility under the securities laws to establish accounting principles, and for overseeing the private sector standards-setting process. The Office works closely with the Financial Accounting Standards Board, to which the SEC has delegated authority for accounting standards setting, as well as the International Accounting Standards Board and the American Institute of Certified Public Accountants.

In addition to its responsibility for accounting standards, the Commission is responsible for the approval or disapproval of auditing rules put forward by the Public Company Accounting Oversight Board, a private-sector regulator established by the Sarbanes-Oxley Act to oversee the auditing profession. The Commission also has thorough-going oversight responsibility for all of the activities of the Public Company Accounting Oversight Board (PCAOB), including approval of its annual budget. To assist the Commission in the execution of these responsibilities, the Office of the Chief Accountant is the principal liaison with the PCAOB. The Office also consults with registrants and auditors on a regular basis regarding the application of accounting and auditing standards and financial disclosure requirements.

. . . .

Office of Compliance Inspections and Examinations

The Office of Compliance Inspections and Examinations administers the SEC's nationwide examination and inspection program for registered self-regulatory organizations, broker-dealers, transfer agents, clearing agencies, investment companies, and investment advisers. The Office conducts inspections to foster compliance with the securities laws, to detect violations of the law, and to keep the Commission informed of developments in the regulated community. Among the more important goals of the examination program is the quick and informal correction of compliance problems. When the Office finds deficiencies, it issues a "deficiency letter" identifying the problems that need to be rectified and monitors the situation until compliance is achieved. Violations that appear too serious for informal correction are referred to the Division of Enforcement.

Office of International Affairs

The SEC works extensively in the international arena to promote cooperation among national securities regulatory agencies, and to encourage the maintenance of high regulatory standards worldwide. The Office of International Affairs assists the Chairman and the Commission in the development and implementation of the SEC's international regulatory and enforcement initiatives. The Office negotiates bilateral and multilateral agreements for Commission approval on such subjects as regulatory cooperation and enforcement assistance, and oversees the implementation of such arrangements. It is also responsible for advancing the Commission's agenda in international meetings and organizations. The Office also conducts a technical assistance program for countries with emerging securities markets, which includes training both in the United States and in the requesting country. Over 100 countries currently participate in this program.

Office of Investor Education and Advocacy

The Office of Investor Education and Advocacy has three main functional areas:

The *Office of Policy* has responsibility for reviewing agency action from the perspective of the individual investor, including conducting investor surveys and focus groups. It also plays a role in the Commission's efforts to help ensure that investor disclosures are written in plain English.

The *Office of Investor Advocacy* responds to questions, complaints, and suggestions from the members of the public. Tens of thousands of investors contact the SEC each year using the agency's online forms or our (800) SEC-0330 hotline (toll-free in U.S.) to ask questions on a wide range of securities-related topics, to complain about problems with their investments or their financial professionals, or to suggest improvements to the agency's regulations and procedures.

The *Office of Investor Education* carries out the SEC's investor education program, which includes producing and distributing educational materials, participating in educational seminars and investor-oriented events, and partnering with federal agencies, state regulators, and others on investor literacy initiatives.

Office of Information Technology

The Office of Information Technology supports the Commission and staff of the SEC in all aspects of information technology. The Office has overall management responsibility for the Commission's IT program including application development, infrastructure operations and engineering, user support, IT program management, capital planning, security, and enterprise architecture. The Office operates the Electronic Data Gathering Analysis and Retrieval (EDGAR) system, which electronically receives, processes, and disseminates more than 500,000 financial statements every year. The Office also maintains a very active website that contains a wealth of information about the Commission and the securities industry, and also hosts the EDGAR database for free public access.

Office of the Executive Director

The Office of the Executive Director assists the Chairman in developing and executing the management policies of the SEC. The Office formulates budget and authorization strategies, supervises the allocation and use of SEC resources, promotes management controls and financial integrity, manages the administrative support offices, and oversees the development and implementation of the SEC's automated information systems.

. . . .

Office of Legislative Affairs and Intergovernmental Relations

The Office of Legislative Affairs and Intergovernmental Relations serves as the agency's formal liaison with the Congress, other Executive Branch agencies, and state and local governments. The staff carefully monitors ongoing legislative activities and initiatives on Capitol Hill that affect the Commission and its mission. Through regular communication and consultation with House and Senate members and staff, the Office communicates legislators' goals to the agency, and communicates the agency's own regulatory and management initiatives to the Congress.

The Office is responsible for responding to congressional requests for testimony of SEC officials, as well as requests for documents, technical assistance, and other information. In addition, the Office monitors legislative and oversight hearings that pertain to the securities markets and the protection of investors. . . .

Office of Public Affairs

The Office of Public Affairs assists the Commission in making the work of the SEC open to the public, understandable to investors, and accountable to taxpayers. It helps every other SEC Division and Office accomplish the agency's overall mission — to protect investors, maintain fair, orderly, and efficient markets, and facilitate capital formation. The Office coordinates the agency's relations with the media and the general public, in this country and around the world.

. . . .

Office of the Secretary

The Secretary of the Commission is appointed by the Chairman, and is responsible for the procedural administration of Commission meetings, rulemaking, practice, and procedure. Among the responsibilities of the Office are the scheduling and recording of public and non-public meetings of the Commission; the administration of the process by which the Commission takes action without a meeting (called the seriatim process); the administration of the duty-officer process (by which a single Commissioner is designated to authorize emergency action); the maintenance of records of Commission actions; and the maintenance of records of financial judgments in enforcement proceedings. The Office also provides advice to the Commission and the staff on questions of practice and procedure.

. . . .

Office of Equal Employment Opportunity

Because the SEC's employees are its most important resource, the Office of Equal Employment Opportunity works to ensure that the agency's professional staff come from diverse backgrounds that reflect the diversity of the investing public. Equal employment opportunity at the SEC is a continuing commitment. To maintain neutrality in resolving disputes, the EEO Office is independent of any other SEC office. The EEO Director reports to the Chairman. The primary mission of the EEO Office is to prevent employment discrimination, including discriminatory harassment, so that all SEC employees have the working environment to support them in their efforts to protect investors, maintain healthy markets, and promote capital formation.

Office of the Inspector General

The Office of the Inspector General conducts internal audits and investigations of SEC programs and operations. Through these audits and investigations, the Inspector General seeks to identify and mitigate operational risks, enhance government integrity, and improve the efficiency and effectiveness of SEC programs.

Office of Administrative Law Judges

The Commission's Office of Administrative Law Judges consists of independent judicial officers who conduct hearings and rule on allegations of securities law violations in cases initiated by the Commission. When the Commission initiates a public administrative proceeding, it refers the case to the Office, where it is assigned to an individual Administrative Law Judge (ALJ). The ALJ then conducts a public hearing that is similar to a non-jury trial in the federal courts. Just as a federal judge can do, an ALJ issues subpoenas, rules on motions, and rules on the admissibility of evidence. At the conclusion of the hearing, the parties submit proposed findings of fact and conclusions of law. The ALJ prepares an initial decision that includes factual findings and legal conclusions that are matters of public record. Parties may appeal an initial decision to the Commission, which can affirm, reverse, modify, set aside or remand for further proceedings. Appeals from Commission action are to a United States Court of Appeals.

The Laws That Govern the Securities Industry

Securities Act of 1933

Often referred to as the "truth in securities" law, the Securities Act of 1933 has two basic objectives:

- require that investors receive financial and other significant information concerning securities being offered for public sale; and
- prohibit deceit, misrepresentations, and other fraud in the sale of securities.

Purpose of Registration

A primary means of accomplishing these goals is the disclosure of important financial information through the registration of securities. This information enables investors, not the government, to make informed judgments about whether to purchase a company's securities. While the SEC requires that the information provided be accurate, it does not guarantee it. Investors who purchase securities and suffer losses [may] have important recovery rights if they can prove that there was [materially] incomplete or inaccurate disclosure of important information.

The Registration Process

In general, securities sold in the U.S. must be registered. The registration forms companies file provide essential facts while minimizing the burden and expense of complying with the law. In general, registration forms call for:

- a description of the company's properties and business;
- a description of the security to be offered for sale;
- information about the management of the company; and
- financial statements certified by independent accountants.

All companies, both domestic and foreign, must file their registration statements electronically. These statements and the accompanying prospectuses become public shortly after filing, and investors can access them using the Electronic Data Gathering, Analysis, and Retrieval System (EDGAR). Registration statements are subject to examination for compliance with disclosure requirements.

Not all offerings of securities must be registered with the Commission. Some exemptions from the registration requirement include:

- private offerings to a limited number of persons or institutions;
- offerings of limited size;
- intrastate offerings; and
- securities of municipal, state, and federal governments.

By exempting many small offerings from the registration process, the SEC seeks to foster capital formation by lowering the cost of offering securities to the public.

Securities Exchange Act of 1934

With this Act, Congress created the Securities and Exchange Commission. The Act empowers the SEC with broad authority over all aspects of the securities industry. This includes the power to register, regulate, and oversee brokerage firms, transfer agents, and clearing agencies as well as the nation's securities self-regulatory organizations (SROs). The various stock exchanges, such as the New York Stock Exchange and the American Stock Exchange, are SROs. The Financial Industry Regulatory Authority [FINRA], which operates the NASDAQ system, is also an SRO.

The Act also identifies and prohibits certain types of conduct in the markets and provides the Commission with disciplinary powers over regulated entities and persons associated with them.

The Act also empowers the SEC to require periodic reporting of information by companies with publicly traded securities. [For example, pursuant to the authority granted by the Securities Exchange Act, the SEC engages in regulating the following activities:]

Corporate Reporting

Companies [having a specified amount of assets and number of shareholders] must file annual and other periodic reports. These reports are available to the public through the SEC's EDGAR database.

Proxy Solicitations

The Securities Exchange Act also governs the disclosure in materials used to solicit shareholders' votes in annual or special meetings held for the election of directors and the approval of other corporate action. This information, contained in proxy materials, must be filed with the Commission in advance of any solicitation to ensure compliance with the disclosure rules. Solicitations, whether by management or shareholder groups, must disclose all important facts concerning the issues on which holders are asked to vote.

Tender Offers

The Securities Exchange Act requires disclosure of important information by anyone acquir[ing] more than 5 percent of a company's securities by direct purchase or tender offer. Such an offer often is extended in an effort to gain control of the company. As with the proxy rules, this allows shareholders to make informed decisions on these critical corporate events.

Insider Trading

The securities laws broadly prohibit fraudulent activities of any kind in connection with the offer, purchase, or sale of securities. These provisions are the basis for many types of disciplinary actions, including actions against fraudulent insider trading. Insider trading is illegal when a person trades a security while in possession of material nonpublic information in violation of a duty to withhold the information or refrain from trading.

Registration of Exchanges, Associations, and Others

The Act requires a variety of market participants to register with the Commission, including exchanges, brokers and dealers, transfer agents, and clearing agencies. Registration for these organizations involves filing disclosure documents that are updated on a regular basis. The exchanges and [FINRA] are identified as self-regulatory organizations (SRO). SROs must create rules that allow for disciplining members for improper conduct and for establishing measures to ensure market integrity and investor protection. SRO proposed rules are published for comment before final SEC review and approval.

Trust Indenture Act of 1939

This Act applies to debt securities such as bonds, debentures, and notes that are offered for public sale. Even though such securities may be registered under the Securities Act, they may not be offered for sale to the public unless a formal agreement between the issuer of bonds and the bondholder, known as the trust indenture, conforms to the standards of this Act.

Investment Company Act of 1940

This Act regulates the organization of companies, including mutual funds, that engage primarily in investing, reinvesting, and trading in securities, and whose own securities are offered to the investing public. The regulation is designed to minimize conflicts of interest that arise in these complex operations. The Act requires these companies to disclose their financial condition and investment policies to investors when stock is initially sold and, subsequently, on a regular basis. The focus of this Act is on disclosure to the investing public of information about the fund and its investment objectives, as well as on investment company structure and operations. It is important to remember that the Act does not permit the SEC to directly supervise the investment decisions or activities of these companies or judge the merits of their investments.

Investment Advisers Act of 1940

This law regulates investment advisers. With certain exceptions, this Act requires that firms compensated for advising others about securities investments register with the SEC and conform to regulations designed to protect investors. . . .

Sarbanes-Oxley Act of 2002

On July 30, 2002, President Bush signed into law the Sarbanes-Oxley Act of 2002 [SOX], which he characterized as "the most far reaching reforms of American business practices since the time of Franklin Delano Roosevelt." The Act mandated a number of reforms to enhance corporate responsibility, [improve] financial disclosures, and combat corporate and accounting fraud. [SOX also] created the "Public Company Accounting Oversight Board," also known as the PCAOB, to oversee the activities of the auditing profession. . . .

Dodd-Frank Wall Street Reform and Consumer Protection Act of 2010

The Dodd-Frank Wall Street Reform and Consumer Protection Act was signed into law on July 21, 2010 by President Barack Obama. The legislation set out to reshape the U.S. regulatory system in a number of areas including but not limited to consumer protection, trading restrictions, credit ratings, regulation of financial products, corporate governance and disclosure, and transparency. . . .

Jumpstart Our Business Startups (JOBS) Act

On April 5, 2010, the Jumpstart Our Business Startups (JOBS) Act was signed into law by President Barack Obama. The JOBS Act requires the SEC to write rules and issue studies on capital formation, disclosure, and registration requirements. Cost-effective access to capital for companies of all sizes plays a critical role in our national economy, and companies seeking access to capital should not be hindered by unnecessary or overly burdensome regulations. . . .

---

§ 1.03 Reminiscing the SEC Years

To help celebrate its fiftieth anniversary, the SEC published a colorful history of its past.[11] The following represents a sampling of this account.

50 Years of the U.S. Securities and Exchange Commission
(Published by the SEC) (1984)

In 1940, *Fortune* magazine called the House of Morgan at 23 Wall Street and the 1778 Pennsylvania Avenue headquarters of the Securities and Exchange Commission "temples" in which lie "the deepest feelings of a community." The building on Wall

---

11. This, of course, is not to imply that the SEC is without its critics. See, e.g., R. Karmel, Regulation by Prosecution—The Securities and Exchange Commission Versus Corporate America (1982); H. Kripke, The SEC and Corporate Disclosure: Regulation In Search of a Purpose (1979); P. Mahoney, Wasting a Crisis—Why Securities Regulation Fails (2015); Labaton, *S.E.C. Facing Deeper Trouble*, New York Times, Dec. 1, 2002, at D1; Macey, *Administrative Agency Obsolescence and Interest Group Formation: A Case Study of the SEC at Sixty*, 15 Cardozo L. Rev. 909 (1994).

Street, Fortune said, "is the chief memorial of a business era that came to an end ten years ago," and the SEC "is a shrine to the outraged feelings of the voters of 1932. . . ."

Working with a rough blueprint in the cold aftermath of the Great Crash of 1929, the architects of the Securities and Exchange Commission managed to create a sound structure which has weathered half a century. First they attended to the groundwork— building a sound regulatory structure—and then turned toward refining and modernizing the system they had constructed.

The SEC's foundation was laid in an era which was particularly ripe for reform. Before the debacle of 1929, there was no public support to regulate the post-World War I surge of securities activity, and what proposals were made to require financial disclosure and prevent the fraudulent sale of stock were never seriously pursued. Tempted by promises of "rags to riches" and easy credit, most investors gave little thought to the inherent dangers in unbridled market operation.

During the 1920s, some 20 million large and small shareholders took advantage of post-war prosperity and set out to make their "killing" on the stock market. It is estimated that of the $50 billion in new securities offered during this period, half proved to be worthless.

The 1920s also signaled the rise of "margin buying," as brokers, backed by capital loans from corporations such as Electric Bond and Share and Standard Oil Company, offered stock to investors in exchange for a small down payment and interest on the balance of the purchase price.

By 1929, a full 40 percent of all investors were margin buyers, many of whom "pyramided" their paper profits, accumulating hundreds of thousands of dollars in profit on comparatively minuscule investments. When prices began to decline and brokers started making "margin calls," many customers were unable to raise the cash to pay back their loans and resorted to selling securities. The act of selling further depressed prices, creating a vicious circle that soon collapsed, bringing the country's business and financial systems to the verge of disaster.

The Great Crash dramatized the need for federal intervention in establishing and maintaining higher standards of business conduct in the capital markets. America's economy was crippled without investor confidence. The goal of restoring that confidence led to the creation of the Securities and Exchange Commission.

Investor confidence, the stock market and the economy all reached their lowest ebb in 1933, as the "Senate Bear Hunt"—the investigation into the exchanges and securities markets—revealed rampant malpractices and abuses in securities financing. The "rubble in the pyramid was exposed," according to Fortune, as Senate Banking and Commerce Committee Counsel Ferdinand Pecora drew testimony from Wall Street traders, banking officials, and executives of institutions such as the House of Morgan. The much publicized hearings and the public support for reform which followed paved the way for the Securities Act of 1933, the first effective federal legislation regulating corporate finance.

. . . .

Although their work on the 1933 Act was over, the drafting team of Cohen, Landis and Corcoran—called Frankfurter's "Happy Hotdogs" by journalists of the day—were eventually to offer further advice on proposed securities legislation. . . .

As Pecora's investigation continued to expose abuses, momentum grew for a bill to regulate the stock exchanges. Approached by a Pecora aide to draft a stock exchange bill, Landis, Cohen and Corcoran turned the initial work over to two young government attorneys who produced 12 drafts of the bill before Cohen shaped the final product. The so-called Rayburn-Fletcher bill, named for its House and Senate sponsors, was introduced February 10, 1934.

The bill drew immediate protest from the press and the financial community. The "drastic stock market bill," said The New York Times, amounted to "autocratic meddling" in an area which should only be supervised by those with long experience in the field. The Wall Street Journal warned of a pervasive movement toward "social control." In an extensive lobbying campaign against the bill, New York Stock Exchange President Richard Whitney claimed the legislative proposals threatened the existence of brokerage firms and guaranteed unemployment for employees in the financial sector.

By spring the bill had undergone considerable change to make it more palatable to the financial community. One of the major amendments to the bill removed oversight of the exchanges from the jurisdiction of the Federal Trade Commission and the Federal Reserve Board, placing it under a separate new commission. Its provisions granted the commission broad power over stock exchanges, requiring registration by most broker-dealers.

A system of continuous disclosure was established for firms issuing securities traded on an exchange, and manipulation of securities prices was outlawed. The new commission was vested with authority over the solicitation of corporate proxies, and officers and directors of listed companies were prohibited from trading in their own securities for short-term profit.

The agency would consist of five commissioners, appointed by the President, no more than three of whom are members of the same political party. When the long legislative battle ended with the bill's passage on June 1, 1934, the Securities and Exchange Commission was born.

. . . .

Four of the President's five appointees to the new Commission came as no surprise. Three were recruited from the Federal Trade Commission: James Landis, whose brilliance, background and reputation for hard work portended his possible chairmanship; FTC Commissioner George Mathews; and FTC Chief Counsel Robert Healy, a former associate justice of the Vermont Supreme Court who had been instrumental in the adoption of the 1933 Act. The fourth selection was Ferdinand Pecora, the relentless prosecutor of the Senate investigation.

The appointment of Joseph Kennedy to the fifth slot on the Commission, for the longest of the staggered one, two, three, four and five-year terms, gave rise to considerable astonishment and criticism. An old friend and loyal supporter of Roosevelt's, Kennedy was a financier and market operator who had played the game and won under the questionable practices of the '20s. Although he was aware of Kennedy's reputation, the President recognized his integrity and saw Kennedy as a man uniquely qualified to [serve as Chairman of the Commission and to] conciliate the business and financial communities.

. . . .

[The second SEC Chairman was William O. Douglas.] In *Go East, Young Man,* Douglas speaks glowingly about the staff of the SEC, which had swelled to 1,800 at the time of his chairmanship, as "honest, idealistic, hard-working, and loyal men and women to the nth degree . . . [N]o taint of unethical conduct ever touched [the commission], nor did partisan politics motivate it. Above all else, the commission's performance was highly professional."

. . . .

The camaraderie that [to some degree] still characterizes the SEC is deeply rooted in the pre-War years, when the agency became a surrogate family to employees working 14 or 16-hour days. Convivial drinks were shared after work in the Oak Lounge of the Powhatan Hotel at 19th and I Streets. At lunchtime, "everyone made a beeline to the Potomac Restaurant," recalled 45-year staffer Oliver App. "For 25 cents, you could get meat, two vegetables, coffee, bread, and the salad bar."

. . . .

The *esprit de corps* among the staff of the Douglas Commission may have had much to do with William O. Douglas himself. The Yakima, Washington native had a sense of humor and personality. . . . The Douglas chairmanship was also a busy and productive one. . . .

. . . .

By 1939 Douglas felt that he had completed his work on the Commission: he had ensured the workability of the 1933, 1934 and 1935 Acts; he had forced the loosely governed New York Stock Exchange to begin reform; and he had conceived and carried to fruition two new pieces of reform legislation. With the offer of a deanship at Yale Law School pending, Douglas informed Roosevelt of his intention to step down as chairman.

Douglas was about to tee off on the ninth hole with several SEC associates one afternoon in March 1939 when a breathless caddy ran up and told Douglas the White House wanted him. "I have a new job for you," Roosevelt informed him after he was ushered into the Oval Office. "It's a mean job, a dirty job, a thankless job." Douglas' heart sank, as Roosevelt described what he believed was the chairmanship of the Federal Communications Commission, an inefficiently-run agency which he knew the President wanted to "clean up."

"It's a job you'll detest," Roosevelt added, with Douglas in silent agreement. "Tomorrow I am sending your name to the Senate as Louis Brandeis' successor." A dumbfounded Douglas had just learned that at age 40, he was about to become the youngest Supreme Court justice in more than a century.

Justice William O. Douglas' replacement for the SEC chairmanship was his close friend Jerome Frank, who had joined the Commission in 1938 to fill the Landis vacancy. A voracious reader, prolific writer and a near-genius, Frank "had the most creative legal mind of anyone in our time," wrote Douglas in Go East, Young Man. [Frank was later appointed to the U.S. Court of Appeals for the Second Circuit.]

. . . .

The high caliber of the SEC staff was reflected in the 1949 Hoover Report on Regulatory Commissions, which recognized the SEC as "an outstanding example of the independent commission at its best." The staff of the 1950s, however, suffered under increasing budget cuts, largely a result of the Eisenhower Administration's commitment to a balanced budget. . . .

"Nobody would take a day off or go on vacation because they were afraid someone would measure their chair to see if it fit them," said Ruth Appleton, who feared the loss of her own job in the 50s, when "it was pretty rough for women lawyers to find jobs." She recalled that on one or two occasions, the staff was forced to take a half-day off without pay to keep from cutting additional positions. [In a more recent article, Professor Roberta S. Karmel, the first woman SEC Commissioner, "believe[s] that to a much greater extent than in other organizations I have worked, the SEC was a meritocracy where hard work and intellectual firepower mattered much more than one's sex." Karmel, *From SEC Enforcement Attorney to Commissioner*, 65 Md. L. Rev. 692, 705 (2006).]

. . . .

The seeds for a strong Enforcement Division were planted in the late 1950's to cope with the rise in boiler-room operations, but it was under [Chairman] Manny Cohen's tutelage that they became firmly rooted. . . . In 1965 [Irving] Pollack became director and recruited Stanley Sporkin as his associate director. The technique developed by Pollack and later fine-tuned by Sporkin . . . is what Pollack called "the valve approach" and Sporkin called "the access strategy": getting the optimal use of the enforcement staff's resources by going after the individuals or firms . . . which "control the valve" or provide access to the criminals.

. . . .

Few of the SEC's activities in the 1970s drew more publicity than the enforcement program run by Stanley Sporkin, who was described in December 1974 by *Fortune* writer Walter Guzzardi, Jr., in "Those Zealous Cops on the Securities Beat," as "a man of considerable charm and spectral eye."

. . . .

Sporkin's style of enforcement has been described by his former coworkers as "creative" and "ingenious." Looking back, Sporkin says he used an "even-handed" approach that enhanced the credibility of the SEC's enforcement program. "Nobody could be out of the reach of the agency, and nobody could 'own' the agency. Yet we had to be fair to people, and treat them fairly and decently," he said. Within the confines of the Commission's budgetary resources, Sporkin employed the "access strategy" which he and his predecessor, Irving Pollack, had developed. [Judge Sporkin, one of this country's preeminent lawyers, subsequently became General Counsel of The Central Intelligence Agency and thereafter a United States District Court Judge in the District of Columbia.]

. . . .

In the mid-1970s, Sporkin led the Commission's crusade against "questionable payments" by corporations—a thrust which was inspired by the Watergate investigations into illegal corporate campaign contributions made during the 1972 election. [This effort ultimately culminated in the enactment by Congress in 1977 of the Foreign Corrupt Practices Act.]

. . . .

The result was what former Enforcement Division attorney Arthur Mathews [who became a superb defense litigator with the Washington, D.C. law firm of Wilmer Cutler & Pickering] called "one of the best things to happen to America in the century." From the first voluntary disclosure by a firm in 1975 to the enactment of the 1977 Foreign Corrupt Practices Act, some 600 corporations voluntarily disclosed such "material information" as overseas and domestic bribery, falsification of records, illegal campaign contributions and undisclosed perquisites. The questionable payments made by more than 50 other corporations were revealed through SEC enforcement actions.

By 1976, some of the world's largest corporations had admitted to questionable payments of some form, including the Lockheed Aircraft Corporation in Japan and the Gulf Oil Corporation, whose undeclared campaign contributions had amounted to millions of dollars. The SEC had successfully shown the need for a reform in corporate record-keeping and had garnered Congressional support to legislate a system of internal accounting controls.

. . . .

Note: The SEC Now

For those who are baseball fans, you may be intrigued that Fay Vincent, a former Commissioner of Baseball, also is a former SEC staffer.

Perhaps the change in attitude with respect to the benefits of efficient government oversight is reflected by the following:

On October 19, 1987, now referred to as Black Monday, the Dow Jones Industrial Average dropped a previously unimaginable 508 points. On that

Monday, $500 billion of paper wealth evaporated. For many, it inevitably brought to mind the collapse of the stock market in 1929 which preceded the Great Depression. The reaction of businessmen to the recent crisis, however, points to one of the many differences between these two historic events. "Unlike their predecessors in the 1920's, who did not think emergency Government measures could help, the businessmen of [today] are calling for Washington to intervene to stabilize the markets." In addition, a Presidential task force studied the October crash and strongly recommended tougher governmental regulation of financial markets. . . . [12]

Note, however, that excessive government regulation remains a concern, prompting calls for the SEC to relax its rules that allegedly impede capital formation. See generally Langevoort, *The SEC as a Bureaucracy: Public Choice, Institutional Rhetoric, and the Process of Policy Formulation*, 47 WASH. & LEE L. REV. 527 (1990) (and sources cited therein).

In his article *Administrative Agency Obsolescence and Interest Group Formation: A Case Study of the SEC at Sixty*, 15 CARDOZO L. REV. 909, 948–949 (1994), Professor Jonathan R. Macey opined that "the SEC has engaged in a wholesale campaign of imperialistic turf expansion." He asserted:

> The picture that emerges . . . is one of the SEC as a highly politicized organization intent on preserving its own bureaucratic turf despite the mounting evidence of its own obsolescence and irrelevance. The SEC's major litigation efforts and regulatory initiatives have been designed to protect the Commission's regulatory turf, rather than to further important areas of public policy.

Likewise, the U.S. Chamber of Commerce issued a critical report on the SEC. The Chamber asserted that, in the post-Enron "highly charged environment," there is "fertile ground to encourage, and even demand, the SEC to expand its enforcement powers, to press expansive theories of liability, and to seek increasingly punitive sanctions in its enforcement actions." U.S. Chamber of Commerce, *Report on the Current Enforcement Program of the Securities and Exchange Commission* at 13 (2006).

Taking issue with the above characterization, Professor David L. Ratner responded:

> No agency is perfect, and the SEC has had its ups and downs over the years. But it is a testament to the prescience of the people who drafted the securities laws back in the early 1930s, and to the quality of the people who have served as Commissioners and staff members over the years, that it has adapted to change without the need for basic amendment of its governing statutes, that it has been free of major scandals, and that it has been an important force for higher ethical standards in an industry which relies heavily

---

12. Introductory Comment, *A Historical Introduction to the Securities Act of 1933 and the Securities Exchange Act of 1934*, 49 OHIO ST. L.J. 329 (1988).

on public confidence. The SEC is one important reason why the securities industry is in so much better shape than other financial service industries, and why the U.S. securities markets are the best securities markets in the world. Obsolete? No. Actually, it is in pretty good shape for a sixty year old.

Ratner, *The SEC at Sixty: A Reply to Professor Macey*, 16 Cardozo L. Rev. 1765, 1779 (1995). *See also*, Symposium, *The SEC at 75*, 78 U. Cin. L. Rev. No. 3 (2009).

Undoubtedly, the Sarbanes-Oxley Act of 2002 and the Dodd-Frank Act of 2010, both enacted in the wake of major financial debacles, signify more extensive SEC regulation for at least the relatively near future.

---

§ 1.04 The Role of Counsel

The role of securities counsel has been described by the SEC as follows:

> Very little of a securities lawyer's work is adversary in character. He [or she] doesn't work in courtrooms where the pressure of vigilant adversaries and alert judges [are] checks. He [or she] works in [the] office where prospectuses, proxy statements, opinions of counsel, and other documents [are prepared] that we, our staff, the financial community, and the investing public must take on faith.[13]

Counsel has been viewed as carrying the "passkey" to the securities markets."[14] For example, the rendering of a lawyer's opinion "is frequently the red or green light to the consummation of a securities transaction."[15] And, as stated by the eminent Judge Friendly: "In our complex society . . . the lawyer's opinion can be [an] instrument for inflicting pecuniary loss more potent than the chisel or the crowbar."[16] Recognizing the importance of counsel's role, the Second Circuit has stated that "effective implementation of [investor] safeguards . . . depends in large measure on the members of the bar who serve in an advisory capacity to those engaged in securities transactions."[17]

---

13. *In re Emmanuel Fields,* [1973 Transfer Binder] Fed. Sec. L. Rep. (CCH) ¶ 79,407, at 83,175 n. 20 (SEC 1973), *aff'd,* 495 F.2d 1075 (D.C. Cir. 1974).

14. Shipman, *The Need for SEC Rules to Govern the Duties and Civil Liabilities of Attorneys Under the Federal Securities Statutes,* 34 Ohio St. L.J. 231 (1973); Sommer, *The Emerging Duties of the Securities Lawyer,* [1973–1974 Transfer Binder] Fed. Sec. L. Rep. (CCH) ¶ 79,631, at 83,689.

15. Gruenbaum, *Corporate/Securities Lawyers: Disclosure, Responsibility and Liability to Investors,* 54 Notre Dame L. Rev. 795, 804 (1979).

16. *United States v. Benjamin,* 328 F.2d 854, 863 (2d Cir. 1964), *cert. denied,* 377 U.S. 953 (1964). Professor Margaret Sachs has authored an insightful article on the securities law decisions of Judge Friendly. See Sachs, *Judge Friendly and the Law of Securities Regulation: The Creation of a Judicial Reputation,* 50 SMU L. Rev. 777 (1997).

17. *SEC v. Spectrum, Ltd.,* 489 F.2d 535, 536 (2d Cir. 1973).

It is quite clear that securities lawyers are being sued with regularity. In this litigious society, corporate and securities counsel must advise with prudence (and should document his/her files). This is particularly true given securities counsel's obligations in the "post-Enron" world. This subject is addressed in Chapter 16.

---

§ 1.05 Internationalization of the Securities Markets

The internationalization of the world's securities markets continues at a rapid pace. As stated in a U.S. House of Representative Report (No. 101-240):

> The major forces driving this trend [toward internationalization] appear to be: rapid technological advances in communications and computer technology; the growing economic interdependence between the U.S. and its major trading partners; the increasing tendency of major investors, particularly mutual funds and pension funds, to diversify their investments on a global basis; and the growing inclination of U.S. and foreign-based firms to rely on foreign debt and equity markets to raise capital.
>
> An abundance of statistics confirms the internationalization trend. . . . Clearly, the participation of U.S. market professionals in foreign markets, and participation by foreigners in our own markets, has risen exponentially in recent years.
>
> The potential gains from globalization are enormous. The expanded opportunities for market participation mean a larger pool of investors, thus increased liquidity in the capital markets and expanding the ability of businesses to raise the necessary capital to be competitive in global markets.
>
> While internationalization carries obvious benefits, it also carries clear risks and challenges. Although the linkage of markets has proceeded rapidly, the harmonization of regulation, surveillance, and enforcement is progressing at a much slower pace. . . .

A number of scholars have reflected on the internationalization of the securities markets. See N. POSER, INTERNATIONAL SECURITIES REGULATION 8–9 (1991) ("Perhaps the most urgent need in the area of international securities regulation is for the establishment of financial responsibility standards for firms that operate in more than one country and for procedures to monitor and enforce these standards."); M. STEINBERG, F. GEVURTZ, & E. CHAFFEE, GLOBAL ISSUES IN SECURITIES LAW 1 (2013) (While "the world has transitioned to transnational securities markets, these markets remain fragmented."); M. STEINBERG, INTERNATIONAL SECURITIES LAW — A CONTEMPORARY AND COMPARATIVE ANALYSIS 2 (1999) ("Effective regulation in an expanding global marketplace poses concerns for participants and securities regulators."); Pinto, *The Internationalization of the Hostile Takeover Market: Its Implications for Choice of Law in Corporate and Securities Law*, 16 BROOKLYN J. INT'L L. 55

(1990) ("More recently, we are witnessing a greater internationalization of [the take-over] market with increasing cross-border acquisition activities, including the rise of international hostile takeovers."); Warren, *Global Harmonization of Securities Laws: The Achievement of the European Communities*, 31 HARVARD INT'L L.J. 185 (1990) ("In recent years . . . the pace of internationalization of securities markets has hastened dramatically, with the greatest surge occurring in just the last decade.").

———

§ 1.06 Selected Securities Law Research Sources[18]

There are a number of useful securities law research sources. These sources include:

Legislative History

Lexis Advance contains the Senate and House committee reports prepared in connection with the 1933 and 1934 Acts. Lexis Advance also offers Congressional Information Service (CIS) legislative history materials for some federal securities statutes.

Westlaw provides the Federal Securities (Legislative History database (Westlaw database identifier 'fsec-lh')), which contains the "legislative history of the federal securities statutes beginning with 1933. This history includes congressional committee reports as reprinted in U.S. Code Congressional and Administrative News beginning with 1948. From 1990 forward, FSEC-LH contains all securities-related congressional committee reports, including reports on bills that did not become law. Presidential signing statements, issued at the time the President signed a bill into law, are also available."

Other sources providing legislative history of the federal securities statutes include:

Corporate Fraud Responsibility: A Legislative History of the Sarbanes-Oxley Act of 2002 (William H. Manz ed. 2003).

Federal Bar Association, *Federal Securities Laws: Legislative History*, 1933–1982 (1983).

_____, *Federal Securities Laws: Legislative History*, 1983–1987 Supplement (1988).

_____, *Federal Securities Laws: Legislative History*, 1987–1990 Supplement (1991).

Government Securities Law: A Legislative History of the Government Securities Act of 1986, Pub. Law No. 99-571 (Bernard D. Reams, Jr. & Carol J. Gray eds. 1989).

Legislative History of the Securities Act of 1933 and Securities Exchange Act of 1934 (J.S. Ellenberger & Ellen P. Mahar eds. 1973).

———

18. This Section was prepared by Gregory Ivy, Esq., Director, Underwood Law Library, Southern Methodist University. I thank Mr. Ivy for his contribution to this Project as well as his expert assistance with respect to my scholarly pursuits for the past several years.

Securities Primary Law Sourcebook (A.A. Sommer, Jr. ed., 1996). Contains the legislative history of the Acts of 1933 and 1934, among many other things.

SEC Issuances

Categories of SEC documents available on the SEC website www.sec.gov are below. Many of these documents are also available on Lexis Advance, Westlaw, and in CCH's Federal Securities Law Reporter.

- Forms and Filings ('EDGAR')

The SEC's EDGAR (Electronic Data Gathering, Analysis, and Retrieval) system "performs automated collection, validation, indexing, acceptance, and forwarding of submissions by companies and others who are required by law to file forms with the U.S. Securities and Exchange Commission (SEC). Its primary purpose is to increase the efficiency and fairness of the securities market for the benefit of investors, corporations, and the economy by accelerating the receipt, acceptance, dissemination, and analysis of time-sensitive corporate information filed with the agency." EDGAR is accessible for free on the SEC's website. Commercial services such as Livedgar, 10-K Wizard, Lexis, and Westlaw provide the same information with value-adding enhancements.

- *Regulatory Actions*
  - Proposed Rules
  - Final Rules
  - Concept Releases
  - Interpretive Releases
  - Policy Statements
  - PCAOB Rulemaking
  - SRO Rulemaking and NMS Plans
  - Exchange Act Exemptive Applications
  - Exemptive Orders
  - Other Commission Orders and Notices
  - Public Petitions and Rulemaking
- *Staff Interpretations*
  - Staff Accounting Bulletins
  - Staff Legal Bulletins
  - Telephone Interpretations
  - Staff No-Action Letters, Interpretive and Exemptive Letters
- *News and Public Statements*
  - News Digest

- Press Releases
- Special Studies
- Speeches and Public Statements
- Testimony
- Investor Complaint Data
- *Litigation*
  - Litigation Releases
  - Administrative Proceedings
  - ALJ Initial Decisions & Orders
  - Reports of Investigations
  - Commission Opinions
  - Trading Suspensions
  - Investor Claims Funds
  - Briefs

Court Decisions

Litigation in the federal district courts involving federal securities laws generally arises when the SEC or investors file civil actions, or when the Department of Justice files criminal actions. The resulting court opinions, orders, and other documents may be published in federal court reports such as the Federal Supplement, Federal Reporter, and United States Reports, as well as Lexis Advance, Westlaw, court websites, CCH's Federal Securities Law Reporter, and securities law newsletters.

Secondary Sources

Services

Federal Securities Law Reporter (Commerce Clearing House (CCH)). This Reporter provides extensive treatment of the federal securities laws. It contains the text of statutes, proposed statutes, regulations, proposed regulations, annotations, court decisions, SEC releases, SEC staff no-action letters, SEC forms, and other SEC-issued pronouncements, as well as CCH editorial explanations.

Blue Sky Law Reporter (Commerce Clearing House (CCH)). This Reporter contains U.S. state (and territorial, e.g., Guam) laws, regulations, decisions, and pronouncements relating to securities at the state (and territorial) level.

Treatises and Books

BADER, W. REECE, SECURITIES ARBITRATION.

BAINBRIDGE, STEPHEN M., SECURITIES LAW: INSIDER TRADING.

BERSON, DAVID & BERSON, SUSAN, THE DODD-FRANK WALL STREET REFORM AND CONSUMER PROTECTION ACT: FROM LEGISLATION TO IMPLEMENTATION TO LITIGATION.

BIALKIN, KENNETH & GRANT, WILLIAM, SECURITIES UNDERWRITING.

BLOOMENTHAL, HAROLD S., & WOLFF, SAMUEL, GOING PUBLIC AND THE PUBLIC CORPORATION.

————, SECURITIES LAW HANDBOOK (annual).

————, SECURITIES AND FEDERAL CORPORATE LAW.

————, INTERNATIONAL CAPITAL MARKETS AND SECURITIES REGULATION.

————, EMERGING TRENDS IN SECURITIES LAW.

BORDEN, ARTHUR M. & YUNIS, JOEL A., GOING PRIVATE.

BOSTELMAN, JOHN T., BUCKHOLZ, ROBERT, & TREVINO, MARC, PUBLIC COMPANY DESKBOOK: SARBANES-OXLEY AND FEDERAL GOVERNANCE REQUIREMENTS.

BRANSON, DOUGLAS M., CORPORATE GOVERNANCE.

BRODSKY, DAVID M. & KRAMER, DANIEL J., FEDERAL SECURITIES LITIGATION: COMMENTARY AND FORMS.

BROMBERG, ALAN R., LOWENFELS, LEWIS D., & SULLIVAN, MICHAEL J., BROMBERG AND LOWENFELS ON SECURITIES FRAUD AND COMMODITIES FRAUD.

BROWN, GARY M., SODERQUIST ON THE SECURITIES LAWS.

BROWN, J. ROBERT, JR., REGULATION OF CORPORATE DISCLOSURE.

CANE, MARILYN BLUMBERG & SHUB, PATRICIA A., SECURITIES ARBITRATION: LAW AND PROCEDURE.

COHN, STUART R., SECURITIES COUNSELING FOR NEW AND DEVELOPING COMPANIES.

FANTO, JAMES A., DIRECTORS' AND OFFICERS' LIABILITY.

FLEISCHER, ARTHUR & SUSSMAN, ALEXANDER R., TAKEOVER DEFENSE.

FRANKEL, TAMAR, THE REGULATION OF MONEY MANAGERS.

————, SECURITIZATION: STRUCTURED FINANCING, FINANCIAL ASSETS POOLS, AND ASSET-BACKED SECURITIES.

FRIEDMAN, HOWARD M., PUBLICLY-HELD CORPORATIONS—A LAWYER'S GUIDE.

————, SECURITIES REGULATION IN CYBERSPACE.

GARNER, BRYAN A., SECURITIES DISCLOSURE IN PLAIN ENGLISH.

GLASER, DONALD, FITZGIBBON, SCOTT & WEISE, STEVEN, LEGAL OPINIONS.

GOLDWASSER, DAN L. & ARNOLD, M. THOMAS, ACCOUNTANTS' LIABILITY.

GOODMAN, AMY, & OLSON, JOHN F., A PRACTICAL GUIDE TO SEC PROXY AND COMPENSATION RULES.

HAFF, ROBERT J., ANALYSIS OF KEY SEC NO-ACTION LETTERS.

————, LIABILITY OF ATTORNEYS AND ACCOUNTANTS FOR SECURITIES TRANSACTIONS.

HAZEN, THOMAS LEE, TREATISE ON THE LAW OF SECURITIES REGULATION.

HICKS, J. WILLIAM, CIVIL LIABILITIES: ENFORCEMENT AND LITIGATION UNDER THE 1933 ACT.

_____, EXEMPTED TRANSACTIONS UNDER THE SECURITIES ACT OF 1933.

JACOBS, ARNOLD S., DISCLOSURE AND REMEDIES UNDER THE SECURITIES LAWS.

_____, MANUAL OF CORPORATE FORMS FOR SECURITIES PRACTICE.

_____, OPINION LETTERS IN SECURITIES MATTERS: TEXT, CLAUSES, LAW.

_____, SECTION 16 OF THE SECURITIES EXCHANGE ACT.

JANVEY, RALPH S., REGULATION OF THE SECURITIES AND COMMODITIES MARKETS.

JOHNSON, CHARLES J., MCLAUGHLIN, JOSEPH & HAUETER, ERIC S., CORPORATE FINANCE AND THE SECURITIES LAWS.

JOHNSON, PHILIP MCBRIDE & HAZEN, THOMAS LEE, COMMODITIES REGULATION.

KARMEL, ROBERTA S., REGULATION BY PROSECUTION — THE SECURITIES AND EXCHANGE COMMISSION VERSUS CORPORATE AMERICA.

KAUFMAN, MICHAEL J., SECURITIES LITIGATION: DAMAGES.

KIRSCH, CHARLES E., INVESTMENT ADVISER REGULATION.

LANGEVOORT, DONALD C., INSIDER TRADING: REGULATION, ENFORCEMENT, AND PREVENTION.

LAWRENCE, GARY, DUE DILIGENCE IN BUSINESS TRANSACTIONS.

LEDERMAN, SCOTT J., HEDGE FUND REGULATION.

LEE, RUBEN, WHAT IS AN EXCHANGE?: THE AUTOMATION, MANAGEMENT, AND REGULATION OF FINANCIAL MARKETS.

LEMKE, THOMAS P. ET AL., REGULATION OF INVESTMENT COMPANIES.

LIPTON, DAVID A., BROKER-DEALER REGULATION.

LIPTON, MARTIN & STEINBERGER, ERICA H., TAKEOVERS AND FREEZEOUTS.

LONG, JOSEPH C., KAUFMAN, MICHAEL J., & WUNDERLICH, JOHN M., BLUE SKY LAW.

LORNE, SIMON M., ACQUISITIONS AND MERGERS: NEGOTIATED AND CONTESTED TRANSACTIONS.

LOSS, LOUIS & SELIGMAN, JOEL, FUNDAMENTALS OF SECURITIES REGULATION.

LOSS, LOUIS, SELIGMAN, JOEL, & PARADES, TROY, SECURITIES REGULATION.

MAHONEY, COLLEEN P. ET AL., THE SEC ENFORCEMENT PROCESS: PRACTICE AND PROCEDURE IN HANDLING AN SEC INVESTIGATION AFTER SARBANES-OXLEY.

MAHONEY, PAUL G., WASTING A CRISIS — WHY SECURITIES REGULATION FAILS.

MATHESON, JOHN, PUBLICLY-TRADED COMPANIES — GOVERNANCE, OPERATION AND REGULATION.

PERINO, MICHAEL A., THE HELLHOUND OF WALL STREET: HOW FERDINAND PECORA'S INVESTIGATION OF THE GREAT CRASH FOREVER CHANGED AMERICAN FINANCE.

PERINO, MICHAEL A., SECURITIES LITIGATION AFTER THE REFORM ACT.

PICKHOLZ, MARVIN G., SECURITIES CRIMES.

POSER, NORMAN S. & FANTO, JAMES A., BROKER-DEALER LAW AND REGULATION.

POSER, NORMAN S., INTERNATIONAL SECURITIES REGULATION.

RICHTER, SCOTT E., SECURITIES LITIGATION: FORMS AND ANALYSIS.

ROBBINS, DAVID E., SECURITIES ARBITRATION PROCEDURE MANUAL.

ROMEO, PETER J. & DYE, ALAN L., SECTION 16 OF THE SECURITIES EXCHANGE ACT OF 1934: TREATISE AND REPORTING GUIDE.

RUSSO, THOMAS A., REGULATION OF THE COMMODITIES FUTURES AND OPTIONS MARKETS.

SARGENT, MARK A., & HONABACH, DENNIS R., PROXY RULES HANDBOOK.

SECURITIES LAW TECHNIQUES: TRANSACTIONS, LITIGATION (A.A. SOMMER, JR. ED.).

SELIGMAN, JOEL, THE SEC AND THE FUTURE OF FINANCE.

_____, THE TRANSFORMATION OF WALL STREET: A HISTORY OF THE SECURITIES AND EXCHANGE COMMISSION AND MODERN CORPORATE FINANCE.

SODERQUIST, LARRY D., UNDERSTANDING THE SECURITIES LAWS.

STEINBERG, MARC I., ATTORNEY LIABILITY AFTER SARBANES-OXLEY.

_____, INTERNATIONAL SECURITIES LAW: A CONTEMPORARY AND COMPARATIVE ANALYSIS.

_____, SECURITIES REGULATION: LIABILITIES AND REMEDIES.

_____, UNDERSTANDING SECURITIES LAW.

_____, COUTURE, WENDY GERWICK, KAUFMAN, MICHAEL J., & MORRISSEY, DANIEL J., SECURITIES LITIGATION — LAW, POLICY, AND PRACTICE.

_____ & FERRARA, RALPH C., SECURITIES PRACTICE: FEDERAL AND STATE ENFORCEMENT.

_____, GEVURTZ, FRANKLIN A., & CHAFFEE, ERIC C., GLOBAL ISSUES IN SECURITIES LAW.

_____ & WANG, WILLIAM, INSIDER TRADING.

THOMAS, RANDALL S. & DIXON, CATHERINE T., ARANOW & EINHORN ON PROXY CONTESTS FOR CORPORATE CONTROL.

TOKER, DONALD L. & HUDSON, ROBERT A., INITIAL PUBLIC OFFERINGS.

VAN ALSTYNE, DEBRA ET AL., PERIODIC REPORTING UNDER THE FEDERAL SECURITIES LAW.

WATERS, MICHAEL D., PROXY REGULATION.

Journals, Newsletters, and Other Periodicals

Andrews Securities Litigation and Regulation Reporter (Andrews Publications). This Reporter contains "selected court documents, including petitions, complaints, briefs, motions, trial court memoranda and other documents from state and federal courts." Available on Westlaw.

Insights: The Corporate and Securities Law Advisor (Aspen Publishers). Available on Lexis Advance.

Mealey's Emerging Securities Litigation (Mealey Publications). Covers "evolving and dynamic areas of securities litigation." Available on Lexis Advance.

The Review of Securities & Commodities Regulation (Thomson/West). Available on Westlaw.

SEC News Digest (Securities and Exchange Commission). This publication "provides daily information on recent Commission actions, including enforcement proceedings, rule filings, policy statements, and upcoming Commission meetings." Available on the SEC website at http://www.sec.gov/news/digest.shtml and on Lexis.

Securities Class Action Alert (Investor's Research Bureau).

Securities Regulation and Law Report (Bureau of National Affairs) (BNA). Available on Westlaw.

Securities Law Review (Thomson Reuters). Available on Westlaw.

Securities Regulation Law Journal (Thomson Reuters). Available on Westlaw.

Periodicals Index: Legal Resource Index (1980-present). This is a nearly comprehensive tool for locating legal periodical articles dating from 1980 to the present. The *Legal Research Index* is available on Lexis Advance and Westlaw and currently indexes more than 850 English-language periodicals.

Continuing Legal Education (CLE) Publications

ALI-ABA Course of Studies Materials. Available on Lexis Advance and Westlaw.

Practising Law Institute, *Commercial Law and Practice* course handbook series. Available on Lexis Advance and Westlaw.

Forms

Regulatory Forms. The SEC's regulatory forms are available from many sources, among the best of which are the SEC's website and CCH's *Federal Securities Law Reporter.* Numerous treatises and CLE publications provide instructions and examples for completing these forms, such as: Weinstein, et al., *SEC Compliance: Financial Reporting and Forms.*

Andrews Securities Litigation and Regulation Reporter. This Reporter contains "selected court documents, including petitions, complaints, briefs, motions, trial court memoranda and other documents from state and federal courts." Available on Westlaw.

Brodsky, David M. & Kramer, Daniel J., Federal Securities Litigation: Commentary and Forms.

Richter, Scott E., Securities Litigation: Forms and Analysis.

Updating Research

KeyCite. Covers SEC decisions and releases, as well as statutes, cases, law reviews, etc. Available on Westlaw.

Shepard's Citations. Coverage includes SEC decisions, reports, and releases, as well as statutes, cases, law reviews, etc. Available on Lexis Advance.

Chapter 2

Definition of a "Security"

§ 2.01 Introduction

The term "security" not only covers instruments commonly known in the investment world as securities, such as stocks and bonds, but may also include novel and unique instruments. Such instruments have included, for example, interests in "pyramid" sales schemes, chinchillas, and whiskey warehouse receipts. Ordinarily, these rather novel types of instruments come within the securities laws because they are held to be "investment contracts."

The term "security" is defined in § 2(a)(1) of the Securities Act of 1933 and § 3(a)(10) of the Securities Exchange Act of 1934. Although the language of these statutes differs somewhat, they have been construed in an identical manner. Fairly broad at first glance, the instruments set forth in the statutory definitions are only the starting point. This is due to the phrase *"unless the context otherwise requires,"* which precedes each of the provisions. This phrase, as will be seen, focuses on the economic reality of the transaction, and hence, is very significant.

Failure on counsel's part to recognize that a "security" is present can be disastrous. As will be seen in the following chapters, absent an exemption, no sale of a security can take place unless a registration statement is in effect. Because the requirements for meeting a particular exemption may be complex, failure on counsel's part to perceive that his/her client's "deal" involves a security often means that the securities are being sold in violation of the securities laws. Under such circumstances, the Securities and Exchange Commission (SEC), state securities commissioner(s), and private parties may bring suit. Even criminal liability, depending on the circumstances, may be imposed. Hence, many deals have been scuttled, parties held liable, and lawyers sued for failure on counsel's part to recognize that a "security" was present. This point is brought home by the following case.

Wartzman v. Hightower Productions, Ltd.

Maryland Court of Special Appeals

53 Md. App. 656, 456 A.2d 82 (1983)

James S. Getty, Judge.

Woody Hightower did not succeed in breaking the Guinness World Record for flagpole sitting; his failure to accomplish this seemingly nebulous feat, however, did generate protracted litigation. . . .

Hightower Productions Ltd. (Hightower) . . . came into being in 1974 as a promotional venture conceived by Ira Adler, Frank Billitz and J. Daniel Quinn. The principals intended to employ a singer-entertainer who would live in a specially constructed mobile flagpole perch from April 1, 1975, until New Year's Eve at which time he would descend in Times Square in New York before a nationwide television audience having established a new world record for flagpole sitting.

The young man selected to perform this feat was to be known as "Woody Hightower". The venture was to be publicized by radio and television exposure, by adopting a theme song and by having the uncrowned champion make appearances from his perch throughout the country at concerts, state fairs and shopping centers.

In November, 1974, the three principals approached Michael Kaminkow of the law firm of Wartzman, Rombro, Rudd and Omansky, P.A., for the specific purpose of incorporating their venture. Mr. Kaminkow, a trial attorney, referred them to his partner, Paul Wartzman.

The three principals met with Mr. Wartzman at his home and reviewed the promotional scheme with him. They indicated that they needed to sell stock to the public in order to raise the $250,000 necessary to finance the project. Shortly thereafter, the law firm prepared and filed the articles of incorporation and Hightower Productions Ltd. came into existence on November 6, 1974. The Articles of Incorporation authorized the issuance of one million shares of stock at the par value of 10 cents per share, or a total of $100,000.00.

Following incorporation, the three principals began developing the project. With an initial investment of $20,000, they opened a corporate account at Maryland National Bank and an office in the Pikesville Plaza Building. Then began the search for "Woody Hightower." After numerous interviews, twenty-three year old John Jordan emerged as "Woody Hightower".

After selecting the flagpole tenant, the corporation then sought a company to construct the premises to house him. This consisted of a seven foot wide perch that was to include a bed, toilet, water, refrigerator and heat. The accommodations were atop an hydraulic lift system mounted upon a flatbed tractor trailer.

. . . .

Hightower employed two public relations specialists to coordinate press and public relations efforts and to obtain major corporate backers. "Woody" received a proclamation from the Mayor and City Council of Baltimore and after a press breakfast at the Hilton Hotel on "All Fools Day" ascended to his home in the sky.

Within ten days, Hightower obtained a live appearance for "Woody" on the Mike Douglas Show, and a commitment for an appearance on the Wonderama television program. The principals anticipated a "snow-balling" effect from commercial enterprises as the project progressed with no substantial monetary commitments for approximately six months.

Hightower raised $43,000.00 by selling stock in the corporation. Within two weeks of "Woody's" ascension, another stockholders' meeting was scheduled, because the corporation was low on funds. At that time, Mr. Wartzman informed the principals that no further stock could be sold, because the corporation was "structured wrong", and it would be necessary to obtain the services of a securities attorney to correct the problem. Mr. Wartzman had acquired this information in a casual conversation with a friend who recommended that the corporation should consult with a securities specialist.

The problem was that the law firm had failed to prepare an offering memorandum and failed to assure that the corporation had made the required disclosures to prospective investors in accordance with the provisions of the Maryland Securities Act. . . . Mr. Wartzman advised Hightower that the cost of the specialist would be between $10,000.00 and $15,000.00. Hightower asked the firm to pay for the required services and the request was rejected.

Hightower then employed substitute counsel and scheduled a shareholders' meeting on April 28, 1975. At that meeting, the stockholders were advised that Hightower was not in compliance with the securities laws; that $43,000.00, the amount investors had paid for issued stock, had to be . . . placed in escrow; that the fee of a securities specialist would be $10,000.00 to $15,000.00 and that the additional work would require between six and eight weeks. In the interim, additional stock could not be sold, nor could "Woody" be exhibited across state lines. Faced with these problems, the shareholders decided to discontinue the entire project.

On October 8, 1975, Hightower filed suit [against the law firm] alleging breach of contract and negligence. . . .

The jury returned a verdict in favor of Hightower in the amount of $170,508.43. . . .

In conclusion, the final comment of Judge Lowe is equally apposite here.

> The unfortunate oversight on which this case was based was a costly one, but it was made by one who was hired precisely for the purpose of averting the consequent losses. It is he, and his firm, who must bear them.

Judgment affirmed.

Problem A

Madison, the sole proprietor of Take It Easy Restaurant in Winslow, Arizona, decides that she would like her business to become another "McDonald's" (but would settle for "Wendy's"). She realizes, however, that this dream will take some time. Her first step is to seek additional capital. She approaches three residents of Winslow—Lewis, Stiles, and Walker—and enters into an agreement with them. The written limited partnership agreement for the duly formed limited partnership provides in part as follows: In return for an investment into the business of $75,000 each by Lewis, Stiles, and Walker, each will become a 10 percent owner of the business and each will receive 10 percent of the restaurant's net profits every six months. The daily management of the business is to be left to Madison and all ordinary decisions are to be hers "so long as reasonably made," but Lewis, Stiles, and Walker each have the right to "advise" her on any matter related to the business and each have "veto" power with respect to certain extraordinary matters. Is a security present?

Problem B

Doolittle, a solar engineer, has invented a heating system that he believes is more economical and efficient than current systems. He needs capital, however, to market the system. Doolittle contacts his good friend Harry Biddle, who has keen financial acumen, for advice. Biddle suggests that Doolittle form a general partnership with Biddle and his absent-minded Uncle Frank who has had no previous business experience. In return for Doolittle's product and his continued work to perfect and market it, Biddle and Uncle Frank (who are "clueless" about solar heating systems) will each contribute $125,000. All parties agree. Is a security present?

Problem C

As a second-year associate at a law firm that specializes in business litigation, you are asked by a partner to do some preliminary research regarding whether the firm should represent the following potential clients who contend that they have been defrauded:

(a) A purchaser of 4,000 shares of stock in a privately held corporation, which represents 40 percent of the stock issued and outstanding. Two of the other shareholders own 2,000 shares (20%) each and the remaining two stockholders own 1,000 shares (10%) each.

(b) A franchisee of an "Augie's" fast food franchise who put up $150,000 for the right to the franchise. All ordering of supplies, menu items, and hours of operation are under the direction of the franchisor.

(c) The purchaser of a condominium unit in a newly built vacation resort complex where the unit is offered for rent 10 months of the year by a central rental pool operator who is not affiliated with, but who is recommended by the promoter.

(d) The purchaser of a one percent interest in a limited liability company (LLC) where the LLC's operating agreement vests managerial authority in the LLC's members.

(e) A federally insured bank that received a promissory note from the recipient of a loan, a privately held company. The note is to mature 11 months after execution and is secured by a pledge of the recipient's customer notes receivable. The borrower is to pay principal and interest on the amount outstanding and intends to use the loan for the company's plant expansion and product diversification.

(f) An employee of a large industrial enterprise who has taken part in a voluntary, contributory pension plan.

(g) A holder of two certificates of deposit, one issued by Pittsgold State Bank of Pittsgold, Kentucky, and the other by a bank located in the Grand Cayman Islands.

(h) A limited partnership comprised of 25 limited partners and one general partner where the limited partners, pursuant to the terms of the limited partnership agreement, have the right to advise the general partner, to vote on certain matters (such as any change in the partnership's line of business), and to remove the general partner upon the approval of two-thirds of the limited partners.

---

§ 2.02 The Meaning of "Investment Contract"

The Supreme Court has construed the definition of a "security" several times in an attempt to clarify the statutory definitions contained in the securities acts. In its decisions, the Court has rejected a literal interpretation of the statutes, adopting instead a more flexible view that looks to the economic reality of the particular plan or scheme addressed. Although not all of the cases are covered here,[1] the more important and timely ones are. In addition, the following materials include discussion of major state and lower federal court decisions in order to highlight the key principles and issues in this area.

Securities and Exchange Commission v. W.J. Howey Co.

United States Supreme Court

328 U.S. 293, 66 S. Ct. 1100, 90 L. Ed. 1244 (1946)

MR. JUSTICE MURPHY delivered the opinion of the Court.

This case involves the application of § 2(1) [now § 2(a)(1)] of the Securities Act of 1933 to an offering of units of a citrus grove development coupled with a contract for cultivating, marketing and remitting the net proceeds to the investor.

The Securities and Exchange Commission instituted this action to restrain the respondents from using the mails and instrumentalities of interstate commerce in

---

1. U.S. Supreme Court decisions not contained in this chapter include: *SEC v. C. M. Joiner Leasing Corp*, 320 U.S. 344 (1943) (holding sale of assignments of oil leasehold subdivisions by parcels constituted sale of securities); *SEC v. Variable Annuity Life Insurance Co. of America*, 359 U.S. 65 (1959) (holding variable annuity contracts to be securities); *SEC v. United Benefit Life Insurance Co.*, 387 U.S. 202 (1967) (holding that a "flexible fund annuity contract" was a security); *Tcherepnin v. Knight*, 389 U.S. 332 (1967) (holding withdrawable capital shares in a savings and loan association to be securities); *Gould v. Ruefenacht*, 471 U.S. 701 (1985) (companion case to *Landreth*, 471 U.S. 681 (1985), holding that common stock, having attributes characteristic of common stock, is a security).

the offer and sale of unregistered and non-exempt securities in violation of § 5(a) of the Act. . . .

Most of the facts are stipulated. The respondents, W. J. Howey Company and Howey-in-the-Hills Service, Inc., are Florida corporations under direct common control and management. The Howey Company owns large tracts of citrus acreage in Lake County, Florida. During the past several years it has planted about 500 acres annually, keeping half of the groves itself and offering the other half to the public "to help us finance additional development." Howey-in-the-Hills Service, Inc. is a service company engaged in cultivating and developing many of these groves, including the harvesting and marketing of the crops.

Each prospective customer is offered both a land sales contract and a service contract, after having been told that it is not feasible to invest in a grove unless service arrangements are made. While the purchaser is free to make arrangements with other service companies, the superiority of Howey-in-the-Hills Service, Inc. is stressed. Indeed, 85% of the acreage sold during the 3-year period ending May 31, 1943, was covered by service contracts with Howey-in-the-Hills Service, Inc.

The land sales contract with the Howey Company provides for a uniform purchase price per acre or fraction thereof, varying in amount only in accordance with the number of years the particular plot has been planted with citrus trees. Upon full payment of the purchase price the land is conveyed to the purchaser by warranty deed. Purchases are usually made in narrow strips of land arranged so that an acre consists of a row of 48 trees. During the period between February 1, 1941, and May 31, 1943, 31 of the 42 persons making purchases bought less than 5 acres each. The average holding of these 31 persons was 1.33 acres and sales of as little as 0.65, 0.7 and 0.73 of an acre were made. These tracts are not separately fenced and the sole indication of ownership is found in small land marks intelligible only through a plat book record.

The service contract, generally of a 10-year duration without option of cancellation, gives Howey-in-the-Hills Service, Inc. a leasehold interest and "full and complete" possession of the acreage. For a specified fee plus the cost of labor and materials, the company is given full discretion and authority over the cultivation of the groves and the harvest and marketing of the crops. The company is well established in the citrus business and maintains a large force of skilled personnel and a great deal of equipment, including 75 tractors, sprayer wagons, fertilizer trucks and the like. Without the consent of the company, the land owner or purchaser has no right of entry to market the crop; thus there is ordinarily no right to specific fruit. The company is accountable only for an allocation of the net profits based upon a check made at the time of picking. All the produce is pooled by the respondent companies, which do business under their own names.

The purchasers for the most part are non-residents of Florida. They are predominantly business and professional people who lack the knowledge, skill and equipment necessary for the care and cultivation of citrus trees. They are attracted by the expectation of substantial profits. . . . Many of these purchasers are patrons of a resort hotel owned and operated by the Howey Company in a scenic section adjacent to the groves. The hotel's advertising mentions the fine groves in the vicinity and the attention of the patrons is drawn to the groves as they are being escorted about the surrounding countryside. They are told that the groves are for sale; if they indicate an interest in the matter, they are then given a sales talk.

It is admitted that the mails and instrumentalities of interstate commerce are used in the sale of the land and service contracts and that no registration statement . . . has ever been filed with the Commission in accordance with the Securities Act of 1933 and the rules and regulations thereunder.[2]

Section 2(1) [now Section 2(a)(1)] of the Act defines the term "security" to include the commonly known documents traded for speculation or investment. This definition also includes "securities" of a more variable character, designated by such descriptive terms as "certificate of interest or participation in any profit-sharing agreement," "investment contract" and "in general, any interest or instrument commonly known as a 'security.'" The legal issue in this case turns upon a determination of whether, under the circumstances, the land sales contract, the warranty deed and the service contract together constitute an "investment contract" within the meaning of § 2(1). . . .

The term "investment contract" is undefined by the Securities Act or by relevant legislative reports. But the term was common in many state "blue sky" laws in existence prior to the adoption of the federal statute and, although the term was also undefined by the state laws, it had been broadly construed by state courts so as to afford the investing public a full measure of protection. Form was disregarded for substance and emphasis was placed upon economic reality. An investment contract thus came to mean a contract or scheme for "the placing of capital or laying out of money in a way intended to secure income or profit from its employment." *State v. Gopher Tire & Rubber Co.*, 146 Minn. 52, 56, 177 N.W. 937, 938. This definition was uniformly applied by state courts to a variety of situations where individuals were led to invest money in a common enterprise with the expectation that they would earn a profit solely through the efforts of the promoter or of someone other than themselves.

By including an investment contract within the scope of § 2(1) of the Securities Act, Congress was using a term the meaning of which had been crystallized by this prior judicial interpretation. It is therefore reasonable to attach that meaning to the term as used by Congress, especially since such a definition is consistent with the statutory aims. In other words, an investment contract for purposes of the Securities

---

2. [To invoke jurisdiction under the federal securities laws, there must be some use of the mails or of the instrumentalities of interstate commerce. This requirement is normally met without difficulty. Use of the telephone in connection with the subject action, for example, is sufficient. — ed.]

Act means a contract, transaction or scheme whereby a person invests his money in a common enterprise and is led to expect profits solely from the efforts of the promoter or a third party, it being immaterial whether the shares in the enterprise are evidenced by formal certificates or by nominal interests in the physical assets employed in the enterprise. [Such a definition] permits the fulfillment of the statutory purpose of compelling full and fair disclosure relative to the issuance of "the many types of instruments that in our commercial world fall within the ordinary concept of a security." H. Rep. No. 85, 73d Cong., 1st Sess., p. 11. It embodies a flexible rather than a static principle, one that is capable of adaptation to meet the countless and variable schemes devised by those who seek the use of the money of others on the promise of profits.

The transactions in this case clearly involve investment contracts as so defined.

. . . .

This conclusion is unaffected by the fact that some purchasers choose not to accept the full offer of an investment contract by declining to enter into a service contract with the respondents. The Securities Act prohibits the offer as well as the sale of unregistered, non-exempt securities. Hence it is enough that the respondents merely offer the essential ingredients of an investment contract.

We reject the suggestion of the Circuit Court of Appeals that an investment contract is necessarily missing where the enterprise is not speculative or promotional in character and where the tangible interest which is sold has intrinsic value independent of the success of the enterprise as a whole. The test is whether the scheme involves an investment of money in a common enterprise with profits to come solely from the efforts of others. If that test be satisfied, it is immaterial whether the enterprise is speculative or non-speculative or whether there is a sale of property with or without intrinsic value. The statutory policy of affording broad protection to investors is not to be thwarted by unrealistic and irrelevant formulae.

Reversed.

Note

The factual setting presented to the Supreme Court in *Howey* has been repeated numerous times. Courts repeatedly look beyond a strict statutory construction and examine the economic reality of the transaction to determine whether a property interest combined with some form of service contract constitutes a security (termed the *"aggregation approach"*). The *Howey* analysis applied by the courts in these cases can usually be broken down into three issues:

First: Are the investors' interests interwoven with those of other investors and/or the promoter for a return on their investment ("common enterprise")?

Second: Is the interest bought in order to obtain a financial return or for other reasons ("expectation of profits")?

And third: Does the investor participate in the venture to such a degree that he/ she is not dependent "solely on the efforts of others" for profits?[3]

There are many appellate and district court decisions dealing with the *Howey* issues. Although decided several decades ago, the following case is illustrative of the seemingly bizarre schemes that have been held to be "investment contracts," and, hence, "securities."

Continental Marketing Corp. v. Securities and Exchange Commission

United States Court of Appeals

387 F.2d 466 (10th Cir. 1967)

David T. Lewis, Circuit Judge.

Continental Marketing Corporation appeals from an order entered by the District Court for the District of Utah preliminarily enjoining the company from offering for sale and selling investment contracts for the "sale, care, management, replacement or resale of live beaver for breeding purposes," in violation of the anti-fraud provisions contained in § 17(a) of the Securities Act of 1933, and § 10(b) of the Securities Exchange Act of 1934, and Rule 10b-5 thereunder. . . . Continental's appeal questions only the finding that the company was engaged in the offer and sale of securities within the meaning of applicable federal laws.

Appellant was organized in 1965 as a Colorado corporation and thereafter represented itself as an integral part of the organized domestic beaver industry. Its sales literature, couched in such glowing terms as "fabulous possibilities" and the "road to riches," presented to the prospective purchaser a history of the development of the beaver industry with specific reference to the activities, both past and present, of co-defendants and illustrated for the benefit of the purchaser a charted explanation of what was available in service after purchase of the beaver from appellant. The chart lines a sale of beaver from appellant (or either of two other defendant sales companies) to the owner purchaser. Thereafter, the owner may care for his own animals with each pair of beaver requiring a private swimming pool, patio, den and nesting box together with the services of a veterinarian, dental technician, breeding specialist, etc. or the owner may choose to place his animals (at a cost of $6 per month per animal) with a professional rancher who is a member of the defendant North American Beaver Association which in turn has available the technical assistance of two ranchers' service companies, also named defendants. All purchasers of beaver were

---

3. *See generally* Arnold, *The Definition of a Security Under the Federal Securities Law Revisited*, 34 Clev. St. L. Rev. 249 (1986); Franco, *The Investment Company Act's Definition of "Security" and the Myth of Equivalence*, 7 Stan. J. Law Bus. & Fin. 1 (2001); Lowenfels & Bromberg, *What Is a Security Under the Federal Securities Laws?*, 56 Alb. L. Rev. 473 (1993); McGinty, *What Is a Security?*, 1993 Wis. L. Rev. 1033.

encouraged not to take possession of the animals and although Continental made over two hundred sales in sixteen states, grossing over a million dollars, all who purchased from appellant elected not to take possession of their beavers and each contracted with one of the ranchers as suggested by appellant.

. . . .

In addition to the more commonly known securities, § 2(1) [now § 2(a)(1)] of the 1933 Act defines a security to include

. . . any . . . certificate of interest or participation in any profit-sharing agreement . . . *investment contract*, . . . or, in general, any interest or instrument commonly known as a 'security,'

. . . .

The appellant points out that in *Howey* both the sales contract of a unit of a citrus grove and the contract for the care and management of the same were executed by the same promoter. We are urged, therefore, to hold that

The judicial definition of the term "investment contract" requires the investment in a common enterprise in which the investor is led to expect profits solely from the efforts of the seller or a third person *owned or controlled by the seller.*

We do not think the element of ownership or control [by the promoter over the third person] is essential. The better approach and the one which the Supreme Court in *Howey* noted was being employed by the state courts is to disregard form for substance and place emphasis on economic reality. The more critical factor is the nature of the investor's participation in the enterprise. If it is one of providing capital with the hopes of a favorable return, then it begins to take on the appearance of an investment contract notwithstanding the fact that there may be more than one party or other than a principal party and his agent on the other end of the transaction or transactions. . . .

The expressed and cited interpretation of the Securities Act amply covers the activities of appellant in the case at bar. Continental's appearance to the public, by design, was that of a representative of the domestic beaver industry, the growth and development of which was necessary to and would bring profit to investors. Purchasers were encouraged to leave their beavers at the ranches where they were located at the time of sale and where they would be "expertly housed, fed and otherwise cared for." They were advised that all they needed to do was buy the beavers, pay ranching fees and reap "geometric profits" as the beavers reproduced and the offspring sold. . . .

Investment by members of the public was a profit-making venture in a common enterprise, the success of which was inescapably tied to the efforts of the ranchers and the other defendants and not to the efforts of the investors. . . . If the structure collapsed, then the purchasers would have little more than a bad investment. Certainly the beavers as mere animals and not as part of the enterprise did not have value consistent with the price many of the purchasers paid. The economic inducement was the faith or hope in the success of the enterprise—the domestic beaver industry— as a whole, and not the value of the animals alone.

In this setting we hold that the transactions in question involved the sale of investment contracts and therefore "securities" within the meaning of the applicable acts and apply, with approval of the High Court, "a flexible rather than a static principle, one that is capable of adaptation to meet the countless and variable schemes devised by those who seek the use of the money of others on the promise of profits."

————————

The Supreme Court's most recent decision on the definition of "security" follows.

Securities and Exchange Commission v. Edwards

United States Supreme Court

540 U.S. 389, 124 S. Ct. 892, 157 L. Ed. 2d 813 (2004)

Justice O'Connor delivered the opinion of the Court.

"Opportunity doesn't always knock . . . sometimes it rings." And sometimes it hangs up. So it did for the 10,000 people who invested a total of $300 million in the payphone sale-and-leaseback arrangements touted by respondent under that slogan. The Securities and Exchange Commission (SEC) argues that the arrangements were investment contracts, and thus were subject to regulation under the federal securities laws. In this case, we must decide whether a moneymaking scheme is excluded from the term "investment contract" simply because the scheme offered a contractual entitlement to a fixed, rather than a variable return.

I

Respondent Charles Edwards was the chairman, chief executive officer, and sole shareholder of ETS, Payphones, Inc. (ETS). ETS, acting partly through a subsidiary also controlled by respondent, sold payphones to the public via independent distributors. The payphones were offered packaged with a site lease, a 5-year leaseback and management agreement, and a buyback agreement. All but a tiny fraction of purchasers chose this package, although other management options were offered. The purchase price for the payphone packages was approximately $7,000. Under the leaseback and management agreement, purchasers received $82 per month, a 14% annual return. Purchasers were not involved in the day-to-day operation of the payphones they owned. ETS selected the site for the phone, installed the equipment, arranged for connection and long-distance service, collected coin revenues, and maintained and repaired the phones. Under the buyback agreement, ETS promised to refund the full purchase price of the package at the end of the lease or within 180 days of a purchaser's request.

In its marketing materials and on its website, ETS trumpeted the "incomparable pay phone" as "an exciting business opportunity," in which recent deregulation had "opened the door for profits for individual pay phone owners and operators."

According to ETS, "very few business opportunities can offer the potential for ongoing revenue generation that is available in today's pay telephone industry."

The payphones did not generate enough revenue for ETS to make the payments required by the leaseback agreements, so the company depended on funds from new investors to meet its obligations. [Generally, a "ponzi scheme" uses funds raised from new investors to satisfy the obligations owed to other investors whose investments predated the funds contributed by the newer investors.] In September 2000, ETS filed for bankruptcy protection. The SEC brought this civil enforcement action the same month. It alleged that respondent and ETS had violated the registration requirements of §§ 5(a) and (c) of the Securities Act of 1933, the antifraud provisions of both § 17(a) of the Securities Act of 1933, and § 10(b) of the Securities Exchange Act of 1934 and Rule 10b-5 thereunder. The District Court concluded that the payphone sale-and-leaseback arrangement was an investment contract within the meaning of, and therefore subject to, the federal securities laws. *SEC v. ETS Payphones, Inc.,* 123 F. Supp. 2d 1349 (ND Ga. 2000). The Court of Appeals reversed. 300 F.3d 1281 (CA11 2002) *(per curiam).* It held that respondent's scheme was not an investment contract, on two grounds. First, it read this Court's opinions to require that an investment contract offer either capital appreciation or a participation in the earnings of the enterprise, and thus to exclude schemes, such as respondent's, offering a fixed rate of return. Second, it held that our opinions' requirement that the return on the investment be "derived solely from the efforts of others" was not satisfied when the purchasers had a contractual entitlement to the return. We conclude that it erred on both grounds.

II

"Congress' purpose in enacting the securities laws was to regulate *investments,* in whatever form they are made and by whatever name they are called." To that end, it enacted a broad definition of "security," sufficient "to encompass virtually any instrument that might be sold as an investment." Section 2(a)(1) of the 1933 Act and § 3(a)(10) of the 1934 Act, in slightly different formulations which we have treated as essentially identical in meaning, define "security" to include "any note, stock, treasury stock, security future, bond, debenture, . . . investment contract, . . . [or any] instrument commonly known as a 'security'." "Investment contract" is not itself defined.

The test for whether a particular scheme is an investment contract was established in our decision in *SEC v. W. J. Howey Co.* We look to "whether the scheme involves an investment of money in a common enterprise with profits to come solely from the efforts of others." This definition "embodies a flexible rather than a static principle, one that is capable of adaptation to meet the countless and variable schemes devised by those who seek the use of the money of others on the promise of profits."

In reaching that result, we first observed that when Congress included "investment contract" in the definition of security, it "was using a term the meaning of which had been crystallized" by the state courts' interpretation of their "blue sky" laws. The state courts had defined an investment contract as "a contract or scheme for 'the placing of capital or laying out of money in a way intended to secure income or profit from its employment,'" and had "uniformly applied" that definition to "a variety of situations where individuals were led to invest money in a common enterprise with the expectation that they would earn a profit solely through the efforts of the promoter or [a third party]." Thus, when we held that "profits" must "come solely from the efforts of others," we were speaking of the profits that investors seek on their investment. . . . We used "profits" in the sense of income or return, to include, for example, dividends, other periodic payments, or the increased value of the investment.

There is no reason to distinguish between promises of fixed returns and promises of variable returns for purposes of the test, so understood. In both cases, the investing public is attracted by representations of investment income, as purchasers were in this case by ETS' invitation to "'watch the profits add up.'" Moreover, investments pitched as low-risk (such as those offering a "guaranteed" fixed return) are particularly attractive to individuals more vulnerable to investment fraud, including older and less sophisticated investors. Under the reading respondent advances, unscrupulous marketers of investments could evade the securities laws by picking a rate of return to promise. We will not read into the securities laws a limitation not compelled by the language that would so undermine the laws' purposes.

Respondent protests that including investment schemes promising a fixed return among investment contracts conflicts with our precedent. We disagree. No distinction between fixed and variable returns was drawn in the blue sky law cases that the *Howey* Court used in formulating the test. . . . Indeed, two of those cases involved an investment contract in which a fixed return was promised. *People v. White*, 124 Cal. App. 548, 550–551, 12 P.2d 1078, 1079 (1932) (agreement between defendant and investors stated that investor would give defendant $5,000 and would receive $7,000 from defendant one year later); *Stevens v. Liberty Packing Corp.*, 111 N. J. Eq. 61, 62–63, 161 A. 193, 193–194 (1932) ("ironclad contract" offered by defendant to investors entitled investors to $56 per year for 10 years on initial investment of $175, ostensibly in sale-and-leaseback of breeding rabbits).

None of our post-*Howey* decisions is to the contrary. In *United Housing Foundation, Inc. v. Forman*, we considered whether "shares" in a nonprofit housing cooperative were investment contracts under the securities laws. We identified the "touchstone" of an investment contract as "the presence of an investment in a common venture premised on a reasonable expectation of profits to be derived from the entrepreneurial or managerial efforts of others," and then laid out two examples of investor interests that we had previously found to be "profits." Those were "capital appreciation resulting from the use of investors' funds" and "participation in earnings resulting from the use of investors' funds." We contrasted those examples, in which "the investor is 'attracted solely by the prospects of a return'" on the investment, with housing cooperative shares, regarding which the purchaser "is motivated by a desire to use or consume the item purchased." Thus, *Forman* supports the commonsense understanding of "profits" in the *Howey* test as simply "financial returns on . . . investments."

Concededly, *Forman*'s illustrative description of prior decisions on "profits" appears to have been mistaken for an exclusive list in a case considering the scope of a different term in the definition of a security, "note." See *Reves*, 494 U.S. at 68 n. 4[4] . . . But that was a misreading of *Forman*, and we will not bind ourselves unnecessarily to passing dictum that would frustrate Congress' intent to regulate all of the "countless and variable schemes devised by those who seek the use of the money of others on the promise of profits."

Given that respondent's position is supported neither by the purposes of the securities laws nor by our precedents, it is no surprise that the SEC has consistently taken the opposite position, and maintained that a promise of a fixed return does not preclude a scheme from being an investment contract. It has done so in formal adjudications and in enforcement actions. . . .

The Eleventh Circuit's perfunctory alternative holding, that respondent's scheme falls outside the definition because purchasers had a contractual entitlement to a return, is incorrect and inconsistent with our precedent. We are considering investment contracts. The fact that investors have bargained for a return on their investment does not mean that the return is not also expected to come solely from the efforts of others. Any other conclusion would conflict with our holding that an investment contract was offered in *Howey* itself. 328 U.S. at 295–296 (service contract entitled investors to allocation of net profits).

We hold that an investment scheme promising a fixed rate of return can be an "investment contract" and thus a "security" subject to the federal securities laws. The judgment of the United States Court of Appeals for the Eleventh Circuit is reversed, and the case is remanded for further proceedings consistent with this opinion.

[A] Profits "Solely" From the Efforts of Others

The Supreme Court in *Howey* stated that one of the requirements for an instrument to be an investment contract is that the investor expect to derive "profits solely from the efforts of the promoter or a third party." A question after *Howey* is how strictly the term "solely" should be construed. Several circuit court decisions have

---

4. [In *Reves*, the Supreme Court stated:

We emphasize that by "profit" in the context of notes, we mean "a valuable return on an investment," which undoubtedly includes interest. We have, of course, defined "profit" more restrictively in applying the *Howey* test to what are claimed to be "investment contracts." *See, e.g., Forman*, 421 U.S. at 852 ("[P]rofit" under the *Howey* test means either "capital appreciation" or "a participation in earnings"). To apply this restrictive definition to the determination whether an instrument is a "note" would be to suggest that notes paying a rate of interest not keyed to the earnings of the enterprise are not "notes" within the meaning of the Securities Act. Because the *Howey* test is irrelevant to the issue before us today, we decline to extend the definition of "profit" beyond the realm in which that definition applies.]

discussed the issue. Two leading cases are the Fifth Circuit's decision in *SEC v. Koscot Interplanetary, Inc.*, 497 F.2d 473 (5th Cir. 1974), and the Ninth Circuit's decision in *SEC v. Glenn W. Turner Enterprises, Inc.*, 474 F.2d 476 (9th Cir. 1973), where the critical inquiry was defined as: "*whether the efforts made by those other than the investor are the undeniably significant ones, those essential managerial efforts which affect the failure or success of the enterprise.*" This *Koscot/Turner* test accordingly rejects a literal interpretation of "solely" and has been widely followed. The Supreme Court, although not expressly adopting this formulation, appears to have acquiesced in this formulation. For example, in *United Housing Foundation, Inc. v. Forman,* 421 U.S. 837, 852 n.16 (1975), the Court paraphrased this aspect of the *Howey* standard, thereby requiring that "profits . . . be derived from the entrepreneurial or managerial efforts of others." We will explore this concept in greater depth through much of this chapter.

The *Continental Marketing* decision set forth in the text above illustrates an important principle: namely, that the party exerting the significant efforts need not be owned or controlled by the seller-promoter. Such a result makes a great deal of sense. Otherwise, even though investors may be unable to exercise meaningful control over the enterprise, promoters could avoid securities law coverage merely by contracting with a nonaffiliated third party to perform the necessary acts. Application of *Howey's* economic reality test prevents this consequence.

[B] "Expectation of Profits"

As will be discussed later in this chapter, in *United Housing Foundation, Inc. v. Forman*, 421 U.S. 837 (1975), the Supreme Court identified two forms of "profit" that meet the *Howey* test: (1) "capital appreciation resulting from the development of the initial investment" and (2) "a participation in earnings resulting from the use of investors' funds." More recently, in *SEC v Edwards,* 540 U.S. 389, 394 (2004), the Supreme Court elaborated that "profit" includes, "for example, dividends, other periodic payments, or the increased value of the investment." Hence, a contractual entitlement to a fixed return meets the *Howey* expectation of profit prong.

Another key point is that the securities laws generally do not apply where the purchaser is principally motivated by a desire to use or consume the particular item acquired. For example, because the plaintiffs in *United Housing* were motivated mainly by the desire to obtain affordable and decent housing, rather than seeking a return on the acquisition, the securities laws were not applicable.

[C] The "Common Enterprise" Requirement

As the Supreme Court pointed out in *Howey*, an essential ingredient for the finding of an investment contract is that there be a "common enterprise." Generally, there are two types of common enterprise: horizontal commonality and vertical commonality.

All courts have held that horizontal commonality is sufficient to meet this aspect of the *Howey* test. Generally, horizontal commonality looks to the relationships that exist between an individual investor and the pool of other investors. Under this standard, a pooling of the interests of the investors is essential to finding the existence of an investment contract. Hence, "no horizontal common enterprise can exist unless there . . . exists between [the investors] themselves some relationship which ties the fortunes of each investor to the success of the overall venture." *Curran v. Merrill Lynch, Pierce, Fenner & Smith*, 622 F.2d 216, 224 (6th Cir. 1980), *aff'd on other grounds*, 456 U.S. 353 (1982).

The lower courts widely disagree, however, on whether "vertical commonality" (a relationship between the investor(s) and the promoter) satisfies the *Howey* common enterprise element. A number of courts hold that only horizontal commonality (and not vertical commonality) satisfies the common enterprise requirement. See, e.g., *Salcer v. Merrill Lynch, Pierce, Fenner & Smith, Inc.*, 682 F.2d 459 (3d Cir. 1982); *Milnarik v. M. S. Commodities, Inc.*, 457 F.2d 274 (7th Cir. 1972).

Another view deems "vertical commonality" to be sufficient. Nonetheless, courts that accept "vertical commonality" themselves differ on the scope of this concept. As explained by one court:

> There is a split in the courts that have applied the "vertical commonality" approach regarding precisely what is necessary to satisfy this standard. The courts applying the more restrictive definition state that "vertical commonality" exists where "the fortunes of the investor are interwoven with and dependent upon the efforts and success of those seeking the investment or third parties." . . . Thus, the Ninth Circuit appears to require that there be a "direct relation between the success or failure of the promoter and that of his investors." *Mordaunt v. Incomco*, 686 F.2d at 817 (9th Cir. 1982). However, absent such a direct relation, the Ninth Circuit will not find "vertical commonality." . . . .
>
> A broader definition of "vertical commonality" seems to have been articulated by [some courts holding] that "the requisite commonality is evidenced by the fact that the fortunes of all investors are inextricably tied to the efficacy of the [promoter's efforts]" . . . Thus, rather than requiring a tie between the fortunes of the investors and the *fortunes* of the promoters, as is necessitated under the restrictive definition of "vertical commonality," the broader definition merely requires a link between the fortunes of the investors and the *effort*s of the promoters. . . .

Mechigian v. Art Capital Corp., 612 F. Supp. 1421, 1427 (S.D.N.Y. 1985). For further discussion, see Chang, *Defining a Common Enterprise in Investment Contracts*, 72 Ohio St. L.J. 59 (2011); Gordon, *Defining a Common Enterprise in Investment Contracts*, 72 Ohio St. L.J. 59 (2011).

The Supreme Court's decision in *Marine Bank v. Weaver*, 455 U.S. 551 (1982), covered later in this chapter, impacts the common enterprise requirement. *See generally*

Mordaunt v. Incomco, 469 U.S. 1115 (1985) (White, J., dissenting from the denial of the petition for a writ of certiorari).

[D] Limited Partnerships

The judicial analysis of whether partnership interests fall within the definition of a security has proceeded along the lines of whether a partnership interest is an "investment contract."

Since state law governing the operation of limited partnerships traditionally prohibited limited partners from performing significant managerial functions, courts usually held that these interests met the *Howey* requirement that profits be derived essentially from the efforts of others. Analysis often focused upon both the terms of the partnership agreement and on the actual extent of managerial participation by the limited partners.

The case law is fairly uniform on this point. See, e.g., *Liberty Property Trust v. Republic Properties Corp.*, 577 F.2d 335 (D.C. Cir. 2009) (limited partnership units in real estate venture were securities); *L & B Hospital Ventures, Inc. v. Healthcare International, Inc.*, 894 F.2d 150 (5th Cir. 1990) (limited partnership interests purchased by physicians who practiced medicine in a hospital held to be securities); *Mayer v. Oil Field Systems Corp.*, 721 F.2d 59 (2d Cir. 1983) (limited partnership interest in energy exploration venture was a security); *Goodman v. Epstein*, 582 F.2d 388 (7th Cir. 1978) (stating that the *Howey* phrase "solely from the efforts of others" should not be read as a strict or literal limitation on the definition of an investment contract and holding that evidence that a limited partner arranged financing for the venture before its inception did not overcome the fact that by state law he could not manage it).

It should be stressed, however, that a court still must make an independent examination of whether the limited partnership interest meets the *Howey* investment contract test. Whether or not a partnership interest is "limited" for state law purposes is significant, but not necessarily determinative. This is illustrated by *Gordon v. Terry*, 684 F.2d 736 (11th Cir. 1982). In that case, a limited partnership was formed for the purposes of buying and selling undeveloped land. The limited partners had explicit voting power on whether or not specific pieces of land should be sold and at what time. The Eleventh Circuit (ruling on a summary judgment motion) held that these interests did not pass the *Howey* test and, hence, were not investment contracts. Similarly, in *Steinhardt Group, Inc. v. Citicorp.*, 126 F.3d 144 (3d Cir. 1997), the Third Circuit held under the facts of that case that "the limited partner retained pervasive control over its investment in the limited partnership such that it cannot be deemed a passive investor under *Howey* and its progeny."

This issue has become more prevalent. Pursuant to applicable limited partnership statutes, limited partners may engage in extensive activities yet retain their limited liability status. For example, under § 303(b) of the Revised Uniform Limited

Partnership Act (RULPA), a limited partner may engage in such actions as "consulting with and advising a general partner" regarding the partnership business, serving as an officer or director of a corporation that is a general partner of the limited partnership, and voting on a number of important subjects, such as "a change in the nature of the business" and "the admission or removal of a general partner." Moreover, if the limited partnership agreement so provides, the limited partner may enjoy a right of approval over *any* matter related to the partnership's business. Even more expansive is the 2001 Uniform Limited Partnership Act, which generally insulates a limited partner from personal liability "even if the limited partner participates in the management and control of the limited partnership."

In sum, interests in a limited partnership generally are securities because limited partners ordinarily rely on the general partners to exercise the essential entrepreneurial or managerial efforts. However, in those situations where limited partners have the capability to exert meaningful efforts, the *Howey* investment contract test may not be met.[5]

[E] General Partnerships

Since general partnerships do not possess the same restrictions on participation in management as limited partnership interests, they usually fail to satisfy the *Howey* "from the efforts of others" test. After all, general partners are viewed as co-owners having the power of ultimate control. Importantly, each general partner is subject to personal liability for the debts of the general partnership. Accordingly, several lower court cases in the 1960s and 1970s applied *Howey* in a fairly literal manner and held that general partnership interests were not securities. See, e.g., *Hirsch v. du Pont*, 396 F. Supp. 1214 (S.D.N.Y. 1975), *aff'd*, 553 F.2d 750 (2d Cir. 1977) ("substantial 'legal rights to a voice in partnership matters' inhered in the general partnership interests: [thus] those interests were not securities, irrespective of the degree to which [the partners] actually chose to exercise their rights.")

In *Williamson v. Tucker*, 645 F.2d 404, 422–429 (5th Cir. 1981), the Fifth Circuit may have "rescued" general partnership interests from being declared outside the scope of the securities laws as a matter of law. That case involved a series of joint ventures, each of which owned an undivided interest in certain real estate. In stating that, under certain circumstances, general partnership or joint venture interests may be securities, the Fifth Circuit reasoned:

> Although general partners and joint venturers may not individually have decisive control over major decisions, they do have the sort of influence which

---

5. *See* Everhard, *The Limited Partnership Interest: Is It a Security? Changing Times*, 17 Del. J. Corp. L. 441 (1992) (asserting that in those situations where "the powers retained by the limited partners are so pervasive that they are in a position to adequately protect themselves, . . . the protections of the federal securities laws are neither appropriate nor necessary").

generally provides them with access to important information and protection against a dependence on others. Moreover, partnership powers are not in the nature of a nominal role in the enterprise which a seller of investment contracts would include in order to avoid the securities laws; on the contrary, one would expect such a promoter to insist on ultimate control over the investment venture. An investor who is offered an interest in a general partnership or joint venture should be on notice, therefore, that his ownership rights are significant, and that the federal securities acts will not protect him from a mere failure to exercise his rights.

It should be clear . . . however, that the mere fact that an investment takes the form of a general partnership or joint venture does not inevitably insulate it from the reach of the federal securities laws. All of these cases presume that the investor-partner is not in fact dependent on the promoter or manager for the effective exercise of his partnership powers. If, for example, the partner has irrevocably delegated his powers, or is incapable of exercising them, or is so dependent on the particular expertise of the promoter or manager that he has no reasonable alternative [but to rely] on that person, then his partnership powers may be inadequate to protect him from the dependence on others which is implicit in an investment contract.

Thus, a general partnership in which some agreement among the partners places the controlling power in the hands of certain managing partners may be an investment contract with respect to the other partners. In such a case the agreement allocates partnership power as in a limited partnership, which has long been held to be an investment contract. Similarly, one would not expect partnership interests sold to large numbers of the general public to provide any real partnership control; at some point there would be so many partners that a partnership vote would be more like a corporate vote, each partner's role having been diluted to the level of a single shareholder in a corporation. Such an arrangement might well constitute an investment contract.

A general partner or joint venturer who lacks the business experience and expertise necessary to intelligently exercise partnership powers may also be dependent on the investment's promoter or manager.

. . . A scheme which sells investments to inexperienced and unknowledgeable members of the general public cannot escape the reach of the securities laws merely by labeling itself a general partnership or joint venture. Such investors may be led to expect profits to be derived from the efforts of others in spite of partnership powers nominally retained by them.

A genuine dependence on others might also exist where the partners are forced to rely on some particular non-replaceable expertise on the part of a promoter or manager. Even the most knowledgeable partner may be left with no meaningful option when there is no reasonable replacement for the investment's manager. For example, investors may be induced to enter a real estate partnership on the promise that the partnership's manager has some unique understanding of the real estate market in the area in which the partnership is to invest; the partners may have the legal right to replace the manager, but they could do so only by forfeiting the management ability on which the success of the venture is dependent. Or investors may purchase joint venture interests in an operating business in reliance on the managing partner's unusual experience and ability in running that particular business; again, a legal right of control would have little value if the partners were forced to rely on the manager's unique abilities. We must emphasize, however, that a reliance on others does not exist merely because the partners have chosen to hire another party to manage their investment. The delegation of rights and duties—standing alone—does not give rise to the sort of dependence on others which underlies the third prong of the *Howey* test. An investor who retains control over his investment has not purchased an interest in a common venture "premised on the reasonable expectation of profits to be derived from the entrepreneurial or managerial efforts of others," even if he has contracted with the vendor for the management of the property. So long as the investor retains ultimate control, he has the power over the investment and the access to information about it which is necessary to protect against any unwilling dependence on the manager. It is not enough, therefore, that partners in fact rely on others for the management of their investment; a partnership can be an investment contract only when the partners are so dependent on a particular manager that they cannot replace him or otherwise exercise ultimate control.

All of this indicates that an investor who claims his general partnership or joint venture interest is an investment contract has a difficult burden to overcome. On the face of a partnership agreement, the investor retains substantial control over his investment and an ability to protect himself from the managing partner or hired manager. Such an investor must demonstrate that, in spite of the partnership form which the investment took, he was so dependent on the promoter or on a third party that he was in fact unable to exercise meaningful partnership powers.

Thus, one would have to show that the reliance on the manager which forms the basis of the partner's expectations was an understanding in the original transaction, and not some subsequent decision to delegate partnership duties. . . .

A general partnership or joint venture interest can be designated a security if the investor can establish, for example, that (1) an agreement among the parties leaves so little power in the hands of the partner or venturer that the arrangement in fact distributes power as would a limited partnership; or (2) the partner or venturer is so inexperienced and unknowledgeable in business affairs that he is incapable of intelligently exercising his partnership or venture powers; or (3) the partner or venturer is so dependent on some unique entrepreneurial or managerial ability of the promoter or manager that he cannot replace the manager of the enterprise or otherwise exercise meaningful partnership or venture powers.

Note

The *Williamson* decision appears to be an expansion of the circumstances under which general partnership or joint venture interests will be found to be securities. Nonetheless, as the *Williamson* court emphasized, "an investor who claims his general partnership or joint venture interest is an investment contract has a difficult burden. . . ." Subsequent decisions applying *Williamson* confirm this concept. See, e.g., *Nunez v. Robin*, 2011 U.S. App. LEXIS 4825 (5th Cir. 2011) (active participation in management by joint venturer meant that joint venture interest was not an investment contract). Nonetheless, depending on the underlying facts and circumstances, this hurdle may be overcome. See, e.g., *SEC v. Shields*, 744 F.2d 633 (10th Cir. 2014) (holding that as alleged by the SEC, applying *Williamson*, joint venture interests were securities).

While a number of subsequent cases have examined general partnership interests under the analysis set forth in *Williamson*, some courts have declined to do so. For example, in *Banghart v. Hollywood General Partnership*, 902 F.2d 805, 808 (10th Cir. 1990), the Tenth Circuit stated:

> [R]egardless of the control actually exercised, if a partnership agreement retains real power in the general partners, then an investment in the general partnership is not a security. Thus, our determination of whether a general partnership interest can be characterized as a security turns on the partnership agreement.
>
> When a partnership agreement allocates powers to general partners that are specific and unambiguous and those powers provide the general partners with access to information and the ability to protect their investment, then the presumption is that the general partnership is not a security. As the [Fourth Circuit] stated, "[e]ven when general partners do not individually have decisive control over major decisions, they do have the sort of influence which generally provides them with access to important information and protection against a dependence on others." . . . The strong presumption that an interest in a general partnership is not a security can only be overcome by evidence that the general partners were rendered passive investors because they were somehow precluded from exercising their powers of control and supervision.

Accord, Rivanna Trawlers Unlimited v. Thompson Trawlers, Inc., 840 F.2d 236 (4th Cir. 1988); *Fargo Partners v. Dain Corp.,* 540 F.2d 912 (8th Cir. 1976). Interestingly, the

Tenth Circuit elected to apply the *Williamson* analysis in a subsequent decision, *SEC v. Shields*, 744 F.3d 633 (10th Cir. 2014).

[F] Limited Liability Partnership (LLP) Interests

With respect to (registered) limited liability partnership (LLP or RLLP) interests, on the other hand, these interests, depending on the circumstances, may be deemed investment contracts. LLPs are general partnerships. By registering with the applicable state regulator and meeting certain other criteria, partners in a LLP are not vicariously liable for the LLP's debts and obligations. Due to this more limited liability exposure, LLP partners are more likely to be passive investors. As stated by the Eleventh Circuit:

> An RLLP partner is liable only for the amount of his or her capital contribution, plus the partner's personal acts, and is not exposed to vicarious liability for the acts of other partners or the acts of the partnership as a whole. This limitation on liability means that RLLP partners have less of an incentive to preserve control than general partners do. While general partners normally wish to preserve control because their personal assets are at risk, RLLP partners have only their investment at risk if they remain passive, and risk personal liability only if they become active.

SEC v. Merchant Capital, 483 F.3d 747, 755–756 (11th Cir. 2007). Likening the powers held by the LLP partners to those of limited partners, the court held that the LLP partners did not exercise essential managerial efforts. Hence, the LLP interests were held to be investment contracts. *See generally* Welle, *When Are Limited Liability Partnership Interests Securities?*, 27 J. Corp. L. 63 (2001).

[G] Limited Liability Company (LLC) Interests

An issue not yet fully resolved is whether interests in a limited liability company (LLC) are securities. An LLC, a creature of statute, is a flexible form of noncorporate business organization that, like a partnership, allows a planner to choose pass-through taxation (without classification as an S corporation). The Internal Revenue Service (IRS) recognizes LLCs as partnerships for tax purposes, thus legitimizing the LLC's pass-through tax structure. Thus, the LLC avoids double taxation and corporate formalities and allows a pass-through of income and loss to its members for tax purposes. Further, LLC investors (referred to as members) may take an unrestricted role in management without sacrificing limited liability.

The *Howey* investment contract test applies to determine whether LLC interests are securities. It may be argued that LLC interests are not investment contracts since most of the state statutes vest management power in the LLC members. This power arguably signifies that LLC members are not relying essentially on the efforts of others. Under this approach, LLC interests are similar to interests in a general partnership and, therefore, ordinarily are not investment contracts. Nonetheless, depending on the provisions contained in the LLC operating documents and the surrounding circumstances (such as the subject member's degree of influence and the expertise required to operate the business), application of the *Williamson* factors may result in the LLC interests satisfying the *Howey* test.

Moreover, a number of courts, pointing to the limited liability protection afforded to LLC members, hold that the *Williamson* analysis has no application in the LLC setting. For example, one court opined:

> In *Williamson*, the court cited a general partner's liability for the obligations of the partnership and his right to control the business . . . as being the "critical factors" to distinguishing a general partnership interest from an investment contract. Because limited liability companies ordinarily do not share these characteristics, there is no justification for a broad presumption against interests in limited liability companies being investment contracts. Extending the *Williamson* presumption for general partnership interests to interests in limited liability companies is not appropriate, given the essential distinctions between the two business forms. We eschew a presumption that interests in limited liability companies are not investment contracts, within the meaning of the securities laws.

AK's Daks Communications, Inc. v. Maryland Securities Division, 771 A. 2d 487, 498 (Md. Ct. Sp. App. 2001).

Consistent with the above analysis—upon examining the economic realities of the underlying transaction—a number of more recent decisions have held that the LLC members in fact were passive investors, thereby signifying that the LLC interests were securities.[6] For example, in *United States v. Leonard*, 529 F.3d 83, 87–91 (2d Cir. 2008), the Second Circuit reasoned:

> Although federal statutes enumerate many different instruments that fit the definition of security, the parties agree that the only category that potentially applies to this case is "investment contract." . . . Appellants suggest that the Little Giant and Heritage units cannot constitute securities because investors never expected profits "solely from the efforts" of the promoters or others.

---

6. *See, e.g., Affco Investments 2001 LLC v. Proskauer Rose LLP*, 625 F.3d 185, 191 (5th Cir. 2010); *United States v. Leonard*, 529 F.3d 83, 89–91 (2d Cir. 2008); *SEC v Friendly Power Company*, 49 F. Supp. 2d 1363 (S.D. Fla. 1999). *See generally*, Goforth, *Why Limited Liability Company Membership Interests Should Not Be Treated as Securities and Possible Steps to Encourage This Result*, 45 Hastings L.J. 1223 (1994); Ribstein, *Form and Substance in the Definition of a "Security": The Case of Limited Liability Companies*, 51 Wash. & Lee. L. Rev. 807 (1994); Sargent, *Are Limited Liability Company Interests Securities?*, 19 Pepp. L. Rev. 1069 (1992); Steinberg & Conway, *The Limited Liability Company as a Security*, 19 Pepp. L. Rev. 1105 (1992); Welle, *Limited Liability Company Interests as Securities: An Analysis of Federal and State Actions Against Limited Liability Companies Under the Securities Laws*, 73 Den. U.L. Rev. 425 (1996).

Following the Ninth Circuit's lead, see *SEC v. Glenn W. Turner Enterprises*, 474 F.2d 476, 482 (9th Cir.1973), we have held that the word "solely" should not be construed as a literal limitation; rather, we "consider whether, under all the circumstances, the scheme was being promoted primarily as an investment or as a means whereby participants could pool their own activities, their money and the promoter's contribution in a meaningful way." . . .

Our consideration of whether the investors in Little Giant and Heritage viewed the units primarily as a passive investment is complicated by the fact that Little Giant and Heritage were each structured as an LLC—a relatively new, hybrid vehicle that combines elements of the traditional corporation with elements of the general partnership while retaining flexibility for federal tax purposes. . . . Although "common stock is the quintessence of a security," . . . and "[n]ormally, a general partnership interest is not considered a 'security,'" because of the sheer diversity of LLCs, membership interests therein resist categorical classification. Thus, an interest in an LLC is the sort of instrument that requires "case-by-case analysis" into the "economic realities" of the underlying transaction.

One of the original promoters of Little Giant and Heritage, Russell Finnegan, testified at trial that the LLCs were structured so as to minimize the possibility that the investment units would constitute securities—"to get into the gray areas of the securities law." Indeed, were we to confine ourselves to a review of the organizational documents, we would likely conclude that the interests in Little Giant and Heritage could not constitute securities because the documents would lead us to believe that members were expected to play an active role in the management of the companies. For example, the sheet titled "Summary of Business Opportunity: Heritage Film Group, LLC" explains:

Each Member is required to participate in the management of the Company retaining one (1) vote for each Unit acquired. Each important decision relating to the business of the Company must be submitted to a vote of the Members.

The purchase of interests in the Company is not a passive investment. While specific knowledge and expertise in the day to day operation of a film producing and distributing company is not required, Members should have such knowledge and experience in general business, investment and/or financial affairs as to intelligently exercise their management and voting rights . . . . Further, each Member is required to participate in the management of the Company by serving on one or more committees established by the Members.

The summary further states that a manager may be chosen to perform certain "ministerial functions," such as keeping books and records, keeping the members informed, and circulating ballots to members, but the members retain the right to replace the manager and appoint his successor upon majority vote. Likewise, the operating agreement for Heritage provides that the "Company shall be managed by the Members. [E]ach Member shall have the right to act for and bind the Company in the ordinary course of its business." Thus, on the face of the documents, Heritage and Little Giant appear to provide far too much investor control to allow the jury to conclude that the units were securities.

In actuality, however, the Little Giant and Heritage members played an extremely passive role in the management and operation of the companies. At trial, members testified that they voted, at most, "a couple of times." Although the organizational documents provided for the formation of a number of committees, only two committees were formed for each of Heritage and Little Giant—a financial committee and a management committee. Of the 250–300 investors in Little Giant, five served on the management committee and seven served on the financial committee. Of the 350–400 investors in Heritage, ten served on the management committee and seven served on the financial committee. Thus, the vast majority of investors in both companies did not actively participate in the venture, exercising almost no control.

Record evidence allowed the jury to conclude that—notwithstanding the language in the organizational documents suggesting otherwise—from the start there could be no "reasonable expectation" of investor control.... Such consideration of the reality of the transaction is consistent with the Supreme Court's repeated instruction to prize substance over form in our evaluation of what constitutes a security....

For one, under the organizational documents, the members' managerial rights and obligations did not accrue until the LLCs were "fully organized." As promoter James Alex testified, so-called "interim managers" initially held legal control rights, and they decided almost every significant issue prior to the completion of fundraising: "The script, the director, the cast, the crew, scoring of it, editing. The entire picture was pretty well preproduced." Thus, the jury could reasonably have found the managerial rights contained in the organizational documents were hollow and illusory.

The jury was also entitled to consider the fact that the members appear not to have negotiated any terms of the LLC agreements. Rather, they were presented with the subscription agreements on a take-it-or-leave-it basis. That they played no role in shaping the organizational agreements themselves raises doubts as to whether the members were expected to have significant control over the enterprise.

Moreover, the members had no particular experience in film or entertainment and therefore would have had difficulty exercising their formal right to take over management of the companies after they were fully organized....

And their number and geographic dispersion left investors particularly dependent on centralized management. We echo the Fifth Circuit in finding that investors may be so lacking in requisite expertise, so numerous, or so dispersed that they become utterly dependent on centralized management, counteracting a legal right of control. See *Williamson v. Tucker*, 645 F.2d 404, 423–24 (5th Cir. 1981). "What matters more than the form of an investment scheme is the 'economic reality' that it represents. The question is whether an investor, as a result of the investment agreement itself or the factual circumstances that surround it, is left unable to exercise meaningful control over his investment." . . .

In sum, upon consideration of the totality of the circumstances, we conclude that the jury could have determined that, notwithstanding the organizational documents drafted to suggest active participation by members, the defendants sought and expected passive investors for Little Giant and Heritage, and therefore the interests that they marketed constituted securities.

[H] Franchises

Conventional franchising agreements (which may also take such forms as dealerships, distributorships, or leasing arrangements) generally have been held not to constitute "investment contracts." The rationale is that pursuant to these arrangements, the franchisee exerts substantial efforts. See, e.g., *Wilkins v. M & H Financial, Inc.*, 621 F.2d 311 (8th Cir. 1980); *Bitter v. Hoby's International, Inc.*, 498 F.2d 183 (9th Cir. 1974); *Lima v. City Investing Co.*, 487 F.2d 689 (3d Cir. 1973). For example, the Tenth Circuit in *Meyer v. Dans un Jardin*, 816 F.2d 533, 535 (10th Cir. 1987), held that the franchise agreement was not a security, explaining:

> It is undeniable that the product, the reputation, and the promotional and managerial expertise developed by the franchisor are material to the success of its franchisees. Benefits expected from the franchisor provide incentives for entering into a franchise agreement rather than undertaking a wholly independent business. But that does not mean the typical franchisee can expect to profit from the investment without regard to the franchisee's own business skills.
>
> Under the franchise agreement here, the plaintiffs were responsible for constructing the franchise store, paying rent, salaries, and advertising expenses, hiring and firing employees, maintaining customer relationships, ordering inventory, and devoting their full time and best efforts to the day-to-day management of the franchise store. The defendants' role was essentially limited to providing merchandise and promotional materials at plaintiffs' expense, conducting training seminars, and assisting plaintiffs in the commencement of their operation. . . .

Nonetheless, it is important to emphasize that the label "franchise" is not determinative. Where the franchisee has not exerted (or has not been granted realistic authority to exercise) substantial managerial rights and responsibilities with respect to the enterprise, an investment contract may be held to exist. *See, e.g., SEC v. Aqua-Sonic Products Corp.,* 687 F.2d 577 (2d Cir. 1982); Securities Act Release No. 5211, [1971–1972 Transfer Binder] Fed. Sec. L. Rep. (CCH) ¶ 98,446 (1971) ("[I]n the Commission's view a security is offered or sold where the franchisee is not required to make significant efforts in the operation of the franchise in order to obtain the promised return."). Moreover, where a franchise agreement is really a pyramid scheme, in which profits are sought from the sale of other "franchises" through the main efforts of the promoter and/or third parties (rather than from the sale of products), an investment contract normally will be recognized. *See, e.g., Piambino v. Bailey,* 610 F.2d 1306 (5th Cir. 1980). See generally, Johnson & Campbell, *Securities Law and the Franchise Agreement,* 1980 UTAH L. REV. 311 (1980).

[I] Condominiums — Property Interests Combined with Service Contracts

The factual setting presented to the Supreme Court in *SEC v. W.J. Howey Co.* has been repeated numerous times in a variety of contexts. Courts repeatedly have looked beyond a strict statutory construction and have examined the economic reality of the transaction to determine whether a property interest combined with some form of service contract constitutes a security (termed the *aggregation approach*).

The *Howey* analysis applied by the courts in these cases can usually be broken down into three issues:

First, are the investors dependent on other investors and/or the promoter for a return on their investment ("common enterprise")?

Second, is the interest bought to obtain a financial return or for other reasons ("expectation of profits")?

Third, do the investors participate in the venture to such a degree that they are not dependent "solely on the efforts of others" for their profits?

The applicability of the securities laws in this context may arise where there is the offer and sale of condominium units, or other units in a real estate development, coupled with an arrangement for the promoter or its designee to perform certain rental services for the purchaser. Such agreements may be held to involve the offer and sale of an investment contract or a participation in a profit-sharing arrangement within the meaning of the securities acts. On this subject, the SEC has expressed the following view in Securities Act Release No. 5347 (1973):

> The offer of real estate as such, without any collateral arrangements with the seller or others, does not involve the offer of a security. When the real estate is offered in conjunction with certain services, a security, in the form

of an investment contract, may be present. The Supreme Court in *Securities and Exchange Commission v. W. J. Howey Co.*, 328 U.S. 298 (1946), set forth what has become a generally accepted definition of an investment contract.... The *Howey* case involved the sale and operation of orange groves. The reasoning, however, is applicable to condominiums.

. . . .

In summary, the offering of condominium units in conjunction with any one of the following will cause the offering to be viewed as an offering of securities in the form of investment contracts:

1. The condominiums, with any rental arrangement or other similar service, are offered and sold with emphasis on the economic benefits to the purchaser to be derived from the managerial efforts of the promoter, or a third party designated or arranged for by the promoter, from rental of the units.

2. The offering of participation in a rental pool arrangement; [or]

3. The offering of a rental or similar arrangement whereby the purchaser must hold his unit available for rental for any part of the year, must use an exclusive rental agent or is otherwise materially restricted in his occupancy or rental of his unit.

In all of the above situations, investor protection requires the application of the federal securities laws.

If the condominiums are not offered and sold with emphasis on the economic benefits to the purchaser to be derived from the managerial efforts of others, . . . an owner of a condominium unit may, after purchasing his unit, enter into a non-pooled rental arrangement with an agent not designated or required to be used as a condition to the purchase, whether or not such agent is affiliated with the offeror, without causing a sale of a security to be involved in the sale of the unit. Further, a continuing affiliation between the developers or promoters of a project and the project by reason of maintenance arrangements does not make the unit a security.

Note that a security may exist in additional situations other than the three classified above in the SEC release. For one such case, see *Hodges v. H & R Investments Ltd.*, 668 F. Supp. 545 (N.D. Miss. 1987) (purchase of condominium coupled with collateral agreements, including a guarantee of rental receipts to the investor by the promoters, held to be a security).

In another decision, the Ninth Circuit expansively applied the *Howey* test to a condominium *resale* coupled with a rental agreement between the purchaser and a rental agent recommended by but not affiliated with the real estate broker. *Hocking v. Dubois*, 885 F.2d 1449 (9th Cir. 1989) (en banc). The decision has raised concerns among real estate brokers that their recommendation of a leasing agent (even if not affiliated with such broker) in connection with the sale as well as resale of a vacation-type condominium may trigger application of the securities laws. In *Hocking*, the Ninth Circuit concluded:

> We agree with defendants and amici that the three-judge panel may have written too broadly its conclusion that so long as a rental pool 'option' exists, all secondary market sales necessarily involve a security. Such a per se rule would be ill-suited to the examination of the economic reality of each transaction required by *Howey*. In the context of isolated resales, each case requires an analysis of how the condominium was promoted to the investor, including any representations made to the investor, and the nature of the investment and the collateral agreements. The investor's intentions and expectations as communicated to the broker would be relevant in determining what investment package was actually offered.
>
> If the *Howey* analysis is undertaken, the securities laws are found to apply, and the application of the securities laws places undue burdens on developers, real estate brokers, or condominium owners, changes in the law should be sought from Congress or the Securities and Exchange Commission. *Howey*, on this record, requires this case to proceed beyond summary judgment.

Id. at 1462. Nonetheless, applying *Howey*, a number of courts more recently have held that the sale of condominium units, coupled with a rental program, were not securities under federal law. *See, e.g., Salameh v. Tarsadia Hotels*, 726 F.3d 1124 (9th Cir. 2013). The following decision provides one such example.

Alunni v. Development Resources Group, LLC

United States Court of Appeals, Eleventh Circuit

445 Fed. Appx. 288, 2011 U.S. App. LEXIS 21792 (2011)

These consolidated appeals arise from the sale of condominium units in the Legacy Dunes condominium complex ("Legacy Dunes") in Kissimmee, Florida. The plaintiffs, who purchased Legacy Dunes units, alleged the defendants violated federal and state securities laws in connection with the sales. The district court concluded the securities laws did not apply to the condominium sales at issue because the sales did not constitute "investment contracts," and thus were not "securities." The district court granted summary judgment to the defendants, and the plaintiffs appealed. After review we affirm.

I. BACKGROUND

A. The Parties

This consolidated appeal involves parties in the Alunni Lawsuit and the Roggenbuck lawsuit, as explained below.

In the Alunni case, Albert Alunni and 97 others (a collection of individuals, trusts, and limited liability companies) brought this lawsuit against 14 defendants involved in the marketing and sale of the Legacy Dunes units. In the Roggenbuck case, the Adrianne Roggenbuck Trust, one limited liability company, and 18 individuals brought a similar lawsuit against 15 defendants. The plaintiffs in both cases purchased one or more condominium units in Legacy Dunes. Most of the plaintiffs live in or around Chicago, Illinois.

The defendants include Development Resources Group, LLC ("DRG"); Legacy Dunes Condominium, LLC ("LDC"); Real Estate Dreams, LLC ("RED"); The Real Estate Investment Group, Ltd. ("REIG"); and Geneva Hospitality Management, LLC ("Geneva"); as well as various officers and principals of DRG, LDC, RED, REIG, and Geneva.

Defendant DRG is an Orlando, Florida-based company engaged in the development and sale of condominium projects in Florida. In January 2006, DRG formed LDC to purchase Legacy Dunes, a 488-unit apartment complex in Kissimmee, Florida, and to convert Legacy Dunes into a condominium.

To market Legacy Dunes, LDC (the owner) entered into a brokerage agreement with RED, a Florida real estate brokerage company. RED, in turn contracted with REIG, an Illinois real estate brokerage company, to market Legacy Dunes to potential buyers in Chicago. REIG's principal is defendant Joseph Aldeguer, who had a Saturday morning radio program in Chicago called "Making Money in Real Estate with Joseph Aldeguer." REIG and Aldeguer promoted Legacy Dunes on Aldeguer's radio show and through real estate workshops in Chicago.

Defendant Geneva is a Wisconsin-based property management company that worked with REIG and Aldeguer at the real estate workshops. Geneva ultimately did not serve as property manager at Legacy Dunes.

B. Purchase and Conversion of Legacy Dunes

In February 2006, LDC contracted to purchase the Legacy Dunes apartment complex, and it consummated the purchase on June 27, 2006. A few days after closing, LDC filed a declaration of condominium, converting Legacy Dunes to a condominium. When LDC did so, it created the Legacy Dunes condominium association, a separate corporation that is not a party in these cases.

LDC controlled the condominium association for three months. On September 30, 2006, LDC turned over control of the Legacy Dunes condominium association to the unit owners.

When LDC bought Legacy Dunes, approximately 94% of the units were occupied by tenants with long-term (one or two year) leases. Before the sale to LDC, Legacy Dunes's owner operated the complex's leasing office.

On June 27, 2006, the day it purchased Legacy Dunes, LDC entered into a contract (the "leasing agreement") with Sovereign Residential Services, LLC ("Sovereign"). The leasing agreement stated that LDC appointed Sovereign as "the sole and exclusive leasing agent" for all Legacy Dunes units offered for lease. The leasing agreement stated that LDC "represents and warrants that all homeowners of

[Legacy Dunes] are required to use [Sovereign] for any leasing of their premise in [Legacy Dunes]." LDC agreed "that all inquiries for any lease(s) or renewal(s) for the leasing of [Legacy Dunes] shall be referred to [Sovereign] and all negotiations connected therewith shall be conducted by or under the direction of [Sovereign]."

The leasing agreement obligated Sovereign to "use reasonable efforts to lease available units within [Legacy Dunes] as expeditiously as possible" at rates approved by LDC, as well as to collect rent from tenants on behalf of the unit owners. LDC paid the entire cost of the rental management services provided by Sovereign.

The leasing agreement with Sovereign was exclusively for long-term (i.e., greater than seven months) leasing of Legacy Dunes units. Although local zoning regulations permitted short-term rentals, Legacy Dunes's declaration of condominium did not. Neither LDC nor DRG ever engaged management for short-term leasing.

The leasing agreement between LDC and Sovereign was for a one-year term and expired in 2007.

C. Marketing and Promotion of Legacy Dunes Condominium Units

In the spring of 2006, LDC, REIG, and Aldeguer began marketing the Legacy Dunes condominium units. Plaintiffs first heard about Legacy Dunes on Aldeguer's radio show, and they were invited to attend real estate workshops at the Mortgage Exchange ("TME"), a mortgage brokerage company in Chicago owned and run by Aldeguer.

Three workshops were held, one each in May, June, and July 2006. About 100 to 150 people attended each workshop, where they were solicited to buy Legacy Dunes units.

At the workshops, plaintiffs were told about Legacy Dunes as a real estate investment opportunity. Both Aldeguer and DRG officer James Wear spoke at the workshops. Aldeguer and Wear told plaintiffs that Legacy Dunes was re-zoned to permit nightly rentals and they planned to convert Legacy Dunes to a hotel, but the process would take time because of the complex's existing tenants.

Plaintiffs were told they would receive immediate income from the long-term tenants who already occupied 94% of the units at Legacy Dunes and that they did not have to manage their units. Specifically, Aldeguer said rental income would be paid without the "headache of being a landlord" . . .

The plaintiffs submitted sworn statements about what they were told at the workshops. Plaintiff Robert Devereaux, for example, was told that (1) Legacy Dunes would be converted to a short-term rental resort (also called "condo hotel" units); (2) the complex "would be managed with 80% of the rental going to the owner of the unit and 20% going to the management company"; and (3) "this would be a totally passive investment with no active participation required of the owners." Plaintiff Sandra Griggs was told "what a great investment property/investment vehicle [a Legacy Dunes unit] would be, especially since (a) it would give owners excellent positive cash flow, and (b) they predicted tremendous continuous appreciation here and in the Orlando area."

At the workshops, the plaintiffs were provided with information about the location of Legacy Dunes, floor plans of typical units, the layout of the complex, and the amenities offered. The plaintiffs were shown photos of the complex, floor plans of various units, and maps of the surrounding area. REIG arranged on-the-spot financing following the workshops.

D. Purchase Agreements

The plaintiffs purchased about 125 of the 488 Legacy Dunes units. The sales were effectuated through written condominium purchase agreements between LDC and the purchasers. Each purchase agreement stated the following in all caps on the top of the first page:

> ORAL REPRESENTATIONS CANNOT BE RELIED UPON AS CORRECTLY STATING THE REPRESENTATIONS OF DEVELOPER. FOR CORRECT REPRESENTATIONS, REFERENCE SHOULD BE MADE TO THIS CONTRACT AND THE DOCUMENTS REQUIRED BY SECTION 718.503 FLORIDA STATUTES TO BE FURNISHED BY DEVELOPER TO A PURCHASER OR LESSEE.

The purchase agreements contained an "entire agreement" clause stating, *inter alia*, that "[n]o agent, representative, salesman or officer of the parties hereto has authority to make, or has made, any statements, agreements, or representations, either oral or in writing, in connection herewith, modifying, adding to, or changing the terms and conditions hereof and neither party has relied upon any representation or warranty not set forth in this Agreement."

The purchase agreements notified the plaintiffs that, if there was a tenant currently residing in the unit purchased, the plaintiffs were buying the unit subject to the lease. Otherwise, the plaintiffs received complete and permanent possession of their units.

Once the existing leases expired, each plaintiff was free to occupy his unit or rent it out to others. All rental income was unit-specific — that is, rental payments were not pooled together and divided among unit owners, but instead each unit owner received the net rental income generated by his own property.

The purchase agreements included an addendum containing, among other things, provisions on long-term rental management agreement, short-term rental, and temporary rental guarantee. The long-term rental management agreement provision stated that LDC agreed "to provide all leasing/concierge services" at LDC's expense until the first of: (1) June, 30, 2007; (2) the day the purchaser of the unit occupied the unit; or (3) the date the purchaser of the unit placed the unit into a short-term rental pool. The provision further stated that owners of Legacy Dunes units "will be required to utilize and retain the leasing management company selected by the Board of Directors" of the condominium association. The provision prohibited plaintiffs from showing their units to prospective tenants without prior approval.

The short-term rental provision stated that (1) LDC acknowledged the unit purchaser's "intent . . . to place the unit associated with this Purchase Agreement into a short term rental pool," and (2) should Legacy Dune's zoning classification not permit short-term rentals within 120 days, LDC would refund $25,000 to the purchaser.

The temporary rental guarantee provision stated that, should the purchaser's unit become unoccupied, LDC would pay the purchaser the rent on the unit at the previous rental rate, less certain costs, during the same period during which LDC provided the leasing/concierge services—i.e., until the first of: (1) June 30, 2007; (2) the date the purchaser of the unit occupied the unit; or (3) the date the purchaser of the unit placed the unit into a short-term rental pool.

The purchase agreements stated that "[t]he nature and extent of the rights and obligations of the Purchaser in acquiring and owning the Unit will be controlled by and subject to the Declaration" of condominium for Legacy Dunes, and "Purchaser agrees to comply with all of the terms, conditions and obligations set forth therein." The plaintiffs acknowledged in the purchase agreement that they had received a copy of the declaration of condominium. The declaration of condominium for Legacy Dunes provided, "A condominium unit shall not be leased for a period of less than seven (7) months or as amended by the Board of Directors."

The plaintiffs signed their purchase agreements and initialed each page of them.

E. Post-Purchase Losses

The plaintiffs purchased their units in Legacy Dunes around September to December 2006. Existing long-leases began to expire, and Legacy Dunes units could not yet be rented on a short-term basis.

The Legacy Dunes unit owners obtained approval for short-term rental of Legacy Dunes units in summer of 2007. As to the short-term leasing of Legacy Dunes units, the plaintiffs could choose their own management company to lease their unit, or they could do so themselves.

After 2007, rentals in Legacy Dunes dropped dramatically, and many plaintiffs went months without having any rental income at all. The units depreciated in value. The plaintiffs struggled to make the payments on their Legacy Dunes units.

. . . .

II. DISCUSSION

A. The Howey Test

The federal securities laws on which the plaintiffs base their claims against defendants—the Securities Act of 1933 and the Securities Exchange Act of 1934—all define "security" as including, among other things, "investment contracts." Although the definition of security extends to things other than investment contracts (e.g., stocks, bonds, and notes), the parties here agree that "investment contract" is the only portion of the definition that arguably applies. Therefore, if the sales of

Legacy Dunes condominium units do not constitute investment contracts, then they are not securities, the securities laws do not apply to the transactions, and the grant of summary judgment to the defendants is appropriate.

. . . .

"A common enterprise exists where the 'fortunes of the investor are interwoven with and dependent upon the efforts and success of those seeking the investment or of third parties.'" . . . We have held that "the fact that an investor's return is independent of that of other investors in the scheme is not decisive" because "the requisite commonality is evidenced by the fact that the fortunes of all investors are inextricably tied to the efficacy of the promoter." . . .

As to the expectation of profits solely from the efforts of others prong, "[w]e have held that 'solely' is not interpreted restrictively." . . . Instead, we "look to the economic reality, focusing on the dependency of the investor on the entrepreneurial or managerial skills of a promoter or other party." . . . "An investor who has the ability to control the profitability of his investment, either by his own efforts or by majority vote in group ventures, is not dependent upon the managerial skills of others." . . . "The fact that the investor has delegated management duties or has chosen to rely on some other party does not establish dependency. The investor must have no reasonable alternative to reliance on that person." . . .

B. Analysis

We agree with the district court that the facts of these lawsuits establish that the plaintiffs' purchase of condominium units in Legacy Dunes did not constitute "investment contracts." The plaintiffs purchased fee simple interests in real estate, subject only to: (1) the condominium declaration and bylaws; (2) each unit's existing long-term leases (for those units that had tenants), until they expired; and (3) a one-year period during which the plaintiffs had to lease their units (if they chose to lease them) through Sovereign, the property management company selected by LDC. Once the existing leases expire, the plaintiffs were free to lease their units or occupy the units themselves. And once the condominium association (in which plaintiffs had representation after LDC turned over control in September 2006) approved short-term leasing in 2007, the plaintiffs were free to choose whatever management company they wished. Moreover, during the one-year period in which the plaintiffs were locked in to using Sovereign as their leasing agent, the plaintiffs had a temporary rent guarantee that paid them the rent on their existing leases even if their units became unoccupied.

Under these facts, neither the "common enterprise" nor the "expectation of profits solely from the efforts of others" prongs of the *Howey* test are satisfied. The fortunes of the plaintiffs were not "inextricably tied" to the defendants' efforts, because once the plaintiffs' rent was no longer guaranteed, they were free to control their units themselves. For the same reason, the plaintiffs were not dependent on management skills of others because they had the ability to control the profitability of their individual condominium units.

Plaintiffs' attempt to analogize their situation to that in *Howey* is unpersuasive. In *Howey*, the Supreme Court found that the sale of units in a citrus grove development, coupled with a ten-year, non-terminable lease-back and service contract for operating the unit in the grove, constituted an investment contract. The Supreme Court noted that: (1) the units were sold in narrow strips that were not separately fenced and "the sole indication of separate ownership [was] found in small land marks intelligible only through a plat book record"; (2) the owners of particular units had no right of entry into the grove and no right to specific fruit; (3) the owners of the units in the grove lived out of state and lacked the requisite knowledge, skill, and equipment to cultivate citrus trees; and (4) the produce was pooled and the grove operator was "accountable only for an allocation of the net profits." The Supreme Court concluded, under the circumstances, that the coupled transaction was an investment contract. . . .

Here, the transfer of rights in land was far from incidental. . . . As opposed to *Howey*, the transaction here was *not* something more than a fee simple interest in land coupled with (temporary) management services by a company selected by the seller. Nor is third-party management absolutely essential here, as it was in *Howey*.

Plaintiffs contend that third-party management was essential because the plaintiffs all lived in the Chicago area or other areas similarly far from the Kissimmee, Florida location of Legacy Dunes. Additionally, they contend that they all purchased their Legacy Dunes units as investments and not for their own use. However, plaintiffs had other options that did not entail the use of third-party management. Even if purchasing the units as an investment, a plaintiff could have chosen to re-sell his unit for a profit either before or after the existing long-term lease expired. Or a plaintiff could have chosen, once the one-year Sovereign exclusivity period ended, to lease his unit himself or through another rental agency. We note in this regard that the real estate rentals at issue here do not entail the kind of specialized knowledge or equipment present in many cases that have found third-party dependency. . . .

The bottom line is that the plaintiffs had some "ability to control the profitability of [their] investment." The fact that the plaintiffs "delegated management duties or [chose] to rely on some other party does not establish dependency."

The plaintiffs argue that the representations made at the real estate workshops run by Aldeguer focused exclusively on the investment character of the Legacy Dunes units and extolled the effort-free profit available from short-term rentals of the units arranged by the promoters' hand-picked management company, Geneva. Although it is true we must consider "the promises and inducements held out to investors . . . in determining whether or not a particular transaction is a security," here the purchase agreements made abundantly clear that oral representations—at the workshops or otherwise—were not part of the parties' agreement. The parties' actual written agreement demonstrated that it was a real estate purchase agreement, that many of the units were subject to existing long-term leases, and short-term leasing was not immediately available. Moreover, the parties' agreement did not contain any guarantee as to rental income past the first year. Despite the defendants' rosy forecasts, what they actually offered plaintiffs was the purchase of real estate—ownership of units in a condominium complex, with a one year required long-term leasing agent and a contemporaneous period of guaranteed rental income. This was a real estate contract, not an investment contract.

[J] The Risk Capital Test

The risk capital test is an important alternative to the *Howey* standard for ascertaining the existence of an investment contract. Although not generally adopted by the federal courts, the test has been embraced by a number of states by statute or case law. Importantly, application of the risk capital test may lead to a finding of a "security" under the applicable state law where the *Howey* test would hold that no security interest is present.

The risk capital test was first recognized by the California Supreme Court in *Silver Hills Country Club v. Sobieski*, 55 Cal.2d 811, 361 P.2d 906, 908, 13 Cal. Rptr. 186 (1961), in an opinion written by Justice Traynor. There, the California Commission of Corporations successfully argued that the offer and sale of memberships in a country club to be operated for profit were securities under California law. The proceeds from such memberships were to be used for club improvements; members and their immediate families were to be entitled to use club facilities. Even though the benefits to be received were non-pecuniary, the court, applying the risk capital test, held that the membership interests were securities. Justice Traynor stated:

> We have here nothing like the ordinary sale of a right to use existing facilities. Petitioners are soliciting the risk capital with which to develop a business for profit. The purchaser's risk is not lessened merely because the interest he purchases is labeled a membership. Only because he risks his capital along with other purchasers can there be any chance that the benefits of club membership will materialize.

The Supreme Court of Hawaii expanded upon the risk capital test in *State Commissioner of Securities v. Hawaii Market Center, Inc.*, 52 Hawaii 642, 649, 485 P.2d 105, 108 (1971). In holding that a franchise marketing scheme constituted a security, the court stated that an investment contract is created under the Hawaii Securities Act whenever:

> (1) An offeree furnishes initial value to an offeror, and

> (2) a portion of this initial value is subjected to the risks of the enterprise, and

> (3) the furnishing of the initial value is induced by the offeror's promises or representations which give rise to a reasonable understanding that a valuable benefit of some kind, over and above the initial value, will accrue to the offeree as a result of the operation of the enterprise, and

(4) the offeree does not receive the right to exercise practical and actual control over the managerial decisions of the enterprise.

As the court approvingly acknowledged, the above standard is derived from Coffey, *The Economic Realities of a "Security": Is There a More Meaningful Formula?*, 18 Case W. Res. L. Rev. 367 (1967). The Hawaii Supreme Court more recently applied this four-pronged test in *In re TriVectra v. Ushijima*, 144 P. 3d 1 (Haw. 2006). The preceding "risk capital" standard has been adopted by a number of other state courts. See, e.g., *Deckebach v. La Vida Charters, Inc.*, 666 F. Supp. 1049 (S.D. Ohio 1987) (applying Ohio law and citing applicable state cases). Moreover, other versions of the risk capital test have been adopted by a number of states by statute. *See, e.g.,* Wash. Rev. Code § 21.20.005(17)(a).

It is important to note that generally under the risk capital test there is no horizontal common enterprise required and the *Howey* "solely" from the efforts of others standard is relaxed.[7]

Moreover, while evidently applying *Howey*, a number of state courts have set forth somewhat different terminology. For example, in holding that life settlement agreements were investment contracts, the Texas Supreme Court held:

> [W]e conclude that an "investment contract" for purposes of the Texas Securities Act means (1) a contract, transaction, or scheme through which a person pays money (2) to participate in a common venture or enterprise (3) with the expectation of receiving profits, (4) under circumstances in which the failure or success of the enterprise, and thus the person's realization of the expected profits, is at least predominately due to the entrepreneurial or managerial, rather than merely ministerial or clerical, efforts of others, regardless of whether those efforts are made before or after the transaction.

Life Partners, Inc. v. Arnold, 464 S.W.3d 660, 667 (Tex. 2015).

Irrespective of whether the risk capital or the *Howey* test is employed, it may be argued that some courts have not adequately focused on the prospective investor's position at the time that the offer and negotiation occur. Instead, such courts too often may concern themselves with the investor's anticipated position after the deal is struck. Yet, because the critical decisions are made at the offer and negotiation stages, it is at these stages that courts should assess whether the interests at stake warrant invocation of the securities laws. Hence, the time of the applicable "offer" and "sale" should be determinative. On this point, *see* Carney & Fraser, *Defining a "Security": Georgia's Struggle with the "Risk Capital" Test*, 30 Emory L.J. 73 (1981). *See generally* Branson & Okamoto, *The Supreme Court's Literalism and the Definition of "Security" in the State Courts*, 50 Wash. & Lee L. Rev. 1043 (1993).

---

7. *See* 49 *Ops. Cal. Att'y. Gen.* 124, CCH Blue Sky L. Rep. ¶ 70,747 (1967) (1954–1971 Transfer Binder).

§ 2.03 The Emphasis on Economic Reality

Before the Supreme Court's decision in *United Housing Foundation, Inc. v. Forman*, 421 U.S. 837 (1975), the Court had held on every occasion it had considered the issue that the interest at bar was a security. In *Forman* the Court emphasized the economic reality of the situation rather than the form in which the transaction was clothed. Relying largely on the phrase, *"unless the context otherwise requires,"* the Court held that the shares of stock involved were not securities.

United Housing Foundation, Inc. v. Forman

United States Supreme Court

421 U.S. 837, 95 S. Ct. 2051, 44 L. Ed. 2d 621 (1975)

MR. JUSTICE POWELL delivered the opinion of the Court.

The issue in these cases is whether shares of stock entitling a purchaser to lease an apartment in Co-op City, a state subsidized and supervised nonprofit housing cooperative, are "securities" within the purview of the Securities Act of 1933 and the Securities Exchange Act of 1934.

I

Co-op City is a massive housing cooperative in New York City. Built between 1965 and 1971, it presently houses approximately 50,000 people on a 200-acre site containing 35 high-rise buildings and 236 town houses. The project was organized, financed, and constructed under the New York State Private Housing Finance Law, commonly known as the Mitchell-Lama Act, enacted to ameliorate a perceived crisis in the availability of decent low-income urban housing. In order to encourage private developers to build low-cost cooperative housing, New York provides them with large long-term, low-interest mortgage loans and substantial tax exemptions. Receipt of such benefits is conditioned on a willingness to have the State review virtually every step in the development of the cooperative. The developer also must agree to operate the facility "on a nonprofit basis," and he may lease apartments only to people whose incomes fall below a certain level and who have been approved by the State.

The United Housing Foundation (UHF), a nonprofit membership corporation established for the purpose of "aiding and encouraging" the creation of "adequate, safe and sanitary housing accommodations for wage earners and other persons of low or moderate income," was responsible for initiating and sponsoring the development of Co-op City. Acting under the Mitchell-Lama Act, UHF organized the Riverbay Corporation (Riverbay) to own and operate the land and buildings constituting Co-op City. Riverbay, a nonprofit cooperative housing corporation, issued the stock that is the subject of this litigation. UHF also contracted with Community Services, Inc. (CSI), its wholly owned subsidiary, to serve as the general contractor and sales agent for the project. As required by the Mitchell-Lama Act, these decisions were approved by the State Housing Commissioner.

To acquire an apartment in Co-op City an eligible prospective purchaser[8] must buy 18 shares of stock in Riverbay for each room desired. The cost per share is $25, making the total cost $450 per room, or $1,800 for a four-room apartment. The sole purpose of acquiring these shares is to enable the purchaser to occupy an apartment in Co-op City; in effect, their purchase is a recoverable deposit on an apartment. The shares are explicitly tied to the apartment: they cannot be transferred to a nontenant; nor can they be pledged or encumbered; and they descend, along with the apartment, only to a surviving spouse. No voting rights attach to the shares as such: participation in the affairs of the cooperative appertains to the apartment, with the residents of each apartment being entitled to one vote irrespective of the number of shares owned.

Any tenant who wants to terminate his occupancy, or who is forced to move out, must offer his stock to Riverbay at its initial selling price of $25 per share. In the extremely unlikely event that Riverbay declines to repurchase the stock, the tenant cannot sell it for more than the initial purchase price plus a fraction of the portion of the mortgage that he has paid off, and then only to a prospective tenant satisfying the statutory income eligibility requirements.

In May 1965, subsequent to the completion of the initial planning, Riverbay circulated an Information Bulletin seeking to attract tenants for what would someday be apartments in Co-op City. After describing the nature and advantages of cooperative housing generally and of Co-op City in particular, the Bulletin informed prospective tenants that the total estimated cost of the project, based largely on an anticipated construction contract with CSI, was $283,695,550. Only a fraction of this sum, $32,795,550, was to be raised by the sale of shares to tenants. The remaining $250,900,000 was to be financed by a 40-year low-interest mortgage loan from the New York Private Housing Finance Agency. After construction of the project the mortgage payments and current operating expenses would be met by monthly rental charges paid by the tenants. While these rental charges were to vary, depending on the size, nature, and location of an apartment, the 1965 Bulletin estimated that the "average" monthly cost would be $23.02 per room, or $92.08 for a four-room apartment.

Several times during the construction of Co-op City, Riverbay, with the approval of the State Housing Commissioner, revised its contract with CSI to allow for increased construction costs. In addition, Riverbay incurred other expenses that had not been reflected in the 1965 Bulletin. To meet these increased expenditures, Riverbay, with the Commissioner's approval, repeatedly secured increased mortgage loans from the State Housing Agency. Ultimately the construction loan was $125 million more than the figure estimated in the 1965 Bulletin. As a result, while the initial purchasing price

---

8. Respondents are referred to herein variously as "purchasers," "owners," or "tenants." Respondents do not hold legal title to their respective apartments, but they are purchasers and owners of the shares of Riverbay which entitles them to occupy the apartments. By virtue of their right of occupancy, respondents are usually described as tenants.

remained at $450 per room, the average monthly rental charges increased periodically, reaching a figure of $39.68 per room as of July 1974.

These increases in the rental charges precipitated the present lawsuit. Respondents, 57 residents of Co-op City, sued in federal court on behalf of all 15,372 apartment owners, and derivatively on behalf of Riverbay, seeking upwards of $30 million in damages, forced rental reductions, and other "appropriate" relief. Named as defendants (petitioners herein) were UHF, CSI, Riverbay, several individual directors of these organizations, the State of New York, and the State Private Housing Finance Agency. The heart of respondents' claim was that the 1965 Co-op City Information Bulletin falsely represented that CSI would bear all subsequent cost increases due to factors such as inflation. Respondents further alleged that they were misled in their purchases of shares since the Information Bulletin failed to disclose several critical facts. On these bases, respondents asserted two claims under the fraud provisions of the federal Securities Act of 1933 [and] the Securities Exchange Act of 1934. . . .

Petitioners, while denying the substance of these allegations, moved to dismiss the complaint on the ground that federal jurisdiction was lacking. They maintained that shares of stock in Riverbay were not "securities" within the definitional sections of the federal Securities Acts . . .

[W]e conclude that the disputed transactions are not purchases of securities within the contemplation of the federal statutes.

II

[Congress] sought to define "the term 'security' in sufficiently broad and general terms so as to include within that definition the many types of instruments that in our commercial world fall within the ordinary concept of a security." H. R. Rep. No. 85, 73d Cong., 1st Sess., 11 (1933). The task has fallen to the Securities and Exchange Commission (SEC), the body charged with administering the Securities Acts, and ultimately to the federal courts to decide which of the myriad financial transactions in our society come within the coverage of these statutes.

In making this determination in the present case we do not write on a clean slate. Well-settled principles enunciated by this Court establish that the shares purchased by respondents do not represent any of the "countless and variable schemes devised by those who seek the use of the money of others on the promise of profits," and therefore do not fall within "the ordinary concept of a security."

A

We reject at the outset any suggestion that the present transaction, evidenced by the sale of shares called "stock," must be considered a security transaction simply because the statutory definition of a security includes the words "any . . . stock." Rather we adhere to the basic principle that has guided all of the Court's decisions in this area:

[I]n searching for the meaning and scope of the word "security" in the Act[s], form should be disregarded for substance and the emphasis should be on economic reality.

Tcherepnin v. Knight, 389 U.S. 332, 336 (1967).

The primary purpose of the Acts of 1933 and 1934 was to eliminate serious abuses in a largely unregulated securities market. The focus of the Acts is on the capital market of the enterprise system: the sale of securities to raise capital for profit-making purposes, the exchanges on which securities are traded, and the need for regulation to prevent fraud and to protect the interest of investors. Because securities transactions are economic in character Congress intended the application of these statutes to turn on the economic realities underlying a transaction, and not on the name appended thereto. Thus, in construing these Acts against the background of their purpose, we are guided by a traditional canon of statutory construction:

[A] thing may be within the letter of the statute and yet not within the statute, because not within its spirit, nor within the intention of its makers.

. . . .

In holding that the name given to an instrument is not dispositive, we do not suggest that the name is wholly irrelevant to the decision whether it is a security. There may be occasions when the use of a traditional name such as "stocks" or "bonds" will lead a purchaser justifiably to assume that the federal securities laws apply. This would clearly be the case when the underlying transaction embodies some of the significant characteristics typically associated with the named instrument.

In the present case respondents do not contend, nor could they, that they were misled by use of the word "stock" into believing that the federal securities laws governed their purchase. Common sense suggests that people who intend to acquire only a residential apartment in a state-subsidized cooperative, for their personal use, are not likely to believe that in reality they are purchasing investment securities simply because the transaction is evidenced by something called a share of stock. These shares have none of the characteristics "that in our commercial world fall within the ordinary concept of a security." Despite their name, they lack what the Court in *Tcherepnin* deemed the most common feature of stock: the right to receive "dividends contingent upon an apportionment of profits." Nor do they possess the other characteristics traditionally associated with stock: they are not negotiable; they cannot be pledged or hypothecated; they confer no voting rights in proportion to the number of shares owned; and they cannot appreciate in value. In short, the inducement to purchase was solely to acquire subsidized low-cost living space; it was not to invest for profit.

B

The Court of Appeals, as an alternative ground for its decision, concluded that a share in Riverbay was also an "investment contract" as defined by the Securities Acts.

Respondents further argue that in any event what they agreed to purchase is "commonly known as a 'security'" within the meaning of these laws. In considering these claims we again must examine the substance—the economic realities of the transaction—rather than the names that may have been employed by the parties. We perceive no distinction, for present purposes, between an "investment contract" and an "instrument commonly known as a 'security.'" In either case, the basic test for distinguishing the transaction from other commercial dealings is

> whether the scheme involves an investment of money in a common enterprise with profits to come solely from the efforts of others.

Howey, 328 U.S., at 301.[9]

This test, in shorthand form, embodies the essential attributes that run through all of the Court's decisions defining a security. The touchstone is the presence of an investment in a common venture premised on a reasonable expectation of profits to be derived from the entrepreneurial or managerial efforts of others. By profits, the Court has meant either capital appreciation resulting from the development of the initial investment . . . or a participation in earnings resulting from the use of investors' funds. . . . In such cases the investor is "attracted solely by the prospects of a return" on his investment. . . . By contrast, when a purchaser is motivated by a desire to use or consume the item purchased — "to occupy the land or to develop it themselves," as the *Howey* Court put it — the securities laws do not apply.

In the present case there can be no doubt that investors were attracted solely by the prospect of acquiring a place to live. . . . Nowhere does the Bulletin seek to attract investors by the prospect of profits resulting from the efforts of the promoters or third parties. . . . It also informs purchasers that they will be unable to resell their apartments at a profit since the apartment must first be offered back to Riverbay "at the price . . . paid for it." In short, neither of the kinds of profits traditionally associated with securities was offered to respondents.

The Court of Appeals recognized that there must be an expectation of profits for these shares to be securities, and conceded that there is "no possible profit on a resale of [this] stock."

. . . The court correctly noted, however, that profit may be derived from the income yielded by an investment as well as from capital appreciation, and then proceeded to find "an expectation of 'income' in at least three ways." Two of these supposed sources of income or profits may be disposed of summarily. We turn first to the

---

9. This test speaks in terms of "profits to come *solely* from the efforts of others." (Emphasis supplied.) Although the issue is not presented in this case, we note that the Court of Appeals for the Ninth Circuit has held that "the word 'solely' should not be read as a strict or literal limitation on the definition of an investment contract, but rather must be construed realistically, so as to include within the definition those schemes which involve in substance, if not form, securities." *SEC v. Glenn W. Turner Enterprises*, 474 F.2d 476, 482, *cert. denied*, 414 U.S. 821 (1973). We express no view, however, as to the holding of this case.

Court of Appeals' reliance on the deductibility for tax purposes of the portion of the monthly rental charge applied to interest on the mortgage. We know of no basis in law for the view that the payment of interest, with its consequent deductibility for tax purposes, constitutes income or profits.[10] These tax benefits are nothing more than that which is available to any homeowner who pays interest on his mortgage.

The Court of Appeals also found support for its concept of profits in the fact that Co-op City offered space at a cost substantially below the going rental charges for comparable housing. Again, this is an inappropriate theory of "profits" that we cannot accept. The low rent derives from the substantial financial subsidies provided by the State of New York. This benefit cannot be liquidated into cash; nor does it result from the managerial efforts of others. In a real sense, it no more embodies the attributes of income or profits than do welfare benefits, food stamps, or other government subsidies.

The final source of profit relied on by the Court of Appeals was the possibility of net income derived from the leasing by Co-op City of commercial facilities, professional offices and parking spaces, and its operation of community washing machines. The income, if any, from these conveniences, all located within the common areas of the housing project, is to be used to reduce tenant rental costs. Conceptually, one might readily agree that net income from the leasing of commercial and professional facilities is the kind of profit traditionally associated with a security investment. But in the present case this income—if indeed there is any—is far too speculative and insubstantial to bring the entire transaction within the Securities Acts. Undoubtedly [these facilities and offices] make Co-op City a more attractive housing opportunity, but the possibility of some rental reduction is not an "expectation of profit" in the sense found necessary in *Howey*.[11]

There is no doubt that purchasers in this housing cooperative sought to obtain a decent home at an attractive price. But that type of economic interest characterizes every form of commercial dealing. What distinguishes a security transaction—and what is absent here—is an investment where one parts with his money in the hope of receiving profits from the efforts of others, and not where he purchases a commodity for personal consumption or living quarters for personal use.

Reversed

---

10. Even if these tax deductions were considered profits, they would not be the type associated with a security investment since they do not result from the managerial efforts of others. . . .

11. Respondents urge us to abandon the element of profits in the definition of security and to adopt the "risk capital" approach articulated by the California Supreme Court in *Silver Hills Country Club v. Sobieski*, 55 Cal. 2d 811, 361 P. 2d 906 (1961). . . . Even if we were inclined to adopt such a "risk capital" approach we would not apply it in the present case. Purchasers of apartments in Co-op City take no risk in any significant sense. If dissatisfied with their apartments, they may recover their initial investment in full.

Note

The *Forman* decision stands for the general proposition that the securities laws do not apply where the purchaser engages in the transaction principally to use or consume the interest acquired. Because the plaintiffs in *Forman* were motivated mainly by the desire to obtain affordable and decent housing, rather than seeking a return on the acquisition, the securities laws were not applicable.

In a more recent decision, Justice Powell, sitting by designation on the Eleventh Circuit, opined that purchases of beachfront lots and equity memberships in an adjacent country club were not securities. The court asserted that the purchasers entered into these transactions "primarily to use them, not to derive profits from the entrepreneurial efforts of the developers." Moreover, "[t]he overall emphasis in the promotional material was clearly placed on enjoying the beauty . . . and the amenities of the club and community." Hence, the court held: "where those who purchase something [have] the primary desire to use or consume it, the security laws do not apply." *Rice v. Branigar Organization, Inc.*, 922 F.2d 788, 790–791 (11th Cir. 1991). See *Bara v. Hamilton Farm Golf Club,* [2009 Transfer Binder] Fed. Sec. L. Rep. (CCH) ¶ 95,377 (D.N.J. 2009) (purchase of golf club memberships not securities under federal law).

As will be seen, however, if an instrument takes on the usual characteristics of traditional stock, the securities laws will apply. This is so even if the purchaser intends to be an active entrepreneur who seeks to "use or consume" the business acquired. *See* § 2.03[B], *infra*.

[A] Forms of Profit

The *Forman* Court identified two forms of "profit" that meet the *Howey* test: (1) "capital appreciation resulting from the development of the initial investment," and (2) "a participation in earnings resulting from the use of investors' funds." In so holding, the Court rejected the plaintiffs' argument that their tax deductions were a form of profit. More recently, in *SEC v. Edwards,* 540 U.S. 389 (2004), the Supreme Court elaborated that "profit" includes, "for example, dividends, other periodic payments or the increased value of the investments." Hence, a contractual entitlement to a fixed return meets the *Howey* expectations-of-profit prong.

[B] The Sale of Business Doctrine

In *Forman*, the Supreme Court stated that the *Howey* "test, in shorthand form, embodies the essential attributes that run through all of the Court's decisions defining a security." Before *Forman*, the Court's decisions involving whether a security was present principally had centered on the meaning of the term "investment contract." Nonetheless, many believed that the above language meant that, in order for a security to be present (such as "stock" or "note"), the *Howey* test must be met.

This issue crystallized in the split that developed among the lower federal courts concerning the "sale of business" doctrine. The issue involved was whether the transfer of stock incidental to the sale of a closely held business constituted a security. The Second, Third, Fourth, and Fifth Circuits rejected the sale of business doctrine, while the Seventh, Ninth, Tenth, and Eleventh Circuits accepted the doctrine. There was persuasive scholarly commentary on both sides of the issue.[12]

For example, in *Golden v. Garafalo*, 678 F.2d 1139 (2d Cir. 1982), the Second Circuit emphatically rejected the sale of business doctrine. The court held that "conventional stock in business corporations is a security within the meaning of the 1933 and 1934 Acts whether or not the underlying transaction involves the sale of a business to one who intends to manage it." The transaction at issue in *Garafalo* involved the sale of 100 percent of the stock of a privately held corporation to buyers who intended to manage the business directly. The court determined that *Forman* laid down a two-part test: The first prong of the test asked whether the shares in question were "stock" and examined whether the instruments possessed the traditional attributes of "stock." Only after the *Forman* Court rejected the shares as being "stock" did it turn to the second prong to evaluate whether the shares were an investment contract under the *Howey* test. According to the Second Circuit in *Garafalo*, Congress created an expansive definition for the term "security" and specifically included all instruments with characteristics that were generally agreed on in the commercial world. "Catch-all phrases such as 'investment contract' were then included to cover unique instruments not easily classified."

On the other hand, in *Fredericksen v. Poloway*, 637 F.2d 1147 (7th Cir. 1981), the Seventh Circuit adopted the sale of business doctrine, holding that if the purchaser of stock in a corporation assumes control over the critical decisions of the corporation, the transaction does not involve the sale of securities. The court stated that "the key to defining the scope of the securities laws is whether the transaction is primarily for commercial (i.e., motivated by a desire to use, consume, occupy, or develop), or for investment purposes." The court rejected a literal interpretation of the statutory definition of a security, finding that the definition, merely because it contained the word "stock," did not apply to every sales transaction involving stock. The court interpreted *Forman* as applying only a one-part "economic reality" test and as looking to substance over form.

Subsequently, in *Sutter v. Groen*, 687 F.2d 197 (7th Cir. 1982), the Seventh Circuit held that "[i]f the purchaser has, or by the purchase in question, acquired more than fifty percent of the common stock of the corporation, his purpose in purchasing the stock will be presumed to have been entrepreneurship rather than investment," and

---

12. *See, e.g.*, Hazen, *Taking Stock of Stock and the Sale of Closely Held Corporations: When Is Stock Not a Security?*, 61 N.C. L. Rev. 393 (1983); Thompson, *The Shrinking Definition of a Security: Why Purchasing All of a Company's Stock Is Not a Federal Security Transaction*, 57 N.Y.U. L. Rev. 225 (1982); Wheatley, *Function Over Form: The Sale of Business Doctrine and the Definition of a Security*, 63 B.U.L. Rev. 1129 (1983).

the securities laws do not apply. The court allowed the presumption to be rebutted if the purchaser's main purpose is proven to be investment.

After these lower court decisions adopting the sale of business doctrine, a number of issues remained open. For example, would the doctrine apply to the sale of stock where:

(a) One 20 percent co-owner, being the largest shareholder, intends to manage the business jointly with the other co-owners?

(b) A co-owner, who otherwise would have the right actively to manage the business, delegates this managerial authority to others?

(c) There are three purchasers, namely, Abel who acquires 51 percent, Berry, who purchases 25 percent, and Casey who acquires 24 percent of the stock. Does it make sense that Berry and Casey may invoke the securities laws but not Abel? How is this any different from a limited partnership where only the limited partners (but not the general partners) normally can invoke the securities laws?

(d) There is a tender offer made by a publicly held corporation for 100 percent of another publicly held corporation's stock. Should the bidder-offeror be able to invoke the federal securities laws if it is defrauded by the offeree ("target") corporation (such as through misrepresentation and nondisclosure of material facts)?

Due to the deep split among the lower federal courts and the important policy issues raised, the Supreme Court resolved the sale of business doctrine issue.

Landreth Timber Company v. Landreth

United States Supreme Court

471 U.S. 681, 105 S. Ct. 2297, 85 L. Ed. 2d 692 (1985)

MR. JUSTICE POWELL delivered the opinion of the Court.

This case presents the question whether the sale of all of the stock of a company is a securities transaction subject to the antifraud provisions of the federal securities laws (the Acts).

I

Respondents Ivan K. Landreth and his sons owned all of the outstanding stock of a lumber business they operated in Tonasket, Washington. The Landreth family offered their stock for sale through both Washington and out-of-state brokers. Before a purchaser was found, the company's sawmill was heavily damaged by fire. Despite the fire, the brokers continued to offer the stock for sale. Potential purchasers were advised of the damage, but were told that the mill would be completely rebuilt and modernized.

Samuel Dennis, a Massachusetts tax attorney, received a letter offering the stock for sale. On the basis of the letter's representations concerning the rebuilding plans, the predicted productivity of the mill, existing contracts, and expected profits, Dennis became interested in acquiring the stock. He talked to John Bolten, a former client who had retired to Florida, about joining him in investigating the offer. After having an audit and an inspection of the mill conducted, a stock purchase agreement was negotiated, with Dennis the purchaser of all of the common stock in the lumber company. Ivan Landreth agreed to stay on as a consultant for some time to help with the daily operations of the mill. Pursuant to the terms of the stock purchase agreement, Dennis assigned the stock he purchased to B & D Co., a corporation formed for the sole purpose of acquiring the lumber company stock. B & D then merged with the lumber company, forming petitioner Landreth Timber Co. Dennis and Bolten then acquired all of petitioner's Class A stock, representing 85% of the equity, and six other investors together owned the Class B stock, representing the remaining 15% of the equity.

After the acquisition was completed, the mill did not live up to the purchasers' expectations. Rebuilding costs exceeded earlier estimates, and new components turned out to be incompatible with existing equipment. Eventually, petitioner sold the mill at a loss and went into receivership. Petitioner then filed this suit seeking rescission of the sale of stock and $2,500,000 in damages, alleging that respondents had widely offered and then sold their stock without registering it as required by the Securities Act of 1933. . . . Petitioner also alleged that respondents had . . . made misrepresentations and had failed to state material facts as to the worth and prospects of the lumber company, all in violation of the Securities Exchange Act of 1934.

. . . .

Respondents moved for summary judgment on the ground that the transaction was not covered by the Acts because under the so-called "sale of business" doctrine, petitioner had not purchased a "security" within the meaning of those Acts. The District Court granted respondents' motion and dismissed the complaint for want of federal jurisdiction. It acknowledged that the federal statutes include "stock" as one of the instruments constituting a "security," and that the stock at issue possessed all of the characteristics of conventional stock. Nonetheless, it joined what it termed the "growing majority" of courts that had held that the federal securities laws do not apply to the sale of 100% of the stock of a closely held corporation.

. . .

The United States Court of Appeals for the Ninth Circuit affirmed the District Court's application of the sale of business doctrine. . . . Because the Courts of Appeals are divided over the applicability of the federal securities laws when a business is sold by the transfer of 100% of its stock, we granted certiorari. . . . We now reverse.

II

It is axiomatic that "[t]he starting point in every case involving construction of a statute is the language itself." . . . Section 2(1) [now § 2(a)(1)] of the 1933 Act . . . defines a "security" as including any note, stock, treasury stock, bond, debenture, evidence of indebtedness, certificate of interest or participation in any profit-sharing agreement, collateral-trust certificate, preorganization certificate or subscription, transferable share, investment contract, voting-trust certificate, certificate of deposit for a security, fractional undivided interest in oil, gas, or other mineral rights, . . . or, in general, any interest or instrument commonly known as a "security," or any certificate of interest or participation in, temporary or interim certificate for, receipt for, guarantee of, or warrant or right to subscribe to or purchase, any of the foregoing.[13] As we have observed in the past, this definition is quite broad . . . and includes both instruments whose names alone carry well-settled meaning, as well as instruments of "more variable character [that] were necessarily designated by more descriptive terms," such as "investment contract" and "instruments commonly known as a 'security.'" *SEC v. C.M. Joiner Leasing Corp.*, 320 U.S. 344, 351 (1943). The face of the definition shows that "stock" is considered to be a "security" within the meaning of the Acts. As we observed in *United Housing Foundation, Inc. v. Forman*, most instruments bearing such a traditional title are likely to be covered by the definition.

As we also recognized in *Forman*, the fact that instruments bear the label "stock" is not of itself sufficient to invoke the coverage of the Acts. Rather, we concluded that we must also determine whether those instruments possess "some of the significant characteristics typically associated with" stock, recognizing that when an instrument is both called "stock" and bears stock's usual characteristics, "a purchaser justifiably [may] assume that the federal securities laws apply" . . . . We identified those characteristics usually associated with common stock as (i) the right to receive dividends contingent upon an apportionment of profits; (ii) negotiability; (iii) the ability to be pledged or hypothecated; (iv) the conferring of voting rights in proportion to the number of shares owned; and (v) the capacity to appreciate in value.[14]

Under the facts of *Forman*, we concluded that the instruments at issue there were not "securities" within the meaning of the Acts. That case involved the sale of shares of stock entitling the purchaser to lease an apartment in a housing cooperative. The stock bore none of the characteristics listed above that are usually associated with traditional stock. Moreover, we concluded that under the circumstances, there was

---

13. We have repeatedly ruled that the definitions of "security" in § 3(a)(10) of the 1934 Act and § 2(1) of the 1933 Act are virtually identical and will be treated as such in our decisions dealing with the scope of the term. *Marine Bank v. Weaver*, 455 U.S. 551, 555, n. 3, 102 S. Ct. 1220, 1223, n. 3, 71 L.Ed.2d 409 (1982); *United Housing Foundation, Inc. v. Forman*, 421 U.S. 837, 847, n. 12, 95 S.Ct. 2051, 2058, n. 12, 44 L.Ed.2d 621 (1975).

14. Although we did not so specify in *Forman*, we wish to make clear here that these characteristics are those usually associated with common stock, the kind of stock often at issue in cases involving the sale of a business. Various types of preferred stock may have different characteristics and still be covered by the Acts.

no likelihood that the purchasers had been misled by use of the word "stock" into thinking that the federal securities laws governed their purchases. The purchasers had intended to acquire low-cost subsidized living space for their personal use; no one was likely to have believed that [they were] purchasing investment securities.

In contrast, it is undisputed that the stock involved here possesses all of the characteristics we identified in *Forman* as traditionally associated with common stock. Indeed, the District Court so found. Moreover, unlike in *Forman*, the context of the transaction involved here — the sale of stock in a corporation — is typical of the kind of context to which the Acts normally apply. It is thus much more likely here than in *Forman* that an investor would believe he was covered by the federal securities laws. Under the circumstances of this case, the plain meaning of the statutory definition mandates that the stock be treated as "securities" subject to the coverage of the Acts.

Reading the securities laws to apply to the sale of stock at issue here comports with Congress' remedial purpose in enacting the legislation to protect investors by "compelling full and fair disclosure relative to the issuance of 'the many types of instruments that in our commercial world fall within the ordinary concept of a security.'" *SEC v. W.J. Howey Co.*, 328 U.S., at 299 . . . . Although we recognize that Congress did not intend to provide a comprehensive federal remedy for all fraud, we think it would improperly narrow Congress' broad definition of "security" to hold that the traditional stock at issue here falls outside the Acts' coverage.

III

Under other circumstances, we might consider the statutory analysis outlined above to be a sufficient answer compelling judgment for petitioner. Respondents urge, however, that language in our previous opinions, including *Forman*, requires that we look beyond the label "stock" and the characteristics of the instruments involved to determine whether application of the Acts is mandated by the economic substance of the transaction. Moreover, the Court of Appeals rejected the view that the plain meaning of the definition would be sufficient to hold this stock covered, because it saw "no principled way," to justify treating notes, bonds, and other of the definitional categories differently. We address these concerns in turn.

A

It is fair to say that our cases have not been entirely clear on the proper method of analysis for determining when an instrument is a "security." This Court has decided a number of cases in which it looked to the economic substance of the transaction, rather than just to its form, to determine whether the Acts applied. In *SEC v. C.M. Joiner Leasing Corp.*, for example, the Court considered whether the 1933 Act applied to the sale of leasehold interests in land near a proposed oil well drilling. In holding that the leasehold interests were "securities," the Court noted that "the reach of the Act does not stop with the obvious and commonplace." Rather, it ruled that unusual devices such as the leaseholds would also be covered "if it be proved as matter of fact that they were widely offered or dealt in under terms or courses of dealing which established their character in commerce as 'investment contracts,' or as 'any interest or instrument commonly known as a "security." ' " . . .

SEC v. W.J. Howey Co., . . . further elucidated the *Joiner* Court's suggestion that an unusual instrument could be considered a "security" if the circumstances of the transaction so dictated. At issue in that case was an offering of units of a citrus grove development coupled with a contract for cultivating and marketing the fruit and remitting the proceeds to the investors. The Court held that the offering constituted an "investment contract" within the meaning of the 1933 Act because, looking at the economic realities, the transaction "involve[d] an investment of money in a common enterprise with profits to come solely from the efforts of others." . . .

This so-called "*Howey* test" formed the basis for the second part of our decision in *Forman*, on which respondents primarily rely. As discussed above, . . . the first part of our decision in *Forman* concluded that the instruments at issue, while they bore the traditional label "stock," were not "securities" because they possessed none of the usual characteristics of stock. We then went on to address the argument that the instruments were "investment contracts." Applying the *Howey* test, we concluded that the instruments likewise were not "securities" by virtue of being "investment contracts" because the economic realities of the transaction showed that the purchasers had parted with their money not for the purpose of reaping profits from the efforts of others, but for the purpose of purchasing a commodity for personal consumption.

Respondents contend that *Forman* and the cases on which it was based require us to reject the view that the shares of stock at issue here may be considered "securities" because of their name and characteristics. Instead, they argue that our cases require us in every instance to look to the economic substance of the transaction to determine whether the *Howey* test has been met. According to respondents, it is clear that petitioner sought not to earn profits from the efforts of others, but to buy a company that it could manage and control. Petitioner was not a passive investor of the kind Congress intended the Acts to protect, but an active entrepreneur, who sought to "use or consume" the business purchased just as the purchasers in *Forman* sought to use the apartments they acquired after purchasing shares of stock. Thus, respondents urge that the Acts do not apply.

We disagree with respondents' interpretation of our cases. First, it is important to understand the contexts within which these cases were decided. All of the cases on which respondents rely involved unusual instruments not easily characterized as "securities." Thus, if the Acts were to apply in those cases at all, it would have to have been because the economic reality underlying the transactions indicated that the instruments were actually of a type that falls within the usual concept of a security. In the case at bar, in contrast, the instrument involved is traditional stock, plainly within the statutory definition. There is no need here, as there was in the prior cases, to look beyond the characteristics of the instrument to determine whether the Acts apply.

Contrary to respondents' implication, the Court has never foreclosed the possibility that stock could be found to be a "security" simply because it is what it purports to be. . . . Nor does *Forman* require a different result. Respondents are correct that in *Forman* we eschewed a "literal" approach that would invoke the Acts' coverage simply because the instrument carried the label "stock." *Forman* does not, however, eliminate the Court's ability to hold that an instrument is covered when its characteristics bear out the label.

Second, we would note that the *Howey* economic reality test was designed to determine whether a particular instrument is an "investment contract," not whether it fits within *any* of the examples listed in the statutory definition of "security." Our cases are consistent with this view. Moreover, applying the *Howey* test to traditional stock and all other types of instruments listed in the statutory definition would make the Acts' enumeration of many types of instruments superfluous. Finally, we cannot agree with respondents that the Acts were intended to cover only "passive investors" and not privately negotiated transactions involving the transfer of control to "entrepreneurs." The 1934 Act contains several provisions specifically governing tender offers, disclosure of transactions by corporate officers and principal stockholders, and the recovery of short-swing profits gained by such persons. Eliminating from the definition of "security" instruments involved in transactions where control passed to the purchaser would contravene the purposes of these provisions. . . . Thus, the structure and language of the Acts refute respondents' position.

B

We now turn to the Court of Appeals' concern that treating stock as a specific category of "security" provable by its characteristics means that other categories listed in the statutory definition, such as notes, must be treated the same way. Although we do not decide whether coverage of notes or other instruments may be provable by their name and characteristics, we do point out several reasons why we think stock may be distinguishable from most if not all of the other categories listed in the Acts' definition.

Instruments that bear both the name and all of the usual characteristics of stock seem to us to be the clearest case for coverage by the plain language of the definition. First, traditional stock "represents to many people, both trained and untrained in business matters, the paradigm of a security." . . . Thus persons trading in traditional stock likely have a high expectation that their activities are governed by the Acts. Second, as we made clear in *Forman*, "stock" is relatively easy to identify because it lends itself to consistent definition. Unlike some instruments, therefore, traditional stock is more susceptible of a plain meaning approach.

. . . .

. . . We here expressly leave until another day the question whether "notes" or "bonds" or some other category of instrument listed in the definition might be shown "by proving [only] the document itself." . . . [The Court subsequently addressed this issue in the *Reves* decision — see § 2.05[A], *infra*.] We hold only that "stock" may be viewed as being in a category by itself for purposes of interpreting the scope of the Acts' definition of "security."

IV

We also perceive strong policy reasons for not employing the sale of business doctrine under the circumstances of this case. By respondents' own admission, application of the doctrine depends in each case on whether control has passed to the purchaser. It may be argued that on the facts of this case, the doctrine is easily applied, since the transfer of 100% of a corporation's stock normally transfers control. We think even that assertion is open to some question, however, as Dennis and Bolten had no intention of running the sawmill themselves. Ivan Landreth apparently stayed on to manage the daily affairs of the business. Some commentators who support the sale of business doctrine believe that a purchaser who has the ability to exert control but chooses not to do so may deserve the Acts' protection if he is simply a passive investor not engaged in the daily management of the business. In this case, the District Court was required to undertake extensive fact-finding, and even requested supplemental facts and memoranda on the issue of control, before it was able to decide the case.

More importantly, however, if applied to this case, the sale of business doctrine would also have to be applied to cases in which less than 100% of a company's stock was sold. This inevitably would lead to difficult questions of line-drawing. The Acts' coverage would in every case depend not only on the percentage of stock transferred, but also on such factors as the number of purchasers and what provisions for voting and veto rights were agreed upon by the parties. [Hence,] coverage by the Acts would in most cases be unknown and unknowable to the parties at the time the stock was sold. These uncertainties attending the applicability of the Acts would hardly be in the best interests of either party to a transaction. . . . Respondents argue that adopting petitioner's approach will increase the workload of the federal courts by converting state and common law fraud claims into federal claims. We find more daunting, however, the prospect that parties to a transaction may never know whether they are covered by the Acts until they engage in extended discovery and litigation over a concept as often elusive as the passage of control. . . .

V

In sum, we conclude that the stock at issue here is a "security" within the definition of the Acts, and that the sale of business doctrine does not apply. The judgment of the United States Court of Appeals for the Ninth Circuit is therefore

Reversed

Note

Reconciling the Supreme Court's decision in *Landreth Timber* with the economic reality approach, the Court in a subsequent case reasoned: "*Landreth Timber* does not signify a lack of concern with economic reality; rather it signals a recognition that stock is, as a practical matter, always an investment if it has the economic characteristics traditionally associated with stock." *Reves v. Ernst & Young*, 494 U.S. 56,

62 (1990). *See Gould v. Ruefenacht*, 471 U.S. 701 (1985) (companion case following *Landreth Timber's* rationale).

Subsequent cases continue to address the issue concerning the security law status of instruments called stock. *See, e.g., Great Rivers Cooperative of S.E. Iowa v. Farmland Industries, Inc.*, 198 F.3d 685 (8th Cir. 2000) (equity interests in capital credits issued by agricultural cooperative association held not a security); *Seger v. Federal Intermediate Credit Bank of Omaha*, 850 F.2d 468 (8th Cir. 1988) (applying *Forman* criteria, lender's Class B "stock" did not have characteristics normally associated with such an instrument and, hence, was not a security); *One-O-One Enterprises, Inc. v. Caruso*, 848 F.2d 1283 (D.C. Cir. 1988) (option to purchase stock deemed a security relying on *Landreth*); *McVay v. Western Plains Service Corporation*, 823 F.2d 1395 (10th Cir. 1987) (interpreting *Forman*, loan participation certificates held not to be "stock" within scope of the securities laws because such certificates "lack[ed] any of the basic attributes of true stock").

As a last point, the Supreme Court's decision in *Landreth* rejected the sale of business doctrine under federal law. The states may interpret their respective securities laws in a different manner. Several states follow *Landreth*. *See, e.g., Andrews v. Browne*, 276 Va. 141, 662 S.E. 2d 58 (Va. 2008) (sale of stock in a closely held company is a security under the Virginia Securities Act). On the other hand, a number of states adhere to the sale of business doctrine. *See, e.g., Doherty v. Kahn*, 289 Ill. App. 3d 544, 682 N.E. 2d 163 (Ill. App. 1997).

[C] Employee Pension Plans

In *International Brotherhood of Teamsters v. Daniel*, 439 U.S. 551 (1979), the Supreme Court applied the "economic reality" concept to constrict, rather than to broaden, the definition of "investment contract." Specifically, the Court held that interests in a noncontributory, compulsory pension plan are not investment contracts and, hence, not securities. In a noncontributory, compulsory pension plan, the employer contributes the necessary payments, not the employee who ultimately benefits from the plan. The Court applied the *Howey* test for an investment contract. Concentrating on the economic reality of the plan, the Court observed that "an employee is selling his labor primarily to obtain a livelihood, not making an investment" and, therefore, concluded that the *Howey* test's "investment of money" element was not satisfied. Moreover, the employer's contributions to the fund were not the equivalent of an "investment" by the employee because no fixed relationship existed between the employer's contributions and the employee's potential benefits. The Court also found that the pension fund's assets did not depend on profits yielded by the efforts of others. To the contrary, the vast majority of the income generated derived from the employer's contributions and thus was independent of the efforts of the fund's managers. In addition, actual receipt of benefits from the fund depended on whether employees met certain individual eligibility requirements, not on the financial success of the fund itself.

The *Daniel* Court further supported its holding by concluding that the enactment of ERISA, which expressly regulates pension plans, eliminated the need for coverage under the securities laws:

> The existence of this comprehensive legislation governing the use and terms of employee pension plans severely undercuts all arguments for extending the Securities Acts to noncontributory, compulsory pension plans. Congress believed that it was filling a regulatory void when it enacted ERISA, a belief which the SEC actively encouraged. Not only is the extension of the Securities Acts . . . not supported by the language and history of those Acts, but in light of ERISA it serves no general purpose.
>
> . . . Whatever benefits employees might derive from the effect of the Securities Acts are now provided in more definite form through ERISA.

On the other hand, voluntarily contributory pension plans may be securities. *See Uselton v. Commercial Lovelace Motor Freight, Inc.*, 940 F.2d 564 (10th Cir. 1991); Securities Act Release Nos. 6188 (1980), 6281 (1981). *But see Matassarin v. Lynch*, 174 F.3d 549 (5th Cir. 1999) (interest in a mandatory employer-funded employee option plan held not a security); *Conrad v. Colgate Palmolive Co.*, 686 F.2d 1230 (7th Cir. 1982) (contributory voluntary pension plans are not securities). *See generally* Bromberg, *The Employee Investor & ESOPS and Other Employee Benefit Plans as Securities,* 19 Sec. Reg. L.J. 325 (1992).

---

§ 2.04 The Presence of Other Regulation and the Implications of *Weaver*

Although not a primary consideration but one of inferential support, the Supreme Court in *Daniel* asserted that there was no need to define the plaintiff's interest as a security because such pension plans are thoroughly regulated today under ERISA. The presence of other federal regulation is now of paramount significance in view of the Supreme Court's subsequent decision in *Marine Bank v. Weaver*, 455 U.S. 551 (1982). *Weaver* also has important implications due to the investment contract analysis that the Court employed in the latter portion of the opinion.

Marine Bank v. Weaver

United States Supreme Court

455 U.S. 551, 102 S. Ct. 1220, 71 L. Ed. 2d 409 (1982)

CHIEF JUSTICE BURGER delivered the opinion of the Court.

We granted certiorari to decide whether two instruments, a conventional certificate of deposit and a business agreement between two families, could be considered securities under the antifraud provisions of the federal securities laws.

I

Respondents, Sam and Alice Weaver, purchased a $50,000 certificate of deposit from petitioner Marine Bank on February 28, 1978. The certificate of deposit has a 6-year maturity, and it is insured by the Federal Deposit Insurance Corporation. The Weavers subsequently pledged the certificate of deposit to Marine Bank on March 17, 1978, to guarantee a $65,000 loan made by the bank to Columbus Packing Co. Columbus was a wholesale slaughterhouse and retail meat market which owed the bank $33,000 at that time for prior loans and was also substantially overdrawn on its checking account with the bank.

In consideration for guaranteeing the bank's new loan, Columbus' owners, Raymond and Barbara Piccirillo, entered into an agreement with the Weavers. Under the terms of the agreement, the Weavers were to receive 50% of Columbus' net profits and $100 per month as long as they guaranteed the loan. It was also agreed that the Weavers could use Columbus' barn and pasture at the discretion of the Piccirillos, and that they had the right to veto future borrowing by Columbus.

The Weavers allege that bank officers told them Columbus would use the $65,000 loan as working capital but instead it was immediately applied to pay Columbus' overdue obligations. The bank kept approximately $42,800 to satisfy its prior loans and Columbus' overdrawn checking account. All but $3,800 of the remainder was disbursed to pay overdue taxes and to satisfy other creditors; the bank then refused to permit Columbus to overdraw its checking account. Columbus became bankrupt four months later. Although the bank had not yet resorted to the Weavers' certificate of deposit at the time this litigation commenced, it acknowledged that its other security was inadequate and that it intended to claim the pledged certificate of deposit.

These allegations were asserted in a complaint filed in the Federal District Court for the Western District of Pennsylvania in support of a claim that the bank violated § 10(b) of the Securities Exchange Act of 1934.

We hold that neither the certificate of deposit nor the agreement between the Weavers and the Piccirillos is a security under the antifraud provisions of the federal securities laws.

II

The definition of "security" in the Securities Exchange Act of 1934 is quite broad. The Act was adopted to restore investors' confidence in the financial markets,[15] and the term "security" was meant to include "the many types of instruments that in our commercial world fall within the ordinary concept of a security." The statutory definition excludes only currency and notes with a maturity of less than nine months. It includes ordinary stocks and bonds, along with the "countless and variable schemes devised by those who seek the use of the money of others on the promise of profits...."

---

15. Fitzgibbon, *What Is a Security? A Redefinition Based on Eligibility to Participate in the Financial Markets*, 64 MINN. L. REV. 893, 912–918 (1980).

SEC v. W. J. Howey Co., 328 U.S. 293, 299 (1946). Thus, the coverage of the antifraud provisions of the securities laws is not limited to instruments traded on securities exchanges and over-the-counter markets, but extends to uncommon and irregular instruments. We have repeatedly held that the test "'is what character the instrument is given in commerce by the terms of the offer, the plan of distribution, and the economic inducements held out to the prospect.'" . . . .

The broad statutory definition is preceded, however, by the statement that the terms mentioned are not to be considered securities if "the context otherwise requires. . . ." Moreover, we are satisfied that Congress, in enacting the securities laws, did not intend to provide a broad federal remedy for all fraud.

III

The Court of Appeals concluded that the certificate of deposit purchased by the Weavers might be a security. Examining the statutory definition, the court correctly noted that the certificate of deposit is not expressly excluded from the definition since it is not currency and it has a maturity exceeding nine months.[16] It concluded, however, that the certificate of deposit was the functional equivalent of the withdrawable capital shares of a savings and loan association held to be securities in *Tcherepnin v. Knight*, 389 U.S. 332 (1967). The court also reasoned that, from an investor's standpoint, a certificate of deposit is no different from any other long-term debt obligation. Unless distinguishing features were found on remand, the court concluded that the certificate of deposit should be held to be a security.

Tcherepnin is not controlling. The withdrawable capital shares found there to be securities did not pay a fixed rate of interest; instead, purchasers received dividends based on the association's profits. Purchasers also received voting rights. In short, the withdrawable capital shares in *Tcherepnin* were much more like ordinary shares of stock and "the ordinary concept of a security," than a certificate of deposit.

The Court of Appeals also concluded that a certificate of deposit is similar to any other long-term debt obligation commonly found to be a security. In our view, however, there is an important difference between a bank certificate of deposit and other long-term debt obligations. This certificate of deposit was issued by a federally regulated bank which is subject to the comprehensive set of regulations governing the banking industry.[17] Deposits in federally regulated banks are protected by the reserve,

---

16. The definition of a "security" in the 1934 Act . . . includes the term, "certificate of deposit, for a security." However, this term does not refer to certificates of deposit such as the Weavers purchased. Instead, "certificate of deposit, for a security" refers to instruments issued by protective committees in the course of corporate reorganizations. *Canadian Imperial Bank of Commerce v. Fingland*, 615 F.2d 465, 468 (CA7 1980).

17. In *Teamsters v. Daniel*, 439 U.S. 551 (1979), we held that a noncontributory, compulsory pension plan was not a security. One of our reasons for our holding in *Daniel* was that the pension plan was regulated by the Employee Retirement Income Security Act of 1974 (ERISA): "The existence of this comprehensive legislation governing the use and terms of employee pension plans severely undercuts all arguments for extending the Securities Acts to noncontributory, compulsory pension plans." Since ERISA regulates the substantive terms of pension plans, and also requires certain

reporting, and inspection requirements of the federal banking laws; advertising relating to the interest paid on deposits is also regulated. In addition, deposits are insured by the Federal Deposit Insurance Corporation. Since its formation in 1933, nearly all depositors in failing banks insured by the FDIC have received payment in full, even payment for the portions of their deposits above the amount insured.

We see, therefore, important differences between a certificate of deposit purchased from a federally regulated bank and other long-term debt obligations. The Court of Appeals failed to give appropriate weight to the important fact that the purchaser of a certificate of deposit is virtually guaranteed payment in full, whereas the holder of an ordinary long-term debt obligation assumes the risk of the borrower's insolvency. The definition of "security" in the 1934 Act provides that an instrument which seems to fall within the broad sweep of the Act is not to be considered a security if the context otherwise requires. It is unnecessary to subject issuers of bank certificates of deposit to liability under the antifraud provisions of the federal securities laws since the holders of bank certificates of deposit are abundantly protected under the federal banking laws. We therefore hold that the certificate of deposit purchased by the Weavers is not a security.

IV

The Court of Appeals also held that a finder of fact could conclude that the separate agreement between the Weavers and the Piccirillos is a security. Examining the statutory language, the court found that the agreement might be a "certificate of interest or participation in any profit-sharing agreement" or an "investment contract." It stressed that the agreement gave the Weavers a share in the profits of the slaughterhouse which would result from the efforts of the Piccirillos. Accordingly, in that court's view, the agreement fell within the definition of "investment contract" stated in *Howey*, because "the scheme involves an investment of money in a common enterprise with profits to come solely from the efforts of others."

Congress intended the securities laws to cover those instruments ordinarily and commonly considered to be securities in the commercial world, but the agreement between the Weavers and the Piccirillos is not the type of instrument that comes to mind when the term "security" is used and does not fall within "the ordinary concept of a security." The unusual instruments found to constitute securities in prior cases involved offers to a number of potential investors, not a private transaction as in this case. In *Howey*, for example, 42 persons purchased interests in a citrus grove during a 4-month period. In *C. M. Joiner Leasing*, [where] offers to sell oil leases were sent to over 1,000 prospects. . . . we noted that a security is an instrument in which there is "common trading." . . . The instruments involved in *C. M. Joiner Leasing* and *Howey* had equivalent values to most persons and could have been traded publicly.

---

disclosures, it was unnecessary to subject pension plans to the requirements of the federal securities laws as well.

Here, in contrast, the Piccirillos distributed no prospectus to the Weavers or to other potential investors, and the unique agreement they negotiated was not designed to be traded publicly. The provision that the Weavers could use the barn and pastures of the slaughterhouse at the discretion of the Piccirillos underscores the unique character of the transaction. Similarly, the provision that the Weavers could veto future loans gave them a measure of control over the operation of the slaughterhouse not characteristic of a security. Although the agreement gave the Weavers a share of the Piccirillos' profits, if any, that provision alone is not sufficient to make that agreement a security. Accordingly, we hold that this unique agreement, negotiated one-on-one by the parties, is not a security.[18]

V

Whatever may be the consequences of these transactions, they did not occur in connection with the purchase or sale of "securities."[19] ...

Note

Do you agree with the *Weaver* Court's analysis with respect to the certificate of deposit issue? Consider the following:

> [T]he likelihood of abuse is relevant *only* to the issues of registration and reporting under the federal securities acts, *not* to whether the antifraud provisions should apply. Fraudulent misconduct in the context of *any* securities transaction will give rise to civil or criminal liability, or both. Furthermore ... the likelihood of abuse should play no part in determining what is, and what is not, a security. Although the context in which a particular transaction occurs may exempt it from certain of the Acts' requirements, that context does not alter the nature of the instrument itself. Phrased differently, if an instrument or transaction meets the Acts' definition of "security," it always will remain a security, regardless of whether the registration or reporting requirements apply.

Steinberg & Kaulbach, *The Supreme Court and the Definition of "Security": The "Context" Clause, "Investment Contract" Analysis, and Their Ramifications*, 40 Vand. L. Rev. 489, 513 (1987).

The *Weaver* decision raises a number of important, yet at this time unresolved, issues.

---

18. Cf. *Great Western Bank & Trust v. Kotz*, 532 F.2d 1252, 1260–1262 (CA9 1976) (Wright, J., concurring) (unsecured note, the terms of which were negotiated face-to-face, given to a bank in return for a business loan, is not a security).

19. It does not follow that a certificate of deposit or business agreement between transacting parties invariably falls outside the definition of a "security" as defined by the federal statutes. Each transaction must be analyzed and evaluated on the basis of the content of the instruments in question, the purposes intended to be served, and the factual setting as a whole.

1. Regarding the *presence of other federal regulation*, does *Weaver* mean that:

(a) All employee pension plans, including voluntary contributory plans, are not securities?

(b) Certificates of Deposit, issued by financial institutions that are (i) subject to extensive regulation, and/or (ii) the CDs of which are insured are not securities? (See discussion in § 2.05[B], *infra*.)

(c) Wherever there is substantial regulation of the particular interest under federal and/or state law, there is no need for coverage under the federal securities laws?

2. Regarding the *investment contract analysis* employed in *Weaver*, does the Court imply that:

(a) No private one-on-one transaction involving a novel or unique instrument is a security? [A number of courts have so held. *See, e.g., Mace Neufeld Productions, Inc. v. Orion Pictures Corp.*, 860 F.2d 944 (9th Cir. 1988) (agreement between two parties that "was unique, private, and never intended to be publicly traded" held not to be a security).]

(b) The instrument must be capable of mass distribution in order for there to be a security? [See discussion in § 2.05[A], *infra*.]

(c) The risk capital test has been implicitly rejected?

(d) Only horizontal commonality (and not vertical commonality) is sufficient to satisfy the common enterprise element of the *Howey* investment contract test? Note, however, that the Supreme Court subsequently denied the petition for a writ of certiorari in *Mordaunt v. Incomco*, 469 U.S. 1115 (1985), which raised the vertical commonality issue. Hence, the issue remains unsettled. In *Mordaunt*, Justice White, dissenting from the denial of the petition, surveyed the divergent views among the lower courts concerning the requisite commonality and opined that "[i]n light of the clear and significant split in the Circuits, I would grant certiorari."

Interestingly, the *Weaver* Court declined to rely on *Howey*. Hence, the question arises whether *Weaver* has modified the *Howey* investment contract test. For example, one court, interpreting *Howey* in light of *Weaver*, has explained that an investment contract "means a contract, transaction or scheme whereby a person (1) invests his money (2) in a common enterprise and (3) is led to expect profits (4) solely from the efforts of the promoter or a third party, and (5) risks loss." *Dooner v. NMI Limited*, 725 F.2d 153, 158 (S.D.N.Y. 1989).

Not surprisingly, *Weaver* has been subject to severe criticism. For example, one respected authority opined: "The Court's rationale for its holding, if an answer to a law examination including the identical question, would probably have been graded F by 95 percent of the securities regulation professors in the United States." H. Bloomenthal, 1982 Securities Law Handbook xlvii (1982). Do you agree? Consider the following:

[T]he result should not turn on whether a "prospectus" is distributed. The *Weaver* Court's implication in this regard is the product of hopelessly circular logic: if a prospectus is required only upon first determining that a security is involved, how can "security" be defined in terms of whether a prospectus is distributed?

[Also,] whether a particular instrument is publicly traded is immaterial if it otherwise fits the definition of "security." An instrument's susceptibility to public trading may be evidence of its character in commerce, but the Court made clear in its very first decision construing the definition of "security" that the Acts' scope does not end with the "obvious or commonplace."[20]

§ 2.05 Debt Securities

[A] Notes

Reves v. Ernst & Young

United States Supreme Court

494 U.S. 56, 110 S. Ct. 945, 108 L.Ed.2d 47 (1990)

JUSTICE MARSHALL delivered the opinion of the Court.

This case presents the question whether certain demand notes issued by the Farmer's Cooperative of Arkansas and Oklahoma are "securities" within the meaning of § 3(a)(10) of the Securities Exchange Act of 1934. We conclude that they are.

I

The Co-Op is an agricultural cooperative that, at the time relevant here, had approximately 23,000 members. In order to raise money to support its general business operations, the Co-Op sold promissory notes payable on demand by the holder. Although the notes were uncollateralized and uninsured, they paid a variable rate of interest that was adjusted monthly to keep it higher than the rate paid by local financial institutions. The Co-Op offered the notes to both members and nonmembers, marketing the scheme as an "Investment Program." Advertisements for the notes, which appeared in each Co-Op newsletter, read in part: "YOUR CO-OP has more than $11,000,000 in assets to stand behind your investments. The Investment is not Federal[ly] insured but it is . . . Safe . . . Secure . . . and available when you need it." Despite these assurances, the Co-Op filed for bankruptcy in 1984. At the time of the filing, over 1,600 people held notes worth a total of $10 million.

After the Co-Op filed for bankruptcy, petitioners, a class of holders of the notes, filed suit against Arthur Young & Co., the firm that had audited the Co-Op's financial

---

20. Steinberg & Kaulbach, *supra*, 40 Vanderbilt L. Rev. at 521–22.

statements (and the predecessor to respondent Ernst & Young). Petitioners alleged, *inter alia*, that Arthur Young had intentionally failed to follow generally accepted accounting principles in its audit, specifically with respect to the valuation of one of the Co-Op's major assets, a gasohol plant. Petitioners claimed that Arthur Young violated these principles in an effort to inflate the assets and net worth of the Co-Op. Petitioners maintained that, had Arthur Young properly treated the plant in its audits, they would not have purchased demand notes because the Co-Op's insolvency would have been apparent. On the basis of these allegations, petitioners claimed that Arthur Young had violated the antifraud provisions of the 1934 Act as well as Arkansas' securities laws.

Petitioners prevailed at trial on both their federal and state claims, receiving a $6.1 million judgment. Arthur Young appealed, claiming that the demand notes were not "securities" under either the 1934 Act or Arkansas law, and that the statutes' antifraud provisions therefore did not apply. A panel of the Eighth Circuit, agreeing with Arthur Young on both the state and federal issues, reversed. *Arthur Young & Co. v. Reves*, 856 F.2d 52 (1988). We granted certiorari to address the federal issue, and now reverse the judgment of the Court of Appeals.

II

A

This case requires us to decide whether the note issued by the Co-Op is a "security" within the meaning of the 1934 Act. Section 3(a)(10) of that Act is our starting point. . . .

The fundamental purpose undergirding the Securities Acts is "to eliminate serious abuses in a largely unregulated securities market." . . . In defining the scope of the market that it wished to regulate, Congress painted with a broad brush. It recognized the virtually limitless scope of human ingenuity, especially in the creation of "countless and variable schemes devised by those who seek the use of the money of others on the promise of profits," . . . and determined that the best way to achieve its goal of protecting investors was "to define 'the term "security" in sufficiently broad and general terms so as to include within that definition the many types of instruments that in our commercial world fall within the ordinary concept of a security.'" . . . Congress therefore did not attempt precisely to cabin the scope of the Securities Acts.[21] Rather, it enacted a definition of "security" sufficiently broad to encompass virtually any instrument that might be sold as an investment.

Congress did not, however, "intend to provide a broad federal remedy for all fraud." . . . Accordingly, "[t]he task has fallen to the Securities and Exchange Commission (SEC), the body charged with administering the Securities Acts, and ultimately

---

21. We have consistently held that "[t]he definition of a security in § 3(a)(10) of the 1934 Act, is virtually identical [to the 1933 Act's definition] and, for present purposes, the coverage of the two Acts may be considered the same." *United Housing Foundation, Inc. v. Forman*, 421 U.S. 837, 847, n.12 (1975) (citations omitted). We reaffirm that principle here.

to the federal courts to decide which of the myriad financial transactions in our society come within the coverage of these statutes." . . . In discharging our duty, we are not bound by legal formalisms, but instead take account of the economics of the transaction under investigation. . . . Congress' purpose in enacting the securities laws was to regulate *investments*, in whatever form they are made and by whatever name they are called.

A commitment to an examination of the economic realities of a transaction does not necessarily entail a case-by-case analysis of every instrument, however. Some instruments are obviously within the class Congress intended to regulate because they are by their nature investments. In *Landreth Timber Co. v. Landreth*, 471 U.S. 681 (1985), we held that an instrument bearing the name "stock" that, among other things, is negotiable, offers the possibility of capital appreciation, and carries the right to dividends contingent on the profits of a business enterprise is plainly within the class of instruments Congress intended the securities laws to cover. *Landreth Timber* does not signify a lack of concern with economic reality; rather, it signals a recognition that stock is, as a practical matter, always an investment if it has the economic characteristics traditionally associated with stock. Even if sparse exceptions to this generalization can be found, the public perception of common stock as the paradigm of a security suggests that stock, in whatever context it is sold, should be treated as within the ambit of the Acts.

We made clear in *Landreth Timber* that stock was a special case, explicitly limiting our holding to that sort of instrument. Although we refused finally to rule out a similar *per se* rule for notes, we intimated that such a rule would be unjustified. Unlike "stock," we said, " 'note' may now be viewed as a relatively broad term that encompasses instruments with widely varying characteristics, depending on whether issued in a consumer context, as commercial paper, or in some other investment context." . . . While common stock is the quintessence of a security, and investors therefore justifiably assume that a sale of stock is covered by the Securities Acts, the same simply cannot be said of notes, which are used in a variety of settings, not all of which involve investments. Thus, the phrase "any note" should not be interpreted to mean literally "any note," but must be understood against the backdrop of what Congress was attempting to accomplish in enacting the Securities Acts.[22]

Because the *Landreth Timber* formula cannot sensibly be applied to notes, some other principle must be developed to define the term "note." A majority of the Courts of Appeals that have considered the issue have adopted, in varying forms, "investment

---

22. An approach founded on economic reality rather than on a set of *per se* rules is subject to the criticism that whether a particular note is a "security" may not be entirely clear at the time it is issued. Such an approach has the corresponding advantage, though, of permitting the SEC and the courts sufficient flexibility to ensure that those who market investments are not able to escape the coverage of the Securities Acts by creating new instruments that would not be covered by a more determinate definition. One could question whether, at the expense of the goal of clarity, Congress overvalued the goal of avoiding manipulation by the clever and dishonest. If Congress erred, however, it is for that body, and not this Court, to correct its mistake.

versus commercial" approaches that distinguish, on the basis of all of the circumstances surrounding the transactions, notes issued in an investment context (which are "securities") from notes issued in a commercial or consumer context (which are not). . . .

The Second Circuit's "family resemblance" approach [,on the other hand,] begins with a presumption that *any* note with a term of more than nine months is a "security." Recognizing that not all notes are securities, however, the Second Circuit has also devised a list of notes that it has decided are obviously not securities. Accordingly, the "family resemblance" test permits an issuer to rebut the presumption that a note is a security if it can show that the note in question "bear[s] a strong family resemblance" to an item on the judicially crafted list of exceptions . . . or convinces the court to add a new instrument to the list.

In contrast, the Eighth and District of Columbia Circuits apply the test we created in *SEC v. W. J. Howey Co.*, 328 U.S. 293 (1946), to determine whether an instrument is an "investment contract" to the determination whether an instrument is a "note." Under this test, a note is a security only if it evidences "(1) an investment; (2) in a common enterprise; (3) with a reasonable expectation of profits; (4) to be derived from the entrepreneurial or managerial efforts of others." . . .

We reject the approaches of those courts that have applied the *Howey* test to notes; *Howey* provides a mechanism for determining whether an instrument is an "investment contract." The demand notes here may well not be "investment contracts," but that does not mean they are not "notes." To hold that a "note" is not a "security" unless it meets a test designed for an entirely different variety of instrument "would make the Acts' enumeration of many types of instruments superfluous," . . . and would be inconsistent with Congress' intent to regulate the entire body of instruments sold as investments. . . .

The other two contenders—the "family resemblance" and "investment versus commercial" tests—are really two ways of formulating the same general approach. Because we think the "family resemblance" test provides a more promising framework for analysis, however, we adopt it. The test begins with the language of the statute; because the Securities Acts define "security" to include "any note," we begin with a presumption that every note is a security.[23] We nonetheless recognize that this presumption cannot be irrebuttable. As we have said, Congress was concerned with regulating the investment market, not with creating a general federal cause of action for fraud. In an attempt to give more content to that dividing line, the Second Circuit

---

23. The Second Circuit's version of the family resemblance test provided that only notes *with a term of more than nine months* are presumed to be "securities." No presumption of any kind attached to notes of less than nine months duration. The Second Circuit's refusal to extend the presumption to *all* notes was apparently founded on its interpretation of the statutory exception for notes with a maturity of nine months or less. Because we do not reach the question of how to interpret that exception, we likewise express no view on how that exception might affect the presumption that a note is a "security."

has identified a list of instruments commonly denominated "notes" that nonetheless fall without the "security" category. See *Exchange Nat. Bank*, [544 F.2d 1126, 1138 (2d. Cir. 1976)] (types of notes that are not "securities" include "the note delivered in consumer financing, the note secured by a mortgage on a home, the short-term note secured by a lien on a small business or some of its assets, the note evidencing a 'character' loan to a bank customer, short-term notes secured by an assignment of accounts receivable, or a note which simply formalizes an open-account debt incurred in the ordinary course of business (particularly if, as in the case of the customer of a broker, it is collateralized)"); *Chemical Bank*, [726 F.2d 930, 939 (2d Cir. 1984)] (adding to list "notes evidencing loans by commercial banks for current operations").

We agree that the items identified by the Second Circuit are not properly viewed as "securities." More guidance, though, is needed. It is impossible to make any meaningful inquiry into whether an instrument bears a "resemblance" to one of the instruments identified by the Second Circuit without specifying what it is about *those* instruments that makes *them* non-"securities." Moreover, as the Second Circuit itself has noted, its list is "not graven in stone," . . . and is therefore capable of expansion. Thus, some standards must be developed for determining when an item should be added to the list.

An examination of the list itself makes clear what those standards should be. In creating its list, the Second Circuit was applying the same factors that this Court has held apply in deciding whether a transaction involves a "security." First, we examine the transaction to assess the motivations that would prompt a reasonable seller and buyer to enter into it. If the seller's purpose is to raise money for the general use of a business enterprise or to finance substantial investments and the buyer is interested primarily in the profit the note is expected to generate, the instrument is likely to be a "security." If the note is exchanged to facilitate the purchase and sale of a minor asset or consumer good, to correct for the seller's cash-flow difficulties, or to advance some other commercial or consumer purpose, on the other hand, the note is less sensibly described as a "security." See, e.g., *Forman*, 421 U.S. at 851 (share of "stock" carrying a right to subsidized housing not a security because "the inducement to purchase was solely to acquire subsidized low-cost living space; it was not to invest for profit"). Second, we examine the "plan of distribution" of the instrument to determine whether it is an instrument in which there is "common trading for speculation or investment." . . . Third, we examine the reasonable expectations of the investing public: The Court will consider instruments to be "securities" on the basis of such public expectations, even where an economic analysis of the circumstances of the particular transaction might suggest that the instruments are not "securities" as used in that transaction. [See] *Landreth Timber,* 471 U. S. at 687, 693 (relying on public expectations in holding that common stock is always a security). . . . Finally, we examine whether some factor such as the existence of another regulatory scheme significantly reduces the risk of the instrument, thereby rendering application of the Securities Acts unnecessary.

We conclude, then, that in determining whether an instrument denominated a "note" is a "security," courts are to apply the version of the "family resemblance" test that we have articulated here: a note is presumed to be a "security," and that presumption may be rebutted only by a showing that the note bears a strong resemblance (in terms of the four factors we have identified) to one of the enumerated categories of instrument. If an instrument is not sufficiently similar to an item on the list, the decision whether another category should be added is to be made by examining the same factors.

B

Applying the family resemblance approach to this case, we have little difficulty in concluding that the notes at issue here are "securities." Ernst & Young admits that "a demand note does not closely resemble any of the Second Circuit's family resemblance examples." ... Nor does an examination of the four factors we have identified as being relevant to our inquiry suggest that the demand notes here are not "securities" .... The Co-Op sold the notes in an effort to raise capital for its general business operations, and purchasers bought them in order to earn a profit in the form of interest.[24] Indeed, one of the primary inducements offered purchasers was an interest rate constantly revised to keep it slightly above the rate paid by local banks and savings and loans. From both sides, then, the transaction is most naturally conceived as an investment in a business enterprise rather than as a purely commercial or consumer transaction.

As to the plan of distribution, the Co-Op offered the notes over an extended period to its 23,000 members, as well as to nonmembers, and more than 1,600 people held notes when the Co-Op filed for bankruptcy. To be sure, the notes were not traded on an exchange. They were, however, offered and sold to a broad segment of the public, and that is all we have held to be necessary to establish the requisite "common trading" in an instrument. See, *e.g., Landreth Timber, supra* (stock of closely held corporation not traded on any exchange held to be a "security"); *Tcherepnin,* 389 U.S., at 337 (nonnegotiable but transferable "withdrawable capital shares" in savings and loan association held to be a "security"); *Howey,* 328 U.S., at 295 (units of citrus grove and maintenance contract "securities" although not traded on an exchange).

The third factor—the public's reasonable perceptions—also supports a finding that the notes in this case are "securities". We have consistently identified the

---

24. We emphasize that by "profit" in the context of notes, we mean "a valuable return on an investment," which undoubtedly includes interest. We have, of course, defined "profit" more restrictively in applying the Howey test to what are claimed to be "investment contracts." See, e.g., Forman, 421 U.S. at 852 ("[P]rofit under the Howey test means either "capital appreciation" or "a participation in earnings"). To apply this restrictive definition to the determination whether an instrument is a "note" would be to suggest that notes paying a rate of interest not keyed to the earnings of the enterprise are not "notes" within the meaning of the Securities Act. Because the Howey test is irrelevant to the issue before us today, we decline to extend the definition of "profit" beyond the realm in which that definition applies. [Compare this language to the Supreme Court's interpretation of "profit" subsequently in SEC v. Edwards, contained in § 2.02, supra — ed.]

fundamental essence of a "security" to be its character as an "investment." The advertisements for the notes here characterized them as "investments," and there were no countervailing factors that would have led a reasonable person to question this characterization. In these circumstances, it would be reasonable for a prospective purchaser to take the Co-Op at its word.

Finally, we find no risk-reducing factor to suggest that these instruments are not in fact securities. The notes are uncollateralized and uninsured. Moreover, unlike the certificates of deposit in *Marine Bank*, which were insured by the Federal Deposit Insurance Corporation and subject to substantial regulation under the federal banking laws, and unlike the pension plan in *Teamsters v. Daniel*, which was comprehensively regulated under the Employee Retirement Income Security Act of 1974, . . . the notes here would escape federal regulation entirely if the [Securities] Acts were held not to apply.

The court below found that "[t]he demand nature of the notes is very uncharacteristic of a security," . . . on the theory that the virtually instant liquidity associated with demand notes is inconsistent with the risk ordinarily associated with "securities." This argument is unpersuasive. Common stock traded on a national exchange is the paradigm of a security, and it is as readily convertible into cash as is a demand note. The same is true of publicly traded corporate bonds, debentures, and any number of other instruments that are plainly within the purview of the Acts. The demand feature of a note does permit a holder to eliminate risk quickly by making a demand, but just as with publicly traded stock, the liquidity of the instrument does not eliminate risk all together. Indeed, publicly traded stock is even more readily liquid than are demand notes, in that a demand only eliminates risk when and if payment is made, whereas the sale of a share of stock through a national exchange and the receipt of the proceeds usually occur simultaneously.

We therefore hold that the notes at issue here are within the term "note" in § 3(a)(10).

. . . .

IV

For the foregoing reasons, we conclude that the demand notes at issue here fall under the "note" category of instruments that are "securities" under the 1933 and 1934 Acts. We also conclude that, even under a respondent's preferred approach to § 3(a)(10)'s exclusion for short-term notes, these demand notes do not fall within the exclusion. Accordingly, we reverse the judgment of the Court of Appeals and remand the case for further proceedings consistent with this opinion.

JUSTICE STEVENS, concurring.

While I join the Court's opinion, an important additional consideration supports my conclusion that these notes are securities notwithstanding the statute's exclusion for currency and commercial paper that has a maturity of no more than nine months. . . . The Courts of Appeals have been unanimous in rejecting a literal reading of that exclusion. They have instead concluded that "when Congress spoke of notes with a maturity not exceeding nine months, it meant commercial paper, not investment securities." *Sanders v. John Nuveen & Co.*, 463 F.2d 1075, 1080 (CA7 1972). . . . This view was first set out in an opinion by Judge Sprecher, *ibid.*, and soon thereafter endorsed by Chief Judge Friendly. *Zeller v. Bogue Electric Manufacturing Corp.*, 476 F.2d 795, 800 (CA2 1973). . . . Others have adopted the same position since. . . .

In my view such a settled construction of an important federal statute should not be disturbed unless and until Congress so decides. . . .

Indeed, the agreement among the Court of Appeals is made all the more impressive in this case because [it is] buttressed by the views of the Securities and Exchange Commission. . . . We have ourselves referred to the exclusion for notes with a maturity not exceeding nine months as an exclusion for "commercial paper." *Securities Industries Assn. v. Board of Governors of Federal Reserve System*, 468 U.S. 137, 150–152 (1984). Perhaps because the restriction of the exclusion to commercial paper is so well established, respondents admit that they did not even argue before the Court of Appeals that their notes were covered by the exclusion. A departure from this reliable consensus would upset the justified expectations of both the legal and investment communities.

Moreover, I am satisfied that the interpretation of the statute expounded by Judge Sprecher and Judge Friendly was entirely correct. As Judge Friendly has observed, the exclusion for short term notes must be read in light of the prefatory language in § 2 of the 1933 Act and § 3 of the 1934 Act. See *Exchange Nat. Bank of Chicago v. Touche Ross & Co.*, 544 F.2d 1126, 1131–1132 and, nn. 7–10 (CA2 1976). Pursuant to that language, definitions specified by the Acts may not apply if the "context otherwise requires." *Marine Bank v. Weaver*, 455 U.S. 551, 556 (1982) (the "broad statutory definition is preceded, however, by the statement that the terms mentioned are not to be considered securities if 'the context otherwise requires . . .'") . . . The context clause thus permits a judicial construction of the statute which harmonizes the facially rigid terms of the nine-month exclusion with the evident intent of Congress. The legislative history of § 3(a)(3) of the 1933 Act indicates that the exclusion was intended to cover only commercial paper, and the SEC has so construed it. As the Courts of Appeals have agreed, there is no apparent reason to construe § 3(a)(10) of the 1934 Act differently. . . .

For these reasons and those stated in the opinion of the Court, I conclude that the notes issued by respondents are securities within the meaning of the 1934 Act.

CHIEF JUSTICE REHNQUIST, with whom JUSTICE WHITE, JUSTICE O'CONNOR, and JUSTICE SCALIA join, concurring in part and dissenting in part.

I join part II of the Court's opinion, but dissent from part III and the statements of the Court's judgment in parts I and IV. In Part III, the court holds that these notes were not covered by the statutory exemption for "any note. . . . which has a maturity at the time of issuance of not exceeding nine months." Treating demand notes as if they were a recent development in the law of negotiable instruments, the Court says "if it is plausible to regard a demand note as having an immediate maturity because demand *could* be made immediately, it is also plausible to regard the maturity of a demand note as being in excess of nine months because demand *could* be made many years or decades into the future. Given this ambiguity, the exclusion must be interpreted in accordance with its purpose." . . .

But the terms "note" and "maturity" did not spring full blown from the head of Congress in 1934. Neither are demand notes of recent vintage. "Note" and "maturity" have been terms of art in the legal profession for centuries, and a body of law concerning the characteristics of demand notes, including their maturity, was in existence at the time Congress passed the 1934 Act.

In construing any terms whose meanings are less than plain, we depend on the common understanding of those terms at the time of the statute's creation. . . . Contemporaneous editions of legal dictionaries defined "maturity" as "[t]he time when a . . . note becomes due." . . . Pursuant to the dominant consensus in the case law, instruments payable on demand were considered immediately "due" such that an action could be brought at any time without any other demand than the suit. See, e.g., M. Bigelow, The Law of Bills, Notes, And Checks § 349, p. 265 (3d ed. W. Lile rev. 1928); 8 C.J., Bills and Notes § 602, p. 406 & n.83 (1916). . . .

. . . [I]n the absence of some compelling indication to the contrary, the maturity date exemption must encompass demand notes because they possess "maturity at the time of issuance of not exceeding nine months."

The legislative history of the 1934 Act—under which this case arises—contains nothing which would support a restrictive reading of the exemption in question. Nor does the legislative history of § 3(a)(3) of the 1933 Act support the asserted limited construction of the exemption in § 3(a)(10) of the 1934 Act. . . .

. . . Although I do not doubt that both the 1933 and 1934 Act exemptions encompass short-term commercial paper, the expansive language in the statutory provisions is strong evidence that, in the end, Congress meant for commercial paper merely to be a subset of a larger class of exempted short-term instruments.

. . . .

. . . The fairest reading of the exemption in light of the context clause is that the situation described in the exemption—notes with maturities at issue of less than nine months—is one contextual exception Congress especially wanted courts to recognize. Such a reading does not render the context clause superfluous; it merely leaves it to the judiciary to flesh out additional "context clause" exceptions.

. . . .

In sum, there is no justification for looking beyond the plain terms of § 3(a)(10), save for ascertaining the meaning of "maturity" with respect to demand notes. That inquiry reveals that the co-op's demand notes come within the purview of the section's exemption for short-term securities. I would therefore affirm the judgment of the Court of Appeals, though on different reasoning.

Note

Since *Reves*, the lower federal courts frequently have interpreted the "family resemblance" test. Compare *SEC v. Zada*, 787 F.3d 375 (6th Cir. 2015) (applying family resemblance test and holding promissory notes to be securities); and *Trust Co. of Louisiana v. N.N.P. Inc.,* 104 F.3d 1478 (5th Cir. 1997) (same), with *Bass v. Janney Montgomery Scott, Inc.*, 210 F.3d 577 (6th Cir. 2000) (promissory notes held not to be securities); *Banco Espanol de Credito v. Security Pacific National Bank,* 973 F.2d 51 (2d Cir. 1992) (sales of loan participations held not a security). For articles addressing *Reves* and its ramifications, *see, e.g.*, Couture, *The Securities Acts' Treatment of Notes Maturing in Less Than Nine Months: A Solution to the Enigma,* 31 Sec. Reg. L.J. 496 (2003); Gordon, *Interplanetary Intelligence About Promissory Notes as Securities,* 69 Tex. L. Rev. 383 (1990); Kerr & Eisenhauer, *Reves Revisited,* 19 Pepp. L. Rev. 1123 (1992); Steinberg, *Notes as Securities: Reves and Its Implications,* 51 Ohio St. L.J. 675 (1990); Warren, *The Treatment of Reves "Notes" and Other Securities Under State Blue Sky Law,* 47 Bus. Law. 321 (1991).

In her article, Professor Kerr addresses the lower court decisions that have been handed down after *Reves*. She (and her coauthor) observe that the factors enunciated in *Reves* "are ambiguous enough to be given a variety of interpretations." With respect to whether the factors are to be balanced, the authors opine that in adopting the family resemblance test "*Reves* provides no indication whether these factors should be balanced . . . or whether each factor must be satisfied in order to rebut the presumption of coverage under the Act. Most courts seem to have adopted a balancing approach." Kerr & Eisenhauer, *supra.* 19 Pepp. L. Rev. at 1153, 1157.

In his article, Professor Warren addresses state blue sky law treatment of notes. Although a number of states follow the family resemblance test enunciated in *Reves*, other standards may be applicable. These include the risk capital test, the investment versus commercial test, and the *Howey* test. *See* Warren, *supra*, 47 Bus. Law. at 325–329.

As another point, the significance of the *Reves* dissent—that notes of less than nine months' duration are not "notes" within federal securities law coverage—is greatly minimized by the Supreme Court's subsequent decision in *SEC v. Edwards,* contained in § 2.02, *supra*. In other words, even if the dissent's approach eventually "wins" on this issue, such debt instruments, nonetheless, may well be "investment contracts" under the expanded definition of "profit" embraced in *Edwards* (e.g., the receipt of "periodic payments").

[B] Certificates of Deposit

The definitive case in this area is *Marine Bank v. Weaver*, 455 U.S. 551 (1982), where the court focused on the existence of depositor insurance and the pervasive federal regulation over banking. Accordingly, the Court held that a certificate of deposit purchased from a federally regulated bank is not a security. See § 2.04, *supra*. Given the widespread impact of the Federal Deposit Insurance Co. and other federal insurance, the *Marine Bank* holding would in practical terms seem to have wide impact. Note, however, that application of the federal securities laws to a CD issued by a state chartered non-federally insured bank or a foreign bank may not be foreclosed by *Weaver*.

A number of post-*Weaver* decisions help highlight the policy questions involved. For example, in *Wolf v. Banco Nacional de Mexico*, 739 F.2d 1458 (9th Cir. 1984), the Ninth Circuit was faced with the issue of whether a certificate of deposit in Mexican pesos in a Mexican bank was a security under U.S. law. The district court, relying on *Weaver's* emphasis on the protection given to depositors by the federal banking laws, held that, since the Mexican deposits were outside the U.S. banking regulatory system, *Weaver* did not compel a finding that these were not securities. Reversing, the Ninth Circuit held that the Mexican CD was not a security, in that the issuing bank was sufficiently regulated and repayment in full was virtually guaranteed, stating: "When a [domestic or foreign] bank is sufficiently well regulated that there is virtually no risk that insolvency will prevent it from repaying the holder of one of its certificates of deposit in full, the certificate is not a security for purposes of the federal securities laws."

In another case, *Tafflin v. Levitt*, 865 F.2d 595, 599 (4th Cir. 1989), *aff'd on other grounds,* 493 U.S. 455 (1990), the Fourth Circuit applied *Weaver* to state regulation. In holding that Maryland's regulatory and insurance system with respect to state-chartered savings and loans compelled the conclusion that the certificates of deposit were not securities, the court reasoned:

> [W]e agree with the district court that there was a comprehensive regulatory and insurance system applicable to Old Court [Savings & Loan] so that its certificates of deposit did not fall within the statutory definition. Maryland law vested supervisory authority over state-chartered savings and loan associations in the Director of the Division of Savings and Loan Associations, and the Board of Savings and Loan Commissioners. Deposits in the member associations, of which Old Court was one, were insured.
>
> We recognize of course that in the case of Old Court and others, the Maryland system viewed in hindsight was ineffective. Whether the holders of Old Court's certificates of deposit will ever be paid in full is problematic. . . . But we do not think that *Marine Bank* depends upon the effectiveness of the regulatory scheme as it may have been administered. . . . At the time Old Court issued the certificates of deposit giving rise to this litigation, there had been no breakdown in Maryland's then regulatory scheme, and neither Old Court nor [the insurer] was insolvent.

. . . .

Thus, we conclude that application of *Marine Bank* depends upon the comprehensiveness of the scheme of regulation, and by that test we think that the Maryland system qualified to render the certificate of deposit not "securities." . . .

Not all courts agree with the foregoing cases. For example, the Tenth Circuit in *Holloway v. Peat, Marwick, Mitchell & Co.*, rejected *Weaver's (Marine Bank's)* functional regulation approach to state regulation. In holding passbook savings accounts and thrift certificates (issued by a financial institution subject to state oversight) to be securities, the court asserted that "under the supremacy clause [of the U.S. Constitution] our focus must be on federal regulation; state regulatory schemes cannot displace the [Securities] Acts." 900 F.2d 1485, 1488 (10th Cir. 1990). *See also, Sanderson v. Roethenmund*, 682 F. Supp. 205 (S.D.N.Y. 1988) (international certificates of deposit held to be securities). Moreover, the Eighth Circuit construed *Weaver* so as not to bar securities law coverage when the investment in the certificates of deposit was not guaranteed. *Olson v. E.F. Hutton & Co.*, [1991–1992 Transfer Binder] Fed. Sec. L. Rep. (CCH) ¶ 96,554 (8th Cir. 1992).

Chapter 3

Primary Issuer Transactional Exemptions from Registration

§ 3.01 Introduction

The general rule is that, absent an exemption, all offers or sales of securities must be registered pursuant to § 5 of the Securities Act of 1933 ("Securities Act" or "1933 Act"). Note that the securities law antifraud provisions apply irrespective of whether an exemption from registration exists.

There are two general types of exemptions: transactional exemptions and securities exempt from registration. The latter covers specific securities or categories of securities that are never required to be registered under § 5, largely due to the intrinsic character or nature of the issuer itself. These exempt securities include, for example, certain short-term promissory notes or bills of exchange, securities issued or guaranteed by municipalities, state or federal governments, and securities issued by nonprofit, religious, educational, or charitable organizations.[1]

Moreover, some securities, although exempt from the 1933 Act's registration requirements, come under the supervision of another federal or state governmental authority. For example, with respect to securities issued by national banks, the Comptroller of the Currency has developed a regulatory framework somewhat similar, yet many think not as rigorous, as that developed by the Securities and Exchange Commission ("SEC"). On the other hand, the securities of bank holding companies are not exempt securities under the federal securities laws.[2]

§ 3.02 Why Perfect a Transactional Exemption?

It is the transactional exemptions that play the important role in this context and comprise the material in this chapter. Before delving into the pertinent issues, one may ask: What's the "big deal"? Why not simply register the offer or sale under § 5 of the 1933 Act? The answers are several. In order to register an offer or sale under

---

1. *See* §§ 3(a)(2) through 3(a)(8) of the Securities Act for a listing of the exempt securities.
2. *See generally* 3 L. Loss, J. Seligman & T. Paredes, Securities Regulation 70–74 (4th ed. 2008).

§ 5, and have what is called a "public offering" or "to go public,"[3] a registration statement must be filed with the Securities and Exchange Commission (SEC). In addition, the final prospectus, which is part of the registration statement, must be timely provided to the purchaser.[4] The registration statement (the prospectus which is a part thereof) is no ordinary document. The disclosures required are detailed and complex. Indeed, the costs of preparing the registration statement, including accountant, attorney, investment banker and printer fees, can easily run into the hundreds of thousands of dollars.

The costs and nature of the registration statement are due largely to § 11 of the 1933 Act which, in practical effect, imposes a "due diligence" requirement upon specified parties, including the issuer's directors and certain of its executive officers, the underwriters, and experts, including accountants (with respect to those portions of the registration statement that an accountant "expertises"). Attorneys, unless they act as experts,[5] are not subject to § 11 liability. Counsel, nonetheless, is integrally involved in the registration process. He/she frequently is delegated by the issuer, underwriter, or other parties potentially liable under § 11 to perform the requisite "due diligence" on their behalf. Other fundamental aspects of counsel's role in this process involve drafting the language contained in the registration statement, advising whether certain disclosures should or must be made, and acting as informal mediator among the various parties involved.

The concept of "due diligence," its significance, and the steps that must be taken to fulfill this mandate are addressed in Chapter 7. In theory, "due diligence" is a defense that may be asserted by the subject party rather than an affirmative obligation. It is certainly true that if the statements made in the registration statement are true or if no lawsuit is ultimately brought, no liability will be incurred for failure to exercise due diligence. If an action is instituted and a material misstatement or omission is shown, however, liability often may be avoided under § 11 only by proving the performance of due diligence. In the realities of corporate practice, therefore, due diligence is a necessity rather than a discretionary function.

The "due diligence" requirement is given "teeth" by the liability consequences. In general, if there is a material misrepresentation or nondisclosure in the *non-expertised* portion of the registration statement, parties subject to § 11 liability—except experts and the issuer (which has no due diligence defense)—often can avoid such liability only by showing that they had exercised "due diligence," i.e., that they

---

3. The terms "public offering" and "going public" are often not synonymous. In short, the initial public offering ("IPO") made by an enterprise constitutes "going public." On the other hand, a successful corporation which has gone public decades ago may make public offerings of its securities on a periodic basis. For further discussion, *see* Chapter 4.

4. This assertion somewhat simplifies the pertinent requirements. We will explore the prospectus delivery requirements in depth in Chapter 4.

5. Counsel acts as an expert, for example, if he/she proffers an opinion contained or referred to in the registration statement. An accountant, by certifying financial statements contained in the registration statement, is a party who frequently is sued as an expert under § 11. *See* §§ 7.03-7.04 *infra*.

had conducted a reasonable investigation and, after such investigation, had no reason to believe and did not believe that the registration statement contained any materially false or misleading statement.[6]

With respect to the *expertised* portion of the registration statement, non-experts are not required to investigate. They only need to show that they had no reason to believe and did not believe that the expertised portion of the registration statement contained any materially false or misleading statement. Moreover, experts are potentially liable under § 11 only for those portions of the registration statement that they themselves "expertised." They can avoid § 11 liability by showing that, with respect to such expertised portion of the registration statement, they had conducted a reasonable investigation and, after such investigation, had no reason to believe and did not believe that such expertised portion of the registration statement contained any materially false or misleading statement.

While the issuer is the only party that has no "due diligence" defense under § 11, it may be insolvent. The result is that aggrieved plaintiffs seek redress against the "deep pockets," frequently the underwriters and the accountants. Because of the severe financial ramifications, which can amount to several million dollars, parties potentially subject to § 11 liability, at least in the initial public offering (IPO) context, seek to ensure that meaningful due diligence is performed.

Accordingly, the costs of having a "registered" offering under the Securities Act frequently will be substantial.[7] For a start-up venture or a business in severe financial difficulty, the costs of a public offering normally will prove prohibitive. Moreover, it is next to impossible successfully to consummate a registered offering unless receptive investment bankers can be retained to underwrite the offering and the financial markets are favorable.[8] These conditions are exacerbated in cases where enterprises with little or no previous earnings history seek to "go public." However, as some of the high-tech and research companies have shown, these problems are not insurmountable.[9]

Even if a financially successful registered offering can be made, it may be advisable for the client nonetheless to perfect a transactional exemption. By refraining

---

6. The § 11 liability issues are discussed at length in Chapter 7.

7. The SEC has lessened this financial burden to a degree for smaller companies. *See* Chapters 4 and 5.

8. The role of the underwriter in the registered offering process is addressed in Chapter 4. Although the underwriter's role in public offerings receives by far greater attention, the success of certain exempt offerings depends, to a large extent, upon the efforts of the underwriter or placement agent. *See, e.g., Sanders v. John Nuveen & Co.*, 619 F.2d 1222 (7th Cir. 1980), *cert. denied*, 450 U.S. 1005 (1981).

9. Irrespective of the enterprise's earnings and future prospects, the climate of the financial markets often determines whether a public offering can be brought "to market." *See* Conner, *Underpricing in the Initial Public Offering: A Solution for Severely Affected Issuers*, 40 Sec. Reg. L.J. 423 (2012); Driebusch and Farrell, *IPO Market Flashes Red for Stocks*, Wall St. J., April 1, 2016, at C1; Kelly & Hennessey, *Finally, an IPO! But It Surely Isn't a Mania*, Wall St. J., Feb. 15, 2003, at C1.

from undertaking an initial public offering (IPO) and thereby "going public," the enterprise essentially is keeping its financial affairs and related matters private among its various participants. By "going public," however, the enterprise, pursuant to the disclosure requirements of the securities laws, will be hanging its dirty linen out for public viewing.[10] The enterprise, pursuant to certain provisions of the Securities Exchange Act, such as § 12(g) or § 15(d), will be required to file annual, quarterly, and other periodic reports with the SEC as well as to provide periodic reports to its shareholders and the pertinent self-regulatory organizations.

Until recently, the Exchange Act required enterprises with 500 or more equity owners and $10 million in total assets to register with the SEC as a public reporting company even if the enterprise never had a registered offering. Many start-ups, as a result of issuing stock to employees, vendors, venture capitalists, and others, soon reached these thresholds. To relieve such companies from the burden of filing periodic reports with the SEC and, presumably, to aid in capital formation, in 2012 Congress passed the Jumpstart Our Business Startups Act or JOBS Act, as it is commonly known. Under this law, an enterprise need not register with the SEC unless its equity securities are held by either 2,000 persons or "500 persons who are not accredited investors." In either case, excluded are equity securities held of record by persons who acquired such securities by means of an exempt "crowd-funding" offering or pursuant to an exempt transaction under an employee compensation plan. The term "accredited investors" is considered later in this Chapter. Suffice it to say for now that it includes investors who are relatively wealthy.

By "going public," other sections of the Exchange Act, such as the record-keeping and internal accounting control provisions,[11] also will become applicable. Moreover, the certification, internal control, and other requirements of the Sarbanes-Oxley Act of 2002, as well as the corporate governance mandates of the Dodd-Frank Act of 2010, must be implemented.[12] Hence, the enterprise, by having a registered offering, will be faced not only with public scrutiny but saddled with high accounting and legal fees as well as the persistent threat of litigation due to the consequences of public disclosure.

For the above reasons, as well as others (such as, by taking the corporation public, the insiders may potentially risk loss of control through a hostile takeover),[13] it may be advisable and indeed necessary to procure a transactional exemption. It should not be surprising that, given the above, the vast majority of offerings are made

---

10. *See, e.g., Schlick v. Penn-Dixie Cement Corp.*, 507 F.2d 374, 384 (2d Cir. 1974).

11. Section 13(b) of the 1934 Act, also known as the accounting provisions of the Foreign Corrupt Practices Act of 1977 which were enacted as an amendment to the Exchange Act, generally requires subject registrants to maintain reasonably accurate books and records and internal accounting controls. The provisions were passed by Congress in the aftermath of the revelation that several hundred American corporations had paid millions of dollars into domestic political slush funds and as bribes to foreign officials for the purpose of procuring or retaining business in the particular foreign country.

12. The Sarbanes-Oxley Act is covered throughout this text, including in Chapter 5.

13. The pros and cons of "going public" are addressed in § 4.05 *infra*.

under a transactional exemption rather than a registered offering pursuant to § 5 of the Securities Act. In many situations, therefore, counsel will seek the viability of a transactional exemption before advising that a registered offering go forward. Hence, we begin our study of the offering process with the transactional exemptions.

§ 3.03 Transactional Exemptions — Introductory Points

A number of introductory comments are in order.

First, the exemptions we are examining are transactionally based. Hence, for each separate *transaction*, an exemption from registration must be perfected.

Second, the relevant parties for the purposes of this Chapter who are seeking to come within the transactional exemptions are primary issuers of securities. For example, a corporation issuing authorized but unissued stock or a limited partnership issuing interests to its participants would each be viewed as a primary issuer while a shareholder who seeks to transfer his/her shares to another would not be so viewed.[14]

Third, accordingly, persons seeking to resell their stock must have a registration statement filed with the SEC unless they likewise perfect an exemption. The exemption that normally would be invoked in this context is § 4(a)(1) of the Securities Act, which exempts from the registration requirements of § 5 transactions made by any person "other than an issuer, underwriter, or dealer." The subject of resales is the focus of Chapter 6.

Fourth, the party seeking the exemption has the burden of proving that it has perfected the exemption. This burden is carried by such party establishing that it has satisfied the necessary conditions for invoking the exemption. Failure to carry this burden signifies that no transactional exemption has been perfected, resulting in liability under the Securities Act for failure to register the offer or sale in question.

Such failure to register gives rise to SEC and perhaps criminal liability for violation of § 5 and to private recovery under § 12(a)(1) of the 1933 Act. Generally, § 12(a)(1) grants to the purchaser the right to rescind the transaction in an action brought against the seller for violation of § 5. In effect, the provision imposes strict liability upon the seller for failure to comply with § 5's registration requirements. Generally, the state securities laws have similar provisions.[15]

Fifth, consistent with the federal securities laws in general, the interstate commerce requirement must be met in order for federal jurisdiction to be invoked in the transactional exemption context. This requirement normally is met without difficulty.

---

14. The subject of resales is addressed in Chapter 6.

15. *See* §§ 7.06, 7.09, 9.08 *infra*.

Use of the mail or any means or instrumentality of interstate commerce is sufficient. An intrastate telephone call, for example, satisfies the federal jurisdictional requirement.[16]

Sixth, even if a transactional exemption has been perfected, thereby obviating the need to register the offering, the antifraud provisions of the securities acts nonetheless apply. The antifraud provisions most frequently invoked are § 17(a) of the Securities Act, § 10(b) of the Exchange Act, and Rule 10b-5 promulgated by the SEC pursuant to its § 10(b) rulemaking authority.[17]

Seventh, as a final important point, federal law is not the only source of regulation in this setting. The state "blue sky" laws also frequently apply and present additional dilemmas for the corporate practitioner and his/her client. With certain exceptions, to perfect an exemption, in addition to satisfying the requirements of federal law, the securities regulations of *each* state where *any* offer or sale is made must also be met. Violation of the state blue sky registration provisions may result in civil monetary liability, enforcement action by the pertinent state regulator, and even criminal prosecution. To the credit of the SEC and the states, significant progress has been made in coordinating the federal and state transactional exemption scheme, thereby alleviating much of the burden in complying with this multifaceted regulatory framework. Moreover, as discussed later in this chapter, federal legislation enacted in 1996 preempts state regulation of certain exempt offerings.

---

§ 3.04 Scenarios

Problem A

Madison, the sole proprietor of Take It Easy Restaurants, Inc. (a duly formed Arizona Corporation) located in Winslow, Arizona, decides that she would like her business to become another "McDonald's" (but would settle for "Wendy's"). She realizes, however, that this dream will take some time. Her first step is to seek additional capital. She approaches (who she believes are) three residents of Winslow: Lewis, Stiles (who in fact moved to Yakima, Washington, six months ago but spends the winter in Winslow), and Walker, each of whom is nonaccredited, and enters into an agreement with them. The only written disclosure provided is the agreement stating as follows: "In return for an investment of $90,000 each by Lewis, Stiles, and Walker into the business (or a total of $270,000), Lewis, Stiles, and Walker each will purchase common stock from Take It Easy Restaurants, Inc. and thereby become a stockholder owning 10 percent of the common stock of the business. In addition, on a

---

16. *See, e.g., Lennerth v. Mendenhall,* 234 F. Supp. 59 (N.D. Ohio 1964).

17. Section 10(b) is addressed in Chapter 8 while § 17(a) is covered in § 9.03.

quarterly basis, Lewis, Stiles and Walker each will receive 10 percent of the restaurant's net profits. The daily management of the business is to be left to Madison and all decisions are to be hers." Madison (who will own 70 percent of the common stock) also states orally that she anticipates net profits to exceed $100,000 annually because of increased customer interest and a more appetizing menu. Seven months later the profits are not as Madison anticipated. Lewis and Stiles are willing to "ride the tide" but Walker wants out of the venture. After Madison refuses to give Walker his money back, Madison comes to you seeking advice. Has Madison, on behalf of Take It Easy Restaurants, perfected a transactional exemption from registration? If so, which exemption(s)? If she has procured an exemption, is there any other basis upon which your client may be liable?

Problem B

Two years later, the business needs additional capital. Madison approaches her attorney, Dillard, a securities practitioner, who in turn consults an investment banker acquaintance, Vincent, who he knows from previous "deals." Dillard and Vincent concur that a Regulation D offering is the route to take. Pursuant thereto, Vincent contacts 53 persons with whom he has previously done business to generate interest. He suggests that they invite their friends and business acquaintances to a seminar that he will conduct on the Take It Easy Restaurants offering. A week later Vincent holds the seminar, with 137 persons attending. Subsequently, 32 of these persons purchase securities, investing $50,000 each. Moreover, Dillard and Vincent highly recommend the deal to some of their wealthy acquaintances, 10 of whom invest $100,000 each. An offering circular is distributed to all of the nonaccredited investors except two who are inadvertently overlooked. Ten months later, seven investors (six of whom received the offering circular and are non-accredited purchasers) want out of the deal. They have come to you for guidance. Presuming there are no antifraud violations, has Take It Easy Restaurants perfected a transactional exemption from registration? If so, which exemption(s)?

With the benefit of hindsight, would it have been wiser to have made the sale of the securities solely to accredited investors? Why or why not?

Problem C

Seven years later, to the delight of Madison and the other investors, Take It Easy Restaurants, Inc. is prospering at record levels. The number of restaurants has increased from one to 10 throughout Arizona. Madison believes that it is time to expand Take It Easy Restaurants to other states. She approaches her broker situated in Phoenix, Howard F. Tweed, of Gouche, Billard & Thomas. He advises that another private offering is the appropriate route and thereupon calls his colleagues in Gouche, Billard & Thomas' Dallas, Denver, Oklahoma City, and Salt Lake City offices to orchestrate the offering. The respective brokers contact 630 existing clients of Gouche, Billard & Thomas and inquire whether these individuals are interested in investing in the offering. Subsequently, 275 detailed private placement memoranda (PPMs) are mailed to those expressing interest.

Ultimately, 44 individuals purchase common stock in the offering, totaling $8.2 million. Four such individuals had incomes of more than $500,000 during each of the past five years, three others are multimillionaires, and four others each purchase $200,000 worth of the securities offered. The other 33 purchasers all purchase less than $50,000 worth of the stock, have annual incomes of less than $175,000 and net worth of less than $1 million.

The SEC subsequently brings suit against Take It Easy Restaurants, Madison, and Gouche, Billard & Thomas for failure to comply with the registration provisions of §5. The defendants contend that they perfected a transactional exemption from registration. The matter is being tried before you, a federal district court judge sitting in Denver. Which way do you rule? Why?

Problem D

Presume that, five years later, Take It Easy Restaurants, Inc. is a successful enterprise, having locations in several states. Madison wishes to raise additional capital for expansion. The decision is reached to make the offering open only to "accredited" purchasers. Which exemptions are available? Should prospective investors be solicited by means of general solicitation, including the Internet? What is your advice as counsel as to the amount and type of information that Take It Easy Restaurants (the corporate issuer) should provide to each "accredited" purchaser?

---

§ 3.05 The Statutory Private Offering Exemption — Section 4(a)(2)

Section 4(a)(2) of the Securities Act exempts from the registration requirements "transactions by an issuer not involving any public offering." There is no monetary limit to the amount of funds that can be raised under this exemption. The provision's legislative history expresses Congress' intent to exempt those transactions from registration "where there is no practical need for [such] application . . . [or] where the public benefits are too remote." H.R. Rep. No. 85, 73d Cong., 1st Sess. 5 (1933).

As construed, federal courts have looked to a number of factors in determining the availability of the §4(a)(2) private offering exemption. Undoubtedly, the starting point is the Supreme Court's seminal decision in *Securities and Exchange Commission v. Ralston Purina Co.*

Securities and Exchange Commission v. Ralston Purina Co.

United States Supreme Court

346 U.S. 119, 73 S. Ct. 981, 97 L. Ed. 2d 1494 (1953)

MR. JUSTICE CLARK delivered the opinion of the Court.

Section 4(1) [now § 4(a)(2)] of the Securities Act of 1933 exempts "transactions by an issuer not involving any public offering" from the registration requirements of § 5. We must decide whether Ralston Purina's offerings of treasury stock to its "key employees" are within this exemption. On a complaint brought by the Commission under § 20(b) of the Act seeking to enjoin respondent's unregistered offerings, the District Court held the exemption applicable and dismissed the suit. The Court of Appeals affirmed. The question has arisen many times since the Act was passed; an apparent need to define the scope of the private offering exemption prompted certiorari.

Ralston Purina manufactures and distributes various feed and cereal products. Its processing and distribution facilities are scattered throughout the United States and Canada, staffed by some 7,000 employees. At least since 1911 the company has had a policy of encouraging stock ownership among its employees; more particularly, since 1942 it has made authorized but unissued common shares available to some of them. Between 1947 and 1951, the period covered by the record in this case, Ralston Purina sold nearly $2,000,000 of stock to employees without registration and in so doing made use of the mails.

In each of these years, a corporate resolution authorized the sale of common stock "to employees . . . who shall, without any solicitation by the Company or its officers or employees, inquire of any of them as to how to purchase common stock of Ralston Purina Company." A memorandum sent to branch and store managers after the resolution was adopted advised that "[t]he only employees to whom this stock will be available will be those who take the initiative and are interested in buying stock at present market prices." Among those responding to these offers were employees with the duties of artist, bakeshop foreman, chow loading foreman, clerical assistant, copywriter, electrician, stock clerk, mill office clerk, order credit trainee, production trainee, stenographer, and veterinarian. The buyers lived in over fifty widely separated communities scattered from Garland, Texas, to Nashua, New Hampshire, and Visalia, California. The lowest salary bracket of those purchasing was $2,700 in 1949, $2,435 in 1950 and $3,107 in 1951. The record shows that in 1947, 243 employees bought stock, 20 in 1948, 414 in 1949, 411 in 1950, and the 1951 offer, interrupted by this litigation, produced 165 applications to purchase. No records were kept of those to whom the offers were made; the estimated number in 1951 was 500.

The company bottoms its exemption claim on the classification of all offerees as "key employees" . . . . Its position on trial was that

> A key employee . . . is not confined to an organization chart. It would include an individual who is eligible for promotion, an individual who especially

influences others or who advises others, a person whom the employees look to in some special way, an individual, of course, who carries some special responsibility, who is sympathetic to management and who is ambitious and who the management feels is likely to be promoted to a greater responsibility.

That an offering to all of its employees would be public is conceded.

The Securities Act nowhere defines the scope of §4[(a)(2)'s] private offering exemption. Nor is the legislative history of much help in staking out its boundaries. . . .

Decisions under comparable exemptions in the English Companies Acts and state "blue sky" laws, the statutory antecedents of federal securities legislation, have made one thing clear—to be public an offer need not be open to the whole world. . . .

Exemption from the registration requirements of the Securities Act is the question. The design of the statute is to protect investors by promoting full disclosure of information thought necessary to informed investment decisions. The natural way to interpret the private offering exemption is in light of the statutory purpose. Since exempt transactions are those as to which "there is no practical need for [the bill's] application," the applicability of §4[(a)(2)] should turn on whether the particular class of persons affected needs the protection of the Act. An offering to those who are shown to be able to fend for themselves is a transaction "not involving any public offering."

The Commission would have us go one step further and hold that "an offering to a substantial number of the public" is not exempt under §4[(a)(2)]. We are advised that "whatever the special circumstances, the Commission has consistently interpreted the exemption as being inapplicable when a large number of offerees are involved." But the statute would seem to apply to a "public offering" whether to few or many. It may well be that offerings to a substantial number of persons would rarely be exempt. Indeed nothing prevents the Commission, in enforcing the statute, from using some kind of numerical test in deciding when to investigate particular exemption claims. But there is no warrant for superimposing a quantity limit on private offerings as a matter of statutory interpretation.

The exemption, as we construe it, does not deprive corporate employees, as a class, of the safeguards of the Act. We agree that some employee offerings may come within §4[(a)(2)], e.g., one made to executive personnel who because of their position have access to the same kind of information that the Act would make available in the form of a registration statement.[18] Absent such a showing of special circumstances,

---

18. This was one of the factors stressed in an advisory opinion rendered by the Commission's General Counsel in 1935.

> I also regard as significant the relationship between the issuer and the offerees. Thus, an offering to the members of a class who should have special knowledge of the issuer is less likely to be a public offering than is an offering to the members of a class of the same size who do not have this advantage. This factor would be particularly

employees are just as much members of the investing "public" as any of their neighbors in the community. . . .

Keeping in mind the broadly remedial purposes of federal securities legislation, imposition of the burden of proof on an issuer who would plead the exemption seems to us fair and reasonable. Agreeing, the court below thought the burden met primarily because of the respondent's purpose in singling out its key employees for stock offerings. But once it is seen that the exemption question turns on the knowledge of the offerees, the issuer's motives, laudable though they may be, fade into irrelevance. The focus of inquiry should be on the need of the offerees for the protections afforded by registration. The employees here were not shown to have access to the kind of information which registration would disclose. The obvious opportunities for pressure and imposition make it advisable that they be entitled to compliance with § 5.

Reversed.

Case Law after Ralston Purina

The lower federal courts subsequent to *Ralston Purina* have had numerous occasions to construe the § 4(a)(2) exemption. Although the principles emerging from these cases are not crystal-clear, the following points can be made:

First, as construed by some courts, the § 4(a)(2) exemption turns on whether *all offers* (rather than actual purchases) are made in accordance with the exemption. A single noncomplying offer may invalidate the entire offering. For example, the Fifth Circuit has stated: "[W]e have held that the defendant must establish that each and every offeree either had the same information that would have been available in a registration statement or had access to such information."[19] When appropriate, the subject issuer may demand the signing of a non-disclosure agreement (NDA) by the prospective investor as a condition to receiving the pertinent information.

Second, although the courts and the SEC have not placed a finite number on how many offers can permissibly be made under the § 4(a)(2) exemption, it is clear that certain limits, depending on the circumstances, apply.[20]

Third, related to the above point, is that, pursuant to the § 4(a)(2) exemption, the issuer cannot engage in general solicitation or advertising. The limits of what conduct constitutes general solicitation so as to make unavailable the § 4(a)(2) exemption at times are unclear. For instance, a seminar held for an offering where 25 existing

---

important in offerings to employees, where a class of high executive officers would have a special relationship to the issuer which subordinate employees would not enjoy. 11 Fed. Reg. 10952.

19. *Swensen v. Engelstad*, 626 F.2d 421, 425–426 (5th Cir. 1980). See *Mark v. FSC Securities Corp.*, 870 F.2d 331, 334 (6th Cir. 1989).

20. *See Ralson Purina*, 346 U.S. at 125.

clients of adequate sophistication attend should be permitted, while a seminar for a particular offering open to all clients of a major broker-dealer (e.g., Merrill Lynch) should be deemed general solicitation.[21]

Fourth, an issuer should take certain precautions against resales, such as obtaining written commitments by purchasers that they are acquiring for investment purposes (called an investment letter), placing appropriate legends on the certificates, and issuing stop transfer instructions. These procedures help the issuer perfect the § 4(a)(2) exemption in the event that purchasers subsequently resell their stock. It may well be, however, that the absence of these steps does not nullify an otherwise valid § 4(a)(2) exemption if no distribution in fact takes place.[22]

Fifth, all offerees must be financially sophisticated or be advised by someone who has the requisite acumen (called an offeree representative). Under case law, individual wealth (unlike the Rule 506 exemption) does not make one sophisticated for § 4(a)(2) private placement purposes.[23] Use of a questionnaire by an issuer to ascertain an investor's financial sophistication is customary.

Sixth, irrespective of whether an offeree (or offeree representative) has financial acumen, "[s]ophistication is not a substitute for access to the [type of] information that a registration statement would disclose."[24] In short, if offerees have not received the type of information that registration would elicit, they cannot bring any alleged "sophistication" to bear in deciding whether or not to invest.[25] Hence, all offerees must be provided with the type of information (not necessarily identical) that would be contained in a registration statement or have access to such information.

Ascertaining which offerees have "access" to registration-type information may be problematic. Relevant factors include high-level executive status in the enterprise, family ties, a privileged relationship based upon prior business dealings between the parties, and economic bargaining power that enables an offeree effectively to obtain the registration-type information.[26]

Moreover, some courts have looked to two additional factors in determining whether the § 4(a)(2) exemption has been perfected: the number of units offered and

---

21. The SEC has issued no-action letters in this context. *See* § 3.11[B]. *See also,* Cohn, *Securities Markets for Small Issuers: The Barrier of Federal Solicitation and Advertising Prohibitions,* 38 U. FLA. L. REV. 1 (1986).

22. *See Livens v. William D. Witter, Inc.,* 374 F. Supp. 1104, 1110 (D. Mass. 1974); Schneider, *The Statutory Law of Private Placements,* 14 REV. SEC. REG. 870, 881 (1981)

23. *See Doran v. Petroleum Management Corp.,* 545 F.2d 893, 903 (5th Cir. 1977). For a more relaxed standard, see *Acme Propane, Inc. v. Tenexco, Inc.,* 844 F.2d 1317, 1321 (7th Cir. 1988).

24. *Doran,* 545 F.2d at 902. *See United States v. Custer Channel Wing Corp.,* 376 F.2d 675, 678 (4th Cir. 1967).

25. *See Hill York Corp. v. American International Franchises, Inc.,* 448 F.2d 680, 690 (5th Cir. 1971).

26. *See Doran v. Petroleum Management Corp.,* 545 F.2d 893, 903 (5th Cir. 1977); Schneider, *supra* note 22, at 877.

the size of the offering.[27] These factors, however, often are irrelevant. For example, the offer and sale by an issuer of one million corporate debentures for $500 million to five sophisticated institutional investors (such as insurance companies), having effective access to registration-type information, normally should be within the § 4(a)(2) private offering exemption.

Note that, with respect to § 4(a)(2) offerings, state regulation also applies. In addition, states have authority to prosecute or to provide redress for fraud. Interestingly, enactment of the National Securities Markets Improvement Act of 1996 preempts state regulation of SEC "rules or regulations issued under section 4(2) [now § 4(a)(2)]." See § 18(b)(4)(D) of the Securities Act. Nonetheless, states may continue to impose their own requirements for private offerings that are exempt under the statute itself (namely, the § 4(a)(2) *statutory* exemption).

§ 3.06 Rule 506 of Regulation D

The SEC adopted Regulation D, including Rule 506, more than three decades ago. Rule 506 may well be the most widely used exemption. As formulated, Rule 506 has certain key criteria that are addressed in the following materials. Historically, an important criterion has been that, in order to perfect the Rule 506 exemption, no advertising or general solicitation is permitted. This firm mandate remained effective until the JOBS Act was enacted in 2012. Today, advertising and general solicitation are allowed if all purchasers are accredited investors.

Pursuant to the JOBS Act, as discussed later in this Section, an issuer may engage in general solicitation and advertising so long as all the purchasers in the offering are accredited investors. For those issuers who elect to use general solicitation and advertising, they nonetheless must adhere to the other applicable provisions of Regulation D (including, for example, restrictions on the resale of securities sold pursuant to Rule 506).

For issuers who wish to sell securities to nonaccredited purchasers or who elect not to engage in advertising or general solicitation, they may elect to conduct their offerings under traditional Rule 506. Accordingly, the following materials will focus on the SEC's adoption of Regulation D as well as the most recent changes to Rule 506. The materials also will address a number of issues that remain significant in the Rule 506 exemption framework.

---

27. *See, e.g., SEC v. Continental Tobacco Co.*, 463 F.2d 137, 158 (5th Cir. 1978). *See generally* American Bar Association, *Section 4(2) and Statutory Law—A Position Paper by the Federal Regulation of Securities Committee*, 31 Bus. Law. 485 (1975).

[A] Traditional Rule 506

Regulation D — Revision of Certain Exemptions from Registration Under the Securities Act of 1933 for Transactions Involving Limited Offers and Sales

SEC Securities Act Release No. 6389 (1982)[28]

Regulation D is a series of . . . rules, designated Rules 501-506 that establishes three exemptions from the registration requirements of the Securities Act and replaces exemptions that currently exist under Rules 146, 240, and 242. The regulation is designed to simplify existing rules and regulations, to eliminate any unnecessary restrictions that those rules and regulations place on issuers, particularly small businesses, and to achieve uniformity between state and federal exemptions in order to facilitate capital formation consistent with the protection of investors.

Rules 501-503 set forth definitions, terms, and conditions that apply generally throughout the regulation. The exemptions of Regulation D are contained in Rules 504-506. Rules 504 and 505 replace Rules 240 and 242, respectively, and provide exemptions from registration under § 3(b) of the Securities Act. Rule 506 succeeds Rule 146 and relates to transactions that are deemed to be exempt from registration under § 4(2) [now § 4(a)(2)] of the Securities Act.

. . . .

Rule 506 takes the place of Rule 146. As under its predecessor, Rule 506 is available to all issuers for offerings sold to not more than 35 purchasers. Accredited investors, however, do not count towards that limit. Rule 506 requires an issuer to make a subjective determination that each [nonaccredited] purchaser meets certain sophistication standards, a provision that narrows a similar requirement as to all offerees under Rule 146. The new exemption retains the concept of the purchaser representative so that unsophisticated purchasers may participate in the offering if a purchaser representative is present. [Also,] Rule 506 prohibits any general solicitation or general advertising. [Note that the JOBS Act enacted in 2012 permits general solicitation and advertising so long as all the purchasers in the offering are accredited investors.]

. . . .

PRELIMINARY NOTES

Regulation D contains six preliminary notes. The first preliminary note reminds issuers that Regulation D offerings, although exempt from § 5 of the Securities Act, are not exempt from antifraud or civil liability provisions of the federal securities laws. The note also reminds issuers conducting Regulation D offerings of their

---

28. Note that certain additions have been made in this Release to reflect subsequent SEC amendments to Regulation D — ed.

obligation to furnish whatever material information may be needed to make the required disclosure not misleading.

Note 2 underscores an issuer's obligation to comply with applicable state law and highlights certain areas of anticipated differences between Regulation D at the federal and state levels. [Note that state regulation of Rule 506 offerings was subsequently preempted by Congress. Nonetheless, the states still retain authority if any such offering involves fraudulent conduct.]

Note 3 makes clear that reliance on any particular exemption in Regulation D does not act as an election. An issuer may always claim the availability of any other applicable exemption. . . .

The fourth note specifies that Regulation D is available only to the issuer of the securities and not to its affiliates or others for resales of the issuer's securities. The note further provides that Regulation D exemptions are only transactional. . . .

Preliminary Note 5 . . . confirms the availability of Regulation D for business combinations.

The sixth note provides that the regulation is not available for use in a plan or scheme to evade the registration requirements of the Securities Act.

RULE 501 — DEFINITIONS AND TERMS USED IN REGULATION D

. . . .

Accredited investor

The introductory language to the proposed definition provided that investors were accredited only if "the issuer and any person acting on the issuer's behalf with respect to such investors have reasonable grounds to believe and do believe, after reasonable inquiry" that the investors came within one of the categories in the definition. It was pointed out that this formulation appeared to bar from the definition someone who actually was accredited but in whom the issuer did not have the requisite belief. The regulation as adopted permits accreditation for investors who are qualified in fact.

The following subsections review the . . . categories of accredited investor in Rule 501(a):

a. Institutional Investors. Rule 501(a)(1) repeats the listing of institutional investors included in § 2(a)(15)(i) of the Securities Act. . . .

[T]he Commission believes it is appropriate to extend accredited investor status to [institutional investors and] any ERISA plan with total assets in excess of $5,000,000.

b. Private Business Development Companies. This category applies to private business development companies as defined in § 202(a)(22) of the Investment Advisers Act of 1940 (the "Advisers Act") [with total assets in excess of $5,000,000]. . . .

c. Tax Exempt Organizations. Proposed Rule 501(a)(3) created a category of accredited investor for college or university endowment funds with assets in excess of $25 million. Upon further consideration and based on commentary the Commission has determined that this category can be expanded to all organizations that are described as exempt organizations in Section 501(c)(3) of the Internal Revenue Code [26 U.S.C. 501(c)(3)]. Additionally, the Commission has lowered the asset level to $5 million.

d. Directors, Executive Officers and General Partners. Rule 501(a)(4) provides that certain insiders of the issuer are accredited investors. As proposed, the category pertained only to directors and executive officers. A number of comment letters recommended that the provision be modified to cover general partners of limited partnerships. The category thus has been revised to include general partners of issuers, as well as directors, executive officers and general partners of those general partners.

e. $150,000 Purchasers. . . . Under this provision a person is an accredited investor upon the purchase of at least $150,000 of the securities if the total purchase price does not exceed 20 percent of the investor's net worth at the time of sale. For natural persons, the joint net worth of the investor and the investor's spouse may be used in measuring the ratio of purchase to net worth. The purchase may be made by one or a combination of four specified methods: cash; marketable securities; an unconditional obligation to pay cash or marketable securities within five years of sale; or a cancellation of indebtedness. [*This provision relating to the "big ticket" $150,000 accredited purchaser subsequently was repealed by the SEC.*]

. . . .

f. $1,000,000 Net Worth Test. This category extends accredited investor status to any natural person whose net worth at the time of purchase exceeds $1,000,000. Net worth may be either the individual worth of the investor or the joint net worth of the investor and the investor's spouse. [As subsequently amended, the $1 million net worth level *excludes* the value of one's primary residence. In addition, the SEC must periodically review this $1 million level to determine whether adjustment of the $1 million amount is appropriate. See § 413(a) of the Dodd-Frank Act of 2010; Securities Act Release No. 9287 (2011).]

g. $200,000 Income Test. A natural person who has an income in excess of $200,000 in each of the last two years and who reasonably expects an income in excess of $200,000 in the current year is an accredited investor. [This provision subsequently was amended to include joint income (with one's spouse) greater than $300,000 in each of the last two years and the reasonable expectation of joint income in excess of $300,000 for the current year.]

. . . The test is no longer keyed to the federal income tax return. Further, the requisite income level must have been sustained over the two most recent years and the investor must reasonably expect continuation of an adequate level in the year of the investment. Also, the term "adjusted gross income" has been changed to "income".

Use of the term "income" will permit the inclusion of certain deductions and additional items of income which, as noted above, were excluded in the proposed concept of adjusted gross income. Accordingly, the appropriate income level has been raised to $200,000.

. . . .

h. Entities Made up of Certain Accredited Investors. The proposed definition of accredited investor did not take into account an entity owned entirely by accredited investors. Rule 501(a)(8) of the final regulation extends accredited investor status to entities in which all the equity owners are accredited investors under Rule 501(a)(1), (2), (3), (4), (6), or (7).

[The SEC subsequently expanded the definition of "accredited investor" to include other supposedly sophisticated investors, such as savings and loan associations, credit unions, broker-dealers, and certain trusts, partnerships, corporations, and government pension plans with total assets greater than $5,000,000.]

RULE 502 — GENERAL CONDITIONS TO BE MET

Rule 502 sets forth general conditions that relate to all offerings under Rules 504 through 506. These cover guidelines for determining whether separate offers and sales constitute part of the same offering under principles of integration, requirements as to specific disclosure requirements in Regulation D offerings, and limitations on the manner of conducting the offering and on the resale of securities acquired in the offering. [Note that the Commission added a substantial compliance concept in Rule 508, discussed in § 3.08.]

. . . .

Integration. Rule 502(a) provides that all sales that are part of the same Regulation D offering must be integrated. The rule provides a safe harbor for all offers and sales that take place at least six months before the start of or six months after the termination of the Regulation D offering, so long as there are no offers and sales, excluding those to employee benefit plans, of the same securities within either of these six month periods. [Note that the SEC in 2007 proposed to decrease this time period from six months to 90 days. See Securities Act Release No. 8828 (2007). To date, this proposal has not been adopted.]

. . . .

Information Requirements. Rule 502(b) provides when and what type of disclosure must be furnished in Regulation D offerings. If an issuer sells securities under Rule 504 or only to accredited investors, then Regulation D does not mandate any specific disclosure.[Note, however, that, with respect to Rule 504 offerings, the applicable state securities laws set forth the pertinent disclosure requirements.] If securities are sold under Rule 505 or 506 to investors that are not accredited, then Rule 502 requires delivery of the information specified in [that Rule] to all [non-accredited] purchasers. . . .

... The balance of Rule 502(b)(2) provides for the treatment of exhibits, the right of purchasers that are not accredited to receive [material written] information which was furnished to accredited investors, and, in offerings involving nonaccredited investors, the right of ... purchasers to ask questions of the issuer concerning the offering, and a specific obligation by the issuer to disclose all material differences in terms or arrangements as between security holders in a business combination or exchange offer. ...

Manner of offering. Rule 502(c) prohibits the use of general solicitation or general advertising in connection with Regulation D offerings, except [for certain offerings] under Rule 504 [and Rule 506].

. . .

Limitations on resale. Securities acquired in a Regulation D offering, with the exception of [certain] offerings under Rule 504, have the status of securities acquired in a transaction under Section 4(2) [now § 4(a)(2)] of the Securities Act [and, hence, are restricted securities]. As further provided in Rule 502(d), [and as subsequently amended,] the issuer shall exercise reasonable care to assure that purchasers of securities are not underwriters, which reasonable care [may include such actions as] inquiry as to investment purpose, disclosure of resale limitations and placement of a legend on the certificate.

RULE 503 — FILINGS OF NOTICE OF SALES

The Commission is adopting a uniform notice of sales form for use in offerings under both Regulation D and Section 4(6) [now § 4(a)(5)] of the Securities Act. ... As with the predecessor forms, issuers will furnish information on Form D mainly by checking appropriate boxes. The form requires an indication of the exemptions being claimed.

[As subsequently amended by the SEC, the timely filing of the Form D is not a condition for perfecting a Reg. D exemption. However, if the issuer is enjoined for failing to file the Form D, such failure acts as a disqualification for the issuer to use a Reg. D exemption in the future. The Commission, in its discretion, may waive any such disqualification.]

[Note, moreover, that the Financial Industry Regulatory Authority [FINRA] requires, with certain exceptions, any member broker-dealer to submit to FINRA a copy of any Private Placement Memorandum (PPM) or other offering document used to sell a security in a non-public offering. Hence, for example, a PPM used in a Rule 506 offering sold to accredited and/or nonaccredited individual investors would require the member to submit to FINRA such PPM pursuant to FINRA Rule 5123.]

[Today, the SEC requires the electronic filing of the Form D (see Securities Act Release No. 8891 (2008).]

. . . .

Note

A chart of the Securities Act Limited and Private Offering Exemptions is contained in § 3.10. Reaction of the securities bar to Regulation D has been largely favorable. Remember that Rule 506 acts as a "safe harbor" for the § 4(a)(2) exemption. If the conditions for the Rule 506 exemption are met, then the issuer has come within the private offering exemption.

In short, conditions for the traditional Rule 506 exemption include:

- There is no limit to the aggregate price of the securities offered.

- The doctrine of integration applies, with the proviso that Regulation D provides a "safe harbor" in certain circumstances (see Rule 502(a)). We will discuss the integration concept in further detail in § 3.15.

- There is no express limit to the number of offerees (depending on the circumstances, however, offers to a large number of offerees may be viewed as "general" solicitation and, hence, loss of the traditional Rule 506 exemption).

- The number of purchasers, excluding accredited investors, is limited to 35 persons. The issuer "must reasonably" believe that it has adhered to this requirement.

- Specified disclosure must be provided to all purchasers who are not accredited (see Rule 502(b)).

- There is no requirement that the issuer determine that the purchaser can bear the economic risk of the investment. Financial sophistication determinations, however, must be made for all nonaccredited purchasers. Except for accredited investors, the issuer prior to sale must "reasonably believe" that each purchaser "either alone or with his purchaser representative(s) has such knowledge and experience in financial and business matters that he is capable of evaluating the merits and risks of the prospective investment." Rule 506(b)(2)(ii).

- In traditional Rule 506 offerings, general advertising or solicitation is prohibited (see Rule 502(c)).

- Pursuant to Rule 508, the SEC applies a "substantial compliance" standard to Rule 506 offerings. See § 3.08.

- Any issuer, irrespective of its status as a reporting or nonreporting entity, its size, or its type of business, may use the SEC Rule 506 exemption. Nonetheless, note that "bad actor" disqualifiers apply.

- There are restrictions on resales (see Rule 502(d)). In addition, the issuer is required to provide written disclosure to all nonaccredited purchasers of any such restrictions on resales.

- The Rule 506 exemption, like the Rule 504 and 505 exemptions, is available to the issuer only and not to its affiliates or shareholders.

- In 2013, as directed by the Dodd-Frank Act of 2010, the SEC adopted "bad actor" disqualifications for Rule 506 offerings. Rule 506(d), the bad actor disqualification provision, resembles the bad actor disqualifiers that have been a component of the Regulation A exemptive framework for decades (see § 3.07[D]).Disqualifying events (that preclude the subject issuer from using the Rule 506 exemption for five or 10 years depending on the type of the misconduct) include specified criminal conduct and court injunctions, SEC disciplinary orders (including cease and desist orders), enforcement orders from other regulators (such as state securities regulators, federal banking agencies, and the CFTC), and suspensions or expulsions issued by a self-regulatory organization (SRO). The disqualification provision of Rule 506(d) encompasses: (1) the issuer (including its predecessors and affiliated enterprises); (2) the issuer's directors and certain officers (as well as its general partners and managing members); (3) the issuer's beneficial owners of 20 percent or more of its stock or other equitable ownership interest (e.g., limited partnership units); (4) promoters; (5) investment managers; and (6) individuals or enterprises that for compensation solicit investors (including general partners, officers, directors, and managing members of such compensated solicitor).

Rule 506(d) does provide an exception when the issuer can establish that it did not know and, in its exercise of reasonable care, could not have known that a disqualified person who had engaged in disqualifying conduct participated in the offering. Moreover, upon a showing of good cause, the Commission may waive the Rule 506(d) disqualification.

- Federal legislation enacted in 1996 preempts state regulation of offerings coming within Rule 506.See § 18(b)(4)(D) of the Securities Act. States nonetheless may set forth notice filing requirements and collect fees with respect to such offerings. In 2014, the North American Securities Administrators Association (NASAA) launched an online Electronic Filing Depository that enhances the efficiency of the state filing process for Rule 506 offerings. Note, moreover, that states retain their authority to bring enforcement actions for fraudulent conduct in connection with such offerings. However, with respect to the requisite parameters of the Rule 506 exemption, the states no longer have any role.

- An important concept under Rule 506 (as well as under Rule 505) is that of an "accredited investor." Under Regulation D, accredited investors irrebuttably are deemed to have access to registration-type information and to possess investment sophistication. Under Rule 501, accredited investors include not only certain entities and institutional investors, but also "fat cat" individual investors. These persons include those whose net worth at the time of the purchase exceeds $1 million (excluding the value of one's primary residence) and those who had an individual income exceeding $200,000 in each of the two most recent years (or exceeding $300,000 joint income with one's spouse) and who reasonably anticipate such an income for the current year. The $1 million net worth level must be periodically reviewed by the SEC to determine whether this $1 million amount should be adjusted. See § 413(a) of the Dodd-Frank Act of 2010; Securities Act Release No. 9287 (2011).

- Significantly, in a Rule 505 or 506 offering involving accredited investors, there is no mandated delivery of information to such accredited investors, because Regulation D irrebuttably presumes that these investors can fend for themselves.

- It is noteworthy that Rule 506 expands the § 4(a)(2) private offering exemption in at least two ways. First, unlike § 4(a)(2), which applies to both offers and sales, Rule 506 largely focuses on purchaser (rather than offeree) qualification. Hence, for example, Rule 506, unlike § 4(a)(2), requires that only purchasers meet the financial sophistication standards. Second, institutions and wealthy individuals irrebuttably are deemed under Regulation D to be financially sophisticated and to have access to the type of information that a registration statement would provide. Case law under § 4(a)(2), particularly with respect to wealthy individual investors, disagrees with the SEC's position.

- Irrespective of the Rule 506 exemption, § 4(a)(2) still is the key exemption in certain contexts. For example, under Rule 506, disclosure of specified information must be provided to all purchasers who are not accredited. On the other hand, § 4(a)(2) allows an offeree's access to the applicable information to substitute for the providing of such information. In view of the costs generated in supplying such information, particularly in offerings of relatively small financial amounts, § 4(a)(2) may provide an attractive alternative. However, with respect to offerings made pursuant to the § 4(a)(2) *statutory* exemption (unlike the Rule 506 exemption), the states may continue to impose their own requirements.

See generally J.W. HICKS, LIMITED OFFERING EXEMPTIONS: REGULATION D (2016); ABA Committee on Federal Regulation of Securities, *Law of Private Placements (Non-Public Offerings) Not Entitled to Benefits of Safe Harbors — A Report,* 66 BUS. LAW. 85 (2010); Johnson, *Private Placements: A Regulatory Black Hole,* 35 DEL. J. CORP. L. 151 (2010); Warren, *A Review of Regulation D: The Present Exemption Regimen for Limited Offerings Under the Securities Act of 1933,* 33 AM. U.L. REV. 355 (1984); Sargent, *The New Regulation D: Deregulation, Federalism and the Dynamics of Regulatory Reform,* 68 WASH. U.L.Q. 225 (1990).

———————

As discussed above, federal legislation enacted in 1996 preempts state regulation of Rule 506 offerings. The question arises whether preemption is triggered upon a mere assertion that the subject offering was made pursuant to Rule 506 or that "something more" is required, such as a showing that the Rule 506 exemption indeed was perfected. The courts are divided on this question. The Sixth Circuit's decision representing the prevailing view follows.

Brown v. Earthboard Sports USA, Inc.

United States Court of Appeals, Sixth Circuit

481 F.3d 901 (2007)

. . . .

Brown's first claim on appeal is that the district court erred in holding that federal law preempts his state Blue Sky law claims. [The National Securities Market Improvement Act of 1996] NSMIA, which in pertinent part amended Section 18(a)(1)(A) of the 1933 Securities Act, preempts state regulation with respect to "covered securities." According to Section 18(b)(4)(D) of the 1933 Securities Act, a "covered security" is, *inter alia,* any security exempt from federal securities registration "pursuant to— . . . Commission rules or regulations issued under § 4(2) [now § 4(a)(2)]" of the 1933 Act. The parties agree that the offering was purportedly made "pursuant to" Rule 506 based on Earthboard's 1999 filing.

The parties differ in their interpretation of the effect of Earthbound's 1999 filing for the Rule 506 exemption. Brown claims that an offering must actually meet the conditions established by the SEC regulation in order to qualify as a "covered security" exempted from state registration requirements by NSMIA. He further claims that Earthboard's offering did not, in fact, qualify as a "covered security" under Rule 506. The defendants answer that NSMIA exempts, *inter alia*, all non-public securities from state regulation so long as the company has attempted to qualify for a valid federal exemption or has purported that the securities are offered "pursuant to" an exemption. Moreover, they argue that the Earthboard offering actually qualified for the Rule 506 exemption. The district court held that the simple fact that the 1999 filing had been entered under the rubric of a federal exemption entitled it to federal preemption pursuant to NSMIA. District courts and state courts have split on the question of whether filings must actually qualify for a federal securities registration exemption in order to be entitled to NSMIA preemption. To the best of our knowledge, no federal appeals court has yet ruled on this question. We now agree with those courts that have held that offerings must actually qualify for a valid federal securities registration exemption in order to enjoy NSMIA preemption.

In *Temple v. Gorman,* 201 F. Supp. 2d 1238 (S.D. Fla. 2002), the district court held that Congress broadly preempted state law registration actions in passing NSMIA. In that case, the plaintiffs asserted that their state law claims were not preempted as the securities were not actually exempt because they did not meet Rule 506's (or any other exemption's) requirements. The district court did not dispute that allegation, but noted that Congress's purpose in passing NSMIA was "to further and advance the development of national securities markets and eliminate the costs and burdens of duplicative and unnecessary regulation by, as a general rule, designating the Federal government as the exclusive regulator of national offerings of securities." Based on this "purpose," as stated in the legislative gloss, the *Temple* Court held that

> the securities in this case were offered or sold pursuant to a Commission rule or regulation adopted under section 4(2) [now § 4(a)(2)] . . . . [and] [r]egardless of whether the private placement actually complied with the substantive requirements of Regulation D or Rule 506, the securities sold to Plaintiffs are federal covered securities because they were sold pursuant to those rules.

As such, the *Temple* court held that the state's Blue Sky law was preempted by the fact that the defendants had *attempted* or *purported* to qualify for a legitimate federal exemption. Several district courts have followed *Temple's* reasoning. . . .

Other courts have roundly rejected *Temple's* reasoning. The Supreme Court of Alabama raised the first challenge to *Temple's* broad-preemption reasoning when it required the defendants claiming NSMIA preemption for their offering, which had been sold pursuant to the Rule 506 exemption, to prove that the challenged securities actually qualified for a valid federal exemption. *Buist v. Time Domain Corp.*, 926 So. 2d 290, 295–98 (Ala. 2005).

Several federal district courts have approved *Buist's* line of reasoning. One district court noted that the "plain language" of the securities laws defines a "covered security" as "one that 'is exempt from registration under this title pursuant to . . . Commission rules or regulations.'" *AFA Private Equity Fund 1 v. Miresco Inv. Servs.*, 2005 U.S. Dist. LEXIS 22071, at *26 (E.D. Mich. Sept. 30, 2005). The *Miresco* court required defendants to "present evidence showing that the securities at issue here are exempt from registration under the rules adopted by the SEC under § 4(2)" and held that "it is [the defendant's] burden, as the party relying on the exemption, to establish that the exemption applies and that all conditions of the exemption had been satisfied." Another court noted that

> [t]o the extent that *Temple* can be read to support the principle of broad preemption that the defendants urge, this Court declines to follow that case. . . . This Court has found no authority for [the broad preemption principle] . . . . [and] contrary to *Temple*, most commentators have stated the obvious: a security has to actually be a 'covered security' before federal preemption applies.

Hamby v. Clearwater Consulting Concepts, LLP, 428 F. Supp. 2d 915, 921 n. 2 (E.D. Ark. 2006) (citations omitted). This general line of reasoning has been repeated even more recently:

> The *Temple* court read language into the statute that does not appear there. A security is covered if it is exempt from registration. . . . Nowhere does the statute indicate that a security may satisfy the definition if it is sold pursuant to a putative exemption. If Congress had intended that an offeror's representation of exemption should suffice it could have said so, but did not. Such an intent seems unlikely, in any event; that a defendant could avoid liability under state law simply by declaiming its alleged compliance with Regulation D is an unsavory proposition and would eviscerate the

statute. Nor is it necessary to look to the legislative history; the statute is unambiguous.

Grubka v. WebAccess Int'l, 445 F. Supp. 2d 1259, 1269–71 (D. Colo. 2006). . . .

We likewise reject *Temple's* approach. Under the prevailing view of the Commerce Clause's grant of authority, Congress has clearly been authorized to regulate the trading of securities. This includes the power to preempt contravening state regulations. Congress could in fact decide to occupy the entire field of securities regulation and preempt all state laws as they pertain to securities. Appellees urge us to believe that Congress actually performed a feat only slightly narrower, for to hold that NSMIA preempts state regulation wherever offerings merely *purport* to be filed pursuant to a valid federal registration exemption, or where parties have filed for, but fail to qualify for, an SEC registration exemption, would effectively eviscerate state registration requirements. In such a world, state registration requirements could be avoided merely by adding spurious boilerplate language to subscription agreements suggesting that the offerings were "covered," or by filing bogus documents with the SEC. Congress indubitably possesses the power to accomplish that end.

However, it is dispositive to our inquiry that Congress chose not to include broadly preemptive language when it enacted NSMIA. Instead, the statute plainly restricts its preemptive scope to "covered securities," and it neither defines, nor requires the SEC to define, "covered securities" in a fashion that would actually include all securities. The statute thus does not expressly preempt state laws with respect to non-"covered" securities, nor does the statute's text reveal an implied intent to preempt all state statutes in the field. Moreover, far from defining "covered securities" in a manner that generally incorporates all securities, the SEC has promulgated specific requirements that must be met in order for a security to be "covered." Therefore, we hold that NSMIA preempts state securities registration laws with respect only to those offerings that actually qualify as "covered securities" according to the regulations that the SEC has promulgated.

. . . .

[For further analysis, see Meyer, *Federal Preemption of the Rule 506 Exemption,* 37 SEC. REG. L.J. 122 (2009).]

[B] JOBS Act — Rule 506

In its enactment of the JOBS Act in 2012, seeking to facilitate capital formation, Congress directed the SEC to authorize the use by issuers of advertising and general solicitation in Rule 506 offerings, provided that all purchasers of the subject securities are *accredited investors*. The SEC also was directed to require issuers that engage in advertising and general solicitation in Rule 506 offerings "to take reasonable steps to verify that purchasers of the securities are accredited investors. . . ." (§ 201(a) of the JOBS Act).In addition, Congress added § 4(b) to the Securities Act to provide that:

"Offers and sales under [Rule 506] shall not be deemed public offerings under the Federal securities laws as a result of general advertising or general solicitation."[29] From this legislative fiction, one may inquire how an issuer engages in general solicitation by such means as the radio, newspaper, and Internet—yet the offering is not deemed "public" by statutory mandate.

The meaning of an issuer's obligation to take reasonable steps to *verify* that all purchasers are accredited is provoking comment. In this regard, it would be prudent for an issuer or its agents to maintain adequate records that set forth the "reasonable steps [taken] to verify" that a subject purchaser in fact is an accredited investor.

To elaborate, the use of general solicitation in Rule 506(c) offerings requires issuers "to take reasonable steps to verify that purchasers of the securities are accredited investors, using such methods as determined by the Commission." In 2013, the SEC engaged in rulemaking pursuant to this directive.[30] The objective of the verification requirement is to minimize the risk that the use of general solicitation in Rule 506 offerings will result in the sale of securities to nonaccredited investors. As set forth by the Commission, whether the steps undertaken by an issuer are "reasonable" is an objective determination based on the particular facts and circumstances of the transaction and the subject purchaser. Adhering to a "principles-based method of verification," the SEC stated that issuers should consider the following factors in meeting their reasonable verification obligation under Rule 506(c):

1. the nature of the purchaser and the type of accredited investor that the purchaser claims to be;

2. the amount and type of information that the issuer has about the purchaser; and

3. the nature of the offering, such as the manner in which the purchaser was solicited in the offering, and the terms of the offering, such as a minimum investment amount.

As stated by the Commission, the foregoing factors are interconnected—the more likely a purchaser reasonably appears to qualify as an accredited investor, the fewer steps an issuer would be required to take to verify accredited status, and vice versa. For example, "if the terms of the offering require a high minimum investment amount and a purchaser is able to meet those terms, then the likelihood of that purchaser satisfying the definition of accredited investor may be sufficiently high such that,

---

29. Note that, if certain conditions are satisfied, a person who maintains a platform or mechanism to effect a Rule 506 compliant offering is not required to register as a broker or dealer. These conditions include, for example, that such broker or dealer and its associated persons: "receive no compensation in connection with" the Rule 506 offering; do "not have possession of customer funds or securities in connection with" the Rule 506 offering; and are not "subject to a statutory [bad actor] disqualification. . . ." Section 201(c) of the JOBS Act, adding, § 4(b)(1)-(3) of the Securities Act.

30. Securities Act Release No 9415 (2013). The following discussion is based on and quotes this Release. *See* Sanders, *Understanding the New Rule 506(c) Exemption*, 42 Sec. Reg. L.J. 347 (2014).

absent any facts that indicate that the purchaser is not an accredited investor, it may be reasonable for the issuer to take fewer steps to verify. . . ." Regardless of the particular steps an issuer takes, because it is the issuer's burden to establish that it has perfected an exemption from Securities Act registration, it is important that issuers (or their agents) retain adequate documentation regarding the steps undertaken with respect to verification of accredited investor status.

With respect to accredited investor status for a natural person, the Commission adopted specific non-exclusive methods of verifying his/her accredited investor status (conducted within the prior three months). First, with respect to verification of a natural person as an accredited investor based on his/her income, an issuer is deemed to satisfy the verification requirement by reviewing any Internal Revenue Service (IRS) form that reports the income of such individual and obtaining a written representation from such individual that he/she reasonably expects to reach the requisite individual (or joint spousal) income during the current year.

Second, to verify that a natural person is an accredited investor based on such investor's net worth, an issuer should review documentation of the investor's assets, such as bank statements, brokerage statements, certificates of deposit, and appraisal reports issued by an independent third party. Liabilities also must be assessed, including a consumer (i.e., credit) report from a nationwide consumer reporting agency.

Third, another avenue by which an issuer may satisfy the verification requirement in Rule 506(c) is to obtain a written confirmation from the subject investor's attorney, certified public accountant, registered broker-dealer, or registered investment adviser that such person has taken reasonable steps to verify within the prior three months and has determined that the investor has accredited status. This last avenue likely is the most appealing. Not surprisingly, individuals, and particularly wealthy individuals, disdain providing to others, particularly strangers, their personal financial information. By providing that written confirmation from the investor's CPA is sufficient, this burden becomes far less onerous.

Moreover, the Commission emphasized that the foregoing three methods are non-exclusive. Importantly, this requirement of verification in Rule 506 offerings where an issuer engages in general solicitation is "separate from and independent of the requirement that sales be limited to accredited investors . . . [In other words,] the reasonable verification requirement mandated by Rule 506(c) must be satisfied even if all purchasers happen to be accredited investors."

In view of the above discussion, this new version of Rule 506 permitting advertising and general solicitation should be widely used by issuers. Although the "reasonable steps to verify" requirement has prompted some concerns, it must be kept in mind that issuers (or their agents) already must undertake significant "due diligence" measures to reasonably believe that a person is an accredited investor under Rule 505 and traditional Rule 506. The availability of accessing scores (if not hundreds or even thousands) of accredited investors by such means as the Internet, traditional advertising (e.g., newspapers), and in-person general solicitation (e.g., telemarketer calls) should induce issuers to use this new exemption. Nonetheless, as SEC Chair Mary Jo White stated in late 2015: "Only a small fraction of issuers [thus far had] claimed the new exemption permitting general solicitation."[31] This likely will change as issuers and their agents become more comfortable with this new exemption.

Even assuming that Rule 506(c) offerings eventually become the preferred exemption, this does not signify that the traditional Rule 506 exemption will lose its usefulness. An issuer that cannot successfully sell the entirety of the subject offering solely to accredited purchasers must turn to nonaccredited purchasers to raise the desired funds. Frequently, the most attractive exemption available in this context remains the traditional Rule 506(b) exemption.

Undoubtedly, the JOBS Act's approval of the use of advertising and general solicitation in Rule 506 offerings is a huge change. From a critical perspective, the Statement issued by then-SEC Commissioner Luis A. Aguilar follows:

Increasing the Vulnerability of Investors

By Commissioner Luis A. Aguilar

U.S. Securities and Exchange Commission

Today the Commission considers a Congressional mandate to amend our private placement rules, allowing issuers to offer securities by means of general solicitation and general advertising, provided only that all purchasers are accredited investors.

I cannot support today's proposal, because it presents a framework that is not balanced and that fails to address the acknowledged increased vulnerability of investors. In fact, there is no consideration of any of the commenters' proposals that would have decreased investor vulnerability.

Since at least 1962, the Commission has held that general solicitation and advertising are inconsistent with private offerings of securities. When general solicitation is used, investors need access to the disclosure and other protections that registration affords. In the absence of registration, and the resulting required disclosure, general solicitation and advertising can all too readily become a tool for deception and misinformation.

Investors are the source of capital needed to create jobs and expand business. I value true capital formation and economic growth, which requires investors to have both confidence in the capital markets and access to the information needed to make good investment decisions.

Today, the Commission proposes amendments that would allow the widespread marketing of securities that, by their terms, are only intended for accredited

---

31. *General Solicitations Lag, SEC's White Says, But Little Fraud Plagues Private Offerings*, 47 Sec. Reg. & L. Rep. (BNA) 2067 (2015).

investors. The proposal would permit solicitation and advertisements via billboards, TV, the Internet, radio, and telemarketer calls, among other avenues. Allowing such broad marketing activities under an exemption designed for "private" offerings is a significant change in the securities framework, and it would greatly increase the vulnerability of investors. Given that vulnerability, the Commission should use its expertise to effect the statutory mandate in a way that balances Congressional intent and the Commission's core mission to protect investors.

Unfortunately, today's proposal fails to consider any of the suggestions recommended by investors, investor advocates, and regulators to mitigate risk. For example, the Commission should have proposed at this time, among other recommendations:

- Amending the definition of accredited investor to require consideration of the investor's financial sophistication; and

- Amending Form D notice requirements to enhance the timing and content of the form.

Allowing General Solicitation Exacerbates Investor Vulnerability to Fraudsters

First, let me address why investors will be more vulnerable. When general solicitation is combined with an offering exemption such as Rule 506, no information statement or disclosure is required to be given to investors. Thus, fraud can be easier to effect and much harder to detect.

In this context, it is easy to see that an issuer could use general solicitation and advertising to disseminate false or misleading information. When reliable information is scarce, fraudsters can easily spread false information. Eliminating the ban on general solicitation and advertising may also facilitate boiler-room cold calling and other high-pressure sales techniques. History shows that, when stock promoters are allowed to advertise and solicit the public without any sort of registration or qualification whatsoever, it opens the door to fraudsters and scam artists of every description.

Moreover, how will these fraudsters be caught? The short answer is that many of them will not. The Commission will not be able to discern these frauds as we can now. Currently, general solicitation accompanying a private placement is a clear red flag and jumpstarts an investigation. Going forward, this red flag would be removed, putting investors even more at risk. The proposal fails even to make an attempt to address this yawning gap by improving the content, timing, and compliance of, and with, the Form D Notice Filing.

We have heard repeatedly in a number of contexts that the anti-fraud provisions of federal and state securities laws should be sufficient to protect investors. This is a short-sighted view that has been disproven over and over again. Ask investors what it is like to be defrauded. In most cases, much of investors' monies are long gone by the time a fraud is identified and an action can be brought. It is the Commission's job to prevent investors from being harmed. True investor protection requires mechanisms to deter and prevent fraud before it begins.

Ways to Combat Fraud

Making Sure Investors in Private Placements Can Truly Fend for Themselves

I am now going to walk through several ideas to decrease the vulnerability of investors that could easily have been a part of the Commission's proposal. In fact, it is surprising that these ideas are receiving no airing, given the clear increase in investor vulnerability. One way to combat fraud is to make sure that purchasers truly have the capacity to fend for themselves. Congress identified this issue when it limited general solicitation and advertising under Rule 506 to offerings in which ALL the purchasers are accredited investors. Underscoring the importance of this requirement, the statute calls for the SEC to write rules requiring issuers to verify that purchasers of securities are accredited investors.

Representative Maxine Waters, who introduced the verification requirement in the U.S. House of Representatives, explained the purpose as follows:

"If we are rolling back protections for our targeted audience of sophisticated individuals, we must take steps to ensure that those folks are in fact sophisticated."

However, the effectiveness of this requirement assumes that the purchaser actually has sufficient knowledge and experience in financial and business matters to evaluate the merits and risks of the prospective investment. Currently, a natural person may qualify as an accredited investor solely on the basis of income or net worth, without regard to any investment experience or financial sophistication. Accordingly, as we consider rules that would allow unregistered securities to be marketed to accredited investors through cold calling, Internet promotions, and other forms of solicitation, we must also consider the accredited investor definition at the same time. For example, some commenters have previously suggested that demonstrating actual investment experience would indicate a level of financial sophistication, which could supplement the existing definition.

Form D Filing

A second way to deter fraud is to require the issuer to make a notice filing on Form D a reasonable period of time prior to making any offers or sales using general solicitation or advertising. Currently, the rules require an issuer to file a Form D within 15 days after the first sale in a Regulation D offering, but that requirement is not a condition to the exemption and for practical purposes is essentially voluntary. A true requirement that notice on Form D be made before general solicitation begins would serve three purposes. First, it would prevent any issuer that fails to file a notice from claiming that improper advertising or solicitation activities were intended as part of a legitimate Rule 506 transaction. This could reduce the amount of such activity by issuers seeking to condition the market or otherwise abuse the exemption. Second, it would provide a mechanism for potential investors to identify the source of an offer, facilitating some degree of due diligence. Third, it would provide a mechanism for regulators to be made aware of a "mass marketed" offering before it is launched.

Moreover, the potential value of a filing on Form D could be significantly enhanced, at little expense to the issuer, by modestly expanding the information required to be provided on the form. For example, such basic information as the issuer's Internet website address, the names of any controlling persons, [and] the size of the issuer, . . . In fact, one must wonder why particular issuers would not be willing to disclose such basic information if that were the case.

Additional Potential Reforms

Other commenters have proposed additional ways to address the increased fraud risk posed by general solicitation and advertising in unregistered offerings. For example, the Commission could require that any advertising under our amended rule comply with guidance similar to that applicable to advertising for registered offerings, including a "balanced presentation of risks and rewards" and a requirement that statements in advertising are consistent with representations in any offering documents. Other potential reforms could include:

- Mandatory "cooling-off" periods, within which investors could terminate a purchase without risk;
- "Warning labels" highlighting the risks of investing in unregistered securities; and/or
- Tightened integration rules, so that general solicitation or advertising for one offering could not be used to condition the market or pump up the stock price for another offering.

Clearly, today's proposal fails to address the increased vulnerability of investors. I believe that we cannot fulfill our mandate without robustly addressing the risks posed by unregistered general solicitation with concrete proposals.

---

§ 3.07 The Limited Offering Exemptions

At this time, you may find it helpful to review the SEC Release in § 3.06[A], particularly the discussion focusing on Rules 501, 502, and 503.

The statutory limited offering exemptions are contained in §§ 3(b) and 4(a)(5) of the Securities Act. These exemptions reflect congressional concern that small enterprises should not be unduly burdened in raising capital. Generally, § 4(a)(5) exempts from registration under the 1933 Act offers and sales by any issuer solely to one or more "accredited investors" if the total offering price does not exceed the amount permitted under § 3(b)(1) of the Act (currently $5 million). No advertising or public solicitation is permitted in connection with a § 4(a)(5) offering, and the issuer must file a notice of such sales made pursuant to the exemption with the SEC. *See*

SEC Securities Act Release No. 6256 (1980).This exemption is rarely used today. Note that offerings under § 4(a)(5) ordinarily also are exempt from Securities Act registration pursuant to Rule 506. As discussed above, offerings made in compliance with the Rule 506 exemption preempt state regulation of such offerings. Hence, generally, § 4(a)(5) would be used only when the bad actor disqualifiers preclude an issuer from invoking Rule 506.

Generally, § 3(b)(1) contains an exemption for small offerings, empowering the Commission to exempt from registration any offering of securities where the aggregate amount of such offering does not exceed $5 million during any 12-month period. Pursuant to this authority, the SEC has promulgated a number of exemptions, including Rule 504 of Regulation D. Note that although the National Securities Market Improvement Act of 1996 preempts state regulation of Rule 506 offerings, state regulation continues to apply to Rule 504 offerings.

Moreover, pursuant to the JOBS Act of 2012, § 3(b)(2) directs the SEC, with specified conditions attached, to exempt a *class* of securities from Securities Act registration where the aggregate offering amount of all securities offered and sold under this exemption during the prior 12-month period does not exceed $50 million. As discussed in the following materials, the SEC has promulgated new offering exemptions pursuant to this directive.

[A] Rule 504

The SEC adopted Rule 504 to facilitate the capital raising needs for the small start-up company. The exemption is not available for investment companies and reporting entities under the Exchange Act (i.e., registrants that must file periodic reports with the SEC). "Bad actor" disqualifiers also apply (see discussion in § 3.06). In a Rule 504 offering, the issuer need not determine whether the purchaser is sophisticated; nor does the issuer need to provide a purchaser representative for the unsophisticated. There are no specified federal disclosure requirements in a Rule 504 offering and there is no express limit on the number of offerees and purchasers. Offerings made pursuant to the Rule 504 exemption during any 12-month period have a ceiling of $5 million.[32]

In fact, the Rule 504 offering exemption permits the issuer to conduct, in essence, a "mini-public" offering where general solicitation is permitted and purchasers in such offerings acquire freely transferable securities. In order for general solicitation to be permitted and the securities acquired to be freely transferable, one of the following two conditions must be met:

- the offering is registered under a state law requiring public filing and delivery of a disclosure document before sale. For sales to occur in a state

---

32. *See* Securities Act Release Nos. 6389 (1982), 6758 (1988), 10238 (2016).

that does not mandate such a disclosure document, the offering must be registered in another state with such a provision and the disclosure document filed in that state must be delivered to all purchasers before sale in both states; or

- the securities are issued under a state law exemption that permits general solicitation and general advertising so long as sales are made only to "accredited investors" as that term is defined in Regulation D.[33]

Where neither of these conditions is satisfied, Rule 504 prohibits advertising and general solicitation and deems the securities acquired "restricted." (Generally, *restricted securities* are subject to resale limitations, hence having conditions attached when the investor seeks to resell such securities.) These restrictions were necessary, according to the SEC, to curb abuse of the Rule 504 exemption in the markets for "microcap" enterprises.[34]

Thus, except for the conditions set forth above, Rule 504 may be viewed as a blanket federal exemption from registration for offerings not exceeding $5 million. The SEC believes that the remedial provisions of the federal securities laws, in conjunction with state regulation, are sufficient protection in these smaller offerings.

In 2016, the SEC amended Rule 504. In Securities Act Release No. 10238 (2016), the Commission stated:

> The amendments that we are adopting to Rule 504 will raise the aggregate amount of securities an issuer may offer and sell in any twelve-month period from $1 million to $5 million, which is the maximum statutorily allowed under Section 3(b)(1). The Commission has not raised the 12-month aggregate offering amount limit in Rule 504 since 1988, when the Commission increased the original Rule 504 offering amount limit of $500,000 to $1 million. Adjusted for inflation, the $1 million limit in 1988 would equate to approximately $2 million today. We believe the $5 million limit will facilitate issuers' ability to raise capital. We also believe that our amendments to increase the aggregate offering amount limit in Rule 504 to $5 million may bolster efforts among the states to enter into, or revise existing, regional coordinated review programs that are designed to increase efficiencies associated with the registration of securities offerings in multiple jurisdictions without increasing risks to investors. Increasing the aggregate offering

---

33. Securities Act Release No. 7644 (1999)

34. *Id.* Offerings involving securities of microcap enterprises often are associated with low prices per share, limited public information, thin capitalization, and little, if any, analyst coverage. *See generally* Bradford, *Securities Regulation and Small Business: Rule 504 and the Case for an Unconditional Exemption,* 5 J. SMALL & EMERGING BUS. L. 1 (2001); Cohn, *The Impact of Securities Laws on Emerging Companies: Would the Wright Brothers Have Gotten Off the Ground?* 3 J. SM. & EMER. BUS. LAW 315 (1999); Hass, *Small Issue Public Offerings Conducted Over the Internet: Are They "Suitable" for the Retail Investor?,* 72 S. CALIF. L. REV. 67 (1998).

amount limit from $1 million to $5 million will also increase the flexibility of state securities regulators to set their own limits and to consider whether any additional requirements should be implemented at the state level.

. . . .

In conjunction with our increase to the Rule 504 aggregate offering amount limit, we are also adopting provisions that will disqualify certain bad actors from participation in offerings conducted pursuant to the exemption. We believe that the disqualification provisions that we are adopting, which are substantially similar to related provisions in Rule 506 of Regulation D [see § 3.06 of the text], will create a more consistent regulatory regime across Regulation D and provide additional protections to investors in Rule 504 offerings.

The Rule 504 disqualification provisions will be implemented by reference to the disqualification provisions of Rule 506 of Regulation D. We believe that creating a uniform set of bad actor triggering events across the various exemptions from Securities Act registration should simplify due diligence, particularly for issuers that may engage in different types of exempt offerings. In accordance with the views of several commenters, the bad actor triggering events for Rule 504 will be substantially similar to existing provisions in Regulation D, Regulation A, and Regulation Crowdfunding and will apply to the issuer and other covered persons (such as underwriters, placement agents, and the directors, officers and significant shareholders of the issuer). . . .

[B] Rule 505

The SEC repealed Rule 505 in 2016. See Securities Act Release No. 10238 (2016). Nonetheless, in view of its historical significance, Rule 505 is treated herein.

Rule 505 provided any issuer that is not an investment company with an exemption from registration under § 3(b)(1) of the Securities Act for sales of securities to (what the issuer reasonably believed were) not more than 35 nonaccredited purchasers and to an unlimited number of accredited investors. In aggregation with other offerings made pursuant to exemptions available under § 3(b)(1) (or sold in violation of § 5), an issuer pursuant to Rule 505 was able to raise up to $5 million during any 12-month period. In a Rule 505 offering, general solicitation or advertising was prohibited and restrictions on resales applied. As in Rule 506 offerings, issuers under the Rule 505 exemption were required to provide written disclosure to all nonaccredited purchasers regarding limitations on resale. Note that a substantial compliance standard applied to offerings made pursuant to the Rule 505 exemption.

The availability of the Rule 505 exemption was conditioned upon the disclosure of specified information to nonaccredited purchasers. Unlike Rule 506, however, an issuer utilizing the Rule 505 exemption was not required to make a determination that the purchaser was sophisticated. If unsophisticated, there was no requirement that the investor have a purchaser representative.[35] Finally, the Rule 505 exemption was unavailable to issuers that engaged in certain misconduct ("bad actor" disqualifiers).[36]

Over the years, the Rule 505 exemption was not frequently used. The reason is that issuers preferred the Rule 506 exemption where state regulation of the subject offering is preempted. In Rule 505 offerings, many states elected to impose additional requirements, such as, for example, that the purchase amount not exceed 10 percent of an investor's net worth. Subsequently, in 2016, the SEC elected to revoke the Rule 505 exemption. In Securities Act Release No. 10238 (2016), the Commission reasoned:

> . . . [W]e are repealing Rule 505. After the effective date of the repeal of Rule 505, issuers will no longer be able to make offers and sales of securities in reliance on Rule 505. We believe that amending Rule 504 to increase the aggregate offering amount from $1 million to $5 million will further reduce the incentives to use Rule 505 by issuers contemplating an exempt offering. We also believe that, even if we were to raise the Rule 505 aggregate offering amount limit from $5 million to $10 million, or some higher amount, such a higher limit would not increase the utility of the Rule 505 exemption as compared to Rule 506, which has no limit, given the historical use of Rule 505 as compared to Rule 506. Further, although Rule 505 provides issuers the ability to sell securities to up to 35 non-accredited investors without having to make a finding, as in Rule 506(b)(2)(ii), that such persons have the knowledge and experience in financial matters that they are capable of evaluating the merits and risks of the prospective investment, this provision does not appear to have historically resulted in the Rule 505 exemption being widely utilized.
>
> We believe the flexibility of the requirements of Rule 504, as amended today, as well as the availability of Rule 506(b) and Rule 506(c) will continue to fulfill the original objectives of Regulation D to achieve uniformity between state and federal exemptions in order to facilitate capital formation consistent with the protection of investors. Amended Rule 504 will be available only to non-reporting issuers that are not investment companies or development stage companies for offerings of up to $5 million in a twelve-month period and will permit general solicitation and the issuance of unrestricted

---

35. For further discussion on this point, see Friedman, *On Being Rich, Accredited, and Undiversified: The Lacunae in Contemporary Securities Regulation*, 47 Okla. L. Rev. 291 (1994); Warren, *A Review of Regulation D: The Present Exemption Regimen for Limited Offerings Under the Securities Act of 1933*, 33 Am. U.L. Rev. 355 (1984). *See also*, Bradford, *Transaction Exemptions in the Securities Act of 1933: An Economic Analysis*, 45 Emory L.J. 591 (1996).

36. *See* discussion in § 3.06 of the text discussing the bad actor disqualifiers.

securities in certain limited situations. Rule 506(b) and 506(c) are available [with certain exceptions] to all issuers without any aggregate offering amount limitations. Rule 506(b) prohibits general solicitation and limits sales to no more than 35 non-accredited investors. Rule 506(c) permits general solicitation where all purchasers of the securities are accredited investors and the issuer takes reasonable steps to verify that the purchasers are accredited investors. Securities issued pursuant to Rules 506(b) and 506(c) are deemed restricted securities. . . .

[C] Rule 701

In 1988, the SEC adopted Rule 701 pursuant to § 3(b) of the 1933 Act. In 1999, the Commission increased the monetary amount that may be raised under Rule 701 by invoking its exemptive authority under § 28 of the Securities Act. Generally, Rule 701 provides an exemption from registration for offers and sales of securities for certain compensation benefit plans adopted for the participation of employees, officers, directors, consultants, and advisers of an eligible company. Rule 701's availability is limited because companies eligible to use the exemption must not be subject to the periodic reporting requirements of the Exchange Act. As a preliminary note to the rule makes clear, Rule 701 is designed to facilitate the issuance of securities for compensation. As a consequence, the rule does not exempt offers and sales that are intended to raise capital.[37]

So long as the offering is made solely to eligible purchasers, Rule 701 permits such offerings to be public in nature, thereby permitting general solicitation. However, limitations on resales by purchasers of such securities exist.

In a Rule 701 offering, unless more than $5 million of securities are to be sold, there are no specific disclosure requirements.[38] Where sales exceed the $5 million threshold, the required disclosure consists of:

- a copy of the compensatory benefit plan or contract;
- a copy of the summary plan description required by the Employee Retirement Income Security Act of 1974 ("ERISA") or, if the plan is not subject to ERISA, a summary of the plan's material terms;
- risk factors associated with investment in the securities under the plan or agreement; and
- the financial statements required in an offering statement on Form 1-A under Regulation A.

---

37. Securities Act Release No. 6768 (1988). *See SEC v. Phan*, 500 F.3d 895 (9th Cir. 2007). *See generally* Robbins, *Securities Offerings to Employees, Consultants, and Advisers Under Rule 701*, 31 Rev. Sec. & Comm. Reg. 51 (1998).

38. *See* Securities Act Release No. 7645 (1998).

The monetary amount of securities that can be offered and sold pursuant to Rule 701 during any 12-month period is the greatest of the following:

(1) $1 million, (2) 15 percent of the company's total assets, or (3) 15 percent of the outstanding securities of the class of securities issued.[39]

Because of the exemption's compensatory (rather than capital raising) purpose, offerings made pursuant to Rule 701 are *not* aggregated with offerings made pursuant to the other § 3(b) exemptions. Nor are the monetary ceilings for other offerings made pursuant to the other § 3(b) exemptions affected by Rule 701 offers and sales. Moreover, "integration of offering" problems are minimized because Rule 701 "specifically state[s] that all offers and sales pursuant to its rubric are deemed to be a part of a single, discrete offering; consequently, Rule 701 transactions need not be integrated into any other offering made by the issuer or vice versa."[40]

[D] The Section 3(b)(2) Exemption — Regulation A

Pursuant to the JOBS Act of 2012, § 3(b)(2) directs the SEC, with specified conditions attached, to exempt a class of securities from Securities Act registration where the aggregate offering amount of all securities offered and sold under this exemption during the prior 12-month period does not exceed $50 million. This new exemption has been coined an "expansion of [former] Regulation A" or "Regulation A Plus."[41] Note, however, that, unlike the § 3(b)(1) exemptions (such as Rules 504 and 505), which are transactional exemptions, the JOBS Act § 3(b)(2) provision adds a "*class* of [exempt] securities" to the § 3 exemption framework. If this statutory language is interpreted by the SEC and the courts as clearly set forth, then offers and sales pursuant to the § 3(b)(2) exemption will never have to be registered under the Securities Act. Significantly, however, the JOBS Act does not preempt state regulation of Regulation A *Tier 1 offerings*, namely, offerings of up to $20 million during a 12-month period made pursuant to the requirements of Tier 1 of Regulation A. Without such preemption, it is likely that state registration will be required as well as the application of merit standards in states that embrace this level of substantive review.[42] Tier 1 and Tier 2 Regulation A offerings are discussed later in this subsection.

Pursuant to the JOBS Act, Congress directed the SEC to exempt a class of securities pursuant to § 3(b)(2) that has the following terms and conditions:

---

39. *Id.*

40. For restrictions on resales regarding securities issued in Rule 701 offerings, *see* Chapter 6.

41. *See, e.g.,* Claassen et al., *JOBS Act Will Simplify IPO Process and Private Capital Raising*, 44 Sec. Reg. & L. Rep. (BNA) 823, 825 (2012). Former Regulation A was an exemption from Securities Act registration for non-reporting companies, permitting generalized interstate public offerings of up to $5 million during any 12-month period, including up to $1.5 million in non-issuer resales.

42. The subject of state merit regulation is addressed in § 4.07.

(1) The aggregate offering amount of all securities offered and sold pursuant to this exemption within the prior 12-month period is not to exceed $50 million;

(2) The securities (which must be equity or debt securities or debt securities that are convertible to equity interests) may be offered and sold in a public offering;

(3) The securities are not restricted and, hence, when acquired, are not subject to a "holding" period (see Chapter 6 herein);

(4) Prior to filing a required offering statement with the SEC, the issuer may solicit indications of interest with respect to the contemplated offering;

(5) The issuer using this § 3(b)(2) exemption (namely, Tier 2 of Regulation A) must file with the SEC audited financial statements on an annual basis;

(6) Any person offering or selling securities pursuant to this exemption is subject to the civil liability provisions of § 12(a)(2) (see § 7.07 herein); and

(7) Such other terms and conditions as the SEC deems necessary to protect investors and that are in the public interests, including:

> (a) The electronic filing and providing to investors of an offering statement by the subject issuer, which would include "audited financial statements, a description of the issuer's business operations, its financial condition, its corporate governance principles, its use of investor funds, and other appropriate matters;"

> (b) An issuer providing to investors and filing with the SEC periodic disclosures focusing on the subject issuer and its financial condition, business operations, use of investor funds, corporate governance practices, and other appropriate matters; and

> (c) The applicability of "bad actor" disqualifiers to preclude issuer availability of this exemption.

In 2015, the SEC adopted an updated and expanded Regulation A (Regulation A+) under § 3(b)(2). As stated by the SEC:

> The final rules, often referred to as Regulation A+, provide for two tiers of offerings: *Tier 1*, for offerings of securities of up to $20 million in a 12-month period, with not more than $6 million in offers by selling security-holders that are affiliates of the issuer; and *Tier 2*, for offerings of securities of up to $50 million in a 12-month period, with not more than $15 million in offers by selling security-holders that are affiliates of the issuer. Both Tiers are subject to certain basic requirements while Tier 2 offerings are also subject to additional disclosure and ongoing reporting requirements.

> The final rules also provide for the preemption of state securities law registration and qualification requirements for securities offered or sold to "qualified purchasers" in Tier 2 offerings. Tier 1 offerings will be subject to

federal and state registration and qualification requirements, and issuers may take advantage of the coordinated review program developed by the North American Securities Administrators Association (NASAA).[43]

In adopting the final Regulation A rules, the Commission issued the following summary that highlights many of the key aspects of the Regulation.

Regulation A+
March 25, 2015

Background

Under the Securities Act of 1933, when a company sells securities to potential investors, it must either register the sale of rely on an exemption from registration. [Former] Regulation A [was] a longstanding exemption from registration that [allowed] unregistered public offerings of up to $5 million of securities in any 12-month period, including no more than $1.5 million of securities offered by security-holders of the company. In recent years, Regulation A offerings [were] relatively rare in comparison to offerings conducted in reliance on other Securities Act exemptions or on a registered basis.

The JOBS Act amended the Securities Act to require the Commission to update and expand the Regulation A exemption. In particular, the JOBS Act directed the Commission to:

- Adopt rules that would allow offerings of up to $50 million of securities within a 12-month period.

- Require companies conducting such offerings to file annual audited financial statements with the SEC.

- Adopt additional requirements and conditions that the Commission determines necessary.

        . . . .

Highlights of the Final Rules

The final rules, often referred to as Regulation A+, . . . provide for two tiers of offerings:

- *Tier 1*, which would consist of securities offerings of up to $20 million in a 12-month period, with not more than $6 million in offers by selling security-holders that are affiliates of the issuer.

- *Tier 2*, which would consist of securities offerings of up to $50 million in a 12-month period, with not more than $15 million in offers by selling security-holders that are affiliates of the issuer.

---

43. SEC News Release 2015-49 (2015). *See* Securities Act Release No. 9741 (2015) (Regulation A adopting release). *See generally* Andrews, *The Regulation A+Exemption: Provider of Practical Tiers or Pointless Tears?*, 44 Sec. Reg. L.J. 221 (2016).

In addition to the limits on secondary sales by affiliates, the rules also limit sales by all selling security-holders to no more than 30 percent of a particular offering in the issuer's initial Regulation A offering and subsequent Regulation A offerings for the first 12 months following the initial offering.

For offerings of up to $20 million, the issuer could elect whether to proceed under Tier 1 or Tier 2. Both tiers would be subject to basic requirements as to issuer eligibility, disclosure, and other matters . . . . Both tiers would also permit companies to submit draft offering statements for non-public review by Commission staff before filing, permit the continued use of solicitation materials after filing the offering statement, require the electronic filing of offering materials and otherwise align Regulation A with current practice for registered offerings.

Additional Tier 2 Requirements

In addition to these basic requirements, companies conducting *Tier 2 offerings* would be subject to other requirements, including:

- A requirement to provide audited financial statements.
- A requirement to file annual, semiannual and current event reports.
- A limitation on the amount of securities non-accredited investors can purchase in a Tier 2 offering of no more than 10 percent of the greater of the investor's annual income or net worth.

The staff would also conduct a study and submit a report to the Commission on the impact of both the Tier 1 and Tier 2 offerings on capital formation and investor protection no later than five years following the adoption of the amendments to Regulation A.

. . . .

Eligibility

The exemption would be limited to companies organized in and with their principal place of business in the United States or Canada. The exemption would not be available to companies that:

- Are already SEC reporting companies and certain investment companies.
- Have no specific business plan or purpose or have indicated their business plan is to engage in a merger or acquisition with an unidentified company.
- Are seeking to offer and sell asset-backed securities or fractional undivided interests in oil, gas or other mineral rights.
- Have been subject to any order of the Commission under Exchange Act Section 12(j) [suspending or revoking the registration of a security] entered within the past five years.
- Have not filed ongoing reports required by [SEC] rules during the preceding two years.
- Are disqualified under the "bad actor" disqualification rules.

The rules exempt securities in a Tier 2 offering from the mandatory registration requirements of Exchange Act Section 12(g) if the issuer meets all of the following conditions:

- Engages services from a transfer agent registered with the Commission.
- Remains subject to a Tier 2 reporting obligation.
- Is current in its annual and semiannual reporting at fiscal year-end.
- Has a public float [stock held by non-affiliates] of less than $75 million as of the last business day of its most recently completed semiannual period, or, in the absence of a public float, had annual revenues of less than $50 million as of its most recently completed fiscal year.

An issuer that exceeds the dollar *and* Section 12(g) registration thresholds would have a two-year transition period before it must register its class of securities, provided it timely files all of its ongoing reports required under Regulation A.

Preemption of Blue Sky Law

In light of the total package of investor protections included in amended Regulation A, the rules provide for the preemption of state securities law registration and qualification requirements for securities offered or sold to "qualified purchasers," defined to be any person to whom securities are offered or sold under a Tier 2 offering.

Not surprisingly, state regulators were displeased with the preemption impact of Regulation A Tier 2 offerings and challenged the validity of the Regulation. The U.S. Court of Appeals for the District of Columbia Circuit rejected this challenge. The decision excerpted below focuses on the securities law issues that were raised.

Lindeen v. Securities and Exchange Commission

United States Court of Appeals, District of Columbia Circuit

825 F.3d 646 (2016)

Karen LeCraft Henderson, Circuit Judge:

Pursuant to congressional mandate, the Securities and Exchange Commission (SEC or Commission) created a new class of securities offerings freed from federal-registration requirements so long as the issuers of these securities comply with certain investor safeguards. . . . The SEC also provided that anyone buying a certain subset of the securities [Tier 2 of Regulation A] will be considered a "qualified purchaser." In doing so, the SEC preempted all state registration and qualification requirements for the subset based on the Securities Act provision that exempts from state registration and qualification requirements securities offered or sold to "qualified purchasers."

The petitioners, William F. Gavin and Monica J. Lindeen (collectively, petitioners), are the chief securities regulators for Massachusetts and Montana, respectively. They argue that, because the SEC declined to adopt a qualified-purchaser definition limited to investors with sufficient wealth, revenue or financial sophistication to protect their interests without state protection, Regulation A-Plus fails both parts of the United States Supreme Court's statutory construction standards enunciated in *Chevron, U.S.A., Inc. v. Natural Resources Defense Council, Inc.,* 467 U.S. 837, 842–43 (1984). They also argue that it should be vacated as arbitrary and capricious because the Commission failed to explain adequately how it protects investors. For the following reasons, we deny the consolidated petitions for review.

I. STATUTORY & REGULATORY BACKGROUND

Securities regulation has existed, in one form or another, since the mid-1800s. Before the Great Depression, securities were regulated almost exclusively by the states and, beginning with Kansas in 1911, many states imposed comprehensive securities regulation regimes. Known as "blue-sky" laws, state systems often required not only pre-sale registration of securities but also pre-sale "qualification" or "merit" review of security sales. Generally, state substantive review prohibited securities sales the state deemed unfair, unjust or inequitable. . . .

After the 1929 stock market crash, the Congress began regulating securities at the federal level. Rather than following the state substantive-review model, the Congress chose instead to mandate pre-sale disclosure of material information to investors. It did so by enacting, first, the Securities Act of 1933 (Securities Act), which regulates the sale of securities in the primary market and, second, the Securities Exchange Act of 1934 (Exchange Act), which created the Commission and established rules governing the resale or exchange of securities in the secondary market. Both the Securities Act and the Exchange Act have evolved considerably since they were first enacted. This case arises against the backdrop of amendments to the Securities Act.

Under section 5 of the Securities Act, a company must file a registration statement and a prospectus with the SEC before it offers its securities for sale. Because the section 5 registration process is often prohibitively expensive for small companies, the Congress enacted section 3(b) of the Securities Act, which allows the Commission, through rulemaking, to exempt from federal-registration requirements certain small-dollar offerings, so long as the Commission finds that federal registration is not required to protect both investors and the public interest. In 1936, the SEC exercised its section 3(b) authority to promulgate "Regulation A." . . .

Originally, Regulation A allowed a company to file a less expensive "offering statement," rather than the pricey section 5 registration statement, before offering securities for sale. To further protect investors, Regulation A forbade any securities sale until SEC staff "qualified" the issuing company's offering statement; moreover, Regulation A obligated the issuing company to deliver an offering circular to investors before consummating any sale. After the sale, investors had the protection of federal antifraud statutes, as well as the Securities Act's civil liability provisions for false or misleading statements. . . .

Although section 3(b) exempted Regulation A offerings from federal-registration requirements, the offerings generally remained subject to state registration and merit-review restrictions, which increased compliance costs for the issuing company. This was especially true for a company desiring to issue securities in multiple states with varying substantive criteria.

A. National Securities Markets Improvement Act of 1996 (NSMIA)

Aware of the problems caused by concurrent state and federal regulation, the Congress enacted the National Securities Markets Improvement Act of 1996 (NSMIA). . . . Designed to alleviate the "redundant, costly, and ineffective" dual federal/state regulatory system, . . . the NSMIA designated the federal government to oversee nation-wide securities offerings while allowing the states to retain control over small, regional or intrastate offerings. The NSMIA did so by amending section 18 of the Securities Act to preempt, on a widespread basis, state registration and qualification regimes for some offerings while leaving intact the states' authority to investigate fraud and to assess fees. . . .

The NSMIA achieved this goal by creating a list of "covered" (*i.e.*, preempted) securities. Covered securities include, *inter alia*, securities listed on the New York Stock Exchange or the NASDAQ National Market System and those issued by a registered investment company. The NSMIA also intended the SEC to play a role in determining its preemptive scope. Specifically, it included in its list of covered securities any security sold "to qualified purchasers, as defined by the Commission by rule." It also granted the Commission authority to "define the term 'qualified purchaser' differently with respect to different categories of securities, consistent with the public interest and the protection of investors." In the view of both the House and Senate committees that advanced the NSMIA, "qualified purchasers" would not need state regulatory protection in light of their financial worth and sophistication.

In 2001, the SEC proposed a rule that would have defined "qualified purchaser" universally (*i.e.*, for *any* securities purchase) to mean "accredited investor" as defined by SEC Rule 501(a) of Regulation D. . . . SEC Rule 501(a), in turn, provides a list of persons and entities deemed "accredited investors," all of which possess greater-than-average levels of financial wherewithal. They include, for instance, business entities, banks, trusts and nonprofit organizations with total assets that exceed $5 million, as well as any natural person with a net worth exceeding $1 million. The SEC never finalized the rule using the Rule 501(a) definition.

B. Jumpstart Our Business Startups Act (JOBS Act)

Following the most recent economic recession, in 2012 the Congress passed the Jumpstart Our Business Startups Act (JOBS Act). . . . The JOBS Act was intended to spur job creation and economic growth by increasing small-business access to capital markets. By enacting Title IV of the JOBS Act (Title IV), the Congress meant to resuscitate the SEC's historically underutilized Regulation A. It did so in three ways.

First, Title IV added section 3(b)(2) to the Securities Act, which directed the SEC to revamp Regulation A. Specifically, section 3(b)(2) required the SEC to promulgate a rule adding a new class of securities to section 3's list of those exempt from federal-registration requirements. It also sketched out the rough parameters for this new class. For instance, it mandated that the aggregate offering amount of section 3(b)(2) securities was not to exceed $50 million and the sale of the securities was not to be restricted; it also provided the SEC with authority to create other requirements the Commission deemed necessary to advance the public interest and to protect investors. . . .

Second, Title IV provided that some of the securities issued under the SEC's forthcoming section 3(b)(2) rule were to be exempt from state registration and qualification requirements. Title IV did so by expanding the section 18 "covered securities" list to include securities issued pursuant to section 3(b)(2) so long as the securities were offered or sold either (1) on a national securities exchange or (2) "to a qualified purchaser, as defined by the Commission pursuant to [section 18(b)(3)] with respect to that purchase or sale." . . .

Third, Title IV ordered the Comptroller General to conduct, within three months of the JOBS Act's enactment, a study to determine the effect of state blue-sky laws on Regulation A offerings. The Comptroller General complied and, in July 2012, reported that the limited use of Regulation A was caused, in part, by the cost of complying with state laws.

C. Section 3(b)(2) Rule

. . . .

On March 25, 2015, the SEC released Regulation A-Plus . . . [T]he SEC defined the term ["qualified-purchaser"] as *"any person* to whom securities are offered or sold pursuant to a Tier-2 offering of this Regulation A." . . . As a result, Regulation A-Plus preempted all state registration and qualification requirements for Tier-2 securities either (1) purchased by an "accredited investor" or (2) purchased by anyone else so long as the non-accredited investor refrained from purchasing securities valued at more than 10 per cent of his net worth or annual income.[Note that Tier-1 Regulation A offerings are subject to state regulation.]

As required by [Securities Act] section 2(b), Regulation A-Plus analyzed whether its qualified-purchaser definition protects investors and "promote[s] efficiency, competition, and capital formation." . . . It did so in light of the JOBS Act goal of "expand[ing] the capital raising options available to smaller and emerging companies." . . . After acknowledging that eliminating state-level review might reduce investor protection, the SEC explained that "[s]everal factors could mitigate" the risk, including the "substantial protections" built into Tier-2 offerings—*i.e.*, the 10 per cent purchase cap and the more rigorous financial disclosure requirements for issuers.

. . .

II. ANALYSIS

The petitioners argue that the term qualified purchaser cannot mean "*any* person" to whom Tier-2 securities are offered or sold but instead must limit the universe of purchasers to those with enough financial wealth or sophistication to invest without state-law safeguards. . . . They insist that the SEC's rule fails both at *Chevron* [*Chevron, U.S.A., Inc. v. Natural Resources Defense Council, Inc.*, 467 U.S. 837 (1984)] Step 1 and Step 2. They also argue that Regulation A-Plus must be vacated as arbitrary and capricious. We address their arguments in turn.

A. Chevron Step One

In the petitioners' view, the SEC's qualified-purchaser definition, which does not restrict Tier-2 sales to wealthy and/or sophisticated investors, contravenes the plain meaning of the Securities Act. To succeed, they must demonstrate that the Securities Act "unambiguously foreclosed" the SEC's qualified-purchaser definition. . . . They have not done so.

To discern the Congress's intent, we generally examine the statutory text, structure, purpose and its legislative history. . . . That said, "[t]he starting point for our interpretation of a statute is always its language," . . . and, here, the language of section 18 confirms that the Congress has *not* "directly spoken to the precise question at issue"—namely, the meaning of qualified purchaser in relation to state preemption. Instead, the Congress explicitly authorized the Commission to define the term ("qualified purchaser" is to be "defined by the Commission by rule"), and to adopt different definitions for different types of securities. The explicit grant of definitional authority manifests that the Congress intended the SEC to enjoy broad discretion to decide who may purchase which securities without the encumbrance of state registration and qualification requirements. Exercising this grant, the SEC concluded that all purchasers of Tier-2 securities are qualified so long as non-accredited purchasers limit their purchase to 10 per cent of their annual income or net worth. Nothing in the text of the Securities Act "unambiguously foreclose[s]" the SEC from adopting this definition. . . .

. . . .

Because Regulation A-Plus does not conflict with the Congress's unambiguous intent, it does not falter at *Chevron* Step 1 and, accordingly, we proceed to *Chevron* Step 2.

B. Chevron Step Two

The petitioners also argue that the SEC's qualified-purchaser definition is unreasonable and therefore fails at *Chevron* Step 2. Typically, at *Chevron* Step 2, we defer to the Commission so long as its definition is "based on a permissible construction of the statute." . . . But "[b]ecause Congress has authorized the Commission . . . to prescribe legislative rules, we owe the Commission's judgment more than mere deference or weight." . . . Indeed, where, as here, "there is an express delegation of authority to the agency to elucidate a specific provision of the statute by regulation," we give the regulation "controlling weight unless [it is] arbitrary, capricious, or manifestly contrary to the statute." . . .

The petitioners insist that the SEC's qualified-purchaser definition "is actually 'manifestly contrary to the statute'" because it imposes no restrictions based on investor wealth, income or sophistication. Their *Chevron* Step 2 arguments mirror their *Chevron* Step 1 arguments and, for all of the reasons set out in our *Chevron* Step 1 discussion, we believe the SEC acted reasonably and within its broad definitional authority when it decided that all Tier-2 investors are considered "qualified purchasers."

. . . .

Because the Commission's qualified-purchaser definition is not "arbitrary, capricious, or manifestly contrary to the statute," . . . it does not fail *Chevron* Step 2.

C. APA Review

Finally, the petitioners challenge Regulation A-Plus as arbitrary and capricious, in violation of the [Administrative Procedure Act] APA. A "rule is arbitrary and capricious" if an "agency fail[s] to consider . . . a factor the agency must consider under its organic statute." . . . , [S]ection 2(b) of the Securities Act requires that, if the Commission "consider[s] or determine[s] whether an action is necessary or appropriate in the public interest," it must also "consider, in addition to the protection of investors, whether the action will promote efficiency, competition, and capital formation." This inquiry contemplates that the Commission will "determine as best it can the economic implications of the rule." *Chamber of Commerce v. SEC*, 412 F.3d 133, 143 (D.C. Cir. 2005). In the petitioners' view, the Commission failed to discharge this duty when it "offered only a single paragraph to explain why existing state law and the new rule might lessen the adverse effects of 'blue sky' preemption." . . .

We disagree. By providing a reasoned analysis of how its qualified-purchaser definition strikes the "appropriate balance between mitigating cost and time demands on issuers and *providing investor protections*," the Commission has complied with its statutory obligation. It considered the benefits of blue-sky review, concluding that it "may aid in detecting fraud and facilitating issuer compliance" by providing another level of investor protection. It also considered the costs imposed on issuers by blue-sky review, relying on the Comptroller General's conclusion that state registration and qualification requirements stymied Regulation A's use in recent years. After discussing the Tier-2 protections afforded to investors in the absence of state law review — *e.g.*, federal and state antifraud enforcement authority, enhanced and continuing issuer disclosure requirements and the 10 per cent purchase cap — the SEC concluded that the Tier-2 requirements "reduce[d] the need for, and the expected benefits of, state review." Given the JOBS Act mandate to revitalize Regulation A, the SEC concluded that the potential decrease in investor protection was balanced by the reduced costs for Tier-2 issuers and purchasers.

In the petitioners' view, the rule should nonetheless be vacated because the SEC failed to show that Tier-2's safeguards "will *actually* mitigate the identified costs of preemption." . . . For its part, amicus NASAA faults the SEC for relying on "little to no evidence" regarding the costs of state-law compliance and state-law preemption. But, as noted, Regulation A was rarely used, which means that the Commission did not have the data necessary to quantify precisely the risks of preemption for investors and the costs of state-law compliance for issuers. We do not require the Commission "to measure the immeasurable" and we do not require it to "conduct a rigorous, quantitative economic analysis unless the statute explicitly directs it to do so," . . . Here, we find that the SEC's "discussion of unquantifiable benefits fulfills its statutory obligation to consider and evaluate potential costs and benefits," . . . ; because the SEC articulated "a satisfactory explanation for its action, including a rational connection between the facts found and the choice made" . . . , we uphold Regulation A-Plus.

For the foregoing reasons, the consolidated petitions for review are denied.

So ordered.

Note

After the adoption of Regulation A Plus, questions were raised about whether smaller companies seeking to access the public markets would opt for this alternative rather than conducting an initial public offering (IPO) pursuant to registration under the Securities Act. Although being saddled with greater reporting, disclosure, and internal control requirements, publicly held companies generally enjoy a better following among analysts, broker-dealers, and investors, as well as greater liquidity in the trading of their stock. On the other hand, enterprises opting for Regulation A Plus are able to raise funds at a lower cost than compared to IPOs and the disclosure mandates are less burdensome. To date, IPOs are significantly fewer in 2016 (213 in 2015 compared to a projected 88 for 2016). To some extent, this decrease is being ameliorated by several relatively smaller companies opting for the Regulation A Plus route. (As of September 2016, approximately 50 companies have done so.) Moreover, a number of companies are opting to use Regulation A Plus as a means of turning their customers into shareholders. See *JOBS Act Converting Customers Into Shareholders*, 48 SEC. REG. & L. REP. (BNA) 1848 (2016); *Smaller Companies May Be Opting for Reg A Plus Over IPOs to Raise Funds*, 48 SEC. REG. & L. REP. (BNA) 851 (2016). The extent to which Regulation A Plus will be used by smaller companies, however, remains to be seen.

[E] Rule 1001 — The "California" Exemption

Showing its administrative flexibility, the SEC adopted Rule 1001 to provide a federal exemption from registration in order to coordinate with a California exemption from state registration for small business issuers. Rule 1001 exempts from registration "offers and sales up to $5,000,000 that are exempt from state qualification under paragraph (n) of § 25102 of the California Corporations Code."[44] The Rule 1001 exemption was promulgated by the SEC under § 3(b) of the Securities Act to enhance capital raising by small businesses, while seeking to maintain adequate investor protection. A closer look at the requirements of Rule 1001 reveals that this exemption is broader in certain respects than the exemptions provided by Rules 505 and 506 of Regulation D.

California § 25102(n) limits the exemption to issuers that are California corporations or other business entities that are formed under California law, including partnerships and trusts.[45] In addition, a non-California corporation may use the exemption if more than 50 percent of its outstanding voting securities are held by California residents and at least 50 percent of its property, payroll, and sales, as determined for state tax purposes, can be attributed to California.[46] The California exemption is not available to investment companies subject to the Investment Company Act of 1940.[47]

To perfect the exemption, an eligible issuer must be able to show that "sales of securities are made only to qualified purchasers or other persons the issuer reasonably believes, after reasonable inquiry, to be qualified purchasers."[48] Section 25102(n) sets forth its own definitions of qualified purchasers, which are similar, but not the same as, accredited purchasers under Regulation D. Examples of qualified purchasers include:

- any person purchasing more than $150,000 of securities in the offering; or

- a natural person whose net worth exceeds $500,000, or a natural person whose net worth exceeds $250,000 if such purchaser's annual income exceeds $100,000 — in either case the transaction must involve:

  (a) only one-class voting stock (or preferred stock establishing the same voting rights),

  (b) an amount limited to no more than 10 percent of the purchaser's net worth, and

---

44. Securities Act Release 7285, [1996 Transfer Binder] Fed. Sec. L. Rep. (CCH) ¶ 85,803, at 88,807 (SEC 1996).
45. *See* Cal. Corp. Code § 25102(n)(1).
46. *See* Cal. Corp. Code § 25102(n)(1), 2115.
47. *See* Cal. Corp. Code § 25102(n)(1).
48. Cal. Corp. Code § 25102(n)(2).

(c) a purchaser able to protect his or her own interests (alone or with the guidance of a professional advisor).[49]

The solicitation permitted under California § 25102(n) is less restrictive than that of Rule 505 and traditional Rule 506 of Regulation D (which prohibit general solicitation). An eligible issuer under Rule 1001 is permitted to "test the waters" by distributing to qualified and non-qualified purchasers a written general announcement that contains certain specified information.[50] The SEC has previously accepted this general announcement process in connection with a "mini-public" offering pursuant to the pre-JOBS version of the Regulation A exemption (see § 3.07[D]). However, telephone solicitation is specifically prohibited until it can be determined that the prospective purchaser is deemed qualified.[51] As a general rule, all offers, oral and written, are limited to qualified purchasers.[52]

The California exemption sets forth further requirements. For example, issuers are required to "provide certain purchasers who are natural persons a disclosure document as specified in [SEC] Rule 502 of Regulation D five days prior to any sale or commitment to purchase."[53] In addition, securities issued pursuant to the exemption are "restricted."[54] This resale restriction and the $5,000,000 offering limitation are the only two federal requirements that are imposed independent of California § 25102(n).

The SEC has stated that any state enacting a transaction exemption similar to California's is eligible to receive the same exemption.[55] To date, the SEC has not formally received any request from a state other than California.[56]

---

§ 3.08 Substantial Compliance Standard and Filing of Form D

After the SEC's adoption of Regulation D in 1982, additional criticism was heard. Two major points were: (1) the unduly technical requirement that the Form D must be

---

49. Securities Act Release, *supra* note 44, at 88,007-88,008.

50. For example, such specified information includes:
    (i) The name of the issuer of the securities,
    (ii) The full title of the security to be raised, [and]
    (iii) The anticipated suitability standards for prospective purchasers.
Cal. Corp. Code § 25102(n)(5)(A). The issuer also has the option of providing additional information, such as the nature of the issuer's business, its geographic location, and/or the probable price range of the security being offered. *See* Cal. Corp. Code § 25102(n)(5)(B).

51. *See* Cal. Corp. Code § 25102(n)(6).

52. *See* Securities Act Release 7285, *supra* note 44, at 88,008.

53. *Id.*

54. 17 C.F.R. § 230.1001(c).

55. *See* Securities Act Release 7285, *supra* note 44, at 88,009.

56. *See id. See also*, Bradford, *The SEC's New Regulation CE Exemption: Federal-State Coordination Run Rampant*, 52 U. Miami L. Rev. 429 (1998).

filed with the Commission as a condition of a Regulation D exemption; and (2) the need for a "substantial compliance" standard so that minor and inadvertent errors would not result in loss of a Regulation D exemption. After consideration, the SEC responded to these assertions by adopting a "substantial compliance" standard in Rule 508.

Moreover, the SEC adopted Rule 507, which eliminates the Form D filing requirement as a condition to the pertinent Regulation D exemption. The Commission stated:

> The proposals to eliminate the Form D filing requirement as a condition to every Regulation D exemption and the Rule 507 disqualification provisions were favorably received by the public commenters. These revisions have been adopted without change. The Rule 503 requirement to file a Form D [electronically] within 15 days of the first sale of securities remains, but will no longer be a condition to the establishment of any exemption under Regulation D. Rule 507 will serve as a disqualification to the use of Regulation D for future transactions by any issuer, if it, or a predecessor or affiliate, has been enjoined by a court for violating the filing obligation established by Rule 503. The Commission has the authority to waive a disqualification upon a showing of good cause.[57]

In other words, the timely filing of the Form D with the SEC is not a condition for perfecting a Regulation D exemption. The issuer nonetheless is required to file a Form D electronically, and, if such issuer is enjoined for failing to file the Form D, the failure to do so acts as a disqualification for such issuer to use a Regulation D exemption in the future. In its discretion, the SEC may waive any such disqualification upon a showing of good cause.

As discussed above, the SEC promulgated a "substantial compliance" standard for offerings pursuant to the Rule 504-506 exemptions. As set forth by the Commission, the "substantial compliance" standard contained in Rule 508 may be explained as follows:

> Rule 508 provides that an exemption from the registration requirements will be available for an offer or sale to a particular individual or entity, despite failure to comply with a requirement of Regulation D, if the requirement is not designed to protect specifically the complaining person; the failure to comply is insignificant to the offering as a whole; and there has been a good faith and reasonable attempt to comply with all requirements of the regulation. Rule 508 specifies that the provisions of Regulation D relating to general solicitation, the dollar limits of Rules 504 and 505 and the limits on non-accredited investors in Rules 505 and 506 are deemed significant to every offering and therefore not subject to the Rule 508 defense. Further, the rule specifies that any failure to comply with a provision of Regulation D is actionable by the Commission under the Securities Act.[58]

---

57. Securities Act Release No. 6825 (1989). The electronic filing of the Form D was adopted by the SEC in Securities Act Release No. 8891 (2008).

58. Securities Act Release No. 6825 (1989).

Accordingly, in order to invoke the Rule 508 substantial compliance defense in private litigation, the subject defendant must show that: *first,* the particular requirement is not intended to specifically protect the complainant (e.g., a complainant who is an accredited investor who does not receive information that was required to be but was not provided to a nonaccredited purchaser); *second,* the compliance defect was not significant to the offering as a whole (e.g., only one nonaccredited purchaser failed to receive the requisite information); *and third,* there was a good faith and reasonable effort to adhere to all of Regulation D's mandates (e.g., despite implementing a reasonably effective procedure for compliance, a ministerial error resulted in one nonaccredited purchaser not being provided the requisite information). Nonetheless, even if the above three conditions are met, the substantial compliance defense may not be invoked if: (1) there is impermissible general solicitation, such as in a traditional Rule 506 offering (e.g., one newspaper advertisement is placed for one day by the issuer in the locale's major newspaper); (2) the dollar limits in a Rule 504 offering are violated (e.g., in a Rule 504 offering, $5,000,001 is raised); *or* (3) the number of nonaccredited purchasers in a Rule 506 is exceeded (e.g., in a Rule 506 offering, there are 36 nonaccredited purchasers). Moreover, irrespective of the foregoing, any Regulation D violation, no matter how technical, may result in the SEC bringing suit.[59]

---

§ 3.09 The Web and General Solicitation

Citizen VC No-Action Letter

2015 SEC No-Act. LEXIS 409, 2015 WL 4699193 (SEC Div. Corp. Fin. 2015)

Rules 502(c) and 506(b) under Regulation D

August 3, 2015
David R. Fredrickson, Esq.
Chief Counsel
Division of Corporation Finance
U.S. Securities and Exchange Commission
100 F. Street, NE
Washington, DC 20549

Re: Citizen VC, Inc.
Dear Mr. Fredrickson:

Our client, Citizen VC, Inc. and its affiliates (collectively, *"CitizenVC"*), proposes to offer and sell from time to time, without registration, limited liability company interests (*"Interests"*) of special purpose vehicles *"SPVs"* established and managed by

---

59. *See* Sargent, *The New Regulation D: Deregulation, Federalism, and the Dynamics of Regulatory Reform*, 68 Wash. U.L.Q. 225 (1990).

a wholly owned subsidiary of CitizenVC, Inc. (the *"Manager"*) in order to aggregate investments made by members (*"Members"*) of the CitizenVC online venture capital investment platform (the *"Site"*). The SPVs invest in seed, early-stage, emerging growth and late-stage private companies, and offer accredited investors the SPVs' Interests in reliance upon the exemption provided pursuant to [traditional] Rule 506(b) of Regulation D promulgated under the Securities Act of 1933, as amended (the *"Securities Act"*). CitizenVC does not intend to rely on the exemption from registration provided under [JOBS Act] Rule 506(c), and will not engage in any general solicitation or general advertising. In connection with, and prior to, the offering of the Interests of SPVs, CitizenVC intends to establish pre-existing, substantive relationships with prospective members of the Site in accordance with the policies and procedures described in this letter. We note that current practices among online venture capital and angel investing sites vary substantially in the methodology for establishing a pre-existing, substantive relationship for purposes of complying with Rule 506(b). It is our opinion that the policies and procedures described in this letter will be sufficient to create the necessary relationship between CitizenVC and prospective investors such that the offering and sale of Interests on the Site will not constitute general solicitation or general advertising within the meaning of Rule 502(c) of Regulation D. On behalf of CitizenVC, we request that the staff of the Division of Corporation Finance (the *"Staff"*) concur with our conclusion.

Background

CitizenVC, Inc. is an online venture capital firm that owns and administers a website (http://citizen.vc) that facilitates indirect investment by its pre-qualified, accredited and sophisticated Members in seed, early-stage, emerging growth and late-stage private companies (*"Portfolio Companies"*) through SPVs organized and managed by the Manager. The SPVs are created to invest in specific Portfolio Companies and not as blind pool investment vehicles. Further, the SPVs will purchase equity interests either from the Portfolio Companies or from selling shareholders (subject to the consent of the Portfolio Companies).

CitizenVC is focused on technology, both its own and those of its portfolio companies, and desires to utilize the Internet and the Site to modernize and streamline traditionally offline venture capital investing activities, including presenting Portfolio Company offering materials to its Members and consummating all transactions online.

The Site is hosted on the publicly accessible Internet and CitizenVC is cognizant of the fact that prospective investors may search the Internet and land on its Site. CitizenVC wants to be prepared to accept membership applications from prospective investors with whom a pre-existing relationship has not yet been formed, but with whom it will establish a relationship prior to offering Interests.

CitizenVC has developed qualification policies and procedures that it intends to use to establish substantive relationships with, and to confirm the suitability of, prospective investors that visit the Site. Upon landing on the homepage of the Site,[60] a visitor that wishes to investigate the password protected sections of the Site accessible only to Members must first register and be accepted for membership. In order to apply for membership, CitizenVC requires all prospective investors, as a first step, to complete a generic online "accredited investor" questionnaire. The satisfactory completion of the online questionnaire is, however, only the beginning of Citizen-VC's relationship building process.[61]

Once a prospective investor has completed the online questionnaire and CitizenVC has evaluated the investor's self-certification of accreditation, CitizenVC will initiate the "relationship establishment period." During this period, CitizenVC will undertake various actions to connect with the prospective investor and collect information it deems sufficient to evaluate the prospective investor's sophistication, financial circumstances, and its ability to understand the nature and risks related to an investment in the Interests. Such activities include: (1) contacting the prospective investor offline by telephone to introduce representatives of CitizenVC and to discuss the prospective investor's investing experience and sophistication, investment goals and strategies, financial suitability, risk awareness, and other topics designed to assist CitizenVC in understanding the investor's sophistication; (2) sending an introductory email to the prospective investor; (3) contacting the prospective investor online to answer questions they may have about CitizenVC, the Site, and potential investments; (4) utilizing third party credit reporting services to confirm the prospective investor's identity, and to gather additional financial information and credit history information to support the prospective investor's suitability; (5) encouraging the prospective investor to explore the Site and ask questions about the Manager's investment strategy, philosophy, and objectives; and (6) generally fostering interactions both online and offline between the prospective investor and CitizenVC. Additionally, prospective investors will be advised that every SPV offering will have a significant minimum capital investment requirement for each investor, which will be not less than $50,000 per individual investment, and in some offerings significantly higher. All of the foregoing activities and interactions are specifically designed to create and strengthen a real, substantive relationship between CitizenVC and the prospective investor, and to verify and ensure that the offering of Interests is suitable for them.

---

60. The publicly accessible homepage contains only generic information about Citizen VC. There is no information accessible on the publicly accessible homepage about any of the current SPVs, Portfolio Companies, investment opportunities or offering materials. The publicly accessible homepage is designed so that no reasonable person could construe it as a solicitation for any particular offering.

61. Applicants who cannot attest to their status as "accredited investors" are denied access to the password protected areas of the Site and are not permitted to continue the membership application process.

The duration of the relationship establishment period is not limited by a specific time period.[62] Rather, it is a process based on specific written policies and procedures created to ensure that the offering of Interests is suitable for each prospective investor.

After CitizenVC is satisfied that (i) the prospective investor has sufficient knowledge and experience in financial and business matters to enable it to evaluate the merits and risks of the investment opportunities on the Site, and (ii) it has taken all reasonable steps it believes necessary to create a substantive relationship with the prospective investor, only then will CitizenVC admit the prospective investor as a Member of the Site. Thereafter, CitizenVC will provide the new Member access to the password protected sections of the Site, where the new Member can investigate investment opportunities curated by CitizenVC and the offering materials related thereto. The relationship with a new Member will exist prior to any offering of securities to such new Member.

Once a sufficient number of qualified Members have expressed interest in the private placement investment opportunity of a particular Portfolio Company, those Members will be provided subscription materials for investment in the SPV formed by CitizenVC to aggregate such Members' investments, which materials shall include additional risk disclosure and detailed "accredited investor" certifications and representations. Thereafter, the offering and sale of Interests of such SPV will be consummated. The SPV will then invest such funds in, and become an equity holder of, the Portfolio Company. Each SPV will be managed by the Manager, which shall become a registered investment adviser as required under the Investment Advisers Act of 1940, as amended (the "*IAA*").

Legal Analysis

Section 5 of the Securities Act prohibits the sale of securities by an issuer in the United States without registration or an available exemption, and Section 4(a)(2) of the Securities Act provides an exemption from registration for offerings that do not involve a "public offering". In interpreting what constitutes a "public offering", the Supreme Court in *SEC v. Ralston Purina Co.* [346 U.S. 119 (1953)] established that the standard for determining whether an offering is public or private turns on "whether the particular class of persons affected need[ed] the protection of the [Securities] Act", and further elaborated that "an offering to those [investors] who are shown to be able to fend for themselves is a transaction 'not involving any public offering.'" Over the years, courts have upheld the general proposition that offerings should be considered private when the issuer and the offeree(s) have a pre-existing relationship.

Rule 506(b) of Regulation D provides a safe harbor for issuers to engage in private placements. Private placements undertaken pursuant to Rule 506(b) are limited,

---

62. *See* Lamp Technologies, Inc. No Action Letter (publicly May 29, 1997). In *Lamp*, the Staff implicitly endorsed a waiting period of 30 days between the satisfactory completion of an accreditation questionnaire and the ability of an agent of the issuer to offer securities to such investor without violating the prohibition on general solicitation.

however, by Rule 502(c) of Regulation D, which imposes as a condition on offers and sales under Rule 506(b) that "... neither the issuer nor any person acting on its behalf shall offer or sell the securities by any form of general solicitation or general advertising ..."

Since the adoption of Regulation D, the Staff has issued various interpretive letters ("*No Action Letters*") that have further clarified the contours of the Regulation and established the "important and well-known principle ... [that] a general solicitation is not present when there is a pre-existing, substantive relationship between an issuer, or its [agent], and the offerees."

Through these No Action Letters, the Staff has endorsed the position that an issuer, through its agent (generally, registered brokers-dealers), may establish a pre-existing, substantive relationship with the use of a questionnaire that, once completed by the investor, provides such agent sufficient information to evaluate the investor's sophistication or accreditation. It is less clear from the guidance, however, whether an issuer itself can rely solely on a questionnaire that relates only to "accredited investor" status (particularly in an online transaction) to establish the necessary pre-existing relationship without a waiting period or additional policies and procedures that would establish a pre-existing and substantive relationship. Many of the No Action Letters appear to interpret the use of questionnaires by registered broker-dealers, acting as agents of issuers, as merely one way to collect "sufficient information to evaluate the prospective offerees' sophistication and financial circumstances." But in *Mineral Lands Research & Marketing Corp. No Action Letter* [Dec. 4, 1985], the Staff elaborated that the types of relationships that may be important in establishing that a general solicitation has not taken place are those that would enable "[the issuer or its agent] to be aware of the financial circumstances or sophistication of the persons with whom the relationship exists or that otherwise are of some substance and duration."

Conclusion

We interpret the Staff's No Action Letter guidance to mean that the *quality* of the relationship between an issuer and an investor is the most important factor to be considered in determining whether a pre-existing, substantive relationship has been established for purposes of offerings made in private placements pursuant to Rule 506(b) of Regulation D. It is our opinion that the No Action Letter guidance of the Staff points to establishing a process for issuers to develop substantive relationships with previously unknown investors, and that this process can be undertaken in a manner that will not contravene the prohibition of general solicitation and general advertising under Rule 502(c). The relationship between issuer and investor is not built through a specific duration of time or a short form accreditation questionnaire. Rather, it can be established by adhering to specific policies and procedures both online and offline (where appropriate), which enable the issuer to evaluate the prospective investor's financial sophistication, circumstances, suitability, and his or her ability to understand the nature and risks of the Interests to be offered. It is this substantive relationship that is necessary to execute an offering of securities online in a password protected area that does not violate Rule 502(c).

We understand that issuers and/or their agents relying on Rule 506(b) will have to take additional steps beyond the circulation of a brief accreditation questionnaire in order to create a substantive relationship with their prospective investors. We believe that CitizenVC has developed the appropriate specific policies and procedures through which it will investigate, engage, and communicate with prospective investors to get to know them, understand their financial sophistication, and evaluate whether they are suitable for the investment opportunities available in the password protected areas of the Site. It should be noted that we are not seeking guidance on whether CitizenVC's processes and procedures described herein satisfy all the other elements of a valid Rule 506(b) offering, including, without limitation, whether a particular SPV reasonably believes that the prospective investors participating in such SPV's offering of Interests are accredited investors.

It is our opinion that the substantive relationship building policies and procedures developed by CitizenVC and described in this letter establish a pre-existing, substantive relationship between CitizenVC and its prospective investors such that granting access to such prospective investors in a password protected area of the CitizenVC Site to materials related to the offering of unregistered Interests in SPVs will not involve any form of general solicitation or general advertising, and will enable CitizenVC to offer Interests online without contravening Rule 502(c).We respectfully request the Staff's concurrence with our opinion.

. . . .

Very truly yours,

Daniel I. DeWolf, Esq.

———————

August 6, 2015

Response of the Office of Chief Counsel
Division of Corporation Finance

Re: Citizen VC, Inc.
   Incoming letter dated August 3, 2015

Based on the facts presented, the Division's views are as follows. . . .

You have requested the staff concur in your conclusion that the policies and procedures described in your letter will create a substantive, pre-existing relationship between CitizenVC and prospective investors such that the offering and sale on the Site of Interests in SPVs that will invest in a particular Portfolio Company will not constitute general solicitation or general advertising within the meaning of Rule 502(c) of Regulation D.

We agree that the quality of the relationship between an issuer (or its agent) and an investor is the most important factor in determining whether a "substantive" relationship exists. As the Division has stated before, a "substantive" relationship is one in which the issuer (or a person acting on its behalf) has sufficient information to evaluate, and does, in fact, evaluate, a prospective offeree's financial circumstances and sophistication, in determining his or her status as an accredited or sophisticated investor. *See, e.g., Bateman Eichler, Hill Richards, Inc.* (Dec. 3, 1985). We note your representation that CVC's policies and procedures are designed to evaluate the prospective investor's sophistication, financial circumstances and ability to understand the nature and risks of the securities to be offered. We also agree that there is no specific duration of time or particular short form accreditation questionnaire that can be relied upon solely to create such a relationship. Whether an issuer has sufficient information to evaluate, and does in fact evaluate, a prospective offeree's financial circumstances and sophistication will depend on the facts and circumstances.

In expressing these views, we note your representation that the relationship with new Members will pre-exist any offering, consistent with the Division's previous guidance. In this regard, we note that a prospective Member is not presented with any investment opportunity when being qualified to join the platform. Any investment opportunity would only be presented after the prospective investor becomes a Member. Further, we understand that CVC creates SPVs for investment in particular Portfolio Companies and not as blind pools for a later investment opportunity.

Because this position is based on the representations in your letter, any different facts or conditions might require the Division to reach a different conclusion.

Sincerely,

David R. Fredrickson

Chief Counsel

———————

In an article discussing the *Citizen VC* matter, one source opined:

> Some commentators have reported that the *Citizen VC* guidance significantly changed the overall compliance landscape for [traditional] Rule 506(b) private offerings . . . . They see *Citizen VC* . . . as a compliance roadmap for any issuer to contact an unlimited number of prospective investors via impersonal non-selective means (*e.g.,* the internet) without jeopardizing Rule 506(b) compliance. When undertaken in accordance with the guidance in *Citizen VC*, such activities, they assert, will be deemed not to involve "general solicitation or general advertising" within the meaning of Rule 502(c). Others have a less expansive view about the general applicability of the *Citizen VC* guidance to conventional issuers and companies other than registered broker-dealers or similar third-party financial intermediaries. It is too soon to know the long term compliance effects of *Citizen VC*. . . . [63]

———————

———————

63. Leisner, *General Solicitation under Rule 506(b) after Citizen VC*, 44 Sec. Reg. L.J. 133, 133–34 (2016).

§ 3.10 Chart of Selected Securities Act Exemptions

Item	Rule 504	Rule 506	Rule 701	Reg. A	§ 4(a)(2)
Aggregate Offering Price Limitation	$5,000,000 (12 mos.)	Unlimited	Depending on certain factors, at least $1,000,000 (12 mos.)	Tier 1 — Up to $20 million (12 mos.); Tier 2 — Up to $50 million (12 mos.)	Unlimited
Number of Investors	Unlimited	Traditional Rule 506(b) offerings — 35 plus an unlimited number of accredited investors; JOBS Act — Rule 506(c) offerings — Unlimited number of accredited investors only	Unlimited but must be an eligible purchaser	Unlimited	Uncertain but evidently a finite number of offerees depending on the circumstances
Investor Qualification	None required	Non-accredited purchaser must be financially sophisticated (alone or with representa-tive); accredited investors presumed to be financially sophisticated	Purchaser must be employee, officer, director, consultant or advisor of an eligible company who has acquired the securities as compensation	None required (but limitation on amount of securities non-accredited investors may purchase in a Tier 2 offering)	Exact requirements uncertain; offeree must receive or have access to the type of information that registra-tion would disclose; also, sophistication standards apply — offeree must be financially sophisticated (alone or with representative)
Commission	Permitted	Permitted	Permitted	Permitted	Permitted

Item	Rule 504	Rule 506	Rule 701	Reg. A	§4(a)(2)
Limitations on Manner of Offering	General solicitation and advertising permitted if state registered or sold only to accredited purchasers under applicable state law	No general solicitation or advertising permitted in traditional Rule 506(b) offering; general solicitation and advertising permitted if all purchasers are accredited (JOBS Act—Rule 506(c))	General solicitation and advertising permitted	General solicitation and advertising permitted	No general solicitation or advertising permitted
Limitations on Resale	Not restricted if state registered or sold only to accredited purchasers under applicable state law	Restricted	Restricted	Not Restricted	Restricted
Issuer Qualifications	Among others, no reporting or investment companies; bad actor disqualifiers apply	"Bad Actor" disqualifiers apply	No reporting companies	Among others, no Exchange Act reporting enterprises; bad actor disqualifiers apply	None
Filing with SEC	Form D required but not as a condition of exemption	Form D required but not as a condition of exemption	No notice of sales required	Filings required	No notice of sales required
Information Requirements	No information specified	In a Rule 506(b) offering to nonaccredited purchasers, see SEC Rule 502(b) for information requirements	No information specified except if greater than $5 million sold	As set forth by SEC rule	Investors receive or have access to the type of information that registration would disclose

§ 3.11 The Burden of Proof File, SEC No-Action Letters, and Rescission Offers

[A] Burden of Proof File

As seen from the foregoing materials, different questions may arise regarding a client's compliance with an exemption from registration. As the law stands, the issuer (as the party seeking to perfect an exemption) has the burden to prove that it has satisfied the requirements for invoking an applicable exemption from registration. To satisfy this criteria, the attorney or the issuer (with the guidance of counsel) should maintain a "burden of proof" file. Such a file, if properly maintained, goes a long way toward showing that the issuer conducted the offering in compliance with the conditions for invoking the exemption.

The importance of properly maintaining a burden of proof file is illustrated by the Sixth Circuit's decision in *Mark v. FSC Securities Corporation,* 870 F.2d 331, 337 (6th Cir. 1989). Holding that the defendants had failed to perfect the Rule 506 exemption, the court alluded to the inadequate procedures utilized:

> [T]he documents [introduced at trial] offered no evidence from which a jury could conclude [that] the issuer reasonably believed each purchaser was suitable so as to warrant a Rule 506 exemption. Instead, all that was proved was the sale of twenty-eight limited partnerships, and the circumstances under which those sales were intended to have been made. The mere fact that the limited-partnership interests were sold cannot support a conclusion that they were sold in compliance with the conditions contemplated by Rule 506. The blank subscription document and offeree questionnaire simply do not amount to probative evidence, when it is the answers and information received from purchasers that determines whether the conditions of Rule 506 have been met. Because there was no evidence from which a jury could conclude that the issuer had the requisite belief, nor from which a jury could determine the reasonableness of any such belief, [the issuer] FSC has failed to sustain its burden of proving an exemption under Rule 506 of Regulation D.

For other examples of inadequate procedures resulting in loss of the exemption, see *Western Federal Corporation v. Erickson,* 739 F.2d 1439 (9th Cir. 1984); *Fukuda v. Nethercott,* [2016-2 Transfer Binder] Fed. Sec. L. Rep. (CCH) ¶ 99,233 (D. Utah 2016).

[B] SEC No-Action Letters

Although not specifically related to transactional exemptions from registration, this is a good point to mention the SEC "no-action" letter process. We already have read an SEC no-action letter in § 3.09 with respect to *Citizen VC* and will look at this process again in later chapters.

Under the SEC no-action process, counsel informs the SEC staff in writing of his or her client's contemplated conduct. Such contemplated conduct may involve, for example, questions related to a Regulation D offering, resales of stock, or proxy statements. The staff responds by either issuing a no-action letter or by refusing to issue such a letter. At times, the staff's response communicates solely an enforcement posture — namely, whether the staff would recommend to the Commission that an enforcement action be initiated if the contemplated conduct were undertaken in the manner set forth in the written request. In other staff responses, in addition to the enforcement position taken, the staff may articulate interpretations of applicable SEC rules and regulations as they pertain to the proposed conduct. In either situation, the staff's views are not those of the Commission and are not binding. Notwithstanding the informal status of SEC no-action letters, they unquestionably have great significance and are relied upon by market participants and their attorneys.

Not surprisingly, the SEC staff's refusal to approve a no-action request normally results in the affected parties not engaging in the contemplated conduct. Even if the staff issues a no-action letter, however, that does not ensure that the client's conduct will not be challenged. Private parties are not bound by an SEC no-action letter and may sue irrespective of the issuance of such a letter. Moreover, although unlikely to happen, the SEC retains its discretion to institute an enforcement action even though its staff has issued a no-action letter covering the very same conduct.[64]

Interestingly, an enforcement action against Morgan Stanley & Co. (Admin. Proceeding File No. 3-7473, Release No. 34- 28990 (1991)) may indicate that parties who are not recipients of a specific SEC no-action letter request rely on letters addressed to others on similar (yet not identical) issues at their peril. As stated by one source:

> [I]t appears that the Commission turned a cold shoulder to Morgan Stanley's statement that it had relied on repeated SEC staff interpretive letters which had blessed action *similar* to that taken by Morgan Stanley. If so, in effect, the SEC has warned: no matter how certain the SEC's position appears to be, do not look to SEC staff articulations as an indication of how the Commission itself will respond to your conduct, unless the staff's articulation is precisely on point or is addressed to you.[65]

Hence, unless an SEC no-action letter response is clearly on point, counsel may be ill advised to use such letters as strong guidance to advise his/her client on a similar, though not identical, issue.

---

64. *See New York City Employees' Retirement System v. SEC,* 45 F.3d 7 (2d Cir. 1995); *In re Morgan Stanley & Co.,* Securities Exchange Act Release No. 28990 (1991). *See generally* R. Haft & M. Hudson, *Analysis of Key No-Action Letters* (2015–2016); Lemke, *The SEC No-Action Letter Process,* 42 Bus. Law. 1019 (1987).

65. Pitt & Johnson, Eviscerating the SEC NoAction Process?, 5 Insights No. 5, at 2 (May 1991) (emphasis supplied). See Nagy, *Judicial Reliance on Regulatory Interpretations in SEC No-Action Letters: Current Problems and a Proposed Framework,* 83 Cornell L. Rev. 921 (1998); Rowe, *A SEC Staff 'No-Action' Position: An Impervious Shield Against Liability or a Paper Tiger?,* 6 Insights No. 7, at 21 (July 1992).

[C] Rescission Offers

An ever present fear for securities counsel and his/her client is that a securities law violation has occurred that is material to the transaction. For example, in a Rule 506 offering, suppose that after the transaction "closes," counsel discovers that there are 36 non-accredited purchasers rather than the allotted maximum of 35 or that there was impermissible general solicitation in connection with the offering. Is there any curative action that the issuer may take? Insofar as purchasers are concerned, the issuer may make a "rescission offer" that fully informs the purchasers of all material facts and provides such purchasers with the right to rescind.

Needless to say, counsel who is responsible for the transaction will be in an uncomfortable position. If the "deal" goes forward and the issuer uses the funds, the issuer (and others) will be subject to liability. Moreover, if the mistake happens to be counsel's doing, then malpractice liability may ensue. Note that, even if a rescission offer may cut off a purchaser's right to sue (although it may not), the SEC and state authorities retain their prerogative to bring an enforcement action.

Rescission offers may occur in the private or public offering context. If a rescission offer is made in the private offering setting, an exemption from registration must be perfected. Otherwise, compliance with the Securities Act registration requirements may be necessary.[66] As stated by one source:

> A rescission offer is an offer to rescind a transaction in which a securities violation occurred or is believed to have occurred. The mechanics of the rescission offer may entail an offer to buy or sell securities. Unlike other offerings of securities, however, and regardless of whether the rescission offer is to purchase securities from or sell securities back to the rescission offeree, a rescission offer is treated as both an offer to sell, and an offer to buy the subject securities. Consequently, compliance with [an exemption from registration or] the registration requirements of the Securities Act [will] be necessary. . . . [67]

§ 3.12 The Federal Crowdfunding Exemption

In the JOBS Act, Congress created a crowdfunding exemption from Securities Act registration. Generally, crowdfunding in this context is the use of the Internet to sell

---

66. *See* Bromberg, *Curing Securities Violations: Rescission Offers and Other Techniques,* 1 J. Corp. L. 1 (1975).

67. Rowe, *Rescission Offers Under Federal and State Securities Law,* 12 J. Corp. Law 383 (1987).

securities in small amounts to a large number of investors. The exemption is found in § 4(a)(6) of the Securities Act and the conditions to perfecting this exemption also are found in § 4A(a) and § 4A(b).

[A] Statutory Exemption and SEC Rules — Overview

Section 4(a)(6) exempts offers up to $1 million during a 12-month period so long as the aggregate amount sold to any investor in reliance on this exemption does not exceed a specified amount, based on such investor's annual income or net worth. In this regard, the maximum amount that may be purchased by any investor pursuant to the crowdfunding exemption shall not exceed "(i) the greater of $2,000 or 5 percent of the annual income or net worth of such investor, as applicable, if either the annual income or the net worth of the investor is less than $100,000; and (ii) 10 percent of the annual income or net worth of such investor, as applicable, not to exceed a maximum aggregate amount of $100,000 if either the annual income or net worth of the investor is equal to or more than $100,000."

Securities acquired under this exemption are restricted, thereby having a one-year holding period unless the securities are transferred: to the issuer; to an accredited investor; to a family member; in connection with the death or divorce of the purchaser; or as part of a Securities Act registered offering. Securities issued through this exemption will be deemed "covered securities" and thereby preempt state regulation (except for fraud purposes) of the subject offering.

The § 4(a)(6) exemption may not be used by Exchange Act reporting companies, investment companies, and foreign issuers. In addition, "bad actor" disqualification provisions apply to preclude use of the exemption by subject issuers.

In order for the exemption to be implemented, the SEC adopted applicable rules and regulations. Pursuant to these rules and regulations, the issuer must file with the SEC and must provide to investors and the subject broker-dealer or funding portal specified information, including: financial statements; a description of the issuer's business and its anticipated business plan; the intended use of the proceeds; the target offering amount; a description of the issuer's ownership and capital structure; and risk factor disclosures. Significantly, the issuer may receive the offering proceeds only when the aggregate amount raised meets or exceeds the target offering amount. Liability consequences ensue if the issuer makes a material misrepresentation or half-truth to purchasers in a crowdfunding exempt offering. These liability ramifications are addressed in § 7.08 of the text.

Pursuant to the crowdfunding exemption, the securities must be sold through a registered broker or registered funding portal. Under the statute, these intermediaries are charged with undertaking specified measures to reduce the risk of investors suffering financial loss and with making available to investors pertinent information received from the subject issuer.

[B] SEC Regulation Crowdfunding

In 2015, the SEC adopted Regulation Crowdfunding ("Regulation CF"). The following excerpt of the SEC's release (Securities Act Release No. 9974 (2015)) provides a succinct overview of Regulation CF.

Final Rules Implementing Regulation Crowdfunding

Regulation Crowdfunding, among other things, permits individuals to invest in securities-based crowdfunding transactions subject to certain thresholds, limits the amount of money an issuer can raise under the crowdfunding exemption, requires issuers to disclose certain information about their offers, and creates a regulatory framework for the intermediaries that facilitate the crowdfunding transactions. As an overview, under the final rules:

- An issuer is permitted to raise a maximum aggregate amount of $1 million through crowdfunding offerings in a 12-month period;

- Individual investors, over the course of a 12-month period, are permitted to invest in the aggregate across *all* crowdfunding offerings up to:
  - ○ If either their annual income or net worth is less than $100,000, then the greater of:
    - ■ $2,000 or
    - ■ 5 percent of the lesser of their annual income or net worth.

- If both their annual income and net worth are equal to or more than $100,000, then 10 percent of the lesser of their annual income or net worth; and

- During the 12-month period, the aggregate amount of securities sold to an investor through *all* crowdfunding offerings may not exceed $100,000.

Certain companies are not eligible to use the Regulation Crowdfunding exemption. Ineligible companies include non-U.S. companies, companies that already are Exchange Act reporting companies, certain investment companies, companies that are disqualified under Regulation Crowdfunding's disqualification rules, companies that have failed to comply with the annual reporting requirements under Regulation Crowdfunding during the two years immediately preceding the filing of the offering statement, and companies that have no specific business plan or have indicated their business plan is to engage in a merger or acquisition with an unidentified company or companies.

Securities purchased in a crowdfunding transaction generally cannot be resold for a period of one year. Holders of these securities do not count toward the threshold that requires an issuer to register its securities with the Commission under § 12(g) of the Exchange Act if the issuer is current in its annual reporting obligation, retains the services of a registered transfer agent and has less than $25 million in assets.

Disclosure by Issuers. The final rules require issuers conducting an offering pursuant to Regulation Crowdfunding to file certain information with the Commission and provide this information to investors and the relevant intermediary facilitating the crowdfunding offering. Among other things, in its offering documents, the issuer is required to disclose:

- Information about officers and directors as well as owners of 20 percent or more of the issuer;

- A description of the issuer's business and the use of proceeds from the offering;

- The price to the public of the securities or the method for determining the price, the target offering amount, the deadline to reach the target offering amount, and whether the issuer will accept investments in excess of the target offering amount;

- Certain related-party transactions;

- A discussion of the issuer's financial condition; and

- Financial statements of the issuer that are, depending on the amount offered and sold during a 12-month period, accompanied by information from the issuer's tax returns, reviewed by an independent public accountant, or audited by an independent auditor. An issuer relying on these rules for the first time would be permitted to provide reviewed rather than audited financial statements, unless financial statements of the issuer are available that have been audited by an independent auditor.

Issuers are required to amend the offering document during the offering period to reflect material changes and provide updates on the issuer's progress toward reaching the target offering amount.

In addition, issuers relying on the Regulation Crowdfunding exemption are required to file an annual report with the Commission and provide it to investors.

Crowdfunding Platforms. One of the key investor protections of Title III of the JOBS Act is the requirement that Regulation Crowdfunding transactions take place through an SEC-registered intermediary, either a broker-dealer or a funding portal.[68] Under Regulation Crowdfunding, offerings must be conducted exclusively through a platform operated by a registered broker or a funding portal, which is a new type of SEC registrant. The rules require these intermediaries to:

---

68. Pursuant to §3(a)(80) of the Securities Exchange Act, "funding portal" is defined as follows:

The term "funding portal" means any person acting as an intermediary in a transaction involving the offer or sale of securities for the account of others, solely pursuant to section 4(a)(6) of the Securities Act of 1933, that does not—

(A) offer investment advice or recommendations;

(B) solicit purchases, sales, or offers to buy the securities offered or displayed on its website or portal;

(C) compensate employees, agents, or other persons for such solicitation or based on the sale of securities displayed or referenced on its website or portal;

(D) hold, manage, possess, or otherwise handle investor funds or securities; or

(E) engage in such other activities as the Commission, by rule, determines appropriate.

- Provide investors with educational materials;
- Take measures to reduce the risk of fraud;
- Make available information about the issuer and the offering;
- Provide communication channels to permit discussions about offerings on the platform; and
- Facilitate the offer and sale of crowdfunded securities.

The rules prohibit a funding portal from:

- Offering investment advice or making recommendations;
- Soliciting purchases, sales or offers to buy securities offered or displayed on its platform;
- Compensating promoters and others for solicitations or based on the sale of securities; and
- Holding, possessing, or handling investor funds or securities.

    . . . .

Note

The crowdfunding exemption may well be little used. As Professor Bradford opines, "the new exemption imposes substantial regulatory costs . . . and, therefore, will not be the panacea crowdfunding supporters hoped for. The regulatory cost of selling securities through crowdfunding may still be too high."[69] Professor Cohn views this effort in even more dismal terms: "[D]espite good intentions, the newly-created exemption is fraught with regulatory requirements that go beyond even existing exemptions and raise transaction costs and liability concerns that may substantially reduce the exemption's utility for small capital-raising efforts."[70] The degree to which the new crowdfunding exemption will be invoked is uncertain.

§ 3.13 Intrastate Offerings — Section 3(a)(11), Rule 147, and Rule 147A

Section 3(a)(11) of the Securities Act provides an exemption from federal registration with respect to "[a]ny security which is a part of an issue offered and sold

---

69. Bradford, *The New Federal Crowdfunding Exemption: Promise Unfulfilled,* 40 Sec. Reg. L. J. 195 (2012).

70. Cohn, *The New Crowdfunding Registration Exemption: Good Idea, Bad Execution,* 64 Fla. L. Rev. 1433 (2012). *See* Hanks, *JOBS Act Crowdfunding Provisions Await Clarification by SEC,* 44 Sec. Reg. & L. Rep. (BNA) 1710 (2012); Palmer, *The Intrastate Crowdfunding Exemption: Gaining the Wisdom of Crowds While Avoiding Its Madness,* 43 Sec. Reg. L.J. 279 (2015).

only to persons resident within a single State or Territory, where the issuer of such security is a person resident and doing business, or, if a corporation, incorporated by and doing business within, such State or Territory." The § 3(a)(11) exemption, like the § 3(a)(9) and § 3(a)(10) exemptions to be addressed later in this Chapter, are categorized in the Securities Act as exempt securities rather than transactional exemptions from registration. In practical effect, however, these exemptions come into play only where there is a transaction that meets the criteria of the applicable exemption. For example, the § 3(a)(11) exemption, concerning securities that are offered and sold pursuant to an intrastate offering, is invoked only where there is an offering that meets the exemptive requirements of the statute.

In 1974, the SEC, in order to establish more definitive standards regarding the intrastate exemption, promulgated Rule 147 to serve as a safe harbor. If the conditions of the rule have not been met, the party still may assert the availability of the § 3(a)(11) statutory exemption. In adopting Rule 147, the Commission stated:

> Section 3(a)(11) was intended to allow issuers with localized operations to sell securities as part of a plan of local financing. Congress apparently believed that a company whose operations are restricted to one area should be able to raise money from investors in the immediate vicinity without having to register the securities with a federal agency. In theory, the investors would be protected both by their proximity to the issuer and by state regulation. Rule 147 reflects this Congressional intent and is limited in its application to transactions where state regulation will be most effective. The Commission has consistently taken the position that the exemption applies only to local financing provided by local investors for local companies. To satisfy the exemption, the entire issue must be offered and sold exclusively to residents of the state in which the issuer is resident and doing business. An offer or sale of part of the issue to a single non-resident will destroy the exemption for the entire issue.

> . . . .

> The rule is a nonexclusive rule. However, persons who choose to rely on Section 3(a)(11) without complying with all the conditions of Rule 147 would have the burden of establishing that they have complied with the judicial and administrative interpretations of Section 3(a)(11) in effect at the time of the offering. The Commission also emphasizes that the exemption provided by Section 3(a)(11) is not an exemption from the civil liability provisions. . . . The Commission further emphasizes that Rule 147 [unlike § 3(a)(11)] is available only for transactions by issuers and is not available for secondary offerings.

SEC Securities Act Release No. 5450 (1974).

In 2016, the SEC amended Rule 147 and adopted a new intrastate safe harbor exemption rule—Rule 147A. Key excerpts of the Commission's 2016 release follow.

Exemptions to Facilitate Intrastate and Regional Securities Offerings

SEC Securities Act Release No. 10238 (2016)

We are adopting amendments to modernize Rule 147 under the Securities Act of 1933, which provides a safe harbor for compliance with the Section 3(a)(11) exemption from [federal] registration for intrastate securities offerings. We are also establishing a new intrastate offering exemption under the Securities Act, designated Rule 147A, which will be similar to amended Rule 147, but will have no restriction on offers [out-of-state] and will allow issuers to be incorporated or organized outside of the state in which the intrastate offering is conducted provided certain conditions are met. The amendments to Rule 147 and new Rule 147A are designed to facilitate capital formation, including through offerings relying upon intrastate crowdfunding provisions under state securities laws, while maintaining appropriate investor protections and providing state securities regulators with the flexibility to add additional investor protections they deem appropriate for offerings within their state.

. . . .

I. Introduction and Background

. . . . [We have determined to] retain and modernize Rule 147 under the Securities Act as a safe harbor for intrastate offerings exempt from registration pursuant to Securities Act Section 3(a)(11). These amendments will modernize the safe harbor, while keeping within the statutory parameters of Section 3(a)(11), so that issuers may continue to rely upon the rule for offerings pursuant to state law exemptions, including crowdfunding provisions, that are conditioned upon compliance with Section 3(a)(11) and Rule 147.

Securities Act Section 3(a)(11) provides an exemption from registration under the Securities Act for "[a]ny security which is part of an issue offered and sold only to persons resident within a single State or Territory, where the issuer of such security is a person resident and doing business within, or, if a corporation, incorporated by and doing business within, such State or Territory." In 1974, the Commission adopted Rule 147 under the Securities Act to provide objective standards for local businesses seeking to rely on Section 3(a)(11). The Rule 147 safe harbor was intended to provide assurances that the intrastate offering exemption would be used for the purpose Congress intended in enacting Section 3(a)(11), namely the local financing of companies by investors within the company's state or territory. Rule 147 reflects this Congressional intent and generally relies upon state regulation to effectively protect investors.

Notwithstanding the importance of these limitations, due to developments in modern business practices and communications technology in the years since Rule 147 was adopted, we have determined that it is necessary to update the requirements of Rule 147 to ensure its continued utility. We are also establishing a new intrastate offering exemption under the Securities Act, designated Rule 147A, that will further accommodate modern business practices and communications technology and provide an alternative means for smaller companies to raise capital locally.

We are adopting new Rule 147A pursuant to our general exemptive authority under Section 28 of the Securities Act, and therefore, new Rule 147A will not be subject to the statutory limitations of Section 3(a)(11). Accordingly, Rule 147A will have no restriction on offers, but will require that all sales be made only to residents of the issuer's state or territory to ensure the intrastate nature of the exemption. Rule 147A also will not require issuers to be incorporated or organized in the same state or territory where the offering occurs so long as issuers can demonstrate the in-state nature of their business, which we believe will expand the number of businesses that will be able to seek intrastate financing under Rule 147A, as compared to amended Rule 147. Certain provisions of existing Rule 147 concerning legends and mandatory disclosures to purchasers and prospective purchasers will apply to offerings conducted pursuant to amended Rule 147 and Rule 147A.

As to current Rule 147, nothing in either amended Rule 147 or new Rule 147A will obviate the need for compliance with any applicable state law relating to the offer and sale of securities. Thus, states will retain the flexibility to adopt requirements that are consistent with their respective interests in facilitating capital formation and protecting their resident investors in intrastate securities offerings, including the authority to impose additional disclosure requirements regarding offers and sales made to persons within their state or territory, or the authority to limit the ability of certain bad actors from relying on applicable state exemptions. In addition, both federal and state antifraud provisions will continue to apply to offers and sales made pursuant to amended Rule 147 and new Rule 147A.

. . . .

II. Amendments to Rule 147 and New Rule 147A

A. Explanation of Amendments to Rule 147 and New Rule 147A

. . . .

1. Manner of Offering

. . . .

. . . . [W]e are adopting new Rule 147A to allow issuers to make offers accessible to out-of-state residents, so long as sales are limited to in-state residents. We are also retaining amended Rule 147 as a safe harbor under Section 3(a)(11) to preserve the continued availability of existing state exemptive provisions that are specifically conditioned upon issuer reliance on Section 3(a)(11) and Rule 147. Issuers relying on amended Rule 147 as a safe harbor under Section 3(a)(11) must continue to limit all offers and sales to in-state residents.

We believe offers made over the Internet that can be viewed by a significant number of out-of-state residents are not consistent with Section 3(a)(11) and Rule 147, even if such offers include prominent disclosure stating that sales will be made only to residents of the same state or territory as the issuer. . . .

. . . [W]e believe that the most appropriate means to permit the offer and sale of securities on Internet websites, or using any other form of mass media likely to reach significant numbers of out-of-state residents, is to adopt a new intrastate offering exemption pursuant to the Commission's general exemptive authority under Section 28. Accordingly, new Rule 147A will require issuers to limit sales to in-state residents, but will not limit offers by the issuer to in-state residents. New Rule 147A thereby will permit issuers to engage in general solicitation and general advertising of their offerings, using any form of mass media, including unrestricted, publicly-available Internet websites, so long as sales of securities so offered are made only to residents of the state or territory in which the issuer is resident.

Consistent with the proposal, both Rule 147A and amended Rule 147 will require issuers to include prominent disclosure with all offering materials stating that sales will be made only to residents of the same state or territory as the issuer. We believe this disclosure will help alert potential investors that only residents of the state in which the issuer is located are eligible to participate in the offering. Nothing in this disclosure requirement, however, will prevent state authorities from imposing additional disclosure requirements or other requirements on offers or sales made to persons within their states.

. . . .

2. Elimination of Residence Requirement for Issuers

. . . .

We are adopting changes to the residency requirements for issuers conducting exempt intrastate offerings largely as proposed, but with certain modifications to reflect our decision to retain existing Rule 147 as a safe harbor to the Section 3(a)(11) exemption. Since we are retaining Rule 147 as a safe harbor and since Section 3(a)(11) expressly requires that if the issuer is a corporation that it be "incorporated by and doing business within, such state or territory," we are not eliminating the "residence" requirement in current paragraph (c)(1) of Rule 147. . . . Instead, we are retaining the requirement that an issuer shall be deemed a resident of a state or territory in which it is incorporated or organized for issuers that are incorporated or organized under state or territorial law, such as corporations, limited partnerships and trusts.

In addition, for consistency between the provisions of Rule 147 and new Rule 147A, throughout amended Rule 147, we are replacing the "principal office" requirement with the proposed "principal place of business" requirement. Instead of "principal office," amended Rule 147 and new Rule 147A will refer to the term "principal place of business" to mean the location from which the officers, partners, or managers of the issuer primarily direct, control and coordinate the activities of the issuer. We do not expect this change will significantly alter the scope of existing Rule 147 as we believe "principal place of business" is conceptually similar to principal office location.

Under amended Rule 147, issuers that are incorporated or organized under state or territorial law will be deemed a "resident" of a particular state or territory in which they are both incorporated or organized and have their "principal place of business." . . . Similarly, issuers that are general partnerships, or in the form of another business organization not organized under any state or territorial law, shall be deemed to be a "resident" of the state or territory in which they have their "principal place of business."

[By comparison,] new Rule 147A(c)(1) will rely solely on the principal place of business requirement to determine the state or territory in which the issuer shall be deemed a "resident," not only for corporate issuers, but for all issuers, including issuers that are not organized under any state or territorial law, such as general partnerships. . . .

We are . . . retaining the proposed principal place of business requirement. . . .

To ensure an appropriate connection between the state, issuers and investors, amended Rule 147(d) and Rule 147A(d) will require an issuer to be a resident of the same state where purchasers are resident or where the issuer reasonably believes they are resident. Viewed together, paragraphs (c) and (d) of each of Rules 147 and 147A help to ensure the local intrastate character of the offering by requiring that both issuers and purchasers reside and have their principal place of business (for purchasers, the principal place of business requirement only applies to purchasers who are legal entities) in the same state or territory where the offering takes place.

For situations where an issuer changes its principal place of business to another state after conducting an intrastate offering in reliance on Rule 147 or Rule 147A, we are adopting provisions in both rules that limit the ability of an issuer to conduct a subsequent intrastate offering pursuant to Rule 147 or Rule 147A, until such time as securities sold in reliance on the exemption in the prior state have come to rest in that state. This is consistent with the view that securities sold in an intrastate offering in one state should have to come to rest within such state before purchasers may resell their securities to out-of-state residents. Accordingly, both rules provide that issuers who have previously conducted an intrastate offering pursuant to Rule 147 or Rule 147A will not be able to conduct another subsequent intrastate offering pursuant to either rule in a different state for a period of six months from the date of the last sale in the prior state, which is consistent with the duration of the resale limitation period specified in our amendments to Rule 147(e) and new Rule 147A(e). . . .

B. Common Requirements of the Amendments to Rule 147 and New Rule 147A

Our amendments to Rule 147 and the provisions of new Rule 147A are substantially identical, *except that, as discussed above, new Rule 147A allows an issuer to make offers accessible to out-of-state residents and to be incorporated or organized out-of-state.* [emphasis supplied] Under the rules we adopt today, both amended Rule 147 and new Rule 147A will include the following provisions:

- A requirement that the issuer satisfy at least one "doing business" requirement that will demonstrate the in-state nature of the issuer's business.

- A new "reasonable belief" standard for issuers to rely upon in determining the residence of the purchaser at the time of the sale of securities.

- A requirement that issuers obtain a written representation from each purchaser as to his or her residency.

- The residence of a purchaser that is a non-natural person, such as a corporation, partnership, trust or other form of business organization, will be defined as the location where, at the time of the sale, the entity has its "principal place of business."

- A limit on resales to persons resident within the state or territory of the offering for a period of six months from the date of the sale by the issuer to the purchaser of a security sold pursuant to the exemption.

- An integration safe harbor that will include any prior offers or sales of securities by the issuer, as well as certain subsequent offers or sales of securities by the issuer occurring after the completion of the offering.

- Disclosure requirements, including legend requirements, to offerees and purchasers about the limits on resales.

1. Requirements for Issuers "Doing Business" In-State

. . . .

. . . [W]e are adopting . . . updated and modernized "doing business" requirements in Rule 147 and new Rule 147A to comport with contemporary small business practices. We believe these updated requirements will expand the universe of issuers that may rely on Section 3(a)(11) and the amended Rule 147 safe harbor, as well as new Rule 147A, to conduct exempt intrastate offerings, while continuing to require issuers to have an in-state presence sufficient to justify reliance on these provisions. Given the increasing "interstate" nature of small business activities, we believe it has become increasingly difficult for companies, even smaller companies that are physically located within a single state or territory, to satisfy the issuer "doing business" requirements of current Rule 147(c)(2). Accordingly, we believe these issuer "doing business" requirements, identical for both amended Rule 147 and new Rule 147A, will provide issuers with greater flexibility in conducting intrastate offerings and expand the availability of these two intrastate offering provisions.

. . . [W]e are adopting amendments to Rule 147(c)(2) and including provisions in new Rule 147A(c)(2) that will provide issuers with greater flexibility to satisfy the current "doing business" requirements by adding an alternative test based on the location of a majority of the issuer's employees while retaining the three 80% threshold tests in current Rule 147(c)(2). Furthermore, while the substance of the three

80% threshold requirements of current Rule 147(c)(2) is being retained in the final rules, compliance with any one of the 80% threshold requirements (or the additional test based on the majority of employees) will be sufficient to demonstrate the in-state nature of the issuer's business, as proposed. This is a change from current Rule 147(c)(2), which requires issuers to satisfy all three 80% threshold requirements.

. . . .

[In addition,] we are adding an alternative requirement to the three modified 80% threshold requirements. This requirement, which relates to the location of a majority of the issuer's employees, will provide an additional method by which an issuer may demonstrate that it conducts in-state business sufficient to justify reliance on either Rule 147 or new Rule 147A. For these purposes, we are permitting an issuer to satisfy the "doing business" requirements by having a majority of its employees based in such state or territory. An employee would be based in the same state or territory of the issuer for purposes of this test if such employee is based out of the offices located within such state or territory. For example, if an employee provides services in the Maryland, Virginia and Washington, DC metro area out of the offices of a company in Maryland, the employee would be based in Maryland for purposes of this test. . . . [W]e believe that using a majority of the employees test provides a standard that more accurately captures the increasingly flexible ways that companies structure and conduct their business operations, while still requiring that more employees be located in-state than elsewhere. Current workforce trends, such as telecommuting, whereby employees often work in a different geographical location from their employer, suggest that flexibility is particularly needed in this area. We believe adding this criterion to expand upon the current doing business requirements in Rule 147(c)(2) will provide additional flexibility to issuers by making these requirements more consistent with modern business practices, especially in light of the different roles employees play within smaller companies and the different locations in which employees carry out such roles, while still providing important indicia of the in-state nature of an issuer's business.

2. Reasonable Relief as to Purchaser Residency Status

. . . .

Consistent with . . . the determination of accredited investor status under Regulation D, we are adopting amendments to Rule 147 and a provision in new Rule 147A that will include a reasonable belief standard for the issuer's determination as to the residence of the purchaser at the time of the sale of the securities. Under the final rules, an issuer will satisfy the requirement that the purchaser in the offering be a resident of the same state or territory in which the issuer is resident by either the existence of the fact that the purchaser is a resident of the applicable state or territory, or by establishing that the issuer had a reasonable belief that the purchaser of the securities in the offering was a resident of such state or territory. Under current Rule 147(d), regardless of the efforts an issuer takes to determine that potential investors are residents of the state in which the issuer is resident, the exemption is lost for the entire offering if securities are offered or sold to just one investor that was not in fact a resident of such state. We continue to believe that permitting issuers to sell on the basis of a reasonable belief of a purchaser's in-state residency status will increase the utility of amended Rule 147 and new Rule 147A by providing issuers with additional certainty about the availability of the exemption under Section 3(a)(11) or new Rule 147A while still providing appropriate investor protections.

[In addition,] both amended Rule 147 and new Rule 147A will include a requirement that issuers obtain a written representation from each purchaser as to his or her residence. We are persuaded by those commenters who stated that this requirement should be retained and considered as evidence of, but not be dispositive of, the purchaser's residency. In the context of Section 3(a)(11), the Commission has previously indicated that "[t]he mere obtaining of formal representations of residence . . . should not be relied upon without more as establishing the availability of the exemption." Whether an issuer has formed a reasonable belief that the prospective purchaser is an in-state resident will be determined on the basis of all facts and circumstances. Obtaining a written representation from purchasers of in-state residency status will not, without more, be sufficient to establish a reasonable belief that such purchasers are in-state residents.

In addition to the written representation, other facts and circumstances could include, but will not be limited to, for example, a pre-existing relationship between the issuer and the prospective purchaser that provides the issuer with sufficient knowledge about the prospective purchaser's principal residence or principal place of business so as to enable the issuer to have a reasonable basis to believe that the prospective purchaser is an in-state resident. An issuer may also consider other facts and circumstances when establishing the residency of a prospective purchaser, such as evidence of the home address of the prospective purchaser, as documented by a recently dated utility bill, pay-stub, information contained in state or federal tax returns, any documentation issued by a federal, state, or local government authority, such as a driver's license or identification card, or a public or private database that the issuer has determined is reasonably reliable, including credit bureau databases, directory listings, and public records.

. . . .

3. Residence of Entity Purchasers

. . . .

[W]e are adopting amendments to Rule 147 and a provision in new Rule 147A that will define the residence of a purchaser that is a legal entity, such as a corporation, partnership, trust or other form of business organization, as the location where, at the time of the sale, the entity has its principal place of business. The final rules define a purchaser's "principal place of business," consistent with the definition for determining issuer residency contained in paragraph (c)(1) of Rules 147 and 147A, as the location in which the officers, partners, or managers of the entity primarily direct, control and coordinate its activities. . . .

4. Limitation Resales

. . . .

. . . [W]e are adopting a requirement in amended Rule 147 and new Rule 147A providing that for a period of six months from the date of the sale of the security by the issuer any resale of the security shall be made only to persons resident within the state or territory in which the issuer was resident at the time of the sale of the security by the issuer. We are persuaded by those commenters that indicated that a period of six months is adequate to establish that securities sold in an intrastate offering have "come to rest" in a state by analogizing to provisions of Rule 144, in which a six-month holding period is deemed sufficient to establish a requisite investment intent. In this regard, given the use of a six-month resale restriction in the Rule 144 context, we believe that a similar resale restriction in the intrastate offering context should provide adequate assurance that the securities will come to rest in-state. [Note, however, that the six-month holding period for restricted securities under Rule 144 applies to Exchange Act reporting issuers while a privately-held issuer's restricted securities must be held for 12 months under Rule 144.This subject is discussed in §6.04.]

. . . .

In light of our revision to the resale limitation to focus on the state where the issuer is a resident, we are including additional language in amended Rule 147(e) and new Rule 147A(e) to specify that all resales during this six month resale limitation period will be restricted to the state or territory in which the issuer was a resident at the time of the sale of the security by the issuer to a purchaser. Accordingly, if an issuer were to change its state or territory of residence during the six month resale limitation period, all resales would, nevertheless, continue to be limited to the state or territory in which the issuer resided at the time of the original sale of securities in reliance upon either Rule 147 or Rule 147A.We believe this additional language will preserve the intent of the proposed resale restriction—to help ensure that the securities offered pursuant to an intrastate offering exemption have come to rest within the state of the offering before being resold.

As proposed, an issuer's ability to rely on the respective rules will not be conditioned on a purchaser's compliance with Rule 147(e) and Rule 147A(e). As discussed in the Proposing Release, the application of current Rule 147(e) in the overall scheme of the safe harbor can cause uncertainty for issuers. We continue to believe that removing the condition on purchaser compliance with Rule 147(e) will increase the utility of the exemption by eliminating the uncertainty created in the offering process for issuers under the current rules. . . .

We continue to believe that eliminating this uncertainty should not result in an increased risk of issuer non-compliance with the rules, because issuers will remain subject to requirements relating to, for example, in-state limitations, legends, stop transfer instructions for transfer agents, and offeree and purchaser disclosures, in order to satisfy the exemption at the federal level. In addition, issuers will continue to be subject to the antifraud and civil liability provisions of the federal securities laws, as well as state securities law requirements.

. . . .

5. Integration

. . . .

[W]e are adopting amendments to the integration safe harbor under Rule 147 and providing an identical integration safe harbor provision in new Rule 147A. . . . The integration safe harbor will cover any prior offers or sales of securities by the issuer, as well as certain subsequent offers or sales of securities by the issuer occurring after the completion of an offering pursuant to Rule 147 or Rule 147A, as applicable. Accordingly, offers and sales made pursuant to Rule 147 and 147A will not be integrated with:

- Offers or sales of securities made prior to the commencement of offers and sales of securities pursuant to Rules 147 or 147A; or

- Offers or sales of securities made after completion of offers and sales pursuant to Rules 147 or 147A that are:

    - Registered under the Securities Act, except as provided in Rule 147(h) or Rule 147A(h);

    - Exempt from registration under Regulation A (17 CFR § 230.251 *et seq.*);

    - Exempt from registration under Rule 701 (17 CFR § 230.701);

    - Made pursuant to an employee benefit plan;

    - Exempt from registration under Regulation S (17 CFR §§ 230.901 through 230.905);

    - Exempt from registration under Section 4(a)(6) of the Act (15 U.S.C. 77d(a)(6)); or

    - Made more than six months after the completion of an offering conducted pursuant to Rules 147 or 147A.

. . . . [I]ntegration safe harbors provide issuers, particularly smaller issuers whose capital needs often change, with greater certainty about their eligibility to comply with an exemption from Securities Act registration. Consistent with . . . the approach taken in Rule 251(c) of Regulation A, the safe harbor from integration provided by Rule 147(g) and Rule 147A(g) will expressly provide that any offer or sale made in reliance on the respective rules will not be integrated with any other offer or sale made either before the commencement of, or more than six months after the completion of, the respective intrastate offerings under either Rule 147 or Rule 147A. For transactions that fall within the scope of the safe harbor, issuers will not have to conduct an integration analysis of the terms of any offering being conducted under the other specified provisions in order to determine whether the two offerings would be treated as one for purposes of qualifying for either exemption. . . .

The bright-line integration safe harbor we are adopting in amended Rule 147(g) and new Rule 147A(g) will assist issuers, particularly smaller issuers, in analyzing certain transactions, but will not address the issue of potential offers or sales that occur concurrently with, or close in time after, a Rule 147 or 147A offering. There is no presumption that offerings outside the integration safe harbors should be integrated. Rather, whether concurrent or subsequent offers and sales of securities will be integrated with any securities offered or sold pursuant to amended Rule 147 or new Rule 147A will depend on the particular facts and circumstances, including whether each offering complies with the requirements of the exemption that is being relied upon for the particular offering. . . .

6. Disclosures to Investors

. . . .

. . . [W]e are adopting amendments to Rule 147 and a provision in new Rule 147A that will require issuers to make specified disclosures to offerees and purchasers about the limitations on resale contained in Rules 147(e) and 147A(e), respectively. Issuers will also be required to meet the legend requirement of Rules 147(f)(1)(i) and 147A(f)(1)(i), respectively. Although the disclosure should be prominently disclosed to each offeree and purchaser at the time any offer or sale is made by the issuer to such person, the amendment and new rule will not require that such disclosure be made in writing in all instances.

. . . . We believe the approach we are adopting—requiring issuers to provide the disclosure to offerees in the same manner in which an offer is communicated—will provide appropriate flexibility to issuers in the conduct of their offerings and avoid potential confusion as to when, for example, an oral offer must be followed up with a written disclosure. Requiring the disclosure to be made orally if the offer is made orally also will help ensure that the investor receives the required disclosure when most relevant (i.e., immediately upon learning about the offer). Furthermore, we believe our amendments to Rule 147(f)(3) and the provision in new Rule 147A(f)(3) will maintain appropriate investor protections, especially in light of the new provision requiring issuers to provide written disclosure to all purchasers within a reasonable period of time before the date of sale. We note that this requirement to provide written disclosure a reasonable period of time before the date of sale is consistent with the disclosure delivery requirements of Regulation D and Rule 701. Finally, while we are not adopting commenters' suggestions to require that written disclosure be provided to all offerees, nothing in our rules prevents state regulators, that deem it necessary and appropriate, from requiring such written disclosures for offers to residents within their states. State regulators are in a position to tailor any such rules to their local capital markets in a manner that addresses capital market practices and investor protection measures they deem appropriate for offers and sales to residents of their state.

. . . .

Finally, in order for the required disclosure to offerees and purchasers under amended Rule 147(f) and new Rule 147A(f) to be as clear as possible, and consistent with our revisions to make the issuer's state of residency the focus of the relevant resale restrictions, we are adding a requirement that the issuer identify in this disclosure the particular state or territory in which the issuer was resident at the time of the original sale of the security. Since a small business may change the location of its residence and principal activities within the six-month resale limitation period provided for in amended Rule 147(e) and new Rule 147A(e), we believe this information, which should be readily available to the issuer, will assist purchasers in understanding the implications of the applicable resale restrictions.

. . . .

The following chart summarizes key conditions and requirements for complying with the Rule 147 and 147A intrastate offering exemptions.

SEC Intrastate Offering Exemptions Safe Harbor[71]	
SEC Rule 147	**SEC Rule 147A**
(Legal Authority) — Section 3(a)(11) of Securities Act of 1933.	*(Legal Authority)* — Section 28 of Securities Act of 1933 — general exemptive authority.
(Required Element) Offers and sales are made only to persons resident within the same state or territory in which the issuer is resident and doing business.	*No requirement to limit offers to a single state or territory.*
	(Required Element) Sales must be limited to persons resident within the same state or territory in which the issuer is resident and doing business.
(Required Element) The issuer of the securities shall be incorporated or organized, and shall have its principal place of business in the offering state or territory.	*No requirement as to state or territory of formation of business entity.*
(Required Element) The issuer shall be deemed to have its principal place of business in a state or territory in which the officers, partners, or managers of the issuer primarily direct, control, and coordinate the activities of the issuer.	
(Intrastate Alternative Element) The issuer derived at least 80% of its consolidated gross revenues from the operation of a business or of real property located in or from the rendering of services within the offering state or territory; *or*	
(Intrastate Alternative Element) The issuer had, at the end of its most recent semi-annual fiscal period prior to an initial offer of securities in any offering or subsequent offering pursuant to Rule 147 or Rule 147A, at least 80% of its assets and those of its subsidiaries on a consolidated basis located within such state or territory; *or*	
(Intrastate Alternative Element) The issuer intends to use and uses at least 80% of the net proceeds to the issuer from sales made pursuant to Rule 147 in connection with the operation of a business or of real property, the purchase of real property located in, or the rendering of services within such state or territory; *or*	

---

71. This chart is authored by Mr. John R. Fahy, a superb securities attorney, and is included herein with Mr. Fahy's permission. The chart has been slightly adapted by Professor Steinberg.

(Intrastate Alternative Element) A majority of the issuer's employees are based in such state or territory.
(Required Element) For a period of six months from the date of the sale by the issuer of a security pursuant to Rule 147 or Rule 147A, any resale of the security acquired in the Rule 147 or Rule 147A offering shall be made only to persons resident within the state or territory in which the issuer was resident at the time of the sale of the security, including securities held by a gift recipient.
(Required Element) Issuer shall place a prominent legend on the security certificate or other like document stating that: "Offers and sales of these securities were made under an exemption from registration and have not been registered under the Securities Act of 1933. For a period of six months from the date of the sale by the issuer of these securities, any resale of these securities (or the underlying securities in the case of convertible securities) shall be made only to persons resident within the state or territory of [Illinois] (offering state)."
(Required Element) Issuer shall issue stop transfer instructions to the issuer's transfer agent, if any, with respect to the securities, or, if the issuer transfers its own securities, make a notation in the appropriate records of the issuer.
(Required Element) Issuer shall obtain a written representation from each purchaser as to his or her residence.
(Required Element) The issuer shall, at the time of any offer or sale by it of a security pursuant to Rule 147 and Rule 147A, prominently disclose to each offeree in the manner in which any such offer is communicated and to each purchaser of such security in writing a reasonable period of time before the date of sale, the following: "Sales will be made only to residents of [identify the name of the state or territory in which the issuer is resident—e.g., *Illinois*]. Offers and sales of these securities are made under an exemption from registration and have not been registered under the Securities Act of 1933. For a period of six months from the date of the sale by the issuer of the securities, any resale of the securities (or the underlying securities in the case of convertible securities) shall be made only to persons resident within the state or territory of [Illinois]."

Note

By comparison, the American Law Institute's (ALI) Federal Securities Code sets forth a different approach: The ALI Code labels such offerings "local offerings" and does not confine them to a single state. Section 514 of the ALI Code focuses solely on purchasers of securities rather than offerees. State lines under § 514 no longer are necessarily controlling as the SEC is given authority, after evaluating economic characteristics and population, to define contiguous areas encompassing a number of states or a state and a contiguous foreign country. Moreover, § 514 permits up to five percent of the securities in such an offering to be sold to no more than five percent of all purchasers who neither work nor reside in the localized area.

Prior to consultation with and determination by the SEC to support the ALI Code, § 514 permitted up to 20 percent of the securities in a "local offering" to be sold to no more than five percent of "non-local" purchasers. In view of the provision's objective of facilitating local financing for local businesses, the SEC believed that the percent of securities sold "non-locally" should be decreased. The change to five percent was subsequently made. In SEC Securities Act Release No. 6242 (1980), the SEC announced its support for congressional enactment of the ALI Code, provided that revisions it sought and obtained from the ALI Reporter (the eminent Professor Louis Loss) and his group of advisers were not significantly amended during the legislative process. The ALI Code, however, has not been introduced in either the U.S. House of Representatives or the Senate and its prospects for enactment are dim.

The rationale underlying the ALI approach is that the underpinnings of the "local offering" exemption are met by § 514, namely, "the probability that investors in local enterprise will have adequate familiarity with [such enterprises] and an acknowledgment that [local] issuers will be relatively small and thus less able to bear the burden of federal registration." Deaktor, *Integration of Securities Offerings*, 31 U. Fla. L. Rev. 465, 481 (1979).

Does § 514 of the ALI Code go too far or not far enough? While the five percent level leaves room for an issuer to retain the exemption if it makes a good faith error about a purchaser's residence or place of work, is the ALI Code correct in concentrating on purchasers only, ignoring issuer solicitation of "non-local" offerees if those individuals never purchase? Under the Code, it appears that, within the § 514 exemption, an issuer theoretically could engage in extensive solicitation in distant states so long as the percentage of purchasers and the securities sold come within the five percent level.[72] Is this proper? Moreover, the SEC is given authority under § 514 to define contiguous areas, including states, territories, and foreign countries, that come within the local offering exemption. Does this mean, for example, that the SEC, in its discretion, could define the following areas as within the § 514 exemption: (1) the District of Columbia, Maryland, and Virginia; and (2) Florida, Georgia, and the Bahamas? If so, does this make good policy, particularly in view that this exemption provides for no delivery of information to prospective purchasers, hence leaving any specified disclosure solely to the "local" jurisdiction?

<hr>

§ 3.14 Recapitalizations and Reorganizations— The § 3(a)(9) and § 3(a)(10) Exemptions

Section 3(a)(9) of the Securities Act exempts from the registration requirements certain bona fide recapitalizations, namely: "Except with respect to a security exchanged in a case under Title 11 of the United States Code [also known as the U.S. Bankruptcy Code], any security exchanged by the issuer with its existing security holders exclusively where no commission or other remuneration is paid or given directly or indirectly for soliciting such exchange." For example, a conversion of debentures into stock serves as an example. The exchange must be bona

<hr>

72. On a practical level, the individual states, pursuant to their "blue sky" statutes, may well prohibit such activity.

fide—not merely an attempt to avoid the Securities Act's registration requirements. To come within this exemption, the following requirements must be met: "[1] The issuer of both securities must be the same; [2] . . . [N]o part of the offering may be made to persons other than existing security holders, or even to existing security holders otherwise than by way of the exchange; [and] [3] There may be no paid solicitation."[73]

Section 3(a)(10) generally exempts from registration securities that are issued in exchange for bona fide legal claims, securities, or property interests when a court or other specified tribunal, after conducting an adversary proceeding on the transaction's fairness, grants such approval. Traditionally, the § 3(a)(10) exemption has been invoked in three situations:(1) settlement of private lawsuits; (2) reorganization of insolvent business organizations outside of bankruptcy litigation; and (3) reorganization of solvent business organizations.[74]

In a relatively recent release, the SEC staff set forth the following conditions for compliance with the § 3(a)(10) exemption:

1. The securities must be issued in exchange for securities, claims, or property interests; they cannot be offered for cash.

2. A court or authorized governmental entity must approve the fairness of the terms and conditions of the exchange.

3. The reviewing court or authorized governmental entity must:

[a] find, before approving the transaction, that the terms and conditions of the exchange are fair to those to whom securities will be issued; and

[b] be advised before the hearing that the issuer will rely on the § 3(a)(10) exemption based on the court's or authorized governmental entity's approval of the transaction.

4. The court or authorized governmental entity must hold a hearing before approving the fairness of the terms and conditions of the transaction.

5. A governmental entity must be expressly authorized by law to hold the hearing, although it is not necessary that the law require the hearing.

6. The fairness hearing must be open to everyone to whom securities would be issued in the proposed exchange.

7. Adequate notice must be given to all those persons.

---

73. LOUIS LOSS & JOEL SELIGMAN, SECURITIES REGULATION 1229–30 (3d ed. 1989).

74. *See generally* J.W. HICKS, EXEMPTED TRANSACTIONS UNDER THE SECURITIES ACT OF 1933 § 3.02 (2016); Glanzer, Schiffman & Packman, *Settlement of Securities Litigation Through the Issuance of Securities Without Registration: The Use of § 3(a)(10) in SEC Enforcement Proceedings*, 50 FORDHAM L. REV. 533 (1981); Mann, *The Section 3(a)(10) Exemption: Recent Interpretations*, 22 U.C.L.A. L. REV. 1247 (1975).

8. There cannot be any improper impediments to the appearance by those persons at the hearing.[75]

While both the § 3(a)(9) and § 3(a)(10) exemptions reflect Congress' concern for the financially troubled enterprise that seeks internal readjustment without having to comply with the 1933 Act's costs of registration, an issuer may have a number of motives for utilizing these exemptions. Indeed, the financial status of an issuer does not affect the availability of these exemptions. For example, in practice, the § 3(a)(10) exemption "has been availed of almost exclusively by financially sound issuers involved in reorganization or other exchanges for a variety of legitimate ongoing business purposes."[76]

---

§ 3.15 Integration of Offerings

Under the concept of integration of offerings, what apparently may seem to be separate offerings instead are construed as one integrated offering. Because of the fairly distinct requirements for each exemption, otherwise exempt offerings may not qualify for an exemption once they are integrated, thereby resulting in a violation of the Securities Act's registration requirements. Moreover, if a purported exempt offering is integrated with a registered offering, the exemption will be destroyed, again resulting in liability.

As a general principle, in determining whether offers and/or sales should be integrated, more than 50 years ago, the SEC set forth a five-factor analysis:

(1) Whether the offerings are part of a single plan of financing;

(2) Whether the offerings involve issuance of the same class of securities;

(3) Whether the offerings have been made at or about the same time;

(4) Whether the same type of consideration is received; and

(5) Whether the offerings are made for the same general purposes.

Securities Act Release No. 4552 (1962). Unless a safe harbor from integration (or other guidance negating integration) applies, the SEC and the courts continue to apply this analysis. *See, e.g., Securities and Exchange Commission v. Murphy*, 626 F.2d 633 (9th Cir. 1980) (integrating purportedly separate offerings); *Donohoe v. Consolidated Operating & Production Corporation*, 982 F.2d 1130 (7th Cir. 1992) (applying five-factor

---

75. Staff Legal Bulletin 3A (CF) (issued by the SEC Division of Corporation Finance), Fed. Sec. L. Rep. (CCH) ¶ 60,003 (2008).

76. Ash, *Reorganizations and Other Exchanges Under Section 3(a)(10) of the Securities Act of 1933*, 75 Nw. U. L. Rev. 1, 10 (1980). *See* Hicks, *Recapitalization Under Section 3(a)(9) of the Securities Act of 1933*, 61 Va. L. Rev. 1057, 1060–1061 (1975).

analysis, court held that separate offerings were distinct, and, hence, would not be integrated).

In order to provide greater certainty for issuers, the SEC, pursuant to its rulemaking authority, has adopted integration "safe harbor" rules in certain contexts. For example, Rule 502(a) in part provides:

> Offers and sales that are made more than six months before the start of a Regulation D offering or are made more than six months after completion of a Regulation D offering will not be considered part of that Regulation D offering, so long as during those six month periods there are no offers or sales of securities by or for the issuer that are of the same or a similar class as those offered or sold under Regulation D. . . .

In 2007, the SEC proposed to decrease this six-month period to 90 days. *See* Securities Act Release No. 8828 (2007). To date, this proposal has not been adopted.

Rule 147(b)(2), as another example, has a similar six-month "safe harbor" from integration with respect to the intrastate offering exemption.

Remember that Rules 147(b)(2) and 502(a) are "safe harbor" provisions. If the issuer engages in offers or sales during the six-month period prior to commencement or after completion of the purportedly exempt offerings, the five-factor analysis outlined above will be applied to determine whether the apparently separate offerings should be integrated.

The SEC also has adopted Rule 155, which provides under certain circumstances "safe harbors" from Securities Act integration "for a registered offering following an abandoned private offering, or a private offering following an abandoned registered offering." Securities Act Release No. 7943 (2001). In the Rule 155 adopting release, the SEC stated:

> The new integration safe harbors that we adopt today as new Rule 155 provide clarity and certainty regarding two common situations, and do not otherwise affect traditional integration analyses. Under Rule 155, we provide conditions under which an issuer that begins a private offering but sells no securities will be able to abandon it and begin a registered offering. Any private offering that relies on this integration safe harbor will need to satisfy the conditions of a private offering exemption, so that the private offering is bona fide. In addition, the issuer and any person acting on its behalf will need to terminate all offering activity with respect to the private offering. Any prospectus filed as part of the registration statement will need to include disclosure regarding abandonment of the private offering. The issuer also will need to wait 30 days after abandoning the private offering before filing the registration statement unless securities were offered in the private offering only to persons who were (or who the issuer reasonably believes were) accredited investors or sophisticated.

New Rule 155 also provides an integration safe harbor that will permit an issuer that started a registered offering to withdraw the registration statement before any securities are sold and then begin a private offering. To use the safe harbor, the issuer and any person acting on its behalf will need to wait 30 days after the effective date of withdrawal of the registration statement before commencing the private offering. The issuer must provide each offeree in the private offering with information concerning withdrawal of the registration statement, the fact that the private offering is unregistered and the legal implication of its unregistered status. In addition, any disclosure document used in the private offering must disclose any changes in the issuer's business or financial condition that occurred after the issuer filed the registration statement that are material to the investment decision in the private offering.[77]

Due to the application of these safe harbors from integration of offerings, as well as other recent SEC pronouncements, the risk of such integration of offerings resulting in a Securities Act registration violation has been diminished (although by no means eliminated). As stated by one "Wall Street" securities lawyer, recent SEC guidance does not alter the status quo with respect to intra-Regulation D offerings (such as Rule 506(b) and Rule 506(c) offerings). On the other hand, the SEC has indicated that no such integration of offerings will occur for "concurrent and serial combinations of Rule 506 offerings with each of Regulation A, proposed Rule 147, and Regulation Crowdfunding, so long as solicitation and advertising in one offering does not improperly condition the market for the other [offering(s)]. This unitary framework . . . displaces the Five-Factor Test where it is applied. In addition, updated safe harbors provide air-tight assurance of non-integration in certain other contexts. As a result, companies will face less integration risk, which may unlock significant value in combining different offering methods."[78]

The policies underlying the concept of integration entail important "trade-offs" between investor protection and capital formation. As asserted by one source:

---

77. Note that Rule 152 remains viable after the adoption of Rule 155. As stated by Professor Hicks:

> An important exception to the integration doctrine is found in Rule 152. In 1999, the SEC adopted Rule 155, which addresses the integration of abandoned offerings. The SEC made clear in the Adopting Release that Rule 152 and related SEC staff interpretations as when an offering is deemed "completed" are unaffected by Rule 155. Rule 152 applies to an issuer that sells securities privately under Section 4(2) and then shortly thereafter sells additional securities in a public offering. Technically, Rule 152 is only applicable where the issuer's decision to make a public offering is formed after the completion of the Section 4(2) offering. . . .

J.W. Hicks, Limited Offering Exemptions: Regulation D § 3:9 (2016). *See* Jones, *The Doctrine of Securities Act "Integration"*, 29 Sec. Reg. L.J. 320 (2001).

78. Parsont, *The SEC's Evolving Integration Doctrine: New Guidance on Combining Offering Methods*, 48 Sec. Reg. & L. Rep. (BNA) 35, 36 (2016).

Integration under the 1933 Act is designed to prevent an issuer from avoiding registration of a nonexempt transaction by accomplishing the transaction through two or more ostensibly distinct offerings each of which, if treated as a separate transaction, would conform to the [exemptive provisions]. Presumably, integration is justifiable as a protective device for investors; however, other significant interests are involved. From the issuer's standpoint, the importance of precision in the structure and timing of securities offerings necessitates a clear definition of the circumstances under which integration will be applicable. . . . [A]n issuer uncertain of the applicability of integration to a proposed offering may be forced to forego the proposed offering altogether or to adjust its characteristics significantly to avoid a potential violation of the registration requirements. Either course of action may entail considerable hardship for the issuer.

Deaktor, *Integration of Securities Offerings*, 31 U. Fla. L. Rev. 465, 473-74 (1979).

Is the SEC's five-factor analysis too ambiguous, or is it the best formulation under the circumstances? After all, in many exempt offerings, issuers will have the availability of SEC integration safe harbor rules. Moreover, the SEC staff, in appropriate circumstances, will provide a requester with a "no-action" letter in the "integration" context. The courts, by their use of the SEC's standard, apparently have not found a better alternative.

A subcommittee of the American Bar Association's Section of Corporation, Banking and Business Law issued a Position Paper, setting forth proposed guidelines for identifying discrete offerings that should not be integrated in the partnership offering context. ABA Subcommittee on Partnerships, Trusts, and Unincorporated Associations, *Integration of Partnership Offerings: A Proposal for Identifying a Discrete Offering*, 37 Bus. Law. 1591, 1610 (1982). Generally, under the proposal, "a discrete offering in the partnership context exists when the offering is designed to fund a separate and independent entity that is not financially dependent upon any entity created through any other offering involving a common sponsor." Responding to the subcommittee's proposal, Professor Morrissey has stated:

The American Bar Association's "discrete offering" proposal is merely an elegant attempt to circumvent the registration process by artificially expanding its carefully restricted exemptions. The various financial dealings of issuers are separable, but not on the basis of contrived divisions. Even though closely timed offerings may be "financially independent" in that they have claims to different assets, they are, in reality, part of a continual attempt to fund one business operation. In such situations . . . investors need information about the central enterprise. If a combination of offerings will place the total issuance outside the well-considered exemptions to registration, an SEC registration filing is in order.

Morrissey, *Integration of Securities Offerings — The ABA's "Indiscreet" Proposal*, 26 Ariz. L. Rev. 41, 76-77 (1984).

On the other hand, Professor Wallace views the integration analysis currently applied by the courts and the SEC as posing an undue impediment to capital formation:

> The integration doctrine continues to frustrate issuers engaged in the capital formation process, engulfing them in a sea of ambiguity, uncertainty, and potential liability. Although the doctrine was created out of a legitimate concern that the investor protection mandate of the Securities Act of 1933 not be thwarted, the doctrine's development has left unresolved many serious problems. The integration doctrine has elusive formulas, with subjective, unweighted, and overlapping terms, and the doctrine's safe harbors have arbitrarily derived time intervals. Finally, the application of the doctrine by the courts, the SEC, and the SEC staff has often resulted in vague and inconsistent pronouncements.

Wallace, *Integration of Securities Offerings: Obstacles to Capital Formation Remain for Small Businesses*, 45 Wash. & Lee L. Rev. 883, 989 (1988).[79] *See generally* Bloomenthal, *SEC Exemptions from Registration — A New Look*, 45 U. Cin. L. Rev. 367 (1976); Campbell, *The Overwhelming Case for Elimination of the Integration Doctrine Under the Securities Act of 1993*, 89 Ky. L.J. 289 (2000–2001); Cohn, *Keep Securities Reform Moving: Eliminate the SEC's Integration Doctrine*, 44 Hofstra L. Rev. 3 (2015).

---

§ 3.16 State "Blue Sky" Law Exemptions

With certain exceptions and subject to the preemptive provisions of the National Securities Markets Improvement Act of 1996, unless an exemption from state registration is perfected, any offer or sale within a particular state must be registered. The result is that perfecting a federal exemption from registration frequently is only half the battle. Exemptions often must be found on the state level in any state where the security is offered or sold.

For decades, there was little uniformity between the federal and state exemption framework. The promulgation of the Uniform Limited Offering Exemption by the North American Securities Administrators Association (NASAA) and its subsequent adoption (in whole or substantial part) by several states eased this uniformity problem. With qualifications, the Uniform Limited Offering Exemption exempts offerings sold in compliance with Rules 501–503 and 505 of SEC Regulation D.[80] In certain respects, however, the NASAA Exemption is more protective of investor interests than

---

79. *See* Taylor & Smith, *Exploitation or Opportunity?*, Sports Illustrated, Aug. 12, 1991, at 46, 52 (profiling Professor Perry Wallace "who [playing for the Vanderbilt Commodores] in the winter of 1967–68 became the Southeastern Conference's first black varsity basketball player").

80. Rule 504, discussed in § 3.07[A], leaves solely to the individual states the authority to prescribe disclosure of specified information and certain other requirements with respect to offerings

Regulation D. For example, investor sophistication or suitability standards may apply in Rule 505 offerings (unlike the SEC's 505).

The attitude of certain states in favor of strong investor protection provisions is intriguing when compared to the "race to the bottom" approach[81] taken by some of these very same states under the applicable corporation laws. Perhaps one response is that the state securities laws are designed in part to protect the individual investor against so-called speculative "shady" promoters, while enabling corporation laws favoring management hopefully will induce publicly held companies to incorporate within the respective states, thereby bringing in a welcome source of revenues in the form of franchise fees. Do you agree with this interpretation? What other reason(s) may account for this apparent anomaly?

In Securities Act Release No. 6561 (1984), the SEC stated:

> A dual system of federal-state securities regulation has existed since the adoption of a federal regulatory structure in the Securities Act of 1933 (the "Securities Act"). Issuers attempting to raise capital through securities offerings are responsible for complying with federal securities laws as well as with all the appropriate state regulations. In recent years it has been recognized that there is a need to increase uniformity between federal and state regulatory systems and among the various state systems and to improve cooperation among those regulatory bodies so that capital formation can be made easier while appropriate investor protections are retained.

> The importance of facilitating greater uniformity in securities regulation was endorsed by Congress with the enactment of Section 19(c) of the Securities Act in the Small Business Investment Incentive Act of 1980 (the "Investment Incentive Act"). Section 19(c) authorizes the Commission to cooperate with any association of state securities regulators which can assist in carrying out the declared policy and purpose of Section 19(c). The declared policy of the section is that there should be greater federal and state cooperation in securities matters, including: (1) maximum effectiveness of regulation; (2) maximum uniformity in federal and state regulatory standards; (3) minimum interference with the business of capital formation; and (4) a substantial reduction in costs and paperwork to diminish the burdens of raising investment capital, particularly by small business, and to diminish costs of the administration of the government programs involved. . . .

> Congress specifically acknowledged the need for a uniform limited offering exemption in enacting Section 19(c) of the Securities Act and authorized the Commission to cooperate with NASAA in its development. Working

---

made within the parameters of that exemption. State regulation of offerings under Rule 506 is preempted.

81. *See, e.g.,* Cary, *Federalism and Corporate Law: Reflections Upon Delaware*, 83 YALE L.J. 663 (1974).

with the states, the Commission developed Regulation D, the federal regulation governing exempt limited offerings. Regulation D was adopted by the Commission in March 1982. On September 21, 1983, NASAA endorsed a revised form of the Uniform Limited Offering Exemption ("ULOE") that is intended to coordinate with Regulation D and to be uniform among the states.

ULOE provides a uniform exemption from state registration for small issuers. A small issuer raising capital in a state which has adopted ULOE may take advantage of both a state registration exemption and a federal exemption under Regulation D. . . . Adoption of ULOE by all states is a major priority. The Commission and NASAA hope to encourage [all of the] states to adopt ULOE in order to achieve the goal of uniformity envisioned by the statute.

This accommodation did not entirely persuade the U.S. Congress. In an effort to reduce overlapping regulation and simplify the regulatory framework, Congress enacted the National Securities Markets Improvement Act of 1996. This reallocation of regulatory authority, including the preemption of state regulation of certain exempt offerings, represents a major change in the federal-state relationship in the securities law setting.

In addition to preempting Rule 506 offerings, the 1996 federal legislation defines the following as "covered" securities, thereby providing the SEC with exclusive authority over the registration of such securities:

(1) securities issued by investment companies registered with the Commission under the Investment Company Act of 1940 (Investment Company Act); (2) securities offered or sold to "qualified purchasers," as that term will be defined by Commission rule; (3) all securities that are listed or authorized for listing on the New York Stock Exchange (NYSE), the American Stock Exchange (AMEX), or quoted on the Nasdaq National Market System (NMS), or listed or authorized for listing on any other national securities exchange that the Commission finds has listing standards that are "substantially similar" to these exchanges or Nasdaq. . . . and (4) securities issued in connection with certain specified transactions that are exempt under the Securities Act.[82]

Not surprisingly, states are displeased with having their securities laws and regulations preempted. The most recent example was the state challenge to Regulation A Tier 2 offerings, which was rejected by the U.S. Court of Appeals. This decision,

---

82. Bagnell & Cannon, *The National Securities Markets Improvement Act of 1996: Summary and Analysis*, 25 SEC. REG. L.J. 3, 5–6 (1997). *See* Campbell, *The Impact of NSMIA on Small Issuers*, 53 BUS. LAW 575 (1998); Friedman, *The Impact of NSMIA on State Regulation of Broker-Dealers and Investment Advisers*, 53 BUS. LAW. 511 (1998); Miller & O'Brien, *The National Securities Markets Improvement Act of 1996*, 30 REV. SEC. & COMM. REG. 23 (1997); Sargent, *The National Securities Improvement Act — One Year Later*, 53 BUS. LAW. 507 (1998).

Lindeen v. SEC, 825 F.3d 646 (D.C. Cir. 2016), upholding the validity of Regulation A Tier 2 and its preemption of state law, is in § 3.07[D] of this Chapter.

---

§ 3.17 Regulation S — Offshore Offerings

Although not an exemption from Securities Act registration, adherence to the provisions of Regulation S signifies that the registration mandates of § 5 are not applicable. Regulation S (adopted in Securities Release Act No. 6863 [1990]) represents an attempt by the SEC to clarify the extraterritorial application of the 1933 Act's registration requirements. This effort seeks to ease undue regulatory burdens on issuers and those seeking to resell, thereby fostering a more efficient international securities market.[83]

In Regulation S, the SEC embraced a territorial approach to the extraterritorial application of registration under the Securities Act. This approach is based on the notion that the registration requirements of the Securities Act are intended to protect the U.S. capital markets and all investors in such markets, whether U.S. residents or foreign nationals. Regulation S represents a change in emphasis, from attempting to protect U.S. persons irrespective of where they are located, to protecting the integrity of the U.S. capital markets. For registration purposes, the Commission decided to rely upon the laws in the jurisdictions in which the transactions occur rather than the U.S. Securities Act. The Commission stated: "The territorial approach recognizes the primacy of the laws in which a market is located. As investors choose their markets, they choose the laws and regulations applicable in such markets." Adherence to this approach is premised on the principles of comity and the expectations of participants in the global markets. The territorial approach thus forms the basis of the Regulation S regulatory framework.[84]

Regulation S is comprised of four rules: Rule 901, 902, 903, and 904. Rule 901 contains a general statement that reflects the SEC's new territorial approach. Rule 901(a) states that only offers and sales of securities inside the United States are subject to § 5. This statement reflects a shift from previous SEC policy (namely, that § 5 was to protect all U.S. citizens no matter where such persons lived or invested) to a basically geographical approach under Regulation S.

The primary inquiry under the new regulatory scheme, as stated in Rule 901, is whether the offer and sale of securities occurs "outside the United States." If the offer and sale are outside the United States within the meaning of Rule 901, the registration provisions of § 5 are not applicable; if the offer or sale occurs within the United

---

83. *See* Wolff, *Offshore Distributions Under the Securities Act of 1933: An Analysis of Regulation S*, 23 L. & Pol'y Int'l Bus. 101 (1991–1992).

84. *See* Securities Act Release No. 6863 (1990); Thalacker, *Reproposed Regulation S*, 683 PLI/Corp. 799 (1990).

States, the registration provisions (absent the perfection of an exemption) are applicable. However, determining whether an offer and sale have occurred outside the United States is not necessarily an easy matter to resolve.

The SEC provides that whether an offer and sale are made outside the United States is to be determined on an ad hoc basis. To clarify when an offer and sale will be considered outside the United States, Regulation S provides two nonexclusive safe harbor provisions in Rules 903 and 904. If the offer and sale satisfy the conditions of either of the safe harbor provisions, such transaction will be deemed to have occurred outside the United States and outside the reach of § 5. Hence, perfecting a safe harbor provides assurance that the registration provisions of the Securities Act will not apply.

Regulation S comprises two safe harbor provisions: (1) an issuer safe harbor (Rule 903) and (2) a safe harbor for resales (Rule 904). All offers and sales, whether made in reliance on the issuer or the resale safe harbor, must satisfy two general conditions. In addition, the issuer must satisfy specific conditions that are set out in each safe harbor provision.

General Conditions

The general conditions applicable to all offers and sales, whether based on the issuer or resale safe harbor, are that: (1) the offer or sale is made in an "offshore transaction;" and (2) there are no "direct selling efforts" in the United States in connection with the distribution or resale of the securities.[85] To engage in an "offshore transaction" there can be no offer or sale to a person in the United States and either of two additional requirements must be satisfied. The first of the alternative requirements is that the buyer is outside the United States, or the seller reasonably believes that the buyer is outside of the United States, at the time the buy order is originated.[86] If an employee of an entity formed under the laws of the United States places the buy order while abroad, the requirement that the buyer be outside the United States is satisfied. The second alternative means of satisfying the "offshore transaction" requirement is to execute the transaction on a designated offshore securities market. However, if the seller or its agent knows that the transaction has been pre-arranged with a buyer in the United States, the second alternative will not be satisfied.

The second general condition that must be satisfied in order for an offer and sale to be considered "outside the United States" is that there be no "direct selling efforts"

---

85. Rule 903(a), (b). *See* McLaughlin, *"Directed Selling Efforts" Under Regulation S and the U.S. Securities Analyst*, 24 Rev. Sec. & Comm. Reg. 117 (1991). These two conditions are herein referred to as "general conditions."

86. Reversing the approach in Securities Act Release 4708, Regulation S defines "U.S. Person" as "any natural person resident in the United States," rather than a U.S. citizen regardless of location. Rule 902(o)(1)(i). Therefore, selling to a U.S. citizen living abroad will not automatically prevent the transaction from being considered an offshore transaction. However, Rule 902(i) makes clear that offers and sales specifically targeted at identifiable groups of U.S. citizens abroad, such as members of the armed forces, will not be offshore transactions. Rule 902(i)(2). The phrase "offshore transaction" is defined in Rule 902(i). *Id.*

in the United States. For purposes of the issuer safe harbor, neither the issuer, distributors, nor their respective affiliates may engage in direct selling efforts in the United States. Failure to adhere to this condition will result in loss of the safe harbor for all participants in the offering. "Directed selling efforts" are defined as any activity that could reasonably be expected to have the effect of conditioning the market in the United States for any of the securities being offered in reliance on Regulation S. Specifically, placing advertisements with television or radio stations reaching the United States or in publications with a general circulation in the United States, mailing printed material to U.S. investors, or conducting promotional seminars in the United States are considered "direct selling efforts." Rule 902(b), however, excludes certain types of advertising from the definition of "direct selling efforts." These exceptions include, for example, "tombstone" advertisements that are placed in publications that have less than 20 percent of their total circulation in the United States. Additionally, sellers are permitted to visit and inspect real estate and other facilities located in the United States without engaging in "direct selling efforts."

Issuer Safe Harbor — Rule 903

The "issuer" safe harbor is applicable not only to the actual issuer but also to the issuer's distributors, their respective affiliates, and persons acting on behalf of the foregoing.[87] The safe harbor may be utilized by both U.S. and foreign issuers offering securities outside the United States. Similar to the previous SEC policy, the conditions that must be satisfied to meet the issuer safe harbor differ depending on the type of securities being offered. For purposes of Regulation S, the SEC separates securities into three categories: Category I, Category II and Category III. The categorization of securities is based on the likelihood that the securities will flow back to the United States. As the probability that the securities will flow back to the United States increases, the procedural requirements necessary to avoid registration become more difficult. Under the Regulation S regulatory scheme, Category I securities are subject to the least regulatory restraints and Category III securities are subject to the most.[88]

Category I securities are securities of "foreign issuers" for which there is no "substantial U.S. market interest,"[89] securities offered and sold in "overseas directed

---

87. Rule 903. Therefore, references to the term "issuer" hereinafter will refer to the issuer, its distributors, and any of their respective affiliates, or any person acting on behalf of the foregoing.

88. See SEC Release No. 6863 (1990). *See* Cogan & Kimbrough, *Regulation S Safe Harbors for Offshore Offers, Sales and Resales*, 4 INSIGHTS No. 8, at 3 (1990).

89. Whether a "substantial U.S. market interest" exist depends on the type of security being offered. Generally, if the foreign issuer is offering equity securities, a substantial U.S. market interest is deemed to exist at the commencement of the offering if: (1) the securities exchanges and inter-dealer quotation systems in the United States in the aggregate constitute the single largest market for such securities; or (2) 20 percent or more of the trading of the class of securities took place on a securities exchange or inter-dealer quotation system located in the United States and less than 55 percent of such trading took place in a foreign securities market. Rule 902(n).

offerings,"[90] securities which are backed by the full faith and credit of a "foreign government," and securities sold pursuant to certain employee benefit plans. Because the SEC concluded that these securities were the least likely to flow back to the United States, it put only minimal procedural requirements upon them.[91] Accordingly, to satisfy the issuer safe harbor, an issuer of Category I securities need only satisfy the general conditions described above: (1) an "offshore transaction;" and (2) no "direct selling efforts" in the United States. Under the Category I issuer safe harbor, sales to U.S. investors overseas are permissible. Nonetheless, participants should be cognizant of preliminary note 2 to Regulation S which excludes from the regulation's protection any plan or scheme to evade the registration provisions of the Securities Act. In sum, prior to the promulgation of Regulation S, the applicability of the federal securities laws to offerings falling under Category I was unclear. Today, Regulation S clarifies the reach of the Securities Act's registration requirements in this context and sets forth relatively minimal regulatory burdens with respect to such offerings.

Offerings falling within the second issuer safe harbor, Category II, are those by foreign and U.S. companies that are subject to the Exchange Act's reporting requirements as well as offerings of debt securities by non-reporting foreign issuers. To qualify for the Category II issuer safe harbor, the issuer must satisfy not only the general conditions but must also comply with certain selling restrictions.[92]

There are two types of selling restrictions applicable to offerings of securities falling within Category II: (1) "transactional restrictions" and (2) "offering restrictions." The transactional restrictions prohibit offers and sales of such securities in the United

---

A substantial U.S. market interest in a foreign issuer's debt securities is deemed to exist upon commencement of the offering if: (1) 300 or more U.S. persons are the aggregate record holders of the issuer's debt securities, its non-participating preferred stock and its asset-backed securities; (2) U.S. persons hold $1 billion or more of the outstanding indebtedness of the foreign issuer; or (3) U.S. persons hold 20 percent or more of the outstanding debt securities of the foreign issuer. Rule 902(n)(2).

Definitions for U.S. market interest in warrants, non-participating preferred stock and asset-backed securities are provided in Rule 903. The other members in the issuer's chain of distribution, such as the underwriter and its affiliates, may rely on the written representation of the issuer that it has a reasonable belief that there is no substantial U.S. market interest in its securities. *See* SEC Release No. 6863 (1990).

90. Two types of offerings can qualify as "overseas directed offerings." *See* Rule 902(j). One is an offering of a foreign issuer's securities directed to residents of a single country other than the United States. The other is an offering of non-participating preferred stock, nonconvertible debt securities, and asset-backed securities of a domestic (U.S.) issuer directed to a single foreign country. Under this latter type of offering, the principal and interest of the securities must be denominated in non-U.S. currency. *Id.* When any participant in the issuer's syndicate knows or is reckless in not knowing that a substantial portion of the offering will be sold or resold outside that country, the offering will not qualify as an overseas directed offering. See Rule 904(c).

91. Securities Act Release No. 6863 (1990).

92. The SEC placed these selling restrictions on Category II securities offerings due to the Commission's belief that Category II securities are more likely to flow back to the United States than are the securities included in Category I. See SEC Release No. 6863 (1990).

States or to a "U.S. person"[93] during a restricted period lasting 40 days. Additionally, a distributor selling the securities prior to the end of the restricted period to certain securities professionals (such as dealers) is required to send a "confirmation or other notice" to such professionals advising them that they are subject to the same restrictions on offers and sales that are applicable to the distributor.

In addition, the issuer and its entire distribution syndicate must adhere to certain "offering restrictions" (which basically are procedures) to meet the Category II and Category III issuer safe harbors. These offering restrictions are procedures that impact the entire offering process and that seek to ensure compliance with the conditions imposed. Generally, as currently formulated, the procedures require that all distributors[94] agree in writing that all offers and sales during the applicable restricted period be made only in accordance with a Regulation S safe harbor or pursuant to registration under the Securities Act or an exemption therefrom. Furthermore, the issuer, distributors and their respective affiliates must include statements in all offering materials that the securities have not been registered under the Securities Act and may not be offered or sold in the United States or to U.S. persons unless the securities are registered or an exemption from registration is perfected.

The final safe harbor category, Category III, applies to all securities not within Categories I or II. This category includes offerings of non-reporting U.S. issuers and equity securities of non-reporting foreign issuers when there is a substantial U.S. market interest in such securities. The SEC imposes the most rigorous restrictions on offerings falling within this category due to the Commission's position that these securities have the highest probability of flowing back to the United States.[95]

As is the case in the first two categories of securities, the general conditions that the offer and sale be made in an "offshore transaction" and that there be no "direct selling efforts" in the United States or to a U.S. person are applicable to Category III securities. Moreover, the offering restrictions applicable to Category II offerings discussed above also are applicable to offerings under Category III. However, the transactional restrictions applicable to Category III offerings are more demanding than those required under Category II.

The transactional restrictions applicable to Category III offerings are similar to the restrictions existing (under SEC Securities Act Release 4708) prior to the promulgation of Regulation S. Due to the Commission's belief that debt offerings of Category III securities are less likely to flow back to the United States, the SEC imposes

---

93. Rule 903(c)(2). A "U.S. person" as defined in Rule 902(o) focuses not on U.S. citizenship, but on U.S. residency. SEC Release No. 6863 (1990). Therefore, U.S. investors, distributors and the like residing overseas may engage in their respective activities without the issuer losing the Regulation S safe harbor protection.

94. "Distributor" is defined as "any underwriter, dealer, or other person who participates, pursuant to a contractual arrangement, in the distribution of the securities. . . ." Rule 902(c).

95. Securities Act Release No. 6863 (1990). *See* Bai, *U.S. Registration Requirements for Multi-National Offerings*, (pts. 1 & 2), 25 Rev. Sec. & Comm. Reg. 131, 144 (1992), 25 Rev. Sec. & Comm. Reg. 151, 157 (1992).

less stringent transactional restrictions upon them than it does upon equity securities.

Debt securities offered pursuant to Category III are subject to a 40-day restricted period. During this period the securities may not be sold to U.S. persons or for the account (or benefit) of U.S. persons. The debt securities must be represented by a temporary global security that is not exchangeable for definitive securities until the 40-day restricted period has expired. When the global security is exchanged for the definitive security, certification must be effected that a non-U.S. person owns the security or that a U.S. person purchased securities in a transaction that was exempt from the registration requirements of the Securities Act. If a distributor or other person receiving a selling concession sells prior to the expiration of the 40-day restricted period, it must send a "confirmation or other notice" to the purchaser stating that the purchaser is subject to the same restrictions on offers and sales that apply to the distributor.

The transactional restrictions applicable to equity offerings under the third issuer safe harbor—Category III—are even more demanding than the restrictions applicable to debt securities in the same category. Rule 903(c)(3)(iii) prohibits equity securities offered under Category III from being sold to a U.S. person or for the account (or benefit) of a U.S. person for a period of one year. Furthermore, the purchaser of the security must certify that it is not a U.S. person and is not acquiring the securities for the account (or benefit) of any U.S. person. In addition, the purchaser must agree to resell only if it adheres to one of three conditions, namely, that such resale is made in accordance with Regulation S, pursuant to a registration statement, or under an exemption from registration. If a U.S. issuer is utilizing the Category III safe harbor, it must place a legend on the securities offered stating that all transfers are prohibited except as set forth above. Finally, the issuer is required, either by contract or pursuant to a provision in its bylaws, articles or charter, to refuse to register any transfer not in accordance with the foregoing.

Resale Safe Harbor

The resale safe harbor generally is available only to security holders who are not issuers, affiliates of an issuer, distributors, or affiliates of a distributor. Nonetheless, under certain circumstances, officers and directors of an issuer and securities professionals may use the resale safe harbor.[96] By satisfying all conditions of the resale safe harbor, the registration requirements of the Securities Act can be avoided. In general, other than securities professionals and officers and directors of an issuer, persons may sell in reliance on the resale safe harbor simply by satisfying the general conditions applicable to Regulation S transactions—(1) a resale in an offshore transaction and (2) without direct selling efforts in the United States.

---

96. Without this exception, officers and directors would be considered affiliates and therefore would be unable to utilize the resale safe harbor.

An officer or director may rely on the resale safe harbor if, in addition to meeting the general requirements, the officer or director is an affiliate solely by virtue of his or her position and is paid no special selling compensation in the resale transaction. With respect to securities professionals, they may not knowingly offer or sell securities to U.S. persons during the applicable restricted period. If the securities professional is selling to another securities professional, a trade confirmation or other notice must be sent to such purchaser reciting the applicable restrictions.

The 1998 Regulation S Amendments

In 1998, the SEC adopted amendments to Regulation S.[97] The amendments reflect the Commission's concern with certain abusive and problematic practices in connection with offers, sales, and resales of securities made in offshore transactions purportedly pursuant to Regulation S. The 1998 Regulation S amendments accordingly focus on market participants who purport to conduct legitimate offshore Regulation S placements but actually place the securities offshore in an effort to evade registration requirements. The amendments seek to impede abusive practices in connection with placements of equity securities by U.S. issuers, while "promot[ing] capital formation and efficient, competitive markets." Hence, the amendments "should prevent further abuses . . . but also allow continuous reliance on Regulation S in legitimate offshore offerings."[98]

Thus, the 1998 Regulation S amendments:

1. Classify the equity securities of all U.S. issuers (both reporting and non-reporting companies) placed offshore under Regulation S as "restricted securities" within the meaning of Rule 144;

2. Align the Regulation S restricted period for these equity securities issued by all U.S. enterprises with the Rule 144 holding periods by lengthening from 40 days to one year the period during which persons relying on the Regulation S safe harbor may not sell these securities to U.S. persons, unless pursuant to registration or an exemption therefrom (termed the "distribution compliance period");

3. Impose certification, legending, stop transfer, and other requirements for sales of equity securities by all U.S. (reporting and non-reporting) issuers;

4. Require purchasers of these equity securities sold by U.S. issuers to agree not to engage in hedging transactions with regard to such securities unless such transactions are in compliance with the Securities Act;

---

97. Securities Act Release No. 7505, [1997–1998 Transfer Binder] Fed. Sec. L. Rep. (CCH) ¶ 86,006 (SEC 1998). The SEC also adopted amendments to Regulation S in 2007. *See* Securities Act Release No. 8869 (2007).

98. *See* SEC Release No. 7505, *supra* note 93, at 80,157. These abuses occurred especially with respect to "the securities of thinly capitalized or microcap companies. These types of securities are particularly vulnerable to fraud and manipulation because little information about them is available to investors."

5. Unless certain conditions are satisfied, prohibit the use of promissory notes as payment for these equity securities; and

6. Clarify that offshore resales under Rule 901 or Rule 904 of equity securities of U.S. issuers, classified as "restricted securities" as defined in Rule 144, will not affect the restricted status of those securities or otherwise cleanse the securities of their restricted status.

Facilitating Global Trading

By promulgating Regulation S the SEC has acknowledged the existence of a global economy and the important role of international securities transactions. While not a panacea, Regulation S establishes a uniform U.S. framework with respect to international securities offerings. Moreover, Regulation S decreases some of the ambiguity that existed under the prior regulatory regime. Regulation S, aside from creating a more flexible approach with fewer regulatory burdens, has been used in conjunction with Rule 144A to increase investment in foreign issuers and to expand international securities trading in general.[99]

Adoption of Rule 144A

Securities Act Release No. 6862 (1990)

[This release is contained in §6.06.]

Note

The SEC's amendments to Regulation S thus are "designed to stop abusive practices in connection with offerings of equity securities purportedly made in reliance on Regulation S." Securities Act Release No. 7392 (1997).

Regulation S and Rule 144A should be viewed together with respect to the SEC's role in facilitating use of the U.S. marketplace for foreign companies without implicating the Securities Act's registration provisions. As stated by one commentator:

> Rule 144A is expected to have a dramatic impact on foreign issuers and investors. Foreign companies, previously reluctant to subject themselves to the onerous disclosure obligations associated with a public offering in the United States, presumably will be attracted by the Rule's streamlined private

---

99. *See generally* Berger, *Offshore Distributions of Securities: The Impact of Regulation S*, 3 Transn'l Law. 578 (1990); Bloomenthal, *Distributions Outside the U.S.—Regulation S*, 10 Sec. & Fed. Corp. L. Rep. 161 (1988); Bradley, *Regulation S: Tempest in a Safe Harbor*, 25 Rev. Sec. & Comm. Reg. 185 (1992); Karmel, *SEC Regulation of Multijurisdictional Offerings*, 16 Brook. J. Int'l L. 3 (1990); Longstreth, *Global Securities Markets and the SEC*, 10 U. Pa. J. Int'l Bus. L. 183 (1988); Steinberg & Lansdale, *Regulation S and Rule 144A: Creating A Workable Fiction in an Expanding Global Securities Market*, 29 Int'l Law. 43 (1995).

placement procedures. Foreign investors may also be persuaded to purchase privately-placed securities in the newly liquid secondary market. Rule 144A, together with Regulation S, may globalize the private placement market.[100]

Hence, the interaction of Rule 144A with Regulation S enables foreign issuers to sell their securities into the U.S. without having to comply with § 5's registration mandate. "Although not all U.S. investors have access to this market, the institutional investors who are the United States' principal securities consumers [are] able to purchase a wider selection of foreign securities without going abroad."[101] Therefore, a foreign issuer can comply with Regulation S in issuing its securities and subsequently have such securities enter the U.S. markets by means of Rule 144A.

———————

100. Seldman, *SEC Rule 144A: The Rule Heard Round the Globe B Or the Sounds of Silence?*, 47 Bus. Law. 333, 339–40 (1991).

101. Perrell & Kiernan, *Regulation S and Rule 144A: A Non-US Issuer's Perspective*, IFLR/Corp. Fin. Sp. Supp. 13, 14 (Sept. 1990).

Appendix

Limited Offering Materials

Purchaser Suitability Questionnaire

INVESTOR:

_____

Name

THE FOLLOWING PURCHASER SUITABILITY QUESTIONNAIRE IS TO ENSURE THAT THIS PRIVATE OFFERING IS CONDUCTED IN FULL COMPLIANCE WITH RULE 506 OF REGULATION D PROMULGATED UNDER THE SECURITIES ACT OF 1933, AS AMENDED. THE QUESTIONNAIRE WILL REMAIN ON FILE IN ABSOLUTE CONFIDENCE IN THE OFFICE OF _____, AND, IF APPLICABLE, YOUR BROKER-DEALER AND YOUR REGISTERED REPRESENTATIVE WITH THE FOLLOWING EXCEPTION: THAT THIS QUESTIONNAIRE MAY BE PRESENTED TO SUCH PARTIES AS DEEMED APPROPRIATE OR NECESSARY TO ESTABLISH THAT THE SALE OF THE INTERESTS TO A PURCHASER WILL NOT RESULT IN VIOLATION OF THE EXEMPTION FROM REGISTRATION UNDER THE SECURITIES ACT OF 1933, AS AMENDED, AND APPLICABLE STATE SECURITIES LAWS WHICH ARE BEING RELIED UPON IN CONNECTION WITH THE SALE OF THE INTERESTS.

Instructions: Please complete each question fully and attach additional information, if necessary. If the answer to any question is "None" or "Not Applicable", please so state.

TO. _____

_____

_____

RE: Purchaser Suitability Questionnaire

_____

Ladies and Gentlemen:

In order to induce you to permit me to purchase the Interests in _____, a Texas Limited Partnership (the "Partnership"), I hereby acknowledge and understand that:

1. I am submitting this Purchaser Suitability Questionnaire (the "Questionnaire") in connection with a proposed purchase of an Interest(s) in the Partnership;

2. I understand that this Questionnaire is not an offer to sell securities and that the completion of this Questionnaire will not constitute a purchase of securities;

3. The Interests heretofore offered to me in the Partnership will not be registered under the Securities Act of 1933, as amended (the "Act"), and applicable state securities statutes and regulations (the "State Acts");

4. In order to endure that the offering and sale of the Interests (the "Offering") is exempt from registration under the Act and the State Acts, you are required to have reasonable grounds to believe, and must actually believe, after making reasonable inquiry and prior to making any sale, that all purchasers meet the suitability standards set forth in the Confidential Private Placement Memorandum dated _____ (the "Memorandum");

5. The information provided herein will be relied upon in connection with the determination as to whether I meet the standards imposed by Rule 506 promulgated under the Act, because the Interests offered hereby have not been and will not be registered under the Act and are being sold in reliance upon the exemptions from registration afforded issuers of securities provided by Section 4(a)(2) of the Act, as well as other limited offering exemptions from the securities and broker-dealer registration provisions of applicable state securities statutes and regulations; and

6. All information supplied will be treated in confidence, except that this Questionnaire may be presented to such parties as deemed appropriate or necessary to establish that the sale of the Interests to me will not result in violation of the exemption from registration under the Act and the State Acts which is being relied upon in connection with the sale of the Interests.

PART I. BIOGRAPHICAL INFORMATION

A. Name:_____ Date of Birth:_____

Business Name:_____ Business Address:_____

Business Telephone Number:_____ Business Fax Number:_____

Business email:_____

Residence:

Address:_____

Residence Telephone Number:_____

Spouse Tax Identification Number:_____

Spouse Name:_____ Date of Birth:_____

Business Name:_____ Business Address:_____

Business Telephone Number:_____ Business Fax Number:_____

In which state (i.e., TX) do you hold your:

    (i)DRIVER'S LICENSE:_____:

    (ii)VOTER'S REGISTRATION:_____;

Please submit copy of unexpired driver's license or passport.

B. *Education:*

    1. College or University (Field(s) of Study):

    Doctorate:_____

    Masters:_____

    Bachelors:_____

    2. Other Specialized Education or
    Instruction:_____

Spouse Education:

    1. College or University (Field(s) of Study):

    Doctorate:_____

    Masters:_____

    Bachelors:_____

    2. Other Specialized Education or Instruction:_____

C. *Professional Memberships or Licenses: (Please List)*

_____

D. *History of Occupation:*

    1. Present occupation (with number of years) and employer:

_____

    2. Prior occupations (with number of years for each) and employer:

_____

_____

    3. Are you currently associated with, or do you own more than 10% of the stock of a registered FINRA member firm: (Check as appropriate)   YES____ NO___

    If YES, please provide below the name, address and telephone number of such firm.

_____

    4. Is the Account Holder(s), or any of his/her immediate family members, a control person of any publicly traded corporation (examples of control persons are policy making officers, directors, or 10% shareholders)?   YES____ NO____

    5. Is the Account Holder(s) an employee or related to an employee of the firm, its subsidiaries, or affiliates?   YES:_____ NO:_____

E. Investor Knowledge and Experience

1. Do you have sufficient knowledge and experience in financial and business matters so as to be capable of evaluating the merits and risks associated with investing in the Partnership?

YES:_____ NO: _____

2. Have you read the Memorandum of the Partnership, including all exhibits, appendices supplements (if any) thereto?

YES:_____ NO: _____

3. Do you understand the nature of an investment in the Partnership and the risks associated with such an investment?

YES:_____ NO:_____

4. Do you understand that there is no guarantee of any financial return on this investment and that you run the risk of losing your entire investment?

YES:_____ NO:_____

5. Do you understand that this investment provides limited liquidity since the Interests are not freely transferable and the Partners have limited rights to withdraw capital from or to withdraw as Partners of the Partnership?

YES:_____ NO:_____

6. Do you or the entity proposing to invest in the Partnership have adequate means of providing for your or its current needs and personal contingencies in view of the fact that this investment provides limited liquidity?

YES:_____ NO:_____

7. Are you purchasing these securities for investment and not with the intent to resell them?

YES:_____ NO:_____

8. You have the right, will be afforded an opportunity, and are encouraged to investigate the Partnership and review relevant records and documents pertaining to the General Partner and the Partnership and its business and to ask questions of a qualified representative of the Partnership regarding this investment and the operations and methods of doing business with the partnership.

Have you conducted any such investigation, sought such documents or asked questions of a qualified representative of the Partnership regarding this investment and the operations and methods of doing business of the Partnership?

YES:_____ NO:_____

a. If the answer to question 8 is yes, have you completed such investigation and/ or received satisfactory answers to any questions posed?

YES:_____ NO:_____

9. a. Have you ever invested in securities:

YES:_____ NO:_____

b. Have you ever invested in investment partnerships, venture capital funds, or other nonmarketable or restricted securities?

YES:_____ NO:_____

10. Indicate the frequency of your investments or, if the prospective purchaser is a corporation, partnership, or other entity, your investments on behalf of such entity, in nonmarketable securities (circle appropriate answer):

Often   Occasional   Seldom

PART II. Individuals Only
(This part must be completed by primary investor even if investing as an entity.)

A. *Accredited Investor Status*

1. _____ I am a director or executive officer of _____ or its Affiliates.

2. _____ I am a natural person whose individual net worth, or joint net worth with my spouse, exceeds $1,000,000, excluding the value of my/our primary residence.

3. _____ I am a natural person whose individual income was in excess of $200,000 in each of the two most recent years or joint income with my spouse was in excess of $300,000 in each of those years and I reasonably expect to reach the same income level in the current year.

B. *Accredited Investor Status B Joint Accounts Combine Financial Information*

1. My net worth, excluding home, furnishings, automobiles, and other assets which are not readily marketable, is in excess of: (Please Check One)

$100,000 _____	$400,000 _____	$800,000 _____
$200,000 _____	$500,000 _____	$900,000 _____
$250,000 _____	$600,000 _____	$1,000,000 _____
$300,000 _____	$700,000 _____	$1,000,000+ _____

2. The current market value of my assets which are liquid (readily convertible to cash) exceeds $_____.

3. PERSONAL INCOME TAX INFORMATION:

(a) Two Years Ago: Annual Gross Income $_____

(b) Last Year: Annual Gross Income $_____

(c) Current Year (estimated): Annual Gross Income $_____

4. Describe any other experience you have in accounting or financial matters:

_____

5. Have you previously participated in other private placement investments?

YES: _____ NO: _____ (Check as appropriate). If so, with whom?_____

_____

6. Indicate the types of investments in which you have previously participated (either direct ownership, limited partnerships, etc.) (check applicable):

G Real Estate	G Bonds	G Options
G Oil & Gas Drilling and/or Lease Acquisition	G Equipment Leasing G Agriculture	G Futures G Mutual Funds
G Oil & Gas Production	G Commodities	G Annuities
G Stocks	G Other (please specify) _____	

7. Cash and cash equivalents and liquid securities (includes stock, bonds, government obligations, etc. at fair market value): (Please Check One)

$100,000 _____	$400,000 _____	$800,000 _____
$200,000 _____	$500,000 _____	$900,000 _____
$250,000 _____	$600,000 _____	$1,000,000 _____
$300,000 _____	$700,000 _____	$1,000,000+ _____

8. Equity in all real estate, net of mortgages: (Please Check One)

$100,000 _____	$400,000 _____	$800,000 _____
$200,000 _____	$500,000 _____	$900,000 _____
$250,000 _____	$600,000 _____	$1,000,000 _____
$300,000 _____	$700,000 _____	$1,000,000+ _____

9. Other investments: (Please Check One)

$100,000 _____	$500,000 _____	$1,000,000 _____
$250,000 _____	$750,000 _____	$1,000,000+ _____

10. State your investment objectives by checking the following where applicable:

G Income B generate income from investments

G Appreciation B increase in the value of an asset

G Tax Shelter B legally avoid or reduce tax liabilities

G Other: _____

PART III. Entities Only

A. 1. Name of Entity: _____

2. Address of Principal Office :_____

3. Type of Organization: _____

    If a Partnership, what states are the principal residences of each of the partners: _____

_____

4. Date and Place of Organization: _____

5. Total assets: _____

B. *Accredited Investor Status*

    The undersigned is an entity qualifying as an Accredited Investor as: (Check those that apply)

1. (a) whether acting in its individual or fiduciary capacity:

    (i) _____ a bank as defined in Section 3(a)(2) of the Act;

    (ii) _____ a saving and loan association or other institution as defined in Section 3(a)(5)(A) of the Act;

    (b) _____ a broker-dealer registered pursuant to Section 15 of the Securities Exchange Act of 1934;

    (c) _____ an insurance company as defined in Section 2(a)(13) of the Act;

    (d) (i)_____ an investment company registered under the Investment Company Act of 1940;

    (ii)_____ a business development company as defined in Section 2(a)(48) of the Investment Company Act of 1940;

    (e) _____ a Small Business Investment Company licensed by the U.S. Small Business Administration under Section 301(c) or (d) of the Small Business Investment Act of 1958;

    (f) _____ a plan established and maintained by a state, its political subdivision, or any agency or instrumentality of a state or its political subdivisions for the benefit of employees, if such plan has total assets in excess of $5,000,000;

    (g) _____ an employee benefit plan within the meaning of the Employee Retirement Income Security Act of 1974, if the investment decision is made by the undersigned as a plan fiduciary, as defined in Section 3(21) of such act, which is either a:

    (i) _____ bank;

    (ii) _____ saving and loan association;

    (iii) _____ insurance company; or

    (iv) _____ registered investment advisor;

    (h) _____ an employee benefit plan with total assets in excess of $5,000,000;

(i) _____ a self-directed plan, with investment decisions made solely by persons that are accredited investors;

2. _____ a private business development company as defined in Section 202(a)(22) of the Investment Advisors Act of 1940;

3. _____ an organization described in Section 501(c)(3) of the Internal Revenue Code, corporation, Massachusetts or similar business trust, or partnership not formed for the specific purpose of acquiring the securities offered, with total assets in excess of $5,000,000;

4. _____ any trust, with total assets in excess of $5,000,000, not formed for the specific purpose of acquiring the securities offered, whose purchase is directed by a sophisticated person as described in Rule 506 of Regulation D;

5. _____ an entity in which *all* of the equity owners are Accredited Investors as defined in Regulation D.

PART IV. *Representations and Warrants*
(To Be Completed By All Prospective Participants)

In order to induce you to permit the undersigned to purchase the Interests in the Partnership, I hereby warrant and represent to you that:

1. I have received, carefully read and understood a copy of that certain Confidential Private Placement Memorandum dated _____ (the "Memorandum"), and all exhibits thereto setting forth information relating to the Partnership and the terms and conditions in the Interests, as well as any other information I deemed necessary or appropriate to evaluate the merits and risks of an investment in the Interests;

2. I have had the opportunity to ask questions of and to receive answers from, representatives of the General Partner concerning the terms and conditions of the Offering and the information contained in the Memorandum;

3. I have such knowledge and experience in financial and business matters, that I am capable of evaluating the merits and risks of an investment decision in the program and am capable of making an informed decision;

4. I DO/DO NOT (circle one) intend to utilize the services of a Purchaser Representative to evaluate the merits and risks of an investment;

5. The information contained in this Questionnaire is accurate, true, complete and correct and may be relied upon by you;

6. I will notify you immediately of any material change in any of such information Occurring prior to any purchase of Interests by me.

Dated: _____.

Individual Entity

_____   _____

Signature Print Name

_____   *By:* _____

Print Name   *Signature of Individual Completing*
                                          Questionnaire

_____   _____

Social Security Number   *Print Name of Individual Completing*

_____   *Questionnaire* _____

                                          *Title*_____

                                          Taxpayer Identification Number

                                          _____

Subscription Agreement

The undersigned hereby subscribes for a Limited Partner Interest in _____, a Texas limited partnership (the "Partnership"), in the amount set forth below.

1. *Subscription.* Subject to the terms and conditions hereof, the undersigned hereby irrevocably subscribes for a Limited Partnership interest (the "Partnership Interest") in the Partnership for a total purchase price of $_____.The undersigned hereby tenders with this Subscription Agreement a check payable to the order of ___ _____ or wire transfer, in the amount of $_____.

2. *Closing.* The undersigned understands the General Partner intends to make an initial closing of the Partnership Interests on September, 2016 and thereafter will open the partnership on a quarterly basis for additional capital contributions from existing or new Limited Partners. If you do not accept this subscription, this Subscription Agreement, together with the funds and other documents delivered to the Partnership, shall be promptly returned to the undersigned with interest, if any.

3. *Determination of Compliance.* The undersigned agrees that this subscription is subject to the following terms and conditions:

(a) You shall have the right, in your sole discretion, to accept or reject all or part of this subscription and to determine whether the Subscription Agreement has been properly completed and whether all suitability requirements have been satisfied. If you find this subscription to be defective, deficient or noncomplying, the subscription price will be promptly returned without interest or deduction.

(b) This subscription is not transferable or assignable.

4. *Receipt of Information.* The undersigned hereby acknowledges receipt of the _____ _____ Private Placement Memorandum, and a copy of the Limited Partnership Agreement which governs the rights of Limited Partners and the operation of the Partnership, and the undersigned acknowledges that he has had reasonable time and opportunity to examine those documents. The undersigned further acknowledges that the Partnership is a suitable investment only for sophisticated investors; that the Partnership Interests are being offered and sold under an exemption from registration under the Securities Act of 1933, as amended, and appropriate state securities laws; and that the offering has not been submitted to or reviewed by the Securities and Exchange Commission, the State Securities Board of Texas, the securities regulation agency of any other state or any other governmental agency.

5. *Representation of Purchaser.* The undersigned hereby makes the following representations, declarations, and warranties to you, with the intent that the same be relied upon in determining the suitability of the undersigned to invest in the Partnership:

(a) *Individual Investor:* I am of legal age and a resident of the State of _____; or

(aa) *Partnership, Trust or other Entity:* The investor has been organized in compliance with applicable law of the State of _____, is presently in existence, and has the power to invest in the Partnership.

(b) The undersigned understands that an investment in the Partnership is an illiquid investment, which means that:

(i) The undersigned must bear the economic risk of investment in the Partnership for an indefinite period of time, since the Partnership Interests have not been registered under the Securities Act of 1933 nor any state securities laws and cannot be sold unless the Partnership Interests are either subsequently registered under said Act and applicable state laws (which is neither contemplated by nor required of the Partnership) or an exemption from such registration is available; and

(ii) There is no established market for the Partnership Interests and that it is not anticipated that any public market for the Partnership Interests will develop in the near future.

(c) The undersigned represents that this investment is being made for the account of the undersigned; the undersigned has not offered or sold any portion of the Partnership Interest for which the undersigned hereby subscribes to any other person and has no present intention of dividing such Partnership Interest with others or reselling or otherwise disposing of any portion of such Partnership Interest, either currently or after the passage of a fixed or determinable period of time, or upon the occurrence or nonoccurrence of any predetermined event or circumstance.

(d) The undersigned represents that none of the following has been represented, guaranteed, or warranted to the undersigned by any broker, the

Partnership, their agents or employees, or any other person, expressly or by implication:

(i) The length of time that the undersigned will be required to remain as the owner of the Partnership Interest;

(ii) The profit to be realized, if any, as a result of investment in the Partnership; or

(iii) The past performance or experience on the part of the Partnership, or any partner or affiliate, their partners, salesmen, associates, agents, or employees or of any other person, will in any way indicate the predicted results of the ownership of the Partnership Interest.

(e) The undersigned has adequate means of providing for current needs and possible personal contingencies and has no need for liquidity in the investment in the Partnership. The undersigned is either (i) an "accredited investor" (as indicated in the Private Placement Questionnaire), or (ii) has a personal net worth in excess of three (3) times the amount to be invested in the Partnership and could afford to sustain a loss of the entire investment in the Partnership in the event such loss should occur.

(f) The undersigned has made an independent examination of the investment and has depended on the advice of counsel and accountants to the undersigned and agrees that you have no responsibility with respect to such matters and such advice.

(g) The undersigned understands that the Partnership is newly formed and has no operating history; the undersigned has carefully reviewed and relied solely upon the Private Placement Memorandum and independent investigations made by the undersigned or by representative(s) of the undersigned, if any, in making the decision to purchase the Partnership Interest hereby subscribed for, and the undersigned has a full understanding and appreciation of the risks involved.

(h) The undersigned understands that any offering literature used in connection with this offering has not been prefiled with the Attorney General or Securities Commission of any state and has not been reviewed by the Attorney General or Securities Commission of any state.

(i) The undersigned understands that any and all documents, records and books pertaining to this investment have been made available for inspection by the undersigned, his attorney and/or accountant, and that the books and records of the Partnership will be available, upon reasonable notice, for inspection by investors during reasonable hours at the principal place of business of the Partnership. The undersigned represents that he has had an opportunity to ask questions of and receive answers from the General Partner, or a person or persons acting on its behalf, concerning the terms and conditions of this investment.

6. *Indemnification of the Partnership and the General Partner.* The undersigned understands the meaning and legal consequences of the representations and warranties contained herein, and hereby agrees to indemnify and hold harmless the Partnership, the General Partner, and their agents and employees from and against any and all loss, damage or liability due to or arising out of a breach of any representation or warranty of the undersigned contained in this Subscription Agreement. Notwithstanding any of the representations, warranties, acknowledgments or agreements made herein, the undersigned does not in any manner waive any rights granted to the undersigned under United States Federal or state securities laws.

7. *Power of Attorney.* In order to induce the General Partner to accept the subscription of the undersigned, and in consideration of the General Partner's agreement to serve as General Partner of the Partnership, the undersigned hereby irrevocably constitutes and appoints the General Partner, with full power of substitution, his true and lawful attorney for him and in his name, place and stead for his use and benefit, to execute:

(a) the Partnership Agreement in the form provided to the undersigned or as the same may be thereafter amended;

(b) all amendments to the Certificate of Limited Partnership and Partnership Agreement regarding a change in name of the Partnership, its address, or that of the General Partner or any Partner, or the admission or withdrawal of a Partner;

(c) all amendments adopted in accordance with Section 11.04 of the Partnership Agreement;

(d) all certificates and other instruments necessary to qualify or continue the Partnership in the states where the Partnership may be doing business;

(e) all conveyances or other instruments or documents necessary, appropriate or convenient to effect the dissolution and termination of the Partnership.

The undersigned hereby agrees to be bound by any representations made by the General Partner or its substitutes acting pursuant to this Power of Attorney, and the undersigned hereby waives any and all defenses which may be available to him to contest, negate or disaffirm its actions or the actions of his substitutes under this Power of Attorney. The powers herein granted are granted for the sole and exclusive benefit of the undersigned and not on behalf of any other person, in whole or in part. This Power of Attorney is hereby declared to be irrevocable and a power coupled with an interest which will survive the death, disability, dissolution, bankruptcy or insolvency of the undersigned.

8. *Subscription Not Revocable.* The undersigned hereby acknowledges and agrees that the undersigned is not entitled to cancel, terminate or revoke this Subscription Agreement or any agreements of the undersigned hereunder and that this Subscription Agreement shall survive the dissolution, death or disability of the undersigned.

9. *Representative Capacity*. If an investment in the Partnership is being made by a corporation, partnership, trust or estate, I, the person signing on behalf of the undersigned entity, represent that I have all right and authority, in my capacity as an officer, general partner, trustee, executor or other representative of such corporation, partnership, trust or estate, as the case may be, to make such decision to invest in the Partnership and to execute and deliver this Subscription Agreement on behalf of such corporation, partnership, trust or estate as the case may be, enforceable in accordance with its terms. I also represent that any such corporation, partnership or trust was not formed for the purpose of buying the Partnership Interest hereby subscribed.

10. *Restrictions on Transferability*. The undersigned understands and agrees that the purchase and resale, pledge, hypothecation or other transfer of the Partnership Interest is restricted by certain provisions of the Limited Partnership Agreement of _____ and that the Partnership Interest shall not be sold, pledged, hypothecated or otherwise transferred unless the Partnership Interest is registered under the Securities Act of 1933, as amended, and applicable state securities laws or an exemption from such registration is available.

11. *Number and Gender*. In this Agreement the masculine gender includes the other two genders and the singular includes the plural, where appropriate to the context.

IN WITNESS WHEREOF, the undersigned has executed this Subscription Agreement on the date set forth below.

Date of Execution: _____ __, 2016

IF INDIVIDUAL INVESTOR:

_____

(Signature)

_____

(Printed Name)

IF CORPORATION, PARTNERSHIP, TRUST,

ESTATE OR REPRESENTATIVE:

_____

Name of Investor

By :_____

Name: _____

Title: _____

APPROVED THIS ____ DAY

of_____, 2016.

By: _____

General Partner

Purchaser Representative Questionnaire

The information contained herein is being furnished for consideration by the General Partners in determining whether the sale of Limited Partnership interests in _____, a Texas Limited Partnership (the "Partnership") may be made to:

_____

(Printed or typed name of potential Limited Partner(s))

The undersigned understands that (i) the General Partners will rely upon the information contained herein for purposes of such determination, (ii) the Limited Partnership interests will not be registered under the Securities Act and may not be registered under the securities laws of the Limited Partner's state of residence in reliance upon exemptions from the registration provisions thereof and (iii) this Questionnaire is not an offer of the Limited Partnership interests or any other securities to the undersigned or to the above-named prospective Limited Partner.

The undersigned is acting as Purchaser Representative for the above-named Limited Partner(s) and is furnishing the following representations and information:

1. The undersigned is not an affiliate of the Partnership (as defined hereafter), except as set forth below. (Write "No Exceptions" or set forth exceptions and give details.)

_____

_____

The only permitted exceptions are those stated below: A Purchaser Representative may not be an affiliate of the Partnership (director, officer, or other employee of the Partnership or of the General Partners or beneficial owner of 10% or more of any class of equity interest in the Partnership or of the General Partners), except where the purchaser is:

(a) related to the purchaser representative by blood, marriage or adoption, no more remotely than as a first cousin;

(b) any trust or estate in which the purchaser representative and any persons related to him or her, as specified in subparagraph (a) or (c), collectively have more than 50% of the beneficial interest (excluding contingent interests) or of which the purchaser representative serves as trustee, executor or in any similar capacity; or

(c) any corporation or other organization in which the purchaser representative and any persons related to him or her, as specified in subparagraph (a) or (b), collectively are the beneficial owners of more than 50% of the equity securities (excluding directors' qualifying shares) or equity interests.

2. The undersigned believes that he/she has sufficient knowledge and experience in financial and business matters to be capable of evaluating, alone or together with

other Purchaser Representatives of the purchaser, or together with the purchaser, the relative merits and risks of an investment in the Partnership. Such opinion is based upon the following information; if the undersigned has relied upon, in part, the expertise of additional Purchaser Representatives or others, their names and addresses are indicated below. (Please describe personal investment experience, business experience, profession and education.)

_____

_____

_____

3. There is no material relationship or agreement between the undersigned or any of his/her affiliates and the Partnership or its affiliates which now exists or is mutually understood to be contemplated or which has existed at any time during the previous two years, nor has the undersigned or any of his/her affiliates received any compensation from the Partnership or its affiliates as a result of any such relationship, except as set forth below. *If you and your firm are participating in the solicitation of purchasers in connection with this private placement or any prior offerings by the General Partners or their affiliates, please (a) so state, (b) separately indicate the total compensation to be received and (c) make sure that the purchaser reads, answers and signs the statements at the end of this Purchaser Representative Questionnaire.* (Write "No Exceptions" or set forth exceptions and give details.)

_____

_____

_____

The foregoing information is complete, correct and may be relied upon by the General Partners and the Partnership. The undersigned agrees to promptly advise of any changes in the foregoing information which may occur prior to the termination of the offering.

Signed this ____ day of _____ 2016, at _____

                                          (City and State)

_____   _____

Firm Name   Signature

_____   _____

Street Address   Type or Print Name

_____   _____

City, State and Zip Code   (Area Code) Telephone Number

IMPORTANT NOTE TO PURCHASER:

If the answer to question 3 above is anything other than "No Exceptions," it means that your Purchaser Representative may at some future date have, presently has, or within the past two years had, a material relationship with the Partnership or its affiliates and will receive or has received compensation therefor. Accordingly, you should understand that such person may have a conflict of interest between such Purchaser Representative's impartial representation of you as a purchaser representative and such Purchaser Representative's past, present, or future relationship with the Partnership or its affiliates. After consideration of the effects such a conflict of interest may have upon such Person's acting as your Purchaser Representative and, if such Person is to so act, you should acknowledge that you have been advised in writing by the Purchaser Representative, prior to completion of the Subscription Agreement, of such potential conflict of interest and that you desire such person to act as your Purchaser Representative. I have been advised in writing by my Purchaser Representative, prior to my completion of the Subscription Agreement, of the potential conflict of interest described in question 3 above.

Yes _____

No _____

I desire the above named person to act as my Purchaser Representative.

Yes _____

No _____

Signed this ____ day of _____ 2016, at _____

(City and State)

IF INDIVIDUAL INVESTOR:

_____

(Signature)

_____

(Printed Name)

IF CORPORATION, PARTNERSHIP,

TRUST, ESTATE OR

REPRESENTATIVE:

_____

Name of Investor

By: _____

Name: _____

Title: _____

Chapter 4

The Registration Process

§ 4.01 Overview of the Registration Process

To protect investors and the integrity of the securities markets, the Securities Act of 1933 (Securities Act or 1933 Act) has two basic objectives: (1) to provide investors with adequate and accurate material information concerning securities offered for sale; and (2) to prohibit fraudulent practices in the offer or sale of securities. The registration framework of the Securities Act seeks to meet these goals by imposing certain obligations and limitations upon persons engaged in the offer or sale of securities. For the Securities Act's registration framework to apply, the interstate commerce requirement must be met. This normally is satisfied without difficulty.

Pursuant to § 5, and absent exception otherwise, a public offering of securities requires that a registration statement be filed with the Securities and Exchange Commission (SEC). As a general matter, *with certain key exceptions*, before the registration statement is filed, there can be no offers to sell or offers to buy the securities in question. After the filing of the registration statement, oral offers and certain written offers are permitted. Until the registration statement becomes effective, however, there can be no sale of the securities. Moreover, unless preempted, the registration requirements of the applicable state securities laws must be met. In this regard, SEC registered offerings of securities that are listed (or will be listed such as pursuant to an initial public offering—an IPO) on a national securities exchange are preempted from state registration regulation.

Under federal law, the main purpose of registration is to provide adequate and accurate disclosure of material information concerning the issuer (as well as affiliates and certain other parties) and the securities the issuer (which, for example, may be common stock in a corporation or interests in a limited partnership) proposes to offer. The disclosure of this information, largely in the form of statutory and free writing § 10 prospectuses, enables investors to evaluate the securities offered and thus make informed investment decisions.

The registration of a securities offering with the SEC does not mean that the offering is considered to be a good risk. The Commission does not have the authority to prevent an offering from going to market because it considers the investment to be of a speculative nature. Rather, the main role of the federal securities laws in this setting is to require the accurate disclosure of material information.

On the other hand, a number of states apply "merit" regulation to certain securities offerings. Under this standard, the pertinent state securities administrator can prevent an offering from going forward because it is not "fair, just and equitable." Under merit regulation, therefore, adequate disclosure is not the only criterion. The substantive fairness of the offering also may be scrutinized.

It also should be pointed out that neither the SEC nor the states verify the truthfulness of the disclosures made in the registration statement. That a registration statement becomes effective in no way vouches for the veracity of the information contained therein. In this regard, both federal and state law prohibit materially false and misleading statements, with civil and criminal remedies available to redress such violations. For example, as discussed in Chapter 7, provided certain conditions are met, § 11 of the 1933 Act imposes civil monetary liability against specified persons who fail to establish "due diligence" (except the issuer, which has no due diligence defense) for any misstatement or omission of a material fact contained in a registration statement; § 12(a)(1) provides that a purchaser may rescind or, alternatively, recover damages against any person who offers or sells a security in violation of § 5; § 12(a)(2) likewise grants the purchaser the right to rescind or to recover damages against any person who sells a security by means of a prospectus or oral communication that includes a materially false or misleading statement if such seller fails to establish the exercise of reasonable care; § 17(a), as addressed in Chapter 9, provides a remedy to the SEC (or the U.S. Department of Justice in a criminal proceeding) for redressing any fraudulent or deceptive conduct committed in the offer or sale of securities; and § 24 of the Securities Act provides for criminal penalties for the willful violation of any provision of the Securities Act or any rule or regulation promulgated thereunder by the SEC. Moreover, as discussed in Chapter 8, under certain circumstances, suit also may be brought under § 10(b) of the Securities Exchange Act for any materially false or misleading statement contained in a registration statement.

Section 5 of the Securities Act may be viewed as the central provision of the federal registration framework. *Subject to certain key exceptions*, § 5: prohibits any person from using the mails or any means of interstate commerce to offer a subject security for sale unless a registration statement has been filed with the SEC; and, with respect to any written communication, prohibits offers to sell unless such communication meets the prospectus requirements.[1] Section 5 also prohibits any sale of a subject security unless a registration statement is effective.

Generally, disclosure pursuant to a § 10 statutory prospectus encompasses the issuer, affiliated persons, and the securities to be offered. The § 10 statutory prospectus, among other things, may be viewed as being both a selling and a disclosure document. As a selling document, it is used by underwriters and dealers for the purpose of helping to persuade investors to purchase the securities. Another commonly

---

1. There are a number of exceptions to this general principle. *See* § 4.02 *infra*.

held view is that the § 10 statutory prospectus, as a disclosure document, serves to protect the various parties from liability. From this perspective, information placed in the statutory prospectus traditionally has been conservative, focusing on historically based information and clearly warning prospective investors of any material risks involved.

In the 1970s and 1980s, the SEC's promulgation of Rule 175 and Item 303 of Regulation S-K signaled a new era for facilitating the disclosure of forward-looking statements and other "soft" (rather than historical) information in the § 10 prospectus. Enactment of the Private Securities Litigation Reform Act of 1995 (PSLRA) also induced Exchange Act reporting issuers in their public offerings of securities to engage in disclosure of "forward-looking" or "soft" information. The "free writing" prospectus adopted by the SEC pursuant to the 2005 reforms further encourages issuers to disclose forward-looking information.[2]

§ 4.02 Framework of Section 5

When speaking of making a public offering, the concept of *"in registration"* is sometimes heard. Generally, the term refers to the entire registration period, commencing at least from the time that the issuer reaches an understanding with the managing underwriter prior to the filing of the registration statement to the time that the prospectus delivery requirements terminate in the post-effective period.[3]

From a structural perspective having legal ramifications, § 5 covers three basic periods for making offers and sales of securities during a registered offering: (1) *the pre-filing period;* (2) *the waiting period*; and (3) *the post-effective period.*

Generally, the offering rules will turn on two factors: *(1) the time period, taken into consideration with, (2) the issuer's reporting status.* Thus, to understand which offering activities are permitted by a particular issuer at a given point in time, it is important to understand not only how the SEC defines each time period, but also the Commission's issuer classification framework.

[A] Issuer Classifications

Generally, issuers may be categorized into five tiers consisting of (1) non-reporting issuers, (2) unseasoned issuers, (3) emerging growth companies, (4) seasoned issuers, and (5) well-known seasoned issuers (WKSI):

(1) A *non-reporting issuer* is an issuer that is not required to file reports pursuant to § 13 or § 15(d) of the Securities Exchange Act (Exchange Act). Such issuers

---

2. The "free writing" prospectus is discussed later in this chapter. Rule 175, Item 303 of Regulation S-K, and the treatment of forward-looking information by the Private Securities Litigation Reform Act (PSLRA) are addressed in Chapters 5, 8, and 11 of this text.

3. *See* Securities Exchange Act Release No. 5180 (1971).

include, for example, a privately held company that is conducting an initial public offering (IPO) as well as a voluntary filer (namely, a non-reporting issuer that elects to voluntarily file periodic reports with the SEC).

(2) An *unseasoned issuer* is an issuer that is required to file Exchange Act reports, but does not satisfy the requirements for unlimited use of Form S-3 (or Form F-3) for a primary offering of its securities (e.g., such unseasoned issuer has a public float (those securities held by non-affiliates) of less than $75 million).[4]

[Note that an *"affiliate"* of an issuer is one who controls, is controlled by, or is under common control of, either directly or indirectly through one or more intermediaries, such issuer.]

(3) *An Emerging Growth Company (EGC)* is an issuer with fewer than $1 billion in annual gross revenues during its previous fiscal year and did not have an initial public offering (IPO) of equity securities on or prior to December 8, 2011. This new category of issuer was legislated pursuant to the Jumpstart Our Business Startups Act (JOBS Act), enacted in 2012. Emerging Growth Companies may use specified reduced reporting and disclosure requirements in their IPOs and subsequent periodic reports (e.g., Form 10-Ks) filed pursuant to the Exchange Act. These issuers also may solicit qualified institutional buyers (QIBs) as well as institutional accredited investors, and thus make "offers to sell" in the pre-filing period (prior to the filing of the IPO registration statement with the SEC).

A company ceases to be an emerging growth company upon the *earliest* of the following events: (1) the last day of the company's fiscal year after the fifth anniversary of conducting its IPO; (2) the last day of its fiscal year in which the company's gross revenues were $1 billion or greater; (3) the date on which the company issued, over the prior three-year period, non-convertible debt exceeding $1 billion; or (4) the date on which the company becomes a "large accelerated filer" (see discussion of *"well-known seasoned issuer"* below). Thus, pursuant to the JOBS Act, Congress eased the IPO regime for an emerging growth company as well as its periodic disclosure mandates for up to five years after conducting its IPO.

(4) A *seasoned issuer* is an issuer that qualifies to use Form S-3 (or Form F-3) to register primary offerings of its common stock, but does not meet the well-known seasoned issuer criteria. Generally, a seasoned issuer is one that has timely filed Exchange Act reports for a 12-month period and that has a public float (representing the aggregate market value of the company's voting stock held by non-affiliates) of at least $75 million.[5]

(5) The last category of issuer is the *well-known seasoned issuer (WKSI)*.[6] Such issuers represent the largest amount of capital raised and traded in the U.S. public

---

4. An issuer that is voluntarily filing Exchange Act reports accordingly is considered a non-reporting issuer for purposes of the rules.

5. *See* Securities Act Release No. 6964 (1992); Securities Act Release No. 6383 (1982).

6. This category of issuer was added as a part of the 2005 offering reform initiative to ease the public offering burden on well-known issuers with widely disseminated financial information

capital markets. Because well-known seasoned issuers have such a wide following by market participants, institutional investors and the media, the SEC has determined that these issuers merit the greatest flexibility in regard to their activities during the public offering process.

There are four requirements that must be satisfied in order for an issuer to qualify as a *well-known seasoned issuer (WKSI)*. First, the issuer is required to file reports pursuant to § 13(a) or § 15(d) of the Exchange Act. Second, for an at-the-market offering of equity securities (e.g., common stock) by or on behalf of the issuer, such issuer must meet the registrant requirements of Form S-3 (or Form F-3), which includes the requirement that the issuer be current and timely in its Exchange Act reporting obligations for at least a 12-month period. Third, the issuer must not be an ineligible issuer.[7] And finally, the issuer must either: (1) have a worldwide common equity (e.g., common stock) market capitalization ("public float") of at least $700 million; or (2) have issued at least $1 billion of non-convertible securities, other than common equity, in registered primary offerings for cash (not exchange offers) in the last three years.

If an issuer is a well-known seasoned issuer based on its public float (namely, common stock held by non-affiliates), that issuer can use automatic shelf registration (generally signifying that the registration statement becomes effective immediately upon filing with the SEC) to register any offering of securities (other than an offering in connection with a business combination). On the other hand, an issuer that has attained well-known seasoned issuer status based on its registered non-convertible securities can register any offering for cash with an automatic shelf registration statement if it is eligible to register primary offerings of securities on Form S-3 (or Form F-3). If it is not eligible to use Form S-3 (or Form F-3), such an issuer is limited to using automatic shelf registration for offerings of non-convertible securities (other than common equity) for cash.[8] The subject of automatic shelf registration is discussed in Chapter 5 (§ 5.02).

The following discussion will address how the offering rules vary depending on the status of the issuer and the period(s) in which a subject communication occurs.

---

available to the public. Whether an issuer qualifies as a well-known seasoned issuer is determined annually. Well-known issuer status is determined on the latter of the date the issuer files its most recent shelf registration statement or its most recent amendment thereto, or the date the issuer files its most recent annual report. *See* Securities Act Release No. 8591 (2005).

7. Ineligible issuers include those issuers who: are not current in their periodic reporting; have filed for bankruptcy or insolvency during the past three years; have been subject to a refusal or stop order under the Securities Act during the past three years; have been convicted of a felony or a misdemeanor or have been found to have violated the anti-fraud provisions of the federal securities laws during the past three years; have been blank check companies, shell companies, or issuers of penny stock during the past three years; or are limited partnerships offering securities other than through a firm commitment underwriting.

8. *See* Securities Act Release No. 8591 (2005).

[B] The Pre-Filing Period

[1] Overview

The *pre-filing* period is the period before a registration statement has been filed with the SEC.[9] During this period, *with certain key exceptions*, §5(c) prohibits the use of the mails or any means of interstate commerce to offer to sell or offer to buy the securities to be offered.[10]

Certain activities, however, are not deemed to be an offer to sell or an offer to buy. For example, *§2(a)(3) exempts negotiations and agreements between the issuer and any underwriter or among underwriters who are or will be in privity of contract with the issuer.* Rule 135 permits an issuer to make an announcement of a proposed public offering, provided that only the information specified in the Rule is released. Moreover, pursuant to Rules 137-139, brokers or dealers may publish certain information about specified issuers in the pre-filing period (as well as in the waiting and post-effective periods).

As a general proposition, however, during the pre-filing period, the concept of "making an offer to sell" is given a relatively broad interpretation. Depending on the classification of the subject issuer and the underlying circumstances, publication of information about the issuer or its securities (even where such information does not refer to a forthcoming offering), *prior to the filing of a registration statement*, may be considered to constitute an "offer to sell." Although the publication is not an express offer, it may be viewed as conditioning the public market or stimulating interest in the securities to be registered (more colorfully referred to as "gun-jumping"). Hence, during the pre-filing period, *absent certain exceptions* discussed below, the issuer and other participants must be cautious regarding the publication of information. Nonetheless, the JOBS Act as well as the SEC's 2005 amendments, discussed later in this chapter, permit certain issuers to engage in a wide range of solicitation activities prior to the filing of the registration statement.

[2] Conditioning the Market ("Gun-Jumping")

A major concern in the pre-filing period is that statements made by the issuer and others (even when such statements do not refer to a forthcoming offering) will be construed as "conditioning the market" ("gun-jumping"), and, hence, constitute an "offer to sell" in violation of §5(c). The SEC has issued a number of releases on this issue. In this regard, the Commission has asserted that: "[T]he publication of

---

9. Note that as a result of certain offering rules adopted by the SEC in 2005, pre-filing period communications may be treated differently depending on whether they occurred within the 30-day period leading up to the filing of the registration statement or more than thirty days prior to such filing. *See* Securities Act Release No. 8591 (2005); discussion of Rule 163A in §4.02[B][3] *infra*.

10. Note also that Section 5(a) prohibits the use of the mails or any instrument or means of interstate commerce to sell or to deliver securities for purposes of sale before the effective date of the registration statement.

information and statements, and publicity efforts, made in advance of a proposed financing which have the effect of conditioning the public mind or arousing public interest in the issuer or in its securities constitutes an offer in violation of the Act."[11]

Nonetheless, Congress and the SEC have provided several non-exclusive safe harbors from the § 5 "gun-jumping" prohibitions for specified issuers:

First, as discussed later in this chapter, *well-known seasoned issuers (WKSI)* are exempt entirely from the "gun-jumping" prohibitions *(see Rule 163)*. These issuers may make "offers to sell" the subject securities in the pre-filing period without violating the registration mandates of § 5.[12]

Second, as provided by the JOBS Act enacted in 2012, an *emerging growth company* and persons acting on its behalf are permitted under § 5(d) of the Securities Act to communicate with qualified institutional buyers (QIBs) and accredited institutional investors prior to the filing of the company's registration statement to solicit indications of interest for the proposed offering. Thus, in the pre-filing period, emerging growth companies may "test the waters" to ascertain the extent of institutional investor interest in the contemplated public offering. (As discussed elsewhere in this text, stated succinctly and generally, an accredited institutional purchaser has total assets exceeding $5 million while a qualified institutional buyer (QIB) generally has at least $100 million invested in securities of issuers that are not affiliated with the QIB at the end of its most recent fiscal year.)

Third, also as elaborated upon later in this chapter, by rule, the SEC excludes all communications by or on behalf of any issuer (other than those communications directed at the contemplated offering or made by an offering participant who is an underwriter or dealer) made more than 30 days prior to the filing of the registration statement from the § 5 gun-jumping prohibitions (so long as the subject issuer takes reasonable steps to prevent further dissemination of the information during the 30-day period prior to the filing of the registration statement) *(see Rule 163A)*.[13] Importantly, under Rule 163A, any such communication cannot reference the contemplated offering.

Fourth, subject to certain conditions, *Rule 168* provides a safe harbor to § 5's gun-jumping prohibitions by allowing Exchange Act reporting issuers to continue to publish any regularly released factual business information and forward-looking information without restriction, subject to the antifraud provisions. The purpose of these types of communications is to keep the market informed about the subject company's financial condition rather than to condition the market for new issuances. A Rule 168 communication must be made by or on behalf of the issuer. This means that the issuer or an agent or representative of the issuer (other than an offering participant who is an underwriter or dealer) must authorize the release of the

---

11. Securities Exchange Act Release No. 5180 (1971).
12. Rule 163 is discussed in § 4.02[B][3] *infra*.
13. Rule 163A is discussed in § 4.02[B][3] *infra*.

communication before it is made. In addition, under Rule 168, information will only be considered "regularly released" if the issuer has previously released the same type of information by substantially the same method of release in the ordinary course of its business.[14]

Indeed, one previous release may establish the requisite "regularly released" track record. Excluded from the safe harbor of Rule 168 is the subject issuer's disclosure of information about the registered offering itself. Note, however, as discussed later in this chapter, disclosure of information by the issuer about the registered offering may be protected under other rules, such as Rule 135. Moreover, if the subject issuer is a well-known seasoned issuer or an emerging growth company, communications that focus on the contemplated offering in the pre-filing period are permitted (in the case of emerging growth companies only to QIBs and institutional accredited investors).[15]

Importantly, the Rule 168 safe harbor rule, providing insulation from § 5 liability with respect to factual and forward-looking information, affords Exchange Act reporting issuers with significant relief from the competing pressures of making full disclosure in Exchange Act reports, while simultaneously complying with the gun-jumping provisions. Prior to the adoption of Rule 168, registrants planning a prospective public offering at times may have been required to disclose forward-looking information as part of their periodic Exchange Act filings, with such disclosure possibly being viewed as conditioning the market. Rule 168 should lay to rest reporting issuer concerns over § 5 liability stemming from publication of regularly released forward-looking information.[16]

Pursuant to Rule 169, the fifth safe harbor, all issuers, including non-reporting issuers (such as voluntary filers or IPO issuers), may continue to publish, prior to the filing of the subject registration statement, any regularly released *factual* business information intended for use by persons other than in their capacity as investors or potential investors (such as information directed for the use of customers or suppliers). A communication intended for non-investors and disseminated under this safe harbor is still protected, even if it inadvertently reaches investors. Further, similar to information disseminated under Rule 168, a release in compliance with Rule 169 is not a § 2(a)(10) prospectus and does not violate the general prohibition against pre-filing offers. And, as with Rule 168, the communication must be made by or on behalf of the subject issuer (other than by a participant underwriter or dealer). However, in contrast to Rule 168, non-reporting issuers under Rule 169 may not publish forward-looking information. And, like Rules 163A and 168, the Rule 169

---

14. Note that Rule 168 does not extend to voluntary filers.

15. *See* JOBS Act § 105(c), adding, § 5(d) of the Securities Act; Securities Act Release No. 8591 (2005).

16. *See Chris-Craft Industries, Inc. v. Bangor Punta Corporation*, 426 F.2d 569 (2d Cir. 1970); Securities Act Release No. 8591 (2005).

safe harbor cannot be used to communicate any information about the registered offering itself.[17]

[3] Rules 163 and 163A and Emerging Growth Companies

As the foregoing discussion provides, there are important safe harbors to the § 5(c) prohibition against pre-filing offers. Generally, the safe harbor rules vary depending on the status of the issuer. For example, under Rule 163, *well-known seasoned issuers* (e.g., companies that have a public float of $700 million and have timely filed their Exchange Act reports for the past 12 months[18]) are completely exempt from restrictions on offers during the pre-filing period. Hence, these issuers are completely free of the gun-jumping prohibitions. Such an issuer (or its agent or representative, but not an offering participant like an underwriter or dealer) may communicate in compliance with § 5 at any time by means of unrestricted oral and written communications. Nonetheless, these communications, when considered offers to sell, may be subject to liability under other securities law provisions based on misrepresentation or omission.[19] As discussed later in this chapter, a written offer made by a well-known seasoned issuer pursuant to Rule 163 will constitute a "free writing prospectus."[20]

As discussed above in § 4.02[A], *emerging growth companies* and persons acting on their behalf likewise are exempt from the prohibition against making offers to sell in the pre-filing period, thereby being allowed under § 5(d) of the Securities Act to solicit indications of interest for a proposed offering from qualified institutional buyers (QIBs) and accredited institutional investors. Hence, prior to the filing of a registration statement with the SEC, an emerging growth company may "test the waters" to ascertain the extent of institutional investor interest in the contemplated public offering.

Issuers that are not well-known seasoned issuers or emerging growth companies remain subject to the gun-jumping prohibitions. Importantly, Rule 163A provides protection for these issuers with respect to their communications that occur more than 30 days prior to the filing of the subject registration statement. Effectively, the Rule 163A safe harbor exempts these communications from the definition of "offer" for § 5(c) purposes. For any such communication *not* to be deemed "an offer to sell," several conditions must be met: *first*, a Rule 163A communication cannot reference the contemplated offering; *second*, only a communication made by or on behalf of

---

17. Prior to the adoption of Rules 168 and 169, the Commission took a similar position regarding regularly released factual information. See Securities Act Release Nos. 5180 (1971); 7856 (2000).

18. The definition for "well-known seasoned issuer" is discussed in § 4.02[A] *supra*.

19. A written offer made in connection with a public offering may be deemed a prospectus under Section 2(a)(10) of the Securities Act. If materially false or misleading, such communication may render the issuer liable under Section 12(a)(2) and Section 17(a) of the Securities Act as well as Section 10(b) of the Exchange Act and Rule 10b-5 promulgated thereunder.

20. *See* § 4.02[C][2] *infra*.

the issuer comes within the safe harbor (with the proviso that the subject communication is not made by an offering participant who is an underwriter or dealer); and *third*, the burden is on the issuer to take reasonable steps to prevent circulation of the communication in the 30-day period leading up to the filing of the registration statement.[21] Key challenges facing the SEC in the interpretation of Rule 163A include determining what constitutes an impermissible "reference" to the contemplated public offering in a pre-filing communication, and determining what actions the issuer must take to corral previously released communications during the 30-day period immediately prior to the filing of the registration statement. Nonetheless, as discussed below, an issuer's disclosure of information about the contemplated registered offering in the pre-filing period may be protected under Rule 135.

[4] *Effect of Rule 135*

Rule 135 allows an issuer, subject to certain conditions, to make a public announcement relating to a contemplated public offering of its securities. In this respect, Rule 135 exempts from § 5(c) a notice given by an issuer in the pre-filing period that complies with its provisions. Hence, an issuer notice that adheres to Rule 135 is not deemed to constitute an "offer to sell" Generally, a Rule 135 notice, in addition to containing only certain specified information, must include a legend stating that the notice does not constitute an offer to sell. Note that the Rule prohibits the underwriters from being named in the notice and that judicial authority has interpreted the Rule as setting forth an exclusive list.[22]

Generally, Rule 135 provides that *only* the following may be set forth in the "notice":

(1) The notice includes a statement to the effect that it does not constitute an offer of any securities for sale; and

(2) The notice otherwise includes *no more than* the following information:

    (i)   The name of the issuer;

    (ii) The title, amount, and basic terms of the securities offered;

    (iii) The amount of the offering, if any, to be made by selling security holders;

    (iv) The anticipated timing of the offering;

    (v) A brief statement of the manner and the purpose of the offering without naming the underwriters;

    (vi) Whether the issuer is directing its offering to only a particular class of purchasers;

    (vii) Any statements or legends required by the laws of any state or foreign country of administrative authority. . . .

---

21. *See* Securities Act Release No. 8591 (2005). Note that Rule 163A may not be used in offerings made by a blank check company, shell company, or penny stock issuer. Also, note that separate rules apply to business combination transactions. *See* Rules 165, 424, 425.

22. *See Chris-Craft Industries, Inc. v. Bangor Punta Corporation*, 426 F.2d 569, 574 (2d Cir. 1970) (en banc).

Id. (emphasis added). Additional information may be provided pursuant to Rule 135 for certain types of offerings, including, for example, an exchange offer, a rights offering to existing security holders, and an offering to the subject issuer's employees. See Rule 135(a)(2)(viii)(A)-(D).

Accordingly, an issuer notice that:

(1) goes beyond the parameters of Rule 135,

(2) that cannot invoke the umbrella of another safe harbor provision (such as Rule 163 for well-known seasoned issuers), and

(3) where the information set forth in the notice is not otherwise required by another SEC regulation

may well constitute an "offer to sell" in the pre-filing period, thereby violating § 5(c) of the Securities Act. In this regard, the Second Circuit has opined:

> When it is announced that securities will be sold at some date in the future and, in addition, an attractive description of these securities and of the issuer is furnished, it seems clear that such an announcement provides much the same kind of information as that contained in a prospectus. Doubtless the line drawn between an announcement containing sufficient information to constitute an offer and one which does not must be to some extent arbitrary. A checklist of features that may be included in an announcement which does not also constitute an offer to sell serves to guide the financial community and the courts far better than any judicially formulated "rule of reason" as to what is or is not an offer. Rule 135 provides just such a checklist, and if the Rule is not construed as setting forth an exclusive list, then much of its value as a guide is lost.[23]

Importantly, note that the safe harbors contained in Rules 168, 169, and 163A cannot reference the contemplated public offering. Therefore, issuers that are not well-known seasoned issuers must continue to exercise caution with respect to public announcements in the pre-filing period of contemplated public offerings.

[5] *Transactions Between Market Professionals*

In addition to Rule 135, certain other actions are exempt from constituting an offer to sell or an offer to buy, and, hence, are permitted in the pre-filing period. For example, *pursuant to § 2(a)(3) of the Securities Act*, negotiations and agreements between the underwriter and the issuer or among underwriters who are (or will be) in privity of contract with the issuer are allowed in the pre-filing period.

Importantly, unless otherwise exempted, the prohibitions of § 5 apply to transactions and discussions between market professionals. For example, an "offer to buy" in the pre-filing period by a dealer not in privity with the issuer to an underwriter who is in privity with the issuer constitutes a violation of § 5(c). The prohibitions of

---

23. 426 F.2d at 574.

§ 5 in the waiting and post-effective periods also apply to transactions and discussions between market professionals, unless otherwise exempted.[24]

Turning to another point, an individual investor who contacts his/her broker-dealer in the pre-filing period to buy a few shares of a company's stock to be issued in the public offering normally does not violate § 5. That is because the individual, unless he/she is deemed to be engaged in a "distribution," has the § 4(a)(1) exemption that exempts from the § 5 registration requirements "transactions by any person other than an issuer, underwriter, or dealer."[25] This subject is covered in Chapter 6.

[6] Rules 137, 138, and 139 and Emerging Growth Companies

Rules 137, 138, and 139 permit broker-dealers to engage in specified "safe harbor" activities in the pre-filing period without violating § 5. Rules 137-139 apply as well to the waiting and post-effective periods. The availability and scope of these rules may be contingent on the reporting status of the issuer as discussed below and in § 4.02[A].[26]

Generally, Rules 137, 138 and 139 establish standards for ascertaining the circumstances under which broker-dealers without violating § 5 may publish research reports concerning issuers that propose to conduct a registered public offering.

Rule 137 is directed at brokers or dealers who are *not* participating in the public offering—in other words, those broker-dealers who are not in privity of contract either with the issuer or with any underwriter or other participant of the offering (e.g., nonparticipating broker-dealers that are not purchasing the securities offered from the issuer or from any of the underwriters). This Rule may be invoked for any eligible issuer irrespective of the subject issuer's Exchange Act reporting status. Generally, Rule 137 allows a nonparticipating broker-dealer in the regular course of its business to publish and distribute research reports containing information, recommendations, and opinions concerning the securities of an issuer that intends to file (or has filed) a Securities Act registration statement without such broker-dealer being deemed an underwriter.[27]

Rule 138 permits brokers or dealers who are (or will be) participating in a distribution of an issuer's common stock (or convertible preferred stock or convertible debt securities) to publish or distribute research reports that are confined specifically to the issuer's *non*-convertible fixed income securities (or vice versa). A research report complying with Rule 138 is deemed not to constitute an offer to sell for purposes of:

---

24. *See, e.g., Byrnes v. Faulkner, Dawkins & Sullivan*, 550 F.2d 1303 (2d Cir. 1977).

25. *See* Chapter 6 for further discussion of the Section 4(a)(1) exemption.

26. References will hereafter generally be made only to U.S. issuers who register their Securities Act offerings on such Forms as S-1 or S-3.

27. Note that Rule 137 cannot be used for offerings by ineligible issuers—ineligible issuers include those issuers that are (or during the past three years have been) a blank check company, shell company, or penny stock issuer. Rule 137(d).

§ 2(a)(10) (defining the term "prospectus"); or § 5(c) (prohibiting offers to sell in the pre-filing period by, among others, underwriters and dealers). Any such research report must be disseminated in the regular course of the broker-dealer's business. Unlike Rule 137, Rule 138 applies only to eligible issuers current in their Exchange Act reporting obligations (or to certain non-reporting foreign private issuers that have either equity securities traded on a designated offshore market or that have a world-wide market value of at least $700 million in outstanding common equity held by nonaffiliates).[28]

Provided that its requirements are met, Rule 139 permits a broker or dealer par-ticipating in a distribution of securities that is the subject of a Securities Act regis-tration statement to publish *issuer-specific research reports* focusing on a particular issuer or any class of such issuer's securities. A research report adhering to Rule 139 is not an offer to sell under § 2(a)(10) (defining the term "prospectus") and is not viewed as "gun-jumping" under § 5(c), namely, an illegal offer to sell in the pre-filing period by a participant in the contemplated public offering. Any such research report under Rule 139 must be published or distributed in the regular course of the broker-dealer's business.

With respect to such *issuer-specific research reports*, use of Rule 139 for U.S. issu-ers generally requires that a seasoned (or well-known seasoned) issuer be current in its Exchange Act reporting and is either eligible to file (or has filed) a registration statement on Form S-3 (or Form F-3) based on Form S-3's $75 million minimum public float eligibility provision. Rule 139 requires that for such issuer-specific research reports, any such publication or distribution by the broker or dealer must "not repre-sent the initiation of publication of research reports about such issuer or its securities or reinitiation of such publication following discontinuation. . . ."[29] Perhaps, surpris-ingly, an issuer-specific research report may upgrade the opinion for such security (from "hold" to "buy"). As Professor Joseph Morrissey has asserted: "[I]t seems that a financially interested broker or dealer will be able to take advantage of this [Rule 139] safe harbor to inflate its rating of [a subject] security [when] having great financial incentive to condition the market to increase the price of the securities being offered." Morrissey, *Rhetoric and Reality: Investor Protection and the Securities Regulation Reform of 2005*, 56 Cath. U.L. Rev. 561, 579 (2007).

In addition, the Rule provides a safe harbor for *industry reports* covering the secu-rities of the subject Exchange Act reporting issuer as well as a substantial number of other issuers. Such an industry report, as is the case with issuer-specific research reports, may upgrade the opinion regarding the subject security (e.g., from "hold" to "buy"). Moreover, such an industry report must "includ[e] similar information about the issuer or its securities [as contained] in similar reports." Also, the report

---

28. Like Rule 137, Rule 138 cannot be used for blank check companies, shell companies, and penny stock issuers. Rule 138(a)(ii)(C)(4).

29. Rule 139(a)(iii). Note that under certain conditions, issuer-specific research reports may be issued pursuant to Rule 139 for foreign private issuers. See Rule 139(a)(1)(B).

must include similar information for a substantial number of companies in the issuer's industry (or sub-industry), or, alternatively, contain a comprehensive list of securities that the broker or dealer currently recommends. Last, for such industry reports, Rule 139 mandates that "[t]he analysis regarding the issuer or its securities is given no materially greater space or prominence in the publication than that given to other securities or issuers."[30]

Importantly, due to the enactment of the JOBS Act in 2012, *emerging growth companies* are treated differently from other companies covered by the foregoing rules (namely, Rules 137, 138, and 139). Under the JOBS Act, a broker or dealer, even if it is participating in the contemplated offering, may publish or distribute a research report covering an emerging growth company that is proposing a public offering of its common equity securities in all three periods — the pre-filing, waiting, and post-effective periods. In this regard, the JOBS Act amended § 2(a)(3) of the Securities Act to provide that the issuance of such a research report is not deemed an "offer to sell" under Sections 2(a)(10) and 5(c) of that Act. Hence, although a research report is not deemed an "offer to sell" for registration compliance purposes, it may be deemed an offer to sell for purposes of the antifraud provisions (including § 17(a) of the Securities Act and § 10(b) of the Securities Exchange Act).

As defined in the statute, "research report means a written, electronic, or oral communication that includes information, opinions, or recommendations with respect to securities of an issuer or an analysis of a security or an issuer, whether or not it provides information reasonably sufficient upon which to base an investment decision." In this context, a key point is that, in compliance with the Securities Act registration provisions (including § 5), a broker or dealer may issue a research report containing a "buy" opinion about an *emerging growth company* that is proposing a registered offering (including an IPO), even if such broker or dealer is participating in the offering. The extent to which broker-dealers may "hype" an emerging growth company's financial condition when distributing such a research report remains to be determined. After all, the fraud provisions still apply for investors and the SEC to invoke.

[C] The Waiting Period

[1] Overview

After the registration statement is filed with the Commission, the *waiting period* commences. In this period, subsections (a) and (b) of § 5 are applicable. Section 5(b)(1) prohibits the use of the mails or any means of interstate commerce to transmit any prospectus, unless such prospectus meets the requirements of § 10. Since § 2(a)(10) defines a prospectus to include any written offer, there is no prohibition under

---

30. Rule 139(a)(2)(iv). Like Rules 137 and 138, Rule 139 cannot be used for blank check companies, shell companies, or penny stock issuers.

§ 5 against *verbal offers* during the waiting period. However, the contents and form of written offers are limited by § 2(a)(10) and § 10 as well as SEC rules.

Stated generally, during the waiting period (as well as the post-effective period), written offers may be made by means of a statutory § 10 prospectus, a § 10 free writing prospectus, as well as a tombstone ad (or Rule 134 public notice). Moreover, pursuant to § 5(a), the securities may not be sold nor may offers to buy be accepted unless the registration statement has become effective.

[2] Free Writing Prospectus

A free writing prospectus is a writing that offers for sale the registered offering of securities. Not meeting the detailed disclosure requirements of a statutory § 10(a) final prospectus, *the free writing prospectus during the waiting period generally may be used by the issuer or any other offering participant.* The free writing prospectus may contain information not set forth in the registration statement but must not conflict with such registration statement. Note that the SEC forbids the use of legends in a free writing prospectus that disclaim liability based on the contents of such free writing prospectus.

To begin, under Rule 163, well-known seasoned issuers may use free writing prospectuses during any phase of an offering, including the pre-filing period, without violating § 5. Note, however, that, while a free writing prospectus may be used during the pre-filing period by (or on behalf of) a well-known seasoned issuer, such a communication may not be made during this period by an offering participant who is an underwriter or participating dealer.[31] Such free writing prospectuses must be filed with the SEC and must contain a legend notifying the recipient where the registration statement (if one has been filed) can be located.

Eligible seasoned issuers (for example, issuers that have a $75 million float and that have timely reported under the Exchange Act for a 12-month period but are not well-known seasoned issuers) may use a free writing prospectus only if a registration statement containing a preliminary statutory prospectus has been filed. Such a free writing prospectus must contain a legend identifying how the investor can access or receive the statutory prospectus, a hyperlink to the statutory prospectus, or the URL (Uniform Resource Locator) for the SEC website where the investor can locate the statutory prospectus. Thus, a seasoned (including a well-known seasoned) issuer's use of a free writing prospectus is not conditioned on delivery to the investor of the most recent statutory prospectus.[32]

---

31. *See* Rule 163(a), (c).

32. The legend may contain, for example, an email address through which the statutory prospectus may be requested. *See* Rules 164, 433; Securities Act Release No. 8591 (2005).

Rule 164 provides a cure for unintentional or immaterial failure to include a proper legend in a free writing prospectus so long as the issuer has made a good faith, reasonable effort to comply and the free writing prospectus is amended as soon as possible. After amendment, the free writing prospectus must be retransmitted by substantially the same means and to substantially the same investors as was the original free writing prospectus.

Moreover, under Rule 164, eligible non-reporting issuers (such as an eligible company conducting an initial public offering—IPO) and eligible unseasoned issuers[33] may use a free writing prospectus if a registration statement has been filed with the SEC and the free writing prospectus is accompanied or preceded by the most recent statutory prospectus.[34] One form of "accompaniment" is a hyperlink to the statutory prospectus in an electronic free writing prospectus, thus making it feasible for these types of issuers to use broadly disseminated free writing prospectuses. Once the required statutory prospectus has been provided, an issuer is not required to provide subsequent preliminary statutory prospectuses to an investor unless there has been a material change to the most recent such statutory prospectus. In other words, absent a material change in the most recent statutory preliminary prospectus, a subject issuer is allowed to send an investor who has received a prior statutory prospectus additional free writing prospectuses unaccompanied by the most recent statutory prospectus. However, after the registration statement becomes effective and the "final" statutory prospectus is available, delivery of an earlier "preliminary" prospectus will not suffice. The "final" statutory § 10(a) prospectus must precede or accompany any free writing prospectus thereafter disseminated, even if a preliminary statutory prospectus had already been provided to the investor.[35]

Last, ineligible issuers also may use free writing prospectuses during the waiting and post-effective periods but such prospectuses may provide only a description of the terms of the offering and the securities offered. An ineligible issuer, for example, is an issuer that has not filed the required Exchange Act reports, has filed for bankruptcy, or has been convicted of a felony. Use of such a free writing prospectus by an ineligible issuer is subject to the statutory prospectus delivery requirements set forth above.[36] Moreover, blank check companies, shell companies, and penny stock issuers are excluded and cannot use any type of free writing prospectus.[37]

With certain exceptions, free writing prospectuses must be filed with the SEC.[38] Importantly, free writing prospectuses, unlike § 10(a) statutory prospectuses, are not part of the registration statement and as such are not subject to § 11 liability; however, free writing prospectuses are subject to § 12(a)(2) disclosure liability and the

---

33. Thus, eligible unseasoned Exchange Act reporting companies, as well as companies conducting initial public offerings (IPOs), may use free writing prospectuses during the waiting and post-effective periods subject to the conditions set forth in Rules 164 and 433.

34. *See* SEC Rules 164, 433.

35. *See* Rule 433(b)(2).

36. *See* Securities Act Release No. 8591 (2005).

37. *See* Rule 164(e)(2).

38. *See* Rule 433(d)(1). Rule 433(g) requires issuers using free writing prospectuses to retain for three years any free writing prospectuses that they have not filed with the SEC. This condition allows the SEC to review such free writing prospectuses used in reliance on Rules 164 and 433. Note that Rule 164 provides a cure for the immaterial or unintentional failure to retain a free writing prospectus so long as a good faith, reasonable effort was made to comply with the prospectus retention requirement.

anti-fraud provisions of the federal securities laws, including § 10(b) of the Exchange Act. Furthermore, pursuant to Rule 159A, an issuer meets the definition of "seller" in a primary securities offering for § 12(a)(2) liability purposes in the context of various underwriting arrangements, including firm commitment underwritings. Under this rule, an issuer is deemed a seller and subject to § 12(a)(2) liability regardless of the underwriting method employed to sell such issuer's securities. Under this rule, an issuer thus is a "seller" with respect to any free writing prospectus or other prospectus that is required to be filed with the SEC and is prepared by (or on behalf of) or is used by such issuer.[39] Note, however, there are court decisions that disagree with the SEC's position. See, e.g., *Lone Star Ladies Investment Club v. Schlotzky's Inc.*, 238 F.3d 363, 370 (5th Cir. 2001) (stating that "in a firm commitment underwriting, . . . the public cannot ordinarily hold the issuer liable under § 12, because the public does not purchase from the issuer").

Under Rule 433, an offer of securities on an issuer's website or hyperlinked from an issuer's website to another website is considered a written offer by the issuer and, unless exempt from registration, is deemed a free writing prospectus. Nonetheless, the Rule allows an issuer to publish historical information on its website that is considered neither an offer to sell nor a free writing prospectus, if the information is identified as historical information and is located on a separate section of the issuer's website that contains historical information.

In most cases, underwriters and dealers are not required to file a free writing prospectus that they prepare, use, or to which they refer.[40] However, there is an exception to this Rule: a free writing prospectus used or referred to by an underwriter or other offering participant, and distributed by or on behalf of an offering participant in a manner that is reasonably designed to lead to its broad unrestricted dissemination, must be filed with the SEC before use.[41]

One last point regarding free writing prospectuses is in the context of Regulation FD (discussed in Chapter 11). The Commission has exempted from the operation of Regulation FD certain communications that are made as part of a registered offering, including § 10(b) free writing prospectuses. In effect, the Commission has determined that such communications suffice for public notice purposes and are an adequate substitute for the prescribed Regulation FD procedures.[42]

---

39. *See* Rule 159A for a complete listing of communications that come within the scope of this Rule.

40. *See* Securities Act Release No. 8591 (2005).

41. *See* Rule 433(d)(l)(ii). See generally, Murdock, *Redoing the Statutory Scheme by Rule-Making*, 40 SEC. REG. L.J. 251 (2012); Pena, *The Free-Writing Prospectus: A Six Question Approach for Issuers*, 35 SEC. REG. L.J. 36 (2007).

42. These exceptions focus on communications directly related to the registered offering. Importantly, as the SEC pointed out, "[c]ommunications not contained in our enumerated list of exceptions from Regulation FD—for example, the publication of regularly released factual business information or regularly released forward-looking information or pre-filing communications—are subject to Regulation FD." Securities Act Release No. 8591 (2005).

[3] Confidential SEC Review of IPO Registration Statements Filed by Emerging Growth Companies

Pursuant to the JOBS Act enacted in 2012 and as amended by the FAST Act in 2015, an *emerging growth company* may confidentially submit to the SEC its draft IPO registration statement for nonpublic review by the Commission prior to the company's public filing of such IPO registration statement. Nonetheless, any such confidential draft and amendments thereto must be publicly filed with the SEC at least 15 days before the date on which the company conducts a "road show" for the IPO (see §6(e)(1) of the Securities Act; discussion of "road shows" in 4.02[C][6] below). This provision thus permits an emerging growth company to initiate the IPO filing process without having to publicly disclose sensitive information, thus retaining the option to discontinue the contemplated IPO and thereby maintaining the confidentiality of such sensitive information. However, if the emerging growth company elects to pursue the IPO, it must publicly file the confidential draft submission (and all amendments thereto) as set forth above—namely, at least 15 days before conducting a "road show" for its IPO.

[4] Media

Issuers and offering participants often use the media to deliver information about themselves to the general public through press releases and interviews. Recognizing that the media is a viable instrument for providing information about issuers and offerings to the public, the Commission has adopted certain rules in this setting. Specifically, where information (oral or written) about an issuer or an offering is provided by the issuer or any offering participant to the media and the information is subsequently published and constitutes an offer to sell, it will be considered a free writing prospectus. As such, these communications are allowed, but the issuer is required to file with the SEC such written communications within four business days of their first publication. In order to satisfy this filing requirement, the issuer may file the actual media publication (or all the information provided to the media in lieu of the publication itself), or a transcript of the interview or similar materials that were provided to the media.[43] As discussed in the following two paragraphs, any further obligations imposed on the issuer for a media publication free writing prospectus will depend on whether the issuer prepared or paid for the publication (be it a written publication or a television or radio broadcast).[44]

If an issuer prepares, pays for, or gives other consideration for the preparation or dissemination of a published article, advertisement, or broadcast, or if an issuer uses or refers to such communication, then the issuer must satisfy all of the conditions (discussed above) for that type of issuer using a free writing prospectus. Put another way, non-reporting issuers and reporting unseasoned issuers that have prepared or paid for the article, advertisement, or broadcast must precede or accompany the

---

43. *See* Rule 433(f).
44. *Id. See* Securities Act Release No. 8591 (2005).

communication with a statutory prospectus and file the media piece with the SEC. A seasoned issuer that prepared or paid for the communication only needs to have filed a registration statement with the SEC and to file the media piece. A well-known seasoned issuer, not subject to the gun-jumping prohibition due to Rule 163, may use such a media piece at any time, subject to filing the free writing prospectus with the SEC.

If, on the other hand, the free writing prospectus is prepared and published or broadcast by media persons unaffiliated with the issuer, and the issuer has participated but has not prepared or paid for the publication of such media piece, the issuer's (other than a well-known seasoned issuer[45]) obligation under § 5 is to have filed a registration statement and thereby a statutory prospectus with the SEC (otherwise, publication of such media piece within the 30-day period prior to the filing of the registration statement with the SEC may constitute gun-jumping—see Rule 163A; § 4.02[B][2] herein). Under such circumstances, accompaniment of the statutory prospectus with the publication is not required. The written communication is to be filed with the SEC within four business days after such issuer becomes aware of the communication.[46]

[5] *The Rule 134 Public Notice*

Another avenue available to issuers looking to publish information about a forthcoming public offering *after the filing of a registration statement* is to disseminate a tombstone ad[47] or the more expansive Rule 134 public notice. Under Rule 134, an issuer, for example, may release general information about: its business; the terms of the securities being offered; the underwriter(s) of the offering; details of the offering process; the anticipated schedule of the offering; a description of marketing events; indications of interest and conditional offers to buy; and the security rating that is reasonably expected to be assigned. The principal purpose behind the public notice is to enable the issuer to gauge the level of financial intermediary and investor interest in the prospective offering. Notably, although the availability of Rule 134 is contingent upon the issuer filing a registration statement (which includes a prospectus), the Commission permits use of the Rule prior to ascertaining a bona fide price range of the securities to be offered.

---

45. Well-known seasoned issuers, of course, are not required to have filed a registration statement prior to using a free writing prospectus, including a media piece. See Rule 163. Within 30 days of filing a registration statement, issuers (other than well-known seasoned issuers) using a media publication that is deemed a free writing prospectus may be engaged in gun-jumping. Cf. Rule 163A.

Note also that there exists a limited exception for issuers that are in the media business, allowing such issuers to rely on the unaffiliated media condition under certain circumstances. See Rule 433(f)(3).

46. *See* Rule 433(f); Securities Act Release No. 8591 (2005).

47. The tombstone ad is exempt from the definition of "prospectus" pursuant to Section 2(a)(10)(b) of the Securities Act.

Note, however, that Rule 134 does not allow the issuer to set forth a detailed description of the securities being offered pursuant to the registration statement. If a term sheet is used by the issuer, for example, such communication, although not allowed under Rule 134, will be treated as a free writing prospectus subject to the requirements for free writing prospectuses that are addressed above.[48]

[6] Roadshows

During the waiting period, in addition to oral communications, tombstone ads, Rule 134 public notices, and § 10 prospectuses, issuers and underwriters customarily conduct "roadshows" to prospective institutional investors, securities professionals, and others as a means to present the issuer and the securities offered in a favorable light. These "performances" are used to ascertain what parties are interested in the securities and the extent of such interest.

Recall that during the 30 days leading up to the filing of the registration statement (except for well-known seasoned issuers and emerging growth companies— to QIBs and institutional accredited investors only), among other prohibitions, no written sales literature (so-called "free writing") is allowed (see Rule 163A). During the waiting period, depending on the status of the issuer, written offering materials that generally may be used include a § 10 prospectus (such as a statutory or free writing prospectus), a tombstone ad, or a Rule 134 public notice. Because roadshows frequently occur during the waiting period and involve the use of the Internet and other electronic media, it is important to determine how the Commission treats such media in light of the restrictions against written offers.

Historically, through a number of no-action letters, the SEC staff had acquiesced in the view that roadshow media did not constitute a § 2(a)(10) prospectus and allowed the use of electronic media by issuers and underwriters to conduct roadshows for audiences consisting of sophisticated investors and securities professionals.[49] However, recognizing that roadshows have evolved from live, real-time productions made primarily to institutional investors to, at times, recorded media reproductions to larger, less sophisticated audiences, the Commission has taken a more detailed approach as to what constitutes written offers and prospectuses.

Pursuant to SEC rules, the conducting of real-time roadshows to live audiences that also are transmitted graphically in real-time (such as in real-time by means of the Internet) are not deemed written communications or free writing prospectuses.[50] On the other hand, "[r]oadshows that do not originate live, in real-time to a live

---

48. *See* SEC Securities Act Release 8591 (2005).

49. *See, e.g., In re Charles Schwab & Co.,* 1999 WL 1038050 (Nov. 12, 1999); *In re Private Financial Network,* [1997 Transfer Binder] Fed. Sec. L. Reg. (SEC) & 77,332 (March 12, 1997).

50. Note that, if visual aids (such as slides) are used as part of a live in real-time roadshow, such visual aids are not a free writing prospectus. However, such a roadshow is an offer to sell the securities subject to Section 12(a)(2) and other liability provisions. *See* Securities Act Release No. 8591 (2005).

audience and are graphically transmitted [such as by being retransmitted by electronic mail] are electronic roadshows that will be considered written communications and, therefore, free writing prospectuses."[51] With one exception,[52] these electronic roadshows that constitute free writing prospectuses are not required to be filed with the SEC.[53]

[7] SEC's Power of Acceleration

Under § 8(a) of the Securities Act, a registration statement becomes effective the twentieth day after it is filed with the SEC. Significantly, the filing of any amendment commences the 20-day waiting period anew. Moreover, customarily, an issuer, particularly in an initial public offering, files its registration statement with a legend (referred to as the "delaying amendment" pursuant to Rule 473) voluntarily waiving this 20-day period in favor of waiting until the SEC elects to clear the registration statement. Note that an exception to this general rule is that well-known seasoned issuers may opt for automatic shelf registration (discussed in Chapter 5) whereby such registration statement becomes effective immediately upon filing with the SEC.[54]

Pursuant to § 8(a), the Commission has the power of acceleration, meaning, for example, that it can determine to have the registration statement become effective immediately after the last amendment is filed. In practice, this power of acceleration along with the issuer's waiver of the 20-day period referred to above may give the Commission a good deal of leverage. Imagine if an issuer, after filing its last amendment, would have to wait 20 days before being able to have the registered securities sold. In many situations, given the volatile nature of the financial markets, the offering, 20 days later, no longer may find a receptive audience. The end result is that the Commission staff may be able to "persuade" the issuer and affiliated parties to disclose more information than they otherwise would prefer.

The SEC has reduced its leverage in this context by, for example, adopting Rule 430A. Under Rule 430A, issuers engaging in offerings of securities for cash no longer are required to file a pre-effective "pricing" amendment (i.e., information relating to price and the underwriting syndicate). Today, specified changes can be made with respect to such matters as price and volume information after the registration statement's effective date, provided that such changes do not materially alter the disclosure contained in the registration statement.

With respect to Rule 430A, the SEC has pointed out that the Rule does not alter an issuer's disclosure obligations. According to the Commission, Rule 430A is

---

51. *Id. See* Rule 433(d)(8)(ii).

52. The one exception is that such an electronic roadshow must be filed with the SEC by a nonreporting issuer (such as an issuer conducting an IPO) "unless the issuer . . . makes at least one version of [the] roadshow available without restriction by means of graphic communication to any person, including any potential investor in the securities . . . ." Rule 433(d)(8).

53. *See* Rule 433(d)(8)(i); Securities Act Release No. 8591 (2005).

54. *See* Rule 415(a)(5)(i); Securities Act Release No. 8591 (2005).

intended to "minimize the risk of disruption of a registrant's marketing schedule caused by the need to file a pricing amendment and wait until the registration statement is declared effective."[55] Note, moreover, that pursuant to the 2005 amendments, registration statements filed by well-known seasoned issuers pursuant to the SEC's automatic shelf registration process (discussed in Chapter 5) become effective immediately upon filing with the Commission.

Significantly, as a condition to granting acceleration, the SEC may require the respective parties to undertake certain actions. For example, under Item 512(h) of Regulation S-K, in order to request acceleration of the effective date of the registration statement, the issuer must disclose, inter alia, any arrangement to indemnify any director, officer or controlling person of the issuer against liabilities arising under the Securities Act. Moreover, a subject issuer, pursuant to Item 510 of Regulation S-K, also must disclose that such indemnification with respect to a director, officer, or controlling person of the issuer, "in the opinion of the Securities and Exchange Commission . . . is against public policy as expressed in the [Securities] Act and is, therefore, unenforceable."

[D] The Post-Effective Period

[1] Overview

After the registration statement becomes effective, the *post-effective* period commences. Sales of the subject securities now may be made. Written offers continue to be regulated by the SEC offering rules discussed above, such as use of the free writing prospectus.[56]

The contents of the final statutory prospectus are specified in § 10(a). Unlike the preliminary prospectus, which is used in the waiting period (see Rule 430), the statutory final prospectus is used after the registration statement becomes effective. This is because the preliminary prospectus has certain incomplete information. During the post-effective period, the § 10(a) final statutory prospectus must be provided or be accessible to purchasers of the subject securities.[57]

[2] Access Equals Delivery

As part of its effort to modernize the offering process, and in acknowledgment of the vast availability of Internet access to the investing public, the SEC adopted an "access equals delivery" framework to the § 5 prospectus delivery requirement in the post-effective period.[58] Under the access equals delivery approach, and subject to

---

55. Securities Act Release No. 6714 (1987). *See* Securities Act Release No. 6964 (1992).

56. *See* discussion § 4.02[C][2] *supra*.

57. *See* Rules 172, 173; Securities Act Release No. 8591 (2005).

58. Securities Act Rule 172.

certain exceptions,[59] investors are presumed to have access to the Internet. Accordingly, issuers and other offering participants, such as dealers, may satisfy the prospectus delivery requirement by posting the final statutory prospectus on a readily accessible website. Thus, the § 5 requirement that a final statutory prospectus precede or accompany the delivery of the securities for sale or accompany a sale confirmation has been eliminated — provided that the final statutory prospectus is timely filed with the Commission and is posted on a readily accessible website.[60] Moreover, in recognition that actual physical delivery aided investors in tracing their purchase to a specific registration statement, thereby preserving their § 11 right of action for any material disclosure deficiency in such registration statement, the SEC adopted a notification rule requiring dealers or underwriters to provide a notice to purchasers that their purchase was pursuant to a registration statement.[61] Such a notice typically provides as follows:

> THIS NOTICE IS PROVIDED TO YOU, IN LIEU OF THE FINAL PROSPECTUS, PURSUANT TO SECURITIES ACT RULE 173 TO THE EXTENT THAT THE SALE WAS MADE PURSUANT TO A REGISTRATION STATEMENT OR IN A TRANSACTION IN WHICH A FINAL PROSPECTUS WOULD HAVE BEEN REQUIRED TO HAVE BEEN DELIVERED IN THE ABSENCE OF SECURITIES ACT RULE 172. YOU CAN REQUEST A COPY OF THE FINAL PROSPECTUS (WHICH NEED NOT BE PROVIDED BEFORE SETTLEMENT) FROM US BY CALLING 866-___-____.

For further discussion, see Morrissey, *Rhetoric and Reality: Investor Protection and the Securities Regulation Reform of 2005*, 56 Cath. U.L. Rev. 561 (2007); Murdock, *Redoing the Statutory Scheme by Rule-Making*, 40 Sec. Reg. L.J. 251 (2012); Pena, *The Free-Writing Prospectus: A Six Question Approach for Issuers*, 33 Sec. Reg. L.J. 36 (2006); Rasmussen, *Let's Not Jump the Gun: An Analysis of the Current State of Section 5 and Recent SEC Actions Involving Section 5 Violations*, 44 Sec. Reg. L.J. 159 (2016).

[E] Chart of Time Periods

The following Chart will help clarify the conduct permitted as well as prohibited during the pre-filing, waiting, and post-effective periods. Note that the Chart simplifies a number of the requirements and should be used for ease of reference purposes.

---

59. Rule 172 does not apply to tender offers or business combination transactions, and is unavailable to registered investment and business development companies.

60. *See* Securities Act Release No. 8591 (2005).

61. *See* Rule 173(a) (providing that "each underwriter or dealer . . . shall provide to each customer from it, not later than two business days following the completion of such sale, a copy of the final prospectus or, in lieu of such prospectus, a notice to the effect that the sale was made pursuant to a registration statement or in a transaction in which a final prospectus would have been required to have been delivered in the absence of Rule 172").

Time Period

Pre-Filing	Waiting	Post-Effective
Offers to sell as well as offers to buy are prohibited—see §§ 2(a)(3), 5(c). Exception for well-known seasoned issuers—WKSI (see Rule 163) and emerging growth companies—EGC (to QIBs and accredited institutional investors)—see § 5(d).	Oral offers and written offers by means of a § 10 prospectus are permitted—see §§ 2(a)(10), 5(b)(1), 10(b), Rules 164, 430, 431, 433.	Sales may be made only if a statutory § 10(a) prospectus has been provided or is accessible to the purchaser—see §§ 2(a)(10), 5(b), 10(a), Rules 172, 173.
More than 30 days before filing date: Written and oral communications are permitted by any issuer as long as they do not reference the offering and subject to certain other restrictions—see Rule 163A.	May make written offers under Rule 164 using a free writing prospectus as long as Rule 433 is complied with and the issuer satisfies applicable "accompaniment" requirements—see Rules 164, 433.	Final prospectus requirements may be satisfied by providing "access" to the statutory prospectus in lieu of actual delivery—see Rules 172, 173.
Sales are prohibited—see §§ 2(a)(3), 5(a).	For seasoned and well-known seasoned issuers, no requirement that use of free writing prospectus is conditioned on actual delivery of preliminary statutory prospectus; rather, a legend must be used stating where the preliminary statutory prospectus can be accessed—see Rules 164, 433.	Use of free-writing prospectuses in the post-effective period permitted under certain circumstances—see §§ 2(a)(10), 5(b)(1), 10(a), Rules 164, 172, 173, 430A, 433.
Negotiations and agreements between the issuer and any underwriter or among underwriters who are or will be in privity with the issuer are permitted—see § 2(a)(3).		Both the "tombstone ad" and the "public notice" may be used—see § 2(a)(10), Rule 134.
All issuers may make an announcement of a proposed public offering in compliance with Rule 135.	Eligible unseasoned issuers and eligible non-reporting issuers may use a free writing prospectus only if accompanied or preceded by the most recent statutory prospectus—See Rule 164, 433.	
All issuers may continue to publish regularly released factual information (including as well in the Waiting and Post-Effective Periods)—see Rules 168, 169.	Both the "tombstone ad" and the "public notice" may be used—see § 2(a)(10), Rule 134.	Securities may be sold and offers to buy may be accepted only in the post-effective period—see §§ 2(a)(3), 5(a).
Exchange Act Reporting Issuers may continue to publish forward-looking information (including as well in the Waiting and Post Effective Periods)—see Rule 168.	Sales are prohibited—see § 5(a).	

Pre-Filing

Pursuant to Rules 137-139 and §2(a)(3), a broker or dealer may publish certain information about specified issuers, including emerging growth companies. This is also the case in the waiting and post-effective periods.

Emerging Growth Companies may "test the waters" and communicate with QIBs and institutional accredited investors regarding proposed offering—see §5(d).

Well-known Seasoned Issuers may make offers to sell and may use free writing prospectuses—see Rule 163.

§ 4.03 Scenarios

Problem A

Texxon, incorporated in Delaware, is a publicly held company engaged in energy exploration and development. Its principal offices are in Houston, Texas. Its common stock is listed on the New York Stock Exchange. The company, pursuant to the requirements of the Securities Exchange Act, files annual reports and other periodic documents with the Securities and Exchange Commission. The company's public float is $550 million and it has gross revenues exceeding $3 billion. For each question, ask whether your answer would be different if Texxon: (1) were a well-known seasoned issuer, (2) an emerging growth company, or (3) not a reporting company.

Assume that Texxon plans to make a public offering of common stock but no registration statement has been filed with the SEC at this time.

(1) The president of Texxon in Houston telephones Jean Better and Sons, Inc., an investment bank in New York City, to discuss Texxon's proposed public offering. Representatives of Texxon and Jean Better thereafter meet in Houston, and tentatively agree that Jean Better and Sons, Inc. will serve as principal underwriter for the issue. They also negotiate the number of shares to be offered, underwriting discounts and dealer allowances, subject to market conditions. They record this agreement in a memorandum. Did their acts violate §5?

(2) Jean Better and Sons, Inc. arranges a full page notice in the Wall Street Journal announcing that Texxon proposes to offer 400,000 shares of common stock pursuant to a public offering and that Jean Better will serve as the principal underwriter.

The announcement also describes the planned use of the proceeds, the plans of management, and that the price of the stock will be at or near market level when the registration statement becomes effective. Is this announcement in violation of § 5?

(3) Texxon mails to 5,000 accredited institutional investors a glossy brochure touting its forthcoming registered offering, its sound financial condition, and its future forecasted earnings.

(4) Texxon issues a press release announcing the forthcoming public offering. The use of the proceeds are described as follows: "In conjunction with major contracts that Texxon anticipates it will receive, the proceeds will be used to finance research and development in energy-related fields." Is this press release a violation of § 5?

(5) Abner, Sykes and Co., a dealer in Arkansas, telephones Jean Better in New York and asks to be a member of the retail selling group of the Texxon public offering when issued. Jean Better accepts the proposal. Has either party (or both) violated § 5?

(6) Jean Better and Sons, Inc., by means of the mails and telephone, invites other investment bankers to join in the registered offering of Texxon's common stock. The interested underwriters sign an agreement among themselves to purchase the stock on certain terms and authorize Jean Better to execute an agreement with Texxon on their behalf. Jean Better does so and mails each underwriter a copy of the agreement. Is this permissible?

Assume the registration statement has been filed with the SEC but it is not yet effective.

(7) A participating dealer, Goulash & Baker, Inc., in New York, telephones a customer in Florida to inform her of Texxon's forthcoming public offering. The customer expresses an interest. Thereupon, the dealer mails her a glossy brochure. A legend contained in the brochure sets forth the website address where the preliminary prospectus can be accessed. Are there any violations by either party?

(8) Abel, Brown and Crest, a dealer not participating in the Texxon public offering, mails its monthly newsletter to customers advising them to purchase Texxon common stock. Has any violation of § 5 occurred?

(9) Texxon places the preliminary prospectus on its website and provides direct access via a hyperlink to a favorable research report on the Company issued by Jean Better and Sons, Inc. When reviewing the Texxon preliminary prospectus, an investor can click on a box marked "Jean Better & Sons Research Report" and be linked to Jean Better and Sons' website where the research report is available. Has Texxon violated § 5?

(10) A sales representative for Jean Better and Sons, Inc. telephones a customer, Mr. Bankroll, to set up a lunch date. At lunch, they discuss the forthcoming issue of Texxon. Bankroll indicates his willingness to buy Texxon stock on a when-issued basis. Has any violation of § 5 occurred? Is the representative's response material?

Assume that Texxon's registration statement is now effective.

(11) Refer to the facts set out in Question (10) above. Assume the sales representative subsequently mails Mr. Bankroll a brochure highlighting the history and development of Texxon, along with a statutory prospectus and a confirmation of his purchase of Texxon stock pursuant to the public offering. Is this a violation of § 5?

(12) Immediately after the registration statement goes effective, Texxon places the statutory § 10(a) prospectus on its website. Jean Better and Sons, Inc., then confirms by mail the sale of Texxon stock to purchasers. The confirmation sets forth that the purchaser may obtain a copy of the final statutory prospectus by calling a toll-free number. Does this meet the prospectus delivery requirements of § 5?

(13) Texxon places a copy of the § 10(a) statutory prospectus, as well as supplemental sales literature, on its website. Both the statutory prospectus and the sales literature can be accessed from the same menu, are clearly identified on the menu, and appear in proximity to each other on the menu. Thus, the sales literature may be accessed by an investor prior to viewing the statutory prospectus. In this situation, is the sales literature permissible?

(14) Texxon places its sales literature in a discussion forum located on the World Wide Web. The Texxon sales literature contains a hyperlink to the Company's statutory prospectus. This allows an investor, while viewing the sales literature, to click on a box marked "statutory (final) prospectus" and be linked directly to the Texxon website. The Texxon statutory prospectus promptly will appear on the investor's computer screen. Is this permissible?

Problem B

Fifteen years ago, Linda Luck founded Gloss, Inc., a cosmetic company created to market Gloss Cosmetics, an all-natural line of beauty products. The operation grew from a small retail store in Southern California to a West Coast enterprise. Bolstered by her rapid success, Luck would like to market her cosmetics line throughout the United States; however, this expansion would require a large capital investment. Gloss, Inc. has already had five private offerings and now Luck considers "going public" with Gloss, Inc. She consults you, her attorney, for advice. What are the consequences of going public? How would you advise Luck?

Assume Gloss, Inc. has been a public company for the past eight years, with Luck maintaining her controlling interest. The public float of Gloss, Inc. is $125 million. The American public has responded enthusiastically to Gloss products, and business is booming. Luck is anxious to expand further, including the national marketing of a fairly new line of products, "Gloss For Men." In conjunction with the further development and marketing of "Gloss For Men," the Gloss board of directors plans a public offering to raise the required capital. Two weeks before the registration statement is to be filed, Luck receives a telephone call from a reporter of "Business Man," a nationally distributed weekly magazine targeted at the young male professional. "Business Man" would like to do an article within the next week on Gloss, Inc.'s line of products for men and asks Luck for some factual background material. Luck responds that she is in the middle of a meeting and will not be available until tomorrow. Luck then calls you, her attorney, and asks whether she should provide "Business Man" with the information that the magazine has requested. What are your concerns? What do you advise?

§ 4.04 The Materially False and Misleading Prospectus

In *SEC v. Manor Nursing Centers, Inc.*, 482 F.2d 1082, 1098 (2d Cir. 1972), the Second Circuit considered whether material misrepresentations or nondisclosures contained in a statutory prospectus signified that, in addition to incurring antifraud liability, the prospectus failed to meet the requirements of § 10(a) of the Securities Act and, hence, violated § 5(b)(2) of that Act. In that case, the violations were premised on the defendants' failure to amend or supplement the prospectus to reflect changes that occurred in the post-effective period that made the previous information furnished materially false and misleading. The Second Circuit held that § 5(b)(2) had been violated, stating:

> We hold that implicit in the statutory provision that the prospectus contain certain information is the requirement that such information be true and correct. A prospectus does not meet the requirements of § 10(a), therefore, if information required to be disclosed is materially false and misleading. Appellants violated § 5(b)(2) by delivering Manor securities for sale accompanied by a prospectus which did not meet the requirements of § 10(a) in that the prospectus contained materially false and misleading statements with respect to information required by § 10(a) to be disclosed.

The Manor Nursing analysis is subject to criticism because it imposes essentially strict liability, thereby nullifying the due diligence and reasonable care defenses contained in §§ 11 and 12(a)(2) of the Securities Act (see Chapter 7). For this reason, a number of courts have limited its holding to apply only where the prospectus or a like document is egregiously incomplete or permeated with misrepresentations.[62] Other courts, in analogous situations, have completely rejected *Manor Nursing's* rationale.[63]

One such case is *SEC v. Southwest Coal & Energy Company*, 624 F.2d 1312, 1319 (5th Cir. 1980). There, the SEC relied by analogy on *Manor Nursing*, arguing that the issuer had never properly qualified for the then Regulation B exemption since its

---

62. *See, e.g., Byrnes v. Faulkner Dawkins & Sullivan*, 413 F. Supp. 453 (S.D.N.Y. 1976), *aff'd on other grounds*, 550 F.2d 1303 (2d Cir. 1977).

63. *See, e.g., SEC v. Blazon Corp.*, 609 F.2d 960 (9th Cir. 1979).

Schedule D offering sheets were materially false and misleading. Such materially defective offering sheets, the SEC asserted, did not meet Regulation B's initial filing requirements, thereby violating § 5(a) and 5(c). The Fifth Circuit rejected this contention, reasoning that such an interpretation would impose strict liability and vitiate the defenses available under other provisions of the securities laws (e.g., §§ 11, 12(a)(2), and 17(a) of the Securities Act and § 10(b) of the Exchange Act). The court stated:

> That an offering sheet which formally complies with the disclosure requirements of Schedule D is misleading in some respect, should not automatically render void *ab initio* a Regulation B exemption obtained on the basis of that offering. Rather, representations and material nondisclosures may be adequately dealt with under the pertinent antifraud provisions expressly designed for that purpose, instead of under § 5(a), (c) which is more appropriately focused upon failures to adhere to the prescribed formal mechanisms or procedures.

The view expressed above, on balance, is correct. To hold that a § 5 violation occurs whenever a security is sold pursuant to a materially false or misleading statement in the prospectus or like document, such as an offering circular, would negate the defenses otherwise available. Such a result is one that Congress did not intend.

On the other hand, if the thrust of *Manor Nursing* is confined to issuers of registered offerings, then the decision may be viewed as compatible with § 11. Hence, because § 11 holds issuers strictly liable for making material misrepresentations or nondisclosures in a registration statement, the *Manor Nursing* rationale may be consistent with the framework of § 11, provided that it is limited only to issuers. Nonetheless, an issuer sued under § 11 has an important defense that is not available in a private action based on a registration violation—establishing that the disclosure violation did not cause the financial loss—in other words, showing lack of loss causation (see Chapter 7 herein).

In this regard, the Commission has certain enforcement powers if the registration statement is materially false or misleading. The most significant such power is the "stop order" pursuant to § 8(d) of the Securities Act. See McLucas, *Stop Order Proceedings Under the Securities Act of 1933: A Current Assessment*, 40 Bus. Law. 515 (1980).

---

§ 4.05 The Decision to "Go Public" — Pros and Cons

The advantages of an enterprise going public and having its initial public offering (IPO) include:

1. The funds obtained from the offering may be used for capital formation purposes as well as for retiring existing indebtedness.

2. The insiders may sell a substantial portion of their stock and thereby become (if they are not already) millionaires.

3. A public offering, by improving the company's financial position, will enable the company to have access to capital on more favorable terms.

4. The funds desired from the offering may enable the company to expand by acquiring other businesses.

5. By offering stock remuneration packages tied to a public market, the enterprise will be in a better position to hire and retain quality personnel.

6. By having a public market for its stock, the company may become better known, thereby possibly resulting in improved profits.

On the other hand, perceived disadvantages of going public include:

1. The costs of an IPO, particularly when compared to other methods of procuring funds, are high.

2. Due to shareholder concern for the short-term, management may discount long-term strategies in order to put emphasis on the company's stock price.

3. The company may be required to disclose financial and operational information it otherwise would have kept confidential, thereby placing it in a possible competitive disadvantage compared to its privately held competitors.

4. Management, through its sale of stock, may lose control of the enterprise and become subject to a hostile takeover.

5. By going public, the enterprise becomes a reporting company under the Securities Exchange Act (see Chapter 5). Such a consequence may be viewed as having several disadvantages, including:

   a. The company now must file periodic and annual reports, comply with the internal accounting controls and recordkeeping mandates of the Foreign Corrupt Practices Act (even if all of the company's operations are domestic), be subject to the federal proxy provisions, as well as a number of other requirements.

   b. The company becomes subject to the rigors of the Sarbanes-Oxley Act of 2002 (SOX) and the Dodd-Frank Act of 2010. For example, applicable requirements include: chief executive officer and chief financial officer certification of the subject company's periodic reports with the SEC; the implementation of sufficient internal controls; delineating the composition and functions of audit and compensation committees; and prohibition of company loans to directors and executive officers.

   c. The expenses of complying with Exchange Act and SOX requirements will be substantial.

    d. Insiders lose some of their privacy as their salaries, perquisites, and transactions with the issuer must be disclosed pursuant to SEC rules.

    e. Due to such mandated disclosure, there is a greater risk of shareholder litigation.

    f. Insiders are subject to the short-swing six-month trading provisions of § 16 of the Exchange Act, thereby resulting in some loss of liquidity and potential liability.

Given the above, the decision to go public may be challenging. Moreover, the registration process — including the planning, preparation, structuring, and timing of a public offering — is a major undertaking for all parties concerned.

---

§ 4.06 The Registered Offering — A Look at the Process

The advantages and disadvantages of going public are addressed in § 4.05. The process of the initial public offering and the ramifications thereof are described in this Section and in Chapter 5.

In brief, and put simplistically, the process of a public offering may be analogized to the sale of commercial goods. In a public offering, the distribution chain normally is as follows: Issuer — Underwriters — Participating Dealers — Investors/Purchasers (who may be individuals or institutions). Generally speaking, the larger in dollar size and the greater the geographical area where the selling activity takes place, the larger the number of underwriters and dealers who will comprise the distribution chain to effectuate the offering. Note the similarity to the sale of commercial goods: Manufacturer — Wholesalers — Retailers — Consumers. As with the sale of commercial goods where wholesalers may sell directly to the public, underwriters also may bypass the "dealer-link" and sell the securities directly to investors. This may occur, for example, when an underwriter (such as UBS) has a national retail brokerage capacity with which to market the securities directly to investors.

Underwriting agreements for the most part are on a "firm commitment" basis. This means that the underwriters agree to purchase the securities from the issuer (at a discount) with the intent to resell them to participating dealers and/or investors. Although the underwriters incur the risk of "being stuck" with the securities if there is insufficient buyer interest, this risk is minimized due to that, during the "waiting" period (when, regardless of the status of the subject issuer, offers can be made), purchaser interest can be estimated with a fair degree of accuracy. And, importantly, the underwriters' obligations normally are subject to several conditions, including various "outs" to not close should certain material adverse changes arise prior to the closing date. Thus, the underwriters customarily are not obligated until the "eve" of the offering's effective date when the underwriting agreement is finalized to, inter alia, determine the desired number of shares to be offered and fix the offering price per share. By that time, there exists a strong indication of the market's likely response to the offering.[64]

Another type of underwriting agreement is on a "best efforts" basis. In this situation, the underwriters act as agents for the issuer. Rather than purchasing the securities outright from the issuer and incurring the risk of insufficient investor interest in such securities or the specter of a "bear" market, the underwriters, acting as agent for the issuer, locate buyers utilizing their "best efforts." These types of offerings may be used for start-up or financially troubled enterprises where there is a substantial degree of uncertainty regarding the offering's, as well as the company's, ultimate success. Because investors may wish some degree of comfort when they part with their money in these types of offerings, such offerings frequently may be made on "a part or none" or "an all or nothing" basis. This means that, unless the requisite number of shares as stated in the registration statement are sold to bona fide purchasers and the proceeds are received by a specified date, all funds must be returned to the prospective investors.[65]

In either a "firm commitment" or "best efforts" underwriting arrangement, the obligations of the underwriters normally are subject to various contractual conditions, called "outs." Pursuant to such an arrangement, for example, underwriters may have the right not to close the "deal" if specified material adverse changes (MACs) arise before the closing date (such as the presence of adverse market conditions) or if the issuer fails to comply with its specified representations and warranties. Moreover, the underwriters condition their obligations by bargaining for the receipt of certain legal opinions and/or representations from counsel for the issuer.[66]

A word should be said about the underwriting syndicate and dealer group. The syndicate is headed by the main underwriter or main underwriters (for example, there may be more than one main underwriter in a fairly large offering). These underwriters generally are the ones to negotiate with the issuer and are delegated by the other underwriters in the syndicate to perform the due diligence functions. To effectuate the desired distribution, the main underwriter(s) will locate and bring in other underwriters who desire to take part in the offering. Generally, these "lower-tier" underwriters in the offering will purchase a significantly smaller number of shares from the issuer than the main underwriter(s). Although all underwriters are

---

64. *See* C. Johnson, J. McLaughlin, and E. Haueter, Corporate Finance and the Securities Laws (5th ed. 2015); Schneider, Manko & Kant, *Going Public: Practice, Procedure and Consequences*, 27 Vill. L. Rev. 1, 24 (1981).

65. *See* Rule 10b-9, 17 C.F.R. § 240.10b-9; Securities Exchange Act Release No. 11532 (1975). *See generally* Frelich & Janvey, *Understanding "Best Efforts" Offerings*, 17 Sec. Reg. L.J. 151 (1989).

66. *See* Schneider, Manko & Kant, *Going Public: Practice, Procedure and Consequences*, 27 Vill. L. Rev. 1, 24 (1981). Such opinions, representations, or statements from counsel raise serious liability concerns. See generally D. Glaser, S. FitzGibbon & S. Weise, *Legal Opinions* (3d. ed. 2015); Rice & Steinberg, *Legal Opinions in Securities Transactions*, 16 J. Corp. L. 375 (1991).

jointly and severally liable for material misstatements in the registration statement, § 11(e) of the Securities Act mitigates this potentially harsh effect somewhat by limiting an underwriter's damages to the dollar amount of the securities offered by such underwriter to the public. Moreover, § 11(f) expressly permits a party to recover contribution.[67]

Members of the dealer group ("participating" dealers), as discussed earlier in this Chapter, are not in privity of contract with the issuer. These are broker-dealers, who for one reason or another (such as inability or a conscious desire not to commit the necessary funds), are not members of the underwriting syndicate but who nonetheless deem it in their financial interests to become a "participant" in the offering. Hence, they purchase from underwriters an allocated number of shares offered and resell them to their customers; their profit is the difference between the purchase price from the underwriters and the price of resale to their customers. Although dealers are not subject to § 11 liability, they may incur liability under other provisions by, for example, making material misstatements or violating the registration requirements.

Note—IPOs

Although having its slow periods, the IPO market has had its moments of glory. *See* Jarzemsky, *Strong Demand for IPOs Rolls On*, WALL ST. J., Sept. 2, 2014, at C1; Kessler, *Easy Money and the IPO Boom*, WALL ST. J., May 27, 2011, at A15. Recent IPOs have included such well-known companies as Alibaba, General Motors, Groupon, Hyatt Hotels, and Facebook. *See* Emshwiller, *Family Squabbles Surface in Hyatt IPO*, WALL ST. J., Oct. 19, 2009, at B1; Raice, *Facebook Sets Historic IPO*, WALL ST. J., Feb. 2, 2012, at A1; Smith & Raice, *Groupon Discounts IPO*, WALL ST. J., Oct. 20, 2011, at B1; Terlep & Smith, *GM Stock Sale in High Gear*, WALL ST. J., Nov. 18, 2010, at A1. The Alibaba offering "marked the biggest IPO the world has ever seen—bigger than Facebook's or General Motors'." TIME, Dec. 22, 2014, at 136.

Criticism of IPO pricing prevails—both at the low and high end. For example, Facebook stock fell 11 percent on its first full day of trading after its IPO—reportedly due to a hefty initial offering price and too many shares being offered to retail individual investors. *See* Bunge, Lucchetti & Chon, *Investors Pummel Facebook*, WALL ST. J., May 22, 2012, at A1. At the other extreme, one notable premium in an IPO was that of Alteon, Inc., a developer of drugs. On the first day of trading, Alteon's stock increased from its initial offering price of $15 a share to $28.75 a share, representing a 92 percent gain. This astounding gain was viewed by some market players as a prime example of "speculative excesses in biotech stocks." Moreover, given this 92 percent gain, one might wonder how the company's executives "could still be

---

67. Such contribution is allowed "unless the person who has become liable was, and the other [person] was not, guilty of fraudulent misrepresentation." Section 11(f)(1).

speaking to its lead underwriter, Baltimore's Alex. Brown & Sons, after shareholders reaped more than $41 million that could have been the company's if the initial public offering had been priced higher." Newman, *Biotech Stock Alteon Skyrockets in IPO*, WALL ST. J., Nov. 4, 1991, at C1. For more recent examples, the price of Alibaba's stock "soared" 38 percent on its first day of trading. And the price of Nutonix "more than doubled in its first day of trading" in September 2016. *See* Driebusch & Farrell, *Technology Shares Pep Up IPO Market*, WALL ST. J., Oct. 26, 2016, at A1; Driebusch & Scaggs, *Alibaba Puts Wind at Market's Back*, WALL ST. J., Sept. 22, 2014, at C1.

To what extent are IPOs underpriced under prevailing practice? In a survey of 114 IPOs conducted between February 1, 2011 and August 11, 2011, the author found that underpricing was not common. Irrespective of the lack of prevalent underpricing, legitimate concerns nonetheless remain. During the survey period, "seventeen stocks (14.91% of the total IPOs conducted) were underpriced by more than 25% of their value. These IPOs include: Qihoo 360 Technology (134.48%), LinkedIn (109.44%), Zillow (78.85%), Teavana (63.53%), Francesca's (62.65%), Zipcar (55.56%), Yandex NV (55.36%), HomeAway (48.93%), Cornerstone OnDemand (46.69%), Dunkin Brands (46.58%), Epocrates (37.25%), Phoenix New Media (34.09%), Endocyte (28.83%), Renren (28.64%), Responsys (28.33%), RPX (25.68%), and 21 Vianet Group (25.33%). These issuers . . . left a substantial amount of cash on the table because of their underpriced IPOs. LinkedIn Corporation's and Qihoo 360 Technology's IPOs, in particular, drew significant media attention and debate about underpricing in IPOs." Conner, *Underpricing in the Initial Public Offering: A Solution for Severely Affected Issuers*, 40 SEC. REG. L.J. 423, 425–426 (2012). *See* Couture, *Price Fraud*, 63 BAYLOR L. REV. 1 (2011) (analyzing the alleged underpricing in IPOs by issuers and underwriters).

---

§ 4.07 State Blue Sky Law — Is There Merit to Merit Regulation?

Generally, under state Blue Sky law, as under the federal securities laws, every security offered to be sold in the applicable state must be registered or exempt from registration. Note an important caveat: If the securities offered are or will be listed on a national securities market, such as the New York Stock Exchange or are or will be traded on the NASDAQ National Market, offerings of such securities are exempt from state registration requirements.

Traditionally, there are three types of registration that states may require. The first type of registration, registration by coordination, is available to the issuer when a registered offering is being made under the Securities Act of 1933. This method of registration only requires the filing of a specified number of copies (e.g., three) of the current federal prospectus as well as any additional information required by the state securities administrator. A second type of registration, registration by notification, requires the filing of a short-form registration statement and is available generally only when an issuer and its predecessors have had a seasoned business for at least five years (e.g., no default and average net earnings). The third type of registration, registration by qualification, mandates full disclosure and may authorize the state securities administrator to engage in merit regulation. As the following discussion indicates, under merit regulation, the state securities administrator can prevent an offering from going forward because it is not "fair, just and equitable." *See* T. Hazen, The Law of Securities Regulation §8.2 (6th ed. 2009); J. Long, M. Kaufman, and J. Wunderlich, Blue Sky Law §1.04 (2016).

Although many states reject merit regulation, a number of others adhere to this approach. In states adopting merit regulation, full and fair disclosure alone is not enough. Rather, the offering also must be deemed "fair, just, and equitable." The debate over merit regulation generally focuses on whether full disclosure of material information concerning an offering is sufficient to protect investors, the propriety of paternalistic government regulation, and the economic costs versus benefits of such a system of regulation. *See generally* Sargent, *The Challenge to Merit Regulation*, 12 Sec. Reg. L.J. 276, 367 (1984) (reviewing states which have changed from a merit to a disclosure mode of regulation).

Generally, merit regulation is used to describe the securities laws of those states that, "in addition to requiring full disclosure, have granted their administrators power to analyze the securities to be offered, the terms of the offering, and the business of the issuer for purposes of determining, according to certain formal and informal rules, whether the securities are too speculative for public sale." J. Mofsky, Blue Sky Restrictions on New Business Promotions 7–8 (1971).

In "tough" merit regulation states, offerings will be denied registration or conditions imposed (such as requiring escrow of insider proceeds for a certain period of time or until specified contingencies are met) where:

(1) the promoters have invested insufficient equity capital in relation to the total capitalization that will exist after the completion of the proposed public offering; or

(2) there is an excessive amount of "cheap stock"—shares issued to promoters and insiders at prices significantly less than the proposed public offering price—in the registrant's capital structure; or

(3) an excessive number of options and warrants have been issued, or are reserved for issuance, in relation to the total capital structure that will exist after completion of the offering; or

(4) the proposed public offering price is too high in relation to the market price, if a market exists, or in relation to the issuer's earnings history, or other factors; or

(5) the underwriter's commissions and/or the selling expenses of the proposed offering are excessive; or

(6) voting rights of the shares being offered to the public are inequitable; or

(7) the issuer's historical earnings, calculated in accordance with generally accepted accounting principles, are insufficient to cover the interest charges on debt securities being registered or the preferred dividend on preferred shares being registered.

Tyler, *More About Blue Sky*, 39 Wash. & Lee L. Rev. 899, 903 (1982). On the other hand, note the following:

> [Merit] rules have been criticized on the grounds that seasoned firms, not subject to the rules, are in effect granted a comparative advantage in raising capital over newly promoted ventures. Newly promoted firms must either adjust the terms of their offerings and their capital structures to the merit rules of particular states or be precluded from publicly offering their securities in those states. Some firm will thus always be at the margin where, for financial and legal reasons, corporate promoters are unwilling to make the adjustment, and a decision not to offer securities in a particular state will be made. Of course, there are [several] states that do not have merit rules, and it has been argued that a proposed offering could always be made there, thus avoiding merit regulation altogether. But practical considerations, relating mainly to the local nature of many small offerings, often foreclose capital formation any place except specific areas where the firm and its promoters are well known. . . .

Mofsky & Tollison, *Demerit in Merit Regulation*, 60 Marq. L. Rev. 367 (1977). For a broad attack on blue sky regulation in general and merit regulation specifically, see Campbell, *An Open Attack on the Nonsense of Blue Sky Regulation*, 10 J. Corp. L. 553, 519 (1985). Upon examining the present regulatory framework, Professor Campbell asserts that "millions of dollars are spent each year on a system of [state] regulation that provides no significant protection to investors and retards capital formation." *See generally* Symposium, *Blue Sky Anniversary Edition*, 50 Washburn L.J. No. 3 (2011) (commemorating the 100th anniversary of the Kansas blue sky law); American Bar Association, Section of Corporation, Banking and Business Law, *Report on State Regulation of Securities Offerings*, 41 Bus. Law. 785 (1986); Brandi, *Securities Practitioners and Blue Sky Laws: A Survey of Comments and a Ranking of States by Stringency of Regulation*, 10 J. Corp. L. 689 (1985); Makens, *Who Speaks for the Investor? An Evaluation of the Assault on Merit Regulation*, 13 U. Balt. L. Rev. 435 (1984); Sargent, *State Disclosure Regulation and the Allocation of Regulatory Responsibilities*, 46 Md. L. Rev. 1027 (1987); Warren, *Legitimacy in the Securities Industry: The Role of Merit Regulation*, 53 Brook. L. Rev. 129 (1987).

Chapter 5

Disclosure, Materiality, and the Sarbanes-Oxley and Dodd-Frank Acts

This chapter examines key issues underlying concepts of disclosure and materiality under the federal securities laws. Issues addressed encompass the SEC's integrated disclosure framework, "plain English" principles, the policies underlying the mandatory disclosure system, disclosure of forward-looking information, and the application of materiality principles, including what is called *qualitative materiality*. In addition, this chapter focuses on key provisions of the Sarbanes-Oxley Act of 2002 and the Dodd-Frank Act of 2010.

§ 5.01 The Integrated Disclosure Framework

[A] Overview

The SEC's integrated disclosure system was adopted to ameliorate the expenses and duplication that were prevalent as a result of two different reporting mandates under the 1933 Act and the 1934 Act. In seeking to make disclosure as uniform as practicable under the two Acts, the SEC promulgated Regulation S-K and Regulation S-X (accounting rules), which act as the key sources for ascertaining the disclosures required to be made.

This is not to imply, however, that the disclosures contained in the various documents prepared pursuant to SEC mandates are identical. For example, with respect to the annual report on Form 10-K and the annual report to shareholders, the SEC took the following position:

> The Commission has determined to require only portions of the Form 10-K and the annual report to security holders to have equivalent disclosure because these documents are not necessarily used in an identical manner. Disclosure requirements in annual reports evolved in the context of shareholders making voting decisions. The [disclosure in the] Form 10-K . . . has been more detailed.[1]

---

1. Securities Act Release No. 6231 (1980).

Hence, under the Commission's integrated disclosure framework, registrant reporting has been simplified in that: "(1) disclosure requirements are made uniform under the Securities Act and the Exchange Act; [and] (2) Exchange Act periodic reporting is used to satisfy much of the disclosure necessary in Securities Act registration statements. . . ."[2]

This emphasis on Exchange Act periodic disclosure under the integrated disclosure system induced the SEC to require that a majority of the registrant's directors sign the annual Form 10-K. Such a signature requirement was necessary, according to the Commission, in order to encourage directors "to devote the needed attention in reviewing the Form 10-K and to seek the involvement of other professionals to the degree necessary to give themselves sufficient comfort."[3]

The integrated disclosure process, although calling for meaningful non-duplicative information, has evoked important liability concerns. These liability issues, related to the concept of "due diligence," are addressed in Chapter 7.

The SEC releases that follow further explain the integrated disclosure framework.

[B] Framework and Rationale

Proposed Comprehensive Revision to System for Regulation of Securities Offerings

Securities Act Release No. 6235 (1980)

The Commission's integration program involves a comprehensive evaluation of the disclosure policies and procedures underlying the Securities Act of 1933 and the Securities Exchange Act of 1934 with a view toward integrating the information systems under those Acts so that investors and the marketplace are provided meaningful, non-duplicative information periodically and when securities are sold to the public, while the costs of compliance for public companies are decreased.

The shape of the program will be influenced by the answers to two fundamental questions:

(1) What information is material to investment decisions in the context of public offerings of securities; and

(2) Under what circumstances and in what form should such material information be disseminated and made available by companies making

---

2. SEC Securities Act Release No. 6331 (1981). Note that under the Electronic Data Gathering, Analysis, and Retrieval System (EDGAR), registrants must submit to the SEC virtually all documents (such as filings) electronically. *See generally* Westerberg, *EDGAR*, 26 Rev. Sec. & Comm. Reg. 173 (1993).

3. SEC Securities Act Release No. 6231 (1980). *See* Brown, *Deregulation and the Annual Report to Shareholders*, 15 Sec. Reg. L.J. 423 (1988). Moreover, chief executive officers and chief financial officers are subject to certification requirements. *See* § 5.04[B] of this chapter.

public offerings of securities to the various participants in the capital market system?

The task of identifying what information is material to investment and voting decisions is a continuing one in the field of securities regulation. Integration, as a concept, involves a conclusion as to equivalency between transactional (Securities Act) and periodic (Exchange Act) reporting. If a subject matter is material information (other than a description of the transaction itself), then it will be material both in the distribution of securities and to the trading markets. Moreover, requirements governing the description of such subject matters should be the same for both purposes. . . . This principle of equivalency has led to the development and expansion of *Regulation S-K*, a technical device designed to state in one place uniform requirements which both Securities Act and Exchange Act items incorporate by reference. . . .

Integration consists, however, of more than just the notion of equivalency of reportable material information under both Acts. It involves answers to the second question posed above: Under what circumstances and to whom should this information be made available? Equivalency alone might be read to suggest that all the information contained, for example, in a Form 10-K should also be reiterated in all prospectuses.

However, the concept of integration also proceeds from the observation that information is regularly being furnished to the market through periodic reports under the Exchange Act. This information is evaluated by professional analysts and other sophisticated users, is available to the financial press and is obtainable by any other person who seeks it for free or at nominal cost. To the extent that the market accordingly acts efficiently, and this information is adequately reflected in the price of a registrant's outstanding securities, there seems little need to reiterate this information in a prospectus in the context of a distribution. The fact of market availability of information for sophisticated users also allows the exploration of other values in addition to cost reductions afforded through non-duplication: in particular, readability and effective communication in specific contexts.

Set forth below as additional background information for these proposals is a review of the evolution of the Securities Act and the Exchange Act, the nature of and participants in the securities marketplace, and recent technological advances.

A. BACKGROUND

1. The Law

The Securities Act and the Exchange Act were enacted as separate legislation and in response to different needs. The Securities Act was intended to prevent frauds in the sale of securities by providing full and fair disclosure in the context of public offerings of securities. The Exchange Act was enacted to regulate brokers and dealers and securities markets. The disclosure framework of the Exchange Act contemplated in 1934 pertained primarily to classes of securities traded on stock exchanges. While both statutes were designed to provide disclosure to investors and the marketplace, the framework of the Securities Act was transaction oriented, i.e., the focus was upon the public offering of securities by any company. The framework of the Exchange Act was status oriented, i. e., the focus was upon issuers with a class of securities listed and traded on an exchange. Also, the two frameworks operated independently. Information required in the Securities Act context was not modified because of the existence of Exchange Act reporting and was only triggered by public offerings at varying times.

While the disparate orientations of the two statutes still exist, the gap between the disclosure frameworks has significantly narrowed since 1934. In 1936, § 15(d) was added to the Exchange Act to provide that under certain circumstances the continuous reporting system would apply to unlisted companies with respect to classes of their securities for which a registration statement had become effective under the Securities Act. Thus, § 15(d) expanded investor protection under the Exchange Act to the over-the-counter market, but only on a fragmentary basis.

The disparity between Exchange Act disclosure requirements for listed and unlisted classes of securities was not resolved until the passage of the Securities Acts Amendments of 1964 which brought many more companies into the continuous reporting system of the Exchange Act. With the passage of § 15(d) and the 1964 amendments, all issuers of a certain size and issuers with certain characteristics selling securities to the public pursuant to an effective registration statement were subjected to the registration and reporting obligations of the Exchange Act. . . . These amendments not only closed a gap under the Exchange Act, but also narrowed the gap between the disclosure framework under the Securities Act — information concerning the issuer and the transaction given only in the context of the public offering — and that under the Exchange Act — continuous disclosure about the issuer. . . . [T]he Commission's efforts will attempt to redress this legislative [gap] by establishing an integrated system of disclosure which will provide investor protection both in public offerings and in the securities markets, at a minimum burden to public companies.

2. Nature of the Securities Markets

The basic issues relating to Securities Act disclosure, i.e., the type of information that should be available and the dissemination of that information, must also be considered in light of the composition of today's markets. The participants in the markets, and therefore the users of the information made available to the markets, are varied and have correspondingly varied needs. They include the professional analyst, the institutional investor, the financial press, and the individual investor.

The professional analysts, widespread throughout the country, constantly digest and synthesize market and company-specific information. These professionals use, and often implore the Commission to require, increasingly complex and sophisticated information. The influx of institutional investors, and their financial advisors, also contributes to the constituency for technical but important statistical data. To a large extent, these professionals act as essential conduits in the flow of information to the ordinary investor. . . .

In addition, this country has a uniquely active and responsive financial press which facilitates the broad dissemination of highly timely and material company-oriented information to a vast readership. The information needs of the individual investor must be considered in this context, recognizing that information reaches the individual investor through both direct and indirect routes.

It is incumbent upon the Commission to consider the entire community of users of company information . . . and to maintain a balance between the needs of the more and less sophisticated users.

3. Technological Advances

The instant proposals are also evidence of an awareness by the Commission of the increasingly easy availability of Exchange Act information through improved technological means. Computerization and electronics are progressing to such a level that information necessary to trading markets is becoming available on a timely and inexpensive basis. Additionally, a large volume of such information can be synthesized, analyzed and presented quickly and in almost any format desired by the user. [As other materials in this chapter describe, technological advances continue to enhance investor access to corporate information.]

B. MATERIALITY OF DISCLOSURE UNDER THE SECURITIES ACT

As noted above, the determination of what information is material to an investment decision in the context of a public offering is a critical question in establishing an integrated system of disclosure. Prior to the adoption of *Regulation S-K* in 1977, there were disparate informational requirements between Securities Act registration forms and Exchange Act reporting forms. Regulation S-K reflects the perception of equivalency discussed above—that information necessary for investment or voting decisions (other than that relating to the transaction itself) should be similar for distribution and for trading markets. With that acknowledgment, the Commission is in a position to develop what information is material, then to determine under what circumstances this information must be reiterated in a prospectus.

Regulation S-K has been designed as the repository for the Commission's requirements for standard and integrated disclosure requirements. . . . The Regulation represents the first step in the definition of [corporate-related] information which is material to an investment or voting decision, whether that decision is under the purview of the Securities Act or the Exchange Act. Accordingly, the multiplication of disclosure item requirements in Regulation S-K is a recognized prerequisite to full integration of the registration and reporting requirements under the two Acts. Consequently, in addition to the present Regulation S-K items pertaining to disclosures regarding an issuer's business, property, directors and executive officers, their remuneration and security ownership, and legal proceedings, the

Commission has adopted six more item requirements. These new items will ensure uniform disclosure under both Acts of information regarding market price of the issuer's common stock, selected financial data, management's discussion and analysis of the issuer's financial condition, supplementary financial information, and exhibits. . . .

Amendments to Annual Report Form; Integration of Securities Acts Disclosure Systems

Securities Act Release No. 6231 (1980)

Form 10-K

Introduction. The Commission today is adopting and proposing major changes in the Securities Act and Exchange Act disclosure systems. These changes are designed to improve the disclosure made to investors and other users of financial information, to facilitate the integration of the two disclosure systems into the single disclosure system long advocated by many commentators, and to reduce current impediments to combining informal security holder communications, such as annual reports to security holders, with official Commission filings.

This release deals with format and content changes in the Form 10-K [filed annually with the SEC] and in the annual report to security holders. Under the system in effect as a result of these changes, minimum disclosure requirements have been developed by the Commission for the Form 10-K and the annual report to security holders. . . .

The Commission has determined to require only portions of the Form 10-K and the annual report to security holders to have equivalent disclosure because these documents are not necessarily used in an identical manner. Disclosure requirements in annual reports evolved in the context of shareholders making voting decisions. The Form 10-K . . . has been more detailed. The Commission recognizes that the information content in Form 10-K not only was originally formulated for a specialized use, but that within those groups which have utilized the Form there are different constituencies. Those constituencies which have been the most frequent users of Form 10-K information are institutional investors, professional security analysts and sophisticated individual investors. The Commission believes that it continues to be appropriate to focus primarily on these frequent user constituencies in formulating Form 10-K requirements, but that such a focus would not be appropriate in formulating requirements for the annual report to security holders.

. . . .

Form 10-K [contains] a basic information package which most, if not all, investors expect to be furnished. Further, it has become apparent that this basic [Form 10-K] information package, . . . developed to support the current information requirements of an active trading market, is virtually identical to the similar information package independently developed in connection with the registration and sale of newly issued shares under the Securities Act. The essential content of these Form 10-K and registration statement information packages includes audited financial statements, a summary of selected financial data appropriate for trend analysis, and a meaningful description of the registrant's business and financial condition.

The restructured Form 10-K which the Commission is adopting today is specifically designed to segregate the basic information package contained in that Form from proxy related or supplemental information. In this regard, the new Form 10-K is structured in four parts. The first part retains the detailed disclosure requirements relating to business, properties, legal proceedings and beneficial ownership. . . . The second part consists of the basic disclosure package which is common to both Securities Act and Exchange Act filings. The third part consists of the traditional proxy disclosure information relating to directors and executive officers and management remuneration. Finally, the fourth part contains requirements for financial statement schedules. . . .

Annual Report to Security Holders

In a [prior] release, the Commission amended [specified rules] to require that annual reports to security holders contain a variety of information, including certified financial statements, a summary of operations, a management analysis, a brief description of the issuer's business, a lines of business breakdown, an identification of the issuer's directors and executive officers, and an identification of the principal market in which securities entitled to vote were traded. These requirements were based on substantially similar requirements in the then existing Form 10-K. In requiring this new information, the Commission made the following statement:

> The annual report to security holders has long been recognized as the most effective means of communication between management and security holders. Such reports are readable because they generally avoid legalistic and technical terminology and present information in an understandable, and often innovative, form. . . . The Commission believes it is in the public interest that all security holders be provided with meaningful information regarding the business, management, operations and financial position of the issuer and that the annual report to security holders is the most suitable vehicle presently available for providing this information.

The Commission continues to believe that all security holders should be provided with meaningful information and that the changes in the Form 10-K requirements on which the annual report to security holder requirements were based should also be made in the annual report because of the importance of the disclosure. This results in a uniformity of the minimum disclosure package in the annual report to security holders and in Form 10-K. This uniformity has been achieved by adopting uniform financial statement requirements, by amending Regulation S-X, by adopting new provisions in Regulation S-K and by adopting several changes in [SEC rules]. The equivalency of the minimum disclosure package in both documents not only satisfies shareholder and investor needs, it also should avoid duplication by allowing issuers to use the disclosure in the annual report to security holders to satisfy some of the requirements of Form 10-K and, if they choose, when selling securities to the public. . . . The Commission is aware that increasing the amount of required disclosure in annual security holder reports involves a risk that readability may be impaired. Although it is difficult to predict with certainty what the effect may be, the Commission does not believe that the changes implemented today should or will have general adverse consequences. . . .

[C] Securities Act Registration Forms

To implement the integrated disclosure system, the Commission has in place two registration forms, Form S-1 and Form S-3.[4] These forms serve as the basic framework for registered offerings under the Securities Act. Incorporation by reference from 1934 Act reports is permitted in varying degrees on both Forms.

[1] Form S-1

The registration statement for the first category is Form S-1. Form S-1 is to be used by enterprises engaging in an initial public offering (IPO), registrants in the Exchange Act reporting system that are ineligible to use Form S-3, and other registrants who choose to utilize Form S-1.[5] An eligible Form S-1 issuer may incorporate by reference from Exchange Act reports into its Securities Act registration statement when it: (1) has filed at least one annual report; (2) is current in its Exchange Act reporting obligations; and (3) has made its Exchange Act reports readily accessible on a website maintained by or for such registrant. This access may be achieved by means of the registrant having on its website a hyperlink to the reports filed on EDGAR, with such reports being accessible through the SEC's website or through a third-party website.[6] [Note that under EDGAR (the Electronic Data Gathering, Analysis, and Retrieval System), registrants must submit to the SEC virtually all documents (such as filings) electronically.]

Pursuant to legislation enacted in 2015, the FAST Act (Fixing America's Surface Transportation Act) allows a smaller reporting company to incorporate by reference in its Form S-1 registration statement any SEC reports filed after such registration

---

4. The SEC eliminated a third form, Form S-2, as part of its 2005 initiative to streamline the registration process. Prior to the 2005 offering reform, incorporation by reference was only allowed on Forms S-2 and S-3. *See* Securities Act Release No. 8591 (2005).

5. The SEC expanded the Form S-3 eligibility requirements for primary offerings of equity securities to now permit issuers that have timely filed their Exchange Act reports and whose equity securities are listed on a national securities exchange (and that are not shell companies) to use Form S-3. *See* Securities Act Release No. 8878 (2007).

6. *See* Securities Act Release No. 8591 (2005). Note that incorporation by reference may not be used by blank check companies, shell companies, or issuers conducting penny stock offerings.

statement's effective date. A "smaller reporting company" is defined in SEC Rule 405 to mean an issuer whose public float is less than $75 million or had revenues during its most recent fiscal year of less than $50 million. [Note that the SEC has proposed to raise the financial threshold to $250 million public float or annual revenues less than $100 million. Securities Act Release No. 10107 (2016).]

Adopting interim final rules to implement this directive of the FAST Act (Securities Act Release No. 10003 (2016)), the SEC stated:

> ... [The FAST Act requires the Commission to revise Form S-1 to permit a smaller reporting company [SRC] to incorporate by reference into its registration statement any documents filed by the issuer subsequent to the effective date of the registration statement. ...

> . . . .

> The amendment [we have adopted pursuant to] the FAST Act to permit forward incorporation by reference by SRCs in Form S-1 will further integrate disclosures under the Securities Act and the Exchange Act and increase regulatory simplification. Forward incorporation by reference will eliminate the need to update information in a filing that has become stale or is incomplete. The amendment should decrease the existing filing burdens by reducing multiple disclosure filings, thereby allowing SRCs to satisfy Form S-1 disclosure requirements and access capital markets at a lower cost. ...

> [As addressed above in this subsection of the textbook,] there are eligibility requirements for any issuer to use historical incorporation by reference on Form S-1 for documents filed before the effective date of the registration statement. These requirements will not be affected as a result of these amendments. Smaller reporting companies must meet each of these existing eligibility requirements and conditions to use forward incorporation by reference on Form S-1. For example, to be eligible to use forward incorporation by reference, smaller reporting companies will be required to be current by having filed (a) an annual report for its most recently completed fiscal year; and (b) all required Exchange Act reports and materials during the 12 months immediately preceding filing of the Form S-1 (or such shorter period that the smaller reporting company was required to file such reports and materials). Smaller reporting companies that are blank check companies, shell companies (other than business combinations related shell companies) or issuers for offerings of penny stocks will not be permitted to forward incorporate by reference into a Form S-1. In addition, the ability to forward incorporate by reference will be conditioned on the smaller reporting company making its incorporated Exchange Act reports and other materials readily available and accessible on a web site maintained by or for the issuer and disclosing in the prospectus that such materials will be provided upon request.

> . . . .

[Thus,] the same eligibility requirements that currently apply to any issuer to use historical incorporation by reference on Form S-1 will apply to forward incorporation by reference by SRCs. Using these well-established eligibility requirements should provide certainty to issuers and investors about when forward incorporation by reference may be used. Requiring the SRCs to be current in their filing requirements will ensure that only issuers with a demonstrated ability to comply with Exchange Act reporting requirements are eligible to forward incorporate by reference. . . .

[2] Form S-3

With respect to *Form S-3*, the SEC has explained:

Form S-3, in reliance on the efficient market theory, allows maximum use of incorporation by reference of Exchange Act reports [into Securities Act registration statements] and requires the least disclosure to be presented in the prospectus. . . . Generally, the Form S-3 prospectus [which can be used in primary offerings of common stock by an issuer which has timely filed in the Exchange Act reporting system for twelve months, has a class of common stock (or similar equity security) traded on a national securities exchange, and is not (and has not been for the prior twelve months) a shell company] will present the same transaction-specific information as will be presented in a Form S-1 prospectus. Information concerning the registrant will be incorporated by reference from its Exchange Act reports. The prospectus will not be required to present any information concerning the registrant unless there has been a material change in the registrant's affairs which has not been reported in an Exchange Act filing or unless the Exchange Act reports incorporated by reference do not reflect certain restated financial statements or other financial information.[7]

To emphasize, the use of the Form S-3 registration statement has been greatly expanded by the SEC. Today, for primary offerings of equity securities (such as common stock), Form S-3 generally can be used by issuers that have timely filed Exchange Act reports for the prior 12 months, have a class of equity securities traded on a national securities exchange (such as the New York Stock Exchange or Nasdaq), and are not (and have not been for at least 12 months) a shell company. For issuers that meet the foregoing conditions but have less than $75 million of voting stock outstanding held by non-affiliates ("public float"), no more than one-third of the public float may be offered by such issuers in primary offerings during any 12-month period. See Securities Act Release No. 8878 (2007).

The rationale largely underlying incorporation by reference of Exchange Act reports into Securities Act registration statements is that information regularly

---

7. SEC Securities Act Release No. 6383 (1982). See Securities Act Release Nos. 6964 (1992), 8878 (2007). For mergers and certain other reorganizations, the Form S-4 registration statement may be used. The Form S-4 is discussed in Chapter 6.

furnished to the securities markets through 1934 Act periodic reports is digested by the marketplace and reflected in the price of the issuer's securities, thereby eliminating the need to reiterate such information in the public offering context. Hence, this theory postulates that the securities markets, by analyzing the available information and accurately valuing the information in setting the price for the security, are efficient. The efficient market theory has received Supreme Court approbation with respect to the issue of "reliance" in §10(b) litigation (discussed in Chapter 8).

For mergers and certain other reorganizations, the Form S-4 registration statement may be used. The Form S-4 is discussed in Chapter 6.

[3] Critical Analysis

Note that the FAST Act and the SEC's 2007 amendments expanding the scope of the Form S-3 contradict the Commission's principal rationale for the Form's adoption. In promulgating the Form S-3 in 1982, the SEC "reli[ed] on the efficient market theory, allow[ing] a maximum use of incorporation of Exchange Act reports and requir[ing] the least disclosure to be presented in the prospectus and delivered to investors." As then adopted, the Form S-3 could be used in primary at-the-market offerings of common stock only if the subject issuer had filed its Exchange Act reports for at least a 36-month period and had a public float of $150 million (or alternatively, a public float of $100 million and three million share trading volume on an annual basis). In 1992, still adhering to the efficient market rationale, the Commission lowered the Form S-3 criteria for issuers having such equity offerings to a 12-month reporting history and $75 million public float.

The U.S. Supreme Court has given its approbation to the efficient market theory in the securities litigation context. In ascertaining whether a subject security trades in an efficient market, lower courts view Form S-3 eligibility as a relevant criterion. Given this history underlying the Form S-3's adoption and implementation, the SEC's expansion of Form S-3 to encompass issuers that may not be traded in an efficient market is a significant departure. Indeed, the FAST Act legislation, as well as the Commission's 2007 amendments, may be viewed as an effort to facilitate capital raising while asserting that any security listed on a national securities exchange is by definition traded in an efficient market. This rationalization, however, contravenes established doctrine that the critical inquiry is the market for that particular stock, not the location where such stock trades.

[D] Ways that a Company Becomes Subject to the Exchange Act's Reporting Requirements

Generally, an issuer becomes subject to the reporting requirements (such as quarterly and annual reports filed with the SEC) of the Securities Exchange Act upon the occurrence of any of the following: (1) The company has a registered public offering under the Securities Act (see §15(d) of the Exchange Act); (2) The company has its securities listed on a national stock exchange, such as the New York Stock Exchange (see § 12(b) of the Exchange Act); (3) The company has utilized Regulation A Plus Tier 2 and now has the public float, asset value, and number of shareholders requiring that it be subject to Exchange Act reporting requirements; or (4) The company has more than $10 million in total assets and a class of equity securities "held of record by [at least] either 2,000 persons or 500 persons who are not accredited investors. . . ." As to this last category, excluded are equity securities held of record by persons who acquired such securities by means of an exempt "crowdfunding" offering or pursuant to an exempt transaction under an employee compensation plan (see § 12(g) of the Exchange Act; Securities Act Release No. 10075 (2016)).

Another way that a private company can "go public" is by utilizing a reverse merger. As set forth in an *Investor Bulletin: Reverse Mergers* issued by the SEC:

Many private companies, including some whose operations are located in foreign countries, seek to access the U.S. capital markets by merging with existing public companies. These transactions are commonly referred to as "reverse mergers" or "reverse takeovers (RTOs)."

What Is a Reverse Merger?

In a reverse merger transaction, an existing public "shell company," which is a public reporting company with few or no operations, acquires a private operating company—usually one that is seeking access to funding in the U.S. capital markets. Typically, the shareholders of the private operating company exchange their shares for a large majority of the shares of the public company. Although the public shell company survives the merger, the private operating company's shareholders gain a controlling interest in the voting power and outstanding shares of stock of the public shell company. Also, typically, the private operating company's management takes over the board of directors and management of the public shell company. The assets and business operations of the post-merger surviving public company are primarily, if not solely, those of the former private operating company.

Why Pursue a Reverse Merger?

A private operating company may pursue a reverse merger in order to facilitate its access to the capital markets, including the liquidity that comes with having its stock quoted on a market or listed on an exchange. Private operating companies generally have access only to private forms of equity, while public companies potentially have access to funding from a broader pool of public investors. A reverse merger often is perceived to be a quicker and cheaper method of "going public" than an initial public offering (IPO). The legal and accounting fees associated with a reverse merger tend to be lower than for an IPO. And while the public shell company is required to report the reverse merger in a Form 8-K filing with the SEC, there are no registration requirements under the Securities Act of 1933 as there would be for an

IPO. In addition, being public may give a company increased value in the eyes of potential acquirers.

Under what circumstances can a company that is within the Exchange Act reporting framework "exit" and thereby become a privately held company? Generally, domestic companies may exit if the number of record holders of the subject class of equity securities drops below 300.[8]

[E] Reduced Disclosure Requirements for Certain Issuers

In an effort to foster capital formation and not to saddle ostensibly smaller companies with undue burdens, certain disclosure accommodations have been made for certain issuers.

Perhaps the most important category of issuers afforded such relief are the *emerging growth companies.*

[1] Emerging Growth Companies

Pursuant to the JOBS Act (2012), *emerging growth companies* enjoy reduced disclosure requirements both when conducting public offerings and in their periodic reporting obligations under the Exchange Act. By way of example, *an emerging growth company:*

- may opt to provide two (rather than three) years of audited financial statements and less extensive disclosure with respect to Management's Discussion and Analysis of Financial Condition and Results of Operation (MD&A) in the subject company's IPO registration statement offering common equity securities;

- is not required to obtain an auditor's report with respect to the quality and reliability of such company's internal control over financial reporting;

- may provide reduced disclosure with respect to information relating to the payment of executive compensation;

- may decline to provide advisory votes by its shareholders on such matters as "say on pay" and executive compensation "golden parachute" arrangements;

- as discussed in Chapter 4, may make offers to sell in the pre-filing period to accredited institutional investors and qualified institutional buyers (QIBs);

---

8. Note that banks, bank holding companies, and savings and loan holding companies are given somewhat different treatment: For example, under § 12(g), such an enterprise becomes an Exchange Act reporting company when it has total assets exceeding $10 million and a class of equity security held of record by at least 2,000 persons (without consideration to the number of investors who are not accredited). Notably, these companies have more relaxed "exit" requirements, allowing such termination when there are less than 1,200 persons who are record holders of the subject class of securities. *See* Securities Act Release No. 10075 (2016).

- pursuant to the FAST Act of 2015, the SEC is directed to further reduce disclosure requirements for emerging growth companies.

Note that an emerging growth company may decline to adopt any of the foregoing accommodations and be subject to the same requirements as other publicly held companies. However, with respect to the *reduced financial accounting standards*, if an emerging growth company decides to comply with these standards to the same extent as larger publicly held companies, it must make its election and inform the SEC of this determination at the time that the company is first obligated to file a registration statement or to file a periodic report with the Commission. Once an emerging growth company opts to forego these reduced financial accounting standards, it cannot change its position thereto so long as such company remains an emerging growth company.

Thus far, while some emerging growth companies are taking advantage of the reduced standards authorized by the JOBS Act (particularly the solicitation of accredited institutional investors in the pre-filing period, initial confidential filing with the SEC of the registration statement, and less disclosure of executive compensation), they "are shunning the law's relaxed financial reporting and accounting standards because they believe there is a stigma attached to them [and because] they don't want to risk turning off investors by including less comprehensive disclosures than other public companies. . . ." Holzer, *Some Firms Shun Looser IPO Rules*, Wall St. J., Nov. 15, 2012, at C1, C2. See Nayeri, *Did the JOBS Act Do Its Job?*, 42 Sec. Reg. L.J. 317 (2014).

Importantly, as a final point in this context, a publicly held company that had its initial public offering (IPO) on or before December 8, 2011 does not qualify as an emerging growth company. This is because the JOBS Act specifically excludes an issuer from being an emerging growth company "if the first sale of common equity securities of such issuer pursuant to an effective registration statement under the Securities Act of 1933 occurred on or before December 8, 2011." (§ 101(d) of the JOBS Act.)

[2] Smaller Reporting Companies

Aside from the JOBS Act, the SEC on its own had provided "scaled" (namely, reduced) disclosure for smaller publicly held companies. In 1992, as part of its Small Business Initiatives, the SEC adopted Regulation S-B to provide more simplified disclosure, thereby facilitating access of small business issuers to the public securities markets.[9] In 2007, the SEC rescinded Regulation S-B. Importantly, at that time, the Commission adopted amendments to the disclosure and reporting requirements under the Securities Act and the Exchange Act to expand the number of issuers that qualify for "scaled" disclosure accommodations for smaller reporting companies. At that time, the Commission estimated that nearly 5,000 companies were eligible to

---

9. Securities Act Release No. 6949 (1992).

use "scaled" disclosure, representing about 13 percent of Exchange Act reporting companies.[10]

Today, smaller reporting companies (defined in § 5.01[C][1] of this Chapter) have reduced disclosure obligations. These requirements will be further decreased in view of the FAST Act's directive that the SEC adopt regulations that lessen a smaller reporting company's disclosure obligations to a greater degree. These "scaled" disclosure items include: description of the company's business; selected financial data; management's discussion and analysis of financial condition and results of operation (MD&A); information relating to market risk; executive compensation; related party transactions; and corporate governance. These smaller reporting companies may elect to follow the reduced (scaled) disclosure items set forth above on an item-by-item basis.

Note

On another matter, Regulation S-K is the central source for determining a publicly held company's disclosure obligations under the federal securities laws. It is not, however, the only source. For example, in the securities offering setting, Rule 408 of Regulation C provides:

> In addition to the information expressly required to be included in a registration statement, there shall be added such further material information, if any, as may be necessary to make the required statements, in the light of the circumstances under which they are made, not misleading.

Rule 12b-20, promulgated under the Exchange Act, contains a similar requirement with respect to reports filed with the SEC pursuant to the Exchange Act.

Moreover, it may be argued that because the issuer itself is selling securities in the offering context, a disclosure obligation arises between the issuer and purchasers of the securities. Hence, it may be posited that in the Securities Act registration setting, if the information is material, it must be disclosed. As will be seen in later chapters, however, this view has not been widely accepted: materiality of the information alone does not trigger a duty to disclose.

[F] Shelf Registration

One of the SEC's significant actions with respect to the integrated disclosure framework is its adoption of Rule 415, the "shelf" registration rule. Generally, Rule 415 focuses on the Securities Act registration of securities to be offered or sold on a delayed or continuous basis in the future. The thrust of shelf registration is that it allows qualified issuers to raise capital in an expedited manner to capture favorable market

---

10. Securities Act Release No. 8876 (2007).

conditions while benefiting from significant cost savings in the form of reduced legal, accounting, and other fees. In a shelf registered offering, information from Exchange Act reports is incorporated by reference into the subject registration statement. As stated by one source:

> Shelf registration offerings have become an essential part of the capital raising markets in the United States. . . . [They] allow for more rapid and repeated access to the markets; once effective, the shelf registration allows an issuer to access the markets at any time and on extremely short notice, often as little as a few hours, without any further SEC review. The benefits of shelf registration include lowering compliance costs, promoting innovative distributions, and decreasing the cost of capital. . . . The flexibility afforded by shelf registration in terms of timing an offering allows a registrant to move quickly to take advantage of "market windows" and, for example, obtain favorable interest rates on debt before market conditions change.

> Indeed, rapid access to the markets was an important factor motivating the adoption of integrated disclosure and the wider use of shelf registration. . . . Preparation of traditional registration statements . . . generally begin several weeks in advance of the proposed offering. By contrast, offerings under shelf registration by design take [far] less time. . . . [11]

Currently, only issuers qualified to register securities on Form S-3 (or Form F-3) are eligible to conduct primary at-the-market offerings of equity securities by means of shelf registration. Other issuers that may use Form S-3 for other types of offerings include those that make: "offerings on a continuing basis of securities issued on exercise of outstanding options or warrants or conversion of other securities; [certain debt offerings;] offerings on a continuous basis under dividend reinvestment plans; offerings on a continuous basis under employee benefit plans; and offerings solely on behalf of selling security holders." Securities Act Release Nos. 6499 (1983), 8591 (2005). *See generally* Banoff, *Regulatory Subsidies, Efficient Markets and Shelf Regulation—An Analysis of Rule 415,* 70 Va. L. Rev. 135 (1984).

Generally, there is no limit on the amount of securities that can be registered pursuant to a shelf registration statement.[12] The underwriters of the offering are not required to be identified in the shelf registration statement. Such a registration statement can be used for up to three years (subject to limited extension). Moreover, the Commission has made shelf registration even more useful for well-known seasoned issuers by way of "automatic" shelf registration under which the shelf registration statement becomes effective immediately upon filing with the SEC. As set forth by the SEC:

---

11. Amici Curiae Brief of the Securities Industry Association and the Bond Market Association at pages 1, 3–4, in *In re Worldcom, Inc. Securities Litigation,* 346 F. Supp. 2d 628 (S.D.N.Y. 2004).

12. As discussed earlier in this chapter, eligible issuers that do not have a $75 million float may register on Form S-3 in primary offerings no more than one-third of their public float during any 12-month period. *See* Securities Act Release No. 8878 (2007).

In addition to the updating of the shelf registration process described above, we are adopting rules to establish a significantly more flexible version of shelf registration for offerings by well-known seasoned issuers. This version of shelf registration, which we refer to as "automatic shelf registration," involves filings on Form S-3 or Form F-3. The automatic shelf registration rules . . . will allow eligible well-known seasoned issuers substantially greater latitude in registering and marketing securities. The automatic shelf registration process will continue to enable the issuer, as with other shelf registrants, to take down securities off a shelf registration statement from time to time. Automatic shelf registration is not mandatory; a well-known seasoned issuer may continue to file any other registration statement it is eligible to use or engage in any exempt offering or offerings of exempt securities available to it.

For well-known seasoned issuers, we believe that the modifications we are adopting will facilitate immediate market access and promote efficient capital formation, without at the same time diminishing investor protection. Most significantly, the new rules will provide the flexibility to take advantage of market windows, to structure securities on a real-time basis to accommodate issuer needs or investor demand, and to determine or change the plan of distribution of securities as issuers elect in response to changing market conditions. We hope that providing these automatic shelf issuers more flexibility for their registered offerings, coupled with the liberalized communications rules we are adopting, will encourage these issuers to raise their necessary capital through the registration process.

Under our automatic shelf registration process, eligible well-known seasoned issuers may register unspecified amounts of different specified types of securities on immediately effective Form S-3 or Form F-3 registration statements. Unlike other issuers registering primary offerings on Form S-3 or Form F-3, the automatic shelf registration process allows eligible issuers to add additional classes of securities and to add eligible majority-owned subsidiaries as additional registrants after an automatic shelf registration statement is effective. . . . Thus, these issuers have significant latitude in determining the types and amounts of their securities or those of their eligible subsidiaries that can be offered without any potential time delay or other obstacles imposed by the registration process. . . .

Securities Act Release No. 8591 (2005). As will be addressed in Chapter 7 of this text, shelf registration raises significant liability concerns.

---

§ 5.02 Plain English Disclosure Requirements

In 1998, the SEC adopted the plain English disclosure rules primarily to address concerns that disclosure documents were too complicated to be effectively used by many individual investors. The principal focus of these rules is clarity of prospectus disclosure. Because prospectuses are drafted in significant part to avoid liability that may ensue from a public offering, language used in prospectuses traditionally has been often highly technical and legalistic. This complexity, in turn, impairs the ability of investors to make knowledgeable judgments regarding the merits of the securities being offered. Under the plain English disclosure rules, the Commission requires issuers to write the cover pages, summary, and risk factors portions of prospectuses in plain English. Further, the SEC has provided specific guidance on how to make the entire prospectus clear, concise, and understandable.[13]

The plain English rule (Rule 421) sets forth requirements with respect to the front and back cover pages, the summary, and the risk factors portions of the prospectus. These requirements include:

- Short sentences;
- Definite, concrete, everyday language;
- Active voice;
- Tabular presentation or bullet lists for complex material, whenever possible;
- No legal jargon or highly technical business terms; and
- No multiple negatives.[14]

In addition to the specific portions of the prospectus discussed above, Rule 421(b) mandates that the entire prospectus be "clear, concise, and understandable." Pertinent standards to be followed in prospectus preparation include:

- Present information in clear, concise sections, paragraphs, and sentences . . . ;
- Use descriptive headings and subheadings;
- Avoid frequent reliance on glossaries or defined terms as the primary means of explaining information in the prospectus . . . ; and
- Avoid legal and highly technical business terminology.[15]

The SEC makes clear, however, that certain business terms are often necessary to describe companies in certain industries (e.g., high-tech corporations). Therefore,

---

13. Securities Act Release No. 7497 (1998).

14. *Id.* Rule 421(d)(2), 17 C.F.R. § 230.421(d)(2).

15. Rule 421(b) 17 C.F.R. § 230.421(b). Further, Rule 421(b) and Securities Act Release No. 7497 (1998) list the following drafting styles that the SEC believes make the prospectus harder to understand:
- Legalistic or overly complex presentations that make the substance of the disclosure difficult to understand;
- Vague "boilerplate" explanations that are imprecise and readily subject to differing interpretations;
- Complex information copied directly from legal documents without any clear and concise explanation of the provision(s); and
- Disclosure repeated in different sections of the document that increases the size of the document but does not enhance the quality of the information.

the Commission proposes that, if certain technical terms are necessary, prospectuses attempt to clearly define the meaning of those terms the first time that they are used. Further, the Commission recognizes that sophisticated investors may want to read certain documents relating to the company in their entirety. For example, investors may wish to read the specific language of a contract that is highly pertinent to the company's future. In these situations, the Commission sets forth that information relating to such documents must be presented and explained in a clear fashion.[16]

See Francis, *To Be Clear, SEC Reviewers Want Filings in Plain English, Period*, WALL ST. J., Sept. 13–14, 2014, at A1 ("Every year, SEC lawyers and accountants review several thousands of the more than half-million documents that companies file with the agency. And while they are primarily on the prowl for accounting inconsistencies and breaches of securities regulations, they also chase down typos, sentence fragments, jargon, puffery and sloppy punctuation.").

---

§ 5.03 Concepts of Disclosure

This section addresses three timely subjects in the securities regulation field: (1) the debate surrounding the securities acts' mandatory disclosure system; (2) issuer disclosure of forward-looking information; and (3) issuer disclosure of qualitative, in addition to quantitative, information.

[A] The Mandatory Disclosure Debate

The propriety of Congress' enactment of a mandatory securities law disclosure system has generated much debate over the last two decades. As discussed throughout this chapter, issuers must disclose specified information when publicly offering securities pursuant to the Securities Act's registration framework. Moreover, once an issuer engages in a public offering, it is required under the Securities Exchange Act to provide the SEC and its shareholders with annual and other periodic reports. Whether such a mandatory disclosure system is appropriate and the type of information that should be subject to compelled disclosure have been subject to debate.

Critics of the mandatory disclosure system argue that the system produces considerable costs yet few benefits.[17] As stated decades ago by Professor Homer Kripke:

---

16. Securities Act Release No. 7497 (1998). *See generally*, B. GARNER, SECURITIES DISCLOSURE IN PLAIN ENGLISH (1999); Robbins & Rothenberg, *Writing Risk Factor Disclosure in Exchange Act Reports*, 39 REV. SEC. & COMM. REG. 87 (2006).

17. *See, e.g.*, H. Manne, *Insider Trading and the Stock Market* (1966); Benston, *The Value of the SEC's Accounting Disclosure Requirements*, 44 ACCT. REV. 515 (1969); Stigler, *Public Regulation of the Securities Markets*, 37 J. BUS. 117 (1964).

> [T]he Commission's disclosure system cannot be given high marks either for performance or on a cost/benefit basis. . . . The system was founded not on disclosure of "all material facts," but on disclosure of events in the past which the Commission could objectively verify. This historical perspective was assumed for the inefficient purpose of preventing blatant securities fraud and for the less apparent purpose of protecting the Commission from criticism for issues that turn sour. In recent years, while the Commission has shown commendable willingness to try to modernize the system, development and economic theory have outrun adaptation of the system.[18]

Today, some of the sting of Professor Kripke's rebuke has been lessened by the SEC's increasing support for enhanced disclosure of "soft" or "forward-looking" information.[19] Nonetheless, it may be asserted that undue reliance on mandatory disclosure is not without costs and weaknesses. Indeed, one authority, assessing whether disclosure should give way to more substantive regulation that impacts normative conduct more directly, opines that "[o]ne of the most significant problems with relying on a disclosure-based system to protect securities markets and investors is the flawed assumption that investors are purely rational actors who can utilize the disclosure effectively to make optimal investment decisions."[20]

Proponents of a mandatory disclosure system assert that, in the absence of such a system: (1) some registrants would engage in fraudulent disclosure practices; (2) insider perquisites and salaries, as well as underwriter costs, would be excessive; (3) current state laws and self-regulatory oversight by themselves would be inadequate for enforcement purposes; (4) the threat of civil and criminal actions would not induce the appropriate level of disclosure; and (5) investors would lose confidence in the integrity of the securities markets.[21]

Additionally, it is argued that mandatory disclosure obligations comprise an economically efficient mechanism for achieving information discovery. As stated by one source:

> Absent mandatory disclosure duties, information traders would engage in duplicative efforts to uncover nonpublic information. The cost of these efforts would be extremely high because information traders, as outsiders, lack access to the management of the firm. Disclosure duties pass these costs to the individual firm. For the firm, the cost of obtaining firm-specific

---

18. Kripke, *Fifty Years of Securities Regulation in Search of a Purpose*, 21 San Diego L. Rev. 257 (1984).

19. *See, e.g.,* discussion in § 5.05 *infra*.

20. Ripken, *The Dangers and Drawbacks of the Disclosure Antidote: Toward a More Substantive Approach to Securities Regulation*, 58 Baylor L. Rev. 139, 147–148 (2006). *See* Morrissey, *The Securities Act at Its Diamond Jubilee: Renewing the Case for a Robust Registration Requirement,* 11 U. Pa. J. Bus. L. 749 (2009).

21. *See* Seligman, *The Historical Need for a Mandatory Corporate Disclosure System,* 9 J. Corp. 1, 9 (1979).

information is rather minimal; indeed, it is a mere by-product of managing the firm.[22]

A further point that should be raised is the impact that disclosure under the federal securities laws has on normative corporate conduct. As this author has stated:

> Although the rationale underlying disclosure is not based primarily on influencing corporate internal affairs but rather on providing shareholders and the marketplace with sufficient information to make intelligent decisions and to be apprised of significant developments, there is little question that disclosure has a substantial impact on the normative conduct of corporations. In this regard, the Commission's disclosure policies . . . have not only had an effect of deterring unlawful or questionable conduct but have played a positive role in influencing the establishment of improved standards of conduct.[23]

[B] Disclosure of "Forward-Looking" Information

Although continuing to strongly support the need for a mandatory disclosure system, the Commission has responded to Professor Kripke and other critics by taking certain actions. Perhaps the most important was the adoption of the integrated disclosure system discussed. A second was the Commission's promulgation of

---

22. Goshen & Parchomovsky, *The Essential Role of Securities Regulation,* 55 Duke L.J. 711, 738 (2006) (also opining that the specific disclosure format, as mandated by SEC rule, further decreases the costs of analyzing information and comparing such information to the data provided by other enterprises). *See generally* Brown, *Corporate Governance, the Securities and Exchange Commission and the Limits of Disclosure,* 57 Cath. U.L. Rev. 45 (2007); Coffee, *Market Failure and the Economic Case for a Mandatory Disclosure System,* 70 Va. L. Rev. 717 (1984); Easterbrook & Fischel, *Mandatory Disclosure and the Protection of Investors,* 70 Va. L. Rev. 669 (1984); Fanto, *The Absence of Cross-Cultural Communications: SEC Mandatory Disclosure and Foreign Corporate Governance,* 17 Nw. J. Int'l L. & Bus. 119 (1996); Fox, *Retaining Mandatory Securities Disclosure: Why Issuer Choice Is Not Investor Empowerment,* 85 Va. L. Rev. 1335 (1997); Hannes, *Comparisons Among Firms: (When) Do They Justify Mandatory Disclosure?,* 29 J. Corp. L. 699 (2004); Hu, *Too Complex to Depict? Innovation, "Pure Information," and the SEC Disclosure Paradigm,* 90 Tex. L. Rev. 1601 (2012); Karmel, *Disclosure Reform — The SEC Is Riding Off in Two Directions at Once,* 71 Bus. Law. 781 (2016); Palmiter, *Toward Disclosure Choice in Securities Offerings,* 1991 Colum. Bus. L. Rev. 1 (1991); Romano, *Empowering Investors: A Market Approach to Securities Regulation,* 107 Yale L.J. 2359 (1998).

23. M. Steinberg, Corporate Internal Affairs: A Corporate and Securities Law Perspective 29 (1983). *See* R. Stevenson, Corporations and Information — Secrecy, Access and Disclosure 81–82 (1980) ("Today the disclosure requirements of the securities laws are used, in a variety of ways, for the explicit purpose of influencing a wide range of corporate primary behavior. . . ."); Ripken, *supra* note 20, at 152 (arguable that disclosure rules serve to indirectly affect corporate decisionmaking); Weiss, *Disclosure and Corporate Accountability,* 34 Bus. Law. 575 (1979) ("[O]ne of the central themes of the system by which large corporations are governed [is] that corporate decisionmaking be regulated through mandatory disclosure requirements rather than direct government intervention.")

Securities Act Rule 175 (and Exchange Act Rule 3b-6), providing a "safe harbor" for projections.[24] A third is the SEC's adoption of Item 303 of Regulation S-K focusing on Management Discussion & Analysis (MD&A).[25] In this regard, the area encompassing issuer affirmative disclosure obligations (including such subjects as disclosure of "soft" information, merger negotiations, and "bad" news) is addressed at length in Chapter 11. And a fourth major development is the enactment of the Private Securities Litigation Reform Act of 1995. A key aspect of this Act is the providing of a safe harbor from liability in private actions for certain forward-looking statements made by publicly held companies (for further discussion, see Chapters 8, 11).

Whereas "hard" information emphasizes historical data, "soft" information often focuses on forward-looking statements, such as projections, forecasts, and predictions. Until the mid-1970s, the SEC and the courts discouraged and even prohibited the disclosure of soft information. The major concern had been that investors, particularly the unsophisticated, might attach too much significance to information that is of questionable reliability.[26]

[1] Adoption of SEC Rule 175

With the adoption of Rule 175 under the Securities Act, the SEC recognized that the flow of "soft" information to the marketplace may enable more informed investment decisions to be made. Generally, Rule 175 (as well as Rule 3b-6 under the Exchange Act) encourages issuer use of financial projections in 1933 Act registration statements, 1934 Act reports, annual reports to shareholders, and other documents filed with the SEC. The rule establishes a "safe harbor" from liability for parties who invoke the rule.

Under Rule 175, "a safe harbor [is recognized] from the applicable liability provisions of the federal securities laws for statements [made by or on behalf of an issuer or by an outside reviewer retained by such issuer] relating to or containing (1) projections of reserves, income (loss), earnings (loss) per share or other financial items, such as capital expenditures, dividends, or capital structure, (2) management plans and objectives for future company operations, and (3) future economic performance included in management's statements." In providing this "safe harbor," Rule 175 precludes liability for the making of issuer forward-looking statements unless the plaintiff establishes that any such statement was made or reaffirmed without a reasonable basis or was disclosed other than in good faith.[27]

It may be argued that the SEC went too far in permitting a first-time public issuer conducting its IPO to include "safe harbor" projections in its registration statement.

---

24. *See* Securities Act Release No. 6084 (1979).
25. *See* SEC Financial Reporting Release No. 36 (1989).
26. *See, e.g., Gerstle v. Gamble-Skogmo, Inc.*, 478 F.2d 1281, 1294 (2d Cir. 1973).
27. Securities Act Release No. 6084 (1979).

Indeed, issuers in Regulation A offerings also are entitled to invoke Rule 175.[28] Unlike established reporting companies, many such issuers are start-up companies with no previous substantial earnings history. In any event, these issuers have not been widely followed in the market. Hence, the SEC may have thrown caution to the wind for the sake of encouraging projections. It can be argued, however, that, if such first-time issuers make projections with no previous earnings history, such projections are not within Rule 175's "safe harbor" because they are not made in "good faith" and "with a reasonable basis."

The above argument, however, is unlikely to succeed. Projections for issuers engaged in IPOs or Regulation A offerings clearly are permitted within the confines of the safe harbor rule. Moreover, pursuant to legislation enacted by Congress in 1995, the safe harbor provisions have been broadened to encompass certain oral and written statements, even if not filed with the SEC, by an Exchange Act reporting company and those acting on its behalf (see Chapters 8, 11).

[2] Management Discussion and Analysis ("MD&A")

Responding further to criticism that the Commission slighted the importance of forward-looking information, the SEC adopted Item 303 of Regulation S-K. Item 303 pertains to "Management Discussion and Analysis of Financial Condition and Results of Operation" (MD&A). This provision plays a significant role in the mandatory disclosure of forward-looking information in certain situations. As stated by one source, "the MD&A has become a major, if not the major, item of narrative disclosure that is studied, together with the financial statements, for investment decision and analysis purposes."[29]

Pursuant to the MD&A, the SEC has asserted that a disclosure obligation exists "where a trend, demand, commitment, event or uncertainty is both presently known to management and reasonably likely to have material effects on the registrant's financial condition or results of operation."[30] In circumstances where a trend, demand, commitment, event or uncertainty is known, the subject company's management must consider the following:

1. Is the known trend, demand, commitment, event or uncertainty likely to come to fruition? If management determines that it is not reasonably likely to occur, no disclosure is required.

2. If management cannot make that determination, it must evaluate objectively the consequences of the known trend, demand, commitment, event or uncertainty, on the assumption that it will come to fruition.

---

28. *See* Securities Act Release No. 6949 (1992).

29. Schneider, *MD&A Disclosure*, 22 Rev. Sec. & Comm. Reg. 149, 150 (1989).

30. SEC Financial Reporting Release No, 36, 6 Fed. Sec. L. Rep. (CCH) ¶ 73,193, at 62,842 (1989).

> *Disclosure is then required unless management determines that a material effect on the registrant's financial condition or results of operations is not reasonably likely to occur.*[31]

The SEC has instituted enforcement actions when it has deemed the MD&A deficient. Private litigants also have brought suit on this basis, at times with success. In view of these significant liability concerns, preparation of the MD&A demands careful planning, adequate time for reflection, and communication among the participants of the disclosure "team."[32] The SEC's "MD&A" Adoption Release is set forth below and is followed by a recent Second Circuit decision on this subject.

MD&A Release

SEC Financial Reporting Release No. 36 (1989)

Evaluation of Disclosure — Interpretive Guidance Introduction

The MD&A requirements are intended to provide, in one section of a filing,[33] material historical and prospective textual disclosure enabling investors and other users to assess the financial condition and results of operations of the registrant, with particular emphasis on the registrant's prospects for the future. As the Concept Release states:

> The Commission has long recognized the need for a narrative explanation of the financial statements, because a numerical presentation and brief accompanying footnotes alone may be insufficient for an investor to judge the quality of earnings and the likelihood that past performance is indicative of future performance. MD&A is intended to give the investor an opportunity to look at the company through the eyes of management by providing both a short and long-term analysis of the business of the company. The Item asks management to discuss the dynamics of the business and to analyze the financials. [See Securities Act Release Nos. 6711 (1987), 8350 (2003).]

As the Commission has stated, "[i]t is the responsibility of management to identify and address those key variables and other qualitative and quantitative factors which are peculiar to and necessary for an understanding and evaluation of the individual company."

-----

31. *Id.* (emphasis supplied). *See* Securities Exchange Act Release No. 8350, [2003–2004 Transfer Binder] Fed. Sec. L. Rep. (CCH) ¶ 87,127 (2003) (setting forth guidelines to assist registrants and issuers in "preparing MD&A disclosure that is easier to follow and understand, and in providing information that more completely satisfies our previously enumerated principal objectives of MD&A").

32. *See e.g., In the Matter of Caterpillar, Inc.,* Administrative Proceeding No. 3-7692 (SEC 1992). *See also,* Schneider, *supra* note 29, at 150.

33. The MD&A should contain a discussion of all the material impacts upon the registrant's financial condition or results of operations, including those arising from disclosure provided elsewhere in the filing.

The Commission has determined that interpretive guidance is needed. . . .

Prospective Information

Several specific provisions in Item 303 require disclosure of forward-looking information. MD&A requires discussions of "known trends or any known demands, commitments, events or uncertainties that will result in or that are reasonably likely to result in the registrant's liquidity increasing or decreasing in any material way." Further, descriptions of known material trends in the registrant's capital resources and expected changes in the mix and cost of such resources are required. Disclosure of known trends or uncertainties that the registrant reasonably expects will have a material impact on net sales, revenues, or income from continuing operations is also required. Finally, the Instructions to Item 303 state that MD&A "shall focus specifically on material events and uncertainties known to management that would cause reported financial information not to be necessarily indicative of future operating results or of future financial condition."[34]

[T]he distinction between prospective information that is required to be disclosed and voluntary forward-looking disclosure is an area requiring additional attention. This critical distinction is explained in the Concept Release:

> Both required disclosure regarding the future impact of presently known trends, events or uncertainties and optional forward-looking information may involve some prediction or projection. The distinction between the two rests with the nature of the prediction required. *Required disclosure is based on currently known trends, events, and uncertainties that are reasonably expected to have material effects*, such as: A reduction in the registrant's product prices; erosion in the registrant's market share; changes in insurance coverage; or the likely non-renewal of a material contract. In contrast, optional forward-looking disclosure involves *anticipating a future trend or event or anticipating a less predictable impact of a known event, trend or uncertainty.*

The rules establishing a safe harbor for disclosure of "forward-looking statements" define such statements to include statements of "future economic performance contained in" MD&A. These safe harbors apply to required statements concerning the future effect of known trends, demands, commitments, events or uncertainties, as well to optional forward-looking statements.[35]

A disclosure duty exists where a trend, demand, commitment, event or uncertainty is both presently known to management and reasonably likely to have material effects on the registrant's financial condition or results of operation. Registrants preparing

---

34. 17 CFR 229.303(a), Instruction 3. The data known to management which may trigger required forward-looking disclosure is hereinafter referred to as "known trends, demands, commitments, events, or uncertainties."

35. Rule 175(c) under the Securities Act of 1933 ("Securities Act"), 17 CFR 230.175(c), and Rule 3b-6(c) under the Exchange Act, 17 CFR 240.3b-6.

their MD&A disclosure should determine and carefully review what trends, demands, commitments, events or uncertainties are known to management. . . .

Where a trend, demand, commitment, event or uncertainty is known, management must make two assessments:

(1) Is the known trend, demand, commitment, event or uncertainty likely to come to fruition? If management determines that it is not reasonably likely to occur, no disclosure is required.

(2) If management cannot make that determination, it must evaluate objectively the consequences of the known trend, demand, commitment, event or uncertainty, on the assumption that it will come to fruition. Disclosure is then required unless management determines that a material effect on the registrant's financial condition or results of operations is not reasonably likely to occur.[36]

Each final determination resulting from the assessments made by management must be objectively reasonable, viewed as of the time the determination is made.[37]

Application of these principles may be illustrated using a common disclosure issue which was considered in the review of a number of Project registrants: designation as a potentially responsible party ("PRP") by the Environmental Protection Agency (the "EPA") under The Comprehensive Environmental Response, Compensation, and Liability Act of 1980 ("Superfund").

> *FACTS*: A registrant has been correctly designated a PRP by the EPA with respect to cleanup of hazardous waste at three sites. No statutory defenses are available. The registrant is in the process of preliminary investigations of the sites to determine the nature of its potential liability and the amount of remedial costs necessary to clean up the sites. Other PRPs also have been designated, but the ability to obtain contribution is unclear, as is the extent of insurance coverage, if any. Management is unable to determine that a material effect on future financial condition or results of operations is not reasonably likely to occur.

Based upon the facts of this hypothetical case, MD&A disclosure of the effects of the PRP status, qualified to the extent reasonably practicable, would be required. For MD&A purposes, aggregate potential costs must be considered in light of the joint

---

36. (Emphasis supplied). MD&A mandates disclosure of specified forward-looking information, and specifies its own standard for disclosure—*i.e.*, reasonably likely to have material effect. This specific standard governs the circumstances in which Item 303 requires disclosure. The probability/magnitude test for materiality approved by the Supreme Court in *Basic, Inc. v. Levinson*, 108 S. Ct. 978 (1988), is inapposite to Item 303 disclosure.

37. Where a material change in a registrant's financial condition (such as a material increase or decrease in cash flows) or results of operations appears in a reporting period and the likelihood of such changes was not discussed in prior reports, the Commission staff as part of its review of the current filing will inquire as to the circumstances existing at the time of the earlier filings to determine whether the registrant failed to discuss a known trend, demand, commitment, event or uncertainty as required by Item 303.

and several liability to which a PRP is subject. Facts regarding whether insurance coverage may be contested, and whether and to what extent potential sources of contributions or indemnification constitute reliable sources of recovery may be factored into the determination of whether a material future effect is not reasonably likely to occur.

Panther Partners Inc. v. Ikanos Communications, Inc.
United States Court of Appeals, Second Circuit
681 F.3d 114 (2012)

BARRINGTON D. PARKER, Circuit Judge:

Plaintiff Panther Partners Inc. ("Panther") appeals an order of the United States District Court for the Southern District of New York, denying leave to amend its complaint alleging violations of §§ 11, 12(a)(2), and 15 of the Securities Act of 1933. The proposed complaint alleged that defendant Ikanos Communications Inc. ("Ikanos" or the "Company") was required to disclose, and failed adequately to disclose, in connection with a March 2006 secondary offering of its securities (the "Secondary Offering"), known defects in the Company's semiconductor chips. We hold that the proposed complaint stated a claim because it plausibly alleged that the defects constituted a known trend or uncertainty that the Company reasonably expected would have a material unfavorable impact on revenues. *See* Item 303 of SEC Regulation S-K, 17 C.F.R. § 229.303(a)(3)(ii). Accordingly, we vacate the judgment of the district court and remand with instructions to permit the filing of the amended complaint.

Background

In this putative securities class action, Panther alleges that Ikanos and various of its officers, directors, and underwriters violated §§ 11, 12(a)(2), and 15 of the Securities Act by failing to disclose known defects in the Company's VDSL (very-high-bit-rate digital subscriber line) Version Four chips. Ikanos is a publicly-traded company that develops and markets programmable semiconductors. The semiconductors enable fiber-fast broadband services over telephone companies' existing copper lines. Ikanos's customers are primarily large original equipment manufacturers ("OEMs") in the communications industry that incorporate Ikanos's products into their products, which are then sold to telecommunications carriers. All of Ikanos's revenues derive from the sale of semiconductor chip sets.

In 2005, Ikanos sold its VDSL Version Four chips to Sumitomo Electric and NEC, its two largest customers and the source of 72% of its 2005 revenues. Sumitomo Electric and NEC then incorporated the chips into products that were in turn sold to NTT and installed in NTT's network.

Ikanos learned in January 2006 that there were quality issues with the chips. In particular, the chips had developed a problem called "Kirkendahl voiding" (Kirkendahl voiding is caused by the mingling of alloys between a gold wire and aluminum pad, causing the connection between the components to fail over time though different temperature exposures), traceable to a third-party assembling company in China to which Ikanos had switched the majority of its assembly work during the third and fourth quarters of fiscal year 2005. In the weeks leading up to the Secondary Offering, the defect issues became more pronounced as Ikanos received an increasing number of complaints from Sumitomo Electric and NEC. The thrust of the complaints was that the chips that had been installed in the NTT network were defective and were causing the network to fail, and that end-users who had subscribed to NTT's television, Internet and telephone services were losing signals and access to their subscribed services. According to Ikanos's former Director of Quality and Reliability, the defects "were a substantial problem for [Ikanos] to resolve in order to appease Sumitomo Electric and NEC and to retain them as customers," in part because Ikanos knew it would be unable to determine which of the chip sets it sold to these customers actually contained defective chips. Panther alleges that Ikanos's Board of Directors met and discussed the defect issue at the time it arose, and Company representatives regularly traveled to Japan to meet with Sumitomo and NEC representatives to evaluate the problem and to discuss possible solutions.

Panther goes on to allege that Ikanos did not disclose the magnitude of the defect issue in either the Registration Statement or the Prospectus for the Secondary Offering. Instead, the Registration Statement simply cautioned in generalized terms that

> [h]ighly complex products such as those that [Ikanos] offer[s] frequently contain defects and bugs, particularly when they are first introduced or as new versions are released. In the past we have experienced, and may in the future experience, defects and bugs in our products. If any of our products contains defects or bugs, or have reliability, quality or compatibility problems, our reputation may be damaged and our OEM customers may be reluctant to buy our products, which could harm our ability to retain existing customers and attract new customers. In addition, these defects or bugs could interrupt or delay sales or shipment of our products to our customers.

> . . . .

Some 5.75 million shares of Ikanos stock were sold in the Secondary Offering at $20.75 per share, raising more than $120 million. The individual defendants sold stock valued at $7.3 million.

Ikanos ultimately determined that the chips had an "extremely high" failure rate of 25–30%. In June 2006, three months after the Secondary Offering, the Company reached an agreement with Sumitomo Electric and NEC to replace at Ikanos's expense all of the units sold—not just the units containing observably defective chips. This recall resulted in the return of hundreds of thousands of chip sets whose cost had to be written off.

In July 2006, the Company reported a net loss of $2.2 million for the second quarter, causing the price of its shares to drop over 25% from $13.85 to $10.24. Three months later, in October 2006, it reduced its expected third-quarter revenues from $40-$43 million to $36–37 million, citing "product delays and manufacturing constraints" involving its fourth-and fifth-generation chip sets. The share price dropped almost 30%, from $10.94 to $7.76, on the news, and analysts lowered their fourth-quarter revenue projections from $45 million to $25 million. Three weeks later, Chief Executive Officer and Board Chairman Rajesh Vashist resigned. Two days later, Ikanos announced third-quarter revenues of $36.7 million and revised revenue estimates for the fourth quarter down further to $21–24 million. Shortly thereafter, plaintiff filed its initial complaint, alleging, among other things, that in contravention of Item 303 of SEC Regulation S-K, defendants failed to disclose the "known . . . uncertaint[y]" that the VDSL Version Four chips were defective and were causing system failures where they were deployed. [The district court dismissed the complaint and denied leave to amend the complaint.]

Discussion

Sections 11 and 12(a)(2) of the Securities Act impose liability on certain participants in a registered securities offering when the registration statement or prospectus contains material misstatements or omissions. The provisions are "notable both for the limitations on their scope as well as the *in terrorem* nature of the liability they create." . . . Section 11 imposes strict liability on issuers and . . . negligence liability on underwriters, "[i]n case any part of the registration statement, when such part became effective, contained an untrue statement of a material fact or omitted to state a material fact required to be stated therein or necessary to make the statements therein not misleading." Section 12(a)(2) imposes liability under similar circumstances for misstatements or omissions in a prospectus. . . . Neither scienter, reliance, nor loss causation is an element of § 11 or § 12(a)(2) claims . . . [Sections 11 and 12(a)(2) are covered in Chapter 7 of this text.]

One of the potential bases for liability under §§ 11 and 12(a)(2) is an omission in contravention of an affirmative legal disclosure obligation. In this case, Item 303 of SEC Regulation S-K provides the basis for Ikanos's alleged disclosure obligation. The Regulation, as we have seen, requires registrants to "[d]escribe any known trends or uncertainties . . . that the registrant reasonably expects will have a material . . . unfavorable impact on . . . revenues or income from continuing operations." Instruction 3 to paragraph 303(a) provides that "[t]he discussion and analysis shall focus specifically on material events and uncertainties known to management that would cause reported financial information not to be necessarily indicative of future operating results or of future financial condition." . . . According to the SEC's interpretive release regarding Item 303, the Regulation imposes a disclosure duty "where a trend, demand, commitment, event or uncertainty is both [1] presently known to management and [2] reasonably likely to have material effects on the registrant's financial condition or results of operations." . . . We believe that, viewed in the context of Item 303's disclosure obligations, the defect rate, in a vacuum, is not what is at issue. Rather, it is the manner in which uncertainty surrounding that defect rate, generated by an increasing flow of highly negative information from key customers, might reasonably be expected to have a material impact on future revenues.

Litwin v. Blackstone Group, L.P., [634 F.3d 706 (2d Cir. 2011)], decided after the district court denied Panther leave to file the [complaint], is instructive on this point. There, investors sued Blackstone, an asset management company, under §§ 11 and 12(a)(2) for omitting from a registration statement and prospectus information regarding negative trends in the real estate market. Blackstone's real estate investments accounted for approximately 22.6% of its assets under management. Reversing the district court's dismissal of the complaint, we held that plaintiffs adequately alleged that Blackstone was required by Item 303 to disclose the trend, "already known and existing at the time of the IPO," because it "was reasonably likely to have a material impact on Blackstone's financial condition." In so holding, we emphasized that

> the key information that plaintiffs assert should have been disclosed is whether, and to what extent, the particular known trend, event, or uncertainty might have been reasonably expected to materially affect Blackstone's investments. . . . Again, the focus of plaintiffs' claims is the required disclosures under Item 303 — plaintiffs are not seeking the disclosure of the . . . downward trend in the real estate market. . . . Rather, plaintiffs claim that Blackstone was required to disclose the manner in which that then-known trend, event, or uncertainty might reasonably be expected to materially impact Blackstone's future revenues.

> . . . .

We hold that the [Complaint] plausibly alleges that the defect issue, and its potential impact on Ikanos's business, constituted a known trend or uncertainty that Ikanos reasonably expected would have a material unfavorable impact on revenues or income from continuing operations. [The Complaint] alleges that, before the Secondary Offering, Ikanos was receiving an increasing number of calls from Sumitomo Electric and NEC alerting Ikanos to the fact that its chips were defective and were causing network failures. The [Complaint] also alleges that the "defect issues," which were becoming "more pronounced," were a "substantial problem for [Ikanos] to resolve" — so much so that members of Ikanos's Board of Directors were discussing the issue, and representatives from the Company were flying to Japan to meet with Sumitomo Electric and NEC. [Importantly,] the [Complaint] adds the critical allegations (1) that these customers accounted for 72% of Ikanos's revenues in 2005 and (2) that Ikanos knew at the time it was receiving an increasing number of calls from these customers that it would be unable to determine which chip sets contained defective chips. The [Complaint] then articulates the plausible inference to be drawn from these facts: that Ikanos "knew that . . . the chips that it had sold to . . . its largest customers and the largest source of its revenues were defective, . . . and that it [may] therefore have to accept returns of *all* of the chips that it had sold to these two important customers." . . .

The reasonable and plausible inferences from these allegations are not simply that Ikanos quite possibly would have to replace and write off a large volume of chip sets, but also that it had jeopardized its relationship with clients who at that time accounted for the vast majority of its revenues. It is true that, as alleged, Ikanos did not recall and undertake to replace all the chip sets until June 2006. Nor was the precise 25–30% chip failure rate determined until after the Secondary Offering. But neither of these facts undermines the plausible inference that, at a time when it was receiving an increasing number of calls from these customers and its Board of Directors was discussing the issue, Ikanos was aware of the "uncertainty" that it might have to accept returns of a substantial volume, if not all, of the chips it had delivered to its major customers. It goes without saying that such "known uncertainties" could materially impact revenues.

In light of these allegations, the Registration Statement's generic cautionary language that "[h]ighly complex products such as those that [Ikanos] offer[s] frequently contain defects and bugs" was incomplete and, consequently, did not fulfill Ikanos's duty to inform the investing public of the particular, factually-based uncertainties of which it was aware in the weeks leading up to the Secondary Offering.

. . . .

Conclusion

The judgment of the district court is vacated, and the case remanded with instructions to grant Panther leave to file the [complaint].

───────────

Note

Note that Item 303 (MD&A) of Regulation S-K has a broader materiality reach than SEC Rule 10b-5 and other remedial provisions, such as §§ 11, 12, and 17(a) of the Securities Act. As stated by one appellate court:

> Because the materiality standards for Rule 10b-5 and Reg. SK-303 differ significantly, the demonstration of a violation of the disclosure requirements of Item 303 does not lead inevitably to the conclusion that such disclosure would be required under Rule 10b-5. Such a duty to disclose must be separately shown [under Rule 10b-5]. . . . [W]e thus hold that a violation of [Reg.] SK-303's reporting requirements does not automatically give rise to a material omission under Rule 10b-5. . . .

Oran v. Stafford, 226 F.3d 275, 288 (3d Cir. 2000) (citations omitted). For two more recent appellate court decisions on this subject, compare *Stratte-McClure v. Morgan Stanley and Co.*, 776 F.3d 94 (2d Cir. 2015) (holding that Reg. S-K Item 303 omission may be a Rule 10b-5 material omission if U.S. Supreme Court standard for § 10(b) materiality met); *In re NVIDIA*, 768 F.3d 1046 (9th Cir. 2014) (opining that Reg. S-K Item 303's standard of materiality is "much broader" than the U.S. Supreme Court's test for § 10(b) materiality and that, accordingly, the disclosure required under Item 303 is not necessarily required under § 10(b)). *See generally* Crawford and Galaro, *A Rule 10b-5 Private Right of Action for MD&A Violations*, 43 Sec. Reg. L.J. 245 (2015). The U.S. Supreme Court has granted a petition for certiorari to determine the § 10(b) liability parameters for an issuer's failure to comply with the disclosure requirements of Item 303. *See Leidos, Inc. v. Indiana Public Retirement System.*

[C] Private Securities Litigation Reform Act

Provisions of the Private Securities Litigation Reform Act of 1995 (PSLRA) encourage the disclosure of forward-looking information. Because the issues relating to disclosure of financial projections and other types of forward-looking information are more suitably addressed in Chapter 8 (which focuses on Exchange Act § 10(b) litigation) and Chapter 11 (which highlights issuer affirmative disclosure obligations), the 1995 legislation's impact in this arena is explored in these later chapters.

[D] The Concept of Materiality

Matrixx Initiatives, Inc. v. Siracusano

United States Supreme Court

563 U.S. 27, 131 S. Ct. 1309, 179 L. Ed. 2d 398 (2011)

JUSTICE SOTOMAYOR delivered the opinion of the Court.

This case presents the question whether a plaintiff can state a claim for securities fraud under § 10(b) of the Securities Exchange Act of 1934 and SEC Rule 10b-5, based on a pharmaceutical company's failure to disclose reports of adverse events associated with a product if the reports do not disclose a statistically significant number of adverse events. Respondents, plaintiffs in a securities fraud class action, allege that petitioners, Matrixx Initiatives, Inc., and three of its executives (collectively Matrixx), failed to disclose reports of a possible link between its leading product, a cold remedy, and loss of smell, rendering statements made by Matrixx misleading. Matrixx contends that respondents' complaint does not adequately allege that Matrixx made a material misrepresentation or omission or that it acted with scienter because the complaint does not allege that Matrixx knew of a statistically significant number of adverse events requiring disclosure. We conclude that the materiality of adverse event reports cannot be reduced to a bright-line rule. Although in many cases reasonable investors would not consider reports of adverse events to be material information, respondents have alleged facts plausibly suggesting that reasonable investors would have viewed these particular reports as material. Respondents have also alleged facts "giving rise to a strong inference" that Matrixx "acted with the required state of mind." We therefore hold, in agreement with the Court of Appeals for the Ninth Circuit, that respondents have stated a claim under § 10(b) and Rule 10b-5.

I

A

Through a wholly owned subsidiary, Matrixx develops, manufactures, and markets over-the-counter pharmaceutical products. Its core brand of products is called Zicam.

All of the products sold under the name Zicam are used to treat the common cold and associated symptoms. At the time of the events in question, one of Matrixx's products was Zicam Cold Remedy, which came in several forms including nasal spray and gel. The active ingredient in Zicam Cold Remedy was zinc gluconate. Respondents allege that Zicam Cold Remedy accounted for approximately 70 percent of Matrixx's sales.

Respondents initiated this securities fraud class action against Matrixx on behalf of individuals who purchased Matrixx securities between October 22, 2003, and February 6, 2004 [on the NASDAQ National Market]. The action principally arises out of statements that Matrixx made during the class period relating to revenues and product safety. Respondents claim that Matrixx's statements were misleading in light of reports that Matrixx had received, but did not disclose, about consumers who had lost their sense of smell (a condition called anosmia) after using Zicam Cold Remedy. Respondents' consolidated amended complaint alleges the following facts, which the courts below properly assumed to be true.

In 1999, Dr. Alan Hirsch, neurological director of the Smell & Taste Treatment and Research Foundation, Ltd., called Matrixx's customer service line after discovering a possible link between Zicam nasal gel and a loss of smell "in a cluster of his patients." Dr. Hirsch told a Matrixx employee that "previous studies had demonstrated that intranasal application of zinc could be problematic." He also told the employee about at least one of his patients who did not have a cold and who developed anosmia after using Zicam.

In September 2002, Timothy Clarot, Matrixx's vice president for research and development, called Miriam Linschoten, Ph.D., at the University of Colorado Health Sciences Center after receiving a complaint from a person Linschoten was treating who had lost her sense of smell after using Zicam. Clarot informed Linschoten that Matrixx had received similar complaints from other customers. Linschoten drew Clarot's attention to "previous studies linking zinc sulfate to loss of smell." Clarot gave her the impression that he had not heard of the studies. She asked Clarot whether Matrixx had done any studies of its own; he responded that it had not but that it had hired a consultant to review the product. Soon thereafter, Linschoten sent Clarot abstracts of the studies she had mentioned. Research from the 1930's and 1980's had confirmed "[z]inc's toxicity." Clarot called Linschoten to ask whether she would be willing to participate in animal studies that Matrixx was planning, but she declined because her focus was human research.

By September 2003, one of Linschoten's colleagues at the University of Colorado, Dr. Bruce Jafek, had observed 10 patients suffering from anosmia after Zicam use. Linschoten and Jafek planned to present their findings at a meeting of the American Rhinologic Society in a poster presentation entitled "Zicam Induced Anosmia." The American Rhinologic Society posted their abstract in advance of the meeting. The presentation described in detail a 55-year old man with previously normal taste and smell who experienced severe burning in his nose, followed immediately by a loss of smell, after using Zicam. It also reported 10 other Zicam users with similar symptoms.

Matrixx learned of the doctors' planned presentation. Clarot sent a letter to Dr. Jafek warning him that he did not have permission to use Matrixx's name or the names of its products. Dr. Jafek deleted the references to Zicam in the poster before presenting it to the American Rhinologic Society. The following month, two plaintiffs commenced a product liability lawsuit against Matrixx alleging that Zicam had damaged their sense of smell. By the end of the class period on February 6, 2004, nine plaintiffs had filed four lawsuits. Respondents allege that Matrixx made a series of public statements that were misleading in light of the foregoing information. In October 2003, after they had learned of Dr. Jafek's study and after Dr. Jafek had presented his findings to the American Rhinologic Society, Matrixx stated that Zicam was "'poised for growth in the upcoming cough and cold season'" and that the company had "'very strong momentum.'"[38] Matrix further expressed its expectation that revenues would "be up in excess of 50% and that earnings, per share for the full year [would] be in the 25 to 30 cent range." In January 2004, Matrixx raised its revenue guidance, predicting an increase in revenues of 80 percent and earnings per share in the 33-to-38-cent range.

In its Form 10-Q filed with the SEC in November 2003, Zicam warned of the potential "material adverse effect" that could result from product liability claims, "whether or not proven to be valid." It stated that product liability actions could materially affect Matrixx's "product branding and goodwill," leading to reduced customer acceptance. It did not disclose, however, that two plaintiffs had already sued Matrixx for allegedly causing them to lose their sense of smell.

On January 30, 2004, Dow Jones Newswires reported that the Food and Drug Administration (FDA) was "looking into complaints that an over-the-counter common-cold medicine manufactured by a unit of Matrixx Initiatives, Inc. (MTXX) may be causing some users to lose their sense of smell" in light of at least three product liability lawsuits. Matrixx's stock fell from $13.55 to $11.97 per share after the report. In response, on February 2, Matrixx issued a press release that stated:

> "All Zicam products are manufactured and marketed according to FDA guidelines for homeopathic medicine. Our primary concern is the health and safety of our customers and the distribution of factual information about our products. Matrixx believes statements alleging that intranasal Zicam products caused anosmia (loss of smell) are completely unfounded and misleading.

> "In no clinical trial of intranasal zinc gluconate gel products has there been a single report of lost or diminished olfactory function (sense of smell). Rather, the safety and efficacy of zinc gluconate for the treatment of symptoms related to the common cold have been well established in two double-blind, placebo controlled, randomized clinical trials. In fact, in neither study were there any reports of anosmia related to the use of this compound. The

---

[38]. At oral argument, counsel for the United States, which submitted an *amicus curiae* brief in support of respondents, suggested that some of these statements might qualify as nonactionable "puffery." This question is not before us, as Matrixx has not advanced such an argument.

overall incidence of adverse events associated with zinc gluconate was extremely low, with no statistically significant difference between the adverse event rates for the treated and placebo subsets.

"A multitude of environmental and biologic influences are known to affect the sense of smell. Chief among them is the common cold. As a result, the population most likely to use cold remedy products is already at increased risk of developing anosmia. Other common causes of olfactory dysfunction include age, nasal and sinus infections, head trauma, anatomical obstructions, and environmental irritants."

The day after Matrixx issued this press release, its stock price bounced back to $13.40 per share.

On February 6, 2004, the end of the class period, Good Morning America, a nationally broadcast morning news program, highlighted Dr. Jafek's findings. (The complaint does not allege that Matrixx learned of the news story before its broadcast.) The program reported that Dr. Jafek had discovered more than a dozen patients suffering from anosmia after using Zicam. It also noted that four lawsuits had been filed against Matrixx. The price of Matrixx stock plummeted to $9.94 per share that same day. Zicam again issued a press release largely repeating its February 2 statement.

On February 19, 2004, Matrixx filed a Form 8-K with the SEC stating that it had "convened a two-day meeting of physicians and scientists to review current information on smell disorders" in response to Dr. Jafek's presentation. According to the Form 8-K, "In the opinion of the panel, there is insufficient scientific evidence at this time to determine if zinc gluconate, when used as recommended, affects a person's ability to smell." A few weeks later, a reporter quoted Matrixx as stating that it would begin conducting "'animal and human studies to further characterize these post-marketing complaints.'"

On the basis of these allegations, respondents claimed that Matrixx violated § 10(b) of the Securities Exchange Act and SEC Rule 10b-5 by making untrue statements of fact and failing to disclose material facts necessary to make the statements not misleading in an effort to maintain artificially high prices for Matrixx securities.

B

Matrixx moved to dismiss respondents' complaint, arguing that they had failed to plead the elements of a material misstatement or omission and scienter. The District Court granted the motion to dismiss. Relying on *In re Carter-Wallace, Inc., Securities Litigation*, 220 F.3d 36 (CA2 2000), it held that respondents had not alleged a statistically significant correlation between the use of Zicam and anosmia so as to make failure to public[ly] disclose complaints and the University of Colorado study a material omission. The District Court similarly agreed that respondents had not stated with particularity facts giving rise to a strong inference of scienter. It noted that the complaint failed to allege that Matrixx disbelieved its statements about

Zicam's safety or that any of the defendants profited or attempted to profit from Matrixx's public statements.

The Court of Appeals reversed. 585 F.3d 1167 (CA9 2009). Noting that " '[t]he determination [of materiality] requires delicate assessments of the inferences a "reasonable shareholder" would draw from a given set of facts and the significance of those inferences to him,' " the Court of Appeals held that the District Court had erred in requiring an allegation of statistical significance to establish materiality. It concluded, to the contrary, that the complaint adequately alleged "information regarding the possible link between Zicam and anosmia" that would have been significant to a reasonable investor. Turning to scienter, the Court of Appeals concluded that "[w]ithholding reports of adverse effects of and lawsuits concerning the product responsible for the company's remarkable sales increase is 'an extreme departure from the standards of ordinary care,' " giving rise to a strong inference of scienter.

We granted certiorari, and we now affirm.

II

Section 10(b) of the Securities Exchange Act makes it unlawful for any person to "use or employ, in connection with the purchase or sale of any security . . . any manipulative or deceptive device or contrivance in contravention of such rules and regulations as the Commission may prescribe as necessary or appropriate in the public interest or for the protection of investors." SEC Rule 10b-5 implements this provision by making it unlawful to, among other things, "make any untrue statement of a material fact or to omit to state a material fact necessary in order to make the statements made, in the light of the circumstances under which they were made, not misleading." We have implied a private cause of action from the text and purpose of § 10(b). See *Tellabs, Inc. v. Makor Issues & Rights, Ltd.*, 551 U. S. 308, 318 (2007).

To prevail on their claim that Matrixx made material misrepresentations or omissions in violation of § 10(b) and Rule 10b-5, respondents must prove "(1) a material misrepresentation or omission by the defendant; (2) scienter; (3) a connection between the misrepresentation or omission and the purchase or sale of a security; (4) reliance upon the misrepresentation or omission; (5) economic loss; and (6) loss causation." *Stoneridge Investment Partners, LLC v. Scientific-Atlanta, Inc.*, 552 U. S. 148, 157 (2008). Matrixx contends that respondents have failed to plead both the element of a material misrepresentation or omission and the element of scienter because they have not alleged that the reports received by Matrixx reflected statistically significant evidence that Zicam caused anosmia. We disagree.

A

We first consider Matrixx's argument that "adverse event reports that do not reveal a statistically significant increased risk of adverse events from product use are not material information."

1

To prevail on a § 10(b) claim, a plaintiff must show that the defendant made a statement that was "*misleading* as to a *material* fact."[39] In *Basic* [485 U.S. 224 (1988)], we held that this materiality requirement is satisfied when there is "a substantial likelihood that the disclosure of the omitted fact would have been viewed by the reasonable investor as having significantly altered the "total mix" of information made available." We were "careful not to set too low a standard of materiality," for fear that management would "bury the shareholders in an avalanche of trivial information.'" . . .

Basic involved a claim that the defendant had made misleading statements denying that it was engaged in merger negotiations when it was, in fact, conducting preliminary negotiations. The defendant urged a bright-line rule that preliminary merger negotiations are material only once the parties to the negotiations reach an agreement in principle. We observed that "[a]ny approach that designates a single fact or occurrence as always determinative of an inherently fact-specific finding such as materiality, must necessarily be overinclusive or underinclusive." We thus reject the defendant's proposed rule, explaining that it would "artificially exclud[e] from the definition of materiality information concerning merger discussions, which would otherwise be considered significant to the trading decisions of a reasonable investor."

Like the defendant in *Basic*, Matrixx urges us to adopt a bright-line rule that reports of adverse events[40] associated with a pharmaceutical company's products cannot be material absent a sufficient number of such reports to establish a statistically significance that the product is in fact causing the events.[41] Absent statistical significance, Matrixx argues, adverse event reports provide only "anecdotal" evidence that "the user of a drug experienced an adverse event at some point during or following the use of that drug." Accordingly, it contends, reasonable investors would not consider such reports relevant unless they are statistically significant because only then do they "reflect a scientifically reliable basis for inferring a potential causal link between product use and the adverse event."

---

[39]. Under the Private Securities Litigation Reform Act of 1995 (PSLRA), when a plaintiff's claim is based on alleged misrepresentations or omissions of a material fact, "the complaint shall specify each statement alleged to have been misleading, [and] the reason or reasons why the statements is misleading." 15 U.S.C. § 78u-4(b)(1).

[40]. The FDA defines an "[a]dverse drug experience" as "[a]ny adverse event associated with the use of a drug in humans, whether or not considered drug related." 21 CFR § 314.80(a) (2010). Federal law imposes certain obligations on pharmaceutical manufacturers to report adverse events to the FDA. During the class period, manufacturers of over-the-counter drugs such as Zicam Cold Remedy had no obligation to report adverse events to the FDA. In 2006, Congress enacted legislation to require manufacturers of over-the-counter drugs to report any "serious adverse event" to the FDA within 15 business days. *See* 21 U.S.C. §§ 379aa(b), (c).

[41]. "A study that is statistically significant has results that are unlikely to be the result of random error" . . .

As in *Basic*, Matrixx's categorical rule would "artificially exclud[e]" information that "would otherwise be considered significant to the trading decision of a reasonable investor." Matrixx's argument rests on the premise that statistical significance is the only reliable indication of causation. This premise is flawed: As the SEC points out, "medical researchers . . . consider multiple factors in assessing causation." Brief for United States as *Amicus Curiae* 12. Statistically significant data are not always available. For example, when an adverse event is subtle or rare, "an inability to obtain a data set of appropriate quality or quantity may preclude a finding of statistical significance." Moreover, ethical considerations may prohibit researchers from conducting randomized clinical trials to confirm a suspected causal link for the purpose of obtaining statistically significant data.

A lack of statistically significant data does not mean that medical experts have no reliable basis for inferring a causal link between a drug and adverse events. As Matrixx itself concedes, medical experts rely on other evidence to establish an inference of causation. See Brief for Petitioners 44B45, n. 22.[42] We note that courts frequently permit expert testimony on causation based on evidence other than statistical significance. . . . We need not consider whether the expert testimony was properly admitted in those cases, and we do not attempt to define here what constitutes reliable evidence of causation. It suffices to note that, as these courts have recognized, "medical professionals and researchers do not limit the data they consider to the results of randomized clinical trials or to statistically significant evidence."

The FDA similarly does not limit the evidence it considers for purposes of assessing causation and taking regulatory action to statistically significant data. In assessing the safety risk posed by a product, the FDA considers factors such as "strength of the association," "temporal relationship of product use and the event," "consistency of findings across available data sources," "evidence of a dose-response for the effect," "biologic plausibility," "seriousness of the event relative to the disease being treated," "potential to mitigate the risk in the population," "feasibility of further study using observational or controlled clinical study designs," and "degree of benefit the product provides, including availability of other therapies." . . . It does not apply any single metric for determining when additional inquiry or action is necessary, and it certainly does not insist upon 'statistical significance.'"

Not only does the FDA rely on a wide range of evidence of causation, it sometimes acts on the basis of evidence that suggests, but does not prove, causation. For example, the FDA requires manufacturers of over-the-counter drugs to revise their labeling

---

[42]. Matrixx and its *amici* list as relevant factors the strength of the association between the drug and the adverse effects; a temporal relationship between exposure and the adverse event; consistency across studies; biological plausibility; consideration of alternative explanations; specificity (*i.e.*, whether the specific chemical is associated with the specific disease); the dose-response relationship; and the clinical and pathological characteristics of the event. Brief for Petitioners 44B45, n. 22; Brief for Consumer Healthcare Products Assn. et al. as *Amici Curiae* 12B13. These factors are similar to the factors the FDA considers in taking action against pharmaceutical products.

"to include a warning as soon as there is reasonable evidence of an association of a serious hazard with a drug; a causal relationship need not have been proved." More generally, the FDA may make regulatory decisions against drugs based on postmarketing evidence that gives rise to only a suspicion of causation. . . . Attaining a prominent degree of suspicion is much more likely, and may be considered a sufficient basis for regulatory decisions."

This case proves the point. In 2009, the FDA issued a warning letter to Matrixx stating that "[a] significant and growing body of evidence substantiates that the Zicam Cold Remedy intranasal products may pose a serious risk to consumers who use them." The letter cited as evidence 130 reports of anosmia the FDA had received, the fact that the FDA had received few reports of anosmia associated with other intranasal cold remedies, and "evidence in the published scientific literature that various salts of zinc can damage olfactory function in animals and humans." It did not cite statistically significant data.

Given that medical professionals and regulators act on the basis of evidence of causation that is not statistically significant, it stands to reason that in certain cases reasonable investors would as well. As Matrixx acknowledges, adverse event reports "appear in many forms, including direct complaints by users to manufacturers, reports by doctors about reported or observed patient reactions, more detailed case reports published by doctors in medical journals, or larger scale published clinical studies." As a result, assessing the materiality of adverse event reports is a "fact-specific" inquiry, that requires consideration of the source, content, and context of the reports. This is not to say that statistical significance (or the lack thereof) is irrelevant—only that it is not dispositive of every case.

Application of *Basic*'s "total mix" standard does not mean that pharmaceutical manufacturers must disclose all reports of adverse events. Adverse event reports are daily events in the pharmaceutical industry; in 2009, the FDA entered nearly 500,000 such reports into its reporting system. . . . The fact that a user of a drug has suffered an adverse event, standing alone, does not mean that the drug caused that event. The question remains whether a *reasonable* investor would have viewed the nondisclosed information "'as having *significantly* altered the "total mix" of information made available.'" . . . . For the reasons just stated, the mere existence of reports of adverse events—which says nothing in and of itself about whether the drug is causing the adverse events—will not satisfy this standard. Something more is needed, but that something more is not limited to statistical significance and can come from "the source, content, and context of the reports." This contextual inquiry may reveal in some cases that reasonable investors would have viewed reports of adverse events as material even though the reports did not provide statistically significant evidence of a causal link.[43]

---

[43]. We note that our conclusion accords with views of the SEC, as expressed in an *amicus curiae* brief filed in this case. *See* Brief for United States as *Amicus Curiae* 11B12; *see also TSC Industries, Inc. v. Northway, Inc.*, 426 U. S. 438, 449, n. 10 (1976) ("[T]he SEC's view of the proper balance

Moreover, it bears emphasis that § 10(b) and Rule 10b-5(b) do not create an affirmative duty to disclose any and all material information. Disclosure is required under these provisions only when necessary "to make . . . statements made, in the light of the circumstances under which they were made, not misleading." 17 CFR § 240.10b-5(b); see also *Basic*, 485 U.S., at 239, n. 17 ("Silence, absent a duty to disclose, is not misleading under Rule 10b-5"). Even with respect to information that a reasonable investor might consider material, companies can control what they have to disclose under these provisions by controlling what they say to the market.

2

Applying *Basic*'s "total mix" standard in this case, we conclude that respondents have adequately pleaded materiality. This is not a case about a handful of anecdotal reports, as Matrixx suggests. Assuming the complaint's allegations to be true, as we must, Matrixx received information that plausibly indicated a reliable causal link between Zicam and anosmia. That information included reports from three medical professionals and researchers about more than 10 patients who had lost their sense of smell after using Zicam. Clarot told Linschoten that Matrixx had received additional reports of anosmia. (In addition, during the class period, nine plaintiffs commenced four product liability lawsuits against Matrixx alleging a causal link between Zicam use and anosmia.) Further, Matrixx knew that Linschoten and Dr. Jafek had presented their findings about a causal link between Zicam and anosmia to a national medical conference devoted to treatment of diseases of the nose.[44] Their presentation described a patient who experienced severe burning in his nose, followed immediately by a loss of smell, after using Zicam, suggesting a temporal relationship between Zicam use and anosmia.

Critically, both Dr. Hirsch and Linschoten had also drawn Matrixx's attention to previous studies that had demonstrated a biological causal link between intranasal application of zinc and anosmia. Before his conversation with Linschoten, Clarot, Matrixx's vice president of research and development, was seemingly unaware of these studies, and the complaint suggests that, as of the class period, Matrixx had not conducted any research of its own relating to anosmia. . . . Accordingly, it can reasonably be inferred from the complaint that Matrixx had no basis for rejecting Dr. Jafek's findings out of hand.

---

between the need to insure adequate disclosure and the need to avoid the adverse consequences of setting too low a threshold for civil liability is entitled to consideration").

[44]. Matrixx contends that Dr. Jafek and Linschoten's study was not reliable because they did not sufficiently rule out the common cold as a cause for their patients' anosmia. We note that the complaint alleges that, in one instance, a consumer who did not have a cold lost his sense of smell after using Zicam. More importantly, to survive a motion to dismiss, respondents need only allege "enough facts to state a claim to relief that is plausible on its face." *Bell Atlantic Corp. v. Twombly*, 550 U.S. 544, 570 (2007). For all the reasons we state in the opinion, respondents' allegations plausibly suggest that Dr. Jafek and Linschoten's conclusions were based on reliable evidence of a causal link between Zicam and anosmia.

We believe that these allegations suffice to "raise a reasonable expectation that discovery will reveal evidence" satisfying the materiality requirement, and to "allo[w] the court to draw the reasonable inference that the defendant is liable for the misconduct alleged." ... The information provided to Matrixx by medical experts revealed a plausible causal relationship between Zicam Cold Remedy and anosmia. Consumers likely would have viewed the risk associated with Zicam (possible loss of smell) as substantially outweighing the benefit of using the product (alleviating cold symptoms), particularly in light of the existence of many alternative products on the market. Importantly, Zicam Cold Remedy allegedly accounted for 70 percent of Matrixx's sales. Viewing the allegations of the complaint as a whole, the complaint alleges facts suggesting a significant risk to the commercial viability of Matrixx's leading product.

It is substantially likely that a reasonable investor would have viewed this information " 'as having significantly altered the "total mix" of information made available.' " Matrixx told the market that revenues were going to rise 50 and then 80 percent. Assuming the complaint's allegations to be true, however, Matrixx had information indicating a significant risk to its leading revenue-generating product. Matrixx also stated that reports indicating that Zicam caused anosmia were " 'completely unfounded and misleading' " and that " 'the safety and efficacy of zinc gluconate for the treatment of symptoms related to the common cold have been well established.' " Importantly, however, Matrixx had evidence of a biological link between Zicam's key ingredient and anosmia, and it had not conducted any studies of its own to disprove that link. In fact, as Matrixx later revealed, the scientific evidence at that time was " 'insufficient ... to determine if zinc gluconate, when used as recommended, affects a person's ability to smell.' "

Assuming the facts to be true, these were material facts "necessary in order to make the statements made, in the light of the circumstances under which they were made, not misleading." We therefore affirm the Court of Appeals' holding that respondents adequately pleaded the element of a material misrepresentation or omission.

. . . .

For the reasons stated, the judgment of the Court of Appeals for the Ninth Circuit is

Affirmed.

---

[1] Qualitative Materiality — Disclosure Relating to "Integrity" or "Competency"

Materiality under the federal securities laws signifies that the misstated or omitted fact, if accurately disclosed, would have been considered important by a reasonable investor in making his/her voting or investment decision. At times, a subject event or circumstance may give rise to difficult materiality determinations. For example, the probability and magnitude in regard to the consummation of certain corporate developments, such as the successful completion of merger negotiations, may be "contingent or speculative in nature." To ascertain whether such contingent developments are material, the probability/magnitude test is utilized. This test postulates that materiality "will depend at any given time upon a balancing of both the indicated probability that the event will occur and the anticipated magnitude of the event in light of the totality of the company activity." *Basic, Inc. v. Levinson,* 485 U.S. 224, 232, 238 (1988).

Purely qualitative information focusing on "insider" (such as director) conduct, unlike quantitative information, does not necessarily impact significantly on the earnings, assets, or economic viability of the registrant. Rather, such information more directly relates to the integrity and competency of corporate management. Under the Commission's rules and judicial decisions, disclosure is required, for example, of certain self-dealing transactions engaged in by management[45] as well as adjudicated illegalities[46] and certain other events (such as the imposition of an SEC injunction).[47] Absent self-dealing, an adjudicated illegality, or mandated disclosure called for by a specific rule, the question is whether the registrant must disclose qualitative information that is not economically material. Note that, if the pertinent information is economically material, then it likely must be disclosed pursuant to such mandates as Item 303 (MD&A) of Regulation S-K.

The case that follows focuses on qualitative materiality in the proxy solicitation setting. Given the adoption of the integrated disclosure system and the court's language, the decision's rationale should extend to the registered offering context.

Gaines v. Haughton

United States Court of Appeals, Ninth Circuit

645 F.2d 761 (1981)

ELY, Circuit Judge.

Ora E. Gaines, the plaintiff-appellant herein, appeals from an order of dismissal and summary judgment for defendants (Lockheed Aircraft Corporation and a number of former and present directors and officers of Lockheed) in a shareholder lawsuit alleging both derivative claims of breach of fiduciary duty/waste of corporate assets and class action claims of federal securities violations. . . .

FACTS

From as early as 1961 to as late as 1975, Lockheed engaged in the practice of hiring "consultants" and "foreign sales agents" and paying them large fees and commissions in connection with foreign sales of Lockheed aircraft and equipment. Approximately

---

45. *See, e.g., Maldonado v. Flynn,* 597 F.2d 789 (2d Cir. 1979); Items 402, 404 of Regulation S-K.

46. *See, e.g., SEC v. Savoy Industries,* 587 F.2d 1149 (D.C. Cir. 1978); Item 401(f) of Regulation S-K.

47. *See* Item 401(f)(3) of Regulation S-K.

$30–38 million was paid directly to foreign governments and officials during this period.[48] Shortly after the existence of these clandestine, "off the books" questionable payments were revealed by the Securities and Exchange Commission (SEC) and United States Senate proceedings in July-August 1975. . . . [Thereafter,] Gaines — an individual Lockheed shareholder — commenced this lawsuit in the United States District Court for the Central District of California. . . . [The basis of the claim under § 14(a) is Lockheed's and the board of directors' nondisclosure of these practices.]

Gaines' federal class action claims seek a permanent injunction barring Lockheed from making further improper or undisclosed payments, filing materially false or misleading proxy materials or periodic financial reports, or maintaining any undisclosed accounts. Gaines also seeks a declaration invalidating past elections, removing certain directors, appointing a special master to investigate the payments made, approving new proxy materials, requiring amendment of prior filings, and requiring an accounting of payments made. . . .

. . . We draw a sharp distinction . . . between allegations of director misconduct involving breach of trust or self-dealing — the nondisclosure of which is presumptively material — and allegations of simple breach of fiduciary duty/waste of corporate assets — the nondisclosure of which is never material for § 14(a) purposes. . . . The distinction between "mere" bribes and bribes coupled with kickbacks to the directors makes a great deal of sense, indeed, is fundamental to a meaningful concept of materiality under § 14(a) and the preservation of state corporate law. . . .

There are clearly instances of illegal conduct by director-nominees, unrelated to self-dealing . . . which would have to be disclosed, especially if they involved criminal convictions. . . . Our holding is limited to existing directors' duty under § 14(a) to disclose noncriminal conduct in proxy solicitations for their re-election. . . . [moved to text from footnote]

Many corporate actions taken by directors in the interest of the corporation might offend and engender controversy among some stockholders. Investors share the same diversity of social and political views that characterizes the polity as a whole. The tenor of a company's labor relations policies,[49] economic decisions to relocate or close established industrial plants, commercial dealings with foreign countries which are disdained in certain circles, decisions to develop (or not to develop) particular natural resources or forms of energy technology, and the promulgation of

---

[48]. There are no allegations that Lockheed made improper payments to *domestic* officials or that any federal criminal laws were violated by the foreign payments. *See* Special Review Committee Report at 7–15. The Foreign Corrupt Practices Act of 1977, Pub. L. No. 95-213, 91 Stat. 1494, codified at 15 U.S.C. §§ 78m, 78dd-1, 78dd-2, 78ff, was signed into law after the conclusion of the scenario herein. . . .

[49]. *Amalgamated Clothing and Textile Workers Union v. J.P. Stevens & Co.*, 475 F. Supp. 328 (S.D.N.Y. 1979), is perhaps the quintessential example of shareholders' creative — and inappropriate — use of the federal securities laws to attempt to regulate the normative content of corporate policies and management business decisions. . . .

corporate personnel policies that reject (or embrace) the principle of affirmative action, are just a few examples of business judgments, soundly entrusted to the broad discretion of the directors, which may nonetheless cause shareholder dissent and provoke claims of "wasteful," "unethical," or even "immoral" business dealings. Should corporate directors have a duty under § 14(a) to disclose all such corporate decisions in proxy solicitations for their re-election? We decline to extend the duty of disclosure under § 14(a) to these situations. While we neither condone nor condemn these and similar types of corporate conduct (including the now-illegal practice of questionable foreign payments), we believe that aggrieved shareholders have sufficient recourse to state law claims against the responsible directors and, if all else fails, can sell or trade their stock in the offending corporation in favor of an enterprise more compatible with their own personal goals and values.

Absent credible allegations of self-dealing by the directors or dishonesty [or specified other misconduct, such as adjudicated illegalities] or deceit which inures to the direct, personal benefit of the directors — a fact that demonstrates a betrayal of trust to the corporation and shareholders and the director's essential unfitness for corporate stewardship — we hold that director misconduct of the type traditionally regulated by state corporate law need not be disclosed in proxy solicitations for director elections. This type of mismanagement, unadorned by self-dealing, is simply not material or otherwise within the ambit of the federal securities laws. . . . A contrary holding would place an unwarranted premium on the form rather than the substance of a shareholder's complaint and, moreover, would represent a move toward the federalization of corporate law that the Supreme Court has repeatedly and emphatically rejected.[50]

Note — Qualitative Materiality and the SEC's Proxy Disclosure Enhancements

For a more recent federal appellate court decision that restrictively interprets this aspect of qualitative materiality, see *Greenhouse v. MCG Capital Corp.,* 392 F.3d 650 (4th Cir. 2004) (CEO's fabrication of educational background falsely stating that he had completed college held not material). Compare Norris, *Radio Shack Chief Resigns After Lying,* N.Y. TIMES, Feb. 21, 2006, at C1 (reporting that the CEO of Radio Shack resigned after "revelation that he had lied to the company about his education by claiming two college degrees when he had none"); Weaver, *Abbott Executive's*

---

[50]. In *Santa Fe Industries, Inc. v. Green,* 430 U.S. 462, 477–80 (1977), the Supreme Court refused to find an implied cause of action under Rule 10b-5 [in that case] because the essence of the complaint was a breach of fiduciary duty of the type traditionally regulated by state law. Expanding implied causes of action under the federal securities law to encompass tangentially implicated instances of mismanagement would, the Court said, exceed Congress' intent, pose a danger of vexatious shareholder litigation, and create potentially insoluble conflicts between state and federal standards. . . . *See generally,* Ferrara & Steinberg, *A Reappraisal of Santa Fe: Rule 10b-5 and the New Federalism,* 129 U. PA. L. REV. 263.

Credentials Misstated, Wall St. J., Sept. 29–30, 2012, at B3 (stating that "Abbott continues to stand behind [the executive]").

As stated by one court:

> While the fact that a corporation's employees engaged in illegal conduct may well be material to the reasonable investor for several obvious reasons, the obligation to disclose uncharged illegal conduct will not arise from the materiality of this information alone. Rather . . . a duty to disclose uncharged illegal conduct arises when it is necessary to disclose this conduct under the terms of a statute or regulation *or* when it is necessary to disclose this conduct in order to prevent statements the corporation does make from misleading the public.[51]

For a state court decision holding that the type of qualitative information present in *Gaines* in fact must be disclosed to prospective investors, see *Bridwell v. State,* 804 S.W.2d 900 (Tex. Ct. Crim. App. 1991).

In an amicus curiae memorandum supporting the (unsuccessful) petition for rehearing en banc before the Ninth Circuit, the SEC expressed its disagreement with the court's decision in *Gaines.* The Commission stated:

> In holding that management conduct is presumptively material if it involves self-dealing, the [*Gaines*] panel acknowledges that certain misconduct of directors is "directly relevant to a determination of whether they are qualified to exercise stewardship of the company," . . . and thus is important to shareholders in determining whether to re-elect such directors. The panel's opinion provides no explanation of why no other type of director misconduct, regardless of its bearing on the same qualifications, can ever be material. The Commission submits that, like self-dealing, the misconduct alleged in this case bears a sufficient nexus to "a determination of whether [directors] are qualified to exercise stewardship of the company" that its materiality may not be foreclosed as a matter of law.

> Plaintiff alleges that certain of Lockheed's officers and directors knew and participated in substantial and pervasive illegal practices. Such allegations of illegal conduct of corporate affairs certainly are not so obviously unimportant to a reasonable shareholder's evaluation of the fitness of nominees to serve as directors that they may be dismissed as a matter of law. These alleged practices raise substantial questions regarding the "character and integrity of the officers relevant to their management of the corporation," which shareholders might well consider important. . . .

> Further, the alleged magnitude of the illegal practices, and their centrality to Lockheed's business operations, indicate the pervasiveness of the integrity problem, rendering it even more likely that shareholders would consider

---

51. *In re Axis Capital Holdings Ltd. Securities Litigation,* 456 F. Supp. 2d 576, 587 (S.D.N.Y. 2006).

such matters important and indeed that shareholders would question the very business competence of directors who have engaged in or fostered such conduct. . . .

See generally Williams, *The Securities and Exchange Commission and Corporate Social Transparency*, 112 HARV. L. REV. 1199 (1999).

The SEC has adopted proxy disclosure enhancements. *See* Securities Exchange Act Release No. 61175 (2009). As set forth in the SEC release adopting the amendments, these proxy disclosure enhancements include:

- To the extent that risks arising from a company's compensation policies and practices for employees are reasonably likely to have a material adverse effect on the company, discussion of the company's compensation policies or practices as they relate to risk management and risk-taking incentives that can affect the company's risk and management of that risk;

- Reporting of the aggregate grant date fair value of stock awards and option awards granted in the fiscal year in the Summary Compensation Table and Director Compensation Table to be computed in accordance with Financial Accounting Standards Board Accounting Standards Codification Topic 718, Compensation B Stock Compensation ("FASB ASC Topic 718"), rather than the dollar amount recognized for financial statement purposes for the fiscal year, with a special instruction for awards subject to performance conditions;

- Disclosure of the qualification of directors and nominees for director, and the reasons that person should serve as a director of the company at the time at which the relevant filing is made with the Commission; the same information would be required in the proxy materials prepared with respect to nominees for director nominated by others;

- Disclosure of any directorships held by each director and nominee at any time during the past five years at any public company or registered investment company;

- Disclosure regarding the consideration of diversity in the process by which candidates for director are considered for nomination by a company's nominating committee;

- [More detailed] disclosure of other legal actions involving a company's executive officers, directors, and nominees for director, and lengthening the time during which such disclosure is required from five to ten years;

- Disclosure about a company's board leadership structure and the board's role in the oversight of risk;

- Disclosure about the fees paid to compensation consultants and their affiliates under certain circumstances; and

- Disclosure of the vote results from a meeting of shareholders on Form 8-K generally within four business days of the meeting.

[2] Qualitative Economic Materiality

Staff Accounting Bulletin (SAB) No. 99 (1999) focuses on the concept of materiality in preparing financial statements and performing audits of such financial statements. SAB 99 asserts that exclusive reliance on specified quantitative benchmarks (such as 5%) to evaluate materiality is inappropriate. Hence, in given situations, even a two percent overstatement of earnings, for example, may be deemed material. Although limited to financial statement disclosure, the parameters of SAB 99 may extend to narrative portions of SEC disclosure documents. The SEC staff set forth the following list of considerations that may render material a quantitatively small misrepresentation of a financial statement item:

- Whether the misstatement arises from an item capable of precise measurement or whether it arises from an estimate and, if so, the degree of imprecision inherent in the estimate;
- Whether the misstatement masks a change in earnings or other trends;
- Whether the misstatement hides a failure to meet analysts' consensus expectations for the enterprise;
- Whether the misstatement changes a loss into income or vice versa;
- Whether the misstatement concerns a segment or other portion of the registrant's business that has been identified as playing a significant role in the registrant's operations or profitability;
- Whether the misstatement affects the registrant's compliance with regulatory requirements;
- Whether the misstatement affects the registrant's compliance with loan covenants or other contractual requirements;
- Whether the misstatement has the effect of increasing management's compensation—for example, by satisfying requirements for the award of bonuses or other forms of incentive compensation; and
- Whether the misstatement involves concealment of an unlawful transaction.

The following case serves as an important example of the issues surrounding qualitative economic materiality.

Ganino v. Citizens Utilities Company

United States Court of Appeals, Second Circuit

228 F.3d 154 (2000)

KATZMAN, Circuit Judge:

The plaintiffs-appellants appeal from a final judgment of the United States District Court for the District of Connecticut granting the defendants-appellees' motion to dismiss the Second Amended Complaint (the "Complaint") for failure to state a claim under Sections 10(b) . . . of the Securities Exchange Act of 1934 (the

"Exchange Act"), and Rule 10b-5 promulgated thereunder. The district court held [that] the misrepresentations regarding certain payments amounting to 1.7% of total annual revenue were immaterial as a matter of law. . . . For the reasons that follow, we reverse in part, vacate in part, and remand with instructions.

I. BACKGROUND

A. Factual Background

The plaintiffs in this action purchased or acquired the common stock of Citizens Utilities Company ("Citizens" or the "Company"), the corporate defendant, between May 7, 1996 and August 7, 1997 (the "Class Period"). Alleging that Citizens' share price was fraudulently inflated during the Class Period, the plaintiffs seek to represent the class of all purchasers of Citizens common stock during the Class Period in this action against Citizens and three of its senior officers. The following allegations are drawn from their Complaint, which we accept as true for purposes of this appeal.

Citizens is a publicly traded communications and public services company. As of 1995, Citizens had reported over fifty consecutive years of increased revenue, earnings, and earnings per share, a fact which it emphasized in its public comments. In 1995, however, Citizens would not receive approximately $38 million in revenue from Pacific Bell. In order to continue to report increased earnings, the Company had to find another source of revenue.

That replacement source was Hungarian Telephone & Cable Corporation ("HTCC"), a U.S. Company which provides telephone services in Hungary under telecommunications concessions from the Hungarian government. The concession contracts require HTCC to meet certain construction milestones. Failure to do so would subject HTCC to fines, reduction of its exclusivity period, or abrogation of the contracts. Unprofitable since its inception, HTCC by 1995 lacked the necessary funds to satisfy its contractual requirements and began looking for a source of financing. Beginning in May 1995, HTCC and Citizens (through a wholly owned subsidiary of Citizens) entered into a series of agreements under which Citizens agreed in 1995 to make and/or guarantee loans to HTCC. In consideration for these loans and guarantees, Citizens received substantial fees (the "Financial Support Fees" or the "Fees"), consisting primarily of HTCC stock and options. In addition, Citizens also provided management consulting services to HTCC.

1. Allegations of Material Misrepresentations

Although Citizens earned and received approximately $10.1 million in Financial Support Fees from HTCC in 1995, Citizens, according to the Complaint, fraudulently recognized this sum as 1996 first and second quarter income without proper disclosure. Because Citizens' 1995 annual financial statement ("1995 Form 10-K") filed with the Securities and Exchange Commission (the "SEC") stated that Citizens "ha[d] been compensated for . . . guarantees and financial support [to HTCC]," investors were allegedly misled into believing that the $10.1 million booked in 1996 was new income, unrelated to the 1995 HTCC loan and guarantee transactions.

a. May 7, 1996 Announcement of 1996 First Quarter Financial Results and First Quarter Form 10-Q

On May 7, 1996, Citizens publicly announced an after-tax net income of $38.9 million for the first quarter of 1996, up 15% from the corresponding period in 1995. These results were reflected in its 1996 first quarter financial statement ("First Quarter Form 10-Q"). The defendants did not disclose that "as much as $6.9 million of the $38.9 million . . . was HTCC related income which was deceptively 'stored' by Citizens" until the first quarter of 1996. According to the Complaint, the defendants also concealed the fact that this $6.9 million made up most if not all of the reported 15% increase during the first quarter of 1996.

b. August 15, 1996 Press Release and 1996 Second Quarter Form 10-Q

On August 15, 1996, Citizens issued another press release announcing "record . . . profits for the three-and six-month periods ended June 30, 1996," with the second quarter's net income of $46.3 million representing a 10% increase over the comparable period in the preceding year. Citizens attributed this growth to "continuous above-average growth in volume and profitability in each of its sectors, particularly telecommunications." These results were reflected in its 1996 second quarter financial report ("Second Quarter Form 10-Q"). The Complaint charges that the August 15, 1996 press release and the 1996 Second Quarter Form 10-Q both failed to disclose that "approximately $10 million of the $85.1 million of reported income for the six months ended June 30, 1996 was HTCC related income" which should have been recognized in 1995. The Complaint states that the defendants also concealed the fact that this approximately $10 million accounted for the full 10% increase in income for the first six months of 1996 over the comparable period in 1995.

c. Subsequent Financial Statements and Press Releases

The $10.1 million of Financial Support Fees were also reported as part of the year-to-date earnings in Citizens' 1996 Third Quarter Form 10-Q, 1996 Form 10-K, and accompanying press releases. An additional $11.2 million of Fees were booked in the last quarter of 1996 and reflected in the 1996 year-end statement ("1996 Form 10-K"). In total, the Fees at issue added up to approximately $22 million, or 1.7% of Citizens' total revenue for 1996. As with the Form 10-Qs for the first two quarters of 1996, the defendants did not disclose in the Third Quarter Form 10-Q, 1996 Form 10-K, and accompanying press releases that the reported income included HTCC Fees earned and received in 1995.

On April 30, 1997, Citizens issued a press release announcing lower than expected earnings for the first quarter of 1997. These results were reflected in the Company's 1997 First Quarter Form 10-Q. Neither document attributed the drop in income to the decrease in HTCC Fees. Instead, according to the Complaint, the press release misleadingly focused on rising expenses. Beginning in or about May 1997, industry analysts began to report weaknesses in Citizens' earnings position. Their predictions were confirmed by Citizens in August 1997 with the filing of its 1997 Second Quarter Form 10-Q, which also disclosed that the reported income for the first two quarters of 1996 included material income from HTCC.

. . . .

B. Procedural History

The district court granted the defendants' motion to dismiss. See *Ganino v. Citizens Utilities Co.*, 56 F. Supp.2d 222 (D. Conn. 1999). Focusing on the issue of materiality, the court quoted a newspaper article which observed that " '[m]ost auditors—and their corporate clients—define materiality as any event or news that might affect a company's earnings, positively or negatively, by 3% to 10% . . . . [it] has become standard practice in corporate America. Thus, if a particular charge or event doesn't meet the 3% to 10% level, companies feel they don't have to disclose it.' " . . . Applying this 3% to 10% range, the court held that "the amount in issue here—1.7% of Citizens' revenues for the relevant time period, pursuant to GAAP— is immaterial as a matter of law."

. . . .

II. DISCUSSION

We review de novo a district court's dismissal of a complaint pursuant to Rule 12(b)(6), accepting all factual allegations in the complaint as true and drawing all reasonable inferences in the plaintiffs' favor. . . .

Materiality

At the pleading stage, a plaintiff satisfies the materiality requirement . . . by alleging a statement or omission that a reasonable investor would have considered significant in making investment decisions. . . . It is not sufficient to allege that the investor might have considered the misrepresentation or omission important. On the other hand, it is not necessary [for the plaintiff] to assert that the investor would have acted differently if an accurate disclosure was made. An omitted fact may be immaterial if the information is trivial, or is "so basic that any investor could be expected to know it." . . . Therefore, whether an alleged misrepresentation or omission is material necessarily depends on all relevant circumstances of the particular case.

Materiality is a mixed question of law and fact. We have held that, when presented with a Rule 12(b)(6) motion, "a complaint may not properly be dismissed . . . on the ground that the alleged misstatements or omissions are not material unless they are so obviously unimportant to a reasonable investor that reasonable minds could not differ on the question of their importance."

a. Numerical Benchmark

The district court held that the alleged misrepresentations of the HTCC Fees as having been received in 1996 were immaterial as a matter of law because the Fees amounted to only 1.7% of Citizens' 1996 total revenue. The plaintiffs and the SEC, as amicus curiae, contend that the court's exclusive reliance on a single numerical or percentage benchmark to determine materiality was error. Their position is supported by ample authority. In *Basic, Inc. v. Levinson,* 485 U.S. 224 (1988) [contained in Chapter 11], the Supreme Court expressly rejected the use of a numerical formula:

> A bright-line rule indeed is easier to follow than a standard that requires the exercise of judgment in the light of all the circumstances. But ease of application alone is not an excuse for ignoring the purposes of the Securities Acts and Congress' policy decisions. Any approach that designates a single fact or occurrence as always determinative of an inherently fact-specific finding such as materiality, must necessarily be overinclusive or underinclusive.

Following *Basic,* we have consistently rejected a formulaic approach to assessing the materiality of an alleged misrepresentation. . . . With respect to financial statements, the SEC [staff] has commented that various "[q]ualitative factors may cause misstatements of quantitatively small amounts to be material." . . . Of particular relevance to this action are the following:

- whether the misstatement masks a change in earnings or other trends
- whether the misstatement hides a failure to meet analysts' consensus expectations for the enterprise.

Unlike, for example, a rule promulgated by the SEC pursuant to its rulemaking authority, SAB No. 99 does not carry with it the force of law. . . . Nonetheless, because SEC staff accounting bulletins "constitute a body of experience and informed judgment," and SAB No. 99 is thoroughly reasoned and consistent with existing law — its non-exhaustive list of factors is simply an application of the well-established *Basic* analysis to misrepresentations of financial results — we find it persuasive guidance for evaluating the materiality of an alleged misrepresentation.

The two Court of Appeals cases cited by the district court support the approach we take here. In *Parnes v. Gateway 2000, Inc.,* 122 F.3d 539 (8th Cir. 1997), the Eighth Circuit held that the alleged misrepresentations, which amounted to 2% of total assets, were immaterial as a matter of law "[t]aken in context." The court did not rely on the single numerical benchmark, but also took into consideration the fact that the case involved a high-risk/high-yield investment, and that the risk factors had been prominently disclosed in a prospectus. Similarly, in *Glassman v. Computervision Corp.,* 90 F.3d 617 (1st Cir. 1996), the First Circuit Court of Appeals considered whether a 3% to 9% drop in quarterly revenue was immaterial as a matter of law. It stated, in dicta, that "[w]here a variable, although material, is of only minor predictive value, disclosure of a rough estimate of that variable's value can obviate the need for more specific disclosure." The clear implication of this statement is that a 3% to 9% drop may be material depending on the circumstances. To the extent that the two district court decisions also cited in the opinion below adopted a bright-line test for materiality, we disagree with their approach.

. . . .

c. Relevant Timeframe

We next consider the relevant timeframe. The plaintiffs, joined by the SEC, maintain that the court should have considered the impact of the alleged misrepresentations on all misstated items in the financial statement for all relevant periods, not only for the year as a whole. In this case, the Complaint alleged that substantial portions of the income reported during the first two quarters of 1996 were in fact the 1995 Fees. Accordingly, the plaintiffs and the SEC contend that the court should have assessed the impact of the Fees on Citizens' quarterly income. The defendants argue that the court correctly compared the Fees to annual results only, because the plaintiffs theorized that the defendants deferred recognition of the Fees in order to maintain Citizens' annual growth trend.

We reject the defendants' contention. Materiality is determined in light of the circumstances existing at the time the alleged misstatement occurred. . . . Thus, we held in *Kaiser-Frazer Corp. v. Otis & Co.*, 195 F.2d 838, 843 (2d Cir. 1952), that an overstatement of fourth quarter earnings was not rendered immaterial simply because profits for the year as a whole were not affected by the misrepresentation because "the prospective purchaser was entitled to a full disclosure of all the facts that were known to the Corporation at the time the [financial statement] was issued." See also *Glassman*, 90 F.3d at 633 (comparing quarterly results); *SEC v. Keller Indus., Inc.*, 342 F.Supp. 654, 657 n. 5 (S.D.N.Y. 1972) (recognizing that a publicly filed interim quarterly report can be actionable under Rule 10b-5 if it contains material misstatements).

Citizens' own press releases implicitly acknowledge the significance of quarterly financial statements. For example, its May 7, 1996 press release touted first quarter results as a predictor of annual performance, stating that the Company was "well on its way toward its 52nd consecutive year of increased revenues, net income and earnings per share." . . . Therefore, we think it appropriate to compare the Fees to not only annual, but also quarterly financial results.

d. This Complaint

Applying the foregoing principles to this action, we conclude that the Complaint alleged material misrepresentations in the 1996 First and Second Quarter Form 10-Qs and corresponding press releases, namely, the alleged misrepresentation of $10.1 million of Fees received in 1995 as 1996 income. The $6.9 million of 1995 Fees booked during the first quarter of 1996 equaled 17.7% of Citizens' reported after-tax net income ($38.9 million), and 11.7% of its pre-tax net income ($58.78 million) for that quarter. The $10.1 million reflected in the 1996 Second Quarter Form 10-Q amounted to 11.9% of after-tax net income ($85.15 million), and 8% of pre-tax net income ($126.62 million) for the first six months of 1996. We believe it is inappropriate to determine at this stage of the litigation that these substantial amounts, both in absolute terms and as percentages of total net income for the respective quarters, were immaterial as a matter of law.

Aside from the magnitude of the overstatements, the Complaint alleged that the defendants deceptively stored the Fees until 1996 in order to manage the Company's 1995 and 1996 income, and that they did so in order to conceal Citizens' failure to meet analysts' expectations and to sustain its 51-year earnings trend. The Complaint asserted that the $6.9 million of Fees reported in the First Quarter Form 10-Q accounted for "a substantial portion, if not all, of the increase in income for the first quarter 1996 compared to the first quarter of 1995[.]" Moreover, according to the Complaint, analysts' projections of Citizens' "income for the first six (6) months of 1996 were met and exceeded only as a result of th[e] additional HTCC-related income, and the increase in income for the first six months of 1996 compared to the first six months of 1995 was due entirely to the income recognized from HTCC." Viewed in this context, it cannot be said that no reasonable investor would have considered the misreporting of 1995 Fees as 1996 income to be significant or to have altered the total mix of information affecting their investment decisions. We therefore conclude that the Complaint alleged material misrepresentations. . . .

———————

In a more recent decision addressing qualitative economic materiality, the Second Circuit opined:

> "[W]e have consistently rejected a formulaic approach to assessing the materiality of an alleged misrepresentation." *Ganino*, 228 F.3d at 162; *see also ECA & Local 134 IBEW Joint Pension Trust v. JP Morgan Chase Co.,* 553 F.3d 187, 204 (2d Cir. 2009) ("While *Ganino* held that bright-line numerical tests for materiality are inappropriate, it did not exclude analysis based on, or even emphasis of, quantitative considerations.") In both *Ganino* and *ECA & Local 134,* we cited with approval SEC Staff Accounting Bulletin No. 99, 64 Fed. Reg. 45,150 (1999) [hereinafter SAB No. 99], which provides relevant guidance regarding the proper assessment of materiality.
>
> As the SEC [staff] stated,
>
>> The use of a percentage as a numerical threshold, such as 5%, may provide the basis for a preliminary assumption that . . . a deviation of less than the specified percentage with respect to a particular item . . . is unlikely to be material. . . . But quantifying, in percentage terms, the magnitude of a misstatement . . . cannot appropriately be used as a substitute for a full analysis of all relevant considerations.
>
> SAB No. 99, 64 Fed. Reg. at 45,151; *see also ECA & Local 134,* 533 F.3d at 204 (noting that a "five percent numerical threshold is a good *starting place* for assessing . . . materiality" (emphasis added)). Accordingly, a court must consider "both 'quantitative' and 'qualitative' factors in assessing an item's materiality,"

and that consideration should be undertaken in an integrative manner. *See . . .* SAB No. 99, 64 Fed. Reg. at 45,152 ("Qualitative factors may cause misstatements of quantitatively small amounts to be material. . . .").

Litwin v. Blackstone Group, L.P., 634 F.3d 706, 717 (2d Cir. 2011). *See generally* Couture, *Materiality and a Theory of Legal Circularity,* 17 U. Pa. J. Bus. L. 453 (2015); Hodges, *The Qualitative Considerations of Materiality: The Emerging Relationship Between Materiality and Scienter,* 30 Sec. Reg. L.J. 4 (2002).

[E] Environmental Disclosure

In 2010, the SEC issued an interpretive release providing guidance with respect to the MD&A in the context of disclosure related to climate change. The SEC release follows.

Commission Guidance Regarding Disclosure Related to Climate Change

Securities and Exchange Commission

Securities Act Release No. 9106 (2010)

The Securities and Exchange Commission ("SEC" or "Commission") is publishing this interpretive release to provide guidance to public companies regarding the Commission's existing disclosure requirements as they apply to climate change matters.

I. Background and Purpose of Interpretive Guidance

A. Introduction

Climate change has become a topic of public discussion in recent years. Scientists, government leaders, legislators, regulators, businesses, including insurance companies, investors, analysts and the public at large have expressed heightened interest in climate change. International accords, federal regulations, and state and local laws and regulations in the U.S. address concerns about the effects of greenhouse gas emissions on our environment, and international efforts to address the concerns on a global basis continue. The Environmental Protection Agency is taking action to address climate change concerns, and Congress is considering climate change legislation. Some business leaders are increasingly recognizing the current and potential effects on their companies' performance and operations, both positive and negative, that are associated with climate change and with efforts to reduce greenhouse gas emissions. Many companies are providing information to their peers and to the public about their carbon footprints and their efforts to reduce them.

This release outlines our views with respect to our existing disclosure requirements as they apply to climate change matters. This guidance is intended to assist companies in satisfying their disclosure obligations under the federal securities laws and regulations.

B. Background

1. Recent Regulatory, Legislative and Other Developments

In the last several years, a number of state and local governments have enacted legislation and regulations that result in greater regulation of greenhouse gas emissions. Climate change related legislation is currently pending in Congress. The House of Representatives has approved one version of a bill, and a similar bill was introduced in the Senate in the fall of 2009. This legislation, if enacted, would limit and reduce greenhouse gas emissions through a "cap and trade" system of allowances and credits, among other provisions.

The Environmental Protection Agency has been taking steps to regulate greenhouse gas emissions. On January 1, 2010, the EPA began, for the first time, to require large emitters of greenhouse gases to collect and report data with respect to their greenhouse gas emissions. This reporting requirement is expected to cover 85% of the nation's greenhouse gas emissions generated by roughly 10,000 facilities. In December 2009, the EPA issued an "endangerment and cause or contribute finding" for greenhouse gases under the Clean Air Act, which will allow the EPA to craft rules that directly regulate greenhouse gas emissions.

Some members of the international community also have taken actions to address climate change issues on a global basis, and those actions can have a material impact on companies that report with the Commission. One such effort in the 1990s resulted in the Kyoto Protocol. Although the United States has never ratified the Kyoto Protocol, many registrants have operations outside of the United States that are subject to its standards. Another important international regulatory system is the European Union Emissions Trading System (EU ITS), which was launched as an international "cap and trade" system of allowances for emitting carbon dioxide and other greenhouse gases, based on mechanisms set up under the Kyoto Protocol. In addition, the United States government is participating in ongoing discussions with other nations, including the recent United Nations Climate Conference in Copenhagen, which may lead to future international treaties focused on remedying environmental damage caused by greenhouse gas emissions. Those accords ultimately could have a material impact on registrants that file disclosure documents with the Commission.

The insurance industry is already adjusting to these developments. A 2008 study listed climate change as the number one risk facing the insurance business. Reflecting this assessment, the National Association of Insurance Commissioners recently promulgated a uniform standard for mandatory disclosure by insurance companies to state regulators of financial risks due to climate change and actions taken to mitigate them. We understand that insurance companies are developing new actuarial models and designing new products to reshape coverage for green buildings, renewable energy, carbon risk management and directors' and officers' liability, among other actions.

2. Potential Impact of Climate Change Related Matters on Public Companies

For some companies, the regulatory, legislative and other developments noted above could have a less significant effect on operating and financial decisions, including those involving capital expenditures to reduce emissions and, for companies subject to "cap and trade" laws, expenses related to purchasing allowances where reduction targets cannot be met. Companies that may not be directly affected by such developments could nonetheless be indirectly affected by changing prices for goods or services provided by companies that are directly affected and that seek to reflect some or all of their changes in costs of goods in the prices they charge. For example, if a supplier's costs increase, that could have a significant impact on its customers if those costs are passed through, resulting in higher prices for customers. New trading markets for emission credits related to "cap and trade" programs that might be established under pending legislation, if adopted, could present new opportunities for investment. These markets also could allow companies that have more allowances than they need, or that can earn offset credits through their businesses, to raise revenue through selling these instruments into those markets. Some companies might suffer financially if these or similar bills are enacted by the Congress while others could benefit by taking advantage of new business opportunities.

In addition to legislative, regulatory, business and market impacts related to climate change, there may be significant physical effects of climate change that have the potential to have a material effect on a registrant's business and operations. These effects can impact a registrant's personnel, physical assets, supply chain and distribution chain. They can include the impact of changes in weather patterns, such as increases in storm intensity, sea-level rise, melting of permafrost and temperature extremes on facilities or operations. Changes in the availability or quality of water, or other natural resources on which the registrant's business depends, or damage to facilities or decreased efficiency of equipment can have material effects on companies. Physical changes associated with climate change can decrease consumer demand for products or services; for example, warmer temperatures could reduce demand for residential and commercial heating fuels, service and equipment.

For some registrants, financial risks associated with climate change may arise from physical risks to entities other than the registrant itself. For example, climate change-related physical changes and hazards to coastal property can pose credit risks for banks whose borrowers are located in at-risk areas. Companies also may be dependent on suppliers that are impacted by climate change, such as companies that purchase agricultural products from farms adversely affected by droughts or floods.

3. Current Sources of Climate Change Related Disclosures Regarding Public Companies

There have been increasing calls for climate-related disclosures by shareholders of public companies. This is reflected in the several petitions for interpretive advice submitted by large institutional investors and other investor groups. The New York Attorney General's Office recently has entered into settlement agreements with three energy companies under its investigation regarding their disclosures about their greenhouse gas emissions and potential liabilities to the companies resulting from climate change and related regulation. The companies agreed in the settlement agreements to enhance their disclosures relating to climate change and greenhouse gas emissions in their annual reports filed with the Commission.

Although some information relating to greenhouse gas emissions and climate change is disclosed in SEC filings, much more information is publicly available outside of public company disclosure documents filed with the SEC as a result of voluntary disclosure initiatives or other regulatory requirements. . . .

II. Historical Background of SEC Environmental Disclosure

The Commission first addressed disclosure of material environmental issues in the early 1970s. The Commission issued an interpretive release stating that registrants should consider disclosing in their SEC filings the financial impact of compliance with environmental laws, based on the materiality of the information. [Securities Act Release No. 5170 (1971)] Throughout the 1970s, the Commission continued to explore the need for specific rules mandating disclosure of information relating to litigation and other business costs arising out of compliance with federal, state and local laws that regulate the discharge of materials into the environment or otherwise relate to the protection of the environment. These topics were the subject of several rule-making efforts, extensive litigation, and public hearings, all of which resulted in the rules that now specifically address the disclosure of environmental issues. The Commission adopted these rules, which we discuss below, in final and current form in 1982, after a decade of evaluation and experience with the subject matter. [Securities Act Release No. 6383 (1982)]

Earlier, beginning in 1968, we began to develop and fine-tune our requirements for management to discuss and analyze their company's financial conditions and results of operations in disclosure documents filed with the Commission. During the 1970s and 1980s, materiality standards for disclosure under the federal securities laws also were more fully articulated. Those standards provide that information is material if there is a substantial likelihood that a reasonable investor would consider it important in deciding how to vote or make an investment decision, or, put another way, if the information would alter the total mix or available information. In the articulation of the materiality standards, it was recognized that doubts as to materiality of information would be commonplace, but that, particularly in view of the prophylactic purpose of the securities laws and the fact that disclosure is within management's control, "it is appropriate that these doubts be resolved in favor of those the statute is designed to protect." With these developments, registrants had clearer guidance about what they should disclose in their filings.

More recently, the Commission reviewed its full disclosure program relating to environmental disclosures in SEC filings in connection with a Government

Accountability Office review. The Commission also has had the opportunity to consider the thoughtful suggestions that many organizations have provided us recently about how the Commission could direct registrants to enhance their disclosure about the climate change related matters.

III. Overview of Rules Requiring Disclosure of Climate Change Issues

When a registrant is required to file a disclosure document with the Commission, the requisite form will largely refer to the disclosure requirements of Regulation S-K and Regulation S-X. Securities Act Rule 408 and Exchange Act Rule 12b-20 require a registrant to disclose, in addition to the information expressly required by Commission regulation, "such further material information, if any, as may be necessary to make the required statements, in light of the circumstances under which they are made, not misleading." In this section, we briefly describe the most pertinent non-financial statement disclosure rules that may require disclosure related to climate change; in the following section, we discuss their application to disclosure of certain specific climate change related matters.

A. Description of Business

Item 101 of Regulation S-K requires a registrant to describe its business and that of its subsidiaries. The Item lists a variety of topics that a registrant must address in its disclosure documents, including disclosure about its form of organization, principal products and services, major customers, and competitive conditions. The disclosure requirements cover the registrant and, in many cases, each reportable segment about which financial information is presented in the financial statements. If the information is material to individual segments of the business, a registrant must identify the affected segments.

Item 101 expressly requires disclosure regarding certain costs of complying with environmental laws. In particular, Item 101(c)(1)(xii) states:

> Appropriate disclosure also shall be made as to the material effects that compliance with Federal, State and local provisions which have been enacted or adopted regulating the discharge of materials into the environment, or otherwise relating to the protection of the environment, may have upon the capital expenditures, earnings and competitive position of the registrant and its subsidiaries. The registrant shall disclose any material estimated capital expenditures for environmental control facilities for the remainder of its current fiscal year and its succeeding fiscal year and for such further periods as the registrant may deem material.

B. Legal Proceedings

Item 103 of Regulation S-K requires a registrant to briefly describe any material pending legal proceeding to which it or any of its subsidiaries is a party. A registrant also must describe material pending legal actions in which its property is the subject of the litigation. If a registrant is aware of similar actions contemplated by governmental authorities, Item 103 requires disclosure of those proceedings as well. A registrant need not disclose ordinary routine litigation incidental to its business or other types of proceedings when the amount in controversy is below thresholds designated in this Item.

Instruction 5 to Item 103 provides some specific requirements that apply to disclosure of certain environmental litigation. Instruction 5 states:

> Notwithstanding the foregoing, an administrative or judicial proceeding (including, for purposes of A and B of this Instruction, proceedings which present in large degree the same issues) arising under any Federal, State or local provisions that have been enacted or adopted regulating the discharge of materials into the environment or primary for the purpose of protecting the environment shall not be deemed "ordinary routine litigation incidental to the business" and shall be described if:
>
> (A) Such proceeding is material to the business or financial condition of the registrant;
>
> (B) Such proceeding involves primarily a claim for damages, or involves potential monetary sanctions, capital expenditures, deferred charges or charges to income and the amount involved, exclusive of interest and costs, exceeds 10 percent of the current assets of the registrant and its subsidiaries on a consolidated basis; or
>
> (C) A governmental authority is a party to such proceeding and such proceeding involves potential monetary sanctions, unless the registrant reasonably believes that such proceeding will result in no monetary sanctions, or in monetary sanctions, exclusive of interest and costs, of less than $100,000; provided, however, that such proceedings which are similar in nature may be grouped and described generically.

C. Risk Factors.

Item 503(c) of Regulation S-K requires a registrant to provide where appropriate, under the heading "Risk Factors," a discussion of the most significant factors that make an investment in the registrant speculative or risky. Item 503(c) specifies that risk factor disclosure should clearly state the risk and specify how the particular risk affects the particular registrant; registrants should not present risks that could apply to any issuer or any offering.

D. Management's Discussion and Analysis [MD&A].

Item 303 of Regulation S-K requires disclosure known as the Management's Discussion and Analysis of Financial Condition and Results of Operations, or MD&A. The MD&A requirements are intended to satisfy three principal objectives:

- to provide a narrative explanation of a registrant's financial statements that enables investors to see the registrant through the eyes of management;
- to enhance the overall financial disclosure and provide the context within which financial information should be analyzed; and

- to provide information about the quality of, and potential variability of, a registrant's earnings and cash flow, so that investors can ascertain the likelihood that past performance is indicative of future performance.

MD&A disclosure should provide material historical and prospective textual disclosure enabling investors to assess the financial condition and results of operations of the registrant, with particular emphasis on the registrant's prospects for the future. Some of this information is itself non-financial in nature, but bears on registrants' financial condition and operating performance.

The Commission has issued several releases providing guidance on MD&A disclosure, including on the general requirements of the item and its application to specific disclosure matters. Over the years, the flexible nature of this requirement has resulted in disclosures that keep pace with the evolving nature of business trends without the need to continuously amend the text of the rule. Nevertheless, we and our staff continue to remind registrants, through comments issued in the filing review process, public statements by staff and Commissioners and otherwise, that the disclosure provided in response to this requirement should be clear and communicate to shareholders management's view of the company's financial condition and prospects.

Item 303 includes a broad range of disclosure items that address the registrant's liquidity, capital resources and results of operations. Some of these provisions, such as the requirement to provide tabular disclosure of contractual obligations, clearly specify the disclosure required for compliance. But others instead identify principles and require management to apply the principles in the context of the registrant's particular circumstances. For example, registrants must identify and disclose known trends, events, demands, commitments and uncertainties that are reasonably likely to have a material effect on financial condition or operating performance. This disclosure should highlight issues that are unreasonably likely to cause reported financial information not to be necessarily indicative of future operating performance or of future financial condition. Disclosure decisions concerning trends, demands, commitments, events, and uncertainties generally should involve the:

- consideration of financial, operational and other information known to the registrant;

- identification, based on this information, of known trends and uncertainties; and

- assessment of whether these trends and uncertainties will have, or are reasonably likely to have, a material impact on the registrant's liquidity, capital resources or results of operations.

The Commission has not quantified, in Item 303 or otherwise, a specific future time period that must be considered in assessing the impact of a known trend, event or uncertainty that is reasonably likely to occur. As with any other judgment required by Item 303, the necessary time period will depend on a registrant's particular circumstances and the particular trend, event or uncertainty under consideration. For example, a registrant considering its disclosure obligation with respect to its liquidity needs would have to consider the duration of its known capital requirements and the periods over which cash flows are managed in determining the time period of its disclosure regarding future capital sources. In addition, the time horizon of a known trend, event or uncertainty may be relevant to a registrant's assessment of the materiality of the matter and whether or not the impact is reasonably likely. As with respect to other subjects of disclosure, materiality "with respect to contingent or speculative information or events . . . 'will depend at any given time upon a balancing of both the indicated probability that the event will occur and the anticipated magnitude of the event in light of the totality of the company activity.'" [*Basic, Inc. v. Levinson*, 485 U.S. 224, 238 (1988), quoting, *Texas Gulf Sulfur Co.*, 401 F.2d 833, 849 (2d Cir. 1968)].

The nature of certain MD&A disclosure requirements places particular importance on a registrant's materiality determinations. The Commission has recognized that the effectiveness of MD&A decreases with the accumulation of unnecessary detail or duplicative or uninformative disclosure that obscures material information. Registrants drafting MD&A disclosure should focus on material information and eliminate immaterial information that does not promote understanding of registrants' financial condition, liquidity and capital resources, changes in financial condition and results of operations. While these materiality determinations may limit what is actually disclosed, they should not limit the information that management considers in making its determinations. Improvements in technology and communications in the last two decades have significantly increased the amount of financial and non-financial information that management has and should evaluate, as well as the speed with which management receives and is able to use information. While this should not necessarily result in increased MD&A disclosure, it does provide more information that may need to be considered in drafting MD&A disclosure. In identifying, discussing and analyzing known material trends and uncertainties, registrants are expected to consider all relevant information even if that information is not required to be disclosed, and, as with any other disclosure judgments, they should consider whether they have sufficient disclosure controls and procedures to process this information.

Analyzing the materiality of known trends, events or uncertainties may be particularly challenging for registrants preparing MD&A disclosure. As the Commission explained in the 1989 Release, when a trend, demand, commitment, event or uncertainty is known, "management must make two assessments:

- Is the known trend, demand, commitment, event or uncertainty likely to come to fruition? If management determines that it is not reasonably likely to occur, no disclosure is required.

- If management cannot make that determination, it must evaluate objectively the consequences of the known trend, demand, commitment, event or uncertainty, on the assumption that it will come to fruition. Disclosure is then required unless management determines that a material effect on the registrant's financial condition or results of operations is not reasonably likely to occur."

Identifying and assessing known material trends and uncertainties generally will require registrants to consider a substantial amount of financial and non-financial information available to them, including information that itself may not be required to be disclosed.

Registrants should address, when material, the difficulties involved in assessing the effect of the amount and timing of uncertain events, and provide an indication of the time periods in which resolution of the uncertainties is anticipated. In accordance with Item 303(a), registrants must also disclose any other information a registrant believes is necessary to an understanding of its financial condition, changes in financial condition and results of operations.

. . . .

Note

Professor Amy Westbrook has written a number of provocative articles focusing on the failure of the securities laws and the SEC to elicit disclosure about a subject company's operations in sanctioned countries (i.e., State Sponsors of Terrorism — SSTs). Professor Westbrook asserts:

> If information about a company's operations in or with the Sanctioned Countries is important to investors, then the U.S. federal securities laws should be enforced by requiring companies to disclose it. Yet the research . . . shows that the majority of companies are not providing any disclosure. Although the SEC . . . seems to be attempting to elicit disclosure, such efforts have not been effective. Information about activities in and with the Sanctioned Countries is being disclosed at a low rate. To add insult to injury, . . . it is still nearly impossible for investors to find the information they need from publicly available sources, including the SEC. In short, very little information is effectively disclosed.

Westbrook, *What's In Your Portfolio? U.S. Investors Are Unknowingly Financing State Sponsors of Terrorism,* 59 DePaul L. Rev. 1151, 1218 (2010).

Significantly, the Iran Threat Reduction and Syria Human Rights Act of 2012 requires Exchange Act reporting companies to disclose contracts and "dealings" with Iranian or other identified persons. See § 13(r) of the Securities Exchange Act.

---

§ 5.04 The Sarbanes-Oxley Act ("SOX") and Its Implementation

Problem

Frank Romero is CEO of DataZine, Inc., a Nasdaq National Stock Market publicly held corporation that distributes periodicals for professionals of the technology industry. As required by § 302(a) and § 906 of the Sarbanes-Oxley Act, Romero recently certified DataZine's most recent Form 10-Q, filed with the SEC under its mandatory disclosure system. Romero read the entire report and knew of no material misstatement or omission contained within the report that would make it misleading. Unbeknownst to Romero, the report contained multiple material misstatements and omissions: profits for a wholly owned subsidiary of DataZine amounting to nearly 25 percent of DataZine's net profits were inflated by 40 percent due to questionable accounting practices; a major lawsuit filed during the quarter in question against DataZine regarding distribution rights to some of its core periodicals was omitted (if an adverse verdict were to be rendered, the damages incurred likely would exceed 10 percent of DataZine's net profits); and discovery that an enthusiastically "hyped" newly launched product that was touted to "significantly enhance profitability" will not perform as predicted was omitted. Consider the following:

(A) Does the fact that Romero had no personal knowledge of these material misstatements and omissions relieve him of liability for his certification?

(B) DataZine has in place the following procedures: all financial statements supposedly are prepared consistent with Generally Accepted Accounting Principles (GAAP) and the company's annual financial statements are audited by a "national" accounting firm; the audit committee is comprised entirely of outside directors; the chief financial officer (CFO) also must provide a § 302 and § 906 certification; and division heads must provide a statement to Romero that the SEC filing accurately reflects information under their respective domains. Romero has never reviewed this practice to see how effective it actually is. What would you advise Romero about his liability for the misstatement regarding inflated profits due to questionable accounting practices?

(C) All lawsuits that are deemed potentially material by the corporation's general counsel are to be reported to Romero promptly after the general counsel becomes aware of them. Moreover, the general counsel is required to certify a report to Romero regarding the status of all such litigation prior to each SEC filing. Romero has evaluated this process and reviewed the general counsel's report within the past 90 days before the last Form 10-Q filing. He is not aware of the major lawsuit. What would you advise Romero about his liability for the omission regarding the pending litigation about distribution rights?

(D) Romero receives a monthly report from the head of R&D for DataZine that informs him of new products being developed, as well as the status of products that are currently in development. The monthly report contains all test data for developing products. The most recent monthly report was reviewed by Romero before certification this quarter. Romero has previously reviewed monthly reports for effectiveness, but the recent product failure was not included in the most recent monthly report because the report is not designed to track products after initial launch. What would you advise Romero about his liability for the omission of the failure of the newly launched product to perform as predicted?

[A] Introduction

After the enactment of three major acts of federal legislation in 1995,[52] 1996[53] and 1998,[54] seeking to foster capital formation and redress perceived abuses associated with class actions, the election of President George W. Bush portended the continued deregulation of the securities markets and affected players in the process. Instead, the very opposite occurred: After the revelation of major financial debacles that impaired the very foundation of the U.S. capital markets, Congress enacted the most pro-regulatory securities legislation since the passage of the Securities Exchange Act in 1934.

The Sarbanes-Oxley Act of 2002 (SOX) federalizes state corporation law in several ways, going far beyond the disclosure framework that serves as the foundation to federal securities regulation.[55] Regulation of auditors now is at a level never envisioned even in the worst nightmares of the accounting profession. Moreover, chief executive and chief financial officers must "certify" with prudence, taking care to have effective controls in place to help assure the accuracy of their assessments. Overlooked to some degree, yet a surprising mandate in light of previous law, is Congress' direction for the SEC to oversee a continuous issuer disclosure regime.[56]

The U.S. securities markets traditionally have been viewed as premier, serving a vital role in the stability of our economy. Hopefully, the enactment and enforcement

---

52. The Private Securities Litigation Reform Act of 1995 (PSLRA).

53. The National Securities Markets Improvement Act of 1996 (NSMIA).

54. The Securities Litigation Uniform Standards Act of 1998 (SLUSA).

55. For example, directors who serve on an audit committee must be independent (Sarbanes-Oxley Act § 301(m)(3)), CEOs and CFOs must forfeit bonuses if an issuer financial restatement is prepared under certain circumstances (Sarbanes-Oxley Act § 304), and company loans to directors and executive officers are generally prohibited (Sarbanes-Oxley Act § 402).

56. *See* Sarbanes-Oxley Act § 409, *amending*, § 13(l) of the Exchange Act (requiring publicly held companies to "disclose to the public on a rapid and current basis such additional information concerning material changes in the financial condition or operations of the issuer in plain English . . . as the Commission determines, by rule . . . .") This provision is a marked contrast to the previously established periodic disclosure framework. *See* Securities Act Release No. 8090 (2002); Steinberg, *Insider Trading, Selective Disclosure, and Prompt Disclosure: A Comparative Analysis*, 22 U. Pa. J. Int'l L. 635 (2001). For further discussion, *see* Chapter 11.

of the Sarbanes-Oxley Act as well as the Dodd-Frank Act of 2010 will help restore investor confidence in the integrity of our financial markets.[57]

The following discussion highlights key provisions of the Sarbanes-Oxley Act. For ease of organization and understanding, the materials are placed at this point in the text. Please note that, where appropriate, a number of these provisions also are covered elsewhere in this textbook.

[B] Key Provisions

[1] CEO and CFO Certifications

The Sarbanes-Oxley Act enhanced senior corporate management's responsibility to the investing public by requiring that the chief executive officer (CEO) and the chief financial officer (CFO) each certify, among other items, that the company's financial disclosures are a fair and accurate representation of such company's financial position.[58] Under the Act, the CEO and the CFO of all publicly held companies each must provide two separate certifications (pursuant to SOX §§ 302 and 906). Section 302 of the Act covers each registrant annual (Form 10-K) and quarterly (Form 10-Q) report required to be filed under the Exchange Act. The § 302 certification mandates that the CEO and CFO each certify as follows:

1. I have reviewed this annual report on Form 10-K [or periodic report on Form 10-Q] of the Registrant;

2. Based on my knowledge, this report does not contain any untrue statement of a material fact or omit to state a material fact necessary to make the statements made, in light of the circumstances under which such statements are made, not misleading with respect to the period covered by this report;

3. Based on my knowledge, the financial statements, and other financial information included in this report, fairly present in all material respects the financial condition, results of operations and cash flows of the Registrant as of, and for, the periods presented in this report;

4. The Registrant's other certifying officer and I are responsible for establishing and maintaining disclosure controls and procedures and internal control over financial reporting for the Registrant and have:

(a) Designed such disclosure controls and procedures, or caused such disclosure controls and procedures to be designed under our supervision,

---

57. *See generally* J. Bostelman, R. Buckholz & M. Trevino, Public Company Deskbook: Sarbanes-Oxley and Federal Governance Requirements (2d ed. 2011); Branson, *Too Many Bells? Too Many Whistles? Corporate Governance in the Post-Enron, Post-WorldCom Era*, 58 So. Car. L. Rev. 65 (2006); Morrissey, *Catching the Culprits: Is Sarbanes-Oxley Enough?*, 2003 Colum. Bus. L. Rev. 801 (2003); Nicholson, *The Culture of Under-Enforcement: Buried Treasure, Sarbanes-Oxley and the Corporate Pirate*, 5 DePaul Bus. & Comm. L.J. 321 (2007); *Symposium*, 105 Mich. L. Rev. No 8 (2007).

58. Sarbanes-Oxley Act § 302(a).

to ensure that material information relating to the Registrant, including its consolidated subsidiaries, is made known to us by others within those entities, particularly during the period in which this report is being prepared;

(b) Designed such internal control over financial reporting, or caused such internal control over financial reporting to be designed under our supervision, to provide reasonable assurance regarding the reliability of financial reporting and the preparation of financial statements for external purposes in accordance with generally accepted accounting principles;

(c) Evaluated the effectiveness of the Registrant's disclosure controls and procedures and presented in this report our conclusions about the effectiveness of the disclosure controls and procedures, as of a date within 90 days preceding this report; and

(d) Disclosed in this report any change in the Registrant's internal control over financial reporting that occurred during the Registrant's most recent fiscal quarter (the Registrant's fourth fiscal quarter in the case of an annual report) that has materially affected, or is reasonably likely to materially affect, the Registrant's internal control over financial reporting; and

5. The Registrant's other certifying officer and I have disclosed, based on our most recent evaluation of internal control over financial reporting, to the Registrant's auditors and the audit committee of the Registrant's board of directors (or persons performing the equivalent functions):

(a) All significant deficiencies and material weaknesses in the design or operation of internal control over financial reporting which are reasonably likely to adversely affect the Registrant's ability to record, process, summarize and report financial information; and

(b) Any fraud, whether or not material, that involves management or other employees who have a significant role in the Registrant's internal control over financial reporting.

6. The Registrant's other certifying officer and I have indicated in the report whether or not there were significant changes in internal controls or in other factors that could significantly affect internal controls subsequent to the date of their evaluation, including any corrective actions with regard to significant deficiencies and material weaknesses.[59]

The SEC Release focusing on the § 302 certification is contained later in this Section.

---

59. Rule 13a-14(a)/15d-14(a). *See* Sarbanes-Oxley Act § 302(a)(1)-(a)(6).

The § 906 certification, adding § 1350 to the criminal statutes,[60] applies to each Exchange Act report containing financial statements and provides for significant criminal penalties for knowingly false certification. Pursuant to § 906, the CEO and CFO certification each must state that, "based on my knowledge, the periodic report containing the financial statements fully complies with the [Exchange Act periodic reporting] requirements and that information contained in the [subject] periodic report fairly presents, in all material respects, the financial condition and results of operations of the issuer."[61]

These provisions in SOX place CEOs and CFOs in a potentially precarious situation, such as when a company restates its audited financials. Clearly, a CEO or CFO who, with knowledge, falsely certifies any such report is subject to severe penalties. As a defense, the officer may claim that he/she did not know that a statement in the report was materially incorrect. Even assuming that this defense is meritorious, the officer nevertheless is subject to other civil liability based on SOX's mandate that the certifying officer engage in specified affirmative conduct for the establishment and implementation of reasonably effective disclosure controls and procedures. Such liability may arise, for example: in a private § 10(b) action (where recklessness is sufficient scienter); in an SEC enforcement action (where depending on the provision violated, negligence is sufficient); or in a state court suit for breach of fiduciary duty.[62]

[2] Audit Committee

Under the Sarbanes-Oxley Act, the audit committee is defined as a committee established by the board of directors for the purpose of overseeing the accounting and financial reporting processes of the company and the audits of such company's financial statements. Under SOX, if no such committee exists, then the entire board

---

60. 18 U.S.C. § 1350.

61. *Id. See SEC v. Jensen*, 2016 WL 4537377 (9th Cir. 2016) (holding SEC may bring enforcement actions against subject officers who sign off on false or misleading certifications, not just officers who fail to sign the required certifications); *United States v. Scrushy*, [2004–2005 Transfer Binder] Fed. Sec. L. Rep. (CCH) ¶ 93,039 (N.D. Ala. 2004) (upholding constitutionality of § 906 of SOX). *See generally*, Hogan, *The Enron Legacy: Corporate Governance Requirements for a New Era*, 31 SEC. REG. L.J. 142, 143–144 (2003), *interpreting*, 18 U.S.C. § 1350.

62. *See* discussion in Chapters 8, 9, and 15 *infra*. For example, negligence suffices for violations of § 17(a)(2) or 17(a)(3) of the Securities Act and § 13(a) of the Exchange Act. Note that a false certification, without more, is not sufficient to establish the subject officer's scienter. *See Central Laborers' Pension Fund v. Integrated Electrical Services, Inc.*, 497 F.3d 546 (5th Cir. 2007); *Garfield v. NDC Healthcare Corp.*, 466 F.3d 1255 (11th Cir. 2006). *See generally* Alverson, *Sarbanes-Oxley §§ 302 and 906: Corporate Reform or Legislative Redundancy?*, 33 SEC. REG. L.J. 15 (2005); Brockett, *The Sarbanes-Oxley Act of 2002: What It Means For Business Litigators*, 30 SEC. REG. L.J. 360 (2002). For an SEC enforcement action based on an allegedly false Section 302 certification, *see, e.g., SEC v. Rica Foods, Inc.*, 35 SEC. REG. & L. REP. (BNA) 1427 (S.D. Fla. 2003). For a private securities action premised on an allegedly false Section 302 certification, *see, e.g., In re Ramp Corp. Securities Litigation*, [2006 Transfer Binder] Fed. Sec. L. Rep. (CCH) ¶ 93,914 (S.D.N.Y. 2006).

of directors is considered the audit committee; however, all members of the audit committee must be independent. Directors who serve on the audit committee can receive only their director remuneration from the corporation; they cannot serve as consultants or in other roles for which they are compensated.[63]

The audit committee is given the direct responsibility of engaging the auditing firm, preapproving audit as well as non-audit services, and overseeing the auditor's work. Under SOX, the independent auditor is required to directly report to the audit committee. In addition, the audit committee must establish procedures for dealing with internal corporate "whistle-blower" complaints concerning accounting or auditing matters. The audit committee also is vested with the power to employ its own legal counsel and other advisers as the committee deems is necessary to carry out its duties.[64]

[a] Audit Committee Independence

SOX requires that the members of the audit committee be independent—thus precluding a member from being affiliated with the company or its subsidiaries other than his/her membership on the board of directors. This requirement of independence also prohibits an audit committee member from receiving consulting or similar fees. Accordingly, an independent director may receive compensation only for serving as a director and as a board committee member.[65]

The SEC has implemented this aspect of SOX, precluding the national stock exchanges (such as the New York Stock Exchange) from listing the security of any company that fails to comply with the SEC mandates. The SEC requirements, in conjunction with the mandates of SOX, signify that listed companies must adhere to the following standards:

- each member of the listed company's audit committee must be independent from the company and its management;
- the audit committee must have direct responsibility for the appointment, compensation, retention and oversight of the company's independent auditor, and the independent auditor must report directly to the audit committee;
- the audit committee must establish procedures for handling complaints regarding the company's accounting practices;
- the audit committee must have authority to engage advisors as it determines necessary to carry out its duties; and

---

63. Sarbanes-Oxley Act §§ 205(a)(58)(A)-(B), *amending*, §§ 3(a)(58)(A)-(B), 10A(m)(3) of the Exchange Act; Securities Act Release No. 8220 (2003).

64. Sarbanes-Oxley Act §§ 201(h), 202(i), 301(m), *amending*, § 10A(h), (i), (m) of the Exchange Act. Note that the auditors are precluded from engaging in specified non-audit services. SOX §§ 201-203. *See* § 5.08[O] *infra*.

65. *Id.* § 301(m)(3), *amending*, § 10A(m)(3) of the Exchange Act.

- the company must provide appropriate funding for the audit committee to pay the fees of the independent auditor, any outside advisers engaged by the audit committee, and the committee's administrative expenses.[66]

[b] Audit Committee Financial Expert

Under § 407 of SOX, disclosure is required as to whether any member of the audit committee qualifies as a "financial expert." If an audit committee does not have a financial expert, management must explain the reasons for the absence thereof in applicable SEC filings. In charging the SEC with formulating rules to implement this provision, Congress gave some clear guidance. Under SOX, a financial expert must have an understanding of Generally Accepted Accounting Principles (GAAP), experience with respect to the auditing or preparation of financial statements, an understanding of audit committee functions, and experience with internal accounting controls.[67]

Under the rules adopted by the SEC pursuant to SOX's mandate, the term "financial expert" is replaced with the term "audit committee financial expert." In order to be classified as an "audit committee financial expert," an individual must have the knowledge and experience described in the Act, as well as the ability to apply generally accepted accounting principles with respect to the accounting for estimates, accruals and reserves. A person can acquire the status of financial expert through education or through experience as a financial officer, accounting officer, or auditor (or through supervising such person). Significantly, according to the SEC, the designation of an audit committee member as a financial expert does not impose more obligations on that individual than those placed on other audit committee members.[68]

[3] Improper Influence on Audits

The Sarbanes-Oxley Act makes it illegal for any person, whether director, officer, or an individual acting under such person's direction, to fraudulently influence, manipulate, coerce, or mislead any accountant who is engaged in the performance of an audit of the subject registrant's financial statements.[69] Exercising its regulatory authority, the SEC has promulgated the following rule with respect to this provision:

> No officer or director of an issuer, or any other person acting under the direction thereof, shall directly or indirectly take any action to coerce, manipulate, mislead, or fraudulently influence any independent public or certified public accountant engaged in the performance of an audit or review of the

---

66. Akin Gump Strauss Hauer & Feld, LLP Corporate Governance Alert, Dated May 2, 2003. *See* Securities Act Release No. 8220 (2003); Securities Exchange Act Release No. 48745 (2003).

67. Sarbanes-Oxley Act § 407.

68. Securities Act Release No. 8177 (2003). See Item 401(h) of Regulation S-K.

69. Sarbanes-Oxley Act § 303.

financial statements of that issuer that are required to be filed with the Commission . . . if that person knew or should have known that such action, if successful, could result in rendering the issuer's financial statements materially misleading.[70]

[4] Forfeiture of Bonuses and Profits

In the event that a publicly held company must prepare an accounting restatement due to the material noncompliance of such registrant, as a result of misconduct, the CEO and the CFO must reimburse the company for any bonus or other incentive-based compensation. Moreover, under such circumstances, any profits realized from the sale of the registrant's securities received by the subject officer within the 12-month period following the filing with the SEC of the misleading report(s) must be disgorged to the company.[71] Unfortunately, the statute does not explain when an accounting restatement is considered to be "as a result of misconduct." As construed by a number of courts thus far, this provision is one of CEO/CFO no-fault: in the event that an accounting restatement is issued by the company due to misconduct, the company's CEO and CFO must reimburse the company any incentive-based compensation.[72] The Dodd-Frank Act extends the clawback provision to encompass any executive officer and specifies that the issuer "will recover from any [such] current or former executive officer" the excess incentive-based compensation.[73]

[5] Officer and Director Bars

SOX lowers the standard for barring individuals from being officers and directors of publicly held companies. Previously, a court had authority to bar a securities law violator from serving as a director or officer of a publicly held enterprise who was found liable for securities fraud and held to be "substantially unfit." SOX lowers that standard to "unfitness." Accordingly, upon a finding that the subject violator engaged in securities fraud and is deemed unfit to serve as a director or officer of a publicly held company, a bar order is to be entered.[74]

---

70. Exchange Act Rule 13b2-2(b)(1). *See* Securities Exchange Act Release No. 47890 (2003). Note that the SEC rule renders negligent conduct actionable.

71. Sarbanes-Oxley Act § 304.

72. *See SEC v. Jensen*, 835 F.3d 1100 (9th Cir. 2016); *SEC v. Jenkins*, 718 F. Supp. 2d 1070 (D. Ariz. 2010). *See generally* Cherry & Wang, *Clawbacks: Prospective Contract Measures in an Era of Excessive Executive Compensation and Ponzi Schemes,* 94 Minn. L. Rev. 368 (2009); Kelsh, *Section 304 of the Sarbanes-Oxley Act of 2002: The Case for a Personal Culpability Requirement,* 59 Bus. Law. 1005 (2004); Schwartz, *The Clawback Provision of Sarbanes-Oxley: An Underutilized Incentive to Keep the Corporate House Clean,* 64 Bus. Law. 1 (2008).

73. *See* § 954 of the Dodd-Frank Act, *adding,* § 10D of the Securities Exchange Act.

74. Sarbanes-Oxley Act § 305, *amending,* § 20(e) of the Securities Act & 21(d)(2) of the Exchange Act. *See* Barnard, *Rule 10b-5 and the "Unfitness" Question,* 47 Ariz. L. Rev. 9 (2005). For further discussion, *see* Chapter 15 *infra.*

[6] Insider Trading During Blackout Periods

Under the Sarbanes-Oxley Act, executive officers and directors are prohibited from trading any equity security of the issuer, acquired through the scope of employment, during a blackout period, when at least half of the issuer's individual account plan participants are not permitted to trade in the equity security for more than three consecutive business days. Stated generally, SOX also requires that the issuer deliver notice of blackout periods at least 30 days prior to the blackout period, giving proper notice to employees, executives, and the SEC.[75] The SEC has adopted rules governing this prohibition against trading during blackout periods. Under Regulation Blackout Trading Restriction (BTR), a director or executive officer of a publicly held issuer is prohibited from trading, during a blackout period, equity securities that were acquired in connection with such director's or officer's service to the subject issuer.[76]

A violation of § 306(a) of the Act is deemed a violation of the Exchange Act and is subject to SEC enforcement action. Furthermore, an issuer or a security holder may bring on behalf of such issuer an action against the director or officer who violated the blackout period, and seek disgorgement of all profits from the sale of such securities acquired in connection with the director's or officer's service to the issuer. The amount disgorged will be calculated, under Regulation BTR, as the difference between the amount paid for the equity security on the date of the transaction and the amount that would have been received for the security if the transaction had taken place outside of the blackout period.[77]

[7] Disclosure of Off-Balance Sheet Transactions

SOX requires reporting companies to disclose in their financial statements any off-balance sheet transaction, arrangement or obligation that may have a material effect on the financial condition of the corporation. The Act also mandates that the subject financial report reflect all material correcting adjustments that have been identified by the public accountant. Further, the Act requires the SEC to promulgate rules providing that subject companies must present pro forma financial information included in an SEC filing or other public disclosure (such as a press release) in a nonmisleading manner and must reconcile such pro forma financial information with the subject company's financial condition and results of operation under GAAP.[78] Subsequently, the SEC adopted implementing rules, including Regulation G, pursuant to this legislative directive. These rules "address public companies' disclosure or release of certain financial information that is calculated and presented on the basis of methodologies other than in accordance with generally accepted accounting principles (GAAP)."[79]

---

75. Sarbanes-Oxley Act § 306.

76. *See* Securities Exchange Act Release No. 47225 (2003).

77. *Id. See* Sarbanes-Oxley Act § 306; Regulation BTR; W. WANG & M. STEINBERG, INSIDER TRADING §§ 12:1-12:5 (Oxford Univ. Press 2010).

78. Sarbanes-Oxley Act § 401, *amending,* § 13(i)-(j) of the Exchange Act.

79. Securities Act Release No. 8176 (2003). See Regulation G; Item 10 of Regulation S-K.

[8] *Prohibition of Loans to Directors and Executive Officers*

The Sarbanes-Oxley Act prohibits loans by a publicly held company to its executive officers and directors. Certain limited types of loans are permitted if they are extended in the ordinary course of business by the company and are granted to the fiduciary on the same basis as loans provided to the general public.[80]

[9] *Reporting of Insider Transactions*

The Sarbanes-Oxley Act expedites disclosures of sales or purchases of equity securities by directors, officers, and 10 percent shareholders of publicly held registrants. Under SOX, a change in beneficial ownership, with certain exceptions, must be reported by the end of the second business day following the execution of the transaction. Under the statute, the SEC must allow the filing to be electronic, and make the information of such filing publicly accessible. The company must also provide this information in a timely manner by placing the information on the company website not later than the business day after the SEC filing.[81] Subsequently, the SEC promulgated rules requiring mandatory electronic filing of beneficial ownership reports under § 16(a).[82]

[10] *Management and Auditor Assessment of Internal Controls*

SOX requires management to create, maintain, and assess internal controls. Management also must report on the effectiveness of the internal controls. In addition, with certain exceptions, the Act requires the independent auditor to report on whether the company has adequate internal controls.[83] Note that emerging growth companies and smaller reporting companies are exempt from the *auditor's* (but not management's) internal control report.[84]

The SEC has adopted rules mandating that each Exchange Act reporting company (including an emerging growth company and a smaller reporting company) provide in its Form 10-K a report of management addressing the subject company's internal control over financial reporting. The Commission stated:

> As directed by Section 404 of the Sarbanes-Oxley Act of 2002, we are adopting rules requiring companies subject to the reporting requirements of the Securities Exchange Act of 1934, other than registered investment companies, to include in their annual reports a report of management on the company's internal control over financial reporting. The internal

---

80. Sarbanes-Oxley Act § 402, *amending*, § 13(k) of the Exchange Act. For an SEC enforcement based on the loan prohibition of Section 402, *see In the Matter of Goodfellow and Molaris*, Securities Exchange Act Release No. 52865 (2005).

81. Sarbanes-Oxley Act § 403(a).

82. Sarbanes-Oxley Act Release No. 8230 (2003).

83. Sarbanes-Oxley Act § 404.

84. *See* § 103 of the JOBS Act, *amending*, § 404(b) of the Sarbanes-Oxley Act; Securities Act Release No. 9142 (2010), *implementing*, § 989G of the Dodd-Frank Act. Generally, small issuers have a market capitalization of less than $75 million, not counting securities held by affiliates.

control report must include: a statement of management's responsibility for establishing and maintaining adequate internal control over financial reporting for the company; management's assessment of the effectiveness of the company's internal control over financial reporting as of the end of the company's most recent fiscal year; a statement identifying the framework used by management to evaluate the effectiveness of the company's internal control over financial reporting; and a statement that the registered public accounting firm that audited the company's financial statements included in the annual report has issued an attestation report on management's assessment of the company's internal control over financial reporting. Under [these] rules, a company is required to file the registered public accounting firm's attestation report as part of the annual report. Furthermore, . . . management [must] evaluate any change in the company's internal control over financial reporting that occurred during a fiscal quarter that has materially affected, or is reasonably likely to materially affect, the company's internal control over financial reporting.[85]

[11] Senior Financial Officer Code of Ethics

Under SOX, a publicly held company is required to disclose whether or not it has a code of ethics applicable to its senior financial officers. A code of ethics contains standards that set forth ethical behavior. The code of ethics envisioned by SOX should seek to ensure fair and accurate disclosure of financial data, and compliance with governmental rules and regulations. If a company does not have a code of ethics, it is required to explain the reason for such absence in the applicable periodic reports required to be filed pursuant to the Securities Exchange Act.[86]

Implementing this statute, the SEC has mandated that a subject registrant disclose in its annual report whether the company has a written code of ethics for its chief executive officer, chief financial officer, chief accounting officer or comptroller, or individuals performing like functions. The failure by a company to adopt such a written code of ethics and the reasons explaining such failure must be disclosed. Moreover, registrants must disclose any waiver or amendment of its Code of Ethics on either a Form 8-K or on its website.[87]

[12] Real-Time Disclosure

SOX requires publicly held companies, as set forth by SEC rules, to make rapid and current disclosure of material changes in their financial condition or operations. These disclosures must be in plain English.[88] Under this provision, as discussed in

---

85. Securities Act Release No. 8238 (2003). In 2007, the SEC adopted amendments with respect to management's report on internal control over financial reporting. *See, e.g.,* Securities Act Release No. 8808 (2007).

86. Sarbanes-Oxley Act § 406.

87. *See* Item 406 of Regulation S-K; Securities Act Release No. 8177 (2003).

88. Sarbanes-Oxley Act § 409, *amending,* § 13(l) of the Exchange Act.

Chapter 11, the Commission has added several items to be promptly disclosed pursuant to Form 8-K.[89] The SEC also approved rules accelerating the filing date for Form 10-K and 10-Q reports for certain issuers.[90]

[13] Accounting Oversight Board

The Sarbanes-Oxley Act established the Public Company Accounting Oversight Board (PCAOB or Board). The Board's fundamental purpose is to oversee the auditing of public companies in order to help ensure accurate and independent financial reporting by public companies subject to the federal securities laws. The PCAOB is not an agency of the federal government; it is a non-profit corporation formed under the laws of the District of Columbia. The Board has sweeping powers to establish quality control, ethical, and auditing standards for accounting firms. The PCAOB also has the power and authority to inspect, investigate, and bring disciplinary proceedings against public auditing firms.[91]

The SEC has oversight authority over the Board.[92] Such oversight helps to ensure that the policies and rules of the PCAOB are consistent with the objectives of the federal securities laws. The Board is subject to a similar degree and control by the SEC as is the Financial Industry Regulatory Authority (FINRA).[93] The Board must file its proposed rules with the SEC, and the Commission will publish the proposals for public comment. A rule proposed by the PCAOB will not become effective until the SEC has approved such rule. Also, any disciplinary actions taken by the PCAOB are subject to review by the SEC. The SEC has the power to reduce or modify the sanctions imposed by the PCAOB if the SEC finds that the sanctions are not appropriate.[94] After such SEC review, the U.S. Court of Appeals has authority to review the sanctions ordered.[95] In addition, the SEC has the power to

---

89. *See* Securities Exchange Act Release No. 49424 (2004); discussion in Chapter 11. *See generally* Horwich, *New Form 8-K and Real-Time Disclosure,* 37 Rev. Sec. & Comm. Reg. 109 (2004).

90. *See* Securities Exchange Act Release No. 47226 (2003).

91. Sarbanes-Oxley Act § 101(a)-(b). See *Free Enterprise Fund v. Public Company Accounting Oversight Board,* 561 U.S. 477 (2010), where the Supreme Court, with one exception, upheld the constitutionality of the statute creating the PCAOB. The Court held that the "for cause" tenure protection afforded by the statute for PCOAB board members ran afoul of the separation of powers doctrine. Nonetheless, the Court ruled that the unconstitutional tenure provisions were separable from the remaining provisions of the statute. Accordingly, the PCAOB may conduct its functions as set forth by the statute but PCOAB board members may be removed "at will" by the SEC. For an article prior to the Supreme Court's decision asserting that the statute was unconstitutional, *see* Nagy, *Playing Peekaboo with Constitutional Law: The PCAOB and Its Public/Private Status,* 80 NOTRE DAME L. REV. 975 (2005).

92. Sarbanes Oxley Act § 107.

93. *See* J. HAMILTON & T. TRAUTMANN, SARBANES-OXLEY ACT OF 2002 at 41 (2002), *citing,* S. Rep. No. 107-205 (2002).

94. Sarbanes-Oxley Act § 107(b)(2), (b)(4), (c)(1), (c)(3). See J. Hamilton & T. Trautmann, *supra* note 93, at 41.

95. Securities Exchange Act § 25(a).

censure the PCAOB and its members, and also has the power to limit the Board's activities.[96]

[14] Auditor Independence

[a] Non-Audit Services

The Sarbanes-Oxley Act focuses on the issue of auditor independence. The Act prohibits a registered public accounting firm that is auditing a publicly held enterprise from engaging in specified non-audit services.[97] These specified prohibited non-audit services include, for example, (1) bookkeeping, (2) appraisal services, (3) actuarial services, (4) management functions or human resources work, (5) broker-dealer, investment adviser or investment banking services, (6) legal services and other expert services unrelated to auditing, (7) internal audit outsourcing, (8) financial information systems design and implementation, and (9) any other service that the PCAOB determines is impermissible.[98]

[b] Audit Committee Pre-Approval of Permitted Non-Audit Services

SOX generally requires pre-approval by the audit committee for any allowable non-audit functions performed by the accounting firm. As long as the auditing firm complies with the Act's mandate for audit committee pre-approval, the subject firm may provide tax services and other allowable non-audit services to its audit clients. Further, SOX provides for a de minimis exception to the pre-approval of non-audit functions.[99]

[c] Audit Partner Rotation

SOX requires the lead or coordinating audit partner (but not the firm itself) to rotate off of an audit engagement every five years, with at least a five-year cooling-off period before a lead auditor may return to a given audit client.[100] In addition, the SEC has issued rules requiring that other audit partners rotate every seven years, with

---

96. Sarbanes-Oxley Act § 107(d). Rules adopted by the PCAOB subsequent to the enactment of the JOBS Act do not apply to an audit of an emerging growth company unless the SEC determines that "the application of such additional requirements is necessary or appropriate in the public interest . . ." JOBS Act § 104, *amending*, § 103(a)(3) of the Sarbanes-Oxley Act.

97. *Id.* § 201(a), *amending*, § 10A(g) of the Exchange Act.

98. *Id. See* Securities Act Release No. 8183 (2003) (adopting rules relating to auditor independence, including prohibition of certain non-audit services).

99. *See* Sarbanes-Oxley Act § 202(A); Securities Act Release No. 8183 (2003). The de minimis exception arises when the total of non-audit services does not exceed five percent of the revenues paid by the registrant to such auditor, the services were not recognized as non-audit services at the time of the engagement, the services are promptly brought to the audit committee's attention, and such non-audit services are approved by the audit committee (or a duly authorized member of the audit committee) prior to the completion of the audit. SOX § 202(B).

100. Sarbanes-Oxley Act § 203, *amending*, § 10A(j) of the Exchange Act.

a minimum cooling-off period of at least two years.[101] If certain conditions are met, "small" firms with fewer than 10 partners and fewer than five SEC audit clients are exempt from the rule.[102]

[d] Report to the Audit Committee

SOX requires the independent public auditor to make timely reports to the audit committee.[103] These reports must include all critical accounting policies and practices to be used, all alternative treatments of financial information within GAAP that have been discussed with management and the ramifications of the use of each such alternative, and any other material written communication between the auditor and management. The audit committee is ultimately responsible for deciding any accounting methodology disagreements between management and the independent public accountants.[104]

[e] Cooling-Off Period

Under SOX, an auditor cannot perform an audit of a company if the registrant's chief executive officer, chief financial officer, controller, or chief accounting officer was employed by the subject auditor during the one-year period prior to the initiation of the audit and participated in any capacity in an audit of such issuer.[105]

[15] Attorney Professional Responsibility

The Sarbanes-Oxley Act requires an attorney who is practicing before the SEC to report evidence of a material violation of the securities laws or breach of fiduciary duty to the company's CEO or chief legal counsel (CLC). If the CEO or CLC does not respond appropriately, adopting appropriate remedial measures, the attorney is required to report evidence of the violation to the audit committee, another committee comprised entirely of outside directors, or the board of directors.[106] The statute also directs the SEC to formulate rules setting forth minimum standards of attorney professional conduct. Subsequently, the SEC promulgated minimum standards of professional conduct (Standards) for attorneys practicing before the Commission.[107] These Standards are addressed in Chapter 16 of this text.

---

101. Securities Act Release No. 8183 (2003).

102. *Id.* In order for such an audit firm to qualify for this exemption, the PCAOB "must conduct a review of all of the firm's engagements subject to the rule at least once every three years." *Id.*

103. Sarbanes-Oxley Act § 204, *amending,* § 10A(k) of the Exchange Act.

104. Sarbanes-Oxley Act §§ 204, 301(B)(2), *amending,* § 10A(k), (m) of the Exchange Act.

105. Sarbanes-Oxley Act § 206, *amending,* 10A(l) of the Exchange Act.

106. Sarbanes-Oxley Act § 307.

107. Securities Exchange Act Release No. 47276 (2003).

[16] Financial Analysts' Conflicts of Interest

SOX addresses securities analysts and possible conflicts of interest arising from their duties. The Act directs the SEC to formulate rules that enhance the objectivity of analyst research reports and increase investor confidence in analyst research.[108] Responding to this directive, the SEC promulgated Regulation AC. Regulation AC requires, for example, that research analysts: certify the truthfulness of the views expressed in public appearances as well as contained in their research reports; and disclose in such certification any compensation received that is directly or indirectly related to the specific recommendations or views set forth in public appearances or their research reports. Regulation AC contains a number of exemptions, such as excluding from the Regulation's mandates foreign securities analysts, non-registered investment advisers, and the media.[109] In this regard, the Commission also approved extensive self-regulatory rules that, for example: prohibit tying a research analyst's remuneration to the firm's procurement of specific banking transactions; forbid a research analyst to provide favorable analysis on a company in return for investment banking engagements; and prohibit a firm from retaliating against a research analyst who publishes a research report that is detrimental to the firm's present or prospective investment banking relationship with a subject corporation.[110]

[17] Remedies and Criminal Penalties

The following discussion highlights key remedies and civil penalties that were enacted pursuant to the Sarbanes-Oxley Act.

[a] Statute of Limitations

As addressed in Chapter 8, SOX extends the statute of limitations for pursuing a private claim based on fraud, deceit, or manipulation to two years after discovery of the relevant facts constituting the violation and in no event more than five years after the violation occurs.[111] The previous statute of limitations was that suit had to be brought within one year after discovery of the facts constituting the violation and in no event more than three years after such violation.[112]

[b] Whistleblower Civil Remedy

SOX creates a private cause of action for an employee of a publicly held company who has been discharged or incurred retaliatory treatment because he/she has been

---

108. Sarbanes-Oxley Act § 501(a). *See* Hilgers, *Analyzing Wall Street Research Analyst Conflicts of Interest,* 31 Sec. Reg. L.J. 427 (2003).

109. *See* Securities Act Release No. 8193 (2003).

110. *See* Securities Exchange Act Release Nos. 45908 (2002), 48252 (2003).

111. 28 U.S.C. § 1658.

112. *See* discussion § 8.09[B] *infra.*

a whistleblower by providing information regarding conduct reasonably believed to violate a rule or regulation of the SEC, or provision of federal law relating to fraud, including but not limited to mail fraud, wire fraud, bank fraud, and securities fraud. An employee so situated is entitled to all necessary relief, including reinstatement, back pay, interest, compensation for any special damages, litigation costs, attorney's fees and expert fees.[113]

The Dodd-Frank Act expands upon these whistleblower provisions whereby whistleblowers who satisfy the statute's requirements are entitled to be awarded monetary amounts of 10 percent to 30 percent if a money penalty exceeding $1 million is levied.[114] In promulgating rules implementing this statute, the SEC stated that the Dodd-Frank Act

> established a whistleblower program that requires the Commission to pay an award . . . to eligible whistleblowers who voluntarily provide the Commission with original information about a violation of the federal securities laws that lead to the successful enforcement of a covered judicial or administrative action, or a related action. Dodd-Frank also prohibits retaliation by employers against individuals who provide the Commission with information about possible securities violations.[115]

[c] Insider Trading During Blackouts — Disgorgement of Profits

As discussed earlier in this Section, SOX forbids an executive officer or director of a publicly held company from trading subject securities during any mandatory blackout period applicable to a registrant's employee pension plan. If this provision is violated, the Act authorizes the company or shareholders of the company (by derivative suit) to procure the disgorgement of any profit realized by the officer or director.[116]

[d] No Discharge of Securities Fraud Debts in Bankruptcy

SOX amends the Bankruptcy Code to prohibit individuals from receiving a discharge of debts attributable to a judgment or settlement of federal or state securities fraud claims.[117] The statute seeks to prevent corporate insiders "from sheltering their

---

113. Sarbanes-Oxley Act § 806, *amending*, 18 U.S.C. § 1514A. *See* Steinberg & Kaufman, *Minimizing Corporate Liability Exposure When the Whistle Blows in the Post Sarbanes-Oxley Era*, 30 J. Corp. L. 445 (2005).

114. Dodd-Frank Act § 922 *amending*, § 21 of the Exchange Act.

115. Securities Exchange Act Release No. 64545 (2011). *See* Pearlman & Mertineit, *SEC's Rules Implementing Dodd-Frank's Bounty Provisions Provide Whistleblowers with a Dangerous Weapon*, 39 Sec. Reg. L.J. 141 (2011).

116. Sarbanes-Oxley Act § 306.

117. Sarbanes-Oxley Act § 803, *amending*, § 523(a) of the Bankruptcy Code.

assets under the umbrella of bankruptcy and protecting [such assets] from judgments and settlements arising from federal and state securities law violations."[118]

[e] Court Order Freezing Certain Extraordinary Payments

SOX grants to the SEC the authority to seek and procure a court order freezing extraordinary payments made to a corporate officer or director during a Commission investigation involving possible violation of the federal securities laws.[119] According to the Ninth Circuit, the statute "gives the SEC authority to ensure that assets of an issuer of securities which have been fraudulently obtained are not dissipated [by the subject insider(s)] during the investigation and litigation of securities fraud cases."[120] At this point, neither the statute nor the SEC has defined the term "extraordinary payments."

[f] Fair Funds Provision

SOX, as amended by the Dodd-Frank Act, authorizes the SEC, when disgorgement and/or civil money penalties are ordered against a subject party in an enforcement action, to establish a fund for the benefit of investors that will help offset their losses due to the illegalities committed.[121] For example, in the *WorldCom* matter, the Second Circuit affirmed the district judge's approval of the Commission's proposal to distribute, pursuant to the SOX "Fair Fund" provision, $750 million to aggrieved WorldCom investors.[122]

[g] SEC Equitable Relief

Prior to Sarbanes-Oxley, the SEC largely relied on the inherent equitable authority of the federal courts to procure equitable relief in its enforcement actions.[123] Types of equitable relief obtained by the Commission have included, for example, disgorgement, ordering of an accounting, appointment of a receiver, asset freeze and restructuring of the board of directors.[124] Any question as to the propriety of such relief[125]

---

118. J. Hamilton & T. Trautmann, *supra* note 93, at 83, *citing*, remarks of Sen. John McCain, Cong. Rep., July 10, 2002, at S6529.

119. Sarbanes-Oxley Act § 1103, *amending*, § 21C(c) of the Exchange Act.

120. *SEC v. Genstar TV Guide International*, 367 F.3d 1087, 1090–1091 (9th Cir. 2004).

121. Sarbanes-Oxley Act § 308.

122. *See Official Committee of Unsecured Creditors of WorldCom Inc. v. SEC*, 467 F.3d 73 (2d Cir. 2006).

123. *See, e.g.*, *Deckert v. Independent Shares Corp.*, 311 U.S. 282 (1940); *SEC v. Posner*, 16 F.3d 500 (2d Cir. 1994); *SEC v. Wencke*, 622 F.2d 1363, 1369 (9th Cir. 1980) (stating that "[t]he federal courts have inherent equitable authority to issue a variety of 'ancillary relief' measures in actions brought by the SEC to enforce the federal securities laws").

124. *See, e.g.*, *SEC v. Interlink Data Network of Los Angeles Inc.*, 77 F.3d 1201 (9th Cir. 1996); *SEC v. Commonwealth Chemical Securities, Inc.*, 574 F.2d 90 (2d Cir. 1978); *SEC v. Current Financial Services, Inc.*, 783 F. Supp. 1441 (D.D.C. 1992); *SEC v. Mattel, Inc.*, 1974 WL 449 (D.D.C. 1974).

125. A number of sources questioned the propriety of certain types of such relief. *See, e.g.*, Dent, *Ancillary Relief in Federal Securities Law: A Study in Federal Remedies,* 67 MINN. L. REV. 865 (1983).

has been resolved by the Sarbanes-Oxley Act. Section 21(d)(5) of the Exchange Act, as amended by SOX, provides: "In any action or proceeding brought or instituted by the Commission under any provision of the securities laws, the Commission may seek, and any Federal court may grant, any equitable relief that may be appropriate or necessary for the benefit of investors."[126]

[h] Criminal Sanctions

SOX enhances several criminal sanctions under Title VIII (Corporate Fraud and Accountability Act of 2002), Title IX (the White Collar Crime Penalty Enhancement Act of 2002), and Title XI (the Corporate Fraud Accountability Act of 2002). Under these enhancements, it is a crime, punishable for up to 20 years, to "knowingly alter, destroy, mutilate, conceal, cover-up or make a false entry in any record, document, or tangible object with the intent to impede, obstruct or influence the investigation or proper administration of any matter within the jurisdiction of any department or agency of the United States. . . ."[127] Another enhancement makes securities fraud a separate criminal offense, punishable for up to 25 years' imprisonment. This statute encompasses any person who "knowingly executes or attempts to execute a scheme . . . to defraud any person in connection with any security of an [Exchange Act reporting] issuer or to obtain by false or fraudulent . . . representations . . . any money or property in connection with the purchase or sale of any security of an [Exchange Act reporting] issuer. . . ."[128] The Sarbanes-Oxley Act also sets forth that attempts and conspiracies to commit such offenses as mail fraud, wire fraud, and the new securities fraud are criminally punishable.[129] Finally, SOX increases the punishment for mail and wire fraud from imprisonment of the previous five years to 20 years.[130]

[C] CEO and CFO Certifications

Certification of Disclosure in Companies' Quarterly and Annual Reports

Securities and Exchange Commission

Securities Act Release No. 8124 (2002)

I. Introduction

On July 30, 2002, the Sarbanes-Oxley Act of 2002 (the "Act") was enacted. Section 302 of this Act, entitled "Corporate Responsibility for Financial Reports,"

---

126. Sarbanes-Oxley Act § 305(b), *amending,* § 21(d)(5) of the Exchange Act.

127. 18 U.S.C. § 1519. *See Yates v. United States,* 134 S. Ct. 1074 (2015) (ruling that § 1519's prohibition against shredding a "tangible object" covers objects "used to record or preserve information").

128. 18 U.S.C. § 1348.

129. 18 U.S.C. § 1341, 1343, 1344, 1347, 1348.

130. 18 U.S.C. § 1349.

requires the Commission to adopt final rules . . . . under which the principal executive officer or officers and the principal financial officer or officers, or persons providing similar functions, of an issuer each must certify the information contained in the issuer's quarterly and annual reports. Section 302 also requires these officers to certify that: they are responsible for establishing, maintaining and regularly evaluating the effectiveness of, the issuer's internal controls; they have made certain disclosures to the issuer's auditors and the audit committee of the board of directors about the issuer's internal controls; and they have included information in the issuer's quarterly and annual reports about their evaluation and whether there have been significant changes in the issuer's internal controls or in other factors that could significantly affect internal controls subsequent to the evaluation.

. . . .

In light of Congress' directive in Section 302 of the Act, we are adopting rules that implement the certification mandated by the Act . . . .

While Section 302 of the Act requires an issuer's principal executive and financial officers to make specific certifications regarding their responsibilities to establish and maintain internal controls, it does not directly address the issuer's responsibility for controls and procedures related to the issuer's Exchange Act reporting obligations. The June Proposals included requirements that companies maintain sufficient procedures to provide reasonable assurances that they are able to collect, process and disclose, within the time periods specified in the Commission's rules and forms, the information required to be disclosed in their Exchange Act reports. We have adopted this requirement largely as proposed. Because of the broad scope of Section 302 of the Act, the new rules are applicable to all types of issuers that file reports under Section 13(a) or 15(d) of the Exchange Act, including foreign private issuers, banks and savings associations, issuers of asset-backed securities, small business issuers and registered investment companies.

II. Certification of Quarterly and Annual Reports

Rule Requirements

As adopted, new Exchange Act Rules 13a-14 and 15d-14 require an issuer's principal executive officer or officers and the principal financial officer or officers, or persons performing similar functions, each to certify in each quarterly and annual report, including transition reports, filed or submitted by the issuer under Section 13(a) or 15(d) of the Exchange Act that:

- he or she has reviewed the report;
- based on his or her knowledge, the report does not contain any untrue statement of a material fact or omit to state a material fact necessary in order to make the statements made, in light of the circumstances under which such statements were made, not misleading with respect to the period covered by the report;
- based on his or her knowledge, the financial statements, and other financial information included in the report, fairly present in all material respects the

financial condition, results of operations and cash flows of the issuer as of, and for, the periods presented in the report;

- he or she and the other certifying officers:

  [1] are responsible for establishing and maintaining "disclosure controls and procedures" . . . ;

  [2] have designed such disclosure controls and procedures to ensure that material information is made known to them, particularly during the period in which the periodic report is being prepared;

  [3] have evaluated the effectiveness of the issuer's disclosure controls and procedures as of a date within 90 days prior to the filing date of the report; and

  [4] have presented in the report their conclusions about the effectiveness of the disclosure controls and procedures based on the required evaluation as of that date;

- he or she and the other certifying officers have disclosed to the issuer's auditors and to the audit committee of the board of directors (or persons fulfilling the equivalent function):

  [1] all significant deficiencies in the design or operation of internal controls (a pre-existing term relating to internal controls regarding financial reporting) which could adversely affect the issuer's ability to record, process, summarize and report financial data and have identified for the issuer's auditors any material weaknesses in internal controls; and

  [2] any fraud, whether or not material, that involves management or other employees who have a significant role in the issuer's internal controls; and

- he or she and the other certifying officers have indicated in the report whether or not there were significant changes in internal controls or in other factors that could significantly affect internal controls subsequent to the date of their evaluation, including any corrective actions with regard to significant deficiencies and material weaknesses.

For purposes of the new rules, "disclosure controls and procedures" are defined as controls and other procedures of an issuer that are designed to ensure that information required to be disclosed by the issuer in the reports filed or submitted by it under the Exchange Act is recorded, processed, summarized and reported, within the time periods specified in the Commission's rules and forms. "Disclosure controls and procedures" include, without limitation, controls and procedures designed to ensure that information required to be disclosed by an issuer in its Exchange Act reports is accumulated and communicated to the issuer's management, including its principal executive and financial officers, as appropriate to allow timely decisions regarding required disclosures.

. . . .

§ 5.05 The Dodd-Frank Act—Corporate Governance

Continuing the trend of the Sarbanes-Oxley Act of 2002, the Dodd-Frank Act of 2010 likewise impacts aspects of corporate governance that traditionally have been within the purview of state corporate law.

[A] Key Provisions

Key provisions of the Dodd-Frank Act affecting corporate governance include:

(1) "Say on Pay"—Pursuant to § 14A of the Securities Exchange Act, an *advisory vote* by a reporting issuer's shareholders on *executive compensation* is required. This mandatory non-binding shareholder vote—"Say on Pay Resolution"—calls for disclosure of compensation disclosure and analysis (CD&A) by the subject issuer to its stockholders. The CD&A must address in a meaningful way such issuer's executive compensation policies and determinations.

(2) "Golden Parachutes"—Golden parachutes generally are generous severance benefits that high level executives receive upon a "change in control" of the company. Section 14A of the Exchange Act requires that a subject company hold a non-binding shareholder vote on golden parachute arrangements.

(3) Pay Versus Performance Disclosure—Pursuant to § 14(i) of the Exchange Act, the SEC must adopt rules to require a reporting company to disclose in its proxy solicitation materials for its annual shareholder meeting the payment of executive compensation as compared to the subject company's financial performance.[131]

(4) Dual Roles: CEO as Chairman of Board of Directors?—Section 14B of the Exchange Act mandates that the SEC adopt rules that require a reporting company to explain in its annual proxy statement why it has determined for the same person to act as both chief executive officer (CEO) and chairman of its board of directors, or, in the alternative situation, why the subject company has determined that different persons serve as CEO and chairman of its board of directors.

(5) Internal Pay Equity Disclosure (Focus on the CEO)—The Dodd-Frank Act (§ 953(b)) directs the SEC to amend Item 402 (entitled "Executive Compensation") of Regulation S-K requiring a subject company to disclose: (a) the median of the annual total compensation paid to all employees (excluding the CEO); (b) the CEO's annual total compensation; and (c) the ratio of the median compensation of all employees as set forth in (a) above to the CEO's annual total compensation.

(6) Disclosure of "Hedging"—Pursuant to Section 14(j) of the Exchange Act, the SEC is directed to adopt rules mandating that a reporting company disclose in the

---

131. *See Swanson v. Weil*, [2012–2013 Transfer Binder] Fed. Sec. L. Rep. (CCH) ¶ 97,045 (D. Colo. 2012) (applying Delaware law, court held that approval of executive compensation package prior to shareholder advisory "say on pay" vote did not negate application of the business judgment rule).

proxy solicitation materials for its annual shareholder meeting whether the company allows its directors or employees to hedge such company's equity securities.

(7) Restrictions on Voting by Non-Beneficial Holders—Section 6(b) of the Exchange Act sets forth that the rules of any national securities exchange may not permit any member (e.g., a broker-dealer firm) that does not beneficially own a subject security from voting that security on specified matters (such as an election of directors) unless authorized to do so by the beneficial owner of such security.

(8) Independent Compensation Committee—Section 10A of the Exchange Act directs the SEC to prohibit the national securities exchanges (such as the New York Stock Exchange) from listing (with certain exceptions) any equity security of any issuer that does not have a compensation committee comprised entirely of independent directors. This directive follows that set forth in the Sarbanes-Oxley Act requiring that a reporting company's audit committee be comprised entirely of independent directors. The exchanges have adopted standards requiring that listed companies have a compensation committee comprised solely of independent directors.[132]

(9) "Clawback" Entitlement—Expanding the scope of the "clawback" provision contained in Section 304 of the Sarbanes-Oxley Act, Section 954 of the Dodd-Frank Act mandates that a subject-company's former and current executives (not limited to the CEO and CFO) repay to the company any excessive incentive-driven compensation based on the restatement of such company's financial statements. No showing of culpability or fault is required to be proven for recovery of such excessive compensation. The statute directs subject companies to adopt procedures and policies to recover this excessive compensation which implicitly is premised on the principle of unjust enrichment.

[B] Proxy Access Rule

Pursuant to the Dodd-Frank Act (§ 971, amending, § 14(a) of the Exchange Act), the SEC is authorized to adopt appropriate rules whereby shareholders are granted access to a subject company's proxy statement in order to nominate candidates for such company's board of directors. Pursuant to that authorization, the SEC adopted the proxy access rules. See Securities Exchange Release No. 62764 (2010). These rules generally entitled the largest shareholder or largest group of shareholders, who own at least three percent of the shares entitled to be voted and who have held such shares for at least three years, to nominate the greater of one director-candidate or up to 25 percent of the total number of directors who serve on such company's board of directors. To qualify, no such shareholder (or group) may intend to change control of the issuer or seek a greater number of seats on the board of directors than the proxy access rules permit. If more than one shareholder (or group of shareholders) qualify

---

132. *See* Securities Exchange Act Release No. 48745 (2003).

(namely, owning more than three percent of the subject issuer's shares and holding such shares for at least three years), then only the shareholder (or group) with the largest ownership percentage may invoke the proxy "access" entitlement.

The proxy access rules were declared invalid in *Business Roundtable v. SEC,* 647 F.3d 1144 (D.C. Cir. 2011). This decision is contained in Chapter 9, §9.04[E].

Chapter 6

Resales and Reorganizations

§ 6.01 Introduction

As seen from the foregoing materials, the Securities Act of 1933 was enacted in large part to help promote the dissemination of adequate and reliable information to the investing public in the distribution process. To achieve this objective, § 5 requires registration for any sale of a security unless such sale is exempt from the registration provisions. The party seeking to invoke an exemption from registration has the burden of proving that such exemption has been perfected.

We have examined the exemptions for issuers in Chapter 3. Attention now turns to exemptions for resales by persons other than an issuer. We begin by addressing § 4(a)(1), which provides the most important exemption in this context. By its terms, § 4(a)(1) exempts from the registration requirements of § 5 "*transactions* by any person *other than* an *issuer, underwriter or dealer.*" Hence, as a general proposition, the § 4(a)(1) exemption permits individual investors to resell their securities without registration, provided such resales are viewed as "transactions" (rather than as part of a "distribution") and such persons are not deemed "underwriters."

Because § 4(a)(3) and § 4(a)(4) exempt most transactions by broker-dealers, the problems that arise under § 4(a)(1) generally involve underwriters. Underwriter status necessarily renders the § 4(a)(1) exemption unavailable.

In this chapter, we focus on the federal provisions relating to resales and reorganizations. Significantly, the National Securities Markets Improvement Act of 1996 (NSMIA) preempts state regulation of §§ 4(a)(1), 4(a)(3), 4(a)(4), and 4(a)(7) of the Securities Act. Note, however, that state regulation is federally preempted with respect to the § 4(a)(1) and § 4(a)(3) exemptions only if the issuer of the subject security is an Exchange Act reporting company. *See* § 18(b)(4) of the Securities Act.

Problem A

Abbott, an entrepreneur who privately owns his own successful business called "Abbott's Outfitters," is enthusiastic about the prospects of Sher & Good, Inc., a popular ice cream franchiser, distributor, and manufacturer. Pursuant to Sher & Good's first registered public offering, Abbott shows his enthusiasm by purchasing 190,000 shares for $1.9 million ($10 per share), representing 15 percent of the shares offered. Although not an officer or director of Sher & Good, Abbott has a long-term business relationship and friendship with the company's largest shareholder, who also is the CEO and Chair of the Board of Directors of the company.

Ten months after all shares in the offering were sold, Abbott is in financial difficulty as his business (Abbott's Outfitters) is in dire need of additional capital. Abbott wishes to remain the sole owner of Abbott's Outfitters and will not consider any type of private offering. Moreover, interest rates for commercial loans currently are high. He concludes that his only logical alternative is to dispose of his 190,000 shares of Sher & Good, Inc. which are now selling in the Nasdaq stock market for $16.50 per share. Before going ahead with his plans, Abbott prudently consults with you as to the legality of the contemplated sales. What do you advise?

Presume the same facts as above except that, instead of purchasing the shares of Sher & Good in a registered public offering, Abbott acquired them in a Rule 506 offering under Regulation D. Different result? Is it relevant whether Sher & Good is a privately or publicly held company?

Problem B

Assume that you are counsel to Patterson & Bellweather, a regional broker-dealer. Abbott contacts his broker at Patterson & Bellweather and directs the broker to sell his 190,000 shares of Sher & Good at periodic intervals during the next six months (in order to maintain as orderly a price as possible). The broker and Abbott come to you before carrying out the directive. What do you advise? What are your concerns? Does it matter whether Abbott is a director of Sher & Good?

Problem C

Your client, a privately held company, desires to form a stock benefit plan for its 56 employees. Two key conditions are that the company retain its privately held status and that the stock received by the employees pursuant to the Plan be nonrestricted ("free" stock). What do you advise the client? Draft a short memo highlighting the key issues and concerns.

---

§ 6.02 The Concept of Underwriter

The concept of underwriter is fundamental to the framework of the 1933 Act. Congress contemplated that underwriters would play an integral role in both the initial and secondary distribution process. Underwriter status subjects applicable parties to the provisions of § 5 and results in liability exposure for material misrepresentations and nondisclosures contained in the registration statement.

Section 2(a)(11) of the Securities Act defines an "*underwriter*" as "any person who has purchased from an issuer with a view to, or offers or sells for an issuer in connection with, the distribution of any security, or participates or has a direct or indirect participation in any such undertaking, or participates or has a participation in the direct or indirect underwriting of any such undertaking, but such term shall not include a person whose interest is limited to a commission from an underwriter or dealer not in excess of the usual and customary distributors' or sellers' commission." The term "*distribution*" has been described as "the entire process by which in the course of a public offering the block of securities is dispersed and ultimately comes to rest in the hands of the investing public." *SEC v. Kern*, 425 F.3d 143, 153 (2d Cir. 2005), quoting, *In re Lewisohn Copper Corp*, 38 SEC 226, 234 (1958).

In this regard, see SEC Rules 141 and 142, which, in effect, exclude from underwriter status: (1) distributors and dealers who receive a commission from an underwriter or dealer not in excess of the usual and customary distributors' or sellers' commissions (Rule 141); and (2) those persons who, under the circumstances delineated in the rule, purchase for investment purposes all or a specified portion of the securities remaining unsold after the lapse of a defined period of time (Rule 142).

For the purposes of § 2(a)(11) only (i.e., who should be regarded as an "underwriter"), the term "*issuer*" is defined to include a person who *controls* the issuer. Rule 405 defines control as "the possession, direct or indirect, of the power to direct or cause the direction of the management and policies of a person, whether through the ownership of voting securities, by contract, or otherwise." Significantly, the inclusion of control persons within the definition of "issuer" for § 2(a)(11) purposes signifies that sales by directors and executive officers create the risk that some party involved in the transaction is an "underwriter."

An examination of § 2(a)(11) reveals that a person can become an underwriter in the following ways:

> *(1) By purchasing from the issuer with a view toward distribution;*
>
> *(2) By offering or selling for an issuer in connection with a distribution;*
>
> *(3) By participating, directly or indirectly, in the distribution or underwriting effort;*
>
> *(4) By selling securities of the issuer on behalf of a control person in connection with the distribution of any security; and*
>
> *(5) By purchasing securities of the issuer from a control person with a view toward distribution.*

If a person falls within any of these categories, he/she will be deemed to be an underwriter. Note the lack of guidance § 2(a)(11) provides. For example: What evidence shows intent to distribute? What circumstances constitute participation? What power must a person possess to be in control? The answers to these questions are necessarily based on the individual circumstances of each case. Judicial decisions are fairly scarce, and not surprisingly, have not eliminated fears of inadvertent underwriter status. Moreover, beyond Rule 144 (which will be examined in §6.04), the SEC has promulgated few rules or regulations in this area.

[A] The Presumptive Underwriter Doctrine

In a registered offering of securities, an individual, a few investors, or an institution may purchase a substantial portion of the offering and thereafter resell the securities to the public.[1] At least two problems may arise: First, the purchasers may hold the securities until the information in the registration statement becomes outdated (but note that concern is minimal when the issuer timely files its periodic reports, such as its Form 10-Ks and 10-Qs, pursuant to the Exchange Act); and second, the purchasers, perhaps seeking to take advantage of the rapid price increase normally associated with a "hot issue,"[2] may sell large quantities of the subject securities in a "distribution" within a short period. If the §4(a)(1) or §4(a)(7) exemption were to apply, these sales would be free of the registration requirements, including, of course, the prospectus access/delivery obligation. Concerned with the lack of disclosure in this context, the SEC formulated (*and later abandoned*) the presumptive underwriter doctrine.

Under the presumptive underwriter doctrine, one who purchases more than 10 percent of the securities offered in a registered offering may be deemed an underwriter unless such person establishes sufficient investment intent. The doctrine was criticized by pension and employee benefit plans, life insurance companies, and other institutional investors. In fear of the doctrine, a number of institutional investors significantly limited their purchases of securities in registered public offerings.

The SEC evidently abandoned the presumptive underwriter doctrine more than 30 years ago. As stated by the Commission's then-Director of the Division of Corporation Finance, Linda C. Quinn:

> For many years, a concept known as the "presumptive underwriter" doctrine existed. That doctrine assumed that a purchaser of a relatively large amount of securities covered by a registration statement (at one point 10 percent) was buying with a view to distribution and, therefore, should be deemed a statutory underwriter. The theory was most subjective, most difficult of explanation, and presented considerable problems both in compliance, as well as administration. In 1983, in the American Council of Life Insurance letter, the "presumptive underwriter" doctrine was for all

---

1. *See* Ahrenholz & Van Valkenberg, *The Presumptive Underwriter Doctrine: Statutory Underwriter Status for Investors Purchasing a Substantial Portion of a Registered Offering*, 1973 Utah L. Rev. 773 (1973).

2. Generally, a "hot issue" is an issuance of securities that, shortly after the registration statement has gone effective, is trading in the aftermarket at a substantially higher price than the registered offering price.

intents and purposes abandoned. . . . Nothing in the Securities Act compelled the view that a person acquiring a substantial part of an offering should be treated differently from any other investor with a large position in the issuer, unless the purchaser becomes an affiliate as a result of the purchases.[3] [Note that an *"affiliate"* of an issuer generally is one who controls, is controlled by, or is under common control with, either directly or indirectly, such issuer.]

***

[B] Purchasing from an Issuer with a View Toward Distribution

A person who has acquired "restricted securities" from an issuer often has obtained the securities pursuant to the §4(a)(2) private offering exemption or pursuant to Rule 506 of Regulation D. One problem is that when an issuer sells unregistered securities to one or more persons in a non-public transaction, it is possible that the transfer is in reality a public offering in disguise—a two-step, indirect distribution in which the transferees function as "underwriters" for the issuer.

An affiliate of the issuer selling either restricted or nonrestricted securities faces a similar problem—because of his or her close connection with the issuer, an affiliate, absent the exercise of utmost care, may be unable to invoke the §4(a)(1) exemption in any resale transaction involving securities of the issuer.

As discussed earlier in this chapter, if a person is deemed to be an "underwriter," he/she cannot rely on the exemption from registration provided by §4(a)(1) of the Securities Act to protect the resale transaction. Generally, although §4(a)(1) exempts ordinary transactions such as a private resale of securities, it does so only with respect to "transactions by any person other than an issuer, *underwriter*, or dealer." The dilemma for persons holding *restricted securities* of an issuer and for affiliates of an issuer (regardless whether such affiliates seek to sell restricted or nonrestricted securities) comes into focus upon examining the statutory definition of "underwriter." Section 2(a)(11) of the Act defines an "underwriter" to include any person who "has purchased" securities from the issuer "with a view to . . . the *distribution* of any security."

Section 2(a)(11) does not provide an objective standard for determining whether a person acquiring securities from an issuer is taking with a view toward investment or with a view toward resale. For a non-affiliate holding *restricted securities*, a resale in purported reliance upon §4(a)(1) carries the risk that such seller will be deemed to be an "underwriter" within the meaning of §2(a)(11), and therefore, unable to claim the desired exemption. For an affiliate who intends to sell any securities of the

---

3. Address by Linda C. Quinn before the ABA's Federal Regulation of Securities Committee (Nov. 22, 1986), *discussed in* Barron, *The SEC Staff Finally Abandons the "Presumptive Underwriter" Doctrine*, 15 SEC. REG. L.J. 246 (1987).

issuer, *restricted or not*, the same risk is present. As will be discussed in § 6.04, provided that the requirements of Rule 144 are met, the Rule provides a safe-harbor to persons holding restricted securities of an issuer and to affiliates of an issuer who seek to resell either restricted or nonrestricted securities.

The following case illustrates how one court determined "investment intent."

United States v. Sherwood

United States District Court, Southern District of New York

175 F. Supp. 480 (1959)

Sugarman, J.

The crucial issue [in this prosecution for criminal contempt] is, "Were the shares of Canadian Javelin Limited sold by Sherwood required to be registered before sale thereof by him?"

The prosecution theory is alternatively, first, that a registration statement was required to be filed because Sherwood was a statutory underwriter when he acquired his shares because he purchased them from an issuer with a view to distribution thereof, or second, that Sherwood was required to file a registration statement because when he made the sales complained of, he was a "control person."

The evidence does not sustain the second charge that Sherwood was at the time of the sales a "control person." To the contrary, although Sherwood dominated 8% of the total issued stock, he was unable to secure representation on the board of directors; he had had a falling-out with John Christopher Doyle, who appears to have been the dominant figure in the management of Canadian Javelin Limited, and Sherwood was unable to free the bulk of his shares for distribution until Doyle consented thereto. . . .

As to the first contention, that Sherwood was a statutory underwriter, on this record I am not satisfied beyond a reasonable doubt that at the time Sherwood took his shares from the issuer through Doyle, he purchased them with a view to the distribution thereof.

Defendant points to the long period between his purchase of and the first sale from his block of Canadian Javelin Limited shares. From this, he argues that:

> From such behavior, it is impossible to infer the intention to distribute, *at the time of acquisition*, that is necessary under the Act to qualify Sherwood as an underwriter within the meaning of the Act. His retention of the shares for a minimum of two full years after he personally had obtained physical possession of them belies any inference that he had originally acquired them "with a view to distribution," and is inconsistent with any such intention.

On the proof before me it appears that Sherwood took the [full] ownership of the block of shares. . . . The passage of two years before the commencement of [transactions involving] these shares is an insuperable obstacle to my finding that Sherwood took these shares with a view to distribution thereof, in the absence of any relevant evidence from which I could conclude he did not take the shares for investment. No such evidence was offered at the trial. In fact, the only reference to Sherwood's intention with regard to the block of stock which he received appears when government counsel was cross-examining Sherwood's Canadian counsel, Courtois. The testimony, if anything, indicates Sherwood's intention not to sell his stock. Courtois' testimony on this score is as follows:

A. I remember asking Mr. Sherwood if he had any intention of selling any of his shares or disposing of his holdings in Canadian Javelin.

Q. And what was his answer?

A. His answer was no because he said for the time being he had a large block and he thought as such it had some value.

. . . [Motion to sanction defendant Sherwood for criminal contempt is denied.]

***

The Holding Period, Change in Circumstances Defense, and Sales By Pledgees

(1) **Holding Period**: *Sherwood* is an example of a "rule of thumb" for determining investment intent. From that decision, as well as subsequent developments, it generally was viewed that the SEC normally would not initiate an enforcement action against a party who was not a "control" person and who held the restricted securities for at least two years prior to sale. As we will see, Rule 144 significantly shortens this period if certain criteria are met. See § 6.04.

Perhaps surprisingly, however, where another available exemption (such as Rule 144) is not available, this two-year holding period remains relevant. In a recent decision, *SEC v. Big Apple Consulting USA, Inc.*, 783 F.3d 786, 807 (11th Cir. 2015) (citations omitted), the appellate court reasoned:

The definition of "underwriter" in the Securities Act is expansive. An "underwriter" is "any person who has purchased from an issuer with a *view to*, or *offers or sells for* an issuer in connection with, *the distribution* of any security. . . ." 15 U.S.C. § 77b(a)(11) (emphasis added). In its motion for summary judgment, the SEC argued and the district court found that the relevant defendants were underwriters "because they obtained CyberKey stock *with a view to distribution*." (Emphasis added.) . . . .

Whether the relevant defendants' receipt of the unregistered shares was made "with a view to" distribution focuses on their investment intent at the time of acquisition. Thus, there is a distinction between acquiring shares from the issuer with an investment purpose and acquiring shares for the purpose of reselling them. Because it is difficult to discern a party's intent at the time of purchase with respect to downstream sales of unregistered shares, courts and commentators have typically focused on the amount of time a security holder holds on to shares prior to reselling them. . . . Courts have generally agreed that a two-year holding period is sufficient to negate the inference that the security holder did not acquire the securities with a "view to distribute." . . .

(2) Restrictive Legends—Change in Circumstances: Restrictive legends normally are placed on securities acquired in an unregistered offering of restricted securities (e.g., pursuant to Rule 506). Subject parties may claim that these restrictive legends establish their investment intent at the time of purchase. Not surprisingly, the courts have rejected this contention, holding that the purchase of stock from an issuer under an investment restriction is by no means a conclusive defense to underwriter status.

On the other hand, "change in circumstances" in certain situations may serve as a valid defense to such status. When invoking the change in circumstances defense, the subject party asserts that it bought the stock with investment intent but that subsequent unforeseen changes compelled the earlier than planned sale of the stock. Nonetheless, the defense may be difficult to establish. As the Tenth Circuit reasoned in *G. Eugene England Foundation v. First Federal Corporation*, [1976–1977 Transfer Binder] Fed. Sec. L. Rep. (CCH) ¶ 95,837, at 91,015 (10th Cir. 1973):

> The original taking of the stock under an investment restriction is not conclusive that First Federal was not an underwriter. In *Gilligan, Will & Co. v. SEC*, 267 F.2d 461 (2d Cir. 1959), the Commission's finding that Gilligan, Will & Co. and its partners were underwriters [and hence violated § 5] was upheld in the face of the challenge that the securities had been taken with an investment intention and held for some ten months under that restriction. The court there recognized that allowance of such course of dealing "would be to permit a dealer who speculatively purchases an unregistered security in the hope that the financially weak issuer had . . . turned the corner, to unload on the unadvised public what [it] later determines to be an unsound investment without the disclosure sought by the securities laws, although it is in precisely such circumstances that disclosure is most necessary and desirable." The trial court here correctly found that no change in circumstances . . . had occurred.

But see Lectmor v. VTR, Inc., [1969–1970 Transfer Binder] Fed. Sec. L. Rep. (CCH) ¶ 92,707 (S.D.N.Y. 1970), where the court ruled that dismissal from employment and the return of indictments constituted a sufficient change in circumstances to avoid underwriter status.

Note, moreover, that at the time that the SEC adopted Rule 144 (discussed in § 6.04), the Commission stated that:

> [T]he "change in circumstances" concept should no longer be considered as one of the factors in determining whether a person is an underwriter . . . since the circumstances of the seller are unrelated to the need of investors

for the protections afforded by the registration [requirement] and other provisions of the Act.

Securities Act Release No. 5223 (1972). Nonetheless, the Preliminary Note to Rule 144 currently provides:

> [P]rior to and since the adoption of Rule 144, subsequent acts and circumstances have been considered to determine whether the purchaser took the securities "with a view to distribution" at the time of the acquisition. Emphasis has been placed on factors such as the length of time the person held the securities and whether there has been an unforeseeable change in circumstances of the holder. Experience has shown, however, that reliance upon such factors alone has led to uncertainty in the application of the registration provisions of the Act.

Hence, the change in circumstances doctrine evidently remains intact. Moreover, the SEC does not have the authority to abolish a judicial doctrine by administrative fiat. *See* T. Hazen, The Law of Securities Regulation 217–218 (6th ed. 2009) (to the extent that the change in circumstances defense is a valid test in terms of the statutory definition of one who purchases with an intent to redistribute, the SEC cannot by administrative fiat change the meaning of the statute); M. Steinberg, Understanding Securities Law § 6.04[B] (6th ed. 2014). On policy grounds, should a "change in circumstances" be recognized as a valid defense to underwriter status?

(3) Sales by Pledgees: The inadvertent underwriter problem (with the prospect of rendering the § 4(a)(1) exemption unavailable) also arises in connection with sales by pledgees (e.g., banks) of securities pledged by control persons (as well as restricted securities pledged by either control persons or nonaffiliates). Note that a "pledge" of stock is itself a "sale" under the Securities Act. See *Rubin v. United States*, 449 U.S. 424 (1981).

For example, if the pledgor (e.g., a control person) defaults on a bank loan secured by the pledge, can the pledgee (i.e., the bank) sell the securities pledged without being deemed an underwriter? In *SEC v. Guild Films Co., Inc.*, 279 F.2d 485 (2d Cir. 1960), the pledgor, a controlling shareholder, pledged as collateral for a loan from a bank a substantial block of securities that bore a restrictive legend on the face of the securities. After the shareholder defaulted on the loan, the bank, knowing of the restrictive legend, sold some of the securities without a registration statement being filed. The Second Circuit held that the bank was an underwriter. Even though the bank may have taken the securities as collateral and had not directly dealt with the issuer, "the bank knew that [it] had been given unregistered stock and that the issuer had specifically forbidden that the stock be sold." Hence, to avoid § 5 liability, the bank had to retain the securities pledged, invoke an exemption (e.g., § "4(1½)", § 4(a)(7), Rule 144, Rule 144A), or induce the issuer to file a registration statement.

Language contained in the *Guild Films* case may be criticized as being unduly onerous upon good faith pledgees. By concluding that a good faith pledgee participates in a distribution or takes with the view to distribute whenever a pledgor defaults, it may be asserted that the Second Circuit's rationale unfairly hampers legitimate commercial activity. On the other hand, it may be argued that the key issue is not the pledgee's culpability in facilitating the sale of securities to the investing public but rather whether such sales should be permitted by the pledgee where the effect is to place into the hands of uninformed investors securities which have never been part of a registered offering. To purchasers of such securities who have not received adequate disclosure, the pledgee's good faith is of little solace.[4]

In this regard, the potentially harsh results of the *Guild Films* decision on legitimate commercial activity may be mitigated in practice by a pledgee bank's use of: (1) a covenant by the pledgor to register the securities ("a registration covenant") in the event of the pledgor's default (in all likelihood, such a covenant would not be worth the paper it was written on); (2) the invocation of an exemption from registration, such as the § 4(a)(7) or the § "4(1½)" exemption (see § 6.05); and (3) a more circumspect approach to accepting pledgor securities as collateral.

The thrust of the *Guild Films* decision evidently remains good law. The continued vitality of the court's broad language as it relates to good faith pledgees, however, is open to question. As the First Circuit opined, "[t]here is considerable support for the . . . view that a good faith pledgee who sells unregistered shares at a foreclosure sale is not an 'underwriter.'" *A.D.M. Corporation v. Thompson*, [1982–1983 Transfer Binder] Fed. Sec. L. Rep. (CCH) ¶ 99,206 (1st Cir. 1983) (and SEC "no-action" letters cited therein). Nonetheless, the SEC continues to adhere to the view that, under certain circumstances, the pledgee's sale of the securities pledged creates underwriter status.[5]

[C] Participating in the Underwriting Effort

Based on the Second Circuit's decision in the case that follows, the making of continual solicitations resulting in a distribution of securities renders the § 4(a)(1)

---

4. *See generally* Rice, *The Effects of Registration on the Disposition of Pledged Securities*, 21 Stan. L. Rev. 1607, 1618 (1969) (The author expresses disagreement with *Guild Films* if "the court's reference to good faith . . . extends to the lender's ignorance of the pledgor's status as a statutory underwriter. [Under the court's language,] a lender who accepts unregistered stock in pledge from a statutory underwriter, wholly unaware of any restrictions on transferability and even reasonably believing the stock to be registered, may well become a participant in the distribution upon foreclosure and public sale."); Sargent, *Pledges and Foreclosure Rights Under the Securities Act of 1933*, 45 Va. L. Rev. 885, 894 (1959) ("Regardless of the bona fides of the pledge, realistically the pledgee never intends 'investment' . . . . [I]n a very real sense, virtually every pledgee intends to sell or distribute if the pledgor defaults on the underlying loan.").

5. *See In re DG Bank (Schweiz) AG*, [1991–1992 Transfer Binder] Fed. Sec. L. Rep. (CCH) ¶ 84,945 (SEC 1992); T. Hazen, The Law of Securities Regulation 214–216 (6th ed. 2009); Hueter, *The Plight of the Pledgee Under Rule 144*, 3 Sec. Reg. L.J. 111 (1975). Compare *Seattle-First National Bank v. Carlstedt*, [1984 Transfer Binder] Fed. Sec. L. Rep. (CCH) ¶ 91,499 (W.D. Okla. 1984). *See generally Rubin v. United States*, 449 U.S. 424 (1981) (holding that a pledge of stock given as collateral for a loan is an "offer or sale" of a security within the meaning of § 17(a) of the Securities Act).

exemption unavailable, regardless of a person's motive or relationship with the issuer. This is so even if the party is a volunteer and receives no compensation for its efforts.

Securities and Exchange Commission v. Chinese Consolidated Benevolent Association

United States Court of Appeals, Second Circuit

120 F.2d 738 (1941)

Augustus N. Hand, Circuit Judge.

The Securities and Exchange Commission seeks to enjoin the defendant from the use of any instruments of interstate commerce or of the mails in disposing, or attempting to dispose, of Chinese Government bonds for which no registration statement has ever been made.

The defendant is a New York corporation organized for benevolent purposes having a membership of 25,000 Chinese. On September 1, 1937, the Republic of China authorized the issuance of $500,000,000 in 4% Liberty Bonds, and on May 1, 1938 authorized a further issue of $50,000,000 in 5% bonds. In October, 1937, the defendant set up a committee which has had no official or contractual relation with the Chinese government for the purpose of:

(a) Uniting the Chinese in aiding the Chinese people and government in their difficulties.

(b) Soliciting and receiving funds from members of Chinese communities in New York, New Jersey and Connecticut, as well as from the general public in those states, for transmission to China for general relief.

All the members of the committee were Chinese and resided in New York City. Through mass meetings, advertising in newspapers distributed through the mails, and personal appeals, the committee urged the members of Chinese communities in New York, New Jersey and Connecticut to purchase the Chinese government bonds referred to and offered to accept funds from prospective purchasers for delivery to the Bank of China in New York as agent for the purchasers. At the request of individual purchasers and for their convenience the committee received some $600,000 to be used for acquiring the bonds, and delivered the moneys to the New York agency of the Bank of China, together with written applications by the respective purchasers for the bonds which they desired to buy. . . . Neither the committee, nor any of its members, has ever made a charge for their activities or received any compensation from any source. The Bank of China has acted as an agent in the transactions and has not solicited the purchase of bonds or the business involved in transmitting the funds for that purpose.

No registration statement under the Securities Act has ever been made covering any of the Chinese bonds advertised for sale. Nevertheless, the defendant has been a medium through which over $600,000 has been collected from would-be purchasers and through which bonds in that amount have been sold to residents of New York, New Jersey and Connecticut.

. . . .

It should be observed at the outset that the Commission is not engaged in preventing the solicitation of contributions to the Chinese government, or its citizens. Its effort is only to prevent the sale of Chinese securities through the mails without registry. If that cannot be prevented there is nothing to stop Germany, Italy, Japan, or any other nation, as well as China, from flooding our markets with securities without affording purchasers the information which the Securities Act intends to render available for investors in foreign bond issues.

. . . .

We think that the defendant has violated Section 5(a) of the Securities Act when read in connection with Section 2(3) [now § 2(a)(3)] because it engaged in selling unregistered securities issued by the Chinese government when it solicited offers to buy the securities "for value". The solicitation of offers to buy the unregistered bonds, either with or without compensation, brought defendant's activities literally within the prohibition of the statute. Whether the Chinese government as issuer authorized the solicitation, or merely availed itself of gratuitous and even unknown acts on the part of the defendant whereby written offers to buy, and the funds collected for payment, were transmitted to the Chinese banks does not affect the meaning of the statutory provisions which are quite explicit. In either case the solicitation was equally for the benefit of the Chinese government and broadly speaking was for the issuer in connection with the distribution of the bonds.

. . . .

Under Section 4(1) [now § 4(a)(1)] the defendant is not exempt from the registration requirements if it is "an underwriter". The court below reasons that it is not to be regarded as an underwriter since it does not sell or solicit offers to buy "for an issuer in connection with, the distribution" of securities. In other words, it seems to have been held that only solicitation authorized by the issuer in connection with the distribution of the Chinese bonds would satisfy the definition of underwriter contained in Section 2(11) [now § 2(a)(11)] and that defendant's activities were never for the Chinese government but only for the purchasers of the bonds. Though the defendant solicited the orders, obtained the cash from the purchasers and caused both to be forwarded so as to procure the bonds, it is nevertheless contended that its acts could not have been for the Chinese government because it had no contractual arrangement or even understanding with the latter. But the aim of the Securities Act is to have information available for investors. This objective will be defeated if buying orders can be solicited which result in uninformed and improvident purchases. It can make no difference as regards the policy of the Act whether an issuer has solicited orders through an agent, or has merely taken advantage of the services of a person interested for patriotic reasons in securing offers to buy. The aim of the issuer is to promote the distribution of the securities, and of the

Securities Act is to protect the public by requiring that [investors] be furnished with adequate information. . . . Accordingly, the words "[sell] for an issuer in connection with the distribution of any security" ought to be read as covering continual solicitations, such as the defendant was engaged in, which normally would result in a distribution of issues of unregistered securities within the United States. Here a series of events were set in motion by the solicitation of offers to buy which culminated in a distribution that was initiated by the defendant. We hold that the defendant acted as an underwriter.

There is a further reason for holding that Section 5(a)(1) forbids the defendant's activities in soliciting offers to buy the Chinese bonds. Section 4(1) was intended to exempt only trading transactions between individual investors with relation to securities already issued and not to exempt distributions by issuers. The words of the exemption in Section 4(1) are: "Transactions by any person other than an issuer, underwriter, or dealer. . . ." The issuer in this case was the Republic of China. The complete transaction included not only solicitation by the defendant of offers to buy, but the offers themselves, the transmission of the offers and the purchase money through the banks to the Chinese government, the acceptance by that government of the offers and the delivery of the bonds to the purchaser or the defendant as his agent. The argument on behalf of the defendant incorrectly assumes that Section 4(1) [now § 4(a)(1)] applies to the component parts of the entire transaction we have mentioned and thus exempts defendant unless it is an underwriter for the Chinese Republic. Section 5(a)(1), however, broadly prohibits sales of securities irrespective of the character of the person making them. The exemption is limited to "*transactions*" by persons other than "issuers, underwriters, or dealers". It does not in terms or by fair implication protect those who are engaged in steps necessary to the *distribution* of security issues. To give Section 4(1) the construction urged by the defendant would afford a ready method of thwarting the policy of the law and evading its provisions.

. . . .

The decree is reversed with directions to the District Court to deny the defendant's motion to dismiss and to issue the injunction as prayed for in the bill of complaint.

Notes and Questions

(1) Notice that the defendant in *Chinese Consolidated Benevolent Ass'n.* was a volunteer and received no compensation. According to the court, continual solicitations resulting in a distribution of securities normally confers underwriter status, irrespective of a person's motive or relationship with the issuer. Such a finding necessarily involves a detailed factual inquiry on an ad hoc basis. Where there is available precedent, however, counsel may have some relatively firm basis upon which to advise. Is this sufficient or should there be more explicit guidelines in place, for example, the promulgation of SEC rules on the subject?

(2) *SEC v. Allison*, [1982 Transfer Binder] Fed. Sec. L. Rep. (CCH) ¶ 98,774 (N.D. Cal. 1982), raised the issue of inadvertent involvement in the distribution process. The defendants argued that, while they may have participated in the distribution, they did not have an intent to distribute. The court disagreed, holding that proof of intent is unnecessary when the defendant participates in the distribution. The court stated: "When, as in this case, a defendant's actions were necessary to and a substantial factor in an illegal securities distribution, the defendant is a participant and thus an underwriter irrespective of the defendant's intent." A more recent case holding likewise is *SEC v. Lybrand*, 200 F.Supp. 2d 384 (S.D.N.Y. 2002). *See also*, *SEC v. Olins*, [2009–2010 Transfer Binder] Fed. Sec. L. Rep. (CCH) ¶ 95,641 (N.D. Cal. 2010) (holding that defendants purchased with a view toward distribution and hence were underwriters, thereby violating § 5 when they sold their shares without registration); *Peck v. Pacific CMA, Inc.*, 2007 U.S. Dist. LEXIS 40435 (D. Colo. 2007) (finding that the defendants' business history evidenced their intent to purchase from the subject company having the intent to resell, hence rendering them underwriters).

(3) *Zicklin v. Breuer*, 534 F. Supp. 745, 747 (S.D.N.Y. 1982), is an example of the uncertainty generated by the definition of "underwriter" in § 2(a)(11). The court found that Bankers Trust purchased shares on behalf of its customers of a public offering, acted as an important link in the chain of distribution, and issued reports touting the shares to its customers at the time it was buying and selling securities for its customers' accounts. Nevertheless, the court found that, as a matter of law, the bank was not an underwriter. The court reasoned:

> From my review of the uncontested facts, Bankers Trust was merely acting in a manner characteristic of the practices of the so-called "trust and estates" department of any commercial bank. [Bankers Trust] serves as the account manager for certain of its customers on the investment advisory accounts they maintain at the bank. As a part of that service, Bankers Trust issues reports describing and recommending certain securities . . . and buys and sells shares for [customers'] accounts. Bankers Trust maintains a relationship with its customers; in no manner did it have a relationship with [the issuer], [the principal underwriter], or the underwriting itself. Plaintiff, therefore, must properly plead some greater nexus between the investment management department of Bankers Trust and this underwriting of securities before such liability can attach. Otherwise, all commercial banks could potentially be the hostage of well-pleaded . . . complaints and speculative and inferential affidavits.

Is the court's holding consistent with that of the Second Circuit in the *Chinese Consolidated Benevolent Ass'n* case? Is the decision correct as a matter of policy? It may be argued that a key distinction is that the defendants in the Second Circuit case acted with the intent to benefit the issuer while Bankers Trust acted on behalf of its customers, owing them certain duties. Is this a relevant distinction?

§ 6.03 Distributions by Controlling Persons or Affiliates

The concept of "control" is crucial to the understanding of secondary distributions. For the purposes of determining who is an "underwriter," § 2(a)(11) defines the term "issuer" to include a controlling person. Therefore, underwriter status is accorded to any person who sells securities on behalf of a controlling person in connection with the distribution of any security.

The possibility of inadvertent underwriter status is ever-present because of the ambiguities associated with the meaning of "control." Moreover, the inclusion of control persons within the definition of "issuer" for § 2(a)(11) purposes signifies that sales of securities by directors and executive officers create the risk that some party involved in the transaction is an "underwriter," irrespective of whether the securities are restricted or unrestricted. *Indeed, control person status has been found to exist based on such factors as*

- *percentage of stock ownership;*
- *director or officer position held; and*
- *relationships with insiders.*

Because directors and executive officers frequently are shareholders and have relatively close relationships with other key insiders, this problem of potential underwriter status is a very practical and widespread one.

[A] The Meaning of "Control"

The lack of a precise definition for control frustrates counselors and corporate planners. A.A. Sommer Jr.,[6] who was a widely respected corporate practitioner and former SEC Commissioner, addressed the problem of defining control:

> Like so many key notions, the imprecise limits of the term ["control"] have been limned through the painstaking process of rule, interpretation, judicial decision and ad hoc determination in [SEC] "no action letters." Out of these there has come no mathematical standard, no slide rule computation, no certain rule which can infallibly guide counsel and client in making this most important determination—a determination which can be costly if wrongly made. . . . [I]t has become axiomatic that in

---

6. From the author's personal experience, Al Sommer distinguished himself as an excellent securities attorney and very supportive of "beginning" lawyers. Irrespective of whether one was a major partner in a "blue chip" firm or a junior associate in a lesser known firm, Mr. Sommer consistently was courteous and supportive. Needless to say, that is very refreshing.

deciding who is a "controlling person" the entire situation within the corporation at the time of determination, together with some of the history of the corporation, must be considered; single factors—shareholdings, offices held, titles, conduct—are rarely determinative, at least not in the close cases. . . .

Sommer, *Who's "In Control"?—S.E.C.*, 21 Bus. Law. 559 (1966). The above excerpt aptly expresses the uncertainty that surrounds the concept of control. The Commission, in an effort to alleviate some of the uncertainty, promulgated Rule 405 which defines "control."

Rule 405 defines control as "the possession, direct or indirect, of the power to direct or cause the direction of the management and policies of a person, whether through the ownership of voting securities, by contract, or otherwise." Rule 405 focuses on a person's ability to direct the management and policies of the corporation. Use of Rule 405 to define control in the § 2(a)(11) context, however, has been criticized by commentators. See 7B J.W. Hicks, Exempted Transactions Under the Securities Act of 1933 § 9.03[2][a] (2016); Campbell, *Defining Control in Secondary Distributions*, 18 B.C. Ind. & Com. L. Rev. 37 (1976).

These commentators suggest that an appropriate definition of control should stress a person's ability to compel the issuer to register an offering. They assert that Congress never intended a person to be deemed an issuer for § 2(a)(11) purposes when that person did not possess the power to effect registration. Moreover, they argue that the SEC's use of Rule 405 to define control fails to relieve uncertainty. The following case provides a startling example of the ambiguities relating to the concept of "control."

Pennaluna & Company v. Securities and Exchange Commission

United States Court of Appeals, Ninth Circuit

410 F.2d 861 (1969)

Merrill, Circuit Judge.

Pursuant to § 25 of the Securities Exchange Act of 1934 . . . petitioners seek review of an order of the Securities and Exchange Commission.

Pennaluna & Company was a [registered broker-dealer] operating in Wallace and Kellogg, Idaho, and Spokane, Washington. . . . It dealt primarily in securities issued by mining companies and for the most part traded on a wholesale basis with other broker-dealers. . . .

At issue in these proceedings are alleged violations of registration and antifraud provisions.

. . . .

VIOLATIONS OF REGISTRATION PROVISIONS

This case does not involve a primary distribution by the issuing company. Rather, we are here dealing with alleged secondary distributions of stock by a controlling person through various underwriters, with none of the transactions registered as required by § 5 of the Securities Act of 1933.

A. Violations by Pennaluna

With respect to the violations charged against [the broker-dealer] Pennaluna, the dispute centers in major part around [its sale of] two large blocks of unregistered Silver Buckle shares.

. . . .

Pennaluna is charged with being an underwriter as to [Silver Buckle] shares. . . .

By the basic definition in § 2(11) [now § 2(a)(11)], one "who [purchases] from an issuer with a view to, or offers or sells for an issuer in connection with, the distribution of any security" is an underwriter. It [is clear that Pennaluna] did not purchase from or sell for Silver Buckle, the actual issuer. It is necessary, therefore, to determine whether Pennaluna purchased from or sold for a person included in the term "issuer" for the purpose of § 2(11): "any person directly or indirectly controlling or controlled by the issuer, or any person under direct or indirect common control with the issuer."[7]

The Commission found that at the time of the sales in question Magnuson was a person controlling Silver Buckle and was therefore an "issuer" as that term is used in § 2(11); . . . that as to the stock in question [Magnuson] effected public distributions through Pennaluna; and that Pennaluna acted as underwriter in effecting these [trades]. The petitioners dispute these contentions.

1. Burden of Proof

At the outset, petitioners contend that the Commission erroneously imposed upon them the burden of establishing a lack of control by Magnuson.

It is well recognized as a general proposition that one who claims an exemption from the broad registration requirement of § 5 has the burden of proving that the exemption applies. . . .

Petitioners do not dispute this as a general proposition. They would, however, limit it to a primary distribution where the shares come from the issuing company. They concede that in such a case the distribution carries a presumptive need for registration. Where the shares do not come from the issuing company, however, petitioners

---

7. Rule 405 provides:

The term "control" (including the terms "controlling", "controlled by" and "under common control with") means the possession, direct or indirect, of the power to direct or cause the direction of the management and policies of a person, whether through the ownership of voting securities, by contract or otherwise.

contend that there is no presumptive need and that the Commission should bear the burden of establishing that the shares came from a controlling person and thus of establishing the existence of an "issuer" under § 2(11).

The holding of *SEC v. Culpepper,* 270 F.2d 241 (2d Cir. 1959), is to the contrary and we agree with that holding. . . . Petitioners' result would place upon the Commission the burden of proving the need for registration in all secondary distributions. The congressional concern over such distributions, made clear from legislative history,[8] strongly indicates that the presumptive need for registration implicit in § 5 extends to all secondary distributions. . . .

While the congressional concern reached to all secondary distributions of significant proportions, it was obvious that it could not impose upon a seller other than the issuing corporation the duty of registering his stock unless the shareholder was in a position to require the issuing corporation to seek registration. "Control" of the corporation thus became an essential factor in cases of secondary distribution.

In the light of this purpose a practical test for control has been suggested: "Is a particular person in a position to obtain the required signatures of the issuer and its officers and directors on a registration statement?" 1 L. Loss, *Securities Regulations* 557 (2d ed. 1961).

Where a secondary distribution of significant proportions is involved it is not unreasonable, in our judgment, to impose upon the seller the burden of establishing his inability to secure the necessary corporate action.

2. Magnuson's Control of Silver Buckle

Silver Buckle was organized in 1947 with F. Scott, its organizer, serving as president and director throughout its corporate existence. . . . Magnuson was the holder of [less than 2% of outstanding] shares. He was not an officer or director [of Silver Buckle]. The SEC has found him to be a controlling person on that date [May 1962] and that his control continued throughout the life of Silver Buckle. Although conceding that he later occupied a position of control, petitioners strenuously assert that he was not in such a position [at that time].

"Control" is not to be determined by artificial tests, but is an issue to be determined from the particular circumstances of the case. . . . Under Rule 405, it is not

---

8. H.R. Rep. No. 85, 73d Cong., 1st Sess., 13–14 (1933):

Its [§ 2(a)(11)] second function is to bring within the provisions of the bill redistribution whether of outstanding issues or issues sold subsequently to the enactment of the bill. All the outstanding stock of a particular corporation may be owned by one individual or a select group of individuals. At some future date they may wish to dispose of their holdings and to make an offer of this stock to the public. Such a public offering may possess all the dangers attendant upon a new offering of securities. Wherever such a redistribution reaches significant proportions, the distributor is treated as equivalent to the original issuer and, if he seeks to dispose of the issue through a public offering, he becomes subject to the Act.

necessary that one be an officer, director, manager, or even shareholder to be a controlling person. Further, control may exist although not continuously and actively exercised.

. . . The Commission scrutinized [Magnuson's] prior relations with those individuals who clearly constituted the Silver Buckle control group. It concluded that his connection with two important subsidiary corporations, the group's reliance upon his assistance, their close relationship in enterprises other than Silver Buckle, and the freedom with which the group felt able to call upon him for assistance in their efforts to retain control supported the conclusion that [Magnuson] was a member of the Silver Buckle control group during the period from May, 1962, on. We cannot say that this conclusion was without sufficient foundation. . . .

[*Affirmed in part; reversed in part.*]

Note

The foregoing decision illustrates that, *based on relationships alone*, one can be a control person. This can be the case even if one does not have a director or officer position with the corporation and owns a small percentage (or relatively few shares) of the corporation. For more recent cases holding that the subject defendants were affiliates or control persons, see *SEC v. Cavanaugh,* 445 F.3d 105 (2d. Cir. 2006); *SEC v. Kern,* 425 F.3d 143 (2d. Cir. 2005); *SEC v. Zenergy International, Inc.,* 2015 WL 5731652 (N.D. Ill. 2015).

[B] Contractual Agreements to Sell

As the foregoing material observes, only the issuer can register a secondary public offering. This consequence is not unduly onerous, according to proponents, because a controlling person has the leverage for inducing the issuer to file a registration statement and to elicit adequate disclosure on the part of such an issuer. Because of the ambiguities associated with the concept of control, a person who may be viewed as an affiliate may contract with the issuer when he/she acquires the stock for the right of demand registration, thereby granting the control person the contractual right to demand that the issuer file a 1933 Act registration statement when the person wishes to dispose of his/her stock. If the purported "control person" does not have such leverage, he/she may settle for the right of "piggy-back" registration. This right, looking to the terms of the covenant negotiated, authorizes the control person to sell ("piggy-back") his/her stock or a portion thereof at the time that the issuer elects to file a registration statement. *See* O'Hare, *Institutional Investors, Registration Rights, and the Specter of Liability Under Section 11 of the Securities Act of 1933,* 1996 Wis. L. Rev. 217 (1996).

[1] Provision of Rule 15c2-11 Information

In any event, such "control person" should insist that the issuer covenant to provide Rule 15c2-11 information. Generally, Rule 15c2-11 prohibits broker-dealers from publishing a quotation for any security unless specified information is available with respect to the issuer and the security. In effect, the rule prevents the widespread distribution of securities without certain minimal information being publicly available. Hence, the following information is required to be reasonably current and to be made reasonably available by the subject broker or dealer upon the request of a prospective purchaser:

(i) the exact name of the issuer and its predecessor (if any);

(ii) the address of its principal executive offices;

(iii) the state of incorporation, if it is a corporation;

(iv) the exact title and class of the security;

(v) the par or stated value of the security;

(vi) the number of shares or total amount of the securities outstanding as of the end of the issuer's most recent fiscal year;

(vii) the name and address of the transfer agent;

(viii) the nature of the issuer's business;

(ix) the nature of products or services offered;

(x) the nature and extent of the issuer's facilities;

(xi) the name of the chief executive officer and members of the board of directors;

(xii) the issuer's most recent balance sheet and profit and loss and retained earnings statements;

(xiii) similar financial information for such part of the two preceding fiscal years as the issuer or its predecessor has been in existence;

(xiv) whether the broker or dealer or any associated person is affiliated, directly or indirectly with the issuer;

(xv) whether the quotation is being published or submitted on behalf of any other broker or dealer, and, if so, the name of such broker or dealer; and

(xvi) whether the quotation is being submitted or published directly or indirectly on behalf of the issuer, or any director, officer or any person, directly or indirectly the beneficial owner of more than 10 percent of the outstanding units or shares of any equity security of the issuer, and, if so, the name of such person, and the basis for any exemption under the federal securities laws for any sales of such securities on behalf of such person.

Importantly, if the control person induces the issuer to disseminate Rule 15c2-11 information, the "current information" requirement of Rule 144, which provides a safe harbor in the resale context, will be satisfied. See §6.04.

[2] Letter from Issuer's Counsel

Note, moreover, that when restricted securities are involved, the securities will contain a restrictive legend or stop transfer instructions. To have the securities transaction consummated, including removal of the legends or "stops," "the issuer's securities law counsel (or other designated 'point person' for the issuer) [must] authorize [by written communication] the transfer agent to transfer the stock into the 'street name' of the selling securities broker-dealer firm, free of legends and free of stops." Barron, *Control and Restricted Securities*, 28 SEC. REG. L.J. 74, 75 (2000).

[3] Additional Pitfalls

As a final point, even where the control person in a secondary distribution induces the issuer to file a *registration statement*, there remain significant pitfalls. One particular concern is disclosure. For example, where all or a part of the proceeds of the offering will be paid to selling shareholders rather than to the issuer, the registration statement must carefully disclose this consequence.[9] Another problem is that shareholders effecting a secondary registered offering may be tempted to manipulate the price of the stock. The SEC, aware of the potential for abuse, has brought enforcement actions in this context and has promulgated a number of rules designed to curtail such manipulative activity.[10]

[C] PIPES

A relatively recent development with respect to the registration of secondary offerings concerns "PIPES" (Private Investments in Public Equity). Generally, PIPES involve the purchase of securities in an issuer private placement (such as pursuant to §4(a)(2) or Rule 506), the issuer's subsequent registration of the restricted stock with the SEC, and, upon effectiveness of the registration statement, the ability of the PIPE investors to resell immediately their stock into the public markets. PIPES frequently are priced at a discount to the then current public market price (such as that quoted on the Nasdaq). As an additional "sweetener," PIPE investors may receive "warrants" priced attractively that may be exercised at some point in the future.

If structured improperly, PIPES can cause significant shareholder dilution. Moreover, because the price of a subject issuer's stock often drops once a PIPE transaction becomes known, insider trading concerns have developed. Nonetheless, PIPES may be viewed as providing a useful means for obtaining capital for smaller publicly held companies that experience difficulty raising funds due to their inability to

---

9. *See, e.g.*, Item 507 of SEC Regulation S-K; *In the Matter of Universal Camera Corp.*, 19 S.E.C. 648 (1945).

10. *See, e.g.*, SEC Regulation M; *In the Matter of Hazel Bishop, Inc.*, 40 S.E.C. 718 (1961).

undertake traditional private or public offerings or procure loans on favorable terms from financial institutions.

During the past decade, tens of billions of dollars have been raised in PIPE deals. In response, the SEC has become more vigorous in scrutinizing the disclosures made in these arrangements, thereby signifying that PIPES may become less popular. *See SEC v. Lyon*, 529 F. Supp. 2d 444 (S.D.N.Y 2008); Burns, *SEC Slows Flow of PIPE Deals to a Trickle*, Wall St. J. (online), Dec. 27, 2006); Lerner, *Disclosing Toxic PIPES*, 58 Bus. Law. 655 (2003); Sjostrom, *PIPES*, 2 Entre. Bus. L.J. 381 (2007); Steinberg & Obi, *Examining the Pipeline: A Contemporary Assessment of Private Investments in Public Equity ("PIPES")*, 11 U. Pa. J. Bus. L. 1 (2008); A Friedland Capital White Paper, *Overview: Private Investment in Public Equity ("PIPES")* (July 25, 2005), available at www.friedlandworldwide.com.

[D] Effecting a Distribution

The Securities Act does not explicitly hold the conduct of controlling persons illegal when they effect a distribution of unregistered shares through an underwriter. Of course, what a statute fails expressly to do a court can accomplish through construing the statute's pertinent language, legislative history, and policy rationales. In *United States v. Wolfson*, 405 F.2d 779 (2d Cir. 1968), the Second Circuit held that a group of controlling persons, Wolfson and his cohorts, violated § 5 because they effected an unregistered distribution of securities through several unwitting brokerage houses.

The Court observed that the § 4(a)(1) exemption "by its terms exempts only transactions." Hence, because Wolfson and his cronies were effecting a "distribution," they could not avail themselves of the § 4(a)(1) exemption. As the Seventh Circuit more recently stated:

> Section 4(1) [now § 4(a)(1)] provides an exemption for *transactions, not individuals*. It was created to exempt routine trading *transactions* with respect to securities already issued and *not to exempt distributions* by issuers or acts of others who engage in steps necessary to such distributions.

SEC v. Holschuh, 694 F.2d 130, 137–138 (7th Cir. 1982) (emphasis added). See *SEC v. Kern*, 425 F.3d 143, 152–153 (2d Cir. 2005); *SEC v. Murphy*, 626 F.2d 633, 648 (9th Cir. 1980). As an additional point from the *Wolfson* case, the six brokerage houses, although unable to invoke the § 4(a)(1) exemption, were not subject to the § 5 requirements due to the § 4(a)(4) exemption. The court supported this conclusion by finding that each of the unwitting brokerage houses effected only transactions (unaware of the "distribution"), the transactions were solicited by Wolfson, and the transactions were executed in the over-the-counter market. (For an interesting article on Louis Wolfson, see Weinberger, *What's in a Name?—The Tale of Louis Wolfson's Affirmed*, 39 Hofstra L. Rev. 645 (2011)).

An earlier case, *Ira Haupt & Co.*, 23 S.E.C. 589 (1946), had the effect of making brokers wary of selling a controlling person's shares. Schulte controlled Park & Tilford, Inc. He gave a series of sell orders, involving around 200 shares per order, to his broker Haupt. During a six-month period, 93,000 shares were sold pursuant to these orders. Haupt was charged with violating § 5 for its role in effecting the unregistered offering. Haupt proffered two defenses. *First*, Haupt argued that its sales of Park & Tilford shares were not a distribution because there was no plan to sell a specified number of shares. The Commission rejected this defense, finding that the facts and circumstances clearly put Haupt on notice that a distribution was anticipated.

Second, the broker Haupt claimed the § 4(a)(4) exemption, which, *inter alia*, exempts "brokers' transactions executed upon customers' orders on any exchange. . . ." In rejecting this defense, the SEC reasoned that the § 4(a)(4) exemption does not exempt brokers from § 5 when they act as underwriters in a "distribution." The SEC defined a "distribution" as "[t]he entire process by which in the course of a public offering the block of securities is dispersed and ultimately comes to rest in the hands of the investing public." Here, *Haupt* was effecting a "distribution" rather than engaging in a "transaction." As will be discussed later in the chapter, to alleviate some of the concern generated by the *Haupt* decision, the SEC promulgated Rule 144.

[E] Broker-Dealer Reasonable Inquiry

The SEC adopted Rule 144 in 1972. As will be examined in § 6.04, Rule 144 provides a safe harbor for both the broker and the individual in the resale context.

A broker-dealer must focus on seeking to ensure that it is not selling on behalf of a control person in connection with a distribution or otherwise participating in a distribution. In this setting, "reasonable inquiry" by a broker-dealer is a necessity. As the SEC has stated:

> A dealer who offers to sell, or is asked to sell a substantial amount of securities must take whatever steps are necessary to be sure that this is a transaction not involving an issuer, person in a control relationship with an issuer, or an underwriter. For this purpose, it is not sufficient for him merely to accept self-serving statements of his sellers and their counsel without reasonably exploring the possibility of contrary facts.
>
> The amount of inquiry called for necessarily varies with the circumstances of particular cases. A dealer who is offered a modest amount of a widely traded security by a responsible customer, whose lack of relationship to the issuer is well known to him, may ordinarily proceed with considerable confidence. On the other hand, when a dealer is offered a substantial block of a little-known security, either by persons who appear reluctant to disclose exactly where the securities came from, or where the surrounding

circumstances raise a question as to whether or not the ostensible sellers may be merely intermediaries for controlling persons or statutory underwriters, then searching inquiry is called for.

Securities Act Release No. 4445 (1962). In a subsequent release, the Commission elaborated:

> While the amount of inquiry called for necessarily varies with the circumstances of particular cases, all registered broker-dealers should establish minimum standard procedures to prevent and detect violations of the federal securities laws and to ensure that the firm meets its continuing responsibility to know both its customers and the securities being sold. There should be written supervisory procedures that cover sales as well as purchases. These must be made known to salesmen and be sufficient to reveal promptly to supervisory officials transactions which may, when examined individually or in the aggregate, indicate that sales in a security should be halted immediately pending further inquiry.
>
> Registered broker-dealers should also establish standard procedures as an initial step in their general investigation into the background of prospective customers and the source of the securities to be traded. In the case of a new customer, a new account form identifying the customer and describing his financial condition and investment objectives should be completed before sales are made. A firm should not permit accounts to be opened by third persons or orders accepted from third persons on behalf of a customer without the customer's express authorization. In addition, registered broker-dealers should make certain routine inquiries of customers, including, for example: whether the customer has direct or indirect connections with any publicly owned company or with the issuer; what his financial condition is (so that the broker-dealer may determine whether it is consistent with the value of the securities to be sold); whether the customer's securities were acquired on the open market; whether he is the true beneficial owner of them; whether he has non-public information about the issuer and whether he is currently selling or attempting to sell the same securities through other brokerage houses.
>
> Basic information concerning the issuer such as its address, business activities, principals, products, assets, financial condition and number of shares of stock outstanding, should be obtained independently as a matter of course. Where public information concerning the company is not available from the Commission or standard research sources, the extent of inquiry required to reasonably assure the broker or dealer that the proposed transaction complies with applicable legal requirements will be correspondingly greater.

Securities Act Release No. 5168 (1972). *See also* Rule 144(g)(3) (defining the term "brokers' transactions" to require, *inter alia*, that the broker, after conducting a "reasonable inquiry," "is not aware of circumstances indicating that the person for whose account the securities are sold is an underwriter with respect to the securities or that the transaction is a part of a distribution of securities of the issuer").

In a more recent release, the Commission once again asserted its position with respect to the appropriate level of a broker's diligence in this setting:

> [A] dealer who offers to sell, or is asked to sell a substantial amount of securities must take whatever steps are necessary, to be sure that this is a transaction not involving an issuer, person in a control relationship with an issuer, or an underwriter. For this purpose, it is not sufficient for him merely to accept self-serving statements of his sellers and their counsel without reasonably exploring the possibility of contrary facts.

In re Transactions in Securities of Laser Arms Corporation by Certain Broker-Dealers, [1990–1991 Transfer Binder] Fed. Sec. L. Rep. (CCH) ¶ 84,724 (SEC 1991). *See* FINRA Regulatory Notice 09-05 (2009) (emphasizing to broker-dealer firms their responsibilities to conduct adequate diligence when participating in unregistered sales of restricted securities). For recent appellate court decisions holding brokers liable under § 5 for failure to conduct a reasonable inquiry in this context, *see Bloomfield v. SEC*, [2016 Transfer Binder] Fed. Sec. L. Rep. (CCH) ¶ 99,083 (9th Cir. 2016); *World Trade Financial Corporation v. SEC*, 739 F.3d 1243 (9th Cir. 2014); *Wonsover v. SEC*, 205 F.3d 408 (D.C. Cir. 2000).

---

§ 6.04 Rule 144

[A] Background

Historically, that a non-affiliate acquired securities pursuant to a § 4(a)(2) private placement exemption did not thereafter preclude such person from reselling the securities. For example, as discussed earlier, a non-affiliate holding restricted securities (e.g., securities acquired pursuant to offerings made under § 4(a)(2) or Rule 506) normally could resell such securities after a substantial holding period, such as two or three years. Moreover, in certain situations, such non-affiliates, who acquired restricted securities allegedly for investment, could resell them pursuant to § 4(a)(1), notwithstanding a relatively recent acquisition date, if the seller could demonstrate a "change of circumstances." Nonetheless, given that the burden of proving the perfection of an exemption is upon the seller, prudent parties exercised utmost caution when disposing of their securities without registration.

The situation for affiliates, and broker-dealers that executed orders to sell securities for the account of affiliates, was even more onerous. As a result of the SEC's 1946 administrative proceeding in *Ira Haupt*, discussed above, it was difficult for the broker to determine whether an affiliate, when disposing of stock, was engaging in a "distribution" of the issuer's securities. The confusion that broker-dealers faced in attempting to determine whether a distribution would occur led the SEC to adopt Rule 154 in 1951.[11] Unfortunately, Rule 154 was of limited value because it was designed for brokers, but offered no protection to those persons on behalf of whom the sale was executed.[12]

After extensive analysis, the "Wheat Report" was issued in 1969.[13] The Report recommended a series of rules that sought to clarify the circumstances under which an affiliate or a non-affiliate could rely upon §4(a)(1) for resale transactions. In 1970, the SEC set forth a single proposed rule as an alternative to the series recommended by the Wheat Report.[14] It was called Proposed Rule 144 and was designed to continue the SEC's efforts towards providing objective standards with respect to the availability of the §4(a)(1) exemption. Finally, after lively debate and extensive public comments and suggestions, the final version of Rule 144 was adopted in 1972.[15]

Generally, Rule 144 acts as a safe harbor from incurring liability under the registration provisions of the Securities Act. It permits the public sale in ordinary trading transactions of supposedly limited amounts of securities owned by persons controlling, controlled by, or under common control with the issuer (i.e., "affiliates"), and by other persons who have acquired "restricted securities" of the issuer. Hence, Rule 144 protects certain resale transactions from the Securities Act's registration mandates when such transactions are engaged in by: (1) "non-affiliated" persons who have acquired securities from either the issuer or an affiliate of the issuer in a transaction not involving a public offering ("restricted securities"), (2) persons who are deemed to be "affiliates" of the issuer at the time they propose to resell any securities of the issuer (irrespective whether such securities are restricted or unrestricted), and (3) brokers who effect transactions in compliance with the Rule.

The safe harbor derived from Rule 144 is important to the functioning of the securities markets. Absent the availability of an exemption, all sales of securities must be registered under §5 of the Act. The exemptions normally available in the resale context are §4(a)(1) for sellers and §4(a)(4) for brokers. Their application under a given set of conditions, however, may be problematic. By creating a safe harbor for perfecting these exemptions, Rule 144 seeks to provide greater clarity in this area.[16]

---

11. *See* Securities Act Release No. 3421 (1951), *as amended by* Securities Act Release No. 3525 (1954).

12. *See* S. Goldberg, *Private Placements and Restricted Securities* §7.1 (rev. ed. 1982).

13. *See Disclosure to Investors — A Reappraisal of Federal Administrative Policies Under the '33 and '34 Acts* (1969) ("Wheat Report").

14. *See* Securities Act Release No. 5087 (1970).

15. Securities Act Release No. 5223 (1972). *See* J.W. Hicks, Exempted Transactions Under the Securities Act of 1933 §10.02[2] (2012).

16. *See* Campbell, *Resales of Securities: The New Rules and the New Approach of the SEC,* 37 Sec. Reg. L.J. 317 (2009); M. Pollock, *Resale of Restricted Securities,* Corporate Practice Series (BNA) No. 46 (1986); Fogelson, *Rule 144 — A Summary Overview,* 37 Bus. Law. 1519 (1981).

[B] Provisions of the Rule

Since its adoption in 1972, Rule 144 has been amended several times and substantially liberalized. The basic purpose of Rule 144, however, has remained the same. Generally, with certain caveats, Rule 144 provides a safe harbor under the §4(a)(1) exemption for investors (e.g., institutional as well as individual investors) who are selling their securities without registration, and for brokers under the §4(a)(4) exemption who are effecting sales of such securities. Rule 144 provides this safe harbor through an objective set of provisions, premised on the rationale that some relaxation of Securities Act disclosure and registration requirements is appropriate with respect to relatively small secondary transactions. If the investor and the broker make the sales in compliance with the conditions set forth in Rule 144, they will not be deemed to be "underwriters" or engaged in a "distribution."[17]

An understanding of certain terms is crucial to an understanding of Rule 144. Rule 144 defines an "affiliate" of an issuer as a "person that directly, or indirectly through one or more intermediaries, controls, or is controlled by, or is under common control with, such an issuer." In addition, Rule 144 defines "restricted" securities as those "securities that are acquired directly or indirectly from the issuer, or from an affiliate of the issuer, in a transaction or chain of transactions not involving any public offering, or securities acquired from the issuer that are subject to the resale limitations of Regulation D under the Act, or securities that are subject to the resale limitations of Regulation D and are acquired in a transaction or chain of transactions not involving any public offering." Hence, such restricted securities include, for example, those acquired in offerings pursuant to §4(a)(2), Rule 505, Rule 506, and Rule 701. By contrast, *non*restricted securities include those securities that were sold pursuant to a Securities Act registered offering, as well as those sold pursuant to Regulation A Plus and a Rule 504 state registered offering.

The foregoing definitions are important. In certain situations, Rule 144 treats affiliates and non-affiliates differently. For example:

- only non-affiliates can resell restricted securities of non-reporting companies free of Rule 144 requirements after holding the securities for one year (see Rule 144(b)(1);[18]

- Rule 144's holding requirements pertain only to restricted securities; and

- affiliates holding nonrestricted securities may resell a specified amount of their securities pursuant to Rule 144 without being subject to a holding period.

Note that Rule 144 does not address the area of non-affiliates selling nonrestricted securities.

---

17. *See* D. Goldwasser, *A Guide to Rule 144* (2d ed. 1978); Ash in 11 H. Sowards, Federal Securities Act §6B.01 (1987); Gilroy & Kaufman in 3 A.A. Sommer, Securities Law Techniques §38.01 (1987).

18. *See* Securities Act Release No. 8869 (2007).

To utilize Rule 144 a person must meet five general requirements, some of which have been eliminated or substantially modified by the SEC in certain circumstances.

First, there must be adequate current information concerning the issuer (see Rule 144(c)). This requirement is in accord with the underlying policy of the Securities Act which is to protect investors through adequate and fair disclosure. The information requirement can be satisfied in either of two ways: (1) the issuer can be subject to and be currently complying with the reporting requirements of the Exchange Act, or (2) if the issuer is not a 1934 Act reporting company, the issuer can publicly make information available pursuant to Exchange Act Rule 15c2-11 (see § 6.03[B] which sets forth the Rule 15c2-11 information requirements). If the purchaser has sufficient leverage, he or she may contract with the issuer that it be required to furnish the Rule 15c2-11 information.

Second, the person seeking to sell the restricted securities (e.g., stock acquired in a Rule 506 offering) must meet the holding period established by Rule 144 (see Rule 144(d)). This holding period is six-months for restricted securities of Exchange Act reporting issuers and one-year for restricted securities of non-reporting issuers. The holding period seeks to ensure that the person assumed an investment stake in the prior purchase(s) and has not acted merely as the issuer's conduit for a sale to the public of unregistered securities.

The holding period runs from the date of purchase from the issuer or an affiliate of the issuer. Hence, a subsequent purchaser's acquisition of stock from a control person will trigger the start of the holding period as will an initial purchase from the issuer. Importantly, note that, in determining the requisite holding period, a non-affiliate may "tack" to his/her holding period those of prior holders who were unaffiliated with the issuer.[19]

---

19. *See* Securities Act Release No. 7390 (1997). In reducing the Rule 144 holding periods, the SEC asserted that this reduction will decrease "compliance burdens and costs without significant impact on investor protection. . . . [A]lso the [amendments] will promote market efficiency, investment and capital formation by reducing the liquidity costs of holding restricted securities and reducing issuers' cost of raising capital through the sale of restricted securities." Accord, Securities Exchange Release No. 8869 (2007).

With respect to "tacking," *see* Securities Act Release No. 6862 (1990). In expanding the "tacking" periods for non-affiliates owning restricted securities, the Commission explained:

> Under Rule 144, as previously in effect, restricted securities generally were required to be held for at least two years before the holder could sell the securities in reliance upon the safe-harbor provisions of Rule 144. Except in limited instances, the holding period of predecessor owners was not combined with, or "tacked" to, the holding period of the person wishing to sell in reliance on Rule 144.

As a result of its reexamination of the tacking concept embodies in Rule 144, the Commission today is amending the Rule to permit holders of restricted securities acquired in a transaction or series of transactions not involving any public offering to add to their own holding period those of prior holders unaffiliated with the issuer. No such tacking will be permitted, however, where the seller has purchased from an affiliate of the issuer whose presence in the chain of title will trigger the commencement of a new holding period. . . .

Third, Rule 144 places restrictions on the amount of sales of common stock or similar equity security *an affiliate* can make during a given period in reliance on the Rule (see Rule 144(e)). This requirement is designed to ensure that a "distribution" does not take place and to lessen the impact of these sales on the trading markets. Generally, *with certain exceptions* (see Rule 144(b)(1) discussed later in this section), sales of such equity securities by an affiliate under Rule 144 during any three-month period cannot exceed the greater of: (1) one percent of the shares of that class outstanding as shown by the most recent statement of the issuer; or (2) the average weekly trading volume reported on all exchanges (and/or through NASDAQ or the consolidated transaction reporting system) for the four weeks preceding the filing of notice as specified in Rule 144(h). Note that the volume limitation for the resale of debt securities (as well as non-convertible preferred stock and asset-backed securities) is set at a higher level. Pursuant to amended Rule 144(e), resales are permitted of such securities "in an amount that does not exceed ten percent of a tranche (or class when the securities are non-participatory, preferred stock) together with all sales of securities of the same tranche sold for the account of the selling security holder within a three-month period." Securities Act Release No. 8869 (2007).

Fourth, under Rule 144, equity securities must be resold by affiliates in ordinary brokerage transactions within the meaning of § 4(a)(4) or in transactions directly with a market maker, without solicitation, or through riskless principal transactions.[20] An affiliate seeking to rely on Rule 144 for the sale of equity securities must not "solicit or arrange for the solicitation of orders to buy securities in anticipation of or in connection with such transactions."[21] The SEC has eliminated these manner of sale requirements with respect to resales of debt securities.

As an additional point, the broker must receive no more than the usual and customary broker's commission. Finally, with respect to sales by an affiliate during a three-month period that exceed 5,000 shares or have a sales price greater than $50,000, notice of each such sale must be filed with the SEC.

The "brokers' transactions" requirement referred to above (see Rule 144(f)) must be distinguished from the requirements with the same name in Rule 144(g). Rule 144(f) is one of the conditions that must be met by a seller intending to rely on the Rule. The broker also must find an exemption for its role in the transaction. Rule 144(g), by defining the term "brokers' transactions" and by delineating aspects of "reasonable inquiry" to be conducted by the broker, greatly assists the broker in meeting Rule 144's safe harbor and thereby perfect the § 4(a)(4) exemption.[22] This subject also was addressed above in § 6.03[E].

---

20. A "riskless principal transaction" is a transaction whereby a broker-dealer, upon receiving a "buy order" from a customer purchases the subject security in the market as principal to effectuate the buy order or, upon receiving a sell order from a customer, sells the subject security in the market as principal to satisfy the sell order.

21. Rule 144(f), 17 C.F.R. § 230.144(f).

22. *See* Securities Act Release Nos. 4445 (1962), 5168 (1972); *In re Transactions in Securities of Laser Arms Corporation by Certain Broker-Dealers,* [1990–1991 Transfer Binder] Fed. Sec. L. Rep.

To invoke the exemption from Securities Act registration provided by Rule 144, all conditions of the rule must be satisfied. Rule 144 is a "safe harbor" and, hence, is nonexclusive. Accordingly, even though a person has not met the conditions of Rule 144, he/she still may seek to invoke another exemption, such as the statutory §4(a)(1) exemption.[23] In the Rule 144 adopting release, however, the SEC asserted that "persons who offer or sell restricted securities without complying with Rule 144 are hereby put on notice by the Commission that . . . they will have a substantial burden of proof that an exemption from registration is available. . . ." See *SEC v. M&A West, Inc.*, 538 F.3d 1043 (9th Cir. 2008); *SEC v. Cavanaugh*, 445 F.3d 105, 114 (2d Cir. 2006).

As will be discussed in the following 2007 SEC Release, Rule 144(b)(1) is the major exception to the foregoing requirements. Under Rule 144(b)(1), a non-affiliate who has held the restricted securities for the requisite amount of time (for example, one year with respect to restricted securities of a non-reporting issuer) may resell such securities free of Rule 144's restrictions. The period is measured from the date of acquisition from the issuer or from an affiliate of the issuer.

Rule 144 Amendments

Securities Act Release No. 8869 (2007)

Rule 144 under the Securities Act of 1933 creates a safe harbor for the sale of securities under the exemption set forth in Section 4(1) [now §4(a)(1)] of the Securities Act. We are shortening the holding period requirement under Rule 144 for "restricted securities" of issuers that are subject to the reporting requirements of the Securities Exchange Act of 1934 to six months. Restricted securities of issuers that are not subject to the Exchange Act reporting requirements will continue to be subject to a one-year holding period prior to any public resale. The amendments also substantially reduce the restrictions applicable to the resale of securities by non-affiliates. In addition, the amendments simplify the Preliminary Note to Rule 144, amend the manner of sale requirements and eliminate them with respect to debt securities, amend the volume limitations for debt securities, increase the Form 144 filing thresholds, and codify several staff interpretive positions that relate to Rule 144. Finally, we are eliminating the presumptive underwriter provision in Securities Act Rule 145, except for transactions involving a shell company, and revising the resale requirements in Rule 145(d). We believe that the amendments will increase the liquidity of privately

---

(CCH) ¶ 84,724 (SEC 1991). In the *Laser Arms* proceeding, the Commission reaffirmed its position with respect to the appropriate level of a broker's diligence in this setting:

> [A] dealer who offers to sell, or is asked to sell a substantial amount of securities must take whatever steps are necessary, to be sure that this is a transaction not involving an issuer, person in a control relationship with an issuer, or an underwriter. For this purpose, it is not sufficient for him merely to accept self-serving statements of his sellers and their counsel without reasonably exploring the possibility of contrary facts.

23. Securities Act Release No. 5223 (1972).

sold securities and decrease the cost of capital for all issuers without compromising investor protection.

. . . .

I. Background

The Securities Act of 1933 ("Securities Act") requires registration of all offers and sales of securities in interstate commerce or by use of the U.S. mails, unless an exemption from the registration requirement is available. Section 4(1) [now §4(a)(1)] of the Securities Act provides such an exemption for transactions by any person other than an issuer, underwriter or dealer.

The definition of the term "underwriter" is key to the operation of the Section 4(1) exemption. Section 2(a)(11) of the Securities Act defines an underwriter as "any person who has purchased from an issuer with a view to, or offers or sells for an issuer in connection with, the distribution of any security, or participates or has a direct or indirect participation in any such undertaking." The Securities Act does not, however, provide specific criteria for determining when a person purchases securities "with a view to . . . the distribution" of those securities. In 1972, the Commission adopted Rule 144 to provide a safe harbor from this definition of "underwriter" to assist security holders in determining whether the Section 4(1) exemption is available for their resale of securities. [Securities Act Release No. 5223 (1972)]

Rule 144 regulates the resale of two categories of securities—restricted securities and control securities. Restricted securities are securities acquired pursuant to one of the transactions listed in Rule 144(a)(3) [such as §4(a)(2) or Rule 506]. Although it is not a term defined in Rule 144, "control securities" is used commonly to refer to securities held by an affiliate of the issuer, regardless of how the affiliate acquired the securities. Therefore, if an affiliate acquires securities in a transaction that is listed in Rule 144(a)(3), those securities are both restricted securities and control securities. A person selling restricted securities, or a person selling restricted or other securities on behalf of the account of an affiliate, who satisfies all of Rule 144's applicable conditions in connection with the transaction, is deemed not to be an "underwriter," as defined in Section 2(a)(11) of the Securities Act. . . .

Since its adoption, we have reviewed and revised Rule 144 several times. We last made major changes in 1997 ("1997 amendments"). [Securities Act Release No. 7391 (1997)] At that time, we shortened the required holding periods for restricted securities. Before the 1997 amendments, security holders could resell restricted securities under Rule 144, subject to limitation, after two years, and persons who were not affiliates and had not been affiliates during the prior three months, could resell restricted securities without limitation after three years. The 1997 amendments changed these two-year and three-year periods to one-year and two-year periods, respectively.

. . . .

Rule 144 states that a selling security holder shall be deemed not to be engaged in a distribution of securities, and therefore not an underwriter, with respect to such securities, thus making available the Section 4(1) exemption from registration, if the resale satisfies specified conditions. The conditions include the following:

- There must be adequate current public information available about the issuer;

- If the securities being sold are restricted securities, the security holder must have held the security for a specified holding period;

- The resale must be within specified sales volume limitations;

- The resale must comply with the manner of sale requirements; and

- The selling security holder must file Form 144 if the amount of securities being sold exceeds specified thresholds.

Rule 144, as it existed before today's amendments, permitted a non-affiliate to publicly resell restricted securities without being subject to the above limitations if the securities had been held for two years or more, provided that the security holder was not, and, for the three months prior to the sale, had not been, an affiliate of the issuer.

[In] July 2007, we again proposed to amend several aspects of Rule 144 and Rule 145, including by further shortening the holding periods (the "2007 Proposing Release"). [Securities Act Release No. 8813 (2007)]. . . .

II. Discussion of Final Amendments

A. Simplification of the Preliminary Note and Text of Rule 144

We are adopting the amendments to the Preliminary Note with some modification from the proposed version. . . . Consistent with the proposal, the revised Preliminary Note clarifies that any person who sells restricted securities, and any person who sells restricted securities or other securities on behalf of an affiliate, shall be deemed not to be engaged in a distribution of such securities and therefore shall be deemed not to be an underwriter with respect to such securities if the sale in question is made in accordance with all the applicable provisions of the rule. The revised Preliminary Note further states that, although Rule 144 provides a safe harbor for establishing the availability of the Section 4(1) exemption, it is not the exclusive means for reselling restricted and control securities. Therefore, Rule 144 does not eliminate or otherwise affect the availability of any other exemption for resales. Consistent with a statement that was included in the original Rule 144 adopting release, we are adding a statement to the Preliminary Note that the Rule 144 safe harbor is not available with respect to any transaction or series of transactions that, although in technical compliance with the rule, is part of a plan or scheme to evade the registration requirements of the Securities Act. We also are adopting plain English changes throughout the rule text substantially as proposed.

B. Amendments to Holding Periods for Restricted Securities

1. Six-Month Rule 144(d) Holding Period Requirement for Exchange Act Reporting Companies

As stated above, in 1997, we reduced the Rule 144 holding periods for restricted securities for both affiliates and non-affiliates. Before the 1997 amendments, security holders could sell limited amounts of restricted securities after holding those securities for two years if they satisfied all other conditions imposed by Rule 144. Under Rule 144(k) [now Rule 144(b)(1)], non-affiliates could sell restricted securities without being subject to any of the conditions in Rule 144 after holding their securities for three years. The 1997 amendments to Rule 144 reduced the two-year Rule 144(d) holding period to one year and amended the three-year Rule 144(k) holding period to two years.

. . . .

The purpose of Rule 144 is to provide objective criteria for determining that the person selling securities to the public has not acquired the securities from the issuer for distribution. A holding period is one criterion established to demonstrate that the selling security holder did not acquire the securities to be sold under Rule 144 with distributive intent. We do not want the holding period to be longer than necessary or impose any unnecessary costs or restrictions on capital formation. After observing the operation of Rule 144 since the 1997 amendments, we believe that a six-month holding period for securities of reporting issuers provides a reasonable indication that an investor has assumed the economic risk of investment in the securities to be resold under Rule 144. *Therefore, we are adopting a six-month holding period for reporting companies. . . .* [emphasis supplied]

Most commenters agreed that shortening the holding period to six months for restricted securities of reporting issuers will increase the liquidity of privately sold securities and decrease the cost of capital for reporting issuers, while still being consistent with investor protection. By reducing the holding period for restricted securities, these amendments are intended to help companies to raise capital more easily and less expensively. For example, by making private offerings more attractive, the amendments may allow some companies to avoid certain types of costly financing structures involving the issuance of extremely dilutive convertible securities. Many commenters supported the proposal to maintain the existing one-year holding period for restricted securities of non-reporting issuers.

Under the amendments that we are adopting, the six-month holding period requirement will apply to the securities of an issuer that has been subject to the reporting requirements of Section 13 or 15(d) of the Exchange Act for a period of at least 90 days before the Rule 144 sale. *Restricted securities of a "non-reporting issuer" will continue to be subject to a one-year holding period requirement.* A non-reporting issuer is one that is not, or has not been for a period of at least 90 days before the Rule 144 sale, subject to the reporting requirements of Section 13 or 15(d) of the Exchange Act.

We believe that different holding periods for reporting and non-reporting issuers are appropriate given that reporting issuers have an obligation to file periodic reports with updated financial information (including audited financial information in annual filings) that are publicly available on EDGAR, the Commission's electronic filing system. Although non-reporting issuers must make some information publicly available before resales can be made under Rule 144, this information typically is much more limited in scope than information included in Exchange Act reports, is not required to include audited financial information, and is not publicly available via EDGAR. For these reasons, we believe that continuing to require security holders of non-reporting issuers to hold their securities for one year is not unduly burdensome and is consistent with investor protection.

2. Significant Reduction of Conditions Applicable to Non-Affiliates

Before adoption of these amendments, both non-affiliates and affiliates were subject to all other applicable conditions of Rule 144, in addition to the Rule 144(d) holding period requirement, including the condition that current information about the issuer of the securities be publicly available, the limitations on the amount of securities that may be sold in any three-month period, the manner of sale requirements and the Form 144 notice requirement. However, pursuant to paragraph (k) of Rule 144 as it existed prior to the amendments that we are adopting, a non-affiliate of the issuer at the time of the Rule 144 sale who had not been an affiliate during the three months prior to the sale, could sell the securities after holding them for two years without complying with these other conditions.

In the 2007 Proposing Release, we proposed to permit non-affiliates to resell their restricted securities freely after meeting the applicable holding period requirement (i.e., six months with respect to a reporting issuer and one year with respect to a non-reporting issuer), except that non-affiliates of reporting issuers still would be subject to the current public information requirement in Rule 144(c) for an additional six months after the end of the initial six-month holding period.

. . . .

We are adopting the amendments for the sale of restricted securities by nonaffiliates after the holding period, as proposed. Under the amendments, after the applicable holding period requirement is met, the resale of restricted securities by a nonaffiliate under Rule 144 will no longer be subject to any other conditions of Rule 144 except that, with regard to the resale of securities of a reporting issuer, the current public information requirement in Rule 144(c) will apply for an additional six months after the six-month holding period requirement is met. Therefore, a non-affiliate will no longer be subject to the Rule 144 conditions relating to volume limitations, manner of sale requirements, and filing Form 144. [See Rule 144(b)(1)] [emphasis supplied]

We believe that the complexity of resale restrictions may inhibit sales by, and imposes costs on, non-affiliates. Because Rule 144 is relied upon by many individuals to resell their restricted securities, we believe that it is particularly helpful to streamline and reduce the complexity of the rule as much as possible while retaining its integrity. We continue to believe that retaining the current public information requirement with regard to resales of restricted securities of reporting issuers for up to one year after the acquisition of the securities is important to help provide the market with adequate information regarding the issuer of the securities. In addition, we generally believe that most abuses in sales of unregistered securities involve affiliates of issuers and securities of shell companies. As discussed below, we are codifying the staff's current interpretive position that Rule 144 cannot be relied upon for the resale of the securities of reporting and non-reporting shell companies.

The final conditions applicable to resales under Rule 144 of *restricted* securities held by affiliates and non-affiliates of the issuer can be summarized as follows:

	Affiliate or Person Selling on Behalf of an Affiliate	**Non-Affiliate (and Has Not Been an Affiliate During the Prior Three Months)**
Restricted Securities of Reporting Issuers	*During six-month holding period*—no resales under Rule 144 permitted. *After six-month holding period*—may resell in accordance with all Rule 144 requirements including: • Current public information, • Volume limitations, • Manner of sale requirements for equity securities, and • Filing of Form 144	*During six-month holding period*—no resales under Rule 144 permitted. *After six-month holding period but before one year*—unlimited public resales under Rule 144 except that the current public information requirement still applies. *After one-year holding period*—unlimited public resales under Rule 144; need not comply with any other Rule 144 requirements.
	Affiliate or Person Selling on Behalf of an Affiliate	**Non-Affiliate (and Has Not Been an Affiliate During the Prior Three Months)**
Restricted Securities of Non-Reporting Issuers	*During one-year holding period* no resales under Rule 144 permitted. *After one-year holding period*—may resell in accordance with all Rule 144 requirements, including: • Current public information, • Volume limitations, • Manner of sale requirements for equity securities, and • Filing of Form 144.	*During one-year holding period*—no resales under Rule 144 permitted. *After one-year holding period*—unlimited public resales under Rule 144; need not comply with any other Rule 144 requirements.

C. Amendments to the Manner of Sale Requirements Applicable to Resales by Affiliates

Before today's amendments, the manner of sale requirements in Rule 144(f) required securities to be sold in "brokers' transactions" or in transactions directly with a "market maker," as that term is defined in Section 3(a)(38) of the Exchange Act. Additionally, the rule prohibits a selling security holder from: (1) soliciting or arranging for the solicitation of orders to buy the securities in anticipation of, or in connection with, the Rule 144 transaction; or (2) making any payment in connection with the offer or sale of the securities to any person other than the broker who executes the order to sell the securities.

In the Proposing Release, we proposed to eliminate the manner of sale requirements for the sale of both equity and debt securities alike, reasoning that the manner of sale requirements are not necessary to satisfy the purposes of Rule 144 and limit the liquidity of the security. . . .

In response to comments, we are adopting amendments to the manner of sale requirements that apply to resales of equity securities of affiliates. We last made substantive amendments to the manner of sale requirements in 1978. [Securities Act Release No. 5979 (1978)] Since then, the growth of technological and other developments directed at meeting the investment needs of the public and reducing the cost of capital for companies have led us to refine the rules governing the trading of securities. We believe that it is appropriate now to adopt two amendments to the manner of sale requirements so that the restrictions better reflect current trading practices and venues.

First, we are adopting a change to Rule 144(f) to permit the resale of securities through riskless principal transactions in which trades are executed at the same price, exclusive of any explicitly disclosed markup or markdown, commission equivalent, or other fee, and the rules of a self-regulatory organization permit the transaction to be reported as riskless. A "riskless principal transaction" is defined as a principal transaction where, after having received from a customer an order to buy, a broker or dealer purchases the securities as principal in the market to satisfy the order to buy or, after having received from a customer an order to sell, sells the security as principal to the market to satisfy the order to sell. We believe that these riskless principal transactions are equivalent to agency trades. As with agency trades, in order to qualify as a permissible manner of sale under the revised rule, the broker or dealer conducting the riskless principal transaction must meet all the requirements of a brokers' transaction, as defined by Rule 144(g), except the requirement that the broker does no more than execute the order or orders to sell the securities as agent for the person for whose account the securities are sold. The broker or dealer must neither solicit nor arrange for the solicitation of customers' orders to buy the securities in anticipation of or, in connection with, the transaction, must receive no more than the usual and customary markup or markdown, commission equivalent, or other fee, and must conduct a reasonable inquiry regarding the underwriter status of the person for whose account the securities are to be sold.

Second, we are amending Rule 144(g) which defines "brokers' transaction" for purposes of the manner of sale requirements. Under the definition of brokers' transactions, a broker must neither solicit nor arrange for the solicitation of customers' orders to buy the securities in anticipation of, or in connection with, the transaction. However, certain activities specified in three subparagraphs of Rule 144(g)[(3)] are deemed not to be a solicitation. We are adding another subparagraph covering the posting of bid and ask quotations in alternative trading systems that will also be deemed not to be a solicitation. This new provision permits a broker to insert bid and ask quotations for the security in an alternative trading system, as defined in Rule 300 Regulation of ATS, provided that the broker has published bona fide bid and ask quotations for the security in the alternative trading system on each of the last 12 business days.

D. Changes to Rule 144 Conditions Related to Resales of Debt Securities by Affiliates

1. Comments Received on Proposed Amendments Relating to Debt Securities

In the 2007 Proposing Release, we proposed to eliminate the manner of sale requirements in Rule 144 with regard to sales of debt securities by affiliates. We also requested comment on whether there were any other conditions in Rule 144, such as the volume limitations, to which debt securities should not be subject. In the 2007 Proposing Release, we included preferred stock and asset-backed securities in the "debt securities" category for purposes of the proposed elimination of the manner of sale requirements.

. . . .

2. No Manner of Sale Requirements Regarding Resales of Debt Securities

We are adopting the amendments to eliminate the manner of sale requirements for resales of debt securities held by affiliates. . . . We agree that, as financial intermediaries, brokers serve an important function as gatekeepers for promoting compliance with Rule 144, and we are concerned that eliminating the manner of sale requirements for equity securities would lead to abuse. However, we do not believe that the fixed income securities market raises the same concerns about abuse, and are persuaded that the manner of sale requirements may place an unnecessary burden on the resale of fixed income securities. Combined with the changes that we are making to the Rule 144(e) volume limitations, these amendments will permit holders of debt securities to rely on Rule 144 to resell their debt securities in a way and amount that was not possible previously.

As proposed, our definition of debt securities in Rule 144 includes non-participatory preferred stock (which has debt-like characteristics) and asset-backed securities (where the predominant purchasers are institutional investors including financial institutions, pension funds, insurance companies, mutual funds and money managers) in addition to other types of nonconvertible debt securities. This definition of debt securities is consistent with the treatment of such securities under Regulation S.

3. Raising Volume Limitations for Debt Securities

We also are adopting amendments to raise the Rule 144(e) volume limitations for debt securities. Before the amendments that we are adopting, under Rule 144(e), the amount of securities sold in a three-month period could not exceed the greater of: (1) one percent of the shares or other units of the class outstanding as shown by the most recent report or statement published by the issuer, or (2) the average weekly volume of trading in such securities, as calculated pursuant to provisions in the rule. . . .

Debt securities generally are issued in tranches. We agree that, prior to our amendments, the volume limitations in Rule 144 constrained the ability of debt holders to rely on Rule 144 for the resales of their securities. For the same reasons that we are eliminating the manner of sale requirements for debt securities, we believe that it is appropriate to adopt an alternative volume limitation that is specifically applicable to resale of debt securities. We are amending Rule 144(e) to permit the resale of debt securities in an amount that does not exceed ten percent of a tranche (or class when the securities are non-participatory preferred stock), together with all sales of securities of the same tranche sold for the account of the selling security holder within a three-month period. We believe that this new ten percent limitation provision will permit a more reasonable amount of trading in debt securities than the one percent limitation has permitted. These revised volume limitations also apply to resales of non-participatory preferred stock or asset-backed securities, which are defined as debt securities for purposes of Rule 144.

E. Increase of the Thresholds that Trigger the Form 144 Filing Requirement for Affiliates

Before today's amendments, Rule 144(h) required a selling security holder to file a notice on Form 144 if the security holder's intended sale exceeded either 500 shares or $10,000 within a three-month period. These filing thresholds had not been modified since 1972. [Securities Act Release No. 5223 (1972)]. . . .

We are adopting increased Form 144 filing thresholds. . . . As proposed, we are raising the dollar threshold to $50,000 to adjust for inflation since 1972. [Query why the SEC declined to adjust for inflation the $1 million net worth /$200,000 annual income level for qualification as an accredited investor under Regulation D adopted in 1982.] After considering the comments, we are raising the share threshold to 5,000 shares, rather than the proposed 1,000 shares. We believe that the 5,000 share threshold is an appropriate alternate threshold for trades in amounts that may not reach the $50,000 dollar threshold, but that merit notice to the market.

. . . .

F. Codification of Several Staff Positions

In the 2007 Proposing Release, we proposed to codify several interpretive positions issued by the staff of the Division of Corporation Finance. . . .

We are adopting all of the codifications substantially as proposed. The codifications should make these interpretations more transparent and readily available to the public.

1. Securities Acquired under Section 4(6) [now § 4(a)(5)] of the Securities Act are Considered "Restricted Securities"

. . . .

Section 4(6) [now § 4(a)(5)] provides for an exemption from registration for an offering that does not exceed $5,000,000 that is made only to accredited investors, that does not involve any advertising or public solicitation by the issuer or anyone acting on the issuer's behalf and for which a Form D has been filed. Because the resale status of securities acquired in Section 4(6) [now § 4(a)(5)] exempt transactions should be the same as securities received in other nonpublic offerings that are included in the definition of restricted securities, we are of the view that securities acquired under Section 4(6) [now § 4(a)(5)] should be defined as restricted securities for purposes of Rule 144. Therefore, we are adopting an amendment to add securities acquired under Section 4(6) [now § 4(a)(5)] of the Securities Act to the definition of restricted securities.

. . . .

6. Treatment of Securities Issued by "Reporting and Non-Reporting Shell Companies"

A *blank check company* is a company that:

- Is in the development stage;
- Has no specific business plan or purpose, or has indicated that its business plan is to merge with or acquire an unidentified third party; and
- Issues penny stock.

Such companies historically have provided opportunity for abuse of the federal securities laws, particularly by serving as vehicles to avoid the registration requirements of the securities laws.

. . .

In 2005, we amended Securities Act Rule 405 to define a *"shell company"* to mean a registrant, other than an asset-backed issuer, that has:

(1) no or nominal operations; and

(2) either:

- no or nominal assets;
- assets consisting solely of cash and cash equivalents; or

- assets consisting of any amount of cash and cash equivalents and nominal other assets.

[In] January 2000, the Division of Corporation Finance concluded in a letter to NASD Regulation, Inc. that Rule 144 is not available for the resale of securities initially issued by companies that are, or previously were, blank check companies. In an effort to curtail misuse of Rule 144 by security holders through transactions in the securities of blank check companies, we proposed to codify this position with some modifications. . . .

We are adopting, as proposed, the amendment to prohibit reliance on Rule 144 for the resale of securities of a company that is a reporting or a non-reporting shell company. Under the amendment rules, [with certain exceptions] Rule 144 will not be available for the resale of securities initially issued by either a reporting or non-reporting shell company or an issuer that has been at any time previously a reporting or non-reporting shell company. . . .

    . . . .

Commentary on Rule 144

Rule 144(b)(1) Applied to Restricted Securities

Rule 144(b)(1) effectively removes all restrictions when *non-affiliates* have held *restricted* securities for the applicable holding period and allows such non-affiliates to freely resell such securities. Rule 144(b)(1) accordingly eases the burdens that were placed on the liquidity of restricted securities.

Consider this result with the SEC's assertion when it adopted Rule 144 in 1972:

> [T]he purpose and underlying policy of the [Securities] Act to protect investors requires . . . that there be *adequate current information concerning the issuer*, whether the resales of securities by persons result in a distribution or are effected in trading transactions. Accordingly, the availability of [Rule 144] is conditioned on the existence of adequate current public information. [24]

The SEC, with its amendments to Rule 144, essentially has nullified the above rationale. One justification proffered is the deregulatory assertion that "[t]he purpose of the amendments is to relax restrictions on resales of securities that are more burdensome than necessary." [25] But nowhere does the Commission adequately explain why such restrictions are "more burdensome than necessary," particularly in view of the investor protection concerns that are highlighted throughout the 1972

---

24. Securities Act Release No. 5223 (1972) (emphasis supplied).
25. Securities Act Release No. 6286 (1981). *See* Securities Act Release Nos. 6488 (1983), 8869 (2008).

Rule 144 adopting release. Hence, Rule 144, as revised, may be viewed as inconsistent with a major objective of the 1933 Act, which is to protect investors by ensuring that their decisions are informed, and also as incompatible with a fundamental premise underlying the rule's adoption.

There is, of course, another side to this issue. In order to promote capital formation and induce investors to take a stake in start-up and similar enterprises, a non-affiliate who holds restricted securities must have a way to resell those securities if he or she chooses. Rule 144 now provides such shareholders with an opportunity to resell their restricted securities after holding them for a minimal period (six months for a reporting issuer and 12 months for a non-reporting issuer). In this way, the revised Rule meets prospective sellers' expectations and facilitates the flow of venture capital into the economy. The prospective purchaser is adequately protected, it may be asserted, by the application of the antifraud provisions. And, if a trading market for the subject issuer's securities should develop, then Rule 15c2-11 information must be made available. Moreover, a prospective buyer is not compelled to purchase the restricted securities. The determination whether to acquire the securities if adequate current issuer information is unavailable should be left to the prospective purchaser, and not foreclosed by government intervention.

Nonetheless, it may be asserted that the SEC revisions to Rule 144 unduly liberalize certain restrictions, while other overly burdensome limitations of the Rule have been virtually ignored by the SEC. If adequate information is not available concerning the issuer, a prospective non-affiliated seller should not be permitted to unload unlimited quantities of restricted securities into the market. The prospective seller should only be allowed to resell the restricted securities in limited volumes over a period of time. In this way, the prospective seller will not have to rely on the unwilling, nonreporting issuer for public information and will not be locked in to the investment, while at the same time, he/she will not be able to dump unlimited amounts of restricted securities into the market.

By promulgating Rule 144(b)(1), the SEC appears to take the position that the unloading of all of a non-affiliate's restricted securities stock after the requisite six-month (for reporting issuers) and 12-month (for non-reporting issuers) holding periods will never constitute a "distribution." Such a position is questionable. Given the substantial amount of restricted stock that a non-affiliate can unload in the marketplace under certain conditions, the SEC's blanket exemption spreads too far.

Moreover, the SEC's amendments to Rule 144 are inconsistent with the disclosure approach of Rules 505 and 506 of Regulation D, covered in Chapter 3 of this text. If the Commission's objective is to ensure the provision of adequate information to "unsophisticated" (unaccredited) investors of restricted securities, it should be irrelevant whether the investor purchased the securities from the issuer (pursuant to Regulation D) or from a shareholder who is not affiliated with the issuer (by means of Rule 144). In either case, the prospective unaccredited purchaser's need for sufficient information to make an intelligent investment decision remains the same. Only in the Rule 505 or 506 Regulation D offering context, however, is the investor entitled to such information. In the Rule 144 setting, by contrast, there is no mandated disclosure when the investor purchases restricted securities from a non-affiliated party (who has met the requisite holding requirement) of an issuer that fails to provide current public information (but note that should a trading market develop for the subject securities, then Rule 15c2-11 information must be made available).

Rule 144 Does Not Cover Non-Restricted Securities Sold by a Non-Affiliate

Rule 144 does not cover a non-affiliate's disposition of nonrestricted stock. Nonetheless, the SEC, by its promulgation of Rule 144(b)(1), appears to take the position that the sale of a non-affiliate's stock is not a separate distribution. Moreover, the assumption of underwriter status may no longer be a pitfall for non-affiliates selling nonrestricted stock due to the SEC's evident abandonment of the presumptive underwriter doctrine. These developments may lead to the conclusion that a non-affiliate can freely resell nonrestricted stock without limitation pursuant to the § 4(a)(1) exemption. The Commission, however, has declined to expressly address this issue.

If the above represents the SEC's position, it is misplaced. In certain circumstances, a non-affiliate can hold a substantial percentage of nonrestricted stock. Permitting such nonaffiliates to freely liquidate their positions conflicts with both the definition of underwriter under § 2(a)(11) and the rationale underlying the § 4(a)(1) transactional exemption. In short, persons who dispose of large percentages of securities in the public markets are, in actuality, engaging in a distribution rather than a transaction and, when they do so after a short holding period, are purchasing from an issuer with a view toward distribution. Support for this assertion may be premised on the fact that, if a substantial security holder were an affiliate, he/she would be subject to the volume limitation requirements of Rule 144(e). Yet, status as an affiliate in this context should not be determinative. At times, an affiliate may have more leverage to induce the issuer to file a registration statement for the securities such affiliate wishes to sell. Nevertheless, the detrimental effect on the capital trading markets and the investing public are identical, irrespective of whether one has affiliate status when reselling large quantities of stock.

The foregoing assertions are reinforced by the following scenario: Company X, for investment purposes, purchases 12 percent of Company Y's "unrestricted" stock over a six-month period on the New York Stock Exchange. Insiders of Company Y, who still retain 51 percent ownership of the public company's stock and are able to elect the entire board of directors, have no desire to share control. Company X, pleased with its investment, increases its ownership interest in Company Y's "unrestricted" stock during a three-year period to 19 percent. One year later, after the insiders reject

Company X's request to have a seat on Company Y's board of directors, Company X elects to sell all of its stock in Company Y on the New York Stock Exchange during a ninety-day period.

Under the above scenario, Company X is not an "affiliate" of Company Y. It is neither in a "control" relationship nor can it compel Company Y to file a registration statement. Being a non-affiliate, its sales, by analogy to Rule 144(b)(1), do not constitute a "distribution." Moreover, again in reference to Rule 144(b)(1) and Rule 144(d), a four-year holding period, as reflected in the illustration, indicates that Company X, not being a control person, acquired and held the securities with investment intent, hence mitigating against the assumption of underwriter status. The policies of the Securities Act, however, demand that Company X, absent registration, should not be able within a fairly short time period to unload its securities on the investing public.

With the promulgation of Rule 144(b)(1) and the evident abandonment of the presumptive underwriter doctrine, the SEC appears to have given the impression that non-affiliates can resell nonrestricted stock without limitation. Non-affiliates and their counsel, however, should not act with the certainty as other parties and transactions that clearly come within Rule 144's scope. Because unlimited sales by non-affiliates should not be permitted for the reasons provided, the SEC should prescribe a safe harbor volume limitation under the § 4(a)(1) exemption for non-affiliates selling nonrestricted stock.

---

§ 6.05 The Section "4(1½)" Exemption

One exemption thus far not discussed is the so-called § "4(1½)" exemption. This exemption, based largely on SEC no-action letters and other SEC pronouncements, seeks to fill a gap in the statutory exemptive scheme. Upon examining this framework, it appears that, until the enactment of § 4(a)(7) in 2015 (discussed in § 6.06), there existed no statutory or regulatory exemption that expressly covered unlimited sales of securities by affiliates (as well as unlimited sales of such securities by non-affiliates) who desired to sell their securities in a *private transaction* after a short holding period. By way of example, Rule 144 neither helps a "control" person who wishes to sell all of his/her stock in a private transaction nor a non-affiliate who has not held restricted securities for a sufficient period to invoke the rule.

Focusing on the § "4(1½)" exemption, the SEC in Securities Act Release No. 6188 (1980), stated:

> In making such private sales, the affiliates presumably would rely on the so-called "Section 4(1½)" exemption. This is a hybrid exemption not specifically provided for in the 1933 Act but clearly within its intended

purpose. The exemption basically would permit affiliates to make private sales of securities held by them so long as some of the established criteria for sales under both Section 4(1) and Section 4(2) of the Act are satisfied.

Unfortunately, the Commission has declined to identify the pertinent "established criteria" of § 4(a)(1) and § 4(a)(2), which must be satisfied in order for a party successfully to invoke the § "4(1½)" exemption. The following material addresses this murky area.

Ackerberg v. Johnson

United States Court of Appeals, Eighth Circuit

892 F.2d 1328 (1989)

BEAM, Circuit Judge.

This appeal arises out of the sale of 16,500 unregistered shares of Vertimag Systems Corporation stock for $99,000. Norman J. Ackerberg brought suit against [among others] Clark E. Johnson, Jr., the chairman of the board of Vertimag, from whom Ackerberg bought most of his shares. . . .

Ackerberg bought the Vertimag shares in March of 1984. Ackerberg bought 12,500 shares from Johnson, who, in addition to being the chairman of the board, was one of the founders of Vertimag and its largest individual stockholder. . . .

The Vertimag transaction began in October of 1983, when Vertimag proposed a private placement of $10,000,000 in securities, to be sold at $6.00 to $6.50 per share. In December of 1983, Ackerberg said that if he could invest around $100,000, he would be interested. . . . Ackerberg [was then given] a ninety-nine page private placement memorandum which contained detailed information about Vertimag.

On March 17, 1984, Ackerberg signed a subscription agreement, prepared by counsel for Vertimag. *[Note that many of the shares purchased by Ackerberg were owned by Johnson, not the issuer.]* Ackerberg testified by deposition that he read and understood this document. Vertimag's counsel stressed to Ackerberg that no sale could be made without the subscription agreement, which agreement informed Ackerberg that the Vertimag securities were unregistered and not readily transferable. . . . Ackerberg also represented in the subscription agreement that his yearly income was in excess of $200,000, that his net worth was over $1,000,000, and that his liquid assets exceeded $500,000. . . .

On August 23, 1988, the district court entered summary judgment in favor of Ackerberg on the § 12(1) [now § 12(a)(1)] claim. . . . [We reverse.]

. . . We agree with Johnson that he is entitled, as a matter of law, to an exemption under § 4(1) [now § 4(a)(1)]. . . .

Johnson argues that he is entitled to an exemption under § 4(1) of the 1933 Act, which provides that the registration requirements of the 1933 Act shall not apply to "transactions by any person other than an issuer, underwriter, or dealer."[26]

It is clear that the applicable and appropriate exemption to be applied in this case is § 4(1). To the extent that Ackerberg argues that both Johnson and the [other] defendants rely on a "§ 4(1½)" exemption, he misunderstands the nature of a § 4(1) exemption. While the term "§ 4(1½) exemption" has been used in the secondary literature, *see, e.g.,* ABA Report, *The Section "4(1½)" Phenomenon: Private Resales of "Restricted" Securities,* 34 Bus. Law. 1961 (1979); Schneider, *Section 4(1½) — Private Resales of Restricted or Control Securities,* 49 Ohio St. L.J. 501 (1988), the term does not properly refer to an exemption other than § 4(1). Rather, the term merely expresses the statutory relationship between § 4(1) [now § 4(a)(1)] and § 4(2) [now 4(a)(2)]. That is, the definition of underwriter, found in § 2(11) [now § 2(a)(11)], depends on the existence of a distribution, which in turn is considered the equivalent of a public offering. Section 4(2) contains the exemption for transactions not involving a public offering. Any analysis of whether a party is an underwriter for purposes of § 4(1) necessarily entails an inquiry into whether the transaction involves a public offering. While the term "4(1½) exemption" adequately expresses this relationship, it is clear that the exemption for private resales of restricted securities is § 4(1). We need not go beyond the statute to reach this conclusion.

We agree with the district court that the burden of providing entitlement to an exemption is on the party claiming entitlement. . . . We disagree, however, that Johnson has failed to meet his burden. In the absence of any finding that this transaction involved a distribution, Johnson has shown that he is not an issuer, underwriter or dealer within the meaning of § 4(1) of the 1933 Act.

The terms "issuer" and "dealer" are defined, respectively, in §§ 2(4) and 2(12) [now §§ 2(a)(4) and 2(a)(12)]. The parties do not seriously argue that Johnson was an issuer or dealer. Clearly he is neither. Rather, Ackerberg contends that Johnson is an underwriter within § 4(1).

When considering whether Johnson is an underwriter, it is helpful to consider that the § 4(1) exemption is meant to distinguish "between distribution of securities and trading in securities." L. Loss & J. Seligman, 2 Securities Regulation 627 (3d ed. 1989). . . .

The statutory definition of "underwriter" is found in § 2(11). "The term 'underwriter' means any person who has purchased from an issuer with a view to, or offers or sells for an issuer in connection with, the distribution of any security." The congressional intent in defining "underwriter" was to cover all persons who might operate as conduits for the transfer of securities to the public. . . . Thus,

---

[26]. [This footnote has been moved to the text — ed.]

"underwriter" is generally defined in close connection with the definition and meaning of "distribution." . . . The term "underwriter" thus focuses on "distribution." Given the statutory definition of "underwriter," the exemption should be available if: (1) the acquisition of the securities was not made "with a view to" distribution; or (2) the sale was not made "for an issuer in connection with" a distribution. . . . Relevant to both inquiries are whether the securities have come to rest in the hands of the security holder and whether the sale involves a public offering.

We begin by considering whether the securities were acquired by Johnson with a view to their distribution. The inquiry depends on the distinction between a distribution and mere trading; so long as Johnson initially acquired his shares from the issuer with an investment purpose and not for the purpose of reselling them, the acquisition was not made "with a view to" distribution. While this determination would at first seem to be a fact-specific inquiry into the security holder's subjective intent at the time of acquisition, the courts have considered the more objective criterion of whether the securities have come to rest. That is, the courts look to whether the security holder has held the securities long enough to negate any inference that his intention at the time of acquisition was to distribute them to the public. Many courts have accepted a two-year rule of thumb to determine whether the securities have come to rest. . . . This two-year rule has been incorporated by the SEC into Rule 144, which provides a safe harbor for persons selling restricted securities acquired in a private placement. . . . [As the materials in the preceding Section of this text discuss, the SEC under Rule 144 has shortened this two-year period to six months for reporting companies and 12 months for nonreporting companies.]

Johnson purchased his securities in 1979 or 1980, when Vertimag Systems was incorporated in California. He did not sell any of these shares to Ackerberg until 1984. . . . Thus, Johnson held his shares for at least four years before selling them to Ackerberg, a period well in excess of the usual two years required to find that the securities have come to rest.

Our second inquiry is whether the resale was made "for an issuer in connection with" a distribution. Whether the sale was "for an issuer" can also be determined by whether the shares have come to rest. That is the best objective evidence of whether a sale is "for an issuer" is whether the shares have come to rest.

To determine whether the sale was made "in connection with" a distribution, however, requires that we consider directly the meaning of "distribution," and thus whether the resale involved a public offering. The definition of "distribution" as used in § 2(11) is generally considered to be synonymous with a public offering. In *Gilligan, Will & Co. v. SEC*, 267 F.2d 461 (2d Cir. 1959), the court explained the connection between "underwriter," "distribution," and "public offering." Since § 2(11) . . . defines an 'underwriter' as 'any person who has purchased from an issuer with a view to . . . the distribution of any security' and since a 'distribution' requires a 'public offering,' . . . the question is whether there was a 'public offering.'" . . .

The case law is equally clear that a public offering is defined not in quantitative terms, but in terms of whether the offerees are in need of the protection which the Securities Act affords through registration. Thus, the Supreme Court held in *SEC v. Ralston Purina*, 346 U.S. 119 (1953), that the proper focus is on the need of the offerees for information. . . .

This circuit has followed *Ralston Purina* by finding that a public offering "turns on the need of the offerees for the protections afforded by registration. . . . If the offerees have access to such information, registration is unnecessary, and the section 4(2) exemption should apply." . . .

That "distribution" should be read in terms of "public offering," and the need of the offerees for information, makes sense in light of the purpose of the 1933 Act as construed by this circuit. . . . Moreover, the parties in this case do not dispute that Ackerberg is a sophisticated investor, not in need of the protections afforded by registration under the 1933 Act. As earlier stated, Ackerberg read and signed a subscription agreement in which he represented that: he had the knowledge and experience in investing to properly evaluate the merits and risks of his purchase of Vertimag securities; he was given full and complete information regarding Vertimag Systems Corporation; he knew that the securities were not registered under the 1933 Act, and were being sold pursuant to exemptions from the 1933 Act; and he knew that the sale was being made in reliance on his representations in the subscription agreement. Ackerberg further represented that his net worth was substantial, and the record clearly shows that Ackerberg is, if not a conscientious investor, at least a prolific one. We, therefore, have no trouble finding that Ackerberg is a sophisticated investor and not in need of the protections afforded by registration under the 1933 Act. Hence, this case involves no public offering, and thus no distribution. Absent a distribution, Johnson cannot be an underwriter within §4(1) [now §4(a)(1)], and is, therefore, entitled to that exemption.

. . . .

Note

As seen from the foregoing, the Commission has declined to specifically identify the pertinent "established criteria" of §4(a)(1) and §4(a)(2), which must be satisfied in order for a party successfully to invoke the § "4(1½)" exemption. However, as seen from *Ackerberg v. Johnson* and SEC pronouncements, certain criteria relevant for perfecting the exemption may be as follows:

- While the source of the § "4(1½)" exemption is § 4(a)(1), the determination of appropriate standards to govern the exemption is primarily derived from § 4(a)(2) authority.

- Advertising and general solicitation are not permitted.

- Although no finite number has been established, there is some limit on the number of offerees and purchasers.

- Whether the prospective seller must hold the restricted securities for a certain length of time (such as one year) is uncertain. The holding point may be more relevant where there is no public information available concerning the issuer or where a large number of shares are sought to be sold to several unsophisticated investors.

- The purchasers' access to registration-type information (or the actual providing of such information), as well as purchaser sophistication, are important factors. As the *Ackerberg* decision above addresses, the offerees' need for protection under the Securities Act registration process is a key criterion.

See Olander & Jacks, *The Section 4(1½) Exemption—Reading Between the Lines of the Securities Act of 1933*, 15 Sec. Reg. L.J. 339 (1988). *See also* Schneider, *Section 4(1½)—Private Resales of Restricted or Control Securities*, 49 Ohio St. L.J. 501 (1988).

---

§ 6.06 The Section 4(a)(7) Exemption

In 2015, pursuant to the FAST Act, Congress enacted § 4(a)(7)—a new statutory exemption from Securities Act registration. Provided its conditions are met, this new statutory provision exempts from Securities Act registration the resale of control as well as restricted and nonrestricted securities to accredited investors. Generally, the requirements of § 4(a)(7) are as follows:

- The seller of the securities must not be the subject issuer or one of its subsidiaries.

- All purchasers of such securities must be accredited investors as that term is defined under Regulation D (as one example, an individual investor having a net worth of $1 million exclusive of primary residence).

- No advertising or general solicitation is permitted.

- The subject securities must have been authorized and outstanding for a minimum of 90 days.

- The selling shareholder (as well as any person receiving compensation for its participation in the offer, solicitation, or sale of the subject securities) is not a "bad actor."

- The issuer is not an ineligible company to invoke this exemption, such as a blank check, shell, or bankrupt company.

- The securities do not constitute all or part of a subject underwriter's unsold allotment of a public offering.

- With limited exceptions (e.g., certain foreign issuers), if the issuer is not a reporting company under the Securities Exchange Act, §4(a)(7)(d)(3) provides that "the seller and a prospective purchaser designated by the seller obtain from the issuer, upon request of the seller, and the seller in all cases makes available to a prospective purchaser," reasonably current specified information. This information, for example, includes: general information regarding the issuer (e.g., nature of its business, services, and products, as well as the identity of its directors and officers); the name of any broker-dealer or other agent being compensated for participating in the offering; and financial information, including the issuer's most recent balance sheet and profit-and-loss statement for the two most recent fiscal years (or for such shorter period that the issuer has been in operation).

- In a situation where the seller of the securities is a control person of the subject enterprise, such control person must describe the nature of the affiliation and certify that it has no reasonable basis to believe that the enterprise is in violation of the securities laws or regulations adopted thereunder.

Securities acquired pursuant to the §4(a)(7) exemption are deemed "restricted" within the meaning of Rule 144 and thus subject to resale restrictions. Also significant is that securities sold pursuant to the §4(a)(7) exemption are defined as "covered securities" and thereby preempted from state registration and qualification regulation. Moreover, because §4(a)(7) provides that it is not the exclusive means for perfecting an exemption from Securities Act registration, the informal §4(1½) exemption should continue to be a viable alternative.

The enactment of §4(a)(7) provides greater certainty to private resales of control and restricted securities as compared to the informal §4(1½) exemption covered in §6.05 above. The exemption will likely be used, for example, in block trades transacted by large shareholders, including sales by: institutional investors, affiliates (including members of the company's "founding family"), and investors who acquired large positions pursuant to exempt offerings (e.g., Rule 506 offerings) made prior to the subject company's IPO.

By setting forth specified requirements, §4(a)(7) should provide comfort to selling shareholders seeking to use the exemption. In certain ways, the §4(a)(7) exemption may be viewed as more flexible than the informal §4(1½) exemption. For example, §4(a)(7) does not limit the number of offerees and purchasers, whereas a large number of such persons under the §4(1½) exemption would present the risk that the offering would be considered a "public" offering and thereby constitute a §5 registration violation.

On the other hand, §4(a)(7) in some respects is more demanding than §4(1½). For example, in order to satisfy the §4(a)(7) exemption: (1) All purchasers must be accredited investors; (2) Specified information upon the request of the prospective seller must be provided to the prospective purchaser and seller—with the distinct possibility that, absent a contractual obligation, the subject issuer will decline to provide such information to a nonaffiliate shareholder who seeks to resell its securities pursuant to this exemption (hence, highlighting the importance of insisting upon the inclusion of a provision in the subscription agreement requiring that the issuer supply this information upon the prospective seller's request); and (3) A control person must certify that such person has no reasonable grounds to believe that the subject issuer is in violation of the securities laws or regulations adopted thereunder.

Even with these added requirements, §4(a)(7) brings needed certainty to the planning and consummation of resales of restricted and control securities within the Securities Act exemption framework. Provided that the conditions of the §4(a)(7) exemption are met, securities acquired thereby will not be deemed to constitute a "distribution" for purposes of §2(a)(11) (which defines the term "underwriter").

Thus, by setting forth specified conditions for satisfying an exemption from registration, §4(a)(7) should be frequently used by: (1) insiders (e.g., affiliates) and large shareholders (such as institutional investors) who desire to resell their securities beyond the volume limits permitted under Rule 144; and (2) to a lesser extent, by those shareholders who wish to promptly sell and have not held their restricted securities for the length of time required to invoke Rule 144. Note that, provided its conditions are met, §4(a)(7) also provides an exemption for nonaffiliates selling a large percentage of an issuer's nonrestricted stock—a situation that Rule 144 does not cover.

As a consequence, §4(a)(7) provides a viable alternative means for significant shareholders to dispose of their securities. However, as contrasted with Rule 144 transactions, where the subject securities frequently are sold into public markets, securities sold pursuant to the §4(a)(7) exemption are solely to accredited purchasers. Hence, it may well be that sophisticated purchasers of securities in transactions exempt under §4(a)(7) will negotiate for a liquidity price discount in view of the lack of a public trading market.

For a timely and comprehensive article addressing the §4(a)(7) exemption, *see* Anthony, *Navigating the New Section 4(a)(7) Private Resale Exemption—Compliance, Utilization, and Market Implications*, 44 Sec. Reg. L.J. 317 (2016).

———————

§ 6.07 Rule 144A

Adoption of Rule 144A

Securities Act Release No. 6862 (1990)

I. *EXECUTIVE SUMMARY*

. . . .

The Commission today is adopting Rule 144A. New Rule 144A provides a non-exclusive safe harbor exemption from the registration requirements of the Securities Act for resales to eligible institutions of any restricted [unregistered] securities that, when issued, were not of the same class as securities listed on a U.S. securities exchange or quoted in the National Association of Securities Dealers Automated Quotation system ("NASDAQ"). With the exception of registered broker-dealers, a qualified institutional buyer ["QIB"] must in the aggregate own and invest on a discretionary basis at least $100 million in securities of issuers that are not affiliated with that qualified institutional buyer.

The Rule as adopted provides for an eligibility threshold of $10 million in securities for broker-dealers that are registered under the Securities Exchange Act of 1934 (the "Exchange Act"), irrespective of whether they are buying for purposes of intermediation or investment. In addition, to facilitate intermediation in this market, the Rule provides that a registered broker-dealer may purchase as riskless principal, as defined in the Rule, for an institution that is itself eligible to purchase under the Rule, or act as agent on a non-discretionary basis in a sale to such an institution.

In addition to meeting the $100 million in securities requirement, banks and savings and loan associations must have a net worth of at least $25 million to be qualified institutional buyers. Because of the unique status of such financial institutions as federally-insured depository institutions, the Commission is of the opinion that such an eligibility test is warranted. To avoid placing U.S. banks at a competitive disadvantage, the net worth test applies to both foreign and domestic banks.

. . . .

Registered broker-dealer affiliates of banks and savings and loan associations, which are subject to direct Commission oversight, would, however, be able to purchase under the Rule on the same terms as other registered broker-dealers. Such registered broker-dealer affiliates would not be required to meet the net worth test.

Where the issuer of the securities to be resold is neither a reporting company under the Exchange Act, nor exempt from reporting pursuant to Rule 12g3-2(b) under the Exchange Act, nor a foreign government eligible to use Schedule B under the Securities Act, availability of the Rule is conditioned on the holder of the security, and a prospective purchaser from the holder, having the right to obtain from the issuer specified limited information about the issuer, and on the purchaser having received such information from the issuer, the seller, or a person acting on either of their behalf, upon request.

Although the Rule imposes no resale restrictions, a seller or any person acting on its behalf must take reasonable steps to ensure that the buyer is aware that the seller may rely on the exemption from the Securities Act's registration requirements afforded by Rule 144A.

II. *NEW RULE 144A*

The Commission views Rule 144A as adopted today as the first step toward achieving a more liquid and efficient institutional resale market for unregistered securities. The Commission intends to monitor the evolution of this market and to revisit the Rule with a view to making any appropriate changes. Among the issues that the Commission would expect to consider would be the nature and number of regular participants in the market, the types of securities traded, the liquidity of the market, the extent of foreign issuer participation in the private market, the effect of the Rule 144A market on the public market, and any perceived abuses of the safe harbor.

. . . .

Rule 144A sets forth a non-exclusive safe harbor from the registration requirements of Section 5 of the Securities Act for the resale of restricted securities to specified institutions by persons other than the issuer of such securities. . . .

By providing that transactions meeting its terms are not "distributions," the Rule essentially confirms that such transactions are not subject to the registration provisions of the Securities Act. In the case of persons other than issuers or dealers, the Rule does this by providing that any such person who offers and sells securities in accordance with the Rule will be deemed not to be engaged in a distribution and therefore not to be an underwriter within the meaning of Sections 2(11) [now §2(a) (11)] and 4(1) [now §4(a)(1)] of the Securities Act. Such persons therefore may rely on the exemption from registration provided by Section 4(1) [now §4(a)(1)] for transactions by persons other than issuers, underwriters or dealers. Dealers have the benefit of an exemption from registration under Section 4(3) [now §4 (a)(3)] of the Securities Act. . . .

Nothing in the Rule removes the need to comply with any applicable state law relating to the offer and sale of securities. Similarly, the Rule does not affect the securities registration requirements of Section 12 of the Exchange Act or the broker-dealer registration requirements of Section 15(a) of the Exchange Act for a broker or dealer who effects private resales.

In the case of securities originally offered and sold under Regulation D of the Securities Act, a person that purchases securities from an issuer and immediately offers and sells such securities in accordance with Rule [144A] is not an "underwriter" within the meaning of Rule 502(d) of Regulation D. Issuers making a Regulation D offering, who generally must exercise reasonable care to assure that purchasers are not underwriters, therefore would not be required to preclude resales under Rule 144A. Similarly, the fact that purchasers of securities from the issuer may purchase such securities with a view to reselling such securities pursuant to the Rule will not affect the availability to such issuer of an exemption under Section 4(2) [now §4(a)(2)] of the Securities Act from the registration requirements of the Securities Act.

Summary of Rule 144A

Rule 144A is directed at providing resale markets in generally three different settings: (1) the sale of debt securities from placement agents to QIBs; (2) resales of restricted securities originally sold pursuant to private or limited offerings, such as pursuant to Rule 506 of Regulation D; and (3) resales of securities of foreign enterprises or of securities originally offered outside of the United States, such as pursuant to Regulation S. Rule 144A's objective generally has been achieved insofar as helping to attract foreign companies to the U.S. capital markets.

As pointed out by the WALL STREET JOURNAL, Rule 144A is being used by issuers to avoid the federal registration requirements. For example, a company seeking to issue debt securities will place such securities with a placement agent pursuant to the §4(a)(2) or Rule 506 exemption who in turn will sell them to QIBs under Rule 144A. Rule 144A is deemed advantageous because such offerings can be effected almost instantaneously and without the rigorous disclosure requirements mandated in registered offerings.[27]

Another approach being utilized is to have the Rule 144A offering followed shortly thereafter by a Securities Act registered offering. Such a registered exchange offering, called an "A/B exchange," involves the issuance of the securities offered pursuant to the SEC registration statement to the Rule 144A holders in exchange for their securities that were acquired by means of Rule 144A.[28]

The requirements of Rule 144A may strike the reader as being complicated. The following is a Summary that hopefully will make the conditions of the Rule more understandable.

Requirements
(1) Resales of restricted securities to qualified institutional buyers (QIBs)
*(e.g., eligible insurance companies, investment companies, employee
benefit plans, venture capital firms)*

Such qualified institutional buyer ("QIB") must have $100 million invested in securities (of issuers that are not affiliated with such buyer) at the conclusion of its most recent fiscal year (goes to amount invested in securities, *not* assets).

---

27. *See* Raghaven, *Private Placement Market is Proving Popular,* WALL ST. J., April 1, 1997, at C14.

28. Bodner & Welsh, *Institutional Buyer Beware: Recent Decisions Reinforce Narrow Range of Remedies Available to QIBs in Rule 144A Offerings,* 36 REV. SEC. & COMM. REG. 1728 (2004) (also stating that "[r]oughly two-thirds to three-quarters of high-yield offerings are now accomplished by a Rule 144A private placement, often followed by an A/B exchange").

(a) In addition to $100 million invested in securities, banks and savings and loan associations must have a net worth of at least $25 million.

(b) Broker-Dealers are not required to meet the $100 million invested in securities standard. Rather, an eligible broker-dealer must own and invest on a discretionary basis at least $10 million of securities of issuers that are not affiliated with such dealer. In addition, a dealer who acts solely in a riskless principal transaction on behalf of a qualified institutional purchaser is itself treated as a QIB, regardless of whether it meets the $10 million invested in securities standard mentioned above.

(2) Qualifying the Prospective Purchaser

It is the seller's responsibility to qualify the prospective purchaser. In other words, the seller or its agent must "reasonably believe" that such purchaser is a QIB. The rule enumerates a number of non-exclusive means to satisfy this requirement, including such purchaser's most recent publicly available annual financial statements and the most recent information appearing in documents publicly filed by such prospective purchaser.

Pursuant to the JOBS Act of 2012, the SEC amended Rule 144A to provide that securities sold pursuant to Rule 144A may be offered to persons who are not qualified institutional buyers (QIBs) — so long as the securities in fact are sold to only those persons who the seller and any person acting on the seller's behalf reasonably believe are QIBs.[29] In such offerings conducted pursuant to Rule 144A, general solicitation and advertising are permitted.[30]

(3) Exclusion of fungible securities from Rule 144A

The "nonfungibility" condition arose due to concern that Rule 144A would result in the development of side-by-side public and private markets for the same class of securities, thereby resulting in loss of liquidity to the established trading markets. Hence, as adopted, Rule 144A is not available for securities that, at the time of their issuance, are of the same class (i.e. fungible) as securities trading on a U.S. exchange or quoted on the Nasdaq stock market. Note that convertible securities, having an effective conversion premium at the time of issuance of less than ten percent, are treated as securities of both the convertible and the underlying securities. Today, Rule 144A securities are traded on a "fully automated web-based platform, . . . [a] centralized electronic system [of the Nasdaq Stock Market] for displaying and accessing trading interest in [Rule] 144A issuers."[31]

---

29. JOBS Act § 201(a)(2); Securities Act Release No. 9415 (2013).

30. JOBS Act § 201(a)(2).

31. *Nasdaq's New 144A Platform Approved by SEC for Launch Aug. 15*, 39 Sᴇᴄ. Rᴇɢ. & L. Rᴇᴘ. (BNA) 1214 (2007).

(4) Resales of Rule 144A Securities

Securities acquired pursuant to a Rule 144A transaction are deemed to be "restricted" securities within the meaning of Rule 144. Hence, the Rule 144 holding periods apply to securities acquired pursuant to a transaction utilizing Rule 144A. Thus, for non-reporting Exchange Act issuers, Rule 144A securities will be freely tradeable by non-affiliates after a one-year holding period.

(5) Provision of Information

Upon request to the issuer, other than certain foreign issuers, a non-reporting Exchange Act issuer must provide to the holder and to the prospective purchaser certain basic information concerning the issuer's business (namely, "a very brief statement of the nature of the business of the issuer and the products and services it offers") and its financial statements (namely, its "most recent balance sheet and profit and loss and retained earnings statements"). Information ordinarily would be obtained by the holder from the issuer pursuant to contractual rights negotiated at the time of issuance.

(6) Notice Requirement

The rule requires that the seller take reasonable steps to notify the QIB that the seller may be relying on Rule 144A as an exemption from registration.

―――――――――

Note

The "provision of information" condition of Rule 144A raised the ire of former SEC Commissioner Edward Fleischman. He contended that the delivery of information requirement will adversely affect "that class of business enterprises most needy of the benefits promised by the Rule and most capable of magnifying those benefits to the advantage of the entire American economy, namely the smaller domestic privately owned issuers. . . ." Elaborating, Commissioner Fleischman explained:

> It is that group [of] companies, that has traditionally obtained its long-term financing in the institutional private placement market, that has become even more dependent on that market today given the withdrawal of many providers of venture capital, and that has most needed the benefits (quicker pace, reduced cost, and greater facility of financing) promised by the new Rule through the removal of the overhang of lawyer-intensive and paperwork-burdened resale transactions.[32]

Another commentator on this condition to Rule 144A likewise asserted:

> . . . [T]he requirement to provide information in certain cases already has caused practitioners problems in arranging Rule 144A transactions. Critics

―――――――――

32. Securities Act Release No. 6862 (1990) (Fleischman, Commr., dissenting in part).

of this requirement say the requirement is inconsistent with the SEC's theory that large institutions can fend for themselves and do not need the SEC prescribing what information they need in order to make an investment decision. . . .

[It has been] correctly predicted that . . . the execution of transactions involving already-issued securities would be interrupted until the purchaser has requested and obtained the information or has decided to abstain from exercising its right to do so.[33]

On the other hand, Rule 144A has raised concerns that it will adversely impact individual investors. To such critics, the SEC's promulgation of Rule 144A represents yet another example of the Commission's solicitousness toward capital formation and institutional investors to the detriment of ordinary investors. In a letter to then SEC Chairman David Breeden, two influential Congressmen, John D. Dingell and Edward J. Markey, expressed their concern:

We strongly endorse what we understand to be the policy goals underlying the Commission's adoption of Rule 144A. The Commission staff is to be commended for its creativity, hard work, and the high quality of its efforts in seeking to enhance the competitiveness of the U.S. in today's global markets. Nonetheless, we are concerned about the specific mechanism established to achieve these goals. In particular, we are concerned about the possible development of a two-tiered securities market for U.S. investors, one public and one private, and the serious negative implications of such a development; the diminished availability of many quality investments to smaller investors and, conversely, the greater likelihood that poor investments will be passed on to unwitting investors through mutual and pension funds or other avenues of leakage, and the rule's diminution of the amount and type of disclosure, particularly with regard to foreign companies about which U.S. investors have historically had little information.[34]

See also Norris, *The SEC and the Death of Disclosure*, N.Y. Times, June 9, 1991, at C5 (offering a critical view that, due to Rule 144A, "institutional investors can buy privately placed securities and trade them freely with other institutions . . . [a]fter minimal financial disclosure.").

In light of the foregoing materials, consider the following: (1) What are the problems that Rule 144A seeks to alleviate? Or, stated differently, what are the key purposes underlying Rule 144A? (2) Does the Rule, as drafted, accomplish these objectives? (3) Are there investor protection concerns that merit further exploration, perhaps even the need to amend the Rule to alleviate these concerns? (4) Has the

---

33. Hanks, *Rule 144A: Easing Restrictions on Trading Unregistered Securities*, N.Y.L.J., May 10, 1990, at 5, 6.

34. Excerpts of the letter are contained and discussed in Barron, *Some Comments on SEC Rule 144A*, 18 Sec. Reg. L.J. 400 (1991).

Rule succeeded in bringing about in this country a liquid and efficient institutional resale market comprised of unregistered securities, thereby giving institutional investors direct access to both domestic and foreign issued securities?

Rule 144A thus far has been most successful in attracting foreign companies to the U.S. capital markets. According to a report authored by the SEC staff, 69 of the first 95 issuers whose securities were sold by means of Rule 144A were foreign entities. The rule, however, is a disappointment for its failure to stimulate a resale market in Regulation D and similar types of offerings.[35] On the other hand, as discussed earlier in this Section, Rule 144A is being used extensively by companies marketing their securities to QIBs. The amount of equity and debt capital raised pursuant to Rule 144A approximates $800 billion annually. Indeed, the Nasdaq Stock Market has implemented a centralized automated trading system for Rule 144A securities.[36]

See generally Bradford, *Rule 144A and Integration*, 20 SEC. REG. L.J. 37 (1992); Rumsey, *Rule 144A and Other Developments in the Resale of Restricted Securities,* 19 Sec. Reg. L.J. 400 (1991); Sjostrom, *The Birth of Rule 144A Equity Offerings,* 56 UCLA L. REV. 409 (2008).

---

§ 6.08 Corporate Reorganizations

[A] In General

Corporations, as well as other entities, frequently engage in reorganizations. State corporation statutes, corporate charters, and similar controlling instruments normally require shareholder approval or consent of mergers, consolidations, transfer of assets and reclassifications of stock. These reorganizations normally result in the exchange of shares or the issuance of new stock. Rule 145(a) makes it clear that when such plans of reorganization are submitted to shareholders for approval, the corporation makes an "offer to sell" within the meaning of § 2(a)(3) of the Securities Act. Rule 145, therefore, has several ramifications.

[B] Rule 145 — Ramifications

Absent an exemption from registration, the sale of securities pursuant to Rule 145 triggers the registration requirements of § 5 as well as due diligence obligations (including the rigorous culpability standards of § 11). Rule 145 transactions may be registered pursuant to the Securities Act on Form S-4. The Form S-4 framework

---

35. *See* 23 Sec. Reg. & L. Rep. (BNA) 1589 (1991).

36. *Nasdaq's New 144A Platform Approved by SEC for Launch Aug. 15*, 39 SEC. REP. & L. REP. (BNA) 1214 (2007).

improves the effectiveness of the business reorganization prospectus by requiring that information be presented in a more accessible and meaningful format.[37]

By triggering the registration requirements, Rule 145 also implicates §5's "gun-jumping" prohibition.[38] Thus, with certain exceptions, communications designed to influence shareholders' votes may be viewed as constituting offers to sell in the pre-filing period and, hence, violations of §5(c). Rule 145(b) provides certain exceptions in this respect. For example, a corporation contemplating a Rule 145 reorganization that will be registered under the Securities Act may communicate to the public basic information, including the issuer's name, a brief description of the business of the parties, and a brief description of the transaction. Compliance with the provisions of Rule 145(b) has the effect of protecting the communication from constituting an "offer to sell" under §2(a)(3) or from being deemed a "prospectus" under §2(a)(10). In this regard, the pre-filing publicity notice permitted under Rule 135 is also available for such transactions.[39]

[C] "Downstream Sales"

The ramifications of Rule 145 do not end after the shareholders approve a plan of reorganization. Rule 145(c) addresses the problem of "downstream sales." Depending on the circumstances, parties to a Rule 145 transaction who publicly sell or publicly offer to sell their securities may be deemed to be engaged in a distribution as well as being deemed underwriters within the meaning of §2(a)(11).[40] These parties can avoid underwriter status, however, by meeting the criteria contained in Rule 145(d).

---

37. *See* Securities Act Release No. 6578 (1985). *See generally* Campbell, *Rule 145: Mergers, Acquisitions and Recapitalizations Under the Securities Act of 1933*, 56 Fordham L. Rev. 277 (1987).

38. For discussion on conditioning the market ("gun-jumping"), *see* §4.02[B][2] *supra*.

39. Rule 135 is addressed in §4.02[B][4] *supra*. SEC Rules 165 and 166 also exempt certain communications regarding business combination transactions from §5 of the Securities Act. Rule 165 is not limited to offerors and may be used by "any other participant that may need to rely on and complies with [Rule 165] in communicating about the transaction." Rule 166 permits communications by participants in a registered offering involving a business combination transaction before the first public announcement of the offering upon a showing that "all reasonable steps within their control [were taken] to prevent further distribution or publication of the communication until either the first public announcement is made or the registration statement related to the transaction is filed [with the Commission.]" *See* Securities Act Release No. 42055, [1999–2000 Transfer Binder] Fed. Sec. L. Rep. (CCH) ¶ 86,215 (SEC 1999).

40. The 2007 amendments to Rule 145 provide that underwriter status will no longer be presumed unless the covered transaction involves a shell company, other than a business combination shell company, as those terms are defined by Rule 405. Rule 405 defines a shell company as a registrant that has either no or nominal assets, or whose assets consist primarily of cash and cash equivalents, while a business combination shell company is a shell company formed solely for the purpose of changing corporate domicile or to complete certain business combination transactions. See Securities Act Release No. 8869 (2007).

As an initial point, for parties who neither are affiliates of the acquired company nor affiliates of the acquiring company, the securities received in a Rule 145 transaction are nonrestricted securities, thereby having no restrictions on resale.

In regard to parties who are affiliates of an entity *acquired* pursuant to a Rule 145 transaction, the SEC, consistent with its Rule 144 modifications, has substantially relaxed the "resale" provisions of Rule 145. As a result, such parties (who are affiliates of the acquired, but not of the acquiring, entity) today have much greater leeway in reselling their securities without fear of assuming underwriter status. Accordingly, persons who are affiliates of the acquired entity that receive securities in registered business combinations and who subsequently transfer such securities will not be deemed underwriters if:

i. The securities are sold in compliance with the provisions of paragraphs (c), (e), (f), and (g) of Rule 144 and at least 90 days have elapsed since the time that such securities were acquired in connection with the transaction; or

ii. The person is a non-affiliate of the issuer (i.e., a non-affiliate of the acquiring company), has been a non-affiliate of the issuer for at least three months, has held the securities for at least a six-month period, and the issuer has complied with the current public reporting requirements of Rule 144(c) (by either being an Exchange Act reporting company or by making adequate information available); or

iii. The party is a non-affiliate of the issuer, has been a non-affiliate of the issuer for at least three months, and has held the securities for at least one year.[41]

Consider the effect of the SEC's amendments to Rule 145 (with respect to persons who were affiliates of an entity acquired in a Rule 145 transaction, who are not affiliates of the acquiring entity, and who have been such non-affiliates for at least three months). First, such non-affiliates of the issuer (i.e., non-affiliates of the acquiring company) can dispose of all of their securities after six months if the issuer has maintained adequate current public information. Second, such non-affiliates, after a one-year holding period, can sell all of their shares even if the issuer is not making adequate current information available (of course, subject to Rule 15c2-11 requiring that specified information must be publicly available in order for a broker-dealer to publish a quotation for such security). Note that the holding period is measured from the date of acquisition from the issuer or from an affiliate of the issuer. "Tacking" of the applicable holding period is permitted when transactions take place between non-affiliates.[42]

The public policy assessments made by the Commission in adopting these revisions can be questioned on much the same basis as was made with respect to the amendments to Rule 144. Undoubtedly, the Commission's amendments to Rule 145

---

41. *See* Securities Act Release Nos. 6508 (1984), 7390 (1997), 8869 (2007).

42. *See* Securities Act Release No. 7390 (1997); Securities Act Release No. 6862 (1990). *See generally*, Campbell, *Resales of Securities: The New Rules and the New Approach of the SEC,* 37 Sec. Reg. L.J. 317 (2008).

are a victory for deregulation and capital formation. Some may claim, however, that the costs are too great: Permitting non-affiliates of the issuer to "dump" their securities on the investing public with relatively little information being available about the issuer (e.g., limited to Rule 15c2-11 information) deals a blow to two fundamental purposes underlying the federal securities laws, namely: to ensure the integrity of the financial marketplace and to enable investors to have adequate information before them so that they can make informed investment decisions.

[D] "Spin-Offs"

Spin-offs have many variations. The "classical" spin-off occurs when a parent corporation distributes shares of a privately held subsidiary as a stock dividend to its current shareholders. In such event, it is only a matter of time before these shares become publicly traded. Absent the availability of an exemption, "spin-offs" thereby may have the effect of evading the registration requirements. Due to this concern, the SEC and the courts have held that this technique, depending on the circumstances, calls for Securities Act registration. Moreover, parent corporations that cause their subsidiaries to engage in such practices may be deemed to be "underwriters."[43]

Defendants, charged with failing to register a "spin-off" offering, have asserted that the stock dividend distributed to shareholders was not an "offer to sell" or "sale" within the meaning of § 2(a)(3) of the Securities Act because it was not "for value," and hence, was not in violation of § 5. The SEC and the courts frequently have rejected this argument, reasoning that the creation of a public market for the spun-off securities constitutes value to the parent corporation when the stockholders dispose of these securities.[44]

In 1997, the SEC's Division of Corporation Finance opined that a spin-off does not require Securities Act registration if the following five conditions are met: (1) shareholders of the parent corporation do not provide any consideration for the spun-off shares; (2) the shares spun-off are distributed pro rata to the parent corporation's shareholders; (3) adequate information about the subsidiary and the spin-off must be provided by the parent corporation to both the stockholders and the securities trading markets; (4) the parent corporation has a valid business purpose justifying the spin-off; and (5) if the parent corporation elects to spin-off restricted securities, it must have held such securities for a requisite period.[45] Note, moreover, that SEC Rule 15c2-11 impedes public trading of securities acquired in unregistered spin-offs by prohibiting broker-dealers from either initiating or continuing to

---

43. *See SEC v. Datronics Engineers, Inc.*, 490 F.2d 250 (4th Cir. 1973), *cert. denied*, 416 U.S. 937 (1974); *SEC v. Harwyn Industries Corp.*, 326 F. Supp. 943 (S.D.N.Y. 1971). *But see Isquith v. Caremark International, Inc.*, 136 F.3d 531 (7th Cir. 1998).

44. *See* cases cited note 43 *supra*.

45. *See* SEC Legal Bulletin No. 4 (Sept. 16, 1997).

provide price quotations for a security unless specified information is available with respect to both the issuer and the security.[46]

[E] Adoption of Form S-4

Business Combination Transactions—Adoption of Registration Form

Securities Act Release No. 6578 (1985)

The Commission announces the adoption of a new form to be used to register securities under the Securities Act of 1933 in connection with business combination transactions. The form applies the principles of the integrated disclosure system to disclosure in the context of mergers and exchange offers. The form is designed to improve the effectiveness of the business combination prospectus by requiring that information be presented in a more accessible and meaningful format.

. . . .

I. Executive Summary

This rulemaking action is part of the Commission's Proxy Review Program and represents the culmination of efforts extending over several years to improve disclosure to investors in business combinations.

This area has been the focus of attention because the documents delivered to security holders in the context of business combinations (mergers and exchange offers) are frequently unwieldy, often 150 or more pages. . . . Form S-4 extends the principles underlying the integrated disclosure system to all business combination registration statements. . . . The Form also extends the principles of integration to the full extent to which they are applied in the context of primary offerings not involving business combinations. [Also,] Form S-4 provides simplified and streamlined disclosure in prospectuses for business combinations whether the transactions are effected by merger or exchange offer.

The integrated disclosure system, on which Form S-4 is based, proceeds from the premise that investors in the primary market need much the same information as investors in the trading market. Integration also specifies the manner in which information should be delivered to investors. Under Forms S-1 . . . and S-3, transaction oriented information must be presented in the prospectus. Company oriented information, however, may be presented in, delivered with, or incorporated by reference

---

46. *See* T. Hazen, *supra* note 5, at 250–253; Bloomenthal, *Market-Makers, Manipulators and Shell Games*, 45 ST. JOHN'S L. REV. 597 (1971); Long, *Control of the Spin-Off Device Under the Securities Act of 1933*, 25 OKLA. L. REV. 317 (1972); Lorne, *The Portfolio Spin-Off and Securities Registration*, 52 TEX. L. REV. 918 (1974); cases cited *supra* note 43.

into the prospectus, depending on the extent to which Exchange Act reports containing the information have been disseminated and assimilated in the market.

. . . .

The prospectus requirements of Form S-4 are divided into four sections. The first section calls for information about the transaction, which will be presented in the prospectus in all cases, and which is designed to make the presentation of the complex transactions that typify business combinations more easily understood by investors. The next two sections specify the information about the businesses involved and prescribe different levels of prospectus presentation and incorporation by reference depending upon which form under the Securities Act the company could use in making a primary offering of its securities not involving a business combination. The last section sets forth the requirements as to voting and management information. All voting information must be presented in the prospectus, while the amount of prospectus presentation for management information, like company information, depends on which form could be used in a primary offering not involving a business combination.

The use of the S-1 [and S-3] approach in Form S-4 reflects the premise that decisions made in the context of business combination transactions and those made otherwise in the purchase of a security in the primary or trading market are substantially similar. At the same time, the Commission recognizes that there are significant differences. In particular, business combination decisions are not of the same volitional nature as other investment decisions. Moreover, typically mergers may give rise to a change in security ownership as a consequence of inaction.

To address the differences in the nature of the investment decision, special provisions have been included in the Form. First, a specifically tailored item covering risk factors, ratio of earnings to fixed charges, certain per share data and other information must be presented in the prospectus regardless of the level of disclosure available to the companies involved. This item, as adopted, has been expanded to reflect commentators' suggestions that the item include: (1) certain additional financial data; and (2) information about regulatory approvals.

While the item highlights certain information discussed more fully elsewhere in the prospectus, or in documents incorporated by reference therein, it is not intended to be a summary of all material information concerning the transaction and the parties thereto. In the case of S-3 companies, where company and management information, including historical financial statements, is not presented in the prospectus, such information will have been furnished to security holders and widely disseminated in the market by means of the company's annual report to security holders. Therefore, this information need not be reiterated in the business combination prospectus. . . .

Chapter 7

Due Diligence and Securities Act Liability

§ 7.01 Introduction

As discussed in the foregoing Chapters (at this point review the discussions in §§ 3.01 and 4.01), a registration statement is required to be utilized in connection with a public offering. As sometimes happens after a successful public financing, start-up companies go broke or the price of an established issuer's stock decreases. When an investor loses substantial sums, he/she may seek recompense. As we all know, however, the securities laws are not an insurance policy. Investment in the stock of an issuer is a risk-taking venture.

There are certain caveats. Although some investors may be more financially sophisticated or have greater access to superior advisers than others, all are entitled under the Securities Act to receive adequate and truthful information concerning the issuer, its associated persons, and the offering. This information provides the investor with the opportunity to make an informed decision whether to purchase the securities.

When a registration statement (including the prospectus, which comprises part of the registration statement) contains a materially false or misleading statement, the policies underlying the securities laws are frustrated. Investors cannot make informed decisions if their decisions are based on erroneous information. Moreover, they will lose confidence in the integrity of the financial marketplace.

In view of the above, investors under certain conditions may recover their losses if they purchase securities pursuant to a registration statement that contains a material misrepresentation or nondisclosure. The provision most likely to be invoked in this context is § 11 of the Securities Act.

Concerning due diligence in the registered offering context, the *BarChris* case (283 F. Supp. 643 (S.D.N.Y. 1968)), still serves as the most appropriate vehicle for focusing on this concept. As *BarChris* illustrates, although technically a defense, due diligence is a necessary function to be performed. The discussion thereafter addresses the various parties who may assert the due diligence defense and the degree of investigation required for each such party, including: directors ("inside" as well as "outside"), signatories of the registration statement, underwriters, accountants (who serve as "experts"), and attorneys (who are not liable under § 11 unless they "expertise" a portion of the registration statement, serve as a director, or act in some other capacity that brings them within the provision's reach).

After analyzing *BarChris* and its ramifications, this Chapter discusses the controversial issue, particularly for underwriters, of due diligence in the integrated disclosure framework. These concerns, as the materials in § 7.08 point out, are accentuated in the shelf registration context. Many critics claim that the SEC's response, principally the adoption of Rule 176, is inadequate. The ultimate resolution reached should accommodate the legitimate concerns of underwriters yet be consistent with investor protection.

The next portion of the Chapter focuses on § 12(a)(2) of the Securities Act, which contains a "reasonable care" defense that, depending on the circumstances, may be similar to § 11's "due diligence" defense. Section 12(a)(2) may be similar to § 11's remedial counterpart where an *unregistered* offering takes on the characteristics of a public offering, including with respect to free writing prospectuses.[1] Moreover, in either the registered or unregistered offering setting, as discussed in Chapter 8 of this text, plaintiffs always can seek to invoke § 10(b) of the Securities Exchange Act.[2]

Finally, the Chapter will examine the remedial provisions afforded by the crowdfunding provision of the JOBS Act. As will be seen, this right of action has many similarities to the § 12(a)(2) remedy.

§ 7.02 The Registered Offering — Framework of Section 11

[A] Persons Subject to Section 11 Liability

Section 11(a) of the Securities Act specifies the classes of persons who may be subject to liability for material misstatements or nondisclosures contained in the registration statement (including the statutory prospectus, which is part of the registration statement). Parties subject to liability include: (1) all persons who sign the registration statement including, pursuant to § 6(a) of the Securities Act, the "issuer, its principal executive officer or officers, its principal financial officer, its controller or principal accounting officer, and the majority of its board of directors or persons performing similar functions"; (2) every director (or person performing similar functions) or general partner of the issuer; (3) every person named with his/her consent in the registration statement as being or about to become a person stated in (2) above; (4) every underwriter of the offering; (5) every expert "who has with his consent been named as having prepared or certified any part of the registration statement, or as having prepared or certified any report or valuation which is used in connection with the registration statement, with respect to the statement in such registration statement, report, or valuation which purports to have been prepared or certified by him";

---

1. *See Gustafson v. Alloyd Company,* 513 U.S. 561 (1995); Securities Release No. 8591 (2005).
2. *See Herman & MacLean v. Huddleston,* 459 U.S. 375 (1983).

and (6) pursuant to § 15(a) of the Securities Act, every control person of the issuer.[3] Due to the statutory language and the exhaustive enumeration of those parties subject to suit under § 11, the courts have refused to impose "aiding and abetting" liability pursuant to this provision.

[B] Elements of the Section 11 Right of Action

Generally, provided that the interstate commerce requirement has been met, a private action for damages under § 11(a) may be brought by "any person acquiring such security" unless it can be shown that, at the time of purchase, the purchaser knew of the misstatement or omission. Privity between the purchaser and the defendant is not required for recovery. Moreover, the § 11 right of action is available in the initial offering setting as well as when those shares (subject to the "tracing" requirement) are subsequently traded in the aftermarket.[4] In addition, a plaintiff bringing suit under § 11 normally need not show reliance upon the misstatement or omission. In fact, the plaintiff need not even have read the prospectus.

Pursuant to § 11(a), however, where the plaintiff acquired the securities more than 12 months after the effective date of the registration statement and if the issuer has made generally available an "earnings statement" covering this 12-month period, the plaintiff must prove reliance on the misstatement or omission. Such reliance may be shown by means other than the actual reading of the prospectus.[5]

Nor is the plaintiff who brings a § 11 action required to prove that the material misrepresentation or nondisclosure "caused" the loss. In this regard, however, § 11(e) permits the defendant to prove that the plaintiff's loss was due to factors other than the material misrepresentation(s) or nondisclosure(s) contained in the registration statement.

Practical limitations, however, at times may have the effect of nullifying the § 11 right of action. For example, § 11 actions have a relatively short statute of limitations. In this respect, § 13 of the Securities Act provides that an action pursuant to § 11 must

---

3. *See* § 15(a) of the Securities Act which provides that "[e]very person who . . . controls any person liable under section 11 or 12, shall also be liable jointly and severally . . . to the same extent [that] such controlled person . . . [is liable] to any [aggrieved] person, unless the controlling person had no knowledge of or reasonable grounds to believe in the existence of the facts [at issue]."

4. The overwhelming majority of courts allow Section 11 to be invoked in the aftermarket by allegedly aggrieved purchasers, provided that the "tracing" requirement is met. However, based on the U.S. Supreme Court's decision in *Gustafson v. Alloyd Co.*, 513 U.S. 561 (1995) (discussed in § 7.09[D]), which limited Section 12(a)(2)'s scope to public offerings, a few courts have confined Section 11's coverage to those securities purchased in the public offering itself. Compare *Hertzberg v. Dignity Partners, Inc.*, 191 F.3d 1076 (9th Cir. 1999) (holding purchasers who traced shares acquired in the aftermarket to the allegedly false registration statement had standing under § 11) and *Schwartz v. Celestial Seasonings, Inc.*, 178 F.R.D. 545 (D. Colo. 1998) (same), with *Gould v. Harris*, 929 F. Supp. 353 (C.D. Cal. 1996) (tracing not recognized to confer § 11 standing).

5. *See* SEC Rule 158 (defining the terms: "earning statement," "made generally available to its security holders," and "effective date of the registration statement" for the purposes of the reliance requirement as set forth in the final paragraph of § 11(a)).

be brought "within one year after the discovery of the untrue statement or the omission, or after such discovery should have been made by the exercise of reasonable diligence . . . [but] in no event shall any such action be brought . . . more than three years after the security was offered to the public." In practical effect, however, the "tracing" requirement may nullify a plaintiff's invocation of § 11 in the aftermarket context. For example, stockholders lack standing under § 11 with respect to those shares that they are unable to affirmatively trace to the public registered offering. Hence, pursuant to the tracing requirement, plaintiffs must show not that they "might" have purchased shares by means of a deficient registration statement in a particular offering, but that they in fact did purchase such shares pursuant to that specific offering (and registration statement). *See Krim v. pcOrder.com, Inc.,* 402 F.3d 489, 495–496 (5th Cir. 2005), where the Fifth Circuit observed: "[A]ftermarket purchasers seeking standing [under § 11] must demonstrate the ability to 'trace' their shares to the faulty registration [statement]." Given the practical difficulties of "tracing," this requirement is a difficult one for "aftermarket" § 11 plaintiffs. This "already burdensome task of proving tracing has become even more onerous as a growing number of courts have rejected the use of statistical evidence to prove tracing [thereby requiring that tracing be proven to a 100% certainty]. This is true even when the pool of stock on the [secondary] market contains 99.85% registered stock [that can be traced to the subject registered offering]."[6]

To summarize under § 11, a *plaintiff*:

- must have purchased the security where a means or instrumentality of interstate commerce was used in connection with the offer or sale;

- at the time of purchase, must not have known of the misrepresentation or nondisclosure;

- must show that the misrepresentation or nondisclosure was "material," meaning that reasonable investors would have considered the pertinent information important in making their investment decisions;

- need not establish privity;

- can recover for aftermarket purchases, subject to the onerous "tracing" requirement;

- normally need not show reliance upon the misrepresentation or nondisclosure;

---

6. Steinberg & Kirby, *The Assault on Section 11 of the Securities Act: A Study in Judicial Activism,* 63 Rutgers L. Rev. 1, 27 (2010), *citing, Krim v. pcOrder.com,* 402 F.3d 489 (5th Cir. 2005); *In re Quarterback Officer Systems, Inc. Securities Litigation,* 1993 WL 623310 (C.D. Cal. 1993); *In re Elscint Ltd. Securities Litigation,* 674 F. Supp. 374 (D. Mass. 1987). *See generally, Barnes v. Osofsky,* 373 F.2d 269 (2d Cir. 1967); *Newbridge Networks Securities Litigation,* 767 F. Supp. 275 (D.D.C. 1991); *Guenther v. Cooper Life Sciences, Inc.,* 759 F. Supp. 1437 (N.D. Cal. 1990); *Kirkwood v. Taylor,* 590 F. Supp. 1375 (D. Minn. 1984); *McFarland v. Memorex Corp.,* 493 F. Supp. 631 (N.D. Cal. 1980); Murray, *Aftermarket Purchaser Standing Under § 11 of the Securities Act of 1933,* 73 St. John L. Rev. 633 (1999); Sale, *Disappearing Without a Trace: Sections 11 and 12(a)(2) of the Securities Act,* 75 Wash. L. Rev. 429 (2000).

- need not prove that the misrepresentation or nondisclosure "caused" the loss (in other words, causation is presumed once a material misstatement or nondisclosure has been shown by the plaintiff—but may be rebutted by the defendant;

- must bring the action within the time period set forth by § 13's statute of limitations.

See M. STEINBERG, W. COUTURE, M. KAUFMAN, AND D. MORRISSEY, SECURITIES LITIGATION: LAW, POLICY, AND PRACTICE 61–132 (2016).

The case that follows adopts the prevailing view that recognizes "tracing" under § 11.

Hertzberg v. Dignity Partners, Inc.

United States Court of Appeals, Ninth Circuit

191 F.3d 1076 (1999)

This case arises out of alleged misstatements and omissions contained in Appellee Dignity Partners, Inc.'s ("Dignity's") registration statement filed with the Securities and Exchange Commission [SEC] for an initial public offering of Dignity common stock. Dignity was in the business of buying the rights to life insurance proceeds from people with AIDS, paying a lump sum up front and taking over the responsibility for paying the premiums. Shortly after the offering, the fact that AIDS patients were living longer than expected because of new AIDS treatments became public knowledge. As a result of the longer lives of the insured, Dignity posted huge losses, and the stock plummeted.

Plaintiffs/appellants Hertzberg, Derosa, and Feinman ("Hertzberg") are investors who purchased Dignity stock on the open market more than 25 days after the initial offering but before the news of the longer life expectancy or large losses became public knowledge. They brought a class action for several violations of the securities laws by Dignity, including violation of Section 11 of the Securities Act of 1933 ("Securities Act"). Hertzberg claims that Dignity knew of the longer life expectancy but failed to disclose it in the registration statement. The district court dismissed the Section 11 causes of action on the ground that, because appellants had not bought their stock in the initial public offering . . . they did not have standing to bring the claim. . . .

We reverse the district court's holding that the original named plaintiffs lacked standing under Section 11.

. . . .

DISCUSSION

We review the district court's interpretation of Section 11 de novo. In determining the meaning of a statute, we look first to its text. Section 11(a) provides that where a material fact is misstated or omitted from a registration statement accompanying a stock filing with the Securities and Exchange Commission, "any person acquiring such security" may bring an action for losses caused by the misstatement or omission. . . .

The term "any person" is quite broad, and we give words their ordinary meaning. According to Webster's Third New Int'l Dictionary (3d ed. 1986), "any" means "one, no matter what one"; "ALL"; "one or more discriminately from all those of a kind." This broad meaning of "any" has been recognized by this circuit.

The limitation on "any person" is that he or she must have purchased "such security." Clearly, this limitation only means that the person must have purchased a security issued under that, rather than some other, registration statement. [Moreover,] [i]f there is a mixture of pre-registration stock and stock sold under the misleading registration statement, a plaintiff must either show that he purchased his stock in the initial offering or trace his later-purchased stock back to the initial offering.

[Thus, while there may exist] a problem of proof in a case in which stock was issued under more than one registration statement,[7] the only Dignity stock ever sold to the public was pursuant to the allegedly misleading registration statement at issue in this case. Thus, as long as Hertzberg is suing regarding this security, he is "any person purchasing such security," regardless of whether he bought in the initial offering, a week later, or a month after that.

Further, paragraph (e) of Section 11 uses "the amount paid for the security (not exceeding the price at which the security was offered to the public)" as the baseline for measuring damages. Such a provision would be unnecessary if only a person who bought in the actual offering could recover, since, by definition, such a person would have paid "the price at which the security was offered to the public." We will "avoid a reading which renders some words altogether redundant."

Finally, Dignity believes that its reading of Section 11 is supported by the Supreme Court's decision in *Gustafson* [513 U.S. 561 (1995)]. We believe that Dignity is mistaken. In *Gustafson*, the Supreme Court interpreted Section 12 of the Securities Act, rather than Section 11, and limited its decision to determining what was a "prospectus" under Section 12. Dicta in *Gustafson* indicate that a suit under Section 12 may only be maintained by a person who purchased the stock in the offering under the prospectus, but the Court gave no indication that it intended this restriction to apply to Section 11.

Dignity relies on the Supreme Court's statements in *Gustafson* that Section 12 is a companion to Section 11 for its claim that Section 11 applies only to people who purchased their stock in the initial offering. However, while Section 11 and Section 12 are indeed parallel statutes, their wording is significantly different as to who can bring a suit. As already noted, Section 11 permits suit without restriction by "any person acquiring such security." Section 12, by contrast, permits suit against a seller of a security by prospectus only by "the person purchasing such security from him . . ."

---

[7]. [This footnote has been moved to the text. — ed.]

Congress's decision to use "from him" in Section 12 but not in Section 11 must mean that Congress intended a different meaning in the two sections. . . . Further, there is nothing in the reasoning or underlying logic of *Gustafson* that indicates that we should read into Section 11 the express privity requirement of Section 12. [Section 12 is covered later in this Chapter.]

Where the meaning of a statute is clear from the text, we need look no further. However, we note that even if we were to find the wording of the statute ambiguous, the legislative history supports Hertzberg's reading of Section 11.

> The House Report accompanying the version of the bill that ultimately became the Securities Act of 1933 provides: the civil remedies accorded by [Section 11] are given to all purchasers . . . regardless of whether they bought their securities at the time of the original offer or at some later date, provided, of course, that the remedy is prosecuted within the period of limitations provided by section 13.

H.R. Rep. No. 73-85, at 22 (emphasis added). By expressly referring to purchasers who bought their securities "at some later date" other than "at the time of the original offer," the Report makes it clear that purchasers in the aftermarket are intended to have a cause of action under the Section. Similarly, when Congress amended Section 11 in 1934 to add a requirement of proof of reliance on the registration statement if there had been an intervening earning statement, the House Report stated:

> The basis of this provision is that in all likelihood the purchase and price of the security purchased after publication of such an earning statement will be predicated upon that statement rather than upon the information disclosed upon registration.

H.R. Rep. 73-1838 at 41. By referring to purchases after publication of an earning statement, the Report makes clear that purchasers in the aftermarket are within the group of purchasers provided a cause of action by Section 11.

. . . .

Note

Note that in the above case, all of the shares that were available to be purchased in the public trading markets (such as the Nasdaq Stock Market) were issued pursuant to the allegedly materially misleading registration statement. As discussed above, several courts require that "tracing" be proven with 100 percent certainty. In view of this strict mandate, consider the ease with which a company's insiders can introduce non-registered securities into the public markets and thus avoid § 11 liability to secondary market purchasers. For example:

> Stock issued pursuant to Rule 506 is exempt from registration and must only be held for at most twelve months prior to being resold. Issuers and insiders desiring to immunize themselves from Section 11 liability can

cause a small quantity of these unregistered shares to be sold in the public markets shortly after the time of the registered offering. This would pollute the entire pool of stock and render tracing by non-statistical means, in practical effect, nearly impossible. Without statistical tracing, it only takes one non-registered share to render Section 11 inoperative as to aftermarket purchasers.[8]

It may be posited that, if an issuer or its insiders have formulated such a strategy, the negating of a § 11 right of action that otherwise would have been available to secondary market purchasers is a material fact that must be disclosed.

_____

In the following case, the Supreme Court addressed the extent to which statements of opinion or belief are actionable under § 11.

Omnicare, Inc. v. Laborers District Council Construction Industry Pension Fund

United States Supreme Court

___ U.S. ___, 135 S. Ct. 1318, 191 L. Ed. 2d 253 (2015)

Justice KAGAN delivered the opinion of the Court.

Before a company may sell securities in interstate commerce, it must file a registration statement with the Securities and Exchange Commission (SEC). If that document either "contain[s] an untrue statement of a material fact" or "omit[s] to state a material fact . . . necessary to make the statements therein not misleading," a purchaser of the stock may sue for damages. [Section 11(a) of the Securities Act,] 15 U.S.C. § 77k(a). This case requires us to decide how each of those phrases applies to statements of opinion.

I.

The Securities Act of 1933 protects investors by ensuring that companies issuing securities (known as "issuers") make a "full and fair disclosure of information" relevant to a public offering. The linchpin of the Act is its registration requirement. With limited exceptions not relevant here, an issuer may offer securities to the public only after filing a registration statement. That statement must contain specified information about both the company itself and the security for sale. Beyond those required disclosures, the issuer may include additional representations of either fact or opinion.

Section 11 of the Act promotes compliance with these disclosure provisions by giving purchasers a right of action against an issuer or designated individuals (directors, partners, underwriters, and so forth) for material misstatements or omissions in registration statements. As relevant here, that section provides:

_____

8. Steinberg and Kirby, *supra* note 6, at 34.

"In case any part of the registration statement, when such part became effective, contained an untrue statement of a material fact or omitted to state a material fact required to be stated therein or necessary to make the statements therein not misleading, any person acquiring such security . . . [may] sue."

Section 11 thus creates two ways to hold issuers liable for the contents of a registration statement—one focusing on what the statement says and the other on what it leaves out. Either way, the buyer need not prove (as he must to establish certain other securities offenses) that the defendant acted with any intent to deceive or defraud.

This case arises out of a registration statement that petitioner Omnicare filed in connection with a public offering of common stock. Omnicare is the nation's largest provider of pharmacy services for residents of nursing homes. Its registration statement contained (along with all mandated disclosures) analysis of the effects of various federal and state laws on its business model, including its acceptance of rebates from pharmaceutical manufacturers. Of significance here, two sentences in the registration statement expressed Omnicare's view of its compliance with legal requirements:

- "We believe our contract arrangements with other healthcare providers, our pharmaceutical suppliers and our pharmacy practices are in compliance with applicable federal and state laws."

- "We believe that our contracts with pharmaceutical manufacturers are legally and economically valid arrangements that bring value to the healthcare system and the patients that we serve."

Accompanying those legal opinions were some caveats. On the same page as the first statement above, Omnicare mentioned several state-initiated "enforcement actions against pharmaceutical manufacturers" for offering payments to pharmacies that dispensed their products; it then cautioned that the laws relating to that practice might "be interpreted in the future in a manner inconsistent with our interpretation and application." And adjacent to the second statement, Omnicare noted that the Federal Government had expressed "significant concerns" about some manufacturers' rebates to pharmacies and warned that business might suffer "if these price concessions were no longer provided."

Respondents here, pension funds that purchased Omnicare stock in the public offering (hereinafter Funds), brought suit alleging that the company's two opinion statements about legal compliance give rise to liability under § 11. Citing lawsuits that the Federal Government later pressed against Omnicare, the Funds' complaint maintained that the company's receipt of payments from drug manufacturers violated anti-kickback laws. Accordingly, the complaint asserted, Omnicare made "materially false" representations about legal compliance. And so too, the complaint continued, the company "omitted to state [material] facts necessary" to make its representations not misleading. The Funds claimed that none of Omnicare's officers and directors "possessed reasonable grounds" for thinking that the opinions offered were truthful and complete. Indeed, the complaint noted that one of Omnicare's attorneys had warned that a particular contract "carrie[d] a heightened risk" of liability under anti-kickback laws. At the same time, the Funds made clear that in light of § 11's strict liability standard, they chose to "exclude and disclaim any allegation that could be construed as alleging fraud or intentional or reckless misconduct."

The District Court granted Omnicare's motion to dismiss. In the court's view, "statements regarding a company's belief as to its legal compliance are considered 'soft' information" and are actionable only if those who made them "knew [they] were untrue at the time." The court concluded that the Funds' complaint failed to meet that standard because it nowhere claimed that "the company's officers knew they were violating the law." The Court of Appeals for the Sixth Circuit [in an opinion written by the Honorable Guy Cole, with whom the author of this textbook was a summer law clerk for the Vorys law firm in Columbus Ohio] reversed. See 719 F.3d 498 (2013). It acknowledged that the two statements highlighted in the Funds' complaint expressed Omnicare's "opinion" of legal compliance, rather than "hard facts." But even so, the court held, the Funds had to allege only that the stated belief was "objectively false"; they did not need to contend that anyone at Omnicare "disbelieved [the opinion] at the time it was expressed." . . .

We granted certiorari to consider how § 11 pertains to statements of opinion. We do so in two steps, corresponding to the two parts of § 11 and the two theories in the Funds' complaint. We initially address the Funds' claim that Omnicare made "untrue statement[s] of . . . material fact" in offering its views on legal compliance. We then take up the Funds' argument that Omnicare "omitted to state a material fact . . . necessary to make the statements [in its registration filing] not misleading." Unlike both courts below, we see those allegations as presenting different issues. In resolving the first, we discuss when an opinion itself constitutes a factual misstatement. In analyzing the second, we address when an opinion may be rendered misleading by the omission of discrete factual representations. Because we find that the Court of Appeals applied the wrong standard, we vacate its decision.

II.

The Sixth Circuit held, and the Funds now urge, that a statement of opinion that is ultimately found incorrect — even if believed at the time made — may count as an "untrue statement of a material fact." As the Funds put the point, a statement of belief may make an implicit assertion about the belief's "subject matter". To say "we believe X is true" is often to indicate that "X is in fact true." In just that way, the Funds conclude, an issuer's statement that "we believe we are following the law" conveys that "we in fact are following the law" — which is "materially false," no matter what the issuer thinks, if instead it is violating an anti-kickback statute.

But that argument wrongly conflates facts and opinions. A fact is "a thing done or existing" or "[a]n actual happening." Webster's New International Dictionary 782 (1927). An opinion is "a belief[,] a view," or a "sentiment which the mind forms of persons or things." Most important, a statement of fact ("the coffee is hot") expresses certainty about a thing, whereas a statement of opinion ("I think the coffee is hot") does not ("An opinion, in ordinary usage . . . does not imply . . . definiteness . . . or certainty"); 7 Oxford English Dictionary 151 (1933) (an opinion "rests[s] on grounds insufficient for complete demonstration"). Indeed, that difference between the two is so ingrained in our everyday ways of speaking and thinking as to make resort to old dictionaries seem a mite silly. And Congress effectively incorporated just that distinction in § 11's first part by exposing issuers to liability not for "untrue statement[s]" full stop (which would have included ones of opinion), but only for "untrue statement[s] of . . . *fact*."

Consider that statutory phrase's application to two hypothetical statements, couched in ways the Funds claim are equivalent. A company's CEO states: "The TVs we manufacture have the highest resolution available on the market." Or, alternatively, the CEO transforms that factual statement into one of opinion. "I *believe*" (or "I think") "the TVs we manufacture have the highest resolution available on the market." The first version would be an untrue statement of fact if a competitor had introduced a higher resolution TV a month before—even assuming the CEO had not yet learned of the new product. The CEO's assertion, after all, is not mere puffery, but a determinate, verifiable statement about her company's TVs; and the CEO, however innocently, got the facts wrong. But in the same set of circumstances, the second version would remain true. Just as she said, the CEO really did believe, when she made the statement, that her company's TVs had the sharpest picture around. And although a plaintiff could later prove that opinion erroneous, the words "I believe" themselves admitted that possibility, thus precluding liability for an untrue statement of fact. That remains the case if the CEO's opinion, as here, concerned legal compliance. If, for example, she said, "I believe our marketing practices are lawful," and actually did think that, she could not be liable for a false statement of fact— even if she afterward discovered a longtime violation of law. Once again, the statement would have been true, because all she expressed was a view, not a certainty, about legal compliance.

That still leaves some room for § 11's false-statement provision to apply to expressions of opinion. As even Omnicare acknowledges, every such statement explicitly affirms one fact: that the speaker actually holds the stated belief. See . . . W. Keeton, D. Dobbs, R. Keeton, & D. Owen, Prosser and Keeton on the Law of Torts § 109, p. 755 (5th ed. 1984) (Prosser and Keeton) ("[A]n expression of opinion is itself always a statement of . . . the fact of the belief, the existing state of mind, of the one who asserts it"). For that reason, the CEO's statement about product quality ("I believe our TVs have the highest resolution available on the market") would be an untrue statement of fact—namely, the fact of her own belief—if she knew that her company's TVs only placed second. And so too the statement about legal compliance ("I believe our marketing practices are lawful") would falsely describe her own state of mind if she thought her company was breaking the law. In such cases, § 11's first part would subject the issuer to liability (assuming the misrepresentation were material).

In addition, some sentences that begin with opinion words like "I believe" contain embedded statements of fact . . . . Suppose the CEO in our running hypothetical said: "I believe our TVs have the highest resolution available because we use a patented technology to which our competitors do not have access." That statement may be read to affirm not only the speaker's state of mind, as described above, but also an underlying fact: that the company uses a patented technology. . . . Accordingly, liability under § 11's false-statement provision would follow (once again, assuming materiality) not only if the speaker did not hold the belief she professed but also if the supporting fact she supplied were untrue.

But the Funds cannot avail themselves of either of those ways of demonstrating liability. The two sentences to which the Funds object are pure statements of opinion: To simplify their content only a bit, Omnicare said in each that "we believe we are obeying the law." And the Funds do not contest that Omnicare's opinion was honestly held. Recall that their complaint explicitly "exclude[s] and disclaim[s]" any allegation sounding in fraud or deception. What the Funds instead claim is that Omnicare's belief turned out to be wrong—that whatever the company thought, it was in fact violating anti-kickback laws. But that allegation alone will not give rise to liability under § 11's first clause because, as we have shown, a sincere statement of pure opinion is not an "untrue statement of material fact," regardless whether an investor can ultimately prove the belief wrong. That clause, limited as it is to factual statements, does not allow investors to second-guess inherently subjective and uncertain assessments. In other words, the provision is not . . . an invitation to Monday morning quarterback an issuer's opinions.

III.

A

That conclusion, however, does not end this case because the Funds also rely on § 11's omissions provision, alleging that Omnicare "omitted to state facts necessary" to make its opinion on legal compliance "not misleading." As all parties accept, whether a statement is "misleading" depends on the perspective of a reasonable investor: The inquiry (like the one into materiality) is objective. *Cf. TSC Industries, Inc. v. Northway, Inc.*, 426 U.S. 438, 445 (1976) (noting that the securities laws care only about the "significance of an omitted or misrepresented fact to a reasonable investor"). We therefore must consider when, if ever, the omission of a fact can make a statement of opinion like Omnicare's, even if literally accurate, misleading to an ordinary investor.

Omnicare claims that is just not possible. On its view, no reasonable person, in any context, can understand a pure statement of opinion to convey anything more than the speaker's own mindset. As long as an opinion is sincerely held, Omnicare argues, it cannot mislead as to any matter, regardless what related facts the speaker has omitted. Such statements of belief (concludes Omnicare) are thus immune from liability under § 11's second part, just as they are under its first.

That claim has more than a kernel of truth. A reasonable person understands, and takes into account, the difference we have discussed above between a statement of fact and one of opinion. She recognizes the import of words like "I think" or "I believe," and grasps that they convey some lack of certainty as to the statement's content. See, *e.g.*, Restatement (Second) of Contracts § 168, Comment *a*, p. 456 (1979) (noting that a statement of opinion "implies that [the speaker] . . . is not certain enough of what he says" to do without the qualifying language). And that may be especially so when the phrases appear in a registration statement, which the reasonable investor expects has been carefully wordsmithed to comply with the law. When reading such a document, the investor thus distinguishes between the sentences "we believe X is true" and "X is true." And because she does so, the omission of a fact that merely rebuts the latter statement fails to render the former misleading. In other words, a statement of opinion is not misleading just because external facts show the opinion to be incorrect. Reasonable investors do not understand such statements as guarantees, and § 11's omissions clause therefore does not treat them that way.

But Omnicare takes its point too far, because a reasonable investor may, depending on the circumstances, understand an opinion statement to convey facts about how the speaker has formed the opinion—or, otherwise put, about the speaker's basis for holding that view. And if the real facts are otherwise, but not provided, the opinion statement will mislead its audience. Consider an unadorned statement of opinion about legal compliance: "We believe our conduct is lawful." If the issuer makes that statement without having consulted a lawyer, it could be misleadingly incomplete. In the context of the securities market, an investor, though recognizing that legal opinions can prove wrong in the end, still likely expects such an assertion to rest on some meaningful legal inquiry—rather than say, on mere intuition, however sincere. Similarly, if the issuer made the statement in the face of its lawyers' contrary advice, or with knowledge that the Federal Government was taking the opposite view, the investor again has cause to complain: He expects not just that the issuer believes the opinion (however irrationally), but that it fairly aligns with the information in the issuer's possession at the time. Thus, if a registration statement omits material facts about the issuer's inquiry into or knowledge concerning a statement of opinion, and if those facts conflict with what a reasonable investor would take from the statement itself, then § 11's omissions clause creates liability.

An opinion statement, however, is not necessarily misleading when an issuer knows, but fails to disclose, some fact cutting the other way. Reasonable investors understand that opinions sometimes rest on a weighing of competing facts; indeed, the presence of such facts is one reason why an issuer may frame a statement as an opinion, thus conveying uncertainty. Suppose, for example, that in stating an opinion about legal compliance, the issuer did not disclose that a single junior attorney expressed doubts about a practice's legality, when six of his more senior colleagues gave a stamp of approval. That omission would not make the statement of opinion misleading, even if the minority position ultimately proved correct: A reasonable investor does not expect that *every* fact known to an issuer supports its opinion statement.

Moreover, whether an omission makes an expression of opinion misleading always depends on context. Registration statements as a class are formal documents, filed with the SEC as a legal prerequisite for selling securities to the public. Investors do not, and are right not to, expect opinions contained in those statements to reflect baseless, off-the-cuff judgments, of the kind that an individual might communicate in daily life. At the same time, an investor reads each statement within such a document, whether of fact or of opinion, in light of all its surrounding text, including hedges, disclaimers, and apparently conflicting information. And the investor takes into account the customs and practices of the relevant industry. So an omission that renders misleading a statement of opinion when viewed in a vacuum may not do so once that statement is considered, as is appropriate, in a broader frame. The reasonable investor understands a statement of opinion in its full context, and § 11 creates liability only for the omission of material facts that cannot be squared with such a fair reading.

These principles are not unique to § 11: They inhere, too, in much common law respecting the tort of misrepresentation. The Restatement of Torts, for example, recognizes that "[a] statement of opinion as to facts not disclosed and not otherwise known to the recipient may" in some circumstances reasonably "be interpreted by him as an implied statement" that the speaker "knows facts sufficient to justify him in forming" the opinion, or that he at least knows no facts "incompatible with [the] opinion." Restatement (Second) of Torts § 539, p. 85 (1976). When that is so, the Restatement explains, liability may result from omission of facts—for example, the fact that the speaker failed to conduct any investigation—that rebut the recipient's predictable inference. Similarly, the leading treatise in the area explains that "it has been recognized very often that the expression of an opinion may carry with it an implied assertion, not only that the speaker knows no facts which would preclude such an opinion, but that he does know facts which justify it." Prosser and Keeton § 109, at 760. That is especially (and traditionally) the case, the treatise continues, where—as in a registration statement—a speaker "holds himself out or is understood as having special knowledge of the matter which is not available to the plaintiff." . . .

And the purpose of § 11 supports this understanding of how the omissions clause maps onto opinion statements. Congress adopted § 11 to ensure that issuers "tell[ ] the whole truth" to investors. H.R. Rep. No. 85, 73d Cong., 1st Sess., 2 (1933) (quoting President Roosevelt's message to Congress). For that reason, literal accuracy is not enough: An issuer must as well desist from misleading investors by saying one thing and holding back another. Omnicare would nullify that statutory requirement for all sentences starting with the phrases "we believe" or "we think." But those magic words can preface nearly any conclusion, and the resulting statements as we have shown, remain perfectly capable of misleading investors. Thus, Omnicare's view would punch a hole in the statute for half-truths in the form of opinion statements.

And the difficulty of showing that such statements are literally false—which requires proving an issuer did not believe them, would make that opening yet more consequential: Were Omnicare right, companies would have virtual *carte blanche* to assert opinions in registration statements free from worry about § 11. That outcome would ill-fit Congress's decision to establish a strict liability offense promoting "full and fair disclosure" of material information.

Omnicare argues, in response, that applying § 11's omissions clause in the way we have described would have "adverse policy consequences." According to Omnicare, any inquiry into the issuer's basis for holding an opinion is "hopelessly amorphous," threatening "unpredictable" and possibly "massive" liability. And because that is so, Omnicare claims, many issuers will choose not to disclose opinions at all, thus "depriving [investors] of potentially helpful information." . . .

But first, that claim is, just as Omnicare labels it, one of "policy"; and Congress gets to make policy, not the courts. The decision Congress made, for the reasons we have indicated, was to extend § 11 liability to all statements rendered misleading by omission. In doing so, Congress no doubt made § 11 less cut-and-dry than a law prohibiting only false factual statements. Section 11's omissions clause, as applied to statements of both opinion and fact, necessarily brings the reasonable person into the analysis, and asks what she would naturally understand a statement to convey beyond its literal meaning. And for expressions of opinion, that means considering the foundation she would expect an issuer to have before making the statement. All that, however, is a feature, not a bug, of the omissions provision.

Moreover, Omnicare way overstates both the looseness of the inquiry Congress has mandated and the breadth of liability that approach threatens. As we have explained, an investor cannot state a claim by alleging only that an opinion was wrong; the complaint must as well call into question the issuer's basis for offering the opinion. And to do so, the investor cannot just say that the issuer failed to reveal its basis. Section 11's omissions clause, after all, is not a general disclosure requirement; it affords a cause of action only when an issuer's failure to include a material fact has rendered a published statement misleading. To press such a claim, an investor must allege that kind of omission—and not merely by means of conclusory assertions. See *Ashcroft v. Iqbal*, 556 U.S. 662, 678, 129 S. Ct. 1937, 173 L.Ed.2d 868 (2009) ("Threadbare recitals of the elements of a cause of action, supported by mere conclusory statements, do not suffice"). To be specific: The investor must identify particular (and material) facts going to the basis for the issuer's opinion—facts about the inquiry the issuer did or did not conduct or the knowledge it did or did not have— whose omission makes the opinion statement at issue misleading to a reasonable person reading the statement fairly and in context. That is no small task for an investor.

Nor does the inquiry such a complaint triggers ask anything unusual of courts. Numerous legal rules hinge on what a reasonable person would think or expect. In requiring courts to view statements of opinion from an ordinary investor's perspective, § 11's omissions clause demands nothing more complicated or unmanageable.

Indeed, courts have for decades engaged in just that inquiry, with no apparent trouble, in applying the common law of misrepresentation.

Finally, we see no reason to think that liability for misleading opinions will chill disclosures useful to investors. Nothing indicates that § 11's application to misleading factual assertions in registration statements has caused such a problem. And likewise, common-law doctrines of opinion liability have not, so far as anyone knows, deterred merchants in ordinary commercial transactions from asserting helpful opinions about their products. That absence of fallout is unsurprising. Sellers (whether of stock or other items) have strong economic incentives to . . . *sell* (*i.e.*, hawk or peddle). Those market-based forces push back against any inclination to underdisclose. And to avoid exposure for omissions under § 11, an issuer need only divulge an opinion's basis, or else make clear the real tentativeness of its belief. Such ways of conveying opinions so that they do not mislead will keep valuable information flowing. And that is the only kind of information investors need. To the extent our decision today chills *misleading* opinions, that is all to the good: In enacting § 11, Congress worked to ensure better, not just more, information.

B

Our analysis on this score counsels in favor of sending the case back to the lower courts for decision. Neither court below considered the Funds' omissions theory with the right standard in mind — or indeed, even recognized the distinct statutory questions that theory raises. We therefore follow our ordinary practice of remanding for a determination of whether the Funds have stated a viable omissions claim (or, if not, whether they should have a chance to replead).

In doing so, however, we reemphasize a few crucial points pertinent to the inquiry on remand. Initially, as we have said, the Funds cannot proceed without identifying one or more facts left out of Omnicare's registration statement. The Funds' recitation of the statutory language — that Omnicare "omitted to state facts necessary to make the statements made not misleading" — is not sufficient; neither is the Funds' conclusory allegation that Omnicare lacked "reasonable grounds for the belief" it stated respecting legal compliance. At oral argument, however, the Funds highlighted another, more specific allegation in their complaint: that an attorney had warned Omnicare that a particular contract "carrie[d] a heightened risk" of legal exposure under anti-kickback laws. On remand, the court must review the Funds' complaint to determine whether it adequately alleged that Omnicare had omitted that (purported) fact, or any other like it, from the registration statement. And if so, the court must determine whether the omitted fact would have been material to a reasonable investor — *i.e.*, whether "there is a substantial likelihood that a reasonable [investor] would consider it important." . . .

Assuming the Funds clear those hurdles, the court must ask whether the alleged omission rendered Omnicare's legal compliance opinions misleading in the way described earlier — *i.e.*, because the excluded fact shows that Omnicare lacked the basis for making those statements that a reasonable investor would expect. Insofar as the omitted fact at issue is the attorney's warning, that inquiry entails consideration of such matters as the attorney's status and expertise and other legal information available to Omnicare at the time. Further, the analysis of whether Omnicare's opinion is misleading must address the statement's context. That means the court must take account of whatever facts Omnicare *did* provide about legal compliance, as well as any other hedges, disclaimers, or qualifications it included in its registration statement. The court should consider, for example, the information Omnicare offered that States had initiated enforcement actions against drug manufacturers for giving rebates to pharmacies, that the Federal Government had expressed concerns about the practice, and that the relevant laws "could "be interpreted in the future in a manner" that would harm Omnicare's business.

With these instructions and for the reasons stated, we vacate the judgment below and remand the case for further proceedings.

It is so ordered.

Justice SCALIA, concurring in part and concurring in the judgment.

Section 11 of the Securities Act of 1933 imposes liability where a registration statement "contain[s] an untrue statement of a material fact" or "omit[s] to state a material fact necessary to make the statements therein not misleading." I agree with the Court's discussion of what it means for an expression of opinion to state an untrue material fact. But an expression of opinion implies facts (beyond the fact that the speaker believes his opinion) only where a reasonable listener would understand it to do so. And it is only when expressions of opinion *do* imply these other facts that they can be "misleading" without the addition of other "material facts." The Court's view would count far more expressions of opinion to convey collateral facts than I—or the common law—would, and I therefore concur only in part.

. . . .

Note—In re Sanofi Securities Litigation

In a 2016 decision interpreting *Omnicare*, the Second Circuit stated in the *Sanofi Securities Litigation* decision, 816 F.3d 199 (2d Cir. 2016):

> In *Omnicare*, the Supreme Court held that where an investor has alleged that an issuer omitted [disclosing] material information and thereby rendered a statement of opinion misleading,
>
> > [t]he investor must identify particular (and material) facts going to the basis for the issuer's opinion—facts about the inquiry the issuer did or did not conduct or the knowledge it did or did not have—whose omission makes the opinion statement at issue misleading to a reasonable person reading the statement fairly and in context.
>
> . . . [Hence,] *Omnicare* affirmed that liability for making a false statement of opinion may lie if either "the speaker did not hold the belief she professed"

or "the supporting facts she supplied were untrue." But *Omnicare* went on to hold that opinions, though sincerely held and otherwise true as a matter of fact, may nonetheless be actionable if the speaker omits information whose omission makes the statement misleading to a reasonable investor.

The Supreme Court emphasized that meeting the standard under *Omnicare* "is no small task for an investor," and also provided guidance for applying its ruling. The Court noted that a reasonable investor, upon hearing a statement of opinion from an issuer, "expects not just that the issuer believes the opinion (however irrationally), but that it fairly aligns with the information in the issuer's possession at a time." . . .

The Court, however, cautioned against an overly expansive reading of this standard, noting that "[r]easonable investors understand that opinions sometimes rest on a weighing of competing facts," and adding that "[a] reasonable investor does not expect that *every* fact known to an issuer supports its opinion statement." The Court went on to say that a statement of opinion "is not necessarily misleading when an issuer knows, but fails to disclose, some fact cutting the other way."

. . . .

Issuers must be forthright with their investors, but securities law does not impose on them an obligation to disclose every piece of information in their possession. As *Omnicare* instructs, issuers need not disclose a piece of information merely because it cuts against their projections. Given the sophistication of the investors here, the FDA's public preference for double-blind studies, and the absence of a conflict between Defendants' statements and the FDA's comments, we conclude that no reasonable investor would have been misled by Defendants' optimistic statements . . . .

816 F.3d at 209–210, 214 (citations omitted).

Note that the Supreme Court's decision in *Omnicare* has been applied by lower federal courts to other provisions of the securities laws, including § 10(b) and SEC Rule 10b-5.

[C] Defenses

Section 11(b) provides a number of due diligence defenses for persons other than the issuer. Generally, the only defenses available to the issuer, once a plaintiff establishes a prima facie case, are the purchaser's knowledge of the misstatement or omission, lack of causation, in pari delicto, and expiration of the statute of limitations. These defenses, of course, are available to any defendant. Moreover, a non-issuer defendant, who discovers a material misstatement or omission in the registration statement, may avoid liability by taking the action specified in § 11(b)(1) or (2).[9]

---

9. Before the effective date of the registration statement or part thereof in question, he/she (1) resigns from or takes such steps as are permitted by law to resign from, or ceases or refuses to act in,

The *"due diligence" defenses* are contained in § 11(b)(3). As regards the unexpertised portion of the registration statement, a defendant must show that, *after reasonable investigation,* he/she had reason to believe and did believe at the time such part of the registration statement became effective, there was no material misstatement or omission. As regards the "expertised" part, a defendant (other than the responsible expert) need show only that he/she had no reasonable ground to believe and did not believe that the expertised portion of the registration statement was defective. While a non-expert is not required to make an investigation of expertised information, he/she must "have no reasonable ground to believe" such information is inaccurate.[10]

An expert, on the other hand, is required to show that after reasonable investigation, he/she had reasonable grounds to believe and did believe his/her statement to be accurate. In other words, an expert is required to exercise the same standard of care regarding the part expertised by him/her as a non-expert is required to exercise regarding the non-expertised portion of the registration statement. Experts are not subject to liability under § 11 for misstatements or omissions in the unexpertised part of the registration statement merely by reason of their involvement as experts. Note, however, that depending on the facts and circumstances, an expert may incur liability under another rationale (e.g., under state law for aiding and abetting) if the non-expertised portion of the registration statement is materially deficient.

[D] Due Diligence Standard

Section 11(c) provides that the standard of reasonableness by which the concept of "reasonable investigation" is to be measured is that required of "a prudent man in the management of his own property." The "prudent man" standard applies not only to the reasonableness of one's investigation but also to the reasonableness of one's belief.

While opinions may differ as to whether the standard is unitary or elastic, the *BarChris* decision, which is contained in the following materials, unequivocally indicates that the degree of responsibility, and *a fortiori* the extensiveness of the investigation required to establish due diligence, largely will depend upon the type of person and the nature of his/her relationship with the issuer. While *BarChris* let it be known that the statutory due diligence obligations are not to be treated lightly, the decision

---

every office, capacity or relationship ascribed to him/her in the registration statement, and (2) advises the SEC and the issuer in writing of the action taken and disavowing responsibility for such part of the registration statement.

After such part of the registration statement has become effective, (1) if he/she was unaware that it had become effective, and, (2) upon becoming aware of such fact, acts forthwith, (3) advises the SEC in writing as set forth above, and (4) gives reasonable public notice that such part of the registration statement had become effective without her/his knowledge.

10. The same standard applies under § 11(b)(3)(D) to statements in the registration statement purporting to have been made by a public official or purporting to be a copy or extract from a public official document.

did not resolve many of the problems inherent in the vague "reasonable investigation" standard.

Subsequently, the SEC adopted Rule 176, which lists a number of factors to be taken
into account as "circumstances affecting the determination of what constitutes reasonable investigation." These factors are:

(a) The type of issuer;

(b) The type of security;

(c) The type of person;

(d) The office held when the person is an officer;

(e) The presence or absence of another relationship to the issuer when the
person is a director or proposed director;

(f) Reasonable reliance on officers, employees, and others whose duties
should have given them knowledge of the particular facts (in light of the
functions and responsibilities of the particular person with respect to the
issuer and the filing);

(g) When the person is an underwriter, the type of underwriting arrangement, the role of the particular person as an underwriter and the availability of information with respect to the registrant; and

(h) Whether, with respect to a fact or document incorporated by reference,
the particular person had any responsibility for the fact or document at the
time of the filing from which it was incorporated.

Critics contend that these guidelines do little to provide meaningful content to the
"reasonable investigation" standard.[11]

[E] Causation and Reliance

In an action brought pursuant to § 11, causation is presumed (which may be rebutted by the defendant) once a material misstatement or omission has been shown by
the plaintiff to exist. Moreover, the plaintiff-purchaser normally need not establish
reliance.

[F] Materiality and Damages

Section 11 imposes liability only for "material" misstatements or omissions in the
registration statement. Therefore, materiality is a threshold determination. The issue
of materiality is discussed throughout this textbook, including in this Chapter as well
as several others.

Similarly, the plaintiff must have suffered damages compensable within the provisions of § 11(e). The damages formulation set forth in § 11(e) is statutorily

---

11. A checklist of due diligence procedures is contained in the Appendix to this Chapter.

prescribed. That statute sets forth a single formulation that has three components. The triggering of the appropriate component rests on whether the plaintiff continues to hold the security, disposed of the security before suit, or disposed of the security after suit was brought. The measure of damages under § 11(e) is:

> [T]he difference between the amount paid for the security (not exceeding the price at which the security was offered to the public) and (1) the value thereof as of the time suit was brought, or (2) the price at which such security shall have been disposed of in the market before suit, or (3) the price at which such security shall have been disposed of after suit but before judgment if such damages shall be less than the damages representing the difference between the amount paid for the security (not exceeding the price at which the security was offered to the public) and the value thereof as of the time such suit was brought.

As discussed above, the plaintiff is not required to prove that the material misstatement(s) or omission(s) "caused" the loss. The defendant, however, pursuant to § 11(e), can reduce (either in part or totally) the plaintiff's monetary damages by showing that the loss (or portion thereof) was attributable to factors other than the pertinent misrepresentation(s) or nondisclosure(s). The *Akerman* case, which follows, highlights these threshold requirements.

Akerman v. Oryx Communications, Inc.

United States District Court, Southern District of New York

[1984 Transfer Binder] Fed. Sec. L. Rep. (CCH) ¶ 91,680 (S.D.N.Y. 1984),
aff'd, 810 F.2d 344 (2d Cir. 1987)

Defendant Oryx Communications, Inc. ("Oryx"), a Delaware corporation with its principal executive offices in New York City, was incorporated on April 6, 1981, to acquire video rights to American films and to manufacture and sell video cassettes and video discs for home use abroad.

. . . .

To further these goals, Oryx sought to raise approximately $3,000,000 of capital through a public stock offering. Oryx's management filed a registration statement and an accompanying prospectus dated June 30, 1981, with the Securities and Exchange Commission ("SEC"), for a firm commitment offering of 700,000 units. Each unit sold for $4.75 and was composed of one share of common stock and one warrant to purchase common stock at a later date at $5.75.

Shortly after [the public offering], the price of Oryx units began to decline. . . .

Plaintiffs alleged that the decline in Oryx's value was a result of an inaccurate prospectus and registration materials. On November 10, 1981, Oryx had publicly announced that its June 1981 prospectus and registration statement contained certain erroneous figures. This media announcement was followed by a letter to shareholders dated November 12. . . .

On November 25, 1981, the Akerman plaintiffs initiated this action alleging violations of section 11. . . .

The case is far from one of monumental significance, and the theories advanced by plaintiffs' counsel illustrate how legal ingenuity can greatly complicate securities litigation. Even after several rounds of briefing, argument, and amendments, and after the considerable efforts this opinion represents, the proper results on some of the issues presented are far from clear. Although plaintiffs showed that the statements in the Oryx prospectus were theoretically material, defendants have successfully demonstrated that the decline in the value of Oryx stock was in fact caused by factors other than the matters misstated. Plaintiffs are therefore ineligible for damages under section 11(e). . . .

I. Materiality

A fundamental purpose of the Securities Act of 1933 ("the Act") "was to substitute a philosophy of full disclosure for the philosophy of caveat emptor and thus to achieve a high standard of business ethics in the securities industry." *Securities and Exchange Commission v. Capital Gains Research Bureau,* 375 U.S. 180, 186 (1963). The Act mandates disclosure of all material facts relating to the sale or offering of covered securities. As Judge Weinstein wrote in *Feit v. Leasco Data Processing Equipment Corp.,* 332 F. Supp. 544, 549 (E.D.N.Y. 1971), "the prospective purchaser of a new issue of securities is entitled to know what the deal is all about."

. . .

The existence of a misstatement sufficiently serious to be deemed "material" is a threshold issue in any claim under sections 11 and 12(2) of the Securities Act of 1933. The Supreme Court discussed materiality in the context of a Rule 14a-9 proxy violation in *TSC Industries, Inc. v. Northway, Inc.,* 426 U.S. 438 (1976): "[t]he question of materiality . . . is an objective one, involving the significance of an omitted or misrepresented fact to a reasonable investor. . . . An omitted fact is material if there is a substantial likelihood that a reasonable shareholder would consider it important in deciding [whether to purchase the securities or in deciding] how to vote." . . . Courts have widely adopted this formula as the test for materiality in securities law actions.

. . . .

. . . [T]he figures published by Oryx significantly overstated the earnings per share by over one hundred percent. . . . A reasonable investor presented with [accurate] figures might well have questioned whether management was capable of carrying forward its plan, outlined in the Oryx prospectus, of building a video business by capitalizing on contacts and its president's experience in the industry. . . .

Nor can the lack of a significant drop in the price of Oryx's stock after disclosure [of the erroneous figures] by itself establish immateriality as a matter of law. The price of a thinly traded over-the-counter new-issue stock such as Oryx cannot always be counted on to respond to such an announcement. . . .

II. Damages under Section 11

Although plaintiffs may be correct, as a theoretical matter, that the kind of statement Oryx made in its prospectus can be material within the meaning of section 11, they have failed to show that Oryx's statements . . . caused whatever losses plaintiffs may have suffered. Thus, plaintiffs are not entitled to any recovery on their section 11 claims.

Section 11 imposes civil liability for any materially untrue or misleading statements [contained in a registration statement, on, among others,] "every person who signed the registration statement . . . [and] every underwriter with respect to such security." . . . As the issuer, Oryx is strictly liable without regard to scienter. The statute offers three alternative measures of damages: (1) the difference between the amount paid for the security and its value at the time suit is brought; (2) the difference between the purchase price and the price at which the security was disposed of in the market prior to suit; or (3) the difference between the purchase price and the price for which the security is sold after suit, as long as this does not exceed the difference between the purchase price and the price at the time of suit. . . . Section 11(e), however, expressly allows a defendant to limit his liability by showing that the drop in market price is unrelated to the material misstatements.

. . . .

Thus, the statute recognizes that there may be cases in which a misstatement is material to an investor's decision although it has not in fact adversely affected the value of the stock. . . .

Plaintiffs have offered the affidavit of an expert, John Hammerslough, who argues that their entire out-of-pocket loss is attributable to the earnings misstatement. He bases his opinion, however, on allegations that go far beyond the claims in plaintiff's original or proposed amended complaints, and relies on factors inapposite to a section 11(e) defense. Hammerslough concludes: "[i]t is my opinion that if the misstatements and omissions had been revealed prior to the effective date of the Prospectus, the underwriters and the investing public would have concluded that management was either grossly incompetent or fraudulent and, the underwriting would have been canceled, the investments by plaintiffs and others would not have been made, and the damages would not have been incurred." . . . Such observations, however accurate, do not rebut a section 11(e) defense. *That section does not focus on the causal relationship between the misstatement and the original purchase, but rather on the relationship between the misstatement and any subsequent decline in value.* [emphasis supplied]

. . . .

Defendant's motion for judgment on this claim was originally based on a showing that there was no decline in the value of Oryx's securities after the public disclosure on November 10 of the error in its prospectus. A market decline after the announcement of an error is the most obvious evidence of a causal relationship between a misstated fact and a stock's inaccurate valuation. Generally speaking, if the market initially overvalues a stock due to erroneous information, the price will drop upon disclosure to a level that "represents the consensus of buying and selling opinion of the value of the securities as they actually are." . . .

In this case, Oryx stock remained stable in the two-week period between disclosure and the filing of this suit, and for several months thereafter. . . .

Plaintiffs seek alternatively to claim injury based upon depreciation in the stock's price prior to public disclosure of the erroneous information. This argument has at least possible theoretical validity, since disclosure of an error to a group of underwriters, for example, could enable them to force down the price of the stock involved prior to the public disclosure that would put plaintiffs on notice. In this case, the bid price of Oryx fell from $4.00 on October 19 to $3.25 on November 9, the day before the public correction. Plaintiffs attempted to connect this depreciation to the activities of certain corporate officers, SEC officials, accountants, and attorneys who were informed of the misstatements in the course of Oryx's internal investigation during October and early November. After extensive discovery, however, plaintiffs failed to uncover any evidence of insider trading, premature disclosure to investors, or stock manipulation. . . . The evidence at hand forces the conclusion that any decline prior to November 10 was unrelated to disclosure to this limited circle of insiders.

 . . . .

No doubt many independent factors contributed to the stock's decline. . . . The influence of general market factors, however, entitles defendants only to an appropriate reduction of damages. To prevail on this summary judgment motion, which seeks dismissal of the section 11 claims, defendants face "an especially high burden; they [must] prove that the decline in value of [Oryx] stock resulted solely from factors other than the material omissions [or misstatements]." . . . The legislative choice to impose the burden of proof on defendants under section 11(e) represents a judgment that the risk of any uncertainty as to causality must fall upon defendants in order to insure the full disclosure that is the primary goal of the Act. Plaintiffs are in effect entitled to a rebuttable presumption that the decline was related to the nondisclosure. . . .

Although defendants failed in their more general attack on the significance of the alleged discrepancy in performance of the Oryx stock, the court offered them an opportunity to prove by expert, statistical analysis that the alleged discrepancy had insufficient significance to create a genuine issue of material fact. Defendants have since offered convincing proof that the variance is statistically irrelevant. Professors Cyrus Derman and Morton Klein of Columbia University conducted an exhaustive computer analysis of the performance of the stock of the other one hundred companies which went public during May and June of 1981. They found that many other new issue securities suffered equal or greater declines in value between June 1 and November 25, 1981. Oryx, in fact, performed exactly at the statistical median. . . . An additional statistical test indicated that Oryx's stock "behaved over the entire period in a manner consistent with its own inherent variation." . . . Plaintiffs were afforded thirty days to respond to this analysis; they have failed to rebut defendants' evidence persuasively.

Thus, on the record before the court, defendants are entitled to summary judgment on this issue of section 11(e) liability. They have carried their heavy burden of proving that the decline was caused by factors other than the matters misstated in the registration statement. . . . Although plaintiffs initially carried their "minimal burden" of establishing a prima facie case by showing materiality, defendants have come forward with a credible, factually supported demonstration of the lack of any connection between the drop in value of Oryx securities and the misstatements.

. . . .

[G] Contribution and Indemnification

Under § 11, violators generally are subject to joint and several liability. Accordingly, a plaintiff is entitled to recover the entire judgment against any violator. An exception to this framework exists with respect to outside directors who are liable only in proportion to their fault unless they had actual knowledge of the falsity.

In order to distribute judgment and settlement costs among joint violators, the two common techniques used are contribution and indemnification. While indemnification involves a shifting of the entire loss from one defendant to another person, contribution involves a sharing of the damages among the tortfeasors.[12]

Section 11(f) of the Securities Act clearly provides for a right to *contribution* ("unless the person who has become liable was, and the other was not, guilty of fraudulent misrepresentation"). The provision, however, leaves unsettled the extent to which losses are to be shared among the parties. The traditional view is that the parties share the entire loss on a pro rata basis (i.e., equally among the joint tortfeasors irrespective of individual fault). The emerging view is that apportionment of damages should be premised upon a proportionate fault or pro tanto basis.[13] The subject of contribution and the methods of allocating contribution in securities litigation are addressed in Chapter 8.

The right to *indemnification* is far more uncertain. Neither § 11 nor any other provision of the securities laws provide for such a right. The SEC's position, as contained in Item 512(h) of Regulation S-K, is that indemnification of officers, directors, and

---

12. *See generally* Ruder, *Multiple Defendants in Securities Law Fraud Cases: Aiding and Abetting, Conspiracy, In Pari Delicto, Indemnification and Contribution*, 120 U. Pa. L. Rev. 597 (1972).

13. "The pro tanto method mandates that plaintiffs receive the full amount of damages awarded and that the non-settling defendants receive a judgment reduction in the amount paid to the plaintiffs in settlement." Steinberg & Olive, *Contribution and Proportionate Liability Under the Federal Securities Laws in Multidefendant Securities Litigation After the Private Securities Litigation Reform Act of 1995*, 50 SMU L. Rev. 337, 363 (1996).

controlling persons of the registrant for liabilities arising under the Securities Act is against public policy, and, hence, unenforceable. Interestingly, however, the SEC has no such hostility to the procurement of insurance. Rule 461(c) of Regulation C provides that normally "[i]nsurance against liabilities arising under the [Securities] Act, whether the cost of insurance is borne by the registrant, the insured or some other person, will not be considered a bar to acceleration [of the effective date of the registration statement]."[14]

A troubling issue with respect to indemnification is whether the underwriter, pursuant to an indemnity contract with the issuer or its controlling persons, may thereby avoid liability. With respect to intentional securities law violations by the underwriter, the courts have denied indemnification. Generally, the courts reason that, permitting a party to avoid monetary liability for its own reckless or willful misconduct, is contrary to the securities acts' objective of inducing parties to be scrupulous about their disclosure obligations. Moreover, the issuer's indemnification of the underwriter is suspect in that the funds ultimately come out of the shareholders' pockets, the very individuals who were damaged by the misconduct. E.g., *Eichenholtz v. Brennan*, 52 F.3d 478 (3d Cir. 1995); *Globus v. Law Research Serv., Inc.*, 418 F.2d 1276 (2d Cir. 1969). The foregoing reasons also are applicable for prohibiting indemnification where the underwriter has been negligent. Some courts, however, may enforce an indemnity contract where the underwriter's culpability does not surpass that of negligence.[15] The following case focuses on these issues.

Eichenholtz v. Brennan

United States Court of Appeals, Third Circuit

52 F.3d 478 (1995)

. . . .

THE RIGHT TO CONTRIBUTION AND INDEMNIFICATION

(a) Federal Securities Laws

The court agrees with the non-settling defendants that under section 11 of the Securities Act of 1933 (the "1933 Act"), they have an express right to seek contribution for liability under that section. . . .

However, there is no express right to indemnification under the 1933 or 1934 Acts. Further, those courts that have addressed the issue have concluded that there is no implied right to indemnification under the federal securities laws. . . . This circuit has not yet addressed this issue.

---

14. *See generally* Griffith, *Uncovering a Gatekeeper: Why the SEC Should Mandate Disclosure of Details Concerning Directors' and Officers' Liability Insurance Policies*, 154 U. PA. L. REV. 1147 (2006).

15. *See* Comment, *Allocation of Damages Under the Federal Securities Laws*, 60 WASH. U. L.Q. 211 (1982) (and cases cited therein).

As will be explained below, indemnification runs counter to the policies under-lying the 1933 and 1934 Acts. In addition, there is no indication that Congress intended that indemnification be available under the Acts. . . . In drafting the Acts, Congress was not concerned with protecting the underwriters, but rather it sought to protect investors. Here, it is the underwriters, not the victims, who seek indemni-fication. We agree with those courts that have held that there is no implied right to seek indemnification under the federal securities laws.

In addition, in support of its right to seek indemnification from [the issuer] ITB, [the underwriter] First Jersey relies on its underwriting agreements with ITB.

(b) First Jersey's Contractual Right to Indemnification

Each of four separate underwriting agreements between [the issuer] ITB and [the underwriter] First Jersey contains provisions for indemnification. In these provisions, ITB agreed to indemnify First Jersey from any and all loss, liability, claims, damage, and expense arising from any material misstatement, untrue statement, or omission in the public offering.

Generally, federal courts disallow claims for indemnification because such claims run counter to the policies underlying the federal securities acts. The underlying goal of securities legislation is encouraging diligence and discouraging negligence in securities transactions. These goals are accomplished "by exposing issuers and underwriters to the substantial hazard of liability for compensatory damages."

The non-settling defendants argue that the policy of not enforcing indemnifica-tion provisions should not apply in cases, as here, where an underwriter was merely negligent, played a "*de minimis*" role in the public offering at issue, or was being held derivatively or vicariously liable. We disagree.

A number of federal courts have held that this policy against allowing indemni-fication extends to violations of sections 11 and 12(2) [now § 12(a)(2)], where the underwriter is merely negligent in the performance of its duties. We agree. The poli-cies underlying the 1933 and 1934 Acts demand that all underwriters be encouraged to fulfill their duties in a public offering, regardless of their role.

[T]he federal securities laws seek, *inter alia,* to encourage underwriters to conduct thorough independent investigations. Unlike contribution, contractual indemnifi-cation allows an underwriter to shift its entire liability to the issuer before any alle-gation of wrongdoing or a determination of fault. As such, indemnification, it is argued, undermines the role of the underwriter as "investigator and public advocate." If the court enforced an underwriter indemnification provision, it would effectively eliminate the underwriter's incentive to fulfill its investigative obligation. "The stat-ute would fail to serve the prophylactic purpose that . . . underwriters make some reasonable attempt to verify the data submitted to them."

In addition, if the court were to allow the non-settling defendants to avoid sec-ondary or derivative liability "merely by showing ignorance, [it] would contravene the congressional intent to protect the public, particularly unsophisticated investors, from fraudulent practices." As for vicarious liability, "[c]ertain employers . . . assume a higher public duty under the securities laws than do other persons, a duty that requires the affirmative exercise of a high standard of supervision." The public depends upon an underwriter's investigation and opinion, and it relies on such opinions when investing. Denying claims for indemnification would encourage underwriters to exhibit the degree of reasonable care required by the 1933 and 1934 Acts.

The non-settling defendants also argue that it makes no sense to preserve their sections 11 and 12(2) statutory defenses, of due diligence and due care respectively, while they are deprived of the right to seek indemnification. This argument lacks merit.

In order to successfully assert a due care or a due diligence defense, an underwriter must prove that it conducted a reasonable investigation and had a reasonable belief that the information relating to an offering was accurate and complete. These defenses encourage an underwriter to act reasonably; they are not available to a negligent underwriter. Unlike indemnification, the statutory defenses support the policies of the Act. Underwriters will be more likely to act diligently in an effort to assert the defenses.

We conclude that the underwriter [contractual] indemnification agreements between [the underwriter] First Jersey and [the issuer] ITB run counter to the policies underlying the securities acts. Although the nonsettling defendants had a right to contribution, they did not have a right to indemnification. Therefore, the district court did not abuse its discretion in barring and extinguishing any causes of action for indemnification. . . .

Problem A

The board of directors of Jiffy Muffler, Inc., a privately held company situated in Boise, Idaho, determines to "go public" in order to procure sufficient capital to open up 60 additional "shops" throughout Big Sky country. Jiffy's directors are Biddle, Doolittle, Hazelwood, Morris, and Nance. Doolittle is president and chief executive officer. Morris is a local entrepreneur involved in a number of different business ventures who has known Doolittle since high school. His only affiliation with Jiffy Muffler is serving as a director. Biddle is a lawyer whose firm does not do any legal work for the corporation. Hazelwood is an accounting professor at the local college. Nance, one of Doolittle's golfing cronies, rarely attends board meetings and serves as a director as a favor to Doolittle.

The corporation selects: the investment bank Tweed LLP to serve as the main underwriter for the public offering (and a number of other investment bankers also are invited to serve as underwriters); the law firm of Cass, Bass & Bib LLP to serve as counsel for the issuer; and the accounting firm of Harry Abernathy LLP "to expertise" the financial statements to be contained in the registration statement. To assist it in performing its due diligence, Tweed LLP hires the law firm of Ranier & Cascades LLP.

The registration statement is prepared. Some of the representations contained in the registration statement are that: (1) due to the highly competitive nature of the business and Jiffy's short five-year financial history as a private company, the investor must be prepared to lose his/her entire investment; (2) Jiffy made a net profit of $7,575,000 during the past fiscal year (without disclosing that $3,350,000 of that profit was due to selling prime location real estate to the city of Boise in a land condemnation proceeding); and (3) Jiffy's assets include the ownership of 53 muffler shops (when in fact Jiffy owns 52 shops). Moreover, the registration statement, among other deficiencies, overstates the company's revenues for the prior fiscal year by 20 percent.

All of the directors of Jiffy subsequently sign the registration statement. At the time of signing, Hazelwood, Nance, and Morris inform Doolittle that they are relying upon him for the accuracy of the registration statement.

Upon reviewing the registration statement, Jenkins, a partner of Tweed LLP (who is serving as the investment bank), says "the lawyers at Ranier & Cascades tell me that it looks okay." As Jenkins was informed, Armstrong, a senior associate at Ranier & Cascades, had "kicked the tires," inspecting Jiffy's physical facilities and other matters. Among other actions, Armstrong, along with a partner of the firm McHenry, had questioned Jiffy's directors and officers, examined major contracts, and the corporation's minutes.

After conducting an audit, the accounting firm of Harry Abernathy LLP "expertises" the certified financial statements, which are included in the registration statement. Unknown to the accounting firm, Jiffy's financial records were altered by Doolittle to overstate revenues received during the past year by 20 percent.

Shortly after the public offering, Jiffy goes bankrupt. Purchasers of Jiffy stock in the registered offering bring suit seeking recovery pursuant to § 11 (as well as other provisions). Are the purchasers likely to be successful on their § 11 claims? Against which parties? Why?

Problem B

Suppose that Jiffy Muffler, Inc. (rather than going bankrupt as stated above) prospers. Through the years, the company has had several public offerings. Its stock is traded on the New York Stock Exchange and the company qualifies as an S-3 issuer. Madison, Jiffy's fairly new chief executive, decides that the time has come to take advantage of the SEC's "shelf" registration rule for at-the-market offerings of equity securities. She also informs Tweed LLP, Jiffy's traditional investment banker, that it better be competitive or the deal will go to another investment banker.

Six months later, seeing a market "window," Jiffy decides to take some of the equity securities "off-the-shelf," naming the investment bank Day & Thomas LLP as its main underwriter. The offering is completed within a single business day. Unknown to Day & Thomas, the registration statement fails to disclose that Jiffy had been sued for compensatory and punitive damages seeking over $50 million in a class action suit filed in New York state court five days earlier for muffler defects. In addition, the Exchange Act filed documents incorporated by reference into the registration statement substantially overstate the number of Jiffy Muffler shops.

Shortly after the termination of the "shelf" offering, the price of Jiffy common stock decreases from $37 to $22 per share. Calhoun, a purchaser in the shelf offering, brings suit naming, among others, the issuer Jiffy and the underwriter Day & Thomas as defendants. At an early stage, Jiffy elects to settle.

Is the investment bank Day & Thomas subject to liability under § 11? What are (and what should be) the standards to be applied to ascertain the § 11 liability of an underwriter such as Day & Thomas in this context?

———————

Problem C

Jack and Jill Milton seek to find a suitable investment to help enable them to afford the lifestyle to which they are rapidly becoming accustomed. They approach their lawyer, Samuels, about their predicament. He responds that an acquaintance of his, Wallace, is the "promoter" for a forthcoming limited partnership offering that seems to be a good investment.

The offering qualifies for the § 3(a)(11) intrastate federal exemption and the securities being offered have been registered (pursuant to a duly filed registration statement) on the state level. Samuels accompanies the Miltons over to Wallace's place of business where they listen to Wallace "speak up" the deal. During the discussion, Samuels asks Wallace several questions concerning the investment. The Miltons also are given an offering circular that Samuels had no part in preparing. Upon reviewing the offering circular at the Miltons' request and after making further inquiry of Wallace, Samuels asserts that "this deal is the best I've seen for people like you. Even aside from its tax advantages, this is a tremendous investment. You'd be making a big mistake not to get a piece of this action." Unknown to Samuels and the Miltons, the prospectus contains material misrepresentations.

The Miltons, pursuant to the offering, invest $100,000 in the limited partnership by mailing the subscription agreement and check for $100,000 to Wallace. Six months later, Wallace absconds to the Bahamas with the proceeds from the offering, leaving the limited partnership insolvent. The Miltons, angry at Samuels, come to you about recovering their $100,000. What do you advise? Under § 12(a)(2) of the Securities Act, is the case against Samuels worth pursuing? Would it matter if Samuels received a "finder's fee" of $10,000 from Wallace for introducing the Miltons to Wallace?

———————

§ 7.03 Due Diligence in the Registered Offering Context

Although handed down a half-century ago, the seminal case on due diligence in the § 11 context is *Escott v. BarChris Construction Corporation*. While reading the decision, consider whether the court's approach adequately takes into account business realities. Does *BarChris* reflect an accommodation between the interests of entrepreneurs and investors? What due diligence steps should potential § 11 defendants routinely take to help guard against their being held liable for a materially false or misleading statement contained in a registration statement?

Escott v. BarChris Construction Corporation

United States District Court, Southern District of New York

283 F. Supp. 643 (1968)

McLean, District Judge.

This is an action by purchasers of convertible subordinated fifteen year debentures of BarChris Construction Corporation (BarChris). . . .

The action is brought under Section 11 of the Securities Act of 1933 (15 U.S.C. § 77k). Plaintiffs allege [and the district court ruled] that the registration statement with respect to these debentures filed with the Securities and Exchange Commission, which became effective on May 16, 1961, contained material false statements and material omissions.

Defendants fall into three categories: (1) the persons who signed the registration statement; (2) the underwriters, consisting of eight investment banking firms, led by Drexel & Co. (Drexel); and (3) BarChris's auditors, Peat, Marwick, Mitchell & Co. (Peat, Marwick).

The signers, in addition to BarChris itself, were the nine directors of BarChris, plus its controller, defendant Trilling, who was not a director. Of the nine directors, five were officers of BarChris, i.e., defendants Vitolo, president; Russo, executive vice president; Pugliese, vice president; Kircher, treasurer; and Birnbaum, secretary. Of the remaining four, defendant Grant was a member of the firm of Perkins, Daniels, McCormack & Collins, BarChris's attorneys. He became a director in October 1960. Defendant Coleman, a partner in Drexel, became a director on April 17, 1961 as did Auslander, who [was] not otherwise connected with BarChris.

Defendants . . . have pleaded the defenses open to them under Section 11 of the Act. . . . [S]ome background facts should be mentioned. At the time relevant here, BarChris was engaged primarily in the construction of bowling alleys, somewhat euphemistically referred to as "bowling centers." These were rather elaborate affairs. They contained not only a number of alleys or "lanes," but also, in most cases, bar and restaurant facilities.

The introduction of automatic pin setting machines in 1952 [when bowling became "kingpin"[16]] gave a marked stimulus to bowling. It rapidly became a popular sport, with the result that "bowling centers" began to appear throughout the country in rapidly increasing numbers. BarChris benefitted from this increased interest in bowling. Its construction operations expanded rapidly. It is estimated that in 1960 BarChris installed approximately three per cent of all lanes built in the United States. It was thus a significant factor in the industry, although two large established companies, American Machine & Foundry Company [AMF] and Brunswick, were much larger factors.

BarChris's sales increased dramatically from 1956 to 1960. According to the prospectus, net sales, in round figures, in 1956 were some $800,000, in 1957 $1,300,000, in 1958 $1,700,000. In 1959 they increased to over $3,300,000, and by 1960 they had leaped to over $9,165,000.

For some years the business had exceeded the managerial capacity of its founders. Vitolo and Pugliese are each men of limited education. Vitolo did not get beyond high school. Pugliese ended his schooling in seventh grade. Pugliese devoted his time to supervising the actual construction work. Vitolo was concerned primarily with obtaining new business. Neither was equipped to handle financial matters.

Rather early in their career they enlisted the aid of Russo, who was trained as an accountant. He eventually became executive vice president of BarChris. In that capacity he handled many of the transactions which figure in this case.

In 1959 BarChris hired Kircher, a certified public accountant who had been employed by Peat, Marwick. He started as controller and became treasurer in 1960. In October of that year, another ex-Peat, Marwick employee, Trilling, succeeded Kircher as controller. At approximately the same time Birnbaum, a young attorney, was hired as house counsel. He became secretary on April 17, 1961.

. . . .

Under [its] financing method, BarChris was compelled to expend considerable sums in defraying the cost of construction before it received reimbursement. As a consequence, BarChris was in constant need of cash to finance its operations, a need which grew more pressing as operations expanded.

. . . .

By early 1961, BarChris needed additional working capital. The proceeds of the sale of the debentures involved in this action were to be devoted, in part at least, to fill that need.

---

[16]. [*See* Ip, *AMF Bowling Basks in Spotlight as IPO Gets Warm Welcome*, WALL ST. J., Nov. 5, 1997, at C1. *But see* Palank, *Heavy Debt, Changing Ways Push AMF to Bowl for Dollars*, WALL ST. J., Nov. 14, 2012, at B1 (stating that AMF, "the world's largest operator of bowling alleys, filed for bankruptcy-court protection").]

The registration statement of the debentures, in preliminary form, was filed with the Securities and Exchange Commission on March 30, 1961. A first amendment was filed on May 11 and a second on May 16. The registration statement became effective on May 16. The closing of the financing took place on May 24. On that day BarChris received the net proceeds of the financing.

By that time BarChris was experiencing difficulties in collecting amounts due from some of its customers. Some of them were in arrears in payments due to factors on their discounted notes. As time went on those difficulties increased. Although BarChris continued to build alleys in 1961 and 1962, it became increasingly apparent that the industry was overbuilt. Operators of alleys, often inadequately financed, began to fail. Precisely when the tide turned is a matter of dispute, but at any rate, it was painfully apparent in 1962.

In May of that year BarChris made an abortive attempt to raise more money by the sale of common stock. It filed with the Securities and Exchange Commission a registration statement for the stock issue which it later withdrew. In October 1962 BarChris came to the end of the road. On October 29, 1962, it filed in this court a petition for an arrangement under Chapter XI of the Bankruptcy Act. BarChris defaulted in the payment of the interest due on November 1, 1962 on the debentures.

The Debenture Registration Statement

.... [T]he various falsities and omissions ... [in the Debenture Registration Statement] were as follows:

   1960 Earnings

   (a) *Sales*

As per prospectus	$ 9,165,320
Correct figure	$ 8,511,420
Overstatement	$ 653,900

   (b) *Net Operating Income*

As per prospectus	$ 1,742,801
Correct figure	$ 1,496,196
Overstatement	$ 246,605

   (c) *Earnings per Share*

As per prospectus	$ .75
Correct figure	$ .65
Overstatement	$ .10

      . . . .

   Earnings Figures for Quarter Ending March 31, 1961

      . . . .

Gross Profit

As per prospectus	$ 483,121
Correct figure	$ <u>252,366</u>
Overstatement	$ 230,755

Backlog as of March 31, 1961

As per prospectus	$ 6,905,000
Correct figure	$ <u>2,415,000</u>
Overstatement	$ 4,490,000

. . . .

The "Due Diligence" Defenses

Section 11(b) of the Act provides that:

> . . . no person, other than the issuer, shall be liable . . . who shall sustain the burden of proof— . . . (3) that (A) as regards any part of the registration statement not purporting to be made on the authority of an expert . . . he had, after reasonable investigation, reasonable ground to believe and did believe, at the time such part of the registration statement became effective, that the statements therein were true and that there was no omission to state a material fact required to be stated therein or necessary to make the statements therein not misleading; . . . and (C) as regards any part of the registration statement purporting to be made on the authority of an expert (other than himself) . . . he had no reasonable ground to believe and did not believe, at the time such part of the registration statement became effective, that the statements therein were untrue or that there was an omission to state a material fact required to be stated therein or necessary to make the statements therein not misleading. . . .

Section 11(c) defines "reasonable investigation" as follows:

> In determining, for the purpose of paragraph (3) of subsection (b) of this section, what constitutes reasonable investigation and reasonable ground for belief, the standard of reasonableness shall be that required of a prudent man in the management of his own property.

Every defendant, except BarChris itself, to whom, as the issuer, these defenses are not available, and except Peat, Marwick, whose position rests on a different statutory provision, has pleaded these affirmative defenses. Each claims that (1) as to the part of the registration statement purporting to be made on the authority of an expert (which, for convenience, I shall refer to as the "expertised portion"), he had no reasonable ground to believe and did not believe that there were any untrue statements or material omissions, and (2) as to the other parts of the registration statement, he made a reasonable investigation, as a result of which he had reasonable ground to believe and did believe that the registration statement was true and that no material fact was omitted. As to each defendant, the question is whether he has sustained the burden of proving these defenses. Surprising enough, there is little or no judicial authority on this question. . . .

Before considering the evidence, a preliminary matter should be disposed of. The defendants do not agree among themselves as to who the "experts" were or as to the parts of the registration statement which were expertised. Some defendants say that Peat, Marwick was the expert; others say that BarChris's attorneys, Perkins, Daniels, McCormack & Collins, and the underwriters' attorneys, Drinker, Biddle & Reath, were also the experts. On the first view, only those portions of the registration statement purporting to be made on Peat, Marwick's authority were expertised portions. On the other view, everything in the registration statement was within this category, because the two law firms were responsible for the entire document.

The first view is the correct one. To say that the entire registration statement is expertised because some lawyer prepared it would be an unreasonable construction of the statute. Neither the lawyer for the company nor the lawyer for the underwriters is an expert within the meaning of § 11. The only expert, in the statutory sense, was Peat, Marwick, and the only parts of the registration statement which purported to be made upon the authority of an expert were the portions which purported to be made on Peat, Marwick's authority.

The parties also disagree as to what those portions were. Some defendants say that it was only the 1960 figures (and the figures for prior years, which are not in controversy here). Others say in substance that it was every figure in the prospectus. . . .

Here again, the more narrow view is the correct one. The registration statement contains a report of Peat, Marwick as independent public accountants dated February 23, 1961. This relates only to the consolidated balance sheet of BarChris and consolidated subsidiaries as of December 31, 1960, and the related statement of earnings and retained earnings for the five years then ended. This is all that Peat, Marwick purported to certify. It is perfectly clear that it did not purport to certify the 1961 figures, some of which are expressly stated in the prospectus to have been unaudited.

I turn now to the question of whether defendants have proved their due diligence defenses. The position of each defendant will be separately considered.

Russo

Russo was, to all intents and purposes, the chief executive officer of BarChris. He was a member of the executive committee. He was familiar with all aspects of the business. He was personally in charge of dealings with the factors. He acted on BarChris's behalf in making the financing agreements with Talcott and he handled the negotiations with Talcott in the spring of 1961. He talked with customers about their delinquencies.

. . . .

It was Russo who arranged for the temporary increase in BarChris's cash [on deposit with] banks on December 31, 1960, a transaction which borders on the fraudulent. He was thoroughly aware of BarChris's stringent financial condition in May 1961. He had personally advanced large sums to BarChris of which $175,000 remained unpaid as of May 16.

In short, Russo knew all the relevant facts. He could not have believed that there were no untrue statements or material omissions in the prospectus. Russo has no due diligence defenses.

Vitolo and Pugliese

They were the founders of the business who stuck with it to the end. Vitolo was president and Pugliese was vice president. Despite their titles, their field of responsibility in the administration of BarChris's affairs during the period in question seems to have been less all-embracing than Russo's. Pugliese in particular appears to have limited his activities to supervising the actual construction work.

Vitolo and Pugliese are each men of limited education. It is not hard to believe that for them the prospectus was difficult reading, if indeed they read it at all.

But whether it was or not is irrelevant. The liability of a director who signs a registration statement does not depend upon whether or not he read it or, if he did, whether or not he understood what he was reading.

And in any case, Vitolo and Pugliese were not as naive as they claim to be. They were members of BarChris's executive committee. At meetings of that committee BarChris's affairs were discussed at length. They must have known what was going on. Certainly they knew of the inadequacy of cash in 1961. They knew of their own large advances to the company which remained unpaid. They knew that they had agreed not to deposit their checks until the financing proceeds were received. They knew and intended that part of the proceeds were to be used to pay their own loans.

All in all, the position of Vitolo and Pugliese is not significantly different, for present purposes, from Russo's. They could not have believed that the registration statement was wholly true and that no material facts had been omitted. And in any case, there is nothing to show that they made any investigation of anything which they may not have known about or understood. They have not proved their due diligence defenses.

Kircher

Kircher was treasurer of BarChris and its chief financial officer. He is a certified public accountant and an intelligent man. He was thoroughly familiar with BarChris's financial affairs. He knew the terms of BarChris's agreements with Talcott. He knew of the customers' delinquency problem. He participated actively with Russo in May 1961 in the successful effort to hold Talcott off until the financing proceeds came in. He knew how the financing proceeds were to be applied and he saw to it that they were so applied. He arranged the officers' loans and he knew all the facts concerning them.

Moreover, as a member of the executive committee, Kircher was kept informed as to those branches of the business of which he did not have direct charge.

Kircher worked on the preparation of the registration statement. He conferred with Grant [BarChris's outside counsel] and on occasion with Ballard [underwriters' counsel]. He supplied information to them about the company's business. He read the prospectus and understood it. He knew what it said and what it did not say.

Kircher's contention is that he had never before dealt with a registration statement, that he did not know what it should contain, and that he relied wholly on Grant, Ballard and Peat, Marwick to guide him. He claims that it was their fault, not his, if there was anything wrong with it. He says that all the facts were recorded in BarChris's books where these "experts" could have seen them if they had looked. He says that he truthfully answered all their questions. In effect, he says that if they did not know enough to ask the right questions and to give him the proper instructions, that is not his responsibility.

There is an issue of credibility here. In fact, Kircher was not frank in dealing with Grant and Ballard. He withheld information from them. But even if he had told them all the facts, this would not have constituted the due diligence contemplated by the statute. Knowing the facts, Kircher had reason to believe that the expertised portion of the prospectus, i.e., the 1960 figures, was in part incorrect. He could not shut his eyes to the facts and rely on Peat, Marwick for that portion.

As to the rest of the prospectus, knowing the facts, he did not have a reasonable ground to believe it to be true. On the contrary, he must have known that in part it was untrue. Under these circumstances, he was not entitled to sit back and place the blame on the lawyers for not advising him about it.

Kircher has not proved his due diligence defenses.

Trilling

Trilling's position is somewhat different from Kircher's. He was BarChris's controller. He signed the registration statement in that capacity, although he was not a director.

Trilling entered BarChris's employ in October 1960. He was Kircher's subordinate. When Kircher asked him for information, he furnished it. . . .

Trilling was not a member of the executive committee. He was a comparatively minor figure in BarChris. The description of BarChris's "management" [in] the prospectus does not mention him. He was not considered to be an executive officer.

Trilling may well have been unaware of several of the inaccuracies in the prospectus. But he must have known of some of them. As a financial officer, he was familiar with BarChris's finances and with its books of account. . . . In the light of these facts, I cannot find that Trilling believed the entire prospectus to be true.

But even if he did, he still did not establish his due diligence defenses. He did not prove that as to the part of the prospectus expertised by Peat, Marwick he had no reasonable ground to believe that it was untrue. He also failed to prove, as to the parts of the prospectus not expertised by Peat, Marwick, that he made a reasonable investigation which afforded him a reasonable ground to believe that it was true. As far as appears, he made no investigation. He did what was asked of him and assumed that others would properly take care of supplying accurate data as to the other aspects of the company's business. This would have been well enough but for the fact that he signed the registration statement. As a signer, he could not avoid responsibility by leaving it up to others to make it accurate. Trilling did not sustain the burden of proving his due diligence defenses.

Birnbaum

Birnbaum was a young lawyer, admitted to the bar in 1957, who, after brief periods of employment by two different law firms and an equally brief period of practicing in his own firm, was employed by BarChris as house counsel and assistant secretary in October 1960. Unfortunately for him, he became secretary and a director of BarChris on April 17, 1961, after the first version of the registration statement had been filed with the Securities and Exchange Commission. He signed the later amendments, thereby becoming responsible for the accuracy of the prospectus in its final form.

Although the prospectus, in its description of "management," lists Birnbaum among the "executive officers" and devotes several sentences to a recital of his career, the fact seems to be that he was not an executive officer in any real sense. He did not participate in the management of the company. As house counsel, he attended to legal matters of a routine nature. Among other things, he incorporated subsidiaries, with which BarChris was plentifully supplied. . . . He was thus aware of that aspect of the business.

One of Birnbaum's more important duties, first as assistant secretary and later as full-fledged secretary, was to keep the corporate minutes of BarChris and its subsidiaries. This necessarily informed him to a considerable extent about the company's affairs. . . .

It seems probable that Birnbaum did not know of many of the inaccuracies in the prospectus. He must, however, have appreciated some of them. In any case, he made no investigation and relied on the others to get it right. Unlike Trilling, he was entitled to rely upon Peat, Marwick for the 1960 figures, for as far as appears, he had no personal knowledge of the company's books of account or financial transactions. But he was not entitled to rely upon Kircher, Grant and Ballard for the other portions of the prospectus. As a lawyer, he should have known his obligations under the statute. He should have known that he was required to make a reasonable investigation of the truth of all the statements in the unexpertised portion of the document which he signed. Having failed to make such an investigation, he did not have reasonable ground to believe that all these statements were true. Birnbaum has not established his due diligence defenses except as to the audited 1960 figures.

Auslander

Auslander was an "outside" director, i.e., one who was not an officer of BarChris. He was chairman of the board of Valley Stream National Bank in Valley Stream, Long Island. In February 1961 Vitolo asked him to become a director of BarChris. Vitolo gave him an enthusiastic account of BarChris's progress and prospects. As an inducement, Vitolo said that when BarChris received the proceeds of a forthcoming issue of securities, it would deposit $1,000,000 in Auslander's bank.[17]

In February and early March 1961, before accepting Vitolo's invitation, Auslander made some investigation of BarChris. He obtained Dun & Bradstreet reports which contained sales and earnings figures for periods earlier than December 31, 1960. He caused inquiry to be made of certain of BarChris's banks and was advised that they regarded BarChris favorably. He was informed that inquiry of Talcott had also produced a favorable response.

On March 3, 1961, Auslander indicated his willingness to accept a place on the board. Shortly thereafter, on March 14, Kircher sent him a copy of BarChris's annual report for 1960. Auslander observed that BarChris's auditors were Peat, Marwick. They were also the auditors for the Valley Stream National Bank. He thought well of them.

Auslander was elected a director on April 17, 1961. The registration statement in its original form had already been filed, of course without his signature. On May 10, 1961, he signed a signature page for the first amendment to the registration statement which was filed on May 11, 1961. This was a separate sheet without any document attached. Auslander did not know that it was a signature page for a registration statement. He vaguely understood that it was something "for the SEC."

Auslander attended a meeting of BarChris's directors on May 15, 1961. At that meeting he, along with the other directors, signed the signature sheet for the second amendment which constituted the registration statement in its final form. Again, this was only a separate sheet without any document attached. Auslander never saw a copy of the registration statement in its final form.

At the May 15 directors' meeting, however, Auslander did realize that what he was signing was a signature sheet to a registration statement. This was the first time that he had appreciated that fact. A copy of the registration statement in its earlier form as amended on May 11, 1961 was passed around at the meeting. Auslander glanced at it briefly. He did not read it thoroughly.

At the May 15 meeting, Russo and Vitolo stated that everything was in order and that the prospectus was correct. Auslander believed this statement.

---

[17]. After BarChris received the financing proceeds, it deposited in the Valley Stream National Bank not $1,000,000, but $150,000 in a checking account and $150,000 in a six-months' time deposit. The checking account was reduced to approximately $12,000 within a few weeks.

In considering Auslander's due diligence defenses, a distinction is to be drawn between the expertised and non-expertised portions of the prospectus. As to the former, Auslander knew that Peat, Marwick had audited the 1960 figures. He believed them to be correct because he had confidence in Peat, Marwick. He had no reasonable ground to believe otherwise.

As to the non-expertised portions, however, Auslander is in a different position. He seems to have been under the impression that Peat, Marwick was responsible for all the figures. This impression was not correct, as he would have realized if he had read the prospectus carefully. Auslander made no investigation of the accuracy of the prospectus. He relied on the assurance of Vitolo and Russo, and upon the information he had received in answer to his inquiries back in February and early March. These inquiries were general ones, in the nature of a credit check. The information which he received in answer to them was also general, without specific reference to the statements in the prospectus, which was not prepared until some time thereafter.

It is true that Auslander became a director on the eve of the financing. He had little opportunity to familiarize himself with the company's affairs. The question is whether, under such circumstances, Auslander did enough to establish his due diligence defense with respect to the non-expertised portions of the prospectus.

Although there is a dearth of authority under § 11 on this point, an English case under the analogous Companies Act is of some value. In *Adams v. Thrift*, [1915] 1 Ch. 557, *aff'd*, [1915] 2 Ch. 21, it was held that a director who knew nothing about the prospectus and did not even read it, but who relied on the statement of the company's managing director that it was "all right," was liable for its untrue statements.

. . . .

Section 11 imposes liability in the first instance upon a director, no matter how new he is. He is presumed to know his responsibility when he becomes a director. He can escape liability only by using that reasonable care to investigate the facts which a prudent man would employ in the management of his own property. In my opinion, a prudent man would not act in an important matter without any knowledge of the relevant facts, in sole reliance upon representations of persons who are comparative strangers and upon general information which does not purport to cover the particular case. To say that such minimal conduct measures up to the statutory standard would, to all intents and purposes, absolve new directors from responsibility merely because they are new. This is not a sensible construction of Section 11, when one bears in mind its fundamental purpose of requiring full and truthful disclosure for the protection of investors.

I find and conclude that Auslander has not established his due diligence defense with respect to the misstatements and omissions in those portions of the prospectus other than the audited 1960 figures.

. . . .

Grant

Grant became a director of BarChris in October 1960. His law firm was counsel to BarChris in matters pertaining to the registration of securities. Grant drafted the registration statement for the stock issue in 1959 and for the warrants in January 1961. He also drafted the registration statement for the debentures. In the preliminary division of work between him and Ballard, the underwriters' counsel, Grant took initial responsibility for preparing the registration statement, while Ballard devoted his efforts in the first instance to preparing the indenture.

Grant is sued as a director and as a signer of the registration statement. This is not an action against him for malpractice in his capacity as a lawyer. Nevertheless, in considering Grant's due diligence defenses, the unique position which he occupied cannot be disregarded. As the director most directly concerned with writing the registration statement and assuring its accuracy, more was required of him in the way of reasonable investigation than could fairly be expected of a director who had no connection with this work.

There is no valid basis for plaintiffs' accusation that Grant knew that the prospectus was false in some respects and incomplete and misleading in others. Having seen him testify at length, I am satisfied as to his integrity. I find that Grant honestly believed that the registration statement was true and that no material facts had been omitted from it.

In this belief he was mistaken, and the fact is that for all his work, he never discovered any of the errors or omissions which have been recounted at length in this opinion, with the single exception of Capitol Lanes. He knew that BarChris had not sold this alley and intended to operate it, but he appears to have been under the erroneous impression that Peat, Marwick had knowingly sanctioned its inclusion in sales because of the allegedly temporary nature of the operation.

Grant contends that a finding that he did not make a reasonable investigation would be equivalent to a holding that a lawyer for an issuing company, in order to show due diligence, must make an independent audit of the figures supplied to him by his client. I do not consider this to be a realistic statement of the issue. There were errors and omissions here which could have been detected without an audit. The question is whether, despite his failure to detect them, Grant made a reasonable effort to that end.

Much of this registration statement is a scissors and paste-pot job. Grant lifted large portions from the earlier prospectuses, modifying them in some instances to the extent that he considered necessary. But BarChris's affairs had changed for the worse by May 1961. Statements that were accurate in January were no longer accurate in May. Grant never discovered this. He accepted the assurances of Kircher and Russo that any change which might have occurred had been for the better, rather than the contrary.

It is claimed that a lawyer is entitled to rely on the statements of his client and that to require him to verify their accuracy would set an unreasonably high standard. This is too broad a generalization. It is all a matter of degree. To require an audit would obviously be unreasonable. On the other hand, to require a check of matters easily verifiable is not unreasonable. Even honest clients can make mistakes. The statute imposes liability for untrue statements regardless of whether they are intentionally untrue. The way to prevent mistakes is to test oral information by examining the original written record.

There were things which Grant could readily have checked which he did not check. For example, he was unaware of the provisions of the agreements between BarChris and Talcott. He never read them. Thus, he did not know, although he readily could have ascertained, that BarChris's contingent liability on Type B leaseback arrangements was 100 per cent, not 25 per cent. He did not appreciate that if BarChris defaulted in repurchasing delinquent customers' notes upon Talcott's demand, Talcott could accelerate all the customer paper in its hands, which amounted to over $3,000,000.

As to the backlog figure, Grant appreciated that scheduled unfilled orders on the company's books meant firm commitments, but he never asked to see the contracts which, according to the prospectus, added up to $6,905,000. Thus, he did not know that this figure was overstated by some $4,490,000.

. . . On the subject of minutes, Grant knew that minutes of certain meetings of the BarChris executive committee held in 1961 had not been written up. Kircher, who had acted as secretary at those meetings, had complete notes of them. Kircher told Grant that there was no point in writing up the minutes because the matters discussed at those meetings were purely routine. Grant did not insist that the minutes be written up, nor did he look at Kircher's notes. If he had, he would have learned that on February 27, 1961 there was an extended discussion in the executive committee meeting about customers' delinquencies, that on March 8, 1961 the committee had discussed the pros and cons of alley operation by BarChris, that on March 18, 1961 the committee was informed that BarChris was constructing or about to begin constructing twelve alleys for which it had no contracts, and that on May 13, 1961 Dreyfuss, one of the worst delinquents, had filed a petition in [bankruptcy].

Grant knew that there had been loans from officers to BarChris in the past because that subject had been mentioned in the 1959 and January 1961 prospectuses. In March Grant prepared a questionnaire to be answered by officers and directors for the purpose of obtaining information to be used in the prospectus. The questionnaire did not inquire expressly about the existence of officers' loans. At approximately the same time, Grant prepared another questionnaire in order to obtain information on proxy statements for the annual stockholders' meeting. This questionnaire asked each officer to state whether he was indebted to BarChris, but it did not ask whether BarChris was indebted to him.

Despite the inadequacy of these written questionnaires, Grant did, on March 16, 1961, orally inquire as to whether any officers' loans were outstanding. He was assured by Russo, Vitolo and Pugliese that all such loans had been repaid. Grant did not ask again. He was unaware of the new loans in April. He did know, however, that, at

Kircher's request, a provision was inserted in the indenture which gave loans from individuals priority over the debentures. Kircher's insistence on this clause did not arouse his suspicions.

It is only fair to say that Grant was given to understand by Kircher that there were no new officers' loans and that there would not be any before May 16. It is still a close question, however, whether, under all the circumstances, Grant should have investigated further, perhaps by asking Peat, Marwick, in the course of its S-1 review, to look at the books on this particular point. I believe that a careful man would have checked.

. . . .

As far as customers' delinquencies is concerned, although Grant discussed this with Kircher, he again accepted the assurances of Kircher and Russo that no serious problem existed. He did not examine the records as to delinquencies, although BarChris maintained such records.

. . . .

Grant was entitled to rely on Peat, Marwick for the 1960 figures. He had no reasonable ground to believe them to be inaccurate. But the matters which I have mentioned were not within the expertised portion of the prospectus. As to this, Grant, was obliged to make a reasonable investigation. I am forced to find that he did not make one. After making all due allowances for the fact that BarChris's officers misled him, there are too many instances in which Grant failed to make an inquiry which he could easily have made which, if pursued, would have put him on his guard. In my opinion, this finding on the evidence in this case does not establish an unreasonably high standard in other cases for company counsel who are also directors. Each case must rest on its own facts. I conclude that Grant has not established his due diligence defenses except as to the audited 1960 figures.

The Underwriters and Coleman

The underwriters other than Drexel made no investigation of the accuracy of the prospectus. . . . [The other underwriters] all relied upon Drexel as the "lead" underwriter.

Drexel did make an investigation. The work was in charge of Coleman, a partner of the firm, assisted by Casperson, an associate. Drexel's attorneys acted as attorneys for the entire group of underwriters. Ballard did the work, assisted by Stanton [a junior associate].

On April 17, 1961 Coleman became a director of BarChris. He signed the first amendment to the registration statement filed on May 11 and the second amendment, constituting the registration statement in its final form, filed on May 16. He thereby assumed a responsibility as a director and signer in addition to his responsibility as an underwriter.

The facts as to the extent of the investigation that Coleman made may be briefly summarized. He was first introduced to BarChris on September 15, 1960.

Thereafter he familiarized himself with general conditions in the industry, primarily by reading reports and prospectuses of the two leading bowling alley builders, American Machine & Foundry Company and Brunswick. These indicated that the industry was still growing. He also acquired general information on BarChris by reading the 1959 stock prospectus, annual reports for prior years, and an unaudited statement for the first half of 1960. He inquired about BarChris of certain of its banks and of Talcott and received favorable replies.

The purpose of this preliminary investigation was to enable Coleman to decide whether Drexel would undertake the financing. It did not have direct reference to any specific registration statement for at that time, of course, none had been prepared. Coleman was sufficiently optimistic about BarChris's prospects to buy 1,000 shares of its stock, which he did in December 1960.

On January 24, 1961, Coleman held a meeting with Ballard, Grant and Kircher, among others. By that time Coleman had about decided to go ahead with the financing, although Drexel's formal letter of intent was not delivered until February 9, 1961 (subsequently revised on March 7, 1961). At this meeting Coleman asked Kircher how BarChris intended to use the proceeds of the financing. In reply to this inquiry, Kircher wrote a letter to Coleman dated January 30, 1961 outlining BarChris's plans. This eventually formed the basis of the application of proceeds section in the prospectus.

Coleman continued his general investigation. He obtained a Dun & Bradstreet report on BarChris on March 16, 1961. He read BarChris's annual report for 1960 which was available in March.

By mid-March, Coleman was in a position to make more specific inquiries. By that time Grant had prepared a first draft of the prospectus, consisting of a marked-up copy of the January 1961 warrant prospectus. Coleman attended three meetings to discuss the prospectus with BarChris's representatives. The meetings were held at Perkins, Daniels' office on March 20, March 23 and March 24, 1961. Those present included Grant or his partner McCormack and Kircher for the company, and Coleman, Casperson and Ballard for the underwriters. Logan [Peat, Marwick's manager of the 1960 audit], was present at one of the meetings.

At these discussions, which were extensive, successive proofs of the prospectus were considered and revised. . . . Coleman and Ballard asked pertinent questions and received answers which satisfied them. . . .

After Coleman was elected a director on April 17, 1961, he made no further independent investigation of the accuracy of the prospectus. He assumed that Ballard was taking care of this on his behalf as well as on behalf of the underwriters.

In April 1961 Ballard instructed Stanton to examine BarChris's minutes for the past five years and also to look at "the major contracts of the company."[18] Stanton went to BarChris's office for that purpose on April 24. He asked Birnbaum for the

---

[18]. [This footnote has been moved to the text. — ed.]

minute books. He read the minutes of the board of directors and discovered interleaved in them a few minutes of executive committee meetings in 1960. He asked Kircher if there were any others. Kircher said that there had been other executive committee meetings but that the minutes had not been written up.

Stanton read the minutes of a few BarChris subsidiaries. His testimony was vague as to which ones. . . . Stanton was a very junior associate. He had been admitted to the bar in January 1961, some three months before. This was the first registration statement he had ever worked on.

As to the "major contracts," all that Stanton could remember seeing was an insurance policy. Birnbaum told him that there was no file of major contracts. Stanton did not examine the agreements with Talcott. He did not examine the contracts with customers. He did not look to see what contracts comprised the backlog figure. Stanton examined no accounting records of BarChris. His visit, which lasted one day, was devoted primarily to reading the directors' minutes.

On April 25 Ballard wrote to Grant about certain matters which Stanton had noted on his visit to BarChris the day before, none of which Ballard considered "very earth shaking." . . .

On May 9, 1961, Ballard came to New York and conferred with Grant and Kircher.

. . . .

It must be remembered that this conference took place only one week before the registration statement became effective. Ballard did nothing else in the way of checking during that intervening week.

Ballard did not insist that the executive committee minutes be written up so that he could inspect them, although he testified that he knew from experience that executive committee minutes may be extremely important. If he had insisted, he would have found the minutes highly informative. . . . Ballard did not ask to see BarChris's schedule of delinquencies or Talcott's notices of delinquencies, or BarChris's correspondence with Talcott.

Ballard did not examine BarChris's contracts with Talcott. He did not appreciate what Talcott's rights were under those financing agreements or how serious the effect would be upon BarChris of any exercise of those rights.

Ballard did not investigate the composition of the backlog figure to be sure that it was not "puffy." He made no inquiry after March about any new officers' loans, although he knew that Kircher had insisted on a provision in the indenture which gave loans from individuals priority over the debentures. He was unaware of the seriousness of BarChris's cash position and of how BarChris's officers intended to use a large part of the proceeds. . . .

Like Grant, Ballard, without checking, relied on the information which he got from Kircher. He also relied on Grant who, as company counsel, presumably was familiar with its affairs.

The formal opinion which Ballard's firm rendered to the underwriters at the closing on May 24, 1961 made clear that this is what he had done. The opinion stated ([italics] supplied):

> In the course of the preparation of the Registration Statement and Prospectus by the Company, we have had numerous conferences with representatives of and counsel for the Company and with its auditors and we have raised many questions regarding the business of the Company. Satisfactory answers to such questions were in each case given us, and all other information and documents we requested have been supplied. *We are of the opinion that the data presented to us are accurately reflected in the Registration Statement and Prospectus* and that there has been omitted from the Registration Statement no material facts included in such data. *Although we have not otherwise verified the completeness or accuracy of the information furnished to us*, on the basis of the foregoing and with the exception of the financial statements and schedules (which this opinion does not pass upon), we have no reason to believe that the Registration Statement or Prospectus contains any untrue statement of any material fact or omits to state a material fact required to be stated therein or necessary in order to make the statements therein not misleading.

Coleman testified that Drexel had an understanding with its attorneys that "we expect them to inspect on our behalf the corporate records of the company including, but not limited to, the minutes of the corporation, the stockholders and the committees of the board authorized to act for the board." Ballard manifested his awareness of this understanding by sending Stanton to read the minutes and the major contracts. It is difficult to square this understanding with the formal opinion of Ballard's firm which expressly disclaimed any attempt to verify information supplied by the company and its counsel.

In any event, it is clear that no effectual attempt at verification was made. The question is whether due diligence required that it be made. Stated another way, is it sufficient to ask questions, to obtain answers which, if true, would be thought satisfactory, and to let it go at that, without seeking to ascertain from the records whether the answers in fact are true and complete?

I have already held that this procedure is not sufficient in Grant's case. Are underwriters in a different position, as far as due diligence is concerned?

The underwriters say that the prospectus is the company's prospectus, not theirs. Doubtless this is the way they customarily regard it. But the Securities Act makes no such distinction. The underwriters are just as responsible as the company if the prospectus is false. And prospective investors rely upon the reputation of the underwriters in deciding whether to purchase the securities.

. . . .

In a sense, the positions of the underwriter and the company's officers are adverse. It is not unlikely that statements made by company officers to an underwriter to induce him to underwrite may be self-serving. They may be unduly enthusiastic. As in this case, they may, on occasion, be deliberately false.

The purpose of Section 11 is to protect investors. To that end the underwriters are made responsible for the truth of the prospectus. If they may escape that responsibility by taking at face value representations made to them by the company's management, then the inclusion of underwriters among those liable under § 11 affords the investors no additional protection. To effectuate the statute's purpose, the phrase "reasonable investigation" must be construed to require more effort on the part of the underwriters than the mere accurate reporting in the prospectus of "data presented" to them by the company. It should make no difference that this data is elicited by questions addressed to the company officers by the underwriters, or that the underwriters at the time believe that the company's officers are truthful and reliable. In order to make the underwriters' participation in this enterprise of any value to the investors, the underwriters must make some reasonable attempt to verify the data submitted to them. They may not rely solely on the company's officers or on the company's counsel. A prudent man in the management of his own property would not rely on them.

It is impossible to lay down a rigid rule suitable for every case defining the extent to which such verification must go. It is a question of degree, a matter of judgment in each case. In the present case, the underwriters' counsel made almost no attempt to verify management's representations. I hold that was insufficient.

On the evidence in this case, I find that the underwriters' counsel did not make a reasonable investigation of the truth of those portions of the prospectus which were not made on the authority of Peat, Marwick as an expert. Drexel is bound by their failure. It is not a matter of relying upon counsel for legal advice. Here the attorneys were dealing with matters of fact. Drexel delegated to them, as its agent, the business of examining the corporate minutes and contracts. It must bear the consequences of their failure to make an adequate examination.

The other underwriters, who did nothing and relied solely on Drexel and on the lawyers, are also bound by it. It follows that although Drexel and the other underwriters believed that those portions of the prospectus were true, they had no reasonable ground for that belief, within the meaning of the statute. Hence, they have not established their due diligence defense, except as to the 1960 audited figures.

The same conclusions must apply to Coleman. Although he participated quite actively in the earlier stages of the preparation of the prospectus, and contributed questions and warnings of his own, in addition to the questions of counsel, the fact is that he stopped his participation toward the end of March 1961. He made no investigation after he became a director. When it came to verification, he relied upon his counsel to do it for him. Since counsel failed to do it, Coleman is bound by that failure. Consequently, in his case also, he has not established his due diligence defense except as to the audited 1960 figures.

Peat, Marwick

Section 11(b) provides:

> Notwithstanding the provisions of subsection (a) no person . . . shall be liable as provided therein who shall sustain the burden of proof—. . . . (3) that . . . (B) as regards any part of the registration statement purporting to be made upon his authority as an expert . . . (i) he had, after reasonable investigation, reasonable ground to believe and did believe, at the time such part of the registration statement became effective, that the statements therein were true and that there was no omission to state a material fact required to be stated therein or necessary to make the statements therein not misleading. . . .

This defines the due diligence defense for an expert. Peat, Marwick has pleaded it.

The part of the registration statement purporting to be made upon the authority of Peat, Marwick as an expert was, as we have seen, the 1960 figures. But because the statute requires the court to determine Peat, Marwick's belief, and the grounds thereof, "at the time such part of the registration statement became effective," for the purposes of this affirmative defense, the matter must be viewed as of May 16, 1961, [which was the registration statement's effective date] and the question is whether at that time Peat, Marwick, after reasonable investigation, had reasonable ground to believe and did believe that the 1960 figures were true and that no material fact had been omitted from the registration statement which should have been included in order to make the 1960 figures not misleading. In deciding this issue, the court must consider not only what Peat, Marwick did in its 1960 audit, but also what it did in its subsequent "S-1 review." The proper scope of that review must also be determined.

. . . .

The 1960 Audit

Peat, Marwick's work [concerning BarChris] was in . . . charge of a member of the firm, Cummings, and more immediately in charge of Peat, Marwick's manager, Logan. Most of the actual work was performed by a senior accountant, Berardi, who had junior assistants, one of whom was Kennedy.

Berardi was then about thirty years old. He was not yet a C.P.A. He had had no previous experience with the bowling industry. This was his first job as a senior accountant. He could hardly have been given a more difficult assignment.

After obtaining a little background information on BarChris by talking to Logan and reviewing Peat, Marwick's work papers on its 1959 audit, Berardi examined the results of test checks of BarChris's accounting procedures which one of the junior accountants had made, and he prepared an "internal control questionnaire" and an "audit program." Thereafter, for a few days subsequent to December 30, 1960, he inspected BarChris's inventories and examined certain alley construction. Finally, on January 13, 1961, he began his auditing work which he carried on substantially continuously until it was completed on February 24, 1961. Toward the close of the work, Logan reviewed it and made various comments and suggestions to Berardi.

It is unnecessary to recount everything that Berardi did in the course of the audit. We are concerned only with the evidence relating to what Berardi did or did not do with respect to those items which I have found to have been incorrectly reported in the 1960 figures in the prospectus. More narrowly, we are directly concerned only with such of those items as I have found to be material.

Capitol Lanes

First and foremost is Berardi's failure to discover that Capitol Lanes had not been sold. This error affected both the sales figure and the liability side of the balance sheet. Fundamentally, the error stemmed from the fact that Berardi never realized that Heavenly Lanes and Capitol were two different names for the same alley. In the course of his audit, Berardi was shown BarChris's contract file. He examined the contracts in the file and made a list of them. The file must have included a contract with an outside purchaser for Heavenly Lanes, although no such contract was ever produced at the trial, for Berardi included Heavenly on his list. . . .

The evidence is conflicting as to whether BarChris's officers expressly informed Berardi that Heavenly and Capitol were the same thing and that BarChris was operating Capitol and had not sold it. I find that they did not so inform him.

Berardi did become aware that there were references here and there in BarChris's records to something called Capitol Lanes. He also knew that there were indications that at some time BarChris might operate an alley of that name. . . .

. . . .

Berardi testified that he inquired of Russo about Capitol Lanes and that Russo told him that Capitol Lanes, Inc. was going to operate an alley some day but as yet it had no alley. Berardi testified that he understood that the alley had not been built and that he believed that the rental payments were on vacant land.

I am not satisfied with this testimony. If Berardi did hold this belief, he should not have held it. The entries as to insurance and as to "operation of alley" should have alerted him to the fact that an alley existed. He should have made further inquiry on the subject. It is apparent that Berardi did not understand this transaction.

In any case, he never identified this mysterious Capitol with the Heavenly Lanes which he had included in his sales and profit figures. The vital question is whether he failed to make a reasonable investigation which, if he had made it, would have revealed the truth.

Certain accounting records of BarChris, which Berardi testified he did not see, would have put him on inquiry. One was a job cost ledger card for job no. 6036, the job number which Berardi put on his own work sheet for Heavenly Lanes. This card read "Capital Theatre (Heavenly)." In addition, two accounts receivable cards each showed both names on the same card, Capitol and Heavenly. Berardi testified that he looked at the accounts receivable records but that he did not see these particular cards. He testified that he did not look on the job cost ledger cards because he took the costs from another record, the costs register.

The burden of proof on this issue is on Peat, Marwick. Although the question is a rather close one, I find that Peat, Marwick has not sustained that burden. Peat, Marwick has not proved that Berardi made a reasonable investigation as far as Capitol Lanes was concerned and that his ignorance of the true facts was justified.

. . . .

The S-1 Review

The purpose of reviewing events subsequent to the date of a certified balance sheet (referred to as an S-1 review when made with reference to a registration statement) is to ascertain whether any material change has occurred in the company's financial position which should be disclosed in order to prevent the balance sheet figures from being misleading. The scope of such a review, under generally accepted auditing standards, is limited. It does not amount to a complete audit.

Peat, Marwick prepared a written program for such a review. I find that this program conformed to generally accepted auditing standards. Among other things, it required the following:

1. Review minutes of [meetings of] stockholders, directors and committees. . . .

2. Review latest interim financial statements and compare with corresponding statements of preceding year. Inquire regarding significant variations and changes.

. . . .

4. Review the more important financial records and inquire regarding material transactions not in the ordinary course of business and any other significant items.

. . . .

6. Inquire as to changes in material contracts. . . .

. . . .

10. Inquire as to any significant bad debts or accounts in dispute for which provision has not been made.

. . . .

14. Inquire as to . . . newly discovered liabilities, direct or contingent. . . .

Berardi made the S-1 review in May 1961. He devoted a little over two days to it, a total of 20 hours. He did not discover any of the errors or omissions pertaining to the state of affairs in 1961 which I have previously discussed at length, all of which were material. The question is whether, despite his failure to find out anything, his investigation was reasonable within the meaning of the statute.

What Berardi did was to look at a consolidating trial balance as of March 31, 1961 which had been prepared by BarChris, compare it with the audited December 31,

1960 figures, discuss with Trilling certain unfavorable developments which the comparison disclosed, and read certain minutes. He did not examine any "important financial records" other than the trial balance. As to minutes, he read only what minutes Birnbaum gave him, which consisted only of the board of directors' minutes of BarChris. He did not read such minutes as there were of the executive committee. He did not know that there was an executive committee, hence he did not discover that Kircher had notes of executive committee minutes which had not been written up. He did not read the minutes of any subsidiary.

In substance, what Berardi did is similar to what Grant and Ballard did. He asked questions, he got answers which he considered satisfactory, and he did nothing to verify them. For example, he obtained from Trilling a list of contracts. The list included Yonkers and Bridge. Since Berardi did not read the minutes of subsidiaries, he did not learn that Yonkers and Bridge were intercompany sales. . . . Since Berardi did not look at any contract documents, and since he was unaware of the executive committee minutes of March 18, 1961 (at that time embodied only in Kircher's notes), he did not learn that BarChris had no contracts for these jobs. . . .

Berardi noticed that there had been an increase in notes payable by BarChris. Trilling admitted to him that BarChris was "a bit slow" in paying its bills. Berardi recorded in his notes of his review that BarChris was in a "tight cash position." Trilling's explanation was that BarChris was experiencing "some temporary difficulty."

Berardi had no conception of how tight the cash position was. He did not discover that BarChris was holding up checks in substantial amounts because there was no money in the bank to cover them. He did not know of the loan from Manufacturers Trust Company or of the officers' loans. Since he never read the prospectus, he was not even aware that there had ever been any problem about loans from officers.

During the 1960 audit Berardi had obtained some information from factors, not sufficiently detailed even then, as to delinquent notes. He made no inquiry of factors about this in his S-1 review. Since he knew nothing about Kircher's notes of the executive committee meetings, he did not learn that the delinquency situation had grown worse. He was content with Trilling's assurance.

. . . .

There had been a material change for the worse in BarChris's financial position. That change was sufficiently serious so that the failure to disclose it made the 1960 figures misleading. Berardi did not discover it. As far as results were concerned, his S-1 review was useless.

Accountants should not be held to a standard higher than that recognized in their profession. I do not do so here. Berardi's review did not come up to that standard. He did not take some of the steps which Peat, Marwick's written program prescribed. He did not spend an adequate amount of time on a task of this magnitude. Most important of all, he was too easily satisfied with glib answers to his inquiries.

This is not to say that he should have made a complete audit. But there were enough danger signals in the materials which he did examine to require some further investigation on his part. Generally accepted accounting standards required such further investigation under these circumstances. . . .

Here again, the burden of proof is on Peat, Marwick. I find that that burden has not been satisfied. I conclude that Peat, Marwick has not established its due diligence defense.

. . . .

§ 7.04 Analysis of Due Diligence in View of *BarChris*

Strictly speaking, "due diligence" is a defense that may be asserted by the subject party rather than an affirmative obligation. If the statements made in the registration statement are true or, alternatively, if no lawsuit is brought, no liability will be incurred for an individual's failure to exercise due diligence. On the other hand, if an action is instituted and a material misstatement or omission is shown, liability often may be avoided under § 11 only by proving the performance of due diligence. For this reason, as a practical matter, due diligence is a necessity.

Is the *BarChris* court's graduated approach to determining liability under § 11 consistent with the statutory language? While a literal reading may imply a unitary standard, the section's application is open to interpretation. Arguably, the extensiveness of the investigation required to meet one's due diligence defense depends upon the standard of care appropriate for a particular defendant in view of his/her position, relationship with the issuer, and involvement in the preparation of the registration statement. Hence, the action to be taken in order to meet one's due diligence obligation may vary according to the above factors. The concept "in like position" is a necessary implication in ascertaining whether that standard has been met. *BarChris* supports this analysis. The following discussion addresses the concept of due diligence for various categories of § 11 defendants.

Directors

In analyzing the due diligence defense raised by the defendant directors, *BarChris* draws a distinction between inside and outside directors, and between inside directors based upon the extent of their knowledge of or access to the pertinent facts. Certainly one would expect a director who also serves as the principal executive officer to be required to perform more diligently than an outside director who otherwise has no relationship with the issuer. As another example, publicly held corporations must establish executive, compensation, and other key committees, comprised of three directors who, in many cases, make decisions that otherwise would be within the province of the entire board of directors. Depending upon the circumstances, an inordinate hardship would be imposed upon directors not serving on those committees if they were held to the same degree of responsibility.

BarChris indicates that, while less may be required of certain directors in order to meet their due diligence obligations, reasonable investigation still requires affirmative action. Hence, outside directors must endeavor to make some type of an independent verification of the information contained in the registration statement. Clearly, a director who makes no effort to investigate will not be able to sustain his/her burden of establishing that he/she acted with due diligence. As stated more recently in *WorldCom,* "directors are not excused from performing a meaningful due diligence investigation due to the involvement of professionals, such as underwriters and auditors." *In re WorldCom, Inc. Securities Litigation,* [2005–2006 Transfer Binder] Fed. Sec L. Rep. (CCH) ¶ 93,137, at 95,781 (S.D.N.Y. 2005).

It may be asserted that an *outside director* should: seek to attend board of director meetings regarding the offering; review the registration statement with care (probing relevant corporate personnel and counsel on the factual contents and representations made therein); review the Exchange Act filed documents that are incorporated by reference into the registration statement; with the aid of competent advisers, assess the abilities of management as well as the company's reputation; ask questions and follow up if necessary. Although the performance of the foregoing actions may not guarantee absolution from liability, it should provide persuasive evidence that the outside director met his/her due diligence obligations.

In one such case, an outside director met his due diligence defense under § 11. See *Weinberger v. Jackson,* [1990–1991 Transfer Binder] Fed. Sec. L. Rep. (CCH) ¶ 95,693, at 98,256 (N.D. Cal. 1990). The court reasoned:

> Defendant Valentine was an outside director. The only cause of action now pending against him is under section 11.
>
> Section 11(b)(3) provides the so called "due diligence" defense. That is an affirmative defense which requires that a defendant show that "he had, after reasonable investigation, reasonable ground to believe and did believe" that there were no material misstatements or omissions. Section 11(c) imposes the measure of "reasonableness" as that of a reasonably prudent person managing his own property. Valentine's motion for summary judgment contends that there is no genuine issue of material fact [because he has] met those standards. This court agrees.
>
> Since Valentine was an outside director, he was not obliged to conduct an independent investigation into the accuracy of all the statements contained in the registration statement. He could rely upon the reasonable representations of management, if his own conduct and level of inquiry were reasonable under the circumstances. He was reasonably familiar with the company's business and operations. He regularly attended board meetings at which the board discussed every aspect of the company's business. And he reviewed

the company's financial statements. He was familiar with the company's development of its new product lines. He was involved with various company decisions. He reviewed six drafts of the registration statement and saw nothing suspicious or inconsistent with the knowledge that he had acquired as a director. And he discussed certain aspects of the registration statement with management. . . .

Plaintiffs argue that Valentine did not make specific inquiries of the company's management with respect to the representations contained in the prospectus. But he had no duty to do so as long as the prospectus statements were consistent with the knowledge of the company which he had reasonably acquired in his position as director. He was also given comfort by the fact that the prospectus and the information in it were reviewed by underwriters, counsel and accountants. This met the standards of due diligence and reasonable inquiry. . . .

Note that outside directors are liable only in proportion to their fault under § 11 unless they had actual knowledge of the falsity. Hence, an outside director who is deemed two percent responsible for the violation is liable for damages on that proportional fault basis unless he/she acted with actual knowledge (e.g., damages of $50 million, such outside director's liability is $1 million).

Signatories

Persons who sign the registration statement (at least a majority of the directors and certain high level officers of the issuer) may be held to stringent due diligence obligations. This is despite the fact that, had they not signed, their respective duties of investigation, particularly in the case of officers not holding directorships, may have differed. The rationale for holding signatories, particularly those who are inside directors or who otherwise hold principal corporate offices (even if not directors), to a strict standard of due diligence is that prospective investors reasonably may assume, that by signing the registration statement, such signatories represent that it is an accurate statement of the information contained therein.

To a large extent, *BarChris* may be viewed as treating "inside" signatories in effect as guarantors of the accuracy of the registration statement.[19] Interestingly, however, Congress specifically rejected a proposal that would have made directors guarantors in this context.[20] On the other hand, it may be said that *BarChris* "does not deny the [due diligence] defense [to such inside signatories], but recognizes the obvious difficulty of establishing it."[21]

---

19. Accord, *Feit v. Leasco Data Processing Equipment Corp.*, 332 F. Supp. 544 (E.D.N.Y. 1971). *See* Folk, *Civil Liabilities Under the Federal Securities Acts: The BarChris Case*, 55 Va. L. Rev. 1 (1969).

20. *See* H.R. Rep. No. 85, 73d Cong., 1st Sess. 5 (1933); H.R. Rep. No. 152, 73d Cong., 1st Sess. 26 (1933); Landis, *The Legislative History of the Securities Act of 1933*, 28 Geo. Wash. L. Rev. 29, 48 (1959).

21. Folk, *supra* note 19, 55 Va. L. Rev. at 22.

Attorneys

Due diligence is a concern for lawyers who are involved in a registered offering. For example, counsel may: (1) serve as a director of the issuer; (2) act as an expert within the meaning of § 11(a)(4) (e.g., by rendering a legal opinion that is contained in the registration statement); and (3) perform due diligence investigations on behalf of a client (e.g., an underwriter) in its stead.

In *BarChris,* the young attorney, Birnbaum, while not a director at the time the registration statement originally was filed, was a director when he signed the later amendments. He thereby subjected himself to § 11 liability as a director and as a signatory. Unfortunately, Birnbaum made no investigation whatsoever and relied on the statements of others. The court noted that, while Birnbaum was not an executive officer in any real sense, he was named as such in the prospectus. Further, by virtue of his duties as in-house counsel and keeper of the corporate minutes, he had considerable information about the corporation's affairs. While not aware of many of the inaccuracies in the prospectus, as a lawyer he must have appreciated some of them. He should have known his statutory obligations and made a reasonable investigation.

Would Birnbaum have been held liable had he not been a signatory? The court's opinion indicates that he would have been liable. In this regard, note that his liability would have been based upon his status as a director and not as an attorney. However, the fact that Birnbaum was an attorney was taken into consideration in determining whether he had conducted a reasonable investigation.

Grant, the issuer's outside counsel, was liable both as a director and as a signatory. The court took into account his role of being primarily responsible as issuer's counsel for drafting the registration statement, reasoning that "more was required of him in the way of reasonable investigation than could fairly be expected of a director who had no connection with this work." The court indicated that, by its holding, it was not seeking to establish an unduly onerous standard for outside counsel who also serves as a director. Rather, each case must turn on its own facts. Here, even taking into account that BarChris' officers had misled Grant, "there ... [were] too many instances in which Grant failed to make an inquiry which, if pursued, would have put him on his guard."

Counsel who renders a formal legal opinion that is included in the registration statement with his/her consent is considered an "expert" within the ambit of § 11. For example, counsel may proffer an opinion that: (1) the company and its subsidiaries are duly incorporated; (2) licenses are in order; and (3) the company's securities are validly issued under state law and are non-assessable. Such opinions rarely are problematic. More difficult issues arise when counsel proffers an opinion that is critical to the "deal." For example, opinions by tax counsel regarding the deductibility under the federal tax laws of certain investments have been the focus of considerable attention by the Treasury Department, the SEC, the U.S. Department of Justice, and the American Bar Association.

A different question is presented where an attorney, acting as counsel for either the issuer or the underwriter, furnishes a "comfort opinion." A comfort opinion essentially is a statement that, based on counsel's participation in the preparation of the registration statement and conferences with representatives of the issuer, underwriters and accountants, he/she has no reason to believe that the registration statement violates § 11. In order not to be subject to § 11 liability, counsel should ensure that neither the opinion nor its contents appear in the registration statement.

It is clear that an attorney who renders legal advice or assists in the preparation of the registration statement does not thereby become an expert within the meaning of § 11. In *Herman & MacLean v. Huddleston*, 459 U.S. 375, 386 n.22 (1983), the Supreme Court observed that "certain individuals who play a part in preparing the registration statement generally cannot be reached by a § 11 action. These include . . . lawyers not acting as experts." Note, however, as will be discussed later in this chapter as well as in Chapter 8, attorneys can be held liable under certain circumstances for violating § 12(a)(2) of the Securities Act and § 10(b) of the Exchange Act.

In practice, the issuer, directors, and underwriters frequently task their due diligence investigations (or portions thereof) to counsel. Such tasking, as *BarChris* made clear, is appropriate. In effect, while counsel seeks to perform an adequate investigation on behalf of his/her client, it is the client, and not counsel, who will be held liable under § 11 if counsel fails to meet the requisite standard of care. In such instances, counsel may be confronted with a legal malpractice suit, but that is a separate matter.

What should counsel do in order to ensure that his/her client's due diligence obligations are met? (See Appendix to this Chapter.) Because persons potentially liable under § 11 have different due diligence obligations depending on such factors as their position, relationship with the issuer, and involvement in the preparation of the registration statement, counsel should stand in his/her client's shoes. The extensiveness of the investigation appropriately may range from that required of an outside director to the extensive verification required of underwriters in the traditional public offering setting.

Accountants

Suits against accountants under § 11 typically relate to the certified financial statements contained in the registration statement. To the extent that the registration statement is inaccurate in any respect other than the part expertised by them, the accountants are not subject to § 11 liability (although they may be liable under other statutes and state common law). An issue raised in *BarChris* was whether accountants should be held to a higher standard of care under § 11 than would be necessary to conform to standards in their profession.

The Seventh Circuit's decision in *Hochfelder v. Ernst & Ernst*, 503 F.2d 1100, 1107–1108, 1113 (7th Cir. 1974), *rev'd on other grounds*, 425 U.S. 185 (1976), is instructive on the standards by which an accountant's audit must be judged. The court, essentially agreeing with *BarChris*, held that accountants generally "are required to meet only the standard of care expected of persons holding themselves out as skilled accountants." Accord, *SEC v. Arthur Young & Co.*, 590 F.2d 785 (9th Cir. 1979).

The Seventh Circuit, however, relying on Judge Learned Hand's opinion in *The T.J. Hooper*, 60 F.2d 737 (2d Cir. 1932), went on to assert that compliance with GAAS (Generally Accepted Auditing Standards)[22] does not provide automatic insulation from liability. As the court pointed out, a determination must be made whether the prevailing professional practice constitutes reasonable prudence. Hence, while compliance with GAAS may strongly suggest that the requisite standard of care has been met, "[c]ourts must in the end say what is required; there are precautions so imperative that even their universal disregard will not excuse their omission." 503 F.2d at 1113 n.16 (quoting, *The T.J. Hooper*, 60 F.2d at 740).

Generally, with respect to accountants' liability under § 11, the lead of *BarChris* concerning the proper standard of care has been followed. Accordingly, it appears that compliance with GAAS normally will provide a shield to charges of carelessness. Note, however, that:

> It is vitally important to point out that this shield only relates to an accountant's care in obtaining essential underlying facts. Compliance with GAAS will not be a shield to liability where an unreasonable judgment is made on the basis of adequate information properly obtained. The decisions scrutinizing accountants' audit procedures have at the same time considered the reasonableness of the judgments made on the basis of the information unearthed during the audit.

> In addition, compliance with GAAS will not act as a shield from liability for misleading presentation of information obtained during the course of a properly conducted audit. In other words, the "investigative" portion of the audit, in which the accountant obtains evidential matter to support the information ultimately presented in financial statements, is only the first step in the evaluation of liability. The next step is to scrutinize the judgments made by the accountant on the basis of the information obtained, and the final step is to scrutinize the fairness of the financial statements taken as a whole.

---

22. As the Ninth Circuit has pointed out:

> "Generally Accepted Accounting Principles" (GAAP) establish guidelines relating to the process by which the transactions and events of a business entity are measured, recorded, and classified in accordance with a conventional format. GAAS [Generally Accepted Auditing Standards] thus differs from GAAP; the former involves how an auditor goes about obtaining information, while the latter involves the format in which to present the information.

SEC v. Arthur Young & Co., 590 F.2d 785, 789 n.4 (9th Cir. 1979). As to GAAS, the court further stated: "'Generally Accepted Auditing Standards' (GAAS) are general standards of conduct relating to the auditor's professional qualities as well as to the judgments exercised by him in the performance of his examination and the issuance of his report." *Id.* at 788 n.2.

When financial statements are alleged to be false or misleading, carelessness at any of the three levels can lead to liability.[23]

Underwriters

A significant aspect of *BarChris* is its impact upon underwriters. A rigorous degree of investigation was imposed for a number of reasons. First, the underwriter is uniquely situated to verify the accuracy of the contents of the registration statement. Not only do underwriters have access to information, they have the necessary leverage in the traditional Securities Act registration framework to compel the issuer to fulfill its disclosure duties. Second, the investing public relies upon the reputation of the underwriter and upon its participation in the offering as an endorsement of the correctness of the registration statement. As stated by the SEC:

> An underwriter . . . occupies a vital position in an offering. The underwriter stands between the issuer and the public purchasers, assisting the issuer in pricing and, at times, in structuring the financing and preparing disclosure documents. Most importantly, its role is to place the offered securities with public investors. By participating in an offering, an underwriter makes an implied representation about the securities. Because the underwriter holds itself out as a securities professional, and especially in light of its position vis-à-vis the issuer, this recommendation itself implies that the underwriter has a reasonable basis for belief in the truthfulness and completeness of the key representations made in any disclosure documents used in the offerings.[24]

In *Feit v. Leasco Data Processing Equipment Corp.*, 332 F. Supp. 544, 581–582 (E.D.N.Y. 1971), the court asserted:

> [C]ourts must be particularly scrupulous in examining the conduct of underwriters since they are supposed to assume an opposing posture with respect to management. . . . In light of this adverse position they must be expected to be alert to exaggerations and rosy outlooks and chary of assurances by the issuer. Their duty is to the investing public under Section 11 . . . and that duty cannot be taken lightly.

The court recognized, however, that an underwriter cannot be expected to possess the intimate knowledge of corporate affairs that inside directors would possess, and consequently its duty to investigate should be considered in view of its more limited access. The court emphasized, nonetheless, that an underwriter is expected to exercise a high degree of care in the course of its investigation. Not only must underwriters make an independent verification of management's representations, they must play the devil's advocate.

---

23. Gruenbaum & Steinberg, *Accountants' Liability and Responsibility: Securities, Criminal and Common Law*, 13 Loy. L.A.L. Rev. 247, 260 (1980).

24. Securities Exchange Act Release No. 26100 (1988).

In another decision, the underwriter was deemed to have satisfied its due diligence defense. As set forth by the court, the underwriter conducted the following investigation:

> After reviewing the record, this court concludes that there is no genuine issue of material fact that the underwriters did meet the standards required of them by section 11. . . . Their investigation of [the issuer] was conducted primarily by the managing underwriters. It was conducted by experienced people, who were assisted by attorneys and accountants. The underwriters reviewed the industry, the company, the company's management, and the company's past and projected manufacturing, sales and financial performance. The underwriters had over twenty meetings with various management personnel, covering all aspects of the company's business. Company personnel were specifically questioned about the development and scheduled availability of products, related operating systems and applications software. The underwriters also contacted many of [the issuer's] suppliers, customers, and distributors, who were asked extensive questions about the company's operations. The underwriters reviewed company documents including operating plans, product literature, corporate records, financial statements, contracts, and lists of distributors and customers. They examined trade journals and other industry-related publications to ascertain industry trends, market trends and competitive information. They also made physical inspections of the company's facilities. When any negative or questionable information was developed as a result of their investigation, the underwriters discussed it with the appropriate persons and arrived at informed decisions and opinions. The underwriters also obtained written representations from the selling stockholders and the company that as of the closing date of the public offering, there were no misstatements or omissions.
>
> As a result of that investigation and due diligence, the underwriters reasonably believed the accuracy of the information contained in the prospectus, including the information alleged to be misrepresented or omitted here. The underwriters had no knowledge of any misrepresentations or omissions, and their work met the standards of the diligence and reasonable investigation required by section 11. . . .

Weinberger v. Jackson, [1990–1991 Transfer Binder] Fed. Sec. L. Rep. (CCH) ¶ 95,693, at 98,255 (N.D. Cal. 1990). *See also In re Facebook, Inc. IPO Securities and Derivative Litigation*, 312 F.R.D. 332 (S.D.N.Y. 2015) (certifying class action § 11 claims against underwriters and other defendants); *In re Worldcom, Inc. Securities Litigation*, 346 F. Supp. 2d 628 (S.D.N.Y. 2004) (holding issues of material fact existed whether underwriters met their § 11 due diligence defense); *In re International Rectifier Securities Litigation*, [1997 Transfer Binder] Fed. Sec. L. Rep. (CCH) ¶ 99,469 (C.D. Cal. 1997) (holding underwriters met due diligence defense); *In re Donaldson, Lufkin & Jenrette Securities Corp.*, [1992 Transfer Binder] Fed. Sec. L. Rep. (CCH) ¶ 85,035 (SEC 1992)

(SEC enforcement action against underwriter for failing to adequately investigate where registration statement contained disclosure deficiency).

As discussed in depth later in this Chapter, in recognition of possible limitations on the underwriter's ability to investigate in certain circumstances, the SEC adopted Rule 176.[25]

Consider the due diligence defense for underwriters who are not the managing underwriter(s) for a registered offering. These underwriters normally rely on the managing underwriter(s) to perform adequate due diligence. It would be prudent for such underwriters to satisfy themselves that: (1) the managing underwriter(s) assessed the accuracy and adequacy of the information contained in the registration statement in a reasonably thorough manner by means of conducting a reasonable investigation; and (2) that they themselves had reasonable grounds for believing that such registration statement did not contain a material misrepresentation or nondisclosure.

How should an underwriter (or legal counsel designated by an underwriter) proceed in order to perform adequate due diligence? A due diligence checklist is contained as an Appendix to this Chapter and may be examined at this time.

Since *BarChris* was handed down, there have been relatively few decisions interpreting § 11's due diligence defense. The case that follows provides a worthwhile example.

In re Software Toolworks Inc. Securities Litigation

United States Court of Appeals, Ninth Circuit

38 F.3d 1078 (1994)

Opinion of HALL, Circuit Judge.

In this case, we consider the securities fraud claims raised by disappointed investors in Software Toolworks, Inc., who appeal the district court's summary judgment in favor of auditors Deloitte & Touche and underwriters Montgomery Securities and Paine Webber, Inc. We affirm in part, reverse in part, and remand.

---

25. *See generally* Chapman, *Underwriters' Due Diligence Revisited*, 35 Rev. Sec. & Comm. Reg. 207 (2002); Diamond and Travis, *Pitfalls and Risks Regarding Qualified Independent Underwriters*, 42 Sec. Reg. & L. Rep. (BNA) 1253 (2010); Freilich & Janvey, *Understanding "Best Efforts" Offerings*, 17 Sec. Reg. L.J. 151 (1989); Frerichs, *Underwriter Due Diligence Within the Integrated Disclosure System—If It Isn't Broken, Don't Fix It*, 16 Sec. Reg. L.J. 386 (1989); Greene, *Determining the Responsibilities of Underwriters Distributing Securities Within an Integrated Disclosure System*, 56 Notre Dame Law. 755 (1981); Horwich, *Section 11 of the Securities Act: The Cornerstone Needs Some Tuckpointing*, 58 Bus. Law. 1 (2002); Roin & Lewis, *Due Diligence Investigations: A Litigator's Perspective*, 34 Rev. Sec. & Comm. Reg. 209 (2001); Committee on Federal Regulation on Securities, *Report of the Task Force on Sellers' Due Diligence and Similar Defenses Under the Federal Securities Laws*, 48 Bus. Law. 1185 (1993).

I.

In July 1990, Software Toolworks, Inc., a producer of software for personal computers and Nintendo game systems, conducted a public offering of common stock at $18.50 a share, raising more than $71 million. After the offering, the market price of Toolworks' shares declined steadily until, on October 11, 1990, the stock was trading at $5.40 a share. At that time, Toolworks issued a press release announcing substantial losses and the share price dropped another fifty-six percent to $2.375.

The next day, several investors ("the plaintiffs") filed a class action alleging that Toolworks, auditor Deloitte & Touche ("Deloitte"), and underwriters Montgomery Securities and Paine Webber, Inc. ("the Underwriters") had issued a false and misleading prospectus and registration statement in violation of Sections 11 and 12(2) [now § 12(a)(2)] of the Securities Act of 1933 ("the 1933 Act"). . . . Specifically, the plaintiffs claimed that the defendants had (1) falsified audited financial statements for fiscal 1990 by reporting as revenue sales to *original equipment manufacturers* ("OEMs") with whom Toolworks had no binding agreements, (2) fabricated large consignment sales in order for Toolworks to meet financial projections for the first quarter of fiscal 1991 ("the June quarter"), and (3) lied to the Securities and Exchange Commission ("SEC") in response to inquiries made before the registration statement became effective.

Toolworks and its officers quickly settled with the plaintiffs for $26.5 million. After the completion of discovery, the district court granted summary judgment. . . .

We conduct de novo review of the district court's grant of summary judgment. In so doing, we are mindful that, although materiality and scienter are both fact-specific issues which should ordinarily be left to the trier of fact, summary judgment may be granted in appropriate cases. . . .

II.

We first address the plaintiffs' claim against the Underwriters under section 11 . . . of the 1933 Act. Section 11 imposes liability "[i]n case any part of [a] registration statement . . . contain[s] an untrue statement of a material fact or omit[s] to state a material fact required to be stated therein or necessary to make the statements therein not misleading." . . .

Liability under section 11 . . . properly may fall on the underwriters of a public offering. Underwriters, however, may absolve themselves from liability by establishing a "due diligence" defense. Under section 11, underwriters must prove that they "had, after reasonable investigation, reasonable ground to believe and did believe . . . that the statements therein were true and that there was no omission to state a material fact required to be stated therein or necessary to make the statements therein not misleading." . . .

. . . In determining whether an underwriter meets the [§ 11] due diligence test, "the standard of reasonableness shall be that required of a prudent man in the management of his own property."

The district court held that the Underwriters had established due diligence as a matter of law and, accordingly, issued summary judgment against the plaintiffs. . . . On appeal, the plaintiffs contend that due diligence is so fact-intensive that summary judgment is inappropriate even where underlying historical facts are undisputed. The plaintiffs further contend that, in any event, the district court erred by ignoring disputed issues of material fact in this case. We hold that, in appropriate cases, summary judgment may resolve due diligence issues but that, in this case, the district court erred by granting summary judgment in favor of the Underwriters. . . .

A.

The plaintiffs first argue that "due diligence . . . [and] the reasonableness of the defendants' investigation . . . is a question for the jury, even on undisputed facts." We agree, of course, that summary judgment is generally an inappropriate way to decide questions of reasonableness because "the jury's unique competence in applying the 'reasonable man' standard is thought ordinarily to preclude summary judgment." We have, however, squarely rejected the contention that "reasonableness is always a question of fact which precludes summary judgment." Rather, reasonableness "becomes a question of law and loses its triable character if the undisputed facts leave no room for a reasonable difference of opinion." Accordingly, "reasonableness [is] appropriate for determination on [a] motion for summary judgment when only one conclusion about the conduct's reasonableness is possible."

Courts therefore may resolve questions of due diligence in those cases where no rational jury could conclude that the defendant had not acted reasonably. Several courts have, in fact done just that. . . .

The district court, therefore, properly held that "the adequacy of due diligence may be decided on summary judgment when the underlying historical facts are undisputed." . . .

B.

The plaintiffs next assert that, even if summary judgment may resolve due diligence issues in some cases, the district court erred in this case because three "hotly disputed" issues of material fact preclude summary judgment on the question of the Underwriters' due diligence. We consider each in turn.

1.

The plaintiffs first argue that the Underwriters failed to investigate properly Toolworks' Nintendo business. Specifically, the plaintiffs assert that the Underwriters should have discovered that, in contravention of statements in the prospectus, Toolworks had lowered prices on its Nintendo games and had "sold" significant inventory on a consignment basis, giving buyers an unqualified right to return unsold merchandise.

The district court disagreed, noting that the Underwriters had obtained written representation from Toolworks and Deloitte that the prospectus was accurate, had confirmed with Toolworks' customers that the company did not accept returns of non-defective cartridges, and had surveyed retailers to ensure that the company had not lowered its prices. Thus, the court concluded that the Underwriters had, as a matter of law, "performed a thorough and reasonable investigation of Toolworks' Nintendo business." For the following reasons, we agree.

a.

The plaintiffs argue that the prospectus was false and misleading because it stated that Toolworks' "Nintendo software products have not been subject to price reductions," when, in fact, Toolworks had begun a price-cutting promotion days before the offering. The plaintiffs, however, presented no direct evidence that the Underwriters knew of this promotion. Indeed, the record illustrates that Toolworks' management consistently assured the Underwriters that the company would not reduce prices. The plaintiffs nevertheless assert that summary judgment was inappropriate because a jury might infer that the Underwriters knew about the price cuts because Toolworks' management discussed the promotion while on a private plane with the Underwriters. All personnel who were on the plane, however, testified that no conversations regarding price cutting reached the Underwriters. As such, any inference that the Underwriters knew about the sales would not be based in fact and would be unreasonable. The district court properly granted summary judgment in favor of the Underwriters on this issue.

b.

The plaintiffs also claim that the prospectus was false and misleading because it stated that Toolworks "does not currently provide any product return rights to its retail Nintendo customers," when, in fact, the company had booked several consignment sales prior to the offering. Again, however, the plaintiffs offered no direct evidence that the Underwriters knew about the sales, which represented a significant departure from prior Toolworks' policy. In fact, the record illustrates that the Underwriters made a substantial effort to ascertain Toolworks' return policy, both before and after the consignment sales occurred. The plaintiffs nevertheless assert that circumstantial evidence permits an inference that the Underwriters knowingly "watered down" the prospectus' risk-disclosure statement about merchandise returns and ignored a memorandum from one Toolworks customer ("Walmart") describing an unlimited right-of-return. This argument, however, misconstrues the full record.

In the process of drafting the prospectus, the Underwriters did change the risk-disclosure statement. An original draft stated that, "[i]n light of increased competition among the [Nintendo] entertainment titles on the market, it may be necessary for [Toolworks] to modify its return policy." The final version stated only that "[t]here can be no assurance that [Toolworks] will not be subject to product returns in the future." This change, however, is not sufficient to permit a reasonable inference that the Underwriters knew or should have known that Toolworks actually had changed its return policy. In fact, the Underwriters changed the disclosure statement in direct response to assertions by Toolworks' management that the company would never offer return rights and that the prospectus as originally written could prompt customers to seek such concessions in the future.

Moreover, although the Underwriters did receive a memorandum from Walmart describing an unqualified right to return non-defective merchandise, the record illustrates that Walmart never actually had such rights. Upon receiving the Walmart memorandum, the Underwriters called the retailer and confirmed that the statement regarding returns was erroneous (it should have said that Walmart had an unqualified right to return defective merchandise). Thus, in light of this correction, the fact that the actual contract between Toolworks and Walmart provided only for the return of defective items, and the fact that Walmart never returned any undamaged products, an inference that the Underwriters attempted to conceal Toolworks' return policy would be unreasonable. The district court properly granted summary judgment in favor of the Underwriters on this issue.

2.

The plaintiffs next assert that a material issue of fact exists regarding whether the Underwriters diligently investigated, or needed to investigate, Toolworks' recognition of OEM revenue on its financial statements. The plaintiffs claim that the Underwriters "blindly rel[ied]" on Deloitte in spite of numerous "red flags" indicating that the OEM entries were incorrect and that, as a result, the district court erred in granting summary judgment.

An underwriter need not conduct due diligence into the "expertised" parts of a prospectus, such as certified financial statements. Rather, the underwriter need only show that it "had no reasonable ground to believe, and did not believe . . . that the statements therein were untrue or that there was an omission to state a material fact required to be stated therein or necessary to make the statements therein not misleading." The issue on appeal, therefore is whether the Underwriters' reliance on the expertised financial statements was reasonable as a matter of law.

a.

As the first "red flag," the plaintiffs point to Toolworks' "backdated" contract with Hyosung, a Korean manufacturer. During the fourth quarter of fiscal 1990, Toolworks recognized $1.7 million in revenue from an OEM contract with Hyosung. In due diligence, the Underwriters discovered a memorandum from Hyosung "backdat[ing]" the agreement to permit Toolworks to recognize revenue in fiscal 1990. The plaintiffs claim that, after discovering this memorandum, the Underwriters could no longer rely on Deloitte because the accountants had approved revenue recognition for the transaction.

If the Underwriters had done nothing more, the plaintiffs' contention might be correct. The plaintiffs, however, ignore the significant steps taken by the Underwriters after discovery of the Hyosung memorandum to ensure the accuracy of Deloitte's revenue recognition. The Underwriters first confronted Deloitte which explained that it was proper for Toolworks to book [that particular] revenue in fiscal 1990. . . . The

Underwriters then insisted that Deloitte reconfirm, in writing, the Hyosung agreement and Toolworks' other OEM contracts. Finally, the underwriters contacted other accounting firms to verify Deloitte's OEM revenue accounting methods.

Thus, with regard to the Hyosung agreement, the Underwriters did not "blindly rely" on Deloitte. The district court correctly held that, as a matter of law, the Underwriters' investigation of the OEM business was reasonable.

b.

The plaintiffs next assert that the Underwriters could not reasonably rely on Deloitte's financial statements because Toolworks' counsel, Riordan & McKinzie, refused to issue an opinion letter stating that the OEM agreements were binding contracts. This contention has no merit because, contrary to the plaintiffs' assertions, Toolworks had never requested the law firm to render such an opinion. The plaintiffs attempt to infer wrongdoing in such circumstances is patently unreasonable. The district court correctly granted summary judgment in favor of the Underwriters on this issue.

c.

Finally, the plaintiffs assert that, by reading the agreements, the Underwriters should have realized that Toolworks had improperly recognized revenue. Specifically, the plaintiffs claim that several of the contracts were contingent and that it was facially apparent that Toolworks might not receive any revenue under them. As the Underwriters explain, this contention misconstrues the nature of a due diligence investigation:

> [The Underwriters] reviewed the contracts to verify that there was a written agreement for each OEM contract mentioned in the Prospectus — not to analyze the propriety of revenue recognition, which was the responsibility of [Deloitte]. Given the complexity surrounding software licensing revenue recognition, it is absurd to suggest that, in perusing Toolworks' contracts, [the Underwriters] should have concluded that [Deloitte] w[as] wrong, particularly when the OEM's provided written confirmation.

We recently confirmed precisely this point in a case involving analogous facts: "[T]he defendants relied on Deloitte's accounting decisions (to recognize revenue) about the sales. Those expert decisions, which underlie the plaintiffs' attack on the financial statements, represent precisely the type of 'certified' information on which section 11 permits nonexperts to rely." . . .

Thus, because the Underwriters' reliance on Deloitte was reasonable under the circumstances, the district court correctly granted summary judgment on this issue. . . .

3.

The plaintiffs next attack the Underwriters' due diligence efforts for the period after Toolworks filed a preliminary prospectus and before the effective date of the offering. During this time, several significant events transpired. First, Barron's published a negative article about Toolworks that questioned the company's "aggressive accounting." Second, in response to the Barron's article, the SEC initiated a review of Toolworks' prospectus. Third, Toolworks sent two letters responding to the SEC. And, fourth, Toolworks booked several consignment sales that made the company appear to have a prosperous quarter, thereby ensuring success of the offering.

The district court held that the Underwriters satisfied their due diligence obligations during this period primarily by relying on Toolworks' representations to the SEC. For the following reasons, we conclude that disputed issues of material fact exist regarding the Underwriters' efforts and, accordingly, we reverse and remand for a trial on the merits.

a.

The plaintiffs first contend that the Underwriters should have done more to investigate the Barron's allegations of slumping sales and improper accounting. The Underwriters established, however, that they contacted a representative of Nintendo and several large retailers to confirm the strength of the market in response to the Barron's article. Moreover, as explained above, the Underwriters' reliance on Deloitte's accounting decisions was reasonable as a matter of law. Summary judgment was appropriate on this issue.

b.

Next, the plaintiffs raise the issue of Toolworks' July 4, 1990 letter to the SEC, which described the company's June quarter performance. In the letter, Toolworks represented that, although preliminary financial data was not available, Toolworks anticipated revenue for the quarter would be between $21 and $22 million. The plaintiffs claim that Toolworks deliberately falsified these estimates and that the Underwriters knew of this deceit.

The Underwriters claim that they were not involved in drafting the July 4 SEC letter and that, as a result, they have no responsibility for its contents. The plaintiffs presented evidence, however, that the letter was a joint effort of all professionals working on the offering, including the Underwriters. In fact, a Riordan & McKinzie partner, specifically testified that, "[w]hen the letter finally went to the SEC, all parties had been involved in the process of creating it. There had been conference calls discussing it and comments and changes made by a lot of different members of the working group." Others similarly testified that the Underwriters were actively involved in discussions of how to respond to the SEC's inquiries regarding the June quarter.

The Underwriters argue that, even if they participated in initial discussions about the letter, they never knew that Toolworks' financial data actually was available and that, as a result, they could not have known that the letter (and the prospectus) were misleading. Given the Underwriters participation in drafting both documents, however, we think this is an unresolved issue of material fact. A reasonable factfinder could infer that, as members of the drafting group, the Underwriters had access to all information that was available and deliberately chose to conceal the truth. We therefore hold that summary judgment was inappropriate on this issue.

c.

After suffering lagging sales in the first two months of the June quarter, Toolworks booked several large consignment sales in late June, the quarter's final month, thereby enabling the company to meet its earning projections. Toolworks later had to reverse more than $7 million of these sales in its final financial statements for the quarter. The plaintiffs presented evidence that the Underwriters knew that Toolworks had performed poorly in April, that Toolworks had no orders for the month as of June 8, that the June quarter is traditionally the slowest of the year for Nintendo sales, and that the late June sales accounted for more revenue than the cumulative total of Toolworks' Nintendo sales for the prior two and a half months. For its due diligence investigation of these sales, however, the Underwriters did little more than rely on Toolworks' assurances that the transactions were legitimate. A reasonable inference from this evidence is that Toolworks fabricated the June sales to ensure that the offering would proceed and that the Underwriters knew, or should have known, of this fraud. As a result, we conclude that summary judgment regarding the Underwriters' diligence on this issue was also inappropriate.

C.

Thus, we hold that the district court properly granted summary judgment in favor of the Underwriters on the section 11 issues regarding their due diligence investigation into Toolworks' Nintendo sales practices and description of OEM revenue. The district court erred, however, by granting summary judgment on the section 11 claims regarding the July 4 SEC letter and Toolworks' June quarter results. We remand for a trial on the merits of those claims.

. . . .

Affirmed in part, Reversed in part.

---

§ 7.05 Impact of the Integrated Disclosure System

[At this point, review the materials on "The Integrated Disclosure Framework" contained in § 5.01.]

Circumstances Affecting the Determination of What Constitutes Reasonable Investigation and Reasonable Grounds for Belief under Section 11 of the Securities Act

Securities Act Release No. 6335 (1981)

. . . .

Concerns Regarding Responsibilities Under the Integrated Disclosure System

The Securities Act was conceived in order to "bring back public confidence" which had been eviscerated by the widespread securities frauds of the 1920's. According to James Landis, one of the drafters of the Securities Act, the lengthy Senate hearings on corporate financing which preceded adoption of the Act, "indicted a system as a whole that had failed miserably in imposing those essential fiduciary standards that should govern persons whose function it was to handle other people's money." The resulting Securities Act imposed high standards of care on all persons involved in public offerings of securities. The legislative history indicates that the Congressional intent in adopting the Securities Act was to impose standards of "[h]onesty, care and competency" upon those who participate in the preparation of the registration statement or the distribution to public investors of the securities registered thereunder.

The statute generally requires that new public issues of securities be registered with the Commission. The signers of the registration statement, the issuer's directors or partners, the underwriters, the accountants and certain other persons are made civilly liable by Section 11(a) of the Securities Act for any untrue statement of a material fact which is contained in an effective registration statement or for any omission to state a material fact required to be stated therein or necessary to avoid making the statements therein misleading. Section 11(b) of the Securities Act provides that each person, other than the issuer, will not be held liable, however, if he can sustain the burden of proof that his conduct, under the circumstances, was reasonable. Specifically, subsection 11(b)(3) permits the defendant to prove that he made a reasonable investigation of and had reasonable grounds to believe in the accuracy of the non-expertised portions of the registration statement or, with respect to any part presented upon the authority of an expert other than the defendant, that he had no reasonable ground to believe and did not believe there was a material omission or misstatement.

Underwriters and others have expressed concern regarding their ability to discharge fully their responsibilities under Section 11 with respect to registration statements incorporating substantial information from periodic reports. Historically, preparation of the traditional Form S-1 registration statement began many weeks in advance of the proposed offering due to the time required to assemble and verify the information required to be set forth in the registration statement and prospectus. During this time, underwriters, directors and others conducted the necessary due diligence inquiries which, as a matter of prudence, were substantially completed before the initial filing of the registration statement. In contrast, integrated short form registration statements rely, to the maximum extent possible, on information contained in previously filed

Exchange Act reports or in the annual report to security holders. Information actually set forth in the short form registration statement pertains primarily to the proposed transaction, the use of proceeds and the updating of information in incorporated documents. Preparation time is reduced sharply, as is the period of time between the issuer's decision to undertake a securities offering and the filing of the registration statement with the Commission. [Today, shelf registration enables an issuer to conduct a public offering on very short notice, frequently as little as a few hours.]

Some commentators are fearful that this reduction in preparation time, together with competitive pressures, will restrict the ability of responsible underwriters to conduct what would be deemed to be a reasonable investigation, pursuant to Section 11, of the contents of the registration statement. They believe that issuers may be reluctant to wait for responsible underwriters to finish their inquiry, and may be receptive to offers from underwriters willing to do less.

Some underwriters also object to utilizing information in periodic reports for registration purposes, because it has been composed by persons without consultation with the underwriters who may, in turn, be held, in the context of a registration statement, to a higher standard of civil liability than that to which the original preparers may have been subject. Moreover, there is a perception that issuers may be reluctant to modify previously filed documents in instances where the underwriters question the quality of the disclosure and that this reluctance, again coupled with competitive pressures, will hinder due diligence activities. [Note that SEC Rule 412 is designed to alleviate concerns regarding the modification of disclosures made in previously filed SEC documents. Among other things, the rule sets forth that a modifying or superseding statement made in an SEC filed document is not deemed an admission that the statement that undergoes such change violates the federal securities laws.]

Moreover, because Section 11 imposes liability for omissions or misstatements of material fact in any part of the registration statement when that part became effective, there has been concern that liability could be asserted based on information in a previously filed document which was accurate when filed but which had become outdated and subsequently was incorporated by reference into a registration statement.

[Subsequently adopted Rule 415], allowing shelf registration, also has caused apprehension. Commentators on the rule believed that insufficient consideration had been given to the responsibilities of the persons involved in a shelf registration . . . under the Rule. For example, a shelf offering [may] involve automatic incorporation by reference into the registration statement of Exchange Act reports for a substantial period of time because the offering may be made on a delayed or continuous basis. In addition, if an underwriter is brought into a shelf offering after the initial effective date of the registration statement, the late-arriving underwriter would be responsible for the accuracy of the contents of the registration statement as of the time of his entry into the transaction. Although incorporation by reference of subsequently filed documents and changes in underwriters can occur in any offering, they may be more likely to occur in shelf offerings, which may continue over a substantial period and contemplate a variety of offering techniques for the registered securities. [Shelf registration is covered in Chapter 5, § 5.01[F].]

. . . .

Due Diligence in an Integrated Disclosure System

As discussed earlier, the Securities Act imposes a high standard of conduct on specific persons, including underwriters and directors, associated with a registered public offering of securities. Under Section 11, they must make a reasonable investigation and have reasonable grounds to believe the disclosures in the registration statement are accurate. As the Court stated in *Escott v. BarChris Construction Corporation:*

> In order to make the underwriter's participation in this enterprise of any value to the investors, the underwriters must make some reasonable attempt to verify the data submitted to them. They may not rely on the company's officers or on the company's counsel. A prudent man in the management of his own property would not rely on them.

The principal goal of integration is to simplify disclosure and reduce unnecessary repetition and redelivery of information which has already been provided, not to alter the roles of participants in the securities distribution process as originally contemplated by the Securities Act. The integrated disclosure system, past and proposed, is thus not designed to modify the responsibility of underwriters and others to make a reasonable investigation. Information presented in the registration statement, whether or not incorporated by reference, must be true and complete in all material respects and verified where appropriate. Likewise, nothing in the Commission's integrated disclosure system precludes conducting adequate due diligence. This point can be demonstrated by addressing the two principal concerns which have been raised.

First, . . . commentators have expressed concern about the short time involved in document preparation. There also may be a substantial reduction in the time taken for pre-effective review at the Commission. As to the latter point, however, commentators . . . themselves noted that due diligence generally is performed prior to filing with the Commission. . . . As to the former point, there is nothing which compels an underwriter to proceed prematurely with an offering. Although, as discussed below, [it] may wish to arrange [its] due diligence procedures over time for the purpose of avoiding last minute delays in an offering environment characterized by rapid market changes, in the final analysis the underwriter is never compelled to proceed with an offering until [it] has accomplished [its] due diligence.

The second major concern relates to the fact that documents, prepared by others, often at a much earlier date, are incorporated by reference into the registration statement. Again, it must be emphasized that due diligence requires a reasonable investigation of all the information presented therein and any information incorporated by reference. If such material contains a material misstatement, or omits a material fact, then, in order to avoid liability, a subsequent document must be filed to correct the earlier one, or the information must be restated correctly in the registration statement. Nothing in the integrated disclosure system precludes such action.

The Commission specifically rejects the suggestion [advanced by the Securities Industry Association (SIA)] that the underwriter needs only to read the incorporated materials and discuss them with representatives of the registrant and named experts. Because the registrant would be the sole source of virtually all information, this approach would not, in and of itself, include the element of verification required by the case law and contemplated by the statute.

Thus, verification in appropriate circumstances is still required, and if a material misstatement or omission has been made, correction by amendment or restatement must be made. For example, a major supply contract on which the registrant is substantially dependent should be reviewed to avoid the possibility of inaccurate references to it in the prospectus. On the other hand, if the alleged misstatement in issue turns on an ambiguity or nuance in the drafted language of an incorporated document, making it a close question as to whether a violation even has been committed, then the fact that a particular defendant did not participate in preparing the incorporated document, when combined with judgmental difficulties and practical concerns in making changes in prepared documents, would seem to be an appropriate factor in deciding whether "reasonable belief" in the accuracy of statements existed and thus in deciding whether to attach liability to a particular defendant's conduct.

In sum, the Commission strongly affirms the need for due diligence and its attendant vigilance and verification. The Commission's efforts towards integration of the Securities Act and the Exchange Act relate solely to elimination of unnecessary repetition of disclosure, not to the requirements of due diligence which must accompany any offering. Yet, in view of the fact that court decisions to date have construed due diligence under factual circumstances not involving an integrated system, and in order to encourage a focus on a flexible approach to due diligence rather than a rigid adherence to past practice, the Commission believes that it would be helpful to codify its prior statements so that courts and others may fully understand the new system [*see, e.g.*, SEC Rule 176].

Techniques of Due Diligence in an Integrated Disclosure System

Although the basic requirements of due diligence do not change in an integrated system, the manner in which due diligence may be accomplished can properly be expected to vary from traditional practice in some cases. To this end, underwriters and others can utilize various techniques. Historical models of due diligence have focused on efforts during the period of activity associated with preparing a registration statement, but the integrated disclosure system requires a broader focus. Issuers, underwriters and their counsel will necessarily be reevaluating all existing practices connected with effectuating the distribution of securities to develop procedures compatible with the integrated approach to registration.

In view of the compressed preparation time and the volatile nature of the capital markets, underwriters may elect to apply somewhat different, but equally thorough, investigatory practices and procedures to integrated registration statements. Unless the underwriter intends to reserve a specified period of time for investigation after the registration statement has been prepared but before filing, it will be necessary to develop in advance a reservoir of knowledge about the companies that may select the underwriter to distribute their securities registered on short form registration statements. To a considerable extent, broker-dealers already take this approach when they provide financial planning and investment advisory services to the investing public, as well as financial advice to companies themselves.

Extensive data about seasoned companies can be obtained with little effort. The periodic reports filed pursuant to the Exchange Act contain a wealth of information relating to a subject issuer's financial performance, competitive position and future prospects. Other material developments are promptly reported on Form 8-K. Careful review of these filings on an on-going basis not only facilitates a general familiarity with each issuer but should permit the underwriter to identify factors critical to the continuing success of the company. In many cases the underwriters also have available analysts' reports to evaluate the issuer and its industry. With greater knowledge, the underwriter will be better prepared to question incomplete explanations, descriptions or reasoning and generally will be more sensitive to detecting and assessing material developments. The process of verification should be expedited as a result.

The issuer's investor relations program provides another opportunity for enhancing the underwriter's familiarity with the company. In particular, analysts' and brokers' meetings allow underwriters or potential underwriters to question members of management and to evaluate their skills and abilities. Discussion at such sessions can address recent transactions, events and economic results in relation to other companies in the same industry. When combined with the practice of furnishing detailed written analyses of material corporate events, these sessions can duplicate certain steps traditionally undertaken by the underwriter and issuer only during the preparation of the registration statement.

For directors, their continuing involvement in their company's activities must be considered. They receive reports, request information from management, meet periodically, and analyze, plan and participate in the company's business. These activities provide a strong basis for their evaluation of disclosure in a registration statement, and for considering what further due diligence is necessary on their part. In particular, their roles in reviewing the company's Form 10-K annual report and other Exchange Act filings are relevant to their due diligence for a registration statement incorporating those filings.

By developing a detailed familiarity with the company and the periodic reports it files with the Commission, the underwriter and others can minimize the number of additional tasks that must be performed in the context of a subsequent registered offering in order to meet the statutory standard of due diligence. When the short form registration statement is being prepared, the underwriter's investigation then can proceed expeditiously and can be concluded at the earliest appropriate point in time. By way of comparison, a first time offering by a new or relatively unseasoned issuer requires the underwriter and other subject persons to engage in extensive data collection, analysis and independent inquiry during the preparation period for the long form registration statement.

In sum, under the Exchange Act a great deal of information about registered companies is both regularly furnished to the marketplace and also carefully analyzed by investment bankers, directors and others. Although perhaps not traditionally seen in this light, a close following of this information by investment bankers can be an important part of due diligence in the case of an underwritten offering and should expedite the remaining due diligence inquiries and verification.

Issuers eligible for short-form registration also can undertake specific steps designed to minimize the need for elaborate original investigations by underwriters immediately prior to the public distribution of newly registered securities. These actions could include (1) involvement of directors and underwriters in the preparation of the Form 10-K, (2) similar involvement by counsel for the underwriting group, (3) early discussions with underwriters about major new developments and (4) early coordination, well in advance, with respect to offerings contemplated during a given year.

The Commission believes it is crucial that issuers carefully consider what is required for underwriters and others to accomplish their investigation and cooperate with them in their efforts to satisfy their statutory obligations. The financing plans of issuers must take these practical requirements into account.

. . . .

Conclusion

Prior to enactment of the Securities Act in 1933, there was little information available about the new issues of securities offered for sale to the public. Today, however, a wealth of accounting and other company-specific information is rapidly disseminated throughout increasingly efficient securities markets. Because the securities markets absorb previously filed information about seasoned issuers, the Commission has determined to permit such issuers to satisfy certain disclosure requirements of the Securities Act by incorporating by reference into the registration statement pertinent information, updated where necessary, from previously filed Exchange Act reports. Although an efficient market conveys information expeditiously, it has no capacity to authenticate information. Therefore, the Commission rejects any notion that investors no longer rely upon the underwriter and others to perform an investigatory function.

In re Worldcom, Inc. Securities Litigation

United States District Court, Southern District of New York

346 F. Supp. 2d 628 (2004)

Cote, District Judge

. . . .

Beginning in the 1980s, the SEC embarked on a "program to integrate the disclosure requirements of the Securities Act and the Securities Exchange Act of 1934." The chief purpose of the integrated disclosure system was to furnish investors with "meaningful, nonduplicative information both periodically and when securities distributions are made to the public," while decreasing "costs of compliance for public companies." . . .

Although earlier steps toward integration had been taken, the SEC aimed in the early 1980s to integrate the two acts, "primarily by incorporating by reference Exchange Act reports into Securities Act registration statements." The push to incorporate by reference was motivated by the growing recognition that "for companies in the top tier, there is a steady stream of high quality corporate information continually furnished to the market and broadly digested, synthesized and disseminated." . . . The SEC reasoned that top-tier companies should be able to incorporate their Exchange Act filings by reference, since these disclosures, along with "other communications by the registrant, such as press releases, ha[ve] already been disseminated and accounted for by the market place." Those eligible include issuers who, among other things, either have substantial equity "floats" or rated debt securities. Incorporation by reference was implemented by introducing a new, shortened registration form — Form S-3 — for use by "companies which are widely followed by professional analysts." In a Form S-3 registration, the registrant's Form 10-K from the most recently concluded fiscal year and all subsequent periodic Exchange Act filings between the end of that fiscal year and the termination of the offering are required to be incorporated by reference. Given the reduced length of the form, the process of filing a Form S-3 is known as short-form registration.

Short-form registration was accompanied by related changes in shelf registration, the process by which securities are registered to be offered or sold on a delayed or continuous basis. [See the discussion on shelf registration in Chapter 5, § 5.01[F]]. The purpose of shelf registration is to allow a single registration statement to be filed for a series of offerings. Shelf registration aims to afford the issuer the "procedural flexibility" to vary "the structure and terms of securities on short notice" and "time its offering to avail itself of the most advantageous market conditions."

. . . .

Together, the mechanism of incorporation by reference and the expansion of shelf registration significantly reduced the time and expense necessary to prepare public offerings, thus enabling more "rapid access to today's capital markets." As the SEC recognized, these changes affected the time in which underwriters could perform their investigations of an issuer. Underwriters had weeks to perform due diligence for traditional registration statements. By contrast, under a short-form registration regime, "[p]reparation time is reduced sharply" thanks to the ability to incorporate by reference prior disclosures. . . .

These two innovations triggered concern among underwriters. Members of the financial community worried about their ability "to undertake a reasonable investigation with respect to the adequacy of the information incorporated by reference from periodic reports filed under the Exchange Act into the short form registration statements utilized in an integrated disclosure system." Specifically, underwriters expressed concern that

> this reduction in preparation time, together with competitive pressures, will restrict the ability of responsible underwriters to conduct what would be deemed to be a reasonable investigation, pursuant to Section 11, of the contents of the registration statement. . . . [I]ssuers may be reluctant to wait for responsible underwriters to finish their inquiry, and may be receptive to offers from underwriters willing to do less.

. . . . Because an [issuer] could select among competing underwriters when offering securities through a shelf registration, some questioned whether an underwriter could "afford to devote the time and expense necessary to conduct a due diligence review before knowing whether it will handle an offering and that there may not be sufficient time to do so once it is selected." Others doubted whether they would have the chance "to apply their independent scrutiny and judgment to documents prepared by registrants many months before an offering." . . . .

Because of concerns like those described here, the SEC introduced Rule 176 in 1981 "to make explicit what circumstances may bear upon the determination of what constitutes a reasonable investigation and reasonable ground for belief as these terms are used in Section 11(b)." . . . Rather than give underwriters a "safe harbor from liability for statements made in incorporated Exchange Act reports," the SEC turned to the American Law Institute's proposed Federal Securities Code for guidance. Rule 176, which largely mirrors Section 1704(g) of the [ALI] Code, provides in relevant part:

> In determining whether or not the conduct of a person constitutes a reasonable investigation or a reasonable ground for belief meeting the standard set forth in section 11(c), relevant circumstances include, with respect to a person other than the issuer:
>
> (a) The type of issuer;
>
> (b) The type of security;
>
> (c) The type of person;
>
> . . . .

(f) Reasonable reliance on officers, employees, and others whose duties should have given them knowledge of the particular facts (in the light of the functions and responsibilities of the particular person with respect to the issuer and the filing);

(g) When the person is an underwriter, the type of underwriting arrangement, the role of the particular person as an underwriter and the availability of information with respect to the registrant; and

(h) Whether, with respect to a fact or document incorporated by reference, the particular person had any responsibility for the fact or document at the time of the filing from which it was incorporated.

. . . [T]he SEC's own commentary on the rule makes clear that Rule 176 did not alter the fundamental nature of underwriters' due diligence obligations. . . . At the time Rule 176 was finalized, the SEC took care to explain that integrated disclosure was intended to "simplify disclosure and reduce unnecessary repetition and redelivery of information," not to "modify the responsibility of underwriters and others to make a reasonable investigation." Instead, emphasizing that "nothing in the Commission's integrated disclosure system precludes conducting adequate due diligence," the SEC advised underwriters concerned about the time pressures created by integrated disclosure to "arrange [their] due diligence procedures over time for the purpose of avoiding last minute delays in an offering environment characterized by rapid market changes." It also reminded them that an underwriter is "never compelled to proceed with an offering *until he has accomplished his due diligence.*" . . . And the SEC warned underwriters that the verification "required by the case law and contemplated by the statute" would still be required in appropriate circumstances. [More] recently, the SEC recalled that it "expressly rejected the consideration of competitive timing and pressures when evaluating the reasonableness of an underwriter's investigation." . . .

The SEC's intent to maintain high standards for underwriter due diligence is confirmed by its many discussions of appropriate due diligence techniques in the integrated disclosure system. In proposing Rule 176, the SEC acknowledged that different investigatory methods would be needed "in view of the compressed preparation time and the volatile nature of the capital markets." Nonetheless, it emphasized that such techniques must be *"equally thorough."* . . . Among the strategies recommended by the SEC were the development of a "reservoir of knowledge about the companies that may select the underwriter to distribute their securities registered on short form registration statements" through a "careful review of [periodic Exchange Act] filings on an ongoing basis," consultation of analysts' reports, and active participation in the issuer's investor relations program, especially analysts and brokers meetings. . . .

At the time the SEC finalized the shelf registration rule two years later, it again recognized that "the techniques of conducting due diligence investigations of registrants qualified to use short form registration . . . would differ from due diligence investigations under other circumstances." Nonetheless, it stressed the use of "anticipatory and continuous due diligence programs" to augment underwriters' fulfillment of their due diligence obligations. Among other practices, the SEC approvingly noted the increased designation of one law firm to act as underwriters' counsel, which "facilitates continuous due diligence by ensuring on-going access to the registrant on the underwriters' behalf"; the holding of "Exchange Act report 'drafting sessions,'" which allow underwriters "to participate in the drafting and review of periodic disclosure documents before they are filed"; and "periodic due diligence sessions," such as meetings between prospective underwriters, their counsel, and management shortly after the release of quarterly earnings. . . .

In 1998, the SEC proposed expanding Rule 176 to "identify [specified] due diligence practices that the Commission believes would enhance an underwriter's due diligence investigation when conducting an expedited offering." SEC Rel. 7606A, 63 Fed. Reg. at 67231. Among these [enumerated] practices were the underwriter's receipt of a SAS 72 comfort letter. Yet the SEC emphasized that "these practices in no way constitute an exclusive list or serve as a substitute for a court's analysis of all relevant circumstances." The 1998 proposal has never been finalized. Even if the proposed changes had been enacted, however, the SEC cautioned that "only a court can make the determination of whether a defendant's conduct was reasonable under all the circumstances of a particular offering." . . .

It must be noted that academics and practitioners alike have asserted that the current regime for underwriter liability under Section 11 no longer makes sense. Professor Coffee, for one, has observed that "it is not clear that the underwriter today still performs the classic gatekeeping function. . . . Many argue that serious due diligence efforts are simply not feasible within the time constraints of shelf registration. Given these constraints, they claim that the solution lies in downsizing the threat under section 11." 52 Bus. Law. 1195, 1211 (1997). Another professor has remarked that "there is a strong practical case to be made for absolving underwriters of all inquiry obligations short of recklessness. . . . As underwriter involvement diminishes in significance relative to the deal as a whole, it becomes that much more problematic to apply a negligence-based standard in the first place." Langevoort, 63 Law and Contemp. Probs. 45, 67 (2000). A third asserts that in today's capital markets, "it is reasonable to question whether the underwriter's 'due diligence' role is justified at all. . . . *[F]or shelf registrations, disinterested advance due diligence is the exception not the rule.*" Partnoy, 79 Wash. U.L.Q. 491, 522 (2001) [emphasis supplied].

[Moreover, as asserted by the Securities Industry Association (SIA) and the Bond Market Association as amici curiae in this case:

> [T]he integrated disclosure system and the shelf registration rule as they now exist provide the context in which the reasonableness of the underwriters' investigation and belief must be evaluated. The prudent man standard must be interpreted from the point of view of a prudent man who has

determined to buy securities in a shelf offering recognizing the timing and manner of such offering and the qualifications that the issuer must meet even to be eligible to use the shelf registration process. In light of the existence of Rule 415 permitting shelf offerings, it would be unfair to penalize an underwriter who participates in a shelf offering of an appropriate issuer for not conducting the type of due diligence required for a non-qualifying issuer. To do so would be to read the due diligence defense out of the statute.]

[On the other hand, as discussed in Chapter 5 of this text, the use of Form S-3 has been greatly expanded. Today, for primary offerings of equity securities (such as common stock), Form S-3 generally can be used by issuers that have timely filed Exchange Act reports for the prior twelve months, have a class of equity security traded on a national securities exchange (such as the New York Stock Exchange or Nasdaq), and are not (and have not been for at least twelve months) a shell company. For those issuers that meet the foregoing conditions but have less than $75 million of voting stock outstanding held by non-affiliates ("public" float), no more than one-third of the public float may be offered by such issuers in primary offerings during any twelve-month period. See Securities Act Release No. 8878 (2007).]

[Similar to the position advocated by the SIA and Bond Counsel Association,] a Task Force of experienced counsel to underwriters concludes that the "'integrated disclosure system' and the expansion of shelf registration statements have called into question whether underwriters any longer 'sponsor' an issue in a meaningful way, as opposed to delivering advice and distribution services." *Task Force Report*, 48 Bus. Law. 1185, 1239 (1993). Similarly, the ABA Committee on Federal Regulation on Securities has complained to the SEC that

> [t]he benefits of 'on demand' financing . . . are undermined by continuing to impose on financial intermediaries and other 'gatekeepers' the responsibility to take the time necessary to do a sufficient due diligence investigation to assure quality disclosure without recognizing and making allowances for their difficulty or even inability to do so. It is not possible for underwriters and others to meet this standard in the current financing environment.

. . . . Thus, academics and practitioners have called for a reexamination of underwriters' liability under Section 11 on the grounds that "Congress's assumptions in 1933 and 1934 about registrants working with individual underwriters in a relatively leisurely atmosphere are at odds with today's competition by multiple underwriters for highspeed transactions." Implicit in these calls for a legislative change is the recognition that current law continues to place a burden upon an underwriter to conduct a reasonable investigation of non-expertised statements in a registration statement, including an issuer's interim financial statements.

. . . .

Note—Appointment of Underwriters' Counsel and Director Signature on Form 10-K

Appointment of Underwriters' Counsel

In *WorldCom*, the federal district court observed that in the shelf registration framework the designation of one law firm to conduct continuous due diligence acting as underwriters' counsel has been approvingly noted by the SEC. In this regard, the Commission stated: "The trend toward appointment of a single law firm to act as underwriters' counsel is a particularly significant development. . . . Registrants appoint the law firm to act as underwriters' counsel either with or without consulting the prospective participating underwriters." Securities Act Release No. 6499 (1983).

Accordingly, pursuant to the designation, counsel acts on behalf of the prospective underwriters in fulfilling such underwriters' continuous due diligence functions. Because counsel normally is selected by the issuer, conflicts of interest dilemmas arise. Nonetheless, the designation of counsel for the underwriters by the issuer is an accepted technique. Perhaps surprisingly, this approach has not been as extensively utilized as the SEC had envisioned. As observed by the New York City Bar Association's Task Force Report on the "Lawyer's Role in Corporate Governance" (2007) (Executive Summary at page 14): When the Commission adopted the integrated disclosure framework, "it expected that many eligible issuers, in collaboration with their chosen underwriters and their lawyers, would adopt 'continuous' due diligence programs. However, the number of companies today using such continuous due diligence programs appears not to be extensive, and opinions vary on their effectiveness."

A recent study concludes otherwise. After analyzing survey data gathered from securities attorneys regarding the practice of issuers designating underwriters' counsel in shelf-registered offerings, the author concluded:

> The assertion that continuous due diligence programs are not extensively used in shelf-registered offerings is not supported by empirical data. To determine whether, and to what extent, issuers appoint "underwriters' counsel" in shelf-registered offerings, the author surveyed 104 securities law practitioners on a nationwide basis. The survey results indicate that the use of underwriters' counsel for the purpose of conducting continuous due diligence in the shelf registration environment is common. This article accordingly provides empirical evidence that underwriters have significantly adapted their due diligence investigations to the shelf registration environment and integrated disclosure system by implementing the use of underwriters' counsel . . . .[26]

---

26. Bedotto, *If It Ain't Broke, Don't Fix It: The Frequent Use of "Underwriters' Counsel" in Shelf-Registered Offerings Scraps the Need for Underwriter Due Diligence Reforms*, 42 Sec. Reg. L.J. 293, 294 (2014).

Thus, in the automatic shelf registration setting, what feasible steps should an underwriter take to help establish its due diligence defense in the event that the registration statement contains material misrepresentations or omissions? These offerings frequently are completed in a matter of hours. To a significant extent, many issuers designate underwriter's counsel to conduct ongoing due diligence. Moreover, when an underwriter has a relationship with an issuer, certain steps should be taken on a continual basis. These steps (which may be taken by underwriter's counsel) include:

- Maintaining a "reservoir of knowledge" about the issuer and its industry;
- Keeping a due diligence file on the issuer that includes material contracts, leases, bank and loan documents, and employment agreements;
- Monitoring the issuer's SEC filings, including familiarizing itself with the issuer's Form 8-K, 10-K, and 10-Q filings;
- Regularly reviewing meeting minutes of the issuer's board of directors as well as board committees;
- Engaging in drafting sessions with the issuer;
- Conducting periodic interviews with the issuer's key management, and holding periodic due diligence meetings with the issuer to discuss its business;
- Being familiar with the issuer's financial statements, and holding periodic discussions with the issuer's independent auditors.

Even in situations when there is not designated underwriter's counsel and the selected underwriter does not have an ongoing relationship with the issuer, the following steps should be taken in the automatic shelf registration framework:

- Holding a due diligence conference call with the issuer and its key management, the issuer's counsel, and other appropriate personnel;
- Speaking with the company's auditor;
- Contacting in-house counsel to the issuer or the issuer's outside counsel to inquire about material developments, including pending or ongoing litigation;
- Inquiring about the loss or gain of material contracts, personnel, or other material changes in the issuer's business since the filing of the company's last Form 10-Q;
- Communicating with the issuer regarding the feasibility of the offering timeline;
- If the company's auditor is receptive, obtaining a "comfort letter" from such auditor; and
- Conducting internet searches for uncovering news articles and other information about the issuer and its affiliates, including its directors, officers, and control persons.

Director Signature on Form 10-K

Turning to another issue in this discussion, as part of its integrated disclosure framework, the SEC mandates that a majority of a registrant's directors sign the Form 10-K. In Securities Act Release No. 6231 (1980), the Commission reasoned:

> [A] requirement for the signatures [on the Form 10-K] of a majority of a registrant's directors—in addition to those of its principal executive officer, its principal financial officer, and its controller or principal accounting officer—is an appropriate one under the circumstances. The Commission believes that just as its rules and the administrative focus of the Division of Corporation Finance are being realigned to reflect the shift in emphasis toward relying on periodic disclosure under the Exchange Act, so too the attention of the private sector, including management, directors, accountants, and attorneys, must also be refocused towards Exchange Act filings if a sufficient degree of discipline is to be instilled in the system to make it work. With an expanded signature requirement, the Commission anticipates that directors will be encouraged to devote the needed attention to reviewing the Form 10-K and to seek the involvement of other professionals to the degree necessary to give themselves sufficient comfort. In the Commission's view, this added measure of discipline is vital to the disclosure objectives of the federal securities laws, and outweighs the potential impact, if any, of the signature on legal liability.

Concerns have been expressed that the director signature requirement for the Form 10-K may result in greater liability exposure. For example, the signing of the Form 10-K by a subject director arguably may signify that the director was a "cause" of the filing, failed to act in "good faith," and/or acted with "scienter," thereby giving rise to a host of both SEC and private liability concerns. At this point, it appears that the signature requirement, at least to some extent, has induced directors to scrutinize the Form 10-K and to seek the advice of corporate counsel in this exercise to a much greater degree than previously was the practice. Enactment of the Sarbanes-Oxley Act and Dodd-Frank Acts should encourage such greater scrutiny by directors. Moreover, (as discussed in Chapter 5) pursuant to the Sarbanes-Oxley Act, the registrant's chief executive officer and chief financial officer must make "certifications" concerning the accuracy of the disclosures made and the efficacy of internal controls with respect to such registrant's Exchange Act periodic SEC filings.

As a last point in this regard, consider the following statement:

> It has been argued that retaining due diligence obligations in a system of integrated disclosure proves that the Commission does not really believe in efficient markets. There is, however, no obvious contradiction between efficiency and due diligence. A market which immediately processes all publicly available information can also process a lie. Investors can be efficiently defrauded. The role of the underwriter is to verify the accuracy of

information already impounded in price—in short, to discover the lie. To the extent underwriters actually do discover lies, or deter issuers from telling them, they produce a benefit.[27]

§ 7.06 Section 12(a)(1) of the Securities Act

Section 12(a)(1) of the Securities Act gives teeth to § 5 by providing the purchaser of securities with an express private right of action against his/her seller if such seller offers or sells a security in violation of § 5. In an action brought under § 12(a)(1), the purchaser may seek rescission or, if he/she no longer owns the securities, damages. Section 12(a)(1) (as well as § 12(a)(2)) does not provide a plaintiff with a choice of remedies. *See Wigand v. Flo-Tek, Inc.*, 609 F.2d 1028, 1035 (2d Cir. 1979): "If the plaintiff owns the stock, he is entitled to rescission but not damages. If the plaintiff no longer owns the stock, he is entitled to damages but not rescission."

If a violation of § 5 has been committed by the seller, the purchaser ordinarily is entitled to recovery. In other words, strict liability is imposed against the seller. The exercise of reasonable care or bona fide but unsuccessful efforts to perfect an exemption from registration are irrelevant. Hence, upon the purchaser establishing a prima facie case that the seller violated § 5, a seller may avoid liability only, for example, by showing that the offering qualifies for an exemption or that the purchaser is *in pari delicto*. The statute of limitations for § 12(a)(1) actions is one year. See § 13 of the Securities Act. Interestingly, a number of courts have required the plaintiff to plead compliance with this limitations period.

§ 7.07 Section 12(a)(2) of the Securities Act

Aggrieved purchasers of securities acquired in a public offering by an issuer or its controlling shareholder(s) may seek to invoke § 12(a)(2) of the Securities Act. Generally, § 12(a)(2) affords an express right of action to a purchaser against his/her seller for rescission, or damages if the securities have been disposed of, where the purchaser acquired the securities by means of a prospectus or oral communication (that relates

---

27. Banoff, *Regulatory Subsidies, Efficient Markets, and Shelf Registration: An Analysis of Rule 415*, 70 Va. L. Rev. 135, 180–181 (1984). *See* Fox, *Shelf Registration, Integrated Disclosure, and Underwriter Due Diligence: An Economic Analysis*, 70 Va. L. Rev. 1005 (1984); Leahy, *What Due Diligence Dilemma? Re-Envisioning Underwriters' Continuous Due Diligence After* WorldCom, 30 Cardozo L. Rev. 2001 (2009); Maynard, *Blue Sky Regulation of Rule 415 Shelf-Registered Primary Offerings: The Need for a Limited Form of Federal Preemption*, 22 Ariz. St. L.J. 89 (1990); Michaels, *No Fraud? No Problem: Outside Director Liability for Shelf Offerings Under Section 11 of the Securities Act of 1933*, 28 Rev. Bank & Fin. L. 339 (2008–2009).

to a prospectus) that contained a material misstatement or half-truth. Proof of reliance is not required. Indeed, to recover under § 12(a)(2), "a plaintiff need not prove that he ever received the misleading prospectus."[28] Accordingly, § 12(a)(2)'s terms "do not require that the particular sale to an individual plaintiff directly be by means of the prospectus alleged to be misleading." Rather, it is sufficient that "the seller sold by means of a misleading prospectus securities of which those purchased by the plaintiff were a part." With respect to oral communications that relate to a prospectus, however, a different result might follow.[29] See *National Credit Union Administration Board v. RBS Securities, Inc.*, ___ F. Supp. 2d ____ (D. Kan. 2015) (denying motion to dismiss § 12(a)(2) claim alleging materially misleading statements contained in a free writing prospectus).

Section 12(a)(2) provides the seller with a "quasi due diligence" defense. Once the purchaser has established a prima facie case, the onus is shifted to the seller to establish that he/she did not know, and in the exercise of reasonable care could not have known, of the untruth or omission.

In general terms, a comparison between the § 12(a)(2) right of action with that provided under § 11 reveals the following: *First*, similar to § 11 which applies only to registered offerings, due to the Supreme Court's restrictive decision in *Gustafson v. Alloyd Company*, 513 U.S. 561 (1995) (contained herein in § 7.07[B]), the § 12(a)(2) remedy likewise is limited to purchasers of securities in a public offering by an issuer or its controlling shareholder(s). Clearly, the § 12(a)(2) remedy is available in registered offerings, including with respect to free writing prospectuses.

Although not resolved, the Supreme Court's decision in *Gustafson* suggests that § 12(a)(2) also may apply in offerings that take on a public nature but are exempt from Securities Act registration pursuant to § 3 of that Act. Such offerings may include those public offerings that are state registered but exempt from federal registration pursuant to Regulation A Plus, Rule 504, § 3(a)(11) or Rule 147. Note that prior to the *Gustafson* decision, lower courts uniformly held that § 12(a)(2) was available in issuer private offerings exempt from registration (such as pursuant to § 4(a)(2) or Rule 506 of Regulation D);[30] and there existed a split of authority whether the remedy was available in private secondary transactions.[31] Today, it is clear that § 12(a)(2) does not apply to private offerings.

---

28. *Sanders v. John Nuveen & Co., Inc.*, 619 F.2d 1222, 1226 (7th Cir. 1980), *cert. denied*, 450 U.S. 1005 (1981).

29. *Id.* at 1226-27, 1227 n.8.

30. *See, e.g., Abell v. Potomac Insurance Company*, 858 F.2d 1104 (5th Cir. 1988).

31. Compare *Ballay v. Legg Mason Wood Walker, Inc.*, 925 F.2d 682 (3d Cir. 1991) (limiting § 12(2) to initial offerings), with *Pacific Dunlop Holdings, Inc. v. Allen & Co., Inc.*, 993 F.2d 578 (7th Cir. 1993) (holding that § 12(2) extends to secondary transactions). *See generally* Loss, *The Assault on Section 12(2)*, 105 Harv. L. Rev. 908 (1992); Maynard, *Liability Under Section 12(2) of the Securities Act of 1933 for Fraudulent Trading in Post-Distribution Markets*, 32 Wm. & Mary L. Rev. 847 (1991); Weiss, *The Courts Have It Right: Securities Act Section 12(2) Applies Only to Public Offerings*, 48 Bus. Law. 1 (1992).

Second, similar to § 11, pursuant to § 12(b), a defendant may avoid all or part of the damages that otherwise would be incurred by proving that all or part of the depreciation in the value of the securities in question resulted from factors unrelated to the material misstatements(s) or omission(s).

Third, § 12(a)(2) extends liability only to those who "sold" the securities to the allegedly aggrieved purchasers. On the other hand, § 11 specifically enumerates those parties who are subject to liability under that provision. In this regard, note that a dealer, although not subject to § 11 liability, may be liable under § 12 as a "seller" in a registered offering.

Hence, in contrast to the specific categories of possible defendants listed in § 11, § 12(a)(2) by its terms subjects only "sellers" to potential liability. In this respect, depending on the underlying circumstances, underwriters may not be within the reach of § 12(a)(2). As the Eleventh Circuit has observed: "Since § 12 does not provide for underwriter liability per se, an underwriter must also be a seller of the security in question to be liable under the section."[32]

Significantly, in its 2005 offering rule amendments, the SEC enunciated that an issuer in a registered primary offering, as well as an issuer that provides a free writing prospectus, is deemed a "seller" for purposes of § 12. *See* Rule 159A; Securities Act Release No. 8591 (2005). The SEC's position is contrary to some case law. *See, e.g., Lone Star Ladies Investment Club v. Schlotsky's, Inc.*, 238 F.3d 363, 370 (5th Cir. 2001) (holding that "in a firm commitment underwriting, such as this one, the public cannot ordinarily hold the issuer liable under section 12, because the public does not purchase from the issuer").

In adopting Rule 159A, as part of its 2005 offering reforms, the SEC reasoned in Securities Act Release No. 8591 (2005):

> We believe there currently is unwarranted uncertainty as to issuer liability under Section 12(a)(2) for issuer information in registered offerings using certain types of underwriting arrangements. As a result, there is a possibility that issuers may not be held liable under Section 12(a)(2) to purchasers in the initial distribution of the securities for information contained in the issuer's prospectus included in its registration statement. This also could be the case for other communications that are offers by or on behalf of an issuer, including issuer free writing prospectuses. When an issuer registers securities to be sold in a primary offering, the registration covers the offer and sale of its securities to the public. The issuer is selling its securities to the public, although the form of underwriting of such offering, such as a firm commitment underwriting, may involve the sale first by the issuer to the underwriter and then the sale by the underwriter to the public. We believe that an issuer offering or selling its securities in a registered offering pursuant to a registration statement containing a prospectus that it has prepared and filed, or

---

32. *Foster v. Jessup and Lamont Securities Co.*, 759 F.2d 838, 845 (11th Cir. 1985).

by means of other communications that are offers made by or on behalf of or used or referred to by the issuer can be viewed as soliciting purchases of the issuer's registered securities. Therefore, we are adopting a rule providing that under Section 12(a)(2) an issuer in a primary offering of securities, regardless of the form of the underwriting arrangement, will be a seller and will be considered to offer or sell the securities to a purchaser in the initial distribution of the securities as to any of the following communications:

- any preliminary prospectus or prospectus of the issuer relating to the offering required to be filed pursuant to Securities Act Rule 424 or Rule 497;

- any free writing prospectus relating to the offering prepared by or on behalf of or used or referred to by the issuer . . . ;

- the portion of any other free writing prospectus . . . relating to the offering containing material information about the issuer or its securities provided by or on behalf of the issuer; and

- any other communication that is an offer in the offering made by the issuer to such purchaser.

This definition of the issuer as a seller is not intended to affect whether any other person offers or sells a security by means of the same prospectus or oral communication for purposes of Section 12(a)(2). A communication by an underwriter or dealer participating in an offering would also not be on behalf of the issuer solely by virtue of that participation. . . . [T]here are circumstances where the involvement of an issuer could be sufficiently extensive (for example under adoption and entanglement theories) that a communication of another person, including [that of] an offering participant, could be by an issuer.

. . . .

While we have adopted the issuer as seller provisions substantially as proposed, we have included language that clarifies that it is aimed only at liability to purchasers in the initial distribution of the securities who were offered or sold the securities by means of the particular communication. Thus, the Rule, as adopted, would not cover purchasers of the issuer's securities in the aftermarket. We have also provided, as noted above, that an underwriter or dealer participating in an offering is not acting on behalf of the issuer solely by virtue of that participation.[33]

Fourth, another distinction between § 11 and § 12(a)(2) lies in the *standard of care defense*. Whereas § 11 establishes an affirmative defense of "reasonable investigation," § 12(a)(2) provides that the seller exercise "reasonable care." This apparently lower

---

33. *See* Gail, *Uncertain Future: Liability Concerns Surrounding the Application of Section 12(a)(2) of the Securities Act of 1933 to Free-Writing Prospectuses After the Enactment of the SEC's Recently Reformed Offering Rules,* 60 SMU L. Rev. 609 (2007).

standard of care is consistent with the general notion that sellers of securities may not be intimately involved with the offering and may not have the same access to information as do potential § 11 defendants. However, as the Seventh Circuit's decision in *Sanders v. John Nuveen & Co.*, 619 F.2d 1222 (7th Cir. 1980), indicates, the degree of care to be exercised by sellers who are within the § 12(a)(2) inner circle may converge with the reasonable investigation standard of § 11. Nonetheless, the SEC more recently has asserted its belief "that the standard of care under Section 12(a)(2) is less demanding than that prescribed by Section 11, or put another way, that Section 11 requires a more diligent investigation than Section 12(a)(2)." Securities Act Release No. 8591 (2005).

[A] The Meaning of "Seller" and the "In Pari Delicto" Defense

Prior to the Supreme Court's decision in *Pinter v. Dahl*, the lower federal courts differed widely as to which parties were regarded as "sellers" under § 12(a)(2) (as well as under § 12(a)(1)). While some courts held that the statute imposes a strict privity requirement, most courts relaxed the privity requirement to some extent. Under one such view, liability was imposed upon persons as "sellers" for being integrally connected with, or substantially involved in, the transaction. Or, as phrased by the Ninth Circuit: "The test [was] whether the injury to the plaintiff flowed directly and proximately from the actions of the defendant."[34]

The Supreme Court resolved the issue of who is a "seller" for § 12 purposes in the following case. Although the decision only addresses this issue under § 12(1) (now § 12(a)(1)), lower federal courts have applied the holding to cases also arising under § 12(2) (now § 12(a)(2)).

Pinter v. Dahl

United States Supreme Court

486 U.S. 622, 108 S. Ct. 2063, 100 L. Ed. 2d 658 (1988)

Justice Blackmun delivered the opinion of the Court.

The questions presented by this case are (a) whether the common-law *in pari delicto* defense is available in private actions brought under § 12(1) [now § 12(a)(1)] of the Securities Act of 1933 for the rescission of the sale of unregistered securities, and (b) whether one must intend to confer a benefit on himself or on a third party in order to qualify as a "seller" within the meaning of § 12(1) [now § 12(a)(1)].

------

34. *SEC v. Seaboard Corp.*, 677 F.2d 1289, 1294 (9th Cir. 1982). *See generally* O'Hara, *Erosion of the Privity Requirement in Section 12(2) of the Securities Act of 1933: The Expanded Meaning of Seller*, 31 UCLA L. Rev. 921 (1984); Schneider, *Section 12 of the Securities Act of 1933: The Privity Requirement in the Contemporary Securities Law Perspective*, 51 Tenn. L. Rev. 235 (1984).

I

The controversy arises out of the sale prior to 1982 of unregistered securities (fractional undivided interests in oil and gas leases) by petitioner Billy J. "B.J." Pinter to respondents Maurice Dahl and Dahl's friends, family, and business associates. Pinter is an oil and gas producer in Texas and Oklahoma, and a registered securities dealer in Texas. Dahl is a California real estate broker and investor, who, at the time of his dealings with Pinter, was a veteran of two unsuccessful oil and gas ventures. In pursuit of further investment opportunities, Dahl employed an oilfield expert to locate and acquire oil and gas leases. This expert introduced Dahl to Pinter. Dahl advanced $20,000 to Pinter to acquire leases, with the understanding that they would be held in the name of Pinter's Black Gold Oil Company and that Dahl would have a right of first refusal to drill certain wells on the leasehold properties. Pinter located leases in Oklahoma, and Dahl toured the properties, often without Pinter, in order to talk to others and "get a feel for the properties." Upon examining the geology, drilling logs, and production history assembled by Pinter, Dahl concluded, in the words of the District Court, that "there was no way to lose."

After investing approximately $310,000 in the properties, Dahl told the other respondents about the venture. Except for Dahl and respondent Grantham, none of the respondents spoke to or met Pinter or toured the properties. Because of Dahl's involvement in the venture, each of the other respondents decided to invest about $7,500.

Dahl assisted his fellow investors in completing the subscription-agreement form prepared by Pinter. Each letter contract signed by the purchaser stated that the participating interests were being sold without the benefit of registration under the Securities Act, in reliance on Securities and Exchange Commission (SEC or Commission) Rule 146 [which has been superseded by Rule 506]. In fact, the oil and gas interests involved in this suit were never registered with the Commission. Respondents' investment checks were made payable to Black Gold Oil Company. Dahl received no commission from Pinter in connection with the other respondents' purchases.

When the venture failed and their interests proved to be worthless, respondents brought suit against Pinter in the United States District Court for the Northern District of Texas, seeking rescission under § 12(1) [now § 12(a)(1)] of the Securities Act for the unlawful sale of unregistered securities.[35]

In a counterclaim, Pinter alleged that Dahl, by means of fraudulent misrepresentations and concealment of facts, induced Pinter to sell and deliver the securities. Pinter averred that Dahl falsely assured Pinter that he would provide other qualified, sophisticated, and knowledgeable investors with all the information necessary

---

[35]. ... In addition to their § 12(1) claim, respondents alleged that Pinter made material misrepresentations regarding the oil and gas properties and his oil experience, thereby entitling them to damages under § 10(b) of the Securities Exchange Act of 1934 and SEC Rule 10b-5 thereunder, and to rescission under § 12(2) of the Securities Act. Respondents also asserted pendent claims under Texas and California law. None of these additional claims is before us.

for evaluation of the investment. Dahl allegedly agreed to raise the funds for the venture from those investors, with the understanding that Pinter would simply be the "operator" of the wells. Pinter also asserted, on the basis of the same factual allegations, that Dahl's suit was barred by the equitable defenses of estoppel and *in pari delicto*.

The District Court, after a bench trial, granted judgment for the respondent-investors. . . .

A divided panel of the Court of Appeals for the Fifth Circuit affirmed. 787 F.2d 985 (1986). The court first held that Dahl's involvement in the sales to the other respondents did not give Pinter an *in pari delicto* defense to Dahl's recovery. . . .

The Court of Appeals next considered whether Dahl was himself a "seller" of the oil and gas interests within the meaning of § 12(1), for if he was, the court assumed, he could be held liable in contribution for the other plaintiffs' claims against Pinter.[36] Citing Fifth Circuit precedent, the court described a statutory seller as "(1) one who parts with title to securities in exchange for consideration or (2) one whose participation in the buy-sell transaction is a substantial factor in causing the transaction to take place." . . . While acknowledging that Dahl's conduct was a "substantial factor" in causing the other plaintiffs to purchase securities from Pinter, the court declined to hold that Dahl was a "seller" for purposes of § 12(1). Instead, the court went on to refine its test to include a threshold requirement that one who acts as a "promoter" be "motivated by a desire to confer a direct or indirect benefit on someone other than the person he has advised to purchase." . . . The court reasoned that "a rule imposing liability (without fault or knowledge) on friends and family members who give one another gratuitous advice on investment matters unreasonably interferes with well-established patterns of social discourse." . . . Accordingly, since the court found no evidence that Dahl sought or received any financial benefit in return for his advice, it declined to impose liability on Dahl for "mere gregariousness."

. . . .

Because of the importance of the issues involved to the administration of the federal securities law, we granted certiorari.

II

The equitable defense of *in pari delicto*, which literally means "in equal fault," is rooted in the common-law notion that a plaintiff's recovery may be barred by his

---

[36]. Because none of the other plaintiffs sought recovery from Dahl, Dahl's liability on their claims is at issue only if contribution is available to Pinter.

Unlike § 11 of the . . . . Securities Act, § 12 does not expressly provide for contribution. The Court of Appeals did not reach the question whether Pinter is entitled to contribution under § 12(1). . . . The parties have not raised or addressed the contribution issue before this Court, and we express no view as to whether a right of contribution exists under § 12(1) of the Securities Act.

own wrongful conduct. . . . Traditionally, the defense was limited to situations where the plaintiff bore "at least substantially equal responsibility for his injury," and where the parties' culpability arose out of the same illegal act. 1 J. Story, Equity Jurisprudence 399–400 (14th ed. 1918). Contemporary courts have expanded the defense's application to situations more closely analogous to those encompassed by the "unclean hands" doctrine, where the plaintiff has participated "in some of the same sort of wrongdoing" as the defendant. See *Perma Life Mufflers, Inc. v. International Parts Corp.,* 392 U.S. 134, 138 (1968). In *Perma Life,* however, the Court concluded that this broadened construction is not appropriate in litigation arising under federal regulatory statutes. Nevertheless, in separate opinions, five Justices recognized that a narrow, more traditional formulation should be available in private actions under the antitrust laws. . . .

In *Bateman Eichler* [471 U.S. 299 (1985)], the Court addressed the scope of the *in pari delicto* defense in the context of an action brought by securities investors under the antifraud provisions of § 10(b) and Rule 10b-5, alleging that the broker-dealer and corporate insider defendants had induced the plaintiffs to purchase large quantities of stock by divulging false and materially incomplete information on the pretext that it was accurate inside information. The defendants argued that the scope should be broader where the private cause of action is implied, as in a § 10(b) action, rather than expressly provided by Congress, as in an antitrust action. The Court rejected this distinction, concluding that "the views expressed in *Perma Life* apply with full force to implied causes of action under the federal securities laws." . . . Accordingly, it held that the *in pari delicto* defense is available "only where (1) as a direct result of his own actions, the plaintiff bears at least substantially equal responsibility for the violations he seeks to redress, and (2) preclusion of suit would not significantly interfere with the effective enforcement of the securities laws and protection of the investing public." . . . The first prong of this test captures the essential elements of the classic *in pari delicto* doctrine. The second prong, which embodies the doctrine's traditional requirement that public policy implications be carefully considered before the defense is allowed, ensures that the broad judge-made law does not undermine the congressional policy favoring private suits as an important mode of enforcing federal securities statutes. Applying this test to the § 10(b) claim before it, the Court concluded that in such tipper-tippee situations, the two factors precluded recognition of the *in pari delicto* defense. *Bateman Eichler,* 472 U.S. at 317 [contained in Chapter 8 of this text].

A

We do not share the Court of Appeals' narrow vision of the applicability of *Bateman Eichler.* Nothing in this Court's opinion in that case suggests that the *in pari delicto* defense is limited to § 10(b) claims. Nor does the opinion suggest that the doctrine applies only when the plaintiff's fault is intentional or willful.

We feel that the Court of Appeals' notion that the *in pari delicto* defense should not be allowed in actions involving strict liability offenses is without support in history or logic. The doctrine traditionally has been applied in any action based on conduct that "transgresses statutory prohibitions." 2 Restatement of Contracts § 598, Comment a (1932). Courts have recognized the defense in cases involving strict liability offenses. . . . The need to deter illegal conduct is not eliminated simply because a statute creates a strict liability offense rather than punishing willful or negligent misconduct. Regardless of the degree of scienter, there may be circumstances in which the statutory goal of deterring illegal conduct is served more effectively by preclusion of suit than by recovery. In those circumstances, the *in pari delicto* defense should be afforded. . . .

B

Under the first prong of the *Bateman Eichler* test, as we have noted above, a defendant cannot escape liability unless, as a direct result of the plaintiff's own actions, the plaintiff bears at least substantially equal responsibility for the underlying illegality. The plaintiff must be an active, voluntary participant in the unlawful activity that is the subject of the suit. . . . Unless the degrees of fault are essentially indistinguishable or the plaintiff's responsibility is clearly greater, the *in pari delicto* defense should not be allowed, and the plaintiff should be compensated. . . . Refusal of relief to those less blameworthy would frustrate the purpose of the securities laws; it would not serve to discourage the actions of those most responsible for organizing forbidden schemes; and it would sacrifice protection of the general investing public in pursuit of individual punishment. . . . In the context of a private action under § 12(1), the first prong of the *Bateman Eichler* test is satisfied if the plaintiff is at least equally responsible for the actions that render the sale of the unregistered securities illegal — the issuer's failure to register the securities before offering them for sale, or his failure to conduct the sale in such a manner as to meet the registration exemption provisions. As the parties and the Commission agree, a purchaser's knowledge that the securities are unregistered cannot, by itself, constitute equal culpability, even where the investor is a sophisticated buyer who may not necessarily need the protection of the Securities Act. . . . [See] L. Loss, Securities Regulation 1694 (2d ed. 1961).[37] Although a court's assessment of the relative responsibility of the plaintiff will

---

[37]. The panel dissent below expressed concern that failure to provide the *in pari delicto* defense in these circumstances would allow sophisticated investors who purchase unregistered securities to place themselves in a no-lose situation. If the venture proves profitable, the buyer comes out ahead. If the investment goes bad, the buyer can sue to recover his investment in a § 12(1) action. See 787 F.2d at 995. The statute, however, permits such maneuvers. *See* Shulman, *Civil Liability and the Securities Act*, 43 YALE L.J. 227, 246–247 (1933) (Schulman); *accord*, L. LOSS, FUNDAMENTALS OF SECURITIES REGULATION 1003, n.74 (2d. ed. 1988) (LOSS). Section 12(1)'s deterrent effect is achieved, to a great extent, by a provision allowing suits for a full year following sale. Thus, the purchaser of unregistered securities may keep his securities and reap his profit if the securities perform well during the year, but rescind the sale if they do not. . . . Although this provision may appear to offend a sense of fair play, allowing the investor to sue, regardless of his knowledge of the violation when he purchased the securities, furthers the interest of the Securities Act: the seller then has strong incentive to comply with the registration disclosure provisions. These provisions are concerned with affording the unsophisticated investor information necessary to make a

necessarily vary depending on the facts of the particular case, courts frequently have focused on the extent to which the plaintiff and the defendant cooperated in developing and carrying out the scheme to distribute unregistered securities. . . . In addition, if the plaintiff were found to have induced the issuer not to register, he well might be precluded from obtaining § 12(1) rescission.

Under the [second] prong of the *Bateman Eichler* test, a plaintiff's recovery may be barred only if preclusion of suit does not offend the underlying statutory policies. The primary purpose of the Securities Act is to protect investors by requiring publication of material information thought necessary to allow them to make informed investment decisions concerning public offerings of securities in interstate commerce. . . . The registration requirements are the heart of the Act, and § 12(1) imposes strict liability for violating those requirements. Liability under § 12(1) is a particularly important enforcement tool, because in many instances a private suit is the only effective means of detecting and deterring a seller's wrongful failure to register securities before offering them for sale. . . .

In our view, where the § 12(1) plaintiff is primarily an investor, precluding suit would interfere significantly with effective enforcement of the securities laws and frustrate the primary objective of the Securities Act. The Commission, too, takes this position. Because the Act is specifically designed to protect investors, even where a plaintiff actively participates in the distribution of unregistered securities, his suit should not be barred where his promotional efforts are incidental to his role as an investor. . . . Thus, the *in pari delicto* defense may defeat recovery in a § 12(1) action only where the plaintiff's role in the offering or sale of nonexempted, unregistered securities is more as a promoter than as an investor.

Whether the plaintiff in a particular case is primarily an investor or primarily a promoter depends upon a host of factors, all readily accessible to trial courts. These factors include the extent of the plaintiff's financial involvement compared to that of third parties solicited by the plaintiff; the incidental nature of the plaintiff's promotional activities; the benefits received by the plaintiff from his promotional activities; and the extent of the plaintiff's involvement in the planning stages of the offering (such as whether the plaintiff has arranged an underwriting or prepared the offering materials). We do not mean to suggest that these factors provide conclusive evidence of culpable promotional activity, or that they constitute an exhaustive list of factors to be considered. The courts are free, in the exercise of their sound discretion, to consider whatever facts are relevant to the inquiry.

C

Given the record in this case, we cannot ascertain whether Pinter may successfully assert an *in pari delicto* defense against Dahl's § 12(1) claim. The District Court's findings in this case are not adequate to determine whether Dahl bears at least

---

knowledgeable investment decision. Permitting the sophisticated investor to recover also serves to protect the unknowing and innocent investor. . . .

substantially equal responsibility for the failure to register the oil and gas interests or to distribute the securities in a manner that conformed with the statutory exemption, and whether he was primarily a promoter of the offering. The findings indicate, on the one hand, that Dahl may have participated in initiating the entire investment, and that he loaned money to Pinter and solicited his associates' participation in the venture, but, on the other hand, that Dahl invested substantially more money than the other investor-respondents, expected and received no commission for his endeavors, and drafted none of the offering documents. Furthermore, the District Court made no findings as to who was responsible for the failure to register or for the manner in which the offering was conducted. Those findings will be made on the remand of this case for further proceedings.

III

What we have said as to the availability to Pinter of the *in pari delicto* defense against Dahl's § 12(1) action does not obviate the need to consider the second question presented by petitioner. We turn now to that issue.

In determining whether Dahl may be deemed a "seller" for purposes of § 12(1), such that he may be held liable for the sale of unregistered securities to the other investor-respondents, we look first at the language of § 12(1). . . . That statute provides, in pertinent part: "Any person who . . . offers or sells a security" in violation of the registration requirement of the Securities Act "shall be liable to the person purchasing such security from him." This provision defines the class of defendants who may be subject to liability as those who offer or sell unregistered securities. But the Securities Act nowhere delineates who may be regarded as a statutory seller, and the sparse legislative history sheds no light on the issue. The courts, on their part, have not defined the term uniformly.

At the very least, however, the language of § 12(1) contemplates a buyer-seller relationship not unlike traditional contractual privity. Thus, it is settled that § 12(1) imposes liability on the owner who passed title, or other interest in the security, to the buyer for value. See L. Loss, *Fundamentals of Securities Regulation* 1016 (2d ed. 1988) (Loss). Dahl, of course, was not a seller in this conventional sense, and therefore may be held liable only if § 12(1) liability extends to persons other than the person who passes title.[38]

---

[38]. The "offers or sells" and the "purchasing such security from him" language that governs § 12(1) also governs § 12(2), which provides a securities purchaser with a similar rescissionary cause of action for misrepresentation. Most courts and commentators have not defined the defendant class differently for purposes of the two provisions. *See, e.g., Pharo v. Smith*, 621 F.2d 656, 665–668, and nn. 6–8 (CA5 1980); Schneider, *Section 12 of the Securities Act of 1933: The Privity Requirement in the Contemporary Securities Law Perspective*, 51 TENN. L. REV. 235, 261, and nn. 144 and 145 (1984). . . .

The question whether anyone beyond the transferor of title, or immediate vendor, may be deemed a seller for purposes of § 12 has been litigated in actions under both § 12(1) and § 12(2). Decisions under § 12(2) addressing the "seller" question are thus relevant to the issue presented to

In common parlance, a person may offer or sell property without necessarily being the person who transfers title to, or other interest in, that property. We need not rely entirely on ordinary understanding of the statutory language, however, for the Securities Act defines the operative terms of § 12(1). Section 2(3) defines "sale" or "sell" to include "every contract of sale or disposition of a security or interest in a security, for value," and the terms "sell," "offer for sale, or "offer" to include "every attempt or offer to dispose of, or solicitation of an offer to buy, a security or interest in a security, for value." Under these definitions, the range of persons potentially liable under § 12(1) is not limited to persons who pass title. The inclusion of the phrase "solicitation of an offer to buy" within the definition of "offer" brings an individual who engages in solicitation, an activity not inherently confined to the actual owner, within the scope of § 12. . . . Indeed, the Court has made clear, in the context of interpreting § 17(a) of the Securities Act, that transactions other than traditional sales of securities are within the scope of § 2(3) and passage of title is not important. See *United States v. Naftalin*, 441 U.S. 768, (1979). We there explained: "The statutory terms ["offer" and "sell"], which Congress expressly intended to define broadly, ... are expansive enough to encompass the entire selling process, including the seller/agent transaction." . . .

Determining that the activity in question falls within the definition of "offer" or "sell" in § 2(3), however, is only half of the analysis. The second clause of § 12(1), which provides that only a defendant "from" whom the plaintiff "purchased" securities may be liable, narrows the field of potential sellers.[39] One important consequence of this provision is that § 12(1) imposes liability on only the buyer's immediate seller; remote purchasers are precluded from bringing actions against remote sellers. Thus, a buyer cannot recover against his seller's seller . . . .

Several courts and commentators have stated that the purchase requirement necessarily restricts § 12 primary liability to the owner of the security. E.g., . . . Abrams, *The Scope of Liability Under Section 12 of the Securities Act of 1933: "Participation" and the Pertinent Legislative Materials*, 15 Ford. Urban L.J. 877 (1987). . . . Thus, an offeror, as defined by § 2(3), may incur § 12 liability only if the offeror also "sells" the security to the plaintiff, in the sense of transferring title for value.

We do not read § 12(1) so restrictively. The purchase requirement clearly confines § 12 liability to those situations in which a sale has taken place. Thus, a prospective buyer has no recourse against a person who touts unregistered securities to him if he does not purchase the securities. The requirement, however, does not exclude solicitation from the category of activities that may render a person liable when a sale has taken place. A natural reading of the statutory language would include in the statutory seller status at least some persons who urged the buyer to purchase. For example, a securities vendor's agent who solicited the purchase

---

us in this case, and, to that extent, we discuss them here. Nevertheless, this case does not present, nor do we take a position on, the scope of a statutory seller for purposes of § 12(2).

   [39]. [This footnote has been moved to the text—ed.]

would commonly be said, and would be thought by the buyer, to be among those "from" whom the buyer "purchased," even though the agent himself did not pass title. . . .

The Securities Act does not define the term "purchase." The soundest interpretation of the term, however, is as a correlative to both "sell" and "offer," at least to the extent that the latter entails active solicitation of an offer to buy. This interpretation is supported by the history of the phrase "offers or sells," as it is used in § 12(1). As enacted in 1933, § 12(1) imposed liability on "[a]ny person who sells a security." The statutory definition of "sell" included "offer" and the activities now encompassed by that term, including solicitation. The words "offer or" were added to § 12(1) by the 1954 amendments to the Securities Act, when the original definition of "sell" in § 2(3) was split into separate definitions of "sell" and "offer" in order to accommodate changes in § 5. Since "sells" and "purchases" have obvious correlative meanings, Congress' express definition of "sells" in the original Securities Act to include solicitation suggests that the class of those from whom the buyer "purchases" extended to persons who solicit him. The 1954 amendment to § 12(1) was intended to preserve existing law, including the liability provisions of the Act. . . . Hence, there is no reason to think Congress intended to narrow the meaning of "purchased from" when it amended the statute to include "solicitation" in the statutory definition of "offer" alone.

The applicability of § 12 liability to brokers and others who solicit securities purchases has been recognized frequently since the passage of the Securities Act. It long has been "quite clear," that when a broker acting as agent of one of the principals to the transaction successfully solicits a purchase, he is a person from whom the buyer purchases within the meaning of § 12 and is therefore liable as a statutory seller. Indeed, courts had found liability on this basis prior to the 1954 amendment of the statute. . . . Had Congress intended liability to be restricted to those who pass title, it could have effectuated its intent by not adding the phrase "offers or" when it split the definition of "sell" in § 2(3).

An interpretation of statutory seller that includes brokers and others who solicit offers to purchase securities furthers the purposes of the Securities Act—to promote full and fair disclosure of information to the public in the sales of securities. In order to effectuate Congress' intent that § 12(1) civil liability be *in terrorem*, the risk of its invocation should be felt by solicitors of purchases. The solicitation of a buyer is perhaps the most critical stage of the selling transaction. It is the first stage of a traditional securities sale to involve the buyer, and it is directed at producing the sale. In addition, brokers and other solicitors are well positioned to control the flow of information to a potential purchaser, and, in fact, such persons are the participants in the selling transaction who most often disseminate material information to investors. Thus, solicitation is the stage at which an investor is most likely to be injured, that is, by being persuaded to purchase securities without full and fair information. Given Congress' overriding goal of preventing this injury, we may infer that Congress intended solicitation to fall under the mantle of § 12(1).

Although we conclude that Congress intended § 12(1) liability to extend to those who solicit securities purchases, we share the Court of Appeals' conclusion that Congress did not intend to impose rescission based on strict liability on a person who urges the purchase but whose motivation is solely to benefit the buyer. When a person who urges another to make a securities purchase acts merely to assist the buyer, not only is it uncommon to say that the buyer "purchased" from him, but it is also strained to describe the giving of gratuitous advice, even strongly or enthusiastically, as "soliciting." Section 2(3) defines an offer as a "solicitation of an offer to buy . . . for value." The person who gratuitously urges another to make a particular investment decision is not, in any meaningful sense, requesting value in exchange for his suggestion or seeking the value the titleholder will obtain in exchange for the ultimate sale. *The language and purpose of § 12(1) suggest that liability extends only to the person who successfully solicits the purchase, motivated at least in part by a desire to serve his own financial interests or those of the securities owner* [emphasis supplied]. If he had such a motivation, it is fair to say that the buyer "purchased" the security from him and to align him with the owner in a rescission action.

B

Petitioner is not satisfied with extending § 12(1) primary liability to one who solicits securities sales for financial gain. Pinter assumes, without explication, that liability is not limited to the person who actually parts title with the securities, and urges us to validate, as the standard by which additional defendant-sellers are identified, that version of the "substantial factor" test utilized by the Fifth Circuit before the refinement espoused in this case. Under that approach, grounded in tort doctrine, a nontransferor § 12(1) seller is defined as one "whose participation in the buy-sell transaction is a substantial factor in causing the transaction to take place." *Pharo v. Smith*, 621 F.2d 656, 667 (CA5 1980). The Court of Appeals acknowledged that Dahl would be liable as a statutory seller under this test.

We do not agree that Congress contemplated imposing § 12(1) liability under the broad terms petitioner advocates. There is no support in the statutory language or legislative history for expansion of § 12(1) primary liability beyond persons who pass title and persons who "offer," including those who "solicit" offers. Indeed, § 12's failure to impose express liability for mere participation in unlawful sales transactions suggests that Congress did not intend that section [to] impose liability on participants collateral to the offer or sale. When Congress wished to create such liability, it had little trouble doing so.

The deficiency of the substantial-factor test is that it divorces the analysis of seller status from any reference to the applicable statutory language and from any examination of § 12 in the context of the total statutory scheme. Those courts that have adopted the approach have not attempted to ground their analysis in the statutory language. Instead, they substitute the concept of substantial participation in the sales transaction, or proximate causation of the plaintiff's purchase, for the words "offers or sells" in § 12. The "purchase from" requirement of § 12 focuses on the defendant's relationship with the plaintiff-purchaser. The substantial-factor test, on the other hand, focuses on the defendant's degree of involvement in the securities transaction and its surrounding circumstances. Thus, although the substantial-factor test undoubtedly embraces persons who pass title and who solicit the purchase of unregistered securities as statutory sellers, the test also would extend § 12(1) liability to participants only remotely related to the relevant aspects of the sales transaction. Indeed, it might expose securities professionals, such as accountants and lawyers, whose involvement is only the performance of their professional services, to § 12(1) strict liability for rescission. The buyer does not, in any meaningful sense, "purchas[e] the security from" such a person.

Further, no congressional intent to incorporate tort law doctrines of reliance and causation into § 12(1) emerges from the language or the legislative history of the statute. Indeed, the strict liability nature of the statutory cause of action suggests the opposite. . . . By injecting these concepts into § 12(1) litigation, the substantial-factor test introduces an element of uncertainty into an area that demands certainty and predictability. As the Fifth Circuit has conceded, the test affords no guidelines for distinguishing between the defendant whose conduct rises to a level of significance sufficient to trigger seller status, and the defendant whose conduct is not sufficiently integral to the sale. . . . None of the courts employing the approach has articulated what measure of participation qualifies a person for seller status, and logically sound limitations would be difficult to develop. As a result, decisions are made on an ad hoc basis, offering little predictive value to participants in securities transactions . . . We find it particularly unlikely that Congress would have ordained *sub silentio* the imposition of strict liability on such an unpredictably defined class of defendants.

Not surprisingly, petitioner makes no attempt to justify the substantial-factor test as a matter of statutory construction. Instead, the sole justification Pinter advances is that extending § 12 liability pursuant to the test protects investors and serves the "remedial purposes" of the Securities Act. . . . [This] Court never has conducted its analysis entirely apart from the statutory language. "The ultimate question is one of congressional intent, not one of whether this Court thinks it can improve upon the statutory scheme that Congress enacted into law." . . . The ascertainment of congressional intent with respect to the scope of liability created by a particular section of the Securities Act must rest primarily on the language of that section. . . . The broad remedial goals of the Securities Act are insufficient justification for interpreting a specific provision "more broadly than its language and the statutory scheme reasonably permit." . . . We must assume that Congress meant what it said.

The substantial-factor test reaches participants in sales transactions who do not even arguably fit within the definitions set out in § 2(3); it "would add a gloss to the operative language of [§ 12(1)] quite different from its commonly accepted meaning." . . . We conclude that Congress did not intend such a gross departure from the statutory language. Accordingly, we need not entertain petitioner's policy arguments. Being merely a "substantial factor" in causing the sale of unregistered securities is not sufficient in itself to render a defendant liable under § 12(1).

C

We are unable to determine whether Dahl may be held liable as a statutory seller under § 12(1). The District Court explicitly found that "Dahl solicited each of the other plaintiffs (save perhaps Grantham) in connection with the offer, purchase, and receipt of their oil and gas interests." We cannot conclude that this finding was clearly erroneous. It is not clear, however, that Dahl had the kind of interest in the sales that make him liable as a statutory seller. We do know that he received no commission from Pinter in connection with the other sales, but this is not conclusive. Typically, a person who solicits the purchase will have sought or received a personal financial benefit from the sale, such as where he "anticipat[es] a share of the profits," . . . or receives a brokerage commission. . . . But a person who solicits the buyer's purchase in order to serve the financial interests of the owner may properly be liable under § 12(1) without showing that he expects to participate in the benefits the owner enjoys.

The Court of Appeals apparently concluded that Dahl was motivated entirely by a gratuitous desire to share an attractive investment opportunity with his friends and associates. . . . This conclusion, in our view, was premature. The District Court made no findings that focused on whether Dahl urged the other purchases in order to further some financial interest of his own or of Pinter. Accordingly, further findings are necessary to assess Dahl's liability.

IV

The judgment of the Court of Appeals is vacated and the case is remanded for further proceedings consistent with this opinion.

It is so ordered.

Note

Hence, under the *Pinter* analysis, a "seller" for purposes of § 12 includes:

> (1) one who owned the security sold to the purchaser, (2) an agent for a vendor (such as a broker) who successfully solicited the purchase, (3) one who solicited the purchase with the intent to personally benefit thereby, and (4) one who, without financial benefit to oneself, solicited the purchase with the motivation to serve the owner's financial interests.

M. Steinberg, Understanding Securities Law 245 (6th ed. 2014).

Note that under the factual scenario present in *Pinter*, § 12(a)(2) no longer will be applicable in such circumstances in view of the Supreme Court's subsequent decision in *Gustafson* (contained in [B] below).

As discussed at the beginning of this Section, although contrary to a number of court decisions, the SEC by rule (Rule 159A) has taken the position that issuers in registered primary offerings, as well as those issuers that provide a free writing prospectus in connection with registered public offerings, are "sellers" under § 12(a)(2). *See* Securities Act Release No. 8591 (2005).

[B] Limited to "Public" Offerings

Prior to the Supreme Court's decision in *Gustafson*, it was the overwhelming, if not unanimous, view of the lower federal courts that § 12(a)(2) applied to initial offerings, irrespective of whether such offerings were public (e.g., registered) or private (e.g., § 4(a)(2) private placement) in nature. Moreover, there existed a split of authority in the lower federal courts as to whether § 12(a)(2) was applicable to the secondary trading markets. In the following case, to the surprise of many, the Supreme Court limited § 12(a)(2)'s scope to public offerings.

Gustafson v. Alloyd Company

United States Supreme Court

513 U.S. 561, 115 S. Ct. 1061, 131 L. Ed. 2d 1 (1995)

JUSTICE KENNEDY delivered the opinion of the Court.

Under § 12(2) [now § 12(a)(2)] of the Securities Act of 1933 buyers have an express cause of action for rescission against sellers who make material misstatements or omissions "by means of a prospectus." The question presented is whether this right of rescission extends to a private, secondary transaction, on the theory that recitations in the purchase agreement are part of a "prospectus."

I

Petitioners Gustafson, McLean, and Butler (collectively Gustafson) were in 1989 the sole shareholders of Alloyd, Inc., a manufacturer of plastic packaging and automatic heat sealing equipment. Alloyd was formed, and its stock was issued, in 1961. In 1989, Gustafson decided to sell Alloyd and engaged KPMG Peat Marwick to find a buyer. In response to information distributed by KPMG, Wind Point Partners II, L.P., agreed to buy substantially all of the issued and outstanding stock through Alloyd Holdings, Inc., a new corporation formed to effect the sale of Alloyd's stock. The shareholders of Alloyd Holdings were Wind Point and a number of individual investors.

. . . .

On December 20, 1989 Gustafson and Alloyd Holdings executed a contract of sale. Alloyd Holdings agreed to pay Gustafson and his coshareholders $18,709,000 for the sale of the stock plus a payment of $2,122,219, which reflected the estimated increase in Alloyd's net worth from the end of the previous year, the last period for which hard financial data were available. Article IV of the purchase agreement, entitled "Representations and Warranties of the Sellers," included assurances that the company's financial statements "present fairly . . . the Company's financial condition" and that between the date of the latest balance sheet and the date the agreement was executed "there ha[d] been no material advserse change in . . . [Alloyd's] financial condition." The contract also provided that if the year-end audit and financial statements revealed a variance between estimated and actual increased value, the disappointed party would receive an adjustment.

The year-end audit of Alloyd revealed that Alloyd's actual earnings for 1989 were lower than the estimates relied upon by the parties in negotiating the adjustment amount of $2,122,219. Under the contract, the buyers had a right to recover an adjustment amount of $815,000, from the sellers. Nevertheless, on February 11, 1991, the newly formed company (now called Alloyd Co., the same as the original company) and Wind Point brought suit in the United States District Court for the Northern District of Illinois, seeking outright rescission of the contract under § 12(2) of the Securities Act of 1933. Alloyd (the new company) claimed that statements made by Gustafson and his coshareholders regarding the financial data of their company were inaccurate, rendering untrue the representations and warranties contained in the contract. The buyers further alleged that the contract of sale was a "prospectus," so that any misstatements contained in the agreement gave rise to liability under § 12(2) of the 1933 Act. Pursuant to the adjustment clause, the defendants remitted to the purchasers $815,000 plus interest, but the adjustment did not cause the purchasers to drop the lawsuit.

Relying on the decision of the Court of Appeals for the Third Circuit in *Ballay v. Legg Mason Wood Walker, Inc.*, 925 F.2d 682 (1991), the District Court granted Gustafson's motion for summary judgment, holding "that section 12(2) claims can only arise out of initial stock offerings."

On review, the Court of Appeals for the Seventh Circuit vacated the District Court's judgment and remanded for further consideration in light of that court's intervening decision in *Pacific Dunlop Holdings Inc. v. Allen & Co. Inc.*, 993 F.2d 578 (1993). In Pacific Dunlop the [Seventh Circuit] reasoned that the inclusion of the term "communication" in the Act's definition of prospectus meant that the term prospectus was defined "very broadly" to include all written communications that offered the sale of a security. Rejecting the view of the Court of Appeals for the Third Circuit in *Ballay*, the Court of Appeals decided that § 12(2)'s right of action for rescission "applies to any communication which offers any security for sale . . . including the stock purchase agreement in the present case." We granted certiorari to resolve this Circuit conflict and we now reverse.

II

The rescission claim against Gustafson is based upon § 12(2) of the 1933 Act. . . . As this case reaches us, we must assume that the stock purchase agreement contained material misstatements of fact made by the sellers and that Gustafson would not sustain its burden of proving due care. On these assumptions, Alloyd would have a right to obtain rescission if those misstatements were made "by means of a prospectus or oral communication." The parties (and the courts of appeals) agree that the phrase "oral communication" is restricted to oral communications that relate to a prospectus. The determinative question, then, is whether the contract between Alloyd and Gustafson is a "prospectus" as the term is used in the 1933 Act.

Alloyd argues that "prospectus" is defined in a broad manner, broad enough to encompass the contract between the parties. This argument is echoed by the dissents. Gustafson, by contrast, maintains that prospectus in the 1933 Act means a communication soliciting the public to purchase securities from the issuer.

Three sections of the 1933 Act are critical in resolving the definitional question on which the case turns: § 2(10) [now § 2(a)(10)], which defines a prospectus; § 10, which sets forth the information that must be contained in a prospectus; and § 12, which imposes liability based on misstatements in a prospectus. In seeking to interpret the term "prospectus," we adopt the premise that the term should be construed, if possible, to give it a consistent meaning throughout the Act. That principle follows from our duty to construe statutes, not isolated provisions.

We begin with § 10. It provides, in relevant part:

> "Except to the extent otherwise permitted or required pursuant to this subsection or subsections (c), (d), or (e) of this section -

> "(1) a prospectus relating to a security other than a security issued by a foreign government or political subdivision thereof, shall contain the information contained in the registration statement. . . ."

Section 10 does not provide that some prospetuses must contain the information contained in the registration statement. Save for the explicit and well-defined exemptions for securities listed under § 3, see 15 U.S.C. § 77c (exempting certain classes of securities from the coverage of the Act), its mandate is unqualified: "a prospectus . . . shall contain the information contained in the registration statement."

Although § 10 does not define what a prospectus is, it does instruct us what a Prospectus cannot be if the Act is to be interpreted as a symmetrical and coherent regulatory scheme, one in which the operative words have a consistent meaning throughout. There is no dispute that the contract in this case was not required to contain the information contained in a registration statement and that no statutory exemption was required to take the document out of § 10's coverage. It follows that the contract is not a prospectus under § 10. That does not mean that a document ceases to be a prospectus whenever it omits a required piece of information. It does mean that a document is not a prospectus within the meaning of that section if, absent an exemption, it need not comply with § 10's requirements in the first place.

An examination of § 10 reveals that, whatever else "prospectus" may mean, the term is confined to a document that, absent an overriding exemption, must include the "information contained in the registration statement." By and large, only public offerings by an issuer of a security, or by controlling shareholders of an issuer, require the preparation and filing of registration statements. It follows, we conclude, that *a prospectus under § 10 is confined to documents related to public offerings by an issuer or its controlling shareholders.* [emphasis supplied]

. . . .

The Securities Act of 1933, like every Act of Congress, should not be read as a series of unrelated and isolated provisions. Only last term we adhered to the "normal rule of statutory construction" that "identical words used in different parts of the same act are intended to have the same meaning." That principle applies here. If the contract before us is not a prospectus for purposes of § 10 — as all must and do concede — it is not a prospectus for purposes of § 12 either.

The conclusion that prospectus has the same meaning, and refers to the same types of communications (public offers by an issuer or its controlling shareholders), in both §§ 10 and 12 is reinforced by an examination of the structure of the 1933 Act. Sections 4 and 5 of the Act together require a seller to file a registration statement and to issue a prospectus for certain defined types of sales (public offerings by an issuer, through an underwriter). Sections 7 and 10 of the Act set forth the information required in the registration statement and the prospectus. Section 11 provides for liability on account of false registration statements; § 12(2) for liability based on misstatements in prospectuses. Following the most natural and symmetrical reading, just as the liability imposed by § 11 flows from the requirements imposed by §§ 5 and 7 providing for the filing and content of registration statements, the liability imposed by § 12(2), cannot attach unless there is an obligation to distribute the prospectus in the first place (or unless there is an exemption).

. . . .

[A]ccepting Alloyd's argument that any written offer is a prospectus under § 12 would require us to hold that the word "prospectus" in § 12 refers to a broader set of communications than the same term in § 10. The Court of Appeals was candid in embracing that conclusion: "[T]he 1933 Act contemplates many definitions of a prospectus. Section 2(10) gives a single, broad definition; section 10(a) involves an isolated, distinct document — a prospectus within a prospectus; section 10(d) gives the Commission authority to classify many." *Pacific Dunlop Holdings Inc v. Allen & Co.*, 993 F.2d, at 584. The dissents take a similar tack. In the name of a plain meaning approach to statutory interpretation, the dissents discover in the Act two different species of prospectuses: formal (also called § 10) prospectuses, subject to both §§ 10 and 12, and informal prospectuses, subject only to § 12 but not to § 10. Nowhere in the statute, however, do the terms "formal prospectus" or "informal prospectus" appear. Instead, the Act uses one term "prospectus" throughout. In disagreement with the Court of Appeals and the dissenting opinions, we cannot accept the conclusion that this single operative word means one thing in one section of the Act and something quite different in another. . . .

B

Alloyd's contrary argument rests to a significant extent on § 2(10) [now § 2(a)(10)], or, to be more precise, on one word of that section. Section 2(10) provides that "[t]he term 'prospectus' means any prospectus, notice, circular, advertisement, letter, or communication, written or by radio or television, which offers any security for sale or confirms the sale of any security." 15 U.S.C. § 77b(10). Concentrating on the word "communication," Alloyd argues that any written communication that offers a security for sale is a "prospectus." Inserting its definition into § 12(2), Alloyd insists that a material misstatement in any communication offering a security for sale gives rise to an action for rescission, without proof of fraud by the seller or reliance by the purchaser. In Alloyd's view, § 2(10) gives the term "prospectus" a capacious definition that, although incompatible with § 10, nevertheless governs in § 12.

The flaw in Alloyd's argument echoed in the dissenting opinions, is its reliance on one word of the definitional section in isolation. To be sure, § 2(10) defines a prospectus as, inter alia, a "communication, written or by radio or television, which offers any security for sale or confirms the sale of any security." The word "communication," however, on which Alloyd's entire argument rests, is but one word in a list, a word Alloyd reads altogether out of context.

. . . .

There is a better reading. From the terms "prospectus, notice, circular, advertisement or letter," it is apparent that the list refers to documents of wide dissemination. In a similar manner, the list includes communications "by radio or television," but not face-to-face or telephonic conversations. Inclusion of the term "communication" in that list suggests that it too refers to a public communication.

When the 1933 Act was drawn and adopted, the term "prospectus" was well understood to refer to a document soliciting the public to acquire securities from the issuer. See Black's Law Dictionary 959 (2d ed. 1910) (defining "prospectus" as a "document published by a company . . . or by persons acting as its agents or assignees, setting forth the nature and objects of an issue of shares . . . and inviting the public to subscribe to the issue"). In this respect, the word prospectus is a term of art, which accounts for Congressional confidence in employing what might otherwise be regarded as a partial circularity in the formal, statutory definition. See 15 U.S.C. § 77b(10) ("The term 'prospectus' means any prospectus . . ."). The use of the term prospectus to refer to public solicitations explains as well Congress' decision in § 12(2) to grant buyers a right to rescind without proof of reliance. See H.R. Rep. No. 85, 73d Cong., 1st Sess., 10 (1933). . . .

C

Our holding that the term "prospectus" relates to public offerings by issuers and their controlling shareholders draws support from our earlier decision interpreting the one provision of the Act that extends coverage beyond the regulation of public offerings, § 17(a) of the 1933 Act. See *United States v. Naftalin*, 441 U.S. 768 (1979).

In *Naftalin*, though noting that "the 1933 Act was primarily concerned with the regulation of new offerings," the Court held that § 17(a) was "intended to cover any fraudulent scheme in an offer or sale of securities, whether in the course of an initial distribution or in the course of ordinary market trading." The Court justified this holding—which it termed "a major departure from th[e] limitation [of the 1933 Act to new offerings]"—by reference to both the statutory language and the unambiguous legislative history. The same considerations counsel in favor of our interpretation of § 12(2).

The Court noted in *Naftalin* that § 17(a) contained no language suggesting a limitation on the scope of liability under § 17(a). See *id.*, at 778 ("the statutory language . . . makes no distinctions between the two kinds of transactions"). Most important for present purposes, § 17(a) does not contain the word "prospectus." In contrast, as we have noted, § 12(2) contains language, i.e. "by means of a prospectus or oral communication," that limits § 12(2) to public offerings. Just as the absence of limiting language in § 17(a) resulted in broad coverage, the presence of limiting language in § 12(2) requires a narrow construction.

Of equal importance, the legislative history relied upon in *Naftalin* showed that Congress decided upon a deliberate departure from the general scheme of the Act in this one instance, and "made abundantly clear" its intent that § 17(a) have broad coverage. . . . No comparable legislative history even hints that § 12(2) was intended to be a free-standing provision effecting expansion of the coverage of the entire statute. The intent of Congress and the design of the statute require that § 12(2) liability be limited to public offerings.

D

It is understandable that Congress would provide buyers with a right to rescind, without proof of fraud or reliance, as to misstatements contained in a document prepared with care, following well established procedures relating to investigations with due diligence and in the context of a public offering by an issuer or its controlling shareholders. It is not plausible to infer that Congress created this extensive liability for every casual communication between buyer and seller in the secondary market. It is often difficult, if not altogether impractical, for those engaged in casual communications not to omit some fact that would, if included, qualify the accuracy of a statement. Under Alloyd's view any casual communication between buyer and seller in the aftermarket could give rise to an action for rescission, with no evidence of fraud on the part of the seller or reliance on the part of the buyer. In many instances buyers in practical effect would have an option to rescind, impairing the stability of past transactions where neither fraud nor detrimental reliance on misstatements or omissions occurred. We find no basis for interpreting the statute to reach so far.

III

The SEC, as amicus, and [a] dissent, rely on what they call the legislative background of the Act to support Alloyd's construction. With a few minor exceptions, however, their reliance is upon statements by commentators and judges written after the Act was passed, not while it was under consideration. Material not available to the lawmakers is not considered, in the normal course, to be legislative history. After-the-fact statements by proponents of a broad interpretation are not a reliable indicator of what Congress intended when it passed the law, assuming extratextual sources are to any extent reliable for this purpose.

. . . .

If legislative history is to be considered, it is preferable to consult the documents prepared by Congress when deliberating. The legislative history of the Act concerning the precise question presented supports our interpretation with much clarity and force. Congress contemplated that §12(2) would apply only to public offerings by an issuer (or a controlling shareholder). The House Report stated: "[t]he bill affects only new offerings of securities . . . It does not affect the ordinary redistribution of securities unless such redistribution takes on the characteristics of a new offering." H.R. Rep. No. 85, 73d Cong., 1st Sess., 5 (1933). The observation extended to §12(2) as well. Part II, §6 of the House Report is entitled "Civil Liabilities." It begins: "Sections 11 and 12 create and define the civil liabilities imposed by the act. . . . Fundamentally, these sections entitle the buyer of securities sold upon a registration statement . . . to sue for recovery of his purchase price." It will be recalled that as to private transactions, such as the Alloyd purchase, there will never have been a registration statement. If §12(2) liability were imposed here, it would cover transactions not within the contemplated reach of the statute.

. . . .

Nothing in the legislative history, moreover, suggests Congress intended to create two types of prospectuses, a formal prospectus required to comply with both §§10 and 12, and a second, less formal prospectus, to which only §12 would be applicable. The Act proceeds by definitions more stable and precise. The legislative history confirms what the text of the Act dictates: §10's requirements govern all prospectuses defined by §2(10) (although, as we pointed out earlier, certain classes of securities are exempted from §10 by operation of §3). . . .

. . . .

In sum, the word "prospectus" is a term of art referring to a document that describes a public offering of securities by an issuer or controlling shareholder. The contract of sale, and its recitations, were not held out to the public and were not a prospectus as the term is used in the 1933 Act.

The judgment of the Court of Appeals is reversed, and the case is remanded for further proceedings consistent with this opinion.

It is so ordered.

JUSTICE THOMAS, with whom JUSTICE SCALIA, JUSTICE GINSBURG, and JUSTICE BREYER join, dissenting.

From the majority's opinion, one would not realize that §12(2) was involved in this case until one had read more than half-way through. In contrast to the majority's approach of interpreting the statute, I believe the proper method is to begin with the provision actually involved in this case, § 12(2), and then turn to the 1933 Act's definitional section, § 2(10), before consulting the structure of the Act as a whole. Because the result of this textual analysis shows that § 12(2) applies to secondary or private sales of a security as well as to initial public offerings, I dissent.

I

A

As we have emphasized in our recent decisions, "[t]he starting point in every case involving construction of a statute is the language itself." *Landreth Timber Co. v. Landreth*, 471 U.S. 681, 685 (1985) (quoting *Blue Chip Stamps v. Manor Drug Stores*, 421 U.S. 723, 756 (1975) (Powell, J., concurring)). Unfortunately, the majority has decided to interpret the word "prospectus" in § 12(2) by turning to sources outside the four corners of the statute, rather than by adopting the definition provided by Congress.

Section 12(2) creates a cause of action when the seller of a security makes a material omission or misstatement to the buyer by means of a prospectus or oral communication. If the seller acted negligently in making the misstatements, the buyer may sue to rescind the sale. I agree with the majority that the only way to interpret § 12(2) as limited to initial offerings is to read "by means of a prospectus or oral communication" narrowly. I also agree that in the absence of any other statutory command, one could understand "prospectus" as "a term of art which describes the transmittal of information concerning the sale of a security in an initial distribution." But the canon that "we construe a statutory term in accordance with its ordinary or natural meaning," applies only "[i]n the absence of [a statutory] definition."

There is no reason to seek the meaning of "prospectus" outside of the 1933 Act, because Congress has supplied just such a definition in § 2(10). That definition is extraordinarily broad:

> "When used in this subchapter, unless the context otherwise requires
>
> ... "(10) The term 'prospectus' means any prospectus, notice, circular, advertisement, letter, or communication, written or by radio or television, which offers any security for sale or confirms the sale of any security." 15 U.S.C. § 77b(10).

For me, the breadth of these terms forecloses the majority's position that "prospectus" applies only in the context of initial distributions of securities. Indeed, § 2(10)'s inclusion of a prospectus as only one of the many different documents that qualify as a "prospectus" for statutory purposes indicates that Congress intended "prospectus" to be more than a mere "term of art." Likewise, Congress' extension of prospectus to include documents that merely confirm the sale of a security underscores Congress' intent to depart from the term's ordinary meaning. Section 2(10)'s definition obviously concerns different types of communications rather than different types of transactions. Congress left the job of exempting certain classes of transactions to §§ 3 and 4, not to § 2(10). We should use § 2(10) to define "prospectus" for the 1933 Act, rather than, as the majority does, use the 1933 Act to define "prospectus" for § 2(10).

The majority seeks to avoid this reading by attempting to create ambiguities in § 2(10). According to the majority, the maxim noscitur a sociis (a word is known by the company it keeps) indicates that the circulars, advertisements, letters, or other communications referred to by § 2(10) are limited by the first word in the list: "prospectus." Thus, we are told that these words define the forms a prospectus may take, but the covered communications still must be "prospectus-like" in the sense that they must relate to an initial public offering. Noscitur a sociis, however, does not require us to construe every term in a series narrowly because of the meaning given to just one of the terms.

The majority uses the canon in an effort to create doubt, not to reduce it. The canon applies only in cases of ambiguity, which I do not find in § 2(10). Noscitur a sociis is a well-established and useful rule of construction where words are of obscure or doubtful meaning; and then, but only then, its aid may be sought to remove the obscurity or doubt by reference to the associated words. There is obvious breadth in "notice, circular, advertisement, letter, or communication, written or by radio or television." To read one word in a long list as controlling the meaning of all the other words would defy common sense; doing so would prevent Congress from giving effect to expansive words in a list whenever they are combined with one word with a more restricted meaning. Section 2(10)'s very exhaustiveness suggests that "prospectus" is merely the first item in a long list of covered documents, rather than a brooding omnipresence whose meaning cabins that of all the following words. The majority also argues that a broad definition of prospectus makes much of § 2(10) redundant. But the majority fails to see that "communication, written or by radio or television" is a catch-all. It operates as a safety net that Congress used to sweep up anything it had forgotten to include in its definition. This is a technique Congress employed in several other provisions of the 1933 and 1934 Acts. See, e.g., 15 U.S.C. § 77b(1) ("term 'security' means any note, stock, treasury stock, bond, debenture . . . or, in general, any interest or instrument commonly known as a 'security'") . . . . In fact, it is the majority's approach that creates redundancies. The majority cannot account for Congress' decision to begin its definition of "prospectus" with the term prospectus, which is then followed by the rest of § 2(10)'s list. As a result, the majority must conclude that the use of the term is a "partial circularity," a reading that deprives the word of its meaning.

. . . .

Note

In view of *Gustafson*, the issue exists whether certain types of exempt offerings that are public in nature come within the scope of § 12(a)(2). Certainly, it would seem that disclosure memoranda delivered to investors in public offerings that are exempt from federal registration by virtue of Regulation A Plus, Rule 504, § 3(a)(11), or Rule 147 constitute prospectuses and thereby implicate § 12(a)(2). Nonetheless, a number of courts after *Gustafson* take the position that § 12(a)(2) is limited to registered public offerings (*see, e.g., Sturm v. Marriott Marquis Corp.,* 26 F. Supp. 2d 1358, 1370 (N.D. Ga. 1998)). Moreover, clearly § 12(a)(2) does not reach private offerings that are within, for example, the § 4(a)(2)/Rule 506 exemption. *See, e.g., Lewis v. Fresne,* 252 F.3d 352 (5th Cir. 2001) (holding that § 12(a)(2) not available in private transaction); *Vannest v. Sage Rutty & Co., Inc.,* 960 F. Supp. 651 (W.D.N.Y. 1997) (holding that § 12(a)(2) per *Gustafson* does not extend to Rule 506 private offering).

Can secondary market participants who can trace the securities purchased to a public offering bring suit under § 12(a)(2)? We have seen that most courts permit such tracing in a § 11 suit. *See, e.g., Hertzberg v. Dignity Partners, Inc.,* 191 F.3d 1076 (9th Cir. 1999) (contained in § 7.01[B]). With respect to "tracing" and "redistributions" under § 12(a)(2), compare *Gould v. Harris,* 929 F. Supp. 353, 359 (C.D. Cal. 1996) (rejecting tracing under § 12(a)(2) and stating that "*Gustafson* eliminated all claims other than those based upon purchases in the initial offering"), with *Brosious v. Children's Place Retail Stores,* 189 F.R.D. 138, 142–143 (D.N.J 1999) (holding that § 12(a)(2) applicable to "redistribution" in aftermarket of public offering that takes on characteristics of a new public offering).[40]

Today, in view of *Gustafson,* plaintiffs' claims that arise from private offerings ordinarily are brought in state, rather than federal, court.

[C] The Reasonable Care Defense

Under § 12(a)(2), the defendant can avoid liability by showing that he/she did not know, and in the exercise of reasonable care could not have known, of the material misstatement or omission. Whether this standard imposes § 11-type due diligence obligations has been met with mixed reaction.

In defining the meaning of *reasonable care* under § 12(a)(2), it is important to distinguish the responsibilities of a so-called traditional underwriter from those of a "mere" seller. For example, to require a seller in a Rule 504 offering for $700,000 to comply with § 11 due diligence would arguably impose too harsh a standard. Moreover, in many such offerings, the subject person may neither have the bargaining

---

40. For further analysis, *see* Bainbridge, *Securities Act Section 12(2) After the Gustafson Debacle,* 50 Bus. Law. 1231 (1995); Fiflis, *Gustafson v. Alloyd Co., Inc.: Judicial vs. Legislative Power,* 23 Sec. Reg. L.J. 423 (1996); Kerr, *Ralson Redux: Determining Which Section 3 Offerings Are Public Under Section 12(2) After Gustafson,* 50 SMU L. Rev. 175 (1996); Maynard, *The Impact of Gustafson and Its Methodology,* 24 Sec. Reg. L.J. 61 (1996); Sale, *Disappearing Without a Trace: Sections 11 and 12(a)(2) of the 1933 Securities Act,* 75 Wash. L. Rev. 429 (2000); Thel, *Section 12(2) of the Securities Act: Does Old Legislation Matter?,* 63 Fordham L. Rev. 1183 (1995); Weiss, *Securities Act Section 12(2) After Gustafson v. Alloyd Co.: What Questions Remain?,* 50 Bus. Law. 1209 (1995).

position to carry out a § 11-type due diligence investigation nor be intimately involved in the preparation of the offering materials.

On the other hand, where an unregistered offering has many of the characteristics frequently associated with an offering that must be registered (and hence triggers § 12(a)(2) application even after *Gustafson*), the "reasonable investigation" standard of § 11 and the "reasonable care" standard of § 12(2) are "similar, if not identical." *In re Software Toolworks Inc.,* 50 F.3d 615, 621 (9th Cir. 1994).

In analyzing the "reasonable care" defense, the Sixth Circuit opined:

> We believe that the following considerations are pertinent to an analysis of whether a § 12(2) seller has established this affirmative defense [of reasonable care]: (1) the quantum of decisional (planning) and facilitative (promotional) participation, such as designing the deal and contacting and attempting to persuade potential purchasers, (2) access to source data against which the truth or falsity of representations can be tested, (3) relative skill in ferreting out the truth (for example, in this case [the seller's] manager had comparatively greater skill in evaluating judgments based on subsidiary facts, since he performed a similar function in the process of investigating the creditworthiness of borrowers), (4) pecuniary interest in the completion of the transaction, and (5) the existence of a relationship of trust and confidence between the plaintiff and the alleged "seller." These are the circumstances that determine whether a person has exercised due care in this context.

Davis v. Avco Financial Services, Inc., 739 F.2d 1057, 1068 (6th Cir. 1984). *See Ambrosino v. Rodman & Renshaw, Inc.,* 972 F.2d 776 (7th Cir. 1992) (although not conclusive, court found relevant that the defendant's "exercise of due diligence had been higher than the custom and practice of the industry at that time"); *Dennis v. General Imaging, Inc.,* 918 F.2d 496, 505 (5th Cir. 1990) (citations omitted) ("While the exact requirements of this duty depend on the nature of the relationship of the seller at issue to his buyer, federal courts agree that a showing by the seller that he made reasonable inquiries into the possibility of fraud of the issuer and discovered nothing wrong or that no fraud could be discovered by the exercise of reasonable care, warrants a denial of liability."); *Sanders v. John Nuveen & Co.,* 619 F.2d 1222, 1228 (7th Cir. 1980), *cert. denied,* 450 U.S. 1005 (1981) ("Since what constitutes reasonable care under § 12(2) depends upon the circumstances, we . . . do not intimate that the duty of a seller under § 12(2) is always the same as that of an underwriter in a registration offering under § 11(a)"); Securities Act Release No. 8591 (2005) (setting forth the SEC's position "that the standard of care under Section 12(a)(2) is less demanding than that prescribed by Section 11, or put another way, that Section 11 requires a more diligent investigation than Section 12(a)(2)").

[D] Indemnification and Contribution

As a general statement, it appears that the vast majority of recent decisions have refused to imply a right of action for either contribution or indemnification under § 12(a)(2) of the Securities Act. These decisions, for example, include: *Baker, Watts & Company v. Miles & Stockbridge*, 876 F.2d 1101 (4th Cir. 1989); *In re Professional Financial Management*, 683 F. Supp. 1283 (D. Minn. 1988); *In re Olympia Brewing Company Securities Litigation*, 674 F. Supp. 597 (N.D. Ill. 1987).

The Supreme Court thus far has not resolved this issue. The leading federal appellate court decision is *Baker Watts & Co. v. Miles & Stockbridge*, 876 F.2d 1101, 1105–06 (4th Cir. 1989). There, the court reasoned:

> There is an express private right of action under § 12(2) on the part of one who purchases a security pursuant to a misleading prospectus. . . . Plaintiff contends that this provision creates further rights to contribution and indemnification on the part of a securities wrongdoer. We disagree.
>
> First, the statute itself does not create such remedies. Indeed, the statute's protection extends to investors who purchase securities based on misleading statements of material fact; it is not solicitous of unsuccessful defendants in a federal securities action. Plaintiff is therefore not "'one of the class for whose *especial* benefit'" § 12(2) was enacted. . . . We thus hesitate to imply any private remedy in plaintiff's favor based on this provision.
>
> Second, the 1933 Act's legislative history and the structure of the federal securities laws do not suggest the recognition of implied rights of contribution and indemnification. There is no indication in the 1933 Act's legislative history, for example, of any congressional intent to create these remedies in § 12(2). This fact, combined with the plain language of the statute, "reinforces our decision not to find such . . . right[s] of action implicit within the section." . . . Moreover, § 11(f) of the 1933 Act and §§ 9(e) and 18(b) of the Securities Exchange Act of 1934 expressly provide rights to contribution in specific circumstances. Congress knows how to define such a right of action in the federal securities laws, and we infer a lack of congressional intent to do so when the particular provision at issue is silent as to the existence of such a remedy. . . .
>
> Third, the underlying purpose of the 1933 Act is "regulatory rather than compensatory." . . . Negligence in the preparation of a securities prospectus was made actionable under § 12(2) of the 1933 Act in order to promote careful adherence to the requirements of the statute. . . . In particular, a right of action for indemnification would frustrate the statute's goal of encouraging diligence and discouraging negligence in securities

transactions. An unsuccessful defendant in a federal securities action therefore cannot "escape loss by shifting his entire responsibility to another party." . . .

It is unclear whether a federal right of action for contribution would promote the general purposes of the federal securities laws. Although some courts have stated that such a remedy may further the deterrent purposes of the 1933 and 1934 Acts, much the same regulatory purpose can be ascribed to the antitrust laws under which no implied private right of action for contribution is recognized. . . . An even greater deterrent effect may exist if a single securities wrongdoer such as Baker, Watts is held liable for the total adverse judgment. *See* . . . Loewenstein, *Implied Contribution Under the Federal Securities Laws: A Reassessment,* 1982 Duke L.J. 543, 556–58. . . . Regardless of whether an implied right to contribution would advance or impair the purposes of the federal securities laws, such policy considerations cannot overcome the intent of Congress. . . . When neither the statute nor its legislative history "reveals a congressional intent to create a private right of action for the benefit of the plaintiff, we need not carry the . . . inquiry further." . . .

In sum, we agree with the district court that Congress clearly did not provide private rights of action for contribution or indemnification in § 12(2). . . .

[E] Affirmative Defense of Section 12(b)

The Private Securities Litigation Reform Act of 1995 (PSLRA) amended § 12 of the Securities Act by adding a new subsection (§ 12(b)). Section 12(b) provides that in actions brought under § 12(a)(2) a defendant may avoid all or part of the damages that otherwise would be incurred by proving that all or part of the depreciation in the value of the securities in question resulted from factors unrelated to the material misstatement(s) or half-truth(s) that were contained in the prospectus or related oral communications.

---

§ 7.08 Section 4A(c) — The "Crowdfunding" Remedy

As addressed in Chapter 3, pursuant to the JOBS Act of 2012, Congress enacted an exemption from Securities Act registration for "crowdfunding" offerings, provided that the conditions of the exemption are met (see §§ 4(6), 4A of the Securities Act). In § 4A(c), an express private remedy is afforded to purchasers of securities acquired in a crowdfunding exempt offering.

The liability framework of § 4A(c) is patterned after § 12(a)(2). The statute generally provides the right to rescission (if the purchaser still owns the securities) or damages (if he/she no longer does) against the issuer based on a materially false or misleading statement in any written or oral communication made by such issuer in an exempt crowdfunding offering. The term "issuer" for purposes of § 4A(c) is broadly defined to encompass such issuer's directors, partners, officers, principal executive officers, principal financial officer, and controller. Like § 12(a)(2), a defendant may avoid liability if he/she affirmatively proves that he/she did not know, and by the exercise of reasonable care could not have known, of the materially false or misleading statement(s). Moreover, like § 12(a)(2), a purchaser who knows of such untruth or omission is not entitled to recover under the statute. Finally, actions brought pursuant to § 4A(c) are subject to the negative causation defense set forth in § 12(b) (which places the loss causation onus on the defendant) and the statute of limitations contained in § 13 (namely, suit must be brought within one year after discovery of the disclosure deficiency but in no event more than three years after the sale of such security).

The language that Congress used in § 4A(c) is far from a model of clarity. Perhaps the most significant ambiguities are: (1) whether such persons as directors, partners, and officers must themselves make the misrepresentation to be subject to liability under the statute or can such persons be held liable for misstatements that are made by the issuer-enterprise itself; and (2) in order to be deemed an "issuer" under the statute do directors, partners, and officers themselves have to offer or sell the subject securities in an exempt crowdfunding offering. The answers to the foregoing are uncertain. As Professor Bradford astutely points out:

> [S]ection 4A(c) could be read to make the non-issuer issuers liable for statements *made by the issuer,* even if they did not personally make any statements. The argument is that "issuer" consists of all the listed people collectively and whenever the collective "issuer" consists of all the listed people collectively and whenever the collective "issuer" makes a false statement everyone in that collective "issuer" is liable. This interpretation would explain how directors, partners, and officers could be liable as issuers, even if they did not offer or sell any securities.[41]

Undoubtedly, a good amount of time will elapse before the answers to the foregoing inquiries are definitively resolved. Until then, provided that the crowdfunding offering exemption is used with frequency, there may be much litigation wherein plaintiffs will advocate a broad construction of the statute while defendants will seek a narrow interpretation.

---

41. Bradford, *The New Federal Crowdfunding Exemption: Promise Unfulfilled,* 40 Sec. Reg. L. J. 195, 212 (2012) (emphasis in original).

§ 7.09 Availability of State Securities Law Remedies

The state blue sky statutes provide an alternative remedial framework for registration violations and for materially false and misleading statements contained in an offering document. Moreover, absent preemption pursuant to the Securities Litigation Uniform Standards Act (see § 9.08), state law claims may be brought with 1933 Act claims in state court with no right of removal to federal court. See § 22(a) of the Securities Act.

In certain situations, the state blue sky laws may be more favorable to plaintiffs. For example, many states have longer statutes of limitations than that contained in § 13 of the Securities Act. Generally, § 13's statute of limitations is one year after the alleged violation for § 12(a)(1) claims and one year after discovery and in no event more than three years after the sale for § 11 and § 12(a)(2) claims. On the other hand, a number of states provide a statute of limitations of three years for registration violations and up to five years for misstatements.

Another example is the definition of "seller" under the state securities laws. A number of state courts have followed the Supreme Court's decision in *Pinter* for defining the term "seller" under the applicable state securities statute. *See, e.g., Allen v. Columbia Financial Management*, 377 S.E. 2d 352 (S.C. App. 1988).

Nonetheless, some states have rejected *Pinter* and have adopted a different definition of "seller." A few states apply a stricter standard, requiring that the person actually pass title to the security to be a seller. See *Rolex Employees Retirement Trust v. Mentor Graphics Corp.*, [1991 Transfer Binder] Fed. Sec. L. Rep. (CCH) ¶ 96,053 (D. Or. 1991) (interpreting Oregon law). On the other hand, some states adhere to the more expansive "substantial factor" test, the standard that was used by the lower federal courts prior to *Pinter*. Under this test, one is deemed a "seller" if his/her acts were a substantial contributive factor in the occurrence of the transaction. The liability net certainly extends farther under this broad definition of "seller." *See FutureSelect Portfolio Management, Inc. v. Tremont Group Holdings, Inc.*, 331 P.3d 29, 38 (Wash. 2014) (defining a "seller" as any person whose acts were a "substantial contributive factor" with respect to the sales transaction).

Significantly, departing from *Gustafson*, a number of states have construed the applicable state securities statute to extend to all types of initial offerings as well as the secondary trading markets. See *Anheuser-Busch Companies, Inc. v. Summit Coffee*, 934 S.W.2d 705 (Tex. App. 1996). Moreover, some states extend liability not only to those who make the sale but also to those who aid the seller in consummating the transaction. *See, e.g., Perkowski v. Megas Corporation*, 55 Ohio App. 3d 234, 536 N.E.2d 378 (1990).

See generally J. Long, M. Kaufman, and J. Wunderlich, Blue Sky Law § 7.07 (2016); Branson, *Collateral Participant Liability Under State Securities Laws*, 19 Pepp. L. Rev. 1027 (1992); Johnson, *Secondary Liability for Securities Fraud: Gatekeepers in State Court*, 36 Del. J. Corp. L. 463 (2011); Steinberg, *The Emergence of State Securities Laws: Partly Sunny Skies for Investors*, 62 U. Cin. L. Rev. 395 (1993).

Appendix

Due Diligence Checklist (Public Offering)

		PROVIDED	NONE	NOT APPLICABLE (SET FORTH REASON)
1.	Articles of Incorporation for the Company and its subsidiaries, as amended	_____	____	_____
2.	Bylaws of the Company and its subsidiaries, as amended	_____	____	_____
3.	Minutes of all Board of Directors and Committee Meetings for the Company and its subsidiaries	_____	____	_____
4.	Minutes of all Stockholders' Meetings for the Company and its subsidiaries	_____	____	_____
5.	Copies of reports, proxy statements, registration statements and similar documents filed with the Securities and Exchange Commission and state securities commissions, together with related correspondence	_____	____	_____
6.	Registration rights agreements with respect to any shares of capital stock or warrants to purchase such shares	_____	____	_____
7.	All other agreements relating to securities of the Company or any of its subsidiaries, including agreements and investment agreements, stock transfer restriction agreements, voting trusts, or any other such agreements	_____	____	_____
8.	Any agreements with regulatory authorities, including any state securities commissions or commissioners, regarding issuance of shares of capital stock of the Company	_____	____	_____
9.	Any statements of the Board of Directors designating preferences, rights, etc., of any class or series of preferred stock	_____	____	_____

		PROVIDED	NONE	NOT APPLICABLE (SET FORTH REASON)
10.	Schedule of all entities in which the Company owns any outstanding voting securities	_____	_____	_____
11.	List of all offices of the Company and its subsidiaries where the Company and its subsidiaries carry on a material amount of business	_____	_____	_____
12.	List of all offices of the Company and its subsidiaries and the states or other jurisdictions where the Company and its subsidiaries carry on a material amount of business	_____	_____	_____
13.	List and brief description of all material domestic and foreign governmental permits, licenses and approvals held by the Company and its subsidiaries, including those issued by customs authorities	_____	_____	_____
14.	Any employee benefit plans or agreements, stock bonus, profit sharing, stock option, stock purchase, savings or retirement plans or agreements, and all collective bargaining, labor, employment or consulting contracts to which the Company or any of its subsidiaries is a party other than those otherwise called for herein	_____	_____	_____
15.	Employment Agreements between the company and key employees, together with amendments thereto	_____	_____	_____
16.	Any partnership or joint venture agreements to which the Company or any of its subsidiaries is a party	_____	_____	_____
17.	All debentures, notes, loans, lines of credit or revolving credit agreements, both secured and unsecured, mortgages, deeds of trust, security agreements, and other documents relating to indebtedness of the Company not otherwise called for herein	_____	_____	_____
18.	All guarantees by the Company or any of its subsidiaries of the indebtedness of others	_____	_____	_____

		PROVIDED	NONE	NOT APPLICABLE (SET FORTH REASON)
19.	A brief description of the Company's insurance programs and policies (including keyman life insurance), together with any legal documents pertaining thereto and a list of claims against such insurance program currently pending	_____	_____	_____
20.	Form of any standard contracts used with the Company employees	_____	_____	_____
21.	Schedule of all loans and advances outstanding (other than routine travel and business expense advances) by the Company or any subsidiary to any officer or director, or control person of the Company or any subsidiaries	_____	_____	_____
22.	Schedule of all loans and advances outstanding by any officer, director, or control person to the company or any subsidiaries	_____	_____	_____
23.	All leases, options to lease or purchase or purchase contracts relating to real property	_____	_____	_____
24.	All material contracts, agreements, notes, or leases not otherwise called for herein to which the Company, its subsidiaries or any of their respective businesses, including any tax sharing agreements with any party	_____	_____	_____
25.	List of major vendors/suppliers	_____	_____	_____
26.	A schedule of all pending or threatened legal, administrative, arbitrative or other proceedings or governmental investigations pending or threatened against the Company or any other party which might result in (a) damages payable by the Company, (b) a permanent injunction against the Company or any of its subsidiaries, (c) a material deterioration of the business prospects of the Company and its subsidiaries, taken as a whole, or (d) a change in zoning or building ordinances materially affecting the property or leasehold interests of the Company:			

	PROVIDED	NONE	NOT APPLICABLE (SET FORTH REASON)
(i) parties;	_____	_____	_____
(ii) nature of the proceedings;	_____	_____	_____
(iii) date commenced; and	_____	_____	_____
(iv) amount of damages or other relief sought	_____	_____	_____
27. Reports of independent certified public accountants relating to management and accounting procedures of the Company ("management letters")	_____	_____	_____
28. Attorneys' responses to auditor's letters of inquiry relating to the Company	_____	_____	_____
29. All news or press releases of the company for the past year	_____	_____	_____
30. A schedule describing any ongoing tax disputes, and copies of revenue agents' reports and correspondence respecting federal or state tax proceedings involving open years or items	_____	_____	_____
31. Copies of any speeches delivered by any officer or director of the Company to securities or financial organizations	_____	_____	_____
32. Copies of any articles published in any financial periodical or newsletter concerning the Company	_____	_____	_____
33. List and brief description of all trademarks, trade names, copyrights, patents and other similar proprietary rights owned by, or used in the business of, the Company or any of its subsidiaries and all registrations relating thereto	_____	_____	_____
34. Agreements, letters of intent and other documents relating to any pending sales or dispositions of any material portions of the Company's assets	_____	_____	_____

Chapter 8

Section 10(b) and Related Issues

§ 8.01 Overview

This chapter explores developments under § 10(b) of the Securities Exchange Act and Rule 10b-5 promulgated thereunder by the SEC (as well as certain related issues). Generally, the antifraud provisions of the securities acts were designed to protect investors, to help ensure fair dealing in the securities markets, and to promote ethical business practices. Consistent with these objectives, § 10(b) makes it unlawful to employ any deceptive or manipulative device "in connection with the purchase or sale of any security." As enacted by Congress, § 10(b) was designed to be a "catch-all" provision and, as such, it reaches a broad range of practices in connection with the purchase or sale of any security, irrespective of whether such security is publicly traded.

The language of § 10(b) does not create an express private remedy for its violation. Neither does the legislative history reveal that Congress intended to create a private right of action under the statute at the time of its passage. Nonetheless, the federal courts have routinely recognized the existence of a private remedy under § 10(b). As the Supreme Court has recognized, "[t]he existence of this implied remedy is simply beyond peradventure."[1]

In order to establish a successful claim under § 10(b), a plaintiff must prove certain elements. Many of these elements are explored in depth in this chapter.

Due to the Supreme Court's decision in *Central Bank of Denver v. First Interstate Bank of Denver*, 511 U.S. 164 (1994), liability under § 10(b) may be imposed in private actions only against primary violators. In *Central Bank of Denver*, the Court held that § 10(b) liability may not be ordered against aiders and abettors in private actions. The SEC, however, may bring enforcement actions against aiders and abettors for alleged violations of § 10(b). See Chapters 10, 15.

Key elements underlying a § 10(b) claim include (by proof of the preponderance of the evidence):

(1) *Requisite Jurisdictional Means*—Establishing the requisite jurisdictional means. This requirement is normally met without difficulty. For example,

---

1. *Herman & MacLean v. Huddleston,* 459 U.S. 375, 380 (1983).

the Tenth Circuit in *Loveridge v. Dreagoux*, 678 F.2d 870, 874 (10th Cir. 1982), held that "proof of intrastate telephonic messages in connection with the employment of deceptive devices or contrivances is sufficient to confer jurisdiction in a § 10(b) and Rule 10b-5 action."

In *Merrill Lynch, Pierce, Fenner & Smith, Inc. v. Manning*, 136 S. Ct. 1562 (2016), the Supreme Court ruled that § 27 of the Securities Exchange Act, which provides federal district courts with exclusive jurisdiction "of all suits in equity and actions at law brought to enforce any liability or duty created by [this Act] or the rules or regulations thereunder," is the same standard as that applied to ascertain if a case "arises under" federal law pursuant to 28 U.S.C. § 1331. Accordingly, the Court held "that the jurisdictional test established by [§ 27] is the same as the one used to decide if a case 'arises under' a federal law [pursuant to 28 U.S.C. § 1331]."

(2) *Plaintiff as Purchaser or Seller*—The status of the plaintiff as a purchaser or seller of the securities. Note that the defendant need not be a purchaser or seller. See § 8.02.

(3) *Manipulative or Deceptive Practice*—Showing that the defendant as a primary participant bears responsibility for a material misrepresentation or nondisclosure or other deceptive or manipulative practice. "Mere" breach of fiduciary duty, standing alone, is insufficient to state a § 10(b) right of action. See § 8.04. Note moreover that where liability is based upon silence (rather than affirmative statement(s)), the plaintiff must prove that the alleged primary violator had a duty to disclose.

(4) *Materiality*—The misrepresentation, half-truth or omitted statement must be material (see § 8.06). The standard for materiality has been set forth by the Supreme Court in *TSC Industries, Inc. v. Northway*, 426 U.S. 438 (1976), in *Basic, Inc. v. Levinson*, 485 U.S. 224 (1988), and more recently in *Matrixx Initiatives, Inc. v. Siracusano*, 121 S. Ct. 1309 (2011):

An omitted fact is material if there is a substantial likelihood that a reasonable shareholder would consider it important in deciding how to vote [or in making an investment decision]. This standard ... does not require proof of a substantial likelihood that disclosure of the omitted fact would have caused the reasonable investor to change his vote [or investment decision]. What the standard does contemplate is a showing of a substantial likelihood that, under all the circumstances, the omitted fact would have assumed actual significance in the deliberations of the reasonable shareholder. Put another way, there must be a substantial likelihood that the disclosure of the omitted fact would have been viewed by the reasonable investor as having significantly altered the "total mix" of information made available.

The subject of materiality is examined at several points in this textbook.

(5) *Defendant's Scienter*—Establishing that the defendant acted with scienter, signifying knowing or intentional misconduct. See § 8.03.

(6) *Plaintiff's Reliance*—Where called for, showing that the plaintiff relied on the alleged misrepresentation and exercised due diligence. See § 8.05.

(7) *Loss Causation*—Establishing causation between the defendant's wrongful conduct and the plaintiff's loss. See § 21D(b)(4) of the Exchange Act; § 8.05.

(8) *"In Connection With"*—Related to the causation requirement, the plaintiff must prove that the manipulative or deceptive practice was "in connection with" the purchase or sale of a security. Generally, in order to meet this requirement, the proscribed practice must touch upon and be integral to the purchase or sale of the security. See *SEC v. Zandford*, 535 U.S. 813 (2002); *Superintendent of Life Insurance v. Bankers Life and Casualty Co.*, 404 U.S. 6 (1971); § 8.05.

(9) *Damages*—Proving the extent of damages suffered. See M. Kaufman, Securities Litigation: Damages (1989 & Supp.); § 8.08.

(10) *Statute of Limitations*—The plaintiff must bring its action within two years after the violation was, or should have been, discovered by the plaintiff and in no event more than five years after the violation. See 28 U.S.C. § 1658(b) (enacted as part of the Sarbanes-Oxley Act of 2002); § 8.09[B].

Note, moreover, that the plaintiff also *must plead fraud with particularity* in its § 10(b) cause of action. Rule 9(b) of the Federal Rules of Civil Procedure provides: "In all averments of fraud or mistake, the circumstances constituting fraud or mistake shall be stated with particularity. Malice, intent, knowledge, and other condition of mind of a person may be averred generally." As applied in the § 10(b) securities law context, § 21D(b) of the Exchange Act generally requires that a plaintiff must specifically plead each alleged misrepresentation or nondisclosure and why such is misleading, and must allege specific facts as to each such disclosure deficiency supporting a "strong inference" that the subject defendant knew that the misstatement or omission was false. For further discussion, see § 8.09[A].

Also, only primary violators are liable in private actions under § 10(b). In *Central Bank of Denver v. First Interstate Bank of Denver*, 511 U.S. 164 (1994), the Supreme Court held that *in private actions § 10(b) liability may not be imposed against aiders and abettors*. The subject of distinguishing between primary and secondary liability is addressed in Chapter 10. In any event, however, the SEC may institute enforcement actions against aiders and abettors for alleged violations of § 10(b).

The defendant may assert a number of *defenses*, including *in pari delicto, laches,* and *waiver*. See *Hecht v. Harris, Upham & Co.*, 430 F.2d 1202 (9th Cir. 1970). The equitable defense of *in pari delicto* is addressed in § 7.06[A] and § 8.09[C].

With respect to a subject defendant's claim for *indemnification*, because the Supreme Court has ruled that scienter (e.g., deliberate or perhaps reckless misconduct) is required to state a successful § 10(b) (and Rule 10b-5) claim under the Exchange Act, it appears that indemnification would frustrate the public policy as well as the statutory underpinnings of the Act and therefore is prohibited in the § 10(b) context.

The right to *contribution* under § 10(b) likewise has been resolved. In the *Musick, Peeler* decision, the Supreme Court recognized such a right to contribution under § 10(b). See 508 U.S. 286 (1993). Subsequently, the Private Securities Litigation Reform Act (PSLRA) codified this right to contribution. See § 8.10.

Problem

Kentach Labs, Inc., a high-tech concern with a brief operating history, had its first, and thus far only, public offering in October 2016, raising $225 million. The registration statement filed with the SEC contained, as is required, a "use of proceeds" section. Unknown to the accountants, counsel, and investment bankers, Kentach's "inside" directors (Stevens, Lyle, and Morris) anticipated that roughly 35 percent of the proceeds would be used to pay off prior debts rather than 90 percent of the proceeds going toward expansion of the business as the registration statement indicated.

Kentach assumed public reporting obligations upon its conducting of the registered offering and having its stock listed on the Nasdaq stock market. Since the 2016 public offering, Kentach has timely filed annual and other periodic reports. The company, however, from 2016 to May 2017, never disclosed that 35 percent of the proceeds received from the offering were used to pay off prior debts. In May 2017, it was revealed that Stevens, Lyle, and Morris had "fudged" or "cooked" Kentach's financial records in order to hide the true use of the proceeds of the 2016 offering.

Kentach is still in business and solvent. The price of its stock, however, has decreased from its initial offering price of $21.00 in October 2016, to a price of $7.25 per share in June 2017. In July 2017, after public revelation of the true use of the proceeds, the price of the stock quickly dropped during a two-week period to $4.60 per share.

Nuval, an electronic engineer by trade, is always interested in expanding her stock portfolio. Although she had never read or seen a Kentach disclosure or offering document, she was somewhat familiar with the company through her profession and had a hunch that the stock was undervalued. In March 2017, she called her broker, Mondal, and asked her whether she knew of any information about the company. Mondal replied that she did not "follow" the company. Upon checking the research reports on the company, Mondal conjectured that Kentach's relatively low market price may have been due to the market's recognition of a disappointing earnings history and that the company would never achieve the growth that financial analysts had forecast when the company went public. Nonetheless, Nuval in April 2017, without having read a Kentach disclosure or offering document, decided to purchase 3,000 shares at $9.50 per share. In August 2017, she brings suit under the federal securities laws (in a class action) against Kentach, Stevens, Lyle, Morris, the attorneys, and the accountants. The price of Kentach stock in August 2017 on the date the lawsuit is brought is $4.35 per share. What result?

---

§ 8.02 Standing: The Purchaser-Seller Requirement

Blue Chip Stamps v. Manor Drug Stores

United States Supreme Court

421 U.S. 723, 95 S. Ct. 1917, 44 L. Ed. 2d 539 (1975)

MR. JUSTICE REHNQUIST delivered the opinion of the Court.

This case requires us to consider whether the offerees of a stock offering, made pursuant to an antitrust consent decree, may maintain a private cause of action for money damages where they allege that the offeror has violated the provisions of Rule 10b-5 of the Securities and Exchange Commission, but where they have neither purchased nor sold any of the offered shares.

I

In 1963 the United States filed a civil antitrust action against Blue Chip Stamp Co. (Old Blue Chip), a company in the business of providing trading stamps to retailers, and nine retailers who owned 90% of its shares. In 1967 the action was terminated by the entry of a consent decree. The decree contemplated a plan of reorganization whereby Old Blue Chip was to be merged into a newly formed corporation, Blue Chip Stamps (New Blue Chip). The holdings of the majority shareholders of Old Blue Chip were to be reduced, and New Blue Chip, one of the petitioners here, was required under the plan to offer a substantial number of its shares of common stock to retailers who had used the stamp service in the past but who were not shareholders in the old company. Under the terms of the plan, the offering to nonshareholder users was to be proportional to past stamp usage and the shares were to be offered in units consisting of common stock and debentures.

The reorganization plan was carried out, the offering was registered with the SEC as required by the 1933 Act, and a prospectus was distributed to all offerees as required by § 5 of that Act. Somewhat more than 50% of the offered units were actually purchased. In 1970, two years after the offering, respondent, a former user of the stamp service and therefore an offeree of the 1968 offering, filed this suit in the United States District Court for the Central District of California. Defendants below . . . are Old and New Blue Chip, eight of the nine majority shareholders of Old Blue Chip, and the directors of New Blue Chip (collectively called Blue Chip).

Respondent's complaint alleged, inter alia, that the prospectus prepared and distributed by Blue Chip in connection with the offering was materially misleading in its overly pessimistic appraisal of Blue Chip's status and future prospects. It alleged that Blue Chip intentionally made the prospectus overly pessimistic in order to discourage respondent and other members of the allegedly large class whom it represents from accepting what was intended to be a bargain offer, so that the rejected shares might later be offered to the public at a higher price. The complaint alleged that class members because of and in reliance on the false and misleading prospectus failed to purchase the offered units. Respondent therefore sought on behalf of the alleged class some $21,400,000 in damages representing the lost opportunity to purchase the units; the right to purchase the previously rejected units at the 1968 price; and in addition, it sought some $25,000,000 in exemplary damages.

The only portion of the litigation thus initiated which is before us is whether respondent may base its action on Rule 10b-5 of the Securities and Exchange Commission without having either bought or sold the securities described in the allegedly misleading prospectus. . . .

II

During the early days of the New Deal, Congress enacted two landmark statutes regulating securities. The 1933 Act was described as an Act to "provide full and fair disclosure of the character of securities sold in interstate and foreign commerce and through the mails, and to prevent frauds in the sale thereof, and for other purposes." The Securities Exchange Act of 1934 (1934 Act) was described as an Act "to provide for the regulation of securities exchanges and of over-the-counter markets operating in interstate and foreign commerce and through the mails, to prevent inequitable and unfair practices on such exchanges and markets, and for other purposes." . . .

The various sections of the 1933 Act dealt at some length with the required contents of registration statements and prospectuses, and expressly provided for private civil causes of action. Section 11(a) gave a right of action by reason of a false registration statement to "any person acquiring" the security, and § 12 of that Act gave a right to sue the seller of a security who had engaged in proscribed practices with respect to prospectuses and communications to "the person purchasing such security from him."

The 1934 Act was divided into two titles. Title I was denominated "Regulation of Securities Exchanges," and Title II was denominated "Amendments to Securities Act of 1933." Section 10 of that Act makes it "unlawful for any person . . . (b) [t]o use or employ, in connection with the purchase or sale of any security registered on a national securities exchange or any security not so registered, any manipulative or deceptive device or contrivance in contravention of such rules and regulations as the Commission may prescribe as necessary or appropriate in the public interest or for the protection of investors." . . .

In 1942, acting under the authority granted to it by § 10(b) of the 1934 Act, the Commission promulgated Rule 10b-5, now providing as follows:

Employment of manipulative and deceptive devices.

It shall be unlawful for any person, directly or indirectly, by the use of any means or instrumentality of interstate commerce, or of the mails or of any facility of any national securities exchange,

(a) To employ any device, scheme, or artifice to defraud,

(b) To make any untrue statement of a material fact or to omit to state a material fact necessary in order to make the statements made, in the light of the circumstances under which they were made, not misleading, or

(c) To engage in any act, practice, or course of business which operates or would operate as a fraud or deceit upon any person, in connection with the purchase or sale of any security.

Section 10(b) of the 1934 Act does not by its terms provide an express civil remedy for its violation. Nor does the history of this provision provide any indication that Congress considered the problem of private suits under it at the time of its passage. . . . Similarly there is no indication that the Commission in adopting Rule 10b-5 considered the question of private civil remedies under this provision. . . .

Despite the contrast between the provisions of Rule 10b-5 and the numerous carefully drawn express civil remedies provided in the Acts of both 1933 and 1934, it was held in 1946 by the United States District Court for the Eastern District of Pennsylvania that there was an implied private right of action under the Rule. *Kardon v. National Gypsum Co.*, 69 F. Supp. 512. This Court had no occasion to deal with the subject until 25 years later, and at that time we confirmed with virtually no discussion the overwhelming consensus of the District Courts and Courts of Appeals that such a cause of action did exist. *Superintendent of Insurance v. Bankers Life & Cas. Co.*, 404 U.S. 6, 13 n. 9 (1971); *Affiliated Ute Citizens v. United States*, 406 U.S. 128, 150–154 (1972). . . .

Within a few years after the seminal *Kardon* decision, the Court of Appeals for the Second Circuit concluded that *the plaintiff class for purposes of a private damage action under § 10(b) and Rule 10b-5 was limited to actual purchasers and sellers of securities. Birnbaum v. Newport Steel Corp.*, [193 F.2d 461 (2d Cir. 1952)]. [emphasis supplied]

. . . For the reasons hereinafter stated, we are of the opinion that *Birnbaum* was rightly decided, and that it bars respondent from maintaining this suit under Rule 10b-5.

III

The panel which decided *Birnbaum* consisted of Chief Judge Swan and Judges Learned Hand and Augustus Hand; the opinion was written by the last named. Since both § 10(b) and Rule 10b-5 proscribed only fraud "in connection with the purchase or sale" of securities, and since the history of § 10(b) revealed no congressional intention to extend a private civil remedy for money damages to other than defrauded purchasers or sellers of securities, in contrast to the express civil remedy provided [for insider short-swing trading] by § 16(b) of the 1934 Act, the court concluded that the plaintiff class in a Rule 10b-5 action was limited to actual purchasers and sellers. . . .

Just as this Court had no occasion to consider the validity of the *Kardon* holding that there was a private cause of action under Rule 10b-5 until 20-odd years later, nearly the same period of time has gone by between the *Birnbaum* decision and our consideration of the case now before us. As with *Kardon*, virtually all lower federal courts facing the issue in the hundreds of reported cases presenting this question over the past quarter century have reaffirmed *Birnbaum's* conclusion that the plaintiff class for purposes of § 10(b) and Rule 10b-5 private damage actions is limited to purchasers and sellers of securities.

In 1957 and again in 1959, the Securities and Exchange Commission sought from Congress amendment of § 10(b) to change its wording from "in connection with the purchase or sale of any security" to "in connection with the purchase or sale of, *or any attempt to purchase or sell*, any security." 103 Cong. Rec. 11636 (1957) (emphasis added). . . . In the words of a memorandum submitted by the Commission to a congressional committee, the purpose of the proposed change was "to make section 10(b) also applicable to manipulative activities in connection with any attempt to purchase or sell any security." . . . Opposition to the amendment was based on fears of the extension of civil liability under § 10(b) that it would cause. Neither change was adopted by Congress.

The longstanding acceptance by the courts, coupled with Congress' failure to reject *Birnbaum's* reasonable interpretation of the wording of § 10(b), wording which is directed toward injury suffered "in connection with the purchase or sale" of securities, argues significantly in favor of acceptance of the *Birnbaum* rule by this Court.

Available evidence from the texts of the 1933 and 1934 Acts as to the congressional scheme in this regard, though not conclusive, supports the result reached by the *Birnbaum* court. . . . When Congress wished to provide a remedy to those who neither purchase nor sell securities, it had little trouble in doing so expressly. Cf. § 16(b) of the 1934 Act, 15 U.S.C. § 78p(b).

Section 28(a) of the 1934 Act . . . which limits recovery in any private damages action brought under the 1934 Act to "actual damages," likewise provides some support for the purchaser-seller rule. While the damages suffered by purchasers and sellers pursuing a § 10(b) cause of action may on occasion be difficult to ascertain, in the main such purchasers and sellers at least seek to base recovery on a demonstrable number of shares traded. In contrast, a putative plaintiff, who neither purchases nor sells securities but sues instead for intangible economic injury such as loss of a noncontractual opportunity to buy or sell, is more likely to be seeking a largely conjectural and speculative recovery in which the number of shares involved will depend on the plaintiff's subjective hypothesis.

One of the justifications advanced for implication of a cause of action under § 10(b) lies in § 29(b) of the 1934 Act, providing that a contract made in violation of any provision of the 1934 Act is voidable at the option of the deceived party. But that justification is absent when there is no actual purchase or sale of securities, or a contract to purchase or sell, affected or tainted by a violation of § 10(b).

The principal express nonderivative private civil remedies, created by Congress contemporaneously with the passage of § 10(b), for violations of various provisions of the 1933 and 1934 Acts are by their terms expressly limited to purchasers or sellers of securities. Thus § 11(a) of the 1933 Act confines the cause of action it grants to "any person acquiring such security" while the remedy granted by § 12 of that Act is limited to the "person purchasing such security." Section 9 of the 1934 Act, prohibiting a variety of fraudulent and manipulative devices, limits the express civil remedy provided for its violation to "any person who shall purchase or sell any security" in a transaction affected by a violation of the provision. Section 18 of the 1934 Act, prohibiting false or misleading statements in reports or other documents required to be filed by the 1934 Act, limits the express remedy provided for its violation to "any person ... who ... shall have purchased or sold a security at a price which was affected by such statement. . . ." It would indeed be anomalous to impute to Congress an intention to expand the plaintiff class for a judicially implied cause of action beyond the bounds it delineated for comparable express causes of action.

Having said all this, we would by no means be understood as suggesting that we are able to divine from the language of § 10(b) the express "intent of Congress" as to the contours of a private cause of action under Rule 10b-5. *When we deal with private actions under Rule 10b-5, we deal with a judicial oak which has grown from little more than a legislative acorn.* [emphasis supplied] Such growth may be quite consistent with the congressional enactment and with the role of the federal judiciary in interpreting it, but it would be disingenuous to suggest that either Congress in 1934 or the Securities and Exchange Commission in 1942 foreordained the present state of the law with respect to Rule 10b-5. It is therefore proper that we consider, in addition to the factors already discussed, what may be described as policy considerations when we come to flesh out the portions of the law with respect to which neither the congressional enactment nor the administrative regulations offer conclusive guidance.

Three principal classes of potential plaintiffs are presently barred by the *Birnbaum* rule. First are potential purchasers of shares, either in a new offering or on the Nation's post-distribution trading markets, who allege that they decided not to purchase because of an unduly gloomy representation or the omission of favorable material which made the issuer appear to be a less favorable investment vehicle than it actually was. Second are actual shareholders in the issuer who allege that they decided not to sell their shares because of an unduly rosy representation or a failure to disclose unfavorable material. Third are shareholders, creditors, and perhaps others related to an issuer who suffered loss in the value of their investment due to corporate or insider activities in connection with the purchase or sale of securities which violate Rule 10b-5. It has been held that shareholder members of the second and third of these classes may frequently be able to circumvent the *Birnbaum* limitation through bringing a derivative action on behalf of the corporate issuer if the latter is itself a purchaser or seller of securities. But the first of these classes, of which respondent is a member, cannot claim the benefit of such a rule.

. . . . There has been widespread recognition that litigation under Rule 10b-5 presents a danger of vexatiousness different in degree and in kind from that which accompanies litigation in general. This fact was recognized by Judge Browning in his opinion for the majority of the Court of Appeals in this case, 492 F.2d, at 141, and by Judge Hufstedler in her dissenting opinion when she said:

> The purchaser-seller rule has maintained the balances built into the congressional scheme by permitting damage actions to be brought only by those persons whose active participation in the marketing transaction promises enforcement of the statute without undue risk of abuse of the litigation process and without distorting the securities market.

Judge Friendly in commenting on another aspect of Rule 10b-5 litigation has referred to the possibility that unduly expansive imposition of civil liability "will lead to large judgments, payable in the last analysis by innocent investors, for the benefit of speculators and their lawyers. . . ."

We believe that the concern expressed for the danger of vexatious litigation which could result from a widely expanded class of plaintiffs under Rule 10b-5 is founded in something more substantial than the common complaint of the many defendants who would prefer avoiding lawsuits entirely to either settling them or trying them. These concerns have two largely separate grounds. The first of these concerns is that in the field of federal securities laws governing disclosure of information even a complaint which by objective standards may have very little chance of success at trial has a settlement value to the plaintiff out of any proportion to its prospect of success at trial so long as he may prevent the suit from being resolved against him by dismissal or summary judgment. The very pendency of the lawsuit may frustrate or delay normal business activity of the defendant which is totally unrelated to the lawsuit. . . .

Congress itself recognized the potential for nuisance or "strike" suits in this type of litigation, and in Title II of the 1934 Act amended § 11 of the 1933 Act to provide that:

> In any suit under this or any other section of this title the court may, in its discretion, require an undertaking for the payment of the costs of such suit, including reasonable attorney's fees. . . .

Senator Fletcher, Chairman of the Senate Banking and Finance Committee, . . . stated in explaining the amendment to § 11(e): "This amendment is the most important of all." . . . Cong. Rec. 8669. Among its purposes was to provide "a defense against blackmail suits." . . .

Where Congress in those sections of the 1933 Act which expressly conferred a private cause of action for damages, adopted a provision uniformly regarded as designed to deter "strike" or nuisance actions, that fact alone justifies our consideration of such potential in determining the limits of the class of plaintiffs who may sue in an action wholly implied from the language of the 1934 Act.

The potential for possible abuse of the liberal discovery provisions of the Federal Rules of Civil Procedure may likewise exist in this type of case to a greater extent than they do in other litigation. The prospect of extensive deposition of the defendant's officers and associates and the concomitant opportunity for extensive discovery of business documents, is a common occurrence in this and similar types of litigation. To the extent that this process eventually produces relevant evidence which is useful in determining the merits of the claims asserted by the parties, it bears the imprimatur of those Rules and of the many cases liberally interpreting them. But to the extent that it permits a plaintiff with a largely groundless claim to simply take up the time of a number of other people, with the right to do so representing an in terrorem increment of the settlement value, rather than a reasonably founded hope that the process will reveal relevant evidence, it is a social cost rather than a benefit. Yet to broadly expand the class of plaintiffs who may sue under Rule 10b-5 would appear to encourage the least appealing aspect of the use of the discovery rules.

Without the *Birnbaum* rule, an action under Rule 10b-5 will turn largely on which oral version of a series of occurrences the jury may decide to credit, and therefore no matter how improbable the allegations of the plaintiff, the case will be virtually impossible to dispose of prior to trial other than by settlement. . . .

The *Birnbaum* rule, on the other hand, permits exclusion prior to trial of those plaintiffs who were not themselves purchasers or sellers of the stock in question. The fact of purchase of stock and the fact of sale of stock are generally matters which are verifiable by documentation, and do not depend upon oral recollection, so that failure to qualify under the *Birnbaum* rule is a matter that can normally be established by the defendant either on a motion to dismiss or on a motion for summary judgment.

Obviously there is no general legal principle that courts in fashioning substantive law should do so in a manner which makes it easier, rather than more difficult, for a defendant to obtain a summary judgment. But in this type of litigation, where the mere existence of an unresolved lawsuit has settlement value to the plaintiff not only because of the possibility that he may prevail on the merits, an entirely legitimate component of settlement value, but because of the threat of extensive discovery and disruption of normal business activities which may accompany a lawsuit which is groundless in any event, but cannot be proved so before trial, such a factor is not to be totally dismissed. The *Birnbaum* rule undoubtedly excludes plaintiffs who have in fact been damaged by violations of Rule 10b-5, and to that extent it is undesirable. But it also separates in a readily demonstrable manner the group of plaintiffs who actually purchased or actually sold, and whose version of the facts is therefore more likely to be believed by the trier of fact, from the vastly larger world of potential plaintiffs who might successfully allege a claim but could seldom succeed in proving it. And this fact is one of its advantages.

The second ground for fear of vexatious litigation is based on the concern that, given the generalized contours of liability, the abolition of the *Birnbaum* rule would throw open to the trier of fact many rather hazy issues of historical fact the proof of which depended almost entirely on oral testimony. We in no way disparage the worth and frequent high value of oral testimony when we say that dangers of its abuse appear to exist in this type of action to a peculiarly high degree.

. . . .

In today's universe of transactions governed by the 1934 Act, privity of dealing or even personal contact between potential defendant and potential plaintiff is the exception and not the rule. The stock of issuers is listed on financial exchanges utilized by tens of millions of investors, and corporate representations reach a potential audience, encompassing not only the diligent few who peruse filed corporate reports or the sizable number of subscribers to financial journals, but the readership of the Nation's daily newspapers. Obviously neither the fact that issuers or other potential defendants under Rule 10b-5 reach a large number of potential investors, or the fact that they are required by law to make their disclosures conform to certain standards, should in any way absolve them from liability for misconduct which is proscribed by Rule 10b-5.

But in the absence of the *Birnbaum* rule, it would be sufficient for a plaintiff to prove that he had failed to purchase or sell stock by reason of a defendant's violation of Rule 10b-5. The manner in which the defendant's violation caused the plaintiff to fail to act could be as a result of the reading of a prospectus, as respondent claims here, but it could just as easily come as a result of a claimed reading of information contained in the financial pages of a local newspaper. Plaintiff's proof would not be that he purchased or sold stock, a fact which would be capable of documentary verification in most situations, but instead that he decided not to purchase or sell stock. Plaintiff's entire testimony could be dependent upon uncorroborated oral evidence of many of the crucial elements of his claim, and still be sufficient to go to the jury. The jury would not even have the benefit of weighing the plaintiff's version against the defendant's version, since the elements to which the plaintiff would testify would be in many cases totally unknown and unknowable to the defendant. The very real risk in permitting those in respondent's position to sue under Rule 10b-5 is that the door will be open to recovery of substantial damages on the part of one who offers only his own testimony to prove that he ever consulted a prospectus of the issuer, that he paid any attention to it, or that the representations contained in it damaged him. The virtue of the *Birnbaum* rule, simply stated, in this situation, is that it limits the class of plaintiffs to those who have at least dealt in the security to which the prospectus, representation, or omission relates. And their dealing in the security, whether by way of purchase or sale, will generally be an objectively demonstrable fact in an area of the law otherwise very much dependent upon oral testimony. In the absence of the *Birnbaum* doctrine, bystanders to the securities marketing process could await developments on the sidelines without risk, claiming that inaccuracies in disclosure caused nonselling in a falling market and that unduly pessimistic predictions by the issuer followed by a rising market caused them to allow retrospectively golden opportunities to pass.

. . . .

We quite agree that if Congress had legislated the elements of a private cause of action for damages, the duty of the Judicial Branch would be to administer the law which Congress enacted; the Judiciary may not circumscribe a right which Congress has conferred because of any disagreement it might have with Congress about the wisdom of creating so expansive a liability. But as we have pointed out, we are not dealing here with any private right created by the express language of § 10(b) or of Rule 10b-5. No language in either of those provisions speaks at all to the contours of a private cause of action for their violation. However flexibly we may construe the language of both provisions, nothing in such construction militates against the *Birnbaum* rule. We are dealing with a private cause of action which has been judicially found to exist, and which will have to be judicially delimited one way or another unless and until Congress addresses the question. Given the peculiar blend of legislative, administrative, and judicial history which now surrounds Rule 10b-5, we believe that practical factors to which we have adverted, and to which other courts have referred, are entitled to a good deal of weight.

Thus we conclude that what may be called considerations of policy, which we are free to weigh in deciding this case, are by no means entirely on one side of the scale. Taken together with the precedential support for the *Birnbaum* rule over a period of more than 20 years, and the consistency of that rule with what we can glean from the intent of Congress, they lead us to conclude that it is a sound rule and should be followed.

[*Reversed.*]

MR. JUSTICE BLACKMUN, with whom MR. JUSTICE DOUGLAS and MR. JUSTICE BRENNAN join, dissenting.

Today the Court graves into stone *Birnbaum's* arbitrary principle of standing. For this task the Court, unfortunately, chooses to utilize three blunt chisels: (1) reliance on the legislative history of the 1933 and 1934 Securities Acts, conceded as inconclusive in this particular context; (2) acceptance as precedent of two decades of lower court decisions following a doctrine, never before examined here, that was pronounced by a justifiably esteemed panel of that Court of Appeals regarded as the "Mother Court" in this area of the law, but under entirely different circumstances; and (3) resort to utter pragmaticality and a conjectural assertion of "policy considerations" deemed to arise in distinguishing the meritorious Rule 10b-5 suit from the meretricious one. In so doing, the Court exhibits a preternatural solicitousness for corporate well-being and a seeming callousness toward the investing public quite out of keeping, it seems to me, with our own traditions and the intent of the securities laws.

The plaintiff's complaint—and that is all that is before us now—raises disturbing claims of fraud. . . .

From a reading of the complaint in relation to the language of § 10(b) of the 1934 Act and of Rule 10b-5, it is manifest that plaintiff has alleged the use of a deceptive scheme "in connection with the purchase or sale of any security." To my mind, the word "sale" ordinarily and naturally may be understood to mean, not only a single, individualized act transferring property from one party to another, but also the generalized event of public disposal of property through advertisement, auction, or some other market mechanism. Here, there is an obvious, indeed a court-ordered, "sale" of securities in the special offering of New Blue Chip shares and debentures to former users. Yet the Court denies this plaintiff the right to maintain a suit under Rule 10b-5 because it does not fit into the mechanistic categories of either "purchaser" or "seller." This, surely, is an anomaly, for the very purpose of the alleged scheme was to inhibit this plaintiff from ever acquiring the status of "purchaser." Faced with this abnormal divergence from the usual pattern of securities frauds, the Court pays no heed to the unremedied wrong . . . .

In adopting Rule 10b-5 in 1942, the Securities and Exchange Commission issued a press release stating: "The new rule closes a loophole in the protections against fraud administered by the Commission by prohibiting individuals or companies from buying securities if they engage in fraud in their purchase." SEC Release No. 3230 (May 21, 1942). To say specifically that certain types of fraud are within Rule 10b-5, of course, is not to say that others are necessarily excluded. That this is so is confirmed by the apparently casual origins of the Rule, as recalled by a former SEC staff attorney in remarks made at a conference on federal securities laws several years ago:

> It was one day in the year 1943, I believe. I was sitting in my office in the S.E.C. building in Philadelphia [where the SEC had its headquarters during World War II] and I received a call from Jim Treanor who was then the Director of the Trading and Exchange Division. He said, "I have just been on the telephone with Paul Rowen," who was then the S.E.C. Regional Administrator in Boston, "and he has told me about the president of some company in Boston who is going around buying up the stock of his company from his own shareholders at $4.00 a share, and he has been telling them that the company is doing very badly, whereas, in fact, the earnings are going to be quadrupled and will be $2.00 a share for this coming year. Is there anything we can do about it?" So he came upstairs and I called in my secretary and I looked at Section 10(b) and I looked at Section 17 [of the Securities Act of 1933], and I put them together, and the only discussion we had there was where "in connection with the purchase or sale" should be, and we decided it should be at the end.
>
> We called the Commission and we got on the calendar, and I don't remember whether we got there that morning or after lunch. We passed a piece of paper around to all the commissioners. All the commissioners read the rule

and they tossed it on the table, indicating approval. Nobody said anything except Sumner Pike who said, "Well," he said, "we are against fraud, aren't we?" That is how it happened.

Remarks of Milton Freeman, Conference on Codification of the Federal Securities Laws, 22 Bus. Law. 793, 922 (1967).

The question under both Rule 10b-5 and its parent statute, § 10(b), is whether fraud was employed — and the language is critical — by "any person . . . in connection with the purchase or sale of any security." On the allegations here, the nexus between the asserted fraud and the conducting of a "sale" is obvious and inescapable, and no more should be required to sustain the plaintiff's complaint against a motion to dismiss.

. . . .

Notes and Questions

(1) Do you agree with the majority or the dissent in the foregoing case? Why? Was the Court correct in addressing policy issues rather than adhering strictly to a statutory analysis, including consideration of any pertinent legislative history?

(2) It is important to emphasize that, in order to bring a § 10(b) private cause of action for damages, *only the plaintiff (not the defendant)* must be a "purchaser" or "seller."

(3) Applying the purchaser-seller requirement, the lower federal courts have recognized standing under § 10(b) in a variety of circumstances, including: in a shareholder derivative action brought on behalf of an allegedly defrauded corporation where the corporation was a purchaser or seller of its securities; in a "forced" sale transaction, such as a share exchange or "freeze-out" merger (see SEC Rule 145, § 6.07 *supra*); where the plaintiff has "pledged" the securities; and where the plaintiff has entered into a contract to buy or sell the securities. For further discussion, *see* T. Hazen, The Law of Securities Regulation 453–456 (6th ed. 2009); Chaffee, *Standing Under Section 10(b) and Rule 10b-5: The Continued Validity of the Forced Seller Exception to the Purchaser-Seller Requirement,* 11 U. Pa. J. Bus. L. 965 (2009).

(4) Should the *Blue Chip* purchaser-seller requirement apply where the plaintiff seeks solely injunctive relief? The lower courts are divided on this issue. *See Cowin v. Bresler,* 741 F.2d 410 (D.C. Cir. 1984), holding that the plaintiff must be a purchaser or seller when seeking injunctive relief in a § 10(b) action. The court reasoned that the *Blue Chip* standing requirement was necessary to deter strike suits and the rendering of hazy oral testimony. *Accord, Cartica Management, LLC v. CorpBanca, S.A.,* 50 F. Supp. 3d 477 (S.D.N.Y. 2014). Do you agree? Is the threat of vexatious litigation as severe in an action seeking solely injunctive relief? For a decision going the other way, see *Granada Investment, Inc. v. DWG Corp.,* 717 F. Supp. 533 (N.D. Ohio 1989) (and cases cited therein).

(5) Interestingly, Justice Blackmun's vigorous dissent in *Blue Chip* received coverage in *The Brethren*:

> Brennan thought that Blackmun was continuing to drift away from [Chief Justice Burger's] influence . . . and he was determined to encourage it. . . .
>
> On a major securities case (*Blue Chip Stamps v. Manor Drug Stores*) Blackmun had charged that the majority opinion "graves into stone" with "three blunt chisels" certain arbitrary principles, exhibiting "a preternatural solicitousness for corporate well-being." Brennan readily joined the over-written dissent.

B. Woodward & S. Armstrong, The Brethren: Inside the Supreme Court 362 (1979). For an insightful article on the benefits of private securities litigation, see Ramirez, *The Virtues of Private Securities Litigation: An Historic and Macroeconomic Perspective*, 45 Loy. U. (Chi.) L.J. 669 (2014).

In the following case, the Supreme Court granted standing in a private damages action under § 10(b) where there was the conveyance of an option to purchase stock that was transacted by means of an oral agreement.

The Wharf (Holdings) Limited v. United International Holdings, Inc.

United States Supreme Court

532 U.S. 588, 121 S. Ct. 1776, 149 L. Ed. 2d 845 (2001)

Justice BREYER delivered the opinion of the Court.

This securities fraud action focuses upon a company that sold an option to buy stock while secretly intending never to honor the option. The question before us is whether this conduct violates § 10(b) of the Securities Exchange Act of 1934, which prohibits using "any manipulative or deceptive device or contrivance" "in connection with the purchase or sale of any security." We conclude that it does.

I

Respondent United International Holdings, Inc., a Colorado-based company, sued petitioner The Wharf (Holdings) Limited, a Hong Kong firm, in Colorado's Federal District Court. United said that in October 1992 Wharf had sold it an option to buy 10% of the stock of a new Hong Kong cable system. But, United alleged, at the time of the sale Wharf secretly intended not to permit United to exercise the option. United claimed that Wharf's conduct amounted to a fraud "in connection with the . . . sale of [a] security," prohibited by § 10(b). . . . A jury found in United's favor. The Court of Appeals for the Tenth Circuit upheld that verdict. And we granted certiorari to consider whether the dispute fell within the scope of § 10(b).

The relevant facts, viewed in the light most favorable to the verdict winner, United, are as follows. In 1991, The Hong Kong government announced that it would accept bids for the award of an exclusive license to operate a cable television system in Hong Kong. Wharf decided to prepare a bid. Wharf's chairman, Peter Woo, instructed one of its managing directors, Stephen Ng, to find a business partner with cable system experience. Ng found United. And United sent several employees to Hong Kong to help prepare Wharf's application, negotiate contracts, design the system, and arrange financing.

United asked to be paid for its services with a right to invest in the cable system if Wharf should obtain the license. During August and September 1992, while United's employees were at work helping Wharf, Wharf and United negotiated about the details of that payment. Wharf prepared a draft letter of intent that contemplated giving United the right to become a co-investor, owning 10% of the system. But the parties did not sign the letter of intent. And in September, when Wharf submitted its bid, it told Hong Kong authorities that Wharf would be the system's initial sole owner, although Wharf would also "consider" allowing United to become an investor.

In early October 1992, Ng met with a United representative, who told Ng that United would continue to help only if Wharf gave United an enforceable right to invest. Ng then orally granted United an option with the following terms: (1) United had the right to buy 10% of the future system's stock; (2) the price of exercising the option would be 10% of the system's capital requirements minus the value of United's previous services (including expenses); (3) United could exercise the option only if it showed that it could fund its 10% share of the capital required for at least the first 18 months; and (4) the option would expire if not exercised within six months of the date that Wharf received the license. The parties continued to negotiate about how to write documents that would embody these terms, but they never reduced the agreement to writing.

In May 1993, Hong Kong awarded the cable franchise to Wharf. United raised $66 million designed to help finance its 10% share. In July or August 1993, United told Wharf that it was ready to exercise its option. But Wharf refused to permit United to buy any of the system's stock. Contemporaneous internal Wharf documents suggested that Wharf had never intended to carry out its promise. For example, a few weeks before the key October 1992 meeting, Ng had prepared a memorandum stating that United wanted a right to invest that it could exercise if it was able to raise the necessary capital. A handwritten note by Wharf's Chairman Woo replied, "No, no, no, we don't accept that." In September 1993, after meeting with the Wharf board to discuss United's investment in the cable system, Ng wrote to another Wharf executive, "How do we get out?" In December 1993, after United had filed documents with the Securities Exchange Commission representing that United was negotiating the acquisition of a 10% interest in the cable system, an internal Wharf memo stated that "[o]ur next move should be to claim that our directors got quite upset over these representations . . . Publicly, we do not acknowledge [United's] opportunity" to acquire the 10% interest. In the margin of a December 1993 letter from United discussing its expectation of investing in the cable system, Ng wrote, "[B]e careful, must deflect this! [H]ow?" Other Wharf documents referred to the need to "back ped[al]", and "stall".

These documents, along with other evidence, convinced the jury that Wharf, through Ng, had orally sold United an option to purchase a 10% interest in the future cable system while secretly intending not to permit United to exercise the option, in violation of § 10(b) of the Securities Exchange Act and various state laws. The jury awarded United compensatory damages of $67 million and, in light of "circumstances of fraud, malice, or willful and wanton conduct," punitive damages of $58.5 million on the state-law claims. As we have said, the Court of Appeals upheld the jury's award. And we granted certiorari to determine whether Wharf's oral sale of an option it intended not to honor is prohibited by § 10(b).

II

Section 10(b) of the Securities Exchange Act makes it "unlawful for any person . . . [t]o use or employ, in connection with the purchase or sale of any security . . . , any manipulative or deceptive device or contrivance in contravention of such rules and regulations as the [SEC] may prescribe."

Pursuant to this provision, the SEC has promulgated Rule 10b-5. That Rule forbids the use, "in connection with the purchase or sale of any security," of (1) "any device, scheme, or artifice to defraud"; (2) "any untrue statement of a material fact"; (3) the omission of "a material fact necessary in order to make the statements made . . . not misleading"; or (4) any other "act, practice, or course of business" that "operates . . . as a fraud or deceit."

To succeed in a Rule 10b-5 suit, a private plaintiff must show that the defendant used, in connection with the purchase or sale of a security, one of the four kinds of manipulative or deceptive devices to which the Rule refers, and must also satisfy certain other requirements not at issue here.

In deciding whether the Rule covers the circumstances present here, we must assume that the "security" at issue is not the cable system stock, but the option to purchase that stock. That is because the Court of Appeals found that Wharf conceded this point. That concession is consistent with the language of the Securities Exchange Act, which defines "security" to include both "any . . . option . . . on any security" and "any . . . right to . . . purchase" stock. And Wharf's current effort to deny the concession . . . comes too late and is unconvincing. Consequently, we must decide whether Wharf's secret intent not to honor the option it sold United amounted to a misrepresentation (or other conduct forbidden by the Rule) in connection with the sale of the option.

Wharf argues that its conduct falls outside the Rule's scope for two basic reasons. First, Wharf points out that its agreement to grant United an option to purchase shares in the cable system was an oral agreement. And it says that § 10(b) does not cover oral contracts of sale. Wharf points to *Blue Chip Stamps*, in which this Court construed the Act's "purchase or sale" language to mean that only "actual purchasers or sellers of securities" have standing to bring a private action for damages. Wharf notes that the Court's interpretation of the Act flowed in part from the need to protect defendants against lawsuits that "turn largely on which oral version of a series of occurrences the jury may decide to credit." And it claims that an oral purchase or sale would pose a similar problem of proof and thus should not satisfy the Rule's "purchase or sale" requirement.

Blue Chip Stamps, however, involved the very different question whether the Act protects a person who did not actually buy securities, but who might have done so had the seller told the truth. The Court held that the Act does not cover such a potential buyer, in part for the reason that Wharf states. But United is not a potential buyer; by providing Wharf with its services, it actually bought the option that Wharf sold. And *Blue Chip Stamps* said nothing to suggest that oral purchases or sales fall outside the scope of the Act. Rather, the Court's concern was about "the abuse potential and proof problems inherent in suits by investors who neither bought nor sold, but asserted they would have traded absent fraudulent conduct by others." Such a "potential purchase" claim would rest on facts, including the plaintiff's state of mind, that might be "totally unknown and unknowable to the defendant", depriving the jury of "the benefit of weighing the plaintiff's version against the defendant's version." . . . An actual sale, even if oral, would not create this problem, because both parties would be able to testify as to whether the relevant events had occurred.

Neither is there any other convincing reason to interpret the Act to exclude oral contracts as a class. The Act itself says that it applies to "any contract" for the purchase or sale of a security. Oral contracts for the sale of securities are sufficiently common that the Uniform Commercial Code and statutes of frauds in every State now consider them enforceable. . . . Any exception for oral sales of securities would significantly limit the Act's coverage, thereby undermining its basic purposes.

. . . .

Second, Wharf argues that a secret reservation not to permit the exercise of an option falls outside § 10(b) because it does not "relat[e] to the value of a security purchase or the consideration paid"; hence it does "not implicate [§ 10(b)'s] policy of full disclosure." But even were it the case that the Act covers only misrepresentations likely to affect the value of securities, Wharf's secret reservation was such a misrepresentation. To sell an option while secretly intending not to permit the option's exercise is misleading, because a buyer normally presumes good faith. Cf., e.g., Restatement (Second) of Torts § 530, Comment c (1976) ("Since a promise necessarily carries with it the implied assertion of an intention to perform, it follows that a promise made without such an intention is fraudulent"). For similar reasons, the secret reservation misled United about the option's value. Since Wharf did not intend to honor the option, the option was, unbeknownst to United, valueless.

Finally, Wharf supports its claim for an exemption from the statute by characterizing this case as a "disput[e] over the ownership of securities." Wharf expresses concern that interpreting the Act to allow recovery in a case like this one will permit numerous plaintiffs to bring federal securities claims that are in reality no more than ordinary state breach-of-contract claims—actions that lie outside the Act's basic objectives. United's claim, however, is not simply that Wharf failed to carry out a promise to sell its securities. It is a claim that Wharf sold it a security (the option) while secretly intending from the very beginning not to honor the option. And United proved that secret intent with documentary evidence that went well beyond evidence of a simple failure to perform. . . .

For these reasons, the judgment of the Court of Appeals is affirmed.

---

§ 8.03 Requisite Culpability Level

[A] Private Damages Actions

Ernst & Ernst v. Hochfelder

United States Supreme Court

425 U.S. 185, 96 S. Ct. 1375, 47 L. Ed. 2d 668 (1976)

MR. JUSTICE POWELL delivered the opinion of the Court.

The issue in this case is whether an action for civil damages may lie under § 10(b) of the Securities Exchange Act of 1934 (1934 Act), and Securities and Exchange Commission Rule 10b-5, in the absence of an allegation of intent to deceive, manipulate, or defraud on the part of the defendant.

I

Petitioner, Ernst & Ernst, is an accounting firm. From 1946 through 1967 it was retained by First Securities Company of Chicago (First Securities), a small brokerage firm and member of the Midwest Stock Exchange and of the National Association of Securities Dealers, to perform periodic audits of the firm's books and records. In connection with these audits Ernst & Ernst prepared for filing with the Securities and Exchange Commission (Commission) the annual reports required of First Securities under § 17(a) of the 1934 Act, 15 U.S.C. § 78q(a). It also prepared for First Securities responses to the financial questionnaires of the Midwest Stock Exchange (Exchange).

Respondents were customers of First Securities who invested in a fraudulent securities scheme perpetrated by Leston B. Nay, president of the firm and owner of 92% of its stock. Nay induced the respondents to invest funds in "escrow" accounts that he represented would yield a high rate of return. Respondents did so from 1942 through 1966, with the majority of the transactions occurring in the 1950's. In fact, there were no escrow accounts as Nay converted respondents' funds to his own use immediately upon receipt. These transactions were not in the customary form of dealings between First Securities and its customers. The respondents drew their personal checks payable to Nay or a designated bank for his account. No such escrow accounts were reflected on the books and records of First Securities, and none was shown on its periodic accounting to respondents in connection with their other investments. Nor were they included in First Securities' filings with the Commission or the Exchange.

This fraud came to light in 1968 when Nay committed suicide, leaving a note that described First Securities as bankrupt and the escrow accounts as "spurious." Respondents subsequently filed this action for damages against Ernst & Ernst in the United States District Court for the Northern District of Illinois under § 10(b) of the 1934 Act. The complaint charged that Nay's escrow scheme violated § 10(b) and Commission Rule 10b-5, and that Ernst & Ernst had "aided and abetted" Nay's violations by its "failure" to conduct proper audits of First Securities. As revealed through discovery, respondents' cause of action rested on a theory of negligent nonfeasance. The premise was that Ernst & Ernst had failed to utilize "appropriate auditing procedures" in its audits of First Securities, thereby failing to discover internal practices of the firm said to prevent an effective audit. The practice principally relied on was Nay's rule that only he could open mail addressed to him at First Securities or addressed to First Securities to his attention, even if it arrived in his absence. Respondents contended that if Ernst & Ernst had conducted a proper audit, it would have discovered this "mail rule." The existence of the rule then would have been disclosed in reports to the Exchange and to the Commission by Ernst & Ernst as an irregular procedure that prevented an effective audit. This would have led to an investigation of Nay that would have revealed the fraudulent scheme. Respondents specifically disclaimed the existence of fraud or intentional misconduct on the part of Ernst & Ernst.

. . . .

We granted certiorari to resolve the question whether a private cause of action for damages will lie under § 10(b) and Rule 10b-5 in the absence of any allegation of "scienter" — intent to deceive, manipulate, or defraud.[2] We conclude that it will not and therefore we reverse. [*Note that, if this action were brought today, it would be precluded on two grounds: (1) the expiration of the § 10(b) statute of limitations as set forth in 28 U.S.C. § 1658(b) (see § 8.09[B]); and (2) as secondary liability was plead by the plaintiffs in this action, the exclusion of aider and abettor liability in § 10(b) private actions pursuant to the Supreme Court's Central Bank of Denver decision (see § 10.02).*]

II

Federal regulation of transactions in securities emerged as part of the aftermath of the market crash in 1929. The Securities Act of 1933 (1933 Act) . . . was designed to provide investors with full disclosure of material information concerning public

---

[2]. In this opinion the term "scienter" refers to a mental state embracing intent to deceive, manipulate, or defraud. In certain areas of the law recklessness is considered to be a form of intentional conduct for purposes of imposing liability for some act. We need not address here the question whether, in some circumstances, reckless behavior is sufficient for civil liability under § 10(b) and Rule 10b-5.

offerings of securities in commerce, to protect investors against fraud and, through the imposition of specified civil liabilities, to promote ethical standards of honesty and fair dealing. . . . The 1934 Act was intended principally to protect investors against manipulation of stock prices through regulation of transactions upon securities exchanges and in over-the-counter markets, and to impose regular reporting requirements on companies whose stock is listed on national securities exchanges. . . .

Although § 10(b) does not by its terms create an express civil remedy for its violation, and there is no indication that Congress, or the Commission when adopting Rule 10b-5, contemplated such a remedy, the existence of a private cause of action for violations of the statute and the Rule is now well established. During the 30-year period since a private cause of action was first implied under § 10(b) and Rule 10b-5, a substantial body of case law and commentary has developed as to its elements. Courts and commentators long have differed with regard to whether scienter is a necessary element of such a cause of action, or whether negligent conduct alone is sufficient. In addressing this question, we turn first to the language of § 10(b), for "[t]he starting point in every case involving construction of a statute is the language itself."

A

Section 10(b) makes unlawful the use or employment of "any manipulative or deceptive device or contrivance" in contravention of Commission rules. The words "manipulative or deceptive" used in conjunction with "device or contrivance" strongly suggest that § 10(b) was intended to proscribe knowing or intentional misconduct.

In its *amicus curiae* brief, however, the Commission contends that nothing in the language "manipulative or deceptive device or contrivance" limits its operation to knowing or intentional practices. In support of its view, the Commission cites the overall congressional purpose in the 1933 and 1934 Acts to protect investors against false and deceptive practices that might injure them. The Commission then reasons that since the "effect" upon investors of given conduct is the same regardless of whether the conduct is negligent or intentional, Congress must have intended to bar all such practices and not just those done knowingly or intentionally. The logic of this effect-oriented approach would impose liability for wholly faultless conduct where such conduct results in harm to investors, a result the Commission would be unlikely to support. But apart from where its logic might lead, the Commission would add a gloss to the operative language of the statute quite different from its commonly accepted meaning. The argument simply ignores the use of the words "manipulative," "device," and "contrivance" — terms that make unmistakable a congressional intent to proscribe a type of conduct quite different from negligence. Use of the word "manipulative" is especially significant. It is and was virtually a term of art when used in connection with securities markets. It connotes intentional or willful conduct designed to deceive or defraud investors by controlling or artificially affecting the price of securities.

In addition to relying upon the Commission's argument with respect to the operative language of the statute, respondents contend that since we are dealing with "remedial legislation," it must be construed "not technically and restrictively, but flexibly to effectuate its remedial purposes." They argue that the "remedial purposes" of the Acts demand a construction of § 10(b) that embraces negligence as a standard of liability. But in seeking to accomplish its broad remedial goals, Congress did not adopt uniformly a negligence standard even as to express civil remedies. In some circumstances and with respect to certain classes of defendants, Congress did create express liability predicated upon a failure to exercise reasonable care. *E.g.,* 1933 Act § 11(b) (3)(B) (liability of "experts," such as accountants, for misleading statements in portions of registration statements for which they are responsible). But in other situations good faith is an absolute defense. 1934 Act § 18 (misleading statements in any document filed pursuant to the 1934 Act). And in still other circumstances Congress created express liability regardless of the defendant's fault, 1933 Act § 11(a) (issuer liability for misleading statements in the registration statement).

It is thus evident that Congress fashioned standards of fault in the express civil remedies in the 1933 and 1934 Acts on a particularized basis. Ascertainment of congressional intent with respect to the standard of liability created by a particular section of the Acts must therefore rest primarily on the language of that section. Where, as here, we deal with a judicially implied liability, the statutory language certainly is no less important. In view of the language of § 10(b), which so clearly connotes intentional misconduct, and mindful that the language of a statute controls when sufficiently clear in its context, further inquiry may be unnecessary. We turn now, nevertheless, to the legislative history of the 1934 Act to ascertain whether there is support for the meaning attributed to § 10(b) by the Commission and respondents.

B

Although the extensive legislative history of the 1934 Act is bereft of any explicit explanation of Congress' intent, we think the relevant portions of that history support our conclusion that § 10(b) was addressed to practices that involve some element of scienter and cannot be read to impose liability for negligent conduct alone.

. . . The most relevant exposition of the provision that was to become § 10(b) was by Thomas G. Corcoran, a spokesman for the drafters. Corcoran indicated:

> Subsection (c) [§ 9(c) of H. R. 7852—later § 10(b)] says, "Thou shalt not devise any other cunning devices."
>
> . . . .
>
> Of course subsection (c) is a catch-all clause to prevent manipulative devices. I do not think there is any objection to that kind of clause. The Commission should have the authority to deal with new manipulative devices.

Hearings on H. R. 7852 and H. R. 8720 before the House Committee on Interstate and Foreign Commerce, 73d Cong., 2d Sess., 115 (1934).

This brief explanation of § 10(b) by a spokesman for its drafters is significant. The section was described rightly as a "catchall" clause to enable the Commission "to deal with new manipulative [or cunning] devices." It is difficult to believe that any lawyer, legislative draftsman, or legislator would use these words if the intent was to create liability for merely negligent acts or omissions. Neither the legislative history nor the briefs supporting respondents identify any usage or authority for construing "manipulative [or cunning] devices" to include negligence.

. . . .

C

The 1933 and 1934 Acts constitute interrelated components of the federal regulatory scheme governing transactions in securities. As the Court indicated in *SEC v. National Securities, Inc.*, 393 U.S. 453, 466 (1969), "the interdependence of the various sections of the securities laws is certainly a relevant factor in any interpretation of the language Congress has chosen. . . ."

. . . In each instance that Congress created express civil liability in favor of purchasers or sellers of securities, it clearly specified whether recovery was to be premised on knowing or intentional conduct, negligence, or entirely innocent mistake. . . . For example, § 11 of the 1933 Act unambiguously creates a private action for damages when a registration statement includes untrue statements of material facts or fails to state material facts necessary to make the statements therein not misleading. Within the limits specified by § 11(e), the issuer of the securities is held absolutely liable for any damages resulting from such misstatement or omission. But experts such as accountants who have prepared portions of the registration statement are accorded a "due diligence" defense. In effect, this is a negligence standard. An expert may avoid civil liability with respect to the portions of the registration statement for which he was responsible by showing that "after reasonable investigation" he had "reasonable ground[s] to believe" that the statements for which he was responsible were true and there was no omission of a material fact. § 11(b)(3)(B)(i). The express recognition of a cause of action premised on negligent behavior in § 11 stands in sharp contrast to the language of § 10(b). . . .

We also consider it significant that each of the express civil remedies in the 1933 Act allowing recovery for negligent conduct (see §§ 11, 12(2), 15) . . . is subject to significant procedural restrictions not applicable under § 10(b). Section 11(e) of the 1933 Act, for example, authorizes the court to require a plaintiff bringing a suit under § 11, § 12(2), or § 15 thereof to post a bond for costs, including attorneys' fees, and in specified circumstances to assess costs at the conclusion of the litigation. Section 13 specifies a statute of limitations of one year from the time the violation was or should have been discovered, in no event to exceed three years from the time of offer or sale, applicable to actions brought under § 11, § 12(2), or § 15. . . . We think these procedural limitations indicate that the judicially created private damages remedy under § 10(b) . . . cannot be extended, consistently with the intent of Congress, to actions premised on negligent wrongdoing. Such extension would allow causes of action covered by §§ 11, 12(2), and 15 to be brought instead under § 10(b) and thereby nullify the effectiveness of the carefully drawn procedural restrictions on these express actions. We would be unwilling to bring about this result absent substantial support in the legislative history, and there is none.

D

We have addressed, to this point, primarily the language and history of § 10(b). The Commission contends, however, that subsections (b) and (c) of Rule 10b-5 are cast in language which—if standing alone—could encompass both intentional and negligent behavior. These subsections respectively provide that it is unlawful "[t]o make any untrue statement of a material fact or to omit to state a material fact necessary in order to make the statements made, in the light of the circumstances under which they were made, not misleading . . ." and "[t]o engage in any act, practice, or course of business which operates or would operate as a fraud or deceit upon any person. . . ." Viewed in isolation the language of subsection (b), and arguably that of subsection (c), could be read as proscribing, respectively, any type of material misstatement or omission, and any course of conduct, that has the effect of defrauding investors, whether the wrongdoing was intentional or not.

We note first that such a reading cannot be harmonized with the administrative history of the Rule, a history making clear that when the Commission adopted the Rule it was intended to apply only to activities that involved scienter. More importantly, Rule 10b-5 was adopted pursuant to authority granted the Commission under § 10(b). The rulemaking power granted to an administrative agency charged with the administration of a federal statute is not the power to make law. Rather, it is "the power to adopt regulations to carry into effect the will of Congress as expressed by the statute." Thus, despite the broad view of the Rule advanced by the Commission in this case, its scope cannot exceed the power granted the Commission by Congress under § 10(b). For the reasons stated above, we think the Commission's original interpretation of Rule 10b-5 was compelled by the language and history of § 10(b) and related sections of the Acts. When a statute speaks so specifically in terms of manipulation and deception, and of implementing devices and contrivances—the commonly understood terminology of intentional wrongdoing—and when its history reflects no more expansive intent, we are quite unwilling to extend the scope of the statute to negligent conduct.

. . . .

Reversed.

MR. JUSTICE BLACKMUN, with whom MR. JUSTICE BRENNAN joins, dissenting.

Once again—see *Blue Chip Stamps v. Manor Drug Stores*, 421 U.S. 723, 730 (1975)—the Court interprets § 10(b) of the Securities Exchange Act of 1934 . . . and the Securities and Exchange Commission's Rule 10b-5 . . . restrictively and narrowly and thereby stultifies recovery for the victim. This time the Court does so by confining the statute and the Rule to situations where the defendant has "scienter," that is, the "intent to deceive, manipulate, or defraud." Sheer negligence, the Court says, is not within the reach of the statute and the Rule, and was not contemplated when the great reforms of 1933, 1934, and 1942 were effectuated by Congress and the Commission.

Perhaps the Court is right, but I doubt it. The Government and the Commission doubt it too, as is evidenced by the thrust of the brief filed by the Solicitor General on behalf of the Commission as *amicus curiae*. The Court's opinion, to be sure, has a certain technical consistency about it. It seems to me, however, that an investor can be victimized just as much by negligent conduct as by positive deception, and that it is not logical to drive a wedge between the two, saying that Congress clearly intended the one but certainly not the other.

. . . .

Note

Note that the plaintiffs in *Hochfelder* were able to pursue their § 10(b) actions even though many of the violations occurred several years earlier. This was due to that the primary violator, Nay, engaged in fraudulent concealment, thereby permitting the statute of limitations to be tolled under the law as it stood at that time.

Today, however, in view of 28 U.S.C. § 1658(b) (see § 8.09[B]), fraudulent concealment no longer tolls the statute of limitations. Hence, plaintiffs bringing a § 10(b) action must bring suit within two years after discovery of the violation and in no event later than five years after the violation's occurrence.

Moreover, in *Hochfelder*, the plaintiff alleged that the accounting firm was liable under § 10(b) as an aider and abettor. This route no longer is viable in light of the Supreme Court's decision in *Central Bank of Denver* (see § 10.02) holding that aider and abettor liability may not be imposed in private § 10(b) actions.

Note also that the plaintiff *must plead fraud with particularity* in its § 10(b) cause of action. This issue is addressed later in this chapter (§ 8.09[A]).

[B] SEC Actions for Injunctive Relief

After the Supreme Court's decision in *Hochfelder*, the question remained whether the SEC was required to establish scienter in an action for injunctive relief brought for violations of § 10(b). Because the principal focus of an SEC injunctive proceeding "is to protect the public against harm, not to punish the offender,"[3] it was argued by some authorities that an SEC action under § 10(b) could be premised on negligent conduct. Others, relying upon a statutory linguistic analysis, asserted that

---

3. *SEC v. Coven*, 581 F.2d 1020, 1027–1028 (2d Cir. 1978).

scienter had to be proven under § 10(b), irrespective of the plaintiff's identity.[4] The Supreme Court resolved this issue in *Aaron v. SEC*, 446 U.S. 680 (1980). Largely relying on the literal language of Section 10(b) and its legislative history, the Court concluded that "scienter is an element of § 10(b) and Rule 10b-5, regardless of the identity of the plaintiff or the nature of the relief sought." From an SEC enforcement view, *Aaron* is an important case, further aspects of which are discussed in Chapters 9 and 15.

[C] "Recklessness"

A question left open by both *Hochfelder* and *Aaron* is whether reckless conduct constitutes scienter for § 10(b) purposes. The Supreme Court most recently left this issue unresolved in its 2007 decision in *Tellabs* (contained later in this Chapter, in § 8.09[A]). Nonetheless, it appears that reckless misconduct generally meets the scienter requirement for a number of reasons. First, the lower federal courts overwhelmingly have concluded that recklessness satisfies the scienter requirement. Second, this position is reinforced by the enactment of the Private Securities Litigation Reform Act (PSLRA), which strongly suggests that reckless conduct satisfies § 10(b)'s scienter requirement *except for* forward-looking statements by publicly held companies where the defendant's actual knowledge must be proven (see §§ 8.05[B][2], 11.03). And third, the Dodd-Frank Act of 2010 provides that in SEC enforcement actions the requisite mental state for the imposition of aider and abettor liability is knowing or reckless misconduct (see Chapter 15 herein).

The courts today construe reckless conduct to mean conduct that is "highly unreasonable" and that represents "an extreme departure from the standards of ordinary care . . . to the extent that the danger was either known to the defendant or so obvious that the defendant must have been aware of it."[5] This definition of recklessness appears to be nearly unanimous today under federal securities law.

A few older cases (that evidently are no longer followed) adhered to a less strict standard of recklessness. For example, in *Lanza v. Drexel & Co.*, 419 F.2d 1277, 1306 n. 98 (2d Cir. 1973) (en banc), the Second Circuit opined that reckless conduct exists if the defendant had reasonable grounds to believe material facts existed that were misrepresented or omitted, but nonetheless failed to obtain and disclose such facts although he/she could have done so without extraordinary effort. Another approach, termed the "barely reckless" standard, deemed actionable an allegation that the

---

4. *See generally*, M. Steinberg & R. Ferrara, Securities Practice: Federal and State Enforcement § 5.01 et seq. (2d ed. 2001 & 2016–2017 Supp.); Andre, *The Collateral Consequences of SEC Injunctive Relief: Mild Prophylactic or Perpetual Hazard?*, 1981 Ill. L.F. 625; Hazen, *Administrative Enforcement: An Evaluation of the Securities and Exchange Commission's Use of Injunctions and Other Enforcement Methods*, 31 Hastings L.J. 427 (1979).

5. *See, e.g., In re Ikon Office Solutions, Inc. Securities Litigation*, 277 F. 3d 658, 667 (3d Cir. 2002).

defendant "should have known," with the proviso that such conduct surpasses that of negligence. See *Stern v. American Bankshares Corp.*, 429 F. Supp. 818 (E.D. Wis. 1977).

[D] State Court Reaction

Due to the Supreme Court's decisions in the federal securities law area that have had the effect of making a plaintiff's task in establishing a successful cause of action under § 10(b) more difficult, counsel may deem it wise to consider bringing state common law or state securities law claims. In this regard, in construing their respective Blue Sky statutes, some state courts have declined to follow the Supreme Court's lead in *Hochfelder* and *Aaron*, thereby holding that scienter is not required to be shown. For example, the Washington Supreme Court in *Kittilson v. Ford*, 93 Wash. 2d 223, 608 P.2d 264 (1980), a civil action for damages, rejected the *Hochfelder* scienter standard. In distinguishing *Hochfelder* and holding that negligence is sufficient to impose liability, the *Kittilson* court reasoned:

> We believe the holding in *Ernst & Ernst v. Hochfelder* [is] inapplicable to our Securities Act. First, the "manipulative or deceptive" language of Section 10(b) of the 1934 Act is not included in the Washington Act. Secondly, in contrast to the federal scheme, the language of Rule 10b-5 is not derivative but is the statute in Washington. Finally, no legislative history similar or analogous to Congressional legislative history exists in Washington.

See *Merrill Lynch, Pierce, Fenner & Smith v. Bryne*, 320 So. 2d 436 (Dist. Ct. App. Fla. 1975), *writ discharged*, 341 So. 2d 498 (Fla. 1977) (scienter not required to be shown under blue sky antifraud statute). *But see Ohio v. American Equitel Corp.*, 60 Ohio Misc. 7, 395 N.E.2d 1355 (Ct. C.P. Ohio 1979) (requiring scienter to be shown). *See generally*, J. Long, M. Kaufman, & J. Wunderlich, Blue Sky Law § 7.01 (2016).

---

§ 8.04 The "Deception" or "Manipulation" Requirement

[A] Rejection of a Federal Fiduciary Approach

Santa Fe Industries, Inc. v. Green

United States Supreme Court

430 U.S. 462, 97 S. Ct. 1292, 51 L. Ed. 2d 480 (1977)

MR. JUSTICE WHITE delivered the opinion of the Court.

The issue in this case involves the reach and coverage of § 10(b) of the Securities Exchange Act of 1934 and Rule 10b-5 thereunder in the context of a Delaware short-form merger transaction used by the majority stockholder of a corporation to eliminate the minority interest.

I

In 1936, petitioner Santa Fe Industries, Inc. (Santa Fe), acquired control of 60% of the stock of Kirby Lumber Corp. (Kirby), a Delaware corporation. Through a series of purchases over the succeeding years, Santa Fe increased its control of Kirby's stock to 95%; the purchase prices during the period 1968–1973 ranged from $65 to $92.50 per share. In 1974, wishing to acquire 100% ownership of Kirby, Santa Fe availed itself of §253 of the Delaware Corporation Law, known as the "short-form merger" statute. Section 253 permits a parent corporation owning at least 90% of the stock of a subsidiary to merge with that subsidiary, upon approval by the parent's board of directors, and to make payment in cash for the shares of the minority stockholders. The statute does not require the consent of, or advance notice to, the minority stockholders. However, notice of the merger must be given within 10 days after its effective date, and any stockholder who is dissatisfied with the terms of the merger may petition the Delaware Court of Chancery for a decree ordering the surviving corporation to pay him the fair value of his shares, as determined by a court-appointed appraiser subject to review by the court.

Santa Fe obtained independent appraisals of the physical assets of Kirby—land, timber, buildings, and machinery—and of Kirby's oil, gas, and mineral interests. These appraisals, together with other financial information, were submitted to Morgan Stanley & Co. (Morgan Stanley), an investment banking firm retained to appraise the fair market value of Kirby stock. Kirby's physical assets were appraised at $320 million (amounting to $640 for each of the 500,000 shares); Kirby's stock was valued by Morgan Stanley at $125 per share. Under the terms of the merger, minority stockholders were offered $150 per share.

The provisions of the short-form merger statute were fully complied with. The minority stockholders of Kirby were notified the day after the merger became effective and were advised of their right to obtain an appraisal in Delaware court if dissatisfied with the offer of $150 per share. They also received an information statement containing, in addition to the relevant financial data about Kirby, the appraisals of the value of Kirby's assets and the Morgan Stanley appraisal concluding that the fair market value of the stock was $125 per share.

Respondents, minority stockholders of Kirby, objected to the terms of the merger, but did not pursue their appraisal remedy in the Delaware Court of Chancery. Instead, they brought this action in federal court on behalf of the corporation and other minority stockholders, seeking to set aside the merger or to recover what they claimed to be the fair value of their shares. The amended complaint asserted that, based on the fair market value of Kirby's physical assets as revealed by the appraisal included in the information statement sent to minority shareholders, Kirby's stock was worth at least $772 per share. The complaint alleged further that the merger took place without prior notice to minority stockholders; that the purpose of the merger was to appropriate the difference between the "conceded pro rata value of the physical assets," and the offer of $150 per share—to "freez[e] out the minority stockholders at a wholly inadequate price," and that Santa Fe, knowing the appraised value of the physical assets, obtained a "fraudulent appraisal" of the stock from Morgan Stanley and offered $25 above that appraisal "in order to lull the minority stockholders into erroneously believing that [Santa Fe was] generous." This course of conduct was alleged to be "a violation of Rule 10b-5 because defendants employed a 'device, scheme, or artifice to defraud' and engaged in an 'act, practice or course of business which operates or would operate as a fraud or deceit upon any person, in connection with the purchase or sale of any security.'" . . .

The District Court dismissed the complaint for failure to state a claim upon which relief could be granted. . . .

A divided Court of Appeals for the Second Circuit reversed. 533 F.2d 1283 (1976). It first agreed that there was a double aspect to the case: first, the claim that gross undervaluation of the minority stock itself violated Rule 10b-5; and second, that "without any misrepresentation or failure to disclose relevant facts, the merger itself constitutes a violation of Rule 10b-5" because it was accomplished without any corporate purpose and without prior notice to the minority stockholders. . . . The Court of Appeals' view was that, although the Rule plainly reached material misrepresentations and nondisclosures in connection with the purchase or sale of securities, neither misrepresentation nor nondisclosure was a necessary element of a Rule 10b-5 action. . . .

We granted the petition for certiorari challenging this holding because of the importance of the issue involved to the administration of the federal securities laws. We reverse.

II

. . . .

To the extent that the Court of Appeals would rely on the use of the term "fraud" in Rule 10b-5 to bring within the ambit of the Rule all breaches of fiduciary duty in connection with a securities transaction, its interpretation would, like the interpretation rejected by the Court in *Ernst & Ernst*, "add a gloss to the operative language of the statute quite different from its commonly accepted meaning." . . .

The language of § 10(b) gives no indication that Congress meant to prohibit any conduct not involving manipulation or deception. Nor have we been cited to any evidence in the legislative history that would support a departure from the language of the statute. . . . Thus the claim of fraud and fiduciary breach in this complaint states a cause of action under any part of Rule 10b-5 only if the conduct alleged can be fairly viewed as "manipulative or deceptive" within the meaning of the statute.

III

It is our judgment that the transaction, if carried out as alleged in the complaint, was neither deceptive nor manipulative and therefore did not violate either § 10(b) of the Act or Rule 10b-5.

As we have indicated, the case comes to us on the premise that the complaint failed to allege a material misrepresentation or material failure to disclose. The finding of the District Court, undisturbed by the Court of Appeals, was that there was no "omission" or "misstatement" in the information statement accompanying the notice of merger. On the basis of the information provided, minority shareholders could either accept the price offered or reject it and seek an appraisal in the Delaware Court of Chancery. Their choice was fairly presented, and they were furnished with all relevant information on which to base their decision.[6]

. . . .

It is also readily apparent that the conduct alleged in the complaint was not "manipulative" within the meaning of the statute. "Manipulation" is "virtually a term of art when used in connection with securities markets." The term refers generally to practices, such as wash sales, matched orders, or rigged prices, that are intended to mislead investors by artificially affecting market activity. . . . Section 10(b)'s general prohibition of practices deemed by the SEC to be "manipulative" — in this technical sense of artificially affecting market activity in order to mislead investors — is fully consistent with the fundamental purpose of the 1934 Act "to substitute a philosophy of full disclosure for the philosophy of caveat emptor. . . ." Indeed, nondisclosure is usually essential to the success of a manipulative scheme. No doubt Congress meant to prohibit the full range of ingenious devices that might be used to manipulate securities prices. But we do not think it would have chosen this "term of art" if it had meant to bring within the scope of § 10(b) instances of corporate mismanagement such as this, in which the essence of the complaint is that shareholders were treated unfairly by a fiduciary.

IV

The language of the statute is, we think, "sufficiently clear in its context" to be dispositive here but even if it were not, there are additional considerations that weigh

---

[6]. In addition to their principal argument that the complaint alleges a fraud under clauses (a) and (c) of Rule 10b-5, respondents also argue that the complaint alleges nondisclosure and misrepresentation in violation of clause (b) of the Rule. Their major contention in this respect is that the majority stockholder's failure to give the minority advance notice of the merger was a material nondisclosure, even though the Delaware short-form merger statute does not require such notice. . . . But respondents do not indicate how they might have acted differently had they had prior notice of the merger. Indeed, they accept the conclusion of both courts below that under Delaware law they could not have enjoined the merger because an appraisal proceeding is their sole remedy in the Delaware courts for any alleged unfairness in the terms of the merger. Thus, the failure to give advance notice was not a material nondisclosure within the meaning of the statute or the Rule. . . .

heavily against permitting a cause of action under Rule 10b-5 for the breach of corporate fiduciary duty alleged in this complaint. Congress did not expressly provide a private cause of action for violations of § 10(b). Although we have recognized an implied cause of action under that section in some circumstances, we have also recognized that a private cause of action under the antifraud provisions of the Securities Exchange Act should not be implied where it is "unnecessary to ensure the fulfillment of Congress' purposes" in adopting the Act. As we noted earlier, the Court repeatedly has described the "fundamental purpose" of the Act as implementing a "philosophy of full disclosure"; once full and fair disclosure has occurred, the fairness of the terms of the transaction is at most a tangential concern of the statute. As in *Cort v. Ash*, 422 U.S. 66, 80 (1975), we are reluctant to recognize a cause of action here to serve what is "at best a subsidiary purpose" of the federal legislation.

A second factor in determining whether Congress intended to create a federal cause of action in these circumstances is "whether 'the cause of action [is] one traditionally relegated to state law. . . .'" The Delaware Legislature has supplied minority shareholders with a cause of action in the Delaware Court of Chancery to recover the fair value of shares allegedly undervalued in a short-form merger. Of course, the existence of a particular state-law remedy is not dispositive of the question whether Congress meant to provide a similar federal remedy, but we conclude that "it is entirely appropriate in this instance to relegate respondent and others in his situation to whatever remedy is created by state law." . . .

The reasoning behind a holding that the complaint in this case alleged fraud under Rule 10b-5 could not be easily contained. It is difficult to imagine how a court could distinguish, for purposes of Rule 10b-5 fraud, between a majority stockholder's use of a short-form merger to eliminate the minority at an unfair price and the use of some other device, such as a long-form merger, tender offer, or liquidation, to achieve the same result; or indeed how a court could distinguish the alleged abuses in these going private transactions from other types of fiduciary self-dealing involving transactions in securities. The result would be to bring within the Rule a wide variety of corporate conduct traditionally left to state regulation. In addition to posing a "danger of vexatious litigation which could result from a widely expanded class of plaintiffs under Rule 10b-5," *Blue Chip Stamps v. Manor Drug Stores*, 421 U.S., at 740, this extension of the federal securities laws would overlap and quite possibly interfere with state corporate law. Federal courts applying a "federal fiduciary principle" under Rule 10b-5 could be expected to depart from state fiduciary standards at least to the extent necessary to ensure uniformity within the federal system. Absent a clear indication of congressional intent, we are reluctant to federalize the substantial portion of the law of corporations that deals with transactions in securities, particularly where established state policies of corporate regulation would be overridden. As the Court stated in *Cort v. Ash*: "Corporations are creatures of state law, and investors commit their funds to corporate directors on the understanding that, except where federal law expressly requires certain responsibilities of directors with respect to stockholders, state law will govern the internal affairs of the corporation."

We thus adhere to the position that "Congress by § 10(b) did not seek to regulate transactions which constitute no more than internal corporate mismanagement." ... There may well be a need for uniform federal fiduciary standards to govern mergers such as that challenged in this complaint. But those standards should not be supplied by judicial extension of § 10(b) and Rule 10b-5 to "cover the corporate universe."[7]

The judgment of the Court of Appeals is reversed, and the case is remanded for further proceedings consistent with this opinion.

So ordered.

MR. JUSTICE BRENNAN dissents and would affirm for substantially the reasons stated in the majority and concurring opinions in the Court of Appeals, 533 F.2d 1283 (CA2 1976).

———————

Note

On the 50th year anniversary of Rule 10b-5, Professor Ratner opined:

How should the SEC celebrate the anniversary of its most famous piece of handiwork? I have a suggestion: The agency should repeal it. Not only was the rule probably an unauthorized exercise of the SEC's rule-making power in the first place, but 50 years of erratic interpretation by the courts have made it an unworkable tool with which to achieve any legitimate objective of federal securities law.

... [I]n recent years through a combination of broad and narrow interpretations by the courts, [Rule 10b-5] has become a haphazard provision — difficult to apply to some of the principal abuses with which Congress was concerned, but applicable to many other actions that could not conceivably have been within congressional intent.

Ratner, *Repeal SEC's Anti-Fraud Rule*, LEGAL TIMES, May 25, 1992, at 22. *See* Fallone, *Section 10(b) and the Vagaries of Federal Common Law: The Merits of Codifying the Private Cause of Action Under a Structuralist Approach*, 1997 ILL. L. REV. 71; Loewenstein, *The Supreme Court, Rule 10b-5 and the Federalization of Corporate Law*, 39 IND. L. REV. 17 (2005); Thompson & Sale, *Securities Fraud as Corporate Governance: Reflections Upon Federalism*, 56 VAND. L. REV. 859 (2003).

———————

———————

[7]. Cary, *Federalism and Corporate Law: Reflections Upon Delaware*, 83 YALE L. J. 663, 700 (1974) (footnote omitted). Professor Cary argues vigorously for comprehensive federal fiduciary standards, but urges a "frontal" attack by a new federal statute rather than an extension of Rule 10b-5. He writes: "It seems anomalous to jig-saw every kind of corporate dispute into the federal courts through the securities acts as they are presently written."

[B] Federal Disclosure Requirements Based on State Law Claims

Santa Fe is one of the more important decisions that the Supreme Court has handed down in the federal securities law area. Had the decision gone the other way, garden variety suits for breach of fiduciary duty (irrespective of whether there had been adequate disclosure) would have been actionable under § 10(b). *Santa Fe* thus signifies that, in the corporate mismanagement context, a federal claim under § 10(b) must allege a material deception or manipulation. Although theoretically applicable, "manipulation" will seldom be invoked in the corporate mismanagement-nondisclosure setting because the Supreme Court has construed that word as a term of art encompassing market operations.

After *Santa Fe,* however, a number of federal courts have recognized a § 10(b) right of action where the material omission(s), if there had been adequate disclosure, would have enabled shareholders to take corrective steps to avoid financial loss, such as procuring a state court injunction against the contemplated action. Hence, to a certain extent, federal claims under § 10(b) based partially on breach of fiduciary duty under state law still survive. The Supreme Court alluded to but did not address the viability of this rationale in the following case.

Virginia Bankshares, Inc. v. Sandberg

United States Supreme Court

501 U.S. 1083, 111 S. Ct. 2749, 115 L.Ed.2d 929 (1991)

[This decision is contained in § 9.04, which addresses § 14(a) of the 1934 Act. The case also is relevant for our discussion here and may be covered at this time.]

Note

For articles on *Santa Fe* and its progeny, *see, e.g.,* Gelb, *Rule 10b-5 and Santa Fe— Herein of Sue Facts, Shame Facts, and Other Matters,* 87 W. Va. L. Rev. 189 (1985); Gorman, *At the Intersection of Supreme Court and Circuit Street: The Focus of Section 10(b) and Santa Fe's Footnote Fourteen,* 7 J. Corp. L. 199 (1981); Hazen, *Corporate Mismanagement and the Federal Securities Act's Anti-Fraud Provisions: A Familiar Path with Some New Detours,* 20 B.C.L. Rev. 819 (1979); Steinberg & Reese, *The Supreme Court, Implied Rights of Action and Proxy Regulation,* 54 Ohio St. L.J. 67 (1993).

[C] Manipulation

Manipulative acts or practices are prohibited under the federal securities laws.[8] As stated by the Supreme Court, manipulation implicates "intentional or willful conduct designed to deceive or defraud investors by controlling or artificially affecting the price of securities."[9] As set forth by the Supreme Court in a subsequent decision, manipulation encompasses "practices, such as wash sales, matched orders or rigged prices, that are intended to mislead investors by artificially affecting market activity."[10] Nonetheless, such fictitious devices (e.g., wash sales or matched orders) are not essential to a finding of manipulation. As the SEC and a number of courts have stated, the alleged manipulator's intentional creation of a false impression of market activity is sufficient.[11] To identify conduct that is "unrelated to the natural forces of supply and demand,"[12] courts assess whether the subject transactions convey "a false pricing signal to the market."[13] In this context, manipulative conduct may be distinguished from lawful activity by inquiring whether the alleged violator "inject[ed] inaccurate information into the marketplace or creat[ed] a false

---

8. *See, e.g.,* § 17(a) of the Securities Act; §§ 9(a), 10(b), 15(c) of the Securities Exchange Act; SEC Regulation M. Note that a private plaintiff in a § 9 or § 10(b) claim must allege the illegal manipulative activity with particularity pursuant to the pleading requirements of the Private Securities Litigation Reform Act (PSLRA). *See ATSI Communications, Inc. v. The Shaar Fund, Ltd.,* 493 F. 3d 87, 102 (2d Cir. 2007).

Generally, § 15(c) of the Exchange Act addresses deceptive and manipulative conduct by broker-dealers. See *SEC v. Resch-Cassin & Co.,* 362 F. Supp. 964 (S.D.N.Y. 1973); Securities Exchange Act Release No. 3505 (1943). Regulation M relaxes certain restrictions on offering participants when the SEC deems the risk of manipulation to be small. See Adoption of Regulation M, Securities Exchange Act Release No. 38067 (1996) (stating that "Regulation M significantly eases regulatory burdens on offering participants by (i) eliminating the trading restrictions for underwriters of actively traded securities, (ii) reducing the scope of coverage for other securities, (iii) reducing restrictions on issuer plans, (iv) providing a more flexible framework for stabilizing transactions, and (v) deregulating rights offerings").

9. *Ernst & Ernst v. Hochfelder,* 425 U.S. 185, 199 (1976).

10. *Santa Fe Industries, Inc. v. Green,* 430 U.S. 462, 476 (1977). Wash sales are transactions that involve no change in beneficial ownership, while matched orders are orders for the purchase or sale of a security with the knowledge that corresponding orders for substantially the same size and price have been or will be entered at substantially the same time, either by the same person or by different parties. Such transactions can be used to create a false appearance of active trading in the subject security. *See Ernst & Ernst,* 425 U.S. at 205 n. 25. *See also* § 9(a)(1) of the Securities Exchange Act (describing prohibited practices).

11. *See, e.g., ATSI Communications, Inc. v. The Shaar Fund, Ltd.,* 493 F. 3d 87 (2d Cir. 2007); *Pagel, Inc., v. SEC,* 803 F. 2d 942 (8th Cir. 1986); In re *Halsey, Stuart & Co.,* 30 SEC 106 (SEC 1949).

12. *Mobil Corp. v. Marathon Oil, Corp.,* 669 F. 2d 366, 374 (6th Cir. 1981). *See Gurary v. Winehouse,* 190 F. 3d 37, 45 (2d Cir. 1999).

13. *ATSI Communications, Inc. v. The Shaar Fund, Ltd.,* 493 F. 3d 87, 100 (2d Cir. 2007). *See Regents of the University of California v. Credit Suisse First Boston,* 482 F. 3d 372, 390 (5th Cir. 2007); *Markowski v. SEC,* 274 F. 3d 525, 529 (D.C. Cir. 2001); *SEC v. First Jersey Securities, Inc.,* 101 F. 3d 1450, 1466 (2d Cir. 1996); *Sullivan & Long, Inc. v. Scattered Corp.,* 47 F. 3d 857, 861 (7th Cir. 1995).

impression of supply and demand for the security . . . for the purpose of artificially depressing or inflating the price of the security."[14]

Note that in private and SEC actions manipulation is actionable under both § 9 of the Exchange Act and § 10(b) of that Act. For example, to prove manipulation under § 9(a)(2) of the Exchange Act, the following must be shown: "(1) that the defendant [acting with scienter] effected a series of transactions in a security . . . , (2) creating actual or apparent active trading in such security, or raising or depressing the price of such security, (3) for the purpose of inducing the purchase or sale of such security by others."[15] As a generalization, manipulation under § 10(b) may be easier to prove than under § 9(a). For example, the Third Circuit opined that "Section 10(b), unlike Section 9(a), does not require that a plaintiff prove the allegedly unlawful activities had an effect on the price of the stock. Although any damages that the plaintiff "would be entitled to recover under his Section 10(b) and Rule 10b-5 claim would be contingent on proving that [the defendant's] conduct actually depressed prices, proof of price movement is not necessary to establish a violation of Section 10(b) and Rule 10b-5."[16]

---

§ 8.05 Causation and Related Requirements

[A] Overview

Proof of reliance normally is required to help prove the causal connection between the defendant's wrongdoing and the complainant's loss. In some circumstances, as seen by the materials that follow, a plaintiff enjoys a presumption of reliance that the defendant can rebut (for example, by showing that the plaintiff would not have

---

14. *GFL Advantage Fund, Ltd. v. Colkitt*, 272 F. 3d 189, 207 (3d Cir. 2001), *quoted in, ATSI Communications*, 493 F. 3d at 101.

15. McLucas & Angotti, *Market Manipulation*, 22 Rev. Sec. & Comm. Reg. 103, 105 (1989). *See Chemetron Corp v. Business Foods, Inc.*, 682 F. 2d 1149, 1163–1164 (5th Cir. 1982), *vacated and remanded on other grounds*, 460 U.S. 1007 (1983) (stating that "[t]o make out a violation of subsection 9(a)(1) in a private action under subsection 9(e), a plaintiff must prove the existence of (1) a wash sale or matched orders in a security (2) done with scienter (3) for the purpose of creating a false or misleading appearance of active trading in that security (4) on which the plaintiff relied (5) that affected plaintiff's purchase or selling price").

16. *GFL Advantage Fund, Ltd. v. Colkitt*, 272 F.3d 189, 206 (3d Cir. 2001), citing, *Chemetron Corp. v. Business Funds, Inc.*, 718 F.2d 725, 728 (5th Cir. 1983). For commentary on manipulation, *see* A. Bromberg & L. Lowenfels, Securities Fraud & Commodities Fraud §§ 6:55 et seq., 7:73 et seq., (2015); Fischel & Ross, *Should the SEC Prohibit "Manipulation" in Financial Markets?*, 105 Harv. L. Rev. 503 (1991); Howard, *Frontrunning in the Marketplace: A Regulatory Dilemma*, 19 Sec. Reg. L.J. 263 (1989); Multer, *Open Market Manipulation under SEC Rule 10b-5 and Its Analogues*, 39 Sec. Reg. L.J. 97 (2011); Poser, *Stock Market Manipulation and Corporate Control Transactions*, 40 U. Miami L. Rev. 671 (1986); Thel, *Regulation of Manipulation Under Section 10(b): Securities Prices and the Text of the Securities Exchange Act of 1934*, 1988 Colum. Bus. L. Rev. 359 (1988).

acted differently had he/she known of the nondisclosure). As the Supreme Court stated in *Affiliated Ute Citizens v. United States*, 406 U.S. 128, 153–154 (1972):

> Under the circumstances of this case involving primarily a failure to disclose, positive proof of reliance is not a prerequisite to recovery. All that is necessary is that the facts withheld be material in the sense that a reasonable investor [would] have considered them important in the making of this decision. . . . This obligation to disclose and this withholding of a material fact establish the requisite element of causation in fact.

An analysis of the reliance requirement and its relationship to the causation and plaintiff "due diligence" requirements was set forth as follows by a federal appellate court:

Reliance and Causation

Reliance and causation are related concepts. In the common law deceit action from which the Rule 10b-5 claim is derived, it was necessary for the plaintiff to show reliance on the defendant's fraudulent representations as a prerequisite to recovery. Establishing reliance, however, merely proves that the plaintiff was induced to act by the defendant's conduct. It is a non sequitur to conclude that the representation that induced action necessarily caused the consequences of that action. . . . [T]he general statement of the elements of recovery under Rule 10b-5 requires proof both that the plaintiff relied on the misstatement and that the misstatement was the cause of his loss.

In Affiliated Ute Citizens of Utah v. United States, . . . the Supreme Court held that in some circumstances affirmative proof of reliance is not necessary. It distinguished the three subparagraphs of Rule 10b-5, pointing out that the first and third subparagraphs are not restricted to the misstatement or omission of a material fact but forbid a "course of business" or a "device, scheme, or artifice" that operates as a fraud. If a person who has an "affirmative duty under the Rule to disclose" a material fact to the holder of a security devises a plan to induce the holder to sell the securities without disclosing to him material facts that reasonably [would] be expected to influence his decision to sell, positive proof of reliance, it held, is not a prerequisite to recovery.

. . . .

While *Affiliated Ute* relieves the investor in certain circumstances of the necessity of proving affirmatively that he relied on a prospectus or other representation, it does not eliminate the reliance element from the Rule 10b-5 case altogether. . . . In *Rifkin v. Crow*, 574 F.2d 256, 262 (5th Cir. 1978), we restated our understanding of the *Affiliated Ute* rationale as it relates to proof of reliance in a Rule 10b-5 action:

> [W]here a 10b-5 action alleges defendant made positive misrepresentations of material information, proof of reliance by the plaintiff upon the misrepresentation is required. Upon an absence of proof on the issue, plaintiff loses. On

the other hand, where a plaintiff alleges deception by defendant's nondisclosure of material information, the *Ute* presumption obviates the need for plaintiff to prove actual reliance on the omitted information. Upon a failure of proof on the issue, defendant loses. But this presumption of reliance in nondisclosure cases is not conclusive. If defendant can prove that plaintiff did not rely, that is, that plaintiff's decision would not have been affected even if defendant had disclosed the omitted facts, then plaintiff's recovery is barred.

Thus, reliance is an issue in all Rule 10b-5 cases. The difference between misrepresentation and non-disclosure cases relates only to whether proof of reliance is a prerequisite to recovery or whether proof of nonreliance is an affirmative defense. . . .

It is, therefore, necessary to characterize the facts in a Rule 10b-5 case as involving either primarily a failure to disclose, implicating the first or third subparagraph of the Rule and invoking the *Affiliated Ute* presumption of reliance, or, on the other hand, primarily a misstatement or failure to state a fact necessary to make those statements made not misleading, classified under the second subparagraph of the Rule and as to which no presumption of reliance is applicable. . . . This case, involving alleged misstatements and omissions in a prospectus published pursuant to a public offering, cannot properly be characterized as an omissions case of the type for which the *Affiliated Ute* presumption was fashioned. The defendants did not "stand mute" in the face of a duty to disclose as did the defendants in *Affiliated Ute*. . . . They undertook instead to disclose relevant information in an offering statement now alleged to contain certain misstatements of fact and to fail to contain other facts necessary to make the statements made, in light of the circumstances, not misleading. This is not a case in which difficulties of proof of reliance require the application of the *Affiliated Ute* presumption. Because the plaintiffs were not entitled to a presumption of reliance, a jury finding that the plaintiffs relied upon the misstatements and omissions in the prospectus was essential to the plaintiffs' recovery.

. . . .

The district court compounded its failure to submit the reliance issue to the jury by failing also to submit the question of causation. Causation is related to but distinct from reliance. Reliance is a causa sine qua non, a type of "but for" requirement: had the investor known the truth he would not have acted.[17] Courts sometimes consider the reliance components of the Rule 10b-5 action to be a part of the causation element. . . . In this context, the term "transaction causation" is used to describe the requirement that the defendant's fraud must precipitate the investment decision. Reliance is necessarily closely related to "transaction causation." On the other hand,

---

[17]. [This footnote has been moved to the text. — ed.]

"loss causation" refers to a direct causal link between the misstatement and the claimant's economic loss. . . .

Causation requires one further step in the analysis: even if the investor would not otherwise have acted, was the misrepresented fact a proximate cause of the loss? . . . The plaintiff must prove not only that, had he known the truth, he would not have acted, but in addition that the untruth was in some reasonably direct, or proximate, way responsible for his loss. . . . If the investment decision is induced by misstatements or omissions that are material and that were relied on by the claimant, but are not the proximate reason for his pecuniary loss, recovery under the Rule is not permitted. . . . Absent the requirement of causation, Rule 10b-5 would become an insurance plan for the cost of every security purchased in reliance upon a material misstatement or omission. . . .

Huddleston v. Herman & MacLean, 640 F.2d 534, 547–549 (5th Cir. 1981), *aff'd in part and rev'd in part, on other grounds*, 459 U.S. 375 (1983).

Note that § 21D(b)(4) of the Exchange Act expressly requires that a plaintiff prove loss causation in any private action arising under that Act.

Do you agree with the court's analysis that a presumption of reliance should not apply in cases of "half-truths" coming within subparagraph (2) of Rule 10b-5? Can it be argued that a determination on an ad hoc basis of whether an alleged fraud involves half-truths or "pure" nondisclosures at times may be a cumbersome task, giving rise to conjecture? Moreover, is the plaintiff's task equally as challenging in seeking to establish positive proof of reliance, regardless whether the case involves "pure" nondisclosures or half-truths?

[B] The "In Connection With" Requirement

Securities and Exchange Commission v. Zandford

United States Supreme Court

535 U.S. 813, 122 S. Ct. 1899, 153 L. Ed 2d 1 (2002)

Opinion of the Court delivered by STEVENS, Associate Justice

The Securities and Exchange Commission (SEC) filed a civil complaint alleging that a stockbroker violated both § 10(b) of the Securities Exchange Act of 1934 and the SEC's Rule 10b-5, by selling his customer's securities and using the proceeds for his own benefit without the customer's knowledge or consent. The question presented is whether the alleged fraudulent conduct was "in connection with the purchase or sale of any security" within the meaning of the statute and the rule.

I

Between 1987 and 1991, respondent was employed as a securities broker in the Maryland branch of a New York brokerage firm. In 1987, he persuaded William Wood, an elderly man in poor health, to open a joint investment account for himself and his mentally retarded daughter. According to the SEC's complaint, the "stated investment objectives for the account were 'safety of principal and income.'" The Woods granted respondent discretion to manage their account and a general power of attorney to engage in securities transactions for their benefit without prior approval. Relying on respondent's promise to "conservatively invest" their money, the Woods entrusted him with $419,255. Before Mr. Wood's death in 1991, all of the money was gone.

In 1991, the National Association of Securities Dealers (NASD) [now FINRA] conducted a routine examination of respondent's firm and discovered that on over 25 separate occasions, money had been transferred from the Woods' account to accounts controlled by respondent. In due course, respondent was indicted in the United States District Court for the District of Maryland on 13 counts of wire fraud in violation of 18 U.S.C. § 1343. The first count alleged that respondent sold securities in the Woods' account and then made personal use of the proceeds. Each of the other counts alleged that he made wire transfers between Maryland and New York that enabled him to withdraw specified sums from the Woods' accounts. Some of those transfers involved respondent writing checks to himself from a mutual fund account held by the Woods, which required liquidating securities in order to redeem the checks. Respondent was convicted on all counts, sentenced to prison for 52 months, and ordered to pay $10,800 in restitution.

After respondent was indicted, the SEC filed a civil complaint in the same District Court alleging that respondent violated § 10(b) and Rule 10b-5 by engaging in a scheme to defraud the Woods and by misappropriating approximately $343,000 of the Woods' securities without their knowledge or consent. The SEC moved for partial summary judgment after respondent's criminal conviction, arguing that the judgment in the criminal case estopped respondent from contesting facts that established a violation of § 10(b). Respondent filed a motion seeking discovery on the question whether his fraud had the requisite "connection with" the purchase or sale of a security. The District Court refused to allow discovery and entered summary judgment against respondent. It enjoined him from engaging in future violations of the securities laws and ordered him to disgorge $343,000 in ill-gotten gains.

The Court of Appeals for the Fourth Circuit reversed the summary judgment and remanded with directions for the District Court to dismiss the complaint. 238 F.3d 559 (2001). It first held that the wire fraud conviction, which only required two findings— (1) that respondent engaged in a scheme to defraud and (2) that he used interstate wire communications in executing the scheme—did not establish all the elements of a § 10(b) violation. Specifically, the conviction did not necessarily establish that his fraud was "in connection with" the sale of a security. The court then held that the civil complaint did not sufficiently allege the necessary connection because the sales of the Woods' securities were merely incidental to a fraud that "lay in absconding with the proceeds" of sales that were conducted in "a routine and customary fashion." Respondent's "scheme was simply to steal the Woods' assets" rather than to engage "in manipulation of a particular security." Ultimately, the court refused "to stretch the language of the securities fraud provisions to encompass every conversion or theft that happens to involve securities." . . .

We granted the SEC's petition for a writ of certiorari to review the Court of Appeals' construction of the phrase "in connection with the purchase or sale of any security."

. . . .

II

Section 10(b) of the Securities Exchange Act makes it "unlawful for any person . . . [t]o use or employ, in connection with the purchase or sale of any security . . . , any manipulative or deceptive device or contrivance in contravention of such rules and regulations as the [SEC] may prescribe." Rule 10b-5, which implements this provision, forbids the use, "in connection with the purchase or sale of any security," of any device, scheme, or artifice to defraud or any other "act, practice, or course or business that operates . . . as a fraud or deceit." Among Congress' objectives in passing the Act was "to insure honest securities markets and thereby promote investor confidence" after the market crash of 1929. More generally, Congress sought "'to substitute a philosophy of full disclosure for the philosophy of *caveat emptor* and thus to achieve a high standard of business ethics in the securities industry.'"

Consequently, we have explained that the statute should be "construed 'not technically and restrictively, but flexibly to effectuate its remedial purposes.'" In its role enforcing the Act, the SEC has consistently adopted a broad reading of the phrase "in connection with the purchase or sale of any security." It has maintained that a broker who accepts payment for securities that he never intends to deliver, or who sells customer securities with intent to misappropriate the proceeds, violates § 10(b) and Rule 10b-5. This interpretation of the ambiguous text of § 10(b), in the context of formal adjudication, is entitled to deference if it is reasonable. For the reasons set forth below, we think it is. While the statute must not be construed so broadly as to convert every common-law fraud that happens to involve securities into a violation of § 10(b), neither the SEC nor this Court has ever held that there must be a misrepresentation about the value of a particular security in order to run afoul of the Act.

The SEC claims respondent engaged in a fraudulent scheme in which he made sales of his customer's securities for his own benefit. Respondent submits that the sales themselves were perfectly lawful and that the subsequent misappropriation of the proceeds, though fraudulent, is not properly viewed as having the requisite connection with the sales; in his view, the alleged scheme is not materially different from a simple theft of cash or securities in an investment account. We disagree.

According to the complaint, respondent "engaged in a scheme to defraud" the Woods beginning in 1988, shortly after they opened their account, and that scheme continued throughout the 2-year period during which respondent made a series of transactions that enabled him to convert the proceeds of the sales of the Woods' securities to his own use. The securities sales and respondent's fraudulent practices were not independent events. This is not a case in which, after a lawful transaction had been consummated, a broker decided to steal the proceeds and did so. Nor is it a case in which a thief simply invested the proceeds of a routine conversion in the stock market. Rather, respondent's fraud coincided with the sales themselves.

Taking the allegations in the complaint as true, each sale was made to further respondent's fraudulent scheme; each was deceptive because it was neither authorized by, nor disclosed to, the Woods. With regard to the sales of shares in the Woods' mutual fund, respondent initiated these transactions by writing a check to himself from that account, knowing that redeeming the check would require the sale of securities. Indeed, each time respondent "exercised his power of disposition for his own benefit," that conduct, "without more," was a fraud. In the aggregate, the sales are properly viewed as a "course of business" that operated as a fraud or deceit on a stockbroker's customer.

Insofar as the connection between respondent's deceptive practices and his sale of the Woods' securities is concerned, the case is remarkably similar to *Superintendent of Ins. of N.Y. v. Bankers Life & Casualty Co.*, 404 U.S. 6 (1971). In that case the directors of Manhattan Casualty Company authorized the sale of the company's portfolio of treasury bonds because they had been "duped" into believing that the company would receive the proceeds of the sale. We held that "Manhattan was injured as an investor through a deceptive device which deprived it of any compensation for the sale of its valuable block of securities." In reaching this conclusion, we did not ask, as the Fourth Circuit did in this case, whether the directors were misled about the value of a security or whether the fraud involved "manipulation of a particular security." In fact, we rejected the Second Circuit's position in *Superintendent of Ins. of N.Y. v. Bankers Life & Casualty Co.*, 430 F.2d 355, 361 (1970), that because the fraud against Manhattan did not take place within the context of a securities exchange it was not prohibited by § 10(b). We refused to read the statute so narrowly, noting that it "must be read flexibly, not technically and restrictively." Although we recognized that the interests in "'preserving the integrity of the securities markets,'" was one of the purposes animating the statute, we rejected the notion that § 10(b) is limited to serving that objective alone. . . .

Like the company directors in *Bankers Life*, the Woods were injured as investors through respondent's deceptions, which deprived them of any compensation for the sale of their valuable securities. They were duped into believing respondent would "conservatively invest" their assets in the stock market and that any transactions made on their behalf would be for their benefit for the "'safety of principal and income.'" The fact that respondent misappropriated the proceeds of the sales provides persuasive evidence that he had violated § 10(b) when he made the sales, but misappropriation is not an essential element of the offense. Indeed, in *Bankers Life*, we flatly stated that it was "irrelevant" that "the proceeds of the sale that were due the seller were misappropriated." It is enough that the scheme to defraud and the sale of securities coincide.

The Court of Appeals below distinguished *Bankers Life* on the ground that it involved an affirmative misrepresentation, whereas respondent simply failed to inform the Woods of his intent to misappropriate their securities. We are not persuaded by this distinction. Respondent was only able to carry out his fraudulent scheme without making any affirmative misrepresentation because the Woods had entrusted him to make transactions in their best interest without prior approval.

Under these circumstances, respondent's fraud represents an even greater threat to investor confidence in the securities industry than the misrepresentation in *Bankers Life*. Not only does such a fraud prevent investors from trusting that their brokers are executing transactions for their benefit, but it undermines the value of a discretionary account like that held by the Woods. The benefit of a discretionary account is that it enables individuals, like the Woods, who lack the time, capacity, or know-how to supervise investment decisions, to delegate authority to a broker who will make decisions in their best interests without prior approval. If such individuals cannot rely on a broker to exercise that discretion for their benefit, then the account loses its added value. Moreover, any distinction between omissions and misrepresentations is illusory in the context of a broker who has a fiduciary duty to her clients.

More recently, in *Wharf (Holdings) Ltd. v. United Int'l Holdings, Inc.*, 532 U.S. 588 (2001), our decision that the seller of a security had violated § 10(b) focused on the secret intent of the seller when the sale occurred. The purchaser claimed "that Wharf sold it a security (the option) while secretly intending from the very beginning not to honor the option." Although Wharf did not specifically argue that the breach of contract underlying the complaint lacked the requisite connection with a sale of securities, it did assert that the case was merely a dispute over ownership of the option, and that interpreting § 10(b) to include such a claim would convert every breach of contract that happened to involve a security into a violation of the federal securities laws. We rejected that argument because the purchaser's claim was not that the defendant failed to carry out a promise to sell securities; rather, the claim was that the defendant sold a security while never intending to honor its agreement in the first place. Similarly, in this case the SEC claims respondent sold the Woods' securities while secretly intending from the very beginning to keep the proceeds. In *Wharf*, the fraudulent intent deprived the purchaser of the benefit of the sale whereas here the fraudulent intent deprived the seller of that benefit, but the connection between the deception and the sale in each case is identical.

In *United States v. O'Hagan*, 521 U.S. 642 (1997), we held that the defendant had committed fraud "in connection with" a securities transaction when he used misappropriated confidential information for trading purposes. We reasoned that "the fiduciary's fraud is consummated, not when the fiduciary gains the confidential information, but when, without disclosure to his principal, he uses the information to purchase or sell securities. The securities transaction and the breach of duty thus coincide. This is so even though the person or entity defrauded is not the other party to the trade, but is, instead, the source of the nonpublic information." The Court of Appeals distinguished *O'Hagan* by reading it to require that the misappropriated information or assets not have independent value to the client outside the securities market. We do not read *O'Hagan* as so limited. In the chief passage cited by the Court of Appeals for this proposition, we discussed the Government's position that "[t]he misappropriation theory would not . . . apply to a case in which a person defrauded a bank into giving him a loan or embezzled cash from another, and then used the proceeds of the misdeed to purchase securities," because in that situation "the proceeds would have value to the malefactor apart from their use in a securities transaction, and the fraud would be complete as soon as the money was obtained." Even if this passage could be read to introduce a new requirement into § 10(b), it would not affect our analysis of this case, because the Woods' securities did not have value for respondent apart from their use in a securities transaction and the fraud was not complete before the sale of securities occurred.

As in *Bankers Life, Wharf,* and *O'Hagan,* the SEC complaint describes a fraudulent scheme in which the securities transactions and breaches were therefore "in connection with" securities sales within the meaning of § 10(b). Accordingly, the judgment of the Court of Appeals is reversed, and the case is remanded for further proceedings consistent with this opinion.

It is so ordered.

[C] Justifiable Reliance

The plaintiff's due diligence requirement generally requires that the plaintiff's reliance be justifiable. The following factors are relevant in determining whether the plaintiff's reliance was justifiable:

> (1) the sophistication and expertise of the plaintiff in financial and securities matters; (2) the existence of longstanding business or personal relationships; (3) access to the relevant information; (4) the existence of a fiduciary relationship; (5) concealment of the fraud; (6) the opportunity to detect the fraud; (7) whether the plaintiff initiated the stock transaction or sought to expedite the transaction; and (8) the generality or specificity of the misrepresentations.

Ashland Inc. v. Morgan Stanley & Co., Inc., 652 F.3d 333, 338 (2d Cir. 2011). This approach represents the prevailing view.

In *Dupuy v. Dupuy,* 551 F.2d 1005, 1014–1020 (5th Cir. 1977), the Fifth Circuit recognized two policy rationales for this requirement: "First, general principles of equity suggest that only those who have pursued their own interests with care and good faith should qualify for the judicially created private 10b-5 remedies. Second, by requiring plaintiffs to invest carefully, the court promotes the anti-fraud policies of the Acts and engenders stability in the markets." In view of the Supreme Court's decision in *Hochfelder* (see § 7.03[A] *supra*), the Fifth Circuit in *Dupuy* opined:

> We consider that *Ernst & Ernst v. Hochfelder* prompts a change in the law of due diligence, as it is applicable in 10b-5 cases. Both tort law and federal securities policy support imposing on the plaintiff only a standard of care not exceeding that imposed on the defendant. Although the "scienter" requirement may still be unsettled, the Supreme Court has imposed on defendants a standard not stricter than recklessness. In this case, then, the question should not be whether [plaintiff] acted unreasonably by failing to

investigate the condition of Lori Corporation. Instead, the Court should ask whether [plaintiff] intentionally refused to investigate in disregard of a risk known to him or so obvious that he must be taken to have been aware of it, and so great as to make it highly probable that harm would follow.

Two interesting issues that surface in securities litigation are: (1) whether a plaintiff justifiably relies on allegedly false oral statements when the written offering documents, such as a prospectus, are accurate; and (2) whether the inclusion of adequate cautionary language in the written offering documents will render the plaintiff's reliance on the accompanying forward-looking information (e.g., projections) contained in the written materials unjustified. Both of these issues also may be viewed from the perspective of materiality, signifying that the alleged misrepresentations may be deemed immaterial as a matter of law. The following materials address these scenarios.

Myers v. Finkle

United States Court of Appeals, Fourth Circuit

950 F.2d 165 (1991)

WILKINS, Circuit Judge.

Arthur R. Myers, II, his wife, Mary J. Myers, and their son, Arthur R. Myers, III, instituted this action against an accounting firm and its partners (collectively "Finkle"). The Myers alleged violations of section 10(b) of the Securities Exchange Act of 1934 [as well as other provisions.]

I.

For purposes of our review, the following summary of facts is presented in a light most favorable to the Myers. In 1977 Finkle began performing accounting services for the Myers that included preparation of their individual and corporate income tax returns. In 1981 Finkle advised the Myers that they could reduce their income tax liability by investing in real estate limited partnerships as tax shelters. Recommending specific partnerships in which Finkle had a financial interest, Finkle assured the Myers that the investments would result in an "economic profit" in addition to tax benefits. The Myers relied on this advice and followed Finkle's recommendations.

From 1981 to 1985 the Myers invested over $4.8 million in 15 real estate limited partnerships specifically recommended by Finkle. For each investment, the partnership sent the Myers a private placement memorandum describing the risks and prospects of the real estate project being developed by that limited partnership. The private placement memoranda were generally sent to the Myers after Finkle presented them with the necessary investment documents for execution and the investment transaction was completed. The Myers took substantial deductions for tax purposes as a result of losses incurred by the partnerships, but did not realize any monetary return on their investments. The limited partnerships are now in severe financial distress. The Myers claim as damages the amount of their investments, lost use of the funds invested, and consequential damages. . . .

II.

Summary judgment is proper if there is no genuine issue of material fact and the moving party is entitled to judgment as a matter of law. . . . In determining whether this showing has been made, the court must assess the evidence in a light most favorable to the party opposing the motion. . . .

Section 10(b) of the 1934 Act prohibits the use of any manipulative or deceptive device or contrivance in connection with the purchase or sale of any security. . . . "The elements of a Rule 10b-5 cause of action are: (1) the defendant made a false statement or omission of material fact (2) with scienter (3) upon which the plaintiff justifiably relied (4) that proximately caused the plaintiff's damages." . . .

For purposes of this appeal, Finkle concedes that the Myers have established all elements of their claim except justifiable reliance. The Myers contend that this concession, coupled with the existence of material issues of fact regarding the justifiable reliance element, made summary judgment inappropriate. A determination of whether an investor may be justified in relying on oral representations that conflict with contemporaneous written statements in the investor's possession requires a consideration of all relevant factors, including:

> (1) [t]he sophistication and expertise of the plaintiff in financial and securities matters; (2) the existence of long standing business or personal relationships; (3) access to relevant information; (4) the existence of a fiduciary relationship; (5) concealment of the fraud; (6) the opportunity to detect the fraud; (7) whether the plaintiff initiated the stock transaction or sought to expedite the transaction; and (8) the generality or specificity of the misrepresentations.

. . . . Because no single factor is dispositive, consideration of all factors is necessary.

In determining whether the Myers were justified in relying on Finkle's oral representations, we are presented with [the] factual situation in which the oral representations are contradicted by warnings contained in the private placement memoranda. The Myers concede that they "did not study" these documents. In our view, knowledge of information should be imputed to investors who fail to exercise caution when they have in their possession documents apprising them of the risks attendant to the investments. Investors are charged with constructive knowledge of the risks and warnings contained in the private placement memoranda. . . . Consequently, in evaluating the various factors relevant to justifiable reliance, the conduct of the Myers must be examined as if they were aware of the warnings.

The first factor regarding justifiable reliance involves a consideration of the sophistication of the Myers and their experience in financial and investment matters. A review of the affidavits addressing this issue demonstrates their contradictions: in summary, the Myers claim to be inexperienced in investment matters and to have been unfamiliar with tax shelters, while Finkle claims that the Myers have a substantial net worth and operate a successful family-owned seafood business. The district court expressly acknowledged that "[t]he level of the Myers' sophistication is a material issue of fact as to which there is a genuine dispute." . . . However, the court viewed the Myers' apparent wealth as dispositive of the issue of sophistication. We disagree. While wealth may be an important factor, other criteria such as age, education, professional status, investment experience, and business background may also be relevant. . . . *See generally* Fletcher, *Sophisticated Investors Under the Federal Securities Laws,* 1988 Duke L.J. 1081, 1149–53 (listing numerous factors relevant to a determination of sophistication). [Cf. SEC Regulation D defining an individual to be an "accredited investor" because of such person's financial wealth and deeming such person irrebutably to possess financial sophistication.]

The district court also ruled that Finkle did not owe a fiduciary duty to the Myers and that the Myers did not have long-standing business or personal relationships with Finkle. . . . The Myers allege that they were social friends of Robert Finkle and other partners of the firm and that members of the firm spent considerable amounts of time working closely with the Myers on business matters. They further allege that Finkle rendered accounting services to them for four years prior to the initiation of the investment transactions and served as their accountants for a total of at least ten years. While Finkle conceded several of these facts and contested others, the Myers presented sufficient evidence to raise a genuine issue of material fact on this issue.

The evidence is also contradictory regarding the Myers' access to relevant information. The Myers allege that the subscription documents were sent to them for their signature in blank immediately prior to tax deadlines, thus precluding careful consideration of the information they contained. They additionally claim that they did not receive private placement memoranda for the offerings until several months after they signed the subscription documents and invested in the limited partnerships. Finkle contends that the memoranda and other offering materials were provided to the Myers prior to each investment and that financial projections were reviewed with the Myers or their representative. While we express no opinion as to how these disputed factual issues will ultimately be resolved, it would be improper to attribute knowledge of the memoranda to them prior to a determination of whether they had meaningful access to the documents. . . .

Finally, the Myers have raised issues of fact regarding whether they initiated or sought to expedite the transactions. Finkle claims that the Myers initiated the transactions by indicating an interest in avoiding tax liability by investing in the partnerships. However, the Myers contend that for each transaction Finkle called them during the final preparation stage of their tax returns, advised them to invest in the partnerships, and directed them to promptly execute and return the subscription documents.

We conclude that of the eight factors to be weighed in determining whether reliance was justified, the Myers have raised genuine issues of material fact regarding at least five. While the issues presented ultimately may be resolved against them, resolution by summary judgment was thus inappropriate.

. . . .

REVERSED IN PART, AFFIRMED IN PART, AND REMANDED.

Brown v. E.F. Hutton Group, Inc.

United States Court of Appeals, Second Circuit

991 F.2d 1026 (1993)

JACOBS, Circuit Judge.

. . . .

BACKGROUND

Plaintiffs-appellants are approximately 400 presumably unsophisticated, income-oriented investors in a limited partnership called the Hutton/Indian Wells 1983 Energy Income Fund, Ltd. (the "Partnership"). According to the Partnership's prospectus (the "Prospectus"), it was organized to acquire properties upon which existing oil and gas wells are located and to provide regular cash distributions to investors from sales of oil and gas produced from those properties.

After their investments allegedly became worthless, the plaintiffs-appellants (the "Limited Partners") brought suit in the United States District Court for the Southern District Court for the Southern District of New York against Hutton, the Indian Wells Production Company and related entities (collectively, the "defendants"). In their amended complaint, the Limited Partners assert two claims arising under § 10(b). . . .

A. *Allegations in the Amended Complaint*

The district court, for purposes of Hutton's summary judgment motion and without objection from Hutton, accepted as true the following allegations from the amended complaint: (a) that each of the more than 400 Limited Partners was unsophisticated; (b) that each Limited Partner told a Hutton account executive that his or her investment objectives included some combination of income, capital appreciation, tax benefits and savings; and (c) that the Hutton account executives gave oral assurance to each Limited Partner that the Partnership had either no risk or low risk. Hutton's motion did, however, contest the Limited Partners' allegations that they made their purchases in *justifiable reliance* on the brokers' oral representations . . . .

B. *The Offering Materials*

As the Limited Partners contend, the Brochure depicts the Partnership's financial outlook in bright terms. In this regard, the Brochure distinguishes the Partnership from prototypically risky oil and gas investments by emphasizing that the purchase of "only producing oil and gas properties" eliminates exploration risk. The Brochure's disclosure concerning other risks is by reference to the Prospectus. The jacket of the Brochure contains the following caution:

> The use of this material is authorized only when preceded or accompanied by a prospectus for Hutton Indian Wells Energy Income Fund, Ltd. Prospective investors are encouraged to read the prospectus, including the section entitled "Risk Factors."

Although the Brochure again and again references the risk disclosure sections in the Prospectus, nowhere does the Brochure quote or otherwise recite the cautionary statements in the Prospectus.

After a review of the Brochure in its entirety there can be no doubt that it is a selling tool. In contrast, the Prospectus' disclosure of the Partnership's risks is thorough and materially complete, if not decidedly glum. The cover of the Prospectus warns that "[n]o person has been authorized to give any information or to make any representations, other than those contained in this prospectus, and if given or made, such information or representations must not be relied upon." The first page of the prospectus states:

THIS OFFERING INVOLVES CERTAIN RISKS

See "RISK FACTORS"

The "RISK FACTORS" section takes up roughly three single spaced pages. It is prominently featured immediately after the opening "SUMMARY OF OFFERING" section. The "RISK FACTORS" section states at the outset that "[t]here can be no assurance that properties selected will produce oil or gas in the quantities or at the cost anticipated, or that they will not cease producing entirely." It ends by disclosing the Limited Partners' potential obligations in the event the Partnership is "involuntarily liquidated because of insolvency." The "RISK FACTORS" section is divided by headings entitled "General Risks" and "Specific Risks", and by fourteen subheadings entitled "Risks Inherent in Oil and Gas Operations", "Competition and Markets", "Regulation", "Operating and Environmental Hazards", "General Partners' Limited Prior Activities", "Diversification", "Lack of Opportunity to Review Partnership Properties", "Conflicts of Interest", "Limitations on Cash Distributions", "Limited Transferability", "Limited Liquidity", "Loss of Limited Liability", "Distribution of Partnership Properties", and "Partnership Liquidation". The "RISK FACTORS" section also directs the potential investor to numerous other sections of the Prospectus.

There is little in the Prospectus to tranquilize the investor. . . .

In addition, the Prospectus warns that the Limited Partners would "own no direct interest in any oil and gas properties or other assets owned by the Partnership"; that "[t]here will be no ready market" for the Partnership units; and that there is "no assurance that the Partnership will have the financial resources to honor its repurchase commitments."

DISCUSSION

. . . .

§ 10(b) UNSUITABILITY CLAIM

In granting Hutton's motion for summary judgment on the Limited Partners' § 10(b) unsuitability claim, the district court concluded that "the offering materials are not misleading as a matter of law, or, to the same effect, that plaintiffs' reliance on certain portions of the materials was not reasonable as a matter of law." The district court also concluded that the Limited Partners could not have reasonably relied on the alleged *oral* representations by Hutton account executives. Based on our review of the facts and the law, we believe the district court reached the proper result.

This Court [has] recognized the viability of a § 10(b) unsuitability claim . . . . A plaintiff must prove (1) that the securities purchased were unsuited to the buyer's needs; (2) that the defendant knew or reasonably believed the securities were unsuited to the buyer's needs; (3) that the defendant recommended or purchased the unsuitable securities for the buyer anyway; (4) that, with scienter, the defendant made material misrepresentations (or, owing a duty to the buyer, failed to disclose material information) relating to the suitability of the securities; and (5) that the buyer justifiably relied to its detriment on the defendant's fraudulent conduct. Scienter may be inferred by finding that the defendant knew or reasonably believed that the securities were unsuited to the investor's needs, misrepresented or failed to disclose the unsuitability of the securities, and proceeded to recommend or purchase the securities anyway. A plaintiff's burden with respect to the reliance element of an unsuitability claim, as in other § 10(b) and Rule 10b-5 actions, may vary depending on whether the claim alleges fraudulent representations or fraudulent omissions.

Analytically, an unsuitability claim is a subset of the ordinary § 10(b) fraud claim in which a plaintiff must allege, *inter alia*, (1) material misstatement(s) or omission(s), (2) indicating an intent to deceive or defraud, (3) in connection with the purchase or sale of a security. For purposes of this summary judgment motion we accept as true (as did the district court) the Limited Partners' allegations that the Partnership investment was incompatible with their needs for income, capital appreciation and savings, and we consider the aspects of the investment relating to those needs to be material facts as a matter of law.

For the purpose of our review, we will not take the Supplement into consideration. . . . [emphasis supplied]

A. DISCLOSURE OF SUITABILITY

The first count of the amended complaint generally asserts that Hutton's account executives' oral recommendations of the Partnership as a low risk, conservative investment misled the Limited Partners into purchasing unsuitable securities. The Limited Partners acknowledge that Hutton sent the Brochure and Prospectus, and that they received those documents; they insist, however, that the Brochure and Prospectus (a) fail to state expressly that the Partnership is unsuited to an investor who seeks an opportunity for "no risk", "low risk" or "conservative" capital appreciation, income or savings, and (b) understate, obscure or elide discussion of the real risks of the investment. We disagree.

We find that the Limited Partners' reliance on the oral statements presumptively made by Hutton as to the low risk, conservative character of the investment is not justified as a matter of law and that the alleged oral statements are contradicted by the offering materials sent to the Limited Partners. We find further that the information available to the Limited Partners about the suitability of their investments was materially complete and not misleading.

An investor may not justifiably rely on a misrepresentation if, through minimal diligence, the investor should have discovered the truth. . . . Under this standard, § 10(b) liability will not be imposed when an investor's conduct rises to the level of recklessness. To determine whether an investor acted recklessly, and therefore without justifiable reliance, no single factor is dispositive, and all relevant factors must be considered and balanced. . . . In *Royal American* we considered the plaintiff's sophistication and expertise in finance and in the subject matter of the securities transaction; the plaintiff's representation by counsel; the plaintiff's opportunity to detect the fraud; whether the fraud was concealed; and the nature of the fraud. 885 F.2d at 1016. This Court has never established a list of all relevant factors, although many courts have been guided by the following:

> (1) The sophistication and expertise of the plaintiff in financial and securities matters; (2) the existence of longstanding business or personal relationships; (3) access to the relevant information; (4) the existence of a fiduciary relationship; (5) concealment of the fraud; (6) the opportunity to detect the fraud; (7) whether the plaintiff initiated the stock transaction or sought to expedite the transaction; and (8) the generality or specificity of the misrepresentations.

> . . . .

The Limited Partners assert, and we agree, that the opinion below does not fully recite the district court's consideration of all relevant factors in reaching its conclusion that justifiable reliance cannot be established. The Limited Partners therefore suggest that we remand the case to permit the district court to set forth its analysis more explicitly. We decline this invitation. Since we have not previously required that the district court recite its factor-by-factor balancing of the relevant considerations, and since the undisputed facts in the extensive record in this case are more than adequate for this Court to apply the test in the first instance, we shall proceed to do so in the interests of judicial economy.

Although for present purposes we presume that the Limited Partners are unsophisticated investors and that the brokers initiated the transactions, the other relevant factors preclude a conclusion that the alleged reliance could have been justifiable. Initially, we note that none of the Limited Partners allege the existence of a fiduciary relationship or of a longstanding business or personal relationship with Hutton or its brokers. The dominant considerations here, however, are that the

Hutton brokers forwarded the offering materials to the Limited Partners; that the offering materials detailed the investment characteristics bearing upon suitability; that they did so in comprehensive and understandable language; and that the offering materials thereby contradicted the brokers' alleged general assurances.

Specifically, with respect to the Partnership's risks, the Brochure directs the potential investor to the Prospectus, the single most important document and perhaps the primary resource an investor should consult in seeking that information.[18] The Prospectus in turn indicates that the Partnership could collapse altogether depending on a variety of factors and developments, none of which is dismissed as remote. The first paragraph of the Prospectus' "RISK FACTORS" section tells prospective investors that their profits depend on the Partnership's purchase of properties that—assuming they produced oil or gas in the quantity and at the cost anticipated in the first place—may cease production altogether; and that whatever oil or gas may be produced would be sold in a regulated market that fluctuates and had been recently sinking. These warnings are reinforced in the Prospectus by disclosures concerning risks inherent in oil and gas operations, the highly competitive character of the venture, the management's limited experience in acquiring oil or gas producing properties, the Partnership's limited financial resources and technical staff relative to its competition, and the potential for substantial uninsured losses. No reasonable investor reviewing the disclosure documents could fail to appreciate that the Partnership could result in a total loss.

The disclosure of risks adequately informed the Limited Partners that the investment was not suitable for the purpose of generating low risk capital appreciation or income, and the disclosure of the investment's limited transferability and liquidity adequately informed the Limited Partners that the investment was not a suitable savings vehicle. Thus, the information made available to the Limited Partners accurately reflected the suitability of the investment (or lack thereof) for the individual investors; the Limited Partners' asserted reliance on the brokers' alleged oral statements, without further inquiry, was therefore reckless and unjustifiable.

We also find that the Brochure and Prospectus provided the Limited Partners with full and objective disclosure of non-misleading factual material. That is all they were entitled to receive. There is no requirement that written offering materials counteract the enticements of salesmen by anticipating each sales pitch and rebutting it explicitly.

CONCLUSION

As a matter of law, the facts adduced by the Limited Partners cannot support a finding that the Limited Partners justifiably relied on the Hutton account executives'

---

[18]. The Prospectus' express warning to potential investors that they not rely on information or representations obtained elsewhere further establishes its primacy as the source of risk disclosures. However, we agree with the Limited Partners that, despite this warning, information or representations outside of the Prospectus may be material and justify reliance. As stated by the Tenth Circuit, "we do not imply that the defendants can disclaim responsibility for their misrepresentations simply by disclosing the risks in the memorandum and therein warning investors not to rely on representations not contained within the memorandum." 708 F.2d at 1518.

alleged assurance of suitability, or a finding that the Brochure and Prospectus contained material omissions or misrepresentations concerning the suitability of the investment. The Limited Partners, having thus failed to make a showing "sufficient to establish the existence of an element essential to that party's case, and on which that party will bear the burden of proof at trial," ... cannot maintain their unsuitability claim and Hutton is entitled to a judgment as a matter of law.

Accordingly, we find that the district court properly granted Hutton's motion for summary judgment, properly dismissed both pendent state law claims and properly denied reargument.

The judgments of the district court appealed from are affirmed.

Note

Do you agree with the Second Circuit's rationale in *Brown*, given that the investors were unsophisticated? With respect to "seasoned" investors and the costs associated with this type of litigation, Judge Kozinski's dissenting opinion in *Layman v. Combs*, 981 F.2d 1093 (9th Cir. 1993), follows:

> The right to make contracts is more than just a socially useful convention; it's an important aspect of personal autonomy. By contract, we can order some of the most important aspects of our existence: housing, health care, education, the pursuit of a profession or vocation, sometimes even marriage. Having the power to bind ourselves in exchange for similar concessions from others gives us a significant measure of control over our lives.

> Signing a contract does not, of course, guarantee we will be better off. A system of mutual, free exchange gives us only the opportunity to better ourselves; business acumen, diligence and luck will affect the final tally. The right to contract therefore means the right to take chances, to play hunches, to make mistakes; it means having to live by our decisions, no matter how they turn out: "Wise or not, a deal is a deal." ...

> More fundamentally, I question the majority's solicitude for these subscribers. These weren't mom and pop investors who mortgaged their retirement to buy palladium mines in Zanzibar. They weren't forced into the contract by economic duress; they weren't badgered by salesmen who pounded down their doors on Saturday morning. These were seasoned business people who commanded considerable resources. Many of them had substantial experience with horse breeding; some had already been doing business with Spendthrift.[19] Most retained independent investment

[19]. Typical is Robert Stratmore, an attorney who specialized in equestrian law and transactions, who grossed more than $15 million in thoroughbred trading the year of the Spendthrift offering and who holds lifetime breeding rights to Triple Crown winner Seattle Slew. As defendants point out in their briefs, other subscribers included international fashion mogul Calvin Klein;

advisers and lawyers, and took their sweet time buying into the deal. They risked what they warranted were disposable resources, hoping to get even richer. They gambled—and they lost.

. . . The whole point of requiring a written prospectus that conforms to the SEC's precise guidelines is to ensure that the parties rely on unbiased written data, not on half-whispered oral representations. Letting parties warrant that they are relying only on those offering materials serves this policy admirably: It forces potential subscribers to look closely at the written materials and avoids the ambiguity and claims of fraud inevitably fostered by collateral oral promises. The warranty, moreover, focuses on reliance, the key element in establishing liability under Rule 10b-5. . . . Reliance is, by its nature, subjective; it's easily fabricated or distorted, particularly after the deal sours. Letting parties agree about what they will and will not consider in making a sophisticated, face-to-face securities investment would avoid the cost, uncertainty and delay of securities litigation that now turns on inherently unknowable mental processes.

Much is at stake here for everyone involved. This litigation—although it resulted in a complete defense victory, mostly on summary judgment—devoured a staggering quantity of productive resources. The record consists of 50 cubic feet of paper and weighs over half a ton. There were 4500 entries in the docket sheets below, including almost 400 orders and rulings by the district court. Fifty-seven briefs, consisting of nearly 1800 pages, were filed on appeal, yielding three published opinions. Some 200 attorneys contributed to this conflagration, supported by legions of paralegals, summer associates and other staff. The attorneys' fees, for the seven defendants who requested them, amounted to more than $3.5 *million*. This says nothing of the fees incurred by the 13 plaintiffs and the 14 defendants who didn't request reimbursement; it doesn't take into account other litigation expenses such as photocopying, telephone, facsimile and messenger charges; deposition transcripts; airfares, limousines and hotel rooms; power meals in swank restaurants. *See generally* Gibbs, *Skadden Calls Fee Routine; Florida Calls It Gouging*, American Lawyer, July/Aug. 1991, at 19 (billing dispute involving, among other things, a $17 fee for courier delivery of a 75-cent newspaper).

Chasing down ephemeral oral representations may be great fun for the lawyers—and so profitable too—but it does nothing to ensure the integrity or regularity of our securities markets. To the contrary, fear of this type of scorched earth litigation—the juridical equivalent of the firebombing of Dresden—will only discourage people like the sellers from entering into such transactions. That the plaintiffs were able to inflict major financial damage on their adversaries, using as their launch vehicle a case so thin it

---

Zenya Yoshida, Japan's largest and most prominent horse breeder; and the Layman family who has been involved with thoroughbred horses for over thirty years.

was never allowed to reach the jury, will surely send a chill down the spine of anyone contemplating selling securities—or engaging in any other type of business—in our litigation-minded society. Assuming, as we must, that our national interest is served when financial markets function efficiently, unbeclouded by the risk of kamikaze litigation, a clear statement that we *will* enforce a subscriber's warranty he hasn't considered matters outside the offering materials would have an entirely salutary effect.

Doing so would inflict no injustice. The subscribers were sophisticated and obviously wielded substantial bargaining power. They got legal and financial advice galore before committing to the deal. Had they relied on oral representations made by the sellers, they could (and should) have said so before the money was paid and the securities delivered. . . .

The Seventh Circuit takes a more restrictive approach to this subject, reasoning that, as a matter of law, such oral statements in conflict with written disclosures do not meet the materiality threshold and that a plaintiff's reliance on such oral statements is unjustified. In *Acme Propane, Inc. v. Tenexco, Inc.*, 844 F.2d 1317, 1325 (7th Cir. 1988), the court stated: "[W]ritten words govern oral ones in order to reward truthful disclosures and facilitate accurate assessment of risk. . . . We keep in mind the need to deter deceit, both oral and written, and so we shall insist that the written words be true, clear, and complete, in order to be dispositive."

Moreover, does the Seventh Circuit's language in *Eckstein v. Balcor Film Investors*, 8 F.3d 1121, 1131–1132 (7th Cir. 1993), give promoters free license to lie in their glossy sales brochures so long as the written offering memorandum is accurate? Consider the following:

The '33 Act [and SEC rules under certain conditions] permit issuers, underwriters, and dealers to engage in "free writing" . . . and to furnish promotional literature to investors. . . . Only the registration statement need be self-contained. A prospectus is a subset of the information contained in the registration statement, and the sales brochures are a subset of the information in the prospectus (plus the customary effort to sell the securities). If the sales literature had to contain all the warnings that appear in the prospectus, the privilege of distributing supplemental sales literature would be all but meaningless. Federal law establishes a regime in which the prospectus contains the comprehensive description of the securities. Other literature can be brief precisely because an inquiring investor has the prospectus to turn to. Federal law also establishes a rule for resolving conflicts: in the event statements in sales brochures and the prospectus do not agree, the prospectus wins. . . . The plaintiffs do not contend that the risk disclosures in the prospectus were buried or indigestible; to the contrary, they were prominent and blunt. . . . Failure to disclose important things in supplemental literature is not fraud when those things appear in the prospectus. . . .

[D] The "Bespeaks Caution" and Related Doctrines

The "bespeaks caution" doctrine may be viewed from both "materiality" and "reliance" perspectives. The doctrine, *which does not extend to statements of historical fact*, provides that where a disclosure document, such as an offering document or SEC Form 10-K, contains "statements of *future* forecasts, projections and expectations with adequate cautionary language, those statements are not actionable as securities fraud."[20] Hence, under the "bespeaks caution" doctrine, adequate cautionary statements make reliance on the projections or other soft information unreasonable and renders the statements, when read in conjunction with the cautionary language, immaterial.

The Third Circuit in *In re Donald J. Trump Casinos Litigation*, 7 F.3d 357 (3d Cir. 1993), analyzed the "bespeaks caution" doctrine as follows:

> The district court applied what has come to be known as the "bespeaks caution" doctrine. In so doing it followed the lead of a number of courts of appeals which have dismissed securities fraud claims under Rule 12(b)(6) because cautionary language in the offering document negated the materiality of an alleged misrepresentation or omission. . . . We are persuaded by the [reasoning] of these cases and will apply bespeaks caution to the facts before us. The application of bespeaks caution depends on the specific text of the offering document or other communication at issue, i.e., courts must assess the communication on a case-by-case basis. Nevertheless, we can state as a general matter that, when an offering document's forecasts, opinions or projections are accompanied by meaningful cautionary statements, the forward-looking statements will not form the basis for a securities fraud claim if those statements did not affect the "total mix" of information the document provided investors. In other words, cautionary language, if sufficient, renders the alleged omissions or misrepresentations immaterial as a matter of law.

> The bespeaks caution doctrine is, as an analytical matter, equally applicable to allegations of both affirmative misrepresentations and omissions concerning soft information. Whether the plaintiffs allege a document contains an affirmative prediction/opinion which is misleading or fails to include a forecast or prediction which failure is misleading, the cautionary statements included in the document may render the challenged predictive statements or opinions immaterial as a matter of law. Of course, a vague or blanket (boilerplate) disclaimer which merely warns the reader that the investment has risks will ordinarily be inadequate to prevent misinformation. To suffice, the

---

20. *In re Donald J. Trump Casinos Securities Litigation*, 793 F. Supp. 543, 544 (D.N.J. 1992), *aff'd*, 7 F. 3d 357 (3d Cir. 1993) (emphasis supplied). *See Livid Holdings Ltd. v. Salomon Smith Barney Inc.*, 416 F. 3d 940, 948 (9th Cir. 2005) (holding that "extension of the bespeaks caution doctrine to statements of historical fact is inappropriate"). Accord, *Iowa Public Employees' Retirement System v. MF Global, Ltd.*, 620 F. 3d 137 (2d Cir. 2010).

cautionary statements must be substantive and tailored to the specific future projections, estimates or opinions in the prospectus which the plaintiffs challenge.

Because of the abundant and meaningful cautionary language contained in the prospectus, we hold that the plaintiffs have failed to state an actionable claim regarding the statement that the Partnership believed it could repay the bonds. We can say that the prospectus here truly bespeaks caution because, not only does the prospectus generally convey the riskiness of the investment, but its warnings and cautionary language directly address the substance of the statement the plaintiffs challenge. That is to say, the cautionary statements were tailored precisely to address the uncertainty concerning the Partnership's prospective inability to repay the bondholders.

The Private Securities Litigation Reform Act — Safe Harbor for Certain Forward-Looking Statements

The Private Securities Litigation Reform Act amended the Securities Act by adding a new §27A and further amended the Exchange Act by adding a new §21E. The new sections generally provide 1934 Act reporting companies (as well as those acting on their behalf and underwriters with respect to information furnished by or derived from information provided by such companies) with a safe harbor from liability in private actions for certain forward-looking statements (e.g., projections). The safe harbor is applicable to both forward-looking written and oral statements, so long as: (1) the statement is identified as a forward-looking statement and is accompanied by meaningful cautionary statements, thus codifying the "bespeaks caution" doctrine; (2) the statement lacks materiality; *or* (3) the plaintiff fails to prove that the statement was made with actual knowledge of its falsity (irrespective of whether cautionary language is included). This safe harbor applies only to private actions and not to SEC enforcement actions.

The safe harbor also contains specific provisions for oral forward-looking statements made by an issuer or those acting on its behalf under (1) above. Such oral forward-looking statements are protected if such statements are accompanied by appropriate cautionary language and identify "readily available" documentation that set forth important factors that could cause results to differ materially from those projected. The legislation provides that such documentation is to be deemed "readily available" if it is either filed with the SEC or otherwise generally disseminated. The applicability of the safe harbor provisions are subject to enumerated exclusions in the form of certain excluded issuers (e.g., penny stock issuers) and certain statements in specific instances (e.g., tender offers).

In addition, the safe harbor section specifies that its provisions do not impose a duty to update a forward-looking statement. It is unclear whether this language is meant to eliminate the "duty to update" any forward-looking statement or merely to clarify that no implied "duty to update" may be gleaned from this section. Hence, the breadth of this language will be developed by the courts.

For an example of a company's press release that conveys to recipients that forward-looking statements are contained therein, see the following:

> This press release includes "forward-looking" statements within the meaning of the U.S. Securities Acts. All of the statements contained in this press release, other than statements of historical fact, should be considered forward-looking statements, including but not limited to, any statements which may concern (i) the Company's strategies, objectives and plans for expansion of its operations, product and services, (ii) the Company's beliefs and expectations regarding actions that may be taken by regulatory authorities having oversight of the Company, and (iii) the Company's beliefs and expectations of its future operating results. Although the Company believes the expectation reflected in these forward-looking statements are reasonable, it can give no assurance that these expectations will prove to have been correct. All subsequent written and oral forward-looking statements by or attributable to the Company or persons acting on its behalf are expressly qualified in their entirety by this qualification. Investors are cautioned not to place undue reliance on these forward-looking statements, which speak only as of the date hereof and are not intended to give any assurance as to future results. The Company undertakes no obligation to publicly release any revisions to these forward-looking statements to reflect events or circumstances after the date hereof or to reflect the occurrence of unanticipated events.

In regard to this legislatively enacted safe harbor for forward-looking information, the following Joint Explanatory Statement of the Conference Committee is useful.

A Statutory Safe Harbor for Forward-Looking Statements

The Conference Committee has adopted a statutory "safe harbor" to enhance market efficiency by encouraging companies to disclose forward-looking information. This provision adds a new section 27A to the 1933 Act and a new section 21E of the 1934 Act which protects from liability in private lawsuits certain "forward-looking" statements made by persons specified in the legislation.

The Conference Committee has crafted a safe harbor that differs from the safe harbor provisions in the House and Senate passed bills. The Conference Committee safe harbor, like the Senate safe harbor, is based on aspects of SEC Rule 175 and the judicial created "bespeaks caution" doctrine. It is a bifurcated safe harbor that permits greater flexibility to those who may avail themselves of safe harbor protection. There is also a special safe harbor for issuers who make oral forward-looking statements.

The first prong of the safe harbor protects a written or oral forward-looking statement that is: (i) identified as forward-looking, and (ii) accompanied by meaningful cautionary statements identifying important factors that could cause actual results to differ materially from those projected in the statement.

Under this first prong of the safe harbor, boilerplate warnings will not suffice as meaningful cautionary statements identifying important factors that could cause actual results to differ materially from those projected in the statement. The cautionary statements must convey substantive information about factors that realistically could cause results to differ materially from those projected in the forward-looking statement, such as, for example, information about the issuer's business.

As part of the analysis of what constitutes a meaningful cautionary statement, courts should consider the factors identified in the statements. "Important" factors means the stated factors identified in the cautionary statement must be relevant to the projection and must be of a nature that the factor or factors could actually affect whether the forward-looking statement is realized.

The Conference Committee expects that the cautionary statements identify important factors that could cause results to differ materially—but not all factors. Failure to include the particular factor that ultimately causes the forward-looking statement not to come true will not mean that the statement is not protected by the safe harbor. The Conference Committee specifies that the cautionary statements identify "important" factors to provide guidance to issuers and not to provide an opportunity for plaintiff counsel to conduct discovery on what factors were known to the issuer at the time the forward-looking statement was made.

The use of the words "meaningful" and "important factors" are intended to provide a standard for the types of cautionary statements upon which a court may, where appropriate, decide a motion to dismiss, without examining the state of mind of the defendant. The first prong of the safe harbor requires courts to examine only the cautionary statement accompanying the forward-looking statement. Courts should not examine the state of mind of the person making the statement.

Courts may continue to find a forward-looking statement immaterial—and thus not actionable under the 1933 Act and the 1934 Act—on other grounds. To clarify this point, the Conference Committee includes language in the safe harbor provision that no liability attaches to forward-looking statements that are "immaterial."

The safe harbor seeks to provide certainty that forward-looking statements will not be actionable by private parties under certain circumstances. Forward-looking statements will have safe harbor protection if they are accompanied by a meaningful cautionary statement. A cautionary statement that misstates historical facts is not covered by the safe harbor; it is not sufficient, however, in a civil action to allege merely that a cautionary statement misstates historical facts. The plaintiff must plead with particularity all facts giving rise to a strong inference of a material misstatement in the cautionary statement to survive a motion to dismiss.

The second prong of the safe harbor provides an alternative analysis. This safe harbor also applies to both written and oral forward-looking statements. Instead of examining the forward-looking and cautionary statements, this prong of the safe harbor focuses on the state of mind of the person making the forward-looking statement. A person or business entity will not be liable in a private lawsuit for a forward-looking statement unless a plaintiff proves that person or business entity made a false or misleading forward-looking statement with actual knowledge that it was false or misleading. The Conference Committee intends for this alternative prong of the safe harbor to apply if the plaintiff fails to prove the forward-looking statement (1) if made by a natural person, was made with the actual knowledge by that person that the statement was false or misleading; or (2) if made by a business entity, was made by or with the approval of an executive officer of the entity with actual knowledge by that officer that the statement was false or misleading.

The Conference Committee recognizes that, under certain circumstances, it may be unwieldy to make oral forward-looking statements relying on the first prong of the safe harbor. Companies who want to make a brief announcement of earnings or a new product would first have to identify the statement as forward-looking and then provide cautionary statements identifying important factors that could cause results to differ materially from those projected in the statement. As a result, the Conference Committee has provided for an optional, more flexible rule for oral forward-looking statements that will facilitate these types of oral communications by an issuer while still providing to the public information it would have received if the forward-looking statement was written. The Conference Committee intends to limit this oral safe harbor to issuers or the officers, directors, or employees of the issuer acting on the issuer's behalf.

This legislation permits covered issuers, or persons acting on the issuer's behalf, to make oral forward-looking statements within the safe harbor. The person making the forward-looking statement must identify the statement as a forward-looking statement and state that results may differ materially from those projected in the statement. The person must also identify a "readily available" written document that contains factors that could cause results to differ materially. The written information identified by the person making the forward-looking statements must qualify as a "cautionary statement" under the first prong of the safe harbor (i.e., it must be a meaningful cautionary statement or statements that identify important factors that could cause actual results to differ materially from those projected in the forward-looking statement.) For purposes of this provision, "readily available" information refers to SEC filed documents, annual reports and other widely disseminated materials, such as press releases.

Who and what receives safe harbor protection

The safe harbor provision protects written and oral forward-looking statements made by issuers and certain persons retained or acting on behalf of the issuer. The Conference Committee intends the statutory safe harbor protection to make more information about a company's future plans available to investors and the public. The safe harbor covers underwriters, but only insofar as the underwriters provide forward looking information that is based on or "derived from" information provided by the issuer. Because underwriters have what is effectively an adversarial relationship with issuers in performing due diligence, the use of the term "derived from" affords underwriters some latitude so that they may disclose adverse information that the issuer did not necessarily "provide." The Conference Committee does not intend the safe harbor to cover forward-looking information in connection with a broker's sales practices.

The Conference Committee adopts the SEC's present definition, as set forth in Rule 175, of forward-looking information, with certain additions and clarifying changes. The definition covers: (i) certain financial items, including projections of revenues, income and earnings, capital expenditures, dividends, and capital structure; (ii) management's statement of future business plans and objectives, including with respect to its products or services; and (iii) certain statements made in SEC required disclosures, including management's discussion and analysis and results of operations; and (iv) any statement disclosing the assumptions underlying the forward-looking statement.

The Conference Committee has determined that the statutory safe harbor should not apply to certain forward-looking statements. Thus, the statutory safe harbor does not protect forward-looking statements: (1) included in financial statements prepared in accordance with generally accepted accounting principles; (2) contained in an initial public offering registration statement; (3) made in connection with a tender offer; (4) made in connection with a partnership, limited liability company or direct participation program offering; or (5) made in beneficial ownership disclosure statements filed with the SEC under Section 13(d) of the 1934 Act.

. . . .

Moreover, the Committee has determined to extend the statutory safe harbor only to forward-looking information of certain established issuers subject to the reporting requirements of section 13(a) or section 15(d) of the 1934 Act. Except as provided by SEC rule or regulation, the safe harbor does not extend to an issuer who: (a) during the three year period preceding the date on which the statement was first made, has been convicted of a felony or misdemeanor described in clauses (i) through (iv) of Section 15(b)(4) or is the subject of a decree or order involving a violation of the securities laws; (b) makes the statement in connection with a "blank check" securities offering, "rollup transaction," or "going private" transaction; or (c) issues penny stock.

. . . .

This legislation also makes clear that nothing in the safe harbor provision imposes any duty to update forward-looking statements.

The Conference Committee does not intend for the safe harbor provisions to replace the judicial "bespeaks caution" doctrine or to foreclose further development of that doctrine by the courts.

The safe harbor

The legislation provides that, on any motion to dismiss the complaint based on the application of the safe harbor, the court shall consider the statements cited in the complaint and statements identified by the defendant in its moving papers, including any cautionary statements accompanying the forward-looking statement that are not subject to material dispute. The applicability of the safe harbor provisions under subsection (c)(1)(B) shall be based on the "actual knowledge" of the defendant and does not depend on the use of cautionary language. [By comparison,] the applicability of the safe harbor provisions under subsections (c)(1)(A) and (c)(2) shall be based upon the sufficiency of the cautionary language under those provisions and does not depend on the state of mind of the defendant. In the case of a complaint based on an oral forward looking statement in which information concerning factors that could cause actual results to differ materially is contained in "readily available" written documents, the court shall consider statements in [such] readily available written documents.

Asher v. Baxter International, Inc.

United States Court of Appeals, Seventh Circuit

377 F.3d 727 (2004)

Easterbrook, Circuit Judge.

Baxter International, a manufacturer of medical products, released its second-quarter financial results for 2002 on July 18 of that year. Sales and profits did not match analysts' expectations. Shares swiftly fell from $43 to $32. This litigation followed; plaintiffs contend that the $43 price was the result of materially misleading projections on November 5, 2001, projections that Baxter reiterated until the bad news came out on July 18, 2002. Plaintiffs want to represent a class of all investors who purchased during that time either in the open market or by exchanging their shares of Fusion Medical Technologies. (Baxter acquired Fusion in a stock-for-stock transaction; plaintiffs think that Baxter juiced up the market price so that it could secure Fusion in exchange for fewer of its own shares.) Bypassing the question whether the suit could proceed as a class action, the district court dismissed the complaint for failure to state a claim on which relief may be granted. The court did not doubt that the allegations ordinarily would defeat a motion under Fed. R. Civ. P. 12(b)(6). Still, it held, Baxter's forecasts come within the safe harbor created by the Private Securities Litigation Reform Act of 1995. The PSLRA creates rules that judges must enforce at the outset of the litigation; plaintiffs do not question the statutes' application before discovery but do dispute the district court's substantive decision.

Baxter's projection, repeated many times (sometimes in documents filed with the SEC, sometimes in press releases, sometimes in executives' oral statements), was that during 2002 the business would yield revenue growth in the "low teens" compared with the prior year, earnings-per-share growth in the "mid teens," and "operational cash flow of at least $500 million." Baxter often referred to these forecasts as "our 2002 full-year commitments," which is a strange locution. No firm can make "commitments" about the future—Baxter can't *compel* its customers to buy more of its products—unless it plans to engage in accounting shenanigans to make the numbers come out right no matter what happens to the business. But nothing turns on the word; the district court took these "commitments" as "forward-looking statements," and plaintiffs do not quarrel with that understanding. What they do say is that the projections were too rosy, and that Baxter knew it. That charges the defendants with stupidity as much as with knavery, for the truth was bound to come out quickly, but the securities laws forbid foolish frauds along with clever ones.

According to the complaint, Baxter's projections were materially false because (1) its Renal Division had not met its internal budgets in years; (2) economic instability in Latin America adversely affected Baxter's sales in that part of the world; (3) Baxter closed plants in Ronneby, Sweden and Miami Lakes, Florida that had been its principal source of low-cost dialysis products; (4) the market for albumin (blood-plasma) products was "over-saturated," resulting in lower prices and revenue for the BioSciences Division; (5) sales of that division's IGIV immunoglobin products had fallen short of internal predictions; and (6) in March 2002 the BioScience Division had experienced a sterility failure in the manufacture of a major product, resulting in the destruction of multiple lots and a loss exceeding $10 million. The district court assumed, as shall we, that failure to disclose these facts would create problems but for the statutory safe harbor, though items (2) and (4) at least are general business matters rather than Baxter's secrets, and the securities laws do not require issuers to disclose the state of the world, as opposed to facts about the firm. Item (3) also was public knowledge (Baxter issued a press release announcing the closings and a substantial charge against earnings)—though the cost of products that had been made at these plants may have been secret. Whether all firm-specific non-disclosure add up to a material non-disclosure—and whether Baxter had some non-public information about those matters that seem to be general information—are topics we need not tackle.

. . . The statutory safe harbor forecloses liability [regardless of the defendant's state of mind] if a forward-looking statement "is accompanied by meaningful cautionary statements identifying important factors that could cause actual results to differ materially from those in the forward-looking statement" . . . The fundamental problem is that the statutory requirement of "meaningful cautionary statements" is not itself meaningful. What must the firm say? Unless it is possible to give a concrete and reliable answer, the harbor is not "safe"; yet a word such as "meaningful" resists a concrete rendition and thus makes administration of the safe harbor difficult if not impossible. . . . A safe harbor matters only when the firm's disclosures (including the accompanying cautionary statements) are false or misleadingly incomplete; yet whenever that condition is satisfied, one can complain that the cautionary statement must have been inadequate. The safe harbor loses its function. Yet it would be unsound to read the statute so that the safe harbor never works. . . .

Baxter provided a number of cautionary statements throughout the class period. This one, from its 2001 Form 10-K filing—a document to which many of the firm's press releases and other statements referred—is the best illustration:

> "Statements throughout this report that are not historical facts are forward-looking statements. These statements are based on the company's current expectations and involve numerous risks and uncertainties. Some of these risks and uncertainties are factors that affect all international businesses, while some are specific to the company and the health care arenas in which it operates.

> "Many factors could affect the company's actual results, causing results to differ materially, from those expressed in any such forward-looking statements. These factors include, but are not limited to, interest rates; technological advances in the medical field; economic conditions; demand and market acceptance risks for new and existing products, technologies and health care services; the impact of competitive products and pricing; manufacturing capacity; new plant start-ups; global regulatory, trade and tax policies; regulatory, legal or other developments relating to the company's Series A, AF, and AX dialyzers; continued price competition; product development risks, including technological difficulties; ability to enforce patents; actions of regulatory bodies and other government authorities; reimbursement policies of government agencies; commercialization factors; results of product testing; and other factors described elsewhere in this report or in the company's other filings with the Securities and Exchange Commission. Additionally, as discussed in Item 3—'Legal Proceedings,' upon the resolution of certain legal matters, the company may incur charges in excess of presently established reserves. Any such change could have a material adverse effect on the company's results of operations or cash flows in the period in which it is recorded.

> "Currency fluctuations are also a significant variable for global companies, especially fluctuations in local currencies where hedging opportunities are unreasonably expensive or unavailable. If the United States dollar strengthens significantly against most foreign currencies, the company's ability to realize projected growth rates in its sales and net earnings outside the United States could be negatively impacted.

> "The company believes that its expectations with respect to forward-looking statements are based upon reasonable assumptions within the bounds of its knowledge of its business operations, but there can be no assurance that the actual results or performance of the company will conform to

any future results or performance expressed or implied by such forward-looking statements."

The district court concluded that these are "meaningful cautionary statements identifying important factors that could cause actual results to differ materially from those in the forward-looking statement." They deal with Baxter's business specifically, mentioning risks and product lines. Plaintiffs offer two responses. First, they contend that the cautionary statements did not cover any of the six matters that (in plaintiffs' view) Baxter had withheld. That can't be dispositive; otherwise the statute would demand prescience. As long as the firm reveals the principal risks, the fact that some other event caused problems cannot be dispositive. Indeed, an unexpected turn of events cannot demonstrate a securities problem at all, as there cannot be "fraud by hindsight." The other response is that the cautionary statement did not follow the firm's fortunes: plants closed but the cautionary statement remained the same; sterilization failures occurred but the cautionary statement remained the same; and bad news that (plaintiffs contend) Baxter well knew in November 2001 did not cast even a shadow in the cautionary statement.

. . . That leaves the question whether these statements satisfy the statutory requirement that they adequately "identify[ ] important factors that could cause actual results to differ materially from those in the forward-looking statement."

The parties agree on two propositions, each with support in decisions of other circuits. First, "boilerplate" warnings won't do; cautions must be tailored to the risks that accompany the particular projections. Second, the cautions need not identify what actually goes wrong and causes the projections to be inaccurate; prevision is not required. . . . Unfortunately, these principles don't decide any concrete case—for that matter, the statutory language itself does not decide any concrete case. It is the result of a compromise between legislators who did not want any safe harbor (or, indeed any new legislation), and those who wanted a safe harbor along the lines of the old Rule 175 that did not require any cautionary statements but just required the projection to have a reasonable basis. Rule 175 was limited to statements in certain documents filed with the SEC; proponents of the PSLRA wanted to extend this to all statements, including oral declarations and press releases. As is often the situation, a compromise enabled the bill to pass but lacks much content; it does not encode a principle on which political forces agreed as much as it signifies conflict about both the scope and the wisdom of the safe harbor. Compromises of this kind lack spirit. Still, the language was enacted, and we must make something of it.

Plaintiffs say that Baxter's cautions were boilerplate, but they aren't. Statements along the lines of "all businesses are risky" or "the future lies ahead" come to nothing other than caveat emptor (which isn't enough); these statements, by contrast, at least included Baxter-specific information and highlighted some parts of that business that might cause problems. For its part, Baxter says that mentioning these business segments demonstrates that the caution is sufficient; but this also is wrong, because then any issuer could list its lines of business, say "we could have problems in any of these," and avoid liability for statements implying that no such problems were on the horizon even if a precipice was in sight.

What investors would like to have is a full disclosure of the assumptions and calculations *behind* the projections; then they could apply their own discount factors. For reasons covered [elsewhere], however, this is not a sensible requirement. Many of the assumptions and calculations would be more useful to a firm's rivals than to its investors. Suppose, for example, that Baxter had revealed its sterility failure in the BioSciences Division, the steps it had taken to restore production, and the costs and prospects of each. Rivals could have used that information to avoid costs and hazards that had befallen Baxter, or to find solutions more quickly. . . . Baxter's shareholders would have been worse off. Similarly Baxter might have added verisimilitude to its projections by describing its sales policies and the lowest prices it would accept from major customers, but disclosing reservation prices would do more to help the customers than to assist the investors.

. . . .

Whether or not Baxter could have made the cautions more helpful by disclosing assumptions [or] methods, none of these is required. The PSLRA does not require the *most* helpful caution; it is enough to "identify important factors that could cause actual results to differ materially from those in the forward-looking statement." This means that it is enough to point to the principal contingencies that could cause actual results to depart from the projection. The statute calls for issuers to reveal the "important factors" but not to attach probabilities to each potential bad outcome, or to reveal in detail what could go wrong; as we have said, that level of detail might hurt investors (by helping rivals) even as it improved the accuracy of stock prices. (Requiring cautions to contain elaborate detail also would defeat the goal of facilitating projections, by turning each into a form of registration statement. Undue complexity would lead issuers to shut up, and stock prices could become even less accurate. Incomplete information usually is better than none, because market professionals know other tidbits that put the news in context.) Moreover, "[i]f enterprises cannot make predictions about themselves, then securities analysts, newspaper columnists, and charlatans have protected turf. There will be predictions aplenty outside the domain of the securities acts, predictions by persons whose access to information is not as good as the issuer's. When the issuer adds its information and analysis to that assembled by outsiders, the *collective* assessment will be more accurate even though a given projection will be off the mark." . . .

Yet Baxter's chosen language may fall short. There is no reason to think — at least, no reason that a court can accept at the pleading stage, before plaintiffs have access to discovery — that the items mentioned in Baxter's cautionary language were those that at the time were the (or any of the) "important" sources of variance. The problem is not that what actually happened went unmentioned; issuers need not anticipate all sources of deviations from expectations. Rather, the problem is that there is no reason (on this record) to conclude that Baxter mentioned those sources of variance that (at the time of the projection) were the principal or important risks. For all we can tell, the major risks Baxter objectively faced when it made its forecasts were exactly those that, according to the complaint, came to pass, yet the cautionary statement mentioned none of them. Moreover, the cautionary language remained fixed even as the risks changed. When the sterility failure occurred in spring 2002, Baxter left both its forecasts and cautions as is. When Baxter closed the plants that (according to the complaint) were its least-cost sources of production, the forecasts and cautions continued without amendment. This raises the possibility—no greater confidence is possible before discovery—that Baxter omitted important variables from the cautionary language and so made projections more certain than its internal estimates at the time warranted. Thus this complaint could not be dismissed under the safe harbor, though we cannot exclude the possibility that if after discovery Baxter establishes that the cautions did reveal what were, *ex ante*, the major risks, the safe harbor may yet carry the day.

Baxter urges us to affirm the judgment immediately, contending that the full truth had reached the market despite any shortcomings in its cautionary statements. If this is so, however, it is hard to understand the sharp drop in the price of its stock. A "truth-on-the-market" defense is available in principle, but not at the pleading state. Likewise one must consider the possibility that investors looked at all of the projections as fluff and responded only to the hard numbers; on this view it was a reduction in Baxter's growth rate, not the embarrassment of a projection, that caused the price to decline in July 2002; again it is too early in the litigation to reach such a conclusion. It would be necessary to ask, for example, whether the price rose relative to the rest of the market when Baxter made its projections; if not, that might support an inference that the projections were so much noise.

Nor has the time arrived to evaluate Baxter's contention that its projections panned out, so there was no material error. Baxter insists that all of the projections dealt with the entire calendar year 2002, and that by year-end performance was up to snuff—close enough to the projections that any difference was immaterial. Once again, it is inappropriate to entertain such an argument at the pleading stage. The district court will need to determine whether all of the forward-looking statements referenced calendar 2002 as a whole, rather than anticipated improvements quarter-by-quarter over the preceding year. It will be necessary to evaluate whether differences between the projections and the outcome were material under the standard of *Basic*. Finally it may be necessary to explore what Baxter's full-year results actually were; plaintiff's reply brief accuses Baxter of using gimmicks to report extra revenue in 2002 at the expense of later years. The implication is that Baxter may have overstated its 2002 results. Whether that is so cannot be determined on the pleadings, even when supplemented with the documents that Baxter has filed with the SEC.

Reversed and Remanded.

Note

As more recently summarized by the Second Circuit:

> To be protected under the first prong of the safe harbor, a forward-looking statement must be both identified as such and "accompanied by meaningful cautionary statements identifying important factors that could cause actual results to differ materially from those in the forward-looking statement. . . ."

> The safe harbor provision also requires dismissal if the plaintiffs do not "prove that the forward-looking statement . . . was . . . made or approved by [an executive officer or the board of directors or committee thereof] with *actual knowledge* by that [person] that the statement was false or misleading." . . . [B]ecause the safe harbor specifies an "actual knowledge" standard for forward-looking statements, "the scienter requirement for forward looking statements is stricter than for statements of current fact. Whereas liability for the latter requires a showing of either knowing falsity or recklessness, liability for the former attaches only upon proof of knowing falsity."

Slayton v. American Express Company, 604 F.2d 758, 769, 773 (2d Cir. 2010). Similarly, as set forth by the District of Columbia Circuit in *In re: Harmon International, Inc. Securities Litigation*, 791 F.3d 90, 102–103 (D.C. Cir. 2015) (quotations and citations omitted):

> The requirement for "meaningful" cautions calls for substantive company-specific warnings based on a realistic description of the risks applicable to the particular circumstances. Thus, cautionary statements must be substantive and tailored to the specific future projections, estimates or opinions in the [statements] which the plaintiffs challenge. That cautionary language must be tailored to the forward-looking statement that it accompanies follows from the statutory requirement that cautionary language must warn of what "could cause actual results to differ materially *from those in the forward-looking statement.*"

> By contrast, mere boilerplate—This is a forward-looking statement: caveat emptor—does not meet the statutory standard because by its nature it is general and ubiquitous, not tailored to the specific circumstances of a business operation, and not of "useful quality." So too, generalized warnings that forward-looking statements are not guarantees of future performance and involve known and unknown risks and other factors that could cause actual results to be materially different from any future results expressed or implied by them, because such a statement is not specific regarding the business at issue. The Conference Report, in keeping with Congress's intent to "enhance market efficiency by encouraging companies to disclose forward-looking information," states that "boilerplate warnings will not suffice as meaningful cautionary statements identifying important

factors that could cause actual results to differ materially from those projected in the statement."

At the same time, cautionary language cannot be "meaningful" if it is misleading in light of historical facts, that were established at the time the statement was made. Such statements are neither significant nor of useful quality or purpose. Indeed, the Conference Report states that "[a] cautionary statement that misstates historical facts is not covered by the safe harbor." A warning that identifies a potential risk, but "impl[ies] that no such problems were on the horizon even if a precipice was in sight," would not meet the statutory standard for safe harbor protection. If a company were to warn of the potential deterioration of one line of its business, when in fact it was established that that line of business had already deteriorated, then, as the Second Circuit explained, its cautionary language would be inadequate to meet the safe harbor standard. By analogy, the safe harbor would not protect from liability a person "'who warns his hiking companion to walk slowly because there might be a ditch ahead when he knows with near certainty that the Grand Canyon lies one foot away.'" . . . [T]here is an important difference between warning that something "*might*" occur and that something "*actually* had" occurred.

Because Congress required that cautionary statements warn of "important factors that could cause actual results to differ," the cautionary language need not necessarily "mention *the* factor that ultimately belies a forward-looking statement." That is, Congress did not require the cautionary statement warn of "*all*" important factors, so long as "an investor has been warned of risks of a significance similar to that actually realized," such that the investor "is sufficiently on notice of the danger of the investment to make an intelligent decision about it according to her own preferences for risk and reward." Perfect clairvoyance may be impossible because of events beyond a company's control of which it was unaware. . . .[21]

---

21. For legal commentary on the "bespeaks caution" doctrine as well as the federal legislation providing a safe harbor for certain forward-looking statements, *see, e.g.*, Barondes, *The Bespeaks Caution Doctrine: Revisiting the Application of Federal Securities Law to Opinions and Estimates*, 19 J. Corp. L. 243 (1994); Couture, *Mixed Statements: The Safe Harbor's Rocky Shore*, 39 Sec. Reg. L.J. 257 (2011); Horwich, *Cleaning the Murky Safe Harbor for Forward-Looking Statements*, 35 J. Corp. L. 519 (2010); Langevoort, *Disclosures That "Bespeak Caution,"* 49 Bus. Law. 481 (1994); O'Hare, *Good Faith and The Bespeaks Caution Doctrine: It's Not Just a State of Mind*, 58 U. Pitt. L. Rev. 619 (1997); Ripken, *Predictions, Projections, and Precautions: Conveying Cautionary Warnings in Corporate Forward-Looking Statements*, 2005 U. Ill. L. Rev. 929 (2005); Symposium, 51 Bus. Law. No. 4 (1996); Symposium, 33 San Diego L. Rev. No. 3 (1996); Symposium, 24 Sec. Reg. L.J. No. 2 (1996). *See also*, Ahdieh, *The Strategy of Boilerplate*, 104 Mich. L. Rev. 1033 (2006).

[E] "Fraud on the Market" Theory

Basic, Inc. v. Levinson

United States Supreme Court

485 U.S. 224, 108 S. Ct. 978, 99 L. Ed. 2d 194 (1988)

JUSTICE BLACKMUN delivered the opinion of the Court.

This case requires us to apply the materiality requirement of § 10(b) of the Securities Exchange Act of 1934 and the Securities and Exchange Commission's Rule 10b-5 in the context of preliminary corporate merger discussions. We must also determine whether a person who traded a corporation's shares on a securities exchange after the issuance of a materially misleading statement by the corporation may invoke a rebuttable presumption that, in trading, he relied on the integrity of the price set by the market.

I

Prior to December 20, 1978, Basic Incorporated was a publicly traded company primarily engaged in the business of manufacturing chemical refractories for the steel industry. As early as 1965 or 1966, Combustion Engineering, Inc., a company producing mostly alumina-based refractories, expressed some interest in acquiring Basic, but was deterred from pursuing this inclination seriously because of antitrust concerns it then entertained. In 1976, however, regulatory action opened the way to a renewal of Combustion's interest. . . .

Beginning in September 1976, Combustion representatives had meetings and telephone conversations with Basic officers and directors, including petitioners here, concerning the possibility of a merger. During 1977 and 1978, Basic made three public statements denying that it was engaged in merger negotiations. On December 18, 1978, Basic asked the New York Stock Exchange to suspend trading in its shares and issued a release stating that it had been "approached" by another company concerning a merger. On December 19, Basic's board endorsed Combustion's offer of $46 per share for its common stock, and on the following day publicly announced its approval of Combustion's tender offer for all outstanding shares.

Respondents are former Basic shareholders who sold their stock after Basic's first public statement of October 21, 1977, and before the suspension of trading in December 1978. Respondents brought a class action against Basic and its directors, asserting that the defendants issued three false or misleading public statements and thereby were in violation of § 10(b) of the 1934 Act and of Rule 10b-5. Respondents alleged that they were injured by selling Basic shares at artificially depressed prices in a market affected by petitioners' misleading statements and in reliance thereon.

The District Court adopted a presumption of reliance by members of the plaintiff class upon petitioners' public statements that enabled the court to conclude that common questions of fact or law predominated over particular questions pertaining to individual plaintiffs. See Fed. Rule Civ. Proc. 23(b)(3). The District Court therefore certified respondents' class. . . .

The United States Court of Appeals for the Sixth Circuit affirmed the class certification.

. . . .

The Court of Appeals joined a number of other circuits in accepting the "fraud-on-the-market theory" to create a rebuttable presumption that respondents relied on petitioners' material misrepresentations, noting that without the presumption it would be impractical to certify a class under Fed. Rule Civ. Proc. 23(b)(3).

We granted certiorari to resolve the split among the Courts of Appeals as to the standard of materiality applicable to preliminary merger discussions, and to determine whether the courts below properly applied a presumption of reliance in certifying the class, rather than requiring each class member to show direct reliance on Basic's statements.

. . . .

IV

A

We turn to the question of reliance and the fraud-on-the-market theory. Succinctly put:

> "The fraud on the market theory is based on the hypothesis that, in an open and developed securities market, the price of a company's stock is determined by the available material information regarding the company and its business. . . . Misleading statements will therefore defraud purchasers of stock even if the purchasers do not directly rely on the misstatements. . . . The causal connection between the defendants' fraud and the plaintiffs' purchase of stock in such a case is no less significant than in a case of direct reliance on misrepresentations." *Peil v. Speiser*, 806 F.2d 1154, 1160–1161 (CA3 1986).

Our task, of course, is not to assess the general validity of the theory, but to consider whether it was proper for the courts below to apply a rebuttable presumption of reliance, supported in part by the fraud-on-the-market theory.

This case required resolution of several common questions of law and fact concerning the falsity or misleading nature of the three public statements made by Basic, the presence or absence of scienter, and the materiality of the misrepresentations, if any. In their amended complaint, the named plaintiffs alleged that in reliance on Basic's statements they sold their shares of Basic stock in the depressed market created by petitioners. . . . *Requiring proof of individualized reliance from each member of the proposed plaintiff class effectively would have prevented respondents from proceeding with a class action, since individual issues then would have overwhelmed the common ones.* [emphasis supplied] The District Court found that the presumption of reliance created by the fraud-on-the-market theory provided "a practical resolution to the problem of balancing the substantive requirement of proof of reliance in securities cases against the procedural requisites of [Fed. Rule Civ. Proc.] 23." The District Court thus concluded that with reference to each public statement and its impact upon the open market for Basic shares, common questions predominated over individual questions, as required by Fed. Rule Civ. Proc. 23(a)(2) and (b)(3).

Petitioners and their *amici* complain that the fraud-on-the-market theory effectively eliminates the requirement that a plaintiff asserting a claim under Rule 10b-5 prove reliance. They note that reliance is and long has been an element of common-law fraud, see e.g., *Restatement (Second) of Torts* § 525 (1977); Prosser and Keeton on *The Law of Torts* § 108 (5th ed. 1984), and argue that because the analogous express right of action includes a reliance requirement, § 18(a) of the 1934 Act, . . . so too must an action implied under § 10(b).

We agree that reliance is an element of a Rule 10b-5 cause of action. . . . Reliance provides the requisite causal connection between a defendant's misrepresentation and a plaintiff's injury. . . . There is, however, more than one way to demonstrate the causal connection. Indeed, we previously have dispensed with a requirement of positive proof of reliance, where a duty to disclose material information had been breached, concluding that the necessary nexus between the plaintiff's injury and the defendant's wrongful conduct had been established. See *Affiliated Ute Citizens v. United States*, 406 U.S. at 153–154 [1972]. . . . [Has the Court here mistakenly viewed reliance as the requisite causal connection between a defendant's misrepresentation and the plaintiff's loss rather than to the plaintiff's investment decision?]

The modern securities markets, literally involving millions of shares changing hands daily, differ from the face-to-face transactions contemplated by early fraud cases, and our understanding of Rule 10b-5's reliance requirement must encompass these differences.

> "In face-to-face transactions, the inquiry into an investor's reliance upon information is into the subjective pricing of that information by that investor. With the presence of a market, the market is interposed between seller and buyer and, ideally, transmits information to the investor in the processed form of a market price. Thus the market is performing a substantial part of the valuation process performed by the investor in a face-to-face transaction. The market is acting as the unpaid agent of the investor, informing him that given all the information available to it, the value of the stock is worth the market price." *In re LTV Securities Litigation*, 88 F.R.D. 134, 143 (ND Tex. 1980).

. . . .

B

Presumptions typically serve to assist courts in managing circumstances in which direct proof, for one reason or another, is rendered difficult. *See, e.g.,* D. Louisell &

C. Mueller, *Federal Evidence* 541–542 (1977). The courts below accepted a presumption, created by the fraud-on-the market theory and subject to rebuttal by petitioners, that persons who had traded Basic shares had done so in reliance on the integrity of the price set by the market, but because of petitioners' material misrepresentations that price had been fraudulently depressed. Requiring a plaintiff to show a speculative state of facts, *i.e.,* how he would have acted if omitted material information had been disclosed . . . or if the misrepresentation had not been made, . . . would place an unnecessarily unrealistic evidentiary burden on the Rule 10b-5 plaintiff who has traded on an impersonal market.

Arising out of considerations of fairness, public policy, and probability, as well as judicial economy, presumptions are also useful devices for allocating the burdens of proof between parties. . . . The presumption of reliance employed in this case is consistent with, and, by facilitating Rule 10b-5 litigation, supports, the congressional policy embodied in the 1934 Act. In drafting that Act, Congress expressly relied on the premise that securities markets are affected by information, and enacted legislation to facilitate an investor's reliance on the integrity of those markets:

> "No investor, no speculator, can safely buy and sell securities upon the exchanges without having an intelligent basis for forming his judgment as to the value of the securities he buys or sells. The idea of a free and open public market is built upon the theory that competing judgments of buyers and sellers as to the fair price of a security brings [sic] about a situation where the market price reflects as nearly as possible a just price. Just as artificial manipulation tends to upset the true function of an open market, so the hiding and secreting of important information obstructs the operation of the markets as indices of real value."

See *Lipton v. Documation, Inc.,* 734 F.2d 740, 748 (CA11 1984), *cert. denied,* 469 U.S. 1132 (1985).

The presumption is also supported by common sense and probability. Recent empirical studies have tended to confirm Congress' premise that the market price of shares traded on well-developed markets reflects all publicly available information, and, hence, any material misrepresentations. It has been noted that "it is hard to imagine that there ever is a buyer or seller who does not rely on market integrity. Who would knowingly roll the dice in a crooked crap game?" *Schlanger v. Four-Phase Systems Inc.,* 555 F. Supp. 535, 538 (SDNY 1982). Indeed, nearly every court that has considered the proposition has concluded that where materially misleading statements have been disseminated into an impersonal, well-developed market for securities, the reliance of individual plaintiffs on the integrity of the market price may be presumed. Commentators generally have applauded the adoption of one variation or another of the fraud-on-the-market theory. An investor who buys or sells stock at the price set by the market does so in reliance on the integrity of that price. Because most publicly available information is reflected in market price, an investor's reliance on any public material misrepresentations, therefore, may be presumed for purposes of a Rule 10b-5 action.

C

The Court of Appeals found that petitioners "made public, material misrepresentations and [respondents] sold Basic stock in an impersonal, efficient market. Thus the class, as defined by the district court, has established the threshold facts for proving their loss." 786 F.2d at 751. The court acknowledged that petitioners may rebut proof of the elements giving rise to the presumption, or show that the misrepresentation in fact did not lead to a distortion of price or that an individual plaintiff traded or would have traded despite his knowing the statement was false.

Any showing that severs the link between the alleged misrepresentation and either the price received (or paid) by the plaintiff, or his decision to trade at a fair market price, will be sufficient to rebut the presumption of reliance. For example, if petitioners could show that the "market makers" were privy to the truth about the merger discussions here with Combustion, and thus that the market price would not have been affected by their misrepresentations, the causal connection could be broken: the basis for finding that the fraud had been transmitted through market price would be gone. Similarly, if, despite petitioners' allegedly fraudulent attempt to manipulate market price, news of the merger discussions credibly entered the market and dissipated the effects of the misstatements, those who traded Basic shares after the corrective statements would have no direct or indirect connection with the fraud. Petitioners also could rebut the presumption of reliance as to plaintiffs who would have divested themselves of their Basic shares without relying on the integrity of the market. For example, a plaintiff who believed that Basic's statements were false and that Basic was indeed engaged in merger discussions, and who consequently believed that Basic stock was artificially underpriced, but sold his shares nevertheless because of other unrelated concerns, *e.g.*, potential antitrust problems, or political pressures to divest shares of certain businesses, could not be said to have relied on the integrity of a price he knew had been manipulated.

V

In summary:

1. We specifically adopt, for the § 10(b) and Rule 10b-5 context, the standard of materiality set forth in *TSC Industries, Inc. v. Northway, Inc.*, 426 U.S. at 449 [1976].

. . . .

5. It is not inappropriate to apply a presumption of reliance supported by the fraud-on-the-market theory.

6. That presumption, however, is rebuttable.

7. The District Court's certification of the class here was appropriate when made but is subject on remand to such adjustment, if any, as developing circumstances demand.

The judgment of the Court of Appeals is vacated and the case is remanded to that court for further proceedings consistent with this opinion.

It is so ordered.

THE CHIEF JUSTICE, JUSTICE SCALIA, and JUSTICE KENNEDY took no part in the consideration or decision of this case.

JUSTICE WHITE, with whom JUSTICE O'CONNOR joins, concurring in part and dissenting in part.

I join Parts I-III of the Court's opinion, as I agree that the standard of materiality we set forth in *TSC Industries* . . . should be applied to actions under § 10(b) and Rule 10b-5. But I dissent from the remainder of the Court's holding because I do not agree that the "fraud-on-the-market" theory should be applied in this case.

Even when compared to the relatively youthful private cause-of-action under § 10(b), see *Kardon v. National Gypsum Co.,* 69 F. Supp. 512 (ED Pa. 1946), the fraud-on-the-market theory is a mere babe. Yet today, the Court embraces this theory with the sweeping confidence usually reserved for more mature legal doctrines. In so doing, I fear that the Court's decision may have many adverse, unintended effects as it is applied and interpreted in the years to come.

. . . .

In general, the case law developed in this Court with respect to § 10(b) and Rule 10b-5 has been based on doctrines with which we, as judges, are familiar: common-law doctrines of fraud and deceit. . . . Even when we have extended civil liability under Rule 10b-5 to a broader reach than the common law had previously permitted, we have retained familiar legal principles as our guideposts. . . . The federal courts have proved adept at developing an evolving jurisprudence of Rule 10b-5 in such a manner. But with no staff economists, no experts schooled in the "efficient-capital-market hypothesis," no ability to test the validity of empirical market studies, we are not well equipped to embrace novel constructions of a statute based on contemporary microeconomic theory.

. . . [T]he Court today ventures into this area beyond its expertise, beyond—by its own admission—the confines of our previous fraud cases. Even if I agreed with the Court that "modern securities markets . . . involving millions of shares changing hands daily" require that the "understanding of Rule 10b-5's reliance requirement" be changed, I prefer that such changes come from Congress in amending § 10(b). The Congress, with its superior resources and expertise, is far better equipped than the federal courts for the task of determining how modern economic theory and global financial markets require that established legal notions of fraud be modified. In choosing to make these decisions itself, the Court, I fear, embarks on a course that it does not genuinely understand, giving rise to consequences it cannot foresee.

For while the economists' theories which underpin the fraud-on-the-market presumption may have the appeal of mathematical exactitude and scientific certainty, they are—in the end—nothing more than theories which may or may not prove accurate upon further consideration. Even the most earnest advocates of economic analysis of the law recognize this. *See, e.g.,* Easterbrook, *Afterword: Knowledge and Answers,* 85 Colum. L. Rev. 1117, 1118 (1985). Thus, while the majority states that, for purposes of reaching its result it need only make modest presumptions about the way in which "market professionals generally" do their jobs, and how the conduct of market professionals affects stock prices, I doubt that we are in much of a position to assess which theories aptly describe the functioning of the securities industry.

Consequently, I cannot join the Court in its effort to reconfigure the securities laws, based on recent economic theories, to better fit what it perceives to be the new realities of financial markets. I would leave this task to others more equipped for the job than we.

At the bottom of the Court's conclusion that the fraud-on-the-market theory sustains a presumption of reliance is the assumption that individuals rely "on the integrity of the market price" when buying or selling stock in "impersonal, well-developed market[s] for securities." Even if I was prepared to accept (as a matter of common sense or general understanding) the assumption that most persons buying or selling stock do so in response to the market price, the fraud-on-the-market theory goes further. For in adopting a "presumption of reliance," the Court *also* assumes that buyers and sellers rely—not just on the market price—but on the "*integrity*" of that price. It is this aspect of the fraud-on-the-market hypothesis which most mystifies me.

To define the term "integrity of the market price," the majority quotes approvingly from cases which suggest that investors are entitled to "'rely on the price of a stock as a reflection of its value.'" ... But the meaning of this phrase eludes me, for it implicitly suggests that stocks have some "true value" that is measurable by a standard other than their market price. While the Scholastics of Medieval times professed a means to make such a valuation of a commodity's "worth," I doubt that the federal courts of our day are similarly equipped.

Even if securities had some "value"—knowable and distinct from the market price of a stock—investors do not always share the Court's presumption that a stock's price is a "reflection of [this] value." Indeed, "many investors purchase or sell stock because they believe the price *inaccurately* reflects the corporation's worth." *See* Black, *Fraud on the Market: A Criticism of Dispensing with Reliance Requirements in Certain Open Market Transactions,* 62 N.C. L. Rev. 435, 455 (1984) (emphasis added). If investors really believed that stock prices reflected a stock's "value," many sellers would never sell, and many buyers never buy (given the time and cost associated with executing a stock transaction). As we recognized just a few years ago: "[I]nvestors act on inevitably incomplete or inaccurate information; [consequently] there are always winners and losers; but those who have 'lost' have not necessarily been defrauded." ... Yet today, the Court allows investors to recover who can show little more than that they sold stock at a lower price than what might have been.

I do not propose that the law retreat from the many protections that § 10(b) and Rule 10b-5, as interpreted in our prior cases, provide to investors. But any extension of these laws, to approach something closer to an investor insurance scheme, should come from Congress, and not from the courts.

II

Congress has not passed on the fraud-on-the-market theory the Court embraces today. That is reason enough for us to abstain from doing so. But it is even more troubling that, to the extent that any view of Congress on this question can be inferred indirectly, it is contrary to the result the majority reaches.

. . . .

A . . . congressional policy that the majority's opinion ignores is the strong preference the securities laws display for widespread public disclosure and distribution to investors of material information concerning securities. This congressionally-adopted policy is expressed in the numerous and varied disclosure requirements found in the federal securities law scheme.

Yet observers in this field have acknowledged that the fraud-on-the-market theory is at odds with the federal policy favoring disclosure. . . . The conflict between Congress' preference for disclosure and the fraud-on-the-market theory was well expressed by a jurist who rejected the latter in order to give force to the former:

> "[D]isclosure . . . is crucial to the way in which the federal securities laws function. . . . [T]he federal securities laws are intended to put investors into a position from which they can help themselves by relying upon disclosures that others are obligated to make. This system is not furthered by allowing monetary recovery to those who refuse to look out for themselves. If we say that a plaintiff may recover in some circumstances even though he did not read and rely on the defendants' public disclosures, then no one need pay attention to those disclosures and the method employed by Congress to achieve the objective of the 1934 Act is defeated." *Shores v. Sklar*, 647 F.2d, at 483 [CA5 1981 en banc] (Randall, J., dissenting).

It is no surprise, then, that some of the same voices calling for acceptance of the fraud-on-the-market theory also favor dismantling the federal scheme which mandates disclosure. But to the extent that the federal courts must make a choice between preserving effective disclosure and trumpeting the new fraud-on-the-market hypothesis, I think Congress has spoken clearly—favoring the current pro-disclosure policy. We should limit our role in interpreting § 10(b) and Rule 10b-5 to one of giving effect to such policy decisions by Congress.

. . . .

In sum, I think the Court's embracement of the fraud-on-the-market theory represents a departure in securities law that we are ill-suited to commence—and even less equipped to control as it proceeds. As a result, I must respectfully dissent.

Note — Halliburton I *and* Amgen

The Court's decision in *Basic* recognizes the necessity of the class action in § 10(b) litigation. If the majority had required proof of reliance by each individual plaintiff, the class action mechanism apparently would have been unavailable. As stated by a federal district court in a pre-*Basic* decision, "[t]he necessity of individual proof ordinarily precludes a § 10(b) and Rule 10b-5 claim from being asserted as a class action."[22] Hence, the Supreme Court's recognition of the fraud-on-the-market theory helps to ensure that ordinary investors have a viable remedy when they allegedly are defrauded in the impersonal securities markets.[23]

After *Basic*, the Supreme Court has addressed the fraud-on-the-market theory in three cases. In *Halliburton I*, 131 S. Ct. 2179, 2182 (2011), the Supreme Court rejected a restrictive interpretation that had been embraced by the Fifth Circuit. That appellate court ruled that a plaintiff must prove loss causation at the class certification stage in order to invoke the presumption of reliance under the fraud-on-the-market theory. Conveying that the Fifth Circuit had misconstrued *Basic*, the Supreme Court opined:

> It is undisputed that securities fraud plaintiffs must prove certain things in order to invoke *Basic*'s rebuttable presumption of reliance. It is common ground, for example, that plaintiffs must demonstrate that the alleged misrepresentations were publicly known (else how would the market take them into account?), that the stock traded in an efficient market — and that the relevant transaction took place between the time the misrepresentations were made and the time the truth was revealed. . . .
>
> According to the Court of Appeals, [Plaintiff] EPI Fund also had to establish loss causation at the certification stage to "trigger the fraud-on-the-market presumption." . . . The Court of Appeals' requirement is not justified by *Basic* or its logic. To begin, we have never before mentioned loss

---

22. *Gibb v. Delta Drilling Company*, 104 F.R.D. 59, 65 (N.D. Tex. 1984).

23. *See generally* Black, *The Strange Case of Fraud on the Market: A Label in Search of a Theory*, 52 Alb. L. Rev. 923 (1988); Carney, *The Limits of the Fraud on the Market Theory*, 44 Bus. Law. 1259 (1989); Couture, *Price Impact Possibilities*, 44 Sec. Reg. L.J. 255 (2016); Fischel, *Efficient Capital Markets, The Crash, and the Fraud on the Market Theory*, 74 Cornell L. Rev. 907 (1989); Gilson & Kraakman, *The Mechanisms of Market Efficiency*, 70 Va. L. Rev. 549 (1984); Gordon & Kornhauser, *Efficient Markets, Costly Information, and Securities Research*, 60 N.Y.U. L. Rev. 761 (1985); Langevoort, *Theories, Assumptions, and Securities Regulation: Market Efficiency Revisited*, 140 U. Pa. L. Rev. 851 (1992); Macey, *The Fraud on the Market Theory: Some Preliminary Issues*, 74 Cornell L. Rev. 923 (1989); Matheson, *Corporate Disclosure Obligations and the Parameters of Rule 10b-5: Basic, Inc. v. Levinson and Beyond*, 14 J. Corp. L. 1 (1988); Padfield, *Who Should Do the Math: Materiality Issues in Disclosures that Require Investors to Calculate the Bottom Line*, 34 Pepp. L. Rev. 927 (2007); Sachs, *Materiality and Social Change: The Case for Replacing "the Reasonable Investor" with "the Least Sophisticated Investor" in Inefficient Markets*, 81 Tulane L. Rev. 473 (2006); Stout, *The Unimportance of Being Efficient: An Economic Analysis of Stock Market Pricing and Securities Regulation*, 87 Mich. L. Rev. 613 (1988); Wang, *Some Arguments That the Stock Market Is Not Efficient*, 19 U.C. Davis L. Rev. 341 (1986).

causation as a precondition for invoking *Basic*'s rebuttable presumption of reliance. The term "loss causation" does not even appear in our *Basic* opinion. And for good reason: Loss causation addresses a matter different from whether an investor relied on a misrepresentation, presumptively or otherwise, when buying or selling stock.

> We have referred to the element of reliance in a private rule 10b-5 action as "transaction causation," not loss causation. . . . Consistent with that description, when considering whether a plaintiff has relied on a misrepresentation, we have typically focused on facts surrounding the investor's decision to engage in the transaction. Under *Basic*'s fraud-on-the-market doctrine, an investor presumably relies on a defendant's misrepresentation if that "information is reflected in [the] market price" of the stock at the time of the relevant transaction.

In the second case, *Amgen, Inc. v. Connecticut Retirement Plans and Trust Funds*, 133 S. Ct. 1184, 1191 (2013), the Supreme Court held that proof of materiality neither is a prerequisite to class certification nor to the invocation of the fraud-on-the-market presumption of classwide reliance. As stated by the Court:

> Rule 23(b)(3) [of the Federal Rules of Civil Procedure] requires a showing that *questions* common to the class predominate, not that those questions will be answered, on the merits, in favor of the class. Because materiality is judged according to an objective standard, the materiality of Amgen's alleged misrepresentations and omission is a question common to all members of the class [plaintiff] would represent. The alleged misrepresentations and omissions, whether material or immaterial, would be so equally for all investors composing the class. As vital, the plaintiff class's inability to prove materiality would not result in individual questions predominating. Instead, a failure of proof on the issue would end the case, given that materiality is an essential element of the class members' securities-fraud claims. As to materiality, therefore, the class is entirely cohesive: It will prevail or fail in unison. In no event will the individual circumstances of particular class members bear on the inquiry.

The Court's rationale in *Amgen* is based on two key concepts: first, materiality is an objective standard and, accordingly, is established through evidence that is common to all members of the class; second, unlike the element of reliance where—even when the subject security is not traded in an efficient market, a plaintiff may prove individual reliance—failure to establish materiality will terminate the litigation. As the Court stated: "A failure of proof on the *common* question of materiality ends the litigation. . . ." Or, as the Court stated somewhat differently at a different point in its opinion: "A failure of proof on the issue of materiality . . . not only precludes a plaintiff from invoking the fraud-on-the-market presumption of classwide reliance; it also establishes as a matter of law that the plaintiff cannot prevail on the merits of her Rule 10b-5 claim." (133 S. Ct. at 1196, 1199).

Consistent with this rationale, the *Amgen* Court also ruled that defendants may not introduce at the class certification stage rebuttal evidence offered to prove the immateriality of the allegedly deficient disclosures. The Court reasoned that "even a definitive rebuttal on the issue would not undermine the predominance of questions common to the class." Rather, such proof of rebuttal is appropriate at the summary judgment or trial stage of the litigation.

The *Amgen* Court also rejected the defendants' policy arguments. With respect to the assertion that not requiring proof of materiality at the class certification stage would cause the "extraction of extortionate settlements of frivolous claims," the Court asserted that the Private Securities Litigation Reform Act of 1995 (PSLRA) responded to perceived abuses in plaintiff class action litigation by enacting meaningful limitations (including heightened pleading requirements, providing a "safe harbor" for forward-looking statements, imposing further restrictions on the appointment (and compensation) of lead plaintiffs, limiting the award of damages and attorneys' fees, requiring the imposition of sanctions for frivolous litigation, and authorizing a stay of discovery when a motion to dismiss is pending). Significantly, in taking these measures to curb abusive private securities-fraud actions, Congress declined to undo the fraud-on-the-market presumption of classwide reliance.

Similarly, the Court rejected Amgen's argument that requiring proof of materiality prior to class certification would conserve judicial resources. Rather, according to the Court, if adopted, a "mini-trial" at the class-certification stage on the issue of materiality would be necessitated that "would entail considerable expenditures of judicial time and resources, costs scarcely anticipated by [FRCP 23]. . . ." Last, the Court rejected that private securities fraud class actions should be confined in order to mitigate the "vexatious" nature of such litigation. Exercising judicial restraint, the Court opined: "We have no warrant to encumber securities-fraud litigation by adopting an atextual requirement of precertification proof of materiality that Congress, despite its extensive involvement in the securities field, has not sanctioned." (133 S. Ct. at 1201, 1202).

Most recently, the Court revisited the continued validity of the fraud-on-the-market theory for § 10(b) class actions in *Halliburton II*. That decision follows.

Halliburton Co. v. Erica P. John Fund, Inc.

United States Supreme Court

___ U.S. ___, 134 S. Ct. 2398, 189 L. Ed. 2d 339 (2014)

Chief Justice Roberts delivered the opinion of the Court.

Investors can recover damages in a private securities fraud action only if they prove that they relied on the defendant's misrepresentation in deciding to buy or sell a company's stock. In *Basic Inc. v. Levinson*, 485 U. S. 224 (1988), we held that investors could satisfy this reliance requirement by invoking a presumption that the price of stock traded in an efficient market reflects all public, material information — including material misstatements. In such a case, we concluded, anyone who buys or sells the stock at the market price may be considered to have relied on those misstatements.

We also held, however, that a defendant could rebut this presumption in a number of ways, including by showing that the alleged misrepresentation did not actually affect the stock's price — that is, that the misrepresentation had no "price impact." The questions presented are whether we should overrule or modify *Basic*'s presumption of reliance and, if not, whether defendants should nonetheless be afforded an opportunity in securities class action cases to rebut the presumption at the class certification stage, by showing a lack of price impact.

I

Respondent Erica P. John Fund, Inc. (EPJ Fund), is the lead plaintiff in a putative class action against Halliburton and one of its executives (collectively Halliburton) alleging violations of section 10(b) of the Securities Exchange Act of 1934 and Securities and Exchange Commission Rule 10b-5. According to EPJ Fund, between June 3, 1999, and December 7, 2001, Halliburton made a series of misrepresentations regarding its potential liability in asbestos litigation, its expected revenue from certain construction contracts, and the anticipated benefits of its merger with another company — all in an attempt to inflate the price of its stock. Halliburton subsequently made a number of corrective disclosures, which, EPJ Fund contends, caused the company's stock price to drop and investors to lose money.

EPJ Fund moved to certify a class comprising all investors who purchased Halliburton common stock during the class period. The District Court found that the proposed class satisfied all the threshold requirements of Federal Rule of Civil Procedure 23(a): It was sufficiently numerous, there were common questions of law or fact, the representative parties' claims were typical of the class claims, and the representatives could fairly and adequately protect the interests of the class. And except for one difficulty, the court would have also concluded that the class satisfied the requirement of Rule 23(b)(3) that "the questions of law or fact common to class members predominate over any questions affecting only individual members." The difficulty was that [Fifth] Circuit precedent required securities fraud plaintiffs to prove "loss causation" — a causal connection between the defendants' alleged misrepresentations and the plaintiffs' economic losses — in order to invoke *Basic*'s presumption of reliance and obtain class certification. Because EPJ Fund had not demonstrated such a connection for any of Halliburton's alleged misrepresentations, the District Court refused to certify the proposed class. The United States Court of Appeals for the Fifth Circuit affirmed the denial of class certification on the same ground. . . .

We granted certiorari and vacated the judgment, finding nothing in "*Basic* or its logic" to justify the Fifth Circuit's requirement that securities fraud plaintiffs prove loss causation at the class certification stage in order to invoke *Basic*'s presumption of reliance. *Erica P. John Fund, Inc. v. Halliburton Co.*, [131 S. Ct. 2179] (2011) (*Halliburton I*). "Loss causation," we explained, "addresses a matter different from whether an investor relied on a misrepresentation, presumptively or otherwise, when buying or selling a stock." We remanded the case for the lower courts to consider "any further arguments against class certification" that Halliburton had preserved.

On remand, Halliburton argued that class certification was inappropriate because the evidence it had earlier introduced to disprove loss causation also showed that none of its alleged misrepresentations had actually affected its stock price. By demonstrating the absence of any "price impact," Halliburton contended, it had rebutted *Basic*'s presumption that the members of the proposed class had relied on its alleged misrepresentations simply by buying or selling its stock at the market price. And without the benefit of the *Basic* presumption, investors would have to prove reliance on an individual basis, meaning that individual issues would predominate over common ones. The District Court declined to consider Halliburton's argument, holding that the *Basic* presumption applied and certifying the class under Rule 23(b)(3).

The Fifth Circuit affirmed. 718 F.3d 423 (2013). The court found that Halliburton had preserved its price impact argument, but to no avail. While acknowledging that "Halliburton's price impact evidence could be used at the trial on the merits to refute the presumption of reliance," the court held that Halliburton could not use such evidence for that purpose at the class certification stage. . . .

We once again granted certiorari, this time to resolve a conflict among the Circuits over whether securities fraud defendants may attempt to rebut the *Basic* presumption at the class certification stage with evidence of a lack of price impact. We also accepted Halliburton's invitation to reconsider the presumption of reliance for securities fraud claims that we adopted in *Basic*.

II

Halliburton urges us to overrule *Basic*'s presumption of reliance and to instead require every securities fraud plaintiff to prove that he actually relied on the defendant's misrepresentation in deciding to buy or sell a company's stock. Before overturning a long-settled precedent, however, we require "special justification," not just an argument that the precedent was wrongly decided. . . . . Halliburton has failed to make that showing.

A

Section 10(b) of the Securities Exchange Act of 1934 and the Securities and Exchange Commission's Rule 10b-5 prohibit making any material misstatement or omission in connection with the purchase or sale of any security. Although section 10(b) does not create an express private cause of action, we have long recognized an implied private cause of action to enforce the provision and its implementing regulation. To recover damages for violations of section 10(b) and Rule 10b-5, a plaintiff must prove "'(1) a material misrepresentation or omission by the defendant; (2) scienter; (3) a connection between the misrepresentation or omission and the purchase or sale of a security; (4) reliance upon the misrepresentation or omission; (5) economic loss; and (6) loss causation.'" . . . .

The reliance element "'ensures that there is a proper connection between a defendant's misrepresentation and a plaintiff's injury.'" . . . "The traditional (and most direct) way a plaintiff can demonstrate reliance is by showing that he was aware of a company's statement and engaged in a relevant transaction—e.g., purchasing common stock—based on that specific misrepresentation."

In *Basic*, however, we recognized that requiring such direct proof of reliance "would place an unnecessarily unrealistic evidentiary burden on the Rule 10b-5 plaintiff who has traded on an impersonal market." That is because, even assuming an investor could prove that he was aware of the misrepresentation, he would still have to "show a speculative state of facts, i.e., how he would have acted . . . if the misrepresentation had not been made." . . .

We also noted that "[r]equiring proof of individualized reliance" from every securities fraud plaintiff "effectively would . . . prevent[ ] [plaintiffs] from proceeding with a class action" in Rule 10b-5 suits. If every plaintiff had to prove direct reliance on the defendant's misrepresentation, "individual issues then would . . . overwhelm[ ] the common ones," making certification under Rule 23(b)(3) inappropriate.

To address these concerns, *Basic* held that securities fraud plaintiffs can in certain circumstances satisfy the reliance element of a Rule 10b-5 action by invoking a rebuttable presumption of reliance, rather than proving direct reliance on a misrepresentation. The Court based that presumption on what is known as the "fraud-on-the-market" theory, which holds that "the market price of shares traded on well-developed markets reflects all publicly available information, and, hence, any material misrepresentations." The Court also noted that, rather than scrutinize every piece of public information about a company for himself, the typical "investor who buys or sells stock at the price set by the market does so in reliance on the integrity of that price"—the belief that it reflects all public, material information. As a result, whenever the investor buys or sells stock at the market price, his "reliance on any public material misrepresentations . . . may be presumed for purposes of a Rule 10b-5 action." . . .

Based on this theory, a plaintiff must make the following showings to demonstrate that the presumption of reliance applies in a given case: (1) that the alleged misrepresentations were publicly known, (2) that they were material, (3) that the stock traded in an efficient market, and (4) that the plaintiff traded the stock between the time the misrepresentations were made and when the truth was revealed. . . .

At the same time, *Basic* emphasized that the presumption of reliance was rebuttable rather than conclusive. Specifically, "[a]ny showing that severs the link between the alleged misrepresentation and either the price received (or paid) by the plaintiff, or his decision to trade at a fair market price, will be sufficient to rebut the presumption of reliance." So for example, if a defendant could show that the alleged misrepresentation did not, for whatever reason, actually affect the market price, or that a plaintiff would have bought or sold the stock even had he been aware that the stock's price was tainted by fraud, then the presumption of reliance would not apply. In either of those cases, a plaintiff would have to prove that he directly relied on the defendant's misrepresentation in buying or selling the stock.

B

Halliburton contends that securities fraud plaintiffs should always have to prove direct reliance and that the *Basic* Court erred in allowing them to invoke a presumption of reliance instead. According to Halliburton, the *Basic* presumption contravenes congressional intent and has been undermined by subsequent developments in economic theory. Neither argument, however, so discredits *Basic* as to constitute "special justification" for overruling the decision.

1

Halliburton first argues that the *Basic* presumption is inconsistent with Congress's intent in passing the 1934 Exchange Act. Because "[t]he Section 10(b) action is a 'judicial construct that Congress did not enact,'" this Court, Halliburton insists, "must identify—and borrow from—the express provision that is 'most analogous to the private 10b-5 right of action.'" . . . According to Halliburton, the closest analogue to section 10(b) is section 18(a) of the [Exchange] Act, which creates an express private cause of action allowing investors to recover damages based on misrepresentations made in certain regulatory filings. That provision requires an investor to prove that he bought or sold stock "in reliance upon" the defendant's misrepresentation. In ignoring this direct reliance requirement, the argument goes, the *Basic* Court relieved Rule 10b-5 plaintiffs of a burden that Congress would have imposed had it created the cause of action.

EPJ Fund contests both premises of Halliburton's argument, arguing that Congress has affirmed *Basic*'s construction of section 10(b) and that, in any event, the closest analogue to section 10(b) is not section 18(a) but section 9, 15 U. S. C. § 78i— a provision that does not require actual reliance.

We need not settle this dispute. In *Basic,* the dissenting Justices made the same argument based on section 18(a) that Halliburton presses here. . . . The *Basic* majority did not find that argument persuasive then, and Halliburton has given us no new reason to endorse it now.

2

Halliburton's primary argument for overruling *Basic* is that the decision rested on two premises that can no longer withstand scrutiny. The first premise concerns what is known as the "efficient capital markets hypothesis." *Basic* stated that "the market price of shares traded on well-developed markets reflects all publicly available information, and, hence, any material misrepresentations." From that statement, Halliburton concludes that the *Basic* Court espoused "a robust view of market efficiency" that is no longer tenable, for "'overwhelming empirical evidence' now 'suggests that capital markets are not fundamentally efficient.'" . . . To support this contention, Halliburton cites studies purporting to show that "public information is often not incorporated immediately (much less rationally) into market prices." . . .

Halliburton does not, of course, maintain that capital markets are always ineffi-cient. Rather, in its view, *Basic*'s fundamental error was to ignore the fact that "'efficiency is not a binary, yes or no question.'"... The markets for some securities are more efficient than the markets for others, and even a single market can process different kinds of information more or less efficiently, depending on how widely the information is disseminated and how easily it is understood. Yet *Basic*, Halliburton asserts, glossed over these nuances, assuming a false dichotomy that renders the pre-sumption of reliance both underinclusive and overinclusive: A misrepresentation can distort a stock's market price even in a generally inefficient market, and a misrepresentation can leave a stock's market price unaffected even in a generally effi-cient one.

Halliburton's criticisms fail to take *Basic* on its own terms. Halliburton focuses on the debate among economists about the degree to which the market price of a company's stock reflects public information about the company—and thus the degree to which an investor can earn an abnormal, above-market return by trading on such information. That debate is not new. Indeed, the *Basic* Court acknowledged it and declined to enter the fray, declaring that "[w]e need not determine by adjudi-cation what economists and social scientists have debated through the use of sophis-ticated statistical analysis and the application of economic theory."... To recognize the presumption of reliance, the Court explained, was not "conclusively to adopt any particular theory of how quickly and completely publicly available information is reflected in market price." The Court instead based the presumption on the fairly modest premise that "market professionals generally consider most publicly announced material statements about companies, thereby affecting stock market prices." *Basic*'s presumption of reliance thus does not rest on a "binary" view of mar-ket efficiency. Indeed, in making the presumption rebuttable, *Basic* recognized that market efficiency is a matter of degree and accordingly made it a matter of proof.

The academic debates discussed by Halliburton have not refuted the modest prem-ise underlying the presumption of reliance. Even the foremost critics of the efficient-capital markets hypothesis acknowledge that public information generally affects stock prices.... Halliburton also conceded as much in its reply brief and at oral argument.... Debates about the precise degree to which stock prices accurately reflect public information are thus largely beside the point. "That the ... price [of a stock] may be inaccurate does not detract from the fact that false statements affect it, and cause loss," which is "all that *Basic* requires."... Even though the efficient capital markets hypothesis may have "garnered substantial criticism since *Basic*," Halliburton has not identified the kind of fundamental shift in economic theory that could justify overruling a precedent on the ground that it misunderstood, or has since been over-taken by, economic realities.....

Halliburton also contests a second premise underlying the *Basic* presumption: the notion that investors "invest 'in reliance on the integrity of [the market] price.'" Hal-liburton identifies a number of classes of investors for whom "price integrity" is supposedly "marginal or irrelevant." The primary example is the value investor, who believes that certain stocks are undervalued or overvalued and attempts to "beat the market" by buying the undervalued stocks and selling the overvalued ones. . . . If many investors "are indifferent to prices," Halliburton contends, then courts should not presume that investors rely on the integrity of those prices and any misrepresentations incorporated into them.

But *Basic* never denied the existence of such investors. As we recently explained, *Basic* concluded only that "it is reasonable to presume that most investors—knowing that they have little hope of outperforming the market in the long run based solely on their analysis of publicly available information—will rely on the security's market price as an unbiased assessment of the security's value in light of all public information." . . .

In any event, there is no reason to suppose that even Halliburton's main counterexample—the value investor—is as indifferent to the integrity of market prices as Halliburton suggests. Such an investor implicitly relies on the fact that a stock's market price will eventually reflect material information—how else could the market correction on which his profit depends occur? To be sure, the value investor "does not believe that the market price accurately reflects public information *at the time he transacts*." But to indirectly rely on a misstatement in the sense relevant for the *Basic* presumption, he need only trade stock based on the belief that the market price will incorporate public information within a reasonable period. The value investor also presumably tries to estimate *how* undervalued or overvalued a particular stock is, and such estimates can be skewed by a market price tainted by fraud.

C

The principle of *stare decisis* has "'special force'" "in respect to statutory interpretation" because "'Congress remains free to alter what we have done.'" . . . So too with *Basic*'s presumption of reliance. Although the presumption is a judicially created doctrine designed to implement a judicially created cause of action, we have described the presumption as "a substantive doctrine of federal securities-fraud law." . . . That is because it provides a way of satisfying the reliance element of the Rule 10b-5 cause of action. As with any other element of that cause of action, Congress may overturn or modify any aspect of our interpretations of the reliance requirement, including the *Basic* presumption itself. Given that possibility, we see no reason to exempt the *Basic* presumption from ordinary principles of *stare decisis*.

To buttress its case for overruling *Basic*, Halliburton contends that, in addition to being wrongly decided, the decision is inconsistent with our more recent decisions construing the Rule 10b-5 cause of action. As Halliburton notes, we have held that "we must give 'narrow dimensions . . . to a right of action Congress did not authorize when it first enacted the statute and did not expand when it revisited the law.'" . . . Yet the *Basic* presumption, Halliburton asserts, does just the opposite, *expanding* the Rule 10b-5 cause of action. . . .

Not so. In *Central Bank and Stoneridge*, we declined to extend Rule 10b-5 liability to entirely new categories of defendants who themselves had not made any material, public misrepresentation. Such an extension, we explained, would have eviscerated the requirement that a plaintiff prove that he relied on a misrepresentation made *by the defendant*. The *Basic* presumption does not eliminate that requirement but rather provides an alternative means of satisfying it. While the presumption makes it easier for plaintiffs to prove reliance, it does not alter the elements of the Rule 10b-5 cause of action and thus maintains the action's original legal scope.

Halliburton also argues that the *Basic* presumption cannot be reconciled with our recent decisions governing class action certification under Federal Rule of Civil Procedure 23. Those decisions have made clear that plaintiffs wishing to proceed through a class action must actually prove—not simply plead—that their proposed class satisfies each requirement of Rule 23, including (if applicable) the predominance requirement of Rule 23(b)(3). According to Halliburton, *Basic* relieves Rule 10b-5 plaintiffs of that burden, allowing courts to presume that common issues of reliance predominate over individual ones.

That is not the effect of the *Basic* presumption. In securities class action cases, the crucial requirement for class certification will usually be the predominance requirement of Rule 23(b)(3). The *Basic* presumption does not relieve plaintiffs of the burden of proving—before class certification—that this requirement is met. *Basic* instead establishes that a plaintiff satisfies that burden by proving the prerequisites for invoking the presumption—namely, publicity, materiality, market efficiency, and market timing. The burden of proving those prerequisites still rests with plaintiffs and (with the exception of materiality) must be satisfied before class certification. *Basic* does not, in other words, allow plaintiffs simply to plead that common questions of reliance predominate over individual ones, but rather sets forth what they must prove to demonstrate such predominance.

Basic does afford defendants an opportunity to rebut the presumption of reliance with respect to an individual plaintiff by showing that he did not rely on the integrity of the market price in trading stock. While this has the effect of "leav[ing] individualized questions of reliance in the case," there is no reason to think that these questions will overwhelm common ones and render class certification inappropriate under Rule 23(b)(3). That the defendant might attempt to pick off the occasional class member here or there through individualized rebuttal does not cause individual questions to predominate.

Finally, Halliburton and its amici contend that, by facilitating securities class actions, the *Basic* presumption produces a number of serious and harmful consequences. Such class actions, they say, allow plaintiffs to extort large settlements from defendants for meritless claims; punish innocent shareholders, who end up having to pay settlements and judgments; impose excessive costs on businesses; and consume a disproportionately large share of judicial resources.

These concerns are more appropriately addressed to Congress, which has in fact responded, to some extent, to many of the issues raised by Halliburton and its *amici*. Congress has, for example, enacted the Private Securities Litigation Reform

Act of 1995 (PSLRA), 109 Stat. 737, which sought to combat perceived abuses in securities litigation with heightened pleading requirements, limits on damages and attorney's fees, a "safe harbor" for certain kinds of statements, restrictions on the selection of lead plaintiffs in securities class actions, sanctions for frivolous litigation, and stays of discovery pending motions to dismiss. And to prevent plaintiffs from circumventing these restrictions by bringing securities class actions under state law in state court, Congress also enacted the Securities Litigation Uniform Standards Act of 1998, 112 Stat. 3227, which precludes many state law class actions alleging securities fraud. Such legislation demonstrates Congress's willingness to consider policy concerns of the sort that Halliburton says should lead us to overrule *Basic*.

III

Halliburton proposes two alternatives to overruling *Basic* that would alleviate what it regards as the decision's most serious flaws. The first alternative would require plaintiffs to prove that a defendant's misrepresentation actually affected the stock price—so-called "price impact"—in order to invoke the *Basic* presumption. It should not be enough, Halliburton contends, for plaintiffs to demonstrate the general efficiency of the market in which the stock traded. Halliburton's second proposed alternative would allow *defendants* to rebut the presumption of reliance with evidence of a lack of price impact, not only at the merits stage—which all agree defendants may already do—but also *before* class certification. [emphasis supplied]

A

As noted, to invoke the *Basic* presumption, a plaintiff must prove that: (1) the alleged misrepresentations were publicly known, (2) they were material, (3) the stock traded in an efficient market, and (4) the plaintiff traded the stock between when the misrepresentations were made and when the truth was revealed. . . . Each of these requirements follows from the fraud-on-the-market theory underlying the presumption. If the misrepresentation was not publicly known, then it could not have distorted the stock's market price. So too if the misrepresentation was immaterial—that is, if it would not have "'been viewed by the reasonable investor as having significantly altered the "total mix" of information made available,'" . . . —or if the market in which the stock traded was inefficient. And if the plaintiff did not buy or sell the stock after the misrepresentation was made but before the truth was revealed, then he could not be said to have acted in reliance on a fraud-tainted price.

The first three prerequisites are directed at price impact—"whether the alleged misrepresentations affected the market price in the first place." In the absence of price impact, *Basic*'s fraud-on-the-market theory and presumption of reliance collapse. The "fundamental premise" underlying the presumption is "that an investor presumptively relies on a misrepresentation so long as it was reflected in the market price at the time of his transaction." If it was not, then there is "no grounding for any contention that [the] investor[ ] indirectly relied on th[at] misrepresentation[ ] through [his] reliance on the integrity of the market price." . . .

Halliburton argues that since the *Basic* presumption hinges on price impact, plaintiffs should be required to prove it directly in order to invoke the presumption. Proving the presumption's prerequisites, which are at best an imperfect proxy for price impact, should not suffice.

Far from a modest refinement of the *Basic* presumption, this proposal would radically alter the required showing for the reliance element of the Rule 10b-5 cause of action. What is called the *Basic* presumption actually incorporates two constituent presumptions: First, if a plaintiff shows that the defendant's misrepresentation was public and material and that the stock traded in a generally efficient market, he is entitled to a presumption that the misrepresentation affected the stock price. Second, if the plaintiff also shows that he purchased the stock at the market price during the relevant period, he is entitled to a further presumption that he purchased the stock in reliance on the defendant's misrepresentation.

By requiring plaintiffs to prove price impact directly, Halliburton's proposal would take away the first constituent presumption. Halliburton's argument for doing so is the same as its primary argument for overruling the *Basic* presumption altogether: Because market efficiency is not a yes-or-no proposition, a public, material misrepresentation might not affect a stock's price even in a generally efficient market. But as explained, *Basic* never suggested otherwise; that is why it affords defendants an opportunity to rebut the presumption by showing, among other things, that the particular misrepresentation at issue did not affect the stock's market price. For the same reasons we declined to completely jettison the *Basic* presumption, we decline to effectively jettison half of it by revising the prerequisites for invoking it.

B

Even if plaintiffs need not directly prove price impact to invoke the *Basic* presumption, Halliburton contends that defendants should at least be allowed to defeat the presumption at the class certification stage through evidence that the misrepresentation did not in fact affect the stock price. We agree.

1

There is no dispute that defendants may introduce such evidence at the merits stage to rebut the *Basic* presumption. *Basic* itself "made clear that the presumption was just that, and could be rebutted by appropriate evidence," including evidence that the asserted misrepresentation (or its correction) did not affect the market price of the defendant's stock. . . .

Nor is there any dispute that defendants may introduce price impact evidence at the class certification stage, so long as it is for the purpose of countering a plaintiff's showing of market efficiency, rather than directly rebutting the presumption. As EPJ Fund acknowledges, "[o]f course . . . defendants can introduce evidence at class certification of lack of price impact as some evidence that the market is not efficient." . . .

After all, plaintiffs themselves can and do introduce evidence of the *existence* of price impact in connection with "event studies"—regression analyses that seek to show that the market price of the defendant's stock tends to respond to pertinent publicly reported events. . . . In this case, for example, EPJ Fund submitted an event study of various episodes that might have been expected to affect the price of Halliburton's stock, in order to demonstrate that the market for that stock takes account of material, public information about the company. The episodes examined by EPJ Fund's event study included one of the alleged misrepresentations that form the basis of the Fund's suit. . . .

Defendants—like plaintiffs—may accordingly submit price impact evidence prior to class certification. What defendants may not do, EPJ Fund insists and the Court of Appeals held, is rely on that same evidence prior to class certification for the particular purpose of rebutting the presumption altogether.

This restriction makes no sense, and can readily lead to bizarre results. Suppose a defendant at the certification stage submits an event study looking at the impact on the price of its stock from six discrete events, in an effort to refute the plaintiffs' claim of general market efficiency. All agree the defendant may do this. Suppose one of the six events is the specific misrepresentation asserted by the plaintiffs. All agree that this too is perfectly acceptable. Now suppose the district court determines that, despite the defendant's study, the plaintiff has carried its burden to prove market efficiency, but that the evidence shows no price impact with respect to the specific misrepresentation challenged in the suit. The evidence at the certification stage thus shows an efficient market, on which the alleged misrepresentation had no price impact. And yet under EPJ Fund's view, the plaintiffs' action should be certified and proceed as a class action (with all that entails), even though the fraud-on-the-market theory does not apply and common reliance thus cannot be presumed.

Such a result is inconsistent with *Basic*'s own logic. Under *Basic*'s fraud-on-the-market theory, market efficiency and the other prerequisites for invoking the presumption constitute an indirect way of showing price impact. As explained, it is appropriate to allow plaintiffs to rely on this indirect proxy for price impact, rather than requiring them to prove price impact directly, given *Basic*'s rationales for recognizing a presumption of reliance in the first place.

But an indirect proxy should not preclude direct evidence when such evidence is available. As we explained in *Basic*, "[a]ny showing that severs the link between the alleged misrepresentation and . . . the price received (or paid) by the plaintiff . . . will be sufficient to rebut the presumption of reliance" because "the basis for finding that the fraud had been transmitted through market price would be gone." And without the presumption of reliance, a Rule 10b-5 suit cannot proceed as a class action: Each plaintiff would have to prove reliance individually, so common issues would not "predominate" over individual ones, as required by Rule 23(b)(3). Price impact is thus an essential precondition for any Rule 10b-5 class action. While *Basic* allows plaintiffs to establish that precondition indirectly, it does not require courts to ignore a defendant's direct, more salient evidence showing that the alleged misrepresentation did not actually affect the stock's market price and, consequently, that the *Basic* presumption does not apply.

2

The Court of Appeals relied on our decision in *Amgen* in holding that Halliburton could not introduce evidence of lack of price impact at the class certification stage. The question in *Amgen* was whether plaintiffs could be required to prove (or defendants be permitted to disprove) materiality before class certification. Even though materiality is a prerequisite for invoking the *Basic* presumption, we held that it should be left to the merits stage, because it does not bear on the predominance requirement of Rule 23(b)(3). We reasoned that materiality is an objective issue susceptible to common, classwide proof. We also noted that a failure to prove materiality would necessarily defeat every plaintiff's claim on the merits; it would not simply preclude invocation of the presumption and thereby cause individual questions of reliance to predominate over common ones. In this latter respect, we explained, materiality differs from the publicity and market efficiency prerequisites, neither of which is necessary to prove a Rule 10b-5 claim on the merits.

EPJ Fund argues that much of the foregoing could be said of price impact as well. Fair enough. But price impact differs from materiality in a crucial respect. Given that the other *Basic* prerequisites must still be proved at the class certification stage, the common issue of materiality can be left to the merits stage without risking the certification of classes in which individual issues will end up overwhelming common ones. And because materiality is a discrete issue that can be resolved in isolation from the other prerequisites, it can be wholly confined to the merits stage.

Price impact is different. The fact that a misrepresentation "was reflected in the market price at the time of [the] transaction"—that it had price impact—is "*Basic*'s fundamental premise." . . . It thus has everything to do with the issue of predominance at the class certification stage. That is why, if reliance is to be shown through the *Basic* presumption, the publicity and market efficiency prerequisites must be proved before class certification. Without proof of those prerequisites, the fraud-on-the-market theory underlying the presumption completely collapses, rendering class certification inappropriate.

But as explained, publicity and market efficiency are nothing more than prerequisites for an indirect showing of price impact. There is no dispute that at least such indirect proof of price impact "is needed to ensure that the questions of law or fact common to the class will 'predominate.'" . . . That is so even though such proof is also highly relevant at the merits stage.

Our choice in this case, then, is not between allowing price impact evidence at the class certification stage or relegating it to the merits. Evidence of price impact will be before the court at the certification stage in any event. The choice, rather, is between limiting the price impact inquiry before class certification to indirect evidence, or allowing consideration of direct evidence as well. As explained, we see no reason to artificially limit the inquiry at the certification stage to indirect evidence of price impact. Defendants may seek to defeat the *Basic* presumption at that stage through direct as well as indirect price impact evidence.

* * *

More than 25 years ago, we held that plaintiffs could satisfy the reliance element of the Rule 10b-5 cause of action by invoking a presumption that a public, material misrepresentation will distort the price of stock traded in an efficient market, and that anyone who purchases the stock at the market price may be considered to have done so in reliance on the misrepresentation. We adhere to that decision and decline to modify the prerequisites for invoking the presumption of reliance. But to maintain the consistency of the presumption with the class certification requirements of Federal Rule of Civil Procedure 23, defendants must be afforded an opportunity before class certification to defeat the presumption through evidence that an alleged misrepresentation did not actually affect the market price of the stock.

Because the courts below denied Halliburton that opportunity, we vacate the judgment of the Court of Appeals for the Fifth Circuit and remand the case for further proceedings consistent with this opinion.

It is so ordered.

[Note that this case subsequently settled for $100 million. See 49 Sec. Reg. & L. Rep. (BNA) 29 (2017).]

Justice Ginsburg, with whom Justice Breyer and Justice Sotomayor join, concurring.

Advancing price impact consideration from the merits stage to the certification stage may broaden the scope of discovery available at certification. But the Court recognizes that it is incumbent upon the defendant to show the absence of price impact. The Court's judgment, therefore, should impose no heavy toll on securities-fraud plaintiffs with tenable claims. On that understanding, I join the Court's opinion.

Justice Thomas, with whom Justice Scalia and Justice Alito join, concurring in the judgment.

The implied Rule 10b-5 private cause of action is "a relic of the heady days in which this Court assumed common-law powers to create causes of action." . . . We have since ended that practice because the authority to fashion private remedies to enforce federal law belongs to Congress alone. . . . Absent statutory authorization for a cause of action, "courts may not create one, no matter how desirable that might be as a policy matter."

Basic Inc. v. Levinson, 485 U. S. 224 (1988), demonstrates the wisdom of this rule. *Basic* presented the question how investors must prove the reliance element of the implied Rule 10b-5 cause of action—the requirement that the plaintiff buy or sell stock in reliance on the defendant's misstatement—when they transact on modern, impersonal securities exchanges. Were the Rule 10b-5 action statutory, the Court could have resolved this question by interpreting the statutory language. Without a statute to interpret for guidance, however, the Court began instead with a particular policy "problem": for investors in impersonal markets, the traditional reliance requirement was hard to prove and impossible to prove as common among plaintiffs bringing 10b-5 class-action suits. With the task thus framed as "resol[ving]" that "'problem'" rather than interpreting statutory text, the Court turned to nascent economic theory and naked intuitions about investment behavior in its efforts to fashion a new, easier way to meet the reliance requirement. The result was an evidentiary presumption, based on a "fraud on the market" theory, that paved the way for class actions under Rule 10b-5.

Today we are asked to determine whether *Basic* was correctly decided. The Court suggests that it was, and that *stare decisis* demands that we preserve it. I disagree. Logic, economic realities, and our subsequent jurisprudence have undermined the foundations of the *Basic* presumption, and *stare decisis* cannot prop up the façade that remains. *Basic* should be overruled.

. . . .

*   *   *

. . . *Basic* should be overruled in favor of the straightforward rule that "[r]eliance by the plaintiff upon the defendant's deceptive acts"—actual reliance, not the fictional "fraud-on-the-market" version—"is an essential element of the § 10(b) private cause of action."

*   *   *

. . . . *Basic* took an implied cause of action and grafted on a policy-driven presumption of reliance based on nascent economic theory and personal intuitions about investment behavior. The result was an unrecognizably broad cause of action ready made for class certification. Time and experience have pointed up the error of that decision, making it all too clear that the Court's attempt to revise securities law to fit the alleged "new realities of financial markets" should have been left to Congress.

---

[1] Characteristics of an Efficient Market

In order for the presumption of the efficient market theory to apply, the subject security must be traded in an *efficient* market. In making this determination, the principal focus is on the market for that particular security and not on the location (such as the New York Stock Exchange or the Nasdaq Stock Market) where such security trades. Hence, for fraud-on-the-market purposes, the market for each security is distinct, leading to the conclusion that a stock exchange (or over-the-counter market) can be efficient for some securities listed on such exchange, but not for others.

Therefore, what factors generally comprise an efficient market to support the *Basic* presumption of reliance? In *Unger v. Amedisys, Inc.*, 401 F.3d 316, 323 (5th Cir. 2005), the Fifth Circuit looked to the following factors:

Courts have relied on several factors to determine whether a stock is traded in an "efficient market": (1) the average weekly trading volume expressed as a percentage of total outstanding shares; (2) the number of securities analysts following and reporting on the stock; (3) the extent to which market makers and arbitrageurs trade in the stock; (4) the company's eligibility to file SEC registration Form S-3 (as opposed to Form S-1 . . .); (5) the existence of empirical facts "showing a cause and effect relationship between unexpected corporate events or financial releases and an immediate response in the stock price" [evidently, the most important factor]; (6) the company's market capitalization; (7) the bid-ask spread for stock sales; and (8) float, the stock's trading volume without counting insider owned stock. . . .

Although this does not represent an exhaustive list, and in some cases one of the above factors may be unnecessary, once a court endeavors to apply these factors, they must be weighed analytically, not merely counted, as each of them represents a distinct facet of market efficiency.

The foregoing factors have been applied by courts with regularity when determining whether a subject security trades in an efficient market. One factor—namely, whether SEC Form S-3 is available—should be deemed far less significant today due to the Commission's expansion of eligibility of the Form S-3 to encompass those issuers that have a public float of less than $75 million, provided that such issuers have a class of equity securities traded on a national securities exchange (see § 5.01[C]).

---

[2] The "Fraud to Enter the Market" Theory

A more expansive version of the fraud-on-the-market theory, called the "fraud to enter the market" theory or "fraud-created-the-market" theory, applies this doctrine to the offering context where no active trading market exists for the issuer's stock. The leading case is *Shores v. Sklar*, 647 F.2d 462 (5th Cir. 1981) (en banc), *cert. denied*, 459 U.S. 1102 (1983), in which the Fifth Circuit sitting en banc adopted the theory, with ten judges dissenting. The Supreme Court has yet to rule on the theory's validity in this context.

In *Shores*, the plaintiff purchased bonds without reading the offering circular. He alleged in a § 10(b) cause of action that the defendants had perpetrated a fraudulent scheme on the investment community by bringing unmarketable securities into the open market. Invoking the fraud to enter the market theory, the court held that an investor is entitled to rely on the integrity of the market to the extent that the securities offered for sale are entitled to be in the marketplace. To recover under this theory, the plaintiff must establish that the bonds would never have been issued or marketed. Proof that the bonds would have been offered at a lower price is not sufficient. Thus, "the fraudulent scheme [must be] so pervasive that without it the issuer would not have issued, the dealer could not have dealt in, and the buyer could not have bought [the securities], because they would not have been offered at any price."

Id. at 464 n.2, 469–471. As subsequently construed by the Fifth Circuit, securities are deemed not entitled to be marketed, "only where the promoters knew the enterprise itself was patently worthless." *Abell v. Potomac Insurance Company*, 858 F.2d 1104, 1121–1122 (5th Cir. 1988), *vacated on other grounds*, 492 U.S. 914 (1988).

While the Fifth Circuit in *Shores* and its progeny examined how the market would have likely responded to the securities being offered absent the fraud, other courts have focused on the integrity of the regulatory process. For example, the Ninth Circuit held that reliance may be presumed if the investor "relie[d], at least indirectly, on the integrity of the regulatory process and the truth of any representations made to the appropriate agencies and the investors at the time of the original issue." *Arthur Young & Co. v. United States District Court*, 549 F.2d 686, 695 (9th Cir. 1977). The Tenth Circuit has adopted a similar approach. *See T.J. Raney & Sons, Inc., v. Fort Cobb, Okla. Irrigation Fuel Authority*, 717 F.2d 1330, 1332 (10th Cir. 1983).

The Seventh Circuit in *Eckstein v. Balcor Film Investors*, 8 F.3d 1121, 1130–1131 (7th Cir. 1993), rejected the *Shores* "fraud to enter the market" theory. The court reasoned:

> *Shores* held that an investor may maintain an action under Section 10(b) by establishing that the fraud permitted the securities to exist in the market — that but for the fraud the securities would have been "unmarketable" — and that the investor relied on their existence. [We reject the *Shores* rationale.] . . . The existence of a security does not depend on, or warrant, the adequacy of disclosure. Many a security is on the market even though the issuer or some third party made incomplete disclosures. Federal securities law does not include "merit regulation." Full disclosure of adverse information may lower the price, but it does not exclude the security from the market. Securities of bankrupt corporations trade freely; some markets specialize in penny stocks. Thus the linchpin of *Shores* — that disclosing bad information keeps securities off the market, entitling investors to rely on the presence of the securities just as they would rely on statements in a prospectus — is simply false.

After rejecting the *Shores* rationale, the Seventh Circuit opted for a different approach. In *Eckstein*, the limited partnership offering was subject to a minimum sale requirement. To prevail on the issue of reliance, the Seventh Circuit required that plaintiffs prove that, absent the fraud, the limited partnership would not have met the minimum sale requirement.

More recently, the Third Circuit rejected the "fraud-created-the-market" theory. In *Malack v. BDO Seidman LLP*, 617 F.3d 743, 749 (3d Cir. 2010), the court reasoned:

> [Plaintiff] asks us to embrace the legal unmarketability approach to the fraud-created-the-market theory. No matter what approach is taken, however, the theory lacks a basis in any of the accepted grounds for creating a presumption.

"Presumptions typically serve to assist courts in managing circumstances in which direct proof, for one reason or another, is rendered difficult." . . . "[C]onsiderations of fairness, public policy, and probability, as well as judicial economy," often underlie the creation of presumptions. . . . Another relevant concern in the creation of a presumption is whether it is "consistent with . . . congressional policy[.]" . . . "Common sense" also plays a role. Courts may also create presumptions "to correct an imbalance resulting from one party's superior access to the proof," where "social and economic policy incline the courts to favor one contention," or "to avoid a[] [factual] impasse" . . . . "Generally, however, the most important consideration in the creation of presumptions is probability. Most presumptions have come into existence primarily because judges have believed that proof of fact B renders the inference of the existence of fact A so probable that it is sensible and time-saving to assume the truth of fact A until the adversary disproves it." . . .

The fraud-created-the-market theory rests on the conjecture that a "[security's] availability on the market [i]s an indication of [its] apparent genuineness[.]" . . . [Plaintiff] points to "common sense and probability" as support for this conjecture, but neither of these considerations bolsters the idea that securities on the market, by the mere virtue of their availability for purchase, are free from fraud. . . . [24]

[F] Loss Causation

Dura Pharmaceuticals, Inc. v. Broudo

United States Supreme Court

544 U.S. 336, 125 S. Ct. 1627, 161 L. Ed. 2d 577 (2005)

Justice Breyer delivered the opinion of the Court.

A private plaintiff who claims securities fraud must prove that the defendant's fraud caused an economic loss. We consider a Ninth Circuit holding that a plaintiff can satisfy this requirement—a requirement that courts call "loss causation"—simply by alleging in the complaint and subsequently establishing that "the price" of the security *on the date of purchase* was inflated because of the misrepresentation." 339 F.3d 933, 938 (2003). In our view, the Ninth Circuit is wrong, both in respect to what the plaintiff must prove and in respect to what plaintiff's complaint here must allege.

---

24. *See generally* Black, *The Strange Case of Fraud on the Market: A Label in Search of a Theory,* 52 ALB. L. REV. 923 (1988); Carney, *The Limits of the Fraud on the Market Theory,* 44 BUS. LAW. 1259 (1989); Herzog, *Fraud Created the Market: An Unwise and Unwarranted Extension of Section 10(b) and Rule 10b-5,* 63 GEO. WASH. L. REV. 359 (1995); Newkirk, *Sufficient Efficiency: Fraud on the Market in the Initial Public Offering Context,* 58 U. CHI. L. REV. 1393 (1991).

I

Respondents are individuals who bought stock in Dura Pharmaceuticals, Inc., on the public securities market between April 15, 1997, and February 24, 1998. They have brought this securities fraud class action against Dura and some of its managers and directors (hereinafter Dura) in federal court. In respect to the question before us, their detailed amended (181 paragraph) complaint makes substantially the following allegations:

(1) Before and during the purchase period, Dura (or its officials) made false statements concerning both Dura's drug profits and future Food and Drug Administration (FDA) approval of a new asthmatic spray device.

(2) In respect to drug profits, Dura falsely claimed that it expected that its drug sales would prove profitable.

(3) In respect to the asthmatic spray device, Dura falsely claimed that it expected the FDA would soon grant its approval.

(4) On the last day of the purchase period, February 24, 1998, Dura announced that its earnings would be lower than expected, principally due to slow drug sales.

(5) The next day Dura's shares lost almost half their value (falling from about $39 per share to about $21).

(6) About eight months later (in November 1998), Dura announced that the FDA would not approve Dura's new asthmatic spray device.

(7) The next day Dura's share price temporarily fell but almost fully recovered within one week.

Most importantly, the complaint says the following (and nothing significantly more than the following) about economic losses attributable to the spray device misstatement: *"In reliance on the integrity of the market, [the plaintiffs] . . . paid artificially inflated prices for Dura securities"* and the plaintiffs suffered *"damage[s]"* thereby.

The District Court dismissed the complaint. In respect to the plaintiffs' drug-profitability claim, it held that the complaint failed adequately to allege an appropriate state of mind, *i.e.,* that defendants had acted knowingly, or the like. In respect to the plaintiffs' spray device claim, it held that the complaint failed adequately to allege "loss causation."

The Court of Appeals for the Ninth Circuit reversed. In the portion of the court's decision now before us—the portion that concerns the spray device claim—the Circuit held that the complaint adequately alleged "loss causation." The Circuit wrote that "plaintiffs establish loss causation if they have shown that the price *on the date of purchase* was inflated because of the misrepresentation." It added that "the injury occurs at the time of the transaction." Since the complaint pleaded "that the price at the time of purchase was overstated," and it sufficiently identified the cause, its allegations were legally sufficient.

Because the Ninth Circuit's views about loss causation differ from those of other Circuits that have considered this issue, we granted Dura's petition for certiorari. . . . We now reverse.

II

Private federal securities fraud actions are based upon federal securities statutes and their implementing regulations. Section 10(b) of the Securities Exchange Act of 1934 forbids (1) the "use or employ[ment] . . . of any . . . deceptive device," (2) "in connection with the purchase or sale of any security," and (3) "in contravention of" Securities and Exchange Commission "rules and regulations." Commission Rule 10b-5 forbids, among other things, the making of any "untrue statement of material fact" or the omission of any material fact "necessary in order to make the statements made . . . not misleading."

The courts have implied from these statutes and Rule a private damages action, which resembles, but is not identical to, common-law tort actions for deceit and misrepresentation. . . . And Congress has imposed statutory requirements on that private action.

In cases involving publicly traded securities and purchases or sales in public securities markets, the action's basic elements include:

(1) *a material misrepresentation (or omission);*

(2) *scienter, i.e.,* a wrongful state of mind;

(3) *a connection with the purchase or sale of a security;*

(4) *reliance,* often referred to in cases involving public securities markets (fraud-on-the-market cases) as "transaction causation;"

(5) *economic loss,* 15 U. S. C. § 78u-4(b)(4); and

(6) *"loss causation," i.e.,* a causal connection between the material misrepresentation and the loss. . . .

Dura argues that the complaint's allegations are inadequate in respect to these last two elements.

A

We begin with the Ninth Circuit's basic reason for finding the complaint adequate, namely, that at the end of the day plaintiffs need only "establish," *i.e.,* prove, that "the price *on the date of purchase* was inflated because of the misrepresentation." In our view, this statement of the law is wrong. Normally, in cases such as this one (*i.e.,* fraud-on-the-market cases), an inflated purchase price will not itself constitute or proximately cause the relevant economic loss.

For one thing, as a matter of pure logic, at the moment the transaction takes place, the plaintiff has suffered no loss; the inflated purchase payment is offset by ownership of a share that *at that instant* possesses equivalent value. Moreover, the logical link between the inflated share purchase price and any later economic loss is not invariably strong. Shares are normally purchased with an eye toward a later sale. But if, say, the purchaser sells the shares quickly before the relevant truth begins to leak out, the misrepresentation will not have led to any loss. If the purchaser sells later after the truth makes its way into the market place, an initially inflated purchase price *might* mean a later loss. But that is far from inevitably so. When the purchaser subsequently resells such shares, even at a lower price, that lower price may reflect, not the earlier misrepresentation, but changed economic circumstances, changed investor expectations, new industry-specific or firm-specific facts, conditions, or other events, which taken separately or together account for some or all of that lower price. (The same is true in respect to a claim that a share's higher price is lower than it would otherwise have been—a claim we do not consider here.) Other things being equal, the longer the time between purchase and sale, the more likely that this is so, *i.e.*, the more likely that other factors caused the loss.

Given the tangle of factors affecting price, . . . logic alone permits us to say that the higher purchase price will *sometimes* play a role in bringing about a future loss. It may prove to be a necessary condition of any such loss, and in that sense one might say that the inflated purchase price suggests that the misrepresentation (using language the Ninth Circuit used), "touches upon" a later economic loss. But, even if that is so, it is insufficient. To "touch upon" a loss is not to *cause* a loss, and it is the latter that the law requires.

For another thing, the Ninth Circuit's holding lacks support in precedent. Judicially implied private securities-fraud actions resemble in many (but not all) respects common-law deceit and misrepresentation actions. . . . The common law of deceit subjects a person who "fraudulently" makes a "misrepresentation" to liability "for pecuniary loss caused" to one who justifiably relies upon that misrepresentation. . . . And the common law has long insisted that a plaintiff in such a case show not only that had he known the truth he would not have acted but also that he suffered actual economic loss.

Given the common-law roots of the securities fraud action (and the common-law requirement that a plaintiff show actual damages), it is not surprising that other courts of appeals have rejected the Ninth Circuit's "inflated purchase price" approach to proving causation and loss. . . .

We cannot reconcile the Ninth Circuit's "inflated purchase price" approach with these views of other courts. And the uniqueness of its perspective argues against the validity of its approach in a case like this one where we consider the contours of a judicially implied cause of action with roots in the common law.

Finally, the Ninth Circuit's approach overlooks an important securities law objective. The securities statutes seek to maintain public confidence in the marketplace. See *United States v. O'Hagan*, 521 U.S. 642, 658 (1997). They do so by deterring fraud, in part, through the availability of private securities fraud actions. *Randall v. Loftsgaarden*, 478 U.S. 647, 664 (1986). But the statutes make these latter actions available, not to provide investors with broad insurance against market losses, but to protect them against those economic losses that misrepresentations actually cause. . . .

The statutory provision at issue here and the paragraphs that precede it emphasize this last mentioned objective. Private Securities Litigation Reform Act of 1995. The statute insists that securities fraud complaints "specify" each misleading statement; that they set forth the facts "on which [a] belief" that a statement is misleading was "formed"; and that they "state with particularity facts giving rise to a strong inference that the defendant acted with the required state of mind." ... And the statute expressly imposes on plaintiffs "the burden of proving" that the defendant's misrepresentations "caused the loss for which the plaintiff seeks to recover." §78u-4(b)(4). [Section 21D(b)(4) of the Securities Exchange Act]

The statute thereby makes clear Congress' intent to permit private securities fraud actions for recovery where, but only where, plaintiffs adequately allege and prove the traditional elements of causation and loss. By way of contrast, the Ninth Circuit's approach would allow recovery where a misrepresentation leads to an inflated purchase price but nonetheless does not proximately cause any economic loss. That is to say, it would permit recovery where these two traditional elements in fact are missing.

In sum, we find the Ninth Circuit's approach inconsistent with the law's requirement that a plaintiff prove that the defendant's misrepresentation (or other fraudulent conduct) proximately caused the plaintiff's economic loss. We need not, and do not, consider other proximate cause or loss-related questions.

B

Our holding about plaintiffs' need to *prove* proximate causation and economic loss leads us also to conclude that the plaintiffs' complaint here failed adequately to *allege* these requirements. . . .

As we have pointed out, the plaintiffs' lengthy complaint contains only one statement that we can fairly read as describing the loss caused by the defendants' "spray device" misrepresentations. That statement says that the plaintiffs "paid artificially inflated prices for Dura's securities" and suffered "damage[s]." The statement implies that the plaintiffs' loss consisted of the "artificially inflated" purchase "prices." The complaint's failure to claim that Dura's share price fell significantly after the truth became known suggests that the plaintiffs considered the allegation of purchase price inflation alone sufficient. The complaint contains nothing that suggests otherwise.

For reasons set forth in Part II-A, *supra*, however, the "artificially inflated purchase price" is not itself a relevant economic loss. And the complaint nowhere else provides the defendants with notice of what the relevant economic loss might be or of what the causal connection might be between that loss and the misrepresentation concerning Dura's "spray device."

We concede that ordinary pleading rules are not meant to impose a great burden upon a plaintiff. But it should not prove burdensome for a plaintiff who has suffered an economic loss to provide a defendant with some indication of the loss and the causal connection that the plaintiff has in mind. At the same time, allowing a plaintiff to forgo giving any indication of the economic loss and proximate cause that the plaintiff has in mind would bring about harm of the very sort the statutes seek to avoid. Cf. H.R. Conf. Rep. No. 104-369, p. 31 (1995) (criticizing "abusive" practices including "the routine filing of lawsuits . . . with only a faint hope that the discovery process might lead eventually to some plausible cause of action"). It would permit a plaintiff "with a largely groundless claim to simply take up the time of a number of other people, with the right to do so representing an *in terrorem* incre- ment of the settlement value, rather than a reasonably founded hope that the [discovery] process will reveal relevant evidence." *Blue Chip Stamps*, 421 U.S., at 741. Such a rule would tend to transform a private securities action into a partial downside insurance policy. . . .

For these reasons, we find the plaintiffs' complaint legally insufficient. We reverse the judgment of the Ninth Circuit, and we remand the case for further proceedings consistent with this opinion.

It is so ordered.

Note — Freddie Mac *(6th Cir. 2016)*

There have been several district and appellate court decisions applying the Supreme Court's decision in *Dura Pharmaceuticals*. For a succinct analysis, see the Sixth Cir- cuit's decision in *OPERS v. Federal Home Loan Mortgage Corp.*, 830 F.3d 376, 384– 385 (6th Cir. 2016) (citations omitted):

> Loss causation is the casual link between the alleged misconduct and the economic harm ultimately suffered by the plaintiff. It partakes of the tradi- tional elements of loss and proximate causation. Any analogy to the com- mon law tort concept, however, would be imperfect because the alleged misstatements do not generally cause a security to drop in value, but rather, the "underlying circumstance that is concealed or misstated." Thus, in the securities fraud context, "a misstatement or omission is the 'proximate cause' of an investment loss if the risk that caused the loss was within the zone of risk *concealed* by the misrepresentations and omissions alleged by a disap- pointed investor."
>
> This court has acknowledged . . . that loss causation can be shown through a corrective disclosure. Under the corrective disclosure theory, . . . the mar- ket reacted negatively to a corrective disclosure of fraud. A decisive major- ity of circuits have also recognized the alternative theory of materialization of the risk, whereby a plaintiff may allege "proximate cause on the ground that negative investor inferences," drawn from a particular event or disclo- sure, "caused the loss and were a foreseeable materialization of the risk con- cealed by the fraudulent statement."
>
> . . . .

We are mindful of the dangerous incentive that is created when the success of any loss causation argument is made contingent upon a defendant's acknowledgement that it misled investors. Our sister circuits are too and have recognized that defendants accused of securities fraud should not escape liability by simply avoiding a corrective disclosure. *See Mass. Ret. Sys. v. CVS Caremark Corp.*, 716 F.3d 229, 240 (1st Cir. 2013) (reasoning . . . that "a defendant's failure to admit to making a misrepresentation or his denial that a misrepresentation was made" should not shield him in the loss causation analysis, lest he avoid liability by simply refusing to concede that a prior misstatement was false).

In light of our applicable precedent and the clear weight of persuasive authority, we join our fellow circuits in recognizing the viability of alternative theories of loss causation and apply materialization of the risk in this case.

[G] State Securities Law

With respect to the issues of causation and reliance, the state securities laws may differ from federal court interpretation of § 10(b). For example, many states dispense with proof of reliance. *See, e.g.*, Cal. Corp. Code §§ 25400, 25500; Ohio Rev. Code Ann. § 1707.43. Construing its state's version of § 10(b), the Florida Supreme Court held that the plaintiff was not required to prove loss causation. *See E.F. Hutton & Company v. Rousseff*, 537 So. 2d 978 (Fla. 1989). The language of the Florida statute is similar to that contained in the blue sky laws of a number of other states. Critical of the Florida Supreme Court's approach, Professor Cane poignantly observed: "It would seem that a plaintiff bringing a suit under [the Florida statute] could rescind [the transaction] without a showing of proximate cause, or any damage, or any scienter on the part of the defendant. . . . Was the intent of the Florida legislature to create a system of investor insurance?"[25]

On the other hand, a number of state courts have rejected the fraud on the market theory in common law fraud actions. By requiring individualized proof of reliance, these state court decisions may nullify the class action mechanism for securities fraud in their jurisdictions. For example, the California Supreme Court rejected *Basic*, asserting that the fraud-on-the-market theory nullified the reliance requirement. *Mirkin v. Wasserman*, 5 Cal. 4th 1082, 858 P.2d 568, 23 Cal. Rptr. 2d 101 (1993). See *Peil v. Speiser*, 806 F.2d 1154, 1163 n.17 (3d Cir. 1986) ("While the fraud on the market theory is good law with respect to the [federal] Securities Acts, no state courts have adopted the theory, and thus direct reliance remains a requirement of a common law securities fraud claim."); *Gaffin v. Teledyne, Inc.*, 611 A.2d 467, 474 (Del. 1992) ("A class action may not be maintained in a purely common law or equitable

---

25. Cane, *Proximate Causation in Securities Fraud Actions for Rescission*, Fla. Bar Bus. Quart. Rep., Vol. 2, No. 2, at 14 (Spring 1989).

fraud case since individual questions of law or fact, particularly as to the element of justifiable reliance, will inevitably predominate over common questions of law or fact.").

§ 8.06 Materiality

In addition to the discussion contained in Chapters 5 and 7, as well as §§ 8.01 and 8.05, this is a good point to review the concept of materiality as set forth in the Supreme Court's decision in *Matrixx Initiatives* and in the Second Circuit's decision in *Ganino*.

Matrixx Initiatives, Inc. v. Siracusano

United States Supreme Court

131 S. Ct. 1309 (2011)

[This case is contained in § 5.03[D] and may be discussed at this point.]

Ganino v. Citizens Utilities Company

United States Court of Appeals, Second Circuit

228 F.3d 154 (2000)

[This case is contained in § 5.03[D][2] and may be discussed at this point.]

§ 8.07 Cumulative Remedies

Under a cumulative interpretation of the securities laws, a party may invoke a remedy even though another statute may provide another remedy for the same conduct. In *Herman & MacLean v. Huddleston*, 459 U.S. 375 (1983), the Supreme Court adopted a cumulative construction to § 10(b), thereby recognizing an implied right of action for damages under § 10(b) despite the apparent availability of an express cause of action under § 11 of the 1933 Act. The Court reasoned that § 10(b) imposes a heavier burden on the plaintiff by mandating that, unlike § 11, the defendant's scienter be proven in order to recover. Moreover, while § 11 applies solely in the registered offering context, § 10(b) is a "catch-all" antifraud provision designed to reach manipulative or deceptive practices in connection with the purchase or sale of any security, whether traded in the primary or secondary markets.

The Supreme Court's language in *Huddleston* strongly suggests that a cumulative approach between § 10(b) and other express rights of action, such as § 12(a)(2) of the Securities Act and § 18(a) of the Exchange Act, is appropriate where the express remedy does not require the plaintiff to prove scienter. In other words, the various procedural restrictions that apply in actions invoking the express remedies (restrictions that are somewhat absent in suits brought under § 10(b)) are counterbalanced by § 10(b)'s scienter requirement. Based in large part on this rationale, the lower courts adhere to a cumulative approach where the express remedy invoked is § 11 or § 12(a)(2) of the Securities Act or § 18(a) of the Exchange Act. *See, e.g., Berger v. Bishop Investment Corp.*, 695 F.2d 302 (8th Cir. 1982); *Wachovia Bank & Trust Co. v. National Student Marketing Corp.* 650 F.2d 342 (D.C. Cir. 1980); *Ross v. A.H. Robins, Co.*, 607 F.2d 545 (2d Cir. 1979).

With respect to § 18(a), that statute provides an express right of action for damages on behalf of a purchaser or seller against any person who makes or causes to be made a materially false or misleading statement in any document filed with the SEC pursuant to the Exchange Act. Because of § 18(a)'s strict reliance and causation requirements, a suit based solely on § 18(a) poses challenging hurdles (see § 9.05). Hence, normally the § 10(b) action is the preferred route. Whether the increasingly intensive focus by institutional and other sophisticated investors on 1934 Act reports, along with the ramifications of the Sarbanes-Oxley Act, will result in more § 18(a) actions being brought remains to be seen.

A more difficult issue is presented when a cumulative approach is sought to be invoked between § 10(b) and § 9 of the Exchange Act. Under § 9 (which provides a private remedy for purchasers and sellers who have been victimized by stock manipulation), the plaintiff in order to recover must prove scienter, reliance, causation, and damages. Moreover, plaintiffs suing under § 9 are subject to rigorous procedural limitations. As one court has observed: "Section 9(e) . . . permits the court to require security for costs, limits damages to losses sustained by reason of the unlawful price manipulation, provides for contribution by persons not joined as defendants in the original action, and permits the court to assess attorneys' fees against either party." *Wolgin v. Magic Marker Corp.*, 82 F.R.D. 168, 180 (E.D. Pa. 1979). Hence, due to the breadth of the § 9 requirements, plaintiffs bringing suit under § 10(b) are subject to no additional burdens. Indeed, when contrasted with the § 9 express remedy, the § 10(b) right of action is more attractive in a number of respects and is not less attractive in any respect.

Nonetheless, cogent reasons exist for recognizing a cumulative remedy in this context. Prior to the enactment of the Dodd-Frank Act of 2010 which amended § 9 to encompass all securities transactions (with the exception of government securities), § 9 applied by its terms only to transactions on a national securities exchange. Today, after the 2010 Dodd-Frank amendments, plaintiffs may invoke § 9 regardless whether the subject securities are traded on a national securities exchange or in the over-the-counter market.[26]

---

26. *See* §§ 762, 763, 929L of the Dodd-Frank Act, *amending*, § 9 of the Securities Exchange Act; CCH, Dodd-Frank Wall Street Reform and Consumer Protection Act: Law, Explanation and Analysis 376 (2010).

The 2010 Dodd-Frank provisions amending § 9 were to provide equality of regulation between the national securities exchanges and the over-the-counter markets. This approach is sound and firmly rooted in the reality of the operations of the securities markets. In this context, an exclusive construction of remedies, denying investors the long established § 10(b) remedy, would insulate from liability practices repugnant to the purposes underlying the federal securities laws. See Siegel, *Interplay Between the Implied Remedy Under Section 10(b) and the Express Causes of Action of the Federal Securities Laws*, 62 B.U. L. Rev. 385 (1982); Steinberg, *The Propriety and Scope of Cumulative Remedies Under the Federal Securities Laws*, 67 Cornell L. Rev. 557 (1982).

---

§ 8.08 Damages

The federal securities laws limit recovery to "actual damages." Although this measure does not necessarily preclude a recovery of damages that exceed out-of-pocket loss, punitive damages may not be awarded. *See Randall v. Loftsgaarden*, 478 U.S. 647 (1986). Moreover, in SEC enforcement actions, disgorgement and monetary penalties may be levied for violations of § 10(b) as well as for violations of other provisions of the securities laws.

The federal courts most frequently have adopted the out-of-pocket measure of damages to redress violations of § 10(b). Other measures of damages that have received judicial approbation in select cases include the benefit-of-the-bargain, rescissionary, disgorgement, and certain hybrids of the various measures. As explained by Professor Kaufman:

> The benefit-of-the-bargain measure is generally understood as the difference between the represented value of the security purchased or sold and the fair value of the security on the date of the trade. Out-of-pocket relief, which has been termed the "traditional" 10b-5 measure of recovery, represents "the difference between the fair value of all that the [plaintiff] received and the fair value of what he would have received had there been no fraudulent conduct." This measure constitutes the disparity between the fair value of the security purchased and the fair value of the consideration paid, generally measured at the time of the transaction. Disgorgement, as it applies to the securities laws, returns to the plaintiff the amount of the defendant's unjust enrichment. Under the disgorgement theory, the plaintiff recovers the defendant's profit resulting from the fraud, rather than the plaintiff's losses. Finally, rescission, by contrast, is the judicial act of undoing a transaction. Rescission typically precedes restitution, which restores each party to its pre-transaction condition.

Kaufman, *No Foul, No Harm: The Real Measure of Damages Under Rule 10b-5*, 39 Cath. U. L. Rev. 29, 31 (1989).

In addition, the Private Securities Litigation Reform Act of 1995 (PSLRA) added a new Section 21D(e) to the Securities Exchange Act. In general, this provision places a limitation on damages in 1934 Act actions where the plaintiff attempts to establish such damages by reference to the market price of a security. In this context, the PSLRA cap limits damages to the difference between the purchase or sale price paid or received by the plaintiff, as applicable, and the mean trading price of the security during the 90-day period beginning on the date on which the information correcting the misstatement or omission that is the basis for the action is disseminated to the market. For these purposes, the "mean trading price" of a security is the average of the daily trading price of such security, determined as of the close of the market each day during the 90-day period referred to above.

An empirical analysis concludes that the PSLRA damages cap is a failure. The author asserts:

> The empirical analysis of . . . securities fraud class action filings [during the survey period] shows that the PSLRA damages cap does not function as intended because stock prices do not necessarily rise in the 90 days after the corrective information is released to the market. In fact, prices frequently tend to fall even lower during that period. While the overall market movement during the 90-day period may explain some of the variation in the stock price, a broad range of company-specific disclosures released during the period may cause the price to rise or fall, even though these disclosures are not remotely connected to the alleged fraud.[27]

§ 8.09 Defenses and Strategic Considerations

This section looks at three defenses that may be asserted in given cases: (1) failure to plead fraud with particularity; (2) noncompliance with § 10(b)'s statute of limitations; and (3) equitable defenses, particularly the concept of *in pari delicto*.

---

27. Pashin, *The PSLRA Cap on Securities Fraud Damages: An Empirical Evaluation of the 90-Day "Bounce-Back,"* 41 Sec. Reg. L.J. 169, 188-89 (2013). *See generally* M. Kaufman, Securities Litigation: Damages (2011 & Supp.); Alexander, *Rethinking Damages in Securities Class Actions*, 48 Stan. L. Rev. 1487 (1996); Black, *Reputational Damages in Securities Litigation*, 35 J. Corp. L. 169 (2009); Easterbrook & Fischel, *Optimal Damages in Securities Cases*, 52 U. Chi. L. Rev. 611 (1985); Grundfest, *Damages and Reliance Under Section 10(b) of the Exchange Act*, 69 Bus. Law. 307 (2014); Lowenfels & Bromberg, *Compensatory Damages in Rule 10b-5 Actions: Pragmatic Justice or Chaos?*, 30 Seton Hall L. Rev. 1083 (2000); Thompson, *"Simplicity and Certainty" in the Measure of Recovery Under Rule 10b-5*, 51 Bus. Law. 1177 (1996); Thompson, *The Measure of Recovery Under Rule 10b-5: A Restitution Alternative to Tort Damages*, 37 Vand. L. Rev. 349 (1984); Comment, *The Measure of Damages Under Section 10(b) and Rule 10b-5*, 46 Md. L. Rev. 1266 (1987).

[A] Pleading Fraud with Particularity

As discussed in §8.01, in addition to pleading fraud with particularity pursuant to Rule 9(b) of the Federal Rules of Civil Procedure, a plaintiff bringing suit under §10(b) also must adhere to §21D(b) of the Exchange Act. Section 21D(b), enacted pursuant to the PSLRA, sets forth:

> (1) A requirement that a plaintiff in the complaint in any private securities fraud action alleging material misstatements and/or omissions "specify each statement alleged to have been misleading; the reason or reasons why the statement is misleading; and if an allegation regarding the statement or omission is made on information and belief, the complaint shall state with particularity all facts on which that belief is formed."

> (2) A requirement that in any private action under the 1934 Act in which the plaintiff "may recover money damages only on proof that the defendant acted with a particular state of mind, the complaint shall, with respect to each such act or omission alleged to violate [the 1934 Act], state with particularity facts giving rise to a strong inference that the defendant acted with the required state of mind."

Moreover, the plaintiff must successfully meet these pleading requirements in order to be entitled to discovery, including the production of documents and the taking of deposition testimony.

As the Joint Explanatory Statement of the Conference Committee for this legislation recognized, the PSLRA's language derives "in part" from the Second Circuit's pleading requirement which is "[r]egarded as the most stringent pleading standard." Nonetheless, the Conference Committee apparently believed that this "stringent pleading standard" was too lax, stating "[b]ecause the Conference Committee intends to strengthen existing pleading requirements, it does not intend to codify the Second Circuit's case law interpreting this pleading standard." In view of the new statute and its accompanying legislative history, the pleading requirement in private securities fraud actions undoubtedly poses a difficult barrier for plaintiffs to hurdle. In the case that follows, the Supreme Court focused on this subject.

Tellabs, Inc. v. Makor Issues & Rights, Ltd.

United States Supreme Court

551 U.S. 308, 127 S. Ct. 2499, 168 L. Ed. 2d 179 (2007)

JUSTICE GINSBURG delivered the opinion of the Court.

This court has long recognized that meritorious private actions to enforce federal antifraud securities laws are an essential supplement to criminal prosecutions and civil enforcement actions brought, respectively, by the Department of Justice and the Securities and Exchange Commission (SEC). Private securities fraud actions, however, if not adequately contained, can be employed abusively to impose substantial costs on companies and individuals whose conduct conforms to the law. As a check against abusive litigation by private parties, Congress enacted the Private Securities Litigation Reform Act of 1995 (PSLRA).

Exacting pleading requirements are among the control measures Congress included in the PSLRA. The Act requires plaintiffs to state with particularity both the facts constituting the alleged violation, and the facts evidencing scienter, *i.e.*, the defendant's intention "to deceive, manipulate, or defraud." This case concerns the latter requirement. As set out in § 21D(b)(2) of the PSLRA, plaintiffs must "state with particularity facts giving rise to a strong inference that the defendant acted with the required state of mind."

Congress left the key term "strong inference" undefined, and Courts of Appeals have divided on its meaning. In the case before us, the Court of Appeals for the Seventh Circuit held that the "strong inference" standard would be met if the complaint "allege[d] facts from which, if true, a reasonable person could infer that the defendant acted with the required intent." 437 F.3d 588, 602 (2006). That formulation, we conclude, does not capture the stricter demand Congress sought to convey in § 21D(b)(2). It does not suffice that a reasonable factfinder plausibly could infer from the complaint's allegations the requisite state of mind. Rather, to determine whether a complaint's scienter allegations can survive threshold inspection for sufficiency, a court governed by § 21D(b)(2) must engage in a comparative evaluation; it must consider, not only inferences urged by the plaintiff, as the Seventh Circuit did, but also competing inferences rationally drawn from the facts alleged. An inference of fraudulent intent may be plausible, yet less cogent than other, nonculpable explanations for the defendant's conduct. To qualify as "strong" within the intendment of § 21D(b)(2), we hold, an inference of scienter must be more than merely plausible or reasonable — *it must be cogent and at least as compelling as any opposing inference of nonfraudulent intent.* [emphasis supplied]

I

Petitioner Tellabs, Inc., manufactures specialized equipment used in fiber optics networks. During the time period relevant to this case, petitioner Richard Notebaert was Tellabs' chief executive officer and president. Respondents (Shareholders) are persons who purchased Tellabs stock between December 11, 2000, and June 19, 2001. They accuse Tellabs and Notebaert (as well as several other Tellabs executives) of engaging in a scheme to deceive the investing public about the true value of Tellabs' stock.

Beginning on December 11, 2000, the Shareholders allege, Notebaert (and by imputation Tellabs) "falsely reassured public investors, in a series of statements . . . that Tellabs was continuing to enjoy strong demand for its products and earning record revenues," when, in fact Notebaert knew the opposite was true. From December 2000 until the spring of 2001, the Shareholders claim, Notebaert knowingly misled the public in four ways. First, he made statements indicating that demand for Tellabs' flagship networking device, the TITAN 5500, was continuing to grow, when in fact demand for that product was waning. Second, Notebaert made statements indicating that the TITAN 6500, Tellabs next-generation networking device, was available for delivery, and that demand for that product was strong and growing when in truth the product was not ready for delivery and demand was weak. Third, he falsely represented Tellabs' financial results for the fourth quarter of 2000 (and, in connection with those results, condoned the practice of "channel stuffing," under which Tellabs flooded its customers with unwanted products). Fourth, Notebaert made a series of overstated revenue projections, when demand for the TITAN 5500 was drying up and production of the TITAN 6500 was behind schedule. Based on Notebaert's sunny assessments, the Shareholders contend, market analysts recommended that investors buy Tellabs' stock.

The first public glimmer that business was not so healthy came in March 2001 when Tellabs modestly reduced its first quarter sales projections. In the next months, Tellabs made progressively more cautious statements about its projected sales. On June 19, 2001, the last day of the class period, Tellabs disclosed that demand for the TITAN 5500 had significantly dropped. Simultaneously, the company substantially lowered its revenue projections for the second quarter of 2001. The next day, the price of Tellabs stock, which had reached a high of $67 during the period, plunged to a low of $15.87.

On December 3, 2002, the Shareholders filed a class action in the District Court for the Northern District of Illinois. . . . Tellabs moved to dismiss the complaint on the ground that the Shareholders had failed to plead their case with the particularity the PSLRA requires. The District Court agreed, and therefore dismissed the complaint without prejudice. . . .

The Court of Appeals for the Seventh Circuit reversed in relevant part. . . .

II

Section 10(b) of the Securities Exchange Act of 1934 forbids the "use or employ, in connection with the purchase or sale of any security . . . , [of] any manipulative or deceptive device or contrivance in contravention of such rules and regulations as the [SEC] may prescribe as necessary or appropriate in the public interest or for the protection of investors." SEC Rule 10b-5 implements § 10(b). . . .

Section 10(b), this Court has implied from the statute's text and purpose, affords a right of action to purchasers or sellers of securities injured by its violation. To establish liability under § 10(b) and Rule 10b-5, a private plaintiff must prove that the defendant acted with scienter, "a mental state embracing intent to deceive, manipulate, or defraud."[28]

---

[28]. We have previously reserved the question whether reckless behavior is sufficient for civil liability under § 10(b) and Rule 10b-5. . . . Every Court of Appeals that has considered the issue has held that a plaintiff may meet the scienter requirement by showing that the defendant acted

In an ordinary civil action, the Federal Rules of Civil Procedure require only "a short and plain statement of the claim showing that the pleader is entitled to relief." Fed. Rule Civ. Proc. 8(a)(2). Although the rule encourages brevity, the complaint must say enough to give the defendant "fair notice of what the plaintiff's claim is and the grounds upon which it rests." [This Rule 8(a)(2) standard also has been made more demanding on plaintiffs, requiring complainants to plead sufficient facts that "plausibly suggest an entitlement to relief." *Ashcroft v. Iqbal*, 129 S. Ct. 1937, 1951 (2009). Accord, *Bell Atlantic Corp. v. Twombly*, 550 U.S. 544 (2007).]

Prior to the enactment of the PSLRA, the sufficiency of a complaint for securities fraud was governed not by Rule 8, but by the heightened pleading standard set forth in Rule 9(b). Rule 9(b) applies to "all averments of fraud or mistake"; it requires that "the circumstances constituting fraud ... be stated with particularity" but provides that "[m]alice, intent, knowledge, and other condition of mind of a person, may be averred generally."

Courts of Appeals diverged on the character of the Rule 9(b) inquiry in § 10(b) cases: Could securities fraud plaintiffs allege the requisite mental state "simply by stating that scienter existed," or were they required to allege with particularity facts giving rise to an inference of scienter? . . .

Setting a uniform pleading standard for § 10(b) actions was among Congress' objectives when it enacted the PSLRA. Designed to curb perceived abuses of the § 10(b) private action—"nuisance filings, targeting of deep-pocket defendants, vexatious discovery requests and manipulation by class action lawyers," *Dabit*, 547 U.S., at 81 (quoting H. R. Conf. Rep. No. 104-369, p. 31 (1995) (hereinafter H. R. Conf. Rep.))—the PSLRA installed both substantive and procedural controls. Notably, Congress prescribed new procedures for the appointment of lead plaintiffs and lead counsel. This innovation aimed to increase the likelihood that institutional investors— parties more likely to balance the interests of the class with the long-term interests of the company—would serve as lead plaintiffs. Congress also "limit[ed] recoverable damages and attorney's fees, provide[d] a 'safe harbor' for forward-looking statements, ... mandate[d] imposition of sanctions for frivolous litigation, and authorize[d] a stay of discovery pending resolution of any motion to dismiss." And in § 21D(b) of the PSLRA, Congress "impose[d] heightened pleading requirements in actions brought pursuant to § 10(b) and Rule 10b-5."

Under the PSLRA's heightened pleading instructions, any private securities complaint alleging that the defendant made a false or misleading statement must: (1) "specify each statement alleged to have been misleading [and] the reason or reasons why the statement is misleading," and (2) "state with particularity facts giving rise to a strong inference that the defendant acted with the required state of mind" . . .

---

intentionally or recklessly, though the Circuits differ on the degree of recklessness required. The question whether and when recklessness satisfies the scienter requirement is not presented in this case.

The "strong inference" standard "unequivocally raise[d] the bar for pleading scienter," and signaled Congress' purpose to promote greater uniformity among the Circuits. But "Congress did not . . . throw much light on what facts . . . suffice to create [a strong] inference," or on what "degree of imagination courts can use in divining whether" the requisite inference exists. . . . While adopting the Second Circuit's "strong inference" standard, Congress did not codify that Circuit's case law interpreting the standard. With no clear guide from Congress other than its "intent[ion] to strengthen existing pleading requirements," H. R. Conf. Rep., p.41, Courts of Appeals have diverged again, this time in construing the term "strong inference." Among the uncertainties, should courts consider competing inferences in determining whether an inference of scienter is "strong"? Our task is to prescribe a workable construction of the "strong inference" standard, a reading geared to the PSLRA's twin goals: to curb frivolous, lawyer-driven litigation, while preserving investors' ability to recover on meritorious claims.

III

A.

We establish the following prescriptions: *First,* faced with a Rule 12(b)(6) motion to dismiss a § 10(b) action, courts must, as with any motion to dismiss for failure to plead a claim on which relief can be granted, accept all factual allegations in the complaint as true.

Second, courts must consider the complaint in its entirely, as well as other sources courts ordinarily examine when ruling on Rule 12(b)(6) motions to dismiss, in particular, documents incorporated into the complaint by reference, and matters of which a court may take judicial notice. The inquiry, as several Courts of Appeals have recognized, is whether *all* of the facts alleged, taken collectively, give rise to a strong inference of scienter, not whether any individual allegation, scrutinized in isolation, meets that standard.

Third, in determining whether the pleaded facts give rise to a "strong" inference of scienter, the court must take into account plausible opposing inferences. The Seventh Circuit expressly declined to engage in such a comparative inquiry. A complaint could survive, that court said, as long as it "alleges facts from which, if true, a reasonable person could infer that the defendant acted with the required intent"; in other words, only "[i]f a reasonable person could not draw such an inference from the alleged facts" would the defendant prevail on a motion to dismiss. But in § 21D(b)(2), Congress did not merely require plaintiffs to "provide a factual basis for [their] scienter allegations." . . . . Instead, Congress required plaintiffs to plead with particularity facts that give rise to a "strong"—*i.e.,* a powerful or cogent—inference. See American Heritage Dictionary 1717 (4th ed. 2000) (defining "strong" as "[p]ersuasive, effective, and cogent"); 16 Oxford English Dictionary 949 (2d ed. 1989) (defining "strong" as "[p]owerful to demonstrate or convince"; cf. *7 id.* at 924 (defining "inference" as "a conclusion [drawn] from known or assumed facts or statements"; "reasoning from something known or assumed to something else which follows from it").

The strength of an inference cannot be decided in a vacuum. The inquiry is inherently comparative: How likely is it that one conclusion, as compared to others, follows from the underlying facts? To determine whether the plaintiff has alleged facts that give rise to the requisite "strong inference" of scienter, a court must consider plausible nonculpable explanations for the defendant's conduct, as well as inferences favoring the plaintiff. The inference that the defendant acted with scienter need not be irrefutable, *i.e.,* of the "smoking-gun" genre, or even the "most plausible of competing inferences" . . . . Recall in this regard that § 21D(b)'s pleading requirements are but one constraint among many the PSLRA installed to screen out frivolous suits, while allowing meritorious actions to move forward. Yet the inference of scienter must be more than merely "reasonable" or "permissible"—it must be cogent and compelling, thus strong in light of other explanations. *A complaint will survive, we hold, only if a reasonable person would deem the inference of scienter cogent and at least as compelling as any opposing inference one could draw from the facts alleged.* [emphasis supplied]

B.

Tellabs contends that when competing inferences are considered, Notebaert's evident lack of pecuniary motive will be dispositive. The Shareholders, Tellabs stresses, did not allege that Notebaert sold any shares during the class period. While it is true that motive can be a relevant consideration, and personal financial gain may weigh heavily in favor of a scienter inference, we agree with the Seventh Circuit that the absence of a motive allegation is not fatal. As earlier stated, allegations must be considered collectively; the significance that can be ascribed to an allegation of motive, or lack thereof, depends on the entirety of the complaint.

Tellabs also maintains that several of the Shareholders' allegations are too vague or ambiguous to contribute to a strong inference of scienter. For example, the Shareholders alleged that Tellabs flooded its customers with unwanted products, a practice known as "channel stuffing." But they failed, Tellabs argues, to specify whether the channel stuffing allegedly known to Notebaert was the illegitimate kind (*e.g.,* writing orders for products customers had not requested) or the legitimate kind (*e.g.,* offering customers discounts as an incentive to buy). . . . We agree that omissions and ambiguities count against inferring scienter, for plaintiffs must "state with particularity facts giving rise to a strong inference that the defendant acted with the required state of mind." We reiterate, however, that the court's job is not to scrutinize each allegation in isolation but to assess all the allegations holistically. In sum, the reviewing court must ask: When the allegations are accepted as true and taken collectively, would a reasonable person deem the inference of scienter at least as strong as any opposing inference?

IV

Accounting for its construction of § 21D(b)(2), the Seventh Circuit explained that the court "th[ought] it wis[e] to adopt an approach that [could not] be misunderstood as a usurpation of the jury's role." . . . In our view, the Seventh Circuit's concern was undue. A court's comparative assessment of plausible inferences, while constantly assuming the plaintiff's allegations to be true, we think it plain, does not impinge upon the Seventh Amendment right to jury trial.[29]

Congress, as creator of federal statutory claims, has power to prescribe what must be pleaded to state the claim, just as it has power to determine what must be proved to prevail on the merits. It is the federal lawmaker's prerogative, therefore, to allow, disallow, or shape the contours of—including the pleading and proof requirements for—§ 10(b) private actions. No decision of this Court questions that authority in general, or suggests, in particular, that the Seventh Amendment inhibits Congress from establishing whatever pleading requirements it finds appropriate for federal statutory claims. . . . [30]

In the instant case, provided that the Shareholders have satisfied the congressionally "prescribe[d] . . . means of making an issue," . . . the case will fall within the jury's authority to assess the credibility of witnesses, resolve any genuine issues of fact, and make the ultimate determination whether Notebaert and, by imputation, Tellabs acted with scienter. We emphasize, as well, that under our construction of the "strong inference" standard, a plaintiff is not forced to plead more than she would be required to prove at trial. A plaintiff alleging fraud in a § 10(b) action, we hold today, must plead facts rendering an inference of scienter *at least as likely* as any plausible opposing inference. At trial, she must then prove her case by a "preponderance of the evidence." Stated otherwise, she must demonstrate that it is *more likely* than not that the defendant acted with scienter.

While we reject the Seventh Circuit's approach to § 21D(b)(2), we do not decide whether, under the standard we have described, the Shareholders' allegations warrant "a strong inference that [Notebaert and Tellabs] acted with the required state of mind." Neither the District Court nor the Court of Appeals had the opportunity to consider the matter in light of the prescriptions we announce today. We therefore vacate the Seventh Circuit's judgment so that the case may be reexamined in accord with our construction of § 21D(b)(2).

The judgment of the Court of Appeals is vacated, and the case is remanded for further proceedings consistent with this opinion.

It is so ordered.

---

[29]. In numerous contexts, gatekeeping judicial determinations prevent submission of claims to a jury's judgment without violating the Seventh Amendment. *See, e.g., Daubert v. Merrell Dow Pharmaceuticals, Inc.,* 509 U.S. 579 (1993) (expert testimony can be excluded based on judicial determination of reliability); *Neely v. Martin K Eby Constr. Co.,* 386 U.S. 317 (1967) (judgment as a matter of law); *Pease v Rathbun-Jones Engineering Co.,* 243 U.S. 273 (1917) (summary judgment).

[30]. Any heightened pleading rule, including Fed. Rule Civ. Proc. 9(b), could have the effect of preventing a plaintiff from getting discovery on a claim that might have gone to a jury, had discovery occurred and yielded substantial evidence. In recognizing Congress' or the Federal Rule makers' authority to adopt special pleading rules, we have detected no Seventh Amendment impediment.

JUSTICE SCALIA, concurring in the judgment.

I fail to see how an inference that is merely "at least as compelling as any opposing inference," can conceivably be called what the statute here at issue requires: a "strong inference." If a jade falcon were stolen from a room to which only A and B had access, could it *possibly* be said that there was a "strong inference" that B was the thief? I think not, and I therefore think that the Court's test must fail. In my view, the test should be whether the inference of scienter (if any) is *more plausible* than the inference of innocence.

. . . .

Note — Group Pleading and Collective Scienter

After *Tellabs*, motions to dismiss are granted with regularity. Indeed, studies have found that in some years, up to around 50 percent of these motions are granted, while another 15 percent to 20 percent of cases are voluntarily dismissed by plaintiffs, signifying that roughly 30 percent to 35 percent of federal securities class actions proceed beyond the motion to dismiss stage.

Notably, in *Tellabs,* the Supreme Court declined to address whether the PSLRA abolished the "group pleading" doctrine. The group pleading doctrine posits that statements in group-published documents, such as SEC corporate filings and press releases made by a subject issuer, are attributable to directors and officers who exercise day-to-day involvement in normal company operations. Since the passage of the PSLRA, courts overwhelmingly have rejected the "group pleading" doctrine, reasoning that recognition of the doctrine is inconsistent with "the PSLRA's requirements that allegations be set forth with particularity concerning 'the defendant' and scienter be pleaded for 'each act or omission' sufficient to give 'rise to a strong inference that the defendant acted with the required state of mind.'" *Winer Family Trust v. Queen,* 503 F.3d 319, 337 (3d Cir. 2007) (citing cases).

Similarly, the collective scienter thereby has been overwhelmingly rejected. See *Pugh v. Tribune Co.,* 521 F.3d 686, 697 (7th Cir. 2008) (stating that "the corporate scienter inquiry must focus on the state of mind of the individual corporate official or officials who make or issue the statement . . . rather than generally to the collective knowledge of all the corporation's officers and employees"); Accord, *Teamsters Local 445 Freight Division Pension Fund v. Dynex Capital, Inc.,* 531 F.3d 190 (2d Cir. 2008); *Southland Securities Corp. v. Inspire Insurance Solutions, Inc.,* 365 F.3d 353 (5th Cir. 2004). *But see Glazer Capital Management LP v. Magistri,* 549 F.3d 736, 744 (9th Cir. 2008) (stating that "in certain circumstances, some form of collective scienter pleading might be appropriate"). *See also* McCaughey & Demers, *Revisiting Corporate Scienter: In Search of a Middle Ground,* 47 SEC. REG. & L. REP. (BNA) 858 (2015) (stating that plaintiffs frequently attempt "to impute the collective knowledge of a corporation's employees and agents to the corporation itself, without having to tie that knowledge to statements or omissions made by the same individual," and that most courts have rejected this theory).

[B] Statute of Limitations

Today, the statute of limitations for § 10(b) claims is two years after discovery of the violation by the plaintiff and in no event more than five years after the violation. 28 U.S.C. § 1658(b). This statute was enacted as part of the Sarbanes-Oxley Act of 2002.

Prior to Sarbanes-Oxley, the § 10(b) statute of limitations situation was as follows: Being an implied right of action, § 10(b) does not provide by its terms for a statute of limitations. In *Lampf, Pleva, Lipkind, Prupis & Petigrow v. Gilbertson*, 501 U.S. 350 (1991), the Supreme Court set forth the then applicable statute of limitations for private actions under § 10(b) of the Exchange Act. Prior to *Lampf*, a majority of the appellate courts opted for the relevant state statute that was most analogous to § 10(b) and Rule 10b-5. Under this framework, the federal courts selected either the appropriate state's limitations period for common law fraud or the limitations period for securities fraud under the applicable blue sky statute.[31] Irrespective of which particular state statute was applied, the result was a lack of predictability, uniformity and certainty, even within individual federal circuits.[32]

In *Lampf*, the Supreme Court chose a one-year after discovery within a three-year period of repose scheme (one year/three year limitations period), selecting § 9(e) of the Exchange Act as the language to govern § 10(b) actions. Significantly, the Court held that the doctrine of equitable tolling was unavailable under § 10(b). In other words, as held by *Lampf*, § 10(b) actions were required to be instituted within one year after a plaintiff's discovery of the violation and in no event more than three years after the violation.

Critics argued that this one year/three year limitations period was too short in cases of fraud. Indeed, the presence of fraudulent concealment may cause the illegal conduct not to be discovered for several years and perhaps even decades (*see, e.g.,* *Hochfelder* in § 8.03). In enacting the Sarbanes-Oxley Act of 2002, Congress responded to this situation.

Interestingly, lengthening the applicable statute of limitations was the one express change that Congress made regarding private rights of action in its enactment of the Sarbanes-Oxley Act. Instead of amending the numerous statutes of limitations provisions set forth in the securities acts, Congress elected to amend 28 U.S.C. § 1658 (which contains a general statute of limitations).[33] As enacted, § 1658(b) provides that:

---

31. *Nesbit v. McNeil*, 896 F.2d 380, 384 (9th Cir. 1990) (applying Oregon two-year statute) with *Reeves v. Teuscher*, 881 F.2d 1495, 1501 (9th Cir. 1989) (applying Washington three-year statute).

32. *Nesbit v. McNeil*, 896 F.2d 380, 384 (9th Cir. 1990) (applying Oregon two-year statute) with *Reeves v. Teuscher*, 881 F.2d 1495, 1501 (9th Cir. 1989) (applying Washington three-year statute).

33. 28 U.S.C. § 1658(a) sets forth a four-year statute of limitations unless otherwise provided by law.

[A] private right of action that involves a claim of fraud, deceit, manipulation, or contrivance in contravention of a regulatory requirement concerning the securities laws. . . . may be brought not later than the earlier of—

(1) 2 years after the discovery of the facts constituting the violation; or

(2) 5 years after such violation.

This statute clearly applies to suits brought for alleged violations of § 10(b). Other federal securities law rights of action that require proof of fraud, deceit, or manipulation likewise are subject to the two-year/five-year statute of limitations.

In the following case, the Supreme Court examines whether the two-year period begins to run when the plaintiff has actual or inquiry notice of the facts constituting the violation.

Merck & Co., Inc. v. Reynolds

United States Supreme Court

559 U.S. 633, 130 S. Ct. 1784, 176 L. Ed. 2d 582 (2010)

JUSTICE BREYER delivered the opinion of the Court.

This case concerns the timeliness of a complaint filed in a private securities fraud action. The complaint was timely if filed no more than two years after the plaintiffs "discover[ed] the facts constituting the violation." 28 U.S.C. § 1658(b)(1). Construing this limitations statute for the first time, we hold that a cause of action accrues (1) when the plaintiff did in fact discover, or (2) when a reasonably diligent plaintiff would have discovered, "the facts constituting the violation"—whichever comes first. We also hold that the "facts constituting the violation" include the fact of scienter, "a mental state embracing intent to deceive, manipulate, or defraud," *Ernst & Ernst v. Hochfelder,* 425 U.S. 185, 194, n. 12 (1976). Applying this standard, we affirm the Court of Appeal's determination that the complaint filed here was timely.

I

The action before us involves a claim by a group of investors (the plaintiffs, respondents here) that Merck & Co. and others (the petitioners here, hereinafter Merck) knowingly misrepresented the risks of heart attacks accompanying the use of Merck's pain-killing drug, Vioxx (leading to economic losses when the risks later became apparent). The plaintiffs brought an action for securities fraud under § 10(b) of the Securities Exchange Act of 1934 [and] SEC Rule 10b-5 . . . .

The applicable statute of limitations provides that a "private right of action" that, like the present action, "involves a claim of fraud, deceit, manipulation, or contrivance in contravention of a regulatory requirement concerning the securities laws . . . may be brought not later than the earlier of—

"(1) 2 years after the discovery of the facts constituting the violation; or

"(2) 5 years after such violation." 28 U.S.C. § 1658(b).

The complaint in this case was filed on November 6, 2003, and no one doubts that it was filed within five years of the alleged violation. Therefore, the critical date for timeliness purposes is November 6, 2001—two years before this complaint was filed. Merck claims that before this date the plaintiffs had (or should have) discovered the "facts constituting the violation." If so, by the time the plaintiffs filed their complaint, the 2-year statutory period in § 1658(b)(1) had run. The plaintiffs reply that they had not, and could not have, discovered by the critical date those "facts," particularly not the facts related to scienter, and that their complaint was therefore timely.

A

We first set out the relevant pre-November 2001 facts, as we have gleaned them from the briefs, the record, and the opinions below.

1. 1990's. In the mid-1990's Merck developed Vioxx. In 1999 the Food and Drug Administration (FDA) approved it for prescription use. Vioxx suppresses pain by inhibiting the body's production of an enzyme called COX-2 (cyclooxygenase-2). COX-2 is associated with pain and inflammation. Unlike some other anti-inflammatory drugs in its class like aspirin, ibuprofen, and naproxen, Vioxx does not inhibit production of a second enzyme called COX-1 (cyclooxygenase-1). COX-1 plays a part in the functioning of the gastrointestinal tract and also inhibits platelet aggregation (associated with blood clots).

2. March 2000. Merck announced the results of a study, called the "VIGOR" study. The study compared Vioxx with another painkiller, naproxen. The study showed that persons taking Vioxx suffered fewer gastrointestinal side effects (as Merck had hoped). But the study also revealed that approximately 4 out of every 1,000 participants who took Vioxx suffered heart attacks, compared to only 1 per 1,000 participants who took naproxen. . . .

Merck's press release acknowledged VIGOR's adverse cardiovascular data. But Merck said that these data were "consistent with naproxen's ability to block platelet aggregation." Merck noted that, since "Vioxx, like all COX-2 selective medicines, does not block platelet aggregation[, it] would not be expected to have similar effects." And Merck added that "safety data from all other completed and ongoing clinical trials . . . showed no indication of a difference in the incidence of thromboembolic events between Vioxx" and either a placebo or comparable drugs. . . .

This theory—that VIGOR's troubling cardiovascular findings might be due to the absence of a benefit conferred by naproxen rather than due to a harm caused by Vioxx—later became known as the "naproxen hypothesis." In advancing that hypothesis, Merck acknowledged that the naproxen benefit "had not been observed previously." Journalists and stock market analysts reported all of the above—the positive gastrointestinal results, the troubling cardiovascular finding, the naproxen hypothesis, and the fact that the naproxen hypothesis was unproved.

3. February 2001 to August 2001. Public debate about the naproxen hypothesis continued. In February 2001, the FDA's Arthritis Advisory Committee convened to consider Merck's request that the Vioxx label be changed to reflect VIGOR's positive gastrointestinal findings. The VIGOR cardiovascular findings were also discussed. In May, 2001, a group of plaintiffs filed a products-liability lawsuit against Merck, claiming that "Merck's own research" had demonstrated that "users of Vioxx were four times likely to suffer heart attacks as compared to other less expensive, medications." In August 2001, the Journal of the American Medical Association wrote that the available data raised a "cautionary flag" and strongly urged that "a trial specifically assessing cardiovascular risk" be done. At about the same time, Bloomberg News quoted a Merck scientist who claimed that Merck had "additional data" that were "very, very reassuring," and Merck issued a press release stating that it stood "behind the overall and cardiovascular safety profile . . . of Vioxx." . . .

4. September and October 2001. The FDA sent Merck a warning letter released to the public on September 21, 2001. It said that, in respect to cardiovascular risks, Merck's Vioxx marketing was "false, lacking in fair balance, or otherwise misleading." At the same time, the FDA acknowledged that the naproxen hypothesis was a "possible explanation" of the VIGOR results. But it found that Merck's "promotional campaign selectively present[ed]" that hypothesis without adequately acknowledging "another reasonable explanation," namely, "that Vioxx may have pro-thrombotic [*i.e.,* adverse cardiovascular] properties." The FDA ordered Merck to send healthcare providers a corrective letter.

After the FDA letter was released, more products-liability lawsuits were filed. Merck's share price fell by 6.6% over several days. By October 1, the price rebounded. On October 9, 2001, the New York Times said that Merck had reexamined its own data and "found no evidence that Vioxx increased the risk of heart attacks." It quoted the president of Merck Research Laboratories as positing "'two possible interpretations'": "'Naproxen lowers the heart rate, or Vioxx raises it.'" Stock analysts, while reporting the warning letter, also noted that the FDA had not denied that the naproxen hypothesis remained an unproven but possible explanation.

B

We next set forth three important events that occurred *after* the critical date.

1. October 2003. The Wall Street Journal published the results of a Merck-funded Vioxx study conducted at Boston's Brigham and Women's Hospital. After examining the medical records of more than 50,000 Medicare patients, researchers found that those given Vioxx for 30-to-90 days were 36% more likely to have suffered a heart attack than those given either a different painkiller or no painkiller at all. (That is to say, if patients given a different painkiller or given no painkiller at all suffered 10 heart attacks, then the same number of patients given Vioxx would suffer 13 or 14 heart attacks.) Merck defended Vioxx and pointed to the study's limitations.

2. September 30, 2004. Merck withdrew Vioxx from the market. It said that a new study had found "an increased risk of confirmed cardiovascular events beginning after 18 months of continuous therapy." A Merck representative publicly described the results as "totally unexpected." Merck's shares fell by 27% the same day.

3. November 1, 2004. The Wall Street Journal published an article stating that "internal Merck e-mails and marketing materials as well as interviews with outside scientists show that the company fought forcefully for years to keep safety concerns from destroying the drug's commercial prospects. The article said that an early e-mail from Merck's head of research had said that the VIGOR "results showed that the cardiovascular events 'are clearly there,'" that it was "'a shame but . . . a low incidence,'" and that it "'is mechanism based as we worried it was.'" It also said that Merck had given its salespeople instructions to "'DODGE'" questions about Vioxx's cardiovascular effects.

C

The plaintiffs filed their complaint on November 6, 2003. As subsequently amended, the complaint alleged that Merck had defrauded investors by promoting the naproxen hypothesis, knowing the hypothesis was false. It said, for example, that Merck "knew, at least as early as 1996, of the serious safety issues with Vioxx," and that a "1998 internal Merck clinical trial . . . revealed that . . . serious cardiovascular events . . . occurred six times more frequently in patients given Vioxx than in patients given a different arthritis drug or placebo."

Merck, believing that the plaintiffs knew or should have known the "facts constituting the violation" at least two years earlier, moved to dismiss the complaint, saying it was filed too late. The District Court granted the motion. The court held that the (March 2001) VIGOR study, the (September 2001) FDA warning letter, and Merck's (October 2001) response should have alerted the plaintiffs to a *"possibility* that Merck had knowingly misrepresented material facts" no later than October 9, 2001, thus placing the plaintiffs on "inquiry notice" to look further. *In re Merck & Co. Securities, Derivative & "ERISA" Litigation,* 483 F. Supp. 2d 407, 423 (NJ 2007) (emphasis added). Finding that the plaintiffs had failed to "show that they exercised reasonable due diligence but nevertheless were unable to discover their injuries," the court took October 9, 2001, as the date that the limitations period began to run and therefore found the complaint untimely.

The Court of Appeals for the Third Circuit reversed. A majority held that the pre-November 2001 events, while constituting "storm warnings," did not suggest much by way of scienter, and consequently did not put the plaintiffs on "inquiry notice," requiring them to investigate further. *In re Merck & Co. Securities, Derivative & "ERISA" Litigation,* 543 F.3d 150, 172 (2008). A dissenting judge considered the pre-November 2001 events sufficient to start the 2-year clock running. *Id.,* at 173 (opinion of Roth, J.).

Merck sought review in this Court, pointing to disagreements among the Court of Appeals. . . . We granted Merck's petition.

II

Before turning to Merck's arguments, we consider a more basic matter. The parties and the Solicitor General agree that § 1658(b)(1)'s word "discovery" refers not only to a plaintiff's *actual* discovery of certain facts, but also to the facts that a reasonably diligent plaintiff would have discovered. We agree. But because the statute's language does not make this interpretation obvious, and because we cannot answer the question presented without considering whether the parties are right about this matter, we set forth the reasons for our agreement in some detail.

We recognize that one might read the statutory words "after the discovery of the facts constituting the violation" as referring to the time a plaintiff *actually* discovered the relevant facts. But in the statute of limitations context, the word "discovery" is often used as a term of art in connection with the "discovery rule," a doctrine that delays accrual of a cause of action until the plaintiff has "discovered" it. The rule arose in fraud cases as an exception to the general limitations rule that a cause of action accrues once a plaintiff has a "complete and present cause of action" . . . This Court long ago recognized that something different was needed in the case of fraud, where a defendant's deceptive conduct may prevent a plaintiff from even *knowing* that he or she has been defrauded. Otherwise, "the law which was designed to prevent fraud" could become "the means by which it is made successful and secure." *Bailey v. Glover*, 21 Wall. 342, 349 (1875). Accordingly, "where a plaintiff has been injured by fraud and remains in ignorance of it without any fault or want of diligence or care on his part, the bar of the statute does not begin to run until the fraud is *discovered*." *Holmberg v. Armbrecht*, 327 U.S. 392, 397 (1946). . . . And for more than a century, courts have understood that "[f]raud is deemed to be discovered . . . when, in the exercise of reasonable diligence, it could have been discovered." . . .

More recently, both state and federal courts have applied forms of the "discovery rule" to claims other than fraud. . . . Legislatures have codified the discovery rule in various contexts. . . . In doing so, legislators have written the word "discovery" directly into the statute. And when they have done so, state and federal courts have typically interpreted the word to refer not only to actual discovery, but also to the hypothetical discovery of facts a reasonably diligently plaintiff would know. . . .

Thus, treatise writers now describe "the discovery rule" as allowing a claim "to accrue when the litigant first knows *or with due diligence should know* facts that will form the basis for an action." . . .

Like the parties, we believe that Congress intended courts to interpret the word "discovery" in § 1658(b)(1) similarly. Before Congress enacted that statute, this Court, having found in the federal securities laws the existence of an implied private § 10(b) action, determined its governing limitations period by looking to other limitations periods in the federal securities laws. *Lampf, Pleva, Lipkind, Prupis & Petigrow* v. *Gilbertson*, 501 U.S. 350 (1991). Noting the existence of various formulations "differ[ing] slightly in terminology," the Court chose the language in 15 U.S.C. § 78i(e), the statutory provision that governs securities price manipulation claims. 501 U.S. at 364, n. 9. And in doing so, the Court said that private § 10(b) actions "must be commenced within one year *after the discovery of the facts constituting the violation* and within three years after such violation." . . .

Subsequently, every Court of Appeals to decide the matter held that "discovery of the facts constituting the violation" occurs not only once a plaintiff *actually* discovers the facts, but also when a hypothetical reasonably diligent plaintiff would have discovered them. . . . Some of those courts noted that other limitations provisions in the federal securities laws explicitly provide that the period begins to run "after the discovery of the untrue statement . . . *or after such discovery should have been made by [the] exercise of reasonable diligence,*" whereas the formulation adopted by the Court in *Lampf* from 15 U.S.C. §78i(e) does not. . . . But, courts reasoned, because the term "discovery" in respect to statutes of limitations for fraud has long been understood to include discoveries a reasonably diligent plaintiff would make, the omission of an explicit provision to that effect did not matter. . . .

In 2002, when Congress enacted the present limitations statute, it repeated *Lampf*'s critical language. The statute says that an action based on fraud "may be brought not later than the earlier of . . . 2 years *after the discovery of the facts constituting the violation*" (or "5 years after such violation"). §804 of the Sarbanes-Oxley Act, 116 Stat. 801, codified at 28 U.S.C. §1658(b) (emphasis added). (This statutory provision does *not* make the linguistic distinction that the concurrence finds in a *different* statute, §77m, and upon which its argument rests. Cf. 29 U.S.C. §1113(2) (statute in which Congress provided that an action be brought "three years after the earliest date on which the plaintiff had *actual knowledge* of the breach or violation" (emphasis added)).) Not surprisingly, the Courts of Appeals unanimously have continued to interpret the word "discovery" in this statute as including not only facts a particular plaintiff knows, but also the facts any reasonably diligent plaintiff would know. . . .

We normally assume that, when Congress enacts statutes, it is aware of relevant judicial precedent. . . . Given the history and precedent surrounding the use of the word "discovery" in the limitations context generally as well as in this provision in particular, the reasons for making this assumption are particularly strong here. We consequently hold that "discovery" as used in this statute encompasses not only those facts the plaintiff actually knew, but also those facts a reasonably diligent plaintiff would have known. And we evaluate Merck's claims accordingly.

III

We turn now to Merck's arguments in favor of holding that petitioners' claims accrued before November 6, 2001. First, Merck argues that the statute does not require "discovery" of scienter-related "facts." . . . We cannot agree, however, that facts about scienter are unnecessary.

The statute says that the limitations period does not begin to run until "discovery of the *facts constituting the violation.*" 28 U.S.C. §1658(b)(1) (emphasis added). Scienter is assuredly a "fact." In a §10(b) action, scienter refers to "a mental state embracing intent to deceive, manipulate, or defraud." *Ernst & Ernst,* 425 U.S., at 194, n. 12. And the "state of a man's mind is as much a fact as the state of his digestion." *Postal Service Bd. of Governors v. Aikens,* 460 U.S. 711, 716 (1983) (quoting *Edgington v. Fitzmaurice,* [1885] 29 Ch. Div. 459, 483).

And this "fact" of scienter "constitut[es]" an important and necessary element of a § 10(b) "violation." A plaintiff cannot recover without proving that a defendant made a material misstatement *with an intent to deceive*— not merely innocently or negligently. . . . Indeed Congress has enacted special heightened pleading requirements for the scienter element of § 10(b) fraud cases. See 15 U.S.C. § 78u-4(b)(2) (requiring plaintiffs to "state with particularity *facts* giving rise to a strong inference that the defendant acted with the required state of mind" (emphasis added)). . . . It would therefore frustrate the very purpose of the discovery rule in this provision— which, after all, specifically applies only in cases "involv[ing] a claim of fraud, deceit, manipulation, or contrivance," § 1658(b) — if the limitations period began to run regardless of whether a plaintiff had discovered any facts suggesting scienter. So long as a defendant concealed for two years that he made a misstatement with an intent to deceive, the limitations period would expire before the plaintiffs had actually "discover[ed]" the fraud.

We consequently hold that facts showing scienter are among those that "constitut[e] the violation." In so holding, we say nothing about other facts necessary to support a private § 10(b) action. Cf. Brief for United States as *Amicus Curiae* 12, n. 1 (suggesting that facts concerning a plaintiff's reliance, loss, and loss causation are not among those that constitute "the violation" and therefore need not be "discover[ed]" for a claim to accrue).

Second, Merck argues that, even if "discovery" requires facts related to scienter, facts that tend to show a materially false or misleading statement (or material omission) are ordinarily sufficient to show scienter as well. But we do not see how that is so. We recognize that certain statements are such that, to show them false is normally to show scienter as well. It is unlikely, for example, that someone would falsely say "I am not married" without being aware of the fact that his statement is false. Where § 10(b) is at issue, however, the relation of factual falsity and state of mind is more context specific. An incorrect prediction about a firm's future earnings, by itself, does not automatically tell us whether the speaker deliberately lied or just made an innocent (and therefore nonactionable) error. Hence, the statute may require "discovery" of scienter-related facts beyond the facts that show a statement (or omission) to be materially false or misleading. Merck fears that this requirement will give life to stale claims or subject defendants to liability for acts taken long ago. But Congress' inclusion in the statute of an unqualified bar on actions instituted "5 years after such violation," § 1658(b)(2), giving defendants total repose after five years, should diminish that fear.

. . . .

We conclude that the limitations period in § 1658(b)(1) begins to run once the plaintiff did discover or a reasonably diligent plaintiff would have "discover[ed] the facts constituting the violation" — whichever comes first. In determining the time at which "discovery" of those "facts" occurred, terms such as "inquiry notice" and "storm warnings" may be useful to the extent that they identify a time when the facts would have prompted a reasonably diligent plaintiff to begin investigating. But the limitations period does not begin to run until the plaintiff thereafter discovers or a reasonably diligent plaintiff would have discovered "the facts constituting the violation," including scienter—irrespective of whether the actual plaintiff undertook a reasonably diligent investigation.

IV

Finally, Merck argues that, even if all its other legal arguments fail, the record still shows that, before November 6, 2001, the plaintiffs had discovered or should have discovered "the facts constituting the violation." In respect to scienter Merck primarily relies upon (1) the FDA's September 2001 warning letter, which said that Merck had "minimized" the VIGOR study's "'potentially serious cardiovascular finding'" and (2) pleadings filed in products-liability actions in September and October 2001 alleging that Merck had "'omitted, suppressed, or concealed material facts concerning the dangers and risks associated with Vioxx'" and "*purposefully* downplayed and/or understated the serious nature of the risks associated with Vioxx." . . .

The FDA's warning letter, however, shows little or nothing about the here-relevant scienter, *i.e.,* whether Merck advanced the naproxen hypothesis with fraudulent intent. The FDA itself described the pro-Vioxx naproxen hypothesis as a "possible explanation" for the VIGOR results, faulting Merck only for failing sufficiently to publicize the alternative less favorable to Merck, that Vioxx might be harmful.

The products-liability complaints' statements about Merck's knowledge show little more. Merck does not claim that these complaints contained any specific information suggesting the fraud alleged here, *i.e.,* that Merck knew the naproxen hypothesis was false even as it promoted it. And, without providing any reason to believe that the plaintiffs had special access to information about Merck's state of mind, the complaints alleged only in general terms that Merck had concealed information about Vioxx and "purposefully downplayed and/or understated" the risks associated with Vioxx—the same charge made in the FDA warning letter.

In our view, neither these two circumstances nor any of the other pre-November 2001 circumstances that we have set forth in Part I-A, *supra*, whether viewed separately or together, reveal "facts" indicating scienter. Regardless of which, if any, of the events following November 6, 2001, constituted "discovery," we need only conclude that prior to November 6, 2001, the plaintiffs did not discover, and Merck has not shown that a reasonably diligent plaintiff would have discovered, "the facts constituting the violation." In light of our interpretation of the statute, our holding in respect to scienter, and our application of those holdings to the circumstances of this case, we must, and we do, reach that conclusion. Thus, the plaintiffs' suit is timely. . . . The judgment of the Court of Appeals is

Affirmed.

Justice Stevens, concurring in part and concurring in judgment.

In my opinion the Court's explanation of why the complaint was timely filed is convincing and correct. In this case there is no difference between the time when the plaintiffs actually discovered the factual basis for their claim and the time when reasonably diligent plaintiffs should have discovered those facts. For that reason, much of the discussion in Part II of the Court's opinion is not necessary to support the Court's judgment. Until a case arises in which the difference between an actual discovery rule and a constructive discovery rule would affect the outcome, I would reserve decision on the merits of Justice Scalia's argument. . . . With this reservation, I join the Court's excellent opinion.

Justice Scalia, with whom Justice Thomas joins, concurring in part and concurring in the judgment.

Private suits under § 10(b) of the Securities Exchange Act of 1934 must be brought within "(1) 2 years after the discovery of the facts constituting the violation" or "(2) 5 years after such violation," whichever comes first. 28 U.S.C. § 1658(b)(1). I agree with the Court that scienter is among the "facts constituting the violation" that a plaintiff must "discove[r]" for the limitations period to begin. I also agree that respondent's suit is timely, but for a reason different from the Court's: Merck has not shown that respondents actually "discover[ed]" scienter more than two years before bringing suit.

In ordinary usage, "discovery" occurs when one actually learns something new. See Webster's New International Dictionary of the English Language 745 (2d ed. 1957) (defining "discovery" as "[f]inding out or ascertaining something previously unknown or unrecognized"). As the Court notes, however, in the context of the statutes of limitations "discovery" has long carried an additional meaning: It also occurs when a plaintiff, exercising reasonable diligence, *should have* discovered the facts giving rise to his claim. . . . Read in isolation, "discovery" in § 1658(b)(1) might mean constructive discovery.

In context, however, I do not believe it can. Section 13 of the Securities Act of 1933, 48 Stat. 84, explicitly established a constructive-discovery rule for claims under §§ 11 and 12 of that Act:

> "No action shall be maintained to enforce any liability created under section 77k or 77*l*(a)(2) of this title unless brought within one year after the discovery of the untrue statement or the omission, or after such discovery should have been made by the exercise of reasonable diligence. . . ." 15 U.S.C. § 77m.

"[D]iscovery in § 77m obviously cannot mean constructive discovery, since that would render superfluous the phrase "or after such discovery should have been made by the exercise of reasonable diligence." With § 77m already on the books, Congress added limitations periods in the 1934 Act, 15 U.S.C. §§ 78i(e), 78r(c), that did not contain similar qualifying language; instead, each established a time bar that runs from "discovery" *simpliciter*. When Congress enacted § 1658(b)(1) in 2002, establishing a limitations period for private actions for "fraud, deceit, manipulation, or contrivance in contravention of a regulatory requirement concerning the securities laws," specifically including the 1933 and 1934 Acts, see 15 U.S.C. § 78c(a)(47), it likewise included no constructive-discovery caveat. To interpret § 1658(b)(1) as imposing a constructive-discovery standard, one must therefore assume, contrary to common sense, that the same word means two very different things in the same statutory context of limitations periods for securities-fraud actions under the 1933 and 1934 Acts.

True, the sensible presumption that a word means the same thing when it appears more than once in the same statutory context—or even in the very same statute is rebuttable. . . . Context may make clear that in one instance the word carries one meaning, and in a second instance another. But nothing in the context of § 77m or § 1658(b)(1) suggests that is the case. Both provisions impose limitations periods for federal-law claims based on various false statements or omissions involving securities. The former applies to false statements or omissions in registration statements, § 77k, and offers to sell securities, § 77l(a)(2); the broad language of the latter ("claim[s] of fraud, deceit, manipulation, or contrivance in contravention of a regulatory requirement concerning the securities laws") covers other "manipulative or deceptive device[s] or contrivance[s]" made "in connection with the purchase or sale" of a security in violation of Securities and Exchange Commission regulations, § 78j(b), including SEC Rule 10b-5. . . . There is good reason, moreover, for providing an actual-discovery rule for private § 10(b) claims but providing (explicitly) a constructive-discovery rule for claims governed by § 77m: The elements of § 10(b) claims, which include scienter, are likely more difficult to discover than the elements of claims under § 77k or § 77l(a)(2), which do not. . . . And a constructive-discovery standard may be easier to apply to the claims covered by § 77m. Determining when the plaintiff should have uncovered an untrue assertion in a registration statement or prospectus is much simpler than assessing when a plaintiff should have learned that the defendant deliberately misled him using a deceptive device covered by § 10(b).

. . . .

. . . . In any event, whether or not a constructive-discovery standard will in many cases yield the same result, actual discovery is what § 1658(b)(1) requires to start the limitations period.

[Merck subsequently settled this class action for $830 million. *See* 46 SEC. REG. & L. REP. (BNA) 161 (2016).]

Note

(1) The Supreme Court's decision in *Merck*, even though rejecting an actual discovery standard, is favorable to plaintiffs. In practice, a diligent plaintiff rarely will possess constructive notice of a particular defendant's scienter and then decline to file suit within the two-year period.

(2) A key issue that has divided the appellate courts is whether the statute of repose for securities claims, such as the five-year statute of repose in § 2462, can be extended under the tolling principle adopted by the Supreme Court in *American Pipe & Construction Co. v. Utah*, 414 U.S. 538 (1974). There, the Supreme Court held that "the commencement of a class action suspends the applicable statute of limitations as to all asserted members of the class who would have been parties had the suit been permitted to continue as a class action." Several appellate courts hold that *American Pipe* does not extend to statutes of repose. *See, e.g., SRM Global Master Fund Limited v. Bear Stearns Companies LLC*, 829 F.3d 173, 177 (2d Cir. 2016) (holding that "*American Pipe* tolling does not apply to § 1658(b)(2)'s five-year statute of repose [because] first, as a statute of repose, § 1658(b)(2) is not subject to equitable tolling, . . . and, second, [that statute] creates a substantive right in defendants to be free from liability after five years"). Other courts disagree, holding that *American Pipe* applies to both the statute of limitations and the statute of repose. The plaintiffs' bar and institutional investors are concerned. As stated by one law firm:

> Limiting the *American Pipe* tolling rule to only one time period for filing claims imposes heavy burdens on investors. In the Second, Sixth and Eleventh Circuits—which cover Alabama, Connecticut, Florida, Georgia, Kentucky, Michigan, New Hampshire, New York, Ohio and Tennessee—institutional investors must now incur the costs and burdens of extensively monitoring dozens of active securities class actions and, in any case in which the fund has a material financial interest, deciding whether to intervene or file opt-out actions to prevent their individual claims from lapsing under the statute of repose. [Note that individual investors, without significant financial resources and having each incurred relatively modest alleged damages, are in a worse predicament.]

Nicholas & Kaplan, *Time Can Fly*, THE ADVOCATE (Bernstein Litowitz Berger & Grossmann, LLP) at 18, 20 (Summer 2016). The U.S. Supreme Court evidently will resolve this issue, granting the petition for certiorari in *California Public Employees' Retirement System v. ANZ Securities Inc.*

(3) Is the Securities and Exchange Commission (SEC) in its enforcement actions subject to a statute of limitations? As will be seen, the answer largely depends on whether the relief sought is remedial or punitive in nature. Compare *SEC v. Rind*, 991 F.2d 1486 (9th Cir. 1990) (no statute of limitations applicable to SEC action seeking injunctive relief), with *SEC v. Bartek*, [2012–2 Transfer Binder] Fed. Sec. L. Rep. (CCH) ¶ 96,963 (5th Cir. 2012) (holding § 2462's five-year statute of limitations applies to injunctions and officer/director bars); and *Johnson v. SEC*, 87 F.3d 484 (D.C. Cir. 1996) (five-year statute of limitations contained in 28 U.S.C. § 2462 applicable where SEC censure and suspension of brokerage supervisor deemed punitive under circumstances at bar). For further coverage of this issue, see § 15.08.

(4) With respect to private actions, a number of state securities law statutes contain a longer statute of limitations than that now provided by § 10(b). For example,

statutes containing a limitations period of three years after discovery of the material misstatement or omission and in no event more than five years after the sale are not uncommon. *See, e.g.,* Texas Securities Act Art. 581-33H(2). Moreover, the vast majority of states apply equitable tolling principles in cases alleging common law fraud. Hence, in an increasing number of cases, a plaintiff's remedy will be limited to violations of state law due to the expiration of the § 10(b) statute of limitations. See § 9.07.[34]

[C] Defense of In Pari Delicto

Bateman Eichler, Hill Richards, Inc. v. Berner

United States Supreme Court

472 U.S. 299, 105 S. Ct. 2622, 86 L. Ed. 2d 215 (1985)

JUSTICE BRENNAN delivered the opinion of the Court.

The question presented by this case is whether the common-law *in pari delicto* defense bars a private damages action under the federal securities laws against corporate insiders and broker-dealers who fraudulently induce investors to purchase securities by misrepresenting that they are conveying material nonpublic information about the issuer.

I

The respondent investors filed this action in the United States District Court for the Northern District of California, alleging that they incurred substantial trading losses as a result of a conspiracy between Charles Lazzaro, a registered securities broker employed by the petitioner Bateman Eichler, Hill Richards, Inc. (Bateman Eichler), and Leslie Neadeau, President of T.O.N.M. Oil & Gas Exploration Corporation (TONM), to induce them to purchase large quantities of TONM over-the-counter stock by divulging false and materially incomplete information about the company on the pretext that it was accurate inside information. Specifically, Lazzaro is alleged to have told the respondents that he personally knew TONM insiders and had learned, inter alia, that (a) "[v]ast amounts of gold had been discovered in Suriname, and TONM had options on thousands of acres in gold-producing regions of Suriname"; (b) the discovery was not publicly known, but would subsequently be announced; (c) TONM was currently engaged in negotiations with other companies to form a joint venture for mining the Surinamese gold, and (d) when this information was made public, "TONM stock, which was then selling from $1.50 to $3.00/share, would

---

34. For further treatment on § 10(b)'s statute of limitations, *see, e.g.,* Kaufman & Wunderlich, *Leave Time for Trouble: The Limitations Periods Under the Securities Laws,* 40 J. Corp. L. 143 (2014); McManus, *Inquiry Notice Under the Statute of Limitations for § 10(b) and Rule 10b-5 Actions,* 29 Sec. Reg. L.J. 376 (2001); Polden, *Drawing the Appropriate Statute of Limitations in Implied Causes of Action Under Rule 10b-5: A General Framework of Familiar Legal Principles,* 40 Drake L. Rev. 221 (1991).

increase in value from $10 to $15/share within a short period of time, and . . . might increase to $100/share" within a year. Some of the respondents aver that they contacted Neadeau and inquired whether Lazzaro's tips were accurate; Neadeau stated that the information was "not public knowledge" and "would neither confirm nor deny those claims," but allegedly advised that "Lazzaro was a very trustworthy and a good man."

The respondents admitted in their complaint that they purchased TONM stock, much of it through Lazzaro, "on the premise that Lazzaro was privy to certain information not otherwise available to the general public." Their shares initially increased dramatically in price, but ultimately declined to substantially below the purchase price when the joint mining venture fell through. Lazzaro and Neadeau are alleged to have made the representations set forth above knowing that the representations "were untrue and/or contained only half-truths, material omissions of fact and falsehoods," intending that the respondents would rely thereon, and for the purpose of "influenc[ing] and manipulat[ing] the price of TONM stock" so as "to profit themselves through the taking of commissions and secret profits." The respondents contended that this scheme violated, inter alia, § 10(b) of the Securities Exchange Act of 1934 and SEC Rule 10b-5 promulgated thereunder. . . .

. . . .

The lower courts have divided over the proper scope of the *in pari delicto* defense in securities litigation. We granted certiorari. We affirm.

II

The common-law defense at issue in this case derives from the Latin, *in pari delicto potior est conditio defendentis:* "In a case of equal or mutual fault . . . the position of the [defending] party . . . is the better one." The defense is grounded on two premises: first, that courts should not lend their good offices to mediating disputes among wrongdoers; and second, that denying judicial relief to an admitted wrongdoer is an effective means of deterring illegality. In its classic formulation, the *in pari delicto* defense was narrowly limited to situations where the plaintiff truly bore at least substantially equal responsibility for his injury, because "in cases where both parties are *in delicto*, concurring in an illegal act, it does not always follow that they stand *in pari delicto*; for there may be, and often are, very different degrees in their guilt." 1 J. Story, Equity Jurisprudence 304–305 (13th ed. 1886) (Story). . . . In addition, the public policy considerations that undergirded the *in pari delicto* defense were frequently construed as precluding the defense even where the plaintiff bore substantial fault for his injury: "there may be on the part of the court itself a necessity of supporting the public interests or public policy in many cases, however reprehensible the acts of the parties may be." 1 Story 305. . . .

In *Perma Life*, we emphasized "the inappropriateness of invoking broad common-law barriers to relief where a private suit serves important public purposes." [392 U.S. 134, 138 (1968)] That case involved a treble-damages action against a Midas Muffler franchisor by several of its dealers, who alleged that the franchise agreement created a conspiracy to restrain trade in violation of the Sherman and Clayton Acts.

The lower courts barred the action on the grounds that the dealers, as parties to the agreement, were *in pari delicto* with the franchisor. In reversing that determination, the opinion for this Court emphasized that there was no indication that Congress had intended to incorporate the defense into the antitrust laws, which "are best served by insuring that the private action will be an ever-present threat to deter anyone contemplating [illegal] business behavior." Accordingly, the opinion concluded that "the doctrine of *in pari delicto*, with its complex scope, contents, and effects, is not to be recognized as a defense to an antitrust action." The opinion reserved the question whether a plaintiff who engaged in "truly complete involvement and participation in a monopolistic scheme"—one who "aggressively support[ed] and further[ed] the monopolistic scheme as a necessary part and parcel of it"—could be barred from pursuing a damages action, finding that the muffler dealers had relatively little bargaining power and that they had been coerced by the franchisor into agreeing to many of the contract's provisions.

. . . .

Bateman Eichler argues that *Perma Life*—with its emphasis on the importance of analyzing the effects that fault-based defenses would have on the enforcement of congressional goals—is of only marginal relevance to a private damages action under the federal securities laws. Specifically, Bateman Eichler observes that Congress expressly provided for private antitrust actions—thereby manifesting a "desire to go beyond the common law in the antitrust statute in order to provide substantial encouragement to private enforcement and to help deter anticompetitive conduct"—whereas private rights of action under § 10(b) of the Securities Exchange Act of 1934 are merely implied from that provision—thereby, apparently, supporting a broader application of the *in pari delicto defense*. Bateman Eichler buttresses this argument by observing that, unlike the Sherman and Clayton Acts, the securities laws contain savings provisions directing that "[t]he rights and remedies provided by [those laws] shall be in addition to any and all other rights and remedies that may exist at law or in equity"—again, apparently, supporting a broader scope for fault-based defenses than recognized in *Perma Life*.

We disagree. Nothing in *Perma Life* suggested that public policy implications should govern only where Congress expressly provides for private remedies; the classic formulation of the *in pari delicto* doctrine itself required a careful consideration of such implications before allowing the defense. Moreover, we repeatedly have emphasized that implied private actions provide "a most effective weapon in the enforcement" of the securities laws and are "a necessary supplement to Commission action." . . . In addition, we have eschewed rigid common-law barriers in construing the securities laws. . . . We therefore conclude that the views expressed in *Perma Life* apply with full force to implied causes of action under the federal securities laws. Accordingly, a private action for damages in these circumstances may be barred on the grounds of the plaintiff's own culpability only where (1) as a direct result of his own actions, the plaintiff bears at least substantially equal responsibility for the violations he seeks to redress, and (2) preclusion of suit would not significantly interfere with the effective enforcement of the securities laws and protection of the investing public.

A

. . . .

We agree that the typically voluntary nature of an investor's decision impermissibly to trade on an inside tip renders the investor more blameworthy than someone who is party to a contract solely by virtue of another's overweening bargaining power. We disagree, however, that an investor who engages in such trading is necessarily as blameworthy as a corporate insider or broker-dealer who discloses the information for personal gain. Notwithstanding the broad reach of § 10(b) and Rule 10b-5, there are important distinctions between the relative culpabilities of tippers, securities professionals, and tippees in these circumstances. The Court has made clear in recent Terms that a tippee's use of material nonpublic information does not violate § 10(b) and Rule 10b-5 unless the tippee owes a corresponding duty to disclose the information. *Dirks v. SEC,* 463 U.S. 646, 654–664 (1983); *Chiarella v. United States,* 445 U.S. 222, 230, n. 12 (1980). That duty typically is "derivative from . . . the insider's duty." *Dirks v. SEC,* [463 U.S.] at 659. . . . In other words, "[t]he tippee's obligation has been viewed as arising from his role as a participant after the fact in the insider's breach of a fiduciary duty" toward corporate shareholders. *Chiarella v. United States,* [445 U.S.] at 230, n.12. In the context of insider trading, we do not believe that a person whose liability is solely derivative can be said to be as culpable as one whose breach of duty gave rise to that liability in the first place.

Moreover, insiders and broker-dealers who selectively disclose material nonpublic information commit a potentially broader range of violations than do tippees who trade on the basis of that information. A tippee trading on inside information will in many circumstances be guilty of fraud against individual shareholders, a violation for which the tipper shares responsibility. But the insider, in disclosing such information, also frequently breaches fiduciary duties toward the issuer itself. And in cases where the tipper intentionally conveys false or materially incomplete information to the tippee, the tipper commits an additional violation: fraud against the tippee. Such conduct is particularly egregious when committed by a securities professional, who owes a duty of honesty and fair dealing toward his clients. Absent other culpable actions by a tippee that can fairly be said to outweigh these violations by insiders and broker-dealers, we do not believe that the tippee properly can be characterized as being of substantially equal culpability as his tippers.

. . . .

B

We also believe that denying the *in pari delicto* defense in such circumstances will best promote the primary objective of the federal securities laws—protection of the investing public and the national economy through the promotion of "a high standard of business ethics . . . in every facet of the securities industry." Although a number of lower courts have reasoned that a broad rule of *caveat tippee* would better serve this goal, we believe the contrary position adopted by other courts represents the better view.

To begin with, barring private actions in cases such as this would inexorably result in a number of alleged fraudulent practices going undetected by the authorities and unremedied. The Securities and Exchange Commission had advised us that it "does not have the resources to police the industry sufficiently to ensure that false tipping does not occur or is consistently discovered," and that "[w]ithout the tippees' assistance, the Commission could not effectively prosecute false tipping—a difficult practice to detect." . . .

Moreover, we believe that deterrence of insider trading most frequently will be maximized by bringing enforcement pressures to bear on the sources of such information—corporate insiders and broker-dealers. . . .

In addition, corporate insiders and broker-dealers will in many circumstances be more responsive to the deterrent pressure of potential sanctions; they are more likely than ordinary investors to be advised by counsel and thereby to be informed fully of the "allowable limits on their conduct." Although situations might well arise in which the relative culpabilities of the tippee and his insider source merit a different mix of deterrent incentives, we therefore conclude that in tipper-tippee situations such as the one before us the factors discussed above preclude recognition of the *in pari delicto* defense.

Lower courts reaching a contrary conclusion have typically asserted that, absent a vigorous allowance of the *in pari delicto* defense, tippees would have, "in effect, an enforceable warranty that secret information is true," and thus no incentive not to trade on that information. These courts have reasoned, in other words, that tippees in such circumstances would be in "the enviable position of 'heads-I-win tails-you-lose'"; if the tip is correct, the tippee will reap illicit profits, while if the tip fails to yield the expected return, he can sue to recover damages.

We believe the "enforceable warranty" theory is overstated and overlooks significant factors that serve to deter tippee trading irrespective of whether the *in pari delicto* defense is allowed. First, tippees who bring suit in an attempt to cash in on their "enforceable warranties" expose themselves to the threat of substantial civil and criminal penalties for their own potentially illegal conduct. Second, plaintiffs in litigation under § 10(b) and Rule 10b-5 may only recover against defendants who have acted with scienter. Thus "if the tip merely fails to 'pan out' or if the information itself proves accurate but the stock fails to move in the anticipated direction, the investor stands to lose all of his investment. Only in the situation where the investor has been deliberately defrauded will he be able to maintain a private suit in an attempt to recoup his money."

. . . .

We therefore conclude that the public interest will most frequently be advanced if defrauded tippees are permitted to bring suit and to expose illegal practices by corporate insiders and broker-dealers to full public view for appropriate sanctions.

. . . .

Note

The Supreme Court revisited the *in pari delicto* defense in *Pinter v. Dahl,* contained in § 7.06[A]. For additional discussion, *see* Gabaldon, *Unclean Hands and Self-Inflicted Wounds: The Significance of Plaintiff Conduct in Actions for Misrepresentation Under Rule 10b-5,* 71 Minn. L. Rev. 317 (1986); Klock, *Promoter Liability and In Pari Delicto,* 17 Sec. Reg. L.J. 53 (1989); Note, *In Pari Delicto Under the Federal Securities Laws,* 72 Cornell L. Rev. 345 (1987).

§ 8.10 Contribution, Proportionate Liability, and Related Issues

[A] *Musick, Peeler*

In *Musick, Peeler & Garrett v. Employers Insurance of Wausau,* 508 U.S. 286 (1993), the Supreme Court recognized an implied right of action for contribution under § 10(b). The Court focused its inquiry on "how the 1934 Congress would have addressed the issue had the [§ 10(b)] action been included as an express provision in the 1934 Act." Of the eight liability provisions contained in the 1933 and 1934 Acts, the Court found that 1934 Act §§ 9 and 18 impose liability upon defendants who occupy a position most similar to § 10(b) defendants for ascertaining entitlement to contribution. Since both §§ 9 and 18 expressly provide for contribution, the Court reasoned that "consistency requires us to adopt a like contribution rule for the right of action existing under Rule 10b-5."[35]

The Court rejected the argument that two of its relatively recent decisions outside of the securities law arena that declined to recognize an action for contribution[36] signified that contribution likewise was inappropriate under § 10(b). The Court reasoned that these cases construed statutory provisions that allowed for express rights of action. While the ramifications of these cases may foreclose recognizing a right to contribution under express securities law remedial provisions that do not by their

---

35. 508 U.S. 294, 297.

36. *See Texas Industries, Inc. v. Radcliff Materials, Inc.,* 481 U.S. 630 (1981) (no right to contribution based on violation of § 1 of the Sherman Act); *Northwest Airlines, Inc. v. Transport Workers,* 451 U.S. 77 (1981) (no right to contribution pursuant to Equal Pay Act and Title VII of the Civil Rights Act of 1964).

terms provide for this right of action (such as with respect to Securities Act § 12(a)(2)), a different analysis applies to implied rights. Here, because the judiciary has implied the § 10(b) private right of action, it is the Court's role to elaborate, define, and shape the contours of this remedy. Applying this analysis, the Court concluded that "[t]hose charged with liability in a [§ 10(b)] action have a right to contribution against other parties who have joint responsibility for the violation."[37]

[B] Contribution, Proportionate Liability and Related Issues Under the Private Securities Litigation Reform Act of 1995

The Private Securities Litigation Reform Act amended the Exchange Act to add new § 21D(g) thereto. This new section: (1) circumscribes the scope of the current joint and several liability scheme; (2) creates a proportionate liability framework for actions brought against multiple defendants under the Exchange Act or against "outside directors" of the issuer whose securities are the subject of an action under § 11 of the Securities Act; and (3) clarifies several issues relating to partial settlements in federal securities actions.

First, the statute limits the application of joint and several liability for damages to apply only if the trier of fact specifically determines that the defendant in question "knowingly committed" a violation of the federal securities laws. The section provides that the term "knowingly committed" requires actual knowledge as the scienter standard and specifically provides that recklessness cannot constitute a knowing violation. Further, the legislation codifies the right to contribution among such joint tortfeasors recognized by the Supreme Court in *Musick, Peeler v. Employers Insurance*, 508 U.S. 286 (1993). Under this framework, the legislation provides that the liability of such defendants is to be premised upon findings of percentage of responsibility as to each jointly and severally liable defendant.

Second, by implication, in all actions wherein the "knowingly committed" scienter standard of recklessness may be shown, the statute creates a proportionate liability scheme and (with certain exceptions) restricts liability for damages solely to that portion of the judgment that corresponds to the percentage of each individual defendant's responsibility for plaintiffs' losses. In addition, if certain individually liable defendants' shares of liability are uncollectible due to insolvency or some other reason, the statute requires additional proportionate contributions either from the jointly and severally liable defendants or, if still uncollectible, from other proportionately liable defendants for those uncollectible shares in certain specified circumstances.

The statute further provides specific guidelines for determining the percentage of each individual defendant's responsibility for damages in the form of directing the court: (1) to instruct the trier of fact to answer special interrogatories; or (2) to itself make special findings with respect to multiple defendants on specific

---

37. 508 U.S. at 291

issues. Such issues are to include, among other things, the percentage of responsibility of each defendant and whether the defendant "knowingly committed" violations so as to properly place that defendant within the joint and several liability scheme.

Third, the statute evidently brings an end to the controversy generated by several decisions addressing issues of partial settlements in federal securities actions by providing for the discharge of all claims for contribution brought by any other persons, whether or not such persons have themselves settled with the plaintiff, against any defendant that has settled any private action at any time prior to judgment. Moreover, the section requires the implementation of a settlement bar order by the court constituting the discharge of all obligations to the plaintiff of the settling defendant "arising out of the action." The legislation makes clear that such bar orders apply to contribution actions brought by and against the settling defendant.

In addition, the statute provides for a new judgment reduction method applicable in multidefendant partial settlement cases. This method serves to reduce the plaintiff's subsequent judgment against any nonsettling defendant by the greater amount of either (1) the proportionate responsibility of the settling defendant as determined by the court or jury, or (2) the amount that such a settling defendant has already paid to the plaintiff pursuant to the respective settlement agreement.

For further discussion, see Langevoort, *The Reform of Joint and Several Liability Under the Private Securities Litigation Reform Act of 1995: Proportionate Liability, Contribution Rights and Settlement Effects,* 51 Bus. Law. 1157 (1996); Steinberg & Olive, *Contribution and Proportionate Liability Under the Federal Securities Laws,* 50 SMU L. Rev. 337 (1996).

---

§ 8.11 Class Action "Reform"

Private Securities Litigation Reform Act Joint Explanatory Statement of the Committee of Conference (1995)

[The Private Securities Litigation Reform Act of 1995] contains provisions to reform abusive securities class action litigation. It amends the Securities Act of 1933 (the "1933 Act") by adding a new section 27 and the Securities Exchange Act of 1934 (the "1934 Act") by adding a new section 21D. These provisions are intended to encourage the most capable representatives of the plaintiff class to participate in class action litigation and to exercise supervision and control of the lawyers for the class. These provisions are intended to increase the likelihood that parties with significant holdings in issuers, whose interests are more strongly aligned with the class of shareholders, will participate in the litigation and exercise control over the selection and actions of plaintiffs' counsel. The legislation also provides that all discovery is stayed during the pendency of any motion to dismiss or for summary judgment. These stay of discovery provisions are intended to prevent unnecessary imposition of discovery costs on defendants.

THE PROFESSIONAL PLAINTIFF AND LEAD PLAINTIFF PROBLEMS

House and Senate Committee hearings on securities litigation reform demonstrated the need to reform abuses involving the use of "professional plaintiffs" and the race to the courthouse to file the complaint.

Professional plaintiffs who own a nominal number of shares in a wide array of public companies permit lawyers readily to file abusive securities class action lawsuits. Floor debate in the Senate highlighted that many of the "world's unluckiest investors" repeatedly appear as lead plaintiffs in securities class action lawsuits. These lead plaintiffs often receive compensation in the form of bounty payments or bonuses.

The Conference Committee believes these practices have encouraged the filing of abusive cases. Lead plaintiffs are not entitled to a bounty for their services. Individuals who are motivated by the payment of a bounty or bonus should not be permitted to serve as lead plaintiffs. These individuals do not adequately represent other shareholders—in many cases the "lead plaintiff" has not even read the complaint.

The Conference Committee believes that several new rules will effectively discourage the use of professional plaintiffs.

Plaintiff certification of the complaint

This legislation requires, in new section 27(a)(2) of the 1933 Act and new section 21D(a)(2) of the 1934 Act, that the lead plaintiff file a sworn certified statement with the complaint. The statement must certify that the plaintiff: (a) reviewed and authorized the filing of the complaint; (b) did not purchase the securities at the direction of counselor in order to participate in a lawsuit; and (c) is willing to serve as the lead plaintiff on behalf of the class. To further deter the use of professional plaintiffs, the plaintiff must also identify any transactions in the securities covered by the class period, and any other lawsuits in which the plaintiff has sought to serve as lead plaintiff in the last three years.

Method for determining the "most adequate plaintiff"

The Conference Committee was also troubled by the plaintiffs' lawyers "race to the courthouse" to be the first to file a securities class action complaint. This race has caused plaintiffs' attorneys to become fleet of foot and sleight of hand. Most often speed has replaced diligence in drafting complaints. The Conference Committee believes two incentives have driven plaintiffs' lawyers to be the first to file. First, courts traditionally appoint counsel in class action lawsuits on a "first come, first serve" basis. Courts often afford insufficient consideration to the most thoroughly researched, but later filed, complaint. The second incentive involves the court's decision as to who will become lead plaintiff. Generally, the first lawsuit filed also determines the lead plaintiff.

The Conference Committee believes that the selection of the lead plaintiff and lead counsel should rest on considerations other than how quickly a plaintiff has filed its complaint. As a result, this legislation establishes new procedures for the appointment of the lead plaintiff and lead counsel in securities class actions in new section 27(a)(3) of the 1933 Act and new section 21D(a)(3) of the 1934 Act.

A plaintiff filing a securities class action must, within 20 days of filing a complaint, provide notice to members of the purported class in a widely circulated business publication. This notice must identify the claims alleged in the lawsuit and the purported class period and inform potential class members that, within 60 days, they may move to serve as the lead plaintiff. Members of the purported class who seek to serve as lead plaintiff do not have to file the certification filing as part of this motion. "Publication" includes a variety of media, including wire, electronic or computer services.

Within 90 days of the published notice, the court must consider motions made under this section and appoint the lead plaintiff. If a motion has been filed to consolidate multiple class actions brought on behalf of the same class, the court will not appoint a lead plaintiff until after consideration of the motion.

The current system often works to prevent institutional investors from selecting counsel or serving as lead plaintiff in class actions. The Conference Committee seeks to increase the likelihood that institutional investors will serve as lead plaintiffs by requiring courts to presume that the member of the purported class with the largest financial stake in the relief sought is the "most adequate plaintiff."

The Conference Committee believes that increasing the role of institutional investors in class actions will ultimately benefit shareholders and assist courts by improving the quality of representation in securities class actions. Institutional investors are America's largest shareholders, with about $9.5 trillion in assets, accounting for 51% of the equity market. According to one representative of institutional investors: "As the largest shareholders in most companies, we are the ones who have the most to gain from meritorious securities litigation."

Several Senators expressed concern during floor consideration of this legislation that preference would be given to large investors, and that large investors might conspire with the defendant company's management. The Conference Committee believes, however, that with pension funds accounting for $4.5 trillion or nearly half of the institutional assets, in many cases the beneficiaries of pension funds—small investors—ultimately have the greatest stake in the outcome of the lawsuit. Cumulatively, these small investors represent a single large investor interest. Institutional investors and other class members with large amounts at stake will represent the interests of the plaintiff class more effectively than class members with small amounts at stake. The claims of both types of class members generally will be typical.

The Conference Committee recognizes the potential conflicts that could be caused by the shareholder with the "largest financial stake" serving as lead plaintiff. As a result, this presumption may be rebutted by evidence that the plaintiff would not fairly and adequately represent the interests of the class or is subject to unique defenses. Members of the purported class may seek discovery on whether the presumptively most adequate plaintiff would not adequately represent the class. The provisions of the bill relating to the appointment of a lead plaintiff are not intended to affect current law with regard to challenges to the adequacy of the class representative or typicality of the claims among the class.

Although the most adequate plaintiff provision does not confer any new fiduciary duty on institutional investors—and the courts should not impose such a duty—the Conference Committee nevertheless intends that the lead plaintiff provision will encourage institutional investors to take a more active role in securities class action lawsuits. Scholars predict that increasing the role of institutional investors will benefit both injured shareholders and courts: "Institutions with large stakes in class actions have much the same interests as the plaintiff class generally; thus, courts could be more confident settlements negotiated under the supervision of institutional plaintiffs were 'fair and reasonable' than is the case with settlements negotiated by unsupervised plaintiffs' attorneys."

Finally, this lead plaintiff provision solves the dilemma of who will serve as class counsel. Subject to court approval, the most adequate plaintiff retains class counsel. As a result, the Conference Committee expects that the plaintiff will choose counsel rather than, as is true today, counsel choosing the plaintiff. The Conference Committee does not intend to disturb the court's discretion under existing law to approve or disapprove the lead plaintiffs' choice of counsel when necessary to protect the interests of the plaintiff class.

The Conference Report seeks to restrict professional plaintiffs from serving as lead plaintiff by limiting a person from serving in that capacity more than five times in three years. Institutional investors seeking to serve as lead plaintiff may need to exceed this limitation and do not represent the type of professional plaintiff this legislation seeks to restrict. As a result, the Conference Committee grants courts discretion to avoid the unintended consequence of disqualifying institutional investors from serving more than five times in three years. The Conference Committee does not intend for this provision to operate at cross purposes with the Amost adequate plaintiff" provision. The Conference Committee does expect, however, that it will be used with vigor to limit the activities of professional plaintiffs.

Limitation on lead plaintiff's recovery

This legislation also removes the financial incentive for becoming a lead plaintiff. New section 27(a)(4) of the 1933 Act and section 21D(a)(4) of the 1934 Act limits the class representative's recovery to his or her pro rata share of the settlement or final judgment. The lead plaintiff's share of the final judgment or settlement will be calculated in the same manner as the shares of the other class members. The Conference Committee recognizes that lead plaintiffs should be reimbursed for reasonable costs and expenses associated with service as lead plaintiff, including lost wages, and grants the court's discretion to award fees accordingly.

IMPROVEMENTS TO SETTLEMENT PROCESS

Restriction on sealed settlement agreements

New section 27(a)(5) of the 1933 Act and section 21D(a)(5) of the 1934 Act generally bar the filing of settlement agreements under seal. The Conference Committee recognizes that legitimate reasons may exist for the court to permit the entry of a settlement or portions of a settlement under seal. A party must show "good cause," i.e., that the publication of a portion or portions of the settlement agreement would result in direct and substantial harm to any party, whether or not a party to the action. The Conference Committee intends "direct and substantial harm" to include proof of reputational injury to a party.

Limitation on attorneys' fees

The House and Senate heard testimony that counsel in securities class actions often receive a disproportionate share of settlement awards.

Under current practice, courts generally award attorney's fees based on the so-called "lodestar" approach — i.e., the court multiplies the attorney's hours by a reasonable hourly fee, which may be increased by an additional amount based on risk or other relevant factors. Under this approach, attorney's fees can constitute 35% or more of the entire settlement awarded to the class. The Conference Committee limits the award of attorney's fees and costs to counsel for a class in new section 27(a)(6) of the 1933 Act and new section 21D(a)(6) of the 1934 Act to a reasonable percentage of the amount of recovery awarded to the class. By not fixing the percentage of fees and costs counsel may receive, the Conference Committee intends to give the court flexibility in determining what is reasonable on a case-by-case basis. The Conference Committee does not intend to prohibit use of the lodestar approach as a means of calculating attorney's fees. The provision focuses on the final amount of fees awarded, not the means by which such fees are calculated.

Improved settlement notice to class members

The House and Senate heard testimony that class members frequently lack meaningful information about the terms of the proposed settlement. Class members often receive insufficient notice of the terms of a proposed settlement and, thus, have no basis to evaluate the settlement. As one bar association advised the Senate Securities Subcommittee, "settlement notices provided to class members are often obtuse and confusing, and should be written in plain English." The Senate received similar testimony from a class member in two separate securities fraud lawsuits: "Nowhere in the settlement notices were the stockholders told of how much they could expect to recover of their losses . . . I feel that the settlement offer should have told the stockholders how little of their losses will be recovered in the settlement, and that this is a material fact to the shareholder's decision to approve or disapprove the settlement."

In new section 27(a)(7) of the 1933 Act and new section 21D(a)(7) of the 1934 Act, the Conference Committee requires that certain information be included in any proposed or final settlement agreement disseminated to class members. To ensure that critical information is readily available to class members, the Conference Committee requires that such information appear in summary form on the cover page of the notice. The notice must contain a statement of the average amount of damages per share that would be recoverable if the settling parties can agree on a figure, or a statement from each settling party on why there is disagreement. It must also explain the attorney's fees and costs sought. The name, telephone number and address of counsel for the class must be provided. Most importantly, the notice must include a brief statement explaining the reason for the proposed settlement.

MAJOR SECURITIES CLASS ACTION ABUSES

Limits on abusive discovery to prevent "fishing expedition" lawsuits

The cost of discovery often forces innocent parties to settle frivolous securities class actions. According to the general counsel of an investment bank, "discovery costs account for roughly 80% of total litigation costs in securities fraud cases." In addition, the threat that the time of key employees will be spent responding to discovery requests, including providing deposition testimony, often forces coercive settlements.

The House and Senate heard testimony that discovery in securities class actions often resembles a fishing expedition. As one witness noted, "once the suit is filed, the plaintiffs' law firm proceeds to search through all of the company's documents and take endless depositions for the slightest positive comment which they can claim induced the plaintiff to invest and any shred of evidence that the company knew a downturn was coming."

The Conference Committee provides in new section 27(b) of the 1933 Act and new section 21D(b)(3) of the 1934 Act that courts must stay all discovery pending a ruling on a motion to dismiss, unless exceptional circumstances exist where particularized discovery is necessary to preserve evidence or to prevent undue prejudice to a party. For example, the terminal illness of an important witness might require the deposition of the witness prior to the ruling on the motion to dismiss.

To ensure that relevant evidence will not be lost, new section 27(b) of the 1933 Act and new section 21D(b)(3) of the 1934 Act make it unlawful for any person, upon receiving actual notice that names that person as a defendant, willfully to destroy or otherwise alter relevant evidence. The Conference Committee intends this provision to prohibit only the willful alteration or destruction of evidence relevant to the litigation. The provision does not impose liability where parties inadvertently or unintentionally destroy what turn out later to be relevant documents. Although this prohibition expressly applies only to defendants, the Conference Committee believes that the willful destruction of evidence by a plaintiff would be equally improper, and that courts have ample authority to prevent such conduct or to apply sanctions as appropriate.

Attorneys' fees awarded to prevailing parties in abusive litigation

The Conference Committee recognizes the need to reduce significantly the filing of meritless securities lawsuits without hindering the ability of victims of fraud to pursue legitimate claims. The Conference Committee seeks to solve this problem by strengthening the application of Rule 11 of the Federal Rules of Civil Procedure in private securities actions.

Existing Rule 11 has not deterred abusive securities litigation. Courts often fail to impose Rule 11 sanctions even where such sanctions are warranted. When sanctions are awarded, they are generally insufficient to make whole the victim of a Rule 11 violation: the amount of the sanction is limited to an amount that the court deems sufficient to deter repetition of the sanctioned conduct, rather than imposing a sanction that equals the costs imposed on the victim by the violation. Finally, courts have been unable to apply Rule 11 to the complaint in such a way that the victim of the ensuing lawsuit is compensated for all attorneys' fees and costs incurred in the entire action.

The legislation gives teeth to Rule 11 in new section 27(c) of the 1933 Act and new section 21D(c) of the 1934 Act by requiring the court to include in the record specific findings, at the conclusion of the action, as to whether all parties and all attorneys have complied with each requirement of Rule 11(b) of the Federal Rules of Civil Procedure.

These provisions also establish the presumption that the appropriate sanction for filing a complaint that violates Rule 11(b) is an award to the prevailing party of all attorney's fees and costs incurred in the entire action. The Conference Report provides that, if the action is brought for an improper purpose, is unwarranted by existing law or legally frivolous, is not supported by facts, or otherwise fails to satisfy the requirements set forth in Rule 11(b), the prevailing party presumptively will be awarded its attorney's fees and costs for the entire action. This provision does not mean that a party who is sanctioned for only a partial failure of the complaint under Rule 11, such as one count out of a 20-count complaint, must pay for all of the attorney's fees and costs associated with the action. The Conference Committee expects that courts will grant relief from the presumption where a de minimis violation of the Rule has occurred. Accordingly, the Conference Committee specifies that the failure of the complaint must be "substantial" and makes the presumption rebuttable.

For Rule 11(b) violations involving responsive pleadings or dispositive motions, the rebuttable presumption is an award of attorneys' fees and costs incurred by the victim of the violation as a result of that particular pleading or motion.

A party may rebut the presumption of sanctions by providing that: (i) the violation was de minimis; or (ii) the imposition of fees and costs would impose an undue burden and be unjust, and it would not impose a greater burden for the prevailing party to have to pay those same fees and costs. The premise of this test is that, when an abusive or frivolous action is maintained, it is manifestly unjust for the victim of the violation to bear substantial attorneys' fees. The Conference

Committee recognizes that little in the way of justice can be achieved by attempting to compensate the prevailing party for lost time and such other measures of damages as injury to reputation. . . . If a party successfully rebuts the presumption, the court then impose[s] sanctions consistent with Rule 11(c)(2). The Conference Committee intends this provision to impose upon courts the affirmative duty to scrutinize filings closely and to sanction attorneys or parties whenever their conduct violates Rule 11(b).

Limitation on attorney's conflict of interest

The Conference Committee believes that, in the context of class action lawsuits, it is a conflict of interest for a class action lawyer to benefit from the outcome of the case where the lawyer owns stock in the company being sued. Accordingly, new section 27(a)(8) of the 1933 Act and new section 21D(a)(9) requires the court to determine whether a lawyer who owns securities in the defendant company and who seeks to represent the plaintiff class in a securities class action should be disqualified from representing the class.

Bonding for payment of fees and expenses

The House hearings on securities litigation reform revealed the need for explicit authority for courts to require undertakings for attorney's fees and costs from parties, or their counsel, or both, in order to ensure the viability of potential sanctions as a deterrent to meritless litigation. Congress long ago authorized similar undertaking in the express private right of action in section 11 of the 1933 Act and in sections 9 and 18 of the 1934 Act. The availability of such undertakings in private securities actions will be an important means of ensuring that the costs under Rule 11 will not become, in practice, a one-way mechanism only usable to sanction parties with deep pockets.

The legislation expressly provides that such undertakings may be required of parties' attorneys in lieu of, or in addition to, the parties themselves. In this regard, the Conference Committee intends to preempt any contrary state bar restrictions that may inhibit attorneys' provision of such undertakings in behalf of their clients. The Conference Committee anticipates, for example, that where a judge determines to require an undertaking in a class action, such an undertaking would ordinarily be imposed on plaintiffs' counsel rather than upon the plaintiff class, both because the financial resources of counsel would ordinarily be more extensive than those of an individual class member and because counsel are better situated than class members to evaluate the merits of cases and individual motions. This provision is intended to effectuate the remedial purposes of the bill's Rule 11 provision.

REQUIREMENTS FOR SECURITIES FRAUD ACTIONS

Heightened pleading standard

Naming a party in a civil suit for fraud is a serious matter. Unwarranted fraud claims can lead to serious injury to reputation for which our legal system effectively offers no redress. For this reason, among others, Rule 9(b) of the Federal Rules of

Civil Procedure requires that plaintiffs plead allegations of fraud with "particularity." The Rule has not prevented abuse of the securities laws by private litigants. Moreover, the courts of appeals have interpreted Rule 9(b)'s requirement in conflicting ways, creating distinctly different standards among the circuits. The House and Senate hearings on securities litigation reform included testimony on the need to establish uniform and more stringent pleading requirements to curtail the filing of meritless lawsuits.

The Conference Committee language is based in part on the pleading standard of the Second Circuit. The standard also is specifically written to conform the language to Rule 9(b)'s notion of pleading with "particularity."

Regarded as the most stringent pleading standard, the Second Circuit requirement is that the plaintiff state facts with particularity, and that these facts, in turn, must give rise to a "strong inference" of the defendant's fraudulent intent. Because the Conference Committee intends to strengthen existing pleading requirements, it does not intend to codify the Second Circuit's case law interpreting this pleading standard. The plaintiff must also specifically plead with particularity each statement alleged to have been misleading. The reason or reasons why the statement is misleading must also be set forth in the complaint in detail. If an allegation is made on information and belief, the plaintiff must state with particularity all facts in the plaintiff's possession on which the belief is formed.

Loss causation

The Conference Committee also requires the plaintiff to plead and then to prove that the misstatement or omission alleged in the complaint actually caused the loss incurred by the plaintiff in new Section 21D(b)(4) of the 1934 Act. For example, the plaintiff would have to prove that the price at which the plaintiff bought the stock was artificially inflated as the result of the misstatement or omission.

DAMAGES

Written interrogatories

In an action to recover money damages, the Conference Committee requires the court to submit written interrogatories to the jury on the issue of defendant's state of mind at the time of the violation. In expressly providing for certain interrogatories, the Committee does not intend to otherwise prohibit or discourage the submission of interrogatories concerning the mental state or relative fault of the plaintiff and of persons who could have been joined as defendants. For example, interrogatories may be appropriate in contribution proceedings among defendants or in computing liability when some of the defendants have entered into settlement with the plaintiff prior to verdict or judgment.

Limitation on "windfall" damages

The current method of calculating damages in 1934 Act securities fraud cases is complex and uncertain. As a result, there are often substantial variations in the damages calculated by the defendants and the plaintiffs. Typically, in an action involving a fraudulent misstatement or omission, the investor's damages are presumed to be the difference between the price the investor paid for the security and the price of the security on the day the corrective information gets disseminated to the market.

Between the time a misrepresentation is made and the time the market receives corrected information, however, the price of the security may rise or fall for reasons unrelated to the alleged fraud. According to an analysis provided to the Senate Securities Subcommittee, on average, damages in securities litigation comprise approximately 27.7% of market loss. Calculating damages based on the date corrective information is disclosed may end up substantially overestimating plaintiff's damages. The Conference Committee intends to rectify the uncertainty in calculating damages in new section 21D(e) of the 1934 Act by providing a "look back" period, thereby limiting damages to those losses caused by the fraud and not by other market conditions.

This provision requires that [the limitation of] plaintiff's damages be calculated based on the "mean trading price" of the security. This calculation takes into account the value of the security on the date plaintiff originally bought or sold the security and the value of the security during the 90-day period after dissemination of any information correcting the misleading statement or omission. . . .

President Clinton vetoed the Private Securities Litigation Reform Act. Subsequently, Congress overrode the President's veto and the Act became law. The President's Veto Message follows.

Presidential Veto Message on the Private Securities Litigation Reform Act

The White House. Office of the Press Secretary. December 20, 1995. Message from President William J. Clinton to the House of Representatives. December 20, 1995.

TO THE HOUSE OF REPRESENTATIVES:

I am returning herewith without my approval H.R. 1058, the "Private Securities Litigation Reform Act of 1995." This legislation is designed to reform portions of the Federal securities laws to end frivolous lawsuits and to ensure that investors receive the best possible information by reducing the litigation risk to companies that make forward-looking statements.

I support these goals. Indeed, I made clear my willingness to support the bill passed by the Senate with appropriate "safe harbor" language, even though it did not include certain provisions that I favor—such as enhanced provisions with respect to joint and several liability, aider and abettor liability, and statute of limitations.

I am not, however, willing to sign legislation that will have the effect of closing the courthouse door on investors who have legitimate claims. Those who are the victims of fraud should have recourse in our courts. Unfortunately, changes made in this bill during conference could well prevent that.

This country is blessed by strong and vibrant markets and I believe that they function best when corporations can raise capital by providing investors with their best good-faith assessment of future prospects, without fear of costly, unwarranted litigation. But I also know that our markets are as strong and effective as they are because they operate—and are seen to operate—with integrity. I believe that this bill, as modified in conference, could erode this crucial basis of our markets' strength.

Specifically, I object to the following elements of this bill. First, I believe that the pleading requirement of the Conference Report with regard to a defendant's state of mind impose an unacceptable procedural hurdle to meritorious claims being heard in Federal courts. I am prepared to support the high pleading standard of the U.S. Court of Appeals for the Second Circuit—the highest pleading standard of any Federal circuit court. But the conferees make crystal clear in the Statement of Managers their intent to raise the standard even beyond that level. I am not prepared to accept that.

The conferees deleted an amendment offered by Senator Specter and adopted by the Senate that specifically incorporated Second Circuit case law with respect to pleading a claim of fraud. Then they specifically indicated that they were not adopting Second Circuit case law but instead intended to "strengthen" the existing pleading requirements of the Second Circuit. All this shows that the conferees meant to erect a higher barrier to bringing suit than any now existing—one so high that even the most aggrieved investors with the most painful losses may get tossed out of court before they have a chance to prove their case.

Second, while I support the language of the Conference Report providing a "safe harbor" for companies that include meaningful cautionary statements in their projections of earnings, the Statement of Managers—which will be used by courts as a guide to the intent of the Congress with regard to the meaning of the bill—attempts to weaken the cautionary language that the bill itself requires. Once again, the end result may be that investors find their legitimate claims unfairly dismissed.

Third, the Conference Report's Rule 11 provision lacks balance, treating plaintiffs more harshly than defendants in a manner that comes too close to the "loser pays" standard I oppose.

I want to sign a good bill and I am prepared to do exactly that if the Congress will make the following changes to this legislation: first, adopt the Second Circuit pleading standards and reinsert the Specter amendment into the bill. I will support a bill that submits all plaintiffs to the tough pleading standards of the Second Circuit, but I am not prepared to go beyond that. Second, remove the language in the Statement of Managers that waters down the nature of the cautionary language that must be included to make the safe harbor safe. Third, restore the Rule 11 language to that of the Senate bill.

While it is true that innocent companies are hurt by frivolous lawsuits and that valuable information may be withheld from investors when companies fear the risk of such suits, it is also true that there are innocent investors who are defrauded and who are able to recover their losses only because they can go to court. It is appropriate to change the law to ensure that companies can make reasonable statements and future projections without getting sued every time earnings turn out to be lower than expected or stock prices drop. But it is not appropriate to erect procedural barriers that will keep wrongly injured persons from having their day in court.

I ask the Congress to send me a bill promptly that will put an end to litigation abuses while still protecting the legitimate rights of ordinary investors. I will sign such a bill as soon as it reaches my desk.[38]

---

§ 8.12 Extraterritorial Reach of Section 10(b)

Morrison v. National Australia Bank Ltd.

United States Supreme Court

561 U.S. 247, 130 S. Ct. 2869, 177 L. Ed. 2d 535 (2010)

Justice Scalia delivered the opinion of the Court.

We decide whether § 10(b) of the Securities Exchange Act of 1934 provides a cause of action to foreign plaintiffs suing foreign and American defendants for misconduct in connection with securities traded on foreign exchanges.

I

Respondent National Australia Bank Limited (National) was, during the relevant time, the largest bank in Australia. Its Ordinary Shares—what in America would be called "common stock"—are traded on the Australian Stock Exchange Limited and on other foreign securities exchanges, but not on any exchange in the United States. There are listed on the New York Stock Exchange, however, National's American Depositary Receipts (ADRs), which represent the right to receive a specified number of National's Ordinary Shares.

---

[38]. For further analysis of the class action "reform" provisions of the Private Securities Litigation Reform Act as well as related issues, *see, e.g.,* Branson, *Running the Gauntlet: A Description of the Arduous, and Now Often Fatal, Journey for Plaintiffs in Federal Securities Law Actions*, 65 U. Cin. L. Rev. 3 (1996); Carleton, Weisbach & Weiss, *Securities Class Action Lawsuits: A Descriptive Study*, 38 Ariz. L. Rev. 491 (1996); Fallone, *Section 10(b) and the Vagaries of Federal Common Law: The Merits of Codifying the Private Cause of Action Under a Structuralist Approach*, 1997 U. Ill. L. Rev. 71; Thomas & Martin, *Using State Inspection Statutes for Discovery in Federal Securities Fraud Actions*, 77 B.U. L. Rev. 69 (1997); Symposium, 51 Bus. Law. No. 4 (1996); Symposium, 106 Colum. L. Rev. No 7 (2006); Symposium, 33 San Diego L. Rev. No. 3 (1996); *Symposium*, 24 Sec. Reg. L.J. No. 2 (1996).

The complaint alleges the following facts, which we accept as true. In February 1998, National bought respondent HomeSide Lending, Inc., a mortgage servicing company headquartered in Florida. HomeSide's business was to receive fees for servicing mortgages (essentially the administrative tasks associated with collecting mortgage payments). The rights to receive those fees, so-called mortgage-servicing rights, can provide a valuable income stream. How valuable each of the rights is depends, in part, on the likelihood that the mortgage to which it applies will be fully repaid before it is due, terminating the need for servicing. HomeSide calculated the present value of its mortgage-servicing rights by using valuation models designed to take this likelihood into account. It recorded the value of its assets, and the numbers appeared in National's financial statements.

From 1998 until 2001, National's annual reports and other public documents touted the success of HomeSide's business, and respondents Frank Cicutto (National's managing director and chief executive officer), Kevin Race (HomeSide's chief operating officer), and Hugh Harris (HomeSide's chief executive officer) did the same in public statements. But on July 5, 2001, National announced that it was writing down the value of HomeSide's assets by $450 million; and then again on September 2, by another $1.75 billion. The prices of both Ordinary Shares and ADRs slumped. After downplaying the July write-down, National explained the September write-down as the result of a failure to anticipate the lowering of prevailing interest rates (lower interest rates lead to more refinancings, *i.e.*, more early repayments of mortgages), other mistaken assumptions in the financial models, and the loss of goodwill. According to the complaint, however, HomeSide, Race, Harris, and another HomeSide senior executive who is also a respondent here had manipulated HomeSide's financial models to make the rates of early repayment unrealistically low in order to cause the mortgage-servicing rights to appear more valuable than they really were. The complaint also alleges that National and Cicutto were aware of this deception by July 2000, but did nothing about it.

As relevant here, petitioners Russell Leslie Owen and Brian and Geraldine Silverlock, all Australians, purchased National's Ordinary Shares in 2000 and 2001, before the write-downs.[39] They sued National, HomeSide, Cicutto, and the three HomeSide executives in the United States District Court for the Southern District of New York for alleged violations of §§ 10(b) and 20(a) [control person liability] of the Securities and Exchange Act of 1934. . . . They sought to represent a class of foreign purchasers of National's Ordinary Shares during a specified period up to the September write-down.

---

[39]. Robert Morrison, an American investor in National's ADRs, also brought suit, but his claims were dismissed by the District Court because he failed to allege damages. *In re National Australia Bank Securities Litigation*, No. 03 Civ. 6537(BSJ), 2006 WL 3844465, *9 (S.D.N.Y., Oct. 25, 2006). Petitioners did not appeal that decision, 547 F. 3d 167, 170, n. 3 (C.A.2 2008) (case below), and it is not before us. Inexplicably, Morrison continued to be listed as a petitioner in the Court of Appeals and here.

Respondents moved to dismiss for lack of subject-matter jurisdiction under Federal Rule of Civil Procedure 12(b)(1) and for failure to state a claim under Rule 12(b)(6). The District Court granted the motion on the former ground, finding no jurisdiction because the acts in this country were, "at most, a link in the chain of an alleged overall securities fraud scheme that culminated abroad. . . ." The Court of Appeals for the Second Circuit affirmed on similar grounds. The acts performed in the United States did not "compris[e] the heart of the alleged fraud." 547 F.3d at 175–176. We granted certiorari. . . .

II

Before addressing the question presented, we must correct a threshold error in the Second Circuit's analysis. It considered the extraterritorial reach of § 10(b) to raise a question of subject-matter jurisdiction, wherefore it affirmed the District Court's dismissal under Rule 12(b)(1). See 547 F.3d, at 177. In this regard it was following Circuit precedent, see *Schoenbaum v. Firstbrook*, 405 F.2d 200, 208, modified on other grounds en banc, 405 F.2d 215 (1968). The Second Circuit is hardly alone in taking this position, see, *e.g.*, *In re CP Ships Ltd. Securities Litigation*, 578 F.3d 1306, 1313 (C.A.11 2009); *Continental Grain (Australia) PTY. Ltd. v. Pacific Oilseeds, Inc.*, 592 F.2d 409, 421 (C.A.8 1979).

But to ask what conduct § 10(b) reaches is to ask what conduct § 10(b) prohibits, which is a *merits question*. Subject-matter jurisdiction, by contrast, "refers to a tribunal's ' "power to hear a case." ' " . . . It presents an issue quite separate from the question whether the allegations the plaintiff makes entitle him to relief. . . . The District Court here had jurisdiction under 15 U.S.C. § 78aa[40] to adjudicate the question whether § 10(b) applies to National's conduct.

In view of this error, which the parties do not dispute, petitioners ask us to remand. We think that unnecessary. Since nothing in the analysis of the courts below turned on the mistake, a remand would only require a new Rule 12(b)(6) label for the same Rule 12(b)(1) conclusion. As we have done before in situations like this, . . . we proceed to address whether petitioners' allegations state a claim.

III

A

It is a "longstanding principle of American law 'that legislation of Congress, unless a contrary intent appears, is meant to apply only within the territorial jurisdiction of the United States.'" . . . . This principle represents a canon of construction, or a presumption about a statute's meaning, rather than a limit upon Congress's power to legislate. . . . It rests on the perception that Congress ordinarily legislates with

---

[40]. Section 78aa provides:

AThe district courts of the United States . . . shall have exclusive jurisdiction of violations of [the Exchange Act] or the rules and regulations thereunder, and of all suits in equity and actions at law brought to enforce any liability or duty created by [the Exchange Act] or the rules and regulations thereunder."

respect to domestic, not foreign matters. Thus, "unless there is the affirmative intention of the Congress clearly expressed" to give a statute extraterritorial effect, "we must presume it is primarily concerned with domestic conditions." . . . The canon or presumption applies regardless of whether there is a risk of conflict between the American statute and a foreign law. . . . When a statute gives no clear indication of an extraterritorial application, it has none.

Despite this principle of interpretation, long and often recited in our opinions, the Second Circuit believed that, because the Exchange Act is silent as to the extraterritorial application of § 10(b), it was left to the court to "discern" whether Congress would have wanted the statute to apply. See 547 F.3d, at 170 (internal quotation marks omitted). This disregard of the presumption against extraterritoriality did not originate with the Court of Appeals panel in this case. It has been repeated over many decades by various courts of appeals in determining the application of the Exchange Act, and § 10(b) in particular, to fraudulent schemes that involve conduct and effects abroad. That has produced a collection of tests for divining what Congress would have wanted, complex in formulation and unpredictable in application.

As of 1967, district courts at least in the Southern District of New York had consistently concluded that, by reason of the presumption against extraterritoriality, § 10(b) did not apply when the stock transactions underlying the violation occurred abroad. See *Schoenbaum v. Firstbrook*, 268 F. Supp. 385, 392 (1967) (citing *Ferraoli v. Cantor*, CCH Fed. Sec. L. Rep. ¶ 91615 (S.D.N.Y. 1965) and *Kook v. Crang*, 182 F. Supp. 388, 390 (S.D.N.Y. 1960)). *Schoenbaum* involved the sale in Canada of the treasury shares of a Canadian corporation whose publicly traded shares (but not, of course, its treasury shares) were listed on both the American Stock Exchange and the Toronto Stock Exchange. Invoking the presumption against extraterritoriality, the court held that § 10(b) was inapplicable (though it incorrectly viewed the defect as jurisdictional). The decision in *Schoenbaum* was reversed, however, by a Second Circuit opinion which held that "neither the usual presumption against extraterritorial application of legislation nor the specific language of [§] 30(b) show Congressional intent to preclude application of the Exchange Act to transactions regarding stocks traded in the United States which are effected outside the United States. . . ." *Schoenbaum*, 405 F.2d, at 206. It sufficed to apply § 10(b) that, although the transaction in treasury shares took place in Canada, they affected the value of the common shares publicly traded in the United States. Application of § 10(b), the Second Circuit found, was "necessary to protect American investors," *id.*, at 206.

The Second Circuit took another step with *Leasco Data Processing Equip. Corp. v. Maxwell*, 468 F.2d 1326 (1972), which involved an American company that had been fraudulently induced to buy securities in England. There, unlike in *Schoenbaum*, some of the deceptive conduct had occurred in the United States but the corporation whose securities were traded (abroad) was not listed on any domestic exchange. *Leasco* said that the presumption against extraterritoriality applies only to matters over which the United States would not have prescriptive jurisdiction to regulate the deceptive conduct in this country, the language of the Act could be read to cover that conduct, and the court concluded that "if Congress had thought about the point," it would have wanted § 10(b) to apply. *Id.*, at 1334-1337.

With *Schoenbaum* and *Leasco* on the books, the Second Circuit had excised the presumption against extraterritoriality from the jurisprudence of § 10(b) and replaced it with the inquiry whether it would be reasonable (and hence what Congress would have wanted) to apply the statute to a given situation. As long as there was prescriptive jurisdiction to regulate, the Second Circuit explained, whether to apply § 10(b) even to "predominately foreign" transactions became a matter of whether a court thought Congress "wished the precious resources of United States courts and law enforcement agencies to be devoted to them rather than leave the problem to foreign countries." *Bersch v. Drexel Firestone, Inc.*, 519 F.2d 974, 985 (1975); see also *IIT v. Vencap, Ltd.*, 519 F.2d 1001, 1017–1018 (C.A.2 1975).

The Second Circuit had thus established that application of § 10(b) could be premised upon either some effect on American securities markets or investors (*Schoenbaum*) or significant conduct in the United States (*Leasco*). It later formalized these two applications into (1) an "effects test," "whether the wrongful conduct had a substantial effect in the United States or upon United States citizens," and (2) a "conduct test," "whether the wrongful conduct occurred in the United States." *SEC v. Berger*, 322 F.3d 187, 192–193 (C.A.2 2003). These became the north star of the Second Circuit's § 10(b) jurisprudence, pointing the way to what Congress would have wished. Indeed, the Second Circuit declined to keep its two tests distinct on the ground that "an admixture or combination of the two often gives a better picture of whether there is sufficient United States involvement to justify the exercise of jurisdiction by an American court." *Itoba Ltd. v. Lep Group PLC*, 54 F.3d 118, 122 (1995). The Second Circuit never put forward a textual or even extratextual basis for these tests. As early as *Bersch*, it confessed that "if we were asked to point to language in the statutes, or even in the legislative history, that compelled these conclusions, we would be unable to respond," 519 F.2d, at 993.

As they developed, these tests were not easy to administer. The conduct test was held to apply differently depending on whether the harmed investors were Americans or foreigners: When the alleged damages consisted of losses to American investors abroad, it was enough that acts "of material importance" performed in the United States "significantly contributed" to that result; whereas those acts must have "directly caused" the result when losses to foreigners abroad were at issue. See *Bersch*, 519 F.2d. at 993. And "merely preparatory activities in the United States" did not suffice "to trigger application of the securities laws for injury to foreigners located abroad." *Id.*, at 992. This required the court to distinguish between mere preparation and using the United States as a "base" for fraudulent activities in other countries. *Vencap*, [519 F.2d] at 1017–1018. But merely satisfying the conduct test was sometimes insufficient without "'some additional factor tilting the scales'" in favor of the application of American law. *Interbrew v. Edperbrascan Corp.*, 23 F. Supp. 2d 425, 432 (S.D.N.Y. 1998) (quoting *Europe & Overseas Commodity Traders, S.A. v. Banque Paribas London*, 147 F.3d 118, 129 (C.A.2 1998)). District courts have noted the difficulty of applying such vague formulations. See, *e.g., In Alstom SA*, 406 F. Supp. 2d 346, 366–385 (S.D.N.Y. 2005). There is no more damning indictment of the "conduct" and "effects" tests than the Second Circuit's own declaration that "the presence or absence of any single factor which was considered significant in other cases . . . is not necessarily dispositive in future cases." *IIT v. Cornfeld*, 619 F.2d 909, 918 (1980). . . .

Other Circuits embraced the Second Circuit's approach, though not its precise application. Like the Second Circuit, they described their decisions regarding the exterritorial application of § 10(b) as essentially resolving matters of policy. See, *e.g., SEC v. Kasser*, 548 F.2d 109, 116 (C.A.3 1977); *Continental Grain*, 592 F.2d, at 421–422; *Gruenthal GmbH v. Hotz*, 712 F.2d 421, 424–425 (C.A.9 1983); *Kauthar SDN BHD v. Sternberg*, 149 F.3d 659, 667 (C.A.7 1998). While applying the same fundamental methodology of balancing interests and arriving at what seemed the best policy, they produced a proliferation of vaguely related variations on the "conduct" and "effects" tests. As described in a leading Seventh Circuit opinion: "Although the circuits . . . seem to agree that there are some transnational situations to which the antifraud provisions of the securities laws are applicable, agreement appears to end at that point." . . .

At least one Court of Appeals has criticized this line of cases and the interpretive assumption that underlies it. In *Zoelsch v. Arthur Andersen & Co.*, 824 F.2d 27, 32 (1987) (Bork, J.), the District of Columbia Circuit observed that rather than courts' "divining what 'Congress would have wished' if it had addressed the problem[, a] more natural inquiry might be what jurisdiction Congress in fact thought about and conferred." Although tempted to apply the presumption against extraterritoriality and be done with it, see *id.*, at 31-32, that court deferred to the Second Circuit because of its "preeminence in the field of securities law" . . .

Commentators have criticized the unpredictable and inconsistent application of § 10(b) to transnational cases. . . . Some have challenged the premise underlying the Courts of Appeals' approach, namely that Congress did not consider the extraterritorial application of § 10(b) (thereby leaving it open to the courts, supposedly, to determine what Congress would have wanted). See, *e.g.,* Sachs, The International Reach of Rule 10b-5: The Myth of Congressional Silence, 28 Colum. J. Transnat'l. 677 (1990) (arguing that Congress considered, but rejected, applying the Exchange Act to transactions abroad). Others, more fundamentally, have noted that using congressional silence as a justification for judge-made rules violates the traditional principle that silence means no extraterritorial application. . . .

The criticisms seem to us justified. The results of judicial-speculation-made-law — divining what Congress would have wanted if it had thought of the situation before the court — demonstrate the wisdom of the presumption against extraterritoriality. Rather than guess anew in each case, we apply the presumption in all cases, preserving a stable background against which Congress can legislate with predictable effects.

B

Rule 10b-5, the regulation under which petitioners have brought suit, was promulgated under § 10(b), and "does not extend beyond conduct encompassed by § 10(b)'s prohibition." . . . Therefore, if § 10(b) is not extraterritorial, neither is Rule 10b-5. On its face, § 10(b) contains nothing to suggest it applies abroad:

> "It shall be unlawful for any person, directly or indirectly, by the use of any means or instrumentality of interstate commerce or of the mails, or of any facility of any national securities exchange . . . [t]o use or employ, in connection with the purchase or sale of any securities registered on a national securities exchange or any security not so registered, . . . any manipulative or deceptive devise or contrivance in contravention of such rules and regulations as the [Securities and Exchange] Commission may prescribe. . . ."

Petitioners and the Solicitor General contend, however, that three things indicate that § 10(b) or the Exchange Act in general has at least some extraterritorial application.

First, they point to the definition of "interstate commerce," a term used in § 10(b), which includes "trade, commerce, transportation, or communication . . . between any foreign country and any State." 15 U.S.C. § 78c(a)(17). But "we have repeatedly held that even statutes that contain broad language in their definitions of 'commerce' that expressly refer to '*foreign* commerce' do not apply abroad." *Aramco*, 499 U.S., at 251. . . . The general reference to foreign commerce in the definition of "interstate commerce" does not defeat the presumption against extraterritoriality.

Petitioners and the Solicitor General next point out that Congress, in describing the purposes of the Exchange Act, observed that the "prices established and offered in such transactions are generally disseminated and quoted throughout the United States and foreign countries." 15 U.S.C. § 78b(2). The antecedent of "such transaction," however, is found in the first sentence of the section, which declares that "transactions in securities as commonly conducted upon securities exchanges and over-the-counter markets are affected with a national public interest." § 78b. Nothing suggests that this *national* public interest pertains to transactions conducted upon *foreign* exchanges and markets. The fleeting reference to the dissemination and quotation abroad of the prices of securities traded in domestic exchanges and markets cannot overcome the presumption against extraterritoriality.

Finally, there is § 30(b) of the Exchange Act, 15 U.S.C. § 78dd(b), which *does* mention the Act's extraterritorial application: "The provisions of [the Exchange Act] or of any rule or regulation thereunder shall not apply to any person insofar as he transacts a business in securities without the jurisdiction of the United States," unless he does so in violation of regulations promulgated by the Securities and Exchange Commission "to prevent . . . evasion of [the Act]." (The parties have pointed us to no regulation promulgated pursuant to § 30(b).) The Solicitor General argues that "[this] exemption would have no function if the Act did not apply in the first instance to securities transactions that occur abroad." . . .

We are not convinced. In the first place, it would be odd for Congress to indicate the extraterritorial application of the whole Exchange Act by means of a provision imposing a condition precedent to its application abroad. And if the whole Act applied abroad, why would the Commission's enabling regulations be limited to those preventing "evasion" of the Act, rather than all those preventing "violation"? The provision seems to us directed at actions abroad that might conceal a domestic violation, or might cause what would otherwise be a domestic violation to escape on a technicality. At most, the Solicitor General's proposed inference is possible; but possible interpretations of statutory language do not override the presumption against extraterritoriality.

The Solicitor General also fails to account for § 30(a), which reads in relevant part as follows:

> "It shall be unlawful for any broker or dealer . . . to make use of the mails or of any means or instrumentality of interstate commerce for the purpose of effecting on an exchange not within or subject to the jurisdiction of the United States, any transaction in any security the issuer of which is a resident of, or is organized under the laws of, or has its principal place of business in, a place within or subject to the jurisdiction of the United States, in contravention of such rules and regulations as the Commission may prescribe. . . ."

Subsection 30(a) contains what § 10(b) lacks: a clear statement of extraterritorial effect. Its explicit provision for a specific extraterritorial application would be quite superfluous if the rest of the Exchange Act already applied to transactions on foreign exchanges — and its limitation of that application to securities of domestic issuers would be inoperative. Even if that were not true, when a statute provides for some extraterritorial application, the presumption against extraterritoriality operates to limit that provision to its terms. See *Microsoft Corp. v. AT&T Corp.*, 550 U.S. 437, 455–456 (2007). No one claims that § 30(a) applies here.

The concurrence claims we have impermissibly narrowed the inquiry in evaluating whether a statute applies abroad. . . . But we do not say, as the concurrence seems to think, that the presumption against extraterritoriality is a "clear statement rule," if by that is meant a requirement that a statute say "this law applies abroad." Assuredly context can be consulted as well. But whatever sources of statutory meaning one consults to give "the most faithful reading" of the text, there is no clear indication of extraterritoriality here. The concurrence does not even try to refute that conclusion, but merely puts forward the same (at best) uncertain indications relied upon by petitioners and the Solicitor General. . . . [T]hose uncertain indications do not suffice.

In short, there is no affirmative indication in the Exchange Act that § 10(b) applies extraterritorially, and we therefore conclude that it does not.

IV

A

Petitioners argue that the conclusion that § 10(b) does not apply extraterritorially does not resolve this case. They contend that they seek no more than domestic application anyway, since Florida is where HomeSide and its senior executives engaged in the deceptive conduct of manipulating HomeSide's financial models; their complaint also alleged that Race and Hughes made misleading public statements there. This is less an answer to the presumption against extraterritorial application than it is an assertion—a quite valid assertion—that that presumption here (as often) is not self-evidently dispositive, but its application requires further analysis. For it is a rare case of prohibited extraterritorial application that lacks *all* contact with the territory of the United States. But the presumption against extraterritorial application would be a craven watchdog indeed if it retreated to its kennel whenever *some* domestic activity is involved in the case. The concurrence seems to imagine just such a timid sentinel, but our cases are to the contrary. . . .

Applying the same mode of analysis here, we think that the focus of the Exchange Act is not upon the place where the deception originated, but upon purchases and sales of securities in the United States. Section 10(b) does not punish deceptive conduct, but only deceptive conduct "in connection with the purchase or sale of any security registered on a national securities exchange or any security not so registered." . . . Those purchase-and-sale transactions are the objects of the statute's solicitude. It is those transactions that the statute seeks to "regulate" . . . ; it is parties or prospective parties to those transactions that the statute seeks to "protec[t]" . . . And it is in our view only *transactions in securities listed on domestic exchanges, and domestic transactions in other securities, to which § 10(b) applies.* [emphasis supplied]

The primacy of the domestic exchange is suggested by the very prologue of the Exchange Act, which sets forth as its object "[t]o provide for the regulation of securities exchanges . . . operating in interstate and foreign commerce and through the mails, to prevent inequitable and unfair practices on such exchanges. . . ." 48 Stat. 881. We know of no one who thought that the Act was intended to "regulat[e]" *foreign* securities exchanges—or indeed who even believed that under established principles of international law Congress had the power to do so. The [Exchange] Act's registration requirements apply only to securities listed on national securities exchanges.

. . . .

Finally, we reject the notion that the Exchange Act reaches conduct in this country affecting exchanges or transactions abroad for the same reason that *Aramco* [499 U.S. 244 (1991)] rejected overseas application of Title VII to all domestically concluded employment contracts or all employment contracts with American employers: The probability of incompatibility with the applicable laws of other countries is so obvious that if Congress intended such foreign application "it would have addressed the subject of conflicts with foreign laws and procedures." 499 U.S., at 256. Like the United States, foreign countries regulate their domestic securities exchanges and securities transactions occurring within their territorial jurisdiction. And the regulation of other countries often differs from ours as to what constitutes fraud, what disclosures must be made, what damages are recoverable, what discovery is available in litigation, what individual actions may be joined in a single suit, what attorney's fees are recoverable, and many other matters. See, *e.g.,* Brief for United Kingdom of Britain and Northern Ireland as *Amicus Curiae* 16–21. The Commonwealth of Australia, the United Kingdom of Great Britain and Northern Ireland, and the Republic of France have filed *amicus* briefs in this case. So have (separately or jointly) such international and foreign organizations as the International Chamber of Commerce, the Swiss Bankers Association, the Federation of German Industries, the French Business Confederation, the Institute of International Bankers, the European Banking Federation, [and] the Australian Bankers' Association. . . . They all complain of the interference with foreign securities regulation that application of § 10(b) abroad would produce, and urge the adoption of a clear test that will avoid that consequence. *The transactional test we have adopted—whether the purchase or sale is made in the United States, or involves a security listed on a domestic exchange—meets that requirement.* [emphasis supplied]

. . . .

Section 10(b) reaches the use of a manipulative or deceptive device or contrivance only in connection with the purchase or sale of a security listed on an American stock exchange, and the purchase or sale of any other security in the United States. This case involves no securities listed on a domestic exchange, and all aspects of the purchases complained of by those petitioners who still have live claims occurred outside the United States. Petitioners have therefore failed to state a claim on which relief can be granted. We affirm the dismissal of petitioners' complaint on this ground.

It is so ordered.

Justice Breyer, concurring in part and concurring in the judgment.

Section 10(b) of the Securities Exchange Act of 1934 applies to fraud "in connection with" two categories of transactions: (1) "the purchase or sale of any security registered on a national securities exchange" or (2) "the purchase or sale of . . . any security not so registered." 15 U.S.C. § 78j(b). In this case, the purchased securities are listed only on a few foreign exchanges, none of which has registered with the Securities and Exchange Commission as a "national securities exchange." The first category therefore does not apply. Further, the relevant purchases of these unregistered securities took place entirely in Australia and involved only Australian investors. And in accordance with the presumption against extraterritoriality, I do not read the second category to include such transactions. Thus, while state law or other federal fraud statutes, see, *e.g.,* 18 U.S.C. § 1341 (mail fraud), § 1343 (wire fraud), may apply to the fraudulent activity alleged here to have occurred in the United States, I believe that § 10(b) does not. This case does not require us to consider other circumstances.

To the extent the Court's opinion is consistent with these views, I join it.

Justice Stevens, with whom Justice Ginsburg joins, concurring in the judgment.

While I agree that petitioners have failed to state a claim on which relief can be granted, my reasoning differs from the Court's. I would adhere to the general approach that has been the law in the Second Circuit, and most of the rest of the country, for nearly four decades.

I

Today the Court announces a new "transactional test," for defining the reach of § 10(b) of the Securities Exchange Act of 1934 and SEC Rule 10b-5. . . . Henceforth, those provisions will extend only to "transactions in securities listed on domestic exchanges . . . and domestic transactions in other securities" . . . If one confines one's gaze to the statutory text, the Court's conclusion is a plausible one. But the federal courts have been construing § 10(b) in a different manner for a long time, and the Court's textual analysis is not nearly so compelling, in my view, as to warrant the abandonment of their doctrine.

The text and history of § 10(b) are famously opaque on the question of when, exactly, transnational securities frauds fall within the statute's compass. As those types of frauds became more common in the latter half of the 20th century, the federal courts were increasingly called upon to wrestle with that question. The Court of Appeals for the Second Circuit, located in the Nation's financial center, led the effort. Beginning in earnest with *Schoenbaum v. Firstbrook*, 405 F.2d 200, rev'd on rehearing on other grounds, 405 F.2d 215 (1968) (en banc), that court strove, over an extended series of cases, to "discern" under what circumstances "Congress would have wished the precious resources of the United States courts and law enforcement agencies to be devoted to [transnational] transactions," 547 F.3d 167, 170 (2008) (internal quotation marks omitted). Relying on opinions by Judge Henry Friendly, the Second Circuit eventually settled on a conduct-and-effects test. This test asks "(1) whether the wrongful conduct occurred in the United States, and (2) whether the wrongful conduct had a substantial effect in the United States or upon United States citizens." *Id.*, at 171. Numerous cases flesh out the proper application of each prong.

The Second Circuit's test became the "north star" of § 10(b) jurisprudence, not just regionally but nationally as well. With minor variations, other courts converged on the same basic approach. See Brief for United States as *Amicus Curiae* 15 ("The courts have uniformly agreed that Section 10(b) can apply to a transnational securities fraud either when fraudulent conduct has effects in the United States or when sufficient conduct relevant to the fraud occurs in the United States"); see also 1 Restatement (Third) of Foreign Relations Law of the United States § 416 (1986) (setting forth conduct-and-effects test). Neither Congress nor the Securities Exchange Commission (Commission) acted to change the law. To the contrary, the Commission largely adopted the Second Circuit's position in its own adjudications.

In light of this history, the Court's critique of the decision below for applying "judge-made rules" is quite misplaced. This entire area of law is replete with judge-made rules, which give concrete meaning to Congress' general commands. . . .

The development of § 10(b) law was hardly an instance of judicial usurpation. Congress invited an expansive role for judicial elaboration when it crafted such an open-ended statute in 1934. And both Congress and the Commission subsequently affirmed that role when they left intact the relevant statutory and regulatory language, respectively, throughout all the years that followed. . . .

. . . .

Thus, while the Court devotes a considerable amount of attention to the development of the case law, it draws the wrong conclusions. The Second Circuit refined its test over several decades and dozens of cases, with the tacit approval of Congress and the Commission and with the general assent of its sister Circuits. That history is a reason we should give additional weight to the Second Circuit's "judge-made" doctrine, not a reason to denigrate it. "The longstanding acceptance by the courts, coupled with Congress' failure to reject [its] reasonable interpretation of the wording of § 10(b), . . . argues significantly in favor of acceptance of the [Second Circuit] rule by this Court." *Blue Chip*, 421 U.S., at 733.

II

. . . .

. . . The text of the Exchange Act indicates that § 10(b) extends to at least some activities with an international component, but again, it is not pellucid as to which ones. The Second Circuit draws the line as follows: § 10(b) extends to transnational frauds "only when substantial acts in furtherance of the fraud were committed within the United States," *SEC v. Berger*, 322 R. 3d 187, 193 (C.A.2 2003), or when the fraud was "'intended to produce'" and did produce "'detrimental effects within'" the United States, *Schoenbaum*, 405 F.2d, at 206.

This approach is consistent with the understanding shared by most scholars that Congress, in passing the Exchange Act, "expected U.S. securities laws to apply to certain international transactions or conduct." Buxbaum, Multinational Class Actions Under Federal Securities Law: Managing Jurisdictional Conflict, 46 Colum. J. Transnat'l L. 14, 19 (2007). . . . It is also consistent with the traditional understanding, regnant in the 1930's as it is now, that the presumption against extraterritoriality does not apply "when the conduct [at issue] occurs within the United States," and has lesser force when "the failure to extend the scope of the statute to a foreign setting will result in adverse effects within the United States" . . . And it strikes a reasonable balance between the goals of "preventing the export of fraud from America," protecting shareholders, enhancing investor confidence, and deterring corporate misconduct, on the one hand, and conserving United States resources and limiting conflict with foreign law, on the other. . . . Thus, while § 10(b) may not give any "clear indication" on its face as to how it should apply to transnational securities frauds, it does give strong clues that it should cover at least some of them. . . . And in my view, the Second Circuit has done the best job of discerning what sorts of transnational frauds Congress meant in 1934—and still means today—to regulate. I do not take issue with the Court for beginning its inquiry with the statutory text, rather than the doctrine in the Courts of Appeals. I take issue with the Court for beginning *and ending* its inquiry with the statutory text, when the text does not speak with geographic precision, and for dismissing the long pedigree of, and the persuasive account of congressional intent embodied in, the Second Circuit's rule.

Repudiating the Second Circuit's approach in its entirety, the Court establishes a novel rule that will foreclose private parties from bringing § 10(b) actions whenever the relevant securities were purchased or sold abroad and are not listed on a domestic exchange. . . . And while the clarity and simplicity of the Court's test may have some salutary consequences, like all bright-line rules it also has drawbacks.

Imagine, for example, an American investor who buys shares in a company listed only on an overseas exchange. That company has a major American subsidiary with executives based in New York City; and it was in New York City that the executives masterminded and implemented a massive deception which artificially inflated the stock price—and which will, upon its disclosure, cause the price to plummet. Or, imagine that those same executives go knocking on doors in Manhattan and convince an unsophisticated retiree, on the basis of material misrepresentations, to invest her life savings in the company's doomed securities. Both of these investors would, under the Court's new test, be barred from seeking relief under § 10(b).

The oddity of that result should give pause. For in walling off such individuals from § 10(b), the Court narrows the provision's reach to a degree that would surprise and alarm generations of American investors—and, I am convinced, the Congress that passed the Exchange Act. Indeed, the Court's rule turns § 10(b) jurisprudence (and the presumption against extraterritoriality) on its head, by withdrawing the statute's application from cases in which there is *both* substantial wrongful conduct that occurred in the United States *and* a substantial injurious effect on United States markets and citizens.

III

. . . .

The Court elects to upend a significant area of securities law based on a plausible, but hardly decisive, construction of the statutory text. In so doing, it pays short shrift to the United States' interest in remedying frauds that transpire on American soil or harm American citizens, as well as to the accumulated wisdom and experience of the lower courts. I happen to agree with the result the Court reaches in this case. But "I respectfully dissent," once again, "from the Court's continuing campaign to render the private cause of action under § 10(b) toothless." *Stoneridge*, 552 U.S., at 175 (Stevens, J., dissenting).

SEC Extraterritorial Reach

Recognizing the devastating impact that the Supreme Court's decision in *Morrison* would have on government enforcement, in its enactment of the Dodd-Frank Wall Street Reform and Consumer Protection Act of 2010, Congress sought to nullify *Morrison's* severe impact in this context. With respect to the extraterritorial reach of the securities laws' antifraud provisions (such as § 17(a) of the Securities Act and § 10(b) of the Exchange Act), the pertinent provisions vest federal court jurisdiction in an action brought by the SEC or the Department of Justice that involves:

(1) conduct within the United States that constitutes significant steps in furtherance of the violation, even if the securities transaction occurs outside the United States and involves only foreign investors; or

(2) conduct occurring outside the United States that has a foreseeable substantial effect within the United States.

This formulation basically adopts in the government enforcement setting the "conduct" and the "effect" test that was embraced by the federal appellate courts prior to *Morrison,* as well as in the concurring opinion of Justice Stevens in *Morrison.* Nevertheless, because the Supreme Court's decision in *Morrison* focused on § 10(b)'s reach (or lack thereof), whether these provisions vesting federal court jurisdiction will be applied as Congress intended remains uncertain.

The following post-*Morrison* decision focuses on the question: At what point does a purchase or sale of securities occur with respect to securities not listed on a U.S. exchange for purposes of § 10(b)'s reach?

Absolute Activist Value Master Fund Limited v. Ficeto

United States Court of Appeals, Second Circuit

677 F.3d 60 (2d Cir. 2012)

. . . .

Domestic Purchases and Sales

1. The Meaning of a Domestic Transaction

While *Morrison* holds that § 10(b) can be applied to domestic purchases or sales, it provides little guidance as to what constitutes a domestic purchase or sale. To determine the meaning of a domestic purchase or sale, we first consider how these terms are defined in the Exchange Act. "The terms 'buy' and 'purchase' each include any contract to buy, purchase, or otherwise acquire." 15 U.S.C. § 78c(a)(13). Similarly, "[t]he terms 'sale' and 'sell' each include any contract to sell or otherwise dispose of." *Id.* § 78c(a)(14). While the Supreme Court has previously noted that these definitions "are for the most part unhelpful" because "they only declare generally that the terms 'purchase' and 'sale' shall include contracts to purchase or sell," . . . these definitions nonetheless suggest that the act of purchasing or selling securities is the act of entering into a binding contract to purchase or sell securities. Put another way, these definitions suggest that the "purchase" and "sale" take place when the parties become bound to effectuate the transaction.

Our decision in *Radiation Dynamics, Inc. v. Goldmuntz*, 464 F.2d 876 (2d Cir. 1972), also lends support to the notion that a securities transaction occurs when the parties incur irrevocable liability. In that case, we held that in the context of a civil trial brought pursuant to Rule 10b-5, the district court correctly instructed the jury that "the time of a 'purchase or sale' of securities within the meaning of Rule 10b-5 is to be determined as the time when the parties to the transaction are committed to one another." " 'Commitment' is a simple and direct way of designating the point at which, in the classic contractual sense, there was a meeting of the minds of the parties; it marks the point at which the parties obligated themselves to perform what they had agreed to perform even if the formal performance of their agreement is to be after a lapse of time." . . .

Given that the point at which the parties become irrevocably bound is used to determine the timing of a purchase and sale, we similarly hold that the point of irrevocable liability can be used to determine the locus of a securities purchase or sale. Thus, in order to adequately allege the existence of a domestic transaction, it is sufficient for a plaintiff to allege facts leading to the plausible inference that the parties incurred irrevocable liability within the United States: that is, that the purchaser incurred irrevocable liability within the United States to take and pay for a security, or that the seller incurred irrevocable liability within the United States to deliver a security. . . .

However, we do not believe this is the only way to locate a securities transaction. After all, a "sale" is ordinarily defined as "[t]he transfer of property or title for a price." Black's Law Dictionary 1454 (9th ed. 2009); see also U.C.C. § 2-106(1) ("A 'sale' consists in the passing of title from the seller to the buyer for a price."). Thus, a sale of securities can be understood to take place at the location in which title is transferred. Indeed, the Eleventh Circuit has held that, in order to survive a motion to dismiss premised on *Morrison*, it is sufficient for the plaintiff to allege that title to the shares was transferred within the United States. See *Quail Cruises Ship Mgmt. Ltd. v. Agencia de Viagens CVC Tur Limitada*, 645 F.3d 1307, 1310–11 (11th Cir. 2011) ("Given that the Supreme Court in *Morrison* deliberately established a bright-line test based exclusively on the location of the purchase or sale of the security, we cannot say at this stage in the proceedings that the alleged transfer of title to the shares in the United States lies beyond § 10(b)'s territorial reach."). *Accordingly, to sufficiently allege a domestic securities transaction in securities not listed on a domestic exchange, we hold that a plaintiff must allege facts suggesting that irrevocable liability was incurred or title was transferred within the United States.* [emphasis supplied]

. . . .

Note

Thus, under the "transactional test" adopted by the Supreme Court in *Morrison,* for § 10(b) to apply (at least in private actions), "the purchase or sale [must be] made in the United States, or [must] involve a security listed on a domestic exchange." 130 S. Ct. at 2886. For further discussion, *see* Steinberg & Flanagan, *Transnational Dealings—Morrison Continues to Make Waves,* 46 Int'l Law. 829 (2012).

Note that, irrespective of *Morrison,* other provisions of the federal securities laws may be invoked in certain situations. For example, § 18(a) of the Exchange Act provides an express private right of action based on a materially false or misleading statement contained in any document filed with the SEC pursuant to the Exchange Act (see § 9.05 *infra*). Hence, a material misrepresentation contained in a Form 10-K or Form 20-F should be actionable under § 18(a) even if the subject transaction (e.g., an investor's purchase of 5,000 shares of stock) took place on the London Stock Exchange.

A second example is § 17(a) of the Securities Act. This statute is a government enforcement provision and evidently does not provide a private right of action. Section 17(a) prohibits fraud or deceit in the offer or sale of securities (see § 9.03 *infra*). Pursuant to this statute, the SEC may bring enforcement action when illegal offers to sell are made in the United States, even if the sale of such securities occurs abroad. Thus, because § 17(a) encompasses both offers and sales, an offer made in this country (even when the sale is consummated abroad) is within § 17(a)'s coverage. *See, e.g., SEC v. Goldman Sachs & Co.,* 790 F. Supp. 2d 147, 165 (S.D.N.Y. 2011).

And, last, recall that in the Dodd-Frank Act of 2010, Congress expanded the SEC's extraterritorial scope to bring enforcement actions based on a formulation similar to the Second Circuit's conduct and effects test. Provided that this statute survives challenges to its validity (as it evidently is based on federal court jurisdiction rather than § 10(b)'s reach), the SEC's enforcement program with respect to combating transnational fraud should not be adversely impacted (at least to a material degree) by the Supreme Court's decision in *Morrison.*

Note that after *Morrison,* in private litigation involving alleged violations of § 10(b), numerous lawsuits have been dismissed that would have survived prior to that Supreme Court decision. *See, e.g., Plumbers Union Local No. 12 Pension Fund v. Swiss Reinsurance Co.,* 2010 U.S. Dist. LEXIS 105720 (S.D.N.Y. 2010) (although trade orders were electronically placed in United States, case dismissed due to the fact that company's stock was listed only on the SWX Swiss Exchange); *In re Alstom SA Securities Litigation,* 741 F. Supp. 2d 469 (S.D.N.Y. 2010) (even though defendant's stock was listed on the New York Stock Exchange, case dismissed because plaintiffs purchased their stock solely on a French stock exchange (the Premier Marche of Euronext Paris)); *Cornwell v. Credit Suisse Group,* 270 F.R.D. 145 (S.D.N.Y. 2010) (dismissing case where investors, although placing their orders from the United States, purchased securities traded on the Swiss Stock Exchange); *Pope Investments II, LLC v. Deheng Law Firm,*

[2012–2 Transfer Binder] Fed. Sec. L. Rep. (CCH) ¶ 96,976 (S.D.N.Y. 2012) (inducement to purchase securities in the United States made by defendant not sufficient to invoke § 10(b) when transaction occurred in China).

The case that follows illustrates this narrow view. It may well be that this narrow construction is erroneous based on language in the Supreme Court's 2016 decision, *RJR Nabisco, Inc. v. European Community*, 136 S. Ct. 2090, 2100 (2016): "In *Morrison* we addressed the question whether § 10(b) . . . applies to misrepresentations made in connection with the purchase or sale of securities traded *only* on foreign exchanges." (emphasis supplied).

City of Pontiac Policemen's and Firemen's Retirement System v. UBS AG

United States Court of Appeals, Second Circuit

752 F.3d 173 (2014)

José A. Cabranes, Circuit Judge:

In this appeal we consider, as a matter of first impression, whether the bar on extraterritorial application of the United States securities laws, as set forth in *Morrison v. National Australia Bank Ltd.*, 561 U.S. 247 (2010), precludes claims arising out of foreign-issued securities purchased on foreign exchanges, but cross-listed on a domestic exchange (the so-called "listing theory"). . . .

We conclude that . . . the Supreme Court's decision in *Morrison* precludes claims brought pursuant to the Securities Exchange Act of 1934 ("Exchange Act") by purchasers of shares of a foreign issuer on a foreign exchange, even if those shares were cross-listed on a United States exchange. . . .

Plaintiffs, a group of foreign and domestic institutional investors, bring this putative class action against UBS AG ("UBS") and a number of UBS officers and directors (together with UBS, "UBS Defendants"), alleging violations of §§ 10(b) and 20(a) of the Exchange Act in connection with the purchase of UBS "ordinary shares" between August 13, 2003 and February 23, 2009 (the "Class Period"). These shares were listed on foreign exchanges and the New York Stock Exchange ("NYSE"). . . .

. . . .

Viability Under Morrison v. National Australia Bank of Claims Based on Foreign Shares Purchased on a Foreign Exchange

Three foreign institutional investors — plaintiffs Union, IFM, and ATP — and one domestic investor — plaintiff OPEB — purchased their UBS (foreign-issued) ordinary shares on a foreign exchange. The District Court, relying on the Supreme Court's decision in *Morrison v. National Australia Bank,* dismissed these claims. We address the claims of the foreign and domestic plaintiffs separately.

1. *"Foreign Cubed" Claims*[41]

Morrison answered in the negative the question "whether [§ 10(b)] provides a cause of action to foreign plaintiffs suing foreign defendants for misconduct in connection with securities traded on foreign exchanges." It held instead that § 10(b) only provided a private cause of action arising out of "[1] transactions in securities listed on domestic exchanges, and [2] domestic transactions in other securities."

Plaintiffs argue that, by its express terms, the *Morrison* bar is limited to claims arising out of securities "*[not] listed* on a domestic exchange." Under plaintiffs' so-called "listing theory," the fact that the relevant shares were cross-listed on the NYSE brings them within the purview of Rule 10(b), under the first prong of *Morrison*—"transactions in securities listed on domestic exchanges." We conclude that, while this language, which appears in *Morrison* and its progeny, taken in isolation, supports plaintiffs' view, the "listing theory" is irreconcilable with *Morrison* read as a whole.

Morrison emphasized that "the focus of the Exchange Act is . . . upon *purchases and sales* of securities in the United States." As the District Court recognized, this evinces a concern with "the location of the securities *transaction* and not the location of an exchange where the security may be dually listed." *Morrison's* emphasis on "*transactions* in securities listed on domestic exchanges," makes clear that the focus of both prongs was domestic transactions of any kind, with the domestic listing acting as a proxy for a domestic transaction. Indeed, the Supreme Court explicitly rejected the notion that the "*national* public interest pertains to transactions conducted upon *foreign* exchanges and markets." Furthermore, in *Morrison,* although the Ordinary Shares at issue were not traded on any domestic exchange, the Court noted that "[t]here are listed on the [NYSE], however, [defendant]'s American Depositary Receipts (ADRs), which represent the right to receive a specified number of [its] Ordinary Shares." This did not affect the Court's analysis of the shares that were purchased on foreign exchanges.

Perhaps most tellingly, in rejecting this Circuit's "conduct and effects" test in favor of a bright-line rule, *Morrison* rejected our prior holding that " 'the Exchange Act [applies] to transactions regarding stocks traded in the United States which are effected outside the United States . . . .'"

In sum, *Morrison* does not support the application of § 10(b) of the Exchange Act to claims by a foreign purchaser of foreign-issued shares on a foreign exchange simply because those shares are also listed on a domestic exchange. Accordingly, we affirm the judgment of the District Court insofar as it dismissed the claims of Union, IFM, and ATP.

---

[41]. A so-called "foreign-cubed" action involves claims in which "(1) foreign plaintiffs [are] suing (2) a foreign issuer in an American court for violations of American securities laws based on securities transactions in (3) foreign countries." . . .

2. "Foreign Squared" Claims

Plaintiff OPEB is a U.S. entity that purchased some of its UBS shares on a foreign exchange by placing a so-called "buy order" in the United States, which was later executed on a Swiss exchange. In addition to advocating the "listing theory," OPEB argues that its purchase satisfies the second prong of *Morrison* because it constitutes a "purchase . . . of [a] security in the United States."

In our decision in *Absolute Activist Value Master Fund Ltd. v. Ficeto* ("*Absolute Activist*"), we explained that "[a] securities transaction is domestic [for purposes of *Morrison's* second prong] when the parties incur irrevocable liability to carry out the transaction within the United States or when title is passed within the United States.'" We must now decide— as an issue of first impression—whether the mere placement of a buy order in the United States for the purchase of foreign securities on a foreign exchange is sufficient to allege that a purchaser incurred irrevocable liability in the United States, such that the U.S. securities laws govern the purchase of those securities. We conclude that it is not.

Plaintiffs argue that "[w]hen a purchaser is a U.S. entity, 'irrevocable liability' is not incurred when the security is purchased on a foreign exchange [; rather it is incurred] in the U.S. where the buy order is placed." As an initial matter, we have made clear that "a purchaser's citizenship or residency does not affect where a transaction occurs." Accordingly, the fact that OPEB was a U.S. entity, does not affect whether the transaction was foreign or domestic. Nor does the allegation that OPEB placed a buy order in the United States that was then executed on a foreign exchange, standing alone, establish that OPEB incurred irrevocable liability in the United States.

Accordingly, we affirm the judgment of the District Court dismissing the claims of OPEB, a domestic purchaser, insofar as its claims were based on purchases of foreign shares on foreign exchanges.

. . . .

§ 8.13 Special Concepts of Fraud for Broker-Dealers

The area of broker-dealer regulation is a key component of securities law. As a consequence, Chapter 13 addresses this subject. Nonetheless, for purposes of introduction, broker-dealer concepts are discussed here.

In the § 10(b) context, as well as under other provisions of the securities laws, such as § 17(a) of the Securities Act, a number of principles have been developed to hold broker-dealers to a fairly strict standard of conduct. One such theory is the shingle theory, which posits that by hanging out its "shingle," a broker-dealer impliedly represents that its conduct and the behavior of its employees will be fair and will comport with professional norms. As the Second Circuit stated in *Hanly v. SEC*, 415 F.2d 589, 596–597 (2d Cir. 1969): "A securities dealer occupies a special relationship to the buyer of securities in that by his position he impliedly represents he has an adequate basis for the opinions he renders." One aspect of this duty, labeled the suitability theory, recognizes an implied representation by the broker that it will recommend only those securities suitable for each customer's investment objectives and economic status.[42]

A number of other implied representations have been recognized as coming within the shingle theory, including:

(1) An implied representation of fair pricing, including any markup or markdown;

(2) An implied representation that the broker-dealer will execute only authorized transactions for its customers;

(3) An implied representation to disclose any special consideration that influences the broker-dealer's recommendation;

(4) An implied representation to execute promptly customers' orders; and

(5) An implied representation that any recommendation made by a broker-dealer to a customer has a reasonable basis.[43]

One may inquire, however, whether aspects of the shingle theory still provide the basis for a § 10(b) action in light of the Supreme Court's holding in *Santa Fe* that deception or manipulation must be shown (see § 8.04). The following decision takes the position that aspects of the shingle theory are no longer viable.

Pross v. Baird Patrick & Co., Inc.

United States District Court, Southern District of New York

585 F. Supp. 1456 (1984)

CONNER, DISTRICT JUDGE.

Plaintiff Arnold Pross ("Pross") . . . commenced this action against his broker, Baird, Patrick & Co., Inc. ("Baird"), alleging violations of Securities and Exchange Commission ("SEC") Rule 10b-5.

. . . .

---

42. See M. Cane & P. Shub, Securities Arbitration: Law and Procedure 132–174 (1991); R. Janvey, Regulation of the Securities and Commodities Markets & 4.01 (1992); D. Lipton, Broker-Dealer Regulation § 3.07 (2012); N. Poser & J. Fanto, Broker-Dealer Law and Regulation (4th ed. 2015); Kerr, *Suitability Standards: A New Look at Economic Theory and Current SEC Disclosure Policy*, 16 Pac. L.J. 805 (1985); Ramirez, *The Professional Obligations of Securities Brokers Under Federal Law: An Antidote for Bubbles?*, 70 U. Cin. L. Rev. 527 (2002).

43. M. Steinberg & R. Ferrara, Securities Practice: Federal and State Enforcement § 2.17 (2d ed. 2001 & 2016–2017 Supp.).

In his complaint, Pross states that he had a nondiscretionary account with Baird. He alleges that during November and December of 1982, Baird made trades for that account in the stock of Nitron, Inc. ("Nitron"), without his prior consent and, indeed, at times contrary to his specific instructions. Pross further alleges that in making the trades, Baird failed "to disclose any facts to [Pross] concerning the corporation whose shares were being traded on his behalf," including the fact that Baird was "making a market" in Nitron stock, and that Baird engaged in the transactions for its own benefit.

In order to state a cognizable claim for fraud under Rule 10b-5, a plaintiff must allege conduct by the defendant which can fairly be viewed as "manipulative or deceptive" within the meaning of § 10(b) of the Securities Exchange Act of 1934. Manipulation is "virtually a term of art when used in connection with the securities markets," and refers narrowly to practices, such as wash sales, matched sales, or rigged prices, which artificially affect market activity in order to mislead investors. However, in situations not involving a manipulative scheme, the conduct alleged as fraudulent must include deception, misrepresentation, or nondisclosure to violate § 10(b) or Rule 10b-5.

Baird's actions, which Pross has alleged to be fraudulent in the instant case, clearly involve no manipulative activity in the technical sense in which that term is used in the securities laws. Thus, Pross must point to some deceptive action, or material misrepresentation or nondisclosure by Baird in order to maintain his claim of a violation of Rule 10b-5. In his complaint and affidavits in opposition to the instant motion, the only material misstatement or omission Pross identifies is Baird's failure to disclose that it was "making a market" in the stock of Nitron at the time that stock was purchased for plaintiff's account. Although failure by a broker to disclose that it is "making a market" in a particular security is a material omission, which nondisclosure by itself establishes reliance, Baird has demonstrated, without contradiction by plaintiff, that it adequately disclosed its market-maker status.

In support of its motion, Baird has shown that immediately following each purchase of Nitron stock, and well prior to the settlement date for each transaction, it sent to Pross a confirmation slip that clearly stated "we make a mkt in this security." . . . In addition, in Pross's monthly statements dated November 26, 1982 and December 31, 1982, Baird reiterated its disclosure that "we make a mkt in this security." . . . Plaintiff has not disputed the evidence that Baird made these disclosures. Thus, under these circumstances, there exists no factual basis for concluding that Baird failed adequately to disclose to Pross that it was making a market in Nitron stock. . . . So long as a broker adequately discloses its status to its customer, "it is not a fraudulent practice for a brokerage firm to act as a market-maker and to sell securities to its customers as a principal." Accordingly, in light of Baird's disclosure of its status, there is no legal basis for Pross's charge that Baird acted improperly in purchasing Nitron securities for his account at a time when Baird was making a market in those shares.

Stripped of its one allegation of nondisclosure, plaintiff's complaint is reduced to a claim that Baird made trades on his behalf which were contrary to his express instructions and in derogation of the parties' brokerage agreement. The only issue to be determined in the instant case is whether the transactions in Nitron stock were authorized. While the conduct in which Baird allegedly engaged was reprehensible, it does not involve the element of deception necessary to be violative of Rule 10b-5. At most, it provides the basis for a claim of breach of fiduciary duty or breach of contract, which, without more, cannot be converted into a fraud claim under § 10(b) and Rule 10b-5. [*But see* for a decision holding that unauthorized trading may constitute "deception" under § 10(b), *Cruse v. Equitable Securities of New York, Inc.,* 678 F. Supp. 1023, 1028 (S.D.N.Y. 1987) (holding that the plaintiff alleged deception under § 10(b) by asserting that "the account was a non-discretionary one and that [the] defendant traded securities for the account without first attaining the requisite authority").]

Although plaintiff's attorney attempts, in his briefs, to convert Pross's claim into something beyond what has been alleged in the complaint, those efforts are unavailing. Pross's claim is simply not like a claim of churning, where a broker abuses his position of control over his client's account to engage in excessive trading in disregard of the client's investment objectives. In a churning case, the broker uses the discretionary authority with which he has been vested to generate excessive commissions for himself, while at the same time leading his customer to believe that he is attempting to fulfill the customer's investment objectives. The instant case, however, involves the entirely different issue whether certain transactions were in fact authorized by plaintiff or by the parties' agreement. While the act of churning an account has long been considered a scheme or artifice to defraud within the meaning of Rule 10b-5, the simple breach of a brokerage agreement, absent some act of deception, misstatement or omission, has not. Pross's claim falls into the latter, not the former category.

. . . .

Note

With respect to the shingle theory under § 10(b), Professor Langevoort has stated:

> The importance of securities brokers and dealers in the investment marketplace is considerable, and federal law imposes extensive strictures on their conduct. Law developed under rule 10b-5 declares that securities professionals owe extensive . . . duties to their customers and clients and that a breach of those duties is fraudulent misconduct. Two theories, which in the end may be indistinguishable, have emerged to explain the fraud basis for reaching what is in essence unfair dealing. One is the "shingle" theory, which states that a broker-dealer, by publicly holding himself out as such, impliedly represents that he will deal fairly with his customers. The other

theory is that such professionals are, as a matter of law, fiduciaries and are held to fiduciary standards and liabilities. Liability for constructive fraud presumably would be included in the latter.[44]

Also, from the broker-dealer perspective, a case earlier in this chapter merits further exploration at this point: *Brown v. E.F. Hutton Group, Inc.*, 991 F.2d 1026 (2d Cir. 1993) (see § 8.05[C]).

---

[44]. Langevoort, *Fraud and Deception by Securities Professionals*, 61 Tex. L. Rev. 1247, 1280 (1983).

Chapter 9

Alternative Provisions

§ 9.01 Introduction

As Chapters 7 and 8 have discussed, § 11 of the Securities Act and § 10(b) of the Exchange Act play an important role in securities litigation. These provisions, however, may be unavailable to a complainant for a number of reasons. For example, the securities may have been purchased in the aftermarket, hence making the § 11 right of action unavailable (unless the plaintiff meets the onerous "tracing" requirement). Or, alternatively, the complainant may be unable to invoke the § 10(b) remedy because the complainant is not a "purchaser" or "seller" or cannot establish that the defendant acted with scienter. Or, as another example, the alleged violation may have occurred in connection with a proxy solicitation or tender offer. Under such circumstances, counsel should focus on the availability of alternative avenues, including the invocation of federal implied remedies as well as state securities and common law remedies.

Moreover, even where a right of action can be successfully established (such as under § 10(b)), counsel, where appropriate, still should assess the viability of remedies afforded by other provisions. For example, recovery may be afforded under § 14(a) based on the defendant's negligence, whereas § 10(b) mandates proof of scienter. As another example, § 29(b) of the Exchange Act (see § 9.06) may provide an aggrieved party with the right to rescind the subject transaction.

As an additional point, plaintiff's counsel always should assess the advisability of seeking relief under the applicable state common and statutory laws (including "Blue Sky" laws).

Problem

Go to the Problem contained in § 8.01. Analyze the Problem from the standpoint of alternative remedies and the likelihood of success for the claims alleged.

---

§ 9.02 Implied Rights of Action — In General

Prior to 1975, the federal courts liberally recognized implied private rights of action, generally looking to whether the granting of an implied remedy would benefit the class sought to be protected by the statute. For example, in *J.I. Case Co. v. Borak*, 377 U.S. 426 (1964), the Supreme Court recognized an implied right of action under § 14(a) of the Exchange Act (the "proxy" provision), reasoning that such an implied right would promote investor protection and serve as a necessary supplement to SEC enforcement action.

The liberal construction to implied rights of action halted with the Supreme Court's decision in *Cort v. Ash*, 422 U.S. 66, 78 (1975). There, the Court formulated a four-pronged standard:

> First, is the plaintiff "one of the class for whose especial benefit the statute was enacted," — that is, does the statute create a federal right in favor of the plaintiff? Second, is there any indication of legislative intent, explicit or implicit, either to create such a remedy or to deny one? Third, is it consistent with the underlying purpose of the legislative scheme to imply such a remedy for the plaintiff? And finally, is the cause of action one traditionally relegated to state law, in an area basically the concern of the States, so that it would be inappropriate to infer a cause of action based solely on federal law?

In subsequent decisions, the Court has embraced the *Cort* formulation with varying levels of enthusiasm. Compare *Cannon v. University of Chicago*, 441 U.S. 677 (1979), with *Touche Ross & Co. v. Redington*, 442 U.S. 560 (1979). Perhaps somewhat ironically (given the pre-1975 broad construction to implied rights), certain members of the Court have criticized the *Cort* standard as being "an open invitation to federal courts to legislate causes of action not authorized by Congress." *Cannon*, 441 U.S. at 731 (Powell, J., dissenting).

The apparent demise of the *Cort* formulation was evidenced by *Transamerica Mortgage Advisors, Inc. v. Lewis*, 444 U.S. 11, 15–16 (1979), where the Court refused to imply a private right of action under the antifraud provision of the Investment Advisers Act (§ 206). There, the Court, relying on its prior decision in *Redington*, 442 U.S. 560 (1979) (holding that no implied private right of action exists under § 17(a) of the Exchange Act), stated that the central inquiry is to examine Congress' intent. Hence, the Court reasoned:

> The question whether a statute creates a cause of action, either expressly or by implication, is basically a matter of statutory construction. While some opinions of the Court have placed considerable emphasis upon the desirability of implying private rights of action in order to provide remedies thought to effectuate the purposes of a given statute, what must ultimately be determined is whether Congress intended to create the private remedy asserted, as our recent decisions have made clear. We accept this as the appropriate inquiry to be made in resolving the issues presented by the case before us.

Thus, in *Lewis* the Court adhered to what has been viewed as a restrictive approach. Some other cases, however, indicate that the *Cort* formulation possibly survives.

California v. Sierra Club, 451 U.S. 287, 293 (1981), a non-securities law case, high-lights the disagreement on the Court concerning the continued viability of *Cort*. There, in declining to imply a right of action under the pertinent statute, the five-member majority adhered to the *Cort* formulation and asserted:

> Combined, these four factors present the relevant inquiries to pursue in answering the recurring question of implied causes of action. Cases subsequent to *Cort* have explained that the ultimate issue is whether Congress intended to create a private right of action, but the four factors specified in *Cort* remain the "criteria through which this intent could be discerned."

Concurring in the judgment, Justice Rehnquist (joined by three other Justices) in a separate opinion believed that "the Court's opinion places somewhat more emphasis on *Cort v. Ash* than is warranted in light of several more recent 'implied right of action' decisions which limit it."

Consistent with Justice Rehnquist's concurrence, more recent Supreme Court decisions such as *Virginia Bankshares*, 501 U.S. 1083 (1991), and *Central Bank of Denver*, 511 U.S. 164 (1994), reflect a return to a more restrictive approach. In *Virginia Bankshares*, for example, the Court approvingly quoted from *Touche Ross v. Redington* that the "central inquiry remains whether Congress intended to create, either expressly or by implication, a private cause of action." Hence, the Court in *Virginia Bankshares* made clear that congressional intent is "accorded primacy among the considerations that might be thought to bear on any decision to recognize a private remedy." Similarly, in *Central Bank of Denver*, the Court focused on the language of the applicable statute as the controlling factor (see § 10.02). Accord, *Alexander v. Sandoval*, 532 U.S. 275, 286–287 (2001) (in finding no private right of action under disparate-impact regulations adopted pursuant to the Civil Rights Act of 1964, stating that "the judicial task is to interpret the statute Congress has passed to determine whether it displays an intent to create not just a private right but also a private remedy [and that] statutory intent . . . is determinative").

Applying the *Cort* four-pronged formulation and its progeny, the lower federal courts have issued several decisions in the federal securities law context. For example, the lower federal courts generally have:

- Refused to recognize an implied right of action under § 6 of the Exchange Act: (i) against a national securities exchange based on the exchange's failure to enforce its own rules, *see, e.g., Walck v. American Stock Exchange, Inc.*, 687 F.2d 778 (3d Cir. 1982); or (ii) against a broker-dealer, listed corporation, or other subject party based on a violation of the SEC's customer-protection rules or the self-regulatory organizations (SRO) rules. *See, e.g., Harris v. TD Ameritrade, Inc.*, 805 F.3d 664 (6th Cir. 2015); *Jablon v. Dean Witter & Co.*, 613 F.2d 677 (9th Cir. 1980). *But see* for a more liberal approach from more than

50 years ago, *Colonial Realty Corp. v. Bache & Co.*, 358 F.2d 178 (2d Cir. 1966).[1]

- Declined to imply a private damages action under §7 of the Exchange Act on behalf of investors against financial institutions and brokers for violation of the margin requirements. Section 7 authorizes the Federal Reserve Board to regulate margin transactions and prohibits violation of the Board's regulations. Generally, the regulations promulgated by the Board under the authority of §7 set the margin rate for securities purchased at 50 percent, meaning that the purchaser must advance the other 50 percent of the purchase price of the securities bought "on margin." See *Walck v. American Stock Exchange, Inc.*, 687 F.2d 778 (3d Cir. 1982).

Declining to imply a private right of action under §7, the Second Circuit reasoned:

> We . . . hold that no private right of action exists under section 7. First, . . . there is simply no evidence that in passing section 7 Congress intended to create a private action. . . . Second, section 7 was clearly not passed for the "especial benefit" of individual investors. The major reason for enacting section 7 was to control the excessive use of credit in securities transactions. . . . Finally, it is doubtful that allowing a private cause of action would be consistent with the underlying purposes of the legislative scheme. As stated above, the underlying purpose of section 7 is to regulate the use of credit in securities transactions. As the addition of section 7(f) makes clear, this regulation is aimed at both lenders and investors. While allowing a private cause of action could conceivably deter violations by lenders, it seems just as conceivable that it could encourage violations by investors seeking to shift the risk of loss.

Bennett v. United States Trust Company of New York, 770 F.2d 308, 313 (2d Cir. 1985).

- In the tender offer setting, implied a private right of action for damages under §14(e) of the Exchange Act on behalf of target corporation shareholders, but not a damages remedy on behalf of an offeror. See *Panter v. Marshall Field & Co.*, 646 F.2d 271 (7th Cir. 1981). *See generally Piper v. Chris-Craft Industries, Inc.*, 430 U.S. 1 (1977) (applying *Cort* defeated tender offeror does not have standing to bring an implied action for damages under §14(e)). Although there is a split of authority, the apparent majority of courts have provided a target under §13(d) as well as under §14(d) and §14(e) with an implied right of action for injunctive relief. *See, e.g., CSX Corporation v. Children's Investment Fund*

---

1. *See generally* Dropkin, *National Securities Exchange Liability to Public Investors: Time to Overcome Inertia?*, 56 Notre Dame Law. 419 (1981); Lashbrooke, *Implying a Cause of Action for Damages: Rule Violations by Registered Exchanges* and *Associations*, 48 U. Cin. L. Rev. 549 (1979).

Management (UK) LLP, 654 F.3d 276, 284 (2d Cir. 2011). The underlying rationale is that the target company is the "only party with both the capability and incentive to pursue [the bidder's] violations." *Indiana National Corp. v. Rich,* 712 F.2d 1180, 1184 (7th Cir. 1983). *See also, Edelson v. Chi'en,* 405 F.3d 620 (7th Cir. 2005) (opining that § 13(d) may be invoked by a plaintiff only in the setting of a tender offer or other share acquisition relating to control).

- Implied private rights of action under certain provisions of the Investment Company Act[2] and the Trust Indenture Act.[3]

---

§ 9.03 Section 17(a) of the Securities Act

In view of *United States v. Naftalin,* 441 U.S. 768 (1979), and *Aaron v. SEC,* 446 U.S. 680 (1980), § 17(a) of the Securities Act is an attractive enforcement weapon for the Securities and Exchange Commission. Unlike § 10(b) of the Exchange Act, where scienter must be shown, the SEC under § 17(a)(2) or § 17(a)(3) need only establish negligence to prove a violation.

If an implied private right of action for damages under § 17(a) were recognized, plaintiffs could renew the arguments that they are now precluded from litigating under § 10(b) due to controlling Supreme Court decisions. For example, do offerees have standing under § 17(a)[4] and may private plaintiffs recover based upon the defendant's negligence? If the answers to the foregoing were answered in the affirmative, § 17(a) would become a "darling" to the plaintiff securities bar. Nonetheless, the near unanimous view today is that no private right of action exists under § 17(a). The Fifth Circuit's decision in *Landry,* contained in the materials that follow, reflects this position.

---

2. *See, e.g., Fogel v. Chestnut,* 668 F.2d 100 (2d Cir. 1981). *But see Northern Financial Advisors, Inc. v. Schwab Investments,* 615 F.3d 1106 (9th Cir. 2010).

3. *See, e.g., Zeiffiro v. First Pennsylvania Banking and Trust Co.,* 623 F.2d 290 (3d Cir. 1980). *See generally,* Johnson, *The "Forgotten" Securities Statute: Problems in the Trust Indenture Act,* 13 Toledo L. Rev. 92 (1981).

For law review articles addressing implied private rights of action under the federal securities laws, *see, e.g.,* Ashford, *Implied Causes of Action Under Federal Law: Calling the Court Back to Borak,* 79 Nw. U. L. Rev. 227 (1984); Frankel, *Implied Rights of Action,* 67 Va. L. Rev. 533 (1981); Grundfest, *Disimplying Private Rights of Action Under the Federal Securities Laws: The Commission's Authority,* 107 Harv. L. Rev. 961 (1994); Hazen, *Implied Private Remedies Under Federal Statutes: Neither a Death Knell nor a Moratorium — Civil Rights, Securities Regulation, and Beyond,* 33 Vand. L. Rev. 1333 (1980); Schneider, *Implying Private Rights and Remedies Under the Federal Securities Acts,* 62 N.C.L. Rev. 853 (1984); Seligman, *The Merits Do Matter,* 108 Harv. L. Rev. 748 (1995); Steinberg, *Implied Private Rights of Action Under Federal Law,* 55 Notre Dame Law. 33 (1979).

4. *See Reid v. Madison,* 438 F. Supp. 332, 335 (E.D. Va. 1977) (offerees granted standing under § 17(a)).

Moreover, in a key respect, § 17(a) has a severe limitation: its prohibitions apply only to the offer or sale of securities. Hence, the provision does not reach fraud committed in the purchase of securities.

[A] General Scope

United States v. Naftalin

United States Supreme Court

441 U.S. 768, 99 S. Ct. 2079, 60 L. Ed. 2d 624 (1979)

MR. JUSTICE BRENNAN delivered the opinion of the Court.

The question presented in this case is whether § 17(a)(1) of the Securities Act of 1933 . . . prohibits frauds against brokers as well as investors. We hold that it does.

Respondent, Neil Naftalin, was the president of a registered broker-dealer firm and a professional investor. Between July and August 1969, Naftalin engaged in a "short selling" scheme. [Generally, "short-selling" may be defined as

> the sale of a security that the seller does not own or that the seller owns but does not deliver. In order to deliver the security to the purchaser, the short seller borrows the security, typically from a broker-dealer or an institutional investor. The short seller closes out the position by returning the security to the lender, usually by purchasing equivalent securities on the open market. In general, short selling is used to profit from an expected downward price movement, or to hedge the risk of a long position in the same or related security.

Janvey, *Short-Selling*, 20 Sec. Reg. L.J. 270, 271–272 (1992).]

[Naftalin] selected stocks that, in his judgment, had peaked in price and were entering into a period of market decline. He then placed with five brokers orders to sell shares of these stocks, although he did not own the shares he purported to sell. Gambling that the price of the securities would decline substantially before he was required to deliver them, respondent planned to make offsetting purchases through other brokers at lower prices. He intended to take as profit the difference between the price at which he sold and the price at which he covered. Respondent was aware, however, that had the brokers who executed his sell orders known that he did not own the securities, they either would not have accepted the orders, or would have required a margin deposit. He therefore falsely represented that he owned the shares he directed them to sell.[5]

Unfortunately for respondent, the market prices of the securities he "sold" did not fall prior to the delivery date, but instead rose sharply. He was unable to make

---

[5]. A broker may mark an order to sell a customer's shares "long" if he "is informed that the seller owns the security ordered to be sold and, as soon as possible without undue inconvenience or expense, will deliver the security . . . . "

covering purchases, and never delivered the promised securities. Consequently, the five brokers were unable to deliver the stock which they had "sold" to investors, and were forced to borrow stock to keep their delivery promises. Then, in order to return the borrowed stock, the brokers had to purchase replacement shares on the open market at the now higher prices, a process known as "buying in."[6] While the investors to whom the stocks were sold were thereby shielded from direct injury, the five brokers suffered substantial financial losses.

The United States District Court for the District of Minnesota found respondent guilty on eight counts of employing "a scheme and artifice to defraud" in the sale of securities, in violation of § 17(a)(1). . . . Although the Court of Appeals for the Eighth Circuit found the evidence sufficient to establish that respondent had committed fraud, 579 F.2d 444, 447 (1978), it nonetheless vacated his convictions. Finding that the purpose of the Securities Act "was to protect investors from fraudulent practices in the sale of securities," . . . the court held that "the government must prove some impact of the scheme on an investor." . . . Since respondent's fraud injured only brokers and not investors, the Court of Appeals concluded that Naftalin did not violate § 17(a)(1). We granted certiorari, . . . and now reverse.

I

Section 17(a) of the Securities Act of 1933, subsection (1) of which respondent was found to have violated, states:

> It shall be unlawful for any person in the offer or sale of any securities by the use of any means or instruments of transportation or communication in interstate commerce or by the use of the mails, directly or indirectly—
>
> (1) to employ any device, scheme, or artifice to defraud, or
>
> (2) to obtain money or property by means of any untrue statement of a material fact or any omission to state a material fact necessary in order to make the statements made, in the light of the circumstances under which they were made, not misleading, or
>
> (3) to engage in any transaction, practice, or course of business which operates or would operate as a fraud or deceit upon the purchaser.

In this Court, *Naftalin* does not dispute that, by falsely representing that he owned the stock he sold, he defrauded the brokers who executed his sales. . . . He contends, however, that the Court of Appeals correctly held that § 17(a)(1) applies solely to frauds directed against investors, and not to those against brokers.

Nothing on the face of the statute supports this reading of it. Subsection (1) makes it unlawful for "any person in the offer or sale of any securities . . . *directly or indirectly . . .* to employ *any* device, scheme, or artifice to defraud. . . ." (Emphasis added.)

---

[6]. If a broker executes a sell order marked "long" and the seller fails to deliver the securities when due, under certain circumstances the broker must "buy in" substitute securities. . . .

The statutory language does not require that the victim of the fraud be an investor—only that the fraud occur "in" an offer or sale.

An offer and sale clearly occurred here. Respondent placed sell orders with the brokers; the brokers, acting as agents, executed the orders; and the results were contracts of sale, which are within the statutory definition. . . . Moreover, the fraud occurred "in" the "offer" and "sale."[7] The statutory terms, which Congress expressly intended to define broadly, . . . are expansive enough to encompass the entire selling process, including the seller/agent transaction. Section 2(3) [now § 2(a)(3)] of the Act . . . states:

> The term "sale" . . . shall include every contract of sale or disposition of a security or interest in a security, for value. The term . . . "offer" shall include *every attempt or offer to dispose of . . . a security* or interest in a security, for value. (Emphasis added.)

This language does not require that the fraud occur in any particular phase of the selling transaction. At the very least, an order to a broker to sell securities is certainly an "attempt to dispose" of them.

Thus, nothing in subsection (1) of § 17(a) creates a requirement that injury occur to a purchaser. Respondent nonetheless urges that the phrase, "upon the purchaser," found only in subsection (3) of § 17(a), should be read into all three subsections. The short answer is that Congress did not write the statute that way. Indeed, the fact that it did not provides strong affirmative evidence that while impact upon a purchaser may be relevant to prosecutions brought under § 17(a)(3), it is not required for those brought under § 17(a)(1). As is indicated by the use of an infinitive to introduce each of the three subsections, and the use of the conjunction "or" at the end of the first two, each subsection proscribes a distinct category of misconduct. Each succeeding prohibition is meant to cover additional kinds of illegalities—not to narrow the reach of the prior sections. . . .

II

The court below placed primary reliance for its restrictive interpretation of § 17(a)(1) upon what it perceived to be Congress' purpose in passing the Securities Act. Noting that both this Court and Congress have emphasized the importance of the statute in protecting investors from fraudulent practices in the sale of securities, . . . the Court of Appeals concluded that "against this backdrop . . . we are constrained to hold that the government must prove some impact of the scheme on an investor."

But neither this Court nor Congress has ever suggested that investor protection was the *sole* purpose of the Securities Act. As we have noted heretofore, the Act

---

[7]. Respondent contends that the requirement that the fraud be "in" the offer or sale connotes a narrower range of activities than does the phrase "in connection with," which is found in § 10(b) of the Securities Exchange Act of 1934. . . . First, we are not necessarily persuaded that "in" is narrower than "in connection with." Both Congress, see H. R. Report No. 85, 73d Cong., 1st Sess., 6 (1933), and this Court, see *Superintendent of Insurance v. Bankers Life & Cas. Co.,* 404 U.S. 6, 10 (1971), have on occasion used the terms interchangeably. But even if "in" were meant to connote a narrower group of transactions than "in connection with," there is nothing to indicate that "in" is narrower in the sense insisted upon by Naftalin.

"emerged as part of the aftermath of the market crash in 1929." . . . Indeed, Congress' primary contemplation was that regulation of the securities markets might help set the economy on the road to recovery. . . . Prevention of frauds against investors was surely a key part of that program, but so was the effort "to achieve a high standard of business ethics . . . *in every facet of the securities industry.*" *SEC v. Capital Gains Bureau,* 375 U. S. 180, 186–187 (1963) (emphasis added). . . .

. . . While investor protection was a constant preoccupation of the legislators, the record is also replete with references to the desire to protect ethical businessmen. . . . Respondent's assertion that Congress' concern was limited to investors is thus manifestly inconsistent with the legislative history.

Moreover, the welfare of investors and financial intermediaries are inextricably linked—frauds perpetrated upon either business or investors can redound to the detriment of the other and to the economy as a whole. . . . Fraudulent short sales are no exception. Although investors suffered no immediate financial injury in this case because the brokers covered the sales by borrowing and then "buying in," the indirect impact upon investors may be substantial. "Buying in" is in actuality only a form of insurance for investors and, like all forms of insurance, has its own costs. Losses suffered by brokers increase their cost of doing business, and in the long run investors pay at least part of this cost through higher brokerage fees. In addition, unchecked short-sale frauds against brokers would create a level of market uncertainty that could only work to the detriment of both investors and the market as a whole. Finally, while the investors here were shielded from direct injury, that may not always be the case. Had the brokers been insolvent or unable to borrow, the investors might well have failed to receive their promised shares. Entitled to receive shares at one price under the purchase agreement, they would have had to buy substitute shares in the market at a higher price. Placing brokers outside the aegis of § 17(a) would create a loophole in the statute that Congress simply did not intend to create.

III

Although the question was not directly presented in the Government's petition for certiorari, respondent asserts a final, independent argument in support of the judgment below. That assertion is that the Securities Act of 1933 was "preoccupied with" the regulation of initial public offerings of securities, and that Congress waited until the Securities Exchange Act of 1934 to regulate abuses in the trading of securities in the "aftermarket." As Naftalin's fraud did not involve a new offering, he contends that § 17(a) is inapplicable, and that he should have been prosecuted for violations of either the specific short-selling regulations promulgated under the 1934 Act, or for violations of the general antifraud proscriptions of the 1934 Act's § 10(b) . . . and the SEC's Rule 10b-5. . . .

Although it is true that the 1933 Act was primarily concerned with the regulation of new offerings, respondent's argument fails because the antifraud prohibition of § 17(a) was meant as a major departure from that limitation. Unlike much of the rest of the Act, it was intended to cover any fraudulent scheme in an offer or sale of securities, whether in the course of an initial distribution or in the course of ordinary market trading. . . . This is made abundantly clear both by the statutory language, which makes no distinctions between the two kinds of transactions, and by the Senate Report. . . . Respondent is undoubtedly correct that the two Acts prohibit some of the same conduct. . . . But "[t]he fact that there may well be some overlap is neither unusual nor unfortunate." . . . It certainly does not absolve Naftalin of guilt for the transactions which violated the statute under which he was convicted.

IV

This is a criminal case, and we have long held that " 'ambiguity concerning the ambit of criminal statutes should be resolved in favor of lenity,' " . . . and that a defendant may not " 'be subjected to a penalty unless the words of the statute plainly impose it.' " . . . In this case, however, the words of the statute do "plainly impose it." Here, "Congress has conveyed its purpose clearly, and we decline to manufacture ambiguity where none exists." . . . The decision of the Court of Appeals for the Eighth Circuit is *Reversed.*

Note

One may certainly question why the prosecution relied solely on § 17(a) rather than invoking § 10(b) of the Exchange Act. Criminal prosecutions brought for violations similar to Naftalin's and based on § 10(b) traditionally have received judicial approbation. E.g., *United States v. Peltz*, 433 F.2d 48 (2d Cir. 1971). Perhaps the prosecutor did not take securities regulation (or consult with anyone who did).

The Supreme Court in *Naftalin* handed down three significant principles regarding § 17(a). First, the protection afforded by § 17(a)(1) extends beyond investors to encompass financial intermediaries. Second, the language of § 17(a) relating to the prohibition of fraud "in" an offer or sale of securities was sufficiently inclusive to cover Naftalin's misconduct. And third, § 17(a) not only applies in the initial offering context but also extends to the secondary trading markets. This last holding is particularly important. Prior to *Naftalin*, some authorities believed that, as part of the Securities Act which is directed at the regulation of initial offerings, § 17(a) was likewise limited to the initial offering context. Hence, with respect to misconduct occurring in the offer or sale of securities, *Naftalin*'s effect is to subject such misconduct to the prohibitions of both § 17(a) and § 10(b). For further discussion, *see* Steinberg, *Section 17(a) of the Securities Act After Naftalin and Redington,* 68 Geo. L.J. 163 (1979).

As described by one authority on this subject, short-selling provides key benefits to the securities markets:

> Short selling provides the market with two important benefits: market liquidity and pricing efficiency. Substantial market liquidity is provided through short selling by market professionals, such as market makers, block

positioners, and specialists, who facilitate the operation of the markets by offsetting temporary imbalances in the supply and demand for securities. To the extent that securities professionals effect short sales in the market, such short sale activities add to the trading supply of stock available to purchasers and reduce the risk that the price paid by investors is artificially high because of a temporary contraction of supply.

Janvey, *Short Selling*, 20 Sec. Reg. L.J. 270, 272–273 (1992).

Naftalin was convicted of fraudulent short-selling. As a congressional report describes, short-seller abuse seems to be prevalent. *See Short-Selling in the Stock Market*, H.R. Rep. No. 102-414, at 7-8, 13, 17 (1992):

For years, investors and company executives (who are often major shareholders also) have complained about short-selling abuses. . . .

Many of the complaints have alleged that short sellers, after establishing a major short position in a particular stock, have aggressively circulated false rumors about the company's [adverse] financial condition, problems with its products, or the health or integrity of its officers in an effort to drive down the stock price. It has also been frequently alleged that some elements of the press assist and cooperate with short sellers by printing very negative stories about the companies the short sellers have targeted.

In many cases short sellers are alleged to have contacted directly a company's major suppliers, customers, lenders, and institutional shareholders, often anonymously or under false pretenses, to aggressively suggest false or misleading "facts" about the company.

. . . .

The committee has found . . . that many of the reports of rumor-spreading abuse are entirely credible and are strongly suggestive of abuse. Moreover, the widespread nature of these reports and the high degree of similarity among them constitute a highly consistent pattern. The committee finds, therefore, that a pattern of abusive and destructive rumormongering, targeted specifically at companies in the equity securities of which some short-selling investors have established major short positions, appears to be occurring.[8]

[B] State of Mind

In *Aaron v. SEC*, 446 U.S. 680 (1980), the Supreme Court, applying a linguistic analysis, held that in SEC actions seeking injunctive relief, scienter must be proven

---

8. *See* Gordon, *Regulation of Short Selling in the U.S.*, 43 Rev. Sec. & Comm. Reg. 179 (2010); *Regulators Take Aim at Halting Rumors Intended to Move Market Price*, 41 Sec. Reg. L. Rep. (BNA) 1170 (2009).

to establish a violation of § 10(b) of the Exchange Act and § 17(a)(1) of the Securities Act. However, to show a violation of § 17(a)(2) or § 17(a)(3), the SEC need only prove the defendant's negligence.

Note the effect of *Aaron*, when considered in light of *Naftalin*. Upon the making of a proper showing (i.e. a reasonable likelihood that, absent the ordering of an injunction, future violations will occur), the SEC can invoke § 17(a)(2) or § 17(a)(3) to obtain injunctive relief based on a defendant's negligent misconduct, which occurred in the offer or sale of securities in either the primary or the secondary trading markets. In view of this consequence, § 17(a) becomes a more appealing enforcement weapon to the SEC in the "offer or sale" context than the traditional antifraud provision, § 10(b), which requires the Commission to prove scienter.

Moreover, based upon legislation enacted in 1990, the SEC now has cease and desist authority (see Chapter 15). This remedy, coupled with the effects of *Naftalin* and *Aaron*, provides the Commission with the authority to issue a cease and desist authority based upon a party's negligent conduct. Hence, § 17(a) is a powerful weapon in the SEC's arsenal.

Based upon a linguistic analysis (as the Supreme Court applied in *Aaron*), the assertion has been made that, if a private damages action were implied under § 17(a), the requisite culpability standard would be that of negligence. *See Landry v. All American Assurance Co.*, 688 F.2d 381, 387 (5th Cir. 1982). On the other hand, the Supreme Court has stressed that it is inappropriate to imply a private right of action that is significantly more expansive than the provisions that Congress expressly chose to provide. Because §§ 11 and 12(a)(2) of the Securities Act subject plaintiffs to certain procedural limitations and have a culpability standard resembling that of negligence, an argument can be made that liability should be imposed pursuant to § 17(a) in private litigation only for actions that are more blameworthy, namely, for intentional or reckless misconduct. *See Ernst & Ernst v. Hochfelder*, 425 U.S. 185 (1976), in § 8.03[A]. Nonetheless, as the following case illustrates, few courts today recognize an implied right of action under § 17(a).

[C] Rejection of an Implied Right of Action

Landry v. All American Assurance Co.

United States Court of Appeals, Fifth Circuit

688 F.2d 381 (1982)

GARZA, CIRCUIT JUDGE.

Below, the unsuccessful plaintiffs sought to try their case under several theories of securities law, but were permitted to proceed under only one. On this appeal it is their contention that the district court erred both in its dismissal of the other claims and the jury instructions given. With the exception of one state law issue, we find that no reversible error was committed and affirm the result below.

I. A Change of Seasons

In the spring of 1974, appellants Bryan Zeringue, Curtis Chauvin and Dr. W. B. Landry learned—later to their detriment—that certain common stock of the St. Charles Bank and Trust Company was to be made available for sale. The circumstances surrounding the sale of that stock gave rise to the present suit. Disagreement between the parties as to the facts is minuscule.

Appellants are two businessmen and a practicing physician who live and work in St. Charles Parish, Louisiana. For years they had banked with the St. Charles Bank and Trust Company [hereinafter referred to as the Bank]. When the Bank formed an "advisory board" in the fall of 1973, appellants Zeringue and Chauvin were asked to serve on it; they accepted. In the spring of 1974, both Zeringue and Chauvin were informed at one of the board's meetings that the Bank's chairman of the board, Charest Thibaut, was thinking of retiring and was willing to sell some of his common stock. Not long thereafter, Dr. Landry was also informed, by one of his patients, that stock in the Bank was to be made available for purchase. That summer, each appellant purchased 1,500 shares of the Bank's common stock at $60 per share for a total of $90,000 apiece, or $270,000 for the total purchase price.

At first, it appeared that the money invested by the appellants was well spent—in January of 1975 a 25% stock dividend was declared, increasing the common stock ownership of each appellant from 1,500 to 1,875 shares.[9] This feeling of euphoria, however, was unfounded. In the fall and winter of 1974, and the spring of 1975, various audits and bank examinations conducted by the Federal Deposit Insurance Corporation and the Louisiana Commissioner of Financial Institutions revealed gross inadequacies and deficiencies in the financial structure of the Bank. As a result of these examinations and actions taken by regulatory authorities, very substantial changes in the Bank's organization were brought about, including the resignation of the Bank's president, C. Therral Ransome, and the Bank's chairman of the board, Charest Thibaut. Other members of the board also resigned or were asked to resign in the spring and summer of 1975. Finally, in December of 1975, the Bank issued a proxy statement in which its precarious financial condition was set out, and in January, 1976, the Bank issued a stock offering to raise needed additional capital. At that time the Bank's common stock was valued at $4 per share—down from the $60 per share paid by appellants in the summer of 1974.

Outraged by the drastic devaluation of their investments, appellants consulted with counsel, and on January 26, 1977, filed suit in federal court alleging that All American Assurance Company, Republic Securities Corporation, Charest Thibaut, Remy F. Gross and C. Therral Ransome had violated § 10(b) of the Securities Exchange Act of 1934 and Rule 10b-5 promulgated thereunder. Specifically, appellants

---

[9]. [Given your knowledge of corporate finance, does this statement make sense?]

contended that the financial statements prepared and issued by the Bank in 1973 and 1974 were inaccurate and grossly misrepresented its financial condition. Furthermore, it was asserted that representations made by the various defendants at advisory board meetings and elsewhere were affirmatively misleading, inaccurate and omitted material information.

On January 29, 1979, appellants amended their complaint so as to expand both the number of defendants and the causes of action asserted. . . . The causes of action asserted were broadened to encompass claims under § 17(a) of the Securities Act of 1933. . . .

Prior to trial, however, the defendants filed motions to dismiss and/or for summary judgment claiming that no private cause of action was created under . . . § 17(a) of the Securities Act of 1933. . . . The trial court agreed and dismissed the counts. . . .

II. The Dismissed Theories for Relief

Implied Private Cause of Action Under § 17(a) of the Securities Act of 1933

Unquestionably, the most far reaching of the issues we resolve today is whether § 17(a) of the federal Securities Act of 1933 creates an implied private cause of action. . . .

Most of [the cases recognizing a § 17(a) private cause of action rely on] Chief Judge Friendly's concurring opinion in *SEC v. Texas Gulf Sulphur Co.,* 401 F.2d 833 (2nd Cir. 1968). . . . Judge Friendly's opinion was primarily concerned with establishing that negligence in the drafting of a press release should not be the basis of civil liability under Rule 10b-5(2). In his discussion of the origins of Rule 10b-5, however, Judge Friendly stated in dicta that while he had considerable doubt as to whether a private remedy under § 17(a) was ever intended, "there seemed little practical point in denying the existence of such an action under § 17" "[o]nce it had been established . . . that an aggrieved buyer has a private action under § 10(b) of the 1934 Act." As subsequent decisions have revealed, this seed fell on very fertile ground. The lack of a clearly articulated standard, however, has resulted in the fragmentation of the district courts with respect to this issue. Nor can it be said that a general consensus exists among the commentators.[10]

Perhaps the main reason for the somewhat awkward development of the law under § 17(a) of the 1933 Act is the fact that it has traditionally lived in the shadow of another area of securities law: Rule 10b-5. Rule 10b-5, adopted under § 10(b) of the Securities and Exchange Act of 1934, is substantially identical to § 17(a). When the judiciary recognized a private cause of action under Rule 10b-5 shortly after its promulgation, cases that might have fit a § 17(a) cause of action were instead decided under Rule 10b-5. This was true even when a plaintiff pleaded a cause of action under both.

---

[10]. Compare Hazen, *A Look Beyond the Pruning of Rule 10b-5: Implied Remedies and Section 17(a) of the Securities Act of 1933*, 64 Va. L. Rev. 641 (1978). . . .

In 1976, however, the Supreme Court severely limited the Rule 10b-5 cause of action in *Ernst & Ernst v. Hochfelder*, 425 U.S. 185 (1976). There the Court established that allegations of the defendant's scienter are an essential element of the plaintiff's cause of action under Rule 10b-5. The Court based its holding on the language of § 10(b) of the 1934 Act, asserting that the narrower language of that section constrained the reach of the broader Rule 10b-5 language.

The law under § 17(a), however, is not so distinct. In *Aaron v. SEC*, 446 U.S. 680 (1980), the Supreme Court was faced with the question of whether the SEC was required to establish scienter as an element of a civil enforcement action to enjoin violations of § 10(b) and Rule 10b-5 of the 1934 Act, and § 17(a) of the 1933 Act. While the Court decided that scienter was a necessary prerequisite under the 1934 Act, its response split with respect to § 17(a):

> The language of § 17(a) strongly suggests that Congress contemplated a scienter requirement under § 17(a)(1), but not under § 17(a)(2) or § 17(a)(3). The language of § 17(a)(1), which makes it unlawful "to employ any device, scheme, or artifice to defraud," plainly evinces an intent on the part of Congress to proscribe only knowing or intentional misconduct. . . .

> By contrast, the language of § 17(a)(2), which prohibits any person from obtaining money or property "by means of any untrue statement of a material fact," is devoid of any suggestion whatsoever of a scienter requirement. . . .

> Finally, the language of § 17(a)(3), under which it is unlawful for any person "to engage in any transaction, practice, or course of business which *operates* or *would operate* as a fraud or deceit," (emphasis added) quite plainly focuses upon the *effect* of particular conduct on members of the investing public, rather than upon the culpability of the person responsible. . . .

> It is our view, in sum, that the language of § 17(a) requires scienter under § 17(a)(1), but not under § 17(a)(2) or § 17(a)(3).

. . . True, the court resolved the issue only with respect to SEC enforcement actions; however, it is doubtful that a different interpretation would be given if an implied private cause of action is found to exist. Given this assumption, § 17(a) suddenly becomes an attractive, viable alternative to actions previously brought under Rule 10b-5, at least as to those based upon negligence. All of this, however, takes for granted that a private cause of action does indeed exist under § 17(a). After analyzing the issue in light of recent Supreme Court decisions, we conclude that it does not.

The question of whether a private cause of action should be implied under § 17(a) operates against a backdrop of long-developing and varied judicial formulations of the circumstances under which implication is appropriate.[11] The most recent test stems from the Supreme Court's decision of *Cort v. Ash*, 422 U.S. 66 (1975). In *Cort*,

---

[11]. *See generally*, Steinberg, *Implied Private Rights of Action Under Federal Law*, 55 Notre Dame Law. 33 (1979). . . .

the Supreme Court unanimously refused to imply a private cause of action for damages against corporate directors and in favor of stockholders for purported violations of a criminal statute prohibiting corporations from making certain campaign contributions. In rejecting the plaintiff's theory that implication was appropriate for violations of this criminal statute, Justice Brennan outlined the following four-part test for determining when a private remedy should be implied:

> First, is the plaintiff "one of the class for whose *especial* benefit the statute was enacted," — that is, does the statute create a federal right in favor of the plaintiff? Second, is there any indication of legislative intent, explicit or implicit, either to create such a remedy or to deny one? Third, is it consistent with the underlying purposes of the legislative scheme to imply such a remedy for the plaintiff? And finally, is the cause of action one traditionally relegated to state law, in an area basically the concern of the States, so that it would be inappropriate to infer a cause of action based solely on federal law?
>
> . . . Combined, these four factors present the relevant inquiries to pursue in resolving the question of whether an implied cause of action exists.

The test set down in *Cort* was more restrictive than any of its predecessors. Notwithstanding this, more recent cases, by their music if not their lyrics, evince a further retreat from the creation of implied causes of action. For example, in *Touche Ross & Co. v. Redington*, 442 U.S. 560, 568–74 (1979), the court observed that examination of the language, legislative history and purpose of a statute are the proper means for resolving the implication issue. Since the first three criteria of the *Cort* standard are the traditional indicia of legislative intent, the *Redington* Court placed special emphasis on these factors. If these three inquiries remain unsatisfied, the *Redington* Court held that courts need not determine whether an implied private right is a cause of action traditionally relegated to state law. In denying private rights under §17(a) of the 1934 Act, the court indicated for the first time that the four elements of the *Cort* test are not of equal weight; the ultimate issue is whether Congress intended to create a private cause of action. . . .

This approach was echoed later that year in *Transamerica Mortgage Advisors, Inc. v. Lewis*, 444 U.S. 11 (1979), where the court premised its analysis of the implication issues upon basic statutory construction. There, the court declined to imply a private remedy under §206 of the Investment Advisers Act of 1940, relying primarily on its understanding of the Act's legislative history. It noted that other sections of the Act provided for criminal penalties, civil action by the SEC, and other administrative sanctions and expressed doubt that Congress merely forgot to mention a private action it meant to confer. Thereafter, the court concluded that if neither the statutory language nor the legislative history revealed congressional intent to imply a private cause of action, the inquiry ends with a denial of private rights. [The Supreme Court's subsequent decisions in *Virginia Bankshares*, 501 U.S. 1083 (1991) (contained in §8.04 *infra*), and in *Central Bank of Denver*, 511 U.S. 164 (1994) (contained in §10.02 *infra*), are consistent with the restrictive approach espoused by both *Redington* and *Lewis*.]

Application of the modified *Cort* test to § 17(a) of the 1933 Act leads this Court to believe that a private cause of action is not implied. As expressed by so many opinions before us, our analysis must begin with the language of the statute itself. . . .

On its face, § 17(a) does not appear to satisfy the first factor of the *Cort* test, for the statutory language does not suggest a private cause of action. The statute merely represents a general censure of fraudulent practices. . . .

Nor can there be said to be any indication of legislative intent, explicit or implicit, to create such a remedy. The legislative history of the 1933 Act makes no mention of civil liability under § 17(a); congressional discussion of civil liability under the Act centers on §§ 11 and 12.

. . . .

It would, therefore, appear that the second *Cort* factor has been answered in the negative.

Under *Transamerica Mortgage Advisors, Inc. v. Lewis*, our analysis could stop here. However, an examination of the remaining *Cort* factors reinforces our result. The third *Cort* factor asks whether "it is consistent with the underlying purposes of the legislative scheme to imply such a remedy for the plaintiffs?" . . . A review of the Act indicates that the answer to this question is also no.

The Securities Act of 1933 contains two express civil liabilities for the protection of purchasers. The first of these is § 11 which prohibits falsehoods and omissions in the registration statement. The second is § 12(2) [now § 12(a)(2)] which protects purchasers from misstatements or omissions in written or oral communications [in public offerings]. Together these sections confer specific private rights upon purchasers. Before a purchaser may successfully bring suit under either of these two sections, however, strict procedural requirements must first be satisfied. Section 17(a)(2) prohibits the same type of conduct as §§ 11 and 12, but has none of the limitations imposed by Congress. The creation of an implied cause of action § 17(a) under these circumstances would effectively frustrate the carefully laid framework of the Act.[12]

---

[12]. *See* 3 L. Loss, Securities Regulation, . . . at 1785.

This brings us to an apparent inconsistency in two Supreme Court decisions. In *Touche Ross & Co. v. Redington*, 442 U.S. 560, 572 (1979), the court noted that when a statute is surrounded by other sections of the same Act which expressly provide private remedies, the inference arises that "when Congress wished to provide a private damages remedy, it knew how to do so and did so expressly." Yet, earlier that term in *Cannon v. University of Chicago*, 441 U.S. 677, 711 (1979), the court commented that "[t]he fact that other provisions of a complex statutory scheme create express remedies has not been accepted as a sufficient reason for refusing to imply an otherwise appropriate remedy in a separate section."

Seemingly, the cases are in conflict; however, the conflict is not irreconcilable:

> As *Redington* implicitly recognizes, it is one thing to create a negative inference for implication solely because other sections of the Act contain express remedies and quite another when the express remedies are directed at the same type of conduct, are intended to benefit the same identifiable class, and are passed contemporaneously with the statute in question. As to the former, no negative inference should be drawn.

Finally, *Cort* rejects implication of a private cause of action for matters traditionally relegated to state courts. . . . Liability for the sorts of transactions arising under § 17(a), however, is not such a matter. The congressional hearings regarding enactment of the Securities Act are replete with testimony regarding the states' inability to deal with securities fraud. In addition, the Securities Act confers concurrent jurisdiction upon federal and state courts, providing strong support for the proposition that § 17(a) matters are not solely within the state sphere.

Summarizing, then, it would appear that the *Cort* test as applied to § 17(a) of the Securities Act of 1933 points away from the implication of a private cause of action. This, together with the Supreme Court's conservative interpretation of the test in recent years, leads us to the conclusion that the district court correctly dismissed this theory of relief.

. . . .

[*Affirmed.*]

Note

A number of older federal court cases recognized an implied right of action for damages under § 17(a). *See, e.g., Valles Salgado v. Piedmont Capital Corp.*, 452 F. Supp. 853 (D.R.I. 1978). Nonetheless, the Fifth Circuit's decision in the foregoing case represents the nearly unanimous view. Decisions handed down during the past three decades by the federal appellate courts hold that there exists no implied right of action under § 17(a). *See, e.g., Bath v. Bushkin, Gaims, Gaines and Jones,* 913 F.2d 817 (10th Cir. 1990); *Sears v. Likens,* 912 F.2d 889 (7th Cir. 1990); *Newcome v. Esrey,* 862 F.2d 1099 (4th Cir. 1988); *Currie v. Cayman Resources Corporation,* 835 F.2d 780 (11th Cir. 1988); *Krause v. Prettyman,* 827 F.2d 346 (8th Cir. 1987); *In re Washington Public Power Supply Securities Litigation,* 823 F.2d 1349 (9th Cir. 1987) (en banc).

> To do so would create the presumption that the implication of private rights of action are disfavored in all circumstances. Without clear guidance from Congress, such an interpretation would be erroneous. There can be little question that in appropriate circumstances Congress is aware of and is supportive of future judicial implication of private remedies. To deny a private right of action in this situation would not only undermine Congress' intent but would also inflict needless injustices upon aggrieved parties. As to the latter, however, a negative inference can properly be drawn. In this instance, Congress expressly focused on the conduct in question and the class to be afforded recompense. Before drawing such an inference, however, courts should assure themselves that the focus of the statute providing the express remedy is directed at the same type of conduct and is intended to benefit the same identifiable class as the statute which the plaintiff seeks to invoke. If the answer to the foregoing is in the affirmative, then for the courts to impliedly expand the scope of this express remedy may well represent judicial legislation in the face of clear congressional intent.

Steinberg, *Implied Private Rights of Action Under Federal Law*, 55 Notre Dame Law. at 47–48. Applying this rationale, the inference once again is against the creation of an implied private cause of action.

§ 9.04 Section 14(a) of the Securities Exchange Act (The Proxy Statute)

Section 14(a) of the Securities Exchange Act and SEC rules and regulations promulgated thereunder regulate the solicitation of proxies with respect to securities registered under § 12 of the Exchange Act. Section 14(a) "was intended to promote 'the free exercise of the voting rights of stockholders' by ensuring that proxies would be solicited with 'explanation to the stockholder of the real nature of the questions for which authority to cast his vote is sought.'"[13]

[A] Overview

From the Supreme Court's decision in *J.I. Case v. Borak*, 377 U.S. 426 (1964), it is clear that an implied private right of action for damages exists under § 14(a) and Rule 14a-9. Rule 14a-9 prohibits the solicitation of proxies that contain any materially false or misleading statement. As construed by the courts, the statute of limitations for § 14(a) claims is one year after the plaintiff knew or should have known of the violation and, in no event, more than three years after such violation. *See DeKalb County Pension Fund v. Transocean Ltd.*, 817 F.3d 393 (2d Cir. 2016).

The availability of an implied right of action under Rule 14a-8, the SEC shareholder proposal rule, is generally recognized. *See, e.g., Roosevelt v. E.I. DuPont De Nemours & Co.*, 958 F.2d 416 (D.C. Cir. 1992). The standard of materiality, as the Supreme Court held in *TSC Industries, Inc. v. Northway, Inc.*, 426 U.S. 438 (1976), is that "there is a substantial likelihood that a reasonable shareholder would consider [such information] important in deciding how to vote." Provided that the misstatement or omission is material and thus had "a significant propensity to affect the voting process" (*Mills v. Electric Auto-Lite Co.*, 396 U.S. 375, 384–385 (1970)), a plaintiff in a derivative or class action under § 14(a) and Rule 14a-9 is not required to show individual reliance on the misleading proxy solicitation. Hence, according to the Supreme Court in *Mills*, upon a finding of materiality, "a shareholder has made a sufficient showing of causal relationship between the violation and the injury for which he seeks redress if . . . he proves that the proxy solicitation itself . . . was an essential link in the accomplishment of the transaction." In the *Virginia Bankshares* case that follows, the Supreme Court elaborated upon § 14(a)'s causation requirement. Nonetheless, this broad approach is tempered by § 21D(b)(4) of the Securities Exchange Act, enacted pursuant to the PSLRA, requiring that loss causation must be proven by the plaintiff.

Regarding the requisite state of mind for liability purposes, § 14(a) and Rule 14a-9, unlike § 10(b), do not by their terms require that deceptive or manipulative conduct be shown. Based partially on this rationale, courts generally apply a negligence

---

13. *Mills v. Electric Auto-Lite Co.*, 396 U.S. 375, 381 (1970), quoting, H.R. Rep. No. 1383, 73d Cong., 2d Sess., 14 (1934).

standard, at least with respect to inside directors and officers. In *Gould v. American-Hawaiian S.S. Co.*, 535 F.2d 761, 777–778 (3d Cir. 1976), the Third Circuit stated:

> The language of Section 14(a) and Rule 14a-9 contains no suggestion of a scienter requirement, merely establishing a quality standard for proxy material. The importance of the proxy provision to informed voting by shareholders has been stressed by the Supreme Court, which has emphasized the broad remedial purpose of the section, implying a need to impose a high standard of care on the individuals involved. And, unlike Sections 10(b) and 18 of the Act, which encompass activity in numerous and diverse areas of securities markets and corporate management, Section 14(a) is specially limited to materials used in soliciting proxies. Given all of these factors the imposition of a standard of due diligence as opposed to actual knowledge or gross negligence is quite appropriate.

Accord, *Gerstle v. Gamble-Skogmo, Inc.*, 478 F.2d 1281 (2d Cir. 1973). *See also, Securities and Exchange Commission v. Das*, 723 F.3d 943 (8th Cir. 2013) (distinguishing that Circuit's prior holding that scienter is required to be shown in § 14(a) claims against outside directors and accountants and holding that negligence sufficient culpability for corporate officers); *Beck v. Dobrowski*, 559 F.3d 680, 682 (7th Cir. 2009) (stating that there "is no required state of mind for a violation of section 14(a) [and that] a proxy solicitation that contains a misleading misrepresentation or omission violates the section even if the issuer believed in perfect good faith that there was nothing misleading in the proxy materials"); *Shidler v. All American Life & Financial Corp.*, 775 F.2d 917 (8th Cir. 1985) (rejecting strict liability in private damages actions under § 14(a)).

Note, moreover, that there exists authority for the proposition that "the objective sufficiency of the disclosure" is the appropriate standard under § 14(a) when injunctive relief (rather than damages) is sought for the reason that "injunctive relief [is] directed to the integrity of [the] stockholder franchise." *Ash v. LFE Corp.*, 525 F.2d 215, 220 (3d Cir. 1975).

On the other hand, a number of courts hold that, in a § 14(a) damages action brought against outside directors and accountants for materially false or misleading financial statements contained in proxy materials, scienter is required to be shown. For example, with respect to accountants, the Sixth Circuit opined in *Adams v. Standard Knitting Mills*, 623 F.2d 422, 428 (6th Cir. 1980):

> Federal courts created the private right of action under Section 14, and they have a special responsibility to consider the consequences of their rulings and to mold liability fairly to reflect the circumstances of the parties. Although we are not called on in this case to decide the standard of liability of the corporate issuers of proxy material, we are influenced by the fact that the accountant here, unlike the corporate issuer, does not directly benefit from the proxy vote and is not in privity with the stockholder. Unlike the corporate issuer, the preparation of financial statements to be appended to proxies and other reports is the daily fare of accountants, and the

accountant's potential liability for relatively minor mistakes would be enormous under a negligence standard.

See SEC v. Shanahan, 646 F.3d 536, 546–547 (8th Cir. 2011) ("We agree with those courts that have concluded that scienter is an element [of a § 14(a) claim] at least for claims against outside directors and accountants."). *But see Herskowitz v. Nutri/ System, Inc.,* 857 F.2d 179 (3d Cir. 1988) (rejecting Adams' rationale and imposing § 14(a) liability against investment banker based on negligence).

Should the requisite culpability standard under § 14(a) depend upon the defendant's identity and relationship to the issuer? Is such an interpretation consistent with *Hochfelder* and *Aaron?* On the other hand, can it be argued persuasively that the Sixth Circuit, by applying an approach akin to that of a "flexible duty" standard, equitably balanced the competing public policy interests at stake? *But see* Note, 56 Notre Dame Law. 579, 586 (1981) (The Sixth Circuit's "interest in protecting outside accountants from excessive liability does not outweigh the countervailing interest of protecting shareholders from misleading proxy materials.").

Plaintiffs may seek to invoke § 14(a) in a variety of factual contexts. For example, the alleged failure to disclose information material to the shareholders' assessment of management's integrity or competence implicates the proxy provisions. *See, e.g., Gaines v. Haughton,* 645 F.2d 761 (9th Cir. 1981), in § 5.03. Certain breach of fiduciary duty claims, patterned after the "lost state remedy" line of cases, may be actionable under § 14(a). *See, e.g., Weisberg v. Coastal States Gas Corp.,* 609 F.2d 650 (2d Cir. 1979).[14] The § 14(a) remedy also comes into play in proxy fights for corporate control. *See, e.g., GAF Corporation v. Heyman,* 724 F.2d 727 (2d Cir. 1983) (contained in Chapter 14). And, as the following case illustrates, § 14(a) may be invoked in connection with merger transactions. Interestingly, because § 14(a) does not have a purchaser-seller standing requirement and because the requisite culpability standard may be that of negligence, plaintiffs may be successful in a § 14(a) right of action where such relief would have been denied under § 10(b).[15]

---

14. Professor Hazen asserts that, provided there is an inadequacy of disclosure, "there are several important areas of corporate mismanagement that properly can be redressed by the proxy rules." Hazen, *Corporate Mismanagement and the Federal Securities Acts Antifraud Provisions: A Familiar Path With Some New Detours,* 20 B.C.L. Rev. 819, 850 (1979).

15. *See generally* R. Thomas & C. Dixon, Aaron & Einhorn on Proxy Contests for Corporate Control (1998); M. Waters, Proxy Regulation (1992); Bainbridge, *Redirecting State Takeover Laws at Proxy Contests,* 1992 Wis. L. Rev. 1071 (1992); Bradford, *The Possible Future of Private Rights of Action for Proxy Fraud: The Parallel Between Borak and Wilko,* 70 Neb. L. Rev. 306 (1991); Fisch, *From Legitimacy to Logic: Reconstructing Proxy Regulation,* 46 Vand. L. Rev. 1129 (1993); Gelb, *Implied Private Rights of Action Under SEC Rule 14a-9 and Rule 10b-5: The Impact of Virginia Bankshares, Inc. v. Sandberg,* 76 Marq. L. Rev. 363 (1993); Steinberg, *Fiduciary Duties and Disclosure Obligations in Proxy and Tender Contests for Corporate Control,* 30 Emory L.J. 169 (1981); *Symposium on Proxy Reform,* 17 J. Corp. L. No. 1 (1991); Thomas, *Judicial Review of Defensive Tactics in Proxy Contests: When Is Using a Rights Plan Right?,* 46 Vand. L. Rev. 503 (1997).

[B] "True Purpose" and Causation

Virginia Bankshares, Inc. v. Sandberg

United States Supreme Court

501 U.S. 1083, 111 S. Ct. 2749, 115 L. Ed. 2d 929 (1991)

JUSTICE SOUTER delivered the opinion of the Court.

Section 14(a) of the Securities Exchange Act of 1934 authorizes the Securities and Exchange Commission to adopt rules for the solicitation of proxies, and prohibits their violation. In *J. I. Case Co. v. Borak,* 377 U.S. 426 (1964), we first recognized an implied private right of action for the breach of § 14(a) as implemented by SEC Rule 14a-9, which prohibits the solicitation of proxies by means of materially false or misleading statements.

The questions before us are whether a statement couched in conclusory or qualitative terms purporting to explain directors' reasons for recommending certain corporate action can be materially misleading within the meaning of Rule 14a-9, and whether causation of damages compensable under § 14(a) can be shown by a member of a class of minority shareholders whose votes are not required by law or corporate by-law to authorize the corporate action subject to the proxy solicitation. We hold that knowingly false statements of reasons may be actionable even though conclusory in form, but that respondents have failed to demonstrate the . . . basis required to extend the § 14(a) private action to such shareholders when any indication of congressional intent to do so is lacking.

I

In December 1986, First American Bankshares, Inc., (FABI), a bank holding company, began a "freeze-out" merger, in which the First American Bank of Virginia (Bank) eventually merged into Virginia Bankshares, Inc., (VBI), a wholly owned subsidiary of FABI. VBI owned 85% of the Bank's shares, the remaining 15% being in the hands of some 2,000 minority shareholders. FABI hired the investment banking firm of Keefe, Bruyette & Woods (KBW) to give an opinion on the appropriate price for shares of the minority holders, who would lose their interests in the Bank as a result of the merger. Based on market quotations and unverified information from FABI, KBW gave the Bank's executive committee an opinion that $42 a share would be a fair price for the minority stock. The executive committee approved the merger proposal at that price, and the full board followed suit.

Although Virginia law required only that such a merger proposal be submitted to a vote at a shareholders' meeting, and that the meeting be preceded by circulation of a statement of information to the shareholders, the directors nevertheless solicited proxies for voting on the proposal at the annual meeting set for April 21, 1987. In their solicitation, the directors urged the proposal's adoption and stated they had approved the plan because of its opportunity for the minority shareholders to achieve a "high" value, which they elsewhere described as a "fair" price, for their stock.

Although most minority shareholders gave the proxies requested, respondent Sandberg did not, and after approval of the merger she sought damages in the United States District Court for the Eastern District of Virginia from VBI, FABI, and the directors of the Bank. She pleaded two counts, one for soliciting proxies in violation of § 14(a) and Rule 14a-9, and the other for breaching fiduciary duties owed to the minority shareholders under state law. Under the first count, Sandberg alleged, among other things, that the directors had not believed that the price offered was high or that the terms of the merger were fair, but had recommended the merger only because they believed they had no alternative if they wished to remain on board. At trial, Sandberg invoked language from this Court's opinion in *Mills v. Electric Auto-Lite Co.*, 396 U.S. 375, 385 (1970), to obtain an instruction that the jury could find for her without a showing of her own reliance on the alleged misstatements, so long as they were material and the proxy solicitation was an "essential link" in the merger process.

The jury's verdicts were for Sandberg on both counts, after finding violations of Rule 14a-9 by all defendants and a breach of fiduciary duties by the Bank's directors. The jury awarded Sandberg $18 a share, having found that she would have received $60 if her stock had been valued adequately.

. . . .

On appeal, the United States Court of Appeals for the Fourth Circuit affirmed the judgments, holding that certain statements in the proxy solicitation were materially misleading for purposes of the Rule, and that respondents could maintain their action even though their votes had not been needed to effectuate the merger. 891 F.2d 1112 (1989). We granted certiorari because of the importance of the issues presented.

II

The Court of Appeals affirmed petitioners' liability for two statements found to have been materially misleading in violation of § 14(a) of the Act, one of which was that "The Plan of Merger has been approved by the Board of Directors because it provides an opportunity for the Bank's public shareholders to achieve a high value for their shares." . . . Petitioners argue that statements of opinion or belief incorporating indefinite and unverifiable expressions cannot be actionable as misstatements of material fact within the meaning of Rule 14a-9, and that such a declaration of opinion or belief should never be actionable when placed in a proxy solicitation incorporating statements of fact sufficient to enable readers to draw their own, independent conclusions.

A

We consider first the actionability *per se* of statements of reasons, opinion or belief. Because such a statement by definition purports to express what is consciously on the speaker's mind, we interpret the jury verdict as finding that the directors' statements of belief and opinion were made with knowledge that the directors did not hold the beliefs or opinion expressed, and we confine our discussion to statements so made.[16] That such statements may be materially significant raises no serious question. The meaning of the materiality requirement for liability under § 14(a) was discussed at some length in *TSC Industries, Inc. v. Northway, Inc.,* 426 U.S. 438 (1976), where we held a fact to be material "if there is a substantial likelihood that a reasonable shareholder would consider it important in deciding how to vote." . . . We think there is no room to deny that a statement of belief by corporate directors about a recommended course of action, or an explanation of their reasons for recommending it, can take on just that importance. Shareholders know that directors usually have knowledge and expertness far exceeding the normal investor's resources, and the directors' perceived superiority is magnified even further by the common knowledge that state law customarily obliges them to exercise their judgment in the shareholders' interest. . . . Naturally, then, the share owner faced with a proxy request will think it important to know the directors' beliefs about the course they recommend, and their specific reasons for urging the stockholders to embrace it.

B

1

But, assuming materiality, the question remains whether statements of reasons, opinions, or beliefs are statements "with respect to . . . material *fact[s]*" so as to fall within the strictures of the Rule. Petitioners argue that we would invite wasteful litigation of amorphous issues outside the readily provable realm of fact if we were to recognize liability here on proof that the directors did not recommend the merger for the stated reason, and they cite the authority of *Blue Chip Stamps v. Manor Drug Stores,* 421 U.S. 723 (1975), in urging us to recognize sound policy grounds for placing such statements outside the scope of the Rule.

We agree that *Blue Chip Stamps* is instructive, as illustrating a line between what is and is not manageable in the litigation of facts, but do not read it as supporting petitioners' position. The issue in *Blue Chip Stamps* was the scope of the class of plaintiffs entitled to seek relief under an implied private cause of action for violating § 10(b) of the Act, prohibiting manipulation and deception in the purchase or sale of certain securities, contrary to Commission rules. This Court held against expanding the class from actual buyers and sellers to include those who rely on deceptive sales practices by taking no action, either to sell what they own or to buy what they do not. We observed that actual sellers and buyers who sue for compensation must identify a specific number of shares bought or sold in order to calculate and limit any ensuing recovery. Recognizing liability to merely would-be

---

[16]. In *TSC Industries, Inc. v. Northway, Inc.,* 426 U.S. 438, 444, n. 7 (1976), we reserved the question whether scienter was necessary for liability generally under § 14(a). We reserve it still.

investors, however, would have exposed the courts to litigation unconstrained by any such anchor in demonstrable fact, resting instead on a plaintiff's "subjective hypothesis" about the number of shares he would have sold or purchased. Hindsight's natural temptation to hypothesize boldness would have magnified the risk of nuisance litigation, which would have been compounded both by the opportunity to prolong discovery, and by the capacity of claims resting on undocumented personal assertion to resist any resolution short of settlement or trial. Such were the premises of policy, added to those of textual analysis and precedent, on which *Blue Chip Stamps* deflected the threat of vexatious litigation over "many rather hazy issues of historical fact the proof of which depended almost entirely on oral testimony. . . . "

Attacks on the truth of directors' statements of reasons or belief, however, need carry no such threats. Such statements are *factual* in two senses: as statements that the directors do act for the reasons given or hold the belief stated and as statements about the subject matter of the reason or belief expressed. In neither sense does the proof or disproof of such statements implicate the concerns expressed in *Blue Chip Stamps*. The root of those concerns was a plaintiff's capacity to manufacture claims of hypothetical action, unconstrained by independent evidence. Reasons for directors' recommendations or statements of belief are, in contrast, characteristically matters of corporate record subject to documentation, to be supported or attacked by evidence of historical fact outside a plaintiff's control. . . .

It is no answer to argue, as petitioners do, that the quoted statement on which liability was predicted did not express a reason in dollars and cents, but focused instead on the "indefinite and unverifiable" term, "high" value, much like the similar claim that the merger's terms were "fair" to shareholders.[17] The objection ignores the fact that such conclusory terms in a commercial context are reasonably understood to rest on a factual basis that justifies them as accurate, the absence of which renders them misleading. Provable facts either furnish good reasons to make a conclusory commercial judgment, or they count against it, and expressions of such judgments can be uttered with knowledge of truth or falsity just like more definite statements, and defended or attacked through the orthodox evidentiary process that either substantiates their underlying justifications or tends to disprove their existence. . . . In

---

[17]. Petitioners are also wrong to argue that construing the statute to allow recovery for a misleading statement that the merger was "fair" to the minority shareholders is tantamount to assuming federal authority to bar corporate transactions thought to be unfair to some group of shareholders. It is, of course, true that we said in *Santa Fe Industries, Inc. v. Green*, 480 U.S. 462, 479 (1977), that "'[c]orporations are creatures of state law, and investors commit their funds to corporate directors on the understanding that, except where federal law *expressly* requires certain responsibilities of directors with respect to stockholders, state law will govern the internal affairs of the corporation,'" *quoting Cort v. Ash*, 422 U.S. 66, 84 (1975). But § 14(a) does impose responsibility for false and misleading proxy statements. Although a corporate transaction's "*fairness*" is not, as such, a federal concern, a proxy statement's claim of fairness presupposes a factual integrity that federal law is expressly concerned to preserve. . . .

this case, whether $42 was "high," and the proposal "fair" to the minority shareholders depended on whether provable facts about the Bank's assets, and about actual and potential levels of operation, substantiated a value that was above, below, or more or less at the $42 figure, when assessed in accordance with recognized methods of valuation.

Respondents adduced evidence for just such facts in proving that the statement was misleading about its subject matter and a false expression of the directors' reasons. Whereas the proxy statement described the $42 price as offering a premium above both book value and market price, the evidence indicated that a calculation of the book figure based on the appreciated value of the Bank's real estate holdings eliminated any such premium. The evidence on the significance of market price showed that KBW had conceded that the market was closed, thin and dominated by FABI, facts omitted from the statement. There was, indeed, evidence of a "going concern" value for the Bank in excess of $60 per share of common stock, another fact never disclosed. However conclusory the directors' statement may have been, then, it was open to attack by garden-variety evidence, subject neither to a plaintiff's control nor ready manufacture, and there was no undue risk of open-ended liability or uncontrollable litigation in allowing respondents the opportunity for recovery on the allegation that it was misleading to call $42 "high."

. . . .

2

Under § 14(a), then, a plaintiff is permitted to prove a specific statement of reason knowingly false or misleadingly incomplete, even when stated in conclusory terms. In reaching this conclusion we have considered statements of reasons of the sort exemplified here, which misstate the speaker's reasons and also mislead about the stated subject matter (e.g., the value of the shares). A statement of belief may be open to objection only in the former respect, however, solely as a misstatement of the psychological fact of the speaker's belief in what he says. In this case, for example, the Court of Appeals alluded to just such limited falsity in observing that "the jury was certainly justified in believing that the directors did not believe a merger at $42 per share was in the minority stockholders' interest but, rather, that they voted as they did for other reasons, e.g., retaining their seats on the board." . . .

The question arises, then, whether disbelief, or undisclosed belief or motivation [called "true purpose"], standing alone, should be a sufficient basis to sustain an action under § 14(a), absent proof by the sort of objective evidence described above that the statement also expressly or impliedly asserted something false or misleading about its subject matter. We think that proof of mere disbelief or belief undisclosed should not suffice for liability under § 14(a), and if nothing more had been required or proven in this case we would reverse for that reason.

On the one hand, it would be rare to find a case with evidence solely of disbelief or undisclosed motivation without further proof that the statement was defective as to its subject matter. While we certainly would not hold a director's naked admission of disbelief incompetent evidence of a proxy statement's false or misleading character, such an unusual admission will not very often stand alone, and we do not substantially narrow the cause of action by requiring a plaintiff to demonstrate something false or misleading in what the statement expressly or impliedly declared about its subject.

On the other hand, to recognize liability on mere disbelief or undisclosed motive without any demonstration that the proxy statement was false or misleading about its subject would authorize § 14(a) litigation confined solely to what one skeptical court spoke of as the "impurities" of a director's "unclean heart." *Stedman v. Storer*, 308 F. Supp. 881, 887 (SDNY 1969) (dealing with § 10(b)). This, we think, would cross the line that *Blue Chip Stamps* sought to draw. While it is true that the liability, if recognized, would rest on an actual, not hypothetical, psychological fact, the temptation to rest an otherwise nonexistent § 14(a) action on psychological enquiry alone would threaten just the sort of strike suits and attrition by discovery that *Blue Chip Stamps* sought to discourage. We therefore hold disbelief or undisclosed motivation, standing alone [so-called "true purpose"], insufficient to satisfy the element of *fact* that must be established under § 14(a).

C

Petitioners' fall-back position assumes the same relationship between a conclusory judgment and its underlying facts that we described in Part II-B-1, *supra*. Thus, . . . petitioners argue that even if conclusory statements of reason or belief can be actionable under § 14(a), we should confine liability to instances where the proxy material fails to disclose the offending statement's factual basis. There would be no justification for holding the shareholders entitled to judicial relief, that is, when they were given evidence that a stated reason for a proxy recommendation was misleading, and an opportunity to draw that conclusion themselves.

The answer to this argument rests on the difference between a merely misleading statement and one that is materially so. While a misleading statement will not always lose its deceptive edge simply by joinder with others that are true, the true statements may discredit the other one so obviously that the risk of real deception drops to nil. Since liability under § 14(a) must rest not only on deceptiveness but materiality as well (i.e., it has to be significant enough to be important to a reasonable investor deciding how to vote). . . . [P]etitioners are on perfectly firm ground insofar as they argue that publishing accurate facts in a proxy statement can render a misleading proposition too unimportant to ground liability.

But not every mixture with the true will neutralize the deceptive. If it would take a financial analyst to spot the tension between the one and the other, whatever is misleading will remain materially so, and liability should follow. . . . The point of a proxy statement, after all, should be to inform, not to challenge the reader's critical wits. Only when the inconsistency would exhaust the misleading conclusion's capacity to influence the reasonable shareholder would a § 14(a) action fail on the element of materiality.

Suffice it to say that the evidence invoked by petitioners in the instant case fell short of compelling the jury to find the facial materiality of the misleading statement neutralized. The directors claim, for example, to have made an explanatory disclosure of further reasons for their recommendation when they said they would keep their seats following the merger, but they failed to mention what at least one of them admitted in testimony, that they would have had no expectation of doing so without supporting the proposal. . . . And although the proxy statement did speak factually about the merger price in describing it as higher than share prices in recent sales, it failed even to mention the closed market dominated by FABI. None of these disclosures that the directors point to was, then, anything more than a half-truth, and the record shows that another fact statement they invoke was arguably even worse. The claim that the merger price exceeded book value was controverted, as we have seen already, by evidence of a higher book value than the directors conceded, reflecting appreciation in the Bank's real estate portfolio. Finally, the solicitation omitted any mention of the Bank's value as a going concern at more than $60 a share, as against the merger price of $42. . . .

III

The second issue before us, left open in *Mills v. Electric Auto-Lite Co.*, is whether causation of damages compensable through the implied private right of action under § 14(a) can be demonstrated by a member of a class of minority shareholders whose votes are not required by law or corporate bylaw to authorize the transaction giving rise to the claim. *J. J. Case Co. v. Borak*, 377 U.S. 426 (1964), did not itself address the requisites of causation, as such, or define the class of plaintiffs eligible to sue under § 14(a). But its general holding, that a private cause of action was available to some shareholder class, acquired greater clarity with a more definite concept of causation in *Mills*, where we addressed the sufficiency of proof that misstatements in a proxy solicitation were responsible for damages claimed from the merger subject to complaint.

Although a majority stockholder in *Mills* controlled just over half the corporation's shares, a two-thirds vote was needed to approve the merger proposal. After proxies had been obtained, and the merger had carried, minority shareholders brought a *Borak* action. The question arose whether the plaintiffs' burden to demonstrate causation of their damages traceable to the § 14(a) violation required proof that the defect in the proxy solicitation had had "a decisive effect on the voting." The *Mills* Court avoided the evidentiary morass that would have followed from requiring individualized proof that enough minority shareholders had relied upon the misstatements to swing the vote. Instead, it held that causation of damages by a material proxy misstatement could be established by showing that minority proxies necessary and sufficient to authorize the corporate acts had been given in accordance with the tenor of the solicitation, and the Court described such a causal relationship by calling the proxy solicitation an "essential link in the accomplishment of the transaction." In the case before it, the Court found the solicitation essential, as contrasted with one addressed to a class of minority shareholders without votes required by law or by-law to authorize the action proposed, and left it for another day to decide whether such a minority shareholder could demonstrate causation.

In this case, respondents address *Mills'* open question by proffering two theories that the proxy solicitation addressed to them was an "essential link" under the *Mills* causation test.[18] They argue, first, that a link existed and was essential simply because VBI and FABI would have been unwilling to proceed with the merger without the approval manifested by the minority shareholders' proxies, which would not have been obtained without the solicitation's express misstatements and misleading omissions. On this reasoning, the causal connection would depend on a desire to avoid bad shareholder or public relations, and the essential character of the causal link would stem not from the enforceable terms of the parties' corporate relationship, but from one party's apprehension of the ill will of the other.

In the alternative, respondents argue that the proxy statement was an essential link between the directors' proposal and the merger because it was the means to satisfy a state statutory requirement of minority shareholder approval, as a condition for saving the merger from voidability resulting from a conflict of interest on the part of one of the Bank's directors, who voted in favor of the merger while also serving as a director of FABI. . . .

Although respondents have proffered each of these theories as establishing a chain of causal connection in which the proxy statement is claimed to have been an "essential link," neither theory presents the proxy solicitation as essential in the sense of *Mills'* causal sequence, in which the solicitation links a directors' proposal with the votes legally required to authorize the action proposed. As a consequence, each theory would, if adopted, extend the scope of *Borak* actions beyond the ambit of *Mills,* and expand the class of plaintiffs entitled to bring *Borak* actions to include shareholders whose initial authorization of the transaction prompting the proxy solicitation is unnecessary.

. . . .

The theory of causal necessity derived from the requirements of Virginia law dealing with postmerger ratification seeks to identify the essential character of the proxy solicitation from its function in obtaining the minority approval that would preclude a minority suit attacking the merger. Since the link is said to be a step in the process of barring a class of shareholders from resort to the state remedy otherwise available, this theory of causation rests upon the proposition of policy that § 14(a) should

---

[18]. Citing the decision in *Schlick v. Penn-Dixie Cement Corp.*, 507 F.2d 374 (CA2 1974), petitioners characterize respondents' proffered theories as examples of so-called "sue facts" and "shame facts" theories. "A 'sue fact' is, in general, a fact which is material to a sue decision. A "'sue decision' is a decision by a shareholder whether or not to institute a representative or derivative suit alleging a state-law cause of action." Gelb, *Rule 10b-5 and* Santa Fe — *Herein of Sue Facts, Shame Facts, and Other Matters,* 87 W. Va. L. Rev. 189, 198, and n.52 (1985). . . . "Shame facts" are said to be facts which had they been disclosed, would have "shamed" management into abandoning a proposed transaction. . . .

provide a federal remedy whenever a false or misleading proxy statement results in the loss under state law of a shareholder plaintiff's state remedy for the enforcement of a state right. Respondents agree with the suggestions of counsel for the SEC and FDIC that causation be recognized, for example, when a minority shareholder has been induced by a misleading proxy statement to forfeit a state-law right to an appraisal remedy . . . or when such a shareholder has been deterred from obtaining an order enjoining a damaging transaction by a proxy solicitation that misrepresents the facts on which an injunction could properly have been issued. [In the instant case, plaintiffs had no right to appraisal under Virginia law.] Respondents claim that in this case a predicate for recognizing just such a causal link exists in Va. Code § 13.1-691(A)(2) (1989), which sets the conditions under which the merger may be insulated from suit by a minority shareholder seeking to void it on account of [the insider's] conflict.

This case does not, however, require us to decide whether § 14(a) provides a cause of action for lost state remedies, since there is no indication in the law or facts before us that the proxy solicitation resulted in any such loss. The contrary appears to be the case. Assuming the soundness of respondents' characterization of the proxy statement as materially misleading, the very terms of the Virginia statute indicate that a favorable minority vote induced by the solicitation would not suffice to render the merger invulnerable to later attack on the ground of the conflict. The statute bars a shareholder from seeking to avoid a transaction tainted by a director's conflict if, *inter alia*, the minority shareholders ratified the transaction following disclosure of the material facts of the transaction and the conflict. . . . Assuming that the material facts about the merger and [the insider's] interests were not accurately disclosed, the minority votes were inadequate to ratify the merger under state law, and there was no loss of state remedy to connect the proxy solicitation with harm to minority shareholders irredressable under state law. Nor is there a claim here that the statement misled respondents into entertaining a false belief that they had no chance to upset the merger, until the time for bringing suit had run out.

IV

The judgment of the Court of Appeals is reversed.

It is so ordered.

JUSTICE SCALIA, concurring in part and concurring in the judgment.

I

As I understand the Court's opinion, the statement "In the opinion of the Directors, this is a high value for the shares" would produce liability if in fact it was not a high value and the Directors knew that. It would not produce liability if in fact it was not a high value but the Directors honestly believed otherwise. The statement "The Directors voted to accept the proposal because they believe it offers a high value" would not produce liability if in fact the Directors' genuine motive was quite different—except that it would produce liability if the proposal in fact did not offer a high value and the Directors knew that.

I agree with all of this. However, not every sentence that has the word "opinion" in it, or that refers to motivation for Directors' actions, leads us into this psychic thicket. Sometimes such a sentence actually represents facts as facts rather than opinions—and in that event no more need be done than apply the normal rules for § 14(a) liability. I think that is the situation here. In my view, the statement at issue in this case is most fairly read as affirming separately both the fact of the Directors' opinion and the accuracy of the facts upon which the opinion was assertedly based. It reads as follows:

> "The Plan of Merger has been approved by the Board of Directors because it provides an opportunity for the Bank's public shareholders to achieve a high value for their shares."

Had it read "because *in their estimation* it provides an opportunity etc." it would have set forth nothing but an opinion. As written, however, it asserts both that the Board of Directors acted for a particular reason *and* that that reason is correct. This interpretation is made clear by what immediately follows: "The price to be paid is about 30% higher than the [last traded price immediately before announcement of the proposal]. . . . [T]he $42 per share that will be paid to public holders of the common stock represents a premium of approximately 26% over the book value. . . . [T]he bank earned $24,767,000 in the year ended December 31, 1986. . . ." These are all facts that support—and that are obviously introduced for the *purpose* of supporting—the factual trust of the "because" clause, i.e., that the proposal gives shareholders a "high value."

If the present case were to proceed, therefore, I think the normal § 14(a) principles governing misrepresentation of fact would apply.

II

. . . .

I concur in the judgment of the Court, and join all of its opinion except Part II.

Note

In light of the *Virginia Bankshares* case, consider the following:

(1) The Supreme Court's decision evidences an unwillingness to predicate securities law liability on undisclosed motive, which is not grounded in materially false or misleading *factual* representations. Hence, nondisclosure of true purpose appears to be not actionable even when management's principal motive is entrenchment. But the duty to disclose "purpose" does not remain completely avoidable. Such a duty arises, for example, in the context of going private transactions under § 13(e) of the Exchange Act, as well as pursuant to Rule 13e-3 and Schedule 13E-3. See § 14.02.

(2) Has the Supreme Court implicitly overruled the "lost state remedy" line of cases or does this theory remain good law? Stated differently, if the plaintiff Sandberg would have been entitled to an injunction under Virginia law to enjoin the merger if the facts had been accurately disclosed, would she have shown the requisite causation to state a § 14(a) claim?

The answer is that the Supreme Court left this issue unresolved. The Court stated: "This case does not . . . require us to decide whether § 14(a) provides a cause of action for lost state remedies, since there is no indication in the law or facts before us that the proxy solicitation resulted in any such loss." Moreover, the four member dissenting opinion authored by Justice Kennedy strongly indicates that causation for § 10(b) and § 14(a) purposes may be shown in this context by establishing that the misrepresentation or nondisclosure deprived such minority shareholders of an otherwise available state law remedy, such as the right to appraisal or to injunctive relief.

Cases decided after *Virginia Bankshares* support the continued viability of the "*lost state remedy*" line of cases. In one such case, the Second Circuit ruled for the plaintiffs, reasoning that the defendant's deficient proxy statement may have induced the plaintiffs to forfeit their appraisal rights. *Wilson v. Great American Enterprises, Inc.*, 979 F.2d 924 (2d Cir. 1992). Similarly, the Third Circuit stated that causation may be shown when the defendant's "misstatement or omission has caused the minority shareholders to forego an opportunity under state law to enjoin a merger." *Scattergood v. Perelman*, 945 F.2d 618 (3d Cir. 1991). Accord, *Howing Company v. Nationwide Corporation*, 927 F.2d 700 (6th Cir. 1992). However, the theory has been rejected by a number of courts. *See, e.g., Isquith v. Caremark Int'l, Inc.*, 136 F.3d 531 (7th Cir. 1998). *See also, Grace v. Rosenstock*, 228 F.3d 40 (2d Cir. 2000) (holding that appraisal sole remedy under New York law where minority stockholders in a cash-out merger challenge the consideration paid and pursue monetary damages and not equitable relief).

(3) For further analysis of *Virginia Bankshares* and its ramifications, see Gelb, *Implied Private Rights of Action Under SEC Rule 14a-9 and Rule 10b-5: The Impact of Virginia Bankshares, Inc. v. Sandberg*, 76 Marq. L. Rev. 363 (1993); Orlinsky, *Virginia Bankshares, Inc. v. Sandberg: The Golden Rule of Section 14(a)*, 47 Bus. Law. 837 (1992); Steinberg & Reece, *The Supreme Court, Implied Rights of Action, and Proxy Regulation*, 54 Ohio St. L.J. 67 (1993).

[C] SEC Proxy Rule Amendments

The SEC's proxy rules seek to facilitate communications among shareholders. In adopting its proxy rule amendments, the Commission reacted to criticism by certain institutional as well as individual shareholders that the then-existing proxy framework unduly favored incumbent management and impeded the exchange of views among shareholders. Whether the SEC's action accommodates the various constituencies is subject to debate.

Regulation of Communications Among Shareholders

Securities and Exchange Commission

Securities Exchange Act Release No. 31326 (1992)

The Securities and Exchange Commission ("Commission") today announces the adoption of amendments to its proxy rules promulgated under Section 14(a) of the Securities Exchange Act of 1934 ("Exchange Act"). By removing unnecessary government interference in discussions among shareholders of corporate performance and other matters of direct interest to all shareholders, these rules should reduce the cost of regulation to both the government and to shareholders. The amendments eliminate unnecessary regulatory obstacles to the exchange of views and opinions by shareholders and others concerning management performance and initiatives presented for a vote of shareholders. The amendments also lower the regulatory costs of conducting a regulated solicitation by management, shareholders and others by minimizing regulatory costs related to the dissemination of soliciting materials. The rules also remove unnecessary limitations on the shareholders' use of their voting rights, and improve disclosure to shareholders in the context of a solicitation as well as in the reporting of voting results.

. . . The Commission is today adopting several amendments to its proxy rules and related disclosure requirements. These changes include:

(1) Rule 14a-2(b) has been amended to create an exemption from the proxy statement delivery and disclosure requirements for communications with shareholders, where the person soliciting is not seeking proxy authority and does not have a substantial interest in the matter subject to a vote or is otherwise ineligible for the exemption. Public notice of written soliciting activity will be required by beneficial owners of more than $5 million of the registrant's securities through publication, broadcast or submission to the Commission of the written soliciting materials;

(2) The definition of "solicitation" in Rule 14a-1 has been amended to specify that a shareholder can publicly announce how it intends to vote and provide the reasons for that decision without having to comply with the proxy rules;

(3) Rule 14a-3 has been amended to add a new paragraph (f), exempting solicitations conveyed by public broadcast or speech or publication from the proxy statement delivery requirements, provided a definitive proxy statement is on file with the Commission;

(4) Rules 14a-3(a) and 14a-4 have been amended to allow registrants and other soliciting parties to commence a solicitation on the basis of a preliminary proxy statement publicly filed with the Commission, so long as no form of proxy is provided to the solicited shareholders until the dissemination of a definitive proxy statement;

(5) Rule 14a-6 has been amended to allow solicitation materials other than the proxy statement and form of proxy to be filed with the Commission in definitive form at the time of dissemination. In addition, preliminary proxy statements are now available for public inspection when filed except in connection with business combinations other than roll-ups and going private transactions;

(6) Rule 14a-7 has been amended to require registrants, in the case of transactions subject to the Commission roll-up or going private rules, to provide shareholders, upon written request and satisfaction of certain conditions, copies of its list of shareholder names, addresses, and position listings, as well as any list of non-objecting or consenting beneficial owners where in possession of the registrant. In all other cases, registrants are required to make an election either to provide a list to, or mail materials for, the requesting shareholders;

(7) Rules 14a-4(a) and (b)(1) have been amended to require that the form of proxy set forth each matter to be voted upon separately in order to allow shareholders to vote individually on each matter;

. . . .

The amendments adopted today reflect a Commission determination that the federal proxy rules have created unnecessary regulatory impediments to communicating among shareholders and others and to the effective use of shareholder voting rights. The Commission has also determined that modifications in the current rules are desirable to reduce these burdens and to achieve the purposes set forth in the Exchange Act.

Underlying the adoption of Section 14(a) of the Exchange Act was a Congressional concern that the solicitation of proxy voting authority be conducted on a fair, honest and informed basis. Therefore, Congress granted the Commission the broad "power to control the conditions under which proxies may be solicited," and to promote "fair corporate suffrage." A necessary element of the Commission's mandate was "to prevent management or others from obtaining authorization for corporate action by means of deceptive or inadequate disclosure in proxy solicitations." This concern with disclosure included preventing the solicitation of proxies "without fairly informing the stockholders of the purposes for which the proxies are to be used."

Prior to a shareholder granting the legal power to someone else — whether management or an outsider — to vote his or her stock, the shareholder needs to know what matters will be voted on, and how the recipient of the proxy intends to vote the shareholder's shares. This fundamental objective is intended to deal with the problems that would arise if a shareholder was advised that his or her shares were going to be voted on the election of directors and auditors, and instead the proxy was used to vote, for example, in favor of a merger with another company owned by insiders on unfavorable terms.

Thus, the description of the matters to be brought before a meeting for a vote (including the election of directors), the material information related to all such matters (including any substantial interest the soliciting person has in the subject matter of the vote), and the specifics on how the proxy recipient proposes to vote on behalf of the proxy giver unless otherwise instructed are core information critical to shareholders as part of the proxy process. Likewise, the terms of the proxy authority solicited and the ability of soliciting shareholders to reach other shareholders are key elements in assuring the fairness of the solicitation of proxy authority. On the whole, the regulatory scheme adopted by the Commission pursuant to the broad authority granted by Section 14(a) has been designed to make sure that management and others who solicit shareholder proxies provide this needed information to shareholders, allow them to instruct the specific use of their proxy and provide them access to other shareholders through mailing or by access to a shareholder list.

. . . .

Note

The SEC's amendments were largely a response to the revitalized shareholder-rights movement. This movement, encompassing institutional as well as individual shareholders, has focused on economic issues. No longer can incumbent management depend upon institutional investors to support its course of action or simply to sell their shares if displeased. Today, when in their economic interests, institutional investors will take issue with management and, if deemed appropriate, will publicly oppose management's stance.

Although the SEC's amendments facilitate communication among shareholders, a number of critics believe that more extensive reforms are necessary. Such proposals, for example, include that: confidential voting be guaranteed; corporate funds for proxy solicitations should be granted exclusively to a committee of the corporation's largest shareholders; and shareholders owning a certain percentage of the corporation's stock (such as three percent) should be authorized to directly nominate prospective directors. *See generally* Brown, *The Shareholder Communication Rules and the Securities and Exchange Commission: An Exercise in Regulatory Utility or Futility?*, 13 J. Corp. L. 683 (1988); Cane, *The Revised SEC Shareholder Proxy Proposal System: Attitudes, Results and Perspectives*, 11 J. Corp. L. 57 (1985); Dent, *Toward Unifying Ownership and Control in the Public Corporation*, 1989 Wis. L. Rev. 881; *Symposium on Proxy Reform*, 17 J. Corp. L. No. 1 (1991).

[D] The Shareholder Proposal Rule

Shareholder Proposals

SEC Division of Corporation Finance

Staff Legal Bulletin No. 14 (2001)

Rule 14a-8 provides an opportunity for a shareholder owning a relatively small amount of a company's securities to have his or her proposal placed alongside management's proposals in that company's proxy materials for presentation to a vote at an annual or special meeting of shareholders. It has become increasingly popular because it provides an avenue for communication between shareholders and companies, as well as among shareholders themselves. The rule generally requires the company to include the proposal unless the shareholder has not complied with the rule's procedural requirements or the proposal falls within one of the 13 substantive bases for exclusion described in the table below.

Substantive Basis	Description
Rule 14a-8(i)(1)	The proposal is not a proper subject for action by shareholders under the laws of the jurisdiction of the company's organization.
Rule 14a-8(i)(2)	The proposal would, if implemented, cause the company to violate any state, federal or foreign law to which it is subject.
Rule 14a-8(i)(3)	The proposal or supporting statement is contrary to any of the Commission's proxy rules, including rule 14a-9, which prohibits materially false or misleading statements in proxy soliciting materials.
Rule 14a-8(i)(4)	The proposal relates to the redress of a personal claim or grievance against the company or any other person, or is designed to result in a benefit to the shareholder, or to further a personal interest, which is not shared by the other shareholders at large.
Rule 14a-8(i)(5)	The proposal relates to operations that account for less than 5% of the company's total assets at the end of its most recent fiscal year, and for less than 5% of its net earnings and gross sales for its most recent fiscal year, and is not otherwise significantly related to the company's business.
Rule 14a-8(i)(6)	The company would lack the power or authority to implement the proposal.
Rule 14a-8(i)(7)	The proposal deals with a matter relating to the company's ordinary business operations.
Rule 14a-8(i)(8)	The proposal relates to an election for membership on the company's board of directors or analogous governing body.
Rule 14a-8(i)(9)	The proposal directly conflicts with one of the company's own proposals to be submitted to shareholders at the same meeting.
Rule 14a-8(i)(10)	The company has already substantially implemented the proposal.

Rule 14a-8(i)(11)	The proposal substantially duplicates another proposal previously submitted to the company by another shareholder that will be included in the company's proxy materials for the same meeting.
Rule 14a-8(i)(12)	The proposal deals with substantially the same subject matter as another proposal or proposals that previously has or have been included in the company's proxy materials within a specified time frame and did not receive a specified percentage of the vote. . . .
Rule 14a-8(i)(13)	The proposal relates to specific amounts of cash or stock dividends.

. . . .

The rule operates as follows:

- the shareholder must provide a copy of his or her proposal to the company by the deadline imposed by the rule;

- if the company intends to exclude the proposal from its proxy materials, it must submit its reason(s) for doing so to the Commission and simultaneously provide the shareholder with a copy of that submission. This submission to the Commission of reasons for excluding the proposal is commonly referred to as a no-action request;

- the shareholder may, but is not required to, submit a reply to us with a copy to the company; and

- we issue a no-action response that either concurs or does not concur in the company's view regarding exclusion of the proposal.

. . . .

Rule 14a-8 contains eligibility and procedural requirements for shareholders who wish to include a proposal in a company's proxy materials. . . .

To be eligible to submit a proposal, Rule 14a-8(b) requires the shareholder to have continuously held at least $2,000 in market value, or 1%, of the company's securities entitled to be voted on the proposal at the meeting for at least one year by the date of submitting the proposal. Also, the shareholder must continue to hold those securities through the date of the meeting. . . .

[E] Shareholder Nomination of Directors — Rule 14a-11

Business Roundtable v. SEC

United States Court of Appeals, District of Columbia Circuit

647 F.3d 1144 (2011)

GINSBURG, *Circuit Judge*: The Business Roundtable and the Chamber of Commerce of the United States, each of which has corporate members that issue publicly traded securities, petition for review of Exchange Act Rule 14a-11. The rule requires public companies to provide shareholders with information about, and their ability to vote for, shareholder-nominated candidates for the board of directors. The petitioners argue the Securities and Exchange Commission promulgated the rule in violation of the Administrative Procedure Act, 5 U.S.C. §551 *et seq.*, because, among other reasons, the Commission failed adequately to consider the rule's effect upon efficiency, competition, and capital formation, as required by Section 3(f) of the Exchange Act and Section 2(c) of the Investment Company Act of 1940. . . . For these reasons and more, we grant the petition for review and vacate the rule.

I. Background

The proxy process is the principal means by which shareholders of a publicly traded corporation elect the company's board of directors. Typically, incumbent directors nominate a candidate for each vacancy prior to the election, which is held at the company's annual meeting. Before the meeting the company puts information about each nominee in the set of "proxy materials"—usually comprising a proxy voting card and a proxy statement—it distributes to all shareholders. The proxy statement concerns voting procedures and background information about the board's nominee(s); the proxy card enables shareholders to vote for or against the nominee(s) without attending the meeting. A shareholder who wishes to nominate a different candidate may separately file his own proxy statement and solicit votes from shareholders, thereby initiating a "proxy contest."

Rule 14a-11 provides shareholders an alternative path for nominating and electing directors. Concerned the current process impedes the expression of shareholders' right under state corporation laws to nominate and elect directors, the Commission proposed the rule, *see* Facilitating Shareholder Director Nominations, 74 Fed. Reg. 29,024, 29,025–26 (2009) (hereinafter Proposing Release), and adopted it with the goal of ensuring "the proxy process functions, as nearly as possible, as a replacement for an actual in-person meeting of shareholders," 75 Fed. Reg. 56,668, 56,670 (2010) (hereinafter Adopting Release). After responding to public comments, the Commission amended the proposed rule and, by a vote of three to two, adopted Rule 14a-11. The rule requires a company subject to the Exchange Act proxy rules, including an investment company (such as a mutual fund) registered under the Investment Company Act of 1940 (ICA), to include in its proxy materials "the name of a person or persons nominated by a [qualifying] shareholder or group of shareholders for election to the board of directors."

To use Rule 14a-11, a shareholder or group of shareholders must have continuously held "at least 3% of the voting power of the company's securities entitled to be voted" for at least three years prior to the date the nominating shareholder or group submits notice of its intent to use the rule, and must continue to own those securities through the date of the annual meeting. The nominating shareholder or group must submit the notice, which may include a statement of up to 500 words in support of each of its nominees, to the Commission and to the company. A company that receives notice from an eligible shareholder or group must include the proffered information about the shareholder(s) and his nominee(s) in its proxy statement and include the nominee(s) on the proxy voting card.

The Commission did place certain limitations upon the application of Rule 14a-11. The rule does not apply if applicable state law or a company's governing documents "prohibit shareholders from nominating a candidate for election as a director." Nor may a shareholder use Rule 14a-11 if he is holding the company's securities with the intent of effecting a change of control of the company. The company is not required to include in its proxy materials more than one shareholder nominee or the number of nominees, if more than one, equal to 25 percent of the number of directors on the board.

The Commission concluded that Rule 14a-11 could create "potential benefits of improved board and company performance and shareholder value" sufficient to "justify [its] potential costs." The agency rejected proposals to let each company's board or a majority of its shareholders decide whether to incorporate Rule 14a-11 in its bylaws, saying that "exclusive reliance on private ordering under State law would not be as effective and efficient" in facilitating shareholders' rights to nominate and elect directors. The Commission also rejected the suggestion it exclude investment companies from Rule 14a-11. The two commissioners voting against the rule faulted the Commission on both theoretical and empirical grounds. . . .

The petitioners sought review in this court in September 2010. The Commission then stayed the final rule . . . pending the outcome of this case.

II. Analysis

Under the APA [Administrative Procedure Act], we will set aside agency action that is "arbitrary, capricious, an abuse of discretion, or otherwise not in accordance with law." 5 U.S.C. § 706(2)(A). We must assure ourselves the agency has "examine[d] the relevant data and articulate[d] a satisfactory explanation for its action including a rational connection between the facts found and the choices made." The Commission also has a "statutory obligation to determine as best it can the economic implications of the rule." . . .

Indeed, the Commission has a unique obligation to consider the effect of a new rule upon "efficiency, competition, and capital formation," and its failure to "apprise itself—and hence the public and the Congress—of the economic consequences of a proposed regulation" makes promulgation of the rule arbitrary and capricious and not in accordance with law. . . .

The petitioners argue the Commission acted arbitrarily and capriciously here because it neglected its statutory responsibility to determine the likely economic consequences of Rule 14a-11 and to connect those consequences to efficiency, competition, and capital formation. They also maintain the Commission's decision to apply Rule 14a-11 to investment companies is arbitrary and capricious.

We agree with the petitioners and hold the Commission acted arbitrarily and capriciously for having failed . . . adequately to assess the economic effects of a new rule. Here the Commission inconsistently and opportunistically framed the costs and benefits of the rule; failed adequately to quantify the certain costs or to explain why those costs could not be quantified; neglected to support its predictive judgments; contradicted itself; and failed to respond to substantial problems raised by commenters. For these and other reasons, its decision to apply the rule to investment companies was also arbitrary. Because we conclude the Commission failed to justify Rule 14a-11, we need not address the petitioners' additional argument the Commission arbitrarily rejected proposed alternatives that would have allowed shareholders of each company to decide for that company whether to adopt a mechanism for shareholders' nominees to get access to proxy materials.

A. Consideration of Economic Consequences

In the Adopting Release, the Commission predicted Rule 14a-11 would lead to "[d]irect cost savings" for shareholders in part due to "reduced printing and postage costs" and reduced expenditures for advertising compared to those of a "traditional" proxy contest. The Commission also identified some intangible, or at least less readily quantifiable, benefits, principally that the rule "will mitigate collective action and free-rider concerns," which can discourage a shareholder from exercising his right to nominate a director in a traditional proxy contest, and "has the potential of creating the benefit of improved board performance and enhanced shareholder value" ... The Commission anticipated the rule would also impose costs upon companies and shareholders related to "the preparation of required disclosure, printing and mailing ..., and [to] additional solicitations," and could have "adverse effects on company and board performance," for example, by distracting management. ... The Commission nonetheless concluded the rule would promote the "efficiency of the economy on the whole," and the benefits of the rule would "justify the costs" of the rule.

The petitioners contend the Commission neglected both to quantify the costs companies would incur opposing shareholder nominees and to substantiate the rule's predicted benefits. They also argue the Commission failed to consider the consequences of union and state pension funds using the rule and failed properly to evaluate the frequency with which shareholders would initiate election contests.

1. Consideration of Costs and Benefits

In the Adopting Release, the Commission recognized "company boards may be motivated by the issues at stake to expend significant resources to challenge shareholder director nominees." Nonetheless, the Commission believed a company's solicitation and campaign costs "may be limited by two factors": first, "to the extent that the directors' fiduciary duties prevent them from using corporate funds to resist shareholder director nominations for no good-faith corporate purpose," they may decide "simply [to] include the shareholder director nominees ... in the company's proxy materials"; and second, the "requisite ownership threshold and holding period" would "limit the number of shareholder director nominations that a board may receive, consider, and possibly contest."

The petitioners object that the Commission failed to appreciate the intensity with which issuers would oppose nominees and arbitrarily dismissed the probability that directors would conclude their fiduciary duties required them to support their own nominees. The petitioners also argue it was arbitrary for the Commission not to estimate the costs of solicitation and campaigning that companies would incur to oppose candidates nominated by shareholders, which costs commenters expected to be quite large. The Chamber of Commerce submitted a comment predicting boards would incur substantial expenditures opposing shareholder nominees through "significant media and public relations efforts, advertising . . . , mass mailings, and other communication efforts, as well as the hiring of outside advisors and the expenditure of significant time and effort by the company's employees." It pointed out that in recent proxy contests at larger companies costs "ranged from $14 million to $4 million" and at smaller companies "from $3 million to $800,000." In its brief the Commission maintains it did consider the commenters' estimates of the costs, but reasonably explained why those costs "may prove less than these estimates."

We agree with the petitioners that the Commission's prediction directors might choose not to oppose shareholder nominees had no basis beyond mere speculation. Although it is possible that a board, consistent with its fiduciary duties, might forgo expending resources to oppose a shareholder nominee—for example, if it believes the cost of opposition would exceed the cost to the company of the board's preferred candidate losing the election, discounted by the probability of that happening—the Commission has presented no evidence that such forbearance is ever seen in practice. To the contrary, the American Bar Association Committee on Federal Regulation of Securities commented:

> If the [shareholder] nominee is determined [by the board] not to be as appropriate a candidate as those to be nominated by the board's independent nominating committee . . . , then the board will be compelled by its fiduciary duty to make an appropriate effort to oppose the nominee, as boards now do in traditional proxy contests. . . .

The Commission's second point, that the required minimum amount and duration of share ownership will limit the number of directors nominated under the new rule, is a reason to expect election contests to be infrequent; it says nothing about the amount a company will spend on solicitation and campaign costs when there is a contested election. Although the Commission acknowledged that companies may expend resources to oppose shareholder nominees, it did nothing to estimate and quantify the costs it expected companies to incur; nor did it claim estimating those costs was not possible, for empirical evidence about expenditures in traditional proxy contests was readily available. Because the agency failed to "make tough choices about which of the competing estimates is most plausible, [or] to hazard a guess as to which is correct," we believe it neglected its statutory obligation to assess the economic consequences of its rule.

. . . .

The petitioners also maintain, and we agree, the Commission relied upon insufficient empirical data when it concluded that Rule 14a-11 will improve board performance and increase shareholder value by facilitating the election of dissident shareholder nominees. The Commission acknowledged the numerous studies submitted by commenters that reached the opposite result. One commenter, for example, submitted an empirical study showing that "when dissident directors win board seats, those firms underperform peers by 19 to 40% over the two years following the proxy contest." . . . The Commission completely discounted those studies "because of questions raised by subsequent studies, limitations acknowledged by the studies' authors, or [its] own concerns about the studies' methodology or scope." . . .

The Commission instead relied exclusively and heavily upon two relatively unpersuasive studies, one concerning the effect of "hybrid boards" (which include some dissident directors) and the other concerning the effect of proxy contests in general, upon shareholder value. [Cernich (2009) Study] . . . Indeed, the Commission "recognize[d] the limitations of the Cernich (2009) study," and noted "its long-term findings on shareholder value creation are difficult to interpret." In view of the admittedly (and at best) "mixed" empirical evidence, we think the Commission has not sufficiently supported its conclusion that increasing the potential for election of directors nominated by shareholders will result in improved board and company performance and shareholder value. . . .

2. Shareholders with Special Interests

The petitioners next argue the Commission acted arbitrarily and capriciously by "entirely fail[ing] to consider an important aspect of the problem," to wit, how union and state pension funds might use Rule 14a-11. Commenters expressed concern that these employee benefit funds would impose costs upon companies by using Rule 14a-11 as leverage to gain concessions, such as additional benefits for unionized employees, unrelated to shareholder value. The Commission insists it did consider this problem, . . . along the way to its conclusion that "the totality of the evidence and economic theory" both indicate the rule "has the potential of creating the benefit of improved board performance and enhanced shareholder value." Specifically, the Commission recognized "companies could be negatively affected if shareholders use the new rules to promote their narrow interests at the expense of other shareholders," but reasoned these potential costs "may be limited" because the ownership and holding requirements would "allow the use of the rule by only holders who demonstrated a significant, long-term commitment to the company," and who would therefore be less likely to act in a way that would diminish shareholder value. The Commission also noted costs may be limited because other shareholders may be alerted, through the disclosure requirements, "to the narrow interests of the nominating shareholder."

The petitioners also contend the Commission failed to respond to the costs companies would incur even when a shareholder nominee is not ultimately elected.

These costs may be incurred either by a board succumbing to the demands, unrelated to increasing value, of a special interest shareholder threatening to nominate a director, or by opposing and defeating such nominee(s). The Commission did not completely ignore these potential costs, but neither did it adequately address them.

Notwithstanding the ownership and holding requirements, there is good reason to believe institutional investors with special interests will be able to use the rule and, as more than one commenter noted, "public and union pension funds" are the institutional investors "most likely to make use of proxy access." . . . Nonetheless, the Commission failed to respond to comments arguing that investors with a special interest, such as unions and state and local governments whose interests in jobs may well be greater than their interest in share value, can be expected to pursue self-interested objectives rather than the goal of maximizing shareholder value, and will likely cause companies to incur costs even when their nominee is unlikely to be elected. . . . By ducking serious evaluation of the costs that could be imposed upon companies from use of the rule by shareholders representing special interests, particularly union and government pension funds, we think the Commission acted arbitrarily.

3. Frequency of Election Contests

In the Proposing Release, the Commission estimated 269 companies per year, comprising 208 companies reporting under the Exchange Act and 61 registered investment companies, would receive nominations pursuant to Rule 14a-11. In the Adopting Release, however, the Commission reduced that estimate to 51, comprising only 45 reporting companies and 6 investment companies, in view of "the additional eligibility requirements" the Commission adopted in the final version of Rule 14a-11. As originally proposed, Rule 14a-11 would have required a nominating shareholder to have held the securities for only one year rather than the three years required in the final rule. . . . In revising its estimate, the Commission also newly relied upon "[t]he number of contested elections and board-related shareholder proposals" in a recent year, which it believed was "a better indicator of how many shareholders might submit a nomination" than were the data upon which it had based its estimate in the Proposing Release.

The petitioners argue the Commission's revised estimate unreasonably departs from the estimate used in the Proposing Release, conflicts with its assertion the rule facilitates elections contests, and undermines its reliance upon frequent use of Rule 14a-11 to estimate the amount by which shareholders will benefit from "direct printing and mailing cost savings" . . .

The Commission was not unreasonable in predicting investors will use rule 14a-11 less frequently than traditional proxy contests have been used in the past. As Commission counsel pointed out at oral argument, there would still be some traditional proxy contests; the total number of efforts by shareholders to nominate and elect directors will surely be greater when shareholders have two paths rather than one open to them. In any event, the final estimated frequency (51) with which shareholders will use Rule 14a-11 does not clearly conflict with the higher estimate in the Proposing Release (269), or the estimate of proposals under Rule 14a-8 (147), both of which were based upon looser eligibility standards.

In weighing the rule's costs and benefits, however, the Commission arbitrarily ignored the effect of the final rule upon the total number of election contests. That is, the Adopting Release does not address whether and to what extent Rule 14a-11 will take the place of traditional proxy contests. Without this crucial datum, the Commission has no way of knowing whether the rule will facilitate enough election contests to be of net benefit. . . .

. . . .

III. Conclusion

For the foregoing reasons, we hold the Commission was arbitrary and capricious in promulgating Rule 14a-11. . . . The petition is granted and the rule is hereby

Vacated.

———————

Note

For critical assessments of the D.C. Circuit's opinion in *Business Roundtable, see, e.g.,* Davidoff, *Proxy Access in Limbo After Court Rules Against It,* N.Y. Times Dealbook, July 27, 2011 (asserting that "the opinion appears to create an almost insurmountable barrier for the SEC by requiring that it provide empirical support amounting to proof that its rules would be effective"); Hayden & Bodie, *The Bizarre Law and Economics of Business Roundtable v. SEC,* 38 J. Corp. L. 101, 120 (2012) ("Commentators have pointed out that [the DC Circuit's] view of the evidence [in *Business Roundtable*] flips the standard of review on its head, by requiring an agency to demonstrate conclusively that its regulation will provide more benefits than costs").

Irrespective of the D.C. Circuit's invalidation of Rule 14a-11, due to institutional shareholder activism, hundreds of publicly held companies today voluntarily provide qualifying large shareholders (who do not seek to exercise control) with the right to nominate a specified number of directors (usually one or two such directors). *See Proxy Access Remains in Spotlight for 2017 Season,* 48 Sec. Reg. & L. Reg. (BNA) 1882 (2016). In addition, the SEC has issued proposed rules that "would require the use of universal proxies that include the names of both registrant and dissident nominees and thus allow shareholders to vote by proxy in a manner that more closely resembles how they can vote in person at a shareholder meeting." *See* Securities Exchange Act Release No. 79164 (2016).

———————

§ 9.05 Section 18 of the Securities Exchange Act

Section 18 provides an express right of action for damages on behalf of an allegedly aggrieved purchaser or seller against any person who makes or causes to be made a materially false or misleading statement in any document filed with the SEC pursuant to the Exchange Act. The statute requires the complainant to prove that, in reliance on such materially false or misleading statement, that he/she purchased or sold the subject security at a price that was affected by the disclosure deficiency. Hence, both reliance and loss causation must be proven.[19] Significantly, to establish the element of reliance, the plaintiff must show that he/she (or his/her designee) actually read the relevant parts of the document in question (either by reading the filed document itself or as the pertinent document was described in another source).[20]

Section 18 allows for contribution and sets forth a one-year/three-year statute of limitations (namely, that suit must be instituted within one year after discovery of the facts constituting the violation and in no event more than three years after the violation's occurrence). Nonetheless, a number of courts hold that § 1658(b)'s two-year/five-year statute of limitations now is the applicable standard in § 18 actions. Under § 18, the defendant has an affirmative defense of showing good faith and lack of knowledge that the subject statement was materially false or misleading.

With respect to § 18, the Second Circuit recently opined:

... Section 18(a) does not require a plaintiff to plead or prove scienter. But it does not necessarily follow that Section 18(a) is not "a private right of action that involves a claim of fraud, deceit, manipulation, or contrivance."

Section 1658(b) does not define "fraud." As a result, we look to its common-law meaning, because "[i]t is a settled principle of interpretation that, absent other indication, Congress intends to incorporate the well-settled meaning of the common-law terms it uses."

. . . .

On its face, Section 18(a) unquestionably "involves a claim of a misrepresentation made ... to induce another person to act." And the Supreme Court has strongly indicated that, in order for a plaintiff to recover under Section 18(a), such a misrepresentation also must have been "made recklessly without belief in its truth," at the very least.

. . . .

---

19. *See Deephaven Private Placement & Trading Ltd. v. Grant Thornton & Co.*, 454 F.3d 1168 (10th Cir. 2006); *In re Supreme Specialists, Inc. Securities Litigation*, 438 F.3d 256 (3d Cir. 2006).

20. *See, e.g., Gould v. Winstar Communications, Inc.*, 692 F.3d 148 (2d Cir. 2012); *In re Digi International*, 6 F. Supp. 2d 1089 (D. Minn. 1998); *In re American Continental Corp. Securities Litigation*, 794 F. Supp. 1424 (D. Ariz. 1992); *Walsh v. Butcher & Sherrerd*, 452 F. Supp. 80 (E.D. Pa. 1978); *Jacobson v. Peat, Marwick, Mitchell & Co.*, 445 F. Supp. 518 (S.D.N.Y. 1977). Note that the SEC has exempted from § 18 coverage financial statements contained in a registrant's quarterly filings on Form 10-Q. See Exchange Act Rule 15(d)-13(e).

We also think it significant that Section 18(a) imposes liability "unless the person sued shall prove that he acted in good faith and had no knowledge that such statement was false or misleading." The presence of this good-faith defense means that, as a practical matter, Section 18(a) actions will generally involve proof of a defendant's state of mind, and recovery will be permitted only where a defendant acted, at a minimum, recklessly. Congress's inclusion of this defense thus further demonstrates that it intended Section 18(a) to reach only fraudulent misrepresentations, rather than negligent or innocent ones.

. . . .

Taken together, these factors lead us . . . in concluding that . . . Section 18(a) is governed by § 1658(b) . . . .

A plaintiff asserting a Section 18(a) claim is, in essence, asserting a fraud claim—a fraud claim with respect to which the defendant, and not the plaintiff, uncharacteristically bears the burden of proof regarding scienter, but a fraud claim no less.

DeKalb County Pension Fund v. Transocean Ltd., 817 F.3d 393, 405–407 (2d Cir. 2016) (citations omitted).

Because of § 18(a)'s strict reliance requirement, the statute in the past was not invoked with frequent success. This result may be changing to some extent because of increasing use of this statute by institutional investors. Because institutional investors (or their designees) read and analyze Exchange Act reports filed by a subject registrant, the reliance requirement should not pose a significant hurdle for such investors.[21] At least according to some courts, however, the individualized proof of reliance mandated by § 18 may preclude class certification, thereby relegating complainants to pursue solely individual actions.[22]

---

§ 9.06 Section 29(b) of the Securities Exchange Act

Although not often invoked since the Exchange Act's passage in 1934, § 29(b) may serve as a powerful weapon for aggrieved litigants. Under the provision's language, every contract formed or performed in contravention of the 1934 Act or any rule or

---

21. *See* Eisenhofer & Grant, *Institutional Investors and Section 18 of the Exchange Act*, 33 Rev. Sec. & Comm. Reg. 54 (2000).

22. Compare *Beebe v. Pacific Realty Trust*, 99 F.R.D. 60 (D. Ore. 1983) (denying class certification due to § 18's reliance requirement), with *Simpson v. Specialty Retail Concepts*, 149 F.R.D. 94 (M.D.N.C. 1993) (certifying class and finding that § 18 common issues prevailed over issue of reliance). *See* Grant & McIntyre, *Class Certification and Section 18 of the Exchange Act*, 35 Rev. Sec. & Comm. Reg. 255 (2002).

regulation prescribed thereunder "shall be void" as regards the rights of the violating party or his/her successor who takes with knowledge. As the Supreme Court has stated, § 29(b) impliedly "confers a 'right to rescind' a contract void under the criteria of the statute."[23]

Taken literally, § 29(b)'s language, to quote Judge Friendly, is "Draconian."[24] Due to the "devastating meaning" of the provision's language, a number of courts have held that § 29(b) merely codifies common law principles of illegal bargain in the application of the Exchange Act.[25]

Some courts, however, have construed § 29(b) according to its language. In these decisions, the provision has been interpreted to provide plaintiffs with the relief sought, namely, the rescission of the subject transaction. The Fifth Circuit's decision in the *Regional Properties* case, 678 F.2d 552 (5th Cir. 1982) (which is contained in this Section), serves as one such illustration.

In light of the relatively little attention that has thus far been given to § 29(b), the provision should be explored in much greater depth. Basically, § 29(b)'s potential impact may be stated as follows:

> With certain limited exceptions, the language of the section provides that a violating party to a contract, or his successor who takes with knowledge, shall have no rights under the contract, even when performance of the contract has been rendered. Conceivably then, § 29(b) subjects every transaction, from a simple purchase or sale of securities, to a complex proxy fight, merger, tender offer, reorganization, or other transaction to which the Exchange Act applies, to its voidability provisions. . . .

> Although [§ 29(b)] has remained relatively dormant, it needs only to be awakened. Once recognized as a potential "sleeping giant," section 29(b) may be recognized as an extremely important remedial provision . . . created by Congress.[26]

---

23. *Transamerica Mortgage Advisors, Inc. v. Lewis*, 444 U.S. 11, 17 (1979). *See Mills v. Electric Auto-Lite Co.*, 396 U.S. 375, 387–88 (1970).

24. *Pearlstein v. Scudder & German*, 429 F.2d 1136, 1149 (2d Cir. 1970) (Friendly, J., dissenting) ("Despite the Draconian language, § 29(b) does not provide a pat legislative formula for solving every case in which a contract and a violation concur.").

25. *See, e.g., Occidental Life Insurance Co. v. Pat Ryan & Associates*, 496 F.2d 1255, 1265 (4th Cir. 1974).

26. Gruenbaum & Steinberg, *Section 29(b) of the Securities Exchange Act of 1934: A Viable Remedy Awakened*, 48 Geo. Wash. L. Rev. 1, 53–54 (1979).

Regional Properties, Inc. v. Financial and Real Estate Consulting Company

United States Court of Appeals, Fifth Circuit

678 F.2d 552 (1982)

ALVIN B. RUBIN, CIRCUIT JUDGE.

Two real estate developers and their affiliated corporations entered into a number of agreements with a securities broker whereby the broker agreed to structure limited partnerships and market the limited partnership interests. The developers discovered that the broker had never registered as a broker-dealer with the SEC and had thus violated the Securities Exchange Act in selling the partnership interests, although the time when they learned of this is disputed. The major question presented is whether, under these circumstances, the developers were entitled to rescind their agreements with the broker under the contract-voiding provision contained in the Act. We hold that the developers were entitled to bring such an action and established a prima facie case for relief, but that the district court erred in failing to rule upon the broker's asserted defenses. We, therefore, remand the case so that the district court may consider and rule upon these defenses.

. . . .

II. REGIONAL'S SECTION 29(b) CLAIMS

Section 29(b) provides, "[e]very contract made in violation of any provision of [the Act] . . . , and every contract . . . the performance of which involves the violation of . . . any provision of [the Act] . . . , shall be void . . . as regards the rights of any person who, in violation of any such provision . . . shall have made or engaged in the performance of any such contract. . . ." Although it has been a part of the Act since its passage in 1934, it has been invoked infrequently. See Gruenbaum & Steinberg, *Section 29(b) of the Securities Exchange Act of 1934: A Viable Remedy Awakened*, 48 Geo. Wash. L. Rev. 1, 1-3 & n.5 . . . . It does not [by its] terms give a party to a contract made in violation of the section a private cause of action to rescind the contract. If it authorizes such an action by implication, the following questions must also be addressed: (1) What are the elements of the cause of action? (2) What defenses, if any, are available against the claim? and (3) What relief is available to a successful claimant?

A. Does Section 29(b) Provide for a Private Cause of Action?

Without expressly considering whether Section 29(b) implies a private cause of action, courts have uniformly either held or assumed that such suits can be brought. . . .

Language in two subsequent Supreme Court decisions tends to affirm this view. In *Mills v. Electric Auto-Lite Co.*, 396 U.S. 375 (1970), the Court stated, in dicta, that the interests of the "innocent party" to a contract are protected by Section 29(b) "giving him the right to rescind." . . . More recently, in *Transamerica Mortgage Advisors,*

Inc. (TAMA) v. Lewis, 444 U.S. 11 (1979), the Court was called upon to determine whether Section 215(b) of the Investment Advisers Act, which is nearly identical to Section 29(b) of the [Securities Exchange] Act, provides a private cause of action. In answering that question in the affirmative, the Court stated:

> By declaring certain contracts void, § 215 by its terms necessarily contemplates that the issue of voidness under its criteria may be litigated somewhere. At the very least Congress must have assumed that § 215 could be raised defensively in private litigation to preclude the enforcement of an investment advisers contract.

> But the legal consequences of voidness are typically not so limited. A person with the power to void a contract ordinarily may resort to a court to have the contract rescinded and to obtain restitution of consideration paid. . . . Moreover, the federal courts in general have viewed such language as implying an equitable cause of action for rescission or similar relief.

> For these reasons we conclude that when Congress declared in § 215 that certain contracts are void, it intended that the customary legal incidents of voidness would follow, including the availability of a suit for rescission . . . , and for restitution.

. . . Therefore, . . . it must be considered as settled that § 29(b), by implication, does provide a private, "equitable cause of action for rescission or similar relief." . . .

B. The Elements of a Section 29(b) Cause of Action

In *Eastside Church*, [391 F.2d 357 (5th Cir. (1981)] we rejected the defendants' argument that a section 29(b) plaintiff must prove a causal connection between its harm and the defendants' violation of the Act. The "Act," we said, "requires only that the [complainant] be in the class of persons the Act was designed to protect. . . . [I]t is sufficient to show merely that the prohibited transactions occurred and that the [complainant was] in the protected class." . . .

To summarize, then, a person can avoid a contract under section 29(b) if he can show that (1) the contract involved a "prohibited transaction," (2) he is in contractual privity with the defendant, and (3) he is "in the class of persons the Act was designed to protect." [emphasis supplied] [See *Berckley Investment Group, Ltd. v. Colkitt*, 455 F.3d 195, 205 (3d Cir. 2006) (adopting the Fifth Circuit's three-part test and also holding that the plaintiff "must demonstrate a direct relationship between the violation at issue and the performance of the contract, i.e., the violation must be inseparable from the performance of the contract rather than collateral or tangential to the contract").]

. . . .

Financial . . . argues that the Court's statement that section 29(b) renders the contract voidable "at the option of the innocent party" somehow erects a "standing" prescription requiring a section 29(b) plaintiff to show that he is an "innocent party" as a prerequisite to suit. While we do not think it is either correct or fruitful to couch this issue in terms of "standing,"[27] we do think the statement demonstrates the Court's intention that a section 29(b) defendant at least be allowed to invoke the traditional equitable defenses, which we discuss in Part II. C., *infra*. Before defenses to an action are relevant, however, the plaintiff must first have proved its case. We, therefore, examine whether Regional did so.

Contractual privity, the first element of the cause of action, is established beyond dispute. In fact, Regional and Financial were the only parties to the contracts. Regional also satisfied the second element, proof that "prohibited transactions occurred." Section 29(b) does not render void only those contracts that "by their terms" violate the Act. . . . If the Act were so limited, it would lead immediately to the inquiry, "What would such a contract look like?" A statute that voided only contracts by which persons have agreed in express terms to violate the Act would be so narrow as to be a waste of the congressional time spent in its enactment.

. . . .

Interpreting Section 29(b) to render voidable those contracts that are either illegal when made or as in fact *performed* not only avoids these problems but also, in our view, most nearly comports with the language used in Section 29(b). . . . Moreover, this interpretation is the one implicitly adopted by *Eastside Church*. There, we allowed a contract for the purchase of bonds, after it had already been performed, to be rescinded by the seller. There was nothing to suggest that the contract "by [its own] terms" violated the Act. We permitted it to be rescinded simply because the purchaser, *in performing the contract*, had in fact violated the Act by doing so without being registered as a broker-dealer. . . . We acknowledged that, from the standpoint of the broker, this was a "harsh"[28] result, but stated that this "seems to be what Congress intended." . . .

The situation here is in all essentials identical to that in *Eastside Church*. Regional sought to avoid certain contracts, perfectly lawful on their face, the performance of which by Financial resulted in a violation of the Act. That these contracts, under

---

[27]. As Gruenbaum & Steinberg have stated, "Section 29(b) is directed . . . at nullifying the rights of the violator, not at the standing of the complainant to assert the right to the remedy created by the section." *Viable Remedy, supra*, 48 GEO. WASH. L. REV. at 33. The Supreme Court has held that "standing" exists if "the plaintiff alleges that the challenged action has caused him injury in fact, economic or otherwise," and if "the interest sought to be protected by the complainant is arguably within the zone of interest to be protected or regulated by the statute . . . in question." *Data Processing Serv. Orgs., Inc. v. Camp*, 397 U.S. 150, 152–53 (1970).

[28]. Judge Friendly has gone so far as to characterize this interpretation as "Draconian." *Pearlstein v. Scudder & German*, 429 F.2d 1136, 1149 (2d Cir. 1970) (Friendly, J., dissenting), *cert. denied*, 401 U.S. 1013 (1971). He suggested, without citing any legislative history or other support, that §29(b) was merely a legislative direction to the courts to employ the common law principles of illegal bargain. . . . In any event, we do not agree with Judge Friendly's statement that our interpretation of §29(b) provides a "pat . . . formula for solving every case in which a contract and a violation concur." Instead, under our interpretation, the violation, to trigger the application of the section, must have occurred in the making or performance of the contract sought to be rescinded.

different circumstances, could have been performed without violating the Act is immaterial. Considering the language of section 29(b), our holding in *Eastside Church*, and the dicta in *Mills*, we conclude that Regional proved the existence of "prohibited transactions," i.e., ones proscribed by section 29(b).

The final element of a section 29(b) cause of action under *Eastside Church* is proof that the complainant was a "member of the class of persons the Act was designed to protect." The statute does not in terms limit the class of persons who may invoke its contractual voidness provisions to investors. While the law was enacted to protect the public interest and the investor, its protection extends beyond those who buy securities. That statutes must be read in the light of their purpose is an admonition not only ancient but wise. That "The letter killeth and the spirit giveth life"[29] is not limited to hermeneutics but extends as well to the interpretation of congressional text. Yet we start with the objective reading for the Congress has many members and the President signs with yet another hand. If what is written is clear and its application leads to no absurd result, we should not seek to obfuscate the obvious.

Section 29(b) renders certain contracts void. It does not limit that invalidity to contracts between issuers and sellers or to those between issuers and investors. The contracts involved here . . . were precisely the kind of contracts "performance of which involve[d] the violation of" a provision of the Act, specifically, section 15(a)(1). . . .

Moreover, we think that application of the letter of the statute in this case does further the Act's purposes. In *Eastside Church*, we emphasized that section 15(a)(1)'s registration requirement is of the utmost importance in effecting the purposes of the Act. It is through the broker registration requirement that some discipline may be exercised over those who may engage in the securities business and by which necessary standards may be established with respect to training, experience, and records.

. . . As we have pointed out, Financial's fees were raised by the sale of the limited partnership interests, paid over to the general partner in the project, and then, in turn, paid by the general partner to Financial. Without splitting hairs over whether Regional, when it signed the subject contracts, could have been considered the "issuer" of the limited partnership interests, or an "investor" in the projects, we conclude that Regional was a "member of the class of persons the Act was designed to protect," and, therefore, satisfied the last of the elements of a section 29(b) action under *Eastside Church*. . . .

C. The Defenses to a Section 29(b) Cause of Action

Having thus decided that Regional did make out a prima facie case under section 29(b), we next must determine whether there exist defenses to such an action and, if so, whether Financial succeeded in proving any. Although the question of the

---

[29]. The Second Epistle of Paul to the Corinthians, iii, 6.

availability of defenses to a § 29(b) action was not discussed in *Eastside Church*, we have no hesitation in holding that there are such defenses and that they, in fact, encompass all the traditional equitable defenses.

The starting points for our discussion are the propositions, too elementary to require citation, that, historically, a suit to void a contract sounded in equity, and that, in suits in equity, equitable defenses, such as laches, estoppel, etc., may be raised. While actions to void a securities broker's contract obviously stem from statute rather than a traditional equitable right, they are equitable in nature. . . .

. . . .

Therefore, because it would be anomalous to hold that, while one equitable defense is available, the others are not, we join with virtually all other courts that have decided this issue and hold that all equitable defenses are available in a § 29(b) cause of action. . . .

Unfortunately, our holding does not dispose of this important part of the case. Although Financial raised a number of defenses below, . . . the district court failed to rule upon, or even mention, any of them. Because a determination of the validity of these defenses depends upon additional fact findings and interpretations of Texas law, both of which can initially be made more easily by the district court than by us, we remand this case to the district court to rule expressly upon Financial's defensive contentions.

. . . .

[Affirmed in part, vacated and remanded in part.]

---

§ 9.07 Racketeer Influenced and Corrupt Organizations Act (RICO)

The 1995 Federal Legislation (PSLRA)

To state a claim for damages under RICO, the complainant first must allege a violation of the substantive RICO statute (18 U.S.C. § 1962), commonly referred to as "criminal RICO." The constituent elements of criminal RICO, as set forth by the Second Circuit, are "(1) that the defendant (2) through the commission of two or more acts (3) constituting a 'pattern' (4) of 'racketeering activity' (5) directly or indirectly invests in, or maintains an interest in, or participates in (6) an 'enterprise' (7) the activities of which affect interstate or foreign commerce." *Moss v. Morgan Stanley*, 719 F.2d 5, 17 (2d Cir. 1983). After adequately alleging the foregoing, a private plaintiff, in order to invoke RICO's civil provisions for treble damages, attorneys' fees and costs, must satisfy a second burden, namely, that he was "injured in his business or property *by reason* of a violation of Section 1962 [criminal RICO]." 18 U.S.C. § 1964(c). Generally, prior to the 1995 legislation, civil RICO provided an express right of action to redress fraud in the sale of securities (as well as for mail and wire fraud).

The Private Securities Litigation Reform Act of 1995 amended § 1964(c) of the Racketeer Influenced and Corrupt Organizations Act ("RICO") to eliminate securities fraud as a predicate act in a civil RICO action. According to the Joint Explanatory Statement of the Conference Committee for the legislation, the Committee also "intend[ed] that a plaintiff may not plead other specified offenses, such as mail or wire fraud, as predicate acts under civil RICO if such offenses are based on conduct that would have been actionable as securities fraud." An exception is made, thereby permitting a civil RICO action to be initiated in this context, when any person has been criminally convicted in connection with the fraud, in which case the statute of limitations commences to run on the date the conviction becomes final. Thus, after the 1995 legislation, civil RICO rarely will be invoked in securities-related litigation.

Nonetheless, a number of states have enacted their own RICO statutes that, under the conditions set forth in these respective statutes, include securities fraud as a predicate act. As stated by Professor Couture:

> . . . [A] new trend has emerged: institutional investors have begun opting out of federal securities class actions, choosing instead to pursue individual actions in state court under state law. An often overlooked implication of this enhanced prominence of state law in securities litigation is that many states have enacted so-called "little-RICO" statutes, which largely mirror the pre-1995 version of federal RICO. This raises the potential for . . . a new wave of racketeering claims premised on securities fraud asserted by opt-out plaintiffs under state RICO statutes.

Couture, *RICO 2.0: State RICO Statutes in Opt-Out Securities Litigation*, 44 Sec. Reg. L.J. 51 (2016).

---

§ 9.08 State Securities and Common Law Remedies

Previous sections of this text have discussed that a plaintiff may seek to invoke state remedies in addition to or in lieu of the federal securities laws (*see, e.g.,* §§ 7.09, 8.03[D], 8.05[F]). The following material further addresses this subject.

The Securities Litigation Uniform Standards Act of 1998

Enactment of the Securities Litigation Uniform Standards Act of 1998 (SLUSA) severely limits the availability of state law redress in class actions. Pursuant to SLUSA, securities class actions[30] involving nationally traded securities,[31] with certain exceptions, must be brought in federal court invoking only federal (and not state) law. A number of important exceptions exist, however, thereby preserving state securities and common law in those situations. For instance, individual as well as derivative actions may be pursued under state law. State law also may be invoked in actions challenging the conduct of a subject company, any of its affiliates, or affected corporate fiduciaries in regard to specified actions — namely, going-private transactions, tender offers, mergers, and the exercise of appraisal rights. Significantly, SLUSA does not preempt the authority of the state securities commissions, thereby empowering the states to conduct their investigatory and enforcement functions.

The Securities Litigation Uniform Standards Act has had a huge impact in drastically curtailing state law application. Before SLUSA's enactment, it was asserted that publicly held corporations were reluctant to disclose forward-looking information,[32] regardless of the safe harbor afforded by the Private Securities Litigation Reform Act of 1995 (PSLRA). The concern remained that the disclosure of such forward-looking information would subject the affected companies to state court class actions.[33] The

---

30. Pursuant to the Securities Litigation Uniform Standards Act of 1998 (SLUSA), a "covered class action" means:

(i) any single lawsuit in which -

(I) damages are sought on behalf of more than 50 persons or prospective class members, and questions of law or fact common to those persons or members of the prospective class, without reference to issues of individualized reliance on an alleged misstatement or omission, predominate over any questions affecting only individual persons or members; or

(II) one or more named parties seek to recover damages on a representative basis on behalf of themselves and other unnamed parties similarly situated, and questions of law or fact common to those persons or members of the prospective class predominate over any questions affecting only individual persons or members; or

(ii) any group of lawsuits filed in or pending in the same court and involving common questions of law or fact, in which -

(I) damages are sought on behalf of more than 50 persons; and

(II) the lawsuits are joined, consolidated, or otherwise proceed as a single action for any purpose.

Section 101 of the Uniform Standards Act, *amending,* § 16(f)(2)(A) of the Securities Act (15 U.S.C. § 77p(f)(2)(A)), and § 28(f)(5)(B) of the Exchange Act (15 U.S.C. § 78bb(f)(5)(B)).

31. The term national traded security or "covered security" is defined as a security that meets the standards set forth in § 18(b) of the Securities Act, 15 U.S.C. § 77(b). These securities include those that are listed for trading on the New York Stock Exchange, American Stock Exchange, and the NASDAQ NMS. Securities issued by registered investment companies also are defined as nationally traded securities.

32. *See* sources cited in Levin & Pritchard, *The Securities Litigation Uniform Standards Act of 1998: The Sun Sets on California's Blue Sky Laws,* 54 Bus. Law. 1, 12 (1998).

33. *See* Grundfest et al., *Securities Class Action Litigation in 1998: A Report to NASDAQ From the Stanford Law School Securities Class Action Clearinghouse,* 1070 PLI/Corp 69 (1998) ("Since passage of the Reform Act [namely, the PSLRA], a substantial portion of class action litigation has shifted from federal to state court in an apparent attempt to evade the Act's provisions."); Grundfest & Perino, *Securities Litigation Reform: The First Years' Experience — A Statistical Analysis of Class Action Securities Fraud Litigation Under the Private Securities Litigation Reform Act of 1995.* Stanford

passage of SLUSA, generally preempting state law in securities class actions implicating nationally traded securities, has provided sufficient comfort to induce many
companies to disclose forward-looking information. Nonetheless, the preservation
of state derivative suits, when considered with the Delaware Supreme Court's decisions focusing on a corporate fiduciary's duty of candor, has not foreclosed state
litigation in the general disclosure context.

See generally J. Hamilton & T. Trautmann, Securities Litigation Uniform
Standards Act of 1998: Law and Explanation (CCH 1998); Casey, *Shutting the
Doors to State Court: The Securities Litigation Uniform Standards Act of 1998*, 27 Sec.
Reg. L.J. 141 (1999); Painter, *Responding to a False Alarm: Federal Preemption of State
Securities Fraud Causes of Action*, 84 Cornell L. Rev. 1 (1998).

Merrill Lynch, Pierce, Fenner & Smith, Inc. v. Dabit

United States Supreme Court

547 U.S. 71, 126 S. Ct. 1503, 164 L. Ed. 2d 179 (2006)

JUSTICE STEVENS delivered the opinion of the Court.

Title I of the Securities Litigation Uniform Standards Act of 1998 (SLUSA) provides that "[n]o covered class action" based on state law and alleging a "misrepresentation or omission of a material fact in connection with the purchase or sale of a
covered security may be maintained in any State or Federal court by any private
party." ... In this case the Second Circuit held that SLUSA only pre-empts state-law
class-action claims brought by plaintiffs who have a private remedy under federal
law. 395 F.3d 25 (2005). A few months later, the Seventh Circuit ruled to the contrary, holding that the statute also pre-empts state-law class-action claims for which
federal law provides no private remedy. *Kircher v. Putnam Funds Trust*, 403 F.3d 478
(2005). The background, the text, and the purpose of SLUSA's pre-emption provision all support the broader interpretation adopted by the Seventh Circuit.

I

Petitioner Merrill Lynch, Pierce, Fenner & Smith, Inc. (Merrill Lynch), is an investment banking firm that offers research and brokerage services to investors. Suspicious that the firm's loyalties to its investment banking clients had produced biased
investment advice, the New York attorney general in 2002 instituted a formal investigation into Merrill Lynch's practices. The investigation sparked a number of private securities fraud actions, this one among them.

Respondent, Shadi Dabit, is a former Merrill Lynch broker. He filed this class action
in the United States District Court for the Western District of Oklahoma on behalf
of himself and all other former or current brokers who, while employed by Merrill

---

Law School (Feb. 27, 1997); *Securities Class Actions Seem to be Moving to State Courts, According to
New Study*, 29 *Sec. Reg. & L. Rep.* (BNA) 311 (1997).

Lynch, purchased (for themselves and for their clients) certain stocks between December 1, 1999, and December 31, 2000. Rather than rely on the federal securities laws, Dabit invoked the District Court's diversity jurisdiction and advanced his claims under Oklahoma state law.

The gist of Dabit's complaint was that Merrill Lynch breached the fiduciary duty and covenant of good faith and fair dealing it owed its brokers by disseminating misleading research and thereby manipulating stock prices. Dabit's theory was that Merrill Lynch used its misinformed brokers to enhance the prices of its investment banking clients' stocks: The research analysts, under management's direction, allegedly issued overly optimistic appraisals of the stock's value; the brokers allegedly relied on the analysts" reports in advising their investor clients and in deciding whether or not to sell their own holdings; and the clients and brokers both continued to hold their stocks long beyond the point when, had the truth been known, they would have sold. The complaint further alleged that when the truth was actually revealed (around the time the New York attorney general instituted his investigation), the stocks' prices plummeted.

Dabit asserted that Merrill Lynch's actions damaged the class members in two ways: The misrepresentations and manipulative tactics caused them to hold onto overvalued securities, and the brokers lost commission fees when their clients, now aware that they had made poor investments, took their business elsewhere.

In July 2002, Merrill Lynch moved to dismiss Dabit's complaint. It argued, first, that SLUSA pre-empted the action and, second, that the claims alleged were not cognizable under Oklahoma law. . . .

Meanwhile, dozens of other suits, based on allegations similar to Dabit's had been filed against Merrill Lynch around the country on both federal- and state-law theories of liability. The Judicial Panel on Multidistrict Litigation transferred all of those cases, along with this one, to the United States District Court for the Southern District of New York for consolidated pretrial proceedings. Merrill Lynch then filed its second motion to dismiss Dabit's complaint. Senior Judge Milton Pollack granted the motion on the ground that the claims alleged fell "squarely within SLUSA's ambit." *In re Merrill Lynch & Co., Inc.,* 2003 WL 1872820, *1 (Apr. 10, 2003).

The Court of Appeals for the Second Circuit, however, vacated the judgment and remanded for further proceedings. 395 F.3d, at 51. It concluded that the claims asserted by holders did not allege fraud "in connection with the purchase or sale" of securities under SLUSA. Although the court agreed with Merrill Lynch that phrase, as used in other federal securities laws, has been defined broadly by this Court, it held that Congress nonetheless intended a narrower meaning here—one that incorporates the "standing" limitation on private federal securities actions adopted in *Blue Chip Stamps v. Manor Drug Stores,* 421 U. S. 723 (1975). Under the Second Circuit's analysis, fraud is only "in connection with the purchase or sale" of securities, as used in SLUSA, if it is alleged by a purchaser or seller of securities. Thus, to the extent that the complaint in this action alleged that brokers were fraudulently induced, not to sell or purchase, but to retain or delay selling their securities, it fell outside SLUSA's preemptive scope.

After determining that the class defined in Dabit's amended complaint did not necessarily exclude purchasers, the panel remanded with instructions that the pleading be dismissed without prejudice. The court's order would permit Dabit to file another amended complaint that defines the class to exclude "claimants who purchased in connection with the fraud and who therefore could meet the standing requirement" for a federal damages action, and to include only those "who came to hold [a Merrill Lynch] stock before any relevant misrepresentation." Under the Second Circuit's analysis, a class action so limited could be sustained under state law. For the reasons that follow, we disagree.

II

The magnitude of the federal interest in protecting the integrity and efficient operation of the market for nationally traded securities cannot be overstated. In response to the sudden and disastrous collapse in prices of listed stocks in 1929, and the Great Depression that followed, Congress enacted the Securities Act of 1933 (1933 Act) and the Securities Exchange Act of 1934 (1934 Act). Since their enactment, these two statutes have anchored federal regulation of vital elements of our economy.

Securities and Exchange Commission (SEC) Rule 10b-5, promulgated in 1942 pursuant to § 10(b) of the 1934 Act, is an important part of that regulatory scheme. The Rule, like § 10(b) itself, broadly prohibits deception, misrepresentation, and fraud "in connection with the purchase or sale of any security." The SEC has express statutory authority to enforce the Rule. Although no such authority is expressly granted to private individuals injured by securities fraud, in 1946 Judge Kirkpatrick of the United States District Court for the Eastern District of Pennsylvania, relying on "the general purpose" of the Rule, recognized an implied right of action thereunder. *Kardon v. National Gypsum Co.*, 69 F. Supp. 512, 514. His holding was adopted by an "overwhelming consensus of the District Courts and Courts of Appeals," and endorsed by this Court in *Superintendent of Ins. of N. Y. v. Bankers Life & Casualty Co.*, 404 U. S. 6 (1971).

A few years after *Kardon* was decided, the Court of Appeals for the Second Circuit limited the reach of the private right of action under Rule 10b-5. In *Birnbaum v. Newport Steel Corp.*, 193 F.2d 461 (1952), a panel composed of Chief Judge Swan and Judges Augustus and Learned Hand upheld the dismissal of a suit brought on behalf of a corporation and a class of its stockholders alleging that fraud "in connection with" a director's sale of his controlling block of stock to third parties violated Rule 10b-5. The court held that the Rule could only be invoked by a purchaser or seller of securities to remedy fraud associated with his or her own sale or purchase of securities, and did not protect those who neither purchased nor sold the securities in question but were instead injured by corporate insiders' sales to third parties. While the *Birnbaum* court did not question the plaintiffs "standing" to enforce Rule 10b-5, later cases treated its holding as a standing requirement. . . .

By the time this Court first confronted the question, literally hundreds of lower court decisions had accepted "*Birnbaum*'s conclusion that the plaintiff class for purposes of § 10(b) and Rule 10b-5 private damages actions is limited to purchasers and sellers." *Blue Chip Stamps*, 421 U. S., at 731–732. Meanwhile, however, cases like *Bankers Life & Casualty Co.* had interpreted the coverage of the Rule more broadly to prohibit, for example, "deceptive practices *touching* [a victim's] sale of securities as an investor." 404 U.S., at 12–13 (emphasis added). . . . The "judicial oak which ha[d] grown from little more than a legislative acorn," as then-Justice Rehnquist described the rules governing private Rule 10b-5 actions, *Blue Chip Stamps*, 421 U. S., at 737, had thus developed differently from the law defining what constituted a substantive violation of Rule 10b-5. Ultimately, the Court had to decide whether to permit private parties to sue for any violation of Rule 10b-5 that caused them harm, or instead to limit the private remedy to plaintiffs who were themselves purchasers or sellers.

Relying principally on "policy considerations" which the Court viewed as appropriate in explicating a judicially crafted remedy, and following judicial precedent rather than "the many commentators" who had criticized the *Birnbaum* rule as "an arbitrary restriction which unreasonably prevents some deserving plaintiffs from recovering damages," the Court in *Blue Chip Stamps* chose to limit the private remedy. The main policy consideration tipping the scales in favor of precedent was the widespread recognition that "litigation under Rule 10b-5 presents a danger of vexatiousness different in degree and in kind from that which accompanies litigation in general." Even weak cases brought under the Rule may have substantial settlement value, the Court explained, because "[t]he very pendency of the lawsuit may frustrate or delay normal business activity." Cabining the private cause of action by means of the purchaser-seller limitation would, in the Court's view, minimize these ill effects. The limitation of course had no application in Government enforcement actions brought pursuant to Rule 10b-5.

III

Policy considerations similar to those that supported the Court's decision in *Blue Chip Stamps* prompted Congress, in 1995, to adopt legislation targeted at perceived abuses of the class-action vehicle in litigation involving nationally traded securities. While acknowledging that private securities litigation was "an indispensable tool with which defrauded investors can recover their losses," the House Conference Report accompanying what would later be enacted as the Private Securities Litigation Reform Act of 1995 (Reform Act), identified ways in which the class action device was being used to injure "the entire U. S. economy." According to the Report, nuisance filings, targeting of deep-pocket defendants, vexatious discovery requests, and "manipulation by class action lawyers of the clients whom they purportedly represent" had become rampant in recent years. Proponents of the Reform Act argued that these abuses resulted in extortionate settlements, chilled any discussion of issuers' future prospects, and deterred qualified individuals from serving on boards of directors.

Title I of the Reform Act, captioned "Reduction of Abusive Litigation," represents Congress' effort to curb these perceived abuses. Its provisions limit recoverable damages and attorney's fees, provide a "safe harbor" for forward-looking statements, impose new restrictions on the selection of (and compensation awarded to) lead plaintiffs, mandate imposition of sanctions for frivolous litigation, and authorize a stay of discovery pending resolution of any motion to dismiss. Title I also imposes heightened pleading requirements in actions brought pursuant to § 10(b) and Rule 10b-5; it "insists that securities fraud complaints 'specify' each misleading statement; that they set forth the facts on which [a] belief that a statement is misleading was 'formed'; and that they 'state with particularity facts giving rise to a strong inference that the defendant acted with the required state of mind.'" *Dura Pharmaceuticals, Inc. v. Broudo*, 544 U. S. 336, 345 (2005).

The effort to deter or at least quickly dispose of those suits whose nuisance value outweighs their merits placed special burdens on plaintiffs seeking to bring federal securities fraud class actions. But the effort also had an unintended consequence: It prompted at least some members of the plaintiffs' bar to avoid the federal forum altogether. Rather than face the obstacles set in their path by the Reform Act, plaintiffs and their representatives began bringing class actions under state law, often in state court. The evidence presented to Congress during a 1997 hearing to evaluate the effects of the Reform Act suggested that this phenomenon was a novel one; state-court litigation of class actions involving nationally traded securities had previously been rare. See H. R. Rep. No. 105-640, p. 10 (1998); S. Rep. No. 105-182, pp. 3–4 (1998). To stem this "shif[t] from Federal to State courts" and "prevent certain State private securities class action lawsuits alleging fraud from being used to frustrate the objectives of" the Reform Act, Congress enacted SLUSA.

IV

The core provision of SLUSA reads as follows:

> "CLASS ACTION LIMITATIONS.—No covered class action based upon the statutory or common law of any State or subdivision thereof may be maintained in any State or Federal court by any private party alleging—
>
> "(A) a misrepresentation or omission of a material fact in connection with the purchase or sale of a covered security; or
>
> "(B) that the defendant used or employed any manipulative or deceptive device or contrivance in connection with the purchase or sale of a covered security."

A "covered class action" is a lawsuit in which damages are sought on behalf of more than 50 people. A "covered security" is one traded nationally and listed on a regulated national exchange. Respondent does not dispute that both the class and the securities at issue in this case are "covered" within the meaning of the statute, or that the complaint alleges misrepresentations and omissions of material facts. The only disputed issue is whether the alleged wrongdoing was "in connection with the purchase or sale" of securities.

Respondent urges that the operative language must be read narrowly to encompass (and therefore pre-empt) only those actions in which the purchaser-seller requirement of *Blue Chip Stamps* is met. Such, too, was the Second Circuit's view. But insofar as the argument assumes that the rule adopted in *Blue Chip Stamps* stems from the text of Rule 10b-5—specifically, the "in connection with" language, it must be rejected. Unlike the *Birnbaum* court, which relied on Rule 10b-5's text in crafting its purchaser-seller limitation, this Court in *Blue Chip Stamps* relied chiefly, and candidly, on "policy considerations" in adopting that limitation. The *Blue Chip Stamps* Court purported to define the scope of a private right of action under Rule 10b-5—not to define the words "in connection with the purchase or sale." Any ambiguity on that score had long been resolved by the time Congress enacted SLUSA. . . .

Moreover, when this Court *has* sought to give meaning to the phrase in the context of § 10(b) and Rule 10b-5, it has espoused a broad interpretation. A narrow construction would not, as a matter of first impression, have been unreasonable; one might have concluded that an alleged fraud is "in connection with" a purchase or sale of securities only when the plaintiff himself was defrauded into purchasing or selling particular securities. After all, that was the interpretation adopted by the panel in the *Birnbaum* case. But this Court, in early cases like *Superintendent of Ins. of N. Y. v. Bankers Life & Casualty Co.*, 404 U. S. 6 (1971), and most recently in *SEC v. Zandford*, 535 U. S. 813, 820, 822 (2002), has rejected that view. Under our precedents, it is enough that the fraud alleged "coincide" with a securities transaction—whether by the plaintiff or by someone else. The requisite showing, in other words, is "deception 'in connection with the purchase or sale of any security,' not deception of an identifiable purchaser or seller." Notably, this broader interpretation of the statutory language comports with the longstanding views of the SEC.

Congress can hardly have been unaware of the broad construction adopted by both this Court and the SEC when it imported the key phrase—"in connection with the purchase or sale"—into SLUSA's core provision. And when "judicial interpretations have settled the meaning of an existing statutory provision, repetition of the same language in a new statute indicates, as a general matter, the intent to incorporate its . . . judicial interpretations as well." . . . Application of that presumption is particularly apt here; not only did Congress use the same words as are used in § 10(b) and Rule 10b-5, but it used them in a provision that appears in the same statute as § 10(b). Generally, "identical words used in different parts of the same statute are . . . presumed to have the same meaning." . . .

The presumption that Congress envisioned a broad construction follows not only from ordinary principles of statutory construction but also from the particular concerns that culminated in SLUSA's enactment. A narrow reading of the statute would undercut the effectiveness of the 1995 Reform Act and thus run contrary to SLUSA's stated purpose, viz., "to prevent certain State private securities class action lawsuits alleging fraud from being used to frustrate the objectives" of the 1995 Act. As the *Blue Chip Stamps* Court observed, class actions brought by holders pose a special risk of vexatious litigation. It would be odd, to say the least, if SLUSA exempted that particularly troublesome subset of class actions from its pre-emptive sweep.

Respondent's preferred construction also would give rise to wasteful, duplicative litigation. Facts supporting an action by purchasers under Rule 10b-5 (which must proceed in federal court if at all) typically support an action by holders as well, at least in those States that recognize holder claims. The prospect is raised, then, of parallel class actions proceeding in state and federal court, with different standards governing claims asserted on identical facts. That prospect, which exists to some extent in this very case, squarely conflicts with the congressional preference for "national standards for securities class action lawsuits involving nationally traded securities."

In concluding that SLUSA pre-empts state-law holder class-action claims of the kind alleged in Dabit's complaint, we do not lose sight of the general "presum[ption] that Congress does not cavalierly pre-empt state-law causes of action." But that presumption carries less force here than in other contexts because SLUSA does not actually pre-empt any state cause of action. It simply denies plaintiffs the right to use the class action device to vindicate certain claims. The Act does not deny any individual plaintiff, or indeed any group of fewer than 50 plaintiffs, the right to enforce any state-law cause of action that may exist.

Moreover, the tailored exceptions to SLUSA's preemptive command demonstrate that Congress did not by any means act "cavalierly" here. The statute carefully exempts from its operation [individual actions,] certain class actions [such as those class actions involving mergers] based on the law of the State in which the issuer of the covered security is incorporated, actions brought by a state agency or state pension plan, actions under contracts between issuers and indenture trustees, and derivative actions brought by shareholders on behalf of a corporation. The statute also expressly preserves state jurisdiction over state agency enforcement proceedings. The existence of these carve-outs both evinces congressional sensitivity to state prerogatives in this field and makes it inappropriate for courts to create additional, implied exceptions.

Finally, federal law, not state law, has long been the principal vehicle for asserting class-action securities fraud claims. See, *e.g.*, H. R. Conf. Rep. No. 105-803, p. 14 (1998) ("Prior to the passage of the Reform Act, there was essentially no significant securities class action litigation brought in State court"). More importantly, while state-law holder claims were theoretically available both before and after the decision in *Blue Chip Stamps*, the actual assertion of such claims by way of class action was virtually unheard of before SLUSA was enacted; respondent and his *amici* have identified only *one* pre-SLUSA case involving a state-law class action asserting holder claims. This is hardly a situation, then, in which a federal statute has eliminated a historically entrenched state-law remedy.

V

The holder class action that respondent tried to plead, and that the Second Circuit envisioned, is distinguishable from a typical Rule 10b-5 class action in only one respect: It is brought by holders instead of purchasers or sellers. For purposes of SLUSA pre-emption, that distinction is irrelevant; the identity of the plaintiffs does not determine whether the complaint alleges fraud "in connection with the purchase or sale" of securities. The misconduct of which respondent complains here — fraudulent manipulation of stock prices — unquestionably qualifies as fraud "in connection with the purchase or sale" of securities as the phrase is defined in *Zandford*, 535 U. S., at 820, 822, and *O'Hagan*, 521 U. S., at 651.

The judgment of the Court of Appeals for the Second Circuit is vacated, and the case is remanded for further proceedings consistent with this opinion.

It is so ordered.

In the following decision, the Supreme Court declined to extend further the preemption rationale enunciated in *Merrill Lynch v. Dabit*. The Court's holding signifies that state class actions involving *uncovered* securities (i.e. securities that are *not* traded nationally) retain their importance.

Chadbourne & Parke LLP v. Troice

United States Supreme Court

___ U.S. ___, 134 S. Ct. 1058, 188 L. Ed. 2d 88 (2014)

JUSTICE BREYER delivered the opinion of the Court.

The Securities Litigation Uniform Standards Act of 1998 (which we shall refer to as the "Litigation Act") forbids the bringing of large securities class actions based upon violations of state law. It says that plaintiffs may not maintain a class action "based upon the statutory or common law of any State" in which the plaintiffs allege "a misrepresentation or omission of a material fact *in connection with the purchase or sale of a covered security*." 15 U.S.C. §78bb(f)(1) (emphasis added). The Act defines "class actions" as those involving more than 50 members. It defines "covered security" narrowly to include only securities traded on a national exchange (or, here irrelevant, those issued by investment companies).

The question before us is whether the Litigation Act encompasses a class action in which the plaintiffs allege (1) that they "purchase[d]" *uncovered* securities (certificates of deposit that are *not* traded on any national exchange), but (2) that the defendants falsely told the victims that the *uncovered* securities were backed by *covered* securities. We note that the plaintiffs do not allege that the defendants' misrepresentations led anyone to buy or to sell (or to maintain positions in) *covered* securities. Under these circumstances, we conclude the Act does not apply.

In light of the dissent's characterization of our holding—which we believe is incorrect—we specify at the outset that this holding does *not* limit the Federal Government's authority to prosecute "frauds like the one here." The Federal Government *has* in fact brought successful prosecutions against the fraudsters at the heart of this litigation, and we fail to understand the dissent's repeated suggestions to the contrary. . . . Rather, as we shall explain, we believe the basic consequence of our holding is that, without limiting the Federal Government's prosecution power in any significant way, it will permit victims of this (and similar) frauds to recover damages under state law. Under the dissent's approach, they would have no such ability.

I

A

The relevant statutory framework has four parts:

(1) Section 10(b) of the underlying regulatory statute, the Securities Exchange Act of 1934. This well-known statutory provision forbids the "use" or "employ[ment]" of "any manipulative or deceptive device or contrivance" "in connection with the purchase or sale of any security."

Securities and Exchange Commission Rule 10b-5 similarly forbids the use of any "device, scheme, or artifice to defraud" (including the making of "any untrue statement of a material fact" or any similar "omi[ssion]") "in connection with the purchase or sale of any security."

For purposes of these provisions, the Securities Exchange Act defines "security" *broadly* to include not just things traded on national exchanges, but also "any note, stock, treasury stock, security future, security-based swap, bond, debenture . . . [or] certificate of deposit for a security." 15 U.S.C. § 78c(a)(10). See also §§ 77b(a)(1), 80a-2(a) (36), 80b-2(a)(18) (providing virtually identical definitions of "security" for the Securities Act of 1933, the Investment Company Act of 1940, and the Investment Advisers Act of 1940).

(2) A statute-based private right of action. The Court has read § 10(b) and Rule 10b-5 as providing injured persons with a private right of action to sue for damages suffered through those provisions' violation. See, *e.g., Blue Chip Stamps v. Manor Drug Stores,* 421 U. S. 723, 730 (1975).

The scope of the private right of action is more limited than the scope of the statutes upon which it is based. See *Stoneridge Investment Partners, LLC* v. *Scientific-Atlanta, Inc.,* 552 U. S. 148 (2008) (private right does not cover suits against "secondary actors" who had no "role in preparing or disseminating" a stock issuer's fraudulent "financial statements"); *Central Bank of Denver, N. A. v. First Interstate Bank of Denver, N. A.,* 511 U. S. 164, 179 (1994) (private right does not extend to actions against "aiders and abettors" of securities fraud); *Blue Chip Stamps, supra,* at 737 (private right extends only to purchasers and sellers, not to holders, of securities).

(3) The Private Securities Litigation Reform Act of 1995 (PSLRA). 109 Stat. 737, 15 U. S. C. §§ 77z-1, 78u-4. This law imposes procedural and substantive limitations

upon the scope of the private right of action available under § 10(b) and Rule 10b-5. It requires plaintiffs to meet heightened pleading standards. It permits defendants to obtain automatic stays of discovery. It limits recoverable damages and attorney's fees. And it creates a new "safe harbor" for forward-looking statements.

(4) The Securities Litigation Uniform Standards Act. 112 Stat. 3227, 15 U. S. C. § 78bb(f)(1)(A). As we said at the outset, this 1998 law forbids any

"covered class action based upon the statutory or common law of any State

. . . by any private party alleging—

"(A) a misrepresentation or omission of a material fact in connection with the purchase or sale of a covered security; or

"(B) that the defendant used or employed any manipulative or deceptive device or contrivance in connection with the purchase or sale of a covered security."

The law defines "covered security" narrowly. It is a security that "satisfies the standards for a covered security specified in paragraph (1) or (2) of section 18(b) of the Securities Act of 1933." § 78bb(f)(5)(E). And the relevant paragraphs of § 18(b) of the 1933 Act define a "covered security" as "[a security] listed, or authorized for listing, on a national securities exchange" . . . . The Litigation Act also specifies that a "covered security" must be listed or authorized for listing on a national exchange "at the time during which it is alleged that the misrepresentation, omission, or manipulative or deceptive conduct occurred."

The Litigation Act sets forth exceptions. It does not apply to class actions with fewer than 51 "persons or prospective class members." It does not apply to actions brought on behalf of a State itself. It does not apply to class actions based on the law "of the State in which the issuer is incorporated." And it reserves the authority of state securities commissions "to investigate and bring enforcement actions."

We are here primarily interested in the Litigation Act's phrase "misrepresentation or omission of a material fact in connection with the purchase or sale of a covered security." Unless this phrase applies to the class actions before us, the plaintiffs may maintain their state-law-based class actions, and they may do so either in federal or state court. Otherwise, their class actions are precluded altogether. See § 78bb(f)(2) (providing for the removal from state to federal court of class actions that meet the specifications of paragraph 1, and for the dismissal of such suits by the district court).

B

1

The plaintiffs in these actions (respondents here) say that Allen Stanford and several of his companies ran a multibillion dollar Ponzi scheme. Essentially, Stanford and his companies sold the plaintiffs certificates of deposit in Stanford International Bank. Those certificates "were debt assets that promised a fixed rate of return." *Roland v. Green,* 675 F.3d 503, 522 (CA5 2012). The plaintiffs expected that Stanford International Bank would use the money it received to buy highly lucrative assets. But instead, Stanford and his associates used the money provided by new investors to repay old investors, to finance an elaborate lifestyle, and to finance speculative real estate ventures.

The Department of Justice brought related criminal charges against Allen Stanford. A jury convicted Stanford of mail fraud, wire fraud, conspiracy to commit money laundering, and obstruction of a Securities and Exchange Commission investigation. Stanford was sentenced to prison and required to forfeit $6 billion. The SEC, noting that the Bank certificates of deposit fell within the 1934 Securities Exchange Act's broad definition of "security," filed a § 10(b) civil case against Allen Stanford, the Stanford International Bank, and related Stanford companies and associates. The SEC won the civil action, and the court imposed a civil penalty of $6 billion.

2

The plaintiffs in each of the four civil class actions are private investors who bought the Bank's certificates of deposit. Two groups of plaintiffs filed their actions in Louisiana state court against firms and individuals who helped sell the Bank's certificates by working as "investment advisers" affiliated with Stanford, or who provided Stanford-related companies with trust, insurance, accounting, or reporting services. (The defendants included a respondent here, SEI Investments Company.) The plaintiffs claimed that the defendants helped the Bank perpetrate the fraud, thereby violating Louisiana state law.

Two other groups of plaintiffs filed their actions in federal court for the Northern District of Texas. One group sued Willis of Colorado (and related Willis companies) and Bowen, Miclette & Britt, two insurance brokers; the other group sued Proskauer Rose and Chadbourne & Parke, two law firms. Both groups claimed that the defendants helped the Bank (and Allen Stanford) perpetrate the fraud or conceal it from regulators, thereby violating Texas securities law.

The Louisiana state-court defendants removed their cases to federal court, and the Judicial Panel on Multi-District Litigation moved the Louisiana cases to the Northern District of Texas. A single federal judge heard all four class actions.

The defendants in each of the cases moved to dismiss the complaints. The District Court concluded that the Litigation Act required dismissal. The court recognized that the certificates of deposit themselves were not "covered securities" under the Litigation Act, for they were not " 'traded nationally [or] listed on a regulated national exchange.' " But each complaint in one way or another alleged that the fraud included misrepresentations that the Bank maintained significant holdings in " 'highly marketable securities issued by stable governments [and] strong multinational companies,' " and that the Bank's ownership of these "covered" securities made investments in the uncovered certificates more secure. The court concluded that this circumstance provided the requisite statutory "connection" between (1) the plaintiffs' state-law fraud claims, and (2) "transactions in covered securities." Hence, the court dismissed the class actions under the Litigation Act.

All four sets of plaintiffs appealed. The Fifth Circuit reversed. It agreed with the District Court that the complaints described misrepresentations about the Bank's investments in nationally traded securities. Still, the "heart, crux, and gravamen of" the "allegedly fraudulent scheme was representing . . . that the [uncovered] CDs were a 'safe and secure' investment that was preferable to other investments for many reasons." The court held that the falsehoods about the Bank's holdings in covered securities were too "'tangentially related'" to the "crux" of the fraud to trigger the Litigation Act. "That the CDs were marketed with some vague references to [the Bank's] portfolio containing instruments that might be [covered by the Litigation Act] seems tangential to the schemes," to the point where the complaints fall outside the scope of that Act. 675 F.3d, at 522.

Defendants in the four class actions sought certiorari. We granted their petitions.

II

The question before us concerns the scope of the Litigation Act's phrase "misrepresentation or omission of a material fact in connection with the purchase or sale of a covered security." §78bb(f)(1)(A). How broad is that scope? Does it extend further than misrepresentations that are material to the purchase or sale of a covered security?

In our view, the scope of this language does not extend further. To put the matter more specifically: A fraudulent misrepresentation or omission is not made "in connection with" such a "purchase or sale of a covered security" unless it is material to a decision by one or more individuals (other than the fraudster) to buy or to sell a *"covered security."* [emphasis supplied] We add that in *Merrill Lynch, Pierce, Fenner & Smith Inc. v. Dabit,* 547 U. S. 71 (2006), we held that the Litigation Act precluded a suit where the plaintiffs alleged a "fraudulent manipulation of stock prices" that was material to and "'coincide[d]' with" third-party securities transactions, while also inducing the plaintiffs to "hold their stocks long beyond the point when, had the truth been known, they would have sold." We do not here modify *Dabit.*

A

We reach this interpretation of the Litigation Act for several reasons. First, the Act focuses upon transactions in covered securities, not upon transactions in uncovered securities. An interpretation that insists upon a material connection with a transaction in a covered security is consistent with the Act's basic focus.

Second, a natural reading of the Act's language supports our interpretation. The language requires the dismissal of a state-law-based class action where a private party alleges a "misrepresentation or omission of a material fact" (or engages in other forms of deception, not relevant here) "in connection with the purchase or sale of a covered security." §78bb(f)(1). The phrase "material fact in connection with the purchase or sale" suggests a connection that matters. And for present purposes, a connection matters where the misrepresentation makes a significant difference to someone's decision to purchase or to sell a covered security, not to purchase or to sell an uncovered security, something about which the Act expresses no concern. Further, the "someone" making that decision to purchase or sell must be a party other than the fraudster. If the only party who decides to buy or sell a covered security as a result of a lie is the liar, that is not a "connection" that matters.

Third, prior case law supports our interpretation. As far as we are aware, every securities case in which this Court has found a fraud to be "in connection with" a purchase or sale of a security has involved victims who took, who tried to take, who divested themselves of, who tried to divest themselves of, or who maintained *an ownership interest* in financial instruments that fall within the relevant statutory definition. . . . We have found no Court case involving a fraud "in connection with" the purchase or sale of a statutorily defined security in which the victims did not fit one of these descriptions. And the dissent apparently has not either.

Although the dissent characterizes our approach as "new," and tries to describe several of our prior cases in a different way, it cannot escape the fact that every case it cites involved a victim who took, tried to take, or maintained an ownership position in the statutorily relevant securities through "purchases" or "sales" induced by the fraud. . . .

Fourth, we read the Litigation Act in light of and consistent with the underlying regulatory statutes, the Securities Exchange Act of 1934 and the Securities Act of 1933. The regulatory statutes refer to persons engaged in securities transactions that lead to the taking or dissolving of ownership positions. And they make it illegal to deceive a person when he or she is doing so. Section 5 of the 1933 Act, for example, makes it unlawful to "offer to sell or offer to buy . . . any security, unless a registration statement has been filed as to such security." Section 17 of the 1933 Act makes it unlawful "in the offer or sale of any securities . . . to employ any device, scheme, or artifice to defraud, or to obtain money or property by means of any untrue statement of a material fact." And § 10(b) of the 1934 Act makes it unlawful to "use or employ, in connection with the purchase or sale of any security . . . any manipulative or deceptive device or contrivance."

Not only language but also purpose suggests a statutory focus upon transactions involving the statutorily relevant securities. The basic purpose of the 1934 and 1933 regulatory statutes is "to insure honest securities markets and thereby promote investor confidence." Nothing in the regulatory statutes suggests their object is to protect persons whose connection with the statutorily defined securities is more remote than words such as "buy," "sell," and the like, indicate. Nor does anything in the Litigation Act provide us with reasons for interpreting its similar language more broadly.

The dissent correctly points out that the federal securities laws have another purpose, beyond protecting investors. Namely, they also seek to protect securities *issuers,* as well as the investment advisers, accountants, and brokers who help them sell financial products, from abusive class-action lawsuits. Both the PSLRA and the Litigation Act were enacted in service of that goal. By imposing heightened pleading standards, limiting damages, and pre-empting state-law suits where the claims pertained to covered securities, Congress sought to reduce frivolous suits and mitigate legal costs for firms and investment professionals that participate in the market for nationally traded securities.

We fail to see, however, how our decision today undermines that objective. The dissent worries our approach will "subject many persons and entities whose profession it is to give advice, counsel, and assistance in investing in the securities markets to complex and costly state-law litigation." To the contrary, the *only* issuers, investment advisers, or accountants that today's decision will continue to subject to state-law liability are those who do not sell or participate in selling securities traded on U. S. national exchanges. We concede that this means a bank, chartered in Antigua and whose sole product is a fixed-rate debt instrument not traded on a U. S. exchange, will not be able to claim the benefit of preclusion under the Litigation Act. But it is difficult to see why the federal securities laws would be—or should be—concerned with shielding such entities from lawsuits.

Fifth, to interpret the necessary statutory "connection" more broadly than we do here would interfere with state efforts to provide remedies for victims of ordinary state law frauds. A broader interpretation would allow the Litigation Act to cover, and thereby to prohibit, a lawsuit brought by creditors of a small business that falsely represented it was creditworthy, in part because it owns or intends to own exchange-traded stock. It could prohibit a lawsuit brought by homeowners against a mortgage broker for lying about the interest rates on their mortgages—if, say, the broker (not the homeowners) later sold the mortgages to a bank which then securitized them in a pool and sold off pieces as "covered securities."

The dissent all but admits this. Its proposed rule is that whenever "the purchase or sale of the securities [including by the fraudster] is what enables the fraud," the Litigation Act pre-empts the suit. In other words, *any time* one person convinces another to loan him money, by pretending he owns nationally traded securities or will acquire them for himself in the future, the action constitutes federal securities fraud, is subject to federal enforcement, and is *also* precluded by the Litigation Act if it qualifies as a "covered class action" under § 78bb(f)(5)(B) (*e.g.,* involves more than 50 members). Leaving aside whether this would work a significant expansion of the scope of liability under the federal securities laws, it unquestionably would limit the scope of protection under state laws that seek to provide remedies to victims of garden-variety fraud.

The text of the Litigation Act reflects congressional care to avoid such results. Under numerous provisions, it purposefully maintains state legal authority, especially over matters that are primarily of state concern. See §§ 78bb(f)(1)(A)-(B) (limiting preclusion to lawsuits involving "covered," *i.e.,* nationally traded, securities); § 78bb(f)(4) (providing that the "securities commission . . . of any State shall retain jurisdiction under the laws of such State to investigate and bring enforcement actions"); § 78bb(f)(3)(B) (preserving States' authority to bring suits of the kind forbidden to private class-action plaintiffs). . . . A broad interpretation of the Litigation Act works at cross-purposes with this state-oriented concern. Cf. *Zandford*, 535 U. S., at 820 (warning against "constru[ing]" the phrase "in connection with" "so broadly as to convert any common-law fraud that happens to involve securities into a violation of § 10(b)"); *Wharf (Holdings) Ltd.*, 532 U. S., at 596 (recognizing that "ordinary state breach-of-contract claims" are "actions that lie outside the [Securities Exchange] Act's basic objectives").

B

Respondents and the Government make two important counterarguments. Respondents point to statements we have made suggesting we should give the phrase "in connection with" a broad interpretation. In *Dabit*, for example, we said that the Court has consistently "espoused a broad interpretation" of "in connection with" in the context of § 10(b) and Rule 10b-5, and we added that the Litigation Act language similarly warranted a "broad construction." In *Bankers Life*, we said that, if a deceptive practice "touch[es]" a securities transaction, it meets § 10(b)'s "in connection with" requirement, 404 U. S., at 12, and in *O'Hagan*, we said the fraud and the purchase or sale of a security must simply "coincide." 521 U. S., at 656. The idea, we explained in *Zandford*, is that the phrase "should be 'construed not technically and restrictively, but flexibly to effectuate its remedial purposes.'" . . .

Every one of these cases, however, concerned a false statement (or the like) that was "material" to another individual's decision to "purchase or s[ell]" a statutorily defined "security" or "covered security." And the relevant statements or omissions were material to a transaction in the relevant securities by or on behalf of someone other than the fraudster.

Second, the Government points out that § 10(b) of the Securities Exchange Act also uses the phrase "in connection with the purchase or sale of any security." And the Government warns that a narrow interpretation of "in connection with" here threatens a similarly narrow interpretation there, which could limit the SEC's enforcement capabilities.

We do not understand, however, how our interpretation could significantly curtail the SEC's enforcement powers. As far as the Government has explained the matter, our interpretation seems perfectly consistent with past SEC practice. For one thing, we have cast no doubt on the SEC's ability to bring enforcement actions against Stanford and Stanford International Bank. The SEC has already done so successfully. As we have repeatedly pointed out, the term "security" under § 10(b) covers a wide range of financial products beyond those traded on national exchanges, apparently including the Bank's certificates of deposit at issue in these cases. No one here denies that, for § 10(b) purposes, the "material" misrepresentations by Stanford and his associates were made "in connection with" the "purchases" of those certificates.

We find it surprising that the dissent worries that our decision will "narro[w] and constric[t] essential protection for our national securities market," and put "frauds like the one here . . . not within the reach of federal regulation." That would be news to Allen Stanford, who was sentenced to 110 years in federal prison after a successful federal prosecution, and to Stanford International Bank, which was ordered to pay billions in federal fines, after the same. Frauds like the one here—including *this fraud itself*—will continue to be within the reach of federal regulation because the authority of the SEC and Department of Justice extends to all "securities," not just to those traded on national exchanges. . . . When the fraudster peddles an uncovered security like the CDs here, the Federal Government will have the full scope of its usual powers to act. The only difference between our approach and that of the dissent, is that we *also* preserve the ability for investors to obtain relief under state laws when the fraud bears so remote a connection to the national securities market that no person actually believed he was taking an ownership position in that market.

Thus, despite the Government's and the dissent's hand wringing, neither has been able to point to an example of any prior SEC enforcement action brought during the past 80 years that our holding today would have prevented the SEC from bringing. . . .

For these reasons, the dissent's warning that our decision will "inhibit" "litigants from using federal law to police frauds" and will "undermine the primacy of federal law in policing abuses in the securities markets" rings hollow. The dissent cannot point to one example of a federal securities action—public or private—that would have been permissible in the past but that our approach will disallow in the future. And the irony of the dissent's position is that federal law would have *precluded* private recovery in these very suits, because § 10(b) does not create a private right of action for investors vis-à-vis "secondary actors" or "aiders and abettors" of securities fraud. . . .

III

Respondents' complaints specify that their claims rest upon their purchases of uncovered, not of covered, securities. Our search for allegations that might bring their allegations within the scope of the Litigation Act reveals the following:

(1) The first set of Texas plaintiffs alleged that they bought certificates of deposit from Stanford International Bank because they were told "the CDs issued by SIB were safer even than U. S. bank-issued CDs" and "could be redeemed at any time," given that the Bank "only invested the money [*i.e.*, the Bank's money obtained from its certificate sale proceeds] in safe, secure, and liquid assets." They claimed Stanford "touted the high quality of SIB's investment portfolio," and such falsehoods were material to their decision to purchase the uncovered certificates.

(2) The second set of Texas plaintiffs contended that they, too, purchased the Bank's certificates on the belief "that their money was being invested in safe, liquid investments." They alleged that the Bank's marketing materials stated it devoted "the greater part of its assets" to "first grade investment bonds (AAA, AA+, AA) and shares of stock (of great reputation, liquidity, and credibility)."

(3) Both groups of Louisiana plaintiffs alleged that they were induced to purchase the certificates based on misrepresentations that the Bank's assets were "'invested in a well-diversified portfolio of highly marketable securities issued by stable governments, strong multinational companies and major international banks.'" And they claimed the "'liquidity/marketability of SIB's invested assets'" was "the most important factor to provide security to SIB clients."

These statements do not allege, for Litigation Act purposes, misrepresentations or omissions of material fact "in connection with" the "purchase or sale of a covered security." At most, the complaints allege misrepresentations about the *Bank's* ownership of covered securities—fraudulent assurances that the Bank owned, would own, or would use the victims' money to buy *for itself* shares of covered securities. But the Bank is an entity that made the misrepresentations. The Bank is the fraudster, not the fraudster's victim. Nor is the Bank some other person transacting (or refraining from transacting) in covered securities. And consequently, there is not the necessary "connection" between the materiality of the misstatements and the statutorily required "purchase or sale of a covered security."

A final point: The District Court found that one of the plaintiffs acquired Bank certificates "with the proceeds of selling" covered securities contained in his IRA portfolio. . . . The plaintiffs, however, did not allege that the sale of these covered securities (which were used to finance the purchase of the certificates) constituted any part of the fraudulent scheme. Nor did the complaints allege that Stanford or his associates were at all interested in how the plaintiffs obtained the funds they needed to purchase the certificates. Thus, we agree with the Court of Appeals that "[u]nlike *Bankers Life* and *Zandford,* where the entirety of the fraud depended upon the tortfeasor convincing the victims of those fraudulent schemes to sell their covered securities in order for the fraud to be accomplished, the allegations here are not so tied with the sale of covered securities." In our view, like that of the Court of Appeals, these sales constituted no relevant part of the fraud but were rather incidental to it.

For these reasons the Court of Appeals' judgment is affirmed.

It is so ordered.

Note—Why Bring State Claims?

There may be several distinct advantages for plaintiffs to bring state blue sky and common law claims. Importantly, many state securities acts provide that, if appropriate, successful plaintiffs may recover reasonable attorneys' fees and punitive damages. Another significant advantage relates to the statute of limitations issue. Although the Sarbanes-Oxley Act extended the statute of limitations for rights of action based on fraud to two years after discovery of the facts constituting the violation and in no event more than five years after the violation, a number of other federal securities remedies have a one-year/three-year limitations period (namely one year from the date that the plaintiff discovered (or should have discovered) the facts constituting the violation and in no event more than three years after the violation).

By contrast, many of the state blue sky statutes contain a longer statute of limitations under "§ 12(a)(2)" types of statutes. For example, Texas has a three-year/five-year limitations period. In other words, the Texas statute provides a statute of limitations barring such an action "more than three years after discovery of the untruth or omission, or after discovery should have been made by the exercise of reasonable diligence; or more than five years after the sale [or purchase]."[34] Other, more flexible statutes of limitations include those of Florida (two-year/five-year),[35] Michigan (two-year/four-year),[36] Ohio (two-year/four-year),[37] California (one-year/four-year),[38] and Pennsylvania (one-year/four-year).[39] As to the outside limit, there appears to be no equitable tolling allowed.[40] Nonetheless, for statutes that contain a flat period (for example, that suit must be brought within two years after the transaction), there is some authority that the statute may be tolled due to the defendant's fraudulent concealment.[41] Moreover, in cases of common law fraud, it is well established that the statute of limitations may be equitably tolled.[42]

Another example is that many state securities statutes provide for monetary damages based on negligent material misrepresentations or omissions made in the initial offering context, as well as in the secondary trading markets.[43] Under federal law, if § 10(b) is invoked, scienter must be shown.[44] In addition, these state securities statutory counterparts are more expansive than § 12(a)(2). Accordingly,

---

34. Tex. Civ. Stat. Ann. Art. 581-33H(2), (3). In addition, the Texas statute provides a limitations period of three years for registration violations. *Id*. Art. 581-33H(1). By contrast, the Securities Act generally provides a one-year statute of limitations for actions brought under § 12(a)(1) for registration violations. See § 13 of the Securities Act.

35. Fla. Stat. Ann. § 95.11(4)(e). Accord, New Mexico Securities Act, N.M. Art. 58-13B-41 (two year/five year).

36. Mich. Comp. Law Ann. § 4510810(e).

37. Ohio Rev. Code Ann. § 1707.43. For the two-year period in the statute, at least under some circumstances, that period "begins to run upon the actual discovery of the defect." *Eastman v. Benchmark Minerals, Inc.,* 34 Ohio App. 3d 255, 258, 518 N.E. 2d 23, 25 (1986).

38. Cal. Corp. Code § 22506.

39. Pa. Stat. Ann. tit. 70 § 1-504(a).

40. *See, e.g.*: SEC v. Seaboard Corp. 677 F.2d 1301, 1308 (9th Cir. 1982) (interpreting California statute); *Gilbert Family Partnership v. NIDO Corporation,* 679 F. Supp. 679, 685 (E.D. Mich. 1988) (interpreting Michigan statute); *Bull v. American Bank & Trust Co.,* 641 F. Supp. 62, 67 (E.D. Pa. 1986) (interpreting Pennsylvania statute).

41. *See, e.g., Barton v. Peterson,* 733 F. Supp. 1482, 1492–1493 (N.D. Ga. 1990) (interpreting Georgia law); *Platsis v. E.F. Hutton & Company, Inc.,* 642 F. Supp. 1277, 1304–1305 (W.D. Mich. 1986), *aff'd*, 829 F.2d 13 (6th Cir. 1987) (construing § 410(e) of the Michigan Uniform Securities Act).

42. *See Willis v. Maverick,* 760 S.W. 2d 542, 644–645 (Tex. 1988); *Lampf, Pleva, Lipkind, Prupis & Pettigrew v. Gilberson,* 501 U.S. 350, 377–378 (1991) (Kennedy, J. dissenting) ("Only a small number of States constrain fraud actions with absolute periods of repose . . . .").

43. *See, e.g., Kittilson v. Ford,* 93 Wash. 2d 223, 608 P. 2d 264 (1980).

44. *Aaron v. SEC*, 446 U.S. 680 (1980); *Ernst & Ernest v. Hochfelder,* 425 U.S. 185 (1976); § 7.02 *supra*.

under a number of these statutes, plaintiffs may have a four or five-year limitations period to bring an action based on negligently made statements in the secondary markets.

Moreover, although some state courts have followed the Supreme Court's decision in *Pinter v. Dahl* for defining who is a "seller" under the applicable state securities statute,[45] a number of states adhere to more expansive standards. For example, the "substantial factor" test was used by several lower federal courts prior to *Pinter* for defining the term "seller" under § 12 of the Securities Act and is still invoked today by a number of state courts.[46] Under this test, one is deemed a "seller" if his/her actions played an integral role or were a substantial contributing factor in the transaction. Certainly, the liability net extends farther under this definition of "seller."

In addition, a number of the state statutes extend liability exposure to those who materially aid in consummating the transaction.[47] This concept of secondary liability is particularly important in view of the U.S. Supreme Court's decision in *Central Bank of Denver* foreclosing aiding and abetting liability in private actions under § 10(b).[48] Indeed, one who materially aids a sale under such a state statute is subject to liability unless he/she meets the reasonable care defense. In effect, this standard may enable a plaintiff successfully to reach certain parties who would avoid liability under the federal securities laws, either because they were not "sellers" under the *Pinter* test or were aiders and abettors rather than primary violators.[49]

There are other key advantages for plaintiffs under certain of the state securities provisions. For example, many states hold that reliance is not required to be shown under the applicable blue sky statute,[50] hence facilitating class action certification.

---

45. *See, e.g., Baker, Watts & Co., v. Miles & Stockbridge*, 95 Md. App. 145, 620 A.2d 356 (1993); *State v. Williams*, 98 N.C. App. 274, 279, 390 S.E.2d 746, 749 (1990); *Biales v. Young*, 432 S.E.2d 482 (S.C. 1993).

46. *See, e.g., FutureSelect Portfolio Management, Inc. v. Tremont Group Holdings, Inc.*, 331 P.3d 29 (Wash. 2014) (defining a seller to include "any party whose acts were a 'substantial contributive factor' to the sale"); *State ex. rel. Mays v. Ridenhour*, 811 P.2d 1220 (Kan. 1991); *Anders v. Dakota Land & Development Co.*, 380 N.W.2d 862, 867–868 (Minn. App. 1980); *Price v. Brydon*, 307 Or. 146, 764 P.2d 1370 (1988); *Hines v. Data Line Systems, Inc.*, 114 Wash. 2d 127, 787 P.2d 8, 20 (1990).

An even more expansive definition of "seller" may have been recognized in *Lutheran Brotherhood v. Kidder Peabody & Co.*, 829 S.W.2d 300, 306 (Tex. App.), *set aside on other grounds*, 840 S.W.2d 384 (Tex. 1992) (stating that Texas' § 12(a)(2) counterpart, Art. 581-33(A)(2) "applies if the defendant was any link in the chain of the selling process").

47. *See, e.g., Ariz. Rev. Stat. Ann. § 44-2003; Or. Rev. Stat. § 59.115(3); Ohio Rev. Code § 1707.43; Sterling Trust Company v. Adderley*, 168 S.W. 3d 835 (Tex. 2005). *See generally* J. LONG, BLUE SKY LAW § 7.08 (2012).

48. *See, e.g., Ariz. Rev. Stat. Ann. § 44-2003; Or. Rev. Stat. § 59.115(3); Ohio Rev. Code § 1707.43; Sterling Trust Company v. Adderley*, 168 S.W. 3d 835 (Tex. 2005). *See generally* J. LONG, BLUE SKY LAW § 7.08 (2012).

49. *See, e.g., Price v. Brydon*, 307 Or. 146, 764 P.2d 1370 (1988) (holding that attorney's actions in an offering could be viewed as materially aiding the sale).

50. *See, e.g., Cal. Corp. Code §§ 25400, 25500; DMK Biodiesel, LLC v. McCoy*, 859 N.W.2d 867 (Neb. 2015); *Mirkin v. Wasserman*, 5 Cal. 4th 1082, 858 P.2d 568, 23 Cal. Rptr. 2d 101 (1993); Ohio Rev. Code § 1707.43; *Roger v. Lehman Bros. Kuhn Loeb, Inc.*, 621 F. Supp. 114, 118 (S.D. Ohio 1985)

Proving loss causation also may be dispensed with by plaintiffs in a number of states.[51] This more relaxed liability framework prompted Professor Cane to poignantly observe:

> It would seem that a plaintiff bringing a suit under [the Florida statute] could rescind [the transaction] without a showing of proximate cause, or any damage, or any scienter on the part of the defendant. . . . Was the intent of the Florida legislature to create a system of investor insurance?[52]

In addition to their state blue sky claims, investors also may emerge victorious when seeking relief on common law fraud, negligent misrepresentation, and breach of fiduciary duty grounds. In the *Virginia Bankshares* case, for example, although ultimately defeated on their federal and state securities law claims, the plaintiffs were awarded hefty damages on their breach of fiduciary duty claims.[53] In some states, even though not a purchaser or seller of stock, a shareholder who held the subject securities may be entitled to bring a common law action for fraud.[54] And, as another example, the Eleventh Circuit held that, although unsuccessful on their federal and state securities law claims, the plaintiffs established a meritorious breach of fiduciary duty claim against their broker. In so holding, the court asserted that "the [federal and state] securities fraud statutes do not co-opt the existence of separate claims under state fiduciary principles."[55]

In conclusion, provided that SLUSA does not preclude the action, the state securities laws are being invoked by plaintiffs with greater frequency. Due to their more flexible construction, many of the state statutes provide the plaintiff with a right of action where such right may be lacking under federal law. Hence, unless preempted by SLUSA, the effect of the federal courts' restrictive approach to the remedial provisions of the Securities Acts has induced plaintiffs more frequently to file their actions in the state courts.

Nonetheless, as discussed earlier in this Section, it must be emphasized that pursuant to the Securities Litigation Uniform Standards Act (SLUSA), state law

---

(interpreting Ohio Rev. Code Ann. § 1707.43); Texas Securities Act, Art. 581-33A(2); *Anderson v. Vinson Exploration, Inc.*, 832 S.W.2d 657 (Tex. App. 1992).

51. *See E.F. Hutton & Company, Inc. v. Rousseff*, 537 So. 2d 978, 981 (Fla. 1989).

52. Cane, *Proximate Causation in Securities Fraud Actions for Rescission*, Fla. Bar Bus. Quart. Rep., Vol. 2, No. 2, at p. 14 (Spring 1989).

53. *See Sandberg v. Virginia Bankshares, Inc.*, 979 F.2d 332, 342–348 (4th Cir. 1992).

54. *See Small v. Fritz Companies*, 65 P.3d 1255 (Cal. 2003) (allowing persons who allegedly were wrongfully induced to hold their stock rather than selling such securities to bring suit based on common law fraud and negligent misrepresentation); *Gutman v. Howard Savings Bank*, 748 F. Supp. 254, 266 (D.N.J. 1990) (interpreting New Jersey law, standing to bring common law fraud claim granted and reliance may be shown in regard thereto where alleged misstatements were made directly to the complainant).

55. *Gochnauer v. A.G. Edwards & Sons, Inc.*, 810 F.2d 1042, 1050 (11th Cir. 1987). See *Malone v. Brincat*, 722 A.2d 5 (Del. 1998); *EBC I Inc. v. Goldman Sachs & Co.*, 799 N.Y.S 2d 170 (Ct. App. 2005) (recognizing breach of fiduciary duty action based on failure to disclose profit-sharing arrangement). *See generally* J. Long, M. Kaufman & J. Wunderlich, Blue Sky Law (2016).

(with certain exceptions) is preempted in class actions involving nationally traded securities. In such circumstances, federal law serves as the sole source for plaintiff redress.

Anheuser-Busch Companies, Inc. v. Summit Coffee Co.

Texas Court of Appeals

934 S.W.2d 705 (1996)

BARBER, Justice.

This is, in part, a securities case. In our original opinion, we held that section 771 [§ 12] of the Securities Act of 1933 applied to private, secondary securities transactions such as the one at issue in this case. . . . We also noted that article 581-33(A)(2) of the Texas Securities Act was "arguably broader" than its federal counterpart, but did not reach the issue of whether it was broader.

The United States Supreme Court vacated our judgment in this case and instructed us to reconsider the case in light of its opinion in *Gustafson v. Alloyd Co.*, 513 U.S. 561 (1995). See *Anheuser-Busch Cos., Inc. v. Summit Coffee Co.*, 115 S. Ct. 1309 (1995). . . .

On remand, [among other arguments, Defendants] Anheuser-Busch and Campbell Taggart assert [that] Summit Coffee's state and federal securities law claims are legally untenable in light of Gustafson. . . .

We need not determine what impact *Gustafson* has on Summit Coffee's federal securities law claims. We conclude the Texas Securities Act is broader than its federal counterpart, applies to the transaction involved in this case, and will support the trial court's judgment.

SECONDARY TRADING

In their fifth point of error and their first contention on remand, Campbell Taggart and Anheuser-Busch argue that the trial court erred as a matter of law in rendering judgment because the state and federal securities acts are inapplicable to a secondary trading transaction.

A. Applicable Law

1. Gustafson v. Alloyd Co. and The Securities Act of 1933

. . . .

In *Gustafson*, the Supreme Court . . . concluded that [§ 12(a)(2)] of the Securities Act of 1933 did not apply to private, secondary transactions. The Supreme Court's opinion is based on the conclusion that the phrase "by means of a prospectus or oral communication" is a phrase of limitation that restricts [§ 12(a)(2)] to public, initial offerings.

2. The Texas Securities Act

[Similar to a number of other states' securities statutes,] Article 581-33(A)(2) of the Texas Securities Act provides in relevant part:

> A person who offers or sells a security . . . by means of an untrue statement of a material fact or an omission to state a material fact necessary in order to make the statements made, in light of the circumstances under which they are made, not misleading, is liable to the person buying the security from him, who may sue either at law or in equity for rescission, or for damages if the buyer no longer owns the security.

. . . As used in the Texas Securities Act, the terms "sale" or "offer for sale" or "sell" "shall include every disposition, or attempt to dispose of a security for value." . . . The term "sell" means "any act by which a sale is made, and the term "sale" or "offer for sale" shall include a subscription, an option for sale, a solicitation of sale, a solicitation of an offer to buy, an attempt to sell, or an offer to sell, directly or by an agent or salesman, by circular, letter, or advertisement or otherwise." The terms "security" or "securities" include stock. . . . Article 581-33(A)(2) . . . "was lifted almost verbatim from" [1933 Act § 12(2)]. However, article 581-33(A)(2) differs from its federal counterpart in that it does not contain the phrase of limitation "by means of a prospectus or oral communication." The language used in the Texas Securities Act is broader than that used in its federal counterpart. Because of this difference between the Texas Securities Act and the Securities Act of 1933, we conclude Gustafson does not control our interpretation of article 581-33(A)(2) of the Texas Securities Act.

The Texas Legislature did not limit article 581-33 to sales of securities "by means of a prospectus or oral communication." Had the Texas Legislature intended to limit the scope of article 581-33(A)(2), it could have used limiting language, as did Congress. Instead, it broadly defined the terms "sale," "sell," and "security." Further, because article 581-33 is remedial in nature in the civil context, it "should be given the widest possible scope." . . . We are to construe the Texas Securities Act "to protect investors." . . . Given the definitions the legislature gave the relevant terms, the purposes of the Texas Securities Act, and the language of article 581-33(A)(2), we conclude that article 581-33(A)(2) applies to private secondary securities transactions.

Anheuser-Busch and Campbell Taggart urge us to interpret article 581-33(A)(2) in accordance with the Supreme Court's interpretation of section [12(2)] despite the differences in the language used in the two statutes. We decline to do so. Interpretations of the Securities Act of 1933 may be "reliable guides" in interpreting the Texas Securities Act when "they contain virtually the same wording." . . . However, where the statutes use materially different language, we base our interpretation on our legislature's language.

B. Application of Law to Facts

Summit Coffee obtained separate, favorable jury findings that Anheuser-Busch and Campbell Taggart violated section [12(2)] and article 581-33(A)(2). The amount of damages was the same under each theory. The trial court made a single award for the violations. Thus, if that portion of the judgment can be supported under either statute, we must overrule Anheuser-Busch's and Campbell Taggart's fifth point of error.

It is undisputed that the subject transaction was accomplished through the sale of securities as those terms are used in the Texas Securities Act. Article 581-33(A)(2) does not contain language limiting its application to public, initial offerings. Therefore, it is irrelevant that the subject transaction was private and secondary. We conclude the subject transaction was within the scope of article 581-33(A)(2). The trial court did not err in rendering judgment for violation of article 581-33(A)(2). We overrule Anheuser-Busch's and Campbell Taggart's fifth point of error.

. . . .

Sterling Trust Co. v. Adderley

Texas Supreme Court

168 S.W.3d 835 (2005)

Justice O'Neill delivered the opinion of the Court.

The Texas Securities Act (TSA) imposes liability on a person who sells securities "by means of an untrue statement of a material fact or an omission to state a material fact," and imposes liability on a person who "materially aids a seller, buyer, or issuer of a security" if the person acts "with intent to deceive or defraud or with reckless disregard for the truth or the law." The trial court and court of appeals interpreted the latter provision to allow aider liability even if the aider was unaware of its role in the securities violation. We conclude, however, that the TSA's requirement of "reckless disregard for the truth or the law" means that an alleged aider is subject to liability only if it rendered assistance to the seller in the face of a perceived risk that its assistance would facilitate untruthful or illegal activity by the primary violator. This standard does not mean that the aider must know of the exact misrepresentations or omissions made by the seller, but it does mean that the aider must be subjectively aware of the primary violator's improper activity. Accordingly, we reverse the court of appeals' judgment and remand this case to the trial court for further proceedings consistent with this opinion.

I

During the early to mid-1990s, Norman Cornelius formed Avalon Custom Homes and a number of related corporate entities (collectively referred to as "Avalon") designed to develop and sell luxury homes. At that time, Cornelius worked as an investment advisor and broker for Sunpoint Securities. Cornelius operated Avalon out of his Sunpoint office and encouraged his brokerage clients to invest their money in Avalon. Cornelius also persuaded members of his church and retirees from

Mrs. Baird's Bakery to invest in Avalon, offering investors promissory notes that bore as much as an eighteen percent rate of return and allowed conversion to Avalon stock.

Many of the investors chose to invest their retirement savings in Avalon. Because certain retirement accounts such as IRAs and lump-sum pension distributions must be held by a third-party trustee to maintain their preferential tax status, Avalon needed a third-party trustee in order to accept such funds. In 1994, Cornelius began recommending that Avalon investors use Sterling Trust Company, a custodian of self-directed IRA accounts, as their IRA custodian. From 1994 until 1997, Sterling served as the exclusive trustee over the retirement money that the investors self-directed to Cornelius.

In 1997, the Securities and Exchange Commission (SEC) filed suit against Cornelius, alleging that Cornelius misrepresented the risks associated with the investments, misrepresented the uses of investment funds, and misrepresented the commingling and misappropriation of funds. Avalon was forced into receivership, and the Avalon investors collectively lost millions of dollars. A number of elderly investors lost their entire retirement savings. The investors sued Cornelius, Sunpoint Securities, Van Lewis (the owner of Sunpoint), and Sterling Trust. After suit was filed, but before the case was tried, Cornelius died and Sunpoint entered receivership. The claims against Sunpoint were severed from the suit as a result of the receivership, but Sunpoint was still included in the charge as a party to which the jury could apportion responsibility.

. . . .

The jury returned a verdict against Cornelius on all counts. On the issues pertaining to Sterling, however, the verdict was mixed. Specifically, the jury found that Sterling was not a "seller" of securities, that Sterling did not conspire to damage the investors, and that Sterling did not commit fraud. However, the jury found that Sterling aided Cornelius's securities violation. . . . The investors [sought] to recover on the aiding-and-abetting finding, and the trial court rendered judgment against Sterling for $6 million in actual damages and $250,000 in exemplary damages. The court of appeals affirmed the trial court's award of actual damages, but reversed the exemplary damages award. We granted Sterling's petition for review to consider the scope of its potential liability to the investors. . . .

II

The Texas Securities Act establishes both primary and secondary liability for securities violations. Primary liability arises when a person "offers or sells a security . . . by means of an untrue statement of a material fact or an omission to state a material fact necessary in order to make the statements made, in the light of the circumstances under which they are made, not misleading." Secondary liability is derivative liability for another person's securities violation; it can attach to either a control person, defined as "[a] person who directly or indirectly controls a seller, buyer, or issuer of a security," or to an aider, defined as one "who directly or indirectly with intent to deceive or defraud or with reckless disregard for the truth or the law materially aids a seller, buyer, or issuer of a security." Both control persons and aiders are jointly and severally liable with the primary violator "to the same extent as if [they] were" the primary violator.

In this case, the jury found that Sterling was secondarily liable as an aider. Sterling argues that the trial court erred by failing to instruct the jury that an alleged aider cannot be held secondarily liable unless it had a "general awareness" of its role in the primary violation. . . .

We disagree . . . [with the lower courts in this case] that the TSA contains no awareness requirement. The statute's history demonstrates that the Legislature intended the TSA to be interpreted in harmony with federal securities law, and the TSA itself instructs that "[t]his Act may be construed and implemented to effectuate its general purpose to maximize coordination with federal and other states' law and administration." When the Legislature added the aider-liability provision to the TSA in 1977, most federal courts considering the issue had held that aider liability could be imposed under the federal securities law only when the aider was generally aware of its role in an improper scheme. . . .

The investors argue that the federal cases are irrelevant because the Texas Legislature chose a different, lesser standard for aider liability under the TSA; specifically, the investors point out that liability may be imposed on an aider who acted "with intent to . . . defraud or with reckless disregard for the truth or the law," and argue that "reckless disregard" may be shown even if the aider had no awareness of its role in an improper scheme. As support for this proposition, the investors point to a Texas court of appeals case which held that a "failure to conduct minimal investigation and inquiry" before rendering assistance with a securities transaction can suffice to create liability under the "reckless disregard" standard.

We disagree that the "reckless disregard" standard either imposes a lesser standard than the "general awareness" requirement or allows liability to be imposed for a mere failure to investigate. Instead, we conclude that the statute's use of the phrase "reckless disregard for the truth or the law" accords with the requirement that an aider must be aware of the primary violator's improper activities before it may be held liable for assisting in the securities violation. The Legislature's use of the phrase "reckless disregard" is consistent with a requirement of subjective awareness; at the time that the Legislature enacted the TSA, this Court had long held that "recklessness" required evidence of "conscious indifference" in the context of gross negligence. The United States Supreme Court has [stated in] a number of civil actions [that] recklessness requires a subjective awareness of, and indifference to, the risk posed by the defendant's conduct. . . .

We conclude that the TSA's scienter requirement of "reckless disregard for the truth or the law" is similarly intended to impose a requirement of "recklessness in its subjective form," and this recklessness must be directly related to the primary violator's securities violation. When the Texas Legislature adopted the aider provision of the

TSA, it explicitly stated that aider liability should be imposed "only if the aider has the requisite scienter." . . .

We therefore hold that the TSA's "reckless disregard for the truth or the law" standard means that an alleged aider can only be held liable if it rendered assistance "in the face of a perceived risk" that its assistance would facilitate untruthful or illegal activity by the primary violator. In order to perceive such a risk, the alleged aider must possess a "'general awareness that his role was part of an overall activity that is improper.'"

We further hold that the trial court's failure to include the subjective awareness requirement in the jury charge was harmful error. The investors assert that no such instruction was needed; they acknowledge that "the TSA aider liability 'reckless disregard for the truth or the law' language is not inconsistent with the federal 'general awareness' language," but argue that the charge's inclusion of the "reckless disregard" requirement was sufficient to instruct the jury on the standard for liability. We disagree. The trial court is required to "submit such instructions and definitions as shall be proper to enable the jury to render a verdict." In this case, the jury may well have thought that "reckless disregard" could be based on evidence of Sterling's negligent handling of accounts even if Sterling had no actual knowledge of Cornelius's improprieties; the plaintiffs themselves created such a risk of misinterpretation by arguing repeatedly at trial that Sterling "either knew fully what Cornelius was doing" or "exercised reckless disregard" by ignoring internal procedures that would have brought Cornelius's activities to light. Ignoring internal procedures that might have alerted Sterling to Cornelius's scheme may be negligence, but it is not "reckless disregard for the truth or the law." Therefore, "consider[ing] the pleadings of the parties, the evidence presented at trial, and the charge in its entirety," we conclude that the absence of an instruction on the subjective awareness requirement "was reasonably calculated [to] and probably did cause the rendition of an improper judgment." . . .

III

Sterling makes two other arguments that it should be absolved of liability for aiding a securities violation. First, it argues that it cannot be liable as an aider "with respect to transactions and persons with which Sterling had no contact." As the court of appeals correctly noted, however, the TSA does not require the aider to have had direct dealing with the defrauded party; indeed, a person who "materially aids a seller" may have no contact at all with the investors.

Sterling also argues that it cannot be liable as an aider because the jury found in Sterling's favor on its affirmative defense that it did not know, and could not have known, of the particular misrepresentations or omissions made by Cornelius. This affirmative defense is available to persons alleged to have committed a primary violation of the securities laws. As noted above, the statute provides that a seller of a security may be held liable if it "offers or sells a security . . . by means of an untrue statement of a material fact or an omission to state a material fact necessary in order to make the statements made, in the light of the circumstances under which they are made, not misleading." The statute permits the seller to avoid liability by proving the affirmative defense that "he (the offeror or seller) did not know, and in the exercise of reasonable care could not have known, of the untruth or omission."

Because the jury was asked whether Sterling should be held liable as a seller, it was also asked if Sterling had established this affirmative defense; specifically, the question asked whether Sterling "did not know, and in the exercise of reasonable care, could not have known of the untruth or omission" made by the seller. The jury found that Sterling lacked such knowledge and thereby absolved Sterling of primary liability as a seller. Sterling argues that this lack of knowledge also establishes that it cannot be liable as an aider. We disagree.

The TSA provides different knowledge requirements for different classes of defendants; one standard applies to sellers, another applies to control persons, and a third standard applies to aiders. As noted above, sellers are absolved of liability if they prove that [having exercised reasonable care] they lacked knowledge of the "untruth or omission." Control persons may invoke a similar, but not identical, lack-of-knowledge defense:

> A person who directly or indirectly controls a seller, buyer, or issuer of a security is liable under Section 33A, 33B, or 33C jointly and severally with the seller, buyer, or issuer, and to the same extent as if he were the seller, buyer, or issuer, unless the controlling person sustains the burden of proof that he did not know, and in the exercise of reasonable care could not have known, of the existence of the facts by reason of which the liability is alleged to exist.

> . . . .

Finally, the knowledge requirement for aiders is different from both the standard for control persons and the standard for sellers:

> A person who directly or indirectly with intent to deceive or defraud or with reckless disregard for the truth or the law materially aids a seller, buyer, or issuer of a security is liable under [TSA] Section 33A, 33B, or 33C jointly and severally with the seller, buyer, or issuer, and to the same extent as if he were the seller, buyer, or issuer.

Instead of requiring the aider to establish lack of knowledge as an affirmative defense, the section on aider liability requires a plaintiff to prove that the aider acted with "intent to deceive or defraud or with reckless disregard for the truth or the law."

The legislative history of this provision reflects that the Legislature intended to apply distinct liability standards to the different categories of defendants. The Legislature's comment to [the statute] states that the provision "derives in part from Uniform Securities Act § 410(b)." Unlike the TSA, however, this section of the Uniform Securities Act applies the same standard to control persons and to aiders:

> Every person who directly or indirectly controls a seller liable [for unlawful sales of securities], every partner, officer, or director of such a seller, . . . every

employee of such a seller who materially aids in the sale, and every broker-dealer or agent who materially aids in the sale are also liable jointly and severally with and to the same extent as the seller, unless the nonseller who is so liable sustains the burden of proof that he did not know, and in exercise of reasonable care could not have known, of the existence of the facts by reason of which the liability is alleged to exist.

Unif. Securities Act § 410(b). . . .

It thus appears that the TSA adopted the Uniform Securities Act's liability standard for control persons but modified its standard for aiders; while the TSA allows a broader class of persons to qualify as aiders, it imposes a stricter scienter restriction on them. For example, the Uniform Securities Act of 1956 limited aider liability to a seller's employees, brokers, or agents, but the TSA permits "[a] person" who provides material aid to be held liable. In contrast to its narrow class of defendants, the Uniform Securities Act imposed a more relaxed scienter requirement, allowing liability to be imposed on an aider if it negligently failed to discover the facts creating liability. Conversely, the TSA creates a broader class of defendants, but requires more than mere negligence to impose liability; the TSA only imposes liability if the aider acted with "intent to deceive or defraud or with reckless disregard for the truth or the law." Furthermore, the TSA places the burden of proof on the plaintiff to prove that the defendant acted with the requisite scienter, while the Uniform Securities Act required the defendant to prove that it acted with reasonable care. Finally, the TSA focuses on the aider's reckless disregard "for the truth or the law," instead of the aider's knowledge "of the existence of the facts by reason of which the liability is alleged." These modifications indicate that the Legislature gave significant consideration to the proper scienter standard for aiders. We decline to imply an additional defense not offered to aiders under the text of the statute.

Sterling argues that the failure to imply such a defense renders the statute illogical and allows secondary violators to be held liable even when a primary violator could escape liability by invoking an affirmative defense. We disagree. First, a secondary violator's liability depends upon the primary violator's culpability; even without an additional affirmative defense, a secondary violator may only be held liable "to the same extent as" the primary violator. Thus, if it were proven that the seller reasonably believed its statements to be true, there would be no primary violation and no derivative liability to attach to the aider. Second, the Legislature did not act illogically by adopting different scienter standards for primary and secondary violators; the different standards make sense in light of the facts that these parties may reasonably be expected to know. A primary violator is the party actually making the misrepresentations or misleading omissions, and it therefore makes sense to focus on whether it knew the statements were untrue. On the other hand, an aider may know that the primary violator is engaging in improper activity, but, if the aider is not involved in the actual sale or offer of the securities, it may not know what particular misrepresentations or misleading omissions were made to the investors. Consequently, it makes sense to predicate liability on the aider's "reckless disregard for the truth or the law" rather than the aider's knowledge of specific misrepresentations or omissions.

The investors acknowledge that Sterling may not have known the exact misrepresentations that Cornelius was making to the investors, but they argue that Sterling did know that Cornelius was operating an illegal pyramid scheme. We agree that knowledge of such an illegal scheme, if proven, could support a finding that Sterling acted "with reckless disregard for the truth or the law" even if Sterling could not have known of the particular misrepresentations made by Cornelius. . . .

We acknowledge that there is some tension between the jury's finding that Sterling acted with "reckless disregard for the truth or the law" and its finding that Sterling did not know and could not have reasonably known of "the untruth or omission" made by Cornelius. However, Sterling does not argue in this Court that the two findings conflict, and Sterling did not seek to have the jury harmonize these two answers in the trial court. . . . Instead, Sterling argues only that its lack of knowledge of Cornelius's "untruth or omission" establishes as a matter of law that it cannot have acted "with reckless disregard for the truth or the law." We disagree. Because the finding referred specifically to knowledge "of the untruth or omission," we conclude that this finding does not establish whether Sterling knew of Cornelius's improper activity in general, and therefore does not necessarily trump the jury's finding that Sterling acted "with intent to deceive or defraud or with reckless disregard for the truth or the law."

In this case, the jury may have agreed that Sterling could not have known what Cornelius was telling the investors but nevertheless believed that Sterling knew that Cornelius was operating an illegal pyramid scheme. Because the jury in this case was asked only whether Sterling knew of "the untruth or omission," the jury's "no" answer does not shed light on whether the jury believed that Sterling knew Cornelius was engaged in illegal activity. Sterling's argument to the jury also focused on whether Sterling had knowledge of Cornelius's statements, not whether it had knowledge of the underlying scheme. Specifically, Sterling argued that the jury must find that Sterling "did not know, and in the exercise of reasonable care, could not have known of the untruth or omission" because Sterling "had no way of knowing what Norman Cornelius was telling or not telling these people." Consequently, we hold that the jury's finding that Sterling "did not know, and in the exercise of reasonable care could not have known of the untruth or omission" is not dispositive of the question of whether Sterling had knowledge of the underlying wrongdoing.

. . . .

[Reversed and remanded]

Bennett v. Hunter Durham

United States Court of Appeals, Sixth Circuit

683 F.3d 734 (2012)

SUTTON, Circuit Judge.

The Kentucky Securities Act imposes liability [, among other persons,] on (1) anyone who "offers or sells a security" in violation of its terms and (2) any "agent" of the seller who "materially aids" the sale of securities, defined as someone who "effect[s] or attempt[s] to effect" the sale. These related cases present the same question: Does the Act impose liability on an attorney who performs traditional legal services for a company offering its securities for sale to the public? The answer is no.

I.

Paul Bennett, Frederick Clayton and their co-plaintiffs invested in oil-and-gas-exploration companies: either Heartland Resources or Mammoth Resource Partners. When the companies' wells produced little oil or gas, the investors lost money. They sued. Claiming Heartland and Mammoth violated state and federal law by selling unregistered securities and by making other material misrepresentations and omissions, they filed a complaint against the two companies and their officers. They did not stop there. They also sued Hunter Durham, the lawyer who represented Heartland and Mammoth in connection with the issuance and sale of the securities. Durham drafted the documents necessary for the deals, including joint-venture agreements and private placement memoranda that provided details about the investment opportunity. He also told the prospective investors he was available to answer their questions. All the while, Bennett and Clayton allege, Durham knew the documents contained material misrepresentations and omissions and that the securities were neither registered nor exempt from registration.

Durham responded that he merely provided traditional legal services in connection with the issuance and sale of the securities, work that the offer-and-sale provisions of the Kentucky securities laws by themselves do not regulate. In Bennett's lawsuit, the district court granted Durham's motion to dismiss the claim. . . . In Clayton's lawsuit, the district court (through a different judge) granted Durham's motions for summary judgment. . . .

II.

Kentucky, like most States, regulates sales and offers of securities through "blue sky" laws, so named because they initially targeted swindlers so brazen and so shameless they would peddle shares of anything, including (allegedly) shares of the sky. Kentucky's law says, as relevant here:

> (1) Any person, who *offers or sells a security* in violation of this chapter . . . or offers or sells a security by means of any untrue statement of material fact or any omission to state a material fact . . . , and who does not sustain the burden of proof that he did not know and in the exercise of reasonable care

could not have known of the untruth or omission[,] is liable to the person buying the security from him. . . .

(4) Every person who *directly or indirectly controls a seller or purchaser* liable under subsection (1) or (2) of this section, *every partner, officer, or director (or other person occupying a similar status or performing similar functions)* or employee of a seller or purchaser who materially aids in the sale or purchase, and every broker-dealer or *agent who materially aids in the sale or purchase* is also liable jointly and severally with and to the same extent as the seller or purchaser, unless [he] sustains the burden of proof that he did not know, and in the exercise of reasonable care could not have known, of the existence of the facts by reason of which the liability is alleged to exist.

Ky. Rev. Stat. § 292.480 (emphases added). These provisions, along with the rest of Kentucky's blue-sky law, derive from the Uniform Securities Act of 1956, a model law authored by the National Conference of Commissioners on Uniform State Laws, a group of state legislators, judges and legal scholars. Thirty-six other States have adopted the Act in whole or in part. Both provisions, Bennett and Clayton maintain, cover Durham's conduct.

A.

Does an attorney who provides legal advice in connection with a securities transaction "offer[ ] or sell[ ] a security," as required to impose liability under subsection (1) of the statute? The customary meaning of the words suggests not, as Durham never offered to sell or sold shares to anyone. His clients sold the shares, and we do not attribute the transactions of a client to its attorney. An attorney may draft an offering memorandum for his client, but that does not mean the attorney, as opposed to the client, offers to sell the securities. The client and its broker-dealers sell the securities. Durham no more "offered" or "sold" these securities than the lawyer representing Magic Johnson's investment group recently "bought" the Los Angeles Dodgers. . . .

Interpretations of the federal Securities Act of 1933 confirm the point. The federal Act likewise reaches "any person who offers or sells a security" in violation of its rules. 15 U.S.C. § 77*l*(a)(1). And the [Supreme] Court likewise has construed it to cover only "persons who pass title and persons who 'offer,' including those who 'solicit' offers." *Pinter v. Dahl*, 486 U.S. 622, 650 (1988). In rejecting a more expansive definition, *Pinter* reasoned that it "might expose securities professionals, such as accountants and lawyers, whose involvement is only the performance of their professional services," to liability, even though "[t]he buyer does not, in any meaningful sense, purchase the security from such a person." . . .

All of this matters not just because the Supreme Court . . . ha[s] interpreted "offer" and "sell" to rule out liability for attorneys performing traditional legal services in connection with a securities offering. What is particularly revealing is that Kentucky based its blue-sky law on the Uniform Securities Act, which itself "is borrowed substantially" from the same federal law (the Securities Act of 1933) construed in

Pinter . . . There is no reason to think the Kentucky courts would construe the words differently. Since *Pinter,* moreover, other state courts have construed their own blue-sky laws the same way. *See, e.g., Meyers v. Lott,* 993 P.2d 609, 613 (Idaho 2000); *Klein v. Oppenheimer & Co.,* 130 P.3d 569, 582 (Kan. 2006); *Wilson v. Misko,* 508 N.W.2d 238, 248 (Neb. 1993); *Biales v. Young,* 432 S.E.2d 482, 484–85 (S.C. 1993); *see also Allstate Indus. Loan Plan, Inc. v. Mihalek,* 555 S.W.2d 585, 586–87 (Ky. 1977) (relying on precedents from other States in construing the Kentucky Securities Act).

That is all well and good, Bennett and Clayton respond, but Durham was not just a lawyer doing his job. That would be a strong argument — if the facts backed it up. They do not. Bennett alleges and Clayton has put forth facts showing only that Durham drafted and *distributed investment documents, made himself available to answer questions from prospective investors* and represented clients in an enforcement proceeding. That is the type of ordinary legal work securities lawyers do every day. [emphasis supplied] [Do you agree with the court's assessment of "ordinary legal work?"]

Bennett and Clayton persist that Durham "went beyond a role of serving as counsel," and "was not merely an attorney and legal advisor." But they do not say how or when or otherwise elaborate on what that means. Even on summary judgment Clayton was able to identify only one plaintiff who spoke to Durham before investing, and the investor testified that Durham answered his questions, not that Durham solicited or offered to sell any securities. . . .

The only other specific factual allegations Bennett and Clayton make — that Durham served as an attorney to Heartland and Mammoth on many different occasions, that he knew the securities sales were illegal, and that Heartland's executives "relied completely" on his advice — change nothing. A lawyer does not become something other than a lawyer by serving the same client multiple times. Still less is that the case because the client follows his advice unquestioningly or because he knowingly drafts false or misleading documents. Of course, an attorney who knowingly drafted false or misleading documents would face *other* problems. He might be liable for fraud, a claim the district court declined to dismiss in Bennett's case but that the parties eventually stipulated to dismiss themselves. Or he might be liable for malpractice or face disciplinary proceedings. But none of this transforms the attorney into someone who "offers or sells a security" for purposes of Ky. Rev. Stat. § 292.480(1). Durham is not liable under this provision as a matter of law.

B.

Does Durham qualify (1) as a "partner, officer, or director (or other person occupying a similar status or performing similar functions)" or (2) as an "agent who materially aid[ed] in the sale or purchase" of securities? Ky. Rev. Stat. § 292.480(4).

The first part of this claim (raised by Clayton, not Bennett) takes little time. That Durham was a "partner, officer, or director" or occupied a similar status and performed similar functions fails for the same reason the last claim failed. Clayton offered no facts on summary judgment from which we could infer that Durham did anything beyond what would be expected of a securities attorney providing run-of-the-mine legal services. Clayton's brief on appeal seeks to add more, but this effort is too little and too late. It is too little because the alleged facts mentioned in the appellate brief — that Heartland's officers and directors "relied completely" on Durham's work and would have "structured [their] sales operation in any way Mr. Durham advised," — suggest only that Heartland's *actual* partners, officers and directors relied heavily on their attorney, not that Durham was the one calling the shots. . . .

The second part of the claim is also flawed. The statute defines the key term — agent — as "any individual other than a broker-dealer who represents a broker-dealer or issuer in *effecting* or *attempting to effect* purchases or sales of securities." Ky. Rev. Stat. § 292.310(1) (emphasis added).

An attorney does not "effect," as opposed to "affect," purchases or sales of securities. "Effect" in this context means "to carry out (a sale, a purchase)," or more generally "to bring about (an event, a result)." Oxford English Dictionary (3d ed. 2008). That language covers salesmen or placement agents who identify potential investors on behalf of the issuer and convince them to buy securities. An attorney performing ordinary legal work, by contrast, is not hired to "carry out" or "bring about" the sale of securities; the attorney's job is to ensure that any such sale, should the client choose to pursue it, complies with the law. The attorney's work, it is true, may be a but-for cause of a later sale of securities, but the statute requires more. It is not enough that the attorney "represents" the issuer in a matter that culminates in the sale of securities; he must represent the issuer "in effecting or attempting to effect" the sale, meaning that carrying out or bringing about the sale must be the job the client hires the attorney to perform. That is not what securities lawyers generally do, and that was not what Durham did even under a view of the evidence most favorable to the plaintiffs.

Case law confirms this reading. In a survey of a half-dozen cases considering the same question, the Maryland Court of Special Appeals noted that the cases "each have one thing in common: they do not impose liability upon an attorney who merely provides legal services or prepares documents for his or her client." . . . To be liable, "the attorney must do something more than act as legal counsel," namely "actively assist in offering securities for sale, solicit offers to buy, or actually perform the sale." . . .

For their part, Bennett and Clayton cite no case holding an attorney liable under the Uniform Securities Act merely for drafting documents, providing advice and *answering client questions.* . . . [emphasis supplied] [Consider — Who is the "client"?]

Legal scholars also agree with our approach. Under the Uniform Securities Act's definition, they say that "the term 'agent' means only individuals who help to sell securities," meaning that "professionals such as attorneys and accountants[ ] would not qualify as agents under this definition unless they became involved in the sales efforts." Jennifer J. Johnson, *Secondary Liability for Securities Fraud: Gatekeepers in State Court*, 36 Del. J. Corp. L. 463, 482–83 (2011); *see also* Douglas M. Branson,

Chasing the Rogue Professional After the Private Securities Litigation Reform Act of 1995, 50 SMU L. Rev. 91, 120 (1996); . . . Marc I. Steinberg & Chris Claassen, *Attorney Liability Under the State Securities Laws: Landscapes and Minefields*, 3 Berkeley Bus. L.J. 1, 23 (2005) ("prevailing view" is that attorneys are not agents under the Uniform Securities Act because they "do not 'effect' the purchase or sale" of securities).

An attorney who performs ordinary legal work, such as drafting documents, giving advice and answering client questions, is not an "agent" under Ky. Rev. Stat. § 292.480(4). Even if we accept all of the facts alleged in the complaint, that is all Durham did.

. . . .

For these reasons, we affirm.

Malone v. Brincat

Delaware Supreme Court

722 A.2d 5 (1998)

HOLLAND, Justice

Doran Malone, Joseph P. Danielle, and Adrienne M. Danielle, the plaintiffs-appellants, filed this individual and class action in the Court of Chancery. The complaint alleged that the directors of Mercury Finance Company ("Mercury"), a Delaware corporation, breached their fiduciary duty of disclosure. The individual defendant-appellee directors are John N. Brincat, Dennis H. Chookaszian, William C. Croft, Clifford R. Johnson, Andrew McNally, IV, Bruce I. McPhee, Fred G. Steingraber, and Phillip J. Wicklander. The complaint also alleged that the defendant-appellee, KPMG Peat Marwick LLP ("KPMG") aided and abetted the Mercury directors' breaches of fiduciary duty. The Court of Chancery dismissed the complaint with prejudice pursuant to Chancery Rule 12(b)(6) for failure to state a claim upon which relief may be granted.

The complaint alleged that the director defendants intentionally overstated the financial condition of Mercury on repeated occasions throughout a four-year period in disclosures to Mercury's shareholders. Plaintiffs contend that the complaint states a claim upon which relief can be granted for a breach of the fiduciary duty of disclosure. Plaintiffs also contend that, because the director defendants breached their fiduciary duty of disclosure to the Mercury shareholders, the Court of Chancery erroneously dismissed the aiding and abetting claim against KPMG.

This Court has concluded that the Court of Chancery properly granted the defendants' motions to dismiss the complaint. That dismissal, however, should have been without prejudice. Plaintiffs are entitled to file an amended complaint. Therefore, the judgment of the Court of Chancery is affirmed in part, reversed in part, and remanded for further proceedings consistent with this opinion.

Facts

Mercury is a publicly-traded company engaged primarily in purchasing install-ment sales contracts from automobile dealers and providing short-term installment loans directly to consumers. This action was filed on behalf of the named plaintiffs and all persons (excluding defendants) who owned common stock of Mercury from 1993 through the present and their successors in interest, heirs and assigns (the "puta-tive class"). The complaint alleged that the directors "knowingly and intentionally breached their fiduciary duty of disclosure because the SEC filings made by the direc-tors and every communication from the company to the shareholders since 1994 was materially false" and that "as a direct result of the false disclosures . . . the Com-pany has lost all or virtually all of its value (about $2 billion)." The complaint also alleged that KPMG knowingly participated in the directors' breaches of their fidu-ciary duty of disclosure.

According to Plaintiffs, since 1994, the director defendants caused Mercury to dis-seminate information containing overstatements of Mercury's earnings, financial performance and shareholders' equity. Mercury's earnings for 1996 were actually only $56.7 million, or $.33 a share, rather than the $120.7 million, or $.70 a share, as reported by the director defendants. Mercury's earnings in 1995 were actually $76.9 million, or $.44 a share, rather than $98.9 million, or $.57 a share, as reported by the director defendants. Mercury's earnings for 1994 were $83 million, or $.47 a share, rather than $86.5 million, or $.49 a share, as reported by the director defendants. Mercury's earnings for 1993 were $64.2 million, rather than $64.9 million, as reported by the director defendants. Shareholders' equity on December 31, 1996 was disclosed by the director defendants as $353 million, but was only $263 million or less. The complaint alleged that all of the foregoing inaccurate information was included or referenced in virtually every filing Mercury made with the SEC and every commu-nication Mercury's directors made to the shareholders during this period of time.

Having alleged these violations of fiduciary duty, which (if true) are egregious, plaintiffs alleged that as a direct result "of [these] false disclosures . . . the company has lost all or virtually all its value (about $2 billion)," and seeks class action status to pursue damages against the directors and KPMG for the individual plaintiffs and common stockholders. The individual director defendants filed a motion to dismiss, contending that they owed no fiduciary duty of disclosure under the circumstances alleged in the complaint. KPMG also filed a motion to dismiss the aiding and abet-ting claim asserted against it.

After briefing and oral argument, the Court of Chancery granted both of the motions to dismiss with prejudice. The Court of Chancery held that directors have no fiduciary duty of disclosure under Delaware law in the absence of a request for shareholder action. In so holding, the Court stated:

> The federal securities laws ensure the timely release of accurate information into the marketplace. The federal power to regulate should not be duplicated or impliedly usurped by Delaware. When a shareholder is damaged merely

as a result of the release of inaccurate information into the marketplace, unconnected with any Delaware corporate governance issue, that shareholder must seek a remedy under federal law.

We disagree, and although we hold that the Complaint as drafted should have been dismissed, our rationale is different.

. . . .

Issue On Appeal

This Court has held that a board of directors is under a fiduciary duty to disclose material information when seeking shareholder action:

> It is well-established that the duty of disclosure represents nothing more than the well-recognized proposition that directors of Delaware corporations are under a fiduciary duty to disclose fully and fairly all material information within the board's control *when it seeks shareholder action.*

The majority of opinions from the Court of Chancery have held that there may be a cause of action for disclosure violations only where directors seek shareholder action. [*See e.g., Kahn v. Roberts*, 679 A.2d 460, 467 (Del. 1996).] The present appeal requires this Court to decide whether a director's fiduciary duty arising out of misdisclosure is implicated in the absence of a request for shareholder action. We hold that directors who knowingly disseminate false information that results in corporate injury or damage to an individual stockholder violate their fiduciary duty, and may be held accountable in a manner appropriate to the circumstances.

Fiduciary Duty

Delaware Corporate Directors

An underlying premise for the imposition of fiduciary duties is a separation of legal control from beneficial ownership. Equitable principles act in those circumstances to protect the beneficiaries who are not in a position to protect themselves. One of the fundamental tenets of Delaware corporate law provides for a separation of control and ownership. The board of directors has the legal responsibility to manage the business of a corporation for the benefit of its shareholder owners. Accordingly, fiduciary duties are imposed on the directors of Delaware corporations to regulate their conduct when they discharge that function.

The directors of Delaware corporations stand in a fiduciary relationship not only to the stockholders but also to the corporations upon whose boards they serve. The director's fiduciary duty to both the corporation and its shareholders has been characterized by this Court as a triad: due care, good faith, and loyalty. That triparte fiduciary duty does not operate intermittently but is the constant compass by which all director actions for the corporation and interactions with its shareholders must be guided.

Although the fiduciary duty of a Delaware director is unremitting, the exact course of conduct that must be charted to properly discharge that responsibility will change in the specific context of the action the director is taking with regard to either the corporation or its shareholders. This Court has endeavored to provide the directors with clear signal beacons and brightly lined-channel markers as they navigate with due care, good faith, and loyalty on behalf of a Delaware corporation and its shareholders. This Court has also endeavored to mark the safe harbors clearly.

Director Communications
Shareholder Reliance Justified

The shareholder constituents of a Delaware corporation are entitled to rely upon their elected directors to discharge their fiduciary duties at all times. Whenever directors communicate publicly or directly with shareholders about the corporation's affairs, with or without a request for shareholder action, directors have a fiduciary duty to shareholders to exercise due care, good faith and loyalty. It follows *a fortiori* that when directors communicate publicly or directly with shareholders about corporate matters the *sine qua non* of directors' fiduciary duty to shareholders is honesty.

According to the appellants, the focus of the fiduciary duty of disclosure is to protect shareholders as the "beneficiaries" of all material information disseminated by the directors. The duty of disclosure is, and always has been, a specific application of the general fiduciary duty owed by directors. The duty of disclosure obligates directors to provide the stockholders with accurate and complete information material to a transaction or other corporate event that is being presented to them for action.

The issue in this case is not whether Mercury's directors breached their duty of disclosure. It is whether they breached their more general fiduciary duty of loyalty and good faith by knowingly disseminating to the stockholders false information about the financial condition of the company. The directors' fiduciary duties include the duty to deal with their stockholders honestly.

Shareholders are entitled to rely upon the truthfulness of all information disseminated to them by the directors they elect to manage the corporate enterprise. Delaware directors disseminate information in at least three contexts: public statements made to the market, including shareholders; statements informing shareholders about the affairs of the corporation without a request for shareholder action; and, statements to shareholders in conjunction with a request for shareholder action. Inaccurate information in these contexts may be the result of violation of the fiduciary duties of care, loyalty or good faith. We will examine the remedies that are available to shareholders for misrepresentations in each of these three contexts by the directors of a Delaware corporation.

State Fiduciary Disclosure Duty
Shareholder Remedy In Action Requested Context

In the absence of a request for stockholder action, the Delaware General Corporation Law does not require directors to provide shareholders with information concerning the finances or affairs of the corporation. Even when shareholder action is sought, the provisions in the General Corporation Law requiring notice to the shareholders of the proposed action do not require the directors to convey substantive information beyond a statutory minimum. Consequently, in the context of a request for shareholder action, the protection afforded by Delaware law is a judicially recognized equitable cause of action by shareholders against directors.

The fiduciary duty of directors in connection with disclosure violations in Delaware jurisprudence was restated in *Lynch v. Vickers Energy Corp.* Del. Supr., 383 A.2d 278 (1978). In *Lynch*, this Court held that, in making a tender offer to acquire the stock of the minority stockholders, a majority stockholder "owed a fiduciary duty . . . which required 'complete candor' in disclosing fully all the facts and circumstances surrounding the tender offer." In *Stroud v. Grace*, [606 A.2d 75 (Del. 1992)], we noted that the language of our jurisprudence should be clarified to the extent that "candor" requires no more than the duty to disclose all material facts when seeking stockholder action. [Hence, the Delaware Supreme Court has adopted the same materiality standard as that provided by the federal securities laws. See *Rosenblatt v. Getty Oil Co.*, 493 A.2d 929, 944 (Del. 1985), adopting materiality standard set forth in *TSC Industries, Inc. v. Northway, Inc.*, 426 U.S. 438, 449 (1976).] An article by Professor Lawrence Hamermesh includes an excellent historical summary of the content, context, and parameters of the law of disclosure, as it has been developed in a series of decisions during the last two decades. [See 49 Vand. L. Rev. 1087 (1996).]

The duty of directors to observe proper disclosure requirements derives from the combination of the fiduciary duties of care, loyalty and good faith. The plaintiffs contend that, because directors fiduciary responsibilities are not "intermittent duties," there is no reason why the duty of disclosure should not be implicated in every public communication by a corporate board of directors. The directors of a Delaware corporation are required to disclose fully and fairly all material information within the board's control when it seeks shareholder action. When the directors disseminate information to stockholders when no stockholder action is sought, the fiduciary duties of care, loyalty and good faith apply. Dissemination of false information could violate one or more of those duties.

An action for a breach of fiduciary duty arising out of disclosure violations in connection with a request for stockholder action does not include the elements of reliance, causation and actual quantifiable monetary damages. Instead, such actions require the challenged disclosure to have a connection to the request for shareholder action. The essential inquiry in such an action is whether the alleged omission or misrepresentation is material. Materiality is determined with respect to the shareholder action being sought.

The directors' duty to disclose all available material information in connection with a request for shareholder action must be balanced against its concomitant duty to protect the corporate enterprise, in particular, by keeping certain financial information confidential. Directors are required to provide shareholders with all information that is material to the action being requested and to provide a balanced, truthful account of all matters disclosed in the communications with shareholders. Accordingly, directors have definitive guidance in discharging their fiduciary duty by an analysis of the factual circumstances relating to the specific shareholder action being requested and an inquiry into the potential for deception or misinformation.

Fraud On Market
Regulated by Federal Law

When corporate directors impart information they must comport with the obligations imposed by both the Delaware law and the federal statutes and regulations of the United States Securities and Exchange Commission ("SEC"). Historically, federal law has regulated disclosures by corporate directors into the general interstate market. This Court has noted that "in observing its congressional mandate the SEC has adopted a 'basic philosophy of disclosure.'" Accordingly, this Court has held that there is "no legitimate basis to create a new cause of action which would replicate, by state decisional law, the provisions of . . . the 1934 Act." In deference to the panoply of federal protections that are available to investors in connection with the purchase or sale of securities of Delaware corporations, this Court has decided not to recognize a state common law cause of action against the directors of Delaware corporations for "fraud on the market." Here, it is to be noted, the claim appears to be made by those who did not sell and, therefore, would not implicate federal securities laws which relate to the purchase or sale of securities.

The historic roles played by state and federal law in regulating corporate disclosures have been not only compatible but complementary. That symbiotic relationship has been perpetuated by the recently enacted federal Securities Litigation Uniform Standards Act of 1998. Although that statute by its terms does not apply to this case, [subject to certain exceptions,] the new statute will require securities class actions involving the purchase or sale of nationally traded securities, based upon false or misleading statements, to be brought exclusively in federal court under federal law. . . .

State Common Law
Shareholder Remedy In Nonaction Context

Delaware law also protects shareholders who receive false communications from directors even in the absence of a request for shareholder action. When the directors are not seeking shareholder action, but are deliberately misinforming shareholders about the business of the corporation, either directly or by a public statement, there is a violation of fiduciary duty. That violation may result in a derivative claim on behalf of the corporation or a cause of action for damages. There may also be a basis for equitable relief to remedy the violation.

Complaint Properly Dismissed

No Shareholder Action Requested

Here the complaint alleges (if true) an egregious violation of fiduciary duty by the directors in knowingly disseminating materially false information. Then it alleges that the corporation lost about $2 billion in value as a result. Then it merely claims that the action is brought on behalf of the named plaintiffs and the putative class. It is a *non sequitur* rather than a syllogism.

The allegation in paragraph 3 that the false disclosures resulted in the corporation losing virtually all its equity seems obliquely to claim an injury to the corporation. The plaintiffs, however, never expressly assert a derivative claim on behalf of the corporation or allege compliance with Court of Chancery Rule 23.1, which requires pre-suit demand or cognizable and particularized allegations that demand is excused. If the plaintiffs intend to assert a derivative claim, they should be permitted to replead to assert such a claim and any damage or equitable remedy sought on behalf of the corporation. Likewise, the plaintiffs should have the opportunity to replead to assert any individual cause of action and articulate a remedy that is appropriate on behalf of the named plaintiffs individually, or a properly recognizable class consistent with Court of Chancery Rule 23. . . .

The Court of Chancery properly dismissed the complaint before it against the individual director defendants, in the absence of well-pleaded allegations stating a derivative, class or individual cause of action and properly assertable remedy. Without a well-pleaded allegation in the complaint for a breach of fiduciary duty, there can be no claim for aiding and abetting such a breach. Accordingly, the plaintiffs' aiding and abetting claim against KPMG was also properly dismissed.

Nevertheless, we disagree with the Court of Chancery's holding that such a claim cannot be articulated on these facts. The plaintiffs should have been permitted to amend their complaint, if possible, to state a properly cognizable cause of action against the individual defendants and KPMG. Consequently, the Court of Chancery should have dismissed the complaint *without* prejudice.

Conclusion

The judgment of the Court of Chancery to dismiss the complaint is affirmed. The judgment to dismiss the complaint with prejudice is reversed. This matter is remanded for further proceedings in accordance with this opinion.

———————

Holmes v. Grubman

Georgia Supreme Court

286 Ga. 636 (2010)

Carley, Presiding Justice.

As of June 1999, Appellants William K. Holmes and four entities controlled by him owned 2.1 million shares in WorldCom, Inc., the major telecommunications company which went bankrupt after the revelation of massive accounting fraud in 2002. In this suit against Appellees Citigroup Global Markets, Inc., f/k/a Salomon Smith Barney & Co., Inc. (SSB), and its financial analyst, Jack Grubman, Appellants allege that, on June 25, 1999, Holmes verbally ordered his broker at SSB to sell all of Appellants' WorldCom stock, which was then being traded at approximately $92 per share. Appellants further allege that the SSB broker convinced Holmes not to sell, based on recent research reports by Grubman and on his reputation, and that Appellees were operating under a conflict of interest, knowing that WorldCom stock was grossly overvalued, but nevertheless promoting it in order to retain WorldCom's lucrative investment banking business. Instead of selling, Holmes purchased additional shares as the stock price declined. In October 2000, Appellants were forced to sell all of their WorldCom shares in order to meet margin calls, resulting in alleged losses of nearly $200 million.

Appellants filed for bankruptcy and, in 2003, brought this action for damages under Georgia law in the United States Bankruptcy Court for the Middle District of Georgia. The case was transferred to the United States District Court for the Southern District of New York and consolidated for pre-trial purposes with the multidistrict WorldCom Securities Litigation. Appellants' third amended complaint included claims of fraud, negligent misrepresentation, negligence in making disclosures, and breach of fiduciary duty. The district court dismissed that complaint for failure to state a claim upon which relief can be granted. *Holmes v. Grubman (In re WorldCom, Inc. Securities Litigation),* 456 F. Supp. 2d 508 (S.D.N.Y. 2006). On appeal, the United States Court of Appeals for the Second Circuit certified the following questions to this court:

(1) Does Georgia common law recognize fraud claims based on forbearance in the sale of publicly traded securities?

(2) With respect to a tort claim based on misrepresentations or omissions concerning publicly traded securities, is proximate cause adequately pleaded under Georgia law when a plaintiff alleges that his injury was a reasonably foreseeable result of defendant's false or misleading statements but does not allege that the truth concealed by the defendant entered the market place, thereby precipitating a drop in the price of the security?

. . . .

Holmes v. Grubman, 568 F.3d 329, 340–341 (2d Cir. 2009).

1. [*Regarding the first question:*] The claims to which the first question refers are often called "holder" claims. Although this Court has never specifically addressed such claims, it is well-settled that one of the elements of the tort of fraud in Georgia is an " 'intention to induce the plaintiff to act *or refrain from acting . . . .*' " This language is consistent with the Restatement (Second) of Torts § 525 (1977) and the general rule that "induced forbearance can be the basis for tort liability." [See] *Small v. Fritz Cos.,* 30 Cal. 4th 167, 132 Cal. Rptr. 2d 490, 65 P. 3d 1255, 1259 (Cal. 2003).

The public policy underlying the actionability of fraud exists regardless of whether plaintiff is induced to act or refrain from action. Lies which deceive and injure do not become innocent merely because the deceived continue to do something rather than begin to do something else. Inducement is the substance of reliance; the form of reliance—action or inaction—is not critical to the actionability of fraud.

The Supreme Court of the United States has held that only actual purchasers or sellers of securities can make a claim pursuant to Rule 10b-5, promulgated by the Securities and Exchange Commission under § 10(b) of the Securities Exchange Act of 1934. *Blue Chip Stamps v. Manor Drug Stores*, 421 U.S. 723, 730–731 (1975). However, that Court also noted that one disadvantage of its holding "is attenuated to the extent that remedies are available to nonpurchasers and nonsellers under state law." Indeed, the Supreme Court recognized that it has "long been established in the ordinary case of deceit that a misrepresentation which leads to a refusal to purchase or to sell is actionable in just the same way as a misrepresentation which leads to the consummation of a purchase or sale." [*Id.*] at 744. Compare *Merrill Lynch, Pierce, Fenner & Smith v. Dabit*, 547 U.S. 71, (2006) (Securities Litigation Uniform Standards Act preempts state-law holder class-action claims).

Furthermore, although Appellees "are immune from [Rule] 10b-5 liability, they should not be immunized from common law liability merely because their alleged fraud occurred in the securities market rather than the real estate or used car market." The Georgia Court of Appeals has acknowledged that "evidence of fraud . . . includ[es] evidence which supported the conclusion that [the plaintiffs] were fraudulently induced into making *and keeping* their investments." (Emphasis supplied.) *Argentum Intl. v. Woods*, 634 S.E. 2d 195 (2006). Most other states that have confronted this issue have concluded that forbearance from selling stock is sufficient reliance to support a cause of action. . . .

Appellees offer several policy grounds for barring holder claims, including, as the Second Circuit noted, "(1) incoherent theories of proximate cause and damages, (2) speculative damages, and (3) unprovable claims of a subjective intent to sell." After reviewing all such policy considerations, we conclude that, although they

> may justify placing limitations on a holder's cause of action, they do not justify a categorical denial of that cause of action. . . . [T]he high court's decision in *Blue Chip Stamps,* while recognizing policy considerations similar to those defendants advance here, did not view those considerations as justification for a total denial of relief to defrauded holders; it reasoned only that the *federal* courts could deny a forum to wronged stockholders who are not sellers or buyers without unjust consequences because these stockholders retained a remedy in *state* courts. (Emphasis in original.).

Small v. Fritz Cos., [65 P. 3d at] 1261. "Persons claiming that, for reasons of policy, they should be immune from liability for intentional fraud bear a very heavy burden of persuasion, one that defendants here have not sustained." [*Id.*] at 1265.

In many of the decisions on which Appellees rely, holder claims were not categorically rejected, but the plaintiffs failed to allege or prove that they specifically desired to sell their stock at a certain time, or causation was not sufficiently alleged or proved. . . . Similarly, although we have determined that holder claims should be recognized under Georgia law, we further conclude that the limitations imposed in other jurisdictions are appropriate. When acknowledging in *Blue Chip Stamps* the continuing viability of common-law holder claims, "[t]he Supreme Court considered the typical fraud context to be one in which the parties knew each other and the alleged misrepresentations occurred through direct communication." . . . Indeed, the Supreme Court distinguished the "universe of transactions governed by the 1934 Act, [where] privity of dealing or even personal contact between potential defendant and potential plaintiff is the exception and not the rule." . . . Accordingly, we conclude that Georgia law permits holder claims

> where, as here, plaintiffs allege that misrepresentations were directed at them to their injury. Although the price of allowing cases like [Appellees'] to go forward may be that some such cases will unfairly waste the Court's time and the defendants' reputation and money, that is a price the common law has always paid.
>
> . . . .
>
> We further agree with those courts which require specific reliance on the defendants' representations: for example, that if the plaintiff had read a truthful account of the corporation's financial status the plaintiff would have sold the stock, how many shares the plaintiff would have sold, and when the sale would have taken place. The plaintiff must allege actions, as distinguished from unspoken and unrecorded thoughts and decisions, that would indicate that the plaintiff actually relied on the misrepresentations.
>
> . . . . Such distinction reinforces the reliance requirement by separating plaintiffs who actually and justifiably relied upon the misrepresentations from the general investing public, who, though they did not so rely, suffered the loss due to the decline in share value. This distinction also separates common law fraud claims, which must prove actual reliance, from federal securities fraud claims, which may rely upon the fraud-on-the-market theory.
>
> . . . .

Although the Second Circuit's first question was limited to fraud claims, the particular phrasing thereof does not prevent us from reformulating or expanding upon the question. We see no reason why our authorization of common fraud claims based on forbearance in the sale of publicly traded securities, along with the limitations articulated above, should not extend to Appellants' other common-law tort claims. In particular, we note that "'(t)he same principles apply to both fraud and negligent misrepresentation cases'" and that "'the only real distinction between negligent misrepresentation and fraud is the absence of the element of knowledge of the falsity of the information disclosed.'" . . . . Thus, we hold that negligent misrepresentation claims, like fraud claims, can be based on forbearance in the sale of publicly traded securities. The direct communication and specific reliance limitations on fraud claims by "holders" also apply to negligent misrepresentation claims. . . .

2. *Regarding the second question*, we initially recognize that this Court is not authorized to determine what allegations are necessary for a pleading to be adequate in a federal diversity action. "'Although state law governs the burden of proving fraud at trial, the procedure for pleading fraud in federal courts in all diversity suits is governed by the special pleading requirements of Federal Rule of Civil Procedure 9(b).'" . . . . Thus, we will address only the burden placed on a plaintiff at trial to prove proximate cause with respect to a tort claim based on misrepresentations or omissions concerning publicly traded securities.

Appellants contend that Georgia law has incorporated neither the loss causation standard from securities law nor the negligence concept of proximate causation into the intentional tort of fraud. For several decades, however, we have held that, in order to recover in tort for fraud, the plaintiff must prove that he sustained loss or damage as the proximate result of the alleged misrepresentations.

Once again, precedent of the Supreme Court of the United States is informative. *Blue Chips Stamps* involved an aspect of federal securities law which differed from the common law. However, the Supreme Court recently adopted common law causation requirements:

> Judicially implied private securities fraud actions resemble in many (but not all) respects common-law deceit and misrepresentation actions. . . . And the common law has long insisted that a plaintiff in such a case show not only that had he known the truth he would not have acted but also that he suffered actual economic loss. . . . Indeed, the Restatement [Second] of Torts, in setting forth the judicial consensus, says that a person who "misrepresents the financial condition of a corporation in order to sell its stock" becomes liable to a relying purchaser "for the loss" the purchaser sustains "when the facts . . . become generally known" and "as a result" share value "depreciate(s)." § 548A, Comment b, at 107. Treatise writers, too, have emphasized the need to prove proximate causation.

Dura Pharmaceuticals v. Broudo, 544 U.S. 336, 343–344 (2005). We find "nothing in the *Dura* court's analysis of the common law loss causation requirements that justifies a different standard for plaintiffs' common law fraud claim under [Georgia] law." . . . "The reasoning of *Dura* . . . is equally applicable to any securities claim, be it statutory or based in the common law, because any such claim for damages requires a showing of proximate cause." . . .

In answer to the second question, we conclude that, with respect to a tort claim based on misrepresentations or omissions concerning publicly traded securities, a plaintiff at trial has the burden of proving that the truth concealed by the defendant entered the marketplace, thereby precipitating a drop in the price of the security.

Having reviewed the already-extensive precedent regarding the parameters of the loss causation standard in *Dura*, we note that while some courts have held that

> the truth could be revealed by the actual materialization of the concealed risk rather than by a public disclosure that the risk exists, any theory of loss causation would still have to identify when the materialization occurred and link it to a corresponding loss.

. . . .

Even if the truth has made its way into the marketplace, *Dura* requires that a plaintiff show that it was this revelation that caused the loss and not one of the 'tangle of factors' that affect price.

. . . .

Chapter 10

Secondary Liability

§ 10.01 Introduction

This chapter focuses on secondary liability under the federal securities laws. Three different theories of liability are highlighted: aiding and abetting, controlling person, and respondeat superior. Importantly, these theories also are applicable under many state securities statutes. This Chapter also focuses on distinguishing primary from secondary conduct.

Problem

Fellow, who is employed as a broker for SZK Securities, Inc., a registered broker-dealer, informs 20 of his customers that he has confidential information that Maxzoid, Inc., a publicly traded company, has been awarded a multi-year mega-dollar contract by the Brazilian government. The news will be made public by Maxzoid the following week. Based on this information, the customers purchase Maxzoid common stock. In fact, Fellow and his cohorts are engaged in a manipulative scheme in connection with Maxzoid stock, and they have no reason to believe in the existence of any such contract.

Fellow is supervised by another broker, Taylor. Over the past six months, Taylor has received complaints from 15 different customers that Fellow is "too aggressive," is "pushy," and has executed trades without the customers' authorization. Taylor informs Fellow of the complaints and tells him to "cool it." He, however, undertakes no further supervision.

SZK Securities has a supervisory monitoring system in place with respect to its representatives. Under this monitoring system, Fellow is not only supervised by Taylor but also must fill out reports on a periodic basis disclosing, among other things, the stock he personally holds and a list of the securities that he is recommending to his customers. In completing the most recent reports, Fellow fails to reveal that he holds a substantial interest in Maxzoid common stock which he purchased at other brokerage firms located in different cities.

After the manipulative scheme is uncovered, Maxzoid common stock drastically declines. The investors bring suit in federal court seeking damages against Fellow, Taylor, and SKZ Securities. (Assume that no pre-dispute arbitration agreement has been executed between any of the plaintiffs and SZK Securities.) The SEC also institutes an enforcement action against these same parties. Discuss the liability of each defendant.

§ 10.02 Aiding and Abetting Liability

Prior to the Supreme Court's decision in *Central Bank of Denver*, 511 U.S. 164 (1994), virtually every lower federal court considering the issue recognized the propriety of aiding and abetting liability under § 10(b) of the Exchange Act, as well as certain other provisions.[1] However, in *Central Bank of Denver*, the Supreme Court held that § 10(b) of the Exchange Act does not provide for the imposition of aiding and abetting liability in private litigation.

Nonetheless, aider and abettor liability principles remain relevant in the securities law context for a number of reasons. For example, the SEC may pursue aiders and abettors for violations of the federal securities laws, with the requisite mental state for the imposition of liability being knowing or reckless misconduct. Moreover, although the Commission's cease and desist power against those who are a "cause" of an alleged violation evidently is more expansive than aider and abettor liability principles, the Commission still may draw on some of these principles to ascertain the parameters of the liability net. And, as a last example, a number of state securities statutes provide for aiding and abetting liability.

Generally, the three elements necessary for aiding and abetting are: (1) a primary securities law violation by another; (2) substantial assistance by the alleged aider and abettor in the commission of the primary violation; (3) and requisite knowledge (namely, knowing or reckless misconduct) on such alleged aider and abettor's part that his/her conduct was improper. In the Dodd-Frank Act of 2010, Congress resolved the requisite mental culpability for imposing liability against aiders and abettors in SEC enforcement actions: namely, proof of knowing or reckless misconduct.

However, as the Supreme Court's *Central Bank of Denver* decision holds, private parties may not invoke aider and abettor liability under § 10(b). The decision's rationale also signifies that aiding and abetting liability may not be implied in private actions under other provisions of the federal securities laws.

Central Bank of Denver v. First Interstate Bank of Denver

United States Supreme Court

511 U.S. 164, 114 S. Ct. 1439, 128 L. Ed. 2d 119 (1994)

JUSTICE KENNEDY delivered the opinion of the Court.

---

1. *See, e.g., IIT v. Cornfeld*, 619 F.2d 909 (2d Cir. 1980); Olson, *The End of the Section 10(b) Aiding and Abetting Liability Fiction*, 8 INSIGHTS No. 6, at 3 (1994) ("The Court's decision overruled decisions from 11 federal courts of appeals which had recognized Section 10(b) aiding and abetting liability.").

As we have interpreted it, § 10(b) of the Securities Exchange Act of 1934 imposes private civil liability on those who commit a manipulative or deceptive act in connection with the purchase or sale of securities. In this case, we must answer a question reserved in two earlier decisions: whether private civil liability under § 10(b) extends as well to those who do not engage in the manipulative or deceptive practice but who aid and abet the violation. . . .

In 1986 and 1988, the Colorado Springs-Stetson Hills Public Building Authority (Authority) issued a total of $26 million in bonds to finance public improvements at Stetson Hills, a planned residential and commercial development in Colorado Springs. Petitioner Central Bank served as indenture trustee for the bond issues.

The bonds were secured by landowner assessment liens, which covered about 250 acres for the 1986 bond issue and about 272 acres for the 1988 bond issue. The bond covenants required that the land subject to the liens be worth at least 160% of the bonds' outstanding principal and interest. The covenants required AmWest Development, the developer of Stetson Hills, to give Central Bank an annual report containing evidence that the 160% test was met.

In January 1988, AmWest provided Central Bank an updated appraisal of the land securing the 1986 bonds and of the land proposed to secure the 1988 bonds. The 1988 appraisal showed land values almost unchanged from the 1986 appraisal. Soon afterwards, Central Bank received a letter from the senior underwriter for the 1986 bonds. Noting that property values were declining in Colorado Springs and that Central Bank was operating on an appraisal over 16 months old, the underwriter expressed concern that the 160% test was not being met.

Central Bank asked its in-house appraiser to review the updated 1988 appraisal. The in-house appraiser decided that the values listed in the appraisal appeared optimistic considering the local real estate market. He suggested that Central Bank retain an outside appraiser to conduct an independent review of the 1988 appraisal. After an exchange of letters between Central Bank and AmWest in early 1988, Central Bank agreed to delay independent review of the appraisal until the end of the year, six months after the June 1988 closing on the bond issue. Before the independent review was complete, however, the Authority defaulted on the 1988 bonds.

Respondents First Interstate and Jack Naber had purchased $2.1 million of the 1988 bonds. After the default, respondents sued the Authority, the 1988 underwriter, a junior underwriter, an AmWest director, and Central Bank for violations of § 10(b) of the Securities Exchange Act of 1934. The complaint alleged that the Authority, the underwriter defendants, and the AmWest director had violated § 10(b). The complaint also alleged that Central Bank was "secondarily liable under § 10(b) for its conduct in aiding and abetting the fraud."

The United States District Court for the District of Colorado granted summary judgment to Central Bank. The United States Court of Appeals for the Tenth Circuit reversed. *First Interstate Bank of Denver, N.A. v. Pring,* 969 F.2d 891 (1992).

The Court of Appeals first set forth the elements of the § 10(b) aiding and abetting cause of action in the Tenth Circuit: (1) a primary violation of § 10(b); (2) recklessness by the aider and abettor as to the existence of the primary violation; and (3) substantial assistance given to the primary violator by the aider and abettor.

Applying that standard, the Court of Appeals found that Central Bank was aware of concerns about the accuracy of the 1988 appraisal. Central Bank knew both that the sale of the 1988 bonds was imminent and that purchasers were using the 1988 appraisal to evaluate the collateral for the bonds. Under those circumstances, the court said, Central Bank's awareness of the alleged inadequacies of the updated, but almost unchanged, 1988 appraisal could support a finding of extreme departure from standards of ordinary care. The court thus found that respondents had established a genuine issue of material fact regarding the recklessness element of aiding and abetting liability. [Note that this standard of "recklessness" prevails today in SEC enforcement actions pursuant to the Dodd-Frank Act of 2010.] On the separate question whether Central Bank rendered substantial assistance to the primary violators, the Court of Appeals found that a reasonable trier of fact could conclude that Central Bank had rendered substantial assistance by delaying the independent review of the appraisal.

Like the Court of Appeals in this case, other federal courts have allowed private aiding and abetting actions under § 10(b). The first and leading case to impose the liability was *Brennan v. Midwestern Life Ins. Co.*, 259 F. Supp. 673 (ND Ind. 1966), aff'd, 417 F.2d 147 (CA7 1969), cert. denied, 397 U.S. 989 (1970). The court reasoned that "[i]n the absence of a clear legislative expression to the contrary, the statute must be flexibly applied so as to implement its policies and purposes." Since 1966, numerous courts have taken the same position. . . .

After our decisions in *Santa Fe Industries, Inc. v. Green*, 430 U.S. 462 (1977), and *Ernst & Ernst v. Hochfelder*, 425 U.S. 185 (1976), where we paid close attention to the statutory text in defining the scope of conduct prohibited by § 10(b), courts and commentators began to question whether aiding and abetting liability under § 10(b) was still available. Professor Fischel opined that the "theory of secondary liability [under § 10(b) was] no longer viable in light of recent Supreme Court decisions strictly interpreting the federal securities laws." Fischel, Secondary Liability under Section 10(b) of the Securities Act of 1934, 69 Calif. L. Rev. 80, 82 (1981). In 1981, the District Court for the Eastern District of Michigan found it "doubtful that a claim for 'aiding and abetting' . . . will continue to exist under § 10(b)." *Benoay v. Decker*, 517 F. Supp. 490, 495, aff'd, 735 F.2d 1363 (CA6 1984). The same year, the Ninth Circuit stated that the "status of aiding and abetting as a basis for liability under the securities laws [wa]s in some doubt." *Little v. Valley National Bank of Arizona*, 650 F.2d 218, 220, n.3. The Ninth Circuit later noted that "[a]iding and abetting and other 'add-on' theories of liability have been justified by reference to the broad policy objectives of the securities acts. The Supreme Court has rejected this justification for an expansive reading of the statutes and instead prescribed a strict statutory construction approach to determining liability under the acts." *SEC v. Seaboard Corp.*, 677 F.2d

1301, 1311, n.12 (1982). The Fifth Circuit has stated: "[I]t is now apparent that open-ended readings of the duty stated by Rule 10b-5 threaten to rearrange the congressional scheme. The added layer of liability . . . for aiding and abetting . . . is particularly problematic. . . . There is a powerful argument that . . . aider and abettor liability should not be enforceable by private parties pursuing an implied right of action." *Akin v. Q-L Investments, Inc.,* 959 F.2d 521, 525 (1992). Indeed, the Seventh Circuit has held that the defendant must have committed a manipulative or deceptive act to be liable under § 10(b), a requirement that in effect forecloses liability on those who do no more than aid or abet a 10b-5 violation. See, e.g., *Barker v. Henderson, Franklin, Starnes & Holt,* 797 F.2d 490, 495 (1986).

We granted certiorari to resolve the continuing confusion over the existence and scope of the § 10(b) aiding and abetting action.

In the wake of the 1929 stock market crash and in response to widespread abuses in the securities industry, the 73d Congress enacted two landmark pieces of securities legislation: the Securities Act of 1933 (1933 Act) and the Securities Exchange Act of 1934 (1934 Act). . . . The 1933 Act regulates initial distributions of securities, and the 1934 Act for the most part regulates post-distribution trading. Together, the Acts "embrace a fundamental purpose . . . to substitute a philosophy of full disclosure for the philosophy of caveat emptor." . . .

The 1933 and 1934 Acts create an extensive scheme of civil liability. The Securities and Exchange Commission (SEC) may bring administrative actions and injunctive proceedings to enforce a variety of statutory prohibitions. Private plaintiffs may sue under the express private rights of action contained in the Acts. They may also sue under private rights of action we have found to be implied by the terms of § 10(b) and § 14(a) of the 1934 Act. This case concerns the most familiar private cause of action: the one we have found to be implied by § 10(b), the general antifraud provision of the 1934 Act. . . .

In our cases addressing § 10(b) and Rule 10b-5, we have confronted two main issues. First, we have determined the scope of conduct prohibited by § 10(b). . . . Second, in cases where the defendant has committed a violation of § 10(b), we have decided questions about the elements of the 10b-5 private liability scheme: for example, whether there is a right to contribution, what the statute of limitations is, whether there is a reliance requirement, and whether there is an in pari delicto defense. . . .

The latter issue, determining the elements of the 10b-5 private liability scheme, has posed difficulty because Congress did not create a private § 10(b) cause of action and had no occasion to provide guidance about the elements of a private liability scheme. We thus have had "to infer how the 1934 Congress would have addressed the issue[s] had the 10b-5 action been included as an express provision in the 1934 Act." . . .

With respect, however, to the first issue, the scope of conduct prohibited by § 10(b), the text of the statute controls our decision. In § 10(b), Congress prohibited manipulative or deceptive acts in connection with the purchase or sale of securities. It envisioned that the SEC would enforce the statutory prohibition through administrative and injunctive actions. Of course, a private plaintiff now may bring suit against violators of § 10(b). But the private plaintiff may not bring a 10b-5 suit against the defendant for acts not prohibited by the text of § 10(b). To the contrary, our cases considering the scope of conduct prohibited by § 10(b) in private suits have emphasized adherence to the statutory language, "'[t]he starting point in every case involving construction of a statute.'" . . . We have refused to allow 10b-5 challenges to conduct not prohibited by the text of the statute.

In Ernst & Ernst, we considered whether negligent acts could violate § 10(b). We first noted that "the words 'manipulative' or 'deceptive' used in conjunction with 'device or contrivance' strongly suggest that § 10(b) was intended to proscribe knowing or intentional misconduct." . . . The SEC argued that the broad congressional purposes behind the Act—to protect investors from false and misleading practices that might injure them—suggested that § 10(b) should also reach negligent conduct. We rejected that argument, concluding that the SEC's interpretation would "add a gloss to the operative language of the statute quite different from its commonly accepted meaning." . . .

In Santa Fe Industries, another case involving "the reach and coverage of § 10(b)," we considered whether § 10(b) "reached breaches of fiduciary duty by a majority against minority shareholders without any charge of misrepresentation or lack of disclosure." . . . We held that it did not, reaffirming our decision in Ernst & Ernst and emphasizing that the "language of § 10(b) gives no indication that Congress meant to prohibit any conduct not involving manipulation or deception." . . .

Later, in Chiarella, we considered whether § 10(b) is violated when a person trades securities without disclosing inside information. We held that § 10(b) is not violated under those circumstances unless the trader has an independent duty of disclosure. In reaching our conclusion, we noted that "not every instance of financial unfairness constitutes fraudulent activity under § 10(b)." We stated that "the 1934 Act cannot be read more broadly than its language and the statutory scheme reasonably permit" . . . .

Our consideration of statutory duties, especially in cases interpreting § 10(b), establishes that the statutory text controls the definition of conduct covered by § 10(b). That bodes ill for respondents, for "the language of Section 10(b) does not in terms mention aiding and abetting." . . . To overcome this problem, respondents and the SEC [as amicus curiae] suggest (or hint at) the novel argument that the use of the phrase "directly or indirectly" in the text of § 10(b) covers aiding and abetting. . . .

The federal courts have not relied on the "directly or indirectly" language when imposing aiding and abetting liability under § 10(b), and with good reason. There is a basic flaw with this interpretation. According to respondents and the SEC, the "directly or indirectly" language shows that "Congress . . . intended to reach all persons who engage, even if only indirectly, in proscribed activities connected with securities transactions." . . . The problem, of course, is that aiding and abetting lia-bility extends beyond persons who engage, even indirectly, in a proscribed activity; aiding and abetting liability reaches persons who do not engage in the proscribed activities at all, but who give a degree of aid to those who do. A further problem with respondents' interpretation of the "directly or indirectly" language is posed by the numerous provisions of the 1934 Act that use the term in a way that does not impose aiding and abetting liability. . . . In short, respondents' interpretation of the "directly or indirectly" language fails to support their suggestion that the text of § 10(b) itself prohibits aiding and abetting. . . .

Congress knew how to impose aiding and abetting liability when it chose to do so. See, e.g., . . . 18 U.S.C. § 2 (general criminal aiding and abetting statute). . . . If, as respondents seem to say, Congress intended to impose aiding and abetting lia-bility, we presume it would have used the words "aid" and "abet" in the statutory text. But it did not. . . .

We reach the uncontroversial conclusion, accepted even by those courts recogniz-ing a § 10(b) aiding and abetting cause of action, that the text of the 1934 Act does not itself reach those who aid and abet a § 10(b) violation. Unlike those courts, how-ever, we think that conclusion resolves the case. It is inconsistent with settled meth-odology in § 10(b) cases to extend liability beyond the scope of conduct prohibited by the statutory text. To be sure, aiding and abetting a wrongdoer ought to be action-able in certain instances. Cf. Restatement (Second) of Torts § 876(b) (1977). The issue, however, is not whether imposing private civil liability on aiders and abettors is good policy but whether aiding and abetting is covered by the statute.

As in earlier cases considering conduct prohibited by § 10(b), we again conclude that the statute prohibits only the making of a material misstatement (or omission) or the commission of a manipulative act. . . . The proscription does not include giving aid to a person who commits a manipulative or deceptive act. We cannot amend the statute to create liability for acts that are not themselves manipulative or deceptive within the meaning of the statute.

Because this case concerns the conduct prohibited by § 10(b), the statute itself resolves the case, but even if it did not, we would reach the same result. When the text of § 10(b) does not resolve a particular issue, we attempt to infer "how the 1934 Congress would have addressed the issue had the 10b-5 action been included as an express provision in the 1934 Act." . . . For that inquiry, we use the express causes of action in the Securities Acts as the primary model for the § 10(b) action. The reason is evident: Had the 73d Congress enacted a private § 10(b) right of action, it likely would have designed it in a manner similar to the other private rights of action in the Securities Acts.

In Musick, Peeler, for example, we recognized a right to contribution under § 10(b). We held that the express rights of contribution contained in §§ 9 and 18 of the Acts were "important . . . feature[s] of the federal securities laws and that consistency require[d] us to adopt a like contribution rule for the right of action existing under

Rule 10b-5."... And in Blue Chip Stamps, we held that a 10b-5 plaintiff must have purchased or sold the security to recover damages for the defendant's misrepresentation. We said that "[t]he principal express private nonderivative civil remedies, created by Congress contemporaneously with the passage of § 10(b)... are by their terms expressly limited to purchasers or sellers of securities."...

Following that analysis here, we look to the express private causes of action in the 1933 and 1934 Acts. In the 1933 Act, § 11 prohibits false statements or omissions of material fact in registration statements; it identifies the various categories of defendants subject to liability for a violation, but that list does not include aiders and abettors. Section 12 prohibits the sale of unregistered, nonexempt securities as well as the sale of securities [in a public offering] by means of a [prospectus containing a] material misstatement or omission [or a materially misleading oral communication relating to such prospectus]; and [§ 12] limits liability to those who offer or sell the security. In the 1934 Act, § 9 prohibits any person from engaging in manipulative practices such as wash sales, matched orders, and the like. Section 16 prohibits short-swing trading by owners, directors, and officers. Section 18 prohibits any person from making misleading statements in reports filed with the SEC. And § 20A, added in 1988, prohibits any person from engaging in insider trading.

This survey of the express causes of action in the Securities Acts reveals that each (like § 10(b)) specifies the conduct for which defendants may be held liable. Some of the express causes of action specify categories of defendants who may be liable; others (like § 10(b)) state only that "any person" who commits one of the prohibited acts may be held liable. The important point for present purposes, however, is that none of the express causes of action in the 1934 Act further imposes liability on one who aids or abets a violation. Cf. 7 U.S.C. § 25(a)(1) (Commodity Exchange Act's private civil aiding and abetting provision).

From the fact that Congress did not attach private aiding and abetting liability to any of the express causes of action in the Securities Acts, we can infer that Congress likely would not have attached aiding and abetting liability to § 10(b) had it provided a private § 10(b) cause of action.... There is no reason to think that Congress would have attached aiding and abetting liability only to § 10(b) and not to any of the express private rights of action in the Act. In Blue Chip Stamps, we noted that it would be "anomalous to impute to Congress an intention to expand the plaintiff class for a judicially implied cause of action beyond the bounds it delineated for comparable express causes of action."... Here, it would be just as anomalous to impute to Congress an intention in effect to expand the defendant class for 10b-5 actions beyond the bounds delineated for comparable express causes of action.

Our reasoning is confirmed by the fact that respondents' argument would impose 10b-5 aiding and abetting liability when at least one element critical for recovery under 10b-5 is absent: reliance. A plaintiff must show reliance on the defendant's misstatement or omission to recover under 10b-5. Were we to allow the aiding and abetting action proposed in this case, the defendant could be liable without any showing that the plaintiff relied upon the aider and abettor's statements or actions. . . . Allowing plaintiffs to circumvent the reliance requirement would disregard the careful limits on 10b-5 recovery mandated by our earlier cases. [How does the Court's approval of the fraud on the market theory for presumption of reliance purposes in *Basic* impact this assertion? See § 8.05[E]].

Respondents make further arguments for imposition of § 10(b) aiding and abetting liability, none of which leads us to a different answer.

The text does not support their point, but respondents and some amici invoke a broad-based notion of congressional intent. They say that Congress legislated with an understanding of general principles of tort law and that aiding and abetting liability was "well established in both civil and criminal actions by 1934." . . . Thus, "Congress intended to include" aiding and abetting liability in the 1934 Act. A brief history of aiding and abetting liability serves to dispose of this argument.

Aiding and abetting is an ancient criminal law doctrine. . . . Though there is no federal common law of crimes, Congress in 1909 enacted what is now 18 U.S.C. § 2, a general aiding and abetting statute applicable to all federal criminal offenses. The statute decrees that those who provide knowing aid to persons committing federal crimes, with the intent to facilitate the crime, are themselves committing a crime. . . .

The Restatement of Torts, under a concert of action principle, accepts a doctrine with rough similarity to criminal aiding and abetting. An actor is liable for harm resulting to a third person from the tortious conduct of another "if he . . . knows that the other's conduct constitutes a breach of duty and gives substantial assistance or encouragement to the other. . . ." Restatement (Second) of Torts § 876(b) (1977); see also W. Keeton, D. Dobbs, R. Keeton, & D. Owen, Prosser and Keeton on Law of Torts 322–324 (5th ed. 1984). The doctrine has been at best uncertain in application, however. As the Court of Appeals for the District of Columbia Circuit noted in a comprehensive opinion on the subject, the leading cases applying this doctrine are statutory securities cases, with the common-law precedents "largely confined to isolated acts of adolescents in rural society." *Halberstam v. Welch*, 705 F.2d 472, 489 (1983). Indeed, in some States, it is still unclear whether there is aiding and abetting tort liability of the kind set forth in § 876(b) of the Restatement. . . .

More to the point, Congress has not enacted a general civil aiding and abetting statute—either for suits by the Government (when the Government sues for civil penalties or injunctive relief) or for suits by private parties. Thus, when Congress enacts a statute under which a person may sue and recover damages from a private defendant for the defendant's violation of some statutory norm, there is no general presumption that the plaintiff may also sue aiders and abettors. . . .

Congress instead has taken a statute-by-statute approach to civil aiding and abetting liability. For example, the Internal Revenue Code contains a full section governing aiding and abetting liability, complete with description of scienter and the penalties attached. . . . The Commodity Exchange Act contains an explicit aiding and abetting provision that applies to private suits brought under that Act. . . .

[Subsequently, Congress enacted provisions authorizing the SEC to bring enforcement actions against aiders and abettors.]

With this background in mind, we think respondents' argument based on implicit congressional intent can be taken in one of three ways. First, respondents might be saying that aiding and abetting should attach to all federal civil statutes, even laws that do not contain an explicit aiding and abetting provision. But neither respondents nor their amici cite, and we have not found, any precedent for that vast expansion of federal law. It does not appear Congress was operating on that assumption in 1934, or since then, given that it has been quite explicit in imposing civil aiding and abetting liability in other instances. We decline to recognize such a comprehensive rule with no expression of congressional direction to do so.

Second, on a more narrow ground, respondents' congressional intent argument might be interpreted to suggest that the 73d Congress intended to include aiding and abetting only in § 10(b). But nothing in the text or history of § 10(b) even implies that aiding and abetting was covered by the statutory prohibition on manipulative and deceptive conduct.

Third, respondents' congressional intent argument might be construed as a contention that the 73d Congress intended to impose aiding and abetting liability for all of the express causes of action contained in the 1934 Act and thus would have imposed aiding and abetting liability in § 10(b) actions had it enacted a private § 10(b) right of action. As we have explained, however, none of the express private causes of action in the Act imposes aiding and abetting liability, and there is no evidence that Congress intended that liability for the express causes of action.

Even assuming, moreover, a deeply rooted background of aiding and abetting tort liability, it does not follow that Congress intended to apply that kind of liability to the private causes of action in the Securities Acts. . . . In addition, Congress did not overlook secondary liability when it created the private rights of action in the 1934 Act. Section 20 of the 1934 Act imposes liability on "controlling persons" — persons who "contro[l] any person liable under any provision of this chapter or of any rule or regulation thereunder." . . . This suggests that "[w]hen Congress wished to create such [secondary] liability, it had little trouble doing so." . . . Aiding and abetting is "a method by which courts create secondary liability" in persons other than the violator of the statute. The fact that Congress chose to impose some forms of secondary liability, but not others, indicates a deliberate congressional choice with which the courts should not interfere.

We note that the 1929 Uniform Sale of Securities Act contained a private aiding and abetting cause of action. And at the time Congress passed the 1934 Act, the blue sky laws of 11 States and the Territory of Hawaii provided a private right of action against those who aided a fraudulent or illegal sale of securities. See Abrams, The Scope of Liability Under Section 12 of the Securities Act of 1933: "Participation" and the Pertinent Legislative Materials, 15 Ford. Urb. L.J. 877, 945, and n. 423 (1987) (listing provisions). Congress enacted the 1933 and 1934 Acts against this backdrop, but did not provide for aiding and abetting liability in any of the private causes of action it authorized.

In sum, it is not plausible to interpret the statutory silence as tantamount to an implicit congressional intent to impose § 10(b) aiding and abetting liability.

When Congress reenacts statutory language that has been given a consistent judicial construction, we often adhere to that construction in interpreting the reenacted statutory language. . . . Congress has not reenacted the language of § 10(b) since 1934, however, so we need not determine whether the other conditions for applying the reenactment doctrine are present.

Nonetheless, the parties advance competing arguments based on other post-1934 legislative developments to support their differing interpretations of § 10(b). Respondents note that 1983 and 1988 committee reports, which make oblique references to aiding and abetting liability, show that those Congresses interpreted § 10(b) to cover aiding and abetting. H.R. Rep. No. 100-910, pp. 27–28 (1988); H.R. Rep. No. 355, p. 10 (1983). But "[w]e have observed on more than one occasion that the interpretation given by one Congress (or a committee or Member thereof) to an earlier statute is of little assistance in discerning the meaning of that statute." . . .

Respondents observe that Congress has amended the securities laws on various occasions since 1966, when courts first began to interpret § 10(b) to cover aiding and abetting, but has done so without providing that aiding and abetting liability is not available under § 10(b). From that, respondents infer that these Congresses, by silence, have acquiesced in the judicial interpretation of § 10(b). We disagree. This Court has reserved the issue of 10b-5 aiding and abetting liability on two previous occasions. *Herman & MacLean v. Huddleston*, 459 U.S., at 379, n. 5; Ernst & Ernst, 425 U.S., at 191–192, n. 7. Furthermore, our observations on the acquiescence doctrine indicate its limitations as an expression of congressional intent. "It does not follow . . . that Congress' failure to overturn a statutory precedent is reason for this Court to adhere to it. It is 'impossible to assert with any degree of assurance that congressional failure to act represents affirmative congressional approval of the [courts'] statutory interpretation. . . . Congress may legislate, moreover, only through passage of a bill which is approved by both Houses and signed by the President. . . . Congressional inaction cannot amend a duly enacted statute." . . .

Central Bank, for its part, points out that in 1957, 1959, and 1960, bills were introduced that would have amended the securities laws to make it "unlawful . . . to aid, abet, counsel, command, induce, or procure the violation of any provision" of the 1934 Act. . . . These bills prompted "industry fears that private litigants, not only the SEC, may find in this section a vehicle by which to sue aiders and abettors," and the bills were not passed. . . . According to Central Bank, these proposals reveal that those Congresses interpreted § 10(b) not to cover aiding and abetting. We have stated, however, that failed legislative proposals are "a particularly dangerous ground on which to rest an interpretation of a prior statute." . . . "Congressional inaction lacks persuasive significance because several equally tenable inferences may be drawn from such inaction, including the inference that the existing legislation already incorporated the offered change." . . .

It is true that our cases have not been consistent in rejecting arguments such as these. . . . As a general matter, however, we have stated that these arguments deserve little weight in the interpretive process. Even were that not the case, the competing arguments here would not point to a definitive answer. We therefore reject them. As we stated last Term, Congress has acknowledged the 10b-5 action without any further attempt to define it. We find our role limited when the issue is the scope of conduct prohibited by the statute. That issue is our concern here, and we adhere to the statutory text in resolving it.

The SEC points to various policy arguments in support of the 10b-5 aiding and abetting cause of action. It argues, for example, that the aiding and abetting cause of action deters secondary actors from contributing to fraudulent activities and ensures that defrauded plaintiffs are made whole.

Policy considerations cannot override our interpretation of the text and structure of the Act, except to the extent that they may help to show that adherence to the text and structure would lead to a result "so bizarre" that Congress could not have intended it. . . . That is not the case here.

Extending the 10b-5 cause of action to aiders and abettors no doubt makes the civil remedy more far-reaching, but it does not follow that the objectives of the statute are better served. Secondary liability for aiders and abettors exacts costs that may disserve the goals of fair dealing and efficiency in the securities markets.

As an initial matter, the rules for determining aiding and abetting liability are unclear, in "an area that demands certainty and predictability." That leads to the undesirable result of decisions "made on an ad hoc basis, offering little predictive value" to those who provide services to participants in the securities business. "[S]uch a shifting and highly fact-oriented disposition of the issue of who may [be liable for] a damages claim for violation of Rule 10b-5" is not a "satisfactory basis for a rule of liability imposed on the conduct of business transactions." . . . Because of the uncertainty of the governing rules, entities subject to secondary liability as aiders and abettors may find it prudent and necessary, as a business judgment, to abandon substantial defenses and to pay settlements in order to avoid the expense and risk of going to trial.

In addition, "litigation under Rule 10b-5 presents a danger of vexatiousness different in degree and in kind from that which accompanies litigation in general." . . . Litigation under 10b-5 thus requires secondary actors to expend large sums even for pretrial defense and the negotiation of settlements. See 138 Cong. Rec. S12605 (Aug. 12, 1992) (remarks of Sen. Sanford) (asserting that in 83% of 10b-5 cases major accounting firms pay $8 in legal fees for every $1 paid in claims).

This uncertainty and excessive litigation can have ripple effects. For example, newer and smaller companies may find it difficult to obtain advice from professionals.

A professional may fear that a newer or smaller company may not survive and that business failure would generate securities litigation against the professional, among others. In addition, the increased costs incurred by professionals because of the litigation and settlement costs under 10b-5 may be passed on to their client companies, and in turn incurred by the company's investors, the intended beneficiaries of the statute.

We hasten to add that competing policy arguments in favor of aiding and abetting liability can also be advanced. The point here, however, is that it is far from clear that Congress in 1934 would have decided that the statutory purposes would be furthered by the imposition of private aider and abettor liability.

At oral argument, the SEC suggested that 18 U.S.C. § 2 is "significant" and "very important" in this case. At the outset, we note that this contention is inconsistent with the SEC's argument that recklessness is a sufficient scienter for aiding and abetting liability. Criminal aiding and abetting liability under § 2 requires proof that the defendant "in some sort associate[d] himself with the venture, that he participate[d] in it as in something that he wishe[d] to bring about, that he [sought] by his action to make it succeed." . . . But recklessness, not intentional wrongdoing, is the theory underlying the aiding and abetting allegations in the case before us. [Note that knowing or reckless misconduct is the applicable standard today as enacted pursuant to the Dodd-Frank Act of 2010.]

Furthermore, while it is true that an aider and abettor of a criminal violation of any provision of the 1934 Act, including § 10(b), violates 18 U.S.C. § 2, it does not follow that a private civil aiding and abetting cause of action must also exist. We have been quite reluctant to infer a private right of action from a criminal prohibition alone; in *Cort v. Ash*, 422 U.S. 66, 80 (1975), for example, we refused to infer a private right of action from "a bare criminal statute." And we have not suggested that a private right of action exists for all injuries caused by violations of criminal prohibitions. . . . If we were to rely on this reasoning now, we would be obliged to hold that a private right of action exists for every provision of the 1934 Act, for it is a criminal violation to violate any of its provisions. And thus, given 18 U.S.C. § 2, we would also have to hold that a civil aiding and abetting cause of action is available for every provision of the Act. There would be no logical stopping point to this line of reasoning: Every criminal statute passed for the benefit of some particular class of persons would carry with it a concomitant civil damages cause of action.

This approach, with its far-reaching consequences, would work a significant shift in settled interpretive principles regarding implied causes of action. We are unwilling to reverse course in this case. We decline to rely only on 18 U.S.C. § 2 as the basis for recognizing a private aiding and abetting right of action under § 10(b).

Because the text of § 10(b) does not prohibit aiding and abetting, we hold that a private plaintiff may not maintain an aiding and abetting suit under § 10(b). The absence of § 10(b) aiding and abetting liability does not mean that secondary actors in the securities markets are always free from liability under the Securities Acts. Any person or entity, including a lawyer, accountant, or bank, who employs a manipulative device or makes a material misstatement (or omission) on which a purchaser or seller of securities relies may be liable as a primary violator under 10b-5, assuming all of the requirements for primary liability under Rule 10b-5 are met. In any complex securities fraud, moreover, there are likely to be multiple violators; in this case, for example, respondents named four defendants as primary violators.

Respondents concede that Central Bank did not commit a manipulative or deceptive act within the meaning of § 10(b). Instead, in the words of the complaint, Central Bank was "secondarily liable under § 10(b) for its conduct in aiding and abetting the fraud." Because of our conclusion that there is no private aiding and abetting liability under § 10(b), Central Bank may not be held liable as an aider and abettor. The District Court's grant of summary judgment to Central Bank was proper, and the judgment of the Court of Appeals is

Reversed.

JUSTICE STEVENS, with whom JUSTICE BLACKMUN, JUSTICE SOUTER, and JUSTICE GINSBURG join, dissenting.

The main themes of the Court's opinion are that the text of § 10(b) of the Securities Exchange Act of 1934 does not expressly mention aiding and abetting liability, and that Congress knows how to legislate. Both propositions are unexceptionable, but neither is reason to eliminate the private right of action against aiders and abettors of violations of § 10(b) and the Securities and Exchange Commission's Rule 10b-5. Because the majority gives short shrift to a long history of aider and abettor liability under § 10(b) and Rule 10b-5, and because its rationale imperils other well established forms of secondary liability not expressly addressed in the securities laws, I respectfully dissent.

In hundreds of judicial and administrative proceedings in every circuit in the federal system, the courts and the SEC have concluded that aiders and abettors are subject to liability under § 10(b) and Rule 10b-5. . . . While we have reserved decision on the legitimacy of the theory in two cases that did not present it, all 11 Courts of Appeals to have considered the question have recognized a private cause of action against aiders and abettors under § 10(b) and Rule 10b-5. The early aiding and abetting decisions relied upon principles borrowed from tort law; in those cases, judges closer to the times and climate of the 73d Congress than we concluded that holding aiders and abettors liable was consonant with the 1934 Act's purpose to strengthen the antifraud remedies of the common law. One described the aiding and abetting theory, grounded in "general principles of tort law," as a "logical and natural complement" to the private § 10(b) action that furthered the Exchange Act's purpose of "creation and maintenance of a post-issuance securities market that is free from fraudulent practices." . . .

The Courts of Appeals have usually applied a familiar three-part test for aider and abettor liability, patterned on the Restatement of Torts formulation, that requires (i) the existence of a primary violation of § 10(b) or Rule 10b-5, (ii) the defendant's knowledge of (or recklessness as to) that primary violation, and (iii) "substantial assistance" of the violation by the defendant. If indeed there has been "continuing confusion" concerning the private right of action against aiders and abettors, that confusion has not concerned its basic structure, still less its "existence." Indeed, in this case, petitioner assumed the existence of a right of action against aiders and abettors, and sought review only of the subsidiary questions whether an indenture trustee could be found liable as an aider and abettor absent a breach of an indenture agreement or other duty under state law, and whether it could be liable as an aider and abettor based only on a showing of recklessness. These questions, it is true, have engendered genuine disagreement in the Courts of Appeals. But instead of simply addressing the questions presented by the parties, on which the law really was unsettled, the Court sua sponte directed the parties to address a question on which even the petitioner justifiably thought the law was settled, and reaches out to overturn a most considerable body of precedent.

. . . .

Even had § 10(b) not been enacted against a backdrop of liberal construction of remedial statutes and judicial favor toward implied rights of action, I would still disagree with the majority for the simple reason that a "settled construction of an important federal statute should not be disturbed unless and until Congress so decides." . . . A policy of respect for consistent judicial and administrative interpretations leaves it to elected representatives to assess settled law and to evaluate the merits and demerits of changing it. Even when there is no affirmative evidence of ratification, the Legislature's failure to reject a consistent judicial or administrative construction counsels hesitation from a court asked to invalidate it. . . . Here, however, the available evidence suggests congressional approval of aider and abettor liability in private § 10(b) actions. In its comprehensive revision of the Exchange Act in 1975, Congress left untouched the sizeable body of case law approving aiding and abetting liability in private actions under § 10(b) and Rule 10b-5. The case for leaving aiding and abetting liability intact draws further strength from the fact that the SEC itself has consistently understood § 10(b) to impose aider and abettor liability since shortly after the rule's promulgation. . . . In short, one need not disagree as an original matter with the many decisions recognizing the private right against aiders and abettors to concede that the right fits comfortably within the statutory scheme, and that it has become a part of the established system of private enforcement. We should leave it to Congress to alter that scheme.

. . . .

As framed by the Court's order redrafting the questions presented, this case concerns only the existence and scope of aiding and abetting liability in suits brought by private parties under § 10(b) and Rule 10b-5. The majority's rationale, however, sweeps far beyond even those important issues. The majority leaves little doubt that the Exchange Act does not even permit the Commission to pursue aiders and abettors in civil enforcement actions under § 10(b) and Rule 10b-5. . . . Aiding and abetting liability has a long pedigree in civil proceedings brought by the SEC under § 10(b) and Rule 10b-5, and has become an important part of the Commission's enforcement arsenal. [Note that in 1995 Congress' enactment of Exchange Act § 20(e) provides the SEC with express authority to pursue aiders and abettors.] Moreover, the majority's approach to aiding and abetting at the very least casts serious doubt, both for private and SEC actions, on other forms of secondary liability that, like the aiding and abetting theory, have long been recognized by the SEC and the courts but are not expressly spelled out in the securities statues.[2] The principle the Court espouses today—that liability may not be imposed on parties who are not within the scope of § 10(b)'s plain language—is inconsistent with long-established Commission and judicial precedent.

. . . .

I respectfully dissent.

Note

Does *Central Bank of Denver* signify that:

(1) Aiding and abetting liability may not be imposed under any provision of the federal securities laws unless the applicable statute expressly provides for such liability?

(2) The decision precludes application of other common law theories of liability under the federal securities laws, such as conspiracy and respondeat superior? In his dissent, Justice Stevens believes that these theories "appear unlikely to survive."

(3) To recover, litigants must now allege misconduct that constitutes primary liability?

(4) The SEC increasingly will use its administrative cease-and-desist powers against those who allegedly are a "cause" of a violation with greater frequency?

(5) Private litigants will invoke the applicable state securities statutes and common law to an increasing degree?

SEC Aiding and Abetting Authority

After *Central Bank of Denver*, many observers believed that the decision's rationale extended to SEC enforcement actions. Cf. *Aaron v. SEC*, 446 U.S. 680 (1980), following the statutory approach set forth in *Ernst & Ernst v. Hochfelder*, 425 U.S. 185 (1976).

---

[2]. The court's rationale would sweep away the decisions recognizing that a defendant may be found liable in a private action for conspiring to violate § 10(b) and Rule 10b-5. *See, e.g., U.S. Industries, Inc. v. Touche Ross & Co.*, 854 F.2d 1223, 1231 (CA 10 1988); . . . Secondary liability is as old as the implied right of action under § 10(b) itself; the very first decision to recognize a private cause of action under the section and rule, *Kardon v. National Gypsum, Co.*, 69 F. Supp. 512 (E.D. Pa. 1946), involved an alleged conspiracy. . . . In addition, many courts . . . have imposed liability in § 10(b) actions based upon respondeat superior and other common-law agency principles. . . . These court decisions likewise appear unlikely to survive the Court's decision.

Both cases are discussed in § 8.03 of the text. Significantly, the Private Securities Litigation Reform Act of 1995 (PSLRA) and the Dodd-Frank Act of 2010 authorize the SEC to pursue aiders and abettors for alleged violations of the federal securities laws.

Central Bank Applied to Other Liability Theories and Statutes

Focusing on another issue, after *Central Bank of Denver,* lower courts almost unanimously have rejected *conspiracy* liability under § 10(b). Drawing upon the majority's rationale, these courts reason that imposing liability premised on conspiracy theory, like that for aiding and abetting, is not within § 10(b)'s scope. In other words, the same analysis applies for excluding § 10(b) claims for conspiracy. *See, e.g., Securities Investor Protection Corp. v. Holmes,* 76 F.3d 388 (9th Cir. 1996).

Moreover, *Central Bank's* rationale extends to other statutes, such as § 14(a) of the Exchange Act, to similarly preclude aiding and abetting as well as conspiracy liability under those provisions.

As will be seen in § 10.05, the propriety of respondeat superior liability remains unsettled. In that Section, we will examine the applicable principles.

Conduct Constituting Primary Liability

The key issue litigated after *Central Bank* is whether the actor's alleged misconduct gives rise to primary liability under § 10(b). In *Central Bank,* the Court stated: "Any person or entity, including a lawyer, accountant or bank, who employs a manipulative device or makes a material misstatement (or omission) on which a purchaser or seller of securities relies may be liable as a primary violator under [rule] 10b-5 . . . ." The following section focuses on this subject.[3]

Before turning to this subject, the following case provides a good illustration of the SEC invoking its aiding and abetting enforcement authority.

Securities and Exchange Commission v. Apuzzo

United States Court of Appeals, Second Circuit

689 F.3d 204 (2012)

Opinion of Rakoff, District Judge [Sitting by Designation].

The Securities and Exchange Commission ("SEC") alleges that defendant Joseph Apuzzo aided and abetted securities law violations through his role in a fraudulent

---

3. For further commentary on the ramifications of *Central Bank of Denver, see, e.g.,* Branson, *Chasing the Rogue Professional After the Private Securities Litigation Reform Act of 1995,* 50 SMU L. Rev. 91 (1996); Maxey, *Competing Duties? Securities Lawyers' Liability After Central Bank,* 64 Fordham L. Rev. 2185 (1996); Redwood, *Toward a More Enlightened Securities Jurisprudence in the Supreme Court? Don't Bank on It Anytime Soon,* 32 Hous. L. Rev. 3 (1995); Seligman, *The Implications of Central Bank,* 49 Bus. Law. 1429 (1994); Steinberg, *The Ramifications of Recent U.S. Supreme Court Decisions on Federal and State Securities Regulation,* 70 Notre Dame L. Rev. 489 (1995); Warren, *The Primary Liability of Securities Lawyers,* 50 SMU L. Rev. 383 (1996).

accounting scheme. In order for a defendant to be liable as an aider and abettor in a civil enforcement action, the SEC must prove: "(1) the existence of a securities law violation by the primary (as opposed to the aiding and abetting) party; (2) 'knowledge' of this violation on the part of the aider and abettor; and (3) 'substantial assistance' by the aider and abettor in the achievement of the primary violation." . . . After Apuzzo moved to dismiss the Complaint, the district court, Thompson, J., granted Apuzzo's motion to dismiss. Although the district court found that the Complaint plausibly alleged that Apuzzo had actual knowledge of the primary violation, it concluded that the Complaint did not adequately allege "substantial assistance." Specifically, the district court held that the "substantial assistance" component required that the aider and abettor proximately cause the harm on which the primary violation was predicated, and that the Complaint did not plausibly allege such proximate causation.

For the reasons set forth below, we hold that to satisfy the "substantial assistance" component of aiding and abetting, the SEC must show that the defendant "in some sort associate[d] himself with the venture, that he participate[d] in it as in something that he wishe[d] to bring about, [and] that he [sought] by his action to make it succeed." *United States v. Peoni,* 100 F.2d 401, 402 (2d Cir. 1938). Applying that test, we hold that the Complaint plausibly alleged that Apuzzo aided and abetted the primary violation, and we therefore reverse the district court.

. . . .

Discussion

Section 20(e) of the Securities Exchange Act of 1934 allows the SEC, but not private litigants, to bring civil actions against aiders and abettors of securities fraud. The SEC may bring such an action against "any person that knowingly provides substantial assistance" to a primary violator of the securities laws. 15 U.S.C. § 78t(e).[4] Specifically, as noted above, the SEC must prove: (1) the existence of a securities law violation by the primary (as opposed to the aiding and abetting) party; (2) knowledge of this violation on the part of the aider and abettor; and (3) "substantial assistance" by the aider and abettor in the achievement of the primary violation. Apuzzo conceded below that the SEC had adequately pleaded the existence of a primary violation, and he does not contest on appeal the district court's finding that the SEC adequately pleaded his actual knowledge of the fraud. Therefore, the only disputed question on appeal is whether the facts alleged plausibly plead that Apuzzo substantially assisted the primary violator in committing the fraud.

---

[4]. The Dodd-Frank Act of 2010 amended § 20(e) to add the words "or recklessly" after "knowingly." Dodd-Frank Wall Street Reform and Consumer Protection Act, Pub. L. No. 111-203, 124 Stat. 1376, § 9290 (codified at 15 U.S.C. § 78t(e)). This amendment does not apply to this case.

In assessing this issue, we draw guidance from the well-developed law of aiding and abetting liability in criminal cases; for if the conduct of an aider and abettor is sufficient to impose criminal liability, *a fortiori* it is sufficient to impose civil liability in a government enforcement action. Nearly seventy-five years ago, Judge Learned Hand famously stated that in order for a criminal defendant to be liable as an aider and abettor, the Government — in addition to proving that the primary violation occurred and that the defendant had knowledge of it — must also prove "that he in some sort associate[d] himself with the venture, that [the defendant] participate[d] in it as in something that he wishe[d] to bring about, [and] that he [sought] by his action to make it succeed." *United States v. Peoni,* 100 F.2d 401, 402 (2d Cir. 1938). The Supreme Court later adopted Judge Hand's formulation. *Nye & Nissen v. United State,* 336 U.S. 613, 619 (1949). In fact, as the Seventh Circuit has recognized, Judge Hand's standard is "[t]he classic formula for aider and abettor liability." *United States v. Irwin,* 149 F.3d 565, 569 (7th Cir. 1998). Judge Hand's standard has thus survived the test of time, is clear, concise, and workable, and governs the determination of aider and abettor liability in securities fraud cases.

While Apuzzo argues that substantial assistance should, instead, be defined as proximate cause, his argument ignores the difference between an SEC enforcement action and a private suit for damages. "Proximate cause" is the language of private tort actions; it derives from the need of a private plaintiff, seeking compensation, to show that his injury was proximately caused by the defendants' actions. But, in an enforcement action, civil or criminal, there is no requirement that the government prove injury, because the purpose of such actions is deterrence, not compensation.

. . . .

. . . [O]ur case law has not always made this distinction with clarity. . . .

We now clarify that, in enforcement actions brought under [§ 20(e),] 15 U.S.C. § 78t(e), the SEC is not required to plead or prove that an aider and abettor proximately caused the primary securities law violation. In fact, the statute under which the SEC here proceeds, 15 U.S.C. § 78t(e), was passed in the wake of *Central Bank* precisely to allow the SEC to pursue aiders and abettors who, under the reasoning of *Central Bank,* were not themselves involved in the making of the false statements that proximately caused the plaintiffs' injuries. This statutory mandate would be undercut if proximate causation were required for aider and abettor liability in SEC enforcement actions.

Indeed, because only the SEC may bring aiding and abetting claims for securities law violations, many if not most aiders and abettors would escape all liability if such a proximate cause requirement were imposed, since, almost by definition, the activities of an aider and abettor are rarely the direct cause of the injury brought about by the fraud, however much they may contribute to the success of the scheme. We therefore welcome the opportunity to clarify that the appropriate standard for determining the substantial assistance component of aider and abettor liability in an SEC civil enforcement action is the Judge Hand standard set forth above.[5]

Applying the test we have laid out above, it is clear that the Complaint plausibly alleges that Apuzzo provided substantial assistance to the primary violator in carrying out the fraud, and therefore we must reverse the district court. Apuzzo associated himself with the venture, participated in it as something that he wished to bring about, and sought by his action to make it succeed. . . .

Apuzzo argues that his participation in the transaction alone is insufficient to demonstrate substantial assistance because, he contends, "there is simply no allegation in the Complaint that these transactions were unusual." This, however, is doubly erroneous, both because Apuzzo's substantial assistance extended beyond his agreement to participate in the transactions and because the well-pleaded allegations of the Complaint aver that these transactions were hardly ordinary transactions. . . .

Moreover, when evaluating whether Apuzzo rendered substantial assistance, we must consider his high degree of actual knowledge of the primary violation (the second component of aiding and abetting). As we have repeatedly held, the three components of the aiding and abetting test "cannot be considered in isolation from one another." . . . Where, as here, the SEC plausibly alleges a high degree of actual knowledge, this lessens the burden it must meet in alleging substantial assistance.

Apuzzo argues that while a high degree of substantial assistance lowers the SEC's burden to prove scienter, the converse is not true. A close look at our case law, however, reveals that Apuzzo is incorrect. . . . Therefore, a high degree of knowledge may lessen the SEC's burden in proving substantial assistance, just as a high degree of substantial assistance may lessen the SEC's burden in proving *scienter*.

It is particularly appropriate to consider the degree of scienter in evaluating substantial assistance in light of the test for substantial assistance that we have laid out above. When determining whether a defendant sought by his actions to make the primary violation succeed, if a jury were convinced that the defendant had a high degree of actual knowledge about the steps he was taking and the role those steps played in the primary violation, they would be well justified in concluding that the defendant's actions, which perhaps could be viewed innocently in some contexts, were taken with the goal of helping the fraud succeed.

As quoted above, the district court found that the Complaint here alleges, in detail, a very high degree of knowledge of the fraud on Apuzzo's part. Considered in light

---

[5]. This is not to suggest that evidence of proximate cause may not be relevant to identifying when an aider and abettor has provided substantial assistance to a primary violator. One who proximately causes a primary violation with actual knowledge of the primary violation will inherently meet the test we have set forth above. Therefore, the SEC *may* prove substantial assistance by demonstrating that the aider and abettor was a proximate cause of the violation. Our recognition of 'proximate cause' as a factor relevant to identifying substantial assistance, however, does not establish proximate cause as a distinct element of an aiding and abetting claim.

of those allegations, the allegations of substantial assistance can no longer be viewed, as Apuzzo argues, as "business as usual," but rather as an effort to purposely assist the fraud and help make it succeed.

. . . .

Conclusion

In sum, applying the standard we have set forth for evaluating substantial assistance, we conclude that the Complaint should not have been dismissed because it adequately alleged that Apuzzo aided and abetted the primary violator in carrying out his fraudulent scheme. We therefore reverse the district court's Opinion and remand for further proceedings consistent with this opinion.

---

§ 10.03 Distinguishing Primary from Secondary Conduct

[A] Rejection of a Broad "Scheme to Defraud" Theory

Stoneridge Investment Partners, LLC v. Scientific-Atlanta, Inc.

United States Supreme Court

552 U.S. 148, 128 S. Ct. 761, 169 L. Ed. 2d 627 (2008)

JUSTICE KENNEDY delivered the opinion of the Court.

We consider the reach of the private right of action the Court has found implied in § 10(b) of the Securities Exchange Act of 1934 and SEC Rule 10b-5. In this suit investors alleged losses after purchasing common stock. They sought to impose liability on entities who, acting both as customers and suppliers, agreed to arrangements that allowed the investors' company to mislead its auditor and issue a misleading financial statement affecting the stock price. We conclude the implied right of action does not reach the customer/supplier companies because the investors did not rely upon their statements or representations. We affirm the judgment of the Court of Appeals.

I

This class-action suit by investors was filed against Charter Communications, Inc., in the United States District Court for the Eastern District of Missouri. Stoneridge Investment Partners, LLC, a limited liability company organized under the laws of Delaware, was the lead plaintiff and is petitioner here.

Charter issued the financial statements and the securities in question. It was a named defendant along with some of its executives and Arthur Andersen LLP, Charter's independent auditor during the period in question. We are concerned, though with two other defendants, respondents here. Respondents are Scientific-Atlanta, Inc., and Motorola, Inc. They were suppliers, and later customers, of Charter.

For purposes of this proceeding, we take these facts, alleged by petitioner, to be true. Charter, a cable operator, engaged in a variety of fraudulent practices so its quarterly reports would meet Wall Street expectations for cable subscriber growth and operating cash flow. The fraud included misclassification of its customer base; delayed reporting of terminated customers; improper capitalization of costs that should have been shown as expenses; and manipulation of the company's billing cutoff dates to inflate reported revenues. In late 2000, Charter executives realized that, despite these efforts, the company would miss projected operating cash flow numbers by $15 to $20 million. To help meet the shortfall, Charter decided to alter its existing arrangements with respondents, Scientific-Atlanta and Motorola. Petitioner's theory as to whether Arthur Andersen was altogether misled or, on the other hand, knew the structure of the contract arrangements and was complicit to some degree, is not clear at this stage of the case. The point, however, is neither controlling nor significant for our present disposition, and in our decision we assume it was misled.

Respondents supplied Charter with the digital cable converter (set top) boxes that Charter furnished to its customers. Charter arranged to overpay respondents $20 for each set top box it purchased until the end of the year, with the understanding that respondents would return the overpayment by purchasing advertising from Charter. The transactions, it is alleged, had no economic substance; but, because Charter would then record the advertising purchases as revenue and capitalize its purchase of the set top boxes, in violation of generally accepted accounting principles, the transactions would enable Charter to fool its auditor into approving a financial statement showing it met projected revenue and operating cash flow numbers. Respondents agreed to the arrangement.

So that Arthur Andersen would not discover the link between Charter's increased payments for the boxes and the advertising purchases, the companies drafted documents to make it appear the transactions were unrelated and conducted in the ordinary course of business. Following a request from Charter, Scientific-Atlanta sent documents to Charter stating—falsely—that it had increased production costs. It raised the price for set top boxes the rest of 2000 by $20 per box. As for Motorola, in a written contract Charter agreed to purchase from Motorola a specific number of set top boxes and pay liquidated damages of $20 for each unit it did not take. The contract was made with the expectation Charter would fail to purchase all the units and pay Motorola the liquidates damages.

To return the additional money from the set top box sales, Scientific-Atlanta and Motorola signed contracts with Charter to purchase advertising time for a price higher than fair value. The new set top box agreements were backdated to make it appear that they were negotiated a month before the advertising agreements. The backdating was important to convey the impression that the negotiations were unconnected, a point Arthur Andersen considered necessary for separate treatment of the transactions. Charter recorded the advertising payments to inflate revenue and operating cash flow by approximately $17 million. The inflated number was shown on financial statements filed with the Securities and Exchange Commission (SEC) and reported to the public.

Respondents had no role in preparing or disseminating Charter's financial statements. And their own financial statements booked the transactions as a wash, under generally accepted accounting principles. It is alleged respondents knew or were in reckless disregard of Charter's intention to use the transactions to inflate its revenues and knew the resulting financial statements issued by Charter would be relied upon by research analysts and investors.

Petitioners filed a securities fraud class action on behalf of purchasers of Charter stock alleging that, by participating in the transactions, respondents violated § 10(b) of the Securities Exchange Act of 1934 and SEC Rule 10b-5.

The District Court granted respondents' motion to dismiss for failure to state a claim on which relief can be granted. The United States Court of Appeals for the Eighth Circuit affirmed. *In re Charter Communications, Inc., Securities Litigation*, 443 F.3d 987 (2006). In its view the allegations did not show that respondents made misstatements relied upon by the public or that they violated a duty to disclose; and on this premise it found no violation of § 10(b) by respondents. At most, the court observed, respondents had aided and abetted Charter's misstatement of its financial results; but it noted, there is no private right of action for aiding and abetting a § 10(b) violation. See *Central Bank of Denver, N.A. v. First Interstate Bank of Denver, N.A.*, 511 U.S. 164, 191 (1994)....

Decisions of the Courts of Appeals are in conflict respecting when, if ever, an injured investor may rely upon § 10(b) to recover from a party that neither makes a public misstatement nor violates a duty to disclose but does participate in a scheme to violate § 10(b). Compare *Simpson v. AOL Time Warner Inc.*, 452 F.3d 1040 (CA9 2006), with *Regents of Univ. of Cal. v. Credit Suisse First Boston (USA), Inc.*, 482 F.3d 372 (CA5 2007). We granted certiorari....

II

....

... In a typical § 10(b) private action a plaintiff must prove (1) a material misrepresentation or omission by the defendant; (2) scienter; (3) a connection between the misrepresentation or omission and the purchase or sale of a security; (4) reliance upon the misrepresentation or omission; (5) economic loss; and (6) loss causation.

In *Central Bank*, the Court determined that § 10(b) liability did not extend to aiders and abettors. The Court found the scope of § 10(b) to be delimited by the text, which makes no mention of aiding and abetting liability. The Court doubted the implied § 10(b) action should extend to aiders and abettors when none of the express causes of action in the Securities Acts included that liability. It added the following:

> "Were we to allow the aiding and abetting action proposed in this case, the defendant could be liable without any showing that the plaintiff relied upon the aider and abettor's statements or actions. . . . Allowing plaintiffs to circumvent the reliance requirement would disregard the careful limits on 10b-5 recovery mandated by our earlier cases."

The decision in *Central Bank* led to calls for Congress to create an express cause of action for aiding and abetting within the Securities Exchange Act. Then-SEC Chairman Authur Levitt, testifying before the Senate Securities Subcommittee, cited *Central Bank* and recommended that aiding and abetting liability in private claims be established. S. Hearing No. 103-759, pp. 13–14 (1994). Congress did not follow this course. Instead, in §104 of the Private Securities Litigation Reform Act of 1995 (PSLRA), 109 Stat. 757, it directed prosecution of aiders and abettors by the SEC. [§20(e) of the Exchange Act,] 15 U.S.C. §78t(e).

The §10(b) implied private right of action does not extend to aiders and abettors. The conduct of a secondary actor must satisfy each of the elements or preconditions for liability; and we consider whether the allegations here are sufficient to do so.

III

The Court of Appeals concluded petitioner had not alleged that respondents engaged in a deceptive act within the reach of the §10(b) private right of action, noting that only misstatements, omissions by one who has a duty to disclose, and manipulative trading practices (where "manipulative" is a term of art, see, *e.g., Santa Fe Industries, Inc. v. Green,* 430 U.S. 462, 476–477 (1977)) are deceptive within the meaning of the rule. If this conclusion were read to suggest there must be a specific oral or written statement before there could be liability under §10(b) or Rule 10b-5, it would be erroneous. Conduct itself can be deceptive, as respondents concede. In this case, moreover, respondents' course of conduct included both oral and written statements, such as the backdated contracts agreed to by Charter and respondents.

A different interpretation of the holding from the Court of Appeals opinion is that the court was stating only that any deceptive statement or act respondents made was not actionable because it did not have the requisite proximate relation to the investors' harm. That conclusion is consistent with our own determination that respondents' acts or statements were not relied upon by the investors and that, as a result, liability cannot be imposed upon respondents.

A

Reliance by the plaintiff upon the defendant's deceptive acts is an essential element of the §10(b) private cause of action. It ensures that, for liability to arise, the "requisite causal connection between a defendant's misrepresentation and a plaintiff's injury" exists as a predicate for liability. We have found a rebuttable presumption of reliance in two different circumstances. First, if there is an omission of a material fact by one with a duty to disclose, the investor to whom the duty was owed need not provide specific proof of reliance. Second, under the fraud-on-the-market doctrine, reliance is presumed when the statements at issue become public. The public information is reflected in the market price of the security. Then it can be assumed that an investor who buys or sells stock at the market price relies upon the statement.

Neither presumption applies here. Respondents had no duty to disclose; and their deceptive acts were not communicated to the public. No member of the investing public had knowledge, either actual or presumed, of respondents' deceptive acts during the relevant times. Petitioner, as a result, cannot show reliance upon any of respondents' actions except in an indirect chain that we find too remote for liability.

B

Invoking what some courts call "scheme liability," see, *e.g., In re Enron Corp. Securities, Derivative, & "ERISA" Litigation*, 439 F. Supp. 2d 692, 723 (SD Tex. 2006), petitioner nonetheless seeks to impose liability on respondents even absent a public statement. In our view this approach does not answer the objection that petitioner did not in fact rely upon respondents' own deceptive conduct.

Liability is appropriate, petitioner contends, because respondents engaged in conduct with the purpose and effect of creating a false appearance of material fact to further a scheme to misrepresent Charter's revenue. The argument is that the financial statement Charter released to the public was a natural and expected consequence of respondents' deceptive acts; had respondents not assisted Charter, Charter's auditor would not have been fooled, and the financial statement would have been a more accurate reflection of Charter's financial condition. That causal link is sufficient, petitioner argues, to apply *Basic's* [485 U.S. 224 (1988)] presumption of reliance to respondents' acts.

In effect petitioner contends that in an efficient market investors rely not only upon the public statements relating to a security but also upon the transactions those statements reflect. Were this concept of reliance to be adopted, the implied cause of action would reach the whole marketplace in which the issuing company does business; and there is no authority for this rule.

As stated above, reliance is tied to causation, leading to the inquiry whether respondents' acts were immediate or remote to the injury. In considering petitioner's arguments, we note § 10(b) provides that the deceptive act must be "in connection with the purchase or sale of any security." Though this phrase in part defines the statute's coverage rather than causation (and so we do not evaluate the "in connection with" requirement of § 10(b) in this case), the emphasis on a purchase or sale of securities does provide some insight into the deceptive acts that concerned the enacting Congress. See Black, Securities Commentary: The Second Circuit's Approach to the 'In Connection With' Requirement of Rule 10b-5, 53 Brooklyn L. Rev. 539, 541 (1987) ("[W]hile the 'in connection with' and causation requirements are analytically distinct, they are related to each other, and discussion of the first requirement may merge with discussion of the second"). In all events we conclude respondents' deceptive acts, which were not disclosed to the investing public, are too remote to satisfy the requirement of reliance It was Charter, not respondents, that misled its auditor and filed fraudulent financial statements; nothing respondents did made it necessary or inevitable for Charter to record the transaction as it did.

The petitioner invokes the private cause of action under § 10(b) and seeks to apply it beyond the securities markets — the realm of financing business — to purchase and supply contracts — the realm of ordinary business operations. The latter realm is governed, for the most part, by state law. It is true that if business operations are used, as alleged here, to affect securities markets, the SEC enforcement power may reach the culpable actors. It is true as well that a dynamic, free economy presupposes a high degree of integrity in all of its parts, an integrity that must be underwritten by rules enforceable in fair, independent, accessible courts. Were the implied cause of action to be extended to the practices described here, however, there would be a risk that the federal power would be used to invite litigation beyond the immediate sphere of securities litigation and in areas already governed by functioning and effective state-law guarantees. Our precedents counsel against this extension. . . . Though § 10(b) is "not 'limited to preserving the integrity of the securities markets,'" *Bankers Life*, 404 U.S., at 12, it does not reach all commercial transactions that are fraudulent and affect the price of a security in some attenuated way.

These considerations answer as well the argument that if this were a common-law action for fraud there could be a finding of reliance. Even if the assumption is correct, it is not controlling. Section 10(b) does not incorporate common-law fraud into federal law. See, *e.g.*, *SEC v. Zandford*, 535 U.S. 813, 820 (2002) ("Section 10(b) must not be construed so broadly as to convert every common-law fraud that happens to involve securities into a violation"). . . . Just as § 10(b) "is surely badly strained when construed to provide a cause of action . . . to the world at large," it should not be interpreted to provide a private cause of action against the entire marketplace in which the issuing company operates.

Petitioner's theory, moreover, would put an unsupportable interpretation on Congress' specific response to *Central Bank* in § 104 of the PSLRA. Congress amended the securities laws to provide for limited coverage of aiders and abettors. Aiding and abetting liability is authorized in actions brought by the SEC but not by private parties. See [§ 20(e) of the Securities Exchange Act,] 15 U.S.C. § 78t(e). Petitioner's view of primary liability makes an aider and abettor liable under § 10(b) if he or she committed a deceptive act in the process of providing assistance. Were we to adopt this construction of § 10(b), it would revive in substance the implied cause of action against all aiders and abettors except those who committed no deceptive act in the process of facilitating the fraud; and we would undermine Congress' determination that this class of defendants should be pursued by the SEC and not by private litigants. . . .

This is not a case in which Congress has enacted a regulatory statute and then has accepted, over a long period of time, broad judicial authority to define substantive standards of conduct and liability. And in accord with the nature of the cause of action at issue here, we give weight to Congress' amendment to the Act restoring aiding and abetting liability in certain cases but not others. The amendment, in our view, supports the conclusion that there is no liability.

The practical consequences of an expansion, which the Court has considered appropriate to examine in circumstances like these, provide a further reason to reject petitioner's approach. In *Blue Chip,* the Court noted that extensive discovery and the potential for uncertainty and disruption in a lawsuit allow plaintiffs with weak claims to extort settlements from innocent companies. [421 U.S.] at 740–741. Adoption of petitioner's approach would expose a new class of defendants to these risks. As noted in *Central Bank,* contracting parties might find it necessary to protect against these threats, raising the costs of doing business. Overseas firms with no other exposure to our securities laws could be deterred from doing business here. This, in turn, may raise the cost of being a publicly traded company under our law and shift securities offerings away from domestic capital markets.

C

The history of the § 10(b) private right and the careful approach the Court has taken before proceeding without congressional direction provide further reasons to find no liability here. The § 10(b) private cause of action is a judicial construct that Congress did not enact in the text of the relevant statutes. Though the rule once may have been otherwise, see *J.I. Case Co. v. Borak,* 377 U.S. 426, 432–433 (1964), it is settled that there is an implied cause of action only if the underlying statute can be interpreted to disclose the intent to create one. . . . This is for a good reason. In the absence of congressional intent the Judiciary's recognition of an implied private right of action

> "necessarily extends its authority to embrace a dispute Congress has not assigned it to resolve. This runs contrary to the established principle that '[t]he jurisdiction of the federal courts is carefully guarded against expansion by judicial interpretation . . . ,' and conflicts with the authority of Congress under Art. III to set the limits of federal jurisdiction." . . .

The determination of who can seek a remedy has significant consequences for the reach of federal power. . . . See *Wilder v. Virginia Hospital Assn.,* 496 U.S. 498, 509, n. 9 (1990) (requirement of congressional intent "reflects a concern, grounded in separation of powers, that Congress rather than the courts controls the availability of remedies for violations of statutes").

Concerns with the judicial creation of a private cause of action caution against its expansion. The decision to extend the cause of action is for Congress, not for us. Though it remains the law, the § 10(b) private right should not be extended beyond its present boundaries. . . .

This restraint is appropriate in light of the PSLRA, which imposed heightened pleading requirements and a loss causation requirement upon "any private action" arising from the Securities Exchange Act. See 15 U.S.C. § 78u-4(b). It is clear these requirements touch upon the implied right of action, which is now a prominent feature of federal securities regulation. . . . Congress thus ratified the implied right of action after the Court moved away from a broad willingness to imply private rights of action. . . . It is appropriate for us to assume that when § 78u-4 was enacted, Congress accepted the § 10(b) private cause of action as then defined but chose to extend it no further.

IV

Secondary actors are subject to criminal penalties and civil enforcement by the SEC. . . . The enforcement power is not toothless. Since September 30, 2002, SEC enforcement actions have collected over $10 billion in disgorgement and penalties, much of it for distribution to injured investors. . . . And in this case both parties agree that criminal penalties are a strong deterrent. In addition some state securities laws permit state authorities to seek fines and restitution from aiders and abettors. All secondary actors, furthermore, are not necessarily immune from private suit. The securities statutes provide an express private right of action against accountants and underwriters in certain circumstances, see [§ 11 of the Securities Act,] 15 U.S.C. § 77k, and the implied right of action in § 10(b) continues to cover secondary actors who commit primary violations.

Here respondents were acting in concert with Charter in the ordinary course as suppliers and, as matters then evolved in the not so ordinary course, as customers. Unconventional as the arrangement was, it took place in the marketplace for goods and services, not in the investment sphere. Charter was free to do as it chose in preparing its books, conferring with its auditor, and preparing and then issuing its financial statements. In these circumstances the investors cannot be said to have relied upon any of respondents' deceptive acts in the decision to purchase or sell securities; and as the requisite reliance cannot be shown, respondents have no liability to petitioner under the implied right of action. This conclusion is consistent with the narrow dimensions we must give to a right of action Congress did not authorize when it first enacted the statute and did not expand when it revisited the law.

The judgment of the Court of Appeals is affirmed, and the case is remanded for further proceedings consistent with this opinion.

It is so ordered.

JUSTICE BREYER took no part in the consideration or decision of this case.

JUSTICE STEVENS, with whom JUSTICE SOUTER and JUSTICE GINSBURG join, dissenting.

Charter Communications, Inc., inflated its revenues by $17 million in order to cover up a $15 to $20 million expected cash flow shortfall. It could not have done so absent the knowingly fraudulent actions of Scientific-Atlanta, Inc., and Motorola, Inc. Investors relied on Charter's revenue statements in deciding whether to invest in Charter and in doing so relied on respondents' fraud, which was itself a "deceptive device" prohibited by § 10(b) of the Securities Exchange Act of 1934. This is enough to satisfy the requirements of § 10(b) and enough to distinguish this case from *Central Bank of Denver, N.A. v. First Interstate Bank of Denver, N.A.*, 511 U.S. 164 (1994).

The Court seems to assume that respondents' alleged conduct could subject them to liability in an enforcement proceeding initiated by the Government, but nevertheless concludes that they are not subject to liability in a private action brought by injured investors because they are, at most, guilty of aiding and abetting a violation of § 10(b), rather than an actual violation of the statute. . . . Furthermore, while the Court frequently refers to petitioner's attempt to "expand" the implied cause of action,—a conclusion that begs the question of the contours of that cause of action—it is today's decision that results in a significant departure from *Central Bank.*

The Court's conclusion that no violation of § 10(b) giving rise to a private right of action has been alleged in this case rests on two faulty premises: (1) the Court's overly broad reading of *Central Bank*, and (2) the view that reliance requires a kind of super-causation—a view contrary to both the Securities and Exchange Commission's (SEC) position in a recent Ninth Circuit case [*Simpson v. AOL Time Warner, Inc.*] and our holding in *Basic Inc. v. Levinson*, 485 U.S. 224 (1988). These two points merit separate discussion.

I

. . . .

What the Court fails to recognize is that this case is critically different from *Central Bank* because the bank in that case did not engage in any deceptive act and, therefore, did not *itself* violate § 10(b). The Court sweeps aside any distinction, remarking that holding respondents liable would "revive in substance the implied cause of action against all aiders and abettors except those who committed no deceptive act in the process of facilitating the fraud." But the fact that Central Bank engaged in no deceptive conduct whatsoever—in other words, that it was at most an aider and abettor—sharply distinguishes *Central Bank* from cases that do involve allegations of such conduct. . . .

. . . .

II

The Court's next faulty premise is that petitioner is required to allege that Scientific-Atlanta and Motorola made it "necessary or inevitable for Charter to record the transactions as it did," in order to demonstrate reliance. . . .

. . . [P]etitioner has . . . alleged that respondents proximately caused Charter's misstatement of income; petitioner has alleged that respondents knew their deceptive acts would be the basis for statements that would influence the market price of Charter stock on which shareholders would rely. Thus, respondents' acts had the foreseeable effect of causing petitioner to engage in the relevant securities transactions. The Restatement (Second) of Torts § 533, pp. 72–73 (1977), provides that "[t]he maker of a fraudulent misrepresentation is subject to liability . . . if the misrepresentation, although not made directly to the other, is made to a third person and the maker intends or has reason to expect that its terms will be repeated or its substance communicated to the other." The sham transactions described in the complaint in this case had the same effect on Charter's profit and loss statement as a false entry directly on its books that included $17 million of gross revenues that had not been received. And respondents are alleged to have known that the outcome of their fraudulent transactions would be communicated to investors.

The Court's view of reliance is unduly stringent and unmoored from authority. The Court first says that if the petitioner's concept of reliance is adopted the implied cause of action "would reach the whole marketplace in which the issuing company does business." The answer to that objection is, of course, that liability only attaches when the company doing business with the issuing company has *itself* violated § 10(b). The Court next relies on what it views as a strict division between the "realm of financing business" and "ordinary business operations." But petitioner's position does not merge the two: A corporation engaging in a business transaction with a partner who transmits false information to the market is only liable where the corporation *itself* violates § 10(b). Such a rule does not invade the province of "ordinary" business transactions.

. . . .

The Court is concerned that such liability would deter overseas firms from doing business in the United States or "shift securities offerings away from domestic capital markets." But liability for those who violate § 10(b) "will not harm American competitiveness; in fact, investor faith in the safety and integrity of our markets *is* their strength. The fact that our markets are the safest in the world has helped make them the strongest in the world." . . .

Accordingly, while I recognize that the *Central Bank* opinion provides a precedent for judicial policymaking decision in this area of the law, I respectfully dissent from the Court's continuing campaign to render the private cause of action under § 10(b) toothless. I would reverse the decision of the Court of Appeals.

III

While I would reverse for the reasons stated above, I must also comment on the importance of the private cause of action that Congress implicitly authorized when it enacted the Securities Exchange Act of 1934. A theme that underlies the Court's analysis is its mistaken hostility towards the § 10(b) private cause of action. The Court's current view of implied causes of action is that they are merely a "relic" of our prior "heady days." Those "heady days" persisted for two hundred years.

During the first two centuries of this Nation's history much of our law was developed by judges in the common-law tradition. A basic principle animating our jurisprudence was enshrined in state constitution provisions guaranteeing, in substance, that "every wrong shall have a remedy." Fashioning appropriate remedies for

the violation of rules of law designed to protect a class of citizens was the routine business of judges. See *Marbury v. Madison,* 1 Cranch 137, 166 (1803). While it is true that in the early days state law was the source of most of those rules, through-out our history—until 1975—the same practice prevailed in federal courts with regard to federal statutes that left questions of remedy open for judges to answer. . . .

Until *Central Bank,* the federal courts continued to enforce a broad implied cause of action for the violation of statutes enacted in 1933 and 1934 for the protection of investors. As Judge Friendly explained [in *Leist v. Simplot,* 638 F.2d 283, 296–297 (2d Cir. 1980)]:

> "During the late 1940's, the 1950's, the 1960's and the early 1970's there was widespread, indeed almost general, recognition of implied causes of action for damages under many provisions of the Securities Exchange Act, including not only the antifraud provisions, §§ 10 and 15(c)(1), but many others. These included the provision, § 6(a)(1), requiring securities exchanges to enforce compliance with the Act and any rule or regulation made there-under, . . . and provisions governing the solicitation of proxies. . . . Writing in 1961, Professor Loss remarked with respect to violations of the antifraud provisions that with one exception 'not a single judge has expressed himself to the contrary.' [L. Loss,] 3 Securities Regulation 1763-64. When damage actions for violation of § 10(b) and Rule 10b-5 reached the Supreme Court, the existence of an implied cause of action was not deemed worthy of extended discussion. . . ."

In light of the history of court-created remedies and specifically the history of implied causes of action under § 10(b), the Court is simply wrong when it states that Congress did not impliedly authorize this private cause of action "when it first enacted the statute." . . . Congress enacted § 10(b) with the understanding that federal courts respected the principle that every wrong would have a remedy. Today's decision simply cuts back further on Congress' intended remedy. I respectfully dissent.

[B] Rule 10b-5(b) — "Makers" of Statements

Janus Capital Group, Inc. v. First Derivative Traders

United States Supreme Court

564 U.S. 135, 131 S. Ct. 2296, 180 L. Ed. 2d 166 (2011)

JUSTICE THOMAS delivered the opinion of the Court.

This case requires us to determine whether Janus Capital Management LLC (JCM), a mutual fund investment adviser, can be held liable in a private action under Securities and Exchange Commission (SEC) Rule 10b-5 for false statements included in its client mutual funds' prospectuses. Rule 10b-5 prohibits "mak[ing] any untrue statement of a material fact" in connection with the purchase or sale of securities.

We conclude that JCM cannot be held liable because it did not make the statements in the prospectuses.

I

Janus Capital Group, Inc. (JCG) is a publicly traded company that created the Janus family of mutual funds. These mutual funds are organized in a Massachusetts business trust, the Janus Investment Fund. Janus Investment Fund retained JCG's wholly owned subsidiary, JCM, to be its investment adviser and administrator. JCG and JCM are the petitioners here.

Although JCG created Janus Investment Fund, Janus Investment Fund is a separate legal entity owned entirely by mutual fund investors. Janus Investment Fund has no assets apart from those owned by the investors. JCM provides Janus Investment Fund with investment advisory services, which include "the management and administrative services necessary for the operation of [Janus] Fun[d]," but the two entities maintain legal independence. At all times relevant to this case, all of the officers of Janus Investment Fund were also officers of JCM, but only one member of Janus Investment Fund's board of trustees was associated with JCM. This is more independence than is required: By statute, up to 60 percent of the board of a mutual fund may be composed of "interested persons." . . .

As the securities laws require, Janus Investment Fund issued prospectuses describing the investment strategy and operations of its mutual funds to investors. The prospectuses for several funds represented that the funds were not suitable for market timing and can be read to suggest that JCM would implement policies to curb the practice.[6] For example, the Janus Mercury Fund prospectus dated February 25, 2002, stated that the fund was "not intended for market timing or excessive trading" and represented that it "may reject any purchase request . . . if it believes that any combination of trading activity is attributable to market timing or is otherwise excessive or potentially disruptive to the Fund." Although market timing is legal, it harms other investors in the mutual fund.

In September 2003, the Attorney General of the State of New York filed a complaint against JCG and JCM alleging that JCG entered into secret arrangements to permit market timing in several funds run by JCM. After the complaint's allegations

---

[6]. Market timing is a trading strategy that exploits time delay in mutual funds' daily valuation system. The price for buying or selling shares of a mutual fund is ordinarily determined by the next net asset value (NAV) calculation after the order is placed. The NAV calculation usually happens once a day, at the close of the major U. S. markets. Because of certain time delays, however, the values used in these calculations do not always accurately reflect the true value of the underlying assets. For example, a fund may value its foreign securities based on the price at the close of the foreign market, which may have occurred several hours before the calculation. But events might have taken place after the close of the foreign market that could be expected to affect their price. If the event were expected to increase the price of the foreign securities, a market-timing investor could buy shares of a mutual fund at the artificially low NAV and sell the next day when the NAV corrects itself upward. See Disclosure Regarding Market Timing and Selective Disclosure of Portfolio Holdings, 68 Fed. Reg. 70402 (proposed Dec. 17, 2003).

became public, investors withdrew significant amounts of money from the Janus Investment Fund mutual funds.[7] Because Janus Investment Fund compensated JCM based on the total value of the funds and JCM's management fees comprised a significant percentage of JCG's income, Janus Investment Fund's loss of value affected JCG's value as well. JCG's stock price fell nearly 25 percent, from $17.68 on September 2 to $13.50 on September 26.

Respondent First Derivative Traders (First Derivative) represents a class of plaintiffs who owned JCG stock as of September 3, 2003. Its complaint asserts claims against JCG and JCM for violations of Rule 10b-5 and § 10(b) of the Securities Exchange Act of 1934. . . . First Derivative alleges that JCG and JCM "caused mutual fund prospectuses to be issued for Janus mutual funds and made them available to the investing public, which created the misleading impression that [JCG and JCM] would implement measures to curb market timing in the Janus [mutual funds]." [As alleged:] "Had the truth been known, Janus [mutual funds] would have been less attractive to investors, and consequently, [JCG] would have realized lower revenues, so [JCG's] stock would have traded at lower prices." . . .

First Derivative contends that JCG and JCM "materially misled the investing public" and that class members relied "upon the integrity of the market price of [JCG] securities and market information relating to [JCG and JCM]." The complaint also alleges that JCG should be held liable for the acts of JCM as a "controlling person" under 15 U.S.C.A. § 78t(a) (§ 20(a) of the [Securities Exchange] Act).

The District Court dismissed the complaint for failure to state a claim. The Court of Appeals for the Fourth Circuit reversed, holding that First Derivative had sufficiently alleged that "JCG and JCM, by participating in the writing and dissemination of the prospectuses, *made* the misleading statements contained in the documents." *In re Mutual Funds Inv. Litigation*, 566 F.3d 111, 121 (2009) (emphasis in original). With respect to the element of reliance, the court found that investors would infer that JCM "played a role in preparing or approving the content of the Janus fund prospectuses," but that investors would not infer the same about JCG, which could be liable only as a "control person" of JCM under § 20(a). . . .

II

We granted certiorari to address whether JCM can be held liable in a private action under Rule 10b-5 for false statements included in Janus Investment Fund's prospectuses. Under Rule 10b-5, it is unlawful for "any person, directly or indirectly, . . . [t]o make any untrue statement of a material fact" in connection with the purchase or sale of securities. To be liable, therefore, JCM must have "made" the material misstatements in the prospectuses. We hold that it did not.

---

[7]. In 2004, JCG and JCM settled these allegations and agreed to reduce their fees by $125 million and pay $50 million in civil penalties and $50 million in disgorgement to the mutual fund investors.

A

The SEC promulgated Rule 10b-5 pursuant to authority granted under § 10(b) of the Securities Exchange Act of 1934. . . . Although neither Rule 10b-5 nor § 10(b) expressly creates a private right of action, this Court has held that "a private right of action is implied under § 10(b)." . . . That holding "remains the law" . . . but "[c]oncerns with the judicial creation of a private cause of action caution against its expansion" . . . Thus, in analyzing whether JCM "made" the statements for purposes of Rule 10b-5, we are mindful that we must give "narrow dimensions . . . to a right of action Congress did not authorize when it first enacted the statute and did not expand when it revisited the law." . . .

1

One "makes" a statement by stating it. When "make" is paired with a noun expressing the action of a verb, the resulting phrase is "approximately equivalent in sense" to that verb. . . . For instance, "to make a proclamation" is the approximate equivalent of "to proclaim," and "to make a promise" approximates "to promise." . . . The phrase at issue in Rule 10b-5, "[t]o make any . . . statement," is thus the approximate equivalent of "to state."

For purposes of Rule 10b-5, the maker of a statement is the person or entity with ultimate authority over the statement, including its content and whether and how to communicate it. Without control, a person or entity can merely suggest what to say, not "make" a statement in its own right. One who prepares or publishes a statement on behalf of another is not its maker. And in the ordinary case, attribution within a statement or implicit from surrounding circumstances is strong evidence that a statement was made by—and only by—the party to whom it is attributed. This rule might best be exemplified by the relationship between a speechwriter and a speaker. Even when a speechwriter drafts a speech, the content is entirely within the control of the person who delivers it. And it is the speaker who takes credit—or blame— for what is ultimately said.

This rule follows from *Central Bank of Denver, N.A. v. First Interstate Bank of Denver, N. A.*, 511 U. S. 164 (1994), in which we held that Rule 10b-5's private right of action does not include suits against aiders and abettors. Such suits—against entities that contribute "substantial assistance" to the making of a statement but do not actually make it—may be brought by the SEC, but not by private parties. A broader reading of "make," including persons or entities without ultimate control over the content of a statement, would substantially undermine *Central Bank*. If persons or entities without control over the content of a statement could be considered primary violators who "made" the statement, then aiders and abettors would be almost nonexistent.

This interpretation is further supported by our recent decision in *Stoneridge*. There, investors sued "entities who, acting both as customers and suppliers, agreed to arrangements that allowed the investors' company to mislead its auditor and issue a misleading financial statement." . . . We held that dismissal of the complaint was proper because the public could not have relied on the entities' undisclosed deceptive acts. Significantly, in reaching that conclusion we emphasized that "nothing [the defendants] did made it necessary or inevitable for [the company] to record the transactions as it did." This emphasis suggests the rule we adopt today: that the maker of a statement is the entity with authority over the content of the statement and whether and how to communicate it. Without such authority, it is not "necessary or inevitable" that any falsehood will be contained in the statement.

Our holding also accords with the narrow scope that we must give the implied private right of action. Although the existence of the private right is now settled, we will not expand liability beyond the person or entity that ultimately has authority over a false statement.

2

The Government contends that "make" should be defined as "create." Brief for United States as *Amicus Curiae* 14–15 (citing Webster's New International Dictionary 1485 (2d ed. 1958) (defining "make" as "[t]o cause to exist, appear, or occur")). This definition, although perhaps appropriate when "make" is directed at an object unassociated with a verb (*e.g.*, "to make a chair"), fails to capture its meaning when directed at an object expressing the action of a verb.

Adopting the Government's definition of "make" would also lead to results inconsistent with our precedent. The Government's definition would permit private plaintiffs to sue a person who "provides the false or misleading information that another person then puts into the statement." Brief for United States as *Amicus Curiae* 13. But in *Stoneridge*, we rejected a private Rule 10b-5 suit against companies involved in deceptive transactions, even when information about those transactions was later incorporated into false public statements. We see no reason to treat participating in the drafting of a false statement differently from engaging in deceptive transactions, when each is merely an undisclosed act preceding the decision of an independent entity to make a public statement.

For its part, First Derivative suggests that the "well recognized and uniquely close relationship between a mutual fund and its investment adviser" should inform our decision. It suggests that an investment adviser should generally be understood to be the "maker" of statements by its client mutual fund, like a playwright whose lines are delivered by an actor. We decline this invitation to disregard the corporate form. Although First Derivative and its *amici* persuasively argue that investment advisers exercise significant influence over their client funds, it is undisputed that the corporate formalities were observed here. JCM and Janus Investment Fund remain legally separate entities, and Janus Investment Fund's board of trustees was more independent than the statute requires. . . . Any reapportionment of liability in the securities industry in light of the close relationship between investment advisers and mutual funds is properly the responsibility of Congress and not the courts. Moreover, just as with the Government's theory, First Derivative's rule would create the broad liability that we rejected in *Stoneridge*.

Congress also has established liability in § 20(a) for "[e]very person who, directly or indirectly, controls any person liable" for violations of the securities laws. First Derivative's theory of liability based on a relationship of influence resembles the liability imposed by Congress for control. To adopt First Derivative's theory would read into Rule 10b-5 a theory of liability similar to — but broader in application than — what Congress has already created expressly elsewhere. We decline to do so. [In an accompanying footnote, the Court stated: "We do not address whether Congress created liability for entities that act through innocent intermediaries in [§ 20(b) of the Exchange Act.]"]

B

Under this rule, JCM did not "make" any of the statements in the Janus Investment Fund prospectuses; Janus Investment Fund did. Only Janus Investment Fund — not JCM — bears the statutory obligation to file the prospectuses with the SEC. . . . The SEC has recorded that Janus Investment Fund filed the prospectuses. . . . There is no allegation that JCM in fact filed the prospectuses and falsely attributed them to Janus Investment Fund. Nor did anything on the face of the prospectuses indicate that any statements therein came from JCM rather than Janus Investment Fund — a legally independent entity with its own board of trustees.[8]

First Derivative suggests that both JCM and Janus Investment Fund might have "made" the misleading statements within the meaning of Rule 10b-5 because JCM was significantly involved in preparing the prospectuses. But this assistance, subject to the ultimate control of Janus Investment Fund, does not mean that JCM "made" any statements in the prospectuses. Although JCM, like a speechwriter, may have assisted Janus Investment Fund with crafting what Janus Investment Fund said in the prospectuses, JCM itself did not "make" those statements for purposes of Rule 10b-5.

* * *

The statements in the Janus Investment Fund prospectuses were made by Janus Investment Fund, not by JCM. Accordingly, First Derivative has not stated a claim against JCM under Rule 10b-5. The judgment of the United States Court of Appeals for the Fourth Circuit is reversed.

It is so ordered.

---

[8]. First Derivative suggests that "indirectly" in Rule 10b-5 may broaden the meaning of "make." We disagree. The phrase "directly or indirectly" is set off by itself in Rule 10b-5 and modifies not just "to make," but also "to employ" and "to engage." We think the phrase merely clarifies that as long as a statement is made, it does not matter whether the statement was communicated directly or indirectly to the recipient. A different understanding of "indirectly" would, like a broad definition of "make," threaten to erase the line between primary violators and aiders and abettors established by *Central Bank*.

In this case, we need not define precisely what it means to communicate a "made" statement indirectly because none of the statements in the prospectuses were attributed, explicitly or implicitly, to JCM. Without attribution, there is no indication that Janus Investment Fund was quoting or otherwise repeating a statement originally "made" by JCM. . . . More may be required to find that a person or entity made a statement indirectly, but attribution is necessary.

Justice Breyer, with whom Justice Ginsburg, Justice Sotomayor, and Justice Kagan join, dissenting.

This case involves a private . . . Rule 10b-5 action brought by a group of investors against Janus Capital Group, Inc., and Janus Capital Management LLC (Janus Management), a firm that acted as an investment adviser to a family of mutual funds (collectively, the Janus Fund or Fund). The investors claim that Janus Management knowingly made materially false or misleading statements that appeared in prospectuses issued by the Janus Fund. They say that they relied upon those statements, and that they suffered resulting economic harm.

Janus Management and the Janus Fund are closely related. Each of the Fund's officers is a Janus Management employee. Janus Management, acting through those employees (and other of its employees), manages the purchase, sale, redemption, and distribution of the Fund's investments. Janus Management prepares, modifies, and implements the Janus Fund's long-term strategies. And Janus Management, acting through those employees, carries out the Fund's daily activities.

Rule 10b-5 says in relevant part that it is unlawful for "any person, directly or indirectly . . . *[t]o make* any untrue statement of a material fact" in connection with the purchase or sale of securities. . . . The specific legal question before us is whether Janus Management can be held responsible under the Rule for having "ma[d]e" certain false statements about the Janus Fund's activities. The statements in question appear in the Janus Fund's prospectuses.

The Court holds that only the Janus Fund, not Janus Management, could have "ma[d]e" those statements. The majority points out that the Janus Fund's board of trustees has "ultimate authority" over the content of the statements in a Fund prospectus. And in the majority's view, only "the person or entity with ultimate authority over the statement, including its content and whether and how to communicate it" can "make" a statement within the terms of Rule 10b-5.

In my view, however, the majority has incorrectly interpreted the Rule's word "make." Neither common English nor this Court's earlier cases limit the scope of that word to those with "ultimate authority" over a statement's content. To the contrary, both language and case law indicate that, depending upon the circumstances, a management company, a board of trustees, individual company officers, or others, separately or together, might "make" statements contained in a firm's prospectus— even if a board of directors has ultimate content-related responsibility. And the circumstances here are such that a court could find that Janus Management made the statements in question.

I

. . . .

The majority finds the complaint fatally flawed . . . because (1) Rule 10b-5 says that no "person" shall "directly or indirectly . . . *make* any untrue statement of a material fact," (2) the statements at issue appeared in the *Janus Fund's* prospectuses, and

(3) only "the person or entity with ultimate authority over the statement, including its content and whether and how to communicate it" can "make" a false statement.

But where can the majority find legal support for the rule that it enunciates? The English language does not impose upon the word "make" boundaries of the kind the majority finds determinative. Every day, hosts of corporate officials make statements with content that more senior officials or the board of directors have "ultimate authority" to control. So do cabinet officials make statements about matters that the Constitution places within the ultimate authority of the President. So do thousands, perhaps millions, of other employees make statements that, as to content, form, or timing, are subject to the control of another.

Nothing in the English language prevents one from saying that several different individuals, separately or together, "make" a statement that each has a hand in producing. For example, as a matter of English, one can say that a national political party has made a statement even if the only written communication consists of uniform press releases issued in the name of local party branches; one can say that one foreign nation has made a statement even when the officials of a different nation (subject to its influence) speak about the matter; and one can say that the President has made a statement even if his press officer issues a communication, sometimes in the press officer's own name. Practical matters related to context, including control, participation, and relevant audience, help determine who "makes" a statement and to whom that statement may properly be "attributed," — at least as far as ordinary English is concerned.

Neither can the majority find support in any relevant precedent. The majority says that its rule "follows from *Central Bank of Denver, N. A. v. First Interstate Bank of Denver, N. A.*, 511 U. S. 164 (1994)," in which the Court "held that Rule 10b-5's private right of action does not include suits against aiders and abettors." . . . But *Central Bank* concerns a different matter. And it no more requires the majority's rule than free air travel for small children requires free air travel for adults.

Central Bank is a case about *secondary* liability, liability attaching, not to an individual making a false statement, but to an individual helping *someone else* do so. . . .

By way of contrast, the present case is about *primary* liability—about individuals who allegedly themselves "make" materially false statements, not about those who help *others* to do so. The question is whether Janus Management is *primarily* liable for violating the Act, not whether it simply helped others violate the Act. The *Central Bank* defendant concededly did *not* make the false statements in question (others did), while here the defendants allegedly *did* make those statements. And a rule (the majority's rule) absolving those who allegedly *did* make false statements does not "follow from" a rule (*Central Bank*'s rule) absolving those who concededly did *not* do so.

The majority adds that to interpret the word "make" as including those "without ultimate control over the content of a statement" would "substantially undermine" *Central Bank*'s holding. Would it? The Court in *Central Bank* specifically wrote that its holding did "not mean that secondary actors in the securities markets are always free from liability under the securities Acts. *Any person or entity, including a lawyer, accountant, or bank, who* employs a manipulative device or *makes a material misstatement* (or omission) on which a purchaser or seller of securities relies *may be liable as a primary violator under 10b-5,* assuming *all* of the requirements for primary liability under Rule 10b-5 are met."

. . . .

Thus, as far as *Central Bank* is concerned, depending upon the circumstances, board members, senior firm officials, officials tasked to develop a marketing document, large investors, or others (taken together or separately) all might "make" materially false statements subjecting themselves to primary liability. The majority's rule does not protect, it *extends, Central Bank*'s holding of no liability into new territory that *Central Bank* explicitly placed outside that holding. And by ignoring the language in which *Central Bank* did so, the majority's rule itself undermines *Central Bank*. Where is the legal support for the majority's "draw[ing] a clean line" that so seriously conflicts with *Central Bank?* Indeed, where is the legal support for the majority's suggestion that plaintiffs must show some kind of "attribution" of a statement to a defendant,—if it means plaintiffs must show, not only that the defendant "ma[d]e" the statement, but something more?

The majority also refers to *Stoneridge,* but that case offers it no help. . . .

It is difficult for me to see how *Stoneridge* "support[s]" the majority's rule. No one in *Stoneridge* disputed the *making* of the relevant statements, the fraudulent contracts and the like. And no one in *Stoneridge* contended that the equipment suppliers were, in fact, the *makers* of the cable company's misstatements. Rather, *Stoneridge* was concerned with whether the equipment suppliers' *separate* statements were sufficiently disclosed in the securities marketplace so as to be the basis for investor reliance. They were not. But this is a different inquiry than whether statements acknowledged to have been disclosed in the securities marketplace and ripe for reliance can be said to have been "ma[d]e" by one or another actor. . . .

The majority adds that its rule is necessary to avoid "a theory of liability similar to—but broader in application than"—§ 20(a)'s liability, for "'[e]very person who, directly or indirectly, controls any person liable'" for violations of the securities laws. . . . But that is not so. This Court has explained that the possibility of an express remedy under the securities laws does not preclude a claim under § 10(b). *Herman & MacLean* v. *Huddleston,* 459 U. S. 375, 388 (1983).

More importantly, a person who is liable under § 20(a) controls another "*person*" *who is* "*liable*" for a securities violation. . . . We here examine whether a person is primarily liable whether they do, or they do not, control another person *who is liable*. That is to say, here, the liability of some "other person" is not at issue.

And there is at least one significant category of cases that § 10(b) may address that derivative forms of liability, such as under § 20(a), cannot, namely, cases in which one actor exploits another as an innocent intermediary for its misstatements. Here, it may well be that the Fund's board of trustees knew nothing about the falsity of the prospectuses. . . . And if so, § 20(a) would not apply.

The possibility of guilty management and innocent board is the 13th stroke of the new rule's clock. What is to happen when guilty management writes a prospectus (for the board) containing materially false statements and fools both board and public into believing they are true? Apparently under the majority's rule, in such circumstances *no one* could be found to have "ma[d]e" a materially false statement — even though under the common law the managers would likely have been guilty or liable (in analogous circumstances) for doing so as *principals* (and not as aiders and abettors). . . .

Indeed, under the majority's rule it seems unlikely that the SEC itself in such circumstances could exercise the authority Congress has granted it to pursue primary violators who "make" false statements or the authority that Congress has specifically provided to prosecute aiders and abettors to securities violations. . . . That is because the managers, not having "ma[d]e" the statement, would not be liable as principals and there would be no other primary violator they might have tried to "aid" or "abet." . . .

If the majority believes, as its footnote hints, that § 20(b) could provide a basis for liability in this case, then it should remand the case for possible amendment of the complaint. "There is a dearth of authority construing Section 20(b)," which has been thought largely "superfluous in 10b-5 cases." . . . Hence respondent, who reasonably thought that it referred to the proper securities law provision, is faultless for failing to mention § 20(b) as well.

In sum, I can find nothing in § 10(b) or in Rule 10b-5, its language, its history, or in precedent suggesting that Congress, in enacting the securities laws, intended a loophole of the kind that the majority's rule may well create.

II

Rejecting the majority's rule, of course, does not decide the question before us. We must still determine whether, in light of the complaint's allegations, Janus Management could have "ma[d]e" the false statements in the prospectuses at issue. In my view, the answer to this question is "Yes." The specific relationships alleged among Janus Management, the Janus Fund, and the prospectus statements warrant the conclusion that Janus Management did "make" those statements.

In part, my conclusion reflects the fact that this Court and lower courts have made clear that at least *sometimes* corporate officials and others can be held liable under Rule 10b-5 for having "ma[d]e" a materially false statement even when that statement appears in a document (or is made by a third person) that the officials do not legally control. In *Herman & MacLean*, for example, this Court pointed out that "certain individuals who play a part in preparing the registration statement," including corporate officers, lawyers, and accountants, may be primarily liable even where "they are not named as having prepared or certified" the registration statement. . . . And as I have already pointed out, this Court wrote in *Central Bank* that a "lawyer, accountant, or bank, who . . . makes a material misstatement (or omission) on which a purchaser or seller of securities relies *may be liable as a primary violator under 10b-5*, assuming *all* of the requirements for primary liability under Rule 10b-5 are met." . . .

Given the statements in our opinions, it is not surprising that lower courts have found primary liability for actors without "ultimate authority" over issued statements. One court, for example, concluded that an accountant could be primarily liable for having "ma[d]e" false statements, where he issued fraudulent opinion and certification letters reproduced in prospectuses, annual reports, and other corporate materials for which he was not ultimately responsible. *Anixter v. Home-Stake Production Co.*, 77 F.3d 1215, 1225–1227 (CA10 1996). In a later case postdating *Stoneridge*, that court reaffirmed that an outside consultant could be primarily liable for having "ma[d]e" false statements, where he drafted fraudulent quarterly and annual filing statements later reviewed and certified by the firm's auditor, officers, and counsel. *SEC v. Wolfson*, 539 F.3d 1249, 1261 (CA10 2008). And another court found that a corporation's chief financial officer could be held primarily liable as having "ma[d]e" misstatements that appeared in a form 10-K that she prepared but did not sign or file. *McConville v. SEC*, 465 F.3d 780, 787 (CA7 2006).

One can also easily find lower court cases explaining that corporate officials may be liable for having "ma[d]e" false statements where those officials use innocent persons as conduits through which the false statements reach the public (without necessarily attributing the false statements to the officials). See, *e.g., In re Navarre Corp. Securities Litigation*, 299 F.3d 735, 743 (CA8 2002) (liability may be premised on use of analysts as a conduit to communicate false statements to market); *In re Cabletron Systems, Inc.*, 311 F.3d 11, 38 (CA1 2002) (rejecting a test requiring legal "control" over third parties making statements as giving "company officials too much leeway to commit fraud on the market by using analysts as their mouthpieces"). . . .

My conclusion also reflects the particular circumstances that the complaint alleges. The complaint states that "Janus Management, as investment advisor to the funds, is responsible for the day-to-day management of its investment portfolio and other business affairs of the funds. Janus Management furnishes advice and recommendations concerning the funds' investments, as well as administrative, compliance and accounting services for the funds." Each of the Fund's 17 officers was a vice president of Janus Management. The Fund has "no assets separate and apart from those they hold for shareholders." . . . Janus Management disseminated the fund prospectuses through its parent company's Web site. Janus Management employees drafted and reviewed the Fund prospectuses, including language about "market timing." . . . And Janus Management may well have kept the trustees in the dark about the true "market timing" facts. . . .

Given these circumstances, as long as some managers, sometimes, can be held to have "ma[d]e" a materially false statement, Janus Management can be held to have done so on the facts alleged here. The relationship between Janus Management and the Fund could hardly have been closer. Janus Management's involvement in preparing and writing the relevant statements could hardly have been greater. And there is a serious suggestion that the board itself knew little or nothing about the falsity of what was said. Unless we adopt a formal rule (as the majority here has done) that would arbitrarily exclude from the scope of the word "make" those who manage a firm—even when those managers perpetrate a fraud through an unknowing intermediary—the management company at issue here falls within that scope. We should hold the allegations in the complaint in this respect legally sufficient.

With respect, I dissent.

Note — Impact of Janus Capital

(1) By limiting Rule 10b-5(b) primary liability to those persons who have ultimate control over the content of the misrepresentation (and "whether and how to communicate it"), the Supreme Court in *Janus Capital* generally foreclosed primary liability under this provision for those who participate in, draft, or render advice with respect to the misrepresentation. Such individuals normally do not have ultimate control over the content of the statement. As a result, advisers, such as attorneys who draft disclosure documents and investment bankers who provide deal-making input, generally are not primary violators under Rule 10b-5(b). Prior to *Janus Capital*, the lower courts were divided on this issue. Today, attorneys, bankers, and accountants will incur primary Rule 10b-5(b) liability exposure ordinarily only when they author an opinion that is transmitted to investors.

The Supreme Court's decision in *Janus Capital* has been interpreted by many sources as applying not only to material misrepresentations and half-truths under Rule 10b-5(b), but also to all three subsections of Rule 10b-5 as well as the statute, § 10(b). In a surprising SEC decision, the Commission set forth a far more expansive interpretation of Rule 10b-5(a) and (c)—at least in the SEC enforcement setting. The SEC opined:

> [W]e conclude that primary liability under Rule 10b-5(a) and (c) encompasses the "making" of a fraudulent misstatement to investors, as well as the drafting or devising of such a misstatement. Such conduct, in our view, plainly constitutes employment of a deceptive "device" or "act." . . .
>
> . . . Janus does not require a different result. In *Janus*, the Court construed only the term "make" in Rule 10b-5(b), which does not appear in subsections (a) and (c); the decision did not even mention, let alone construe, the broader text of those provisions. And the Court never suggested that because the "maker" of a false statement is primarily liable under subsection (b), he cannot *also* be liable under subsections (a) and (c). Nor did the Court indicate that a defendant's failure to "make" a misstatement for purposes of subsection (b) precludes primary liability under the other provisions.

Moreover, our approach is fully consistent with the rationales on which *Janus* rests. The Court began its analysis with a textual basis for its holding, concluding that one who merely "prepares" a statement necessarily is not its "maker," just as a mere speechwriter lacks "ultimate authority" over the contents of a speech. Our approach does not conflict with that logic: Accepting that a drafter is not primarily liable for "making" a misstatement under Rule 10b-5*(b)*, our position is that the drafter would be primarily liable under subsections *(a)* and *(c)* for employing a deceptive "device" and engaging in a deceptive "act."

Our approach is also consistent with the Court's second justification for its holding—that a drafter's conduct is too remote to satisfy the element of reliance in private actions arising under Rule 10b-5. Investors, the Court explained, cannot be said to have relied on "undisclosed act[s]," such as merely drafting a misstatement, that "preced[e] the decision of an independent entity to make a public statement." Again, our analysis fully comports with that logic. Indeed, we do not suggest that the outcome in *Janus* itself might have been different if only the plaintiffs' claims had arisen under Rule 10b-5(a) or (c). As *Janus* recognizes, those plaintiffs may not have been able to show reliance on the drafters' conduct, regardless of the subsection of Rule 10b-5 alleged to have been violated. Thus, our interpretation would not expand the "narrow scope" the Supreme Court "gives to the implied private right of action."

But to say that a claim will not succeed in every case is not to say that there is no claim at all. In contrast to private parties, the Commission need not show reliance as an element of its claims. Thus, even if *Janus* precludes private actions against those who commit "undisclosed" deceptive acts, it does not preclude Commission enforcement actions under Rule 10b-5(a) and (c) against those same individuals.

In the Matter of Flannery and Hopkins, 2014 WL 7145625 (SEC 2014), *rev'd on other grounds,* 810 F.3d 1 (1st Cir. 2015).

(2) The Supreme Court's decision in *Janus Capital* may be construed to insulate from § 10(b) primary liability corporations, their boards of directors, and management when lower-level officers engage in misconduct but have no ultimate authority over the misrepresentations publicly disseminated. This portrayal of "guilty management and innocent board" was made by the dissent in *Janus Capital*: "Apparently, under the majority's rule, in such circumstances, no one could be found to have 'made' a materially false statement." Nonetheless, post-*Janus Capital*, a number of lower courts have applied principles of agency law for primary liability. *See, e.g., In re Merck & Co. Inc. Securities, Derivative & ERISA Litigation,* 2011 U.S. Dist. LEXIS 87578 (D.N.J. 2011) (denying motion to dismiss where a corporate officer "made the statements pursuant to his responsibility and authority to act as an agent of Merck"). *But see SEC v. Kelly,* 2011 U.S. Dist. LEXIS 108805 (S.D.N.Y. 2011)

(ordering dismissal because the defendant was not the "maker" of allegedly false statements).

(3) As discussed above in this Note, *Janus Capital* evidently addressed the situation where statements were disseminated to investors and suit was based on Rule 10b-5(b) — prohibiting a material misrepresentation or half-truth. *Janus Capital* may be distinguished when an action is brought alleging a "scheme to defraud" under Rule 10b-5(a) and (c). Hence, primary § 10(b) liability may be appropriate (pursuant to Rule 10b-5(a) and (c)) "when the scheme encompasses conduct beyond those misrepresentations" that comprise the Rule 10b-5(b) claim. In such circumstances, primary § 10(b) liability may be imposed irrespective whether the defendant "made" a statement. *SEC v. Mercury Interactive LLC*, 2011 U.S. Dist. LEXIS 134580 (N.D. Cal. 2011), quoting, *WPP Luxenbourg Gamma Three Sarl v. Spot Runner, Inc.*, 655 F.3d 1039, 1057 (9th Cir. 2011); *In the Matter of Flannery and Hopkins*, 2014 WL 7145625 (SEC 2014), *rev'd on other grounds*, 810 F.3d 1 (1st Cir. 2015).

(4) Note that auditors have liability exposure under Rule 10b-5(b) because they "make" a statement. The Independent Auditors Report generally states as follows:

> *In our opinion*, the financial statements referred to above [2015 and 2016] present fairly, in all material respects, the financial position of Brittain Company as of December 31, 2015 and December 31, 2016, and the results of its operations and its cash flows for the years then ended in conformity with accounting principles generally accepted in the United States of America. (emphasis supplied)

(5) In *Janus Capital*, reference was made to § 20(b) of the Exchange Act. That statute makes it "unlawful for any person, directly or indirectly, to do any act or thing that it would be unlawful for such person to do under the provisions of this Act or any rule or regulation thereunder through or by means of another person." Or, as stated in the House of Representatives Report, § 20(b) "makes it unlawful for any person to do, through any other person, anything that he is forbidden to do himself." H.R. Rep. No. 73-1383 (1934). Decisions interpreting § 20(b) are sparse. In this setting, § 20(b) may be invoked where, for example, an officer intentionally causes a misleading statement to be communicated to investors by means of an unknowing board of directors. The scope of the statute is yet unresolved.

(6) Depending on the language of other statutes, *Janus Capital* may or may not be applicable. *See, e.g., SEC v. Big Apple Consulting USA, Inc.*, 783 F.3d 786 (11th Cir. 2015) (holding that *Janus* not applicable to § 17(a) of the Securities Act); *SEC v. Mercury Interactive LLC*, 2011 U.S. Dist. LEXIS 134580 (N.D. Cal. 2011) (declining to apply *Janus Capital* to § 17(a) of the Securities Act and § 14(a) of the Exchange Act because the operative language of those statutes do not require that the defendant "make" a statement to incur liability). Also significant is *Prousalis v. Moore*, 751 F.3d 272 (4th Cir. 2014) (holding *Janus* does not apply in criminal cases).

(7) As a final point, note that collateral actors may be held liable in private actions under state securities and common law. Nonetheless, the Securities Litigation

Uniform Standards Act (SLUSA), addressed in Chapter 9, preempts (with certain exceptions) class actions involving nationally traded securities. Therefore, state law applies in individual and derivative actions as well as class actions not implicating a security that is traded on a national exchange.[9]

§ 10.04 Controlling Person Liability

Section 15 of the Securities Act imposes joint and several liability on any person who controls a person liable under § 11 or § 12 "unless the controlling person had no knowledge of or reasonable grounds to believe in the existence of the facts by reason of which the liability of the controlled person is alleged to exist." Section 20(a) of the Exchange Act provides that "every person who . . . controls any person liable under any provision of this title . . . shall also be liable jointly and severally with and to the same extent as such controlled person to any person to whom such controlled person is liable, unless the controlling person acted in good faith and did not directly or indirectly induce the act or acts constituting the violation or cause of action." As has been pointed out, "[t]he reason for this difference in language is hard to fathom, especially since § 15 of the 1933 Act was amended in the bill which enacted the 1934 Act, and harder still to interpret."[10]

The term "control" is not defined in the Securities Acts. Pursuant to Rule 405, however, the Commission has defined the term to encompass "the possession, direct or indirect, of the power to direct or cause the direction of the management and policies of a person." The courts generally are in accord with this standard. For example, as stated by one appellate court, control was established when the defendant "had the requisite power to directly or indirectly control or influence corporate policy."[11] Or, as stated by the Seventh Circuit: "We have looked to whether the alleged control person actually participated in, that is, exercised control over, the operations of the person in general and, then to whether the alleged control person possessed the power or ability to control the specific transaction or activity upon which the primary violation was predicated, whether or not that power was exercised."[12]

As set forth above, § 20(a) absolves the controlling person of liability if he/she acted in good faith and did not directly or indirectly induce the violation. The statutory language places the burden of proof on the controlling person to establish the good

---

9. For decisions focusing in *Janus Capital* and its ramifications, *see, e.g.*, Birdthistle, *The Supreme Court's Theory of the Fund*, 37 J. CORP. L. 771 (2012); Gillman, *Scope of Primary Liability Under Section 10(b) of the Exchange Act and SEC Rule 10b-5 Following Janus Capital Group*, 40 SEC. REG. L. J. 269 (2012); Poser, *Janus Revisited: The Lower Courts Wrestle with a Troubling Supreme Court Decision*, 45 REV. SEC. & COMM. REG. 211 (2012).

10. *See* R. JENNINGS, H. MARSH, & J. COFFEE, SECURITIES REGULATION 1131 (7th ed. 1992).

11. *G.A. Thompson & Co., Inc. Partridge*, 636 F.2d 945, 958 (5th Cir. 1981).

12. *Harrison v. Dean Witter Reynolds, Inc.*, 974 F.2d 873, 881 (7th Cir. 1992).

faith defense. This view has been widely adopted. However, some courts require the complainant to plead "culpable conduct," signifying that the plaintiff must "show that the controlling person was in some meaningful sense a culpable participant" in the securities violation perpetrated by the controlled person—for example, that the controlling person's inaction, such as that a failure adequately to supervise the primary violator "was deliberate and done intentionally to further the fraud."[13]

With respect to the state of mind required to establish liability, the Supreme Court in *Hochfelder* stated that the controlling person provision "contains a state-of-mind condition requiring something more than negligence."[14] According to some courts, plaintiffs alleging a § 20(a) claim "must plead facts showing either conscious misbehavior or recklessness."[15]

In summary, a minority of courts have adopted the "culpable participant" test, requiring the plaintiff to establish that the defendant's conduct, such as lack of supervision, "was deliberate and done intentionally to further the fraud."[16] On the other hand, the apparent majority of courts have adopted a more remedial interpretation. For example, more than 25 years ago, the Second Circuit opined that, in the brokerage house setting, the controlling person must show that "it has maintained and enforced a reasonable and proper system of supervision and internal control over sales personnel."[17]

Haynes v. Anderson & Strudwick, Inc.

United States District Court, Eastern District of Virginia

508 F. Supp. 1303 (1981)

WARRINER, DISTRICT JUDGE.

This consolidated action involves alleged federal securities laws violations. Specifically, plaintiffs Stuart E. Haynes, Jr. (Haynes, Jr.) and Stuart E. Haynes, Sr. (Haynes, Sr.) claim that defendants Anderson & Strudwick, Inc. (Anderson & Strudwick), a Virginia broker-dealer, and Thomas V. Blanton, Jr. (Blanton), a former

---

13. *SEC v. First Jersey Securities, Inc.,* 101 F.3d 1450, 1472 (2d Cir. 1996); *Sharp v. Coopers & Lybrand,* 649 F.2d 175, 185 (3d Cir. 1981).

14. 425 U.S. at 209.

15. *In re Vivendi Universal,* S.A., 381 F. Supp. 2d 158, 189 (S.D.N.Y. 2003).

16. *Sharp v. Coopers & Lybrand,* 649 F.2d 175, 185 (3d Cir. 1981). In a subsequent case, the Third Circuit may have relaxed this test, opining that "[t]he complaint contains no factual support for the conclusion that the [brokerage] firm knew *or should have known* of the [the broker's] misconduct or that any failure to adequately supervise him was to further the fraud." *Ash v. Ameritreat, Inc.,* 189 F.3d 463 (3d Cir. 1999) (emphasis supplied). *See also, SEC v. J.W. Barclay & Co., Inc.,* 442 F.3d 834, 841 n. 8 (3d Cir. 2006).

17. *Marbury Management, Inc. v. Kohn,* 629 F.2d 705, 716 (2d Cir. 1980). More recent Second Circuit case law may be read as requiring that the controlling person's culpability be part of the complainant's prima facie case, thereby implicitly overruling *Marbury Management. See, e.g., In re Lehman Brothers Mortgage-Backed Securities Litigation,* 650 F.3d 167 (2d Cir. 2011).

employee of Anderson & Strudwick, violated [among other provisions] § 10(b) [of] the 1934 Act. . . .

I.

Briefly stated, plaintiffs, in their Complaint, make the following allegations which will be accepted as true for present purposes. In September, 1978, plaintiffs consulted Blanton concerning the purchase of stock in Shoney's, Inc. (Shoney's), and they placed orders with Blanton to purchase specified amounts of Shoney's stock. Upon receipt of their transaction statements in October 1978, plaintiffs learned that Blanton had purchased Shoney's stock in excess of the orders and, in addition, had purchased shares in C.H.B. Foods, Inc. (C.H.B.), for plaintiffs, along with shares in Sierracin Corporation for Haynes, Sr. . . . Upon plaintiffs learning of this transaction, Blanton persuaded them to retain the C.H.B. stock, informing them on the basis of what plaintiffs alleged to be inside information that the price was certain to go up as a result of the imminent takeover of C.H.B. by General Foods Corporation (General Foods). In reliance upon Blanton's advice and representations, plaintiffs retained the C.H.B. stock and requested Blanton to purchase additional shares of C.H.B.

In November, 1978, Blanton solicited plaintiffs to purchase additional shares of C.H.B. Again, in reliance upon Blanton's information, plaintiffs directed Blanton to do so. Haynes, Jr., also claims that in January, 1979, Blanton began making unauthorized purchases of C.H.B. stock on behalf of Haynes, Jr. [He] instructed Blanton not to purchase additional shares of C.H.B. stock because he would not pay for them. Haynes, Jr. was assured by Blanton that it would not be necessary for Haynes, Jr. to pay for the purchases.

When the General Foods acquisition of C.H.B. had not materialized by January 1979, plaintiffs determined to sell their shares of C.H.B. and instructed Blanton accordingly. Blanton again represented to plaintiffs that the acquisition was going to take place and that an increase in the value of the C.H.B. stock was certain. In addition, Blanton disclosed to Haynes, Jr., that he owned several thousand shares of C.H.B. stock himself, so that there was no need for Haynes, Jr., to be concerned. Plaintiffs claim that ultimately Blanton refused to sell their shares of C.H.B. stock.

The takeover of C.H.B. by General Foods did not materialize and in February, 1979, the Securities and Exchange Commission suspended trading in C.H.B. stock. As a result, the price of C.H.B. stock diminished substantially, causing plaintiffs to suffer damages. [The SEC and the U.S. Department of Justice subsequently brought actions that were successful based on stock manipulation.] Plaintiffs claim that throughout the various discussions with and solicitations by Blanton, they were unaware that Blanton's representations concerning C.H.B. were untrue.

II.

Anderson & Strudwick's initial ground for dismissal is that the Complaint's recitation of federal securities law violations fails to mention any involvement by Anderson & Strudwick. Anderson & Strudwick asserts that the only specific conduct and statements plaintiffs allege as violating § 10(b) and Rule 10b-5 are the alleged conduct and statements of Blanton. It is Anderson & Strudwick's contention, then, that from the Complaint the only basis for its liability is under the common law doctrine of respondeat superior. Anderson & Strudwick argues, however, that the doctrine of respondeat superior [as construed by the Fourth Circuit] was supplanted in the federal securities laws by Congress' enactment of "controlling person" provisions in both the 1933 Act and the 1934 Act. Since plaintiffs have failed to state a cause of action under the appropriate controlling person provision, § 20(a) of the 1934 Act, Anderson & Strudwick contends that plaintiffs' Complaint should be dismissed as to the broker-dealer. Plaintiffs, on the other hand, apparently contend that Anderson & Strudwick is subject to liability under . . . § 20(a), the controlling person provision. . . .

. . . With the enactment of § 15 of the 1933 Act and § 20(a) of the 1934 Act, Congress created a new class of defendants in securities cases—those "controlling persons" who could potentially evade liability for securities law violations by exercising their power through "dummy" corporations or by creating some other legal barrier. . . . Controlling persons, such as officers, directors and stockholders had theretofore been unavailable to suit by investors. Thus, the investing public's remedy for violations of the 1933 and 1934 Acts was expanded by the adoption of § 15 and § 20(a), respectively.

The problem encountered with the controlling person liability under § 15 was that it, too, was absolute. Apparently upon the insistence of officers and directors of brokerage firms, § 15 was amended in 1934 to provide a defense to controlling persons where they "had no knowledge of or reasonable ground to believe in the existence of facts" to support a securities law violation. Section 20(a) of the 1934 Act was enacted with a similar defense of "good faith."

. . . The defense [to controlling person liability] should be applied on a sliding scale so that what may be good faith in one case may not necessarily constitute good faith in another. As one commentator has suggested:

> the exculpating standard should be applied with varying degrees of stringency according to the circumstances of the individual case, so as best to accommodate the conflicting interests of the investing public and the business community.

. . . .

For example, the courts are in general agreement that a more stringent supervisory duty should be imposed upon a broker-dealer than upon an officer or director. . . . Thus, in practice it will be more difficult for a broker-dealer to exculpate himself using the good faith defense than for an officer or director. This would seem to be entirely appropriate since the broker-dealer is usually in a better position to prevent the violation of the securities laws. Of course, the courts will also want to take other circumstances into account, such as the egregiousness of the violation, its duration, the agent's experience with the company, evidence of lax applications of safeguards and the like. Admittedly, an investor does not have the same access to the deep pockets of the broker-dealer under § 20(a) and § 15 as he would have had under common law agency principles. Nevertheless, "[i]t is . . . difficult to imagine how a brokerage firm could reasonably argue that an ostrich-head-in-the-sand approach satisfies the requirement of good faith under section 20(a). . . ."

. . . [T]he Court finds that plaintiffs have sufficiently alleged claims for relief against Anderson & Strudwick under § 20(a) of the 1934 Act. Plaintiffs have alleged that Blanton violated § 10(b) of the 1934 Act and Rule 10b-5 promulgated thereunder and that:

> [a]t all times pertinent to the allegations herein, defendant Blanton was in the employ of and under the control of Anderson & Strudwick as a sales representative and was engaged in effecting sales of securities.

. . . This is all that is required to state a claim under § 20(a). . . . The burden of asserting and proving the defense of good faith is on Anderson & Strudwick. . . .

Anderson & Strudwick contends that the allegations are insufficient under § 20(a) because plaintiffs have failed to allege "culpable behavior" on the part of the brokerage firm. . . .

. . . [O]ther courts have . . . held that the burden of proof as to the good faith defense is on the controlling person. Were it otherwise, good faith would not be a defense; its absence would be an element of a § 20(a) cause of action. Since it is not an element of § 20(a), Anderson and Strudwick's argument is untenable. . . .

Note

A number of federal appellate decisions have construed the concept of control person liability under the securities laws. For example, in *Hollinger v. Titan Capital Corp.*, 914 F.2d 1564, 1575–1576 (9th Cir. 1990) (en banc), the Ninth Circuit rejected the assertion that the plaintiff has the burden to establish a broker-dealer's "culpable participation" under the controlling person provisions. Rather, joining the apparently majority position held by the lower federal courts, the Ninth Circuit opined: "According to the statutory language [of § 20(a)], once the plaintiff establishes that the defendant is a 'controlling person,' then the defendant bears the burden of proof to show his good faith." Elaborating, the court reasoned:

> [A] broker-dealer controls a registered representative for the purposes of § 20(a). By recognizing this control relationship, we do not mean that a broker-dealer is vicariously liable under § 20(a) for all actions taken by its registered representatives. Nor are we making the broker-dealer the "insurer" of its representatives . . . . The mere fact that a controlling person relationship exists does not mean that vicarious liability necessarily follows. Section 20(a) provides that the "controlling person" can avoid liability if she acted in good faith and did not directly or indirectly induce the violations. By

making the good faith defense available to controlling persons, Congress was able to avoid what it deemed to be an undesirable result, namely that of insurer's liability, and instead it made vicarious liability under § 20(a) dependent upon the broker-dealer's good faith.

Contrary to the district court's ruling, the broker-dealer cannot satisfy its burden of proving good faith merely by saying that it has supervisory procedures in place, and therefore, it has fulfilled its duty to supervise. A broker-dealer can establish the good faith defense only by proving that it "maintained and enforced a reasonable and proper system of supervision and internal control." . . .

Another major appellate decision on this subject is *Harrison v. Dean Witter Reynolds, Inc.*, 974 F.2d 873, 876–881 (7th Cir. 1992). Adhering to the prevailing approach, the Seventh Circuit rejected the "culpable participant" test under the controlling person provisions. Surveying its prior decisions in this area, the court set forth the following standards:

The district court based its grant of summary judgment on the proposition of law that under Section 20(a) of the 1934 Act the plaintiff must show "the defendant exercised some control over the wrongdoer with respect to the wrongful acts." . . . This is known as the "culpable participant" requirement or test. . . .

In applying the culpable-participant test . . . the district court used a test we have never approved, a test, the rigors of which contravene our prior holdings, and a test expressly overruled, en banc, by the Court of Appeals for the Ninth Circuit in *Hollinger*. . . .

Clearly, we have never approved or used the culpable-participant test, nor have we ever used any similar test to so stingily limit the definition of control person. . . .

We have long viewed the statute as remedial, to be construed liberally, and "requiring only some indirect means of discipline or influence short of actual direction to hold a control person liable." . . . *We have looked to whether the alleged control-person actually participated in, that is, exercised control over, the operations of the person in general and, then, to whether the alleged control-person possessed the power or ability to control the specific transaction or activity upon which the primary violation was predicated, whether or not that power was exercised.* [emphasis added]

Here Harrison alleged and Dean Witter has not disputed that Dean Witter is a broker-dealer and that Kenning and Carpenter were its employees—[Kenning] as a registered representative, vice president, and account executive and [Carpenter] as a registered representative and Kenning's assistant. Additionally, both had assigned office-space at the Boca Raton branch of Dean Witter, a local, office telephone number, an "800" telephone number, and "Dean Witter" business cards, among other indicia of authority. . . .

The alleged facts are sufficient to prevent our finding as a matter of law, either that Dean Witter did not actually exercise control over the operations of Kenning and Carpenter in general or that Dean Witter did not possess the power or ability to control Kenning and Carpenter's transactions upon which the primary violation is predicated. Accordingly, it was error to grant Dean Witter's motion for summary judgment on the basis that Dean Witter was not a controlling person. We leave that determination to the fact finder.

But the analysis does not end here. The statute provides an affirmative defense for controlling persons, one which the defendant bears the burden of proving. . . . Section 20(a) of the 1934 Act provides that a controlling-person defendant is not liable if the defendant can show he or she "acted in good faith and did not directly or indirectly induce the act or acts constituting the violation or cause of action." . . . Thus, once controlling-person status is shown, "a broker-dealer would be liable for its employee's acts under Section 20(a) if it did not maintain a reasonably adequate system of internal supervision and control over the [registered representative] or did not enforce with any reasonable diligence such system . . ."

The alleged facts indicate Dean Witter had rules in place to prevent various types of fraud. For example, . . . the rules required that supervisors ensure an employee's investments were commensurate with his or her resources. Indeed, on more than one occasion the head of Dean Witter's compliance department asked the local branch manager to investigate the heavy volume in Carpenter's account. He did ask Carpenter and Kenning about it, but apparently accepted without further investigation Carpenter's explanation that it was his own money [when it was actually his client's money]. . . . As it turned out, the two lost some $600,000 in roughly their first year at Dean Witter and some $2,000,000 over the ensuing two years without attracting, what they might consider, unwarranted attention. Under the alleged facts of the present case we cannot say, as a matter of law, that Dean Witter acted in good faith and neither directly nor indirectly induced the act or acts constituting the violation. This determination, too, must be left to the fact finder.[18]

Another inquiry is the extent to which the Private Securities Litigation Reform Act's (PSLRA) proportionate liability regimen applies for determining the extent of

---

18. *See* Carson, *The Liability of Controlling Persons Under the Federal Securities Acts*, 72 Notre Dame L. Rev. 263 (1997); Kuehnle, *Secondary Liability Under the Federal Securities Laws — Aiding and Abetting, Conspiracy, Controlling Person and Agency: Common Law Principles and the Statutory Scheme*, 14 J. Corp. L. 313 (1988); Poor & Reed, *The "Control" Quagmire: The Cumbersome Concept of "Control" for the Corporate Attorney*, 44 Sec. Reg. L.J. 101 (2016); Comment, *Control Person Liability: A Repudiation of Culpable Participation*, 37 J. Corp. L. 929 (2012).

liability and (damages) of control persons under § 20(a). In *LaPerriere v. Vesta Insurance Group*, 526 F.3d 715 (11th Cir. 2008), the Eleventh Circuit held that the "PSLRA mandates that joint and several liability of a controlling person with a controlled person primary violator . . . cannot be imposed unless the controlling person has itself knowingly committed a violation of the securities laws. In the absence of such a finding, . . . only proportionate liability [against the controlling person] may be imposed."[19]

As a final point, note that the SEC today may bring enforcement actions based on a control person's violation of § 20(a). Prior to the enactment of the Dodd-Frank Act of 2010, lower courts were divided on this question. By amending § 20(a), § 929P(c) of the Dodd-Frank Act provides this clear authority to the SEC.

---

§ 10.05 Respondeat Superior Liability

In light of the Supreme Court's decision in *Central Bank of Denver*, is *respondeat superior* a viable basis to impose liability under the federal securities laws? Thus far, the lower federal courts generally have held that *respondeat superior* survives.

Nonetheless, one view posits that the *Central Bank* analysis forecloses *respondeat superior* liability. Indeed, Justice Stevens' dissent supports this position. In a decision prior to *Central Bank*, the Fourth Circuit reasoned against the imposition of *respondeat superior* under the federal securities laws, stating:

> Noteworthy in each [controlling person] provision is the inclusion of a defense from liability based on "good faith" or lack of knowledge or reasonable belief. When originally passed by Congress, § 15 of the 1933 Act held controlling persons absolutely liable for § 11 and § 12 violations by controlled persons. Congress, in passing the 1934 Act, amended § 15 of the earlier Act, adding the language beginning at "unless the controlling person had no knowledge of or reasonable ground to believe in the existence of facts by reason of which the liability of the controlled person is alleged to exist." Likewise, the controlling person provision in the [1934] Act, § 20(a), contained the "good faith" defense to liability. Clearly Congress had rejected an insurer's liability standard for controlling persons in favor of a . . . duty to take due care. . . . The intent of Congress reflected a desire to impose liability only on those who fall within its definition of control. . . .

---

19. As set forth in Rapp, *Proportionate Liability of Controlling Persons? The Problematic Integration of the Private Securities Litigation Reform Act and Securities Exchange Act § 20(a)*, 37 Sᴇᴄ. Rᴇɢ. L.J. 93, 94 (2009). *See* Consenza, *Do the PSLRA's Proportionate Liability Provisions Govern Section 20 Control Person Liability?*, 36 Sᴇᴄ. Rᴇɢ. L.J. 268 (2008).

The most obvious manner in which to establish liability as a controlling person is to prove that a person acted under the direction of the controlling person. This most commonly occurs in an employer-employee relationship. The lack of such a relationship is not determinative, however. . . . In order to satisfy the requirement of good faith it is necessary for the controlling person to show that some precautionary measures were taken to prevent an injury caused by an employee. . . .

The primary duty owed by a broker-dealer to the public is to supervise its employees in an adequate and reasonable fashion. While the standards of supervision may be stringent, this does not create absolute liability for every violation of the securities laws committed by a supervised individual. . . . It is required of the controlling person only that he maintain an adequate system of internal control, and that he maintain the system in a diligent manner.[20]

In cases handed down prior to the Supreme Court's *Central Bank of Denver* decision, the overwhelming majority of appellate courts held that *respondeat superior* liability was appropriate under the federal securities laws. These courts reasoned that the controlling person provisions were enacted by Congress to supplement common law agency principles in order to reach individuals (such as intermediate and upper-level supervisors) who had no agency or employment relationship with the primary violator. As to the entity, the imposition of *respondeat superior* liability was proper. *See, e.g., Henricksen v. Henricksen*, 640 F.2d 880 (7th Cir. 1981); *Paul F. Newton & Co. v. Texas Commerce Bank*, 630 F.2d 1111 (5th Cir. 1980); *Marbury Management, Inc. v. Kohn*, 629 F.2d 705 (2d Cir. 1980).

In a Ninth Circuit *en banc* decision, *Hollinger v. Titan Capital Corporation*, 914 F.2d 1564, 1576–1578 (9th Cir. 1990) (en banc), the court reasoned:

Appellants also claim on appeal that the district court erred in granting summary judgment to Titan on appellant's claim that Titan was secondarily liable for Wilkowski's § 10(b) violation under the common law theory of *respondeat superior*. . . . [W]e now join several other circuits in holding that § 20(a) was intended to supplement, and not to supplant, the common law theory of *respondeat superior* as a basis for vicarious liability in securities cases.

In our earlier cases, we had concluded, without much explanation, that § 20(a) supplanted the doctrine of *respondeat superior*. . . .

After reexamination of the issue as an en banc court, we are now satisfied that "the 'controlling person' provision of Section 20(a) was not intended to supplant the application of agency principles in securities cases, and that it was enacted to expand rather than to restrict the scope of liability under the securities laws." . . . Section 20(a), which was modeled after the controlling

20. *Carpenter v. Harris, Upham & Co., Inc.*, 594 F.2d 388, 393–394 (4th Cir. 1979).

person provision of § 15 of the Securities Act of 1933, was intended to "prevent evasion" of the law "by organizing dummies who will undertake the actual things forbidden." In other words § 20(a) was intended to impose liability on controlling persons, such as controlling shareholders and corporate officers, who would not be liable under *respondeat superior* because they were not the actual employers. Thus, in enacting § 20(a), Congress expanded upon the common law, and in doing so, created a defense (the good faith defense) that would be available only to those who, under common law principles of *respondeat superior*, would have faced no liability at all.

Only if both *respondeat superior* and § 20(a) are available is the statutory scheme comprehensive and the public protected by the federal securities laws. "To allow a brokerage firm to avoid secondary liability simply by showing ignorance, purposeful or negligent, of the acts of its registered representative contravenes Congress' intent to protect the public, particularly unsophisticated investors, from fraudulent practices." . . . When both remedies are available, then the agent who personally committed the wrong is primarily liable (based on proof of his actions or omissions, and on scienter when required); the [employer] who acts through the agent (assuming the agent is acting within the scope of his agency) is secondarily liable [under *respondeat superior*], and other persons who are not subject to *respondeat superior* but who nevertheless control the wrongdoer can be held liable under § 20(a). Because the liability of persons under § 20(a) represents an extension of liability, beyond that imposed by the common law, such persons are afforded statutory defenses not available in the principal-agent context. Controlling persons may thus avoid liability under § 20(a) by demonstrating that they acted in "good faith" within the meaning of that section.

More recent decisions continue to recognize *respondeat superior* principles in the federal securities law setting.[21] The following case serves as a post-*Central Bank* example of this position.

---

21. *See, e.g., In re Tronox, Inc. Securities Litigation,* [2010–2011 Transfer Binder] Fed. Sec. L. Rep. (CCH) ¶ 96,001 (S.D.N.Y. 2011); *In re Parmalat Securities Litigation,* 640 F. Supp. 2d 243, 594 F. Supp. 2d 444 (S.D.N.Y. 2009); *In re Brocade Securities Litigation,* 2008 U.S. Dist. LEXIS 38885 (N.D. Cal. 2008). For further discussion, *see, e.g.,* Ferrara & Sanger, *Derivative Liability in Securities Law: Controlling Person Liability, Respondeat Superior, and Aiding and Abetting,* 40 Wash. & Lee L. Rev. 1007 (1983); Musewicz, *Vicarious Employer Liability and Section 10(b): In Defense of the Common Law,* 50 Geo. Wash. L. Rev. 754 (1982).

Seolas v. Bilzerian

United States District Court, District of Utah

951 F. Supp. 978 (1997)

Opinion of WINDER, Chief Judge.

This matter is before the court on Defendant Cimetrix's motion for judgment on the pleadings, or alternatively for summary judgment, on Plaintiff Dr. Waldron K. Seolas' third and eighth claims for relief.

BACKGROUND

Plaintiff has charged Cimetrix with violating § 10(b) of the Exchange Act and Rule 10b-5, and with common-law fraud. . . .

Plaintiff claims that in November or December 1994, Paul A. Bilzerian, acting as an agent for Cimetrix, wrongfully induced Plaintiff and his family to return approximately 215,000 shares of Cimetrix stock back to Cimetrix without monetary consideration. Plaintiff alleges that Bilzerian represented to Plaintiff that he had discovered a discrepancy between Cimetrix shareholder records regarding Plaintiff's holdings and what had been reported in prior filings with the Securities and Exchange Commission. Bilzerian allegedly told Plaintiff that filing corrected SEC reports would not solve the problem. Instead, Plaintiff contends that Bilzerian represented to him that, to protect Cimetrix from an SEC investigation and a decline in the value of Cimetrix stock, Plaintiff and his family would have to return approximately 215,000 shares back to Cimetrix.

Plaintiff now claims that Bilzerian's statements were fraudulent and that he wrongfully induced the transfer of those shares. According to Plaintiff, Bilzerian overstated any possible discrepancy between the shareholder records and the SEC filings, and that if a discrepancy existed, it could have easily been corrected by an amended SEC filing. Plaintiff also contends that there was no danger to Cimetrix whatsoever as a result of such discrepancies. Plaintiff argues that Bilzerian made all of the representations knowing that they were false and for the purpose of pressuring Plaintiff and his family into returning the 215,000 shares to Cimetrix to inflate the value of Bilzerian's own stock options in the company and to use those shares in funding an employee stock option plan without diluting his own interest in Cimetrix.

. . . .

DISCUSSION

. . . .

Cimetrix . . . argues that the Supreme Court's decision in *Central Bank v. First Interstate Bank,* 511 U.S. 164 (1994), extinguishes all forms of secondary or vicarious liability under § 10(b), including liability based on respondeat superior. . . .

Central Bank's Effect on Respondeat Superior

It is well established that § 10(b) implicitly creates a private cause of action against parties who commit a manipulative or deceptive act in connection with the purchase or sale of securities. Before *Central Bank*, it was also well settled that aiding and abetting a § 10(b) violation itself gave rise to a private cause of action under § 10(b). In *Central Bank*, however, the Supreme Court eliminated aiding and abetting liability under § 10(b), holding that § 10(b) "prohibits only the making of a material misstatement (or omission) or the commission of a manipulative act." . . . Section 10(b) liability does not extend "to those who do not engage in the manipulative or deceptive practice, but who aid and abet the violation." . . .

The Supreme Court's primary reasoning in the *Central Bank* decision was that the text of § 10(b) did not provide for aiding and abetting liability. In determining the scope of conduct prohibited by § 10(b) and Rule 10b-5, the text of the statute controls. Thus, because the text of § 10(b) only proscribes "manipulative or deceptive" acts, and "does not in terms mention aiding and abetting," the Court refused to extend § 10(b) liability to a party who did not itself commit a manipulative or deceptive act regardless of whether that party assisted another to commit such an act. This is consistent with the Court's prior rulings concerning attempts by plaintiffs and the SEC to broaden the statute's reach to include conduct not prohibited by § 10(b)'s text. . . .

Besides aiding and abetting liability, a majority of pre-*Central Bank* courts had established that respondeat superior was a viable theory of liability in § 10(b) cases. . . . These courts held that § 20(a) of the 1934 Act, which provides for "controlling person" liability under § 10(b), did not supplant common-law agency principles and was therefore not the exclusive source of secondary liability for § 10(b) violations. Under this view, respondeat superior and other agency theories were valid bases of liability under § 10(b) independent from § 20(a). . . .

Cimetrix now asks this court to extend *Central Bank's* holding to preclude private § 10(b) actions based on respondeat superior. Cimetrix advances the contention that § 10(b) actions "based on respondeat superior and other common-law agency principles" appear "unlikely to survive." 511 U.S. at 200 n.12 (Stevens, J., dissenting). Essentially, Cimetrix argues that a corporation can only be held liable for a § 10(b) violation under the "controlling person" provision in § 20(a).

The court holds, however, that the *Central Bank* decision does not abolish respondeat superior as a theory of liability under § 10(b). The court rejects Cimetrix's position that, because the text of § 10(b) does not specifically mention agency or respondeat superior, the reasoning of *Central Bank* makes these theories of liability unavailable. Unlike the issues in *Central Bank* . . . , the issue in this case—whether respondeat superior is a legitimate basis of liability under § 10(b)—is not a question of defining the scope of affirmative conduct proscribed by the statute. Instead, the issue is "deciding on whose shoulders to place responsibility for conduct indisputably proscribed" by the statute. "The principal is held liable not because it committed some wrongdoing outside the purview of the statute which assisted the wrongdoing prohibited by the statute, but because its status merits responsibility for the tortious actions of its agent." . . .

The Supreme Court's approach in *American Society of Mechanical Engineers v. Hydrolevel Corp.*, 456 U.S. 556 (1982), provides the proper framework to determine whether courts should recognize respondeat superior as a valid basis of liability in § 10(b) cases. In *Hydrolevel*, the Supreme Court confronted a similar issue to the one at hand: whether a principal could be held liable for an agent's violations of the Sherman Act under a theory of apparent authority. As with § 10(b), the text of the Sherman Act does not specifically mention agency as a basis of liability. The Court, however, did not look solely to the text of the Sherman Act in its analysis. Instead, after recognizing that "[t]he apparent authority theory has long been the settled rule in the federal system," the Court inquired whether an agency theory of liability in the context of antitrust statutes was "consistent with the intent behind the antitrust laws" . . . Finding that it was, the Court held that a principal may be held liable for the antitrust violations of its agent. . . . Following this approach, the court will recognize § 10(b) liability based on respondeat superior if such a theory is consistent with the language of and the intent behind the securities laws.

The court finds that the respondeat superior theory of liability is consistent with the language of § 10(b) and the intent of the securities laws to promote full disclosure and discourage fraud in the securities markets. The legislative history supports this finding. . . . So does the conclusion that, by explicitly including corporations in its definition of "person," Congress foresaw that corporations would be held liable under agency principles. As the Third Circuit explained, "in some instances, liability cannot be imposed without reference to agency principles—a corporation can only act through its agents, and therefore only can be bound through application of agency principles." *AT&T*, 42 F.3d at 1431. Indeed, even the Supreme Court, by acknowledging that entities may be primary violators of § 10(b), recognizes the need to apply agency principles to effectuate the purposes of the securities law. The Court stated in *Central Bank*:

> The absence of § 10(b) aiding and abetting liability does not mean that secondary actors in the securities markets are always free from liability under the Securities Acts. Any person or entity, including a lawyer, accountant, or bank, who employs a manipulative device or makes a material misstatement (or omission) on which a purchaser or seller of securities relies may be liable as a primary violator under 10b-5, assuming all of the requirements for primary liability under Rule 10b-5 are met.

. . . If, as the Supreme Court envisions, entities may be held liable under § 10(b) as primary violators, then courts must recognize agency principles . . . ; as stated above, corporations and other entities can act only through their agents.

In sum, "*Central Bank's* discussion of aiding and abetting should not be transplanted into the more settled realm of agency law." . . . Following the Supreme Court's guidance in *Hydrolevel*, the court concludes that the respondeat superior theory of liability in § 10(b) cases is consistent with, and furthers the intent of, the securities laws. Accordingly, Cimetrix's motion for judgment on this issue is denied.

. . . .

Note

How does the concept of collective scienter connect with the doctrine of *respondeat superior*? Consider the following from *Makor Issues & Rights, Ltd. v. Tellabs, Inc.*, 513 F.3d 702, 710 (7th Cir. 2008) (rejecting collective scienter theory):

> The problem with inferring a collective intent to deceive behind the act of a corporation is that the hierarchical and differentiated corporate structure makes it quite plausible that a fraud, though ordinarily a deliberate act, could be the result of a series of acts none of which was both done with scienter and imputable to the company by the doctrine of *respondeat superior*. Someone low in the corporate hierarchy might make a mistake that formed the premise of a statement made at the executive level by someone who was at worst careless in having failed to catch the mistake. A routine invocation of *respondeat superior*, which would impute the mistake to the corporation provided only that it was committed in the course of the employee's job rather than being 'a frolic of his own,' *Joel v. Morrison*, 6 C. & P. 501, 172 Eng. Rep. 1338 (1834), would, if applied to a securities fraud that requires scienter, attribute to a corporation a state of mind that none of its employees had.

---

§ 10.06 Failure to Supervise

In the Matter of Gutfreund, Strauss, and Meriwether

U.S. Securities and Exchange Commission

[1992 Transfer Binder] Fed. Sec. L. Rep. (CCH) ¶ 85,067 (1992)

[This proceeding is contained in Chapter 13.]

Chapter 11

Issuer Affirmative Disclosure Obligations

§ 11.01 Overview

With certain exceptions, there is no affirmative duty for an issuer to disclose material nonpublic information. Despite the unwillingness of the courts and the SEC to recognize such a general mandate, there exist issuer affirmative disclosure requirements in a number of specific circumstances. These circumstances may include:

(1) when SEC rules and regulations require disclosure of specified information;

(2) when mandatory disclosure of forward-looking information is called for by Item 303 of Regulation S-K which pertains to "Management's Discussion and Analysis of Financial Condition and Results of Operation";

(3) when the issuer is purchasing or selling its securities in the markets;

(4) when the information revealed by the issuer contains a material disclosure deficiency at the time that the statement was made; under such circumstances, there exists a "duty to correct";

(5) when the issuer previously has made a public statement that, although accurate when made, continues to be "alive" in the marketplace and has become materially false or misleading as a result of subsequent events; under such circumstances, a "duty to update" may exist;

(6) when material information has been leaked by, or rumors in the marketplace are attributable to, the issuer; and

(7) when selective disclosure of material information has been inadvertently made to investors or analysts, disclosure to the investing marketplace must be promptly made under SEC Regulation FD.

In this regard, the impact of § 409 of the Sarbanes-Oxley Act of 2002 is significant. That statute amended the Exchange Act (see § 13(l)) to require "real time" disclosure by reporting issuers. Such reporting companies must, as the SEC determines by rule, disclose to the public "on a rapid and current basis" any additional information regarding material changes in the financial operations or condition of the subject enterprise. Implementing this directive in 2004, the SEC has developed a more comprehensive framework with respect to "real time" disclosure by Exchange Act reporting companies.

In other situations, the law is less clear with respect to the existence and scope of an issuer's affirmative duty to disclose, such as in the case of "soft" information, merger negotiations, and bad financial news. Moreover, the impact of "safe harbor" provisions with respect to an issuer's disclosure of certain forward-looking information should be addressed in this context. In this regard, see the safe harbors provided by the Private Securities Litigation Reform Act (§ 8.05[C][2]), and by Rule 175 (§ 5.03[B][1]).

In analyzing an issuer's obligations in this setting, the Supreme Court's decision in *Chiarella v. United States*, 445 U.S. 222 (1980), should be kept in focus. There, the Court held that, absent a duty to disclose, silence by a subject party will not incur § 10(b) liability (see § 12.04).

It traditionally has been thought that when an issuer is selling its securities, all material information must be accurately disclosed. This is so even if the pertinent information is not called for by a specific SEC rule or regulation. A number of relatively recent decisions call into question the validity of this position. For example, in *Cooperman v. Individual Inc.*, 171 F.3d 43 (1st Cir. 1999), the First Circuit stated:

Duty to Disclose

Given our determination that the omission of the alleged Board-level conflict [between the chief executive officer (CEO) Amram and a majority of the board of directors] was material, the question remains whether defendants had a duty to disclose this "material fact" in the Company's registration statement.

[T]his court reiterate[s] the well-settled proposition that the "mere possession of material nonpublic information does not create a duty to disclose it." . . . Although in the context of a public offering there is a strong affirmative duty of disclosure, it is clear that an issuer of securities owes no absolute duty to disclose all material information. The issue, rather, is whether the securities law imposes on defendants a "specific obligation" to disclose information of the type that plaintiffs claim was omitted. We thus look to the explicit language of Section 11 to determine whether it imposes on defendants a "specific obligation" to disclose the Board-level conflict that allegedly existed. . . .

[W]e set out the circumstances in which Section 11 imposes a duty of disclosure: Section 11 by its terms provides for the imposition of liability if a registration statement, as of its effective date: (1) "contained an untrue statement of material fact"; (2) "omitted to state a material fact required to be stated therein"; or (3) omitted to state a material fact "necessary to make the statements therein not misleading."

. . . .

Plaintiffs base their claim of nondisclosure on the second and third prongs of the statute. Specifically, plaintiffs claim that: (1) the existence of the Board-level conflict was a material fact required to be stated therein; and (2) disclosure of the Board-level conflict was necessary to make other statements in the registration statement not misleading.

Plaintiffs base their first argument on Regulation S-K, Item 101(a), which identifies some of the information "required to be stated" in registration statements. Item 101(a) requires an issuer, in the context of an IPO, to "[d]escribe the general development of the business of the registrant." Plaintiffs argue that Item 101(a) by its terms "required" the disclosure of the alleged Board-level dispute as to the development of Individual's business. Plaintiffs raise this argument for the first time in a footnote of their appellate brief. By failing to raise the applicability of Item 101(a) in the district court, plaintiffs have waived this argument. "Our law is clear that a party ordinarily may not raise on appeal issues that were not seasonably advanced (and hence, preserved) below." . . . We thus turn to plaintiffs' second argument.

This argument is to the effect that defendants had a "specific obligation" to disclose the Board-level conflict because its omission rendered affirmative statements in the registration statement misleading. In making this argument, plaintiffs point to two sections of the registration statement: (1) the "business model" section, and (2) the "use of proceeds" section.

. . . .

Plaintiffs argue that [the business model section of the prospectus] is materially misleading because it fails to disclose that, at the time the statement was made, Individual's "business model" was the subject of profound disagreement between [the Chief Executive Officer (CEO)] Amram and the majority of the Board. Indeed, according to the complaint, [CEO] Amram's growth through acquisition strategy was directly contrary to the Company's stated "business model" of growing the Company by developing its existing core business. Even accepting these allegations as true—as we must on a motion to dismiss—we conclude that the omission of the conflict between [CEO] Amram and the Board does not render the "business model" section of the prospectus misleading.

In short, the "business model" section of the prospectus, taken as a whole, is true. According to plaintiffs' complaint, the majority of the Board was committed to growing the Company by building on its existing core business. Disclosure of the business strategy supported by a majority of the directors did not obligate defendants also to disclose information about the extent to which each individual Board member supported that model. . . . More specifically, disclosure of the business strategy supported by the majority of the Board did not obligate defendants also to disclose the fact that

[CEO] Amram—a distinct minority of a multi-member Board—opposed that strategy. *[Note that although Amram was a single director, he also was the CEO.]*

The "use of proceeds" section of Individual's prospectus states that a portion of the net proceeds from the IPO will be used for "general corporate purposes," as well as "the acquisition of businesses, services and technologies that are complementary to those of the Company." Plaintiffs argue that this statement is misleading because it fails to disclose that, at the time the statement was made, [CEO] Amram and the Board could not agree on what acquisitions were "complementary to those of the Company" nor on the pace at which such acquisitions should be made. We conclude that the omission of [CEO] Amram's conflict with the majority of the Board did not render the "use of proceeds" section misleading. Like the "business model" section, the "use of proceeds" section of the prospectus is complete and accurate on its face.

First, disclosure of the majority of the Board's intention to use the IPO proceeds for complementary acquisitions did not obligate defendants also to disclose [CEO] Amram's different views concerning the types of acquisitions Individual should pursue. Second, the Company's adherence to the purpose stated in the "use of proceeds" section rendered that section accurate. Indeed, the complaint alleges that [CEO] Amram resigned due to the Board's summary rejection of his proposal that the Company contribute 100,000 shares of Individual stock to Free Spirits Holdings, a non-complementary business combination that [CEO] Amram planned to establish.

In sum, both the "business model" section and the "use of proceeds" section were complete and accurate. Because the omission of the Board-level conflict did not render either section misleading, we agree with the district court that § 11 did not impose on defendants a duty of disclosure.

A more recent decision agrees with the First Circuit's approach, likewise holding that a company's duty to disclose obligation in the registered offering setting is limited. In *J&R Marketing, SEP v. General Motors Corp.,* 549 F.3d 384, 396–397 (6th Cir. 2008), the Sixth Circuit reasoned:

Plaintiffs urge us to impose upon issuers the same duty faced by those who engage in insider trading. When an insider trades in his company's stock, he has a duty to disclose any nonpublic, material information he knows about the company before trading. *See Chiarella v. United States,* 445 U.S. 222 (1980). Plaintiffs claim that we are faced with a similar scenario, where a "person," in this case GMAC, has far superior knowledge and is taking advantage of an uninformed investor.

We reject plaintiffs' invitation to create such a duty on issuers for three reasons. First, the law makes clear what is required. Section 11 and Section 12 impose liability only on those who mislead or misstate in the statements they choose to make. The only duty to speak absent pure silence comes from Section 11 which imposes liability for an issuer's failure to include information "required to be stated" in its registration statement. Plaintiffs have failed to point us to any regulation or statute requiring GMAC to include all nonpublic, material information in its registration statement.

Second, plaintiffs only case regarding insider trading duties applying to issuers does not hold what plaintiffs request we hold. *Shaw v. Digital Equip. Corp.*, 82 F.3d 1194 (1st Cir. 1996) did say that it was "helpful to conceptualize . . . the corporate issuer[] as an individual insider transacting in the company's securities, and to examine the disclosure obligations that would then arise." . . . Despite such helpfulness, however, the First Circuit went on to do what we have done above: look to the statutes and regulations detailing what must be included in a registration statement and determine whether the information plaintiffs claim should have been included falls under those rules. . . .

Third, we have previously rejected such a wide-ranging duty. We have said, "[t]here is no general duty on the part of a company to provide the public with all material information." . . . Indeed, there needs to be "healthy limits" on the duty to disclose. Those "healthy limits" are determined by Congress and the SEC. We are not authorized to impose a wide-ranging duty to disclose anything that a person can allege was nonpublic, material information. . . .

As will be expanded upon in the materials that follow, the courts thus have declined to impose upon corporations a broad duty affirmatively to disclose. Nonetheless, remember that in certain situations SEC rules require that the issuer or registrant affirmatively disclose certain events or transactions.

Problem A

Josie's Restaurants, a publicly held company whose common stock is listed on the Nasdaq Stock Market, is confidentially approached by Natalie's, Inc. Natalie's, a publicly held company with diversified operations, wishes to enter the restaurant business and believes that Josie's is a suitable candidate for a friendly acquisition by means of a merger. After being approached by Natalie's, Josie's requests its investment banker, Abrams Shoe & Kennedy, to undertake a valuation report (relying in part on company-specific internal nonpublic information), looking at such factors as Josie's earnings (past and projected earnings five years into the future), hard assets, cash flow projections, and goodwill. After conducting the study in a five-day period, the investment banker reports to the Josie's board of directors that a price between $23-$25 per share would be a beneficial price for Josie's stock.

Rumors are prevalent in the marketplace that Josie's may be acquired. After the price of Josie's stock increases from $9 to $15 during a three-day period in heavy trading, the Nasdaq's market surveillance personnel calls Josie's general counsel, Balbono, to inquire about the rumors. Balbono replies "no comment" to the Nasdaq personnel. The following afternoon, Josie's issues a press release, stating: "Josie's is not aware of any reason to explain the rapid fluctuation in the price of its common stock." During a three-day period thereafter, Josie's stock decreases to a price of $11 per share.

One week later, Josie's and Natalie's announce a friendly merger proposal whereby Josie's will be merged into Natalie's with Josie's shareholders being cashed-out at $19 per share. Under the terms of the merger proposal, Josie's officers and other high-level employees will retain their positions at slightly higher remuneration levels. At a specially called shareholder meeting, the merger is approved by Josie's shareholders. The investment banker valuation report is not disclosed either in the proxy materials or in any other corporate communication.

Six months later, after the merger is consummated, former shareholders of Josie's bring suit under §§ 10(b), 14(a), and 29(b) of the Securities Exchange Act. What result?

———————

Problem B

You are the outside general counsel for Bambot, Inc. (Bambot), a publicly held company whose stock is traded on the New York Stock Exchange. The company timely filed its most recent Form 10-Q on May 5th.

Among other disclosures made in that Form 10-Q filing, Bambot revealed a pending civil action in which it is named as a defendant. In pertinent part, Bambot, Inc. stated in the filing: "The Company believes that the lawsuit is without merit and is vigorously contesting this action. At this time, the Company believes that the lawsuit will not have a material adverse effect."

On May 29th, Clarence Bambot, the company's founder and chief executive officer, entered the hospital for exploratory tests. Thirty days later, he is still in the hospital.

Moreover, between June 3 and June 24, the company received notification that five of its major customers will not be renewing contracts with Bambot. These contracts all terminate on December 31 and, in aggregate, they account for over twelve percent of Bambot's revenues and profits.

And yet, still, on June 27, Bambot settles the legal action for $95 million. This monetary sum constitutes eight percent of the Company's net assets.

Bambot's management is against making any disclosure of Clarence Bambot's hospitalization, the non-renewal of the five contracts, and the settlement of the lawsuit. What do you advise? Why?

———————

§ 11.02 Real-Time Disclosure

Implementing the directive set forth by the Sarbanes-Oxley Act for the SEC to adopt "a rapid and current" reporting regime with respect to material changes in a subject registrant's financial condition or operations, the Commission promulgated amendments to the Form 8-K. By reorganizing and expanding reportable event requirements within the Form 8-K, registrants have greater responsibility with respect to disclosing particular material events in a timely manner.

Prior to the amendments, Form 8-K disclosure requirements for reportable events were rather limited. Publicly held companies were able to delay the disclosure of many material events until the next periodic report. Since a number of significant disclosures were delayed, certain material events were not timely disclosed. To help correct this problem, the SEC's amendments to the Form 8-K expand the disclosure requirements and shorten the time frame for specified reportable events. *See* Securities Exchange Act Release No. 49424 (2004).

Section 409 of the Sarbanes-Oxley Act requires that "[e]ach issuer reporting under Section 13(a) and 15(d) shall disclose to the public on a rapid and current basis such additional information concerning material changes in the financial condition or operations of the issuer, in plain English, which may include trend and qualitative information and graphic presentations, as the Commission determines, by rule, is necessary or useful for the protection of investors and in the public interest." In accord with § 409, the Form 8-K amendments shorten the filing deadline for companies mandated to disclose a broad array of material events listed within Form 8-K to four business days after the event has occurred. In addition, the Commission adopted a safe harbor to insulate companies from liability under § 10(b) of the Exchange Act if they fail to timely file particular items within the Form 8-K. The specific Form 8-K items covered by the safe harbor are discussed below (*see* note 2 *infra*).

In the Form 8-K amendments, the Commission has categorized the listed items into nine sections. Summarized succinctly, the nine sections are as follows:

Section 1 — Registrant's Business and Operations

Item 1.01 Entry into a Material Definitive Agreement — A company entering into or amending a material definitive agreement, not within the normal course of business, must disclose the date of the agreement, parties involved and their relationship to the company, and a brief description of the agreement's terms and conditions.

Item 1.02 Termination of a Material Definitive Agreement — A company terminating such an agreement must disclose the specifics of the transaction, including, but not limited to, the date of the termination, a brief description of the material circumstances, and any penalty fees.

Item 1.03 Bankruptcy or Receivership — Disclosure is mandated when a receiver or similar authority has been appointed for the subject registrant or its parent enterprise during bankruptcy proceedings or when the government takes control over the company's assets.

Section 2 — Financial Information

Item 2.01 Completion of Acquisition or Disposition of Assets — A subject company or any of its majority-owned subsidiaries must disclose any significant amount of assets that have been acquired or disposed of when not within the normal course of business.

Item 2.02 Results of Operations and Financial Condition — If a subject registrant or any person acting on its behalf makes a public announcement or issues a press release disclosing material non-public information regarding its financial status for a completed quarterly or annual period, generally such registrant must disclose the date of the announcement or release, briefly identify the announcement or release, and provide the text of such announcement or release as an exhibit to the Form 8-K.

Item 2.03 Creation of a Direct Financial Obligation or an Obligation Under an Off-Balance Sheet Arrangement of a Registrant — A company that becomes subject to a material direct financial obligation must disclose the date the obligation began, briefly describe the subject agreement, disclose the amount of the obligation as well as the payment terms and any other material terms of the agreement. If the obligation results from an off-balance sheet arrangement that makes the company directly or contingently liable, the company must also disclose the additional financial liability that may be incurred.

Item 2.04 Trigger Events that Accelerate or Increase a Direct Financial Obligation or an Obligation Under an Off-Balance Sheet Arrangement — A company under a direct financial obligation or an off-balance sheet arrangement that has such obligation accelerated or increased as a result of a triggering event must disclose the specifics of the triggering event, as well as any additional material obligations.

Item 2.05 Costs Associated with Exit or Disposal Activities — When a company commits to an exit or disposal plan, disposes of long-term assets or terminates employees, with respect to which material charges will be incurred pursuant to generally accepted accounting principles, the registrant must disclose the date of the commitment, reasons for the action, and amounts associated with the action that the registrant estimates will be incurred.

Item 2.06 Material Impairments — When a board of directors (or its designees) determines that an asset is materially impaired, the company must disclose the date of the material charge, a description of the impaired assets, reasons for the material charge, and an estimate of the impairment charge.

Section 3 — Securities and Trading Markets

Item 3.01 Notice of Delisting or Failure to Satisfy a Continued Listing Rule or Standard; Transfer of Listing — When a company receives notice regarding material non-compliance with any listing rule or possible delisting, it must disclose the date the notice was received, the rule or standard that the registrant fails to satisfy, and any actions taken by the registrant with respect to the notice. If a company's securities are delisted, it must disclose the date its securities were delisted.

Item 3.02 Unregistered Sales of Equity Securities—A company selling unregistered equity securities must disclose specific information regarding the issuance if such issuance accounts generally for more than one percent of the securities outstanding of the same class.

Item 3.03 Material Modifications to Rights of Security Holders—When a company materially modifies any rights of registered securities, it must disclose a description of the modifications.

Section 4—Matters Related to Accountants and Financial Statements

Item 4.01 Changes in Registrant's Certifying Accountant—A company must disclose when its independent accountant has resigned or been dismissed or when a new independent accountant has been engaged.

Item 4.02 Non-Reliance on Previously Issued Financial Statements or a Related Audit Report or Completed Interim Review—When a board of directors (or its designees) concludes that any previously issued financial statement cannot be relied upon due to error, the registrant must identify the financial statement, the surrounding facts in regard thereto, any discussions with the independent accountant (including the advice given by the accountant), and the circumstances that gave rise to the discovery. Under certain circumstances, the registrant must file the accountant's letter as an exhibit to such registrant's amended Form 8-K.

Section 5—Corporate Governance and Management

Item 5.01 Changes in Control of Registrant—When a change in control of a registrant occurs, a company must disclose the person(s) currently in control, the date and description of the circumstances surrounding the change, and the amount of control that was acquired.

Item 5.02 Departure of Directors or Certain Officers; Election of Directors; Appointment of Certain Officers; Compensatory Arrangements of Certain Officers—When an officer is appointed or a director is elected, the company must disclose his/her name and background, the date of the appointment or election, the committees on which such director will serve and other specified information. When a director resigns, chooses not to be reelected, or is removed due to disagreements with the company, the company must disclose the date the director left, any positions the director held, a brief description of any disagreement that occurred, and any statements made by the director regarding the disagreement.[1]

---

1. For example, the SEC brought an enforcement action against Hewlett-Packard Co. for declining to reveal the reasons for a director's resignation. The director had resigned due to issues raised by the company's investigation of boardroom leaks. *See* CCH Fed. Sec. L. Rep. No. 2278, at 7 (2007). *See generally* Lawton, *H-P Settles Civil Charges in 'Pretexting' Scandal,* Wall St. J., Dec. 8, 2006, at A3; Waldman, Clark & Stecklow, *H-P's Hurd Admits 'Disturbing' Tactics Were Used in Probe,* Wall St. J., Sept. 23, 2006, at A1. With respect to five directors resigning due to disagreement at Affiliated Computer Services, *see* Karnitschnig & Bandler, *A Failed Deal at ACS Sets Off a Board Brawl,* Wall St. J., Nov. 2, 2007, at C1.

On the other hand, when a specified executive officer resigns, retires or is removed, the registrant need only disclose such event and the date thereof. Disclosure is not required concerning the circumstances surrounding the officer's departure. In addition, disclosure is required when the registrant enters into or amends employment and compensation arrangements that are deemed material with specified executive officers.

Item 5.03 Amendments to Articles of Incorporation or Bylaws; Change in Fiscal Year—When a company amends its articles of incorporation, bylaws, or fiscal year-end date, it must disclose the effective date of the amendments and the description of the new provision if the company did not provide such information in its SEC filed proxy or information statement.

Item 5.04 Temporary Suspension of Trading under Registrant's Employee Benefit Plans—No later than four business days after receiving notification that trading of securities in its employee benefit plans has been temporarily suspended, the registrant must provide the specified information called for by Item 504 of Form 8-K.

Item 5.05 Amendments to the Registrant's Code of Ethics, or Waiver of a Provision of the Code of Ethics—A registrant must disclose any amendments to its Code of Ethics and any waivers thereto granted by the registrant.

Section 6 Asset-Backed Securities—The items set forth in Item 6 of Form 8-K apply only to asset-backed securities.

Section 7—Regulation FD

Item 7.01 Regulation FD Disclosure—If an issuer or any person acting on behalf of an issuer selectively discloses any material nonpublic information, Regulation FD (Fair Disclosure) requires the issuer to disclose this information to the public in a timely manner. One way an issuer may publicly disclose this material information is under this Section of Form 8-K. (Regulation FD is covered later in this chapter.)

Section 8—Other Events

Item 8.01 Other Events—A company *may, at its option*, disclose any other information or event not called for by Form 8-K.

Section 9—Financial Statements and Exhibits

Item 9.01 Financial Statements and Exhibits—A registrant must list any financial statement as well as any financial information and exhibits that are filed (or furnished) as part of the subject Form 8-K.

Note

Although the Form 8-K provides a rather detailed list, there is material information within particular items that the SEC does not require a company to disclose pursuant to Form 8-K. For example, under Item 1.02, "Termination of a Material Definitive Agreement," registrants do not have to disclose in the Form 8-K the loss, in the ordinary course of business, of a material contract or a material decline in business relationships with the company's customers. Even though Form 8-K disclosure is not required of this material development, a company must disclose this information in its next Form 10-Q, for example, pursuant to the Management Discussion and Analysis (MD&A) as required under Item 303 of Regulation S-K. Within the MD&A, a company must assess if the loss of a major contract is likely to occur and if so, disclosure will be required due to its material adverse effect on the company.

In not mandating disclosure in Form 8-K of a registrant's loss of a material contract, the Commission believed that such disclosure would create difficulty in determining when the contract terminated and could be used by customers as a negotiation ploy. See Securities Exchange Act Release No. 49424 (2004). Nonetheless, the irretrievable loss of a major contract presumptively is material to investors. Arguably, investors ought to be promptly provided with this information in order to assess whether to purchase, hold, or sell the subject securities.

In addition, the Commission declined to require that a subject company disclose in the Form 8-K the reasons for the resignation or removal of an executive officer. The SEC's rationale was that the revelation of the purported reasons may embarrass the officer or result in a potential defamation suit against the company brought by the officer. *See* Securities Exchange Act Release No. 49424 (2004). Given the importance of an executive officer's resignation and the leverage that institutional investors have to induce issuer disclosure of the reasons underlying the termination, it is surprising that the SEC elected not to mandate a more comprehensive disclosure.

Along with the Form 8-K listed Items, the Commission adopted a safe harbor for selective Items within the Form 8-K to protect against liability under § 10(b) if a company fails to file those particular Items in a timely manner.[2] Note that, although failure to timely file the Form 8-K with respect to these Items will not subject a company to liability under § 10(b), fraud liability may be incurred if the Form 8-K contains any materially false or misleading statement. Moreover, if a company fails to disclose these Items within Form 8-K, the company still may incur liability in an SEC enforcement action under § 13(a) of the Exchange Act (a reporting violation based

---

2. The Form 8-K safe harbor includes:

Item 1.01	Entry into a Material Definitive Agreement
Item 1.02	Termination of a Material Definitive Agreement
Item 2.03	Creation of a Direct Financial Obligation or an Obligation under an Off-Balance Sheet Arrangement of a Registrant
Item 2.04	Trigger Events that Accelerate or Increase a Direct Financial Obligation or an Obligation under an Off-Balance Sheet Arrangement
Item 2.05	Costs Associated with Exit or Disposal Activities
Item 2.06	Material Impairments
Item 4.02(a)	Non-Reliance on Previously Issued Financial Statements or a Related Audit Report or Completed Interim Review (in the case where a company makes the determination and does not receive a notice described in Item 4.02(b) from its independent accountant)
Item 502(e)	Executive Officer Employment and Compensation Arrangements

on negligence) and, in any event, must disclose the information in its next Form 10-Q. Failure to accurately disclose the called-for information in the next Form 10-Q will subject the company to liability exposure under § 10(b). *See* Securities Exchange Act Release No. 49424 (2004).

---

§ 11.03 Impact of the "MD&A" Requirements

With respect to the mandatory disclosure of forward-looking information, Item 303 of Regulation S-K is playing an increasingly important role in requiring such disclosure in certain situations. Indeed, as stated by one noted source, "the MD&A has become a major, if not the major, item of narrative disclosure that is studied, together with the financial statements, for investment decision and analysis purposes."[3] In the following release, the SEC addresses a registrant's disclosure obligations under the "MD&A"—namely, under Item 303 pertaining to "Management's Discussion and Analysis of Financial Condition and Results of Operation."

MD&A Release

Securities and Exchange Commission

SEC Financial Reporting Release No. 36,
6 Fed. Sec. L. Rep. (CCH) ¶¶ 73,192-73,193 (1989)

[At this point, review the MD&A Release contained in § 5.03[B][2].]

In the Matter of Caterpillar, Inc.

Securities and Exchange Commission

Administrative Proceeding No. 3-7692 (1992)

The Commission deems it appropriate and in the public interest that public administrative proceedings be instituted . . . to determine whether Caterpillar Inc. ("Caterpillar") has failed to comply with Section 13(a) of the Exchange Act and Rules 13a-1 and 13a-13 promulgated under the Exchange Act in connection with reports on Form 10-K and Form 10-Q filed with the Commission. . . .

I. FACTS

A. *Respondent*

Caterpillar is incorporated in Delaware and headquartered in Peoria, Illinois, and carries on operations in numerous locations in the United States and around the world. Caterpillar manufactures and markets engines and equipment for

---

3. Schneider, *MD&A Disclosure*, 22 Rev. Sec. & Comm. Reg. 149, 150 (1989).

earthmoving, construction, and materials handling. Its securities are registered with the Commission pursuant to Section 12(b) of the Exchange Act and traded principally on the New York Stock Exchange. Caterpillar has not been the subject of any prior actions brought by or on behalf of the Commission.

B. *Background*

This matter involves Caterpillar's failure in its Form 10-K for the year ended December 31, 1989, and its Form 10-Q for the first quarter of 1990 to comply with Item 303 of Regulation S-K, Management's Discussion and Analysis of Financial Condition and Results of Operations ("MD & A"). Specifically, the MD & A rules required Caterpillar to disclose information about the 1989 earnings of Caterpillar Brazil, S.A. ("CBSA"), its wholly owned Brazilian subsidiary, and uncertainties about CBSA's 1990 earnings.

1. *CBSA's 1989 Results*

Caterpillar has had a Brazilian subsidiary since the 1950's. Nineteen eighty-nine was an exceptionally profitable year for CBSA. That year, without accounting for the effect of integration, CBSA accounted for some 23 percent of Caterpillar's net profits of $497 million, although its revenues represented only 5 percent of the parent company's revenues. In 1989, CBSA's operating profit was in line with prior years but a number of nonoperating items contributed to greater than usual overall profit. Those items included currency translation gains, export subsidies, interest income, and Brazilian tax loss carry-forwards. Many of these gains were caused by the hyperinflation in Brazil in 1989 and the fact that the dollar-cruzado exchange rate lagged behind inflation.

CBSA's financial results were presented on a consolidated basis with the remainder of Caterpillar's operations. Thus, the impact of CBSA's operations on Caterpillar's overall results was not apparent from the face of Caterpillar's financial statements or the notes thereto. [emphasis supplied]

2. *Management's View of CBSA*

Caterpillar was and is a highly integrated organization. Its various divisions and subsidiaries were, and are, very interdependent. . . . Because of that management perspective, the profit contribution of each subsidiary or division has not historically been used as a basis for personnel, product sourcing or disclosure decisions.

In January of 1990, accounting department personnel began to separately analyze CBSA's 1989 results compared with its 1990 forecast. In the process of that analysis, the various components of CBSA's results were aggregated. The result of that analysis was conveyed to top management and then to the board. By the middle of February 1990—i.e., at least two weeks before Caterpillar filed its 1989 Form 10-K—Caterpillar's top management had recognized that, to adequately understand Caterpillar's 1990 forecast, it was necessary to understand CBSA's 1990 forecast. Management also recognized that CBSA's future performance was exceptionally difficult to predict—particularly in light of anticipated sweeping economic reforms to be instituted by a new administration in Brazil—and that there were substantial uncertainties whether CBSA would repeat its exceptional 1989 earnings in 1990. . . .

During the interim between the February board meeting and the next board meeting, held on April 11, 1990, a new administration took office in Brazil. Fernando Collor de Mello, who had been elected president of Brazil in December 1989, was inaugurated on March 15, 1990, "putting an end," as one Brazilian business journal put it, "to weeks of intense speculation as to what economic measures he will actually announce." Collor immediately instituted sweeping economic and monetary changes in an effort to bring Brazil's hyperinflation under control. . . .

When the Caterpillar board met on April 11, management gave presentations in which it discussed, among other things, the likely negative effects the Collor plan would have on CBSA's sales and profits. . . .

Throughout April and May of 1990 Caterpillar continued to monitor the events in Brazil and their effects on CBSA, including the consequences of the Collor plan on Caterpillar. After the initial cash flow problems resulting from the Collor plan were resolved, sales dramatically increased, alternative methods of financing sales were devised, and the currency unexpectedly temporarily appreciated. The effects of these changes on CBSA were not immediately clear. However, after a review of April and May results, the company concluded the new economic policies would cause CBSA to suffer significant losses in 1990. It also concluded that those losses would not likely be balanced by gains in other parts of the world and consolidated results would be lower than originally anticipated.

At 8:00 a.m. on Monday, June 25, 1990, before the beginning of trading, the company voluntarily issued a press release explaining that the anticipated results for 1990 would be substantially lower than previously projected. The press release noted that "more than half of the decrease in forecasted 1990 profit is due to a dramatic decline in results for [CBSA]." At 10:20 a.m. the stock opened at 61 3/8, down 2 1/8 points from the previous Friday's closing price. During a telephone conference with stock analysts beginning at 1:00 p.m. on Monday afternoon, with the stock trading at 59 1/4, Caterpillar revealed CBSA's importance to the company's 1989 earnings and indicated that the parent company's disappointing second quarter results were largely a product of circumstances in Brazil. On Tuesday, June 26, the day after the conference call, Caterpillar opened at 51 3/4, down 9 5/8 points from Monday's opening price.

. . . .

4. *Caterpillar's Disclosure Regarding CBSA*

Neither the 1989 Form 10-K nor the first quarter 1990 Form 10-Q indicated the extent to which CBSA had affected Caterpillar's bottom line in 1989, nor did they indicate that a decline in CBSA's future results could have a material adverse effect on Caterpillar's bottom line in 1990. *Because CBSA was not a separately reported business segment, Caterpillar's consolidated financial statements and accompanying notes for 1989 were not required to and did not disclose the disproportionate effect of CBSA's profits on the parent company's profits.* [emphasis supplied]

Nothing in the MD & A section of the 1989 Form 10-K suggested the disproportionate impact of CBSA's profits on Caterpillar's 1989 overall profitability. Similarly, the 1989 Form 10-K and the Form 10-Q for the first quarter of 1990 did not adequately mention management's uncertainty about CBSA's 1990 performance.

II. APPLICABLE LAW

. . . .

A. Management's Discussion and Analysis as Required by Item 303 of Regulation S-K

For reports on Form 10-K, Item 303(a) requires the registrant to discuss the liquidity, capital resources, and results of operations of the registrant and to "provide such other information that the registrant believes to be necessary to an understanding of its financial condition, changes in financial condition and results of operations." Item 303(a) also specifically requires

> [w]here in the registrant's judgment a discussion of segment information or of other subdivisions of the registrant's business would be appropriate to an understanding of such business, the discussion shall focus on each relevant, reportable segment or other subdivision of the business and on the registrant as a whole.

In discussing results of operations the registrant is to "[d]escribe any unusual or infrequent events or transactions . . . that materially affected the amount of reported income from continuing operations and in each case, indicate the extent to which income was so affected." . . . Furthermore, the registrant is to describe other significant components of revenues or expenses that should be described to allow a reader of the company's financial statements to understand the registrant's results of operations. As a separate component of the discussion of results of operations, the registrant is to discuss "any known trends or uncertainties that have had or that the registrant reasonably expects will have a material favorable or unfavorable impact on net sales or revenues or income from continuing operations." . . .

B. The MD & A Release

In 1989, the Commission determined that additional interpretive guidance was needed regarding a number of areas of MD & A disclosure and published an interpretive release. . . . Drawing on earlier releases, the MD & A Release noted the underlying rationale for requiring MD & A disclosure and management's core responsibility in providing that disclosure: The MD & A is needed because, without such a narrative explanation, a company's financial statements and accompanying footnotes may be insufficient for an investor to judge the quality of earnings and the likelihood that past performance is indicative of future performance. MD & A is intended to give the investor an opportunity to look at the company through the eyes of management by providing both a short and long-term analysis of the business of the company.

. . . .

As to prospective information, the MD & A Release sets forth the following test for determining when disclosure is required:

> Where a trend, demand, commitment, event or uncertainty is known, management must make two assessments:
>
> (1) Is the known trend, demand, commitment, event or uncertainty likely to come to fruition? If management determines that it is not reasonably likely to occur, no disclosure is required.
>
> (2) If management cannot make that determination, it must evaluate objectively the consequences of the known trend, demand, commitment, event or uncertainty, on the assumption that it will come to fruition. Disclosure is then required unless management determines that a material effect on the registrant's financial condition or results of operations is not reasonably likely to occur.

Where the test for disclosure is met, "MD & A disclosure of the effects [of such uncertainty,] quantified to the extent reasonably practicable, [is] required."

C. Analysis

1. Overview

Regulation S-K requires disclosure of information necessary to understand the registrant's financial statements. Caterpillar's failure to include required information about CBSA in the MD & A left investors with an incomplete picture of Caterpillar's financial condition and results of operations and denied them the opportunity to see the company "through the eyes of management."

Specifically, by failing (i) in its Annual Report on Form 10-K for the year ended December 31, 1989 to provide an adequate discussion and analysis of the impact of CBSA on its 1989 results of operations as contained in its financial statements, and (ii) to adequately disclose in its 1989 Form 10-K and in its Quarterly Report on Form 10-Q for the first quarter of 1990 known uncertainties reasonably likely to have a material effect on Caterpillar's future results of operations, due to CBSA's questionable ability to repeat its 1989 performance, Caterpillar violated Section 13(a) of the Exchange Act and Rules 13a-1 and 13a-13 thereunder. . . .

Note

The foregoing proceeding involved the entry of a cease and desist order by consent in which Caterpillar agreed to maintain adequate procedures to comply with the MD&A requirements. In view of SEC enforcement activity and the possibility that private litigation in this area would ensue, some observers contended that rigorous interpretation of the MD&A requirements would present a "gold mine" for the plaintiffs' bar. However, in view of the PSLRA providing for an expansive safe harbor for MD&A disclosures relating to forward-looking information and the imposition of rigorous pleading requirements, this prediction has not eventuated.

Note that Item 303 (MD&A) of Regulation S-K has a broader materiality reach than § 10(b) and SEC Rule 10b-5, as well as other remedial provisions, such as §§ 11, 12, and 17(a) of the Securities Act. As stated by one appellate court:

> Because the materiality standards for Rule 10b-5 and Reg. SK-303 differ significantly, the demonstration of a violation of the disclosure requirements of Item 303 does not lead inevitably to the conclusion that such disclosure would be required under Rule 10b-5. Such a duty to disclose must be separately shown [under Rule 10b-5] . . . [W]e thus hold that a violation of [Reg.] SK-303's reporting requirements does not automatically give rise to a material omission under Rule 10b-5. . . .

Oran v. Stafford, 226 F.3d 275, 288 (3d Cir. 2000) (citations omitted). For two more recent appellate court decisions on this subject, compare *Stratte-McClure v. Morgan Stanley and Co.*, 776 F.3d 94 (2d Cir. 2015) (holding that Reg. S-K Item 303 omission may be a Rule 10b-5 material omission if U.S. Supreme Court standard for § 10(b) materiality is met); *In re NVIDIA*, 768 F.3d 1046 (9th Cir. 2014) (opining that Reg. S-K Item 303's standard of materiality is "much broader" than the U.S. Supreme Court's test for § 10(b) materiality and that, accordingly, the disclosure required under Item 303 is not necessarily required under § 10(b)). *See generally* Crawford and Galaro, *A Rule 10b-5 Private Right of Action for MD&A Violations*, 43 Sec. Reg. L.J. 245 (2015). The U.S. Supreme Court has granted a petition for certiorari to determine the § 10(b) liability parameters for an issuer's failure to comply with the disclosure requirements of Item 303. *See Leidos, Inc. v. Indiana Public Retirement System.*

Moreover, note that Caterpillar's MD&A was reviewed by high-level management, including its chief financial officer and legal counsel. As observed by one source: "The fact that the SEC commenced enforcement proceedings against Caterpillar despite such heavy corporate involvement is a strong warning and underscores the need for careful, ongoing MD&A reviews in both annual and quarterly reports." To Our Clients, from Wachtell, Lipton, Rosen & Katz, *SEC Issues Alert on MD&A Disclosures* (April 8, 1992). Sample procedures for MD&A preparation and review are addressed in Olson & Mueller, *MD&A Emerges from the Cocoon*, Insights No. 5, at pp. 2, 6 (May 1992). *See* Croft, *MD&A: The Tightrope of Disclosure*, 45 So. Car. L. Rev. 477, 483 (1994) ("MD&A would not dictate disclosure until the trend, demand, commitment, event, or uncertainty appeared 'reasonably likely to occur.'"); Herlihy & Katz, *Recent Developments Concerning Disclosure*, 1991 M & A and Corp. Gov. L. Rep. 395, 411 (SEC actions suggest "that any contingent event of substantial magnitude should be disclosed in the MD & A even if the likelihood of its occurrence is remote."); Seamons, *Requirements and Pitfalls of MD&A Disclosure*, 25 Sec. Reg. L.J. 239, 240 (1997) ("Subsequent enforcement [after the *Caterpillar* proceeding] demonstrates that the SEC scrutinizes MD&A compliance closely and institutes actions not only against registrants, but also against personnel responsible for preparing such disclosure."). *See also,* Myers, *An Issuer's Duty to Disclose: Assessing the Liability Standards for Material*

Omissions, 30 Sec. Reg. L.J. 153 (2002); Williams, *The Securities and Exchange Commission and Corporate Social Transparency,* 112 Harv. L. Rev. 1197 (1999).

§ 11.04 Duty to Disclose Forward-Looking or "Soft" Information

[A] The Private Securities Litigation Reform Act

The provisions of the Private Securities Litigation Reform Act relating to disclosure of forward-looking information are addressed in § 8.05[C][2].

[B] Safe Harbor for Projections — Rule 175

Safe Harbor for Projections

[See discussion in § 5.03[B][1] of the text.]

A number of courts have construed the parameters of Rule 175. For example, in *Wielgos v. Commonwealth Edison Co.,* 892 F.2d 509, 513–516 (7th Cir. 1989), the Seventh Circuit stated:

> Forward-looking statements need not be correct; it is enough that they have a reasonable basis. In December 1982, when Commonwealth Edison made the estimates that Wielgos challenges, it used the best available information. Wielgos does not say otherwise. . . .
>
> Inevitable inaccuracy of a projection does not eliminate the safe harbor; Rule 175 does not say that projections qualify only if firms give ranges and identify the variables that will lead to departure. Like Form S-3 and the shelf registration rules, Rule 175 assumes that readers are sophisticated, can understand the limits of a projection—and that if any given reader does not appreciate its limits, the reactions of the many professional investors and analysts will lead to prices that reflect the limits of the information. . . . A belief that investors—collectively if not individually—can look out for themselves and ought to have information that may improve the accuracy of prices even if it turns out to be fallacious in a given instance underlies the very existence of Rule 175.
>
> Until 1978, when it adopted Rule 175, the SEC discouraged firms from making projections or commenting beyond the domain of "hard" information, such as last year's sales. . . . It did this because statements about the future are less reliable than statements about the past. If you view investors as easily misled and unable to appreciate the uncertainty of predictions, you

try to keep such information out of their hands. You will not succeed. Investors value securities because of beliefs about how firms will do tomorrow, not because of how they did yesterday. If enterprises cannot make predictions about themselves, then securities analysts, newspaper columnists, and charlatans have protected turf. There will be predictions aplenty outside the domain of the securities acts, predictions by persons whose access to information is not as good as the issuer's. When the issuer adds its information and analysis to that assembled by outsiders, the *collective* assessment will be more accurate even though a given projection will be off the mark.

Convincing the SEC of the utility of projections is one thing, and convincing enterprises that they ought to make projections is another. What's in it for them? If all estimates are made carefully and honestly, half will turn out too favorable to the firm and the other half too pessimistic. In either case the difference may disappoint investors, who can say later that they bought for too much (if the projection was too optimistic) or sold for too little (if the projection turns out to be too pessimistic). Thus the role of a safe harbor: the firm is not liable despite error.

Safe harbors are not necessarily enough. Harbors could be impossible to enter. Suppose the Commission were to require the issuer to reveal all of the data, assumptions, and methodology behind its projections, so that participants in the market could assess them fully and react appropriately. Data could be proprietary, secrets whose revelation to business rivals could damage the firm and its investors. . . . See Roger J. Dennis, *Mandatory Disclosure Theory and Management Projections: A Law and Economics Perspective*, 46 Md. L. Rev. 1197, 1211–18 (1987). . . .

. . . [S]ecurities laws require issuers to disclose *firm-specific* information; investors and analysts combine that information with knowledge about the competition, regulatory conditions, and the economy as a whole to produce a value for stock. Just as a firm needn't disclose that 50% of all new products vanish from the market within a short time, so Commonwealth Edison needn't disclose the hazards of its business, hazards apparent to all serious observers and most casual ones.

If Commonwealth Edison were doing significantly and unexpectedly worse than the industry as a whole—in completing its reactors or in making estimates about their costs—that might signal the presence of important, firm-specific information that it would have to reveal. Wielgos does not contend that either the estimates or the performance of Commonwealth Edison fall substantially below the norms of the industry. . . .

Because the estimates in question have a reasonable basis once they are understood as projecting forward from past experience rather than trying to predict what new things can go wrong, they are covered by Rule 175 unless, by the time Commonwealth Edison used the estimates by selling the stock on the basis of documents incorporating them, they "no longer [had] a reasonable basis." . . . Wielgos observes that by December 1983 a team of employees had developed a different estimate; Commonwealth Edison responds that although the old estimate was stale, the new one was tentative and subject to review by higher echelons before release. *Panter v. Marshall Field & Co.*, 646 F.2d 271, 291–93 (7th Cir. 1981), holds that firms need not disclose tentative internal estimates, even though they conflict with published estimates, unless the internal estimates are so certain that they reveal the published figures as materially misleading. Estimates in progress in December 1983 were not of that character. . . .

Issuers need not reveal all projections. Any firm generates a range of estimates internally or through consultants. It may reveal the projection it thinks best while withholding others, so long as the one revealed has a "reasonable basis"—a question on which other estimates may reflect without automatically depriving the published one of foundation. Because firms may withhold even completed estimates, they may withhold in-house estimates that are in the process of consideration and revision. Any other position would mean that once the annual cycle of estimation begins, a firm must cease selling stock until it has resolved internal disputes and is ready with a new projection. Yet because large firms are eternally in the process of generating and revising estimates—they may have large staffs devoted to nothing else—a demand for revelation or delay would be equivalent to a bar on the use of projections if the firm wants to raise new capital. Rule 175 is designed to release enterprises from such binds.

. . . .

[C] "Puffing," "Attribution," and Statements of "Fact"

Raab v. General Physics Corporation

United States Court of Appeals, Fourth Circuit

4 F.3d 286 (1993)

OPINION OF WILKINSON, Circuit Judge.

In this case, we must address the impact of the securities laws on a company's predictions of its future business prospects. We hold that the prognostications here are not the specific guarantees necessary to make such predictions material, and accordingly, we affirm the district court's dismissal of the complaint.

I.

General Physics Corporation provides personnel training and technical support services to the domestic nuclear power industry. In addition, the company's DOE Services Group provides services to the Department of Energy (DOE) and to the prime contractors who generally manage and operate DOE nuclear weapons production and waste processing sites. In a 1991 public offering, the company sold four million shares; those shares are traded on the New York Stock Exchange.

On February 20, 1992, Goldman Sachs issued a six-page research report recommending the purchase of General Physics' stock. The report cautioned, however, that:

Fourth-quarter results were adversely impacted by a slowdown in the procurement of new contracts by the Department of Energy (DOE). The decision last fall to reduce U.S. nuclear weapons has Congress and the DOE reevaluating the nuclear weapons complex. As a result, the procurement of some contracts has been delayed. General Physics has indicated that the pace of contract awards has increased significantly in recent weeks.

The report does not identify a source for the statement. On that same day, General Physics announced record revenues for 1991. That announcement did not mention the slowdown in fourth-quarter 1991 earnings and first-quarter 1992 earnings.

On March 30, 1992, General Physics issued its 1991 Annual Report to Shareholders and filed its 1991 Form 10-K with the SEC. These documents did not discuss the slowdown in DOE awards. The Annual Report represented that:

(1) "Regulatory changes resulting from [accidents at Three Mile Island and Chernobyl], combined with the rising importance of environmental restoration and waste management, have created a marketplace for the DOE Services Group with an expected annual growth rate of 10% to 30% over the next several years";

(2) "Helping the DOE prime contractors respond to these directives is expected to be an increasing segment of General Physics' business in 1992"; and

(3) "With experienced management, engineers, scientists and technicians in place, the DOE Services Group is poised to carry the growth and success of 1991 well into the future."

In a press release that same day, General Physics announced that first-quarter earnings were likely to be half of analysts' estimates. The company stated that "[t]he lower than anticipated earnings resulted primarily from administrative delays in contract awards by [DOE] and the resultant increased overhead costs associated with retaining professional staff pending contract awards by the DOE," but that it believed "conditions in the 1st quarter are temporary and that results during the remainder of 1992 should be in line with analysts' current projections."

On June 18, 1992, General Physics issued another press release disclosing that second-quarter earnings would be less than expected because of continuing delays in the award of DOE contracts and costs resulting from the need to retain professional staff pending new contracts. On June 19, General Physics' share price fell thirty-six percent, from $9.125 to $5.875.

[This] action was brought on behalf of a class of all purchasers of General Physics stock from February 20 to June 18, 1992. Plaintiffs alleged violations of § 10(b) of the Securities Exchange Act of 1934 and Rule 10b-5, claiming that General Physics artificially inflated its stock price by not disclosing the full impact of the slowdown in DOE contract awards. The district court dismissed the complaint with prejudice, holding that plaintiffs had failed to plead specific facts supporting their allegations of fraud. Plaintiffs now appeal.

II.

Plaintiffs claim that General Physics misled share purchasers through (A) Goldman Sachs' statement that the pace of contracting had increased in the weeks before the February 20 report; (B) the Annual Report's failure to disclose the contracting slowdown's adverse impact on earnings and the Report's predictions of growth for the DOE group; (C) the statements in the March 30 press release that the contracting slowdown was administrative and temporary and the prediction in that press release that earnings would be consistent with analysts' expectations for the final three quarters of 1992. We will address these allegations in turn.

A.

We do not think that plaintiffs have pled the specific facts required . . . from which the Goldman Sachs research report can be attributed to General Physics, and General Physics cannot be held liable for the independent statement of a third party. The complaint alleges that "the report went on to quote General Physics." The report, however, does not quote General Physics. It says only that "General Physics has indicated." More importantly, nowhere does the complaint plead with any specificity who allegedly supplied this information to Goldman Sachs, how it was supplied, or how General Physics could have controlled the content of the statement. The securities laws require General Physics to speak truthfully to investors; they do not require the company to police statements made by third parties for inaccuracies, even if the third party attributes the statement to General Physics. Without control over Goldman Sachs' report, any statement made by General Physics personnel could be taken out of context, incorrectly quoted, or stripped of important qualifiers. Plaintiffs have thus failed to plead facts from which it could be inferred that General Physics exercised the kind of control over the Goldman Sachs report that would render it liable for statements made therein. *See Elkind v. Liggett & Myers, Inc.,* 635 F.2d 156, 163 (2d Cir. 1980) (no liability absent allegations that company "sufficiently entangled itself with the analysts' forecasts to render those predictions 'attributable to it'").

B.

Plaintiffs next attack the 1991 Annual Report's failure to disclose the adverse impact of the contracting slowdown on first-quarter 1992 earnings and its predictions of growth in the market for the DOE group. Plaintiffs claim that General Physics had a duty to reveal the adverse trend for DOE contracts in order to keep its optimistic predictions of future growth from becoming misleading.

We disagree. Omitting the contract slowdown from the Annual Report is not actionable because the contemporaneous press release of March 30, 1992 informed the market of a slow-down in DOE contracting awards. Plaintiffs rely on fraud on the market to establish reliance in this case; unfortunately for them, the presumption that the market price has internalized all publicly available information cuts both ways. The information available to the market included not only the Annual Report, but also the March 30 press release. "[I]n a fraud on the market case, the defendant's failure to disclose material information may be excused where that information has been made credibly available to the market by other sources." . . . The "other source" in this case was the press release; if the contracting slowdown was material, the market was aware of it, and the price of the shares reflected it. . . .

Moreover, the 1991 Annual Report was about 1991's results, not 1992's prospects. The company obviously had a duty to accurately report the 1991 results. But General Physics' accurate reporting of its past results did not then require the company to speculate on the effect that a contract slowdown at DOE in 1992 would have on its future earnings. *See In re Convergent Technologies Sec. Litig.*, 948 F.2d 507, 513–14 (9th Cir. 1991) (rejecting plaintiffs' contention that accurate reporting of past results "misled investors by implying that [the company] expected the upward first quarter trend to continue throughout the year").

Such predictions as General Physics did make in its Annual Report about future growth are hardly material. The statements in the 1991 Annual Report that plaintiffs challenge include "[r]egulatory changes . . . have created a marketplace for the DOE Services Group with an expected annual growth rate of 10% to 30% over the next several years" and "the DOE Services Group is poised to carry the growth and success of 1991 well into the future." "Soft," "puffing" statements such as these generally lack materiality because the market price of a share is not inflated by vague statements predicting growth. . . .

The whole discussion of growth is plainly by way of loose prediction, and both the range of rates cited, as well as the time for their achievement, are anything but definite. No reasonable investor would rely on these statements, and they are certainly not specific enough to perpetrate a fraud on the market. Analysts and arbitrageurs rely on facts in determining the value of a security, not mere expressions of optimism from company spokesmen. The market gives the most credence to those predictions supported by specific statements of fact, and those statements are, of course, actionable if false or misleading. However, "projections of future performance not worded as guarantees are generally not actionable under the federal securities laws." . . . Statements such as "the DOE Services Group is poised to carry the growth and success of 1991 well into the future" hardly constitute a guarantee.

Notwithstanding our holding that the allegedly false predictions here are not material, we recognize that expressions of belief or opinion concerning *current facts* may be material. . . . We do not believe, however, that this materiality extends so easily to opinions on uncertain future events. In *Virginia Bankshares* [501 U.S. 1083 (1991)], the Supreme Court addressed the materiality of directors' statements that a merger price was "fair" and that it offered "high" value to minority shareholders. The Court held that the statements were material because the plaintiffs provided evidence showing that the assumptions offered by the directors to support those conclusions were arguably false. Because these assumptions were false, the "plaintiff [was] permitted to prove a specific statement of reason knowingly false or misleadingly incomplete, even when stated in conclusory terms." Predictions of future growth stand on a different footing, however, because they will almost always prove to be wrong in hindsight. If a company predicts twenty-five percent growth, that is simply the company's best guess as to how the future will play out. As a statistical matter, twenty percent and thirty percent growth are both nearly as likely as twenty-five. If growth proves less than predicted, buyers will sue; if growth proves greater, sellers will sue. Imposing liability would put companies in a whipsaw, with a lawsuit almost a certainty. Such liability would deter companies from discussing their prospects, and the securities markets would be deprived of the information those predictions offer. We believe that this is contrary to the goal of full disclosure underlying the securities laws, and we decline to endorse it.

C.

Finally, plaintiffs challenge the statements in the March 30 press release that the contracting slowdown was "administrative" and "temporary" and that "results during the remainder of 1992 should be in line with analysts' current projections." Plaintiffs contend that these statements were false when made and had no reasonable basis, given the slowdown in the award of DOE contracts.

The district court concluded that "[e]specially given the amorphous nature of these terms and the well-known vagaries of Government contracting, the Court is of the opinion that the plaintiffs have not alleged sufficient non-conclusory facts under Rule 9(b) to show that the statements were false. . . ." We agree. Plaintiffs have alleged no facts showing that General Physics did not believe that these statements were accurate at the time. "Temporary" is an indeterminate term: it could mean weeks, it could mean months, it could mean years. It is not clear from the complaint that there was a misstatement at all, much less a material one. Government contracting is frequently a cyclical enterprise. Analysts and markets were well aware that the end of the Cold War might affect General Physics' business involving weapons production; General Physics had no duty to advise investors of what was already commonly known. . . .

General Physics' predictions about earnings for the latter three quarters of 1992 proved incorrect, but hindsight does not establish fraud. If it did, any drop in the price of shares would result in lawsuits from disappointed investors. The market has risks; the securities laws do not serve as investment insurance. Every prediction of success that fails to materialize cannot create on that account an action for securities fraud. Like the optimistic statements of the Annual Report, the statement that results "should be in line with analysts' current projections" hardly constitutes a guarantee that earnings would be forthcoming in particular amounts; this forecast, like the others, lacks the specificity necessary to make it material.

. . . .

AFFIRMED.

Note

Decisions like *Raab* and others that embrace the "puffery" defense for corporate fiduciaries have been criticized. Professor O'Hare takes the position that courts

> have failed to recognize that an investor probably would not consider a statement made by a company's Chief Executive Officer in a public document — as opposed to an oral statement made by a securities broker in a selling situation — to be mere "sales talk." Even more troubling, the courts have failed to recognize that an investor would likely attach greater significance to a Chairman's assessment of a present fact than to a prediction of a future event. In short, the courts have significantly expanded the scope of a powerful defense to dismiss potentially meritorious securities fraud actions with little or no analysis or consideration of the effect of their decisions.

O'Hare, *The Resurrection of the Dodo: The Unfortunate Re-emergence of the Puffery Defense in Private Securities Fraud Actions,* 59 Ohio St. L.J. 1697, 1699–1700 (1998). *See* Padfield, *Is Puffery Material to Investors? Maybe We Should Ask Them,* 10 U. Pa. J. Bus. & Emp. L. 339 (2008).

For more recent examples, compare *Scott v. General Motors Company,* 605 Fed. Appx. 52 (2d Cir. 2015) (GM's statements that it "aims to" increase profitability and "believes" that it has "improved inventory management" deemed nonactionable puffery), with *Gross v. GFI Group, Inc.,* 162 F. Supp. 3d 263 (S.D.N.Y. 2016) (Company executive's statement that a prospective acquisition candidate presented "a singular and unique opportunity to optimize value" held not puffery).

Raab was decided by the Fourth Circuit, an appellate court in which plaintiffs generally have not fared favorably. *See* Steinberg & Appel, *A Prolonged Slump for "Plaintiff-Pitchers": The "Narrow Strike Zone" for Securities Plaintiffs in the Fourth Circuit,* 88 N. Car. L. Rev. 1923, 1928 (2010) (stating that during the article's 14-year survey span, 1995–Jan 2009, "[o]f the thirty-seven cases surveyed, with near unanimity, defendants were victorious, either on the merits or due to procedural obstacles to plaintiffs").

[D] Mandatory Disclosure of "Soft" Information

Starkman v. Marathon Oil Co.

United States Court of Appeals, Sixth Circuit

772 F.2d 231 (1985)

Merritt, Circuit Judge.

Like *Radol v. Thomas,* 772 F.2d 244 (6th Cir. 1985), this action arises out of U.S. Steel's November, 1981 acquisition and eventual merger with Marathon Oil Company. The plaintiff here, Irving Starkman, was a Marathon shareholder until selling his shares on the open market for $78 per share on November 18, 1981, the day before U.S. Steel's tender offer for 51% of Marathon's outstanding shares at $125 per share was announced. On October 31, 1981, Mobil Oil had initiated its takeover bid for Marathon, a bid which Marathon actively resisted by urging its rejection by Marathon shareholders and by seeking and eventually finding a "white knight" or alternative, friendly merger partner-tender offeror, U.S. Steel. Starkman claims that Marathon's board violated Rule 10b-5 and its fiduciary duty to him as a Marathon shareholder by failing to disclose various items of "soft" information — information of less certainty than hard facts — in its public statements to shareholders during the period after Mobil's hostile tender offer and prior to Steel's friendly tender offer. In particular, he says that Marathon should have told shareholders that negotiations were underway with U.S. Steel prior to the consummation of those negotiations in an agreement, and that internal and externally-prepared asset appraisals and five-year earnings and cash flow projections should have been disclosed to shareholders so that they could make a fully informed choice whether to sell their shares or gamble on receiving a higher price in a possible Steel-Marathon merger.

The District Court granted summary judgment for Marathon, finding that these items of soft information had either been sufficiently disclosed or were not required to be disclosed because their nondisclosure did not render materially misleading Marathon's other affirmative public statements. For the reasons stated below, we affirm the judgment of the District Court.

I. BACKGROUND

. . . .

In the summer of 1981, Marathon was among a number of oil companies considered to be prime takeover targets. In this atmosphere, Marathon's top level management began preparations against a hostile takeover bid. Harold Hoopman, Marathon's president and chief executive officer, instructed the company's vice presidents to compile a catalog of assets. This document, referred to as the "Strong Report" or "internal asset evaluation," estimated the value of Marathon's transportation, refining and marketing assets, its other equipment and structures, and the value of proven, probable, and potential oil reserves as well as exploratory acreage. Hoopman and John Strong, who was responsible for combining materials received from various divisions into the final report, both testified that the Strong Report was viewed as a "selling document" which placed optimistic values on Marathon's oil and gas reserves so as to attract the interest of prospective buyers and ensure that Marathon could either ward off an attempt to capture Marathon at a bargain price or obtain the best offer available.

In estimating proven, probable, and potential reserves and exploratory acreage, the Strong Report was based on information that was not available to the general public, for example in annual reports, because only the value of proven reserves was normally included in such public documents. The Strong Report defined proven reserves as those actually producing, probable reserves as reserves for properties where some production had been established and additional production was likely, and potential reserves as reserves for properties where production had not yet been established but where geologic evidence supported wildcat drilling. These reserves were valued using a discounted cash flow methodology. . . . This valuation method, a standard procedure for determining the cash value of oil and gas properties, required projections of price and cost conditions prevailing as far as 20 years into the future. For example, the Strong Report assumed that the rate of increase in oil prices would average over 9% per year from 1980–1990.

Using this methodology, the Strong Report valued Marathon's net assets at between $19 billion and $16 billion (depending on which set of interest rates was used to discount back to present value), a per share value of between $323 and $276. The value of oil and gas reserves made up $14 billion of the $19 billion estimate and $11.5 billion of the $16 billion estimate. A similar report using identical methodology was prepared in mid-July 1981 by the investment banking firm of First Boston, which had been hired by Marathon to assist in preparing for potential takeover bids. The First Boston Report was based only upon proven and probable oil reserves and was also intended to be used as a "presentation piece" to avoid a takeover or maximize the price obtained in a takeover. It placed Marathon's value at between $188 and $225 per share.

Some perspective on the values arrived at in the Strong and First Boston reports can be gained from other, publicly available appraisals of Marathon's assets prepared during 1981. The Herold Oil Industry Comparative Appraisal placed Marathon's appraised value at $199 per share, and two other reports by securities analysts said Marathon had an appraised value of between $200 and $210 per share.

Marathon's market value, however, was well below these appraised values. On October 29, 1981, Marathon closed at $63.75 per share. The next day, Mobil Oil announced its tender offer to purchase up to approximately 68% of outstanding Marathon common stock for $85 per share in cash. Mobil proposed to follow the tender offer with a going private or freezeout merger in which the remaining shareholders of Marathon would receive sinking fund debentures worth approximately $85 per share.

On October 31, 1981, Marathon's board of directors met in emergency session and unanimously decided that the Mobil offer was "grossly inadequate" and approved a vigorous campaign to persuade Marathon shareholders not to tender to Mobil, and to simultaneously seek a "white knight." On November 11 and 12, Marathon's Board made public statements to the shareholders recommending rejection of Mobil's bid as "grossly inadequate" and against the best interests of the company. . . .

On November 17, Hoopman and David Roderick, [U.S.] Steel's president, reached agreement on the terms of Steel's purchase of Marathon, and, after Board approval, an agreement was signed on November 18, 1981. Under the terms of the agreement, Steel would make a tender offer for up to 31 million shares (about 51%) of Marathon stock for $125 per share in cash, to be followed by a merger proposal in which each remaining Marathon shareholder would receive one $100 face value, 12 year, 12 1/2 per cent guaranteed note per share of common stock. On November 19, Steel mailed its tender offer to Marathon shareholders, and Hoopman sent a letter to Marathon shareholders describing the two-stage deal and stating the opinion of Marathon's Board that the agreement was fair to Marathon shareholders. Steel's offer was successful, with over 91% of the outstanding shares tendered, and the second stage freezeout merger was approved by a two-thirds majority of the remaining shareholders in February, 1982.

II. MARATHON'S PUBLIC STATEMENTS AND DISPOSITION BELOW

. . . .

Starkman argues that the failure of any of [Marathon's] communications to disclose the Strong and First Boston reports and the five-year earnings and cash flow projections constituted an omission of material facts which rendered these communications materially misleading. . . .

In granting summary judgment for Marathon in the present action, [the district court] found that the net asset values stated in the Strong and First Boston reports were perfectly consistent with Marathon's repeated public assertion that Mobil's bid was "grossly inadequate" in light of the true value of Marathon's assets, and that disclosure of the reports was not required under Rule 10b-5 because "disclosure of information which is consistent with other statements made is obviously not necessary in order to make those statements not misleading" . . .

The District Court summarily disposed of the claim that the five-year earnings and cash flow projections should have been disclosed, concluding that disclosure of such information is simply not required. . . .

III. DISCUSSION

A. Introduction

. . . .

Despite occasional suggestions by commentators, see, e.g., Bauman, *Rule 10b-5 and the Corporation's Affirmative Duty to Disclose,* 67 Geo. L.J. 935 (1979), and the courts, *Zweig v. Hearst Corp.,* 594 F.2d 1261, 1266 (9th Cir. 1979), that Rule 10b-5 imposes an affirmative obligation on the corporation to disclose all material information regardless of whether the corporation has made any other statements, the established view is that a "duty to speak" must exist before the disclosure of material facts is required under Rule 10b-5. . . .

B. Assets, Appraisals and Earnings Projections

We first address Starkman's contention that Marathon should have disclosed the Strong and First Boston reports and the five-year earnings projections and forecasts given to [U.S.] Steel.

. . . .

Since there is no SEC rule specifically requiring the disclosure of this information, we must determine whether Rule 10b-5 requires its disclosure as material information, the nondisclosure of which would render misleading other statements made by Marathon. The starting point in this analysis is the underlying regulatory policy toward disclosure of such information, since regulatory rules reflect careful study of general conditions prevailing in the securities marketplace and provide guidelines upon which corporate officers and directors are entitled to rely.

The SEC's policy toward the inclusion of appraised asset valuations, projections and other "soft" information in proxy materials, tender offers and other disclosure documents has undergone a gradual evolution toward allowing the inclusion of such information in some special contexts, provided that the assumptions and hypotheses underlying predicted values are also disclosed.

In 1976, future earnings projections were deleted from a list of examples of potentially misleading disclosures in proxy statements in the note which followed Rule 14a-9. And, effective July 30, 1979, the SEC adopted a "safe harbor" rule for projections, under which a statement containing a projection of revenues and earnings would not be considered to be a materially misleading misstatement or omission for purposes of liability under the federal securities laws provided the statement was prepared with a reasonable basis and was disclosed in good faith.

With respect to asset appraisals, Rule 13e-3 requires disclosure of the information called for by Items 7, 8, and 9 of Schedule 13E-3 in the context of freezeout mergers. Item 8 of Schedule 13E-3 requires disclosure of factors important in determining the fairness of such a transaction to unaffiliated shareholders, and these factors include liquidation value; Item 9 of that same schedule says that a summary of any *outside* appraisal must be furnished, with the summary including a discussion of the procedures and methods of arriving at the findings and recommendations of the appraisal. However, a 1979 SEC-proposed amendment under which an issuer would have to disclose any projection given to an appraisal furnisher was never adopted. . . .

. . . .

Rather than suggesting a duty to disclose the Strong and First Boston reports, however, our cases firmly establish the rule that soft information such as asset appraisals and projections must be disclosed only if the reported values are virtually as certain as hard facts.

. . . .

Our cases fully support a rule under which a tender offer target must disclose projections and asset appraisals based upon predictions regarding future economic and corporate events only if the predictions underlying the appraisal or projection are substantially certain to hold. An example is when the predictions in fact state a fixed plan of corporate activity. If a target chooses to disclose projections and appraisals which do not rise to this level of certainty, then it must also inform the shareholders as to the basis for and limitations on the projected realizable values.

The Third Circuit has enunciated a different test, under which "courts should ascertain the duty to disclose asset valuations and other soft information on a case by case basis, by weighing the potential aid such information will give the shareholder against the potential harm, such as undue reliance, if the information is released with a proper cautionary note." *Flynn v. Bass Brothers Enterprises,* 744 F.2d at 988. The court listed several factors the courts have considered in determining the reliability of soft information, including the qualifications of those who prepared the appraisal, the degree of certainty of the data on which it was based, and the purpose for which it was prepared.

By its very nature, however, this sort of judicial cost-benefit analysis is uncertain and unpredictable, and it moreover neglects the role of the market in providing shareholders with information regarding the target's value through competing tender offers. Our approach, which focuses on the certainty of the data underlying the appraisal or projection, ensures that the target company's shareholders will receive all essentially factual information, while preserving the target's discretion to disclose more uncertain information without the threat of liability, provided appropriate qualifications and explanations are made.

Under this standard, Marathon plainly had no duty to disclose the Strong and First Boston reports, because these reports contained estimates of the value of probable, potential and unexplored oil and gas reserves which were based on highly speculative assumptions regarding the path of oil and gas prices, recovery rates and the like over a period of thirty to fifty years. Disclosure of such estimated values could well have been misleading without an accompanying mountain of data and explanations. There is no reported case actually holding that disclosure of appraised values of oil and gas reserves is required, and several which agree with our decision that such disclosure is not required.

Similarly, Marathon had no duty to disclose the five-year earnings and cash flow projections given to [U.S.] Steel and First Boston. This information does not rise to the level of substantial certainty triggering a duty to disclose.

. . . .

Accordingly, the judgment of the District Court is affirmed.

Note

Do you agree with the Sixth Circuit's approach? Should shareholders and the marketplace be entitled, with appropriate cautionary notes provided, to assess the usefulness of such "soft" information in reaching their investment and voting decisions?

In *Starkman,* the Sixth Circuit observed that the Third Circuit in *Flynn v. Bass Brothers Enterprises, Inc.,* 744 F.2d 978, 985–988 (3d Cir. 1984), held that, depending on the circumstances to be determined on an ad hoc basis, asset valuations and other "soft" information must be disclosed. In *Flynn,* the Third Circuit reasoned:

As a matter of public policy, the SEC and the courts generally have not required the inclusion of appraised asset valuations, projections, and other "soft" information in proxy materials or tender offers. . . . The reasons underpinning the SEC's long-standing policy against disclosure of soft information stem from its concern about the reliability of appraisals, its fear that investors might give greater credence to the appraisals or projections than would be warranted, and the impracticability of the SEC's examining such appraisals on a case by case basis to determine whether they are sufficiently reliable to merit disclosure. . . .

Although the disclosure of soft information has not been prohibited as a matter of law, this Court in the past has followed the "general rule" that "presentations of future earnings, appraised asset valuations and other hypothetical data" are to be discouraged. . . . In failing to require disclosure, courts have relied on a perceived SEC policy favoring nondisclosure of soft information, the lack of reliability of such information, and the reluctance to impose potentially high liability for nondisclosure, even if desirable as a matter of public policy, because the law discouraged nondisclosure at the time of the alleged violation.

In assessing the need to disclose an appraised asset valuation, courts have considered several indicia of reliability: the qualifications of those who prepared or compiled the appraisal; the degree of certainty of the data on which it was based; the purpose for which it was prepared; and evidence of reliance on the appraisal. . . .

Recently, there have been indications that the law, in response to developing corporate trends, such as the increase in mergers, has begun to favor more disclosure of soft information. In this regard, we note that SEC policy—a primary reason courts in the past have not required the disclosure of soft information—has begun to change [and continues to favor disclosure of soft information].

Part of the reason for this shift in policy is recognition of shareholders' need for such information. One rationale for the initial prohibition of soft information was the fear that potential purchasers of securities would be misled by overly optimistic claims by management. . . . An unintended by-product of such concern, however, was to keep valuable information from those shareholders who had to decide, within the context of a tender offer or merger, whether or not to sell their securities. . . . The present spate of proxy contests and tender offers was not anticipated when the SEC initially formulated its policy of nondisclosure of soft information. . . .

In order to give full effect to the evolution in the law of disclosure, . . . today we set forth the law for disclosure of soft information as it is to be applied from this date on. Henceforth, the law is not that asset appraisals are, as a matter of law, immaterial. Rather, in appropriate cases, such information must be disclosed. Courts should ascertain the duty to disclose asset valuations and other soft information on a case by case basis, by weighing the potential aid such information will give a shareholder against the potential harm, such as undue reliance, if the information is released with a proper cautionary note.

The factors a court must consider in making such a determination are: the facts upon which the information is based; the qualifications of those who prepared or compiled it; the purpose for which the information was originally intended; its relevance to the stockholders' impending decision; the degree of subjectivity or bias reflected in its preparation; the degree to which the information is unique; and the availability to the investor of other more reliable sources of information. . . .

Returning to the Sixth Circuit's decision in *Starkman*, the court observed that— in a going-private transaction implicating SEC Rule 13e-3—asset appraisals rendered by outside sources, such as an investment banker, must be disclosed in the Schedule 13E-3. The Sixth Circuit subsequently construed the disclosure parameters of outside appraisals made in going private transactions in *Howing Company v. Nationwide Corp.,* 972 F.2d 700 (6th Cir. 1992), 927 F.2d 263 (6th Cir. 1991), 826 F.2d 1470 (6th Cir. 1987). In *Howing*, the Sixth Circuit opined:

The issuer in this case . . . choose to rely on the expertise of the [investment bank] First Boston. The problem with defendants adopting the First Boston opinion letter as their disclosure to shareholders is that this one-page letter is itself woefully inadequate when measured against the specific disclosure requirements of the Rule. An issuer cannot insulate itself from [Rule] 13e-3 liability by relying on an investment banker's opinion letter which itself does not comply with the specific disclosure requirements of the Rule.

826 F.2d at 1479. *See* Kofele-Kale, *The SEC's Going-Private Rules—Analysis and Developments,* 19 Sec. Reg. L.J. 139 (1991).[4]

---

4. For a comprehensive review of the diverse approaches of the federal appellate courts to disclosure of "soft" information, see Kerr, *The SEC and the Courts' Approach to Disclosure of Earnings Projections, Asset Appraisals, and Other Soft Information: Old Problems, Changing Views,* 46 Md. L. Rev. 1071 (1987). *See also,* Brudney, *A Note on Materiality and Soft Information Under the Federal Securities Laws,* 75 Va. L. Rev. 723 (1989); Dennis, *A Mandatory Disclosure Theory and Management Projections: A Law and Economics Perspective,* 46 Md. L. Rev. 1197 (1987); Hiler, *The SEC and the Courts' Approach to Disclosure of Earnings Projections, Asset Appraisals, and Other Soft Information,* 46 Md. L. Rev. 1114 (1987); Karjala, *A Coherent Approach to Misleading Corporate Announcements, Fraud, and Rule 10b-5,* 52 Alb. L. Rev. 957 (1988); Poole, *Improving the Reliability of Management Forecasts,* 14 J. Corp. L. 547 (1989); Rosen, *Liability for "Soft Information": New Developments and Emerging Trends,* 23 Sec. Reg. L.J. 3 (1995); Rowe, *Projections, Appraisals, and Other Soft Information,* 23 Rev. Sec. & Comm. Reg. 37 (1990); Schneider & Dubow, *Forward-Looking Information— Navigating in the Safe Harbor,* 51 Bus. Law. 1071 (1996).

§ 11.05 Duty to Update

The duty to update may arise in a number of different circumstances. Generally, such a duty may be present when the issuer previously has made a statement that, although accurate when made, continues to be "alive" in the marketplace and has become materially false or misleading as a result of subsequent events. This duty may be implicated, for example, in the context of merger negotiations, disclosure of "soft" information, and responding to rumors.

Perhaps significantly, the Private Securities Litigation Reform Act of 1995 (PSLRA) specifies that its safe harbor provisions do not impose a duty to update forward-looking statements. It is unclear whether this language is intended to eliminate the "duty to update" in this context or merely to clarify that no implied duty to update may be derived from the PSLRA. Accordingly, the significance of this language will be construed by the courts.

In this regard, it has become customary for companies to seek to eliminate a duty to update their forward-looking statements. A representative illustration provides: *"We undertake no obligation to publicly update or review any forward-looking statements, whether as a result of new information, future developments or otherwise."*

In certain settings, SEC rules specifically mandate a duty to update. In the tender offer context, for instance, SEC Rule 14e-2 calls for the subject company to disclose to its security holders its position toward the takeover bid and inform such security holders of any material change relating to the position previously taken.

Judicial decisions addressing the duty to update from a general perspective are relatively sparse. For example, the First Circuit in *Backman v. Polaroid Corp.,* 910 F.2d 10, 17 (1st Cir. 1990) (en banc), set forth the following: "We may agree that, in special circumstances, a statement, correct at the time, may have a forward intent and connotation upon which parties may be expected to rely." If this situation should materially change, "further disclosure may be called for."

Similarly, the Fifth Circuit in *Rubinstein v. Collins*, 20 F.3d 160, 170 n.41 (5th Cir. 1994), stated that "it appears that defendants have a duty under Rule 10b-5 to correct statements if those statements have become materially misleading in light of subsequent events."

More recently, the Eleventh Circuit in *Finnerty v. Stiefel Laboratories, Inc.*, 756 F.3d 1310, 1317 (11th Cir. 2014) (citations omitted), opined:

> There is, of course, no obligation to update a prior statement about a historical fact. The duty attaches only to forward-looking statements — statements that contain "an implicit factual representation that remain[s] 'alive' in the minds of investors as a continuing representation." Determining if such an implicit representation was present and whether the representation subsequently became misleading involves an assessment of "the meaning of the statement to the reasonable investor and its relationship to

truth." Whether a company came under an obligation to revise a past disclosure is normally an issue for the finder of fact.

In this case, [the defendant company] SLI denies that it had a duty to disclose the preliminary merger negotiations with Sanofi-Aventis. Conversely, [Plaintiff] argues that SLI's August 2007 statements that it "will continue to be privately held, and the Stiefel family will retain control and continue to hold a majority-share ownership of the company" gave rise to a duty to update when SLI considered itself to be a serious acquisition target. The jury, by its verdict, decided this issue in favor of [the Plaintiff]. We conclude that the evidence in the record is sufficient to support this determination.

For further discussion, see Block, Radin & Carlinsky, *A Post-Polaroid Snapshot of the Duty to Correct Disclosure,* 1991 COLUM. BUS. L. REV. 139, 140 (1991) (stating that the duty to update "is one of the primary concerns faced by corporate counsellors today"); Gwyn & Matton, *The Duty to Update the Forecasts, Predictions, and Projections of Public Companies,* 24 SEC. REG. L.J. 366, 367 (1997) (stating that "[i]n those jurisdictions in which the duty to update a forecast, prediction, or projection has been recognized, the individual or corporation that makes such a statement, which is correct when made, will be under a duty to update the statement if material developments make the statement materially misleading"); Rosenblum, *An Issuer's Duty Under Rule 10b-5 to Correct and Update Materially Misleading Statements,* 40 CATH. U. L. REV. 289, 291 (1991) (asserting that the duty to update "applies only to statements that are 'forward-looking'—statements that by their terms purport to continue to be valid beyond the date they are made").

―――――

§ 11.06 Responding to Rumors

The circulation of rumors in the marketplace concerning a material development affecting a particular issuer (e.g., being awarded a major contract or being the subject of a tender offer) is common. The question arises whether an issuer has a duty to respond to rumors under § 10(b) when such rumors are not attributable to the corporation. Alternatively, in such circumstances, should an issuer be required to seek a halt in the trading of its stock? Presuming that § 10(b) does not require an issuer to respond to rumors in the marketplace, should investors be permitted to sue for damages based upon the corporation's violation of certain self-regulatory organization rules (e.g., rules adopted by the stock exchanges) which impose an affirmative duty to disclose?[5] These questions are addressed in the following case.

―――――

―――――

5. The availability of implied rights of actions for damages for breach of self-regulatory rules also is addressed in § 9.02.

State Teachers Retirement Board v. Fluor Corp.

United States Court of Appeals, Second Circuit

654 F.2d 843 (1981)

Lumbard, Circuit Judge.

. . . .

1. *Duty to Disclose or Halt Trading*

State Teachers asserts that Fluor had a duty to disclose the signing of the SASOL II [South African Coal, Oil and Gas Corporation Limited] contract during the week of March 3 when rumors became rampant and the price and volume of its stock shot upward. We disagree. Under all the circumstances, and particularly in light of its agreement with SASOL to make no announcement until March 10, Fluor was under no obligation to disclose the contract. *A company has no duty to correct or verify rumors in the marketplace unless those rumors can be attributed to the company.* [emphasis supplied] There is no evidence that the rumors affecting the volume and price of Fluor stock can be attributed to Fluor. Fluor responded to inquiries from analysts between March 4 and March 6 without comment on the veracity of the rumors and without making any material misrepresentation.

Moreover, even if the facts here give rise to a duty to disclose, there is no showing of any intent to defraud investors or any conduct which was reckless in any degree. Fluor's actions between March 3 and March 6 were made in a good faith effort to comply with the publicity embargo. The record completely lacks any evidence of scienter—a prerequisite to liability under section 10(b). . . .

State Teachers argues that, in any event, Fluor was under a duty to do what it could to halt trading in its stock once it learned that rumors regarding the SASOL II contract were affecting the price of the stock. This issue was not specifically addressed by the district court. State Teachers now argues that once an issuer decides as a matter of business judgment to withhold material information, it then assumes a duty to protect that news from selective disclosure which may disrupt the public market in its stock. In such a circumstance, the issuer must notify the Exchange and request a trading suspension until the news may be made public. State Teachers argues that this duty arises where, as here, the issuer becomes aware that the precise details of the material information are circulating in the market. It submits that this duty (i) is assumed by any issuer who has its stock traded on a public stock exchange and (ii) is consonant with the purpose of the Securities Exchange Act of 1934 to insure the integrity of the marketplace.

Relying on our [prior] decisions . . . State Teachers further argues that an issuer who fails to fulfill this duty to request a halt in trading, knowing that a selling stockholder may suffer a loss, is reckless; therefore, the scienter requirement for liability to attach in a section 10(b) private action is satisfied.

Under the circumstances presented in this case, we find that Fluor had no duty under section 10(b) to notify the Exchange and request that trading in its shares be suspended. Fluor first heard of rumors in the marketplace regarding the SASOL II contract on March 4. At that point, the volume of trading in Fluor stock had increased over previous weeks but there was no significant change in price. It was not until March 6 that the volume of trading in the stock and its price increased dramatically. The record indicates that no one at Fluor knew the reason for these market developments. That day, Fluor told the New York Stock Exchange that the signing of the SASOL II contract might be an explanation for the activity, and it agreed to the suggestion of the Exchange that trading be suspended. There was no trading on March 7. These facts obviate any suggestion that Fluor acted recklessly, much less with the fraudulent intent necessary for liability under section 10(b). Fluor acted scrupulously when it revealed to the Exchange that the signing of the SASOL II contract might be an explanation for what the Exchange perceived as unusual market activity in Fluor stock. Fluor's good faith is further evidenced by its endorsement of the Exchange's decision to halt trading. For us to say that Fluor should have notified the Exchange at some earlier time would be to create a standard of liability under section 10(b) which gives undue weight to hindsight.

In addition to the absence of an intent to defraud investors, the difficulty of establishing causation also supports our conclusion that a section 10(b) claim does not exist here for Fluor's failure to request a halt in trading. Although the Exchange likely would have honored a request by Fluor to halt trading, the decision rests entirely in the hands of the Exchange. It would be impossible for State Teachers to show on the record before us that had Fluor acted sooner to request a halt in trading the Exchange would have suspended trading before March 7.[6]

2. Private Action for Violation of NYSE Listing Agreement and Company Manual

State Teachers argues that Fluor's failure to comply with section A2 of the New York Stock Exchange's Company Manual creates a federal claim. Section A2 of the Company Manual states that a corporation should be prepared to make an immediate announcement of important corporate developments if unusual market activity

---

[6]. Where unusual market activity is the result of rumors, the most effective way to protect the integrity of the market is for the company to disclose information sufficient to dispel these rumors. Our decisions mentioned in this opinion have articulated when a duty to disclose arises under section 10(b). We do not believe an alternative duty to notify the Exchange or request a halt in trading should be imposed in this case. The facts which existed prior to March 7 did not give Fluor reason to believe that stockholders would be better protected if trading was halted than if it were not. Moreover, the Exchange itself has not imposed any specific duty to report rumors or to request a halt in trading. The Company Manual "recommends that its listed companies contact their Liaison Representatives if they become aware of rumors circulating about the company." Also, the Manual recommends that a company notify the Exchange of any news at least ten minutes before it is announced. "If the Exchange receives such notification in time, it will be in a position to consider whether, in the opinion of the Exchange, trading in the security should be halted temporarily." By telling the Exchange about the SASOL contract four days before its announcement, Fluor met its obligation under the Exchange's rules.

occurs prior to its announcement. The Manual specifically leaves to management's judgment, however, the timing of a public release. The Manual further states that "[i]f rumors or unusual market activity indicate that information on impending developments has leaked out, a frank and explicit announcement is clearly required." And, if rumors "are correct, . . . an immediate, candid statement to the public as to the state of negotiations or the state of development of corporate plans . . . must be made directly and openly."

The district court concluded that these Exchange rules did not give rise to an implied federal right of action . . . . We agree with the district court.

. . . .

In the case at bar, we are faced with a corporation's obligations under section A2 of the Exchange's Company Manual to disclose general corporate news. . . . [A] legislative intent to permit a federal claim for violation of the Exchange's Company Manual rules regarding disclosure of corporate news cannot be inferred. . . .

Affirmed in part; reversed in part [on other grounds]; remanded for further proceedings consistent with this opinion.

Note

Do you agree with the Second Circuit regarding an issuer's affirmative duty to respond to rumors in the marketplace? Although recognizing that Fluor had a valid business purpose in not disclosing the SASOL contract, thereby refuting the assertion that it acted with scienter, the Second Circuit also broadly stated that "[a] company has no duty to correct or verify rumors in the marketplace unless those rumors can be attributed to the company." 654 F.2d at 850. On the other hand, the district court in *Fluor* [500 F. Supp. 278 (S.D.N.Y. 1981)] would have imposed liability under § 10(b) based on the company's failure to affirmatively disclose the material nonpublic information if there were present "rampant" rumors in the market, a rapid and substantial increase in the price of the corporation's stock, and the defendants' possession of a high degree of scienter. The district court defined the requisite scienter as involving "a showing that the failure to disclose was motivated by defendants' intent to deceive investors for their own gain." 500 F. Supp. at 292. Although this standard requires affirmative disclosure in certain circumstances, is it too deferential to management? Has the district court correctly construed the scienter requirement? For example, would the goals of the federal securities laws be better promoted if the scienter requirement were met by the plaintiff's showing that the defendants knew of the information and were aware that it was material to investors but nonetheless failed to disclose such information without having a justifiable reason for nondisclosure?

The Second Circuit in *Fluor* stated that the corporation had a justifiable business reason for delaying disclosure of the SASOL contract. In this regard, *Fluor* is consistent with the accepted view that justifications for delaying disclosure by an issuer of material non-public information generally fall into three categories: "delay while corporate officials ascertain and verify information [until] it is 'ripe for disclosure'; delay while a corporation pursues a business opportunity that would be jeopardized by immediate disclosure; and delay because disclosure would expose the corporation to undue and avoidable risk of loss."[7]

In the Second Circuit's decision in *Fluor*, the court addressed the circumstances in which an issuer may have a duty to seek a halt in the trading of its stock. Do you agree with the Second Circuit's position that Fluor acted in good faith and that the plaintiffs failed to establish causation? On the other hand, would it harm the liquidity of our financial markets if issuers were compelled to seek a halt in the trading of their securities for prolonged periods of time whenever there may be a material corporate development on the horizon combined with rumors and substantial price fluctuations in the market?

As discussed in *Fluor*, the rules of the self-regulatory organizations, including the New York and Nasdaq Stock Exchanges, impose affirmative and timely disclosure requirements that are more rigorous than current § 10(b) case law. Violations of these rules, however, although perhaps resulting in SRO disciplinary action, do not provide investors with an implied right of action for damages. See § 9.02. This position may stem from the belief that, where there are no prior inadequate disclosures, no particular SEC disclosure requirements, nor the presence of "insider" trading, disclosure determinations and the timing of such disclosure generally are best left to the discretion of management. Moreover, if regulation is to have a role in this setting, such regulation should be conducted and enforced by the self-regulatory organizations. If this is indeed the rationale, are you in agreement? What are the policy arguments both for and against permitting investors to sue for damages based upon an issuer's breach of an Exchange's rule calling for affirmative and timely disclosure?

To end this discussion, consider the following: On a hot August afternoon, an individual called the market-surveillance department of Nasdaq, identified himself as the chief financial officer of Sybase, Inc. and requested a halt in the trading of Sybase stock on the Nasdaq pending the release of "material news." Trading was promptly halted in Sybase stock for 34 minutes until Nasdaq personnel ascertained that the alleged Sybase caller was an imposter. Once trading resumed, Sybase stock soared eight percent, reportedly based on that the trading halt gave new momentum to takeover rumors. In view of Sybase's experience, the question is raised whether it is that easy for anyone to telephone a stock market, pose as a high-level company spokesperson, and persuade that stock market to halt trading in the company's stock? The WALL STREET JOURNAL reported that it was that simple until the Sybase fiasco. "'I assume that it will never happen again,' said one regulator close to the situation, with

---

7. Vaughn, *Timing of Disclosure*, 13 REV. SEC. REG. 911, 913 (1980). *See* Sheffey, *Securities Law Responsibilities of Issuers to Respond to Rumors and Other Publicity: Reexamination of a Continuing Problem*, 57 NOTRE DAME LAW. 755 (1982).

the same tone that impatient football coaches use when a player fumbles in a big game. In other words: If it happens again, someone is out of a job."[8]

***

§ 11.07 Duty to Disclose Negotiations

Basic, Inc. v. Levinson

United States Supreme Court

485 U.S. 224, 108 S. Ct. 978, 99 L. Ed. 2d 194 (1988)

JUSTICE BLACKMUN delivered the opinion of the Court.

This case requires us to apply the materiality requirement of § 10(b) of the Securities Exchange Act of 1934, and the Securities and Exchange Commission's Rule 10b-5 in the context of preliminary corporate merger discussions. . . .

I

Prior to December 20, 1978, Basic Incorporated was a publicly traded company primarily engaged in the business of manufacturing chemical refractories for the steel industry. As early as 1965 or 1966, Combustion Engineering, Inc., a company producing mostly alumina-based refractories, expressed some interest in acquiring Basic, but was deterred from pursuing this inclination seriously because of antitrust concerns it then entertained. In 1976, however, regulatory action opened the way to a renewal of Combustion's interest. . . .

Beginning in September 1976, Combustion representatives had meetings and telephone conversations with Basic officers and directors, including petitioners here, concerning the possibility of a merger. During 1977 and 1978, Basic made three public statements denying that it was engaged in merger negotiations. On December 18, 1978, Basic asked the New York Stock Exchange to suspend trading in its shares and issued a release stating that it had been "approached" by another company concerning a merger. On December 19, Basic's board endorsed Combustion's offer of $46 per share for its common stock and on the following day publicly announced its approval of Combustion's tender offer for all outstanding shares.

Respondents are former Basic shareholders who sold their stock after Basic's first public statement of October 21, 1977, and before the suspension of trading in December 1978. Respondents brought a class action against Basic and its directors, asserting that the defendants issued three false or misleading public statements and thereby were in violation of § 10(b) of the 1934 Act and of Rule 10b-5. Respondents alleged that they were injured by selling Basic shares at artificially depressed prices in a market affected by petitioners' misleading statements and in reliance thereon.

---

8. Power, *Prank Caller Does a Number on Nasdaq*, WALL ST. J., Aug. 4, 1995, at C1.

... The District Court ... certified respondents' class. On the merits, however, the District Court granted summary judgment for the defendants. It held that, as a matter of law, any misstatements were immaterial: there were no negotiations ongoing at the time of the first statement, and although negotiations were taking place when the second and third statements were issued, those negotiations were not "destined, with reasonable certainty, to become a merger agreement in principle."

The United States Court of Appeals for the Sixth Circuit affirmed the class certification, but reversed the District Court's summary judgment, and remanded the case. 786 F.2d 741 (1986). The court reasoned that while petitioners were under no general duty to disclose their discussions with Combustion, any statement the company voluntarily released could not be " 'so incomplete as to mislead.' " ... In the Court of Appeals' view, Basic's statements that no negotiations were taking place, and that it knew of no corporate developments to account for the heavy trading activity, were misleading. With respect to materiality, the court rejected the argument that preliminary merger discussions are immaterial as a matter of law, and held that "once a statement is made denying the existence of any discussions, even discussions that might not have been material in absence of the denial are material because they make the statement made untrue."

. . . .

We granted certiorari . . . to resolve the split among the Courts of Appeals as to the standard of materiality applicable to preliminary merger discussions, and to determine whether the courts below properly applied a presumption of reliance in certifying the class, rather than requiring each class member to show direct reliance on Basic's statements. [This second issue addressed by the Court is contained in Chapter 8, § 8.05[E]]

II

The 1934 Act was designed to protect investors against manipulation of stock prices. . . . Underlying the adoption of extensive disclosure requirements was a legislative philosophy: "There cannot be honest markets without honest publicity. Manipulation and dishonest practices of the market place thrive upon mystery and secrecy." . . . This Court "repeatedly has described the 'fundamental purpose' of the Act as implementing a 'philosophy of full disclosure.' " . . .

Pursuant to its authority under § 10(b) of the 1934 Act, the Securities and Exchange Commission promulgated Rule 10b-5. Judicial interpretation and application, legislative acquiescence, and the passage of time have removed any doubt that a private cause of action exists for a violation of § 10(b) and Rule 10b-5, and constitutes an essential tool for enforcement of the 1934 Act's requirements. . . .

The Court previously has addressed various . . . requirements for a violation of § 10(b) or of Rule 10b-5. . . . The court also explicitly has defined a standard of materiality under the securities laws, see *TSC Industries, Inc. v. Northway, Inc.,* 426 U.S. 438 (1976), concluding in the proxy-solicitation context that "[a]n omitted fact is material if there is a substantial likelihood that a reasonable shareholder would consider it important in deciding how to vote." . . . Acknowledging that certain information concerning corporate developments could well be of "dubious significance," the Court [in *TSC*] was careful not to set too low a standard of materiality; it was concerned that a minimal standard might bring an overabundance of information within its reach, and lead management "simply to bury the shareholders in an avalanche of trivial information—a result that is hardly conducive to informed decision-making." . . . It further explained that to fulfill the materiality requirement "there must be a substantial likelihood that the disclosure of the omitted fact would have been viewed by the reasonable investor as having significantly altered the 'total mix' of information made available." . . . We now expressly adopt the *TSC Industries* standard of materiality for the § 10(b) and Rule 10b-5 context.

III

The application of this materiality standard to preliminary merger discussions is not self-evident. Where the impact of the corporate development on the target's fortune is certain and clear, the *TSC Industries* materiality definition admits straightforward application. Where, on the other hand, the event is contingent or speculative in nature, it is difficult to ascertain whether the "reasonable investor" would have considered the omitted information significant at the time. Merger negotiations, because of the ever-present possibility that the contemplated transaction will not be effectuated, fall into the latter category.[9]

A

Petitioners urge upon us a Third Circuit test for resolving this difficulty. Under this approach, preliminary merger discussions do not become material until "agreement-in-principle" as to the price and structure of the transaction has been reached between the would-be merger partners. See *Greenfield v. Heublein, Inc.*, 742 F.2d 751, 757 (CA3 1984), *cert. denied*, 469 U.S. 1215 (1985). By definition, then, information concerning any negotiations not yet at the agreement-in-principle stage could be withheld or even misrepresented without a violation of Rule 10b-5.

Three rationales have been offered in support of the "agreement-in-principle" test. The first derives from the concern expressed in *TSC Industries* that an investor not be overwhelmed by excessively detailed and trivial information, and focuses on the substantial risk that preliminary merger discussions may collapse: because such discussions are inherently tentative, disclosure of their existence itself could mislead investors and foster false optimism. . . . The other two justifications for the agreement-in-principle standard are based on management concerns: because the requirement of "agreement-in-principle" limits the scope of disclosure obligations, it helps preserve

---

9. We do not address here any other kinds of contingent or speculative information, such as earnings forecasts or projections. *See generally* Hiler, *The SEC and the Courts' Approach to Disclosure of Earnings Projections, Asset Appraisals, and Other Soft Information: Old Problems, Changing Views*, 46 MD. L. REV. 1114 (1987).

the confidentiality of merger discussions where earlier disclosure might prejudice the negotiations; and the test also provides a usable, bright-line rule for determining when disclosure must be made. . . .

None of these policy-based rationales, however, purports to explain why drawing the line at agreement-in-principle reflects the significance of the information upon the investor's decision. The first rationale, and the only one connected to the concerns expressed in *TSC Industries*, stands soundly rejected, even by a Court of Appeals that otherwise has accepted the wisdom of the agreement-in-principle test. "It assumes that investors are nitwits, unable to appreciate — even when told — that mergers are risky propositions up until the closing." *Flamm v. Eberstadt*, 814 F.2d at 1175 [CA7 1987]. Disclosure, and not paternalistic withholding of accurate information, is the policy chosen and expressed by Congress. We have recognized time and again, a "fundamental purpose" of the various securities acts, "was to substitute a philosophy of full disclosure for the philosophy of *caveat emptor* and thus to achieve a high standard of business ethics in the securities industry." . . . The role of the materiality requirement is not to "attribute to investors a child-like simplicity, an inability to grasp the probabilistic significance of negotiations," . . . but to filter out essentially useless information that a reasonable investor would not consider significant. . . .

The second rationale, the importance of secrecy during the early stages of merger discussions, also seems irrelevant to an assessment whether their existence is significant to the trading decision of a reasonable investor. To avoid a "bidding war" over its target, an acquiring firm often will insist that negotiations remain confidential . . . and at least one Court of Appeals has stated that "silence pending settlement of the price and structure of a deal is beneficial to most investors, most of the time." . . .

We need not ascertain, however, whether secrecy necessarily maximizes shareholder wealth — although we note that the proposition is at least disputed as a matter of theory and empirical research[10] — for this case does not concern the *timing* of a disclosure; it concerns only its accuracy and completeness. We face here the narrow question whether information concerning the existence and status of preliminary merger discussions is significant to the reasonable investor's trading decision. Arguments based on the premise that some disclosure would be "premature" in a sense are more properly considered under the rubric of an issuer's duty to disclose. The "secrecy" rationale is simply inapposite to the definition of materiality.

The final justification offered in support of the agreement-in-principle test seems to be directed solely at the comfort of corporate managers. A bright-line rule indeed is easier to follow than a standard that requires the exercise of judgment in the light of all the circumstances. But ease of application alone is not an excuse for ignoring the purposes of the securities acts and Congress' policy decisions. Any approach that

---

10. *See, e.g.*, Brown, *Corporate Secrecy, the Federal Securities Laws, and the Disclosure of Ongoing Negotiations,* 36 CATH. U. L. REV. 93, 145–155 (1986); Bebchuk, *The Case for Facilitating Competing Tender Offers,* 95 HARV. L. REV. 1028 (1982); *Flamm v. Eberstadt,* 814 F.2d, at 1177, n.2 (citing scholarly debate). . . .

designates a single fact or occurrence as always determinative of an inherently fact-specific finding, such as materiality, must necessarily be over- or under-inclusive. In *TSC Industries* this Court explained: "The determination [of materiality] requires delicate assessments of the inferences a 'reasonable shareholder' would draw from a given set of facts and the significance of those inferences to him. . . ."

We therefore find no valid justification for artificially excluding from the definition of materiality information concerning merger discussions, which would otherwise be considered significant to the trading decision of a reasonable investor, merely because agreement-in-principle as to price and structure has not yet been reached by the parties or their representatives.

B

The Sixth Circuit explicitly rejected the agreement-in-principle test, as we do today, but in its place adopted a rule that, if taken literally, would be equally insensitive, in our view, to the distinction between materiality and the other elements of an action under Rule 10b-5:

> "When a company whose stock is publicly traded makes a statement, as Basic did, that 'no negotiations' are underway, and that the corporation knows of 'no reason for the stock's activity,' and that 'management is unaware of any present or pending corporate development that would result in the abnormally heavy trading activity,' information concerning ongoing acquisition discussions becomes material *by virtue of the statement denying their existence.*
>
> . . . .
>
> In analyzing whether information regarding merger discussions is material such that it must be affirmatively disclosed to avoid a violation of Rule 10b-5, the discussions and their progress are the primary considerations. However, once a statement is made denying the existence of any discussions, even discussions that might not have been material in absence of the denial are material because they make the statement made untrue."

This approach, however, fails to recognize that, in order to prevail on a Rule 10b-5 claim, a plaintiff must show that the statements were *misleading* as to a *material* fact. It is not enough that a statement is false or incomplete, if the misrepresented fact is otherwise insignificant.

C

Even before this Court's decision in *TSC Industries*, the Second Circuit had explained the role of the materiality requirement of Rule 10b-5, with respect to contingent or speculative information or events, in a manner that gave that term meaning that is independent of the other provisions of the Rule. Under such circumstances, materiality "will depend at any given time upon a balancing of both the indicated probability that the event will occur and the anticipated magnitude of the event in light of the totality of the company activity." *SEC v. Texas Gulf Sulphur Co.,*

401 F.2d at 849. Interestingly, neither the Third Circuit decision adopting the agreement-in-principle test nor petitioners here take issue with this general standard. Rather, they suggest that with respect to preliminary merger discussions, there are good reasons to draw a line at agreement on price and structure.

In a subsequent decision, the late Judge Friendly, writing for a Second Circuit panel, applied the *Texas Gulf Sulphur* probability/magnitude approach in the specific context of preliminary merger negotiations. After acknowledging that materiality is something to be determined on the basis of the particular facts of each case, he stated:

> "Since a merger in which it is bought out is the most important event that can occur in a small corporation's life, to wit, its death, we think that inside information, as regards a merger of this sort, can become material at an earlier stage than would be the case as regards lesser transactions — and this even though the mortality rate of mergers in such formative stages is doubtless high."

SEC v. Geon Industries, Inc., 531 F.2d 39, 47-48 (CA2 1976). We agree with that analysis.[11]

Whether merger discussions in any particular case are material therefore depends on the facts. Generally, in order to assess the probability that the event will occur, a factfinder will need to look to indicia of interest in the transaction at the highest corporate levels. Without attempting to catalog all such possible factors, we note by way of example that board resolutions, instructions to investment bankers, and actual negotiations between principals or their intermediaries may serve as indicia of interest. To assess the magnitude of the transaction to the issuer of the securities allegedly manipulated, a factfinder will need to consider such facts as the size of the two corporate entities and of the potential premiums over market value. No particular event or factor short of closing the transaction need be either necessary or sufficient by itself to render merger discussions material.[12]

---

11. The SEC in the present case endorses the highly fact-dependent probability/magnitude balancing approach of *Texas Gulf Sulphur*. It explains: "The *possibility* of a merger may have an immediate importance to investors in the company's securities even if no merger ultimately takes place." . . . The SEC's insights are helpful, and we accord them due deference. . . .

[12]. To be actionable, of course, a statement must be misleading. Silence, absent a duty to disclose, is not misleading under Rule 10b-5. "No comment" statements are generally the functional equivalent of silence. . . . *See also* New York Stock Exchange Listed Company Manual § 202.01, reprinted in 3 CCH Fed. Sec. L. Rep. ¶ 23,515 (premature public announcement may properly be delayed for valid business purpose and where adequate security can be maintained); American Stock Exchange Company Guide §§ 401–405, reprinted in 3 CCH Fed. Sec. L. Rep. ¶¶ 23,124A-23,124E (similar provisions).

It has been suggested that given current market practices, a "no comment" statement is tantamount to an admission that merger discussions are underway. . . . That may well hold true to the extent that issuers adopt a policy of truthfully denying merger rumors when no discussions are underway, and of issuing "no comment" statements when they are in the midst of negotiations. There are, of course, other statement policies firms could adopt; we need not now advise issuers as to what kind of practice to follow, within the range permitted by law. Perhaps more importantly, we

As we clarify today, materiality depends on the significance the reasonable investor would place on the withheld or misrepresented information.[13] The fact-specific inquiry we endorse here is consistent with the approach a number of courts have taken in assessing the materiality of merger negotiations. Because the standard of materiality we have adopted differs from that used by both courts below, we remand the case for reconsideration of the question whether a grant of summary judgment is appropriate on this record.

. . . .

[Vacated and Remanded]

JUSTICE WHITE, with whom JUSTICE O'CONNOR joins, concurring in part and dissenting in part.

I join Parts I-III of the Court's opinion, as I agree that the standard of materiality we set forth in *TSC Industries, Inc. v. Northway, Inc.*, 426 U.S. 438, 449 (1976), should be applied to actions under § 10(b) and Rule 10b-5. But I dissent from the remainder of the Court's holding because I do not agree that the "fraud-on-the-market" theory should be applied in this case. [See § 8.05[E] for Justice White's dissent on this issue.]

―――――――――

Note

It should be emphasized that the Supreme Court's decision in *Basic* interpreted the issue of "materiality" for § 10(b) purposes in the merger/acquisition setting. *Basic did not address when, if ever, a company must affirmatively disclose the existence of such negotiations:* "[T]his case does not concern the *timing* of a disclosure; it concerns only its accuracy and completeness."

At this time, review the SEC's Release on Regulation S-K, Item 303 MD&A disclosure (see §§ 5.03[B], 11.03). Under certain circumstances, Item 303 requires issuers affirmatively to disclose. With respect to Item 303's impact on disclosure of preliminary merger negotiations, the SEC has stated:

> While Item 303 could be read to impose a duty to disclose otherwise non-disclosed preliminary merger negotiations, as known events or uncertainties reasonably likely to have material effects on future financial condition

―――――――――

think that creating an exception to a regulatory scheme founded on a prodisclosure legislative philosophy, because complying with the regulation might be "bad for business," is a role for Congress, not this Court.

[13]. We find no authority in the statute, the legislative history, or our previous decisions, for varying the standard of materiality depending on who brings the action or whether insiders are alleged to have profited. . . .

We recognize that trading (and profit making) by insiders can serve as *an* indication of materiality . . . We are not prepared to agree, however, that "[i]n cases of the disclosure of inside information to a favored few, determination of materiality has a different aspect than when the issue is, for example, an inaccuracy in a publicly disseminated press release." *SEC v. Geon Industries, Inc.*, 531 F.2d 39, 48 (CA2 1976). . . .

or results of operations, the Commission did not intend to apply and has not applied, Item 303 in this manner. As reflected in the various disclosure requirements under the Securities Act and Exchange Act that specifically address merger transactions, the Commission historically has balanced the informational need of investors against the risk that premature disclosure of negotiations may jeopardize completion of the transaction. . . .

The Commission's interpretation of Item 303, as applied to preliminary merger negotiations, incorporates the same policy determinations. Accordingly, where disclosure is not otherwise required, and has not otherwise been made, the MD&A need not contain a discussion of the impact of such negotiations where, in the registrant's view, inclusion of such information would jeopardize completion of the transaction. Where disclosure is otherwise required or has otherwise been made by or on behalf of the registrant, the interests in avoiding premature disclosure no longer exist. In such case, the negotiations would be subject to the same disclosure standards under Item 303 as any other known trend, demand, commitment, event or uncertainty. These policy determinations also would extend to preliminary negotiations for the acquisition or disposition of assets not in the ordinary course of business.

SEC Financial Reporting Release No. 36, 6 Fed. Sec. L. Rep. (CCH) ¶ 73,197 (1989).

It should be pointed out that in the tender offer setting Item 7 of SEC Schedule 14D-9 requires the subject corporation to disclose the existence of merger discussions which are undertaken in response to a tender offer. In such circumstances,

[i]f no agreement in principle has yet been reached, the possible terms of any transaction or the parties thereto need not be disclosed if in the opinion of the Board of Directors of the subject company such disclosure would jeopardize continuation of the negotiations. In such event, disclosure that negotiations are being undertaken or are underway and are in the preliminary stages will be sufficient.

Instruction to Item 7 of Schedule 14D-9, 17 C.F.R. § 240.14d-101.

Is the SEC's position correct? Does it make sense that the SEC by regulation has mandated a disclosure requirement when the subject corporation engages in merger discussions in response to a tender offer but has declined to mandate such a requirement in other contexts (e.g., as in the *Basic* factual situation)?

In the Matter of Carnation Company, [1984–1985 Transfer Binder] Fed. Sec. L. Rep. (CCH) ¶ 83,801 (SEC 1985), the Commission made the following statement, which is consistent with the Supreme Court's reasoning in *Basic*:

Whenever an issuer makes a public comment or responds to an inquiry from a stock exchange official concerning rumors, unusual market activity, possible corporate developments or any other matter, the statement must be materially accurate and complete. If the issuer is aware of nonpublic information concerning acquisition discussions that are occurring at the time the statement is made, the issuer has an obligation to disclose sufficient information concerning the discussions to prevent the statements made from being materially misleading. . . .

. . . [A]n issuer that wants to prevent premature disclosure of nonpublic preliminary merger negotiations can, in appropriate circumstances, give a "no comment" response to press inquiries concerning rumors or unusual market activity. A "no comment" response would not be appropriate where, inter alia, the issuer has made a statement that has been rendered materially false or misleading as a result of subsequent events or market rumors [which] are attributable to leaks from the issuer. . . .

Note the practical effect of the above. Assume that as corporate counsel you represent a client that is engaged in confidential merger negotiations. Your client's common stock is listed on the New York Stock Exchange. During the past two days, rumors have been rampant in the market that your client will be acquired by means of a merger transaction. As a consequence, the price of the stock has increased dramatically during this two-day period. Your client receives a phone call from Exchange personnel requesting a "no material corporate development" statement. How should your client respond to such an inquiry? Further, do you counsel your client to issue a public statement? Why or why not?[14]

---

§ 11.08 Regulation FD

The SEC adopted Regulation FD (Fair Disclosure) in response to the perceived unfairness when companies selectively disclose material nonpublic information to analysts, institutional investors, and other securities market insiders. The Regulation's basic premise provides that "when an issuer, or person acting on its behalf, discloses material nonpublic information to [selective] persons . . . , it must make public disclosure of that information."[15] The timing of when the issuer must make such a public disclosure depends on whether the selective disclosure was intentional or non-intentional. As summarized by the SEC:

Regulation FD (Fair Disclosure) is a new issuer disclosure rule that addresses selective disclosure. The regulation provides that when an issuer,

---

14. *See generally* Branson, *SEC Nonacquiescence in Judicial Decisionmaking: Target Company Disclosure of Acquisition Negotiations*, 46 Md. L. Rev. 1001 (1987); Brown, *Corporate Secrecy, the Federal Securities Laws, and the Disclosure of Ongoing Negotiations*, 36 Cath. U.L. Rev. 93 (1986); Gabaldon, *The Disclosure of Preliminary Merger Negotiations as an Imperfect Paradigm of Rule 10b-5 Analysis*, 62 N.Y.U. L. Rev. 1218 (1987).

15. Selective Disclosure and Insider Trading, Securities Exchange Act Release No. 43154 (2000), 2000 SEC LEXIS 1672 (hereinafter the "Regulation FD Release"). The discussion in this Section is derived from the SEC Release.

or person acting on its behalf, discloses material nonpublic information to certain enumerated persons (in general, securities market professionals and holders of the issuer's securities who may well trade on the basis of the information), it must make public disclosure of that information. The timing of the required public disclosure depends on whether the selective disclosure was intentional or non-intentional; for an intentional selective disclosure, the issuer must make public disclosure simultaneously; for a non-intentional disclosure, the issuer must make public disclosure promptly. Under the regulation, the required public disclosure may be made by filing or furnishing a Form 8-K, or by another method or combination of methods that is reasonably designed to effect broad, non-exclusionary distribution of the information to the public.[16]

Purposes of Regulation FD

The SEC sought to address several concerns by promulgating Regulation FD. First, it believed that issuers often disclose important nonpublic information, such as advance warnings of earnings results, to securities analysts and/or institutional investors before making such information available to the general investing public. The Commission warned that as a result of this practice, the investing public might not believe that they are on an equal playing field with market insiders and may thereby lose confidence in the integrity of the securities markets. Second, the SEC stated that selective disclosure closely resembles the "tipping" of inside information, but noted that the current state of insider trading law may not create liability for an issuer's selective disclosure.[17] Third, the Commission perceived that the integrity of the securities markets was threatened by issuers selectively disclosing information as a means to secure favorable reviews by analysts. Specifically, analysts may feel pressured to report about a company in a positive light or risk losing their access to company

---

16. *Id.* As set forth in the Glossary to M. Steinberg, Understanding Securities Law 518 (6th ed. 2014):

> Regulation FD prohibits publicly-held issuers or individuals acting on their behalf from selectively disclosing material nonpublic information to certain enumerated persons (generally securities market professionals and holders of the issuer's securities who may well trade on the basis of the information) without disclosing the information publicly. If the selective disclosure is intentional, then the issuer must publicly disclose the information simultaneously by filing or furnishing a Form 8-K to the SEC or in a manner reasonably designed to provide broad distribution of the information. If the selective disclosure is unintentional, then the issuer must disclose the information to the public promptly, but in no event after the later of 24 hours or the opening of the next day's trading on the New York Stock Exchange. Violating Regulation FD exposes the issuer to SEC administrative and civil enforcement action, but does not by itself impose any Rule 10b-5 antifraud liability on the issuer or establish a private right of action.

17. "[I]n light of the 'personal benefit' test set forth in the Supreme Court's decision in *Dirks v. SEC*, 463 U.S. 646 (1983), many have viewed issuer selective disclosures to analysts as protected from insider trading liability." Regulation FD Release, *supra* note 15, at n.7. Nevertheless, the Commission reiterated that it would institute enforcement actions based on violations of § 10(b) where selective disclosures violated the insider trading prohibitions.

personnel. Finally, the SEC opined that recent technological advances, particularly in the communications area, no longer pose undue impediments to timely public disclosure.

Scope of Regulation FD

Regulation FD's scope focuses on those who are prohibited from selectively disclosing material nonpublic information and those to whom such selective disclosure is directed. The Regulation prohibits a company, or persons acting on such company's behalf, from selectively disclosing material inside information regarding such company or its securities. For the purpose of the Regulation, an issuer generally includes a company that has a class of securities registered under § 12 of the Exchange Act or is required to file reports under § 15 of that Act.

Regulation FD defines a "person acting on behalf of the issuer" as "any senior official of the issuer . . . or any other officer, employee, or agent of an issuer who regularly communicates with any [enumerated recipient of information discussed below] . . . , or with holders of the issuer's securities."[18] This definition focuses on those whose job function regularly entails the disclosure of company-related information to the enumerated recipients. Selective disclosure by personnel who may occasionally interact with analysts or investors, for example, would not give rise to liability under Regulation FD. Thus, material nonpublic information disclosed in the due course of business to customers and suppliers would be outside the scope of the Regulation. The Commission, however, has noted that a senior official cannot escape liability by directing non-covered personnel to make a selective disclosure of information to someone within the classes of enumerated recipients. In such a case, the senior official would be held responsible for making the selective disclosure under § 20(b) of the Exchange Act. Finally, the definition of a "person acting on behalf of the issuer" specifically excludes an "officer, director, employee, or agent of an issuer who discloses material nonpublic information in breach of a duty of trust or confidence to the issuer." Such conduct would violate the insider trading prohibitions.

Regulation FD applies when material nonpublic information is selectively disclosed to one of four enumerated classes of recipients outside the issuer:

- a broker or a dealer, or a person associated with a broker or dealer;
- an investment adviser, an institutional investment manager, or a person associated with either;
- an investment company or affiliated person thereof; or
- a holder of the issuer's securities, where it is reasonably foreseeable that the holder will purchase or sell the issuer's securities based on the information.

---

18. 17 C.F.R. § 243.101(c). The Regulation defines "senior official" as "any director, executive officer, investor relations or public relations officer, or other person with similar functions." 17 C.F.R. § 243.101(f).

The Regulation expressly excludes, and thus does not apply to, the following: a "person who owes a duty of trust or confidence to the issuer" (e.g., temporary insiders); a "person who expressly agrees to maintain the disclosed information in confidence"; a credit rating agency ("provided the information is disclosed solely for the purpose of developing a credit rating and the entity's ratings are publicly available"); and, with certain exceptions, in connection with "a securities offering registered under the Securities Act." Furthermore, although not specifically referenced, disclosures to the media or communications to government agencies are outside the Regulation's scope.

Meaning of "Material" and "Nonpublic"

Although the Regulation refers to "material" and "nonpublic" information, it does not define those terms. Instead, the SEC relies on case law to define these terms. Thus, information is material if "a reasonable shareholder would consider it important in making an investment decision . . . [and it is] a fact [that there is a substantial likelihood] would have been viewed by the reasonable investor as having significantly altered the total mix of information made available." Information is nonpublic "if it has not been disseminated in a manner making [such information] available to investors generally."

Although the Commission declined to establish a bright-line test for materiality, it offered several examples of information that likely would require issuers to make a materiality determination: (1) earnings information; (2) mergers, acquisitions, tender offers, joint ventures, or changes in assets; (3) new products or discoveries, or developments regarding customers or suppliers; (4) changes in control or in management; (5) change in auditors; (6) events regarding the issuer's securities; and (7) bankruptcies or receiverships. With this or any other information, the key for any materiality determination is on what significance a reasonable investor would place on the information.

Intentional or Non-Intentional Selective Disclosure

Another important issue under Regulation FD involves whether the issuer selectively disclosed the information intentionally or nonintentionally. This assessment focuses on when the issuer must make the information publicly available. If the issuer intentionally and selectively discloses material nonpublic information, then it must disclose the same information simultaneously to the public. But if the selective disclosure is nonintentional, the issuer must disclose the information promptly, which is defined "as soon as reasonably practicable (but in no event after the later of 24 hours or the commencement of the next day's trading on the New York Stock Exchange) after a senior official of the issuer . . . learns that there has been a non-intentional disclosure by the issuer or person acting on behalf of the issuer of information that the senior official knows, or is reckless in not knowing, is both material and non-public."

The standard for determining whether a selective disclosure was "intentional" meshes with the Regulation's definitions of materiality and nonpublic. The

Regulation defines "intentional" to be that "the person making the disclosure either knows, or is reckless in not knowing, that the information he or she is communicating is *both* material and nonpublic." Thus, if an issuer were merely negligent in erroneously judging whether a certain piece of selectively disclosed information is either material or nonpublic, Regulation FD would not impose liability. By using this standard, the Commission seeks to provide "additional protection that issuers need not fear being second-guessed by the Commission in enforcement actions for mistaken judgments regarding materiality in close cases."[19] Nonetheless, the SEC warned that the determination of materiality should take into account all facts and circumstances. Thus, for example, a materiality judgment that might not be reckless in the context of an impromptu answer to an unexpected question at a press conference may be reckless in the context of a prepared written statement where the issuer has more time to evaluate the information it is about to disclose. Furthermore, if an issuer displays a pattern of "mistaken" judgments regarding materiality, that company's credibility would be harmed when it comes to future claims that any particular disclosure was not intentional.

Methods for Making Public Disclosure

Regulation FD provides issuers with flexibility in determining how to publicly disclose material nonpublic information when they have engaged in selective disclosure of such information. Whatever method the issuer chooses must be "reasonably designed to provide broad, non-exclusionary distribution of the information to the public." One clear method that an issuer can use is either to file or furnish a Form 8-K with the SEC.[20] The Regulation also provides that other methods of public disclosure may be acceptable, such as press releases, press conferences, or conferences that the public can attend or listen to by telephone or teleconference. Today, a growing number of companies, including Google and Microsoft, disseminate announcement of corporate earnings exclusively by means of the Internet.[21]

---

19. *See* Regulation FD Release, *supra* note 15 (stating that "in the case of a selective disclosure attributable to a mistaken determination of materiality, liability will arise only if no reasonable person under the circumstances would have made the same determination").

20. 17 C.F.R. ' 243.101(e)(1). With respect to "filing" versus "furnishing" the information on Form 8-K, the SEC stated:

[I]ssuers may choose either to "file" a report under Item 5 of Form 8-K or to "furnish" a report under Item 9 of Form 8-K that will not be deemed "filed." If an issuer chooses to file the information on Form 8-K, the information will be subject to liability under § 18 of the Exchange Act. The information also will be subject to automatic incorporation by reference into the issuer's Securities Act registration statements, which are subject to liability under Sections 11 and 12(a)(2) of the Securities Act. If an issuer chooses instead to furnish the information, it will not be subject to liability under § 11 of the Securities Act or § 18 of the Exchange Act for the disclosure, unless it takes steps to include that disclosure in a filed report, proxy statement, or registration statement. All disclosures on Form 8-K, whether filed or furnished, will remain subject to the antifraud provisions of the federal securities laws.

21. *See Risks, Liabilities Lie in Way of Organizations Trying to Embrace Social Media*, 42 Sec. Reg. & L. Rep. (BNA) 2301 (2012).

In using these alternatives, the issuer must select a method or combination of methods that are reasonably calculated to provide a broad and effective public disclosure given that issuer's particular circumstances. Thus, for example, an issuer cannot rely solely on issuing a press release if it knows that its press releases are not routinely reported by the wire services. Furthermore, the Commission will take into account whether a company deviated from its usual practices for making a public disclosure in determining whether the method of disclosure in any particular case complies with the Regulation.

The SEC, recognizing that a single method of disclosure may not be desirable, offered a model for making a planned disclosure of material information. First, the issuer should issue a press release distributed through regular channels. Second, it should provide adequate notice through a press release and/or website posting of a scheduled conference call to discuss the particular information, giving investors information on the time and date of the call as well as how to access it. Third, the issuer should hold the conference call in an open manner, such that investors can listen to (but not necessarily ask questions during) the conference call either over the telephone or the Internet. The Commission also suggested that companies make taped replays of the conference call available for some time after they take place so as to allow other investors to listen to it.

Exclusions for Registered Offerings

Generally, Regulation FD "does not apply to disclosures made in connection with a securities offering registered under the Securities Act."[22] Nonetheless, a reporting

---

22. Regulation FD Release, *supra* note 15. With respect to communications made in connection with a registered offering that is excluded from Regulation FD coverage, the SEC in Securities Act Release No. 8591 (2005) stated:

[A]s amended, Regulation FD will not apply to disclosures made in the following communications in connection with a registered securities offering that is of the type excluded from the Regulation:

- a registration statement filed under the Securities Act, including a prospectus contained therein;
- a free writing prospectus used after filing of the registration statement for the offering or a communication falling within the exception to the definition of prospectus contained in clause (a) of Securities Act Section 2(a)(10);
- any other Section 10(b) prospectus;
- a notice permitted by Securities Act Rule 135;
- a communication permitted by Securities Act Rule 134; or
- an oral communication made in connection with the registered securities offering after filing of the registration statement for the offering under the Securities Act.

. . . .

In view of our new rules to expand permissible communications, we believe it is appropriate to clarify that the communications excluded from the operation of Regulation FD are, in fact, those communications that are directly related to a registered securities offering. Communications not contained in our enumerated list of exceptions from Regulation FD—for example, the publication of regularly released factual business information or regularly released forward-looking information or pre-filing communications—are subject to Regulation FD. *Id.*

company's *unregistered* offerings are subject to Regulation FD. The Commission noted that in the context of such offerings, the company should either make selectively disclosed information public or secure a confidentiality agreement from the recipient. It also warned public companies undertaking unregistered offerings that if they fail to adhere to Regulation FD, they may risk losing their exemption from registration. A company's failure to adhere to Regulation FD, however, will not cause it to lose the availability of using short-form Securities Act registration Form S-3 or cause its shareholders to lose their ability to sell their securities under Securities Act Rule 144(c).[23]

SEC Enforcement, No Private Remedy

An issuer that allegedly violates Regulation FD will be subject to SEC enforcement action. The Commission, for example, has procured against registrants cease-and-desist orders, injunctions and money penalties. The SEC also has brought enforcement actions against individuals affiliated with issuers that have violated Regulation FD.

The Regulation, however, does not create any private right of action. Furthermore, it expressly does not establish any Rule 10b-5 antifraud liability for cases based "solely" on an issuer's failure to comply with Regulation FD. Nevertheless, Rule 10b-5 liability may still arise if, for example, the company's public disclosure, designed to satisfy Regulation FD, contains a material misstatement or omits material information.

Note

The SEC has brought numerous enforcement actions based on alleged violations of Regulation FD. *See In re Office Depot, Inc.,* Admin. Proc. File No. 3-14094 (SEC 2010); *SEC v. Flowserve,* SEC Litigation Release No. 19154 (D.D.C. 2005); *In the Matter of Raytheon Company,* Securities Exchange Act Release No. 46897 (2002); *In the Matter of Secure Computing Corp.,* Securities Exchange Act Release No. 46895 (2002).

The SEC, however, lost an enforcement proceeding alleging Regulation FD violations in *SEC v. Siebel Systems, Inc.,* 384 F. Supp. 2d 694, 704 (S.D.N.Y. 2005). Critical of the SEC, the court commented:

> The SEC . . . scrutinized, at an extremely heightened level, every particular word used in the statement, including the tense of verbs and the general syntax of each sentence. No support for such an approach can be found in Regulation FD. . . . Such an approach places an unreasonable burden on a company's management and spokespersons to become linguistic experts, or otherwise live in fear of violating Regulation FD should the words they use

---

23. See 17 C.F.R. § 243.103.

later be interpreted by the SEC as connoting even the slightest variance from the company's public statements.[24]

More recently, the Commission issued a Release addressing a corporate executive's use of social media in the Regulation FD context. That Release follows.

In re Netflix, Inc.

Securities and Exchange Commission

Securities Exchange Act Release No. 69279 (2013)

I. Introduction

The Division of Enforcement has investigated whether Netflix, Inc. ("Netflix") and its Chief Executive Officer, Reed Hastings ("Hastings") violated Regulation FD and Section 13(a) of the Securities Exchange Act of 1934 ("Exchange Act"). The Commission has determined not to pursue an enforcement action in this matter. The investigation concerned Hastings's use of his personal Facebook page, on July 3, 2012, to announce that Netflix had streamed 1 billion hours of content in the month of June. Neither Hastings nor Netflix had previously used Hastings's personal Facebook page to announce company metrics, and Netflix had not previously informed shareholders that Hastings's Facebook page would be used to disclose information about Netflix. The post was not accompanied by a press release, a post on Netflix's own web site or Facebook page, or a Form 8-K.

The investigation raised questions regarding: 1) the application of Regulation FD to Hastings's post; and 2) the applicability of the Commission's August 2008 Guidance on the Use of Company Web Sites [Securities Exchange Act Release No. 58288 (2008)] to emerging technologies, including social networking sites, such as Facebook.

Regulation FD and Section 13(a) of the Exchange Act prohibit public companies, or persons acting on their behalf, from selectively disclosing material, nonpublic information to certain securities professionals, or shareholders where it is reasonably foreseeable that they will trade on that information, before it is made available to the general public. The Commission's 2008 Guidance explained that for purposes of complying with Regulation FD, a company makes public disclosure when it distributes information "through a recognized channel of distribution."

---

24. *See* Brown, *First Reg FD Decision Finds SEC's 'Excessive Scrutiny' Chills Disclosure,* 37 SEC. REG. & L. REP. (BNA) 2102 (2005). For further literature on Regulation FD, *see, e.g.,* Conner, *Regulation FD: Its Creation, Its Authority, Its Possible Impact,* 28 SEC. REG. L.J. 5 (2000); Steinberg & Myers, *Lurking in the Shadows: The Hidden Issues of the Securities and Exchange Commission's Regulation FD,* 27 J. CORP. L. 173 (2002); Thompson & King, *Credibility and Information in Securities Markets After Regulation FD,* 79 WASH. U.L.Q. 615 (2001); Wang, *Selective Disclosure by Issuers — Its Legality and Ex Ante Harm,* 42 VA. J. INT'L L. 869 (2002).

In its investigation, the SEC staff learned (and some public commentary further suggested) that there is uncertainty concerning how Regulation FD and the Commission's 2008 Guidance apply to disclosures made through social media channels. Since the issuance of the 2008 Guidance, the use of social media has proliferated and the Commission is aware that public companies are increasingly using social media to communicate with shareholders and the market generally. The ways in which companies may use these social media channels, however, are not fundamentally different from the ways in which the web sites, blogs, and RSS feeds addressed by the 2008 Guidance are used. Accordingly, the Commission deems it appropriate and in the public interest to issue this Report of Investigation ("Report") pursuant to Section 21(a) of the Exchange Act to provide guidance to issuers regarding how Regulation FD and the 2008 Guidance apply to disclosures made through social media channels.[25]

II. Background of Regulation FD and the 2008 Commission Guidance on the Use of Company Web Sites

Regulation FD provides that when an issuer, or a person acting on its behalf, discloses material, nonpublic information to securities market professionals or shareholders where it is reasonably foreseeable that they will trade on the basis of the information, it must distribute that information in a manner reasonably designed to achieve effective broad and non-exclusionary distribution to the public. When the disclosure of material, nonpublic information is intentional, distribution of the same information to the public must be made simultaneously. When the disclosure of material, nonpublic information is inadvertent, distribution of the same information to the public must be made promptly afterwards. Regulation FD was adopted out of concern that issuers were selectively "disclosing important nonpublic information, such as advance warning of earnings results, to securities analysts or selected institutional investors before making full disclosure of the same information to the general public." In our previous statements on Regulation FD, we have recognized that the "regulation does not require use of a particular method, or establish a 'one size fits all' standard for disclosure." We did, however, "caution issuers that a deviation from their usual practices for making public disclosure may affect our judgment as to whether the method they have chosen in a particular case was reasonable." We have since encouraged "honest, carefully considered attempts to comply with Regulation FD."

In August 2008, in response to the changing electronic landscape of issuer disclosure and the wide-spread use of web sites to disseminate information electronically to investors and the market, the Commission issued its 2008 Guidance. As the 2008 Guidance explained, the Commission has "long recognized the vital role of the Internet and electronic communications in modernizing the disclosure system under the

---

[25]. Section 21(a) of the Exchange Act authorizes the Commission to investigate violations of the federal securities laws, and, in its discretion, "to publish information concerning any such violations." This Report does not constitute an adjudication of any fact or issue addressed herein. . . .

federal securities laws and in promoting transparency, liquidity and efficiency in our trading markets." Additionally, the guidance detailed the many steps we have taken over the years to encourage the dissemination of information electronically, "as we believe that widespread access to company information is a key component of our integrated disclosure scheme, the efficient functioning of the markets, and investor protection."

The Commission has not explicitly addressed the application of Regulation FD and the 2008 Guidance to disclosures made through social media channels. The 2008 Guidance was directed primarily at the use of issuer web sites as a method of disseminating information in compliance with Regulation FD. Yet the guidance also contemplated other "push" technology forms of communication such as email alerts and RSS feeds, along with "interactive" communication tools such as blogs. In light of the rapid "development and proliferation of company web sites since 2000" and with the expectation of "continued technological advances," the 2008 Guidance was designed to be flexible and adaptive. Accordingly, the guidance provided issuers with a factor-based framework for analysis, rather than static rules applicable only to web sites.

As explained in the 2008 Guidance, "whether a company's web site is a recognized channel of distribution will depend on the steps that the company has taken to alert the market to its web site and its disclosure practices, as well as the use by investors and the market of the company's web site." The guidance offered a non-exhaustive list of factors to be considered in evaluating whether a corporate web site constitutes a recognized channel of distribution. The central focus of this inquiry is whether the company has made investors, the market, and the media aware of the channels of distribution it expects to use, so these parties know where to look for disclosures of material information about the company or what they need to do to be in a position to receive this information.

III. Facts

Netflix is an on-line entertainment service that provides movies and television programming to subscribers by streaming content through the internet and by distributing DVDs through the mail. Over the last two years, Netflix has stated that it is increasingly focused on expanding its internet streaming business.

On January 4, 2012, Netflix announced by press release that it had streamed two billion hours of content in the fourth quarter of 2011. Netflix also featured the two billion hours streaming metric in the opening paragraph of the January 25, 2012, letter to shareholders signed by Hastings that accompanied Netflix's quarterly financial results included in its earnings release, a copy of which was also furnished on EDGAR on a Current Report on Form 8-K. During Netflix's 2011 year-end and fourth quarter earnings conference call on January 25, 2012, Hastings was asked why this streaming metric was relevant (since Netflix's revenues are derived through fixed subscriber fees, not based on the number of hours of programming viewed). Hastings explained that streaming was "a measure of an engagement and scale in terms of the adoption of our service and use of our service. . . . . It [two billion hours streaming in a quarter] is a great milestone for us to have hit. And like I said, shows widespread adoption and usage of the service." He also stated that although he did not antici-pate that Netflix would regularly report the number of hours of streamed content, Netflix would update the metric "on a milestone basis."

In an early June [2012] posting on Netflix's official blog, Netflix made a brief ref-erence to people "enjoying nearly a billion hours per month of movies and TV shows from Netflix." The blog was technical in nature, announcing a new content delivery network available to Internet Service Providers, and there was no further detail given about the streaming metric. Beyond that, Netflix did not make any milestone announcements regarding streaming hours between January 25, 2012 and the begin-ning of July 2012.

On July 3, 2012, just before 11:00 a.m. Eastern time, Hastings posted the follow-ing message on his personal Facebook page:

> Congrats to Ted Sarados, and his amazing content licensing team. Netflix monthly viewing exceeded 1 billion hours for the first time ever in June. When House of Cards and Arrested Development debut, we'll blow these records away. Keep going, Ted, we need even more!

This announcement represented a nearly 50% increase in streaming hours from Net-flix's January 25, 2012 announcement that it had streamed 2 billion hours over the preceding three-month quarter.

Prior to his post, Hastings did not receive input from Netflix's chief financial offi-cer, the legal department, or investor relations department. Netflix did not file with or furnish to the Commission a Current Report on Form 8-K, issue a press release through its standard distribution channels, or otherwise announce the streaming milestone. Also on July 3, 2012, and after the Facebook post, Netflix issued a press release announcing the date of its second quarter 2012 earnings release but did not mention Hastings's Facebook post. Netflix's stock continued a rise that began when the market opened on July 3, increasing from $70.45 at the time of Hastings's Face-book post to $81.72 at the close of the following trading day.

The announcement of the streaming milestone reached the securities market incrementally. The post was picked up by a technology-focused blog about an hour later and by a handful of news outlets within two hours. Approximately an hour after the post, Netflix sent it to several reporters, but did not disseminate it to the broader mailing list normally used for corporate press releases. After the markets closed early at 1:00 p.m., several articles in the mainstream financial press picked up the story. Research analysts also wrote about the streaming milestone, describing the metric as a positive measure of customer engagement, indicative of a reduction in the rate Netflix is losing customers, or "churn," and possibly suggesting that quarterly subscriber numbers would be at the high end of guidance.[26]

---

[26]. On July 24, 2012, after the close of market, Netflix announced its second quarter earnings, including quarterly subscriber numbers on the low end of guidance. The stock dropped from the previous day's close of $80.39 to $60.28 per share on July 25, 2012.

Facebook members can subscribe to Hastings's Facebook page, which had over 200,000 subscribers at the time of the post, including equity research analysts associated with registered broker-dealers, shareholders, reporters, and bloggers. Neither Hastings nor Netflix had previously used Hastings's Facebook page to announce company metrics. Nor had they taken any steps to make the investing public aware that Hastings's personal Facebook page might be used as a medium for communicating information about Netflix. Instead, Netflix has consistently directed the public to its own Facebook page, Twitter feed, and blog and to its own web site for information about Netflix. In early December 2012, Hastings stated for the public record that "we [Netflix] don't currently use Facebook and other social media to get material information to investors; we usually get that information out in our extensive investor letters, press releases and SEC filings."

IV. Discussion

A fundamental question raised during the staff's investigation was the application of Regulation FD and the 2008 Guidance to issuer disclosures through rapidly changing forms of communication, including social media channels. We do not wish to inhibit the content, form, or forum of any such disclosure, and we are mindful of placing additional compliance burdens on issuers. In fact, we encourage companies to seek out new forms of communication to better connect with shareholders. We also remind issuers that the analysis of whether Regulation FD was violated is always a facts-and-circumstances analysis based on the specific context presented.

We take this opportunity to clarify and amplify two points. First, issuer communications through social media channels require careful Regulation FD analysis comparable to communications through more traditional channels. Second, the principles outlined in the 2008 Guidance—and specifically the concept that the investing public should be alerted to the channels of distribution a company will use to disseminate material information—apply with equal force to corporate disclosures made through social media channels.

A. Disclosures Triggering Regulation FD

Regulation FD applies when an issuer discloses material, non-public information to certain enumerated persons, including shareholders and securities professionals. It prohibits selective disclosure "[w]henever an issuer, or any person acting on its behalf, discloses any material nonpublic information regarding that issuer *to any person* described in paragraph (b)(1) of this section." Although the Regulation FD Adopting Release highlights the Commission's special concerns about selective disclosure of information to favored analysts or investors, the identification of the enumerated persons within Regulation FD is inclusive, and the prohibition does not turn on an intent or motive of favoritism. Nor does the rule suggest that disclosure of material, non-public information to a broader group that includes both enumerated and non-enumerated persons but that still falls short of a public disclosure negates the applicability of Regulation FD. On the contrary, the rule makes clear that public disclosure of material, nonpublic information must be made in a manner that conforms with Regulation FD whenever such information is disclosed to any group that includes one or more enumerated persons.

Accordingly, we emphasize for issuers that all disclosures to groups that include an enumerated person should be analyzed for compliance with Regulation FD. Specifically, if an issuer makes a disclosure to an enumerated person, including to a broader group of recipients through a social media channel, the issuer must consider whether that disclosure implicates Regulation FD. This would include determining whether the disclosure includes material, nonpublic information. Further, if the issuer were to elect not to file a Form 8-K, the issuer would need to consider whether the information was being disseminated in a manner "reasonably designed to provide broad, non-exclusionary distribution of the information to the public."

B. Broad, Non-Exclusionary Distribution of Information to the Public

Our 2008 Guidance was directed primarily at the use of corporate web sites for the disclosure of material, non-public information. Like web sites, corporate social media pages are created, populated, and updated by the issuer. The 2008 Guidance, furthermore, specifically identified "push" technologies, such as email alerts and RSS [Really Simple Syndication] feeds and "interactive" communication tools, such as blogs, which could enable the automatic electronic dissemination of information to subscribers. Today's evolving social media channels are an extension of these concepts, whereby information can be disseminated to those with access. Thus, the 2008 Guidance continues to provide a relevant framework for applying Regulation FD to evolving social media channels of distribution.

Specifically, in light of the direct and immediate communication from issuers to investors that is now possible through social media channels, such as Facebook and Twitter, we expect issuers to examine rigorously the factors indicating whether a particular channel is a "recognized channel of distribution" for communicating with their investors. We emphasize for issuers that the steps taken to alert the market about which forms of communication a company intends to use for the dissemination of material, non-public information, including the social media channels that may be used and the types of information that may be disclosed through these channels, are critical to the fair and efficient disclosure of information. Without such notice, the investing public would be forced to keep pace with a changing and expanding universe of potential disclosure channels, a virtually impossible task.

Providing appropriate notice to investors of the specific channels a company will use for the dissemination of material, nonpublic information is a sensible and expedient solution. It is not expected that this step would limit the channels of communication a company could use after appropriate notice or the opportunity for a company and investors to benefit from technological innovation and changes in communications practices. The 2008 Guidance encourages issuers to consider including in periodic reports and press releases the corporate web site address and disclosures that the company routinely posts important information on that web site. Similarly, disclosures on corporate web sites identifying the specific social media channels a company intends to use for the dissemination of material non-public information would give investors and the markets the opportunity to take the steps necessary to be in a position to receive important disclosures—e.g., subscribing, joining, registering, or reviewing that particular channel. These are some, but certainly not all, of the methods a company could use, with minimal burden, to enable evolving social media channels of corporate disclosure to be used as recognized channels of distribution in compliance with Regulation FD and the 2008 Guidance.

Although every case must be evaluated on its own facts, disclosure of material, nonpublic information on the personal social media site of an individual corporate officer, without advance notice to investors that the site may be used for this purpose, is unlikely to qualify as a method "reasonably designed to provide broad, non-exclusionary distribution of the information to the public" within the meaning of Regulation FD. This is true even if the individual in question has a large number of subscribers, friends, or other social media contacts, such that the information is likely to reach a broader audience over time. Personal social media sites of individuals employed by a public company would not ordinarily be assumed to be channels through which the company would disclose material corporate information. Without adequate notice that such a site may be used for this purpose, investors would not have an opportunity to access this information or, in some cases, would not know of that opportunity, at the same time as other investors.

V. Conclusion

There has been a rapid proliferation of social media channels for corporate communication since the issuance of the Commission's 2008 Guidance. An increasing number of public companies are using social media to communicate with their shareholders and the investing public. We appreciate the value and prevalence of social media channels in contemporary market communications, and the Commission supports companies seeking new ways to communicate and engage with shareholders and the market. This Report is not aimed at inhibiting corporate communication through evolving social media channels. To the contrary, we seek to remind issuers that disclosures to persons enumerated in Regulation FD, even if made through evolving social media channels, must still be analyzed for compliance with Regulation FD. Moreover, we emphasize that the Commission's 2008 Guidance, though largely focused on the use of web sites, is equally applicable to current and evolving social media channels of corporate communication. The 2008 Guidance explained that issuers must take steps sufficient to alert investors and the market to the channels it will use for the dissemination of material, nonpublic information. We believe that adherence to this guidance will help, with minimal burden, to assure compliance with Regulation FD and the fair and efficient operation of the market.

Chapter 12

Insider Trading

§ 12.01 Introduction

[A] Overview

The subject of "insider" trading has been the focus of increased judicial scrutiny, vigorous SEC enforcement, and congressional attention. The Supreme Court has decided three major cases in this area. In *Chiarella v. United States*, 445 U.S. 222 (1980), the Court asserted that the imposition of liability under § 10(b) and Rule 10b-5 for trading on material non-public information must be premised upon a duty to disclose. In *Dirks v. SEC*, 463 U.S. 646 (1983), the Court held that the duty of tippers-tippees to disclose or abstain from trading under § 10(b) and Rule 10b-5 depends on "whether the insider personally will benefit [e.g., by receipt of pecuniary gain or reputational enhancement that will translate into future earnings], directly, or indirectly, from his disclosure. Absent some personal gain, there has been no breach of duty to stockholders. And absent a breach by the insider, there is no derivative breach [by the tippee]."[1] And, in *United States v. O'Hagan*, 521 U.S. 642 (1997), the Court upheld: the misappropriation theory under § 10(b); and (2) the validity of SEC Rule 14e-3.

The decisions in *Chiarella* and *Dirks*, although embracing certain traditional principles that had been adopted by the lower courts and the SEC,[2] render it more difficult for the SEC and private claimants to emerge victorious. Thus far, however, the SEC generally has met this challenge. In both *Chiarella* and *Dirks*, for example, the Court left unresolved the viability of the misappropriation theory. After *Chiarella*, the SEC and the Department of Justice successfully invoked this rationale. For example, in *United States v. Newman*, 664 F.2d 12, 17–18 (2d Cir. 1981), the Second Circuit upheld an indictment on the grounds that the defendants had allegedly misappropriated valuable non-public information entrusted to them in the utmost secrecy. The court found that the defendants had "sullied the reputations" of their employers, investment banks, "as safe repositories of client confidences" and had deceived the

---

1. Although it did not address the "misappropriation" theory in depth, another Supreme Court decision in the insider trading area is *Carpenter v. United States*, 484 U.S. 19 (1987).

2. *See, e.g., SEC v. Texas Gulf Sulphur Co.*, 401 F.2d 833 (2d Cir. 1968) (en banc), *cert. denied*, 394 U.S. 976 (1969) (imposing a duty on corporate officers and directors premised on the equal access theory to disclose or refrain from trading on material non-public information); *In re Cady, Roberts & Co.*, 40 S.E.C. 907 (1961) (same).

clients of these investment banks "whose takeover plans were keyed to target company stock prices fixed by market forces, not artificially inflated through purchases by purloiners of confidential information." Several other appellate courts adopted the misappropriation theory. Ultimately, the Supreme Court in *United States v. O'Hagan*, 521 U.S. 642 (1997), upheld the misappropriation theory, holding that a person who engages in securities trading, using confidential material information in breach of a fiduciary duty owed to the source of the information, violates § 10(b).

Investors trading contemporaneously in the securities markets in such misappropriation cases initially were left without a remedy. In *Moss v. Morgan Stanley*, 719 F.2d 5 (2d Cir. 1983), the Second Circuit, in affirming the dismissal of an action seeking monetary damages for violations of § 10(b), held that the plaintiffs failed to prove that the defendants breached a duty owed to them. In legislation enacted in 1988, however, Congress provided contemporaneous traders with an express right of action against those on the opposite side of the transaction who allegedly engaged in illegal insider trading of the same class of securities.[3]

Another example of the SEC's response to *Chiarella* was its promulgation, pursuant to § 14(e) of the Williams Act, of Rule 14e-3, which seeks to deter insider and tippee trading in the tender offer setting. Generally, the rule, with certain exceptions, contains broad "disclose or abstain from trading" as well as "anti-tipping" provisions. With certain exemptions, Rule 14e-3 applies the disclose-or-abstain provision where an individual is in possession of material information relating to a tender offer and knows or has reason to know that such information is nonpublic and was obtained directly or indirectly from the offeror, the subject corporation, any of their affiliated persons, or any person acting on behalf of either company.

---

3. For more discussion on *Chiarella*, *Dirks*, *O'Hagan*, and their implications, *see, e.g.*, A. Bromberg, L. Lowenfels & M. Sullivan, Securities Fraud & Commodities Fraud §§ 7.4-7.5 (2015); D. Langevoort, Insider Trading: Regulation, Enforcement & Prevention (1992 & supp.); M. Steinberg & W. Wang, Insider Trading (Oxford Univ. Press 3d edition 2010); Aldave, *Misappropriation: A General Theory of Liability for Trading on Nonpublic Information*, 13 Hofstra L. Rev. 101 (1985); Anderson, *Fraud, Fiduciaries, and Insider Trading*, 10 Hofstra L. Rev. 341 (1982); Bainbridge, *Incorporating State Fiduciary Duties Into the Federal Insider Trading Prohibitions*, 52 Wash. & Lee L. Rev. 1189 (1995); Branson, *Discourse on the Supreme Court Approach to SEC Rule 10b-5 and Insider Trading*, 30 Emory L.J. 263 (1981); Conard, *Enterprise Liability and Insider Trading*, 49 Wash. & Lee L. Rev. 913 (1992); Hiler, *Dirks v. SEC—A Study in Cause and Effect*, 43 Md. L. Rev. 292 (1984); Karjala, *Statutory Regulation of Insider Trading in Impersonal Markets*, 1982 Duke L.J. 627 (1982); Langevoort, *Insider Trading and the Fiduciary Principle: A Post-Chiarella Restatement*, 70 Calif. L. Rev. 1 (1982); Levmore, *Securities and Secrets: Insider Trading and the Law of Contracts*, 68 Va. L. Rev. 117 (1982); Nagy, *Insider Trading and the Gradual Demise of Fiduciary Principles*, 94 Iowa L. Rev. 1315 (2009); Painter, Krawiec & Williams, *Don't Ask, Just Tell: Insider Trading After United States v. O'Hagan*, 84 Va. L. Rev. 153 (1998); Ramirez & Gilbert, *The Misappropriation Theory of Insider Trading Under United States v. O'Hagan: Why Its Bark is Worse Than its Bite*, 26 Sec. Reg. L.J. 162 (1998); Symposium, *Insider Trading: Law, Policy, and Theory After O'Hagan*, 20 Cardozo L. Rev. No. 1 (1998); Wang, *Trading on Material, Nonpublic Information on Impersonal Stock Markets: Who is Harmed and Who Can Sue Whom Under SEC Rule 10b-5?*, 54 S. Cal. L. Rev. 1217 (1981).

In the release adopting the rule, the Commission asserted that *Chiarella* did not limit its authority under § 14(e) to prescribe such a mandate regulating insider trading in the tender offer context. Subsequently, the Supreme Court in *United States v. O'Hagan*, 521 U.S. 642 (1997), upheld the validity of Rule 14e-3, at least insofar as applied to the circumstances present in that case.[4]

Congress also has been active in this area by enacting legislation in 1984 and 1988. Due to the difficulty in comprehensively defining "insider trading," Congress elected to leave the further development of this concept to judicial interpretation. Among other provisions, the 1984 legislation amended § 21(d) of the Exchange Act to authorize the SEC to seek the imposition of a civil monetary penalty amounting to three times the profit received or loss avoided due to the violative transaction(s). As provided by the 1988 legislation, under certain conditions, broker-dealers, investment advisers, and others are subject to the treble monetary penalty for illegal inside trades effected by those persons who are under their control.[5]

Given the presence of fiduciary duties in state corporate law, it perhaps is surprising that insider trading law in this country is generally within the province of federal law. Although a few states (such as Delaware and New York) allow derivative suits against alleged inside traders based on perceived harm to the corporation or on the basis of unjust enrichment,[6] state law remedies often are unavailable in this context.[7] This lack of state law redress is due to the lack of an insider's disclosure obligation when transactions occur in the impersonal securities markets and the view that such trading activity does not harm the corporation. Indeed, outside of Delaware, New York and a few other states, even for those states that hold that insiders owe a duty to disclose material information before trading, such "duty attach[es] where

---

4. For commentary on Rule 14e-3, *see, e.g.,* M. STEINBERG & W. WANG, INSIDER TRADING §§ 9.1-9.4 (Oxford Univ. Press 3d edition 2010); Gruenbaum, *The New Disclose or Abstain From Trading Rule: Has the SEC Gone Too Far?*, 5 CORP. L. REV. 350 (1981); Heller, *Chiarella, SEC Rule 14e-3 and Dirks: "Fairness" Versus Economic Theory*, 37 BUS. LAW. 517 (1982); Koprucki, *Market Insiders' Duty Under Section 10(b), Rule 10b-5, and Rule 14e-3 to Disclose Material Nonpublic Market Information*, 50 U. CIN. L. REV. 558 (1981); Loewenstein, *Section 14(e) of the Williams Act and the Rule 10b-5 Comparisons*, 71 GEO. L.J. 1311 (1983)

5. For commentary on the 1984 and 1988 legislation, *see, e.g.,* Aldave, *The Insider Trading and Securities Fraud Enforcement Act of 1988: An Analysis and Appraisal*, 52 ALB. L. REV. 893 (1988); Friedman, *The Insider Trading and Securities Fraud Enforcement Act of 1988*, 68 N. CAR. L. REV. 465 (1990); Langevoort, *The Insider Trading Sanctions Act of 1984 and Its Effect on Existing Law*, 37 VAND. L. REV. 1273 (1984); Silver, *Penalizing Insider Trading: A Critical Assessment of the Insider Trading Sanctions Act of 1984*, 1985 DUKE L.J. 960; Note, *A Critique of the Insider Trading Sanctions Act of 1984*, 71 VA. L. REV. 455 (1985).

6. *See, e.g., Kahn v. Kolberg Kravis Roberts & Co., L.P.*, 23 A. 3d 831 (Del. 2011); *Diamond v. Oreamuno*, 24 N.Y. 2d 494, 248 N.E. 2d 910, 301 N.Y.S. 2d 78 (1969). Moreover, a small number of states prohibit "insider trading" by statute. *See, e.g.,* § 25402 of the California Corporations Code (adopting "access" approach).

7. *See, e.g., Freeman v. Decio*, 584 F.2d 186 (7th Cir. 1978) (applying Indiana law); *Shein v. Chasen*, 313 So. 2d 739 (Fla. 1975).

the insider and the shareholder trade face-to-face; transactions conducted on anonymous exchanges apparently do not qualify."[8]

[B] The Meaning of "Material" and "Nonpublic" Information

Under certain conditions, the federal securities laws prohibit the trading of securities (or "tipping" related thereto) when such person uses *material nonpublic* information. In *SEC v. Mayhew*, 121 F.3d 44 (2d Cir. 1997), the Second Circuit discussed the meaning of *material* and *nonpublic* information:

Nonpublic Information Requirement

Citing articles in the financial press and the fluctuations in the price of Rorer shares prior to his November 1989 conversation with [his source] Piccolino, [defendant] Mayhew argues that the information he received from Piccolino was already public, relieving him of liability.

Of course, trading based on public information does not violate [§ 10(b) or] § 14(e). Information becomes public when disclosed "to achieve a broad dissemination to the investing public generally and without favoring any special person or group," . . . or when, although known only by a few persons, their trading on it "has caused the information to be fully impounded into the price of the particular stock," . . . Moreover, "[t]o constitute non-public information under the act, information must be specific and more private than general rumor." . . . On the other hand, information may be nonpublic within the meaning of the 1934 Act even though it does not reveal all the details of a [particular contingency, event or] tender offer.

Mayhew bases his argument on the widespread media speculation, prior to November 15, 1989, that Rorer was a takeover or merger candidate. As early as April 5, 1988, one article predicted that "Rorer itself ha[d] become a takeover candidate" after its stock price dropped following Rorer's failed attempt to acquire another pharmaceutical company. . . . On May 30, 1989, another article placed Rorer on a "hit list" of six pharmaceutical companies that it predicted were vulnerable takeover targets. . . . On July 31, 1989, an article discussed the rise in Rorer stock due to "speculation about the next takeover target" in the pharmaceutical industry. . . . In contrast, another article indicated that Rorer planned to stay independent. . . .

. . . .

In sum, the aggregate of public information prior to November 15, 1989, was to the effect that Rorer was willing to merge if it found the right partner

---

8. M. Steinberg & W. Wang, Insider Trading § 15:2 (Oxford Univ. Press 3d edition 2010). *See generally* Branson, *Choosing the Appropriate Default Rule—Insider Trading Under State Law,* 45 Ala. L. Rev. 753 (1994); Hazen, *Corporate Insider Trading: Reawakening the Common Law,* 39 Wash. & Lee. L. Rev. 845 (1982).

and that Rorer was discussing this possibility with up to three companies. Privately, Rorer executives took care to keep information about actual merger discussions secret by limiting the persons who knew about specific merger negotiations to top executives and by using codes in related documents.

We agree with the district court that the information Piccolino conveyed to Mayhew went beyond that which had been publicly disseminated. Mayhew learned from Piccolino that Thurman, the president of Rorer's pharmaceuticals business, had confirmed that Rorer was "actually in discussions" toward merger with a candidate or candidates. He also learned that these merger talks were at a "serious" stage—far enough along to warrant PCA's involvement in negotiating a new employment agreement for Rorer's CEO. To a reasonable investor, this combination of new information, acquired privately, transformed the likelihood of a Rorer merger from one that was certainly possible at some future time to one that was highly probable quite soon.

In *Cusimano*, [97 F.3d 663 (2d Cir. 1996),] we held that a corporate insider's confirmation of information on which the financial press had speculated can satisfy the nonpublic requirement in the context of § 10(b). In that case, the *Wall Street Journal* had reported that AT&T and NCR Corporation were discussing ways to integrate their businesses. On the same day that the article was published, an AT&T insider called Cusimano to confirm the contents of the article and predicted that AT&T would acquire NCR. Cusimano subsequently began trading in NCR securities. We held that the tip Cusimano received satisfied the nonpublic requirement of § 10(b) because the confirmation by an insider of the merger speculated in the press made it less likely that nothing would happen. We see no reason to take a different view under similar circumstances in the context of § 14(e), and thus discern no error in the district court's finding that the information passed from Thurman to Piccolino to Mayhew exceeded that in the financial press and, to that extent, was not public.

In the alternative, Mayhew argues that the information he received from Piccolino was public because it was already built into the price of Rorer stock which had risen on speculation of merger and subsequently fallen as rumored mergers did not take place. We agree that the merger rumors in the media, prior to November 15, 1989, had pushed up the price of Rorer shares; however, the fact that, from the investors' perspective, the rumors had not borne fruit was also impounded into the price, causing it to drop. In these circumstances, it was reasonable for the finder of fact to conclude that this new information that (i) serious merger negotiations were actually ongoing, and (ii) had reached the point where the CEO was about to negotiate a new employment contract with the merged entity, had not been impounded into the price of Rorer stock. That conclusion is buttressed by the fact that on January 15, 1989, when the merger discussions were disclosed, the price of Rorer stock rose more than 20 percent from $49.75 to $63 per share.

In sum, we discern no clear error in the district court's finding that the information Mayhew received from Piccolino following the latter's November 15, 1989 luncheon with Thurman, effectively confirming information about which there had been speculation and lending a degree of immediacy to it, was nonpublic.

Materiality Requirement

Mayhew also challenges the district court's materiality finding, arguing that the information he received from Piccolino lacked sufficient specificity to be material. We disagree.

Information is material "'if there is a substantial likelihood that a reasonable [investor] would consider it important in deciding how to [invest].'" *Basic Inc. v. Levinson*, 485 U.S. 224, 231 (1988). . . . The materiality of information is a mixed question of law and fact. . . .

To be material, the information need not be such a reasonable investor would necessarily change his investment decision based on the information, as long as a reasonable investor would have viewed it as significantly altering the "total mix" of information available. . . . Material facts include those "which affect the probable future of the company and those which may affect the desire of investors to buy, sell, or hold the company's securities." . . .

In the context of a merger, where information can be speculative and tenuous, the materiality standard may be difficult to apply. Materiality will, in such cases, depend "upon a balancing of both the indicated probability that the event will occur and the anticipated magnitude of the event in light of the totality of the company activity." . . . Thus, a violation of the securities laws will not be found where "the disclosed information is so general that the recipient thereof is still 'undertaking a substantial economic risk that his tempting target will prove to be a "white elephant."'" . . . However, because a merger is one of the most important events that can occur for a small company, information regarding a merger "can become material at an earlier stage than would be the case as regards lesser transactions." . . . Moreover, where information regarding a merger originates from an insider, the information, even if not detailed, "takes on an added charge just because it is inside information." . . . And a major factor in determining whether information was material is the importance attached to it by those who knew about it. . . .

In this case, it was reasonable for the district court to conclude the information material to Mayhew's and Piccolino's decisions to invest, in Piccolino's case for the first time in options and for the first time in Rorer securities. Although Mayhew had invested in Rorer prior to November 15, 1989, he had sold all his Rorer shares at a loss by that date. After the Thurman-Piccolino luncheon, Mayhew plunged heavily into Rorer stock and options, committing more than half of his portfolio to the investment. Although Mayhew was not given the specific details of the merger, a lesser level of specificity is required because he knew the information came from an insider and that the merger discussions were actual and serious. . . . We see no basis for disturbing the district court's conclusions that a reasonable investor would find the information to have significantly altered the total mix of available information and that the information was thus, material.

Note — Martha Stewart

Interestingly, the issue of materiality was presented with respect to Martha Stewart's trading of the common stock of ImClone Systems Incorporated (ImClone). Ms. Stewart was criminally convicted for making false statements to government officials and for conspiracy (*United States v. Stewart,* 433 F.3d 273 (2d Cir. 2006)). The alleged insider trading violations were a subject of SEC civil enforcement action but not Department of Justice criminal prosecution. Ms. Stewart settled (without admitting or denying) the SEC's civil action against her for alleged illegal insider trading (38 Sec. Reg. & L. Rep. (BNA) 1397 (S.D.N.Y. 2006)). See MARTHA STEWART's LEGAL TROUBLES (J. Heminway ed., 2006). The issue of materiality thus was not resolved. Serving as an expert witness on behalf of Ms. Stewart, the author of this text opined:

> [1] I understand from the Indictment and the Government's opening argument at trial that the Government has insinuated that Ms. Stewart committed insider trading on December 27, 2001 when she sold her shares of ImClone Systems Incorporated (ImClone). As alleged by the Government, one of her motives, if not her primary motive for allegedly lying, conspiring, and obstructing a governmental investigation, was to cover up the allegedly improper trade. Upon review of testimony concerning the conversation [that Ms. Stewart's stock broker] Mr. Faneuil allegedly had with Ms. Stewart and the surrounding circumstances, I conclude that, accepting the Government's evidence as true, Ms. Stewart did not commit illegal insider trading. Based upon the custom and practice of the SEC and the securities industry, Ms. Stewart would have reasonably believed that she was not engaging in illegal insider trading with respect to her sales of ImClone common stock (stock).

> [2] [Ms. Stewart's stock broker] Mr. Faneuil testified that he told Ms. Stewart on December 27, 2001 that Dr. Samuel Waksal, the CEO of ImClone, was trying to sell all of his ImClone stock held at Merrill Lynch & Co., Inc. (Merrill Lynch). He also testified that Ms. Stewart asked for a price quote, he gave a price quote, and then she ordered the sale of her remaining ImClone stock. Accepting this testimony as true, the information Mr. Faneuil gave Ms. Stewart about Dr. Waksal's contemplated sale was not "material" information applying standards of custom and practice as

understood under the federal securities laws. Therefore, this information cannot serve as the basis for an insider trading charge.

[3] Corporate executive officers and directors, including CEOs, sell shares of a subject company's stock for a variety of reasons, many of which have nothing to do with the subject company. It is well known that a CEO of a U.S. publicly-held company may sell stock: because he/she needs money to use for personal or business purpose(s); to ameliorate margin dilemmas in his/her securities account(s); to diversify the CEO's portfolio to include a broader number and type of investments; to convey a gift; to generate cash to repay a loan or for some other obligation; or for tax planning purposes (especially at the end of the year). Normally, these reasons are irrelevant to the subject company and communicate no useful information to investors about the subject company.

[4] As testified to by [Ms. Stewart's stockbroker] Mr. Faneuil, the conversation with Ms. Stewart occurred at the end of the year (i.e., December 27, 2001). This testimony constitutes further support that information about Dr. Waksal's selling was not material. End of the year selling by CEOs and other insiders for tax planning purposes or to provide gifts to family members is a common occurrence.

[5] CEOs may sell stock for reasons that may impact (either positively or negatively) the subject company. For example, a CEO may sell a number of his/her shares of the subject company due to a lack of confidence in the company's future projects. As another example, a CEO may sell shares of the company's stock in response to a third party's tender offer. Dr. Waksal, for instance, sold over 800,000 shares of ImClone stock in October 2001 pursuant to a tender offer made by Bristol Myers Squibb Company (Bristol Myers).

[6] Under custom and practice today, a corporate insider, such as a CEO, would not sell company stock based on material non-public information. Because of sophisticated investigative resources, vigorous government enforcement, and self-imposed corporate insider trading "black-out" periods, insiders who trade on or tip material non-public information act at their peril.

[7] The purported significance of an insider's contemplated sales of subject securities recedes further when the information communicated does not include the number of shares or the percentage of the CEO's holdings that are contemplated to be sold. According to [Ms. Stewart's stock broker] Mr. Faneuil's testimony, he did not tell Ms. Stewart how many shares Dr. Waksal wanted to sell or what percent of Dr. Waksal's ImClone holdings were at Merrill Lynch; indeed, Mr. Faneuil testified that he told Ms. Stewart that he was sure that Dr. Waksal did not have all of his ImClone shares at Merrill Lynch. My understanding is that there is no evidence that Ms. Stewart was aware of either the amount or the percent of ImClone shares that

Dr. Waksal had at Merrill Lynch. A review of the Form 4 filed by Dr. Waksal with the SEC on or about November 13, 2001 and the Form 5 filed by Dr. Waksal with the SEC on or about February 15, 2002, which I understand have been admitted into evidence as Stewart Exhibits AC and AD, reveals that although Dr. Waksal attempted to sell and later transferred 79,797 shares of ImClone stock to his daughter, he still owned over 2.9 million shares of ImClone stock after the transfer. Dr. Waksal thus attempted to dispose of approximately 2.6 of his ImClone stock holdings on or about December 27, 2001. As set forth in this Declaration, under custom and practice today, this information was not material. An additional fact negating materiality is that approximately two months earlier, in late October 2001, Dr. Waksal sold 814,676 shares of ImClone stock pursuant to the Bristol Myers tender offer, representing over twenty percent of his ImClone stock holdings. This sale, of which I understand Ms. Stewart was aware, evidenced that Dr. Waksal was receptive (or at least not adverse) to selling shares of his ImClone stock.

[8] After approximately twenty-five years' experience in the securities law field, including my work at the SEC, I am aware of no case in the history of the federal securities laws, prior to the litigation against Ms. Stewart, in which anyone was charged with civil or criminal insider trading based solely upon a tip that a CEO or other insider was selling his/her securities of the subject corporation.

[9] Such a charge also is incongruous given the legal regime that existed as of December 27, 2001. In December 2001, any subject insider who sold a subject security generally did not have to disclose that trade to the public until the making of an SEC filing by the tenth day of the month following the trade. Even after Congress' enactment of the Sarbanes-Oxley Act of 2002, this information generally is not required to be filed with the SEC until the end of the second business day following the trade. This regimen evidences that an insider's trade standing alone is not material. If an insider's trade standing alone were material, then a subject insider would be required to publicly disclose his/her contemplated sale of subject securities prior to ordering such sale, not after such sale of subject securities has been effected as existing law generally mandates.

[10] If the fact that a corporate insider (such as a CEO) were seeking to sell his/her stock were itself material information, then every insider trade (such as by a CEO) would itself violate the law. Such a sale transaction under this approach would violate Section 10(b) and Rule 10b-5 because (among other reasons): (1) the sale was non-public (subject company shareholders and prospective investors were unaware of the contemplated trade); and (2) the trade was itself material. Such a position, as set forth in this Declaration, is contrary to the custom and practice that prevailed in December 2001 and that remains true today.

[11] Based on the foregoing, and accepting the Government's evidence as true, it is my opinion that: Ms. Stewart did not receive material information; and, on December 27, 2001, it would have been reasonable for Ms. Stewart to believe that her sale of ImClone stock was not illegal insider trading.

Declaration of Marc I. Steinberg in *United States v. Martha Stewart* (dated Feb. 19, 2004).

Interestingly, it bears emphasis that, until roughly three decades ago, many countries did not prohibit insider trading. As an *Economist* survey pointed out in 1989: "West Germany and France assumed until recently that insider trading was what financial life was all about."[9] Even today, although technically illegal, insider trading is less vigorously prosecuted in a number of countries. What significance should be given to the position taken by other countries? Do these countries believe that the discouragement of insider trading through local business norms is sufficient? Or, do some of these countries view insider trading as a legitimate management perk and a means to enhance market efficiency? Nonetheless, given the increasing number of countries that recently have enacted legislation illegalizing insider trading and are actively pursuing alleged violators, evidently the view of insider trading held in the United States has gained international acceptance.[10]

---

§ 12.02 Problems

Problem A

"Red" Calhounse, Organic State University's football coach, has cocktails with an alumnus and her spouse at an alumni function. The alumnus during cocktails tells her spouse that the corporation, of which she is a director, will announce the receipt of a multi-million dollar contract the following week. Calhounse, being privy to the conversation, thereupon purchases 10,000 shares. He sells them three years later at a profit of $80,000. The SEC brings suit. What result and why?

---

9. *A Survey of Europe's Internal Market,* Economist, July 8, 1989, at 15.

10. For scholarship in the international context, *see, e.g.,* Insider Trading: The Laws of Europe, the United States and Japan (E. Gaillard ed. 1992); Banoff, *The Regulation of Insider Trading in the United States, United Kingdom, and Japan,* 9 U. Mich. Yearbook Int'l Stud. 145 (1988); Beny, *Insider Trading Laws and Stock Markets Around the World: An Empirical Contribution to the Theoretical Law and Economics Debate,* 32 J. Corp. L. 237 (2007); Hazen, *Defining Insider Trading—Lessons from the European Community Directive on Insider Trading,* 55 Law & Cont. Prob. 231 (1992); Nasser, *The Morality of Insider Trading in the United States and Abroad,* 52 Okla. L. Rev. 377 (1999); Poser, *Insider Trading in the United Kingdom,* 24 Rev. Sec. & Comm. Reg. 25 (1991); Salbu, *Regulation of Insider Trading in a Global Marketplace: A Uniform Statutory Approach,* 66 Tulane L. Rev. 837 (1992); Steinberg, *Insider Trading Regulation—A Comparative Analysis,* 37 Int'l Law. 153 (2003); Symposium, 19 Dickinson J. Int'l. No. 1 (2000).

Problem B

Thomas, a financial analyst for Z.G. Gold, Inc., an investment banking and brokerage firm, calls Gregory, the chief financial officer of Mak-It Corp., seeking information about Mak-It's earnings during the last quarter, which will be announced the following week. Gregory says "It looks like our earnings will be down quite a bit." Thomas immediately informs his customers who sell Mak-It stock. The SEC brings suit. Who are "proper" defendants? Result?

Problem C

EZ-Tech, Inc. intends to make a tender offer for the shares of LoMar Corporation, a publicly held company whose common stock is traded on the New York Stock Exchange. Before the EZ-Tech tender offer is announced, Liz Meriweather, a lawyer working for Nameth, Shields & Davis, a law firm that represents EZ-Tech, has dinner with her husband Ryan. She informs Ryan that she is exhausted because of the long hours she is working in regard to the forthcoming EZ-Tech tender offer for LoMar. She adds that this information is confidential. The next day Liz and Ryan, unaware of the purchases by the other, each acquire a few thousand shares of LoMar common stock. Ryan's broker T.Y. Little also purchases Lo-Mar stock based on "hints" communicated by Ryan. After public announcement of the EZ-Tech offer, Liz, Ryan and T.Y. each sell their LoMar shares for a substantial profit. The SEC and private parties in separate actions institute suit against Liz, Ryan and T.Y. What result and why? Would the result be different if the contemplated transaction took the form of a merger rather than a tender offer?

---

§ 12.03 Actual Scenarios

Unfortunately, many otherwise upstanding individuals have had their career, reputation, and freedom demolished by engaging in illegal insider trading. For these individuals, the enticement of seemingly "easy money" and greed overtook their moral values and good judgment. The following case, *United States v. Blackwell*, involving a former esteemed professor, illustrates this point in a very poignant way. A second proceeding, which was settled pursuant to consent (with the defendants neither admitting nor denying the SEC's allegations), follows *Blackwell*. This enforcement action, based on alleged illegal insider trading, was brought against two former elite major league baseball players—Baseball Hall of Famer Eddie Murray and Baltimore Orioles' third baseman Doug DeCinces. Mr. DeCinces also has been criminally convicted. From a baseball accomplishment standpoint, Mr. Murray is one of five players (with Hank Aaron, Willie Mays, Rafael Palmeiro, and Alex Rodriguez being the others) in major league history to have more than 3,000 hits and 500 home runs.

United States v. Blackwell

United States Court of Appeals, Sixth Circuit

459 F.3d 739 (2006)

CLAY, Circuit Judge.

Defendant, Roger D. Blackwell, appeals a December 15, 2005 final judgment of the United States District Court for the Southern District of Ohio, convicting Defendant of [among other violations] fourteen counts of insider trading . . . ; sentencing Defendant to seventy-two months of imprisonment; and fining Defendant $1,000,000. For the reasons set forth below, we AFFIRM Defendant's convictions and sentence.

. . . .

Defendant is a former professor at Ohio State University's School of Business, as well as the president of Roger Blackwell and Associates ("RBA") and an investor in Black Jack Enterprises. Between 1991 and 2004 he was married to Kristina Stephan-Blackwell ("Stephan-Blackwell"). The events in this case arise out of the conduct of Defendant and Stephan-Blackwell in 1999, while Defendant was a member of the board of directors of a small natural foods company, Worthington Foods ("WF"). In July 1999, Kellogg Company ("Kellogg") initiated negotiations for a buyout of WF. The buyout occurred in October 1999. Between July and October 1999, however, several of Defendant's friends and family members invested in WF stock. . . .

The increased buying activity in WF stock between July and October 1999 led to an investigation. On December 15, 1999, the National Association of Securities Dealers ("NASD") sent Kellogg a questionnaire on the Kellogg-WF buyout, requesting information on relationships between persons who bought stock between July and October 1999 and persons who knew about the buyout. Pursuant to the NASD inquiry, Kellogg forwarded the list of persons who bought stock to Defendant, and requested that he inform [Kellogg] of any relationships he had with such persons. Defendant responded to the inquiry by stating: "I supplied no information about the transaction to any of the people on the list or anyone else. When asked by anyone about Worthington Foods during this period, I replied that I was not able to comment about the company's stock, as is my standard practice."

On March 16, 2000, the NASD sent a follow-up questionnaire to Kellogg. The follow-up, among other things, explicitly requested that Defendant supply information on his relationships to [certain persons who bought WF stock.] Defendant responded, explaining his relationships to them, but denying that he informed them of the buyout. Defendant stated, and still maintains, that he promoted WF because he believed in its value, but never disclosed the buyout.

On November 2, 2000, the Securities and Exchange Commission ("SEC") issued a subpoena, requiring Defendant to produce various documents and appear to testify before the SEC. Defendant eventually testified before the SEC on January 9, 2001, claiming that he did not disclose any information about the Kellogg-WF buyout to any person. In January 2002, the SEC sent a written inquiry to Defendant.

Defendant responded on January 18, 2002, reiterating his position that he never disclosed any information about the Kellogg-WF buyout. In February 2002, Stephan-Blackwell and her parents testified before the SEC. They denied that Blackwell had given them insider information on the buyout.

In early 2003, Defendant and Stephan-Blackwell began to have marital difficulties. They separated and Stephan-Blackwell moved to New York, where she began dating Terry Lundgren. In the spring of 2004, Stephan-Blackwell's attorney contacted the government about the instant case. Sometime thereafter Stephan-Blackwell learned that the government was considering pressing charges against her for perjury and insider trading. In the summer of 2004, Stephan- Blackwell and the government worked out an immunity deal, in which Stephan- Blackwell and her parents would receive immunity in exchange for Stephan-Blackwell's admission to conspiracy, perjury, and insider trading and testimony against Defendant. Stephan-Blackwell and Defendant finalized their divorce at approximately the same time. Several months later, Stephan-Blackwell and Lundgren became engaged.

In this same time period, [Jack] Kahl [who purchased WF stock] also approached the government about his involvement in the instant case. On May 27, 2004, pursuant to a proffer of immunity, Kahl admitted to the FBI that Defendant tipped him on the Kellogg-WF buyout. Subsequently, Kahl testified before the grand jury. Specifically, Kahl testified that he spoke with Defendant around 12:30 p.m. on his (Kahl's) birthday, September 20, 1999, and that Defendant informed him that Kellogg was going to buy out WF and that Kahl should buy WF stock.

. . . .

At trial, Stephen-Blackwell [and others] testified for the government. Stephan-Blackwell testified that she informed her parents [and others] of the buyout and encouraged them to buy WF stock after discussing the propriety of doing so with Defendant. She further testified that she and Defendant gave her parents money to buy WF stock. Stephan-Blackwell also testified that both she and Blackwell lied to the NASD and SEC about the tipping, and that she coached her mother to lie to the SEC. She further testified that she deleted emails . . . after receiving a SEC subpoena, in order to protect herself and Defendant. According to Stephan-Blackwell, Defendant was aware of the deletions and condoned them. Additionally, she and Blackwell formulated a plan to withhold information and obscure their relationships with parties who bought WF stock.

Significantly, during Stephan-Blackwell's trial testimony, Defendant allegedly mouthed "I hate you" to Stephan-Blackwell. Finding that such conduct would constitute witness intimidation, the district court allowed Defendant to be cross-examined on this issue, during which Defendant denied mouthing anything to Stephan-Blackwell.

. . . .

Jack Kahl testified that Defendant Blackwell informed him of the buyout, and that he bought WF stock on the morning of his birthday, September 20, 1999, based on the tip. Kahl could not remember the exact date that Defendant tipped him but believed it was around his birthday.

Twomley, WF's CEO and chairman of the board in 1999, testified regarding WF, the buyout, and Defendant's knowledge of it as a board member. Twomley further testified that there were rumors, mainly among WF employees, in the summer of 1999 that a bigger company would buy out WF.

Michelle DeStefano, an FBI agent involved in investigating the defendants, testified that subpoenaed phone records evidenced numerous phone calls between the defendants between July and October 1999.

Thereafter, defendants Jack, Voss, Hughes, Stacey, and Blackwell, as well as non-defendants, Dale Blackwell (Defendant's father), Professor Jarrell, and John Adams testified for the defense. All the defendants denied wrongdoing. Specifically, they all denied that Defendant Blackwell informed them of the buyout. Jack, an attorney, and Voss, who has a Ph.D. in economics and formerly was a professor at George Washington University, additionally testified that they had extensive stock market experience and bought WF stock because it appeared to be a good deal.

Professor Jarrell, former chief economist for the SEC, testified that WF stock was undervalued in September 1999, and thus that it was a good buy. He further testified that sophisticated investors would recognize that WF was undervalued and a potential target for a buyout. Professor Jarrell also explained "leakage theory." According to Professor Jarrell, information on mergers and buyouts will often "leak" to the public without insider trading. Companies about to buy out or be bought out give off signals indicating that a future buyout will occur. Sophisticated investors, especially analysts, and research companies looking for these signals, often learn of buyouts before they are publicly announced. Similarly, family members and close friends may notice an insider's increased activity levels and presume that a merger, or some other large transaction, is about to occur. Finally, Adams testified that he saw rumors of the buyout on Yahoo.

Based on the testimony described above, a jury convicted Defendant of insider trading, conspiracy to commit insider trading, conspiracy to obstruct an agency proceeding, and obstruction of an agency proceeding. . . .

[*Affirmed*]

Securities and Exchange Commission v. Mazzo

SEC Litigation Release No. 22451 (C.D. Cal. Aug. 17, 2012)

The Securities and Exchange Commission today announced a second round of charges in an insider trading case involving former professional baseball players and the former top executive at a California-based medical eye products company that was the subject of illegal trading.

The SEC brought initial charges in the case last year, accusing former professional baseball player Doug DeCinces and three others of insider trading on confidential information ahead of an acquisition of Advanced Medical Optics Inc. DeCinces and his three tippees made more than $1.7 million in illegal profits, and they agreed to pay more than $3.3 million to settle the SEC's charges. [Subsequently, in May 2017, Mr. DeCinces was criminally convicted of insider trading.]

Now the SEC is charging the source of those illegal tips about the impending transaction—DeCinces' close friend and neighbor James V. Mazzo, who was the Chairman and CEO of Advanced Medical Optics. The SEC also is charging two others who traded on inside information that DeCinces tipped to them—DeCinces' former Baltimore Orioles teammate Eddie Murray and another friend David L. Parker, who is a businessman living in Utah.

The SEC alleges that Murray made approximately $235,314 in illegal profits after Illinois-based Abbott Laboratories Inc. publicly announced its plan to purchase Advanced Medical Optics through a tender offer. Murray agreed to settle the SEC's charges by paying $358,151. The SEC's case continues against Parker and Mezzo, the latter of whom was directly involved in the tender offer and tipped the confidential information to DeCinces along the way.

According to the SEC's complaint filed in U.S. District Court for the Central District of California, the total unlawful profits resulting from Mazzo's illegal tipping was more than $2.4 million. Once Mazzo began tipping DeCinces with confidential information about the upcoming transaction, DeCinces soon began to purchase Advanced Medical Optics stock in several brokerage accounts. DeCinces bought more and more shares as the deal progressed and as he continued communicating with Mazzo. DeCinces tipped at least five others who traded on the inside information, including Murray, Parker, and the three traders who settled their charges along with DeCinces last year. . . .

According to the SEC's complaint, Mazzo and DeCinces had been close friends for quite some time and lived in the same exclusive gated community in Laguna Beach, Calif. They socialized together with their wives, belonging to the same Orange County country club and vacationing together overseas. They also communicated frequently by e-mail and through phone calls. Mazzo invested in the restaurant business of DeCinces' son, and DeCinces' daughter provided interior decorating services for Mazzo and his wife. Mazzo was directly involved in the impending Advanced Medical Optics/Abbott transaction from its inception in October 2008. With knowledge of confidential information about the deal and his duty not to disclose it, Mazzo illegally tipped DeCinces, who made significant purchases of Advanced Medical Optics shares on Nov. 5, 2008, and continuing up until and near the time of the public announcement of the acquisition.

The SEC alleges that Parker and DeCinces had been friends and business associates at the time of the illegal trading. Between Jan. 6 and Jan. 8, 2009, Parker bought 25,000 shares of Advanced Medical Optics stock on the basis of confidential information received from DeCinces about the impending transaction. Parker made approximately $347,920 when he sold the stock on the same day as the public announcement. Meanwhile on January 7, Murray used all of the available cash in his self-directed brokerage account to purchase 17,000 shares of Advanced Medical Optics stock on the basis of the confidential information that DeCinces communicated to him. Murray sold all of his shares following the public announcement.

Murray agreed to settle the charges against him without admitting or denying the SEC's allegations by consenting to the entry of a final judgment permanently enjoining him from violating Sections 10(b) and 14(e) of the Securities Exchange Act of 1934 and Rules 10b-5 and 14e-3 thereunder. Murray agreed to pay disgorgement of $235,314, prejudgment interest of $5,180, and a penalty of $117,657 for a total of $358,151. . . .

§ 12.04 The Classical Theory

It was not until 1980 that the U.S. Supreme Court resolved, at least to some degree, the contours of insider trading liability under § 10(b). In that case, *Chiarella v. United States,* the Court rejected the "access" approach, which had been adopted by several appellate courts. Indeed, the access approach has been widely embraced by other countries in their regulation of insider trading.[11] Instead, the Court opted for an approach based on the existence of a fiduciary relationship or a relationship of trust and confidence. Notably, in a subsequent decision, *Dirks v. Securities and Exchange Commission,* 463 U.S. 646 (1983) (included in § 12.06), the Supreme Court interpreted its rationale in *Chiarella* to include certain "outsiders" who have a special relationship with the subject company, including attorneys, accountants, consultants, and underwriters. These persons may be treated as insiders if they trade the company's securities while being aware of material nonpublic information acquired during the undertaking of that engagement. As stated by the *Dirks* Court: "The basis for recognizing this fiduciary duty is not simply that such persons acquired nonpublic corporate information, but rather that they have entered into a special confidential relationship in the conduct of the business of the enterprise and are given access to information solely for corporate purposes."

The Supreme Court's decision in *Chiarella* follows.

Chiarella v. United States

United States Supreme Court

445 U.S. 222, 100 S. Ct. 1108, 63 L. Ed. 2d 348 (1980)

MR. JUSTICE POWELL delivered the opinion of the Court.

The question in this case is whether a person who learns from the confidential documents of one corporation that it is planning an attempt to secure control of a

---

11. *See* M. Steinberg, F. Gevurtz & E. Chaffee, Global Issues in Securities Law 63–83 (2013); Steinberg, *Insider Trading Regulation—A Comparative Analysis,* 37 Int'l Law. 153 (2003).

second corporation violates § 10(b) of the Securities Exchange Act of 1934 if he fails to disclose the impending takeover before trading in the target company's securities.

I

Petitioner is a printer by trade. In 1975 and 1976, he worked as a "markup man" in the New York composing room of Pandick Press, a financial printer. Among documents that petitioner handled were five announcements of corporate takeover bids. When these documents were delivered to the printer, the identities of the acquiring and target corporations were concealed by blank spaces or false names. The true names were sent to the printer on the night of the final printing.

The petitioner, however, was able to deduce the names of the target companies before the final printing from other information contained in the documents. Without disclosing his knowledge, petitioner purchased stock in the target companies and sold the shares immediately after the takeover attempts were made public.[12] By this method, petitioner realized a gain of slightly more than $30,000 in the course of 14 months. Subsequently, the Securities and Exchange Commission (Commission or SEC) began an investigation of his trading activities. In May 1977, petitioner entered into a consent decree with the Commission in which he agreed to return his profits to the sellers of the shares. On the same day, he was discharged by Pandick Press.

In January 1978, petitioner was indicted on 17 counts of violating § 10(b) of the Securities Exchange Act of 1934 (1934 Act) and SEC Rule 10b-5. After petitioner unsuccessfully moved to dismiss the indictment, he was brought to trial and convicted on all counts.

The Court of Appeals for the Second Circuit affirmed petitioner's conviction. 588 F.2d 1358 (1978). We granted certiorari and we now reverse.

II

Section 10(b) of the 1934 Act prohibits the use "in connection with the purchase or sale of any security . . . [of] any manipulative or deceptive device or contrivance in contravention of such rules and regulations as the Commission may prescribe." Pursuant to this section, the SEC promulgated Rule 10b-5. . . .

This case concerns the legal effect of the petitioner's silence. The District Court's charge permitted the jury to convict the petitioner if it found that he willfully failed to inform sellers of target company securities that he knew of a forthcoming takeover bid that would make their shares more valuable. In order to decide whether silence in such circumstances violates § 10(b), it is necessary to review the language and legislative history of that statute as well as its interpretation by the Commission and the federal courts.

---

[12]. Of the five transactions, four involved tender offers and one concerned a merger. 588 F.2d 1358, n. 2 (CA2 1978).

Although the starting point of our inquiry is the language of the statute, § 10(b) does not state whether silence may constitute a manipulative or deceptive device. Section 10(b) was designed as a catchall clause to prevent fraudulent practices. But neither the legislative history nor the statute itself affords specific guidance for the resolution of this case. When Rule 10b-5 was promulgated in 1942, the SEC did not discuss the possibility that failure to provide information might run afoul of § 10(b).

The SEC took an important step in the development of § 10(b) when it held that a broker-dealer and his firm violated that section by selling securities on the basis of undisclosed information obtained from a director of the issuer corporation who was also a registered representative of the brokerage firm. In *Cady, Roberts & Co.*, 40 S.E.C. 907 (1961), the Commission decided that a corporate insider must abstain from trading in the shares of his corporation unless he has first disclosed all material inside information known to him. The obligation to disclose or abstain derives from

> [a]n affirmative duty to disclose material information [which] has been traditionally imposed on corporate "insiders," particularly officers, directors, or controlling stockholders. We, and the courts have consistently held that insiders must disclose material facts which are known to them by virtue of their position but which are not known to persons with whom they deal and which, if known, would affect their investment judgment.

The Commission emphasized that the duty arose from (i) the existence of a relationship affording access to inside information intended to be available only for a corporate purpose, and (ii) the unfairness of allowing a corporate insider to take advantage of that information by trading without disclosure.

That the relationship between a corporate insider and the stockholders of his corporation gives rise to a disclosure obligation is not a novel twist of the law. At common law, misrepresentation made for the purpose of inducing reliance upon the false statement is fraudulent. But one who fails to disclose material information prior to the consummation of a transaction commits fraud only when he is under a duty to do so. And the duty to disclose arises when one party has information "that the other [party] is entitled to know because of a fiduciary or other similar relation of trust and confidence between them."[13] In its *Cady, Roberts* decision, the Commission recognized a relationship of trust and confidence between the shareholders of a corporation and those insiders who have obtained confidential information by reason of their position with that corporation. This relationship gives rise to a duty to disclose because of the "necessity of preventing a corporate insider from . . . tak[ing] unfair advantage of the uninformed minority stockholders." . . .

---

[13]. Restatement (Second) of Torts § 551(2)(a) (1976). See James & Gray, *Misrepresentation — Part II*, 37 Md. L. Rev. 488, 523–527 (1978). As regards securities transactions, the American Law Institute recognizes that "silence when there is a duty to . . . speak may be a fraudulent act." ALI, Federal Securities Code § 262(b) (Prop. Off. Draft 1978).

The federal courts have found violations of § 10(b) where corporate insiders used undisclosed information for their own benefit. The cases also have emphasized, in accordance with the common-law rule, that "[t]he party charged with failing to disclose market information must be under a duty to disclose it." Accordingly, a purchaser of stock who has no duty to a prospective seller because he is neither an insider nor a fiduciary has been held to have no obligation to reveal material facts.

. . . .

Thus, administrative and judicial interpretations have established that silence in connection with the purchase or sale of securities may operate as a fraud actionable under § 10(b) despite the absence of statutory language or legislative history specifically addressing the legality of nondisclosure. But such liability is premised upon a duty to disclose arising from a relationship of trust and confidence between parties to a transaction. Application of a duty to disclose prior to trading guarantees that corporate insiders, who have an obligation to place the shareholder's welfare before their own, will not benefit personally through fraudulent use of material, nonpublic information.[14]

III

In this case, the petitioner was convicted of violating § 10(b) although he was not a corporate insider and he received no confidential information from the target company. Moreover, the "market information" upon which he relied did not concern the earning power or operations of the target company, but only the plans of the acquiring company. Petitioner's use of that information was not a fraud under § 10(b) unless he was subject to an affirmative duty to disclose it before trading. In this case, the jury instructions failed to specify any such duty. In effect, the trial court instructed the jury that petitioner owed a duty to everyone; to all sellers, indeed, to the market as a whole. The jury simply was told to decide whether petitioner used material, nonpublic information at a time when "he knew other people trading in the securities market did not have access to the same information."

The Court of Appeals affirmed the conviction by holding that "[a]nyone—corporate insider or not—who regularly receives material nonpublic information may not use that information to trade in securities without incurring an affirmative duty to disclose." . . . Although the court said that its test would include only persons who regularly receive material, nonpublic information, its rationale for that limitation is unrelated to the existence of a duty to disclose. The Court of Appeals, like the trial court, failed to identify a relationship between petitioner and the sellers that could give rise to a duty. Its decision thus rested solely upon its belief that the federal securities laws have "created a system providing equal access to information necessary for reasoned and intelligent investment decisions." . . . The use by

---

[14]. "Tippees" of corporate insiders have been held liable under § 10(b) because they have a duty not to profit from the use of inside information that they know is confidential and know or should know came from a corporate insider, *Shapiro v. Merrill Lynch, Pierce, Fenner & Smith, Inc.*, 495 F.2d 228, 237–238 (CA2 1974). The tippee's obligation has been viewed as arising from his role as a participant after the fact in the insider's breach of a fiduciary duty. . . .

anyone of material information not generally available is fraudulent, this theory suggests, because such information gives certain buyers or sellers an unfair advantage over less informed buyers and sellers.

This reasoning suffers from two defects. First, not every instance of financial unfairness constitutes fraudulent activity under § 10(b). See *Santa Fe Industries, Inc. v. Green*, 430 U. S. 462, 474–477 (1977). Second, the element required to make silence fraudulent—a duty to disclose—is absent in this case. No duty could arise from petitioner's relationship with the sellers of the target company's securities, for petitioner had no prior dealings with them. He was not their agent, he was not a fiduciary, he was not a person in whom the sellers had placed their trust and confidence. He was, in fact, a complete stranger who dealt with the sellers only through impersonal market transactions.

We cannot affirm petitioner's conviction without recognizing a general duty between all participants in market transactions to forgo actions based on material, nonpublic information. Formulation of such a broad duty, which departs radically from the established doctrine that duty arises from a specific relationship between two parties, should not be undertaken absent some explicit evidence of congressional intent.

As we have seen, no such evidence emerges from the language or legislative history of § 10(b). Moreover, neither the Congress nor the Commission ever has adopted a parity-of-information rule. . . .

Section 10(b) is aptly described as a catchall provision, but what it catches must be fraud. When an allegation of fraud is based upon nondisclosure, there can be no fraud absent a duty to speak. We hold that a duty to disclose under § 10(b) does not arise from the mere possession of nonpublic market information. The contrary result is without support in the legislative history of § 10(b) and would be inconsistent with the careful plan that Congress has enacted for regulation of the securities markets.

IV

In its brief to this Court, the United States offers an alternative theory to support petitioner's conviction. It argues that petitioner breached a duty to the acquiring corporation when he acted upon information that he obtained by virtue of his position as an employee of a printer employed by the corporation. The breach of this duty is said to support a conviction under § 10(b) for fraud perpetrated upon both the acquiring corporation and the sellers.

We need not decide whether this theory has merit for it was not submitted to the jury. . . .

. . . Because we cannot affirm a criminal conviction on the basis of a theory not presented to the jury, we will not speculate upon whether such a duty exists, whether it has been breached, or whether such a breach constitutes a violation of § 10(b).

The judgment of the Court of Appeals is

Reversed.

MR. CHIEF JUSTICE BURGER, dissenting.

I believe that the jury instructions in this case properly charged a violation of § 10(b) and Rule 10b-5, and I would affirm the conviction.

I

As a general rule, neither party to an arm's-length business transaction has an obligation to disclose information to the other unless the parties stand in some confidential or fiduciary relation. See W. Prosser, Law of Torts § 106 (2d ed. 1955). This rule permits a businessman to capitalize on his experience and skill in securing and evaluating relevant information; it provides incentive for hard work, careful analysis, and astute forecasting. But the policies that underlie the rule also should limit its scope. In particular, the rule should give way when an informational advantage is obtained, not by superior experience, foresight, or industry, but by some unlawful means. . . .

I would read § 10(b) and Rule 10b-5 to encompass and build on this principle: to mean that a person who has misappropriated nonpublic information has an absolute duty to disclose that information or to refrain from trading.

The language of § 10(b) and of Rule 10b-5 plainly supports such a reading. By their terms, these provisions reach any person engaged in any fraudulent scheme. This broad language negates the suggestion that congressional concern was limited to trading by "corporate insiders" or to deceptive practices related to "corporate information." Just as surely Congress cannot have intended one standard of fair dealing for "white collar" insiders and another for the "blue collar" level. The very language of § 10(b) and Rule 10b-5 "by repeated use of the word 'any' [was] obviously meant to be inclusive."

The history of the statute and of the Rule also supports this reading. The antifraud provisions were designed in large measure "to assure that dealing in securities is fair and without undue preferences or advantages among investors." H. R. Conf. Rep. No. 94-229, p. 91 (1975). These provisions prohibit "those manipulative and deceptive practices which have been demonstrated to fulfill no useful function." S. Rep. No. 792, 73d Cong., 2d Sess., 6 (1934). An investor who purchases securities on the basis of misappropriated nonpublic information possesses just such an "undue" trading advantage; his conduct quite clearly serves no useful function except his own enrichment at the expense of others.

. . . .

II

The Court's opinion, as I read it, leaves open the question whether § 10(b) and Rule 10b-5 prohibit trading on misappropriated nonpublic information. Instead, the Court apparently concludes that this theory of the case was not submitted to the jury. In the Court's view, the instructions given the jury were premised on the erroneous notion that the mere failure to disclose nonpublic information, however acquired, is a deceptive practice. And because of this premise, the jury was not instructed that the means by which Chiarella acquired his informational advantage—by violating a duty owed to the acquiring companies—was an element of the offense.

The Court's reading of the District Court's charge is unduly restrictive. Fairly read as a whole and in the context of the trial, the instructions required the jury to find that Chiarella obtained his trading advantage by misappropriating the property of his employer's customers. . . .

In sum, the evidence shows beyond all doubt that Chiarella, working literally in the shadows of the warning signs in the print shop, misappropriated—stole to put it bluntly—valuable nonpublic information entrusted to him in the utmost confidence. He then exploited his ill-gotten informational advantage by purchasing securities in the market. In my view, such conduct plainly violates § 10(b) and Rule 10b-5. Accordingly, I would affirm the judgment of the Court of Appeals.

MR. JUSTICE BLACKMUN, with whom MR. JUSTICE MARSHALL joins, dissenting.

Although I agree with much of what is said in Part I of the dissenting opinion of The Chief Justice, I write separately because, in my view, it is unnecessary to rest petitioner's conviction on a "misappropriation" theory. The fact that petitioner Chiarella purloined, or, to use The Chief Justice's word, "stole," information concerning pending tender offers certainly is the most dramatic evidence that petitioner was guilty of fraud. He has conceded that he knew it was wrong, and he and his co-workers in the print shop were specifically warned by their employer that actions of this kind were improper and forbidden. But I also would find petitioner's conduct fraudulent within the meaning of § 10(b) of the Securities Exchange Act of 1934 and the Securities and Exchange Commission's Rule 10b-5, even if he had obtained the blessing of his employer's principals before embarking on his profiteering scheme. Indeed, I think petitioner's brand of manipulative trading, with or without such approval, lies close to the heart of what the securities laws are intended to prohibit.

The Court continues to pursue a course, charted in certain recent decisions, designed to transform § 10(b) from an intentionally elastic "catchall" provision to one that catches relatively little of the misbehavior that all too often makes investment in securities a needlessly risky business for the uninitiated investor. Such confinement in this case is now achieved by imposition of a requirement of a "special relationship" akin to fiduciary duty before the statute gives rise to a duty to disclose or to abstain from trading upon material, nonpublic information. The Court admits that this conclusion finds no mandate in the language of the statute or its legislative history. Yet the Court fails even to attempt a justification of its ruling in terms of the purposes of the securities laws, or to square that ruling with the longstanding but now much abused principle that the federal securities laws are to be construed flexibly rather than with narrow technicality.

I, of course, agree with the Court that a relationship of trust can establish a duty to disclose under § 10(b) and Rule 10b-5. But I do not agree that a failure to disclose violates the Rule only when the responsibilities of a relationship of that kind have been breached. As applied to this case, the Court's approach unduly minimizes the importance of petitioner's access to confidential information that the honest investor, no matter how diligently he tried, could not legally obtain. In doing so, it further advances an interpretation of § 10(b) and Rule 10b-5 that stops short of their full implications. Although the Court draws support for its position from certain precedent, I find its decision neither fully consistent with developments in the common law of fraud, nor fully in step with administrative and judicial application of Rule 10b-5 to "insider" trading.

. . . .

Whatever the outer limits of the Rule, petitioner Chiarella's case fits neatly near the center of its analytical framework. He occupied a relationship to the takeover companies giving him intimate access to concededly material information that was sedulously guarded from public access. The information, in the words of *Cady, Roberts & Co.*, was "intended to be available only for a corporate purpose and not for the personal benefit of anyone." Petitioner, moreover, knew that the information was unavailable to those with whom he dealt. And he took full, virtually riskless advantage of this artificial information gap by selling the stocks shortly after each takeover bid was announced. By any reasonable definition, his trading was "inherent[ly] unfai[r]." This misuse of confidential information was clearly placed before the jury. Petitioner's conviction, therefore, should be upheld, and I dissent from the Court's upsetting that conviction.

Note — "Quasi" Insiders

In the *Dirks* decision, contained later in this Chapter (§ 12.08), the Supreme Court interpreted *Chiarella* to include certain "outsiders" within the classical theory of insider trading. This theory has been coined the "quasi" or "temporary" insider theory. Under the Court's rationale, this theory encompasses such persons as attorneys, accountants, consultants, and underwriters who have a special relationship with the subject company. These persons may be treated as insiders if they trade the company's securities while being aware of material nonpublic information acquired during the undertaking of that engagement. As stated by the *Dirks* Court: "The basis for recognizing this fiduciary duty is not simply that such persons acquired nonpublic corporate information, but rather that they have entered into a special confidential relationship in the conduct of the business of the enterprise and are given access to information solely for corporate purposes."

---

§ 12.05 The "Misappropriation" Theory

The Supreme Court's decision in *Chiarella* left unresolved whether § 10(b)'s insider trading prohibition extended to those who breached a duty owed to the source of the information. At least with respect to those who owe a fiduciary duty to the source of the information, the Supreme Court gave its approval to this approach—coined the "misappropriation" theory—in the *O'Hagan* decision that follows. That decision also addressed the scope of Rule 14e-3, which covers insider trading solely in the tender offer setting. The Court's analysis of Rule 14e-3 is covered later in this Chapter.

United States v. O'Hagan

United States Supreme Court

521 U.S. 642, 117 S. Ct. 2199, 138 L.Ed.2d 724 (1997)

Justice GINSBURG delivered the opinion of the Court.

This case concerns the interpretation and enforcement of § 10(b) and § 14(e) of the Securities Exchange Act of 1934, and rules made by the Securities and Exchange Commission pursuant to these provisions, Rule 10b-5 and Rule 14e-3(a). Two prime questions are presented. The first relates to the misappropriation of material, non-public information for securities trading; the second concerns fraudulent practices in the tender offer setting. In particular, we address and resolve these issues: (1) Is a person who trades in securities for personal profit, using confidential information misappropriated in breach of a fiduciary duty to the source of the information, guilty of violating § 10(b) and Rule 10b-5? (2) Did the Commission exceed its rulemaking authority by adopting Rule 14e-3(a), which proscribes trading on undisclosed information in the tender offer setting, even in the absence of a duty to disclose? Our answer to the first question is yes, and to the second question, viewed in the context of this case, no. [The Court's analysis of the Rule 14e-3 issue is contained in § 12.08.]

Respondent James Herman O'Hagan was a partner in the law firm of Dorsey & Whitney in Minneapolis, Minnesota. In July 1988, Grand Metropolitan PLC (Grand Met), a company based in London, England, retained Dorsey & Whitney as local counsel to represent Grand Met regarding a potential tender offer for the common stock of the Pillsbury Company, headquartered in Minneapolis. Both Grand Met and Dorsey & Whitney took precautions to protect the confidentiality of Grand Met's tender offer plans. O'Hagan did no work on the Grand Met representation. Dorsey & Whitney withdrew from representing Grand Met on September 9, 1988. Less than a month later, on October 4, 1988, Grand Met publicly announced its tender offer for Pillsbury stock.

On August 18, 1988, while Dorsey & Whitney was still representing Grand Met, O'Hagan began purchasing call options for Pillsbury stock. Each option gave him the right to purchase 100 shares of Pillsbury stock by a specified date in September 1988. Later in August and in September, O'Hagan made additional purchases of Pillsbury call options. By the end of September, he owned 2,500 unexpired Pillsbury options, apparently more than any other individual investor. O'Hagan also purchased, in September 1988, some 5,000 shares of Pillsbury common stock, at a price just under $39 per share. When Grand Met announced its tender offer in October, the price of Pillsbury stock rose to nearly $60 per share. O'Hagan then sold his Pillsbury call options and common stock, making a profit of more than $4.3 million.

The Securities and Exchange Commission (SEC or Commission) initiated an investigation into O'Hagan's transactions, culminating in a 57-count indictment. The indictment alleged that O'Hagan defrauded his law firm and its client, Grand Met, by using for his own trading purposes material, nonpublic information regarding Grand Met's planned tender offer. According to the indictment, O'Hagan used the profits he gained through this trading to conceal his previous embezzlement and conversion of unrelated client trust funds. . . . A jury convicted O'Hagan on all 57 counts, and he was sentenced to a 41-month term of imprisonment.

A divided panel of the Court of Appeals for the Eighth Circuit reversed all of O'Hagan's convictions. 92 F.3d 612 (1996). Liability under § 10(b) and Rule 10b-5, the Eighth Circuit held, may not be grounded on the "misappropriation theory" of securities fraud on which the prosecution relied. The Court of Appeals also held that Rule 14e-3(a) — which prohibits trading while in possession of material, nonpublic information relating to a tender offer — exceeds the SEC's § 14(e) rulemaking authority because the rule contains no breach of fiduciary duty requirement. The Eighth Circuit further concluded that O'Hagan's mail fraud and money laundering convictions rested on violations of the securities laws, and therefore could not stand once the securities fraud convictions were reversed. . . . We granted certiorari, and now reverse the Eighth Circuit's judgment.

II

We address first the Court of Appeals' reversal of O'Hagan's convictions under § 10(b) and Rule 10b-5. Following the Fourth Circuit's lead, see *United States v. Bryan*, 58 F.3d 933 (1995), the Eighth Circuit rejected the misappropriation theory as a basis for § 10(b) liability. We hold, in accord with several other Courts of Appeals, that criminal liability under § 10(b) may be predicated on the misappropriation theory.

A

[Section 10(b)] proscribes (1) using any deceptive device (2) in connection with the purchase or sale of securities, in contravention of rules prescribed by the Commission. The provision, as written, does not confine its coverage to deception of a purchaser or seller of securities; rather, the statute reaches any deceptive device used "in connection with the purchase or sale of any security."

Pursuant to its § 10(b) rulemaking authority, the Commission has adopted Rule 10b-5. . . . Liability under Rule 10b-5, our precedent indicates, does not extend beyond conduct encompassed by § 10(b)'s prohibition. . . .

Under the "traditional" or "classical theory" of insider trading liability, § 10(b) and Rule 10b-5 are violated when a corporate insider trades in the securities of his corporation on the basis of material, nonpublic information. Trading on such information qualifies as a "deceptive device" under § 10(b), we have affirmed, because "a relationship of trust and confidence [exists] between the shareholders of a corporation and those insiders who have obtained confidential information by reason of their position with that corporation." *Chiarella v. United States*, 445 U.S. 222, 228 (1980).

That relationship, we recognized, "gives rise to a duty to disclose [or to abstain from trading] because of the 'necessity of preventing a corporate insider from . . . tak[ing] unfair advantage of . . . uninformed . . . stockholders.'" . . . The classical theory applies not only to officers, directors, and other permanent insiders of a corporation, but also to attorneys, accountants, consultants, and others who temporarily become fiduciaries of a corporation. See *Dirks v. SEC*, 463 U.S. 646, 655, n. 14 (1983).

The "misappropriation theory" holds that a person commits fraud "in connection with" a securities transaction, and thereby violates § 10(b) and Rule 10b-5, when he misappropriates confidential information for securities trading purposes, in breach of a duty owed to the source of the information. Under this theory, a fiduciary's undisclosed, self-serving use of a principal's information to purchase or sell securities, in breach of a duty of loyalty and confidentiality, defrauds the principal of the exclusive use of that information. In lieu of premising liability on a fiduciary relationship between company insider and purchaser or seller of the company's stock, the misappropriation theory premises liability on a fiduciary-turned-trader's deception of those who entrusted him with access to confidential information.

The two theories are complementary, each addressing efforts to capitalize on non-public information through the purchase or sale of securities. The classical theory targets a corporate insider's breach of duty to shareholders with whom the insider transacts; the misappropriation theory outlaws trading on the basis of nonpublic information by a corporate "outsider" in breach of a duty owed not to a trading party, but to the source of the information. The misappropriation theory is thus designed to "protec[t] the integrity of the securities markets against abuses by 'outsiders' to a corporation who have access to confidential information that will affect th[e] corporation's security price when revealed, but who owe no fiduciary or other duty to that corporation's shareholders." . . .

In this case, the indictment alleged that O'Hagan, in breach of a duty of trust and confidence he owed to his law firm, Dorsey & Whitney, and to its client, Grand Met, traded on the basis of nonpublic information regarding Grand Met's planned tender offer for Pillsbury common stock. This conduct, the Government charged, constituted a fraudulent device in connection with the purchase and sale of securities.[15]

B

We agree with the Government that misappropriation, as just defined, satisfies § 10(b)'s requirement that chargeable conduct involve a "deceptive device or contrivance" used "in connection with" the purchase or sale of securities. We observe, first,

---

[15]. The Government could not have prosecuted O'Hagan under the classical theory, for O'Hagan was not an "insider" of Pillsbury, the corporation in whose stock he traded. Although an "outsider" with respect to Pillsbury, O'Hagan had an intimate association with, and was found to have traded on confidential information from, Dorsey & Whitney, counsel to tender offeror Grand Met. Under the misappropriation theory, O'Hagan's securities trading does not escape Exchange Act sanction, as it would under the dissent's reasoning, simply because he was associated with, and gained nonpublic information from, the bidder, rather than the target.

that misappropriators, as the Government describes them, deal in deception. A fiduciary who "[pretends] loyalty to the principal while secretly converting the principal's information for personal gain," . . . "dupes" or defrauds the principal. See Aldave, *Misappropriation*: *A General Theory of Liability for Trading on Nonpublic Information*, 13 HOFSTRA L. REV. 101, 119 (1984).

We addressed fraud of the same species in *Carpenter v. United States*, 484 U.S. 19 (1987), which involved the mail fraud statute's proscription of "any scheme or artifice to defraud," 18 U.S.C. § 1341. Affirming convictions under that statute, we said in *Carpenter* that an employee's undertaking not to reveal his employer's confidential information "became a sham" when the employee provided the information to his co-conspirators in a scheme to obtain trading profits. A company's confidential information, we recognized in *Carpenter*, qualifies as property to which the company has a right of exclusive use. The undisclosed misappropriation of such information, in violation of a fiduciary duty, the Court said in *Carpenter*, constitutes fraud akin to embezzlement — "'the fraudulent appropriation to one's own use of the money or goods entrusted to one's care by another.'" *Carpenter's* discussion of the fraudulent misuse of confidential information, the Government notes, "is a particularly apt source of guidance here, because [the mail fraud statute] (like Section 10(b)) has long been held to require deception, not merely the breach of a fiduciary duty." . . .

Deception through nondisclosure is central to the theory of liability for which the Government seeks recognition. As counsel for the Government stated in explanation of the theory at oral argument: "To satisfy the common law rule that a trustee may not use the property that [has] been entrusted [to] him, there would have to be consent. To satisfy the requirement of the [Exchange] Act that there be no deception, there would only have to be disclosure." . . .

The misappropriation theory advanced by the Government is consistent with *Santa Fe Industries, Inc. v. Green*, 430 U.S. 462 (1977), a decision underscoring that § 10(b) is not an all-purpose breach of fiduciary duty ban; rather, it trains on conduct involving manipulation or deception. In contrast to the Government's allegations in this case, in *Santa Fe Industries*, all pertinent facts were disclosed by the persons charged with violating § 10(b) and Rule 10b-5; therefore, there was no deception through nondisclosure to which liability under those provisions could attach. Similarly, full disclosure forecloses liability under the misappropriation theory: Because the deception essential to the misappropriation theory involves feigning fidelity to the source of information, if the fiduciary discloses to the source that he plans to trade on the nonpublic information, there is no "deceptive device" and thus no § 10(b) violation — although the fiduciary-turned-trader may remain liable under state law for breach of a duty of loyalty.[16]

---

[16]. Where, however, a person trading on the basis of material, nonpublic information owes a duty of loyalty and confidentiality to two entities or persons — for example, a law firm and its client — but makes disclosure to only one, the trader may still be liable under the misappropriation theory.

We turn next to the § 10(b) requirement that the misappropriator's deceptive use of information be "in connection with the purchase or sale of [a] security." This element is satisfied because the fiduciary's fraud is consummated, not when the fiduciary gains the confidential information, but when, without disclosure to his principal, he uses the information to purchase or sell securities. The securities transaction and the breach of duty thus coincide. This is so even though the person or entity defrauded is not the other party to the trade, but is, instead, the source of the nonpublic information. . . . A misappropriator who trades on the basis of material, nonpublic information, in short, gains his advantageous market position through deception; he deceives the source of the information and simultaneously harms members of the investing public.

The misappropriation theory targets information of a sort that misappropriators ordinarily capitalize upon to gain no-risk profits through the purchase or sale of securities. Should a misappropriator put such information to other use, the statute's prohibition would not be implicated. The theory does not catch all conceivable forms of fraud involving confidential information; rather, it catches fraudulent means of capitalizing on such information through securities transactions.

. . . .

The Government notes another limitation on the forms of fraud § 10(b) reaches: "The misappropriation theory would not . . . apply to a case in which a person defrauded a bank into giving him a loan or embezzled cash from another, and then used the proceeds of the misdeed to purchase securities." . . . In such a case, the Government states, "the proceeds would have value to the malefactor apart from their use in a securities transaction, and the fraud would be complete as soon as the money was obtained." . . . In other words, money can buy, if not anything, then at least many things; its misappropriation may thus be viewed as sufficiently detached from a subsequent securities transaction that § 10(b)'s "in connection with" requirement would not be met.

The dissent's charge that the misappropriation theory is incoherent because information, like funds, can be put to multiple uses misses the point. The Exchange Act was enacted in part "to insure the maintenance of fair and honest markets," and there is no question that fraudulent uses of confidential information fall within § 10(b)'s prohibition if the fraud is "in connection with" a securities transaction. It is hardly remarkable that a rule suitably applied to the fraudulent uses of certain kinds of information would be stretched beyond reason were it applied to the fraudulent use of money.

The dissent does catch the Government in overstatement. Observing that money can be used for all manner of purposes and purchases, the Government urges that confidential information of the kind at issue derives its value only from its utility in securities trading. Substitute "ordinarily" for "only," and the Government is on the mark.

Our recognition that the Government's "only" is an overstatement has provoked the dissent to cry "new theory." . . . Here, . . . Rule 10b-5's promulgation has not been challenged; we consider only the Government's charge that O'Hagan's alleged fraudulent conduct falls within the prohibitions of the rule and § 10(b). In this context, we acknowledge simply that, in defending the Government's interpretation of the rule and statute in this Court, the Government's lawyers have pressed a solid point too far, something lawyers, occasionally even judges, are wont to do.

The misappropriation theory comports with § 10(b)'s language, which requires deception "in connection with the purchase or sale of any security," not deception of an identifiable purchaser or seller. The theory is also well-tuned to an animating purpose of the Exchange Act: to insure honest securities markets and thereby promote investor confidence. . . . Although informational disparity is inevitable in the securities markets, investors likely would hesitate to venture their capital in a market where trading based on misappropriated nonpublic information is unchecked by law. An investor's informational disadvantage vis-a-vis a misappropriator with material, nonpublic information stems from contrivance, not luck; it is a disadvantage that cannot be overcome with research or skill. *See* Brudney, *Insiders, Outsiders, and Informational Advantages Under the Federal Securities Laws*, 93 HARV. L. REV. 322, 356 (1979).

In sum, considering the inhibiting impact on market participation of trading on misappropriated information, and the congressional purposes underlying § 10(b), it makes scant sense to hold a lawyer like O'Hagan a § 10(b) violator if he works for a law firm representing the target of a tender offer, but not if he works for a law firm representing the bidder. The text of the statute requires no such result.[17] The misappropriation at issue here was properly made the subject of a § 10(b) charge because it meets the statutory requirement that there be "deceptive" conduct "in connection with" securities transactions.

C

The Court of Appeals rejected the misappropriation theory primarily on two grounds. First, as the Eighth Circuit comprehended the theory, it requires neither misrepresentation nor nondisclosure. As we just explained, however, deceptive nondisclosure is essential to the § 10(b) liability at issue. Concretely, in this case, "it [was O'Hagan's] failure to disclose his personal trading to Grand Met and Dorsey, in breach of his duty to do so, that ma[de] his conduct 'deceptive' within the meaning of § 10(b)."

---

[17]. As noted earlier, however, the textual requirement of deception precludes § 10(b) liability when a person trading on the basis of nonpublic information has disclosed his trading plans to, or obtained authorization from, the principal—even though such conduct may affect the securities markets in the same manner as the conduct reached by the misappropriation theory. Contrary to the dissent's suggestion, the fact that § 10(b) is only a partial antidote to the problems it was designed to alleviate does not call into question its prohibition of conduct that falls within its textual proscription. Moreover, once a disloyal agent discloses his imminent breach of duty, his principal may seek appropriate equitable relief under state law. Furthermore, in the context of a tender offer, the principal who authorizes an agent's trading on confidential information may, in the Commission's view, incur liability for an Exchange Act violation under Rule 14e-3(a).

Second and "more obvious," the Court of Appeals said, the misappropriation theory is not moored to § 10(b)'s requirement that "the fraud be 'in connection with the purchase or sale of any security.'" According to the Eighth Circuit, three of our decisions reveal that § 10(b) liability cannot be predicated on a duty owed to the source of nonpublic information: *Chiarella v. United States*, 445 U.S. 222 (1980); *Dirks v. SEC*, 463 U.S. 646 (1983); and *Central Bank of Denver, N.A. v. First Interstate Bank of Denver, N. A.*, 511 U.S. 164 (1994). "[O]nly a breach of a duty to parties to the securities transaction," the Court of Appeals concluded, "or, at the most, to other market participants such as investors, will be sufficient to give rise to § 10(b) liability." We read the statute and our precedent differently, and note again that § 10(b) refers to "the purchase or sale of any security," not to identifiable purchasers or sellers of securities.

Chiarella involved securities trades by a printer employed at a shop that printed documents announcing corporate takeover bids. Deducing the names of target companies from documents he handled, the printer bought shares of the targets before takeover bids were announced, expecting (correctly) that the share prices would rise upon announcement. In these transactions, the printer did not disclose to the sellers of the securities (the target companies' shareholders) the nonpublic information on which he traded. For that trading, the printer was convicted of violating § 10(b) and Rule 10b-5. We reversed the Court of Appeals judgment that had affirmed the conviction.

The jury in *Chiarella* had been instructed that it could convict the defendant if he willfully failed to inform sellers of target company securities that he knew of a takeover bid that would increase the value of their shares. Emphasizing that the printer had no agency or other fiduciary relationship with the sellers, we held that liability could not be imposed on so broad a theory. There is under § 10(b), we explained, no "general duty between all participants in market transactions to forgo actions based on material, nonpublic information." Under established doctrine, we said, a duty to disclose or abstain from trading "arises from a specific relationship between two parties."

The Court did not hold in *Chiarella* that the only relationship prompting liability for trading on undisclosed information is the relationship between a corporation's insiders and shareholders. That is evident from our response to the Government's argument before this Court that the printer's misappropriation of information from his employer for purposes of securities trading — in violation of a duty of confidentiality owed to the acquiring companies — constituted fraud in connection with the purchase or sale of a security, and thereby satisfied the terms of § 10(b). The Court declined to reach that potential basis for the printer's liability, because the theory had not been submitted to the jury. But four Justices found merit in it. And a fifth Justice stated that the Court "wisely le[ft] the resolution of this issue for another day." . . .

Chiarella thus expressly left open the misappropriation theory before us today. Certain statements in *Chiarella*, however, led the Eighth Circuit in the instant case to conclude that § 10(b) liability hinges exclusively on a breach of duty owed to a purchaser or seller of securities. The Court said in *Chiarella* that § 10(b) liability "is premised upon a duty to disclose arising from a relationship of trust and confidence between parties to a transaction," and observed that the printshop employee defendant in that case "was not a person in whom the sellers had placed their trust and confidence." These statements rejected the notion that § 10(b) stretches so far as to impose "a general duty between all participants in market transactions to forgo actions based on material, nonpublic information," and we confine them to that context. The statements highlighted by the Eighth Circuit, in short, appear in an opinion carefully leaving for future resolution the validity of the misappropriation theory, and therefore cannot be read to foreclose that theory.

Dirks, too, left room for application of the misappropriation theory in cases like the one we confront. *Dirks* involved an investment analyst who had received information from a former insider of a corporation with which the analyst had no connection. The information indicated that the corporation had engaged in a massive fraud. The analyst investigated the fraud, obtaining corroborating information from employees of the corporation. During his investigation, the analyst discussed his findings with clients and investors, some of whom sold their holdings in the company the analyst suspected of gross wrongdoing.

The SEC censured the analyst for, inter alia, aiding and abetting § 10(b) and Rule 10b-5 violations by clients and investors who sold their holdings based on the nonpublic information the analyst passed on. In the SEC's view, the analyst, as a "tippee" of corporation insiders, had a duty under § 10(b) and Rule 10b-5 to refrain from communicating the nonpublic information to persons likely to trade on the basis of it. This Court found no such obligation, and repeated the key point made in *Chiarella*: There is no " 'general duty between all participants in market transactions to forgo actions based on material, nonpublic information.' " . . .

No showing had been made in *Dirks* that the "tippers" had violated any duty by disclosing to the analyst nonpublic information about their former employer. The insiders had acted not for personal profit, but to expose a massive fraud within the corporation. Absent any violation by the tippers, there could be no derivative liability for the tippee. Most important for purposes of the instant case, the Court observed in *Dirks*: "There was no expectation by [the analyst's] sources that he would keep their information in confidence. Nor did [the analyst] misappropriate or illegally obtain the information. . . ." *Dirks* thus presents no suggestion that a person who gains nonpublic information through misappropriation in breach of a fiduciary duty escapes § 10(b) liability when, without alerting the source, he trades on the information.

Last of the three cases the Eighth Circuit regarded as warranting disapproval of the misappropriation theory, *Central Bank* held that "a private plaintiff may not maintain an aiding and abetting suit under § 10(b)." We immediately cautioned in *Central Bank* that secondary actors in the securities markets may sometimes be chargeable under the securities acts: "Any person or entity, including a lawyer, accountant, or bank, who employs a manipulative device or makes a material misstatement (or omission) on which a purchaser or seller of securities relies may be liable as a primary violator under 10b-5, assuming . . . the requirements for primary liability under Rule 10b-5 are met." The Eighth Circuit isolated the statement just quoted and drew from it the conclusion that § 10(b) covers only deceptive statements or omissions on which purchasers and sellers, and perhaps other market participants, rely. It is evident from the question presented in *Central Bank*, however, that this Court, in the quoted passage, sought only to clarify that secondary actors, although not subject to aiding and abetting liability, remain subject to primary liability under § 10(b) and Rule 10b-5 for certain conduct.

. . . .

In sum, the misappropriation theory, as we have examined and explained it in this opinion, is both consistent with the statute and with our precedent. Vital to our decision that criminal liability may be sustained under the misappropriation theory, we emphasize, are two sturdy safeguards Congress has provided regarding scienter. To establish a criminal violation of Rule 10b-5, the Government must prove that a person "willfully" violated the provision. Furthermore, a defendant may not be imprisoned for violating Rule 10b-5 if he proves that he had no knowledge of the rule. . . . In addition, the statute's "requirement of the presence of culpable intent as a necessary element of the offense does much to destroy any force in the argument that application of the [statute]" in circumstances such as O'Hagan's is unjust.

The Eighth Circuit erred in holding that the misappropriation theory is inconsistent with § 10(b). The Court of Appeals may address on remand O'Hagan's other challenges to his convictions under § 10(b) and Rule 10b-5.

. . . .

Justice THOMAS, with whom THE CHIEF JUSTICE joins, concurring in the judgment in part and dissenting in part.

Today the majority upholds respondent's convictions for violating § 10(b) of the Securities Exchange Act of 1934, and Rule 10b-5 promulgated thereunder, based upon the Securities and Exchange Commission's "misappropriation theory." Central to the majority's holding is the need to interpret § 10(b)'s requirement that a deceptive device be "use[d] or employ[ed], in connection with the purchase or sale of any security." Because the Commission's misappropriation theory fails to provide a coherent and consistent interpretation of this essential requirement for liability under § 10(b), I dissent.

———————

Note

Although upholding the validity of the misappropriation theory in *O'Hagan*, the Court's decision imposes certain limitations on the theory's scope. For example, consider the following:

(1) The arguable unfairness of U.S. insider trading law is seen by the application of §§ 10(b) and 14(e) in concrete factual settings. For any trade that occurs outside of the tender offer context, insider trading liability is premised on the breach of a duty or relationship of trust and confidence. However, with respect to tender offers, the very broad *parity of information rule* is applied. If anyone knows or has reason to know that the material information came directly or indirectly from an inside source, that person cannot trade or convey the information to others. See the discussion on Rule 14e-3 later in this chapter, § 12.09. The result is that an individual can legally trade or go to prison based solely on how a "deal" is structured. For example, if a deal is structured as a merger, share exchange, or sale of assets, then § 10(b) applies. Instead, if the deal is structured as a tender offer, then both § 10(b) and § 14(e) apply. To many, such a framework inherently is inequitable.

(2) Does full disclosure to the source(s) of the material nonpublic information that one intends to trade (or tip) signify that no "deception" exists and, hence, there is no § 10(b) violation? Should it matter whether such person reveals his/her intent to trade (or tip) before or after the receipt of the information from the source to whom such person owes a fiduciary duty? Note that in *SEC v. Rocklage*, 470 F.3d 1 (1st Cir. 2006), even though the wife told her husband she was planning to tip her brother after her husband revealed material nonpublic information to her, the court found that liability was appropriate due to the wife's preexisting agreement with her brother that she would convey the inside information to him. Hence, the court reasoned that the deceptive conduct occurred prior to the wife's receipt of the information and her brother's trading of the securities.

(3) Note that attorneys may incur disciplinary sanctions for trading (or tipping) on inside information. *See generally* Bainbridge, *Insider Trading Under the Restatement of the Law Governing Lawyers*, 19 J. Corp. L. 1 (1993).

(4) Is the misappropriation theory applicable when the source of the information reveals such information with no expectation of confidentiality to one who trades (or tips)? (See *Dirks*, at fn. 14.)

(5) In its adoption of Rule 10b5-2, the SEC sought to clarify and arguably expand the scope of the misappropriation theory. Rule 10b5-2 sets forth a non-exclusive list of three situations in which a recipient of material nonpublic information is defined to have a relationship of trust and confidence under the misappropriation theory, namely, "(1) when such recipient explicitly agreed to maintain the confidentiality of the information; (2) when a reasonable expectation of confidentiality existed due to that the persons who had the communication(s) (including the misappropriator) enjoyed a history, practice, or pattern of sharing confidences; and (3) when the source of the information (i.e., the person providing the information) was a spouse, child, parent, or sibling of the person receiving the information, unless it can be established as an affirmative defense that on the facts and circumstances of the particular family relationship that no reasonable expectation of confidentiality existed."

M. Steinberg, Understanding Securities Law 390 (6th ed. 2014). Rule 10b5-2 is discussed further in this Chapter, § 12.06.

The following decision applies the misappropriation theory in an SEC enforcement action against Mark Cuban, the high-profile owner of the National Basketball Association's (NBA) Dallas Mavericks. Note that the case did proceed to trial and Mr. Cuban was found not liable by the jury.

Securities and Exchange Commission v. Cuban

United States Court of Appeals, Fifth Circuit

620 F.3d 551 (2010)

Higginbotham, Circuit Judge:

This case raises questions of the scope of liability under the misappropriation theory of insider trading. Taking a different view from our able district court brother of the allegations of the complaint, we are persuaded that the case should not have been dismissed . . . and must proceed to discovery.

Mark Cuban is a well-known entrepreneur and current owner of the Dallas Mavericks and Landmark theaters, among other businesses. The SEC brought this suit against Cuban alleging he violated [the federal securities laws] by trading in Mamma.com stock in breach of his duty to the CEO and Mamma.com—amounting to insider trading under the misappropriation theory of liability. The core allegation is that Cuban received confidential information from the CEO of Mamma.com, a Canadian search engine company in which Cuban was a large minority stakeholder, agreed to keep the information confidential, and acknowledged he could not trade on the information. The SEC alleges that, armed with the inside information regarding a private investment of public equity (PIPE) offering, Cuban sold his stake in the company in an effort to avoid losses from the inevitable fall in Mamma.com's share price when the offering was announced.

Cuban moved to dismiss the action. The district court found that, at most, the complaint alleged an agreement to keep the information confidential, but did not include an agreement not to trade. Finding a simple confidentiality agreement to be insufficient to create a duty to disclose or abstain from trading under the securities laws, the court granted Cuban's motion to dismiss. The SEC appeals, arguing that a confidentiality agreement creates a duty to disclose or abstain and that, regardless, the confidentiality agreement alleged in the complaint also contained an agreement not to trade on the information and that agreement would create such a duty.

. . . .

The SEC alleges that Cuban's trading constituted insider trading. . . . The Supreme Court has interpreted section 10(b) [of the Securities Exchange Act] to prohibit insider trading under two complementary theories, the "classical theory" and the "misappropriation theory."

The classical theory of insider trading prohibits a "corporate insider" from trading on material nonpublic information obtained from his position within the corporation without disclosing the information. According to this theory, there exists "a relationship of trust and confidence between the shareholders of a corporation and those insiders who have obtained confidential information by reason of their position with that corporation." Trading on such confidential information qualifies as a "deceptive device" under section 10(b) because by using that information for his own personal benefit, the corporate insider breaches his duty to the shareholders. The corporate insider is under a duty to "disclose or abstain"—he must tell the shareholders of his knowledge and intention to trade or abstain from trading altogether.

There are at least two important variations of the classical theory of insider trading. The first is that even an individual who does not qualify as a traditional insider may become a "temporary insider" if by entering "into a special confidential relationship in the conduct of the business of the enterprise [he/she is] given access to information solely for corporate purposes." Thus underwriters, accountants, lawyers, or consultants are all considered corporate insiders when by virtue of their professional relationship with the corporation they are given access to confidential information. The second variation is that an individual who receives information from a corporate insider may be, but is not always, prohibited from trading on that information as a tippee. "[T]he tippee's duty to disclose or abstain is derivative from that of the insider's duty" and the tippee's obligation arises "from his role as a participant after the fact in the insider's breach of a fiduciary duty." Crucially, "a tippee assumes a fiduciary duty to the shareholders of a corporation not to trade on material nonpublic information only when the insider has breached his fiduciary duty to the shareholders by disclosing the information to the tippee and the tippee knows or should know there has been a breach." The insider breaches his fiduciary duty when he receives a "direct or indirect personal benefit from the disclosure."

Both the temporary-insider and tippee twists on the classical theory retain its core principle that the duty to disclose or abstain is derived from the corporate insider's duty to his shareholders. The misappropriation theory does not rest on this duty. It rather holds that a person violates section 10(b) "when he misappropriates confidential information for securities trading purposes, in breach of a duty owed to the source of the information." The Supreme Court first adopted this theory in *United States v. O'Hagan*. There, a lawyer traded the securities of a company his client was targeting for a takeover. O'Hagan could not be liable under the classical theory as he owed no duty to the shareholders of the target company. Nevertheless, the Court found O'Hagan violated section 10(b). The Court held that in trading the target company's securities, O'Hagan misappropriated the confidential information regarding the planned corporate takeover, breaching "a duty of trust and confidence" he owed to his law firm and client. Trading on such information "involves feigning fidelity to the source of information and thus utilizes a 'deceptive device' as required by section 10(b)." The Court stated that while there is "no general duty between all participants in market transactions to forgo actions based on material nonpublic information," the breach of a duty to the source of the information is sufficient to give rise to insider trading liability. . . . Because the duty flows to the source of the information and not to shareholders "if the fiduciary discloses to the source that he plans to trade on the nonpublic information, there is no "deceptive device" and thus no § 10(b) violation."

While *O'Hagan* did not set the contours of a relationship of "trust and confidence" giving rise to the duty to disclose or abstain and misappropriation liability, we are tasked to determine whether Cuban had such a relationship with Mamma.com. The SEC seeks to rely on Rule 10b5—2(b)(1), which states that a person has "a duty of trust and confidence" for purposes of misappropriation liability when that person "agrees to maintain information in confidence." [Rule 10b5-2 is covered in § 12.06.] In dismissing the case, the district court read the complaint to allege that Cuban agreed not to disclose any confidential information but did not agree not to trade, that such a confidentiality agreement was insufficient to create a duty to disclose or abstain from trading under the misappropriation theory, and that the SEC over-stepped its authority under section 10(b) in issuing Rule 10b5-2(b)(1). We differ from the district court in reading the complaint and need not reach the latter issues.

The complaint alleges that, in March 2004, Cuban acquired 600,000 shares, a 6.3% stake, of Mamma.com. Later that spring, Mamma.com decided to raise capital through a PIPE offering on the advice of the investment bank Merriman Curhan Ford & Co. At the end of June, at Merriman's suggestion, Mamma.com decided to invite Cuban to participate in the PIPE offering. "The CEO was instructed to contact Cuban and to preface the conversation by informing Cuban that he had confidential information to convey to him in order to make sure that Cuban understood— before the information was conveyed to him—that he would have to keep the information confidential." [SEC Complaint at Paragraph 12]

After getting in touch with Cuban on June 28, Mamma.com's CEO told Cuban he had confidential information for him and Cuban agreed to keep whatever information the CEO shared confidential. The CEO then told Cuban about the PIPE offering. Cuban became very upset "and said, among other things, that he did not like PIPEs because they dilute the existing shareholders." "At the end of the call, Cuban told the CEO 'Well, now I'm screwed. I can't sell.'" [SEC Complaint at Paragraph 14]

The CEO told the company's executive chairman about the conversation with Cuban. The executive chairman sent an email to the other Mamma.com board members updating them on the PIPE offering, [stating:]

> Today, after much discussion, [the CEO] spoke to Mark Cuban about this equity raise [the PIPE Offering] and whether or not he would be interested in participating. As anticipated he initially "flew off the handle" and said he would sell his shares (recognizing that he was not able to do anything until we announce the [offering]) but then asked to see the terms and conditions which we have arranged for him to receive from one of the participating investor groups with which he has dealt in the past.

The CEO then sent Cuban a follow up email, writing "'[i]f you want more details about the private placement please contact . . . [Merriman].'"

Cuban called the Merriman representative and they spoke for eight minutes. "During that call, the salesman supplied Cuban with additional confidential details about the PIPE. In response to Cuban's questions, the salesman told him that the PIPE was being sold at a discount to the market price and that the offering included other incentives for the PIPE investors." It is a plausible inference that Cuban learned the off-market prices available to him and other PIPE participants.

With that information and one minute after speaking with the Merriman representative, Cuban called his broker and instructed him to sell his entire stake in the company. Cuban sold 10,000 shares during the evening of June 28, 2004, and the remainder during regular trading the next day.

That day, the executive chairman sent another email to the board, updating them on the previous day's discussions with Cuban, stating, "'we did speak to Mark Cuban ([the CEO] and, subsequently, our investment banker) to find out if he had any interest in participating to the extent of maintaining his interest. His answers were: he would not invest, he does not want the company to make acquisitions, he will sell his shares which he cannot do until after we announce [the PIPE offering].'"

After the markets closed on June 29, Mamma.com announced the PIPE offering. The next day, Mamma.com's stock price fell 8.5% and continued to decline over the next week, eventually closing down 39% from the June 29 closing price. By selling his shares when he did, Cuban avoided over $750,000 in losses. Cuban notified the SEC that he had sold his stake in the company and publicly stated that he sold his shares because Mamma.com "was conducting a PIPE, which issued shares at a discount to the prevailing market price and also would have caused his ownership position to be diluted."

In reading the complaint to allege only an agreement of confidentiality, the [district] court held that Cuban's statement that he was "screwed" because he "[could not] sell" "appears to express his belief, at least at that time, that it would be illegal for him to sell his Mamma.com shares based on the information the CEO provided." But the court stated that this statement "cannot reasonably be understood as an agreement not to sell based on the information." The court found "the complaint asserts no facts that reasonably suggest that the CEO intended to obtain from Cuban an agreement to refrain from trading on the information as opposed to an agreement merely to keep it confidential." Finally, the court stated that "the CEO's expectation that Cuban would not sell was also insufficient" to allege any further agreement.

Reading the complaint in the light most favorable to the SEC, we reach a different conclusion. In isolation, the statement "Well, now I'm screwed. I can't sell" can plausibly be read to express Cuban's view that learning the confidences regarding the PIPE forbade his selling his stock before the offering but to express no agreement not to do so. However, after Cuban expressed to the CEO the view that he could not sell, he gained access to the confidences of the PIPE offering. According to the complaint's recounting of the executive chairman's email to the board, during his short conversation with the CEO regarding the planned PIPE offering, Cuban requested the terms and conditions of the offering. Based on this request, the CEO sent Cuban a follow up email providing the contact information for Merriman. Cuban called the salesman, who told Cuban "that the PIPE was being sold at a discount to the market price and that the offering included other incentives for the PIPE investors." Only after Cuban reached out to obtain this additional information, following the statement of his understanding that he could not sell, did Cuban contact his broker and sell his stake in the company.

The allegations, taken in their entirety, provide more than a plausible basis to find that the understanding between the CEO and Cuban was that he was not to trade, that it was more than a simple confidentiality agreement. By contacting the sales representative to obtain the pricing information, Cuban was able to evaluate his potential losses or gains from his decision to either participate or refrain from participating in the PIPE offering. It is at least plausible that each of the parties understood, if only implicitly, that Mamma.com would only provide the terms and conditions of the offering to Cuban for the purpose of evaluating whether he would participate in the offering, and that Cuban could not use the information for his own personal benefit.[18] It would require additional facts that have not been put before us for us to conclude that the parties could not plausibly have reached this shared understanding. Under Cuban's reading, he was allowed to trade on the information but prohibited from telling others—in effect providing him an exclusive license to trade on the material nonpublic information. Perhaps this was the understanding, or perhaps Cuban mislead the CEO regarding the timing of his sale in order to obtain a confidential look at the details of the PIPE. We say only that on this factually sparse record, it is at least equally plausible that all sides understood there was to be no trading before the PIPE.[19] That both Cuban and the CEO expressed the belief that Cuban could not trade appears to reinforce the plausibility of this reading.

---

[18]. The parties dispute Mamma.com's motive in providing the information to Cuban. Cuban contends that the offering was already oversubscribed and that this demonstrates the sole purpose of the phone call was to prevent Cuban from trading ahead of the offering. We express no opinion on this factual dispute or the potential implications of Cuban's allegations if they are true. At the motion to dismiss stage we must view all the facts in light most favorable to the SEC and assume that Mamma.com had a legitimate reason for contacting Cuban.

[19]. Such an arrangement would raise serious tipper/tippee liability concerns were it explicit. If the CEO knowingly gave Cuban material nonpublic information and arranged so he could trade on it, it would not be difficult for a court to infer that the CEO must have done so for some personal benefit—e.g., goodwill from a wealthy investor and large minority stakeholder. "A reputational benefit that translates into future earnings, a quid pro quo, or a gift to a trading friend or relative all could suffice to show the tipper personally benefitted." *SEC v. Yun*, 327 F.3d 1263, 1277 (11th Cir. 2003). This of course is not to suggest any such improprieties occurred; rather, it simply reinforces the plausibility of the interpretation of the alleged facts as evidencing an understanding that the agreement included an agreement by Cuban not to trade.

. . . [W]e VACATE the judgment dismissing the case and REMAND to the court of first instance for further proceedings including discovery, consideration of summary judgment, and trial, if reached.

———————

§ 12.06 Family and Other Personal Relationships — SEC Rule 10b5-2

After *O'Hagan*, the applicability of the misappropriation theory in the business setting — such as where an employee purloins material nonpublic information from his/her employer — is well established. In the context of family and other personal relationships, however, the misappropriation theory's impact is less certain.

For example, in *United States v. Chestman,* 947 F.2d 551 (2d Cir. 1991), the Second Circuit rejected the government's reliance on the misappropriation rationale under the facts presented when the wife entrusted inside information to her husband. The court asserted that "a fiduciary duty cannot be imposed unilaterally by entrusting a person with confidential information" and that "marriage does not, without more, create a fiduciary relationship." No such duty arose in the case at bar because the inside information was gratuitously communicated to the husband by the wife with no promise by the husband to keep the information confidential. Further, the court concluded that the husband was not part of the family's "inner circle" (which included the wife's parents), signifying that a fiduciary or comparable duty was not present.

So much for "family values." One can understandably be upset by the law giving greater sanctity to a shareholder's relationship with a director of a publicly held company (with whom such shareholder has never spoken or met) than to one's spouse. Evidently by adopting Rule 10b5-2, the SEC agrees with the asserted absurdity of this approach. The Rule provides a nonexclusive list of three situations in which a person is deemed to have a relationship of trust and confidence for purposes of invoking the misappropriation theory when the person receiving the material nonpublic information trades or tips in the following situations: (1) when such recipient agreed to maintain the confidentiality of the information; (2) when a reasonable expectation of confidentiality existed due to the fact that the persons who had the communications(s) (including the misappropriator) enjoyed a history, practice, or pattern of sharing confidences; and (3) when the source of the information (i.e., the person providing such information) was a spouse, child, parent, or sibling of the person receiving the information, unless it can be established as an affirmative defense that on the facts and circumstances of the particular family relationship that no reasonable expectation of confidentiality existed. *See* Securities Exchange Act Release No. 43154 (2000). Query whether the first situation, namely, when the recipient explicitly agreed to maintain the information's confidentiality is unduly broad, thereby exceeding the parameters of the misappropriation theory set forth in *O'Hagan*.

The *Cuban* decision did not expressly address three key issues. *First*, that the scope of Rule 10b5-2 reaches only personal relationships and does not extend to the business context. In its adoption of Rule 10b5-2, the SEC's focus was confined to personal relationships. This issue has yet to be resolved by the courts. *Second*, that the provider of the information must have a *reasonable* expectation of confidentiality. Courts have held that the failure by such a provider to take reasonable precautionary measures, such as the use of nondisclosure agreements (NDAs), mitigates against a finding that the provider had such an expectation of confidentiality. *Third*, whether — (i) a confidentiality agreement (or NDA) standing alone or (ii) a history of sharing confidences — is sufficient to implicate the duty to disclose or refrain from trading (or tipping) as set forth in the Supreme Court's *O'Hagan* decision.

To violate § 10(b), is it necessary for the trader "to use" rather than merely "to possess" the material nonpublic information? For example, after *O'Hagan*, is it a viable defense that the trader had planned to purchase the subject securities on a certain date prior to the time that he/she came into possession of the inside information? The next Section of this Chapter addresses this issue.

----

§ 12.07 "Possession" versus "Use"

When charged with insider trading, a defendant may contend that he/she had planned to purchase or sell the subject securities prior to coming into possession of the inside information. In response, the SEC's position generally has been that mere possession, rather than use, of the material nonpublic information is sufficient to trigger liability under § 10(b). Likewise, the Second Circuit, endorsing the "possession" standard, opined that "material information cannot lie idle in the human brain." *United States v. Teicher,* 987 F.2d 112, 120 (2d Cir. 1993). *But see United States v. Gansman,* 657 F.3d 85, 92 (2d Cir. 2011) (stating that "[i]n prosecuting a putative 'tipper' under the misappropriation theory of insider trading, the government must prove as an element of the offense that the 'tipper' conveyed material nonpublic information to his 'tippee' with the understanding that it would be *used* for securities trading purposes") (emphasis supplied).

Disagreeing, the Ninth and Eleventh Circuits held that proof of use rather than mere possession is consistent with § 10(b)'s scienter requirement. Language in the Supreme Court's decision in *O'Hagan* also supports the "use" approach. 117 S. Ct. at 2208 (stating that, under the misappropriation theory, "the fiduciary's fraud is consummated . . . when without disclosure to his principal, he *uses* the information to purchase or sell securities"). In *SEC v. Adler,* 137 F.3d 1325 (11th Cir. 1998), the Eleventh Circuit held that § 10(b)'s scienter requirement mandates that the Commission establish that the defendant when he/she traded actually "used" the material nonpublic information. Phrased somewhat differently, the SEC must show that the defendant's knowledge of such information constituted a substantial factor in his/her decision to purchase or sell the subject securities at the particular price or at the particular time. Importantly, however, the court held that a defendant's knowing possession of material nonpublic information when trading raises a strong inference of use. Such inference may be rebutted by the defendant establishing that he/she had independent, justifiable reasons for engaging in the particular transactions at that time and in the amount traded. Similarly, the Ninth Circuit in *United States v. Smith*, 155 F.3d 1051 (9th Cir. 1998), adopted the "use" rather than "possession" standard. The court, however, declined to adhere to the Eleventh Circuit's inference of use (upon a showing of knowing possession) due to constitutional reasons arising from a criminal prosecution.

Reacting to the Ninth and Eleventh Circuit decisions, the SEC adopted Rule 10b5-1. Securities Exchange Act Release No. 43154 (2000). The Rule triggers liability exposure when a person purchases or sells securities while "aware" of material nonpublic information. Hence, a trade is deemed to be "on the basis" of material nonpublic information under Rule 10b5-1 if the trader was "aware" of such information at the time of the purchase or sale. The Rule reflects the position that one who is aware of inside information at the time of trading will have inevitably made use of such information. While the awareness standard expands the scope of insider trading liability (as compared to the Ninth and Eleventh Circuits' approaches), the SEC posits that Rule 10b5-1 enhances investor confidence and the integrity of the securities markets.

Under Rule 10b5-1, an affirmative defense generally is available if the trader engages in the specified transaction(s) pursuant to a preexisting plan, contract, or instruction that is binding and specific. Under such circumstances, the inside information was not a factor in the trading decision. More specifically, to establish the affirmative defense, a person must satisfy the following criteria. First, a person must demonstrate that, prior to becoming aware of the inside information, he/she had entered into a binding contract to purchase or sell the security, had provided instructions to another person to execute the trade for the instructing person's account, or had adopted a written plan for trading securities. Second, the person must demonstrate that, with respect to the purchase or sale, the contract, instructions, or plan: expressly specified the amount(s), price(s), and date(s); or did not permit the person to exercise any influence over how, when, or whether to execute the trade(s) (and in the event that any other person exercised such influence, that person was not aware of the material nonpublic information). Third, the person must demonstrate that the trade(s) that occurred were pursuant to the previously established contract, instructions, or plan. This means that the person neither may alter or deviate from the contract, instruction, or plan, nor enter into a corresponding or opposite hedging transaction with respect to those securities. Furthermore, the defense is governed by a good-faith requirement that the person did not enter into the contract, instruction, or plan as part of a scheme to avoid liability under Rule 10b5-1.

Rule 10b5-1 provides another affirmative defense for trading parties that are entities. This defense is available as an alternative to the defense discussed above. Under the provisions of this defense, an entity will not be liable if it demonstrates that the individual responsible for the investment decision on behalf of the entity was not aware of the material inside information, and that the entity had implemented reasonable policies and procedures to prevent insider trading.

Concerns have been voiced that Rule 10b5-1 plans are being abused by corporate executives to facilitate their trading based on material nonpublic information. *See* Pulliam, Eaglesham, & Barry, *Insider-Trading Probe Widens*, WALL ST. J., Dec. 11, 2012, at A1, A6 (stating that the U.S. attorney in Manhattan is investigating a number of trades, "most made under trading plans").[20]

§ 12.08 "Tipper-Tippee" Liability

In securities parlance, a tipper is one who communicates the subject information while a tippee is a recipient of such information. One who both communicates and receives the information is both a tipper and a tippee.

Prior to the U.S. Supreme Court's decision in *Dirks* (which is the next case we study), the prevailing position was that the tippee "stood in the shoes" of his or her tipper—if the tipper could not trade, the tippee, upon receiving the information from the tipper and knowing of the tipper's situation, also could not trade. For example, a tippee, who received material nonpublic information knowing it came from a corporate officer, could not trade in the subject company's securities. This approach still remains valid with respect to Rule 14e-3, which is covered later in this Chapter and evidently represents the position adopted today by most developed countries.

In the *Dirks* decision, the U.S. Supreme Court rejected the above approach, opting for a standard that is premised on a motivational requirement. The decision follows.

Dirks v. Securities and Exchange Commission

United States Supreme Court

463 U.S. 646, 103 S. Ct. 3255, 77 L. Ed. 2d 911 (1983)

JUSTICE POWELL delivered the opinion of the Court.

Petitioner Raymond Dirks received material nonpublic information from "insiders" of a corporation with which he had no connection. He disclosed this information to

---

20. *See generally*, Horwich, *The Legality of Opportunistically Timing Public Disclosures in the Context of SEC Rule 10b5-1*, 71 BUS. LAW. 1113 (2016); Horwich, *The Origin, Application, Validity, and Potential Misuse of Rule 10b5-1*, 62 BUS. LAW. 913 (2007); Karmel, *The Controversy of Possession Versus Use*, N.Y.L.J., Dec. 17, 1998, at 3; McLucas & Walker, *Insider Trading Developments: Do the Adler and Smith Cases Portend Tougher Times for SEC Enforcement?*, 32 REV. SEC. & COMM. REG. 93 (1999); Nagy, *The "Possession" vs. "Use" Debate in the Context of Securities Trading by Traditional Insiders: Why Silence Can Never Be Golden*, 67 U. CIN. L. REV. 1129 (1999).

investors who relied on it in trading in the shares of the corporation. The question is whether Dirks violated the antifraud provisions of the federal securities laws by this disclosure.

I

In 1973, Dirks was an officer of a New York broker-dealer firm who specialized in providing investment analysis of insurance company securities to institutional investors. On March 6, Dirks received information from Ronald Secrist, a former officer of Equity Funding of America. Secrist alleged that the assets of Equity Funding, a diversified corporation primarily engaged in selling life insurance and mutual funds, were vastly overstated as the result of fraudulent corporate practices. Secrist also stated that various regulatory agencies had failed to act on similar charges made by Equity Funding employees. He urged Dirks to verify the fraud and disclose it publicly.

Dirks decided to investigate the allegations. He visited Equity Funding's headquarters in Los Angeles and interviewed several officers and employees of the corporation. The senior management denied any wrongdoing, but certain corporation employees corroborated the charges of fraud. Neither Dirks nor his firm owned or traded any Equity Funding stock, but throughout his investigation he openly discussed the information he had obtained with a number of clients and investors. Some of these persons sold their holdings of Equity Funding securities, including five investment advisers who liquidated holdings of more than $16 million.

While Dirks was in Los Angeles, he was in touch regularly with William Blundell, the Wall Street Journal's Los Angeles bureau chief. Dirks urged Blundell to write a story on the fraud allegations. Blundell did not believe, however, that such a massive fraud could go undetected and declined to write the story. He feared that publishing such damaging hearsay might be libelous.

During the two-week period in which Dirks pursued his investigation and spread word of Secrist's charges, the price of Equity Funding stock fell from $26 per share to less than $15 per share. This led the New York Stock Exchange to halt trading on March 27. Shortly thereafter California insurance authorities impounded Equity Funding's records and uncovered evidence of the fraud. Only then did the Securities and Exchange Commission (SEC) file a complaint against Equity Funding and only then, on April 2, did the Wall Street Journal publish a front-page story based largely on information assembled by Dirks. Equity Funding immediately went into receivership.

The SEC began an investigation into Dirks' role in the exposure of the fraud. After a hearing by an administrative law judge, the SEC found that Dirks had aided and abetted violations of § 17(a) of the Securities Act of 1933, § 10(b) of the Securities Exchange Act of 1934, and SEC Rule 10b-5, by repeating the allegations of fraud to members of the investment community who later sold their Equity Funding stock. The SEC concluded: "Where 'tippees'—regardless of their motivation or occupation—come into possession of material 'information that they know is confidential and know or should know came from a corporate insider,' they must either publicly disclose that information or refrain from trading." Recognizing, however, that Dirks "played an important role in bringing [Equity Funding's] massive fraud to light," the SEC only censured him.

Dirks sought review in the Court of Appeals for the District of Columbia Circuit. The court entered judgment against Dirks "for the reasons stated by the Commission in its opinion." . . .

. . . We now reverse.

. . . .

III

We were explicit in *Chiarella* in saying that there can be no duty to disclose where the person who has traded on inside information "was not [the corporation's] agent, . . . was not a fiduciary, [or] was not a person in whom the sellers [of the securities] had placed their trust and confidence." Not to require such a fiduciary relationship, we recognized, would "depar[t] radically from the established doctrine that duty arises from a specific relationship between two parties" and would amount to "recognizing a general duty between all participants in market transactions to forgo actions based on material, nonpublic information." This requirement of a specific relationship between the shareholders and the individual trading on inside information has created analytical difficulties for the SEC and courts in policing tippees who trade on inside information. Unlike insiders who have independent fiduciary duties to both the corporation and its shareholders, the typical tippee has no such relationships. In view of this absence, it has been unclear how a tippee acquires the duty to refrain from trading on inside information.

Under certain circumstances, such as where corporate information is revealed legitimately to an underwriter, accountant, lawyer, or consultant working for the corporation, these outsiders may become fiduciaries of the shareholders. The basis for recognizing this fiduciary duty is not simply that such persons acquired nonpublic corporate information, but rather that they have entered into a special confidential relationship in the conduct of the business of the enterprise and are given access to information solely for corporate purposes. When such a person breaches his fiduciary relationship, he may be treated more properly as a tipper than a tippee. For such a duty to be imposed, however, the corporation must expect the outsider to keep the disclosed nonpublic information confidential, and the relationship at least must imply such a duty. [This paragraph is contained in a note of the decision.]

A

The SEC's position, as stated in its opinion in this case, is that a tippee "inherits" the *Cady Roberts* obligation to shareholders whenever he receives inside information from an insider:

> In tipping potential traders, Dirks breached a duty which he had assumed as a result of knowingly receiving confidential information from [Equity

Funding] insiders. Tippees such as Dirks who receive non-public material information from insiders become "subject to the same duty as [the] insiders." Such a tippee breaches the fiduciary duty which he assumes from the insider when the tippee knowingly transmits the information to someone who will probably trade on the basis thereof. . . . Presumably, Dirks' informants were entitled to disclose the [Equity Funding] fraud in order to bring it to light and its perpetrators to justice. However, Dirks—standing in their shoes—committed a breach of the fiduciary duty which he had assumed in dealing with them, when he passed the information on to traders.

This view differs little from the view that we rejected as inconsistent with congressional intent in *Chiarella*. In that case, the Court of Appeals agreed with the SEC and affirmed Chiarella's conviction, holding that

[a]nyone—corporate insider or not—who regularly receives material nonpublic information may not use that information to trade in securities without incurring an affirmative duty to disclose.

Here, the SEC maintains that anyone who knowingly receives nonpublic material information from an insider has a fiduciary duty to disclose before trading.

In effect, the SEC's theory of tippee liability in both cases appears rooted in the idea that the antifraud provisions require equal information among all traders. This conflicts with the principle set forth in *Chiarella* that only some persons, under some circumstances, will be barred from trading while in possession of material nonpublic information. . . .

. . . We reaffirm today that "[a] duty [to disclose] arises from the relationship between parties . . . and not merely from one's ability to acquire information because of his position in the market."

Imposing a duty to disclose or abstain solely because a person knowingly receives material nonpublic information from an insider and trades on it could have an inhibiting influence on the role of market analysts, which the SEC itself recognizes is necessary to the preservation of a healthy market. It is commonplace for analysts to "ferret out and analyze information," . . . and this often is done by meeting with and questioning corporate officers and others who are insiders. And information that the analysts obtain normally may be the basis for judgments as to the market worth of a corporation's securities. The analyst's judgment in this respect is made available in market letters or otherwise to clients of the firm. It is the nature of this type of information, and indeed of the markets themselves, that such information cannot be made simultaneously available to all of the corporation's stockholders or the public generally.

B

The conclusion that recipients of inside information do not invariably acquire a duty to disclose or abstain does not mean that such tippees always are free to trade on the information. The need for a ban on some tippee trading is clear. Not only are insiders forbidden by their fiduciary relationship from personally using undisclosed corporate information to their advantage, but they may not give such information to an outsider for the same improper purpose of exploiting the information for their personal gain. Similarly, the transactions of those who knowingly participate with the fiduciary in such a breach are "as forbidden" as transactions "on behalf of the trustee himself." . . . As we noted in *Chiarella*, "[t]he tippee's obligation has been viewed as arising from his role as a participant after the fact in the insider's breach of a fiduciary duty."

Thus, some tippees must assume an insider's duty to the shareholders not because they receive inside information, but rather because it has been made available to them improperly. And for Rule 10b-5 purposes, the insider's disclosure is improper only where it would violate his *Cady, Roberts* duty. Thus, a tippee assumes a fiduciary duty to the shareholders of a corporation not to trade on material nonpublic information only when the insider has breached his fiduciary duty to the shareholders by disclosing the information to the tippee and the tippee knows or should know that there has been a breach. As Commissioner Smith perceptively observed in *Investors Management Co.*: "[T]ippee responsibility must be related back to insider responsibility by a necessary finding that the tippee knew the information was given to him in breach of a duty by a person having a special relationship to the issuer not to disclose the information. . . ." Tipping thus properly is viewed only as a means of indirectly violating the *Cady, Roberts* disclose-or-abstain rule.

C

In determining whether a tippee is under an obligation to disclose or abstain, it thus is necessary to determine whether the insider's "tip" constituted a breach of the insider's fiduciary duty. All disclosures of confidential corporate information are not inconsistent with the duty insiders owe to shareholders. In contrast to the extraordinary facts of this case, the more typical situation in which there will be a question whether disclosure violates the insider's *Cady, Roberts* duty is when insiders disclose information to analysts. In some situations, the insider will act consistently with his fiduciary duty to shareholders, and yet release of the information may affect the market. For example, it may not be clear—either to the corporate insider or to the recipient analyst—whether the information will be viewed as material nonpublic information. Corporate officials may mistakenly think the information already has been disclosed or that it is not material enough to affect the market. Whether disclosure is a breach of duty therefore depends in large part on the purpose of the disclosure. This standard was identified by the SEC itself in *Cady, Roberts*: a purpose of the securities laws was to eliminate "use of inside information for personal advantage." Thus, *the test is whether the insider personally will benefit, directly or indirectly, from his disclosure. Absent some personal gain, there has been no breach of duty to stockholders. And absent a breach by the insider, there is no derivative breach. . . .* [emphasis supplied]

The SEC argues that, if inside-trading liability does not exist when the information is transmitted for a proper purpose but is used for trading, it would be a rare situation when the parties could not fabricate some ostensibly legitimate business justification for transmitting the information. We think the SEC is unduly concerned. In determining whether the insider's purpose in making a particular disclosure is fraudulent, the SEC and the courts are not required to read the parties' minds. Scienter in some cases is relevant in determining whether the tipper has violated his *Cady, Roberts* duty. But to determine whether the disclosure itself "deceive[s], manipulate[s], or defraud[s]" shareholders, the initial inquiry is whether there has been a breach of duty by the insider. This requires courts to focus on objective criteria, i.e., whether the insider receives a direct or indirect personal benefit from the disclosure, such as a pecuniary gain or a reputational benefit that will translate into future earnings. Cf. Brudney, *Insiders, Outsiders, and Informational Advantages Under the Federal Securities Laws*, 93 Harv. L. Rev. 324, 348 (1979) ("The theory . . . is that the insider, by giving the information out selectively, is in effect selling the information to its recipient for cash, reciprocal information, or other things of value for himself. . . ."). There are objective facts and circumstances that often justify such an inference. For example, there may be a relationship between the insider and the recipient that suggests a quid pro quo from the latter, or an intention to benefit the particular recipient. The elements of fiduciary duty and exploitation of non-public information also exist when an insider makes a gift of confidential information to a trading relative or friend. The tip and trade resemble trading by the insider himself followed by a gift of the profits to the recipient.

Determining whether an insider personally benefits from a particular disclosure, a question of fact, will not always be easy for courts. But it is essential, we think, to have a guiding principle for those whose daily activities must be limited and instructed by the SEC's inside-trading rules, and we believe that there must be a breach of the insider's fiduciary duty before the tippee inherits the duty to disclose or abstain. In contrast, the rule adopted by the SEC in this case would have no limiting principle.

IV

Under the inside-trading and tipping rules set forth above, we find that there was no actionable violation by Dirks. It is undisputed that Dirks himself was a stranger to Equity Funding, with no pre-existing fiduciary duty to its shareholders. He took no action, directly or indirectly, that induced the shareholders or officers of Equity Funding to repose trust or confidence in him. There was no expectation by Dirk's sources that he would keep their information in confidence. Nor did Dirks misappropriate or illegally obtain the information about Equity Funding. Unless the insiders breached their *Cady, Roberts* duty to shareholders in disclosing the nonpublic information to Dirks, he breached no duty when he passed it on to investors as well as to the Wall Street Journal.

It is clear that neither Secrist nor the other Equity Funding employees violated their *Cady, Roberts* duty to the corporation's shareholders by providing information to Dirks. The tippers received no monetary or personal benefit for revealing Equity

Funding's secrets, nor was their purpose to make a gift of valuable information to Dirks. As the facts of this case clearly indicate, the tippers were motivated by a desire to expose the fraud. In the absence of a breach of duty to shareholders by the insiders, there was no derivative breach by Dirks. Dirks therefore could not have been "a participant after the fact in [an] insider's breach of a fiduciary duty."

V

We conclude that Dirks, in the circumstances of this case, had no duty to abstain from use of the inside information that he obtained. The judgment of the Court of Appeals therefore is

Reversed.

JUSTICE BLACKMUN, with whom JUSTICE BRENNAN and JUSTICE MARSHALL join, dissenting.

The Court today takes still another step to limit the protections provided investors by § 10(b) of the Securities Exchange Act of 1934. The device employed in this case engrafts a special motivational requirement on the fiduciary duty doctrine. This innovation excuses a knowing and intentional violation of an insider's duty to shareholders if the insider does not act from a motive of personal gain. Even on the extraordinary facts of this case, such an innovation is not justified.

. . . .

No one questions that Secrist himself could not trade on his inside information to the disadvantage of uninformed shareholders and purchasers of Equity Funding securities. Unlike the printer in *Chiarella*, Secrist stood in a fiduciary relationship with these shareholders. As the Court states, corporate insiders have an affirmative duty of disclosure when trading with shareholders of the corporation. This duty extends as well to purchasers of the corporation's securities.

The Court also acknowledges that Secrist could not do by proxy what he was prohibited from doing personally. But this is precisely what Secrist did. Secrist used Dirks to disseminate information to Dirks' clients, who in turn dumped stock on unknowing purchasers. Secrist thus intended Dirks to injure the purchasers of Equity Funding securities to whom Secrist had a duty to disclose. Accepting the Court's view of tippee liability, it appears that Dirks' knowledge of this breach makes him liable as a participant in the breach after the fact.

The Court holds, however, that Dirks is not liable because Secrist did not violate his duty; according to the Court, this is so because Secrist did not have the improper purpose of personal gain. In so doing, the Court imposes a new, subjective limitation on the scope of the duty owed by insiders to shareholders. The novelty of this limitation is reflected in the Court's lack of support for it.

The insider's duty is owed directly to the corporation's shareholders. . . . As *Chiarella* recognized, it is based on the relationship of trust and confidence between the insider and the shareholder. That relationship assures the shareholder that the insider may not take actions that will harm him unfairly. The affirmative duty of disclosure protects against this injury.

. . . .

The fact that the insider himself does not benefit from the breach does not eradicate the shareholder's injury.

. . . It makes no difference to the shareholder whether the corporate insider gained or intended to gain personally from the transaction; the shareholder still has lost because of the insider's misuse of nonpublic information. The duty is addressed not to the insider's motives, but to his actions and their consequences on the shareholder. Personal gain is not an element of the breach of this duty.

. . . .

The improper purpose requirement not only has no basis in law, but it rests implicitly on a policy that I cannot accept. The Court justifies Secrist's and Dirks' action because the general benefit derived from the violation of Secrist's duty to shareholders outweighed the harm caused to those shareholders. . . . Under this view, the benefit conferred on society by Secrist's and Dirks' activities may be paid for with the losses caused to shareholders trading with Dirks' clients.[21]

Although Secrist's general motive to expose the Equity Funding fraud was laudable, the means he chose were not. Moreover, even assuming that Dirks played a substantial role in exposing the fraud, he and his clients should not profit from the information they obtained from Secrist. . . .

. . . The Court's holding is deficient in policy terms not because it fails to create a legal norm out of that ethical norm, but because it actually rewards Dirks for his aiding and abetting.

Dirks and Secrist were under a duty to disclose the information or to refrain from trading on it. I agree that disclosure in this case would have been difficult. I also recognize that the SEC seemingly has been less than helpful in its view of the nature of disclosure necessary to satisfy the disclose-or-refrain duty. The Commission tells persons with inside information that they cannot trade on that information unless they disclose; it refuses, however, to tell them how to disclose. This seems to be a less than sensible policy, which it is incumbent on the Commission to correct. The Court,

---

[21]. This position seems little different from the theory that insider trading should be permitted because it brings relevant information to the market. *See* H. MANNE, INSIDER TRADING AND THE STOCK MARKET 59–76, 111–146 (1966); Manne, *Insider Trading and the Law Professors*, 23 VAND. L. REV. 547, 565–576 (1970). The Court also seems to embrace a variant of that extreme theory, which postulates that insider trading causes no harm at all to those who purchase from the insider.

Both the theory and its variant sit at the opposite end of the theoretical spectrum from the much maligned equality-of-information theory, and never have been adopted by Congress or ratified by this Court. The theory rejects the existence of any enforceable principle of fairness between market participants.

however, has no authority to remedy the problem by opening a hole in the congressionally mandated prohibition on insider trading, thus rewarding such trading.

. . . .

In my view, Secrist violated his duty to Equity Funding shareholders by transmitting material nonpublic information to Dirks with the intention that Dirks would cause his clients to trade on that information. Dirks, therefore, was under a duty to make the information publicly available or to refrain from actions that he knew would lead to trading. Because Dirks caused his clients to trade, he violated § 10(b) and Rule 10b-5. Any other result is a disservice to this country's attempt to provide fair and efficient capital markets. I dissent.

Note

(1) Subsequent to *Dirks*, the SEC has responded tenaciously in an effort to maintain a vigilant enforcement program against insider trading. One route has been to embrace the "quasi-insider" principle that received approbation in *Dirks*. Under this rationale, individuals enjoying a special relationship with the corporation, such as accountants, attorneys, consultants, and underwriters, may be viewed as insiders when they trade on material non-public information that they legitimately received during the course of that relationship. As stated by the *Dirks* Court, "[t]he basis for recognizing this fiduciary duty is not simply that such persons acquired nonpublic corporate information, but rather that they have entered into a special confidential relationship in the conduct of the business of the enterprise and are given access to information solely for corporate purposes." Another approach invoked by the Commission has been to make the showing of "benefit," required by *Dirks*, by proving that the insider disclosed the information for financial gain or made a "gift" of material non-public information to the tippee.

(2) In perhaps a surprising decision, *United States v. Evans,* 486 F.3d 315 (7th Cir. 2007), the Seventh Circuit upheld the conviction of a tippee even though a prior jury had acquitted the tipper of all charges. Given that a tippee's liability is derivative and must be premised on the tipper's breach, the court's decision may be suspect. Nonetheless, the court reasoned that the earlier acquittal of the tipper "did not prevent a properly instructed second jury from finding that [the tipper's] tips were unlawful and that [the tippee,] by knowingly trading on that information, violated the law." Also, contained earlier in this Chapter (§ 12.03), is a case involving a former university professor who was criminally convicted for unlawful tipping to his then-wife and to his then-best friend, see *United States v. Blackwell,* 459 F.3d 739 (6th Cir. 2006).

(3) After *Dirks* was decided, it was perceived that company spokespersons more frequently made selective disclosure of material nonpublic information to favored research analysts. This conduct raised difficult enforcement dilemmas for the Commission. As the SEC stated (Securities Exchange Act Release No. 43154 (2000)): "In light of the 'personal benefit' test set forth in the Supreme Court's decision in *Dirks,*

many have viewed issuer selective disclosure to analysts as protected from insider trading liability." In response to this evident unfairness and "unequal playing field," the SEC adopted Regulation FD (Fair Disclosure). The Regulation's fundamental focus is that when an issuer, or agent acting on its behalf, knowingly selectively discloses material nonpublic information, such issuer must make simultaneous public disclosure of that information. Regulation FD is addressed in Chapter 11, § 11.08.

The Court's decision in *Dirks* has complicated the task of enforcement authorities and, with some frequency, has had in uneven results. Consider the following case involving former University of Oklahoma and Dallas Cowboys' football coach, Barry Switzer. If the merger transaction in that case had instead been structured as a tender offer, Coach Switzer (as we will study in the following section of this Chapter) would have been held liable.

Securities and Exchange Commission v. Switzer

United States District Court, Western District of Oklahoma

590 F. Supp. 756 (1984)

Saffels, District Judge, Sitting by Designation.

This action brought by the Securities and Exchange Commission [hereinafter SEC] was tried to the court on March 19–22, 1984. It involved allegations of violations of Section 10(b) of the Securities Exchange Act of 1934 and violations of Commission Rule 10b-5. On the basis of the following findings of fact and conclusions of law, the court shall enter judgment on behalf of the defendants.

Findings of Fact

The following findings of fact have been stipulated to by all parties and accepted by the court and are set forth as follows.

. . . .

6. Barry L. Switzer resides at 2811 Castlewood Drive, Norman, Oklahoma (73070). At all times mentioned in the complaint, Switzer was the head football coach at the University of Oklahoma in Norman, Oklahoma.

. . . .

13. Texas International Company [hereinafter TIC] is a Delaware corporation with principal offices located in Oklahoma City, Oklahoma. At all times mentioned in the complaint, TIC was engaged in, among other things, exploration for and development of oil and natural gas properties. . . . On or about June 18, 1982, a wholly-owned subsidiary of TIC merged with Phoenix Resources Company [hereinafter Phoenix] and Phoenix became a wholly-owned subsidiary of TIC. At all times mentioned in the complaint prior to the merger, TIC owned in excess of fifty percent (50%) of the common stock of Phoenix, and, by reason of such ownership position, controlled

Phoenix through election of three of the five members of the Phoenix Board of Directors.

14. Prior to the merger, Phoenix, the successor to King Resources Company, was a Maine corporation with principal offices located in Oklahoma City, Oklahoma. At all times mentioned in the complaint prior to the merger, Phoenix engaged in, among other things, exploration for and development of oil and natural gas properties. . . .

. . . .

18. On or about Wednesday, June 10, 1981, after the public announcement [of the merger, defendant] Hoover sold all sixteen thousand five hundred (16,500) shares of Phoenix at prices between Fifty-Nine Dollars ($59) and Sixty-Three and 50/100 Dollars ($63.50) per share; the pre-tax profits realized on the basis of trading over this three-day period [June 8–10] amounted to approximately Two Hundred Sixty-Seven Thousand Seven Hundred Twenty-Eight Dollars ($267,728); and the pre-tax profits paid to and divided by [defendants] Switzer and Smith amounted to approximately One Hundred Ten Thousand Four Hundred Ninety-One Dollars ($110,491).

19. [Defendants] Hodges and Amyx agreed to purchase Phoenix stock through the Hodges, Amyx, Cross and Hodges investment partnership account.

20. On or about Monday, June 8, and Tuesday, June 9, 1981, Amyx, on behalf of the Hodges, Amyx, Cross and Hodges investment partnership, purchased thirteen thousand (13,000) shares of Phoenix at prices between Forty-Three and 50/100 Dollars ($43.50) and Forty-Eight and 50/100 Dollars ($48.50) per share.

21. On or about Wednesday, June 10, and Thursday, June 11, 1981, the Hodges, Amyx, Cross and Hodges investment partnership sold all thirteen thousand (13,000) shares of Phoenix at prices between Fifty-Nine Dollars ($59) and Sixty-Five Dollars ($65) per share; the pre-tax profits realized by the investment partnership on the basis of trading over a four-day period amounted to approximately Two Hundred Five Thousand Fifty-Five Dollars ($205,055); and the pre-tax profits from such trading paid to and divided by [defendants] Switzer and Smith amounted to approximately Eighty-Five Thousand Three Hundred Ten Dollars ($85,310).

. . . .

The following additional facts are found by the court:

. . . .

32. Barry Switzer is a well-recognized "celebrity" in Oklahoma and elsewhere. He has an interest in the oil and gas industry, as he is personally involved in various ventures within the industry.

33. Over the past several years, defendants Switzer, Kennedy, Deem, Smith, Hodges, Amyx and Hoover have acted together in varying combinations of persons (or in various groups of persons) in making investments. . . . Oftentimes, they trade on

rumors or gossip they hear within the investing community. Profits and losses occurring as a result of stock investments made through these partnerships are shared by the members of the partnerships.

34. TIC had been considering various options for either consolidating or separating TIC and Phoenix for some time prior to its approaching Morgan Stanley on June 4 or 5, 1981. Rumors concerning these various options were circulating within the investing oil and gas community prior to June 4 or 5, 1981.

35. On June 6, 1981, four days prior to the public announcement concerning Phoenix, a state invitational secondary school track meet was held at John Jacobs Field on the University of Oklahoma campus. The track meet was a day long event. Several hundred spectators attended, including Barry Switzer, who arrived at the meet between 10:00 and 10:30 a.m. to watch his son compete, and George and Linda Platt, who arrived between 9:00 and 10:00 a.m. to watch their son compete. Soon after Switzer's arrival at the track meet, he and G. Platt recognized and greeted each other. Neither Switzer nor G. Platt knew that the other would be attending the meet. *[G. Platt was Chairman of the Board and the Chief Executive Officer of TIC and served as a director on the Phoenix Board of Directors.]*

36. G. Platt was a supporter of Oklahoma University football and had met Switzer at a few social engagements prior to June of 1981. TIC was a sponsor of Switzer's football show, "Play Back." G. Platt had had season tickets to the OU football games for approximately five years. G. Platt had obtained autographs from Switzer for G. Platt's minor children, and had had his secretary telephone Switzer to request that his season tickets be upgraded. Upgrading of tickets was extended as a courtesy by Switzer to many season ticket holders. On at least two occasions Switzer had phoned G. Platt requesting continued sponsorship by TIC of Switzer's football television program. These calls were made at the urging of Tom Goodgame, General Manager of the television station which then produced "Play Back." As of June 5, 1981, Switzer knew that G. Platt was Chairman of the Board of TIC and further knew that TIC was a substantial shareholder of Phoenix because Switzer was a stockholder in TIC and thereby knew Phoenix was a subsidiary.

37. Neither G. Platt nor his wife Linda are particularly impressed by Switzer. They view him as "just a nice fellow."

38. Upon first greeting each other at the track meet, G. Platt and Switzer exchanged pleasantries. Switzer then departed and continued on through the bleachers.

39. Throughout the course of the day, G. Platt and Linda Platt generally remained in one place in the bleachers. Switzer, however, throughout the day moved around a great deal, at times speaking with his son or other participants and their families, signing autographs and watching the different events on the field. While moving about, Switzer joined the Platts to visit with them about three to five times. During these visits Switzer and the Platts talked about their sons' participation in the meet, the oil and gas business, the economy, football and their respective personal investments.

40. G. Platt and Switzer did not have any conversations regarding Phoenix or Morgan Stanley, nor did they have any conversations regarding any mergers, acquisitions, take-overs or possible liquidations of Phoenix in which Morgan Stanley would play a part. G. Platt did not make any stock recommendations to Switzer, nor did he intentionally communicate material, non-public corporate information to Switzer about Phoenix during their conversations at the track meet. The information that Switzer heard at the track meet about Phoenix was overheard and was not the result of an intentional disclosure by G. Platt.

41. Sometime in the afternoon, after his last conversation with G. Platt, Switzer laid down on a row of bleachers behind the Platts to sunbathe while waiting for his son's next event. While Switzer was sunbathing, he overheard G. Platt talking to his wife about his trip to New York the prior day. In that conversation, G. Platt mentioned Morgan Stanley and his desire to dispose of or liquidate Phoenix. G. Platt further talked about several companies bidding on Phoenix. Switzer also overheard that an announcement of a "possible" liquidation of Phoenix might occur the following Thursday. Switzer remained on the bleachers behind the Platts for approximately twenty minutes then got up and continued to move about.

42. At this time Switzer had no knowledge as to whether the information he had overheard was confidential.

43. G. Platt was not conscious of Switzer's presence on the bleachers behind him that day, nor that Switzer had overheard any conversation.

44. G. Platt had returned home late the previous day from his meetings in New York, and his wife was to leave town for an entire week on the following day. Having minor children, it is the Platts' common practice to try to arrange for G. Platt to be at home when his wife is out of town. The day of the track meet provided the Platts with an opportunity to discuss their respective plans for the up-coming week. During this discussion, G. Platt's prior business activities in New York and his resultant obligations and appointments were mentioned. In addition, when G. Platt appears distracted, it is not uncommon for his wife to inquire of him what is on his mind. On these occasions, he will talk to her about his problems, even though she does not have an understanding of nor interest in business matters. On the day of the track meet, Phoenix was weighing upon the mind of G. Platt, as it had been for the past several years, prompting G. Platt to talk to his wife about it.

45. On June 6, 1981, after the track meet, Switzer returned home and looked up the price of Phoenix in the paper. He then had dinner with [defendant] Sedwyn Kennedy, a close friend of both his and defendant Lee Allan Smith. In the past, they had all made investments through their partnership, SKS. Switzer told Kennedy he had overheard a conversation about the possible liquidation of Phoenix and that it would probably occur or be announced the next Thursday. Switzer told him the source was a gentleman who was an executive with TIC. Switzer did not tell Kennedy the man was G. Platt. Switzer and Kennedy are close friends and have known each other since 1966.

46. By the end of the evening, Switzer and Kennedy had each expressed an intention to purchase Phoenix stock.

. . . .

56. On Sunday, June 7, 1981, . . . Switzer and Smith met with Robert Hoover at his home, where he was having a party. Switzer and Smith arrived separately. Smith first discussed the matter with Hoover and did not mention where he had received the information. Switzer also told Hoover something was going to happen with Phoenix, but did not say from whom he had heard the information.

57. Hoover agreed to purchase Phoenix stock jointly with Smith and Switzer. Hoover advanced the capital and purchased the stock for his account, based on an understanding that any losses or profits would be split, fifty percent (50%) to Hoover, and the remaining fifty percent (50%) to be divided between Smith and Switzer.

58. Hoover purchased sixteen thousand (16,000) shares of Phoenix stock on or about Monday, June 8, or Tuesday, June 9, 1981.

59. G. Platt did not learn of Switzer's purchase or sale of Phoenix stock, or of the conversation Switzer had overheard, until on or about March 10 or 11, 1982. On or about March 10 or 11, 1982, Switzer called G. Platt at Platt's condominium in Snow Mass, Colorado, and asked to meet with him because Switzer said something he had inadvertently done would affect Platt. At the time Switzer was also staying in Snow Mass, Colorado. During this meeting, Switzer told G. Platt, for the first time, that Switzer had been sitting behind G. Platt and his wife at the track meet on June 6, 1981, and had overheard G. Platt's conversation with his wife regarding Phoenix, and that as a result of that overheard conversation, Switzer and other friends of his had subsequently purchased and sold Phoenix stock. G. Platt had heard as early as February of 1982 that Phoenix was under investigation by the SEC. . . .

. . . .

61. G. Platt did not share in the profits made through the transactions in Phoenix stock by Switzer, Kennedy, Deem, Smith, Hodges, Amyx and Hoover, nor did he receive any other financial benefit as a result of those transactions.

62. G. Platt did not receive any direct or indirect pecuniary gain nor any reputational benefit likely to translate into future earnings due to Switzer's inadvertent receipt of the information regarding Phoenix.

63. G. Platt did not make any gift to Switzer at this time, nor has he ever made a gift to Switzer.

64. Neither Switzer, Kennedy, Smith, Deem, Hodges, Amyx nor Hoover has ever been employed by or been an officer or director of Phoenix or TIC, nor have any of these defendants ever had any business relationship with Phoenix or with G. Platt personally. None of these defendants is a relative or personal friend of G. Platt.

65. None of the defendants had a relationship of trust and confidence with Phoenix, its shareholders or G. Platt.

. . . .

Conclusions of Law

Based upon the foregoing findings of fact, the court makes the following conclusions of law.

. . . .

7. [O]nly when a disclosure is made for an "improper purpose" will such a "tip" constitute a breach of an insider's duty, and only when there has been a breach of an insider's duty which the "tippee" knew or should have known constituted such a breach will there be "tippee" liability sufficient to constitute a violation of § 10(b) and Commission Rule 10b-5.

8. In *Dirks*, the court held that a disclosure is made for an "improper purpose" when an insider personally will benefit, directly or indirectly, from his disclosure. That court stated: "Absent some personal gain, there has been no breach of duty to stockholders. And absent a breach by the insider [to his stockholders], there is no derivative breach [by the tippee]."

9. G. Platt did not breach a fiduciary duty to stockholders of Phoenix for purposes of Rule 10b-5 liability nor § 10(b) liability, when he disclosed to his wife at the track meet of June 6, 1981, that there was going to be a possible liquidation of Phoenix.

10. This information was given to Mrs. Platt by G. Platt for the purpose of informing her of his up-coming business schedule so that arrangements for child care could be made.

11. The information was inadvertently overheard by Switzer at the track meet.

12. Rule 10b-5 does not bar trading on the basis of information inadvertently revealed by an insider.

13. The information was not intentionally imparted to Switzer by G. Platt, nor was the disclosure made for an improper purpose.

14. G. Platt did not personally benefit, directly or indirectly, monetarily or otherwise from the inadvertent disclosure.

15. As noted above, *Dirks* set forth a two-prong test for purposes of determining whether a tippee has acquired a fiduciary duty. First, it must be shown that an insider breached a fiduciary duty to the shareholders by disclosing inside information; and, second, it must be shown that the tippee knew or should have known that there had been a breach by the insider.

16. G. Platt did not breach a duty to the shareholders of Phoenix, and thus plaintiff failed to meet its burden of proof as to the first prong established in *Dirks*. Since G. Platt did not breach a fiduciary duty to Phoenix shareholders, Switzer did not acquire nor assume a fiduciary duty to Phoenix's shareholders, and because Switzer

did not acquire a fiduciary duty to Phoenix shareholders, any information he passed on to defendants Smith, Hodges, Amyx, Hoover, Kennedy and Deem was not in violation of Rule 10b-5.

17. Since plaintiff did not meet its burden of proof as to the first prong of the two-prong *Dirks* test, i.e., it was not proved that G. Platt breached a fiduciary duty to the shareholders of Phoenix, tippee liability cannot result from G. Platt's inadvertent disclosure to Switzer.

. . . .

The Supreme Court confirmed the continued validity of the *Dirks* tipper-tippee liability standard in *Salman v. United States*. The decision follows.

Salman v. United States

United States Supreme Court

137 S. Ct. 420 (2016)

JUSTICE ALITO delivered the opinion of the Court.

Section 10(b) of the Securities Exchange Act of 1934 and the Securities and Exchange Commission's Rule 10b-5 prohibit undisclosed trading on inside corporate information by individuals who are under a duty of trust and confidence that prohibits them from secretly using such information for their personal advantage. . . . Individuals under this duty may face criminal and civil liability for trading on inside information (unless they make appropriate disclosures ahead of time).

These persons also may not tip inside information to others for trading. The tippee acquires the tipper's duty to disclose or abstain from trading if the tippee knows the information was disclosed in breach of the tipper's duty, and the tippee may commit securities fraud by trading in disregard of that knowledge. In *Dirks v. SEC*, 463 U.S. 646 (1983), this Court explained that a tippee's liability for trading on inside information hinges on whether the tipper breached a fiduciary duty by disclosing the information. A tipper breaches such a fiduciary duty, we held, when the tipper discloses the inside information for a personal benefit. And, we went on to say, a jury can infer a personal benefit—and thus a breach of the tipper's duty—where the tipper receives something of value in exchange for the tip or "makes a gift of confidential information to a trading relative or friend." . . .

Petitioner Bassam Salman challenges his convictions for conspiracy and insider trading. Salman received lucrative trading tips from an extended family member, who had received the information from Salman's brother-in-law. Salman then traded on the information. He argues that he cannot be held liable as a tippee because the tipper (his brother-in-law) did not personally receive money or property in exchange for the tips and thus did not personally benefit from them. The Court of Appeals disagreed, holding that *Dirks* allowed the jury to infer that the tipper here breached a duty because he made a 'gift of confidential information to a trading relative.' 792

F.3d 1087, 1092 (CA9 2015). . . . Because the Court of Appeals properly applied *Dirks*, we affirm the judgment below.

I

Maher Kara was an investment banker in Citigroup's healthcare investment banking group. He dealt with highly confidential information about mergers and acquisitions involving Citigroup's clients. Maher enjoyed a close relationship with his older brother, Mounir Kara (known as Michael). After Maher started at Citigroup, he began discussing aspects of his job with Michael. At first he relied on Michael's chemistry background to help him grasp scientific concepts relevant to his new job. Then, while their father was battling cancer, the brothers discussed companies that dealt with innovative cancer treatment and pain management techniques. Michael began to trade on the information Maher shared with him. At first, Maher was unaware of his brother's trading activity, but eventually he began to suspect that it was taking place.

Ultimately, Maher began to assist Michael's trading by sharing inside information with his brother about pending mergers and acquisitions. Maher sometimes used code words to communicate corporate information to his brother. Other times, he shared inside information about deals he was not working on in order to avoid detection. Without his younger brother's knowledge, Michael fed the information to others—including Salman, Michael's friend and Maher's brother-in-law. By the time the authorities caught on, Salman had made over $1.5 million in profits that he split with another relative who executed trades via a brokerage account on Salman's behalf.

Salman was indicted on one count of conspiracy to commit securities fraud and four counts of securities fraud. . . . Facing charges of their own, both Maher and Michael pleaded guilty and testified at Salman's trial.

The evidence at trial established that Maher and Michael enjoyed a "very close relationship." Maher "love[d] [his] brother very much," Michael was like "a second father to Maher," and Michael was the best man at Maher's wedding to Salman's sister. Maher testified that he shared inside information with his brother to benefit him and with the expectation that his brother would trade on it. While Maher explained that he disclosed the information in large part to appease Michael (who pestered him incessantly for it), he also testified that he tipped his brother to "help him" and to "fulfil[l] whatever needs he had." For instance, Michael once called Maher and told him that "he needed a favor." Maher offered his brother money but Michael asked for information instead. Maher then disclosed an upcoming acquisition. Although he instantly regretted the tip and called his brother back to implore him not to trade, Maher expected his brother to do so anyway. . . .

For his part, Michael told the jury that his brother's tips gave him "timely information that the average person does not have access to" and "access to stocks, options, and what have you, that I can capitalize on, that the average person would never have or dream of." Michael testified that he became friends with Salman when Maher was courting Salman's sister and later began sharing Maher's tips with Salman. As he explained at trial, "any time a major deal came in, [Salman] was the first on my phone list." Michael also testified that he told Salman that the information was coming from Maher. . . .

After a jury trial in the Northern District of California, Salman was convicted on all counts. He was sentenced to 36 months of imprisonment, three years of supervised release, and over $750,000 in restitution. After his motion for a new trial was denied, Salman appealed to the Ninth Circuit. While his appeal was pending, the Second Circuit issued its opinion in *United States v. Newman*, 773 F.3d 438 (2014). . . . There, the Second Circuit reversed the convictions of two portfolio managers who traded on inside information. The *Newman* defendants were "several steps removed from the corporate insiders" and the court found that "there was no evidence that either was aware of the source of the inside information." The court acknowledged that *Dirks* and Second Circuit case law allow a factfinder to infer a personal benefit to the tipper from a gift of confidential information to a trading relative or friend. But the court concluded that, "[t]o the extent" *Dirks* permits "such an inference," the inference "is impermissible in the absence of proof of a meaningfully close personal relationship that generates an exchange that is objective, consequential, and represents at least a potential gain of a pecuniary or similarly valuable nature." . . .

Pointing to *Newman*, Salman argued that his conviction should be reversed. While the evidence established that Maher made a gift of trading information to Michael and that Salman knew it, there was no evidence that Maher received anything of "a pecuniary or similarly valuable nature" in exchange—or that Salman knew of any such benefit. The Ninth Circuit disagreed and affirmed Salman's conviction. 792 F.3d 1087. The court reasoned that the case was governed by *Dirks*'s holding that a tipper benefits personally by making a gift of confidential information to a trading relative or friend. Indeed, Maher's disclosures to Michael were "precisely the gift of confidential information to a trading relative that *Dirks* envisioned." 792 F.3d at 1092. . . . To the extent *Newman* went further and required additional gain to the tipper in cases involving gifts of confidential information to family and friends, the Ninth Circuit "decline[d] to follow it." . . .

We granted certiorari to resolve the tension between the Second Circuit's *Newman* decision and the Ninth Circuit's decision in this case. . . .[22]

---

[22] *Dirks v. SEC*, 463 U.S. 646 (1983), established the personal-benefit framework in a case brought under the classical theory of insider-trading liability, which applies "when a corporate insider" or his tippee "trades in the securities of [the tipper's] corporation on the basis of material, nonpublic information." *United States v. O'Hagan*, 521 U. S. 642, 651–652 (1997). In such a case, the defendant breaches a duty to, and takes advantage of, the shareholders of his corporation. By contrast, the misappropriation theory holds that a person commits securities fraud "when he misappropriates confidential information for securities trading purposes, in breach of a duty owed to the source of the information" such as an employer or client. *Id.*, at 652. In such a case, the defendant breaches a duty to, and defrauds, the source of the information, as opposed to the shareholders of his corporation. The Court of Appeals observed that this is a misappropriation case, 792 F.3d, 1087, 1092, n. 4 (CA9 2015), while the Government represents that both theories apply on the facts of this case. . . . We need not resolve the question. The parties do not dispute that *Dirks*'s personal-benefit analysis applies in both classical and misappropriation cases, so we will proceed on the assumption that it does.

II

A

In this case, Salman contends that an insider's "gift of confidential information to a trading relative or friend," is not enough to establish securities fraud. Instead, Salman argues, a tipper does not personally benefit unless the tipper's goal in disclosing inside information is to obtain money, property, or something of tangible value. He claims that our insider-trading precedents, and the cases those precedents cite, involve situations in which the insider exploited confidential information for the insider's own "tangible monetary profit." He suggests that his position is reinforced by our criminal-fraud precedents outside of the insider-trading context, because those cases confirm that a fraudster must personally obtain money or property. More broadly, Salman urges that defining a gift as a personal benefit renders the insider-trading offense indeterminate and overbroad: indeterminate, because liability may turn on facts such as the closeness of the relationship between tipper and tippee and the tipper's purpose for disclosure; and overbroad, because the Government may avoid having to prove a concrete personal benefit by simply arguing that the tipper meant to give a gift to the tippee. He also argues that we should interpret *Dirks*'s standard narrowly so as to avoid constitutional concerns. Finally, Salman contends that gift situations create especially troubling problems for remote tippees—that is, tippees who receive inside information from another tippee, rather than the tipper—who may have no knowledge of the relationship between the original tipper and tippee and thus may not know why the tipper made the disclosure. . . .

The Government disagrees and argues that a gift of confidential information to anyone, not just a "trading relative or friend," is enough to prove securities fraud. . . . Under the Government's view, a tipper personally benefits whenever the tipper discloses confidential trading information for a noncorporate purpose. Accordingly, a gift to a friend, a family member, or anyone else would support the inference that the tipper exploited the trading value of inside information for personal purposes and thus personally benefited from the disclosure. The Government claims to find support for this reading in *Dirks* and the precedents on which *Dirks* relied. . . .

The Government also argues that Salman's concerns about unlimited and indeterminate liability for remote tippees are significantly alleviated by other statutory elements that prosecutors must satisfy to convict a tippee for insider trading. The Government observes that, in order to establish a defendant's criminal liability as a tippee, it must prove beyond a reasonable doubt that the tipper expected that the information being disclosed would be used in securities trading. The Government also notes that, to establish a defendant's criminal liability as a tippee, it must prove that the tippee knew that the tipper breached a duty—in other words, that the tippee knew that the tipper disclosed the information for a personal benefit and that the tipper expected trading to ensue. . . .

B

We adhere to *Dirks*, which easily resolves the narrow issue presented here.

In *Dirks*, we explained that a tippee is exposed to liability for trading on inside information only if the tippee participates in a breach of the tipper's fiduciary duty. Whether the tipper breached that duty depends "in large part on the purpose of the disclosure" to the tippee. "[T]he test," we explained, "is whether the insider personally will benefit, directly or indirectly, from his disclosure." Thus, the disclosure of confidential information without personal benefit is not enough. In determining whether a tipper derived a personal benefit, we instructed courts to "focus on objective criteria, *i.e.*, whether the insider receives a direct or indirect personal benefit from the disclosure, such as a pecuniary gain or a reputational benefit that will translate into future earnings." This personal benefit can "often" be inferred "from objective facts and circumstances," we explained, such as "a relationship between the insider and the recipient that suggests a *quid pro quo* from the latter, or an intention to benefit the particular recipient." In particular, we held that "[t]he elements of fiduciary duty and exploitation of nonpublic information also exist *when an insider makes a gift of confidential information to a trading relative or friend.*" *Ibid.* (emphasis added). In such cases, "[t]he tip and trade resemble trading by the insider followed by a gift of the profits to the recipient." We then applied this gift-giving principle to resolve *Dirks* itself, finding it dispositive that the tippers "received no monetary or personal benefit" from their tips to Dirks, "*nor was their purpose to make a gift of valuable information to Dirks.*"

Our discussion of gift giving resolves this case. Maher, the tipper, provided inside information to a close relative, his brother Michael. *Dirks* makes clear that a tipper breaches a fiduciary duty by making a gift of confidential information to "a trading relative," and that rule is sufficient to resolve the case at hand. As Salman's counsel acknowledged at oral argument, Maher would have breached his duty had he personally traded on the information here himself then given the proceeds as a gift to his brother. It is obvious that Maher would personally benefit in that situation. But Maher effectively achieved the same result by disclosing the information to Michael, and allowing him to trade on it. *Dirks* appropriately prohibits that approach, as well. Cf. [*Dirks*] 463 U.S., at 659 (holding that "insiders [are] forbidden" both "from personally using undisclosed corporate information to their advantage" and from "giv[ing] such information to an outsider for the same improper purpose of exploiting the information for their personal gain"), *Dirks* specifies that when a tipper gives inside information to "a trading relative or friend," the jury can infer that the tipper meant to provide the equivalent of a cash gift. In such situations, the tipper benefits personally because giving a gift of trading information is the same thing as trading by the tipper followed by a gift of the proceeds. Here, by disclosing confidential information as a gift to his brother with the expectation that he would trade on it, Maher breached his duty of trust and confidence to Citigroup and its clients—a duty Salman acquired, and breached himself, by trading on the information with full knowledge that it had been improperly disclosed.

To the extent the Second Circuit held that the tipper must also receive something of a "pecuniary or similarly valuable nature" in exchange for a gift to family or friends, *Newman* 773 F.3d, at 452, we agree with the Ninth Circuit that this requirement is inconsistent with *Dirks*.

C

Salman points out that many insider-trading cases—including several that *Dirks* cited—involved insiders who personally profited through the misuse of trading information. But this observation does not undermine the test *Dirks* articulated and applied. Salman also cites a sampling of our criminal-fraud decisions construing other federal fraud statutes, suggesting that they stand for the proposition that fraud is not consummated unless the defendant obtains money or property. . . . Assuming that these cases are relevant to our construction of § 10(b) (a proposition the Government forcefully disputes), nothing in them undermines the commonsense point we made in *Dirks*. Making a gift of inside information to a relative like Michael is little different from trading on the information, obtaining the profits, and doling them out to the trading relative. The tipper benefits either way. The facts of this case illustrate the point: In one of their tipper-tippee interactions, Michael asked Maher for a favor, declined Maher's offer of money, and instead requested and received lucrative trading information.

We reject Salman's argument that *Dirks*'s gift-giving standard is unconstitutionally vague as applied to this case. *Dirks* created a simple and clear "guiding principle" for determining tippee liability, and Salman has not demonstrated that either § 10(b) itself or the *Dirks* gift-giving standard "leav[e] grave uncertainty about how to estimate the risk posed by a crime" or are plagued by "hopeless indeterminacy." . . . At most, Salman shows that in some factual circumstances assessing liability for gift-giving will be difficult. That alone cannot render "shapeless" a federal criminal prohibition, for even clear rules "produce close cases." We also reject Salman's appeal to the rule of lenity, as he has shown "no grievous ambiguity or uncertainty that would trigger the rule's application." . . . To the contrary, Salman's conduct is in the heartland of *Dirks*'s rule concerning gifts. It remains the case that "[d]etermining whether an insider personally benefits from a particular disclosure, a question of fact, will not always be easy for courts." But there is no need for us to address those difficult cases today, because this case involves "precisely the gift of confidential information to a trading relative" that *Dirks* envisioned. . . .

III

Salman's jury was properly instructed that a personal benefit includes "the benefit one would obtain from simply making a gift of confidential information to a trading relative." As the Court of Appeals noted, "the Government presented direct evidence that the disclosure was intended as a gift of market-sensitive information." And, as Salman conceded below, this evidence is sufficient to sustain his conviction under our reading of *Dirks*. . . . Accordingly, the Ninth Circuit's judgment is affirmed.

———————

§ 12.09 Rule 14e-3

Subsequent to the Supreme Court's decision in *Chiarella*, the SEC, in an effort to regulate insider and tippee trading in the tender offer context, adopted Rule 14e-3, which establishes an expansive "disclose or abstain from trading" rule under § 14(e) of the Exchange Act. As adopted, with certain exceptions, Rule 14e-3 applies this disclose-or-abstain provision to the possession of material information relating to a tender offer where the person knows or has reason to know the information is nonpublic and was received directly or indirectly from the offeror, the subject corporation, any of their affiliated persons, or any person acting on behalf of either company. Moreover, the rule contains a broad anti-tipping provision and provides for certain exceptions pertaining to sales to the offeror and to certain activities by multiservice financial institutions.

In the release adopting Rule 14e-3, the Commission asserted that *Chiarella* did not limit its authority under § 14(e) to prescribe such a mandate regulating insider trading in the tender offer context. In *O'Hagan*, the Supreme Court addressed the validity of Rule 14e-3.

United States v. O'Hagan

United States Supreme Court

521 U.S. 642, 117 S. Ct. 2199, 138 L.Ed.2d 724 (1997)

Justice GINSBURG delivered the opinion of the Court.

This case concerns the interpretation and enforcement of § 10(b) and § 14(e) of the Securities Exchange Act of 1934, and rules made by the Securities and Exchange Commission pursuant to these provisions, Rule 10b-5 and Rule 14e-3(a). Two prime questions are presented. The first relates to the misappropriation of material, nonpublic information for securities trading; the second concerns fraudulent practices in the tender offer setting. In particular, we address and resolve these issues: (1) Is a person who trades in securities for personal profit, using confidential information misappropriated in breach of a fiduciary duty to the source of the information, guilty of violating § 10(b) and Rule 10b-5? (2) Did the Commission exceed its rulemaking authority by adopting Rule 14e-3(a), which proscribes trading on undisclosed information in the tender offer setting, even in the absence of a duty to disclose? Our answer to the first question is yes, and to the second question, viewed in the context of this case, no.

[The case's facts and analysis of the misappropriation theory are contained in § 12.05.]

III

We consider next the ground on which the Court of Appeals reversed *O'Hagan*'s convictions for fraudulent trading in connection with a tender offer, in violation of § 14(e) of the Exchange Act and SEC Rule 14e-3(a). A sole question is before us as to these convictions: Did the Commission, as the Court of Appeals held, exceed its rule-making authority under § 14(e) when it adopted Rule 14e-3(a) without requiring a showing that the trading at issue entailed a breach of fiduciary duty? We hold that the Commission, in this regard and to the extent relevant to this case, did not exceed its authority.

. . . .

Section 14(e)'s first sentence prohibits fraudulent acts in connection with a tender offer. This self-operating proscription was one of several provisions added to the Exchange Act in 1968 by the Williams Act. The section's second sentence delegates definitional and prophylactic rulemaking authority to the Commission. Congress added this rulemaking delegation to § 14(e) in the 1970 amendments to the Williams Act.

Through § 14(e) and other provisions on disclosure in the Williams Act, Congress sought to ensure that shareholders "confronted by a cash tender offer for their stock [would] not be required to respond without adequate information." . . . As we recognized in *Schreiber v. Burlington Northern, Inc.*, 472 U.S. 1 (1985), Congress designed the Williams Act to make "disclosure, rather than court imposed principles of 'fairness' or 'artificiality,' . . . the preferred method of market regulation." Section 14(e), we explained, "supplements the more precise disclosure provisions found elsewhere in the Williams Act, while requiring disclosure more explicitly addressed to the tender offer context than that required by § 10(b)." . . .

Relying on § 14(e)'s rulemaking authorization, the Commission, in 1980, promulgated Rule 14e-3(a). That measure provides:

"(a) If any person has taken a substantial step or steps to commence, or has commenced, a tender offer (the 'offering person'), it shall constitute a fraudulent, deceptive or manipulative act or practice within the meaning of section 14(e) of the [Exchange] Act for any other person who is in possession of material information he knows or has reason to know is nonpublic and which he knows or has reason to know has been acquired directly or indirectly from:

"(1) The offering person,

"(2) The issuer of the securities sought or to be sought by such tender offer, or

"(3) Any officer, director, partner or employee or any other person acting on behalf of the offering person or such issuer, to purchase or sell or cause to be purchased or sold any of such securities or any securities convertible into exchangeable for any such securities or any option or right to obtain or to dispose of any of the foregoing securities, unless within a reasonable time prior to any purchase or sale such information and its source are publicly disclosed by press release or otherwise."

As characterized by the Commission, Rule 14e-3(a) is a "disclose or abstain from trading" requirement. The Second Circuit concisely described the rule's thrust:

"One violates Rule 14e-3(a) if he trades on the bases of material nonpublic information concerning a pending tender offer that he knows or has reason to know has been acquired 'directly or indirectly' from an insider of the offeror or issuer, or someone working on their behalf. Rule 14e-3(a) is a disclosure provision. It creates a duty in those traders who fall within its ambit to abstain or disclose, without regard to whether the trader owes a pre-existing fiduciary duty to respect the confidentiality of the information." *United States v. Chestman*, 947 F.2d 551, 557 (1991) (en banc).

In the Eighth Circuit's view, because Rule 14e-3(a) applies whether or not the trading in question breaches a fiduciary duty, the regulation exceeds the SEC's § 14(e) rulemaking authority. In support of its holding, the Eighth Circuit relied on the text of § 14(e) and our decisions in *Schreiber* and *Chiarella*.

The Eighth Circuit homed in on the essence of § 14(e)'s rulemaking authorization: "[T]he statute empowers the SEC to 'define' and 'prescribe means reasonably designed to prevent' 'acts and practices' which are 'fraudulent.'" All that means, the Eighth Circuit found plain, is that the SEC may "identify and regulate," in the tender offer context, "acts and practices" the law already defines as "fraudulent"; but, the Eighth Circuit maintained, the SEC may not "create its own definition of fraud."

This Court, the Eighth Circuit pointed out, held in Schreiber that the word "manipulative" in the § 14(e) phrase "fraudulent, deceptive, or manipulative acts or practices" means just what the word means in § 10(b): Absent misrepresentation or nondisclosure, an act cannot be indicted as manipulative. Section 10(b) interpretations guide construction of § 14(e), the Eighth Circuit added, citing this Court's acknowledgment in Schreiber that § 14(e)'s "'broad antifraud prohibition' ... [is] modeled on the antifraud provisions of § 10(b) ... and Rule 10b-5." ...

For the meaning of "fraudulent" under § 10(b), the Eighth Circuit looked to *Chiarella*. In that case, the Eighth Circuit recounted, this Court held that a failure to disclose information could be "fraudulent" under § 10(b) only when there was a duty to speak arising out of "'a fiduciary or other similar relationship of trust and confidence.'" ... Just as § 10(b) demands a showing of a breach of fiduciary duty, so such a breach is necessary to make out a § 14(e) violation, the Eighth Circuit concluded.

As to the Commission's § 14(e) authority to "prescribe means reasonably designed to prevent" fraudulent acts, the Eighth Circuit stated: "Properly read, this provision means simply that the SEC has broad regulatory powers in the field of tender offers, but the statutory terms have a fixed meaning which the SEC cannot alter by way of an administrative rule." ...

The United States urges that the Eighth Circuit's reading of § 14(e) misapprehends both the Commission's authority to define fraudulent acts and the Commission's power to prevent them. "The 'defining' power," the United States submits, "would be a virtual nullity were the SEC not permitted to go beyond common law fraud (which is separately prohibited in the first [self-operative] sentence of Section 14(e))." ...

In maintaining that the Commission's power to define fraudulent acts under § 14(e) is broader than its rulemaking power under § 10(b), the United States questions the Court of Appeals' reading of Schreiber. Parenthetically, the United States notes that the word before the Schreiber Court was "manipulative"; unlike "fraudulent," the United States observes, "'manipulative' . . . is 'virtually a term of art when used in connection with the securities markets.'" Most tellingly, the United States submits, Schreiber involved acts alleged to violate the self-operative provision in § 14(e)'s first sentence, a sentence containing language similar to § 10(b). But § 14(e)'s second sentence, containing the rulemaking authorization, the United States points out, does not track § 10(b), which simply authorizes the SEC to proscribe "manipulative or deceptive device[s] or contrivance[s]." Instead, § 14(e)'s rulemaking prescription tracks § 15(c)(2)(D) of the Exchange Act, which concerns the conduct of broker-dealers. . . . Since 1938, § 15(c)(2) has given the Commission authority to "define, and prescribe means reasonably designed to prevent, such [broker-dealer] acts and practices as are fraudulent, deceptive, or manipulative." When Congress added this same rulemaking language to § 14(e) in 1970, the Government states, the Commission had already used its § 15(c)(2) authority to reach beyond common law fraud.

We need not resolve in this case whether the Commission's authority under § 14(e) to "define . . . such acts and practices as are fraudulent" is broader than the Commission's fraud-defining authority under § 10(b), for we agree with the United States that Rule 14e-3(a), as applied to cases of this genre, qualifies under § 14(e) as a "means reasonably designed to prevent" fraudulent trading on material, nonpublic information in the tender offer context.[23] A prophylactic measure, because its mission is to prevent, typically encompasses more than the core activity prohibited. As we noted in Schreiber, § 14(e)'s rulemaking authorization gives the Commission "latitude," even in the context of a term of art like "manipulative," "to regulate nondeceptive activities as a 'reasonably designed' means of preventing manipulative acts, without suggesting any change in the meaning of the term 'manipulative' itself." We hold, accordingly, that under § 14(e), the Commission my prohibit acts, not themselves fraudulent under the common law or § 10(b), if the prohibition is "reasonably designed to prevent . . . acts and practices [that] are fraudulent."

. . . .

In adopting the "disclosure or abstain" rule, the SEC explained:

---

[23]. We leave for another day, when the issue requires decision, the legitimacy of Rule 14e-3(a) as applied to Awarehousing," which the Government describes as "the practice by which bidders leak advance information of a tender offer to allies and encourage them to purchase the target company's stock before the bid is announced." As we observed in *Chiarella*, one of the Commission's purposes is proposing Rule 14e-3(a) was "to bar warehousing under its authority to regulate tender offers." The Government acknowledges that trading authorized by a principal breaches no fiduciary duty. The instant case, however, does not involve trading authorized by a principal; therefore, we need not here decide whether the Commission's proscription of warehousing falls within its § 14(e) authority to define or prevent fraud.

"The Commission has previously expressed and continues to have serious concerns about trading by persons in possession of material, nonpublic information relating to a tender offer. This practice results in unfair disparities in market information and market disruption. Security holders who purchase from or sell to such person are effectively denied the benefits of disclosure and the substantive protections of the Williams Act. If furnished with the information, these security holders would be able to make an informed investment decision, which could involve deferring the purchase or sale of the securities until the material information had been disseminated or until the tender offer has been commenced or terminated."

The Commission thus justified Rule 14e-3(a) as a means necessary and proper to assure the efficacy of Williams Act protections.

The United States emphasizes that Rule 14e-3(a) reaches trading in which "a breach of duty is likely but difficult to prove." . . . "Particularly in the context of a tender offer, . . . there is a fairly wide circle of people with confidential information," . . . notably, the attorneys, investment bankers, and accountants involved in structuring the transaction. The availability of that information may lead to abuse, for "even a hint of an upcoming tender offer may send the price of the target company's stock soaring." . . . Individuals entrusted with nonpublic information, particularly if they have no long-term loyalty to the issuer, may find the temptation to trade on that information hard to resist in view of "the very large short-term profits potentially available [to them]." . . .

"[I]t may be possible to prove circumstantially that a person [traded on the basis of material, nonpublic information], but almost impossible to prove that the trader obtained such information in breach of a fiduciary duty owed either by the trader or by the ultimate insider source of the information." . . . The example of a "tippee" who trades on information received from an insider illustrates the problem. Under Rule 10b-5, "a tippee assumes a fiduciary duty to the shareholders of a corporation not to trade on material nonpublic information only when the insider has breached his fiduciary duty to the shareholders by disclosing the information to the tippee and the tippee knows or should know that there has been a breach." *Dirks*, 463 U.S., at 660. To show that a tippee who traded on nonpublic information about a tender offer had breached a fiduciary duty would require proof not only that the insider source breached a fiduciary duty, but that the tippee knew or should have known of that breach. "Yet, in most cases, the only parties to the [information transfer] will be the insider and the alleged tippee." . . .

In sum, it is a fair assumption that trading on the basis of material, nonpublic information will often involve a breach of a duty of confidentiality to the bidder or target company or their representatives. The SEC, cognizant of the proof problem that could enable sophisticated traders to escape responsibility, placed in Rule 14e-3(a) a "disclose or abstain from trading" command that does not require specific proof of a breach of fiduciary duty. That prescription, we are satisfied, applied to this case, is a "means reasonably designed to prevent" fraudulent trading on material, non-public information in the tender offer context. . . . Therefore, insofar as it serves to prevent the type of misappropriation charged against O'Hagan, Rule 14e-3(a) is a proper exercise of the Commission's prophylactic power under § 14(e).

As an alternate ground for affirming the Eighth Circuit's judgment, *O'Hagan* urges that Rule 14e-3(a) is invalid because it prohibits trading in advance of a tender offer — when "a substantial step . . . to commence" such an offer has been taken — while § 14(e) prohibits fraudulent acts "in connection with any tender offer." O'Hagan further contends that, by covering pre-offer conduct, Rule 14e-3(a) "fails to comport with due process on two levels": The rule does not "give fair notice as to when, in advance of a tender offer, a violation of § 14(e) occurs," and it "disposes of any scienter requirement." . . . The Court of Appeals did not address these arguments, and O'Hagan did not raise the due process points in his briefs before that court. We decline to consider these contentions in the first instance. The Court of Appeals may address on remand any arguments O'Hagan has preserved.

. . . .

Note

(1) Does the application of Rule 14e-3 arguably render the insider trading framework in this country unacceptable? Literally, one may be able to retain her profits legally if the subject transaction takes the form of a merger but be subject to imprisonment for the identical conduct if the transaction is structured as a tender offer.

(2) As stated by the Supreme Court in *O'Hagan*, Rule 14e-3 comes into play when "a substantial step" has been taken "in connection with" a tender offer. The Second Circuit's decision in *SEC v. Mayhew*, 121 F.3d 44 (2d Cir. 1997), interpreted this language as follows:

> Mayhew claims that the district court erred in finding that the tip he received was "in connection with" a tender offer because, at the time he received the tip, [the target] Rorer and [the bidder] RPSA had not taken "substantial steps" toward a tender offer as evidenced by the fact that RPSA did not make the tender offer for another two months. Alternatively, Mayhew argues that the two month lag between the tip and tender offer precludes a finding that the tip was "in connection with" a tender offer under section 14(e) as a matter of law.
>
> Liability under Rule 14e-3 attaches only when a "substantial step or steps" have been taken to accomplish a tender offer. We have no difficulty in concluding that, in this case, such steps had been taken. Prior to Mayhew's November 1989 conversation with [his source] Piccolino, Rorer and RPSA had retained a consulting firm, signed confidentiality agreements, and held meetings between top officials. These steps satisfy the substantiality requirement of Rule 14e-3. *See, e.g., SEC v. Maio*, 51 F.3d 623, 636 (7th Cir. 1995)

(meeting of officials "much more serious than any previous discussion between the parties" satisfies substantial steps requirement); *SEC v. Musella*, 578 F. Supp. 425, 443-44 (S.D.N.Y. 1984) (retaining law firm before tender offer is a substantial step); *Camelot Indus. Corp. v. Vista Resources, Inc.*, 535 F. Supp. 1174, 1183 (S.D.N.Y. 1982) (meeting between officers is a substantial step).

Moreover, liability can attach under section 14(e) even though there is a two month lag between the tip and the tender offer. Congress intended section 14(e) to be a broad antifraud remedy in the area of tender offers.... Any arbitrary temporal limit would frustrate that purpose. It would permit parties to freely misuse information regarding a tender offer "up to [that limit], thus defeating in substantial part the very purpose of the Act— informed decisionmaking by shareholders."... Instead, we must decide whether information is "in connection with" a tender offer on the facts of each particular case.

In this case, the nexus between the tip and the tender offer is self-evident. The information disclosed that Rorer was engaged in actual ongoing discussions with a merger candidate or candidates. The information had no value whatsoever except "in connection with" Mayhew's subsequent purchase of securities in anticipation of the tender offer.... Because, at the time Mayhew traded in Rorer's securities, Rorer and RPSA had taken substantial steps toward the tender offer, and because the information concerned the tender offer and derived value from its nexus to the tender offer, we easily conclude that the "in connection with" requirement of section 14(e) is satisfied.

---

§ 12.10 Damages and Penalties

[A] Damages — Section 10(b) Actions

The measure of damages for insider trading in open market transactions under § 10(b) has received diverse treatment from the relatively few courts that have considered the issue. *Shapiro v. Merrill Lynch, Pierce, Fenner & Smith, Inc.*, 495 F.2d 228 (2d Cir. 1974), represents an expansive approach. There, the Second Circuit, relying on *Affiliated Ute Citizens v. United States*, 406 U.S. 128 (1972), stated that "[t]he proper test to determine whether causation in fact has been established in a nondisclosure case is 'whether the plaintiff would have been influenced to act differently than he did if the defendant had disclosed to him the undisclosed fact.'" After finding that causation in fact had been established (notwithstanding that all transactions occurred on a national securities exchange), the court formulated a potentially broad measure of damages:

> [W]e hold that defendants are liable in this private action for damages to plaintiffs who, during the same period that defendants traded in or recommended trading in Douglas common stock, purchased Douglas stock in the open market without knowledge of the material inside information which was in the possession of defendants.

Having so held, the Second Circuit, however, left to the district court's discretion the proper measure of damages, noting its concern with the potential for draconian liability.

In *Fridrich v. Bradford*, 542 F.2d 307 (6th Cir. 1976), the Sixth Circuit rejected the *Shapiro* analysis. Disagreeing with the Second Circuit, the *Fridrich* court found that the plaintiffs had failed to show that their loss was caused by the defendants' inside trading. The Sixth Circuit supported its holding by pointing out that an award of damages to contemporaneous traders in the open market would create a windfall for fortuitous investors while being essentially punitive. Although the court recognized that it could limit the amount of recovery to the defendants' profits, it declined to do so.

Subsequently, in *Elkind v. Liggett & Myers, Inc.*, 635 F.2d 156 (2d Cir. 1980), the Second Circuit, although not expressly rejecting the *Shapiro* rationale, greatly limited the potential damages recovery. There, the court considered three alternative measures of damages: (1) out-of-pocket, (2) market-repercussion, and (3) disgorgement. Rejecting the out-of-pocket measure, the court pointed out that this measure is normally directed toward compensating a trader for damages that are directly traceable to the defendant's perpetration of a fraud upon the trader. In an impersonal open market, however, "uninformed traders . . . are not induced by representations on the part of the tipper or tippee to buy or sell." Second, the Second Circuit observed that the out-of-pocket measure posed serious proof problems as the "value" of the stock traded during the period of nondisclosure can often be hypothetical. Lastly, the court concluded that the out-of-pocket measure had the potential for the imposition of "draconian, exorbitant damages, out of all proportion to the wrong committed."

The *Elkind* court also rejected the market-repercussion theory of damages. This measure would allow recovery of damages caused by erosion of the stock's market price that is traceable to the defendant's wrongful trading. The rationale underlying the theory is that "if the market price is not affected by the [defendant's] trading, the uninformed investor is in the same position as he would have been had the insider abstained from trading." Upon analysis, the Second Circuit rejected this theory due to the difficult problems of proof it would impose on plaintiffs and that adoption of the theory would frequently preclude recovery for an insider's breach of his/her duty to disclose the confidential information prior to trading.

The *Elkind* court thereupon adopted a third alternative, the disgorgement measure of damages. This measure also is the proper measure of damages under § 20A for contemporaneous traders who trade on the opposite side of the transaction from the defendant. Under the *Elkind* formulation, the measure of damages is as follows:

> (1) [T]o allow any uninformed investor, where a reasonable investor would either have delayed his purchase or not purchased at all if he had the benefit of the tipped information, to recover any post-purchase decline in market value of his shares up to a reasonable time after he learns of the tipped information or after there is a public disclosure of it but (2) limit his recovery to the amount gained by the [subject violator] as a result of his selling at the earlier date rather than delaying his sale until the parties could trade on an equal informational basis. . . . Should the intervening buyers, because of the volume and price of their purchases, claim more than the [subject violator's] gain, their recovery (limited to that gain) would be shared *pro rata*. [635 F.2d at 172]

[B] Penalties

A number of different parties may be subject to a variety of monetary penalties under the federal securities laws for engaging in illegal insider trading. These parties may include actual traders, their tippers, as well as broker-dealers and investment advisers (when they fail to take appropriate steps to prevent the insider trading violation(s) or fail to maintain and enforce policies and procedures reasonably designed to prevent the occurrence of such trading). Penalties that may be levied in this context are (1) requiring the subject party to "disgorge" the ill-gotten profits (or loss avoided) in an SEC enforcement action, (2) subjecting individuals to a criminal fine and imprisonment, and (3) in an SEC enforcement action, within a court's discretion, ordering the subject party to pay a treble damages penalty amounting to three times the profit gained or loss avoided. These penalties, together with the imposition of jail terms and the availability of civil damages, are intended to strongly deter insider trading. As an additional measure to combat insider trading, the SEC may award "whistleblower bounties" between 10 and 30 percent of a money penalty that exceeds $1 million to persons who provide "original information" concerning insider trading violations.

To recover monetary penalties against "control persons" in the insider trading context, the SEC must show that such control person "knew or recklessly disregarded the fact that such controlled person was likely to engage in the act or acts constituting the violation and failed to take appropriate steps to prevent such act or acts before they occurred." Moreover:

> If the controlling person is a broker-dealer or investment advisor, [the 1988 legislation] provides the Commission with more potent ammunition for imposing the new monetary penalties. [It] sets forth an affirmative duty on broker-dealers and investment advisors to maintain adequate procedures to protect against insider trading and it defines a separate standard for controlling person liability in reference to that duty. First, [the legislation] added

Section 15(f) of the Exchange Act and Section 204A of the Investment Advisors Act of 1940 which impose an affirmative duty on broker-dealers and investment advisors to maintain "written policies and procedures reasonably designed" to prevent insider trading violations. Second, Section 21A(b)(1)(B) subjects broker-dealers and investment advisors to controlling person liability if they "knowingly or recklessly failed to establish, maintain, or enforce" those procedures and "such failure substantially contributed to or permitted the occurrence" of the insider trading violation.[24]

In enacting the 1988 legislation, Congress declined to define the term "insider trading." Some observers believe that, given the stigma and penalties imposed upon those who allegedly have engaged in insider trading, the term should be defined by statute. A clear definition, proponents claim, would promote commercial certainty and ease the attorney's burden when advising his/her client. Others contend that a statutory definition is unnecessary. They argue that the court-drawn parameters of insider trading have established sufficiently clear guidelines. Moreover, a statutory definition may well be murky, contain loopholes, and be the subject of frequent judicial interpretation.

What is your conclusion? Should Congress enact a statute defining what conduct constitutes illegal insider trading? If so, what should such a statute provide?

[C] Contemporaneous and Option Traders

After the Second Circuit's decision adopting the misappropriation theory in *United States v. Newman*, the question remained whether purchasers and sellers of securities had a cause of action for monetary damages under § 10(b), even though the defrauding parties who misappropriated the inside information owed them no fiduciary duty. In *Moss v. Morgan Stanley, Inc.*, 719 F.2d 5 (2d Cir. 1983), the Second Circuit held that, in order to recover under § 10(b) for monetary damages, it must be shown that the defendant breached a duty owed to the plaintiff. Relying on *Chiarella*, the court asserted that the relationship giving rise to a duty to disclose must be between the parties to the transaction. Hence, because the misappropriators in *Moss* owed no fiduciary duty to the plaintiff, no § 10(b) right of action was available.

In subsequently enacted legislation, Congress nullified the *Moss* decision in this respect. In the Insider Trading and Securities Fraud Enforcement Act of 1988, Congress enacted § 20A of the Exchange Act to provide an express right of action on behalf of "contemporaneous traders" who were trading the same class of securities on the opposite side of the transaction during the time that the allegedly illegal inside trade(s) occurred. Thus, to recover under this express right of action, the plaintiff must be trading contemporaneously with and on the opposite side of the transaction

---

24. Steinberg & Fletcher, *Compliance Programs for Insider Trading*, 47 SMU L. Rev. 1783, 1788–1789 (1994).

from the inside trader. Moreover, the damages available in an action instituted under § 20A on behalf of contemporaneous traders are limited to the profit gained or loss avoided by the defendant's illegal trades.

Importantly, § 20A does not limit a complainant's entitlement to private rights of action under other provisions of the Exchange Act, such as § 10(b). In this regard, a private right of action under § 10(b) may be available against inside traders (as well as their tippers) on behalf of certain noncontemporaneous traders. Such a situation may arise when, due to insider trading that has increased the price of the target company's stock, a bidder must pay more to acquire such stock. In the House Report accompanying the 1988 legislation, the Committee took the position that a § 10(b) right of action exists in the above situation and that a plaintiff should be able to recover the full extent of any actual damages incurred.

Moreover, as part of the Insider Trading Sanctions Act of 1984, Congress added § 20(d) to the Exchange Act. That provision states:

> Wherever communicating, or purchasing or selling a security while in possession of, material nonpublic information would violate, or result in liability to any purchaser or seller of the security under any provision of this Act, or any rule or regulation thereunder, such conduct in connection with a purchase or sale of a put, call, straddle, option, or privilege with respect to such security or with respect to a group or index of securities including such security, shall also violate and result in comparable liability *to any purchaser or seller of that security* under such provision, rule or regulation.

Section 20(d)'s effect is to provide, within the confines of *Chiarella* and *Dirks*, an option-trading plaintiff with a private right of action against an inside trader of options. Note, however, that a distinct issue is presented as to whether an *option* trader has a private cause of action against an inside *stock* trader. Section 20(d) does not resolve this issue. The lower federal courts are divided. Compare *Deutschman v. Beneficial Corp.*, 841 F.2d 502 (3d Cir. 1988) (providing a right of action), with *Laventhal v. General Dynamics Corp.*, 704 F.2d 407 (8th Cir. 1983) (not permitting suit).[25]

---

§ 12.11 The STOCK Act

The STOCK Act (The Stop Trading on Congressional Knowledge Act), enacted in 2012, clarifies that members and employees of Congress, as well as executive and judicial branch officials and their staffs, are subject to the insider trading prohibitions arising under § 10(b). The rationale is that these individuals, because of their

---

25. *See generally* Joo, *Legislation and Legitimation: Congress and Insider Trading in the 1980s*, 82 IND. L.J. 575 (2007).

positions of trust and confidence, have an obligation not to misuse material non-public information for their personal benefit. The Act's impetus for passage may have been due to a report aired by *60 Minutes* in November 2011 that several members of Congress may have engaged in insider trading. As stated in the "Fact Sheet" issued by the White House Office of the Press Secretary (www.whitehouse.gov), the details of the Stock Act are as follows:

> The STOCK Act expressly affirms that Members of Congress and staff are not exempt from the insider trading prohibitions of federal securities laws and gives House and Senate ethics committees authority to implement additional ethics rules. The Act makes clear that Members and staff owe a duty to the citizens of the United States not to misappropriate nonpublic information to make a profit.

> *Increases Transparency in Financial Disclosure Reporting:* The STOCK Act amends the Ethics in Government Act of 1978 to require a government-wide shift to electronic reporting and online availability of public financial disclosure information. The STOCK Act provides additional transparency for Members of Congress, legislative staff and other government employees currently required to make public financial disclosures:

> - *Trading Reporting*: requires that Members of Congress and government employees report certain investment transactions within 45 days after a trade.

> - *Online Availability*: mandates that the information in public financial disclosure reports (currently made available on request) may be made available on agency websites and ultimately through searchable, sortable databases.

> *New Ethics Requirements*

> - *Expands Pension Foreclosure for Corrupt Members:* the Stock Act requires forfeiture of federal pension if a Member of Congress commits one of several corruption offenses while serving as an elected official. Current law forfeits a Member's pension for conviction of offenses committed while serving in Congress. The STOCK Act expands forfeiture to apply to misconduct by Members committed in other federal, state, and local elected offices and adds further federal crimes, including insider trading, for which forfeiture will be required.

> - *Requires Disclosure of Terms of Mortgages:* The STOCK Act will require Members and certain high level government officials to disclose the terms of personal mortgages.

> - *Bans Special Access to Initial Public Offerings (IPOs):* the Stock Act limits participation in IPOs by Members and senior government employees to purchases available to the public generally.

> - *Requires Report on Political Intelligence in the Financial Markets:*

The STOCK Act requires [the U.S. Comptroller General, in consultation with the Congressional Research Service] to produce a report on the role of political intelligence . . . in the financial markets. [Political intelligence means information that is "(1) derived by a person from direct communications with an executive branch employee, a Member of Congress, or an employee of Congress; and (2) provided in exchange for financial compensation to a client who intends, and who is known to intend, to use the information to inform investment decisions." §7(b) of the STOCK Act.]

. . . .

Subsequently, in 2013, Congress amended the STOCK Act to eliminate the requirement that senior congressional aides and executive branch employees post their securities transactions online. These federal employees are still obligated to report within 45 days their securities trades which exceed the $1,000 threshold.[26]

§ 12.12 Section 16 — "Short-Swing" Trading

[A] Overview

Section 16 of the Exchange Act applies to directors, officers, and beneficial owners of more than 10 percent of any class of equity security of an issuer (other than an exempted security), with such class of equity security having been registered pursuant to §12(b) or §12(g) of the Exchange Act. The statute seeks to deter insider trading based on the use of material nonpublic information by such persons. Section 16 contains three key provisions in attempting to meet this objective.

1. Section 16(a) of the Exchange Act requires that, upon becoming an officer, director, or 10 percent equity shareholder of a §12(b) or §12(g) issuer, such individual must file with the SEC (and with the self-regulatory organization (SRO) with which the stock is listed or traded) a report disclosing the number of the corporation's shares beneficially owned. Subsequent reports must be filed on a timely basis (generally within two business days) to reflect changes in the number of shares beneficially owned.

2. Section 16(c) prohibits such insiders to transact short sales in their issuers' equity securities.

3. Generally, "Section 16(b) is designed to permit the corporation or a security holder bringing an action upon behalf of the corporation to recover for the benefit of the corporation short-swing profits arising from the purchase [and sale or sale and purchase] by insiders within any six-month period of equity securities of the company."[27]

Under § 16(b), an irrebuttable presumption is created when "insiders" engage in such short-swing transactions. The profits that the insider gained from the

---

26. *See* 44 Sec. Reg. & L. Rep. (BNA) 597 (2013).
27. H. Bloomenthal, Securities Law 365 (1966).

transaction(s) are recoverable by the issuer in a suit initiated by it, or if it declines to do so, in a properly instituted shareholder's suit expressly authorized by the statute. In view of the broad remedial nature of the statute, a strict formula for computing "profit realized" has been established. Such a formula is designed "to squeeze all possible profits out of stock transactions, and thus to establish a standard so high as to prevent any conflict between the selfish interest of a fiduciary officer, director, or stockholder and the faithful performance of his duty."[28] The formula established matches the lowest price "in" with the highest price "out," thus ensuring recovery of all possible profits. In fact, this formula can yield a profit when in actuality a loss has been suffered.[29]

Moreover, an insider's intent to profit under a transaction that falls within § 16(b)'s scope need not be shown in order for there to be recovery. As the Seventh Circuit (as well as other courts) pointed out, an insider is "deemed capable of structuring his dealings to avoid any possibility of taint and therefore must bear the risks of any inadvertent miscalculation."[30] In some situations, however, the courts, by finding that certain unorthodox transactions do not constitute the predicate purchase or sale, have displayed a judicial reluctance to impose liability under § 16(b) where no congressional purpose would be served.[31]

Suit under § 16(b) must in be instituted within two years after the date that the defendant's profits were realized. In *Credit Suisse Securities (USA) LLC v. Simmonds,* 132 S. Ct. 1414 (2012), the Supreme Court rejected the Ninth Circuit's holding that the § 16(b) limitations period is tolled until the defendant discloses the subject transaction(s) in a § 16(a) report filed with the SEC. Nonetheless, the Court divided 4 to 4 whether § 16(b)'s two-year statute of limitations may be tolled due to fraudulent concealment, signifying that the limitations period would not begin to run until the plaintiff discovered or should have discovered the facts underlying the claim. Hence, an unresolved issue is whether § 16(b)'s statute of limitations establishes a two-year period of repose that cannot be tolled or whether traditional equitable-tolling principles are to be applied to § 16(b) claims.

[B] Pertinent Issues

The issues dealing with the construction of § 16(b) are, at times, complex. The following discussion seeks to highlight the key concepts. For more extensive treatment, other sources should be consulted.[32]

---

28. *Smolowe v. Delendo Corp.,* 136 F.2d 231 (2d Cir. 1943).

29. *See Morales v. Consolidated Oil & Gas, Inc.,* [1982 Transfer Binder] Fed. Sec. L. Rep. (CCH) ¶ 98,796 (S.D.N.Y. 1982).

30. *Bershad v. McDonough,* 428 F.2d 693, 696 (7th Cir. 1970). See *Whiting v. Dow Chemical Co.,* 523 F.2d 680, 687 (2d Cir. 1975) ("[T]he unwary who fall within [§ 16(b's)] terms have no one but themselves to blame.").

31. *See, e.g., Kern County Land Co. v. Occidental Petroleum Corp.,* 411 U.S. 582 (1973).

32. *See, e.g.,* P. ROMEO & A. DYE, SECTION 16 TREATISE AND REPORTING GUIDE (2016).

[1] Beneficial Ownership and the Concept of Attribution

A significant problem that arises with respect to the concepts of attribution and beneficial ownership in the context of § 16(b) is in attempting to determine whether, and the extent to which, a corporate insider will be liable for short-swing trading profits when the securities are held by another person, group, or organization. This issue may arise, for example, within the context of family-related transactions, of a related trust, of a partnership in which the insider is a partner, or of a corporation in which the insider is an officer, director or shareholder. The question becomes one of the responsibility of the corporate insider for the acts of such parties and his/her relationship with these other parties.

The definition of "beneficial owner" for purposes of § 16(b) focuses on whether the insider has a pecuniary interest. Subject to certain exceptions, Rule 16a-1(a)(2) defines "beneficial owner" as "any person who, directly or indirectly, through any contract, arrangement, understanding, relationship or otherwise, has or shares direct or indirect pecuniary interest in the equity securities." Under the SEC rules, a person has such a pecuniary interest when he/she has an opportunity to share in any profit generated from the subject securities transactions. On a non-exclusive basis, the rules provide a number of situations where an individual is deemed to have such an indirect interest. As one example, securities held by a member of an insider's "immediate family," who shares the same household as such insider, creates a presumption (that is rebuttable) that the insider beneficially owns the securities.[33]

Although the SEC's rules define the term "beneficial ownership" for purposes of § 16, they leave a number of issues unresolved. Moreover, the Commission's approach is not binding on the courts. Therefore, case law remains important.

The cases involving beneficial ownership and the concept of attribution have failed to provide clear standards. Nonetheless, two important factors are: (1) whether the insider exercised control over the securities; and (2) the insider's ability to benefit, directly or indirectly, from the profits generated from the short-swing transactions.[34] On the other hand, the Seventh Circuit has applied a more restrictive analysis. Rather than focusing on control over the securities, the court looked to whether the insider stood to receive a direct monetary benefit from the subject transactions. The court held that profit realized by a corporate insider [for purposes of Section 16(b)] means direct pecuniary benefit to the insider. . . . [I]t is not enough that ties of affinity and consanguinity between the . . . recipient and the insider make it likely that the insider will experience an enhanced sense of well-being as a result of the receipt, or will be led to reduce his gift-giving to the recipient.[35]

---

33. *See* Securities Exchange Act Release No. 28869, [1990–1991 Transfer Binder] Fed. Sec. L. Rep. (CCH) ¶ 84,709 (1991).

34. *See, e.g., Whittaker v. Whittaker Corp.*, 639 F.2d 516 (9th Cir. 1981); *Whiting v. Dow Chemical Co.*, 523 F.2d 680, 688 (2d Cir. 1975); *Atamil Corp. v. Pryor*, 405 F. Supp. 1222 (S.D. Ind. 1975).

35. *CBI Industries, Inc. v. Horton*, 682 F.2d 643, 646 (7th Cir. 1982).

[2] Directors — "Deputization"

Directors and any person performing similar functions (irrespective of whether the business organization is incorporated) are subject to § 16(b). A key issue in this setting is whether a business organization can be viewed as a director of another entity by virtue of that organization having a representative on the latter entity's board of directors.

Generally, the courts have answered the above question affirmatively, holding that a corporation may "deputize" one of its directors or other person to serve on a second corporation's board. For example, the Second Circuit in *Feder v. Martin Marietta Corp.*[36] imposed liability based on the deputization theory. There, the court found that the president and chief executive officer of Martin Marietta had been "deputized by or represented" Martin Marietta during the time he served as a director of Sperry Rand. Therefore, the court concluded that Martin Marietta was in effect a director of Sperry Rand and was forced to disgorge the profits it acquired in the short-swing trading of Sperry Rand stock.

[3] Officers

In determining whether an individual is an officer for § 16 purposes, Rule 16a-1(f) focuses on whether such person performs significant policy-making functions. Consistent with this perspective, the rule specifically includes those individuals who clearly hold policy-making duties, such as the company's president, principal financial officer, and any vice-president in charge of a key business division.[37]

The SEC's position on this issue basically follows case law. The focus of the inquiry in ascertaining who is an officer for purposes of § 16 is upon an individual's functions and responsibilities within the organizational structure. This matter can arise in several different settings. Primarily, however, the issue is whether one, lacking in a title representing him/her as an officer, nevertheless in fact had that status; or, conversely, whether one having the title of officer, for example as vice president, had a role so devoid of decision-making functions that he/she could not in reality be called an officer within the meaning of § 16. For example, the Ninth Circuit has opined:

> [T]he title "Vice President" does no more than raise an inference that the person who holds the title has the executive duties and the opportunities for confidential information that the title implies. The inference can be overcome by proof that the title was merely honorary and did not carry with it any of the executive responsibilities that otherwise might be assumed.[38]

---

36. 406 F.2d 260 (2d Cir. 1969). *See Roth v. Pesseus LLC*, 522 F.3d 242 (2d Cir. 2008); *Dreilling v. American Express Co.*, 458 F.3d 942 (9th Cir. 2006).

37. 17 C.F.R. § 240.16A1(F).

38. *Merrill Lynch, Pierce Fenner and Smith v. Livingston*, 566 F.2d 1119, 1122 (9th Cir. 1978).

[4] Ten Percent Beneficial Owners

Unlike the situation for directors and officers, § 16(b) imposes liability on a 10 percent beneficial owner if that person had that status both when the securities were acquired and when they were sold. Hence, in *Foremost-McKesson, Inc. v. Provident Securities Co.*,[39] the Supreme Court held that "in a purchase-sale sequence, a beneficial owner must account for profits only if he was a beneficial owner before the purchase." And, in *Reliance Electric Co. v. Emerson Electric Co.*,[40] the high Court ruled that liability pursuant to § 16(b) normally cannot be based on a beneficial owner's sale of securities which takes place after his/her ownership was reduced to less than ten percent. This is so, even if at the time when the seller owned more than ten percent of the stock, he/she deliberately structured two separate transactions so as to reduce the extent of liability. For example, the first such sale transaction could be arranged so as to result in the beneficial owner holding 9.9 percent of the company's stock. In the second transaction, the beneficial owner could sell the remaining shares. Provided that in such a two-stage transaction the sales are not "legally tied" to one another,[41] the beneficial owner under *Reliance* is liable under § 16(b) only as to the first transaction.

[5] Objective Approach versus Pragmatic Approach

Persons are subject to § 16(b) liability only if they engage in a "purchase" and "sale" or "sale" and "purchase" of a subject security within a six-month period. As such, an insider's liability may turn upon whether there indeed has been a "purchase" and "sale" within § 16(b)'s scope.

The traditional and still commonly used approach is objective. The "objective" approach works in a mechanical fashion. Courts applying it neither will inquire into an insider's reasons for engaging in the transaction nor will they ascertain his/her access to or use of inside information. Consequently, any transaction that can be viewed as a "purchase" or "sale" and brought within the ambit of the statute will result in liability.[42]

Due to its unfair consequences in certain situations, the objective approach is subject to criticism. As a result, the "pragmatic" approach has been employed in certain "unorthodox" transactions, such as stock reclassifications, dealings in options, warrants, and rights, stock conversions, and exchanges pursuant to mergers. As stated by one commentator:

> The pragmatic approach involves a number of elements. First, and most important, it applies only in certain unusual circumstances. If these circumstances exist, then the transaction is characterized as "unorthodox."

---

39. 423 U.S. 232, 250 (1976).

40. 423 U.S. 232, 250 (1976

41. *See Reece Corp. v. Walco National Corp.*, [1981–1982 Transfer Binder] Fed. Sec. L. Rep. (CCH) ¶ 98,289 (S.D.N.Y. 1981).

42. *See, e.g., Park and Tilford, Inc. v. Shulte*, 160 F.2d 984 (2d Cir. 1947).

Unorthodox transactions are ill-defined, but they usually have peculiar features that either make it unfair to apply Section 16(b) or make it difficult to determine whether or when a purchase or sale has taken place.[43]

The pragmatic approach received Supreme Court approbation in *Kern County Land Co. v. Occidental Petroleum Corp.*[44] The Court reasoned:

> In deciding whether borderline transactions are within the reach of the statute, the courts have come to inquire whether the transaction may serve as a vehicle for the veil which Congress sought to prevent—the realization of short-swing profits based upon access to inside information—thereby endeavoring to implement Congressional objectives without extending the reach of the statute beyond its intended limits. . . . [T]he prevailing view is to apply the statute only when its application would serve its goals. . . . [I]n interpreting the terms "purchase" and "sale," courts have properly asked whether the particular type of transaction is one that gives rise to speculative abuse.[45]

Several courts have employed the pragmatic approach in a variety of contexts. Using this approach, § 16(b) liability has been imposed in some cases[46] but not in others.[47] From these cases as well as from the scholarly commentary, key inquiries in applying the pragmatic approach include:

(1) Whether the transaction in question should be characterized as unorthodox?

(2) Did the defendant-insider have control over the timing of the subject transaction?

(3) Did the insider-defendant have access to material nonpublic information, regardless whether such information in fact was used?[48]

---

43. Tomlinson, *Section 16(b): A Single Analysis of Purchases and Sales—Merging the Objective and Pragmatic Analyses*, 1981 DUKE L.J. 941, 947 (1981).

44. 411 U.S. 582 (1973).

45. *Id.* at 594-595 (citations omitted).

46. *See, e.g., Colan v. Mesa Petroleum Co.*, 951 F.2d 1512 (9th Cir. 1991); *Texas International Airlines v. National Airlines, Inc.*, 714 F.2d 533 (5th Cir. 1983).

47. *See, e.g., At Home Corp. v. Cox Communications, Inc.* 446 F.3d 403 (2d Cir. 2006); *Heublein, Inc. v. General Cinema Corp.*, 722 F.2d 29 (2d Cir. 1983).

48. M. STEINBERG & W. WANG, INSIDER TRADING, at § 14.1 et seq. (Oxford Univ. Press 3d ed. 2010); Tomlinson, *supra* note 43, at 949. *See generally* A. JACOBS, SECTION 16 OF THE SECURITIES EXCHANGE ACT (2016); P. ROMEO & A. DYE, SECTION 16 TREATISE AND REPORTING GUIDE (2016); Ferber, *Short-Swing Transactions Under the Securities Exchange Act*, 16 REV. SEC. REG. 801 (1983); Hazen, *The New Pragmatism of Section 16(b) of the Securities Exchange Act of 1934*, 54 N.C. L. REV. 1 (1975); O'Conner, *Toward a More Efficient Deterrence of Insider Trading: The Repeal of Section 16(b)*, 58 FORDHAM L. REV. 309 (1989); Steinberg & Lansdale, *The Judicial and Regulatory Constriction of Section 16(b) of the Securities Exchange Act of 1934*, 68 NOTRE DAME L. REV. 33 (1992); Taylor, *Teaching an Old Law New Tricks: Rethinking Section 16*, 39 ARIZ. L. REV. 1315 (1997); Thel, *The Genius of Section 16: Regulating the Management of Publicly Held Companies*, 42 HASTINGS L.J. 391 (1991); Tomlinson, *Section 16(b): A Single Analysis of Purchases and Sales—Merging the Objective and Pragmatic Analyses*, 1981 DUKE L.J. 941; Wentz, *Refining a Crude Thumb: The Pragmatic Approach to Section 16(b) of the Securities Exchange Act of 1934*, 70 Nw. U. L. REV. 221 (1975).

§ 12.13 Blackout Periods

Under § 306 of the Sarbanes-Oxley Act, officers and directors are prohibited from trading any equity security of the issuer, acquired through the scope of employment, during a blackout period, when at least half of the issuer's individual account plan participants are not permitted to trade in the equity security for more than three consecutive business days. Furthermore, the Act requires that the issuer deliver notice of blackout periods at least 30 days prior to the blackout period, giving proper notice to employees, executives, and the SEC. The SEC has adopted rules governing the prohibition on trading during blackout periods. Under Regulation Blackout Trading Restriction (BTR), during a blackout period, directors and executive officers of domestic issuers, foreign private issuers, banks and savings associations, small business issuers, and their family members, partnerships, corporations, limited liability companies and trusts are prohibited from trading equity securities acquired in connection with the director's or officer's service to an issuer.

A violation of § 306(a) of the Sarbanes-Oxley Act will be considered a violation of the Exchange Act and is subject to SEC enforcement action. Furthermore, an issuer or a security holder may bring on behalf of such issuer an action against the director or officer who violated the blackout period, and seek disgorgement of all profits from the sale of such securities acquired in connection with the director's or officer's service to the issuer. The amount disgorged will be calculated, under Regulation BTR, as the difference between the amount paid for the equity security on the date of the transaction and the amount that would have been received for the security if the transaction had taken place outside the blackout period.

§ 12.14 Regulation FD

[The material on Regulation FD is contained in § 11.08 of this textbook.]

Chapter 13

Financial Intermediaries — Broker-Dealers and Investment Advisers

§ 13.01 Overview

Preceding chapters have discussed the availability of private rights of action under various provisions of the securities acts. Broker-dealers and investment advisers, of course, may be liable for a primary violation of these sections if their conduct falls within the parameters of these provisions. Under § 11(a)(5) of the Securities Act, for example, if a broker-dealer acts as an underwriter with respect to a registered offering, such broker-dealer would be subject to liability for material misstatements or omissions contained in the registration statement (*see, e.g., Feit v. Leasco Data Processing Equip. Corp.*, 332 F. Supp. 544 (E.D.N.Y. 1971)). In response, the broker-dealer may assert the § 11(b)(3) due diligence defense. As an underwriter, however, the broker-dealer would be subject to the heightened due diligence criteria set forth in *Escott v. BarChris Construction Corporation*, 283 F. Supp. 643 (S.D.N.Y. 1968) (see §§ 7.02, 7.03).

Under § 12 of the Securities Act, a broker-dealer would be liable for an offer or sale of securities either in violation of the § 5 registration requirements (§ 12(a)(1)) or by means of a material misrepresentation or half-truth contained in a prospectus (or oral communication relating to such prospectus) (§ 12(a)(2)). Discussion in Chapter 7 focused on the interpretation that the Supreme Court has given to the terms "prospectus" and "seller" under § 12. *Gustafson v. Alloyd Co.*, 513 U.S. 561 (1995); *Pinter v. Dahl*, 486 U.S. 622 (1988) (§ 7.07). A dealer, by definition, would fall within § 12's reach acting as principal. A broker enters the reach of § 12 when, acting as an agent, it successfully solicits the transaction. As with § 11, the broker-dealer has a diligence-based defense against § 12 liability. The broker-dealer may defend by showing that it exercised "reasonable care," a standard that, as applied by some courts, may require a stringent showing. Moreover, the issue of whether § 12(a)(2) may be invoked in the secondary trading markets against such parties as broker-dealers has been resolved by the Supreme Court in *Gustafson* (where the Court held that § 12(2) [now § 12(a)(2)] applies only to public offerings by an issuer or its controlling shareholders).

Broker-dealers and investment advisers are subject to a number of other provisions. For example, § 17(a) serves as an important government enforcement weapon against financial intermediaries who offer or sell securities. See *United States v.*

Naftalin, 441 U.S. 768 (1979), §9.03[A]. Similarly §15(c) of the Exchange Act is a significant resource against broker-dealers who engage in fraud as is §206 of the Investment Advisers Act with respect to investment advisers. Additionally, the insider trading provisions impact the activities of financial intermediaries (see Chapter 12).

Moreover, a broker-dealer may be subject to liability under the §10(b) antifraud provision as well as secondary liability principles. The discussion in Chapter 8 introduced the major issues under §10(b). The material in this Chapter develops special concepts and theories of liability with regard to broker-dealers, many of which proceed under §10(b).

Note that brokers and dealers must register under both federal and state law. Depending on the amount of assets under management, investment advisors must register under federal law or state law.[1] The failure to register may result in government enforcement action, including criminal prosecution. Also, plaintiffs may seek relief in private litigation based on a broker-dealer's failure to register. The Fifth Circuit's decision in *Regional Properties* (see §9.06) serves as an example of relief being afforded to the plaintiffs even where the broker-dealer's failure to register caused the plaintiffs no harm.

Note also that broker-dealer regulation is subject to self-regulatory organization (SRO) oversight. The key SRO regulator is the Financial Industry Regulatory Authority (FINRA). At this time, although proposed legislation has been introduced in Congress (e.g., The Investment Adviser Oversight Act of 2012), investment advisers are not subject to SRO regulation.

Sections 5, 6, 15A, 17A, and 19 of the Securities Exchange Act contain the general federal regulatory framework for SROs. For example, §6 and 15A require adoption of rules governing the admission and conduct of an SRO's members. Sections 19(b) and (g) address the SEC oversight and the SRO enforcement of these rules. If a broker-dealer runs afoul of an SRO rule, such broker-dealer is subject to sanctions. However, private litigants evidently may not sue for damages for broker-dealer violations of SRO rules (see §9.02).

Thus, we already have addressed many aspects of broker-dealer regulation and liability in previous chapters. In studying the issues contained in this chapter, the materials in earlier parts of the text should be consulted. As further illustrations:

(1) An overview of broker-dealer regulation and the shingle theory is contained in §8.13.

(2) With respect to the duty of a broker-dealer to register and certain private liability ramifications for the failure to do so, see the *Regional Properties* case in §9.06.

---

1. *See* Bagnall & Cannon, *The National Securities Markets Improvement Act of 1996: Summary and Analysis,* 25 SEC. REG. L.J. 3, 13–15 (1997) (pointing out that under the 1996 federal legislation "investment advisers with assets under management of $25 million or more and advisers to [SEC] registered investment companies will fall exclusively under [SEC] jurisdiction" but that states still retain their enforcement powers against such advisers or associated persons where fraud has been committed); Friedman, *The Impact of NSMIA on State Regulation of Broker-Dealers and Investment Advisers,* 53 Bus. Law. 511 (1998).

(3) Discussion of short-selling is contained in § 9.03[A] and that of manipulation in § 8.04[C].

(4) Broker-dealer and investment adviser liability for insider trading is addressed in Chapter 12 and the imposition upon a broker-dealer or investment adviser of a treble monetary penalty based upon the illegal inside trading of a controlled person is examined specifically in § 12.09.

(5) Defenses that a broker-dealer and investment adviser may raise, such as *in pari delicto*, are discussed in *Bateman Eichler* (see § 8.09[C]) and *Regional Properties* (see § 9.06).

(6) Secondary liability of broker-dealers and investment advisers for aiding and abetting, as control persons, and under respondeat superior is addressed in § 10.02-10.06.

Moreover, broker-dealers and investment advisers are subject to vigorous SEC oversight, including the bringing of enforcement actions.

Several sources assert that broker-dealers in big-firms receive preferential treatment in SEC enforcement actions, whereas broker-dealers in small firms do not. A relatively recent empirical study supports this position. As stated by the author:

> The analysis shows that big-firm defendants fared better. . . . [W]hen big firms and their staff were engaged in misconduct, the SEC often brought actions based exclusively on corporate liability, without naming any specific individuals as defendants. . . . [Also, in SEC] administrative proceedings, big-firm defendants were more likely than small-firm defendants to receive no industry ban. . . . The gap between big and small firms persists when the analysis is limited to the individual employees of such firms. . . .

Gadinis, *The SEC and the Financial Industry: Evidence from Enforcement Against Broker-Dealers*, 67 Bus. Law. 679, 728 (2012).

For excellent treatises on broker-dealer regulation, *see* D. Lipton, Broker-Dealer Regulation (2015); N. Poser & J. Fanto, Broker-Dealer Law and Regulation (4th edition 2016).

---

§ 13.02 SEC Staff Study on Investment Advisers and Broker-Dealers

Study on Investment Advisers and Broker-Dealers

Staff of the Securities and Exchange Commission (2011)

Background

. . . .

Broker-dealers and investment advisers are regulated extensively, but the regulatory regimes differ, and broker-dealers and investment advisers are subject to different standards under federal law when providing investment advice about securities. Retail investors generally are not aware of these differences or their legal implications. Many investors are also confused by the different standards of care that apply to investment advisers and broker-dealers. That investor confusion has been a source of concern for regulators and Congress.

Section 913 of Title IX of the Dodd-Frank Wall Street Reform and Consumer Protection Act of 2010 (the "Dodd-Frank Act") requires the U.S. Securities and Exchange Commission (the "Commission") to conduct a study (the "Study") to evaluate:

- The effectiveness of existing legal or regulatory standards of care (imposed by the Commission, a national securities association, and other federal or state authorities) for providing personalized investment advice and recommendations about securities to retail customers; and

- Whether there are legal or regulatory gaps, shortcomings, or overlaps in legal or regulatory standards in the protection of retail customers relating to the standards of care for providing personalized investment advice about securities to retail customers that should be addressed by rule or statute.

. . . .

As required by Section 913, the Study describes the considerations, analysis and public and industry input that the Staff considered in making its recommendations, and it includes an analysis of differences in legal and regulatory standards in the protection of retail customers relating to the standards of care for broker-dealers, investment advisers and their associated persons for providing personalized investment advice about securities to retail customers.

The Commission established a cross-Divisional staff task force (the "Staff") to bring a multi-disciplinary approach to the Study. The Commission also solicited comments and data as part of the Study and received over 3,500 comment letters. The Staff reviewed all of the comment letters, and appreciates commenters' thoughtful efforts to inform the Staff and to raise complex issues for consideration. The Staff also met with interested parties representing investors, broker-dealers, investment advisers, other representatives of the financial services industry, academics, state securities regulators, the North American Securities Administrator Association ("NASAA"), and the Financial Industry Regulatory Authority ("FINRA"), which serves as a self-regulatory organization ("SRO") for broker-dealers.

This Study outlines the Staff's findings and makes recommendations to the Commission for potential new rulemaking, guidance, and other policy changes. These recommendations are intended to make consistent the standards of conduct applying when retail customers receive personalized investment advice about securities from broker-dealers or investment advisers. The Staff therefore recommends establishing a uniform fiduciary standard for investment advisers and broker-dealers when providing investment advice about securities to retail customers that is consistent with the standard that currently applies to investment advisers. The recommendations also include suggestions for considering harmonization of the broker-dealer and investment adviser regulatory regimes, with a view toward enhancing their effectiveness in the retail marketplace.

The views expressed in this Study are those of the Staff and do not necessarily reflect the views of the Commission or the individual Commissioners. This Study was approved for release by the Commission.

Current State of the Investment Adviser and Broker-Dealer Industries

Investment Advisers: Over 11,000 investment advisers are registered with the Commission. As of September 30, 2010, Commission-registered advisers managed more than $38 trillion for more than 14 million clients. In addition, there are more than 275,000 state-registered investment adviser representatives and more than 15,000 state-registered investment advisers. Approximately 5% of Commission-registered investment advisers are also registered as broker-dealers, and 22% have a related person that is a broker-dealer. Additionally, approximately 88% of investment adviser representatives are also registered representatives of broker-dealers. A majority of Commission-registered investment advisers reported that over half of their assets under management related to the accounts of individual clients. Most investment advisers charge their clients fees based on the percentage of assets under management, while others may charge hourly or fixed rates.

Broker-Dealers: The Commission and FINRA oversee approximately 5,100 broker-dealers. As of the end of 2009, FINRA-registered broker-dealers held over 109 million retail and institutional accounts. Approximately 18% of FINRA-registered broker-dealers also are registered as investment advisers with the Commission or a state. Most broker-dealers receive transaction-based compensation.

Regulation of Investment Advisers and Broker-Dealers

The regulatory schemes for investment advisers and broker-dealers are designed to protect investors through different approaches. Investment advisers are fiduciaries to their clients, and the regulation under the Advisers Act generally is principles-based. The regulation of broker-dealers governs how broker-dealers operate, for the most part, through the Commission's antifraud authority in the Securities Act of 1933 ("Securities Act") and the Securities Exchange Act of 1934 ("Exchange Act"), specific Exchange Act rules, and SRO rules based on Exchange Act principles, including (among others) principles of fairness and transparency. Certain differences in the regulation of broker-dealers and advisers reflect differences, current and historical, in their functions, while others may reflect differences in the regulatory regime, particularly when investment advisers and broker-dealers are engaging in the same or substantially similar activity. The recommendations listed in the Study are designed to address gaps in the regulatory regime, as well as differences in approach that are no longer warranted, as they relate to providing personalized investment advice about securities to retail customers.

Investment Advisers: An investment adviser is a fiduciary whose duty is to serve the best interests of its clients, including an obligation not to subordinate clients' interests to its own. Included in the fiduciary standard are the duties of loyalty and care. An adviser that has a material conflict of interest must either eliminate that conflict or fully disclose to its clients all material facts relating to the conflict.

In addition, the Advisers Act expressly prohibits an adviser, acting as principal for its own account, from effecting any sale or purchase of any security for the account of a client, without disclosing certain information to the client in writing before the completion of the transaction and obtaining the client's consent.

The states also regulate the activities of many investment advisers. Most smaller investment advisers are registered and regulated at the state level. Investment adviser representatives of state and federally-registered advisers commonly are subject to state registration, licensing or qualification requirements.

Broker-Dealers: Broker-dealers that do business with the public generally must become members of FINRA. Under the antifraud provisions of the federal securities laws and SRO rules, including SRO rules relating to just and equitable principles of trade and high standards of commercial honor, broker-dealers are required to deal fairly with their customers. While broker-dealers are generally not subject to a fiduciary duty under the federal securities laws, courts have found broker-dealers to have a fiduciary duty under certain circumstances. [Note that, under the U.S. Department of Labor's "fiduciary rule" adopted in 2016 (and scheduled to go into effect in 2017), generally brokers must comply with fiduciary standards when recommending investments to their clients in their retirement accounts. Thus, "both brokers and registered investment advisers will be required to adhere to the same fiduciary standard when providing investment advice on retirement accounts." Tergesen, *Adviser Rule: What You Need to Know*, WALL ST. J., April 7, 2016, at C2.] Moreover, broker-dealers are subject to statutory, Commission and SRO requirements that are designed to promote business conduct that protects customers from abusive practices, including practices that may be unethical but may not necessarily be fraudulent. The federal securities laws and rules and SRO rules address broker-dealer conflicts in one of three ways: express prohibition; mitigation; or disclosure.

An important aspect of a broker-dealer's duty of fair dealing is the suitability obligation, which generally requires a broker-dealer to make recommendations that are consistent with the interests of its customer. Broker-dealers also are required under certain circumstances, such as when making a recommendation, to disclose material conflicts of interest to their customers, in some cases at the time of the completion of the transaction. The federal securities laws and FINRA rules restrict broker-dealers from participating in certain transactions that may present particularly acute potential conflicts of interest. At the state level, broker-dealers and their agents must register with or be licensed by the states in which they conduct their business.

Examination and Enforcement Resources

The Commission's Office of Compliance Inspections and Examinations ("OCIE") examines Commission-registered investment advisers using a risk-based approach.

Due, among other things, to an increase in the number of Commission-registered advisers, a decrease in the number of OCIE staff, and a greater focus on more complex examinations, the number and frequency of examinations of these advisers by OCIE has decreased in recent years. . . .

FINRA has primary responsibility for examining broker-dealers. The Commission staff also examines broker-dealers, particularly when a risk has been identified or when evaluating the examination work of an SRO, including FINRA, but generally does not examine broker-dealers on a routine basis. The states are responsible for examining state-registered investment advisers, and they work with FINRA and the Commission on broker-dealer examinations.

The Commission has broad statutory authority under the federal securities laws to investigate violations of the federal securities laws and SRO rules. The Commission's Division of Enforcement investigates potential securities law violations, recommends that the Commission bring civil actions or institute administrative proceedings, and prosecutes these cases on behalf of the Commission. Examples of enforcement actions involving investment advisers include failures to disclose material conflicts of interest, misrepresentations, and other frauds. For broker-dealers, examples include abusive sales practices, failures to disclose material conflicts of interest, misrepresentations, failures to have a reasonable basis for recommending securities, other frauds, [and] failures to reasonably supervise representatives. The Commission may seek remedial sanctions such as censures, suspensions, injunctions and limitations on business, and violators may be required to pay disgorgement and civil penalties.

. . . .

---

§ 13.03 Arbitration

Today, disputes between broker-dealers and their customers normally are subject to arbitration. Until 1987, such disputes were litigated in the courts. The Supreme Court's 1987 decision in *McMahon*, followed by its 1989 ruling in *Rodriguez*, however, had the effect of changing the applicable forum.

[A] Supreme Court Decisions

Shearson/American Express, Inc. v. McMahon

United States Supreme Court
482 U.S. 220, 107 S. Ct. 2332, 96 L. Ed. 2d 185 (1987)

Justice O'CONNOR delivered the opinion of the Court.

This case presents two questions regarding the enforceability of predispute arbitration agreements between brokerage firms and their customers. The first is whether a claim brought under § 10(b) of the Securities Exchange Act of 1934 must be sent to arbitration in accordance with the terms of an arbitration agreement. The second is whether a claim brought under the Racketeer Influenced and Corrupt Organizations Act (RICO) must be arbitrated in accordance with the terms of such an agreement.

I

Between 1980 and 1982, respondents Eugene and Julia McMahon, individually and as trustees for various pension and profit-sharing plans, were customers of petitioner Shearson/American Express Inc. (Shearson), a brokerage firm registered with the Securities and Exchange Commission (SEC or Commission). Two customer agreements signed by Julia McMahon provided for arbitration of any controversy relating to the accounts the McMahons maintained with Shearson. The arbitration provision provided in relevant part as follows:

> "Unless unenforceable due to federal or state law, any controversy arising out of or relating to my accounts, to transactions with you for me or to this agreement or the breach therefor, shall be settled by arbitration in accordance with the rules, then in effect, of the National Association of Securities Dealers, Inc. or the Boards of Directors of the New York Stock Exchange, Inc. and/or the American Stock Exchange, Inc., as I may elect."

In October 1984, the McMahons filed an amended complaint against Shearson and petitioner Mary Ann McNulty, the registered representative who handled their accounts, in the United States District Court for the Southern District of New York. The complaint alleged that McNulty, with Shearson's knowledge, had violated § 10(b) of the Exchange Act and Rule 10b-5 by engaging in fraudulent, excessive trading in respondents' accounts and by making false statements and omitting material facts from the advice given to respondents. The complaint also alleged a RICO claim and state law claims for fraud and breach of fiduciary duties.

Relying on the customer agreements, petitioners moved to compel arbitration of the McMahons' claims pursuant to § 3 of the Federal Arbitration Act, 9 U.S.C. § 3. . . .

. . . .

We granted certiorari to resolve the conflict among the Courts of Appeals regarding the arbitrability of § 10(b) and RICO claims.

II

The Federal Arbitration Act provides the starting point for answering the questions raised in this case. The Act was intended to "revers[e] centuries of judicial hostility to arbitration agreements," *Scherk v. Alberto-Culver Co.* [417 U.S. 506, 511 (1974)] by "plac[ing] arbitration agreements 'upon the same footing as other contracts.'" 417 U.S. at 511. The Arbitration Act accomplishes this purpose by providing that arbitration agreements "shall be valid, irrevocable, and enforceable, save upon such grounds as exist at law or in equity for the revocation of any contract." 9 U.S.C. § 2. The Act also provides that a court must stay its proceedings if it is satisfied that an issue before it is arbitrable under the agreement, § 3; and it authorizes a federal district court to issue an order compelling arbitration if there has been a "failure, neglect, or refusal" to comply with the arbitration agreement, §4.

The Arbitration Act thus establishes a "federal policy favoring arbitration," requiring that "we rigorously enforce agreements to arbitrate." *Dean Witter Reynolds Inc. v. Byrd,* 470 U.S. at 221. This duty to enforce arbitration agreements is not diminished when a party bound by an agreement raises a claim founded on statutory rights. . . . Absent a well-founded claim that an arbitration agreement resulted from the sort of fraud or excessive economic power that "would provide grounds 'for the revocation of any contract,'" the Arbitration Act "provides no basis for disfavoring agreements to arbitrate statutory claims by skewing the otherwise hospitable inquiry into arbitrability."

The Arbitration Act, standing alone, therefore mandates enforcement of agreements to arbitrate statutory claims. Like any statutory directive, the Arbitration Act's mandate may be overridden by a contrary congressional command. The burden is on the party opposing arbitration, however, to show that Congress intended to preclude a waiver of judicial remedies for the statutory rights at issue. If Congress did intend to limit or prohibit waiver of a judicial forum for a particular claim, such intent "will be deducible from [the statute's] text or legislative history," or from an inherent conflict between arbitration and the statute's underlying purposes. . . .

To defeat application of the Arbitration Act in this case, therefore, the McMahons must demonstrate that Congress intended to make an exception to the Arbitration Act for claims arising under RICO and the Exchange Act, an intention discernible from the text, history, or purposes of the statute. We examine the McMahons' arguments regarding the Exchange Act and RICO in turn.

III

When Congress enacted the Exchange Act in 1934, it did not specifically address the question of the arbitrability of § 10(b) claims. The McMahons contend, however, that congressional intent to require a judicial forum for the resolution of § 10(b) claims can be deduced from § 29(a) of the Exchange Act which declares void "[a]ny condition, stipulation, or provision binding any person to waive compliance with any provision of [the Act]."

First, we reject the McMahons' argument that § 29(a) forbids waiver of § 27 of the Exchange Act . . . Section 27 provides in relevant part:

"The district courts of the United States . . . shall have exclusive jurisdiction of violations of this title or the rules and regulations thereunder, and of all suits in equity and actions at law brought to enforce any liability or duty created by this title or the rules and regulations thereunder."

The McMahons contend that an agreement to waive this jurisdictional provision is unenforceable because § 29(a) voids the waiver of "any provision" of the Exchange Act. The language of § 29(a), however, does not reach so far. What the antiwaiver provision of § 29(a) forbids is enforcement of agreements to waive "compliance" with the provisions of the statute. But § 27 itself does not impose any duty with which persons trading in securities must "comply." By its terms, § 29(a) only prohibits waiver of the substantive obligations imposed by the Exchange Act. Because § 27 does not impose any statutory duties, its waiver does not constitute a waiver of "compliance with any provision" of the Exchange Act under § 29(a).

We do not read *Wilko v. Swan*, 346 U.S. 427 (1953), as compelling a different result. In *Wilko*, the Court held that a predispute agreement could not be enforced to compel arbitration of a claim arising under § 12(2) [now § 12(a)(2)] of the Securities Act. . . . The basis for the ruling was § 14 of the Securities Act, which, like § 29(a) of the Exchange Act, declares void any stipulation "to waive compliance with any provision" of the statute. At the beginning of the analysis, the *Wilko* Court stated that the Securities Act's jurisdictional provision was "the kind of 'provision' that cannot be waived under § 14 of the Securities Act." This statement, however, can only be understood in the context of the Court's ensuing discussion explaining why arbitration was inadequate as a means of enforcing "the provisions of the Securities Act, advantageous to the buyer." The conclusion in *Wilko* was expressly based on the Court's belief that a judicial forum was needed to protect the substantive rights created by the Securities Act: "As the protective provisions of the Securities Act require the exercise of judicial direction to fairly assure their effectiveness, it seems to us that Congress must have intended § 14 . . . to apply to waiver of judicial trial and review." *Wilko* must be understood, therefore, as holding that the plaintiff's waiver of the "right to select the judicial forum," was unenforceable only because arbitration was judged inadequate to enforce the statutory rights created by § 12(2).

Indeed, any different reading of *Wilko* would be inconsistent with this Court's decision in *Scherk v. Alberto-Culver Co.* . . . In *Scherk*, the Court upheld enforcement of a predispute agreement to arbitrate Exchange Act claims by parties to an international contract. The *Scherk* Court assumed for purposes of its opinion that *Wilko* applied to the Exchange Act, but it determined that an international contract "involve[d] considerations and policies significantly different from those found controlling in *Wilko*." The Court reasoned that arbitration reduced the uncertainty of international contracts and obviated the danger that a dispute might be submitted to a hostile or unfamiliar forum. At the same time, the Court noted that the advantages of judicial resolution were diminished by the possibility that the opposing party would make "speedy resort to a foreign court." The decision in *Scherk* thus turned on the Court's judgment that under the circumstances of that case, arbitration was an adequate substitute for adjudication as a means of enforcing the parties' statutory rights. *Scherk* supports our understanding that *Wilko* must be read as barring waiver of a judicial forum only where arbitration is inadequate to protect the substantive rights at issue. At the same time, it confirms that where arbitration does provide an adequate means of enforcing the provisions of the Exchange Act, § 29(a) does not void a predispute waiver of § 27—*Scherk* upheld enforcement of just such a waiver.

The second argument offered by the McMahons is that the arbitration agreement effects an impermissible waiver of the substantive protections of the Exchange Act.

Ordinarily, "[b]y agreeing to arbitrate a statutory claim, a party does not forego the substantive rights afforded by the statute; it only submits to their resolution in an arbitral, rather than a judicial, forum." *Mitsubishi Motors Corp. v. Soler Chrysler-Plymouth, Inc.,* 473 U.S. at 628 . . . The McMahons argue, however, that § 29(a) compels a different conclusion. Initially, they contend that predispute agreements are void under § 29(a) because they tend to result from broker overreaching. They reason, as do some commentators, that *Wilko* is premised on the belief "that arbitration clauses in securities sales agreements generally are not freely negotiated." . . . According to this view, *Wilko* barred enforcement of predispute agreements because of this frequent inequality of bargaining power, reasoning that Congress intended for § 14 generally to ensure that sellers did not "maneuver buyers into a position that might weaken their ability to recover under the Securities Act." . . . The McMahons urge that we should interpret § 29(a) in the same fashion.

We decline to give *Wilko* a reading so far at odds with the plain language of § 14, or to adopt such an unlikely interpretation of § 29(a). The concern that § 29(a) is directed against is evident from the statute's plain language: it is a concern with whether an agreement "waive[s] compliance with [a] provision" of the Exchange Act. The voluntariness of the agreement is irrelevant to this inquiry: if a stipulation waives compliance with a statutory duty, it is void under § 29(a), whether voluntary or not. Thus, a customer cannot negotiate a reduction in commissions in exchange for a waiver of compliance with the requirements of the Exchange Act, even if the customer knowingly and voluntarily agreed to the bargain. Section 29(a) is concerned, not with whether brokers "maneuver[ed customers] into" an agreement, but with whether the agreement "weaken[s] their ability to recover under the [Exchange] Act." . . . The former is grounds for revoking the contract under ordinary principles of contract law; the latter is grounds for voiding the agreement under § 29(a).

The other reason advanced by the McMahons for finding a waiver of their § 10(b) rights is that arbitration does "weaken their ability to recover under the [Exchange] Act." That is the heart of the Court's decision in *Wilko*, and respondents urge that we should follow its reasoning. *Wilko* listed several grounds why, in the Court's view, the "effectiveness [of the Act's provisions] in application is lessened in arbitration." First, the *Wilko* Court believed that arbitration proceedings were not suited to cases requiring "subjective findings on the purpose and knowledge of an alleged violator." *Wilko* also was concerned that arbitrators must make legal determinations "without judicial instruction on the law," and that an arbitration award "may be made without explanation of [the arbitrator's] reasons and without a complete record of their proceedings." . . . Finally, *Wilko* noted that the "[p]ower to vacate an award is limited," and that "interpretations of the law by the arbitrators in contrast to manifest disregard are not subject, in the federal courts, to judicial review for error in interpretation." . . . *Wilko* concluded that in view of these drawbacks to arbitration, § 12(2) claims "require[d] the exercise of judicial direction to fairly assure their effectiveness."

As Justice Frankfurter noted in his dissent in *Wilko*, the Court's opinion did not rest on any evidence, either "in the record . . . [or] in the facts of which [it could] take judicial notice," that "the arbitral system . . . would not afford the plaintiff the rights to which he is entitled." Instead, the reasons given in *Wilko* reflect a general suspicion of the desirability of arbitration and the competence of arbitral tribunals — most apply with no greater force to the arbitration of securities disputes than to the arbitration of legal disputes generally. It is difficult to reconcile *Wilko's* mistrust of the arbitral process with the Court's subsequent decisions involving the Arbitration Act. . . .

Indeed, most of the reasons given in *Wilko* have been rejected subsequently by the Court as a basis for holding claims to be nonarbitrable. In *Mitsubishi*, for example, we recognized that arbitral tribunals are readily capable of handling the factual and legal complexities of antitrust claims, notwithstanding the absence of judicial instruction and supervision. Likewise, we have concluded that the streamlined procedures of arbitration do not entail any consequential restriction on substantive rights. Finally, we have indicated that there is no reason to assume at the outset that arbitrators will not follow the law; although judicial scrutiny of arbitration awards necessarily is limited, such review is sufficient to ensure that arbitrators comply with the requirements of the statute. . . .

The suitability of arbitration as a means of enforcing Exchange Act rights is evident from our decision in *Scherk*. Although the holding in that case was limited to international agreements, the competence of arbitral tribunals to resolve § 10(b) claims is the same in both settings. Courts likewise have routinely enforced agreements to arbitrate § 10(b) claims where both parties are members of a securities exchange or the National Association of Securities Dealers (NASD) [today, the SRO is FINRA], suggesting that arbitral tribunals are fully capable of handling such matters. . . . And courts uniformly have concluded that *Wilko* does not apply to the submission to arbitration of existing disputes, . . . even though the inherent suitability of arbitration as a means of resolving § 10(b) claims remains unchanged. . . .

Thus, the mistrust of arbitration that formed the basis for the *Wilko* opinion in 1953 is difficult to square with the assessment of arbitration that has prevailed since that time. This is especially so in light of the intervening changes in the regulatory structure of the securities laws. Even if *Wilko's* assumptions regarding arbitration were valid at the time *Wilko* was decided, most certainly they do not hold true today for arbitration procedures subject to the SEC's oversight authority.

In 1953, when *Wilko* was decided, the Commission had only limited authority over the rules governing self-regulatory organizations (SROs) — the national securities exchanges and registered securities associations — and this authority appears not to have included any authority at all over their arbitration rules. . . . Since the 1975 amendments to § 19 of the Exchange Act, however, the Commission has had expansive power to ensure the adequacy of the arbitration procedures employed by the SROs. No proposed rule change may take effect unless the SEC finds that the proposed rule is consistent with the requirements of the Exchange Act . . . and the Commission has the power, on its own initiative, to "abrogate, add to, and delete from" any SRO rule if it finds such changes necessary or appropriate to further the objectives of the Act. . . . In short, the Commission has broad authority to oversee and to regulate the rules adopted by the SROs relating to customer disputes, including the power to mandate the adoption of any rules it deems necessary to ensure that arbitration procedures adequately protect statutory rights.

In the exercise of its regulatory authority, the SEC has specifically approved the arbitration procedures of the New York Stock Exchange, the American Stock Exchange, and the National Association of Securities Dealers, the organizations mentioned in the arbitration agreement at issue in this case. We conclude that where, as in this case, the prescribed procedures are subject to the Commission's § 19 authority, an arbitration agreement does not effect a waiver of the protections of the Act. While *stare decisis* concerns may counsel against upsetting *Wilko's* contrary conclusion under the Securities Act, we refuse to extend *Wilko's* reasoning to the Exchange Act in light of these intervening regulatory developments. The McMahons' agreement to submit to arbitration therefore is not tantamount to an impermissible waiver of the McMahons' rights under § 10(b), and the agreement is not void on that basis under § 29(a).

. . . .

We conclude, therefore, that Congress did not intend for § 29(a) to bar enforcement of all predispute arbitration agreements. In this case, where the SEC has sufficient statutory authority to ensure that arbitration is adequate to vindicate Exchange Act rights, enforcement does not effect a waiver of "compliance with any provision" of the Exchange Act under § 29(a). Accordingly, we hold the McMahons' agreement to arbitrate Exchange Act claims "enforce[able] . . . in accord with the explicit provisions of the Arbitration Act." . . .

IV

Unlike the Exchange Act, there is nothing in the text of the RICO statute that even arguably evinces congressional intent to exclude civil RICO claims from the dictates of the Arbitration Act. This silence in the text is matched by silence in the statute's legislative history. . . .

In sum, we find no basis for concluding that Congress intended to prevent enforcement of agreements to arbitrate RICO claims. The McMahons may effectively vindicate their RICO claim in an arbitral forum, and therefore there is no inherent conflict between arbitration and the purposes underlying § 1964(c). Moreover, nothing in RICO's text or legislative history otherwise demonstrates congressional intent to make an exception to the Arbitration Act for RICO claims. Accordingly, the McMahons, "having made the bargain to arbitrate," will be held to their bargain. Their RICO claim is arbitrable under the terms of the Arbitration Act.

. . . .

[*Reversed and Remanded*]

Justice BLACKMUN, with whom Justice BRENNAN and Justice MARSHALL join, concurring in part and dissenting in part.

I concur in the Court's decision to enforce the arbitration agreement with respect to respondents' RICO claims and thus join Parts I, II, and IV of the Court's opinion. I disagree, however, with the Court's conclusion that respondents' § 10(b) claims also are subject to arbitration.

Both the Securities Act of 1933 and the Securities Exchange Act of 1934 were enacted to protect investors from predatory behavior of securities industry personnel. In *Wilko v. Swan*, . . . the Court recognized this basic purpose when it declined to enforce a predispute agreement to compel arbitration of claims under the Securities Act. Following that decision, lower courts extended *Wilko's* reasoning to claims brought under § 10(b) of the Exchange Act, and Congress approved of this extension. In today's decision, however, the Court effectively overrules *Wilko* by accepting the Securities and Exchange Commission's newly adopted position that arbitration procedures in the securities industry and the Commission's oversight of the self-regulatory organizations (SROs) have improved greatly since *Wilko* was decided. The Court thus approves the abandonment of the judiciary's role in the resolution of claims under the Exchange Act and leaves such claims to the arbitral forum of the securities industry at a time when the industry's abuses towards investors are more apparent than ever.[2]

. . . .

A

I agree with the Court's observation that, in order to establish an exception to the Arbitration Act, 9 U.S.C. 1 *et seq.*, for a class of statutory claims, there must be "an intention discernible from the text, history, or purposes of the statute." . . . Where the Court first goes wrong, however, is in its failure to acknowledge that the Exchange Act, like the Securities Act, constitutes such an exception. This failure is made possible only by the unduly narrow reading of *Wilko* that ignores the Court's determination there that the Securities Act *was* an exception to the Arbitration Act. . . .

One has only to reread the *Wilko* opinion without the constricted vision of the Court. The Court's misreading is possible because, while extolling the policies of the Arbitration Act, it is insensitive to, and disregards the policies of, the Securities Act.

This Act was passed in 1933, eight years *after* the Arbitration Act, and in response to the market crash of 1929. The Act was designed to remedy abuses in the securities industry, particularly fraud and misrepresentation by securities-industry personnel, that had contributed to that disastrous event. It had as its main goal investor protection, which took the form of an effort to place investors on an equal footing with

---

[2]. . . . *See, e.g.*, Comment, *Predispute Arbitration Agreements Between Brokers and Investors: The Extension of Wilko to Section 10(b) Claims*, 46 Md. L. Rev. 339, 364–366 (1987) [Interestingly, this Comment was written by Mr. Lee Applebaum under the supervision of the author of this textbook]; Brown, Shell, & Tyson, *Arbitration of Customer-Broker Disputes Arising Under the Federal Securities Laws and RICO*, 15 Sec. Reg. L.J. 3. 18–19 (1987) . . .

those in the securities industry by promoting full disclosure of information on investments. See L. Loss, Securities Regulation 36 (1983).

. . . .

In sum, the same reasons that led the Court to find an exception to the Arbitration Act for § 12(2) claims exist for § 10(b) claims as well. It is clear that *Wilko*, when properly read, governs the instant case and mandates that a predispute arbitration agreement should not be enforced as to § 10(b) claims.

B

Even if I were to accept the Court's narrow reading of *Wilko*, as a case dealing only with the inadequacies of arbitration in 1953, I do not think that this case should be resolved differently today so long as the policy of investor protection is given proper consideration in the analysis. Despite improvements in the process of arbitration and changes in the judicial attitude towards it, several aspects of arbitration that were seen by the *Wilko* court to be inimical to the policy of investor protection still remain. Moreover, I have serious reservations about the Commission's contention that its oversight of the SROs' arbitration procedures will ensure that the process is adequate to protect an investor's rights under the securities acts.

. . . .

Even those who favor the arbitration of securities claims do not contend, however, that arbitration has changed so significantly as to eliminate the essential characteristics noted by the *Wilko* Court. Indeed, proponents of arbitration would not see these characteristics as "problems," because, in their view, the characteristics permit the unique "streamlined" nature of the arbitral process. As at the time of *Wilko*, preparation of a record of arbitration proceedings is not invariably required today. Moreover, arbitrators are not bound by precedent and are actually discouraged by their associates from giving reasons for a decision. . . . Judicial review is still substantially limited to the four grounds listed in § 10 of the Arbitration Act and to the concept of "manifest disregard" of the law. . . .

. . . .

Furthermore, there remains the danger that, *at worst,* compelling an investor to arbitrate securities claims puts him in a forum controlled by the securities industry. This result directly contradicts the goal of both securities acts to free the investor from the control of the market professional. . . .

Finally, the Court's complacent acceptance of the Commission's oversight is alarming when almost every day brings another example of illegality on Wall Street. . . . Many of the abuses recently brought to light, it is true, do not deal with the question of the adequacy of SRO arbitration. They, however, do suggest that the industry's self-regulation, of which the SRO arbitration is a part, is not functioning acceptably. . . . Moreover, these abuses have highlighted the difficulty experienced by the Commission, at a time of growth in the securities market and a decrease in the Commission's staff, to carry out its oversight task. Such inadequacies on the part of the

Commission strike at the very heart of the reasoning of the Court, which is content to accept the soothing assurances of the Commission without examining the reality behind them. . . .

. . . .

Justice STEVENS, concurring in part and dissenting in part.

Gaps in the law must, of course, be filled by judicial construction. But after a statute has been construed, either by this Court or by a consistent course of decision by other federal judges and agencies, it acquires a meaning that should be as clear as if the judicial gloss had been drafted by the Congress itself. This position reflects both respect for Congress' role, . . . and the compelling need to preserve the courts' limited resources, see B. Cardozo, The Nature of the Judicial Process 149 (1921).

During the 32 years immediately following this Court's decision in *Wilko v. Swan*, each of the eight circuits that addressed the issue concluded that the holding of *Wilko* was fully applicable to claims arising under the Securities Exchange Act of 1934. This longstanding interpretation creates a strong presumption, in my view, that any mistake that the courts may have made in interpreting the statute is best remedied by the legislative, not the judicial, branch. . . .

Note

Subsequently, in *Rodriguez De Quijas v. Shearson/American Express, Inc.*, 490 U.S. 477, 482–483 (1989), the Supreme Court overruled *Wilko*. Holding that predispute agreements to arbitrate claims under the Securities Act are enforceable, the Court stated:

> [I]n *McMahon* the Court declined to read § 29(a) of the Securities Exchange Act of 1934, the language of which is in every respect the same as that in § 14 of the 1933 Act, to prohibit enforcement of predispute agreements to arbitrate. The only conceivable distinction in this regard between the Securities Act and the Securities Exchange Act is that the former statute allows concurrent federal-state jurisdiction over causes of action and the latter statute provides for exclusive federal jurisdiction. But even if this distinction were thought to make any difference at all, it would suggest that arbitration agreements, which are "in effect, a specialized kind of forum-selection clause," . . . should not be prohibited under the Securities Act, since they, like the provision for concurrent jurisdiction, serve to advance the objective of allowing buyers of securities a broader right to select the forum for resolving disputes, whether it be judicial or otherwise. And in *McMahon* we explained at length why we rejected the *Wilko* Court's aversion to arbitration as a forum for resolving disputes over securities transactions, especially in light of the relatively recent expansion of the Securities and Exchange Commission's authority to oversee and to regulate those arbitration procedures. . . .

. . . .

[B] Aftermath of *McMahon* and *Rodriguez*

In the aftermath of *McMahon* and *Rodriguez*, many believe that securities arbitration favors the industry. As stated in a New York Times article: "The [brokerage] houses basically like the current system because they own the stacked deck."[3] More recently, the Public Investor Arbitration Bar Association asserted: "As long as brokerage firms and investment advisers retain the ability to require investors to resolve disputes in arbitration, FINRA arbitration may be inherently biased against individuals."[4] A U.S. General Accounting Office (GAO) Report on Securities Arbitration (1992), however, did not agree: "GAO's analysis of statistical results of decisions in arbitration cases at both industry-sponsored and independent forums showed no indication of a pro-industry bias in decisions at industry-sponsored forums." Nonetheless, as Professor Wallace points out: "Given the prominence that securities arbitration enjoy[s], probing questions must be asked regarding the effectiveness [and] basic fairness of the procedures that effectuate it."[5]

Even though not finding a pro-industry bias, the GAO report nonetheless was critical, stating that "GAO's review of arbitration procedures showed that arbitration forums lacked internal controls to provide a reasonable level of assurance regarding either the independence of the arbitrators or their competence in arbitrating disputes." Needless to say, such lack of internal controls, as found by the GAO, bring into question the integrity of the arbitration process. A more recent study conducted by Professors Barbara Black and Jill Gross found that "broker-dealer clients involved in arbitration largely believe that arbitrators were competent and understood the issues, but they were less sure that the arbitrators were open-minded, impartial, and properly applying the law." (*Survey Shows Some Clients See Process as Tilted Against Them*, 40 Sec. Reg. & L. Rep. (BNA) 198 (2008)).

Fortunately, certain improvements have been made. For example, in cases having three arbitrators involving a customer dispute, an arbitration panel must consist of a majority of public arbitrators. *And note:* If requested by the aggrieved customer, as would normally occur, the panel *must* be comprised of all public arbitrators. The rules define those who qualify as public arbitrators to exclude, for instance, those persons who currently work or have worked in the securities industry.

The rules also call for: preservation of a record of the proceeding; disclosure to the parties of certain past or existing affiliations of the arbitrators that are likely to

---

3. Galberson, *When the Investor Has a Gripe*, N.Y. Times, March 29, 1987, at 1, 8. *See* Black, *Is Securities Arbitration Fair to Investors?*, 25 Pace L. Rev. 1 (2004); Johnson, *Wall Street Meets the Wild West: Bringing Law and Order to Securities Arbitration*, 84 N.C. L. Rev. 123 (2005).

4. *PIABA, Other Groups Seek Data on Mandatory Arbitration*, 47 Sec. Reg. & L. Rep. (BNA) 164 (2015).

5. Wallace, *Securities Arbitration After McMahon, Rodriguez, and the New Rules: Can Investors' Rights Really Be Protected?*, 43 Vand. L. Rev. 1199, 1202 (1990). *See also*, Guber, *FINRA Arbitration in the Modern Era: A Defense Practitioner's Perspective*, 44 Rev. Sec. & Comm. Reg. 181 (2011) (stating in 2010, in matters that were tried on their merits, claimants received damages in 47 percent of FINRA arbitration proceedings as compared to 37 percent award rate in 2007).

affect their impartiality; adoption of procedures to facilitate the resolution of discovery disputes; and providing in the statement of award the arbitrators' and parties' names, a summary of the relevant issues in controversy, the damages and/or other relief sought and awarded, a statement of any other issues resolved, and the signatures of the arbitrators who concurred in the award.[6] To some extent, investors are having more success, even recovering punitive damages in a number of cases.[7]

[C] *Charles Schwab* Matter

Seeking to expand the parameters of *McMahon* and *Rodriguez*, Charles Schwab & Co., pursuant to a new provision inserted in its predispute arbitration agreements, sought to preclude its customers from participating in judicial class actions. This effort precipitated an enforcement action brought by FINRA whereby Schwab was found liable for violating FINRA rules. *See* FINRA No. 2011029760201 (2014).[8] An excerpt of that decision follows:

> In this case, we consider whether Charles Schwab & Company, Inc. ("Schwab") or the ("Firm") violated NASD and FINRA rules when the Firm included new provisions in predispute arbitration agreements with customers that prevented customers from bringing or participating in judicial class actions and arbitrators from consolidating individual claims filed in FINRA's arbitration forum. In October 2011, Schwab sent amendments to the Firm's customer account agreement to more than 6.8 million customers in their September 2011 month-end account statement.
>
> The amendments included a "Waiver of Class Action or Representative Action" ("Waiver") requiring customers both to waive their right to bring or participate in class actions against Schwab and the authority of arbitrators to consolidate more than one party's claims.
>
> As a result of these provisions, all disputes between Schwab and its customers would be resolved through bilateral arbitration. The amendments

---

6. *See* Securities Exchange Act Release No. 26805 (1989); NASD Discovery Guide, available at http://www.nasd.com/web/groups/med arb/documents/mediation arbitration/nasdw 009420 .pdf.

7. *See Hosier v. Citigroup Markets, Inc.*, 43 Sec. Reg. & L. Rep. (BNA) 827 (2011) (arbitration award of $54 million, including punitive damages of $17 million); Craig, *Merrill Is Told to Pay $7.7 Million Sum*, Wall St. J., Aug. 28, 2002, at C1. *See generally* Symposium, 62 Brooklyn L. Rev. No. 4 (1996); Katsoris, *Roadmap to Securities ADR*, 11 Fordham J. Corp. & Fin. L. 413 (2006); Nichols, *Arbitrator Selection at the NASD: Investor Perception of a Pro-Securities Industry Bias*, 15 Ohio St. J. Disp. Res. 63 (1999); Poser, *Making Securities Arbitration Work*, 50 SMU L. Rev. 277 (1996); Ramirez, *Arbitration and Reform in Private Securities Litigation: Dealing with the Meritorious as Well as the Frivolous*, 40 Wm. & Mary L. Rev. 1055 (1999); Shell, *Arbitration and Corporate Governance*, 67 N.C. L. Rev. 517 (1989).

8. At the time that this decision was handed down, the author of this textbook (Professor Marc I. Steinberg) was a member of FINRA's National Adjudicatory Council (NAC).

were effective upon notification to customers. Once FINRA became aware that Schwab was using these provisions, FINRA's Department of Enforcement ("Enforcement") commenced the investigation that culminated in the proceedings before us.

We are presented with two central questions regarding the enforceability of Schwab's predispute arbitration agreements with its customers. The first is whether NASD and FINRA rules preserve for customers the ability to bring or participate in judicial class actions and FINRA arbitrators the ability to consolidate more than one party's claims in arbitration. The second is whether the Federal Arbitration Act ("FAA"), which applies to arbitrations of commercial transactions, applies to NASD and FINRA arbitration rules and preempts enforcement of those rules.

. . . .

After our independent review, we [conclude] that Schwab violated NASD and FINRA rules with respect to the Waiver in its entirety. For well over twenty years, FINRA has been in the forefront of establishing the rules under which securities industry arbitrations take place. During this time, FINRA and its premerger self-regulatory organizations ("SROs"), NASD and the New York Stock Exchange, revised their rules repeatedly and responsively for arbitrations between customers and firms or associated persons. FINRA's arbitration forum has been the subject of numerous high-profile legal challenges. There can be little doubt that Congress and the federal courts have repeatedly scrutinized the FINRA rules that govern securities arbitration. Nonetheless, Schwab's misconduct in this case demonstrates its attempted piecemeal erosion of FINRA's well-established arbitration rules.

One aspect of FINRA rules that was approved by the SEC is that customer class actions will be litigated in court, while FINRA arbitration will be available for customers to make individual claims against FINRA firms. FINRA has complementary rules to separate class actions from individual claims: one prohibits any class actions in FINRA arbitration, a second prevents FINRA firms from using an arbitration agreement to defeat a putative class action in court. Yet Schwab argues that these FINRA rules, which have been in force since 1992, are invalid. Although Schwab is noncommittal on this point, we understand the logical extent of its theory to be that the SEC's past approval of these rules was invalid at the time, because Congress had not authorized the SEC to approve these types of arbitration rules. We reject this theory as a misreading of the Exchange Act. We uphold these FINRA rules and find that Schwab's inclusion of a mandatory waiver of participation in judicial class actions, as well as its restriction of an arbitrator's power to join together individual claims violates NASD and FINRA rules.

. . . .

[D] Arbitration Today

Arbitration today, although more complex than in yesteryear,[9] remains a relatively informal process. Rather than burdensome pleading requirements as frequently mandated by federal law, a complainant in arbitration need only specify the relevant facts and the remedies sought.[10] Although discovery is permitted to an increasing extent,[11] including written requests for information and document requests,[12] a number of the more costly and time-consuming aspects of discovery found in federal and state court litigation often are not present. Hence, depositions are rarely permitted. Granting of a dispositive motion (such as a motion to dismiss or motion for summary judgment) prior to the formal hearing is infrequent. These informal procedures can be beneficial to investors, including the inapplicability of strict pleading rules.[13]

At the formal hearing, the panel is comprised of all or a majority of public arbitrators. Unlike a judicial proceeding, formal rules of evidence do not apply, thereby allowing the introduction of hearsay.[14] Relevance and materiality are key criteria in the arbitrators' determination relating to the weight given to evidence proffered.[15]

Arbitrators, not being bound by precise legal standards in their decisions, may render awards premised on the standards of applicable self-regulatory organizations' (SROs') standards, industry custom, or even concepts of equity and fairness. Indeed, damages may be awarded to claimants for violations of SRO rules where no monetary remedy is provided for such misconduct under federal or state securities law. Moreover, many arbitrators are not attorneys and, even for those who are lawyers, they may not have expertise in securities law.[16]

Unless all parties jointly request, no written (or "explained") decision is required by the arbitration rules; only the names of the parties (and their representatives), a summary of the issues presented, the relief sought and awarded, statement of other issues resolved (e.g., jurisdictional and fee rulings), the names of the arbitrators, and the signatures of the arbitrators are the key items necessary.

Although not required, the arbitrators may include a rationale underlying the award. See FINRA Code of Arbitration Procedure for Customer Disputes § 12904.

---

9. *See* Report of the Arbitration Policy Task Force to the Board of Governors, National Association of Securities Dealers, Inc., [1995–1996 Transfer Binder] Fed. Sec. L. Rep. (CCH) ¶ 85,735, at 87,463–87,468 (1996) (hereinafter Ruder Report).

10. Securities Industry Conference of Arbitration (SICA), Uniform Code of Arbitration (UCA) § 13.

11. *See* Ruder Report, *supra* note 9, at 87,463.

12. *See supra* note 10, UCA § 20(a)-(c).

13. *See* Ruder Report, *supra* note 9, at 87,468; M. Cane & P. Shub, Securities Arbitration: Law and Procedure 114 (1991).

14. M. Cane & P. Shub, *supra* note 13, at 37; S. Jaffee, Broker-Dealers and Securities Markets: A Guide to the Regulatory Process 19 (1977).

15. *See supra* note 10, UCA § 21; A Bromberg & L. Lowenfels, Securities Fraud and Commodities Fraud §§ 16.01-16.05 (2015).

16. *See* Ruder Report, *supra* note 9, at 87,468–87,469; Johnson *supra* note 3, at 159–170; Sullivan, *The Scope of Modern Arbitral Awards*, 62 Tulane L. Rev. 1113 (2007).

The rationale frequently provided for not requiring written (or "explained") opinions is that mandating such opinions would contravene the policies underlying arbitration which are to provide an expeditious, efficient and informal forum of alternative dispute resolution.[17] Another argument advanced is that requiring written opinions would be time consuming and burdensome, thereby deterring many qualified individuals from agreeing to serve as arbitrators.[18]

There may be another key reason why arbitrators avoid writing opinions: Because the panel's decision can be overturned by a federal court only on narrow grounds, such as bias, misconduct, or manifest disregard of the law,[19] the writing of an opinion draws a road map by which a disgruntled party will have greater likelihood of upsetting the arbitral award. Moreover, being pressed for time, inadequately paid, and not accomplished in authoring written opinions (particularly in a complex area like securities law), any written decision incurs the risk of being viewed with disfavor by a learned federal court. Because arbitrators perceive that they act in good faith, follow the spirit if not the letter of the applicable law, and seek to do justice, they thus are reluctant to explain their rationale in a written opinion. The end product is one that reaches a defined result with no reasoning provided to support such result and with the losing party having little likelihood of overturning such result.[20]

[E] Arbitration in the Registered Offering Context

Although not a broker-dealer topic, this is a good place to discuss the Carlyle Group's IPO registration statement filed with the SEC that contained a compulsory arbitration clause with respect to shareholder disputes. After widespread objections,

---

17. *See, e.g., Raiford v. Merrill Lynch, Pierce, Fenner & Smith Inc.* 903 F.2d 1410, 1413 (11th Cir. 1990); *Sargent v. Paine Webber Jackson & Curtis Inc.,* 882 F.2d 529, 532 (D.C. Cir. 1989); *Sobel v. Hertz, Warner & Co.,* 469 F.2d 1211, 1214 (2d Cir. 1972).

18. *See* Katzler, *Should Mandatory Written Opinions Be Required in All Securities Arbitrations? The Practical and Legal Implications to the Securities Industry,* 45 Am. U. L. Rev. 151, 164 (1995).

19. Section 10 of the Federal Arbitration Act (FAA), 9 U.S.C. § 10. Although error of law is not provided as a basis for vacating an award pursuant to § 10, a number of federal courts have embraced a standard focusing on manifest disregard of the law by the arbitrators as a ground for vacating an award. See *Comedy Club, Inc. v. Improv West Associates,* 553 F.3d 1277 (9th Cir. 2009); Cane and Greenspon, *Securities Arbitration: Bankrupt, Bothered & Bewildered,* 7 Stan. J. L. Bus. & Fin. 131, 148 n. 100 (2002) (citing cases). Nonetheless, the burden to show "manifest disregard" is a high one for aggrieved parties. As stated by the D.C. Circuit, "[t]he 'manifest disregard of the law' standard for overturning an arbitration award is manifestly difficult to satisfy." *Kurke v. Oscar Gruss and Son, Inc.,* 454 F.3d 350, 359 (D.C. Cir. 2006). There is an issue whether the manifest disregard standard survives the Supreme Court's decision in *Hall Street Associates v. Mattel, Inc.,* 552 U.S. 576 (2008), which can be interpreted to hold that the grounds for vacating an arbitration award under § 10(a) of the Federal Arbitration Act are exclusive. See *Citigroup Global Markets, Inv. v. Bacon,* 562 F.3d 349 (5th Cir. 2009); Gross, *Hall Street Blues: The Uncertain Future of Manifest Disregard,* 37 Sec. Reg. L.J. 3 (2009).

20. *See* S. Jaffee, *supra* note 14, at 339; Black & Gross, *The Explained Award of Damocles: Protection or Peril in Securities Arbitration,* 34 Sec. Reg. L.J. 17 (2006); Steinberg, *Securities Arbitration: Better for Investors than the Courts?,* 62 Brooklyn L. Rev. 1503 (1996).

Carlyle opted to withdraw the provision. Nonetheless, it is quite possible that other issuers in the future will seek to include a mandatory arbitration provision in their IPO registration statements.

Not surprisingly, investor reaction has been hostile to inclusion of such compulsory arbitration clauses. For example, in a joint letter to the SEC, such organizations as Public Citizen and the American Federation of Labor, urged that Carlyle's IPO not be permitted to proceed with the inclusion of the mandatory arbitration clause:

> [T]he action could set a precedent leading to widespread adoption of forced arbitration between companies and their shareholders, as companies seek to further insulate themselves from scrutiny and accountability. . . . These clauses would interfere with investors' well-established private rights of action under the securities laws, including implied causes of action under Rule 10b-5 of the 1934 Securities Exchange Act. [44 Sec. Reg. & L. Rep. (BNA) 316 (2012)]

On this subject, Professor Coffee has observed:

> Sooner or later, this confrontation is coming. In the interim, the SEC and the stock exchanges should consider whether they are prepared to list securities that are immunized from judicial oversight. Here, the FAA [Federal Arbitration Act] does not control. Proxy advisers will need to consider what votes they will recommend to their clients on such amendments—and why. Finally, corporate issuers must ask themselves the pricing question: How much will eliminating judicial review impact their stock price? Pricing may prove determinative.

Coffee, *The Death of Stockholder Litigation?*, Nat. L.J. Feb. 13, 2012, at 14. *See* Morrissey, *Will Arbitration End Securities Litigation?*, 40 Sec. Reg. L.J. 159, 163 (2012) (opining that "even conceding that there may be benefits in mandatory arbitration for consumer and employment matters, it should not be condoned when securities fraud is at issue, particularly at public companies").

---

§ 13.04 The Shingle and Related Theories

At this point, review the material contained in § 8.13.

Pross v. Baird, Patrick & Co., Inc.

United States District Court, Southern District of New York
585 F. Supp. 1456 (1984)

[This case is contained in § 8.13.]

Brown v. E.F. Hutton Group, Inc.

United States Court of Appeals, Second Circuit

991 F.2d 1026 (1993)

[This case is contained in § 8.05[C].]

[A] Distinguishing "Puffery" from "Misrepresentation"

Cohen v. Prudential-Bache Securities, Inc.

United States District Court, Southern District of New York

713 F. Supp. 653 (1989)

KRAM, District Judge.

This action is brought to recover damages for alleged violations of the federal securities laws and various related state laws, including common law fraud, breach of contract and breach of fiduciary duty. . . .

BACKGROUND

In her amended complaint, plaintiff alleges that defendant James defrauded her by making material misrepresentations and omissions, as well as by engaging in other deceptive or manipulative activity. Plaintiff, who has no financial training and who retired in 1979, lives on a fixed income of approximately $30,000 a year. At some point in the 1970's plaintiff was introduced by telephone to Diane Capaccio, who later changed her name to Diane James, and who served as financial advisor and securities broker to plaintiff. At this time, plaintiff advised James that her primary investment objective was to make safe investments and to maximize annual yield without jeopardizing her capital. James was working for the Shearson Company at the time plaintiff first met her, but even after James moved to a position with E.F. Hutton, she continued to act as plaintiff's advisor and broker, regularly speaking with her by telephone, encouraging plaintiff to rely on her investment advice, and recommending investments in securities. James acted as broker on the transactions she recommended. James continued to advise plaintiff and act as her broker after James relocated to California and began working for defendant Prudential-Bache Securities, Inc. ("Prudential"). Plaintiff continued to rely on James at all times.

In February, 1986, James urged plaintiff to liquidate certain securities held in plaintiff's Prudential portfolio and in that month did so. In April of that year, James "repeatedly and very strongly urged" plaintiff to invest in a Texas limited partnership known as the CSH-1 Hotel Limited Partnership ("CSH-1"). Plaintiff alleges on information and belief, based on promotional materials obtained, that Prudential acted as the "special limited partner" and promoter of CSH-1. . . . James told plaintiff that she could expect a very strong cash flow without risk, but that she needed to act quickly so as not to lose the opportunity. Plaintiff received an undated memorandum from defendants that stated in part: "TIMELY AND URGENT—PLEASE REVIEW NOW! UNITS

ARE ONLY A FEW LEFT!" The memorandum also promised a tax-free return of 13.4% and stated that investors placed only $7,744.50 at risk before "write-offs", while noting "NO $ AT RISK at any time with write off+cash returned before sale".

In a telephone conversation with plaintiff in April, 1986, James told plaintiff that the monies already in her Prudential account would be sufficient for the entire CSH-1 investment and that the total investment by plaintiff would not be greater than $8500. No mention was made of the need to make any future payments. James, working through Prudential, forwarded a number of documents to plaintiff for her signature. Without understanding the nature of the documents and on the advice of James, plaintiff signed these papers and returned them to Prudential at some point prior to April 15, 1986. She did not make copies and Prudential did not send her any. James later informed plaintiff that payment for the CSH-1 investment was made from her Prudential portfolio. In November of 1986 and May of 1987, plaintiff made payments of $2,984.25 and $3,087.75, respectively, concerning CSH-1 after such payments were demanded. In October, 1987, the Note Collection Department of Manufacturers Hanover Trust Company demanded payment of $8500 respecting CSH-1, but plaintiff did not understand nor pay. On October 23, 1987, plaintiff began receiving notices from the Fireman's Insurance Company of North America demanding payment, advising her that she had signed a promissory note guaranteed by Fireman's Insurance and that she was in default. The note she allegedly signed obligates plaintiff to pay $54,000 plus 11.2% on unpaid principal, for a total of $84,752.50 through 1991.

Plaintiff claims that the defendants never informed her that CSH-1 was a tax shelter designed for high income-bracket persons, inappropriate for investors with moderate fixed income, and that the investment was risky. Plaintiff's counsel became aware of these facts upon receipt of the CSH-1 Subscription Agreement in January, 1988. Plaintiff claims her investment is at risk, especially in light of threats by Fireman's Insurance to sell plaintiff's shares. Plaintiff also asserts that neither defendant ever asked her for a statement of her income, assets or net worth, and never discussed tax shelters with her.

Plaintiff further alleges, on information and belief, that on or about April 25, 1986, James filled out an investor questionnaire form for plaintiff showing plaintiff's gross income (actual or projected) in excess of $100,000 for each year from 1984 through 1989, indicating that thirty percent of her income came from salary, and showing a net worth of $1,180,000. Plaintiff bases this allegation on a copy of the investor questionnaire provided to her counsel by Fireman's Insurance, and plaintiff's conclusion that the handwriting on the form is not plaintiff's, but instead that of James. Plaintiff, after retiring in 1979, states she has earned no salary and receives only $30,000 per year, with a net worth between $90,000 and $150,000. Plaintiff alleges that, at these salary levels, she would not have been accepted for investment in CSH-1.

Plaintiff never authorized James to use these figures or to act as her amanuensis for such purpose. Plaintiff, whose signature purportedly appears at the bottom of the questionnaire, claims that she never signed this questionnaire. In addition, the signature page bearing plaintiff's purported signature was allegedly notarized on April 25, 1986 in California. Plaintiff claims to have been in New York at that time, did not authorize the notarization and was never in California at any relevant time. Moreover, plaintiff alleges, on information and belief, that her signature was also forged on an Investor Bond Indemnification and Pledge Agreement dated April 25, 1986. This agreement was allegedly required before a purchase in CSH-1 would be allowed. Plaintiff claims she never received any income from CSH-1.

DISCUSSION

Section 10(b) Claim

Defendants attack plaintiffs' first claim in a few ways. Defendants generally attack the pleadings, at certain points, for failing to plead fraud with the particularity required . . . .

. . . Reading the complaint as a whole, as the Court should, the Court concludes that plaintiff has stated a claim under section 10(b) for which relief can be granted.

A. Misrepresentations or Omissions

In order to state a claim under section 10(b), the plaintiff must allege (1) material misstatements or omissions, (2) indicating an intent to deceive or defraud (scienter), (3) in connection with the sale or purchase of any security, (4) upon which the plaintiff detrimentally relied. . . . Plaintiff has done so here. Plaintiff alleges that her longstanding investment advisor and broker advised and cajoled her to invest in CSH-1. In order to induce plaintiff's investment, James allegedly told plaintiff that the investment would be risk-free, would not require more than $8500 of her monies and that she could expect a significant tax-free return. A memorandum on the investment confirmed these representations. At the same time, James failed to inform plaintiff that CSH-1 was a high risk tax shelter, designed for investors with significant amounts of income and assets.

1. Materiality and Related Factors

A primary issue presented is whether or not these alleged representations and omissions are material. . . .

Defendants argue that these misrepresentations were not material as a matter of law since the statements amount to no more than mere puffery. As this Court has explained:

> Courts have recognized a category of statements by brokers which are better characterized as 'puffery' than as material misstatements. When a broker calls a bond 'marvelous', *Zerman v. Ball,* 735 F.2d 15, 21 (2d Cir. 1984), or says a stock is so 'red hot' that the investor 'could not lose,' *Rotstein v. Reynolds & Co.,* 359 F. Supp. 109, 113 (N.D. Ill. 1973), or claims that his primary purpose is to make money for the customer, *Bowman v. Hartig,* 334 F. Supp. 1323, 1328 (S.D. N.Y. 1971), the reasonable investor is presumed to understand that this is nothing more than "the common puff of a salesman," not a material factual misstatement.

See *Newman v. L.F. Rothschild*, 651 F. Supp. 160, 163 (S.D.N.Y. 1986) (holding that broker's "I'm the best in the business" statement, among others, is not actionable); *see also Frota v. Prudential-Bache Securities, Inc.*, 639 F. Supp. 1186, 1190 (S.D.N.Y. 1986) (holding that broker's assurances that the account would be properly managed and that he was the investor's confidant were mere puffery). In a subsequent opinion in the *Newman* litigation, Judge Sweet determined that the "inclusion of a specific percentage . . . puts the misrepresentation in a different category from those . . ." determined to be puffery in the earlier decision. *Newman v. L.F. Rothschild*, 662 F. Supp. 957, 959 (S.D.N.Y. 1987). In so stating, the Court determined that the broker's statement that the investor could earn a return of 20% to 30% without risk was actionable. In the present case, plaintiff alleges that James informed her over the telephone that she would receive a very strong cash flow without risk to her initial investment. This statement standing alone approaches the puffery line, but combined with the memorandum sent by defendants promising a return of 13.4% without risk to the investment, the representations are certainly not mere puffery. In addition, and contrary to defendants' argument, the Court does not find that the promise of this return without risk is so unbelievable that an investor could not reasonably rely upon it.

. . . .

B. Forgeries and Alterations

Defendants attack plaintiff's forgery and alteration allegations on the basis that they cannot state a claim for relief under section 10(b) since plaintiff did not know about their existence or contents and thus could not have relied upon them in making an investment decision. Additionally, defendants argue that these allegations do not allege the requisite device, misrepresentation or omission under section 10(b) or Rule 10b-5. Plaintiff argues that the acts complained of fall within section 10(b)'s prohibition of "any manipulative or deceptive device or contrivance" and the prohibitions of Rule 10b-5. . . .

It is true, as defendant argues, that a claim under section 10(b) must allege an element of deception or manipulation. . . .

The Court believes that plaintiff has alleged a claim for relief. . . . Even if the account in the present case were not discretionary, since it appears that consent by plaintiff was necessary prior to investment, the knowing forgery and alteration of documents by defendants has the same effect as the purchase of an unsuitable security in a discretionary account. In both cases, defendants have acted with scienter, a principal requirement, . . . and in both situations the broker is acting on behalf or in the stead of the investor in a fraudulent fashion. . . . In the present case, . . . the alleged misstatements in plaintiff's investor questionnaire were designed not to mislead plaintiff but to advance defendants' alleged fraudulent scheme.

. . . .

[B] State Law

There is the possibility that state law standards may be more relaxed than federal law with respect to such elements as causation, reliance, and scienter. The following case serves as an illustration where relief was afforded investors on state common law grounds where such relief was denied on the federal and state securities law claims.

Gochnauer v. A.G. Edwards & Sons, Inc.

United States Court of Appeals, Eleventh Circuit

810 F.2d 1042 (1987)

GARZA, Senior Circuit Judge:

The issue before us is whether a stockbroker can violate his fiduciary obligations under state common law and still fail to violate the anti-fraud provisions of federal securities law or the Florida "blue sky" securities statute. The district court so held, and after review of governing law we affirm the ruling of the court below.

BACKGROUND

Both parties agree on the findings of fact presented in the district court's order. In April of 1979, plaintiffs/appellants James R. and Patricia M. Gochnauer ("Gochnauers" or "appellants") maintained a securities account with A.G. Edwards & Sons, Inc., a brokerage firm. James Lester was employed as a broker by appellee A.G. Edwards and under the supervision of appellee Gene Roach, branch manager of A.G. Edwards' Ft. Walton Beach office. At that time the Gochnauers' investments were primarily municipal bonds, and since interest rates were high Mr. Gochnauer asked Mr. Lester if other investments could yield more rewarding financial returns. Lester discussed a number of alternative investments with Mr. Gochnauer, including stocks, gold and silver, and option writing. Lester recommended that the Gochnauers consider option writing and consult with John Kerr, a self-styled investment advisor. Lester told Gochnauer that he had known Kerr for a number of years and that Kerr had been successful in the options market. Gochnauer did not meet with Kerr at that time.

Lester made this recommendation of Kerr without investigating Kerr's qualifications, experience, or education. Kerr was not a licensed investment advisor (though Florida law did not require him to be), nor did he have significant financial experience or education in securities trading. Lester's recommendation of Kerr was based on his personal observations of Kerr and discussions with customers and Kerr's stockbroker (also employed at A.G. Edwards) about Kerr's investment success. Kerr was not employed by A.G. Edwards. Lester arranged a meeting a few months later between the Gochnauers and Kerr, and Kerr offered to become the Gochnauers' exclusive investment advisor for their account at A.G. Edwards.

As part of this arrangement, Kerr told the Gochnauers that if he were given authority to trade their account he would *guarantee* them a fifteen percent (15%) return on their investment; if the account lost money or failed to earn a 15% return, Kerr promised he would make good the difference. Lester's comment on this proposed arrangement consisted solely of assuring the Gochnauers that Kerr was a successful investor with an account at A.G. Edwards "of over $100,000," and that Kerr had "a fine home." These were factually correct statements at the time.

The Gochnauers had been provided a prospectus concerning the options writing program, which stated on its cover that option writing was a risky venture. The Gochnauers' previous investment instructions on file with Lester and A.G. Edwards directed the brokers to pursue conservative investments for income and growth; by contrast, option writing can only be described as highly speculative. Lester had given the Gochnauers a number of forms to sign in the event they decided to grant Kerr the trading authority for their account. The Gochnauers signed a "Customer's Option Agreement" which stated that the Gochnauers had been furnished with the options prospectus, had read it, and understood the risks and obligations attendant to options trading. The Gochnauers accepted Kerr's offer and signed a contract assuring them a 15% return on their options writing investment program. The contract between Kerr and the Gochnauers stated that there were no other parties to the agreement. The Gochnauers then liquidated a number of their bonds and, in September, 1979, they placed $36,831 into an exclusive trading account with Kerr, approximately one-half of their life savings.

After substantial losses between September of 1979 and April of 1980, A.G. Edwards inquired of branch manager Roach why an account desiring income and growth was involved in heavy trading and risky option writing. Roach asked Lester, and Lester contacted Kerr and the Gochnauers to consult with them about their investment goals. Lester subsequently changed the instructions on file at A.G. Edwards from "income and growth" to "speculation." The Gochnauers received a financial statement once a month from A.G. Edwards showing the trading activity of their account and the mounting losses.

By the end of the first year the Gochnauers' account had lost approximately $25,000. Rather than demand the 15% return on the contract, the Gochnauers extended the agreement with Kerr for another year. After the two year period, instead of a guaranteed amount of $54,036.00, the balance in the Gochnauers' trading account had fallen to $4,092.18. Over $13,000 in commissions had been paid to Lester and A.G. Edwards due to the high volume of trading that occurred, approximately one-fourth of the losses. . . . Lester, Roach, and A.G. Edwards deny any and all responsibility for this financial debacle and steadfastly refuse to compensate the Gochnauers for the funds lost through this venture. Appellees contend that the Gochnauers were experienced investors and that the contract between Kerr and the Gochnauers expressly excluded appellees, thereby absolving them from any liability. The Gochnauers filed suit to recover their losses.

. . . .

DISCUSSION

The issue is whether a finding of a breach of fiduciary duty necessitates a finding of statutory securities law violations. It is important to separate the two types of claims raised on appeal. The securities fraud claims are based on Section 10(b) of the Securities Exchange Act of 1934, Rule 10b-5 of the Securities and Exchange Commission, and Florida Statute Section 517.301,[21] the state's "blue sky" securities law. The common law breach of fiduciary duty claim is based on Florida common law.

. . . .

A. Securities Law Violations

The trial court correctly sets out the elements for a cause of action under federal securities law. A successful cause of action under Section 10(b) or Rule 10b-5 requires that the plaintiff prove (1) a misstatement or omission (2) of a material fact (3) made with scienter (4) upon which the plaintiff relied (5) that proximately caused the plaintiffs' loss. . . . The Florida statutory requirements are identical to Rule 10b-5, . . . except that the scienter requirement under Florida law is satisfied by a showing of mere negligence, whereas the minimum showing under Rule 10b-5 is reckless disregard. . . .

The trial judge found evidence to satisfy the first three elements essential to prove a statutory violation. The information concerning Kerr's qualifications, education, and experience was found to be material, and the record clearly shows Lester failed to investigate Kerr's abilities as an investment advisor and failed to relate vital information relevant to the options writing investment decision to the Gochnauers. The court also found that Lester's conduct was "an extreme departure from the standards of ordinary care," . . . satisfying the "reckless" scienter requirement of Rule 10b-5.

A showing of plaintiff's reliance on the misrepresented or omitted information is necessary to satisfy the fourth element of a Rule 10b-5 cause of action. This Circuit requires "reasonable reliance" upon the material misrepresentations, a test of subjective reliance tempered by the requirement of "due diligence" on the part of the plaintiff. . . . Not only must an individual actually rely on the information provided, this reliance must be "justifiable," i.e., with the exercise of reasonable diligence one still could not have discovered the truth behind the fraudulent omission or misrepresentation. . . .

After hearing the evidence, the court concluded that the Gochnauers did *not* rely upon the misrepresentations and omissions of Lester with regard to Kerr's qualifications and experience. Mr. Gochnauer stated at trial that he would have relied on Kerr's advice even if he had known Kerr was not a licensed investment advisor. Apparently, the fact that Mr. Gochnauer, Kerr, and Lester were all former Air Force officers forged a bond of respect and trust between the men. The judge concluded, therefore, that

---

[21]. 517.301 provides in pertinent part:
    "It is unlawful . . . (b) to obtain money or property by means of any untrue statement of a material fact or any omission to state a material fact necessary in order to make the statements made, in the light of the circumstances under which they were made, not misleading; . . ."

the Gochnauers failed to show that they would have acted differently had they known the truth regarding Kerr's qualifications. . . .

Because reliance is also a necessary element of a Florida "blue sky" securities violation, the court found no state securities violation either. . . .

. . . The district court's conclusion that no statutory securities violations exist where appellants did not reasonably rely on Lester's material misrepresentations and omissions is supported by the record.

B. Common Law Fiduciary Obligations

The lower court did determine that Lester, and through application of *respondeat superior* doctrine appellees Roach and A.G. Edwards, breached a fiduciary duty of care owed to the Gochnauers. Appellees vigorously contest this conclusion. Without statutory-based reliance, the argument runs, there can be no liability to the Gochnauers because there is no breach of fiduciary duty either. Statutory securities fraud and common law breach of fiduciary duty, say appellees, are exactly the same. We disagree.

. . . .

Fraud is not the same as breach of fiduciary duty. . . . Florida courts recognize a breach of fiduciary duty claim at common law.

The law is clear that a broker owes a fiduciary duty of care and loyalty to a securities investor. . . . Lester's fiduciary responsibilities in the one-time "non-discretionary" decision to employ Kerr as an investment advisor were:

> (1) the duty to recommend [investments] only after studying it sufficiently to become informed as to its nature, price, and financial prognosis; (2) the duty to perform the customer's orders promptly in a manner best suited to serve the customer's interests; (3) the duty to inform the customer of the risks involved in purchasing or selling a particular security; (4) the duty to refrain from self-dealing . . . ; (5) the duty not to misrepresent any material fact to the transaction; and (6) the duty to transact business only after receiving approval from the customer.

. . . The experience and sophistication of the investor are also relevant to determine the extent of the fiduciary duty of care in explaining contemplated securities transactions.

The trial court found that the Gochnauers were not totally novice investors, but neither were they highly sophisticated. Even though the Gochnauers signed an agreement stating that they understood the risks of option trading, it was incumbent upon Lester to fully explain the risks of options trading and comment on the agreement guaranteeing a 15% return on a speculative investment, a highly unusual arrangement to say the least. . . .

The common law focuses on the fiduciary's responsibilities as a "prudent man," i.e., whether the fiduciary conducted an independent investigation of the merits of a particular investment. . . . The focus of the inquiry is how the fiduciary acted in his selection of the investment, and if the fiduciary did breach his duty to his principal, the question then becomes one of causation. Causation is related to but distinct from reliance. The district court found reliance and causation when it explained the breach and concluded "*but for* the breach of duty, the plaintiffs would not have experienced the heavy losses of approximately 25,000" (emphasis added). There is substantial evidence to support this determination and we do not find it clearly erroneous. . . .

Appellees' contention that the district court's finding of insufficient reliance to make out statutory-based securities fraud claims *must* mean that there was no breach of fiduciary duty confuses the issue. As the [U.S.] Supreme Court's decision in *Santa Fe* made clear, the securities fraud statutes do not co-opt the existence of separate claims under state fiduciary principles. The common law of fiduciary obligation is still intact, and appellees' case law arguments based on *fraud* are simply inapposite here. The finding that there was no statutory reliance on Lester's recommendation of Kerr sufficient to make out a claim for securities fraud does not preclude a finding that the Gochnauers relied on Lester's advice to pursue options writing, an unstable and highly speculative investment. Appellees' liability for securities fraud turned on whether the Gochnauers relied on Lester's misrepresentations concerning Kerr's qualifications. Appellees' liability for a breach of fiduciary duty depends upon the extent to which Lester's general advice to invest in options trading caused the Gochnauers to do so—the question of reliance in this instance becomes part of the question of causation. The district court's finding of "but for" causation sufficiently establishes the Gochnauers' reliance upon Lesters' advice to invest in options trading. . . .

. . . .

The federal and state securities violations require reliance upon a material misrepresentation or omission. The judge, on the basis of the evidence before him, found none. The judge did conclude that Lester breached his fiduciary duty as a "prudent broker" in advising the Gochnauers to pursue options writing, a finding that is not clearly erroneous. Both decisions are supported by the law and the evidence in this case.

AFFIRMED.

Note

The vast majority of cases hold that the mere presence of a broker-customer relationship is not sufficient to constitute the broker a fiduciary. Such a relationship normally exists when a discretionary account is maintained, signifying that the customer has vested the broker with the authority to manage the account, including the power to buy and sell securities on the client's behalf. Such a fiduciary relationship also may be found where the broker is deemed to have exercised control (either overtly or covertly) over the account. In a departure from the majority view, a California appellate court held that, irrespective of the investor's sophistication, all brokers are fiduciaries.[22]

Moreover, under the U.S. Department of Labor's "fiduciary rule" adopted in 2016 (and scheduled to go into effect in 2017), generally brokers must comply with fiduciary standards when recommending investments to their clients in their retirement accounts. Thus, "both brokers and registered investment advisers will be required to adhere to the same fiduciary standard when providing investment advice on retirement accounts." Tergesen, *Adviser Rule: What You Need to Know*, WALL ST. J., April 7, 2016, at C2.

———

The following high-profile case construes the contours of a broker's duty to act with due care in the sophisticated investor context.

De Kwiatkowski v. Bear, Stearns & Co., Inc.

United States Court of Appeals, Second Circuit
306 F.3d 1293 (2002)

. . . .

Background

. . .

Kwiatkowski . . . opened an account at Bear Stearns [Bear] in 1988. . . . The account was handled by Bear's "Private Client Services Group," which provides large private investors with enhanced services, including access if requested to the firm's executive and financial experts. . . . Sabini [his broker] was in regular contact with Kwiatkowski. . . . Sabini provided his client with news and market reports, and sometimes sent him Bear market forecasts and investment recommendations.

At first, Kwiatkowski's account at Bear was limited to securities trading. . . . In January 1991, Kwiatkowski opened a futures account at Bear . . . consisting of 4000 Swiss franc short contracts traded on the Chicago Mercantile Exchange ("CME"). . . . Kwiatkowski's futures account at Bear was at all times "nondiscretionary," meaning that Bear executed only those trades that Kwiatkowski directed. . . .

Kwiatkowski's trading strategy reflected his belief in the long-term strength of the U.S. dollar . . . though he . . . understood that the dollar would experience "ups and downs" in the near term.

Kwiatkowski had been an experienced currency trader. . . . As an entrepreneur . . . he developed a background in trading to hedge the risks associated with his company's foreign currency transactions. Kwiatkowski also had experience betting on

———

22. *Duffy v. Cavalier*, 210 Cal. App. 3d 1514, 259 Cal. Rptr. 162 (1989), *adhered to*, 215 Cal. App. 3d 1517, 264 Cal. Rptr. 740 (1989).

the dollar. . . . In 1990 . . . Kwiatkowski lost nearly $70 million . . . when the dollar declined against the German mark and Swiss franc.

Before Kwiatkowski did his first currency transaction at Bear in September 1992, he met with Bear's then-Chief Economist, Lawrence Kudlow, who expressed the view that the dollar was undervalued worldwide and therefore was a good investment opportunity. In the weeks following this meeting, Kwiatkowski executed several trades betting on the rise of the dollar acquiring 16,000 open contracts on the CME. He closed his position in January 1993, having made $219 million in profits in about four months. . . .

. . . In an October 1994 phone call, Sabini told him that "this is the time to buy the dollar." . . . Within a month, Kwiatkowski amassed 65,000 contracts on the franc, pound, yen, and mark—a position with a notional value of $6.5 billion. . . . Kwiatkowski's position amounted to 30 percent of the CME's total open interest in some of the currencies. . . .

. . . Kwiatkowski traded on margin, meaning he put up only a fraction of the $6.5 billion notional value. . . . As the dollar fluctuated, Kwiatkowski's position was "market-to-market," meaning that his profits were added to his margin and his losses were deducted. . . .

In late November or early December, [David] Schoenthal [the head of Bear Stearns Forex] told Bear's Executive Committee that Kwiatkowski's position was too conspicuous on the CME to allow a quick liquidation, and . . . recommended to Kwiatkowski that he move his position to the over-the-counter ("OTC") market. . . . According to Kwiatkowski, Schoenthal told him that, when and if Kwiatkowski needed to liquidate, Schoenthal could get him out of the OTC market "on a dime." . . . Kwiatkowski accepted Schoenthal's recommendation in part: . . . Kwiatkowski moved half of [his position] to the OTC market.

. . . As of December 21, 1994 . . . Kwiatkowski had made profits of $228 million. When the dollar fell a week later, Kwiatkowski lost $112 million in a single day (December 28). . . . [O]n January 9, 1995, Kwiatkowski lost another $98 million. . . . [O]n January 19, he lost $70 million more. . . . Kwiatkowski was still ahead $34 million on his trades since October 28, 1994.

. . . After the December 28 shock, Kwiatkowski told Schoenthal and Sabini [that] he . . . was thinking of closing his position. They advised him that it would be unwise to liquidate during the holiday season. . . . The dollar rebounded on December 29, and Kwiatkowski recouped $50 million of the previous day's losses.

After the January 9 decline, Kwiatkowski spoke with Wayne Angell, Bear's Chief Economist. According to Kwiatkowski, Angell thought that the dollar remained undervalued and would bounce back. . . .

. . . Two salesmen in Bear's futures department . . . who wrote a monthly report . . . announced in their February 1995 issue that they were downgrading the dollar's outlook to "negative" . . . Kwiatkowski testified that he never received this report.

. . . In mid-February, . . . Kwiatkowski instructed Bear to meet future margin calls by liquidating his contracts. As the dollar declined, Bear gradually liquidated Kwiatkowski's position (obtaining his approval of each trade). By . . . March 2, 1995, Kwiatkowski's total position had been reduced to 40,800 contracts in the Swiss franc and the German mark. He had suffered net losses of $138 million in slightly over four months.

Over the next three days, the dollar fell sharply against both the franc and the mark, and Kwiatkowski's remaining contracts were liquidated at a further loss of $116 million.

On . . . Friday, March 3, Bear . . . [had to] liquidate 18,000 of his contracts in order to meet a margin call. . . . At that time, Kwiatkowski expressed interest in liquidating his position altogether. Schoenthal and Sabini advised Kwiatkowski that because market liquidity generally lessens on Friday afternoons, it would be prudent to hold on and take the chance that the dollar would strengthen. According to Kwiatkowski, he relied on this advice in deciding to hold on to the balance of his contracts.

When the overseas markets opened on Sunday (New York time), the dollar fell. . . . By the early hours of Monday, the liquidation was complete. In order to cover his losses, Kwiatkowski was forced to liquidate his securities account and pay an additional $2.7 million in cash. . . .

In all, Kwiatkowski suffered a net loss of $215 million in his currency trading from October 1994 through Monday, March 6, 1995. At trial, Kwiatkowski's expert witness testified that Kwiatkowski could have saved $53 million by liquidating on Friday, March 3 and $116.5 million if Kwiatkowski had liquidated on Wednesday and Thursday, March 1 and 2.

. . . .

All . . . the claims for negligence and breach of fiduciary duty were dismissed in August 1997. . . . Kwiatkowski filed a Second Amended Complaint in October 1998, which re-pleaded the original claims on somewhat different theories. The amended pleading alleged that Bear had failed to give adequate warning about trading risks and adequate advice regarding liquidation of Kwiatkowski's position. Bear again moved for summary judgment on all claims, arguing that under New York law, the duties it owed to a nondiscretionary customer such as Kwiatkowski were limited to the faithful execution of the client's instructions, and did not entail ongoing advice. In November 1999, the district court granted the motion in part, but refused to dismiss the breach of fiduciary duty and negligence claims, citing issues of fact as to whether Bear had undertaken advisory duties notwithstanding that Kwiatkowski's account was at least nominally of the nondiscretionary kind. . . .

. . . At trial, Kwiatkowski contended that Bear had breached its duties in three ways: [1] Bear failed adequately to advise him about the unique risks inherent in his giant currency speculation; [2] Bear failed to provide him with market information and forecasts, generated by Bear personnel, that were more pessimistic about the dollar than views Kwiatkowski was hearing from others at Bear; and [3] Bear should have advised Kwiatkowski well before March 1995 to consider liquidating his position, and specifically should have advised him on Friday, March 3 to liquidate immediately rather than hold on through the weekend.

. . . Bear . . . [argued] that it had owed Kwiatkowski no duty to give advice. Bear's motion was denied. . . .

The jury found Bear liable on the negligence claim, and awarded Kwiatkowski $111.5 million in damages. It found for Bear on the breach of fiduciary duty claim, and for Sabini on both claims. . . . Bear renewed its motion for judgment as a matter of law on the negligence claim. . . .

The district denied the motion, ruling (inter alia) that the evidence supported the finding of an "entrustment of affairs" to Bear that included "substantial advisory functions," and that the services that Bear provided "embodied the full magnitude of 'handling' Kwiatkowski's accounts, with all the considerable implications that such responsibility entailed." . . .

Discussion

We must decide whether the facts of this case support the legal conclusion that Bear Stearns as broker owed its nondiscretionary customer, Kwiatkowski, a duty of reasonable care that entailed the rendering of market advice and the issuance of risk warnings on an ongoing basis. If so, we must decide whether a reasonable juror could find that Bear breached that duty.

I

. . . [A] broker ordinarily has no duty to monitor a nondiscretionary account, or to give advice to such a customer on an ongoing basis. The broker's duties ordinarily end after each transaction is done, and thus do not include a duty to offer unsolicited information, advice, or warnings concerning the customer's investments. A nondiscretionary customer by definition keeps control over the account and has full responsibility for trading decisions. On a transaction-by-transaction basis, the broker owes duties of diligence and competence in executing the client's trade orders, and is obliged to give honest and complete information when recommending a purchase or sale. The client may enjoy the broker's advice and recommendations with respect to a given trade, but has no legal claim on the broker's ongoing attention. . . .

The giving of advice triggers no ongoing duty to do so.

. . . .

III

. . . .

The claim of negligence in this case, however, presupposes an ongoing duty of reasonable care (i.e., that the broker has obligations between transactions). But in establishing a nondiscretionary account, the parties ordinarily agree and understand that the broker has narrowly defined duties that begin and end with each transaction. . . . [I]n the ordinary nondiscretionary account, the broker's failure to offer information and advice between transactions cannot constitute negligence.

. . . .

Kwiatkowski does not claim any unauthorized trading, any omission of information material to a particular transactions, any violation of government or industry regulations concerning risk disclosures at the time he opened his account, or (except for Schoenthal's advice that he not liquidate on Friday, March 3, 1995) any unsound or reckless advise. . . .

In sum, aside from the March liquidation, the claimed negligence is not in the advice that Bear gave, but in advice that Bear did not give. . . .

. . . Kwiatkowski's claim is viable . . . only if there is evidence to support his theory that Bear, notwithstanding its limited contractual duties, undertook a substantial and comprehensive advisory role giving rise to a duty on Bear's part to display the "care and skill that a reasonable broker would exercise under the circumstances."

We conclude that the district court's judgment must be reversed because there was insufficient evidence to support the finding that Bear undertook any role triggering a duty to volunteer advice and warnings between transactions, or that Bear was negligent in performing those services it did provide. Liability cannot rest on Bear's failure to give ongoing market advice that it had no duty to give, on Bear's failure to issue warnings that it had no duty to give . . . or on Bear's failure to foretell the short-term gyration of the dollar.

1. Advice

Kwiatkowski points to the advice he received from Bear, both solicited and unsolicited. . . .

But the giving of advice is an unexceptional feature of the broker-client relationship. . . . [G]iving advice on particular occasions does not alter the character of the relationship by triggering an ongoing duty to advise in the future (or between transactions) or to monitor all data potentially relevant to a customer's investment. . . .

. . . Kwiatkowski characterizes Bear's frequent giving of advice as an "undertaking" that supports a generalized duty of reasonable care to perform ongoing advisory duties not created by contract. The advisory services that Bear advertised and provided to Kwiatkowski, however, were wholly consistent with his status as a nondiscretionary customer; Kwiatkowski bargained for the expertise of the Private Client Services Group, but he simultaneously signed account agreements making clear that he was solely responsible for his own investments. It was thus obviously contemplated that Kwiatkowski would receive a lot of advice from Bear's senior economists and gurus, and that this advice would not amount to Bear's entrustment with the management of the account. It follows that Kwiatkowski cannot reasonably have believed that once he sought and Bear gave advice, Bear had become "account handler."

Any duty by Bear to offer advice therefore could arise only if the law . . . imposes on Bear some special duty as a result of the relationship between the parties—that is, if Kwiatkowski's account deviated from the usual nondiscretionary account in a way that creates a special duty beyond the ordinary duty of reasonable care that applies to a broker's actions in nondiscretionary accounts. The district court alluded to "special circumstances," in particular Kwiatkowski's outsized account, the frequency of broker contacts. . . .

These circumstances made Kwiatkowski's account special . . . but . . . not special in a way that transforms the account relationship. The transformative "special circumstances" recognized in the cases are circumstances that render the client dependent. . . . The law thus imposes additional extra-contractual duties on brokers who can take unfair advantage of their customers' incapacity or simplicity. . . .

Kwiatkowski of course is the very opposite of the naive and vulnerable client who is protected by "special circumstances." He was a special customer chiefly by reason of his vast wealth, his trading experience, his business sophistication, and his gluttonous appetite for risk. These factors weigh strongly against—and not all in favor of—heightened duties on the part of the broker. . . . We therefore conclude that the theory of "special circumstances" does not broaden the scope of Bear's undertaking.

. . . .

2. Risk

When Kwiatkowski opened his account, Bear warned him of the risks of currency trading. Kwiatkowski argues that Bear should have given further specific warnings throughout the relevant period concerning "extraordinary market and liquidity risks" posed by the size of his position, especially in conjunction with market changes and the volatility of the dollar. . . . [Kwiatkowski] grossly understates the warnings Bear in fact issued and the impact such warnings would have had on any reasonable investor, and because (even if Bear failed to give warnings it was obliged to give) as a matter of law, Kwiatkowski's trading losses were not caused by any insufficiency of warnings.

. . . Bear undertook to serve as "futures commission merchant" ("FCM") (for the trades placed on the CME) and as "OTC dealer" (for the trades placed on the over-the-counter market), and in no other capacity. Bear did not in this case contract to serve in an advisory capacity . . . and thus . . . was neither an "investment adviser" as defined by the Investment Advisers Act of 1940 nor a "commodity trading adviser" as defined by the Commodities Exchange Act. . . .

As a policy matter, it makes no sense to discourage the adoption of higher standards than the law requires by treating them as predicates for liability. Courts therefore have sensibly declined to infer legal duties from internal "house rules" or industry norms that advocated greater vigilance than otherwise required by law. . . .

Kwiatkowski can succeed therefore only if the district court was correct that some "special circumstances" justify imposing extraordinary duties on Bear. We have already explained why Kwiatkowski is the very opposite of the type of client protected by that very limited doctrine. We therefore conclude that Bear had no ongoing duty to give advice and warnings concerning his investments.

. . . .

Finally, even if one could say that Bear breached a duty to advise Kwiatkowski of certain additional risks, that breach could not (as a matter of law) have caused Kwiatkowski's losses. Kwiatkowski could have been under no illusions about his situation after January 19, 1995. In the three weeks preceding that date, he had suffered single-day losses of $112 million, $98 million, and $70 million. . . . Yet, despite these blows, he could have walked away on January 19, 1995 with a net profit of $34 million from the three months of trading. At this point . . . there was nothing that Bear could tell him about the risks that he did not know from experience.

. . . Kwiatkowski cites the failure of the firm to mail him the February 1995 Byers-Taylor report downgrading the dollar to "negative." Assuming that Kwiatkowski would have read and been influenced by the report, and assuming further that Bear was obliged to send him that particular report, this argument misconceives the nature of the risk that Kwiatkowski faced and welcomed. Kwiatkowski knew that the dollar would experience short-term "ups and downs," and he certainly knew that market liquidity was variable and that he could experience massive losses quickly. He made and lost millions of dollars virtually every day. Yet Kwiatkowski nevertheless built a position that exposed him to disaster at any moment. . . . Kwiatkowski knew . . . that even within a long-term upswing, a severe enough down-tick could wipe him out. Accordingly, it would be pure speculation to find that the delivery of one long-term forecast would have rendered Kwiatkowski risk-adverse.

Kwiatkowski also argues that he was misled concerning his ability to liquidate quickly by Schoenthal's statement that he could get out of the OTC market "on a dime." . . . There is no dispute that Schoenthal's advice was sound: The OTC market was preferable to the CME (though, as it happened, Kwiatkowski only half-followed this advice). Nothing suggests that Kwiatkowski fared worse because of this move than he would have if he had left his contracts on the CME. He could not reasonably have believed that "on a dime" meant that billions of dollars in contracts could be folded instantaneously and without loss. . . . No one could reasonably bet millions on the idea that it meant immediate liquidity all the time. . . .

3. Liquidation

Kwiatkowski's remaining argument is that Bear negligently handled the liquidation of his account in March 1995. He contends first that Bear should have advised him to liquidate no later than Wednesday, March 1, in order to avoid being forced into liquidation by margin calls over the ensuing weekend. . . . Finally, he charges negligence in Bear's advice that Friday afternoon, March 3, was a dangerous time to start liquidating.

. . . Assuming that Bear did undertake to assist Kwiatkowski and guide him through the liquidation, there is no evidence of negligence in that process. The notion that Bear negligently failed to advise a Wednesday liquidation in order to avoid a forced weekend liquidation presupposes that Bear knew that liquidation would be forced over the weekend. . . . [I]t is the nature of the markets to go up and down. Schoenthal's advice on Friday afternoon was not that Sunday would be a better time to liquidate than Friday; his advice . . . was that the market "may improve next week." . . . There is no suggestion that Schoenthal failed to exercise reasonable care in forming or expressing that view; Kwiatkowski had no reasonable basis for relying on it, if indeed he did; and the fact that Schoenthal turned out to be wrong does not imply negligence. . . . [B]rokers cannot be liable for honest opinions that turn out to be wrong. . . .

Conclusion

For the reasons stated, we reverse the judgment of the district court and remand for entry of judgment dismissing the complaint.

---

§ 13.05 Churning

Nesbit v. McNeil

United States Court of Appeals, Ninth Court
896 F.2d 380 (1990)

FERNANDEZ, Circuit Judge.

Virginia H. Nesbit and the W. Wallace Nesbit Trust ("plaintiffs") brought this action against Steve McNeil and Black & Company, Inc. ("defendants") and alleged that the defendants had churned the plaintiffs' investment accounts. Among other things, plaintiffs sought to recover for violations of the federal securities laws. . . . The jury brought in a verdict against defendants, and awarded damages in the amount of the excess commissions generated by the churning of the plaintiffs' accounts. The district court denied a motion for judgment notwithstanding the verdict, and entered judgment accordingly.

. . . .

We affirm the district court on each of these issues.

BACKGROUND FACTS

Virginia H. Nesbit was a retired school teacher and the widow of W. Wallace Nesbit, a businessman. Upon his death, Mr. Nesbit left a portfolio of securities that were rather conservative although not necessarily highly successful. Those, as well as other assets, were divided between Mrs. Nesbit and the W. Wallace Nesbit Trust ("the Trust"). Mrs. Nesbit was the trustee of the Trust. From then until 1974, the investments remained conservative and did not do very well. By 1974, there had been a significant loss of value. Mrs. Nesbit then opened accounts for herself and the Trust at Black & Company, Inc. They were opened through Steve McNeil, who was the son of a friend of Mrs. Nesbit. The equity in Mrs. Nesbit's account was then $167,463, and the equity in the Trust's account was $44,177. Mrs. Nesbit, who was not knowledgeable in these matters, told the defendants that her investment objectives for herself and the Trust were stability, income and growth. Defendants claim that she told them she wanted to recoup the losses that had been suffered previously.

Defendants then embarked on a course of conduct that extended over a period of eleven and one half years. By the time the accounts were closed out in October of 1985, the equity in Mrs. Nesbit's account was $301,711, and the equity in the Trust's account was $92,844. There can be little dispute that this was a substantial increase in value. However, the activities of defendants during those eleven and one half years are called into question in this case.

Plaintiffs have pointed out that defendants first liquidated some of the securities in plaintiffs' portfolio. Mr. McNeil then embarked on a course of trading that involve 150 issues, one thousand trades, and an overall transaction value of $4,400,000. While the plaintiffs' account values did grow by $182,915 during the period in question, the defendants' commissions came to $250,000. Moreover, the investments chosen by defendants were not the kind of investments that one would purchase if one sought a stable, income-producing portfolio. Rather, they were often speculative in nature and were not income-producing. By the time the accounts terminated, many of the investments had accrued losses.

By 1984, Mrs. Nesbit became concerned about the level of activity in the accounts. She kept in closer contact with Mr. McNeil, and the level of trading decreased, but did not end entirely. She became even more concerned in 1985. At that time she discovered losses in the portfolio when calls were made upon her by lenders to whom she had pledged certain of the securities. Her concerns increased when the handling of the accounts was questioned by Ronald Linn, an analyst at Titan Capital, and were not particularly allayed when visits with Mr. McNeil brought forth an apology and an expression of embarrassment at the list of losing stocks. All of this ultimately led to the closing of the accounts in October of 1985. [Subsequently,] plaintiffs filed this action.

. . . .

DISCUSSION

. . . [T]he principal question before us is whether plaintiffs can recover damages for churning when they have had an increase in portfolio values that exceeds the amount of commissions they were charged. . . .

Sufficiency of the Evidence

The detection and proof of churning is not a simple matter. Churning can only be identified when one considers the whole history of an account, and even then expert testimony is virtually essential. . . . As we explained in *Mihara v. Dean Witter & Co.,* 619 F.2d 814, 820–21 (9th Cir. 1980):

> When a securities broker engages in excessive trading in disregard of his customer's investment objectives for the purpose of generating commission business, the customer may hold the broker liable for churning in violation of Rule 10b-5. . . . In order to establish a claim of churning, a plaintiff must show (1) that the trading in his account was excessive in light of his investment objectives; (2) that the broker in question exercised control over the trading in the account; and (3) that the broker acted with the intent to defraud or with the willful and reckless disregard for the interests of his client.

Plaintiffs presented substantial evidence on each of these elements, as our statement of background facts has shown. This case involves a relatively unsophisticated investor, who relied upon a person in whom she had confidence—the son of a family friend—to handle her portfolio in a safe and income-generating manner. There can be little doubt that Mr. McNeil did exercise a great deal of de facto control over that account, and the mere fact that he told his client what was being done does not change that situation. This case is quite unlike *Brophy v. Redivo,* 725 F.2d 1218 (9th Cir. 1984), where the only real claim was that certain transactions had been executed without plaintiff's permission and even against her directions. Here the gravamen of the complaint is that the defendants used their position to overtrade in the account and to do so in a way that they knew did not meet the client's true investment desires and objectives. . . . In other words, there was a good deal of evidence about the relationship between the parties and Mr. McNeil's control over the account. That is underscored by Mr. McNeil's embarrassment when he was confronted with the condition of certain securities toward the end of the period. His apology showed that he had something to be embarrassed about; he was not simply executing orders at the direction of Mrs. Nesbit. In addition, the testimony of plaintiffs' expert showed that one could infer the necessary degree of scienter arising out of the handling of this account, and demonstrated that there was excessive trading.

Defendants contend that there was insufficient evidence of excessive trading in the account. Relying on this circuit's comments that expert testimony is virtually essential, defendants argue that Nesbit's expert did not present objective statistical evidence of excessive trading. In particular, they complain that the expert did not testify about a turnover ratio for the account as a whole or for an annualized period[23] and that the commission ratio[24] indicated that there was no churning.

---

[23]. The turnover ratio is the ratio of the total cost of the purchases made for the account during a given period of time to the amount invested. 2 A. BROMBERG & L. LOWENFELS, SECURITIES FRAUD AND COMMODITIES FRAUD § 5.7(322).

[24]. The commission ratio is "the ratio of the broker's commissions generated by the account to the size of the customer's investment in that account." 2 A. BROMBERG & L. LOWENFELS, SECURITIES FRAUD AND COMMODITIES FRAUD § 5.7(322).

Although courts often rely on the turnover ratio and commission ratio to indicate excessive trading, no single factor or test identifies excessive trading. *See* 2 A. Bromberg & L. Lowenfels, *Securities Fraud and Commodities Fraud* § 5.7(310) & (322). Certainly these ratios can make the presence of excessive trading fairly obvious. However, that does not mean that lower ratios will preclude a finding of excessive trading.

Here, Mr. Olson testified that in his expert opinion the 1,000 trades, the high amount of commission compared to the value of the account, the volume of trading, and the presence of losing stock that had been held for some time all pointed toward an improper handling of this account, considering the investment objectives of the client. While defendants have presented evidence and arguments to the contrary, we are in no position to say that the jury improperly found against them on this record. We will not second guess the jury's determination of the facts, where, as here, the evidence is in conflict and there is substantial evidence to support the jury's decision.

. . . .

The Measurement of Damages

As we have already noted, defendants obtained commissions of $250,000 from the plaintiffs. The jury found that $134,000 of that constituted excess commissions. At the same time, the value of plaintiffs' accounts increased in the sum of $182,915. Defendants claimed below, and continue to claim, that the plaintiffs' portfolio gain should be offset against the plaintiffs' commission loss, as a result of which plaintiffs can recover no damages whatever. The district court disagreed, and gave the following instruction to the jury: "If you find that the plaintiffs have proven their claims for churning, excessive trading, plaintiffs may recover as damages any commissions they paid as a result of the churning in excess of commissions that would have been reasonable on transactions during the pertinent time period." The district court did not go on to instruct the jury that it could then offset the trading gains against those commission losses. We agree with the district court.

We begin with the rather straightforward principle announced in *Mihara v. Dean Witter & Co., Inc.*, 619 F.2d at 826, where we said that, "While damages for churning are limited to commissions and interest, plaintiff's claim as to the suitability of the securities purchased would also encompass trading losses." As the Fifth Circuit Court of Appeals explained in *Miley v. Oppenheimer & Co., Inc.*, 637 F.2d at 326, there are two separate and distinct possible harms when an account has been churned, and those are:

> First, and perhaps foremost, the investor is harmed by having had to pay the excessive commissions to the broker. . . . Second, the investor is harmed by the decline in the value of his portfolio . . . as a result of the broker's having intentionally and deceptively concluded transactions, aimed at generating fees, which were unsuitable for the investor. The intentional and deceptive mismanagement of a client's account, resulting in a decline in the value of

that portfolio, constitutes a compensable violation of both the federal securities laws and the broker's common law fiduciary duty, regardless of the amount of the commissions paid to the broker.

In the case at hand, the plaintiffs only suffered one of those harms, but there is no reason to find that they should be denied a recovery because their portfolio increased in value, either because of or in spite of the activities of the defendants.

. . . .

Therefore, we must reject defendants' assault on the damage award in this case.

. . . .

CONCLUSION

We have been presented with the rather unusual case of plaintiffs whose portfolios increased while under the guidance and control of the defendants, and who still chose to bring an action to recover commissions that they had paid to those same defendants.

The jury before which this case was tried could have decided that defendants were perfectly honest brokers, who were being victimized by rather greedy clients. The jury did not do so. Instead, it found that plaintiffs were indeed wronged by the defendants' churning of the accounts. That determination was supported by substantial evidence. . . .

As a result, the defendants were properly required to disgorge the inappropriate portion of their commissions, even if the portfolio itself increased in value, since, as we have shown, issues regarding the performance of the portfolio are separate from issues related to excess commissions. . . .

AFFIRMED.

Note

For commentary on the shingle and related theories, *see* N. Poser & J. Fanto, Broker-Dealer Law and Regulation (4th ed. 2016); Karmel, *Is the Shingle Theory Dead?*, 52 Wash. & Lee L. Rev. 1271 (1995); Langevoort, *Fraud and Deception by Securities Professionals*, 61 Tex. L. Rev. 1247 (1983); Poser, *Liability of Broker-Dealers for Unsuitable Recommendations to Institutional Investors*, 2001 BYU L. Rev. 1493 (2001); Ramirez, *The Professional Obligations of Securities Brokers Under Federal Law: An Antidote for Bubbles?*, 70 U. Cin. L. Rev. 527 (2002); Scott, *A Broker-Dealer's Civil Liability to Investors for Fraud: An Implied Private Right of Action Under Section 15(c)(1) of the Securities Exchange Act of 1934*, 63 Ind. L.J. 687 (1988); Winslow & Anderson, *A Model for Determining the Excessive Trading Element in Churning Claims*, 68 N. Car. L. Rev. 327 (1990).

---

§ 13.06 The "Dramshop" Cases

Puckett v. Rufenacht, Bromagen & Hertz, Inc.

Supreme Court of Mississippi
587 So. 2d 273 (1991)

Hawkins, Presiding Justice, for the Court:

Under the provisions of Rule 20 of the Mississippi Supreme Court Rules, the United States Court of Appeals, Fifth Circuit, has by certificate of November 14, 1990, certified questions of law to this Court following its decision in *Puckett v. Rufenacht, Bromagen & Hertz, Inc.*, 903 F.2d 1014 (1990). . . .

FACTS

Read in the light most favorable to the Pucketts, Rufenacht, Bromagen & Hertz, Inc. (RB & H), a Chicago-based commodity brokerage firm, operates a branch office in Hattiesburg, where the Pucketts reside. Dr. Puckett is a retired pathologist who successfully ran his own pathology lab in Hattiesburg, with gross revenues of $8,000,000 per year.

Dr. Puckett had continuously traded some form of securities from 1955–56 to 1984. He had previously traded commodities on two occasions. He traded with Merrill Lynch in the late 1950's or early 1960's and lost about $40,000. He also traded for a couple of weeks with Paine Webber in mid-1984 and lost about $1,000.

The Pucketts learned of RB & H in July, 1984, at a dinner party. Roger Parker, the manager of the Hattiesburg branch of RB&H, made a presentation about trading commodities in order to acquire customers. Both of the Pucketts opened accounts. They filled out applications on which they stated the amount of risk capital available for commodities trading as $25,000 (for Dr. Puckett) and $15,000 (for Ms. Puckett). Both Dr. and Mrs. Puckett signed Risk Disclosure Statements before they traded. Both Pucketts acknowledged by signing that they "examined this document and underst[ood] fully the advice contained therein."

These statements informed the Pucketts of the substantial risk in futures tradings. . . .

The Pucketts' accounts were nondiscretionary. In other words, they made all the trading decisions themselves—RB & H could not make unauthorized trades on their behalf. Dr. Puckett spent several days each week at RB & H's offices where he used a quote machine and a news service provided on a screen. He also received comments from the floor of the Chicago Mercantile Exchange. Dr. Puckett regularly received statements (confirmation slips and monthly account statement) which he reviewed.

According to his own deposition testimony and affidavits, Dr. Puckett understood the risks of trading commodity futures contracts. Dr. Puckett knew that a risk accompanied every trade and that he had to incur this potential risk in order to reap the potential rewards of large gains. . . . Initially, Dr. Puckett was unaware of how quickly the S & P 500 Index could move in a day, but he became aware of this risk when he lost $65,000 trading this contract in one day. He continued after learning of this risk.

Dr. Puckett had both successful and unsuccessful trades throughout the thirty-eight months he traded with RB & H. Parker testified that he never tried to influence Puckett in his choice of trades. Dr. Puckett agreed and testified that the initial idea for each of his trades was his own. Parker always properly carried out Dr. Puckett's orders. Puckett could not identify any statements made or information provided by Parker which was untrue. Dr. Puckett believed that any advice which Parker gave about trades was in good faith, even if it didn't pan out. . . .

The initial risk figures of $25,000 and $15,000 which the Pucketts listed in their customer applications became unimportant to Dr. Puckett once he began trading and he decided to risk more money as time went on. Dr. Puckett knew his losses on the day they were incurred. He generally covered those losses with a check that afternoon or the next morning.

Dr. Puckett occasionally liquidated securities at another firm to cover his losses. On those occasions, RB & H always waited the five days it took the security transaction to clear before cashing his check. Eventually, Dr. Puckett began liquidating his pension plan to cover his commodity trading losses. The checks did not indicate the source of funds and Dr. Puckett never informed Parker that he was funding his losses by liquidating his pension fund.

Dr. Puckett knew that RB & H received a commission for each trade he made. His monthly account statements showed those amounts.

Dr. Puckett quit trading in September, 1987, on the advice of his son. His accountant had informed his son of the state of Dr. Puckett's finances. Dr. Puckett's son told him to stop. By this time, Dr. Puckett had lost over $2,000,000. Dr. Puckett told Parker he was quitting because he had lost enough. He made no complaints about the way his account was handled and promptly paid his last loss.

Thereafter, the Pucketts brought suit to recover trading losses, punitive damages and attorneys' fees. . . .

In response to RB & H's motion for summary judgment, the Pucketts submitted (by affidavit and deposition) the testimony of three expert witnesses (Jordan, Cullen and Giacona) expressing their opinion that Dr. Puckett traded too many different commodities, and he was not adequately informed and experienced to trade S & P futures contracts, that his trading volumes were so high as to be irrational, that he had no trading plan, and there was an extremely high probability that he would lose all he had if he was allowed to continue trading. The experts expressed their opinion that industry standards required a commodities broker to intervene to advise or require a customer such as Dr. Puckett to discontinue trading commodities. According to the experts, by the time RB & H allowed Dr. Puckett to trade S & P futures, Dr. Puckett had already demonstrated that he was unfit to trade any commodity futures, much less S & P futures. The experts concluded that RB & H's actions in permitting and encouraging Dr. Puckett's continued trading—after he had lost substantial sums of money and after RB & H should have recognized the facts demonstrating his unsuitability to trade commodities—violated standards of conduct and the minimum standard of care generally recognized and accepted in the commodities industry.

The trial judge held for RB & H on each of these counts and dismissed the Pucketts' suit with prejudice.

The Court of Appeals affirmed the trial court's disposition on the fraud issues and certified the following question of state law to this Court:

1. Under Mississippi law, what duty of care does a commodities broker owe to a commodities customer in a nondiscretionary account?

   (a) is the duty only properly to execute trades as directed by the customer, or

   (b) is the commodities broker required to exercise that degree of care which a commodities broker of ordinary professional skill and prudence would exercise under similar circumstances?

2. Under Mississippi law, does a fiduciary duty exist between a commodities broker and a commodities customer with a nondiscretionary account? If so, does that duty extend to require a commodities broker to:

   (a) advise a customer to discontinue trading if the commodities broker knows or has reason to know that the customer is trading excessively and irrationally, or

   (b) that the customer lacks the experience and ability to trade the commodities which he is trading, or

   (c) that the customer has already incurred losses which are very high in proportion to the customer's net worth, so that there is a high probability that the customer will lose his entire net worth if he continues to trade commodities. . . .

. . . .

From the facts related by the Court of Appeals, the following [are] uncontradicted:

1. In 1984 at a dinner party attended by the Pucketts, there was a sales pitch by Parker, a representative of RB & H, on futures trading.

2. At that time Dr. Puckett could be accurately characterized as a good businessman with some experience in securities investment and futures trading.

3. The Pucketts were warned before engaging in futures trading by RB & H by a written statement, signed and understood by them, of the substantial risk they were undertaking in futures trading.

4. No person attempted to sell the Pucketts any futures. No person sought to induce them to enter into any of the great number of futures contracts they entered from 1984 until September, 1987, when Dr. Puckett ceased trading in futures.

5. The Pucketts were not asked to trust or put any faith in any employee of RB & H, except to carry out Dr. Puckett's instructions.

6. Dr. Puckett knew his wins and losses each day.

7. Each transaction, each trade in which RB & H was the broker, and there were perhaps hundreds of them, was a separate and distinct contract. The only interest RB & H had in any of these contracts was that of a broker, receiving a commission from each transaction.

In sum, Dr. Puckett's trading objective was to make profits as a speculator in the commodity markets. He never asked Parker whether particular trades or particular trading strategies were suitable for him in terms of his age, financial needs and investment objectives. Nor did Dr. Puckett ever ask Parker for advice on where he should get the funds to use for trading commodity futures, or whether he should lessen his trading at RB & H. Dr. Puckett neither asked for nor was he given any advice or counseling on his trading tactics and strategies, nor is there anything in the related facts suggesting that he ever expected to receive any advice on the wisdom of any trade.

The only sin the defendants can be accused of committing is standing by while Dr. Puckett committed fiscal hara-kiri. It is equally clear and uncontradicted that no representative of RB & H uttered one word of warning or caution as to any of his trades. In view of the Jordan, Cullen and Giacona affidavits, and for purposes of our analysis, we will assume RB & H had reason to believe Dr. Puckett was, at times at least, trading quite foolishly.

The crux of the inquiry to us is whether RB & H can be held liable to the Pucketts under the common law of this State based upon Parker's and its total silence and passivity during Dr. Puckett's protracted self-immolation.

One word encompasses all the grandeur and majesty of western civilization. That word is "freedom." This, of course, is well known to any student of history. Not as well recognized, but equally true is that the absolute concomitant of freedom is responsibility; the former cannot exist unaccompanied by the latter. They are different sides of the same coin.

The laws of the universe do not forgive mistakes. Every cause must have certain effects. Whether motivated by the best or worst intention, a decision is going to have certain consequences. If it was a mistake, someone must suffer.

If a society is to be free, it must demand of every person who, completely on his own, makes a mistake that he has no legal right to shift from his shoulders onto another's the suffering it causes. In our modern society, en masse we are our brothers' keepers; we pay taxes for schools, highways, public health and hundreds of other public programs. On an individual basis, however, no man should be required by law to pay for what was solely and purely another man's mistake.

It may be morally reprehensible for one man to watch another open a window on the twentieth floor of a skyscraper, climb through it and jump out, when he could easily have reached out and stopped him. To impose a legal responsibility upon the bystander to stop him, however, is an entirely different matter.

THE PUCKETTS' ACCOUNT

The Pucketts' account with RB & H was a nondiscretionary account.

A discretionary account is one in which the broker himself on behalf of the investor customer makes and enters into futures contracts. A nondiscretionary account is one in which by definition, the broker is only expected to faithfully carry out the instructions of the customer.

By its very nature, a broker in a discretionary account is a fiduciary in his treatment of his customer's funds to properly advise and properly invest. On the other hand, while a broker in a nondiscretionary account as his customer's agent obviously has a fiduciary duty to properly carry out his customer principal's instructions, ordinarily his fiduciary duty ends there. He has no further duty to advise or counsel as to the wisdom of his customer's trades.

Under the general law from other jurisdictions, the answer to the first question is that a commodities broker in a nondiscretionary account only owes his customer the duty to properly execute trades as directed by him, and has no further duty to call upon his own professional skill and prudence as to the wisdom of any of his customer's trades.

Likewise, from other jurisdictions, the commodities broker has none of the fiduciary duties encompassed in the second certified question to a nondiscretionary account customer.

We believe the decisions from other jurisdictions are sound and their pronounced principles should apply in this state as well. Dr. Puckett over a period of several years no doubt entered into several hundred futures contracts, each of them separate and distinct. He gave instructions to RB & H in turn entered into the contract precisely as instructed, and charged its commission. Having done so, its contractual duty to Dr. Puckett ended there. It was not legally required to offer an umbrella of professional wisdom between contracts, detect a pattern, and advise him as to any futures trade. Nothing in the related facts suggests that RB & H entered into any kind of contractual obligation to professionally advise or warn Dr. Puckett in any way, or that Dr. Puckett understood RB & H to have such an obligation. . . .

THE DIFFICULT QUESTION

There is a more difficult question arising from the facts of this case as related to us, one not specifically asked by the Court of Appeals, but raised by the Pucketts in their brief, and which presents this Court with a dilemma as to whether we should answer it or not.

The question is, conceding the general rule of law that a commodities broker in a nondiscretionary account only owes his customer the duty to properly carry out his instructions, would a custom or standard of the commodities brokers to warn customers who in their professional judgment are making imprudent and foolish futures trades increase the legal duty owed the Pucketts in this case? Conceding the accuracy of the affidavits of Jordan, Cullen and Giacona filed by the Pucketts, there is such a custom or standard recognized by the commodities brokers.

To begin with, there is nothing in the related facts which suggests that the Pucketts knew of any such custom or standard, and therefore did not enter into any of their futures contracts under any assumption of its existence. The Pucketts never understood or believed RB & H had any such contractual or fiduciary obligation resulting from such a custom or standard, because there is nothing in the related facts to suggest they even knew of it. When Dr. Puckett began his course of trading through RB & H, there is nothing to suggest that in his mind he knew or believed this brokerage house had some duty under some trade custom or standard to warn him as to his improvidence. . . .

. . . .

Courts from other jurisdictions have rejected claims similar to the Pucketts seeking damages based solely upon a brokerage firm's in-house rules or a trade custom to warn customer investors of imprudent investments. Such rules "were never intended to protect [the investor] from his own greed, as plaintiff seems to suggest." Instead, they "are designed to protect the broker from being saddled with losses which the investor is not able to cover, as was ultimately the case here." If the violation of the in-house rule or custom were accompanied by fraud, the rule would be otherwise. . . .

We therefore conclude that the trade custom and standard of care elucidated in the Jordan, Cullen and Giacona affidavits, did not increase the duty RB & H owed the Pucketts in this case.

. . . .

PITTMAN, Justice, dissenting:

Believing that the limited fiduciary duty of a commodities broker includes a duty of ordinary care and a duty of loyalty to a customer of a nondiscretionary account, I respectfully dissent.

I first address the extent of a broker's duty to a customer of a nondiscretionary account. I agree with Justice Hawkins that the general law from other jurisdictions is that the duty is a very limited one. Some jurisdictions have found that there is no fiduciary duty unless there are special circumstances or a contract providing such. The Colorado Supreme Court explained that the stockbroker/customer relationship is not per se fiduciary in nature unless there is proof of practical control of a customer's account by a broker. . . . Likewise, the Wisconsin Supreme Court has found that even a broker who provides advice and counsel to a customer with a nondiscretionary account does not have a fiduciary duty to that customer. . . . Other jurisdictions have also refused to impose a fiduciary duty in the case of nondiscretionary accounts. . . .

. . . .

Other jurisdictions have found that there is a fiduciary duty, but only to properly execute trades as directed. In *Index Futures Group, Inc. v. Ross*, 199 Ill. App.3d 468, 145 Ill. Dec. 574, 557 N.E.2d 344 (Ill. App. 1 Dist. 1990), an appellate court of Illinois found that the duty of care owed by a broker carrying a nondiscretionary account for a customer is an exceedingly narrow one, consisting at most of a duty to properly carry out transactions ordered by the customer. And Illinois courts have explained that a commodities broker is the agent of his customer, at least with regard to the execution of a transaction; and, as such, as a matter of law, he owes his customer certain fiduciary duties within the realm of the execution of the transaction. The fiduciary relationship depends on circumstances peculiar to a particular case. Proper execution of trades is the only duty generally imposed upon a commodities broker on a nondiscretionary account.

Clearly in the minority, California has adopted a broadened fiduciary duty of care owed by brokers to all customers, regardless of who controls the account. This duty requires more than merely carrying out the stated objectives of the customer. It can include informing the customer if the orders are improper and unsuitable. *Duffy v. Cavalier*, 259 Cal. Rptr. 162, 171, 210 Cal. App.3d 1514 (Cal. App. 1 Dist. 1989). I am persuaded by the California view.

Recognizing the general law of other jurisdictions, I would follow one of the following two alternatives:

1. If we adopt the majority view of other jurisdictions that there is only a limited duty of a broker to a customer to properly execute trades as directed, I would find that this is one of the "special circumstances" in which the duty should be broadened to include regular assessment of the customer's resources and subsequent financial counsel. Because of Dr. Puckett's advanced age, substantial losses ($65,000 in one day included in a total loss of over $2,000,000 in thirty-eight months), and lack of experience, and because RB & H knew of Dr. Puckett's actions each day since RB & H provided him a desk, quote machine, comments from the floor of the Chicago Mercantile Exchange, and news service screen in the RB & H facility which he used several days each week to make trades, RB & H should have counseled with Dr. Puckett. This is a "special circumstance" in which RB & H owed at least a duty of ordinary care or a limited fiduciary duty.

2. Or, alternatively, I would prefer to see this Court draft its own law rather than adopt the reasoning of other jurisdictions. Since Mississippi law is silent as to the duty of a commodities broker, I would find that even though a broker's duties to a customer of a nondiscretionary account are minimal, such broker does have a duty of ordinary care and loyalty which includes regular assessment of the customer's resources and subsequent financial counseling regarding margin requirements for commodity futures trading accounts with the accompanying risks of liquidation of an undermargined account and liability for account deficits possibly far in excess of the total of margin deposits. Transactions in commodity futures entail a high degree of financial risk,

and even where the account is nondiscretionary and the customer signs a risk disclosure statement containing an acknowledgment of the risk, a broker who is earning a fee from the customer's orders should regularly ascertain the suitability of a customer to make investments, especially where the customer has a lack of experience. The customer of a nondiscretionary account can then exercise independent judgment and take responsibility for all trading decisions. The broker can make an effort to see that the decisions made by the customer, whether wise or unwise, are at least informed decisions.

RB & H should have consulted with Dr. Puckett to find out if he could sustain such losses and how he was covering the losses. (Dr. Puckett was funding his losses by liquidating his pension fund.) RB & H should have then discussed courses of action. At this point, Dr. Puckett could exercise his own judgment and control over his nondiscretionary account. Experts at the trial concluded that RB & H's actions violated standards of conduct and the minimum standard of care generally recognized and accepted in the commodities industry. I conclude that a broker should have a legal duty of care toward all customers. A commodities broker should have a duty to advise a customer to discontinue trading if the broker knows or has reason to know that the customer lacks the experience and ability to trade the commodities which he is trading, or that the customer has already incurred losses which are very high in proportion to the customer's net worth so that there is a high probability that the customer will lose his entire net worth if he continues to trade commodities. A commodities broker should be required to exercise that degree of care which a commodities broker of ordinary professional skill and prudence would exercise under similar circumstances. . . . RB & H did not fulfill this duty.

For an insightful article on this issue, see Smith, *Rethinking a Broker's Legal Objections to Its Customers — The Dramshop Cases*, 30 Sec. Reg. L.J. 51 (2002).

---

§ 13.07 Defenses

Hecht v. Harris, Upham & Co.

United States Court of Appeals, Ninth Circuit
430 F.2d 1202 (1970)

POWELL, Judge.

The cross appeals by Harris, Upham & Co., Harris, Upham & Co., Inc. (appellants), and Mrs. Bertha Hecht (appellee) are from a judgment of the District Court awarding appellee $504,391.02. . . .

In January 1955 Mr. Hecht died leaving an estate of securities to his wife, the appellee, of a net value of $508,532.00. Shortly after Mr. Hecht's death, but before distribution of the estate, a close business and social relationship was formed between Mrs. Hecht and an investment broker, Mr. Asa Wilder (co-defendant below). Mrs. Hecht transferred her separate securities account (net value $42,000) from Walston & Co. to Hooker & Fay, with whom Wilder was then employed. When her husband's estate was distributed to Mrs. Hecht it was likewise placed with Hooker & Fay. In May 1957 Wilder left Hooker & Fay to become a Representative and Commodities Manager of Harris, Upham & Co. at their San Francisco office. The Hecht account, valued at about $533,161.00, was then transferred to appellants.

The account remained with Harris, Upham & Co. until March 1964 when Mrs. Hecht's tax consultants advised her that the account was substantially depleted. At that time the account had a net value of about $251,308.00. Suit was later commenced in District Court against Wilder and Harris, Upham & Co. and others for alleged violations of [the securities laws].

. . . .

WAIVER, LACHES AND ESTOPPEL

This Court held in *Royal Air Properties, Inc. v. Smith*, 312 F.2d 210 (9th Cir. 1962), that since civil liability was judicially implied from violations of Section 10(b), estoppel, waiver and laches should be applicable. It was there stated that "[t]he purpose of the Securities Exchange Act is to protect the innocent investor, not one who loses his innocence and then waits to see how his investment turns out before he decides to invoke the provisions of the Act."

The District Court in the instant case found that:

> All during the course of the account, plaintiff regularly received from Harris, Upham the customary confirmation slips showing each security or commodity transaction as made and requesting immediate notice of any error. She also received from Harris, Upham the customary monthly statements of her account.

> It was the practice of Wilder to be in contact with plaintiff by telephone concerning her account almost every morning of the business week, and also to visit her at her home at least weekly and sometimes several times a week. Also, plaintiff would often telephone Wilder at his office during the day.

> It was the practice of plaintiff to put her confirmation slips on a table in her home, 'separating the buys from the sells', in order to discuss them with Wilder. After the discussions, Wilder would gather up the confirmation slips and statements and take them to his home—although he had duplicates for his own use at the office.

> During the period of the account plaintiff had her own income tax accountants with whom she consulted concerning her personal tax deductions. Wilder supplied schedules to these income tax accountants, which indicated plaintiff's capital gains and losses arising out of her securities transactions. Plaintiff was also represented on occasion by attorneys—including

representation by able and reputable counsel, recommended by Wilder in connection with the distribution of her husband's estate. . . .

The requirements of estoppel are:

> Four elements must be present to establish the defense of estoppel: (1) The party to be estopped must know the facts; (2) he must intend that his conduct shall be acted on or must so act that the party asserting the estoppel has a right to believe it is so intended; (3) the latter must be ignorant of the true facts; and (4) he must rely on the former's conduct to his injury.

To invoke laches as a defense there must be (1) a lack of diligence by the party against whom the defense is asserted, and (2) prejudice to the party asserting the defense. . . . Where these elements are present, the damage to the party asserting the damage is caused by his detrimental reliance on his adversary's conduct. . . .

The waiver of a legal right is "the voluntary or intentional relinquishment of a known right. It emphasizes the mental attitude of the actor." . . .

Although the trial court's opinion does not specifically conclude that plaintiff intentionally relinquished a known right, it is apparent that the opinion contains findings necessary for the application of estoppel and laches to the facts of this case.

To have these findings upset on appeal it must be shown that they are "clearly erroneous" within the meaning of Rule 52(a), Fed. R. Civ. P. . . .

A review of the record does not disclose that the findings are "clearly erroneous". They will not be disturbed on this appeal.

. . . .

Bateman Eichler, Hill Richards, Inc. v. Berner

United States Supreme Court

472 U.S. 299, 105 S. Ct. 2622, 86 L. Ed. 2d 215 (1985)

[This case is contained in § 8.09[C].]

---

§ 13.08 Investment Adviser Fees

Jones v. Harris Associates L.P.

United States Supreme Court

559 U.S. 335, 130 S. Ct. 1418, 176 L. Ed. 2d 265 (2010)

Justice Alito delivered the opinion of the Court.

We consider in this case what a mutual fund shareholder must prove in order to show that a mutual fund investment adviser breached the "fiduciary duty with respect to the receipt of compensation for services" that is imposed by § 36(b) of the Investment Company Act of 1940, 15 U.S.C. § 80a-35(b) (hereinafter § 36(b)).

I

A

The Investment Company Act of 1940 (Act) . . . regulates investment companies, including mutual funds. "A mutual fund is a pool of assets, consisting primarily of [a] portfolio [of] securities, and belonging to the individual investors holding shares in the fund." *Burks v. Lasker,* 441 U.S. 471, 480 (1979). The following arrangements are typical. A separate entity called an investment adviser creates the mutual fund, which may have no employees of its own. The adviser selects the fund's directors, manages the fund's investments, and provides other services. Because of the relationship between a mutual fund and its investment adviser, the fund often " 'cannot, as a practical matter sever its relationship with the adviser. Therefore the forces of arm's-length bargaining do not work in the mutual fund industry in the same manner as they do in other sectors of the American economy.' ". . .

"Congress adopted the [Investment Company Act of 1940] because of its concern with the potential for abuse inherent in the structure of investment companies." *Daily Income Fund,* 464 U.S. [523, 536 (1984)]. Recognizing that the relationship between a fund and its investment adviser was "fraught with potential conflicts of interest," the Act created protections for mutual fund shareholders. Among other things, the Act required that no more than 60 percent of a fund's directors could be affiliated with the adviser and that fees for investment advisers be approved by the directors and the shareholders of the fund. . . .

The growth of mutual funds in the 1950's and 1960's prompted studies of the 1940 Act's effectiveness in protecting investors. Studies commissioned or authored by the Securities and Exchange Commission (SEC or Commission) identified problems relating to the independence of investment company boards and the compensation received by investment advisers. In response to such concerns, Congress amended the Act in 1970 and bolstered shareholder protection in two primary ways.

First, the amendments strengthened the "cornerstone" of the Act's efforts to check conflicts of interest, the independence of mutual fund boards of directors, which negotiate and scrutinize adviser compensation. The amendments required that no more than 60 percent of a fund's directors be "persons who are interested persons," *e.g.,* that they have no interest in or affiliation with the investment adviser.[25] . . .

---

[25]. An "affiliated person" includes (1) a person who owns, controls, or holds the power to vote 5 percent or more of the securities of the investment adviser; (2) an entity which the investment adviser owns, controls, or in which it holds the power to vote more than 5 percent of the securities; (3) any person directly or indirectly controlling, controlled by, or under common control with the investment adviser; (4) an officer, director, partner, copartner, or employee of the investment adviser; (5) an investment adviser or a member of the investment adviser's board of directors; or (6) the depositor of an unincorporated investment adviser. *See* § 80a-2(a)(3). The

These board members are given "a host of special responsibilities." . . . In particular, they must "review and approve the contracts of the investment adviser" annually, and a majority of these directors must approve an adviser's compensation. . . . Second, § 36(b) of the Act imposed upon investment advisers a "fiduciary duty" with respect to compensation received from a mutual fund, 15 U.S.C. § 80a-35(b), and granted individual investors a private right of action for breach of that duty. . . .

The "fiduciary duty" standard contained in § 36(b) represented a delicate compromise. Prior to the adoption of the 1970 amendments, shareholders challenging investment adviser fees under state law were required to meet "common-law standards of corporate waste, under which an unreasonable or unfair fee might be approved unless the court deemed it 'unconscionable' or 'shocking,' " and "security holders challenging adviser fees under the [Investment Company Act] itself had been required to prove gross abuse of trust." *Daily Income Fund*, 464 U.S., at 540, n. 12. Aiming to give shareholders a stronger remedy, the SEC proposed a provision that would have empowered the Commission to bring actions to challenge a fee that was not "reasonable" and to intervene in any similar action brought by or on behalf of an investment company. This approach was included in a bill that passed the House. H. R. 9510, 90th Cong., 1st Sess., § 8(d) (1967); see also S. 1659, 90th Cong., 1st Sess., § 8(d) (1967). Industry representatives, however, objected to this proposal, fearing that it "might in essence provide the Commission with ratemaking authority." *Daily Income Fund*, 464 U.S., at 538.

The provision that was ultimately enacted adopted "a different method of testing management compensation," *id.*, at 539 (quoting S. Rep., at 5 (internal quotation marks omitted)), that was more favorable to shareholders than the previously available remedies but that did not permit a compensation agreement to be reviewed in court for "reasonableness." This is the fiduciary duty standard in § 36(b).

B

Petitioners are shareholders in three different mutual funds managed by respondent Harris Associates L.P., an investment adviser. Petitioners filed this action in the Northern District of Illinois pursuant to § 36(b) seeking damages, an injunction, and rescission of advisory agreements between Harris Associates and the mutual funds. The complaint alleged that Harris Associates had violated § 36(b) by charging fees that were "disproportionate to the services rendered" and "not within the range of what would have been negotiated at arm's length in light of all the surrounding circumstances."

The District Court granted summary judgment for Harris Associates. Applying the standard adopted in *Gartenberg v. Merrill Lynch Asset Management, Inc.*, 694 F.2d

---

Act defines "interested person" to include not only all affiliated persons but also a wider swath of people such as the immediate family of affiliated persons, interested persons, of an underwriter or investment adviser, legal counsel for the company, and interested broker-dealers. § 80a-2(a)(19).

923 (CA2 1982), the court concluded that petitioners had failed to raise a triable issue of fact as to "whether the fees charged . . . were so disproportionately large that they could not have been the result of arm's-length bargaining." The District Court assumed that it was relevant to compare the challenged fees with those that Harris Associates charged its other clients. But in light of those comparisons as well as comparisons with fees charged by other investment advisers to similar mutual funds, the Court held that it could not reasonably be found that the challenged fees were outside the range that could have been the product of arm's-length bargaining.

A panel of the Seventh Circuit affirmed based on different reasoning, explicitly "disapprov[ing] the *Gartenberg* approach." 527 F.3d 627, 632 (2008). Looking to trust law, the panel noted that, while a trustee "owes an obligation of candor in negotiation," a trustee, at the time of the creation of a trust, "may negotiate in his own interest and accept what the settlor or governance institution agrees to pay." *Ibid.* (citing Restatement (Second) of Trusts § 242, and Comment *f*)). The panel thus reasoned that "[a] fiduciary duty differs from rate regulation. A fiduciary must make full disclosure and play no tricks but is not subject to a cap on compensation." 527 F.3d, at 632. In the panel's view, the amount of an adviser's compensation would be relevant only if the compensation were "so unusual" as to give rise to an inference "that deceit must have occurred, or that the persons responsible for [the] decision have abdicated." . . .

The panel argued that this understanding of § 36(b) is consistent with the forces operating in the contemporary mutual fund market. Noting that "[t]oday thousands of mutual funds compete," the panel concluded that "sophisticated investors" shop for the funds that produce the best overall results, "mov[e] their money elsewhere" when fees are "excessive in relation to the results," and thus "create a competitive pressure" that generally keeps fees low. The panel faulted *Gartenberg* on the ground that it "relies too little on markets." . . . And the panel firmly rejected a comparison between the fees that Harris Associates charged to the funds and the fees that Harris Associates charged other types of clients, observing that "[d]ifferent clients call for different commitments of time" and that costs, such as research, that may benefit several categories of clients "make it hard to draw inferences from fee levels." . . .

The Seventh Circuit denied rehearing en banc by an equally divided vote. 537 F.3d 728 (2008). The dissent from the denial of rehearing argued that the panel's rejection of *Gartenberg* was based "mainly on an economic analysis that is ripe for reexamination." 537 F.3d, at 730 (opinion of Posner, J.). Among other things, the dissent expressed concern that Harris Associates charged "its captive funds more than twice what it charges independent funds," and the dissent questioned whether high adviser fees actually drive investors away.

We granted certiorari to resolve a split among the Courts of Appeals over the proper standard under § 36(b).

II

A

Since Congress amended the Investment Company Act in 1970, the mutual fund industry has experienced exponential growth. Assets under management increased from $38.2 billion in 1966 to over $9.6 trillion in 2008. The number of mutual fund investors grew from 3.5 million in 1965 to 92 million in 2008, and there are now more than 9,000 open- and closed-end funds.

During that time, the standard for an investment adviser's fiduciary duty has remained an open question in our Court, but, until the Seventh Circuit's decision below, something of a consensus had developed regarding the standard set forth over 25 years ago in *Gartenberg*. . . . The *Gartenberg* standard has been adopted by other federal courts, and "[t]he SEC's regulations have recognized and formalized, *Gartenberg*-like factors." . . . In the present case, both petitioners and respondent generally endorse the *Gartenberg* approach, although they disagree in some respects about its meaning.

In *Gartenberg*, the Second Circuit noted that Congress had not defined what it meant by a "fiduciary duty" with respect to compensation but concluded that "the test is essentially whether the fee schedule represents a charge within the range of what would have been negotiated at arm's-length in the light of all the surrounding circumstances." 694 F.2d, at 928. The Second Circuit elaborated that, "[t]o be guilty of a violation of § 36(b), . . . the adviser-manager must charge a fee that is so disproportionately large that it bears no reasonable relationship to the services rendered and could not have been the product of arm's-length bargaining." . . . "To make this determination," the Court stated, "all pertinent facts must be weighed," and the Court specifically mentioned "the adviser-manager's cost in providing the service, . . . the extent to which the adviser-manager realizes economies of scale as the fund grows larger, and the volume of orders with must be processed by the manager." Other factors cited by the *Gartenberg* court include (1) the nature and quality of the services provided to the fund and shareholders; (2) the profitability of the fund to the adviser; (3) any "fall-out financial benefits"—those collateral benefits that accrue to the adviser because of its relationship with the mutual fund; (4) comparative fee structure (meaning a comparison of the fees with those paid by similar funds); and (5) the independence, expertise, care, and conscientiousness of the board in evaluating adviser compensation. . . .[26] Observing that competition among advisers for the business of managing a fund may be "virtually non-existent," the Court rejected the suggestion that "the principal factor to be considered in evaluating a fee's fairness is the price charged by other similar advisers to funds managed by them," although the Court did not suggest that this factor could not be "taken into account." The [*Gartenberg*] Court likewise rejected the "argument that the lower fees charged by investment advisers to large pension funds should be used as a criterion for

---

[26]. [This footnote has been moved to the text.]

determining fair advisory fees for money market funds," since a "pension fund does not face the myriad of daily purchases and redemptions throughout the nation which must be handled by [a money market fund]." . . .[27]

B

The meaning of §36(b)'s reference to "a fiduciary duty with respect to the receipt of compensation for services"[28] is hardly pellucid, but based on the terms of that provision and the role that a shareholder action for breach of that duty plays in the overall structure of the Act, we conclude that *Gartenberg* was correct in its basic formulation of what §36(b) requires: to face liability under §36(b), an investment adviser must charge a fee that is so disproportionately large that it bears no reasonable relationship to the services rendered and could not have been the product of arm's length bargaining.

1

We begin with the language of §36(b). As noted, the Seventh Circuit panel thought that the phrase "fiduciary duty" incorporates a standard taken from the law of trusts. Petitioners agree but maintain that the panel identified the wrong trust-law standard. Instead of the standard that applies when a trustee and a settlor negotiate the trustee's fee at the time of the creation of a trust, petitioners invoke the standard that applies when a trustee seeks compensation after the trust is created. A compensation agreement reached at that time, they point out, "'will not bind the beneficiary' if either 'the trustee failed to make a full disclosure of all circumstances affecting the agreement'" which he knew or should have known or if the agreement is unfair to the beneficiary. . . . Respondent, on the other hand, contends that the term "fiduciary" is not exclusive to the law of trusts, that the phrase means different things in different contexts, and that there is no reason to believe that §36(b) incorporates the specific meaning of the term in the law of trusts.

We find it unnecessary to take sides in this dispute. In *Pepper v. Litton,* 308 U.S. 295 (1939), we discussed the meaning of the concept of fiduciary duty in a context that is analogous to that presented here, and we also looked to trust law. At issue in *Pepper* was whether a bankruptcy court could disallow a dominant or controlling shareholder's claim for compensation against a bankrupt corporation. Dominant or

---

[27]. A money market fund differs from a mutual fund in both the types of investments and the frequency of redemptions. A money market fund often invests in short-term money market securities, such as short-term securities of the United States Government or its agencies, bank certificates of deposit, and commercial paper. Investors can invest in such a fund for as little as a day, so, from the investor's perspective, the fund resembles an investment Amore like a bank account than [a] traditional investment in securities." . . .

[28]. Section 36(b) provides as follows:

"[T]he investment adviser of a registered investment company shall be deemed to have a fiduciary duty with respect to the receipt of compensation for services, or of payments of a material nature, paid by such registered investment company, or by the security holders thereof, to such investment adviser." 84 Stat. 1429 (codified at 15 U.S.C. §80a-35(b)).

controlling shareholders, we held, are "fiduciar[ies]" whose "powers are powers [held] in trust." . . . We then explained:

> "Their dealings with the corporation are subjected to rigorous scrutiny and where any of their contracts or engagements with the corporation is challenged the burden is on the director or stockholder not only to prove the good faith of the transaction but also to show its inherent fairness from the viewpoint of the corporation and those interested therein. . . . *The essence of the test is whether or not under all the circumstances the transaction carries the earmarks of an arm's length bargain.* If it does not, equity will set it aside." . . .

We believe that this formulation expresses the meaning of the phrase "fiduciary duty" in § 36(b). The Investment Company Act modifies this duty in a significant way: it shifts the burden of proof from the fiduciary to the party claiming breach, 15 U.S.C. § 80a-35(b)(1), to show that the fee is outside the range that arm's-length bargaining would produce.

The *Gartenberg* approach fully incorporates this understanding of the fiduciary duty as set out in *Pepper* and reflects § 36(b)(1)'s imposition of the burden on the plaintiff. As noted, *Gartenberg* insists that all relevant circumstances be taken into account, as does § 36(b)(2), 84 Stat. 1429 ("[A]pproval by the board of directors . . . shall be given such consideration by the court as deemed appropriate under *all the circumstances*" (emphasis added)). And *Gartenberg* uses the range of fees that might result from arm's-length bargaining as the benchmark for reviewing challenged fees.

2

Gartenberg's approach also reflects § 36(b)'s place in the statutory scheme and, in particular, its relationship to the other protections that the Act affords investors.

Under the Act, scrutiny of investment adviser compensation by a fully informed mutual fund board is the "cornerstone of the . . . effort to control conflicts of interest within mutual funds." *Burks*, 441 U.S., at 482. The Act interposes disinterested directors as "independent watchdogs" of the relationship between a mutual fund and its adviser. To provide these directors with the information needed to judge whether an adviser's compensation is excessive, the Act requires advisers to furnish all information "reasonably . . . necessary to evaluate the terms" of the adviser's contract, 15 U.S.C. § 80a-15(c), and gives the SEC the authority to enforce that requirement. See § 80a-41. Board scrutiny of adviser compensation and shareholder suits under § 36(b), 84 Stat. 1429, are mutually reinforcing but independent mechanisms for controlling conflicts. See *Daily Income Fund*, 464 U.S., at 541 (Congress intended for § 36(b) suits and directorial approval of adviser contracts to act as "independent checks on excessive fees"); *Kamen*, 500 U.S., at 108 ("Congress added § 36(b) to the [Act] in 1970 because it concluded that the shareholders should not have to rely solely on the fund's directors to assure reasonable adviser fees, notwithstanding the increased disinterestedness of the board" . . .).

In recognition of the role of the disinterested directors, the Act instructs courts to give board approval of an adviser's compensation "such consideration . . . as is deemed appropriate under all the circumstances." §80a-35(b)(2). Cf. *Burks*, 441 U.S., at 485 ("[I]t would have been paradoxical for Congress to have been willing to rely largely upon [boards of directors as] 'watchdogs' to protect shareholder interest and yet, where the 'watchdogs' have done precisely that, require that they be totally muzzled").

From this formulation, two inferences may be drawn. First, a measure of deference to a board's judgment may be appropriate in some instances. Second, the appropriate measure of deference varies depending on the circumstances.

Gartenberg heeds these precepts. *Gartenberg* advises that "the expertise of the independent trustees of a fund, whether they are fully informed about all facts bearing on the [investment adviser's] service and fee, and the extent of care and conscientiousness with which they perform their duties are important factors to be considered in deciding whether they and the [investment adviser] are guilty of a breach of fiduciary duty in violation of §36(b)." . . .

III

While both parties in this case endorse the basic *Gartenberg* approach, they disagree on several important questions that warrant discussion.

The first concerns comparisons between the fees that an adviser charges a captive mutual fund and the fees that it charges in its independent clients. As noted, the *Gartenberg* court rejected a comparison between the fees that the adviser in that case charged a money market fund and the fees that it charged a pension fund. 694 F.2d, at 930, n. 3 (noting the "[t]he nature and extent of the services required by each type of fund differ sharply"). Petitioners contend that such a comparison is appropriate, but respondent disagrees. Since the Act requires consideration of all relevant factors, 15 U.S.C. §80a-35(b)(2), we do not think that there can be any categorical rule regarding the comparisons of the fees charged different types of clients. See *Daily Income Fund, supra,* at 537 (discussing concern with investment advisers' practice of charging higher fees to mutual funds than to their other clients). Instead, courts may give such comparisons the weight that they merit in light of the similarities and differences between the services that the clients in question require, but courts must be wary of inapt comparisons. As the panel below noted, there may be significant differences between the services provided by an investment adviser to a mutual fund and those it provides to a pension fund which are attributable to the greater frequency of shareholder redemptions in a mutual fund, the higher turnover of mutual fund assets, the more burdensome regulatory and legal obligations, and higher marketing costs. 527 F.3d, at 634 ("Different clients call for different commitments of time"). If the services rendered are sufficiently different that a comparison is not probative, then courts must reject such a comparison. Even if the services provided and fees charged to an independent fund are relevant, courts should be mindful that the Act does not necessarily ensure fee parity between mutual funds and institutional clients contrary to petitioners' contentions. . . .

By the same token, courts should not rely too heavily on comparisons with fees charged to mutual funds by other advisers. These comparisons are problematic because these fees, like those challenged, may not be the product of negotiations conducted at arm's length. . . .

Finally, a court's evaluation of an investment adviser's fiduciary duty must take into account both procedure and substance. See 15 U.S.C. § 80a-35(b)(2) (requiring deference to board's consideration "as is deemed appropriate under all the circumstances"); cf. *Daily Income Fund*, 464 U.S., at 541 ("Congress intended security holder and SEC actions under § 36(b), on the one hand, and directorial approval of adviser contracts, on the other, to act as independent checks on excessive fees"). Where a board's process for negotiating and reviewing investment-adviser compensation is robust, a reviewing court should afford commensurate deference to the outcome of the bargaining process. See *Burks*, 441 U.S., at 484 (unaffiliated directors serve as "independent watchdogs"). Thus, if the disinterested directors considered the relevant factors, their decision to approve a particular fee agreement is entitled to considerable weight, even if a court might weigh the factors differently. This is not to deny that a fee may be excessive even if it was negotiated by a board in possession of all relevant information, but such determination must be based on evidence that the fee "is so disproportionately large that it bears no reasonable relationship to the services rendered and could not have been the product of arm's-length bargaining." . . .

In contrast, where the board's process was deficient or the adviser withheld important information, the court must take a more rigorous look at the outcome. When an investment adviser fails to disclose material information to the board, greater scrutiny is justified because the withheld information might have hampered the board's ability to function as "an independent check upon the management." . . . "Section 36(b) is sharply focused on the question of whether the fees themselves were excessive." . . . But an adviser's compliance or noncompliance with its disclosure obligations is a factor that must be considered in calibrating the degree of deference that is due a board's decision to approve an adviser's fees.

It is also important to note that the standard for fiduciary breach under § 36(b) does not call for judicial second-guessing of informed board decisions. See *Daily Income Fund, supra*, at 538; see also *Burks*, 441 U.S., at 483 ("Congress consciously chose to address the conflict-of-interest problem through the Act's independent-directors section, rather than through more drastic remedies"). "[P]otential conflicts [of interests] may justify some restraints upon the unfettered discretion of even disinterested mutual fund directors, particularly in their transactions with the investment adviser," but they do not suggest that a court may supplant the judgment of disinterested directors apprised of all relevant information, without additional evidence that the fee exceeds the arm's-length range. In reviewing compensation under § 36(b), the Act does not require courts to engage in a precise calculation of fees representative of arm's-length bargaining. . . . As recounted above, Congress rejected a "reasonableness" requirement that was criticized as charging the courts with rate-setting responsibilities. Congress' approach recognizes that courts are not well suited to make such precise calculations. . . . *Gartenberg*'s "so disproportionately large" standard reflects this congressional choice to "rely largely upon [independent director] 'watchdogs' to protect shareholders interests." . . .

By focusing almost entirely on the element of disclosure, the Seventh Circuit panel erred. See 527 F.3d, at 632 (An investment adviser "must make full disclosure and play no tricks but is not subject to a cap on compensation"). The *Gartenberg* standard, which the panel rejected, may lack sharp analytical clarity, but we believe that it accurately reflects the compromise that is embodied in § 36(b), and it has provided a workable standard for nearly three decades. . . .

IV

For the foregoing reasons, the judgment of the Court of Appeals is vacated, and the case remanded for further proceedings consistent with this opinion.

It is so ordered.

Justice Thomas, concurring.

The Court rightly affirms the careful approach to § 36(b) cases that courts have applied since (and in certain respects in spite of) *Gartenberg v. Merrill Lynch Asset Management, Inc.*, 694 F.2d 923, 928–930 (CA2 1982). I write separately because I would not shortchange the Court's effort by describing it as affirmation of the "*Gartenberg* standard."

The District Court and Court of Appeals in *Gartenberg* created that standard, which emphasizes fee "fairness" and proportionality, 694 F.2d, at 929, in a manner that could be read to permit the equivalent of the judicial rate regulation the *Gartenberg* opinions disclaim, based on the Investment Company Act of 1940's "tortuous" legislative history and a handful of extrastatutory policy and market considerations . . . . Although virtually all subsequent § 36(b) cases cite *Gartenberg*, most courts have correctly declined its invitation to stray beyond statutory bounds. Instead, they have followed an approach (principally in deciding which cases may proceed past summary judgment) that defers to the informed conclusions of disinterested boards and holds plaintiffs to their heavy burden of proof in the manner the Act, and now the Court's opinion, requires. . . .

I concur in the Court's decision to affirm this approach based upon the Investment Company Act's text and our longstanding fiduciary duty precedents. But I would not say that in doing so we endorse the "*Gartenberg* standard." Whatever else might be said about today's decision, it does not countenance the free-ranging judicial "fairness" review of fees that *Gartenberg* could be read to authorize, and that virtually all courts deciding § 36(b) cases since *Gartenberg* (including the Court of Appeals in this case) have wisely eschewed in the post *Gartenberg* precedents we approve.[29]

---

[29]. [For a recent article, see Karnel, *The Challenge of Fiduciary Regulation: The Investment Advisers Act After Seventy-Five Years*, 10 Brooklyn J. Corp., Fin. & Comm. L. 405 (2016).]

§ 13.09 Conflicts of Interest

Broker-dealers perform various functions, including investment banking, broker-age activities, underwriting, research, investment advice, and investment management. Potential conflicts can arise when information gathering and investment decision functions affect the same issuer. The investment banking department could obtain material, nonpublic information on a publicly held issuer while the broker-age section is recommending trades in the same issuer's securities or while the trading department is executing trades in the issuer's securities for the firm's own proprietary accounts or as a market maker.[30]

Moreover, the Sarbanes-Oxley Act, SEC Regulation AC, and self-regulatory organization rules address the objectivity and sufficiency of disclosure of analyst research reports.

[A] In General

Screening (commonly called "Chinese Wall") procedures consist of policies and procedures designed to control the flow of material nonpublic information within a multiservice financial firm.[31] In the broker-dealer context, a Chinese Wall isolates the investment banking department from the brokerage, research, and other departments and also limits the flow of sensitive information on a need-to-know basis.[32] In the case of banks, the Chinese Wall segregates the trust department from the commercial lending as well as the securities underwriting departments.[33]

Although Chinese Wall policies and procedures differ among firms, institutions employ numerous such practices to control the flow of information between departments.[34] In addition to general written policies and educational programs,

---

30. *See, e.g.*, Levine et al., *Multiservice Securities Firms: Coping with Conflicts in a Tender Offer Context*, 23 WAKE FOREST L. REV. 41 (1988); Lipton & Mazur, *The Chinese Wall Solution to the Conflict Problems of Securities Firms*, 50 N.Y.U. L. REV. 459 (1975). The propriety of such procedures as Chinese Walls to limit a broker-dealer's liability has been criticized. For example, Professor Poser opines that "[t]he Chinese Wall . . . makes it difficult . . . for a multiservice firm to fulfill its duty of undivided loyalty to clients." *Poser, Conflicts of Interest Within Securities Firms*, 16 BROOKLYN J. INT'L. 111 (1990).

31. *See* Securities Exchange Act Release No. 17120, [1980 Transfer Binder] Fed. Sec. L. Rep. (CCH) ¶ 82,646, at 83,461 (1980) (hereinafter SEC Rule 14e-3 Release).

32. *See In re Merrill, Lynch, Pierce, Fenner & Smith*, 43 S.E.C. 933, [1967–1969 Transfer Binder] Fed. Sec. L. Rep. (CCH) ¶ 77,629 (1968) (Exhibit A) (providing example of Chinese Wall policy that Merrill Lynch agreed to employ in a settlement of charges of violating the antifraud provisions of the federal securities laws).

33. *See* Board of Governors of the Federal Reserve System, *Policy Statement Concerning the Use of Inside Information*, 43 Fed. Reg. 12,755, 12,756 (March 17, 1978) (hereinafter Federal Reserve Policy).

34. *See* SEC Division of Market Regulation, *Broker-Dealer Policies and Procedures Designed to Segment the Flow and Prevent the Misuse of Material Nonpublic Information,* [1989–1990 Transfer Binder] Fed. Sec. L. Rep. (CCH) ¶ 84,520, at 80,620-80,625 (1990) (hereinafter SEC Division Report).

consideration should be given to the implementation of procedures such as the following: (i) physical separation of departments in different wings or floors of a building; (ii) maintenance of separate accounting systems, records, and support staff; (iii) clearly identifying sensitive documents, employing secure filing systems, and restricting access by persons in departments where a breach of confidentiality could occur, such as a bank's trust department or a broker-dealer's trading section; (iv) limiting attendance at meetings where sensitive topics will be discussed; (v) restricting the transfer of personnel from one department into another; (vi) restricting directors, officers and employees from serving dual roles in more than one market sensitive area, such as the arbitrage and underwriting sections of a broker-dealer; and (vii) using code names in documents to conceal the identity of issuers.[35]

Generally, these policies and procedures focus on the activities of the sections of a firm that will frequently come into possession of material, nonpublic information, such as the investment banking section of a broker-dealer. At times, persons in other departments must be consulted on sensitive matters, such as when an opinion must be obtained from an analyst in the research department. In these instances, the research analyst would be "brought over the wall": the analyst would be required to operate under the same procedures that limit the investment banking section.[36]

[B] The Need for Reinforcement Measures

In addition to the information segregation measures outlined above, the SEC and commentators have focused on the need for financial intermediaries to maintain reinforcement mechanisms. These other procedures, primarily restricted and watch lists, frequently are employed by multiservice financial firms to cope with their conflicting duties and avert the imposition of liability.[37] Internal audits and other enforcement measures are also utilized to ensure compliance and to detect breaches of the wall.[38] When personnel are brought over the wall, they become subject to these reinforcement procedures as well.[39]

To prevent leaks of inside information, the implementation by multiservice financial firms of reinforcement measures are key components of an effective compliance program.[40] Thus, the Commission often describes adequate procedures for financial

---

35. *See* Federal Reserve Policy, *supra* note 33, at 12,756; Doty & Powers, *Chinese Walls: The Transformation of a Good Business Practice*, 26 AM. CRIM. L. REV. 155, 175–177 (1988).

36. *See* Doty & Powers, *supra* note 35, at 175–177.

37. *See* SEC Rule 14e-3 Release, *supra* note 31, at 83,461; Levine et al., *supra* note 30, at 58.

38. *See* Doty & Powers, *supra* note 35, at 175–177.

39. *See id.* at 177 (including restricted lists, limits on employee securities transactions, and internal audits).

40. *See* SEC Division Report, *supra* note 34, at 80,623-80,625.

intermediaries to include Chinese Walls,[41] restricted lists,[42] watch lists,[43] and other procedures[44] designed to prevent violations of the securities laws.

[C] Regulatory Treatment of Chinese Walls

Although no definitive answer has emerged from case law regarding the propriety of screening (or Chinese Wall) procedures to limit a broker-dealer's liability to its investor-clients,[45] the SEC expressed its approval for such procedures in the tender offer setting when it adopted Rule 14e-3. Rule 14e-3 provides a safe harbor to that rule's "disclose or abstain" provision for entities that implement certain policies and procedures. With certain exceptions, Rule 14e-3 generally imposes liability on persons who are in possession of material, nonpublic information relating to a tender offer and who purchase or sell (or tip such information relating to) the subject securities, unless the information and its source are publicly disclosed in a timely manner.[46]

---

41. *See supra* notes 30–40 and accompanying text.

42. *See* Broker-Dealer Internal Control Procedures for High Yield Securities, Report by the SEC Division of Market Regulation, [1993 Transfer Binder] Fed. Sec. L. Rep. (CCH) ¶ 85,251, at 84,680 n. 15 (1993) (hereinafter Commission Division Report):

When an investment banking transaction becomes "public" (through a filing with the Commission or otherwise), firms will add the issuer's securities to a "restricted" list accessible to personnel throughout the firm. Once this is done, most, if not all, trading by proprietary and employee accounts is prohibited for set time periods.... Because the effects of such restrictions are so wide-ranging, securities are not added to the list until deals are made public. Otherwise, adding a security to this list might send a signal both within and outside the firm that a nonpublic transaction is imminent.

43. *Id.* at 84,680 n. 14:

At most firms, the compliance or legal staff maintains a "watch" or "grey" list of securities. A security is added to this list whenever an investment banking engagement is entered into between the broker-dealer and the security's issuer—or in any other instance in which one part of the broker-dealer has received material, nonpublic information concerning the issuer. The compliance or legal staff uses this list to monitor the firm's activities. For example, if a firm employee buys or sells a security on this list, the compliance or legal staff needs to determine if this transaction is indicative of a "breach" of Chinese Wall procedures.

44. *Id.* at 84,680 n. 16:

Many firms have implemented a third type of list for use after a securities is added to the watch or grey list but before the security has been added to the restricted list. If compliance or legal personnel determines that the firm's or employees' activities should in some way be limited, the security is placed on this list. For example, just prior to the public announcement of an investment banking transaction, the compliance or legal staff may instruct the firm's market makers to trade the issuer's securities in a "passive" manner, (i.e., by executing only unsolicited customer trades).

45. *See, e.g., Slade v. Shearson, Hammill & Co.*, [1973–1974 Transfer Binder] Fed. Sec. L. Rep. (CCH) ¶ 94,439 (S.D.N.Y.), *remanded*, 517 F.2d 398 (2d Cir. 1974); *Cotton v. Merrill Lynch, Pierce, Fenner & Smith, Inc.*, 699 F. Supp. 251 (N.D. Okla. 1988); discussion in Steinberg & Fletcher, *Compliance Programs for Insider Trading*, 47 SMU L. Rev. 1783, 1806–1811 (1994).

46. The person must know or have reason to know that the information has been acquired directly or indirectly from certain parties involved in the tender offer, including the offering person, the issuer of the target securities, and any persons acting on their behalf. *See also* SEC Rule

The Rule provides a safe harbor for entities that would otherwise violate its provisions. This safe harbor covers purchases and sales by nonnatural persons, typically multiservice financial institutions, if the entity can show that the individuals making the investment decision did not know the nonpublic information and that the entity had established policies and procedures, reasonable under the circumstances, to ensure that its individuals would not violate Rule 14e-3. In determining the reasonableness of the policies and procedures, the Rule takes into account the nature of the entity's business. Chinese Walls and restricted lists are specifically identified as examples of policies and procedures that may prevent individual decision makers from learning or using such inside information.[47]

[D] SEC Global Research Analyst Settlements

In 2003, the SEC (as well as self-regulators and several state regulators) settled enforcement actions against 10 major broker-dealer firms and two individual research analysts involving research analyst conflicts of interest. In addition to the issuance of injunctions against the defendants, the Settlement included the payment of disgorgement and money penalties, the making of enhanced disclosures in research reports, the providing to their customers of independent research engaged in by independent research firms, allocation of funds for investor education, and the undertaking of structural reforms by the firms subject to the Settlement.[48]

The structural reforms mandated pursuant to the Settlement sought to address the conflicts of interest between research analysts and the investment banking functions of the subject firms. These structural reforms included:

- The firms will separate research and investment banking, including physical separation, completely separate reporting lines, separate legal and compliance staffs, and separate budgeting processes.

- Analysts' compensation cannot be based directly or indirectly upon investment banking revenues or input from investment banking personnel.

- Investment bankers cannot evaluate analysts.

- An analyst's compensation will be based in significant part on the quality and accuracy of the analyst's research.

- Decisions concerning compensation of analysts will be documented.

- Investment bankers will have no role in determining what companies are covered by the analysts.

- Research analysts will be prohibited from participating in efforts to solicit investment banking business, including pitches and roadshows.

17j-1 (requiring registered investment companies to adopt and enforce written codes of ethics, including conflict of interest situations where access persons obtain material nonpublic information).

47. *See* SEC Rule 14e-3 Release, *supra* note 31, at 83,461.

48. *See* SEC Press Release Nos. 2003-54, 2003-55 (2003).

- Firms will implement policies and procedures reasonably designed to assure that their personnel do not seek to influence the contents of research reports for purposes of obtaining or retaining investment banking business.

- Firms will create and enforce firewalls between research and investment banking reasonably designed to prohibit improper communications between the two. Communications should be limited to those enabling research analysts to fulfill a "gatekeeper" role.[49]

The substance of a number of these provisions were adopted as rules issued by the self-regulatory organizations, including the National Association of Securities Dealers (now the Financial Industry Regulatory Authority—FINRA) and the New York Stock Exchange. These SRO rules provide comparable protections as those contained in the Settlement.

In 2010, the Settlement was amended.[50] Nonetheless, the following provisions and firewalls remain in place under the 2010 modification:

- Investment banking input into the research budget is prohibited;

- The physical separation of research analysts and investment banking is required;

- Investment banking is prohibited from having input into company-specific coverage decisions;

- Research oversight committees are required to ensure the integrity and independence of equity research;

- Communications between investment banking personnel and research analysts regarding the merits of a proposed transaction or a potential candidate for a transaction are prohibited unless a chaperone from the firm's legal and compliance department is present;

- Research analysts and investment bankers are prohibited from having any communications for the purpose of having research personnel identify specific potential investment banking transactions; and

- Research analysts must be able to express their views to a commitment committee about a proposed transaction outside the presence of investment bankers working on the deal.[51]

[E] Sarbanes-Oxley Act Provisions

The Sarbanes-Oxley Act of 2002 (SOX) addresses securities analysts and possible conflicts of interest arising from their duties. The Act directs the SEC to formulate

---

49. *SEC Fact Sheet on Global Analyst Research Settlements* (2003), http://www.sec.gov/news /speech/factsheet.htm. *See* Hilgers, *Under the Influence: Analyzing Wall Street Research Analyst Conflicts of Interest and the Responses Designed to Induce Impartiality*, 31 Sec. Reg. L.J. 427 (2003).

50. *See Court Approves Modifications to Global Research Settlement*, SEC Litigation Release No. 21457 (2010).

51. *Id. See FINRA Rule 2711 (Research Analysts and Research Reports)*.

rules that enhance the objectivity of analyst research reports and increase investor confidence in analyst research.[52] Responding to this directive, the SEC promulgated Regulation AC. Regulation AC requires, for example, that research analysts: certify the truthfulness of the views expressed in public appearances as well as contained in their research reports; and disclose in such certification any compensation received that is directly or indirectly related to the specific recommendations or views set forth in public appearances or their research reports. Regulation AC contains a number of exemptions, such as excluding from the Regulation's mandates foreign securities analysts, non-registered investment advisers, and the media.[53] In this regard, the Commission also approved extensive self-regulatory rules that, for example, prohibit tying a research analyst's remuneration to the firm's procurement of specific banking transactions, that forbid a research analyst to provide favorable analysis on a company in return for investment banking engagements, and that prohibit a firm from retaliating against a research analyst who publishes a research report that is detrimental to the firm's present or prospective investment banking relationship with a subject corporation.[54]

[F] Impact of the JOBS Act

With respect to an emerging growth company,[55] the JOBS Act amends the Securities Exchange Act to prohibit the SEC or a national securities exchange from adopting or implementing any regulation in connection with an emerging growth company's initial public offering (IPO) of common equity that:

> (1) Restricts, based on functional role, which associated persons of a broker, dealer, or member of a national securities association, may arrange for communications between an analyst and a potential investor; or

> (2) Restricts a [research] analyst from participating in any communications with the management of an emerging growth company that is also attended by any other associated person of a broker, dealer, or member of a national securities association whose functional role is other than as an analyst.[56]

Note that the foregoing provision applies only with respect to emerging growth companies. Perhaps more important, the SEC's Global Settlement is not impacted by the JOBS Act.[57] Therefore, the structural reforms set forth by the Settlement remain intact—thereby, signifying that the premier global firms (e.g., Goldman

---

52. Sarbanes-Oxley Act § 501(a). *See* Hilgers, note 49 *supra*.

53. *See* Securities Act Release No. 8193 (2003).

54. *See* Securities Exchange Act Release Nos. 45908 (2002), 48252 (2003).

55. For coverage of emerging growth companies, *see* §§ 4.02, 5.03 *supra*.

56. Section 105(b) of the JOBS Act, *amending,* § 15D of the Exchange Act, as set forth in SEC Division of Trading and Markets, *Jumpstart Our Business Startups Act Frequently Asked Questions About Research Analysts and Underwriters* (Aug. 22, 2012).

57. *Id. See* Puopolo, Jacobson & Adams, *The JOBS Act: Improving Access to Capital Markets for Smaller Companies,* 45 REV. SEC. & COMM. REG. 109, 111 (2012).

Sachs, J.P. Morgan Securities, Credit Suisse, First Boston, Merrill Lynch, Citigroup Global Markets, and UBS), as parties to the Settlement, remain subject to the Settlement's terms and conditions (as modified in 2010).[58] As stated by the SEC staff:

> The Global Settlement was not affected by the JOBS Act. Accordingly, analysts of Global Settlement firms are still subject to the provisions of that court order, including the requirement to create and enforce firewalls between research and investment banking personnel reasonably designed to prohibit all communications between the two except as expressly permitted in the court order. Unless an exception to this requirement is applicable, the analyst is not permitted to participate in a communication in the presence of investment banking personnel. In addition, other Commission and SRO rules regarding analysts continue to apply.

> Prior to enactment of Section 105(b) [of the JOBS Act], SRO rules prohibited analysts of non-Global Settlement firms from attending meetings with issuer management that are also attended by investment banking personnel in connection with an IPO, including pitch meetings. Pursuant to Section 105(b), analysts may now attend such meetings, provided that the issuer qualifies as an emerging growth company. Section 105(b) does not, however, permit analysts to engage in otherwise prohibited conduct in such meetings. Section 105(b) does not, for example, affect SRO rules that otherwise prohibit an analyst from engaging in efforts to solicit investment banking business. Section 105(b) also does not affect other prohibitions as discussed below.

> Therefore, before a firm is formally retained to underwrite an offering, analysts of non-Global Settlement firms in attendance at such meetings could, for example, introduce themselves, outline their research program and the types of factors that the analyst would consider in his or her analysis of a company, and ask follow-up questions to better understand a factual statement made by the emerging growth company's management. In addition, after the firm is formally retained to underwrite the offering, analysts at non-Global Settlement firms could, for example, participate in presentations by the management of an emerging growth company to educate a firm's sales force about the company and discuss industry trends, provide information obtained from investing customers, and communicate their views.

> Firms and analysts should be mindful of the antifraud provisions of the federal securities laws, the Global Settlement, and any other Commission or SRO rule that governs research analyst conflicts. An analyst, for example, remains prohibited from changing his or her research as a result of a communication in an effort to obtain investment banking business. In addition, an analyst continues to be prohibited from giving tacit acquiescence

---

58. *See* § 13.09[D] *supra.*

to overtures from the management of an emerging growth company that attempt to create an expectation of favorable research coverage if the analyst's firm is chosen to underwrite the emerging growth company's IPO. Further, an analyst remains prohibited from providing views that are inconsistent with the analyst's personal views about the emerging growth company or its securities, or from making a statement that is misleading taking into consideration the overall context in which the statement was made. Moreover, investment banking personnel remain prohibited from directly or indirectly directing a research analyst to engage in sales or marketing efforts related to an investment banking services transaction. Firms should ensure that they have instituted and enforce appropriate controls to make sure that analysts are not engaging in prohibited conduct, such as solicitation, at any meetings with company management that are also attended by investment banking personnel, or otherwise.[59]

§ 13.10 Secondary Liability

Problem

[Go to the Problem contained in § 10.01.]

[A] Aiding and Abetting Liability

[At this point, review the materials contained in §§ 10.02–10.03.]

[B] Controlling Person Liability

[At this point, review the materials contained in § 10.04.]

Haynes v. Anderson & Strudwick, Inc.

United States District Court, Eastern District of Virginia
508 F. Supp. 1303 (1981)

[This case is contained in § 10.04.]

---

59. SEC Staff Release, note 56 *supra* (also stating that "[t]he examples given above are not exhaustive").

Hollinger v. Titan Capital Corp.

United States Court of Appeals, Ninth Circuit
914 F.2d 1564 (1990) (en banc)

[The pertinent excerpts to this case are contained in § 10.04.]

———————

Harrison v. Dean Witter Reynolds, Inc.

United States Court of Appeals, Seventh Circuit
974 F.2d 873 (1992)

[The pertinent excerpts to this case are contained in § 10.04.]

———————

[C] Respondeat Superior Liability

[At this point, review the materials contained in § 10.05.]

Hollinger v. Titan Capital Corp.

United States Court of Appeals, Ninth Circuit
914 F.2d 1564 (1990) (en banc)

[The pertinent excerpts to this case are contained in § 10.05.]

———————

[D] Failure to Supervise

Section 15(b)(4)(E) and § 15(b)(6)(A) of the 1934 Act authorize the SEC to sanction a broker-dealer and any associated person if such broker-dealer or associated person fails reasonably to supervise another person who commits certain enumerated securities law violations, if such person is subject to his/her supervision. The statute contains a safe-harbor provision, providing a defense if there have been established and implemented adequate procedures that would reasonably be expected to prevent and detect pertinent violations.

In a release titled "Supervisory Responsibilities of Broker-Dealer Management," Securities Exchange Act Release No. 8404 (1968), the SEC asserted that the following supervisory functions should be fulfilled:

> (1) The review of the firm's methods of obtaining customers' accounts, including provisions for assuring that adequate information is obtained as to the customers' objectives, needs and finances. (2) The review of customer accounts, including a review for churning and switching of securities in customers' accounts as well as unsuitable recommendations and sales of unregistered securities. (3) The review of methods of recruiting and training of employees, including provisions for assuring that salesmen will not be

hired unless the firm can adequately service the business created and maintain an appropriate ratio between sales personnel and back office personnel. Attention . . . to the adequate training and compensation of back office personnel. (4) The review of back office operations, i.e., all systems and procedures, including the currency and accuracy of books and records, the status and causes of "fails to receive" and "fails to deliver," net capital, credit extensions and financial reports. Attention also should be given to operations that can or should be automated. Prompt delivery of securities to customers and prompt disbursement of customers' funds should be emphasized. . . . (5) The review of sales techniques and methods of salesmen. Specifically, procedures should be used for the review of salesmen's telephone recommendations to customers, sales correspondence with customers, new issue sales, suitability of recommendations and discretionary accounts.

In *In the Matter of Prudential-Bache Securities, Inc.,* Securities Exchange Act Release No. 22755 (1986), the SEC stated:

> The Commission has repeatedly warned the broker-dealer community that it will not tolerate lax supervisory policies and procedures. The responsibility of broker-dealers to supervise their employees by means of effective, established procedures is a critical component in the federal investor protection scheme regulating the securities markets. In the seminal *Reynolds* case 25 years ago, the Commission observed:
>
> > brokers and dealers are under a duty to supervise the actions of employees and . . . in large organizations it is especially imperative that the system of internal control be adequate and effective . . . [A] contrary rule would encourage ethical irresponsibility by those who should be primarily responsible.
>
> Prudential-Bache lacked adequate procedures to ensure the effectiveness of the regional manager's supervision of the branch managers. As a result, supervisory responsibility for ensuring adherence to the firm's procedures designed to prevent and detect unlawful behavior ended, for all practical purposes, at the level of the branch manager. . . .
>
> The Commission has long recognized that it is not sufficient for a broker-dealer to establish a system of supervisory procedures which rely solely on supervision by branch managers. See *Shearson, Hamill & Co.,* 42 S.E.C. 811 (1965). In *Shearson, Hamill,* the Commission found that the firm abdicated its responsibility of supervision over its organization by excessive reliance on branch managers, and noted that a firm cannot dissipate its managerial responsibilities by geographic fragmentation, stating:
>
> > The need for central control increases, not decreases, as branch offices become more numerous, dispersed and distant . . . It is essential . . . not only that a system of controls adequate to meet the problems inherent in a large and scattered organization be

established but also that such controls be effectively enforced by those in authority.

In the present matters, the fact that branch managers were remiss in their supervision, therefore, does not insulate Prudential-Bache from liability.

The Commission has also stated that "[t]here must be adequate follow-up and review when a firm's own procedures detect irregularities or unusual trading activity in a branch office . . ." A firm must have adequate procedures to assure that trading restrictions issued by its Compliance Department are not ignored by the branch managers or other personnel. A firm's Compliance Department is an important means for assuring adherence by its employees to the federal securities laws. A broker-dealer is not meeting its supervisory obligations under the federal securities laws if its Compliance Department can be disregarded or otherwise rendered ineffective by a branch manager. Similarly, a firm should seek to foster an attitude among its staff of cooperation with and acceptance of actions by the Compliance Department that will on occasion necessarily interfere with retail sales activity. Under no circumstances should a firm continue to tolerate a supervisor who persistently ignores legitimate Compliance Department recommendations or directives.

. . . .

In the Matter of John H. Gutfreund, Thomas W. Strauss, and John W. Meriwether

U.S. Securities and Exchange Commission
[1992 Transfer Binder] Fed. Sec. L. Rep. (CCH) ¶ 85,067 (1992)

I.

The Commission deems it appropriate and in the public interest that public administrative proceedings be and they hereby are instituted against John H. Gutfreund, Thomas W. Strauss, and John W. Meriwether pursuant to Section 15(b) of the Securities Exchange Act of 1934 ("Exchange Act").

II.

In anticipation of the institution of these administrative proceedings, Gutfreund, Strauss, and Meriwether have each submitted Offers of Settlement which the Commission has determined to accept. Solely for the purposes of these proceedings and any other proceedings brought by or on behalf of the Commission or to which the Commission is a party, prior to a hearing pursuant to the Commission's Rules of Practice, and without admitting or denying the facts, findings, or conclusions herein, Gutfreund, Strauss, and Meriwether each consent to entry of the findings, and the imposition of the remedial sanctions, set forth below.

III.

The Commission also deems it appropriate and in the public interest that a report of investigation be issued pursuant to Section 21(a) of the Exchange Act[60] with respect to the supervisory responsibilities of brokerage firm employees in certain circumstances. Donald M. Feuerstein consents to the issuance of this Report, without admitting or denying any of the statements contained herein.

IV.

On the basis of this Order and the Respondents' Offers of Settlement, the Commission finds the following.[61]

A. FACTS

1. Brokerage Firm Involved

Salomon Brothers Inc. ("Salomon") is a Delaware corporation with its principal place of business in New York, New York. At all times relevant to this proceeding, Salomon was registered with the Commission as a broker-dealer pursuant to Section 15(b) of the Exchange Act. Salomon has been a government-designated dealer in U.S. Treasury securities since 1939 and a primary dealer since 1961.

2. Respondents

John H. Gutfreund was the Chairman and Chief Executive Officer of Salomon from 1983 to August 18, 1991. He had worked at Salomon since 1953.

Thomas W. Strauss was the President of Salomon from 1986 to August 18, 1991. During that time period, Strauss reported to Gutfreund. He had worked at Salomon since 1963.

John W. Meriwether was a Vice Chairman of Salomon and in charge of all fixed income trading activities of the firm from 1988 to August 18, 1991. During that period, Meriwether reported to Strauss. During the same period, Paul W. Mozer, a managing director and the head of Salomon's Government Trading Desk, reported directly to Meriwether.

3. Other Individual

Donald M. Feuerstein was the chief legal officer of Salomon Inc. and the head of the Legal Department of Salomon until August 23, 1991. From 1987 until August 23, 1991, the head of Salomon's Compliance Department reported directly to Feuerstein.

4. Summary

In late April of 1991, three members of the senior management of Salomon — John Gutfreund, Thomas Strauss, and John Meriwether — were informed that Paul Mozer,

---

[60]. Section 21(a) of the Exchange Act authorizes the Commission to investigate whether any person has violated the Exchange Act and the rules thereunder and, in its discretion, to publish a report concerning such investigations.

[61]. The findings herein are solely for the purposes of this proceeding and are not binding on any other person or entity named as a respondent in any other proceeding.

the head of the firm's Government Trading Desk, had submitted a false bid in the amount of $3.15 billion in an auction of U.S. Treasury securities on February 21, 1991. The executives were also informed by Donald Feuerstein, the firm's chief legal officer, that the submission of the false bid appeared to be a criminal act and, although not legally required, should be reported to the government. Gutfreund and Strauss agreed to report the matter to the Federal Reserve Bank in New York. Mozer was told that his actions might threaten his future with the firm and would be reported to the government. However, for a period of months, none of the executives took action to investigate the matter or to discipline or impose limitations on Mozer. The information was also not reported to the government for a period of months. During that same period, Mozer committed additional violations of the federal securities laws in connection with two subsequent auctions of U.S. Treasury securities.

The Respondents in this proceeding are not being charged with any participation in the underlying violations. However, as set forth herein, the Commission believes that the Respondents' supervision was deficient and that this failure was compounded by the delay in reporting the matter to the government.

. . . .

B. FINDINGS

1. Legal Principles

Section 15(b)(4)(E) of the Exchange Act authorizes the Commission to impose sanctions against a broker-dealer if the firm has:

> failed reasonably to supervise, with a view to preventing violations [of the federal securities laws], another person who commits such a violation, if such person is subject to his supervision.

Section 15(b)(6) of the Exchange Act incorporates Section 15(b)(4)(E) by reference and authorizes the Commission to impose sanctions for deficient supervision on individuals associated with broker-dealers.

The principles which govern this proceeding are well-established by the Commission's cases involving failure to supervise. The Commission has long emphasized that the responsibility of broker-dealers to supervise their employees is a critical component of the federal regulatory scheme. As the Commission stated in *Wedbush Securities, Inc.* [48 S.E.C. 963, 967 (1988)]: "In large organizations it is especially imperative that those in authority exercise particular vigilance when indications of irregularity reach their attention."

The supervisory obligations imposed by the federal securities laws require a vigorous response even to indications of wrongdoing. Many of the Commission's cases involving a failure to supervise arise from situations where supervisors were aware only of "red flags" or "suggestions" of irregularity, rather than situations where, as here, supervisors were explicitly informed of an illegal act.

Even where the knowledge of supervisors is limited to "red flags" or "suggestions" of irregularity, they cannot discharge their supervisory obligations simply by relying on the unverified representations of employees. Instead, as the Commission has repeatedly emphasized, "[t]here must be adequate follow-up and review when a firm's own procedures detect irregularities or unusual trading activity. . . ." Moreover, if more than one supervisor is involved in considering the actions to be taken in response to possible misconduct, there must be a clear definition of the efforts to be taken and a clear assignment of those responsibilities to specific individuals within the firm.

2. The Failure to Supervise

[I]n April of 1991 three supervisors of Paul Mozer—John Meriwether, Thomas Strauss, and John Gutfreund—learned that Mozer had submitted a false bid in the amount of $3.15 billion in an auction of U.S. Treasury securities. Those supervisors learned that Mozer had said that the bid had been submitted to obtain additional securities for another trading area of the firm. They also learned that Mozer had contacted an employee of the customer whose name was used on the bid and falsely told the individual that the bid was an error. The supervisors also learned that the bid had been the subject of a letter from the Treasury Department to the customer and that Mozer had attempted to persuade the customer not to inform the Treasury Department that the bid had not been authorized. The supervisors were also informed by Salomon's chief legal officer that the submission of the false bid appeared to be a criminal act.

The information learned by the supervisors indicated that a high level employee of the firm with significant trading discretion had engaged in extremely serious misconduct. As [our] cases make clear, this information required, at a minimum, that the supervisors take action to investigate what had occurred and whether there had been other instances of unreported misconduct. While they could look to counsel for guidance, they had an affirmative obligation to undertake an appropriate inquiry. If they were unable to conduct the inquiry themselves or believed it was more appropriate that the inquiry be conducted by others, they were required to take prompt action to ensure that others in fact undertook those efforts. Such an inquiry could have been conducted by the legal or compliance department of the firm, outside counsel, or others who had the ability to investigate the matter adequately. The supervisors were also required, pending the outcome of such an investigation, to increase supervision of Mozer and to place appropriate limitations on his activities.

The failure to recognize the need to take action to limit the activities of Mozer in light of his admitted misconduct is particularly troubling. . . . Although [Meriwether, Strauss and Gutfreund] had previously been informed that a serious violation had in fact been committed by Mozer, they failed for over three months to take any action to place limitations on his activities to deal with that misconduct.

The need to take prompt action was all the more critical in view of the fact that the potential unlawful conduct had taken place in the market for U.S. Treasury securities. The integrity of that market is of vital importance to the capital markets of the United States, as well as to capital markets worldwide, and Salomon occupied a privileged role as a government-designated primary dealer. The failure of the supervisors to take vigorous action to address known misconduct by the head of the firm's Government Trading Desk caused unnecessary risks to the integrity of this important market.

To discharge their obligations, the supervisors should at least have taken steps to ensure that someone within the firm questioned other employees on the Government Trading Desk, such as the desk's clerk or the other managing director on the Desk. Since the supervisors were informed that Mozer had said that he submitted the false bid to obtain additional securities for another trading desk of the firm, they should also have specifically investigated any involvement of that area of the firm in the matter. The supervisors should also have reviewed, or ensured that others reviewed, documentation concerning the February 21, 1991 auction. Such a review would have revealed, at a minimum, that a second false bid had been submitted in the auction and that false trade tickets and customer confirmations had been created in connection with both false bids. Those facts would have raised serious questions about the operations of the Government Trading Desk, and inquiries arising from those questions might well have led to discovery of the additional false bids described above. For instance, two of the other false bids, those submitted in the December 27, 1990 and February 7, 1991 auctions, involved the same pattern of fictitious sales to and from customer accounts and the suppression of customer confirmations used in connection with the February 21, 1991 auction. Inasmuch as Mozer had admitted to committing one apparently criminal act, the supervisors had reason to be skeptical of Mozer's assurances that he had not engaged in other misconduct.

Each of the three supervisors apparently believed that someone else would take the supervisory action necessary to respond to Mozer's misconduct. There was no discussion, however, among any of the supervisors about what action should be taken or about who would be responsible for taking action. Instead, each of the supervisors assumed that another would act. In situations where supervisors are aware of wrongdoing, it is imperative that they take prompt and unequivocal action to define the responsibilities of those who are to respond to the wrongdoing. The supervisors here failed to do that. As a result, although there may be varying degrees of responsibility, each of the supervisors bears some measure of responsibility for the collective failure of the group to take action.

After the disclosure of one unauthorized bid to Meriwether, Mozer committed additional violations in connection with the submission of two subsequent unauthorized customer bids. Had limits been placed on his activities after the one unauthorized bid was disclosed, these violations might have been prevented. While Mozer was told by Meriwether that his conduct was career-threatening and that it would be reported to senior management and to the government, these efforts were not a sufficient supervisory response under the circumstances. The supervisors were required to take action reasonably designed to prevent a repetition of the misconduct that had been disclosed to them. They could, for instance, have temporarily limited Mozer's activities so that he was not involved in the submission of customer bids pending an adequate review of what had occurred in the February 21, 1991 auction, or they could have instituted procedures to require verification of customer bids.

Under the circumstances of this case, the failure of the supervisors to take action to discipline Mozer or to limit his activities constituted a serious breach of their supervisory obligations. Gutfreund, Strauss and Meriwether thus each failed reasonably to supervise Mozer with a view to preventing violations of the federal securities laws.[62]

As Chairman and Chief Executive Officer of Salomon, Gutfreund bore ultimate responsibility for ensuring that a prompt and thorough inquiry was undertaken and that Mozer was appropriately disciplined. A chief executive officer has ultimate affirmative responsibility, upon learning of serious wrongdoing within the firm as to any segment of the securities market, to ensure that steps are taken to prevent further violations of the securities laws and to determine the scope of the wrongdoing. He failed to ensure that this was done. Gutfreund also undertook the responsibility to report the matter to the government, but failed to do so, although he was urged to make the report on several occasions by other senior executives of Salomon. The disclosure was made only after an internal investigation prompted by other events. Gutfreund's failure to report the matter earlier is of particular concern because of Salomon's role in the vitally-important U.S. Treasury securities market. The reporting of the matter to the government was also the only action under consideration within the firm to respond to Mozer's actions. The failure to make the report thus meant that the firm failed to take any action to respond to Mozer's misconduct.

Once improper conduct came to the attention of Gutfreund, he bore responsibility for ensuring that the firm responded in a way that recognized the seriousness and urgency of the situation. In our view, Gutfreund did not discharge that responsibility.

Strauss, as the President of Salomon, was the official within the firm to whom Meriwether first took the matter of Mozer's misconduct for appropriate action. As its president, moreover, Strauss was responsible for the operations of Salomon as a brokerage firm.[63] Though he arranged several meetings to discuss the matter, Strauss failed to direct that Meriwether, Feuerstein, or others within the firm take the steps necessary to respond to the matter. Even if Strauss assumed that Meriwether or Feuerstein had taken the responsibility to address the matter, he failed to follow

---

[62]. Salomon did not have established procedures, or a system for applying those procedures, which together reasonably could have been expected to detect and prevent the violations. The affirmative defense provisions of Section 15(b)(4)(E) thus do not apply in this case.

[63]. As we noted in *Universal Heritage Investments Corporation,* 47 S.E.C. 839, 845 (1982): The president of a corporate broker-dealer is responsible for compliance with all of the requirements imposed on his firm unless and until he reasonably delegates particular functions to another person in that firm, and neither knows nor has reason to know that such person's performance is deficient.

up and ascertain whether action had in fact been taken. Moreover, it subsequently became clear that no meaningful action was being taken to respond to Mozer's misconduct. Under these circumstances, Strauss retained his supervisory responsibilities as the president of the brokerage firm, and he failed to discharge those responsibilities.

Meriwether was Mozer's direct supervisor and the head of all fixed-income trading activities at Salomon. Meriwether had also been designated by the firm as the person responsible for supervising the firm's fixed-income trading activities, including the activities of the Government Trading Desk.

When he first learned of Mozer's misconduct, Meriwether promptly took the matter to senior executives within the firm. In so doing, he took appropriate and responsible action. However, Meriwether's responsibilities did not end with communication of the matter to more senior executives. He continued to bear direct supervisory responsibility for Mozer after he had reported the false bid to others within the firm. As a result, until he was instructed not to carry out his responsibilities as Mozer's direct supervisor, Meriwether was required to take appropriate supervisory action. Meriwether's efforts in admonishing Mozer and telling him that his misconduct would be reported to the government were not sufficient under the circumstances to discharge his supervisory responsibilities.

C. DONALD M. FEUERSTEIN

Donald Feuerstein, Salomon's chief legal officer, was informed of the submission of the false bid by Paul Mozer in late April of 1991, at the same time other senior executives of Salomon learned of that act. Feuerstein was present at the meetings in late April at which the supervisors named as respondents in this proceeding discussed the matter. In his capacity as a legal adviser, Feuerstein did advise Strauss and Gutfreund that the submission of the bid was a criminal act and should be reported to the government, and he urged them on several occasions to proceed with disclosure when he learned that the report had not been made. However, Feuerstein did not direct that an inquiry be undertaken, and he did not recommend that appropriate procedures, reasonably designed to prevent and detect future misconduct, be instituted, or that other limitations be placed on Mozer's activities. Feuerstein also did not inform the Compliance Department, for which he was responsible as Salomon's chief legal officer, of the false bid.

Unlike Gutfreund, Strauss and Meriwether, however, Feuerstein was not a direct supervisor of Mozer at the time he first learned of the false bid. Because we believe this is an appropriate opportunity to amplify our views on the supervisory responsibilities of legal and compliance officers in Feuerstein's position, we have not named him as a respondent in this proceeding. Instead, we are issuing this report of investigation concerning the responsibilities imposed by Section 15(b)(4)(E) of the Exchange Act under the circumstances of this case.

Employees of brokerage firms who have legal or compliance responsibilities do not become "supervisors" for purposes of Sections 15(b)(4)(E) and 15(b)(6) solely because they occupy those positions. Rather, determining if a particular person is a "supervisor" depends on whether, under the facts and circumstances of a particular case, that person has a requisite degree of responsibility, ability or authority to affect the conduct of the employee whose behavior is at issue. Thus, persons occupying positions in the legal or compliance departments of broker-dealers have been found by the Commission to be "supervisors" for purposes of Sections 15(b)(4)(E) and 15(b)(6) under certain circumstances.

In this case, serious misconduct involving a senior official of a brokerage firm was brought to the attention of the firm's chief legal officer. That individual was informed of the misconduct by other members of senior management in order to obtain his advice and guidance, and to involve him as part of management's collective response to the problem. Moreover, in other instances of misconduct, that individual had directed the firm's response and had made recommendations concerning appropriate disciplinary action, and management had relied on him to perform those tasks.

Given the role and influence within the firm of a person in a position such as Feuerstein's and the factual circumstances of this case, such a person shares in the responsibility to take appropriate action to respond to the misconduct. Under those circumstances, we believe that such a person becomes a "supervisor" for purposes of Sections 15(b)(4)(E) and 15(b)(6). As a result, that person is responsible, along with the other supervisors, for taking reasonable and appropriate action. It is not sufficient for one in such a position to be a mere bystander to the events that occurred.

Once a person in Feuerstein's position becomes involved in formulating management's response to the problem, he or she is obligated to take affirmative steps to ensure that appropriate action is taken to address the misconduct. For example, such a person could direct or monitor an investigation of the conduct at issue, make appropriate recommendations for limiting the activities of the employee or for the institution of appropriate procedures, reasonably designed to prevent and detect future misconduct, and verify that his or her recommendations, or acceptable alternatives, are implemented. If such a person takes appropriate steps but management fails to act and that person knows or has reason to know of that failure, he or she should consider what additional steps are appropriate to address the matter. These steps may include disclosure of the matter to the entity's board of directors, resignation from the firm, or disclosure to regulatory authorities.[64]

These responsibilities cannot be avoided simply because the person did not previously have direct supervisory responsibility for any of the activities of the employee. Once such a person has supervisory obligations by virtue of the circumstances of a particular situation, he must either discharge those responsibilities or know that others are taking appropriate action.

---

[64]. Of course, in the case of an attorney, the applicable Code of Professional Responsibility and the Canons of Ethics may bear upon what course of conduct that individual may properly pursue.

V. ORDER

In view of the foregoing, the Commission deems it appropriate and in the public interest to impose the sanctions specified in the Offers of Settlement submitted by John H. Gutfreund, Thomas W. Strauss, and John W. Meriwether.

Accordingly, IT IS HEREBY ORDERED that:

A. John H. Gutfreund be, and he hereby is:

    (i) ordered to comply with his undertaking not to associate in the future in the capacity of Chairman or Chief Executive Officer with any broker, dealer, municipal securities dealer, investment company or investment adviser regulated by the Commission; and

    (ii) ordered to pay to the United States Treasury a civil penalty aggregating $100,000 pursuant to Section 21B(a)(4) of the Exchange Act.

B. Thomas W. Strauss be, and he hereby is:

    (i) suspended from associating with any broker, dealer, municipal securities dealer, investment company or investment adviser for a period of six (6) months; and

    (ii) ordered to pay to the United States Treasury a civil penalty aggregating $75,000 pursuant to Section 21B(a)(4) of the Exchange Act;

C. John W. Meriwether be, and he hereby is:

    (i) suspended from associating with any broker, dealer, municipal securities dealer, investment company or investment adviser for a period of three (3) months; and

    (ii) ordered to pay to the United States Treasury a civil penalty aggregating $50,000 pursuant to Section 21B(a)(4) of the Exchange Act.

. . . .

Note

See generally D. Lipton, Broker-Dealer Regulation (2015); N. Poser, & J. Fanto, Broker-Dealer Law and Regulation (4th edition 2016); R. Ferrara, D. Rivkin & G. Crespi, Stockbroker Supervision (1989); ABA Task Force, *Broker-Dealer Supervision of Registered Representatives and Branch Office Operations*, 44 Bus. Law. 1361 (1989); Dodge, *The Definition of "Supervisor": Urban Muddies the Water*, 40 Sec. Reg. L.J. 117 (2012); Fanto, *The Vanishing Supervisor*, 41 J. Corp. L. 117 (2015); Ferrara & Sanger, *Derivative Liability in Securities Laws: Controlling Person Liability, Respondeat Superior, and Aiding and Abetting*, 40 Wash. & Lee L. Rev. 1007 (1983); Janvey, *The Feuerstein Report of Investigation: Supervisory Responsibilities of Legal and Compliance Officers of Brokerage Firms*, 21 Sec. Reg. L.J. 166 (1993); Lowenfels & Bromberg, *Broker-Dealer Supervision: A Troublesome Area*, 25 Seton Hall

L. Rev. 527 (1994); Uhlenhop, *Critical Elements of an Effective Supervisory Structure*, 30 Rev. Sec. & Comm. Reg. 173 (2005).

---

§ 13.11 Credit Rating Agencies

The Dodd-Frank Act of 2010 made significant changes with respect to the regulation and oversight of credit rating agencies. The Joint Explanatory Statement of the Committee of Conference, Conference Committee Report No. 111-517 (2010), summarized these provisions as follows:

> *Subtitle C—Improvement to the Regulation of Credit Rating Agencies* gives broader powers to the SEC to regulate nationally recognized statistical rating organizations ("NRSROs"). A new Office of Credit Ratings ("Office") is required to examine NRSROs at least once a year and make key findings public. The Office will write new rules, including requiring NRSROs to (1) set up internal controls over the process for determining credit ratings; (2) establish an independent board of directors; (3) make greater disclosures to the public and investors; and (4) develop universal ratings across asset classes and types off issuer. The report also gives the Office the authority to deregister an NRSRO for providing bad ratings over time. New professional standards are established that require ratings analysts to pass qualifying exams and have continuing education.
>
> The report includes provisions to address conflicts of interest. It prohibits compliance officers from working on ratings, methodologies, or sales and prevents other employees from both marketing ratings services and performing the ratings of securities. The subtitle includes an additional conflict of interest mitigation including a new requirement for NRSROs to conduct a one-year look-back review when an NRSRO employee goes to work for an obligor or underwriter of a security or money market instrument subject to a rating by that NRSRO; and report to the SEC when certain employees of the NRSRO go to work for an entity that the NRSRO has rated in the previous twelve months. The SEC shall make such reports publicly available.
>
> To reduce the reliance on ratings, the report amends several statutes to remove references to credit ratings, credit rating agencies and NRSROs. The subtitle includes a requirement that all Federal agencies review their regulations, policies and practices that reference credit ratings, credit rating agencies, and NRSROs. After identifying where the agency relies on or makes these references, the agencies shall modify their regulations by striking these references and substituting a standard of creditworthiness to be established by the agencies.

New provisions address information gathering. NRSROs must consider information in their ratings that comes to their attention from a source other than the organizations being rated, if they find it credible. In addition, the subtitle includes an elimination of the credit rating agency exemption from Regulation Fair Disclosure, commonly known as Reg. FD.

The report also addresses liability measures for the NRSRO. The report allows investors to bring private rights of action against credit rating agencies for a knowing or reckless failure to conduct a reasonable investigation of the facts or to obtain analysis from an independent source. The report also nullifies Rule 436(g) which provides an exemption for credit ratings provided by NRSROs from being considered a part of the registration statement prepared or certified by a person under the "expert liability" regime of Section 7 and Section 11 of the Securities Act of 1933. The subtitle requires all references to "furnish" be replaced with the word "file" in existing law. Information that is "furnished" to the SEC is subject to a lower standard of accuracy and liability than information "filed" with the SEC.

The report also directs the SEC to establish a system that prohibits issuers of structured finance from selecting the NRSRO that will provide the initial credit rating. The system would mandate that initial rating assignments for structured finance securities be made on a random or semi-random basis, unless the SEC determines, after study, that an alternative system of assigning ratings would better protect investors and serve the public interest.

Chapter 14

Corporate Control Acquisitions and Contests

§ 14.01 Introduction

This Chapter addresses three types of corporate control acquisitions or contests: the proxy battle, the going-private transaction, and the hostile tender offer. Although certain aspects of state law are examined, emphasis is placed on federal regulation.

In reading the following materials, one should keep in mind that hostile proxy and tender offer fights, by their nature, are contests for corporate control. In this way, they are quite similar. As Judge Friendly in *Electronic Specialty Company v. International Controls Corp.,* 409 F.2d 937, 948 (2d Cir. 1969), stated:

> [T]ender offers [and] proxy contests . . . are alike in the fundamental feature that they generally are contests. This means that the participants on both sides act, not "in the peace of a quiet chamber," but under the stresses of the marketplace. They act quickly, sometimes impulsively, often in angry response to what they consider, whether rightly or wrongly, to be low blows by the other side. Probably there will no more be a perfect tender offer than a perfect trial. Congress intended to assure basic honesty and fair dealing, not to impose an unrealistic requirement of laboratory conditions that might make the new statute a potent tool for incompetent management to protect its own interests against the desires and welfare of the stockholders. These considerations bear on the kind of judgment to be applied in testing conduct — on both sides — and also on the issue of materiality.

§ 14.02 Going-Private Transactions

Generally, " [a] going-private transaction is a transaction or series of transactions instituted by the controlling shareholders of a publicly held corporation and designed to eliminate or substantially reduce the corporation's outstanding equity, thereby returning the corporation to private ownership."[1] Generally, these transactions often

---

1. Comment, *Regulating Going-Private Transactions: SEC Rule 13e-3,* 80 Colum. L. Rev. 782 (1980). *See generally* Illig, *A Business Lawyer's Biography: Books Every Dealmaker Should Read,* 61 J. Leg. Ed. 585 (2012).

take the form of a cash-out (or more pejoratively "freeze-out" or " squeeze-out") merger and result in compelling the minority stockholders to exchange their shares for cash.[2] Note that going-private transactions also are addressed in Chapter 9 of this text.

Problem

Dy-Gell, Inc. owns 72 percent of the stock of Lyston, Inc. The stock of both companies is publicly held. A majority of the Lyston board of directors also are directors of Dy-Gell. Both boards agree upon a merger proposal whereby Lyston will be merged into Dy-Gell with public shareholders of Lyston being cashed-out at $28.00 per share. Prior to the announcement of the merger proposal, Lyston stock was trading at $23.50 per share.

In subsequent proxy materials to Lyston shareholders, Lyston discloses that it believes that the merger is fair to minority shareholders and provides the reasons for such belief. It fails to disclose, however, that six months earlier an unaffiliated reputable corporation had approached the Lyston board of directors with a tentative offer to purchase the company at $36.00 per share.

Jordan, a shareholder of Lyston, believes that she is being "squeezed-out" solely because Dy-Gell wants to rid itself of unwanted minority shareholders holding Lyston stock. She thereupon votes against the merger and demands "fair value" for her stock. She also brings suit in federal and state court. What result? Why?

[A] State Law

Weinberger v. UOP, Inc.

Delaware Supreme Court

457 A.2d 701 (1983)

MOORE, JUSTICE.

This post-trial appeal was reheard en banc from a decision of the Court of Chancery. It was brought by the class action plaintiff below, a former shareholder of UOP, Inc., who challenged the elimination of UOP's minority shareholders by a cash-out merger between UOP and its majority owner, The Signal Companies, Inc. Originally, the defendants in this action were Signal, UOP, certain officers and directors of those companies, and UOP's investment banker, Lehman Brothers Kuhn Loeb, Inc.[3] The present Chancellor held that the terms of the merger were fair to the plaintiff and

---

2. *Id. See generally* A. Borden & J. Yunis, Going Private (2015); McGuiness & Rehbock, *Going-Private Transactions: A Practitioner's Guide*, 30 Del. J. Corp. L. 437 (2005).

[3]. Shortly before the last oral argument, the plaintiff dismissed Lehman Brothers from the action. Thus, we do not deal with the issues raised by the plaintiff's claims against this defendant.

the other minority shareholders of UOP. Accordingly, he entered judgment in favor of the defendants.

Numerous points were raised by the parties, but we address only the following questions presented by the trial court's opinion:

   1) The plaintiff's duty to plead sufficient facts demonstrating the unfairness of the challenged merger;

   2) The burden of proof upon the parties where the merger has been approved by the purportedly informed vote of a majority of the minority shareholders;

   3) The fairness of the merger in terms of adequacy of the defendants' disclosures to the minority shareholders;

   4) The fairness of the merger in terms of adequacy of the price paid for the minority shares and the remedy appropriate to that issue; and

   5) The continued force and effect of *Singer v. Magnavox Co.*, Del. Supr., 380 A.2d 969, 980 (1977), and its progeny.

In ruling for the defendants, the Chancellor re-stated his earlier conclusion that the plaintiff in a suit challenging a cash-out merger must allege specific acts of fraud, misrepresentation, or other items of misconduct to demonstrate the unfairness of the merger terms to the minority. We approve this rule and affirm it.

The Chancellor also held that even though the ultimate burden of proof is on the majority shareholder to show by a preponderance of the evidence that the transaction is fair, it is first the burden of the plaintiff attacking the merger to demonstrate some basis for invoking the fairness obligation. We agree with that principle. However, where corporate action has been approved by an informed vote of a majority of the minority shareholders, we conclude that the burden entirely shifts to the plaintiff to show that the transaction was unfair to the minority. But in all this, the burden clearly remains on those relying on the vote to show that they completely disclosed all material facts relevant to the transaction.

Here, the record does not support a conclusion that the minority stockholder vote was an informed one. Material information, necessary to acquaint those shareholders with the bargaining positions of Signal and UOP, was withheld under circumstances amounting to a breach of fiduciary duty. We therefore conclude that this merger does not meet the test of fairness, at least as we address that concept, and no burden thus shifted to the plaintiff by reason of the minority shareholder vote. Accordingly, we reverse and remand for further proceedings consistent herewith.

In considering the nature of the remedy available under our law to minority shareholders in a cash-out merger, we believe that it is, and hereafter should be, an appraisal under 8 Del. C. § 262 as hereinafter construed. We therefore overrule *Lynch v. Vickers Energy Corp.*, Del. Supr., 429 A.2d 497 (1981), to the extent that it purports to limit a stockholder's monetary relief to a specific damage formula. But to give full effect to section 262 within the framework of the General Corporation Law we adopt a more liberal, less rigid and stylized, approach to the valuation process than has heretofore been permitted by our courts. While the present state of these proceedings does not admit the plaintiff to the appraisal remedy per se, the practical effect of the remedy we do grant him will be co-extensive with the liberalized valuation and appraisal methods we herein approve for cases coming after this decision.

Our treatment of these matters has necessarily led us to a reconsideration of the business purpose rule announced in the trilogy of *Singer v. Magnavox Co.*, [Del. Supr., 380 A.2d 969 (1977)]; *Tanzer v. International General Industries, Inc.*, Del. Supr., 379 A.2d 1121 (1977); and *Roland International Corp. v. Najjar*, Del. Supr., 407 A.2d 1032 (1979). For the reasons hereafter set forth we consider that the business purpose requirement of these cases is no longer the law of Delaware.

I.

The facts found by the trial court, pertinent to the issues before us, are supported by the record, and we draw from them as set out in the Chancellor's opinion.

Signal is a diversified, technically based company operating through various subsidiaries. Its stock is publicly traded on the New York, Philadelphia and Pacific Stock Exchanges. UOP, formerly known as Universal Oil Products Company, was a diversified industrial company engaged in various lines of business, including petroleum and petro-chemical services and related products, construction, fabricated metal products, transportation equipment products, chemicals and plastics, and other products and services including land development, lumber products and waste disposal. Its stock was publicly held and listed on the New York Stock Exchange.

In 1974 Signal sold one of its wholly-owned subsidiaries for $420,000,000 in cash. *See Gimbel v. Signal Companies, Inc.*, Del. Ch., 316 A.2d 599, *aff'd*, Del. Supr., 316 A.2d 619 (1974). While looking to invest this cash surplus, Signal became interested in UOP as a possible acquisition. Friendly negotiations ensued, and Signal proposed to acquire a controlling interest in UOP at a price of $19 per share. UOP's representatives sought $25 per share. In the arm's length bargaining that followed, an understanding was reached whereby Signal agreed to purchase from UOP 1,500,000 shares of UOP's authorized but unissued stock at $21 per share.

This purchase was contingent upon Signal making a successful cash tender offer for 4,300,000 publicly held shares of UOP, also at a price of $21 per share. This combined method of acquisition permitted Signal to acquire 5,800,000 shares of stock, representing 50.5% of UOP's outstanding shares. . . .

The negotiations between Signal and UOP occurred during April 1975, and the resulting tender offer was greatly oversubscribed. However, Signal limited its total purchase of the tendered shares so that, when coupled with the stock bought from UOP, it had achieved its goal of becoming a 50.5% shareholder of UOP.

Although UOP's board consisted of thirteen directors, Signal nominated and elected only six. Of these, five were either directors or employees of Signal. The sixth, a partner in the banking firm of Lazard Freres & Co., had been one of Signal's representatives in the negotiations and bargaining with UOP concerning the tender offer and purchase price of the UOP shares. However, the president and chief executive officer of UOP retired during 1975, and Signal caused him to be replaced by James V. Crawford, a long-time employee and senior executive vice president of one of Signal's wholly-owned subsidiaries. Crawford succeeded his predecessor on UOP's board of directors and also was made a director of Signal.

By the end of 1977 Signal basically was unsuccessful in finding other suitable investment candidates for its excess cash, and by February 1978 considered that it had no other realistic acquisitions available to it on a friendly basis. Once again its attention turned to UOP.

The trial court found that at the instigation of certain Signal management personnel, including William W. Walkup, its board chairman, and Forrest N. Shumway, its president, a feasibility study was made concerning the possible acquisition of the balance of UOP's outstanding shares. This study was performed by two Signal officers, Charles S. Arledge, vice president (director of planning), and Andrew J. Chitiea, senior vice president (chief financial officer). Messrs. Walkup, Shumway, Arledge and Chitiea were all directors of UOP in addition to their membership on the Signal board.

Arledge and Chitiea concluded that it would be a good investment for Signal to acquire the remaining 49.5% of UOP shares at any price up to $24 each. Their report was discussed between Walkup and Shumway who, along with Arledge, Chitiea and Brewster L. Arms, internal counsel for Signal, constituted Signal's senior management. . . .

The executive committee meeting was set for February 28, 1978. As a courtesy, UOP's president, Crawford, was invited to attend, although he was not a member of Signal's executive committee. On his arrival, and prior to the meeting, Crawford was asked to meet privately with Walkup and Shumway. He was then told of Signal's plan to acquire full ownership of UOP and was asked for his reaction to the proposed price range of $20 to $21 per share. Crawford said he thought such a price would be "generous", and that it was certainly one which should be submitted to UOP's minority shareholders for their ultimate consideration. He stated, however, that Signal's 100% ownership could cause internal problems at UOP. He believed that employees would have to be given some assurance of their future place in a fully-owned Signal subsidiary. Otherwise, he feared the departure of essential personnel. Also, many of UOP's key employees had stock option incentive programs which would be wiped out by a merger. Crawford therefore urged that some adjustment would have to be made, such as providing a comparable incentive in Signal's shares, if after the merger he was to maintain his quality of personnel and efficiency at UOP.

Thus, Crawford voiced no objection to the $20 to $21 price range, nor did he suggest that Signal should consider paying more than $21 per share for the minority interests. Later, at the executive committee meeting the same factors were discussed, with Crawford repeating the position he earlier took with Walkup and Shumway. . . .

Thus, it was the consensus that a price of $20 to $21 per share would be fair to both Signal and the minority shareholders of UOP. Signal's executive committee authorized its management "to negotiate" with UOP "for a cash acquisition of the minority ownership in UOP, Inc. . . . .

[T]he closing price of UOP's common stock on that day was $14.50 per share.

. . . .

Between Tuesday, February 28, 1978 and Monday, March 6, 1978, a total of four business days, Crawford spoke by telephone with all of UOP's non-Signal, i.e., outside, directors. Also during that period, Crawford retained Lehman Brothers to render a fairness opinion as to the price offered the minority for its stock. He gave two reasons for this choice. First, the time schedule between the announcement and the board meetings was short (by then only three business days) and since Lehman Brothers had been acting as UOP's investment banker for many years, Crawford felt that it would be in the best position to respond on such brief notice. Second, James W. Glanville, a long-time director of UOP and a partner in Lehman Brothers, had acted as a financial advisor to UOP for many years. Crawford believed that Glanville's familiarity with UOP, as a member of its board, would also be of assistance in enabling Lehman Brothers to render a fairness opinion within the existing time constraints.

Crawford telephoned Glanville, who gave his assurance that Lehman Brothers had no conflicts that would prevent it from accepting the task. Glanville's immediate personal reaction was that a price of $20 to $21 would certainly be fair, since it represented almost a 50% premium over UOP's market price. Glanville sought a $250,000 fee for Lehman Brothers' services, but Crawford thought this too much. After further discussions Glanville finally agreed that Lehman Brothers would render its fairness opinion for $150,000.

During this period Crawford also had several telephone contacts with Signal officials. In only one of them, however, was the price of the shares discussed. In a conversation with Walkup, Crawford advised that as a result of his communications with UOP's non-Signal directors, it was his feeling that the price would have to be the top of the proposed range, or $21 per share, if the approval of UOP's outside directors was to be obtained. But again, he did not seek any price higher than $21.

Glanville assembled a three-man Lehman Brothers team to do the work on the fairness opinion. These persons examined relevant documents and information concerning UOP, including its annual reports and its Securities and Exchange Commission filings from 1973 through 1976, as well as its audited financial statements for 1977, its interim reports to shareholders, and its recent and historical market prices and trading volumes. In addition, on Friday, March 3, 1978, two members of the Lehman Brothers team flew to UOP's headquarters in Des Plaines, Illinois, to perform a "due diligence" visit, during the course of which they interviewed Crawford as well as UOP's general counsel, its chief financial officer, and other key executives and personnel.

As a result, the Lehman Brothers team concluded that "the price of either $20 or $21 would be a fair price for the remaining shares of UOP". They telephoned this impression to Glanville, who was spending the weekend in Vermont.

On Monday morning, March 6, 1978, Glanville and the senior member of the Lehman Brothers team flew to Des Plaines to attend the scheduled UOP directors meeting. Glanville looked over the assembled information during the flight. The two had with them the draft of a "fairness opinion letter" in which the price had been left blank. Either during or immediately prior to the directors' meeting, the two-page "fairness opinion letter" was typed in final form and the price of $21 per share was inserted.

On March 6, 1978, both the Signal and UOP boards were convened to consider the proposed merger. Telephone communications were maintained between the two meetings. Walkup, Signal's board chairman, and also a UOP director, attended UOP's meeting with Crawford in order to present Signal's position and answer any questions that UOP's non-Signal directors might have. Arledge and Chitiea, along with Signal's other designees on UOP's board, participated by conference telephone. All of UOP's outside directors attended the meeting either in person or by conference telephone.

First, Signal's board unanimously adopted a resolution authorizing Signal to propose to UOP a cash merger of $21 per share as outlined in a certain merger agreement and other supporting documents. This proposal required that the merger be approved by a majority of UOP's outstanding minority shares voting at the stockholders meeting at which the merger would be considered, and that the minority shares voting in favor of the merger, when coupled with Signal's 50.5% interest would have to comprise at least two-thirds of all UOP shares. Otherwise the proposed merger would be deemed disapproved.

UOP's board then considered the proposal. Copies of the agreement were delivered to the directors in attendance, and other copies had been forwarded earlier to the directors participating by telephone. They also had before them UOP financial data for 1974–1977, UOP's most recent financial statements, market price information, and budget projections for 1978. In addition they had Lehman Brothers' hurriedly prepared fairness opinion letter finding the price of $21 to be fair. Glanville, the Lehman Brothers partner, and UOP director, commented on the information that had gone into preparation of the letter.

Signal also suggests that the Arledge-Chitiea feasibility study, indicating that a price of up to $24 per share would be a "good investment" for Signal, was discussed at the UOP directors' meeting. The Chancellor made no such finding, and our independent review of the record, detailed *infra*, satisfies us by a preponderance of the evidence that there was no discussion of this document at UOP's board meeting. Furthermore, it is clear beyond peradventure that nothing in that report was ever disclosed to UOP's minority shareholders prior to their approval of the merger.

After consideration of Signal's proposal, Walkup and Crawford left the meeting to permit a free and uninhibited exchange between UOP's non-Signal directors. Upon their return a resolution to accept Signal's offer was then proposed and adopted. While Signal's men on UOP's board participated in various aspects of the meeting, they abstained from voting. However, the minutes show that each of them "if voting would have voted yes".

On March 7, 1978, UOP sent a letter to its shareholders advising them of the action taken by UOP's board with respect to Signal's offer. This document pointed out, among other things, that on February 28, 1978 "both companies had announced negotiations were being conducted".

Despite the swift board action of the two companies, the merger was not submitted to UOP's shareholders until their annual meeting on May 26, 1978. In the notice of that meeting and proxy statement sent to shareholders in May, UOP's management and board urged that the merger be approved. The proxy statement also advised:

> The price was determined after *discussions* between James V. Crawford, a director of Signal and Chief Executive Officer of UOP, and officers of Signal which took place during meetings on February 28, 1978, and in the course of several subsequent telephone conversations. (Emphasis added.)

In the original draft of the proxy statement the word "negotiations" had been used rather than "discussions". However, when the Securities and Exchange Commission sought details of the "negotiations" as part of its review of these materials, the term was deleted and the word "discussions" was substituted. The proxy statement indicated that the vote of UOP's board in approving the merger had been unanimous. It also advised the shareholders that Lehman Brothers had given its opinion that the merger prior of $21 per share was fair to UOP's minority. However, it did not disclose the hurried method by which this conclusion was reached. As of the record date of UOP's annual meeting, there were 11,488,302 shares of UOP common stock outstanding, 5,688,302 of which were owned by the minority. At the meeting only 56%, or 3,208,652, of the minority shares were voted. Of these, 2,953,812, or 51.9% of the total minority, voted for the merger, and 254,840 voted against it. When Signal's stock was added to the minority shares voting in favor, a total of 76.2% of UOP's outstanding shares approved the merger while only 2.2% opposed it.

By its terms the merger became effective on May 26, 1978, and each share of UOP's stock held by the minority was automatically converted into a right to receive $21 cash.

II.

A.

A primary issue mandating reversal is the preparation by two UOP directors, Arledge and Chitiea, of their feasibility study for the exclusive use and benefit of Signal. This document was of obvious significance to both Signal and UOP. *Using UOP data*, it described the advantages to Signal of ousting the minority at a price range of

$21-$24 per share. [emphasis supplied] Mr. Arledge, one of the authors, outlined the benefits to Signal:

Purpose Of The Merger

1) Provides an outstanding investment opportunity for Signal — (Better than any recent acquisition we have seen.)

2) Increases Signal's earnings.

3) Facilitates the flow of resources between Signal and its subsidiaries — (Big factor — works both ways.)

4) Provides cost savings potential for Signal and UOP.

5) Improves the percentage of Signal's "operating earnings" as opposed to "holding company earnings".

6) Simplifies the understanding of Signal.

7) Facilitates technological exchange among Signal's subsidiaries.

8) Eliminates potential conflicts of interest.

Having written those words, solely for the use of Signal, it is clear from the record that neither Arledge nor Chitiea shared this report with their fellow directors of UOP. We are satisfied that no one else did either. This conduct hardly meets the fiduciary standards applicable to such a transaction.

. . . .

The Arledge-Chitiea report speaks for itself in supporting the Chancellor's finding that a price of up to $24 was a "good investment" for Signal. It shows that a return on the investment at $21 would be 15.7% versus 15.5% at $24 per share. This was a difference of only two-tenths of one percent, while it meant over $17,000,000 to the minority. Under such circumstances, paying UOP's minority shareholders $24 would have had relatively little long-term effect on Signal, and the Chancellor's findings concerning the benefit to Signal, even at a price of $24, were obviously correct. . . .

Certainly, this was a matter of material significance to UOP and its shareholders. Since the study was prepared by two UOP directors, using UOP information for the exclusive benefit of Signal, and nothing whatever was done to disclose it to the outside UOP directors or the minority shareholders, a question of breach of fiduciary duty arises. This problem occurs because there were common Signal-UOP directors participating, at least to some extent, in the UOP board's decision-making processes without full disclosure of the conflicts they faced.

Although perfection is not possible, or expected, the result here could have been entirely different if UOP had appointed an independent negotiating committee of its outside directors to deal with Signal at arm's length. . . . Since fairness in this context can be equated to conduct by a theoretical, wholly independent, board of directors acting upon the matter before them, it is unfortunate that this course apparently was neither considered nor pursued. . . . Particularly in a parent-subsidiary context, a showing that the action taken was as though each of the contending parties had in fact exerted its bargaining power against the other at arm's length is strong evidence that the transaction meets the test of fairness. . . .[4]

B.

In assessing this situation, the Court of Chancery was required to examine what information defendants had and to measure it against what they gave to the minority stockholders, in a context in which "complete candor" is required. In other words, the limited function of the Court was to determine whether defendants had disclosed all information in their possession germane to the transaction in issue. And by "germane" we mean, for present purposes, information such as a reasonable shareholder would consider important in deciding whether to sell or retain stock.

. . . .

This is merely stating in another way the long-existing principle of Delaware law that these Signal designated directors on UOP's board still owed UOP and its shareholders an uncompromising duty of loyalty. . . .

Given the absence of any attempt to structure this transaction on an arm's length basis, Signal cannot escape the effects of the conflicts it faced, particularly when its designees on UOP's board did not totally abstain from participation in the matter. There is no "safe harbor" for such divided loyalties in Delaware. When directors of a Delaware corporation are on both sides of a transaction, they are required to demonstrate their utmost good faith and the most scrupulous inherent fairness of the bargain. . . . The requirement of fairness is unflinching in its demand that where one stands on both sides of a transaction, he has the burden of establishing its entire fairness, sufficient to pass the test of careful scrutiny by the courts. . . .

There is no dilution of this obligation where one holds dual or multiple directorships, as in a parent-subsidiary context. . . . Thus, individuals who act in a dual capacity as directors of two corporations, one of whom is parent and the other subsidiary, owe the same duty of good management to both corporations, and in the absence of an independent negotiating structure or the directors' total abstention from any participation in the matter, this duty is to be exercised in light of what is best for both companies. . . . The record demonstrates that Signal has not met this obligation.

C.

The concept of fairness has two basic aspects: fair dealing and fair price. The former embraces questions of when the transaction was timed, how it was initiated, structured, negotiated, disclosed to the directors, and how the approvals of the directors and the stockholders were obtained. The latter aspect of fairness relates to the economic and financial considerations of the proposed merger, including all relevant factors: assets, market value, earnings, future prospects, and any other elements that affect the intrinsic or inherent value of a company's stock. . . . However, the test for

---

[4]. [This footnote was moved to the text.]

fairness is not a bifurcated one as between fair dealing and price. All aspects of the issue must be examined as a whole since the question is one of entire fairness. However, in a non-fraudulent transaction we recognize that price may be the preponderant consideration outweighing other features of the merger. Here, we address the two basic aspects of fairness separately because we find reversible error as to both.

D.

Part of fair dealing is the obvious duty of candor. . . . Moreover, one possessing superior knowledge may not mislead any stockholder by use of corporate information to which the latter is not privy. . . . Delaware has long imposed this duty even upon persons who are not corporate officers or directors, but who nonetheless are privy to matters of interest or significance to their company. *Brophy v. Cities Service Co.*, Del. Ch., 70 A.2d 5, 7 (1949). With the well-established Delaware law on the subject, and the Court of Chancery's findings of fact here, it is inevitable that the obvious conflicts posed by Arledge and Chitiea's preparation of their "feasibility study", derived from UOP information, for the sole use and benefit of Signal, cannot pass muster.

The Arledge-Chitiea report is but one aspect of the element of fair dealing. How did this merger evolve? It is clear that it was entirely initiated by Signal. The serious time constraints under which the principals acted were all set by Signal. It had not found a suitable outlet for its excess cash and considered UOP a desirable investment, particularly since it was now in a position to acquire the whole company for itself. For whatever reasons, and they were only Signal's, the entire transaction was presented to and approved by UOP's board within four business days. Standing alone, this is not necessarily indicative of any lack of fairness by a majority shareholder. It was what occurred, or more properly, what did not occur, during this brief period that makes the time constraints imposed by Signal relevant to the issue of fairness.

The structure of the transaction, again, was Signal's doing. So far as negotiations were concerned, it is clear that they were modest at best. Crawford, Signal's man at UOP, never really talked price with Signal, except to accede to its management's statements on the subject, and to convey to Signal the UOP outside directors' view that as between the $20-$21 range under consideration, it would have to be $21. The latter is not a surprising outcome, but hardly arm's length negotiations. Only the protection of benefits for UOP's key employees and the issue of Lehman Brothers' fee approached any concept of bargaining.

As we have noted, the matter of disclosure to the UOP directors was wholly flawed by the conflicts of interest raised by the Arledge-Chitiea report. All of those conflicts were resolved by Signal in its own favor without divulging any aspect of them to UOP.

This cannot but undermine a conclusion that this merger meets any reasonable test of fairness. The outside UOP directors lacked one material piece of information generated by two of their colleagues, but shared only with Signal. True, the UOP board had the Lehman Brothers' fairness opinion, but that firm has been blamed by the plaintiff for the hurried task it performed, when more properly the responsibility for this lies with Signal. There was no disclosure of the circumstances surrounding the rather cursory preparation of the Lehman Brothers' fairness opinion. Instead, the impression was given UOP's minority that a careful study had been made, when in fact speed was the hallmark, and Mr. Glanville, Lehman's partner in charge of the matter, and also a UOP director, having spent the weekend in Vermont, brought a draft of the "fairness opinion letter" to the UOP directors' meeting on March 6, 1978 with the price left blank. We can only conclude from the record that the rush imposed on Lehman Brothers by Signal's timetable contributed to the difficulties under which this investment banking firm attempted to perform its responsibilities. Yet, none of this was disclosed to UOP's minority.

Finally, the minority stockholders were denied the critical information that Signal considered a price of $24 to be a good investment. Since this would have meant over $17,000,000 more to the minority, we cannot conclude that the shareholder vote was an informed one. Under the circumstances, an approval by a majority of the minority was meaningless. . . .

Given these particulars and the Delaware law on the subject, the record does not establish that this transaction satisfies any reasonable concept of fair dealing, and the Chancellor's findings in that regard must be reversed.

E.

Turning to the matter of price, plaintiff also challenges its fairness. His evidence was that on the date the merger was approved the stock was worth at least $26 per share. In support, he offered the testimony of a chartered investment analyst who used two basic approaches to valuation: a comparative analysis of the premium paid over market in ten other tender offer-merger combinations, and a discounted cash flow analysis.

In this breach of fiduciary duty case, the Chancellor perceived that the approach to valuation was the same as that in an appraisal proceeding. Consistent with precedent, he rejected plaintiff's method of proof and accepted defendants' evidence of value as being in accord with practice under prior case law. This means that the so-called "Delaware block" or weighted average method was employed wherein the elements of value, i.e., assets, market price, earnings, etc., were assigned a particular weight and the resulting amounts added to determine the value per share. This procedure has been in use for decades. . . . However, to the extent it excludes other generally accepted techniques used in the financial community and the courts, it is now clearly outmoded. It is time we recognize this in appraisal and other stock valuation proceedings and bring our law current on the subject.

While the Chancellor rejected plaintiff's discounted cash flow method of valuing UOP's stock, as not corresponding with "either logic or the existing law" . . . , it is significant that this was essentially the focus, i.e., earnings potential of UOP, of Messrs. Arledge and Chitiea in their evaluation of the merger. Accordingly, the standard "Delaware block" or weighted average method of valuation, formerly employed in appraisal and other stock valuation cases, shall no longer exclusively control such proceedings. We believe that a more liberal approach must include proof of value by any techniques or methods which are generally considered acceptable in the financial community and otherwise admissible in court, subject only to our interpretation of 8 Del. C. § 262(h), *infra*. . . . This will obviate the very structured and mechanistic procedure that has heretofore governed such matters. . . .

> Fair price obviously requires consideration of all relevant factors involving the value of a company. . . .

> Under 8 Del. C. § 262(h), the Court of Chancery:

> shall appraise the shares, determining their *fair* value exclusive of any element of value arising from the accomplishment or expectation of the merger, together with a fair rate of interest, if any, to be paid upon the amount determined to be the *fair* value. In determining such *fair* value, the Court shall take into account *all relevant factors*. . . . (Emphasis added.)

. . . .

It is significant that section 262 now mandates the determination of "fair" value based upon "all relevant factors". Only the speculative elements of value that may arise from the "accomplishment or expectation" of the merger are excluded. We take this to be a very narrow exception to the appraisal process, designed to eliminate use of *pro forma* data and projections of a speculative variety relating to the completion of a merger. But elements of future value, including the nature of the enterprise, which are known or susceptible of proof as of the date of the merger and not the product of speculation, may be considered. When the trial court deems it appropriate, fair value also includes any damages, resulting from the taking, which the stockholders sustain as a class. If that was not the case, then the obligation to consider "all relevant factors" in the valuation process would be eroded. . . .

. . . Clearly, there is a legislative intent to fully compensate shareholders for whatever their loss may be, subject only to the narrow limitation that one cannot take speculative effects of the merger into account.

Although the Chancellor received the plaintiff's evidence, his opinion indicates that the use of it was precluded because of past Delaware practice. While we do not suggest a monetary result one way or the other, we do think the plaintiff's evidence should be part of the factual mix and weighed as such. Until the $21 price is measured on remand by the valuation standards mandated by Delaware law, there can be no finding at the present stage of these proceedings that the price is fair. Given the lack of any candid disclosure of the material facts surrounding establishment of the $21 price, the majority of the minority vote, approving the merger, is meaningless.

The plaintiff has not sought an appraisal, but rescissory damages of the type contemplated by *Lynch v. Vickers Energy Corp.*, Del. Supr., 429 A.2d 497, 505–06 (1981) (*Lynch II*). [Generally, under rescissory damages, the measure of damages is determined at the time of judgment rather than at the time of the merger. Hence, if the value of the stock increases during this period, this benefits the plaintiff. Of course, if the value of the stock decreases during this period, the plaintiff will not seek rescissory damages. — ed.] In view of the approach to valuation that we announce today, we see no basis in our law for *Lynch II's* exclusive monetary formula for relief. On remand the plaintiff will be permitted to test the fairness of the $21 price by the standards we herein establish, in conformity with the principle applicable to an appraisal—that fair value be determined by taking "into account all relevant factors" [*see* § Del. C. § 262(h), *supra*]. In our view this includes the elements of rescissory damages if the Chancellor considers them susceptible of proof and a remedy appropriate to all the issues of fairness before him. . . .

While a plaintiff's monetary remedy ordinarily should be confined to the more liberalized appraisal proceeding herein established, we do not intend any limitation on the historic powers of the Chancellor to grant such other relief as the facts of a particular case may dictate. The appraisal remedy we approve may not be adequate in certain cases, particularly where fraud, misrepresentation, self-dealing, deliberate waste of corporate assets, or gross and palpable overreaching are involved. . . . Under such circumstances, the Chancellor's powers are complete to fashion any form of equitable and monetary relief as may be appropriate, including rescissory damages. Since it is apparent that this long completed transaction is too involved to undo, and in view of the Chancellor's discretion, the award, if any, should be in the form of monetary damages based upon entire fairness standards, i.e., fair dealing and fair price.[5] . . . [Nonetheless,] we return to the well-established principles of *Stauffer v. Standard Brands, Inc.*, Del. Supr., 187 A.2d 78 (1962), and *David J. Greene & Co. v. Schenley Industries, Inc.*, Del.Ch., 281 A.2d 30 (1971), mandating a stockholder's recourse to the basic remedy of an appraisal.

III.

Finally, we address the matter of business purpose. The defendants contend that the purpose of this merger was not a proper subject of inquiry by the trial court. The plaintiff says that no valid purpose existed—the entire transaction was a mere subterfuge designed to eliminate the minority. The Chancellor ruled otherwise, but in so doing he clearly circumscribed the thrust and effect of *Singer*. . . . This has led to the thoroughly sound observation that the business purpose test "may be . . . virtually interpreted out of existence, as it was in *Weinberger*".[6]

The requirement of a business purpose is new to our law of mergers and was a departure from prior case law. . . .

In view of the fairness test which has long been applicable to parent-subsidiary mergers . . . the expanded appraisal remedy now available to shareholders, and the broad discretion of the Chancellor to fashion such relief as the facts of a given case

---

[5]. Under 8 Del. C. § 262(a), (d) & (e), a stockholder is required to act within certain time periods to perfect the right to an appraisal.

[6]. Weiss, *The Law of Take Out Mergers: A Historical Perspective*, 56 N.Y.U.L. Rev. 624, 671, n. 300 (1981).

may dictate, we do not believe that any additional meaningful protection is afforded minority shareholders by the business purpose requirement of the trilogy of *Singer, Tanzer, Najjar,* and their progeny. Accordingly, such requirement shall no longer be of any force or effect.

The judgment of the Court of Chancery, finding both the circumstances of the merger and the price paid the minority shareholders to be fair, is reversed. The matter is remanded for further proceedings consistent herewith. Upon remand the plaintiff's post-trial motion to enlarge the class should be granted.

. . . .

Reversed and Remanded.

Note

The significant costs of complying with the Sarbanes-Oxley Act of 2002 and the Dodd-Frank Act of 2010 have prompted a number of publicly held companies to go private.

A number of states have declined to follow Delaware's approach. For example, in some states, absent fraud or illegality, appraisal is the sole remedy for lack of "entire fairness" in the terms of the merger. *See, e.g., Yanow v. Teal Industries, Inc.,* 178 Conn. 262, 422 A.2d 311 (1979). A few states accomplish this result by statute. *See, e.g.,* Minn. Stat. Ann. §302A.601 (providing that corporations may merge "with or without a business purpose" and that the remedy for lack of "entire fairness" is appraisal). On the other hand, a number of states either follow *Singer* (by retaining the business purpose test) or adhere to the *Weinberger* construction of "entire fairness," including the more expansive approach to valuation. *See, e.g., Alpert v. 28 Williams St. Corp.,* 63 N.Y.2d 557, 473 N.E.2d 19, 483 N.Y.S.2d 667 (1984); *Perl v. IU Int'l Corp.,* 61 Haw. 622, 607 P.2d 1036 (1980); *Masinter v. Webco Co.,* 262 S.E.2d 433 (W.Va. 1980).

The Delaware Supreme Court's decision in *Weinberger* raises a number of intriguing issues, including: (1) the relation of procedural safeguards (such as the establishment of an independent negotiating committee) to the substantive fairness of the transaction, (2) the duty owed by an investment banker in rendering a fairness opinion to be relied upon by the subsidiary's minority shareholders, and (3) implications under federal law, including *Weinberger's* effect on Rule 10b-5 actions (see §§ 8.04[B], 9.04[B]).

In *Glassman v. Unocal Exploration Corporation,* 777 A.2d 242, 248 (Del. 2001), the Delaware Supreme Court declined to apply *Weinberger's* entire fairness standard to short-form mergers. The court held that, "absent fraud or illegality, appraisal is the exclusive remedy available to a minority stockholder who objects to a short-form merger." The decision may be viewed as a retreat from *Weinberger. See* Steinberg, *Short-Form Mergers in Delaware,* 27 Del. J. Corp. L. 489 (2002).

The liability exposure that a corporate director, officer, or legal counsel can incur in the merger and acquisition setting can be enormous. For example, in the following decision, damages of more than $148 million were awarded.

In re Dole Food Co., Inc. Stockholder Litigation

Delaware Court of Chancery

2015 WL 5052214 (2015) ("unpublished opinion")

[In February 2013], the [Dole] Board agreed that [David H.] Murdock would start functioning as CEO, and [C. Michael] Carter would start functioning as President and COO. . . . Carter [also] retained his position as Dole's General Counsel and Corporate Secretary. He also joined the Board. . . .

As a practical matter, responsibility for day-to-day management of Dole passed . . . to Carter in December 2012. Carter was Murdock's only direct report, which meant that the executive team reported to him. His job was to carry out Murdock's plans, and he did so effectively, even ruthlessly. When Carter set a goal for a division, they fell into line. Dole's executives could not envision anyone failing to carry out Carter's instructions. . . .

In November 2013, defendant Murdock paid $13.50 per share to acquire all of the common stock of Dole . . . that he did not already own. Before the transaction, Murdock owned approximately 40% of Dole's common stock, served as its Chairman and CEO, and was its *de facto* controller. . . . The Merger closed on November 1, 2013.

In his initial letter to Dole's board of directors (the "Board"), Murdock offered to pay $12.00 per share. . . . Murdock conditioned his proposal on (i) approval from a committee of the Board made up of disinterested and independent directors (the "Committee") and (ii) the affirmative vote of holders of a majority of the unaffiliated shares. [Nonetheless,] Murdock did not adhere to its substance. He and his right-hand man, C. Michael Carter, sought to undermine the Committee from the start, and they continued their efforts throughout the process.

Before trial, the allegations and evidence regarding Murdock's and Carter's activities, together with the relationships between certain Committee members and Murdock, were sufficient to create triable questions of fact regarding the Committee's independence. The record at trial, however, demonstrated that the Committee carried out its task with integrity. The Committee was assisted in this effort by expert legal counsel and an investment bank—Lazard Frères & Co. LLC ("Lazard")—that likewise acted with integrity. . . .

Because of the diligence of its members and their advisors, the Committee overcame most of Murdock's and Carter's machinations. The Committee negotiated an increase in the price from $12.00 to $13.50 per share, which Lazard opined fell within a range of fairness. Several market indicators supported Lazard's opinion. Stockholders approved the Merger, with the unaffiliated stockholders narrowly voting in favor in a 50.9% majority.

But what the Committee could not overcome, what the stockholder vote could not cleanse, and what even an arguably fair price does not immunize, is fraud. Before Murdock made his proposal, Carter made false disclosures about the savings Dole could realize after selling approximately half of its business in 2012. He also cancelled a recently adopted stock repurchase program for pretextual reasons. These actions primed the market for the freeze-out by driving down Dole's stock price and undermining its validity as a measure of value. Then, after Murdock made his proposal, Carter provided the Committee with lowball management projections. The next day, in a secret meeting that violated the procedures established by the Committee, Carter gave Murdock's advisors and financing banks more positive and accurate data. To their credit, the Committee and Lazard recognized that Carter's projections were unreliable and engaged in Herculean efforts to overcome the informational deficit, but they could not do so fully. Critically for purposes of the outcome of this litigation, the Committee never obtained accurate information about Dole's ability to improve its income by cutting costs and acquiring farms.

By taking these actions, Murdock and Carter deprived the Committee of the ability to negotiate on a fully informed basis and potentially say no to the Merger. Murdock and Carter likewise deprived the stockholders of their ability to consider the Merger on a fully informed basis and potentially vote it down. Murdock's and Carter's conduct throughout the Committee process, as well as their credibility problems at trial, demonstrated that their actions were not innocent or inadvertent, but rather intentional and in bad faith.

Under these circumstances, assuming for the sake of argument that the $13.50 price still fell within a range of fairness, the stockholders are not limited to a fair price. They are entitled to a fairer price designed to eliminate the ability of the defendants to profit from their breaches of the duty of loyalty. This decision holds Murdock and Carter jointly and severally liable for damages of $148,190,590.18, representing an incremental value of $2.74 per share. Although facially large, the award is conservative relative to what the evidence could support.

[B] Federal Regulation

Would the facts as presented in *Weinberger* provide a federal cause of action under SEC Rules 10b-5 and 14a-9? The Supreme Court's 1991 decision in *Virginia Bankshares* sheds light on this issue.

Virginia Bankshares, Inc. v. Sandberg

United States Supreme Court

501 U.S. 1083, 111 S. Ct. 2749, 115 L.Ed.2d 929 (1991)

[This case is contained in § 9.04[B].]

SEC Rules 13e-3 and 13e-4

In addition to § 10(b) of the Exchange Act, §§ 13e-3 and 13e-4 of the Exchange Act and the SEC rules promulgated thereunder (Rules 13e-3 and 13e-4) are the principal federal securities law provisions governing going-private transactions. Rule 13e-3 is a comprehensive rule that prohibits fraudulent, deceptive or manipulative practices in connection with going private transactions and sets forth filing, disclosure, and dissemination requirements.[7] Rule 13e-4 is narrower in scope and applies to an issuer's tender offer for its own securities ("self tenders"). It, like Rule 13e-3, is an antifraud provision and mandates extensive disclosure.[8] Moreover, the same procedural requirements that apply in third-party tender offers pursuant to § 14(d) generally are extended by Rule 13e-4 to issuer self tenders.[9] Note that an issuer self tender which comes under Rule 13e-4 also may be a going-private transaction within Rule 13e-3's reach. Under such circumstances, both Rule 13c-3 and Rule 13e-4 apply.[10]

Rule 13e-3 calls for subject parties to disclose extensive information with respect to a going-private transaction. The disclosures include: (1) a description of both the benefits and detriments of the transaction to the issuer as well as to affiliated and unaffiliated shareholders; (2) disclosure of any report, opinion, or appraisal received from an outside party concerning the going-private transaction; (3) disclosure of any plans by the issuer to merge, reorganize, sell assets or make any other material change after the transaction; (4) disclosure of the source and total amount of funds for the transaction, an estimation of anticipated expenses, a summary of any loan agreements, and arrangements to finance and repay loans; and (5) disclosure of whether the subject parties reasonably believe that the transaction is fair to unaffiliated stockholders and the factors upon which they have that belief.[11]

As to the last disclosure listed above, some commentators assert that, by requiring that the subject parties disclose whether they "reasonably believe" that the going-private transaction is fair, the SEC is engaging in impermissible substantive regulation.[12] In this respect, the Supreme Court's decision in *Schreiber* (discussed in § 14.04[F][2]) is relevant.[13] There, the Supreme Court held that § 14(e) of the Exchange Act is premised on the truthful disclosure of adequate information rather

---

7. *See* Securities Exchange Act Release No. 16075 (1979). *See* A. Borden et al., Going Private (2011).

8. *See* Securities Exchange Act Release No. 16112 (1979). *See also*, Securities Exchange Act Release No. 42055 (1999).

9. *See* Securities Exchange Act Release No. 54684 (2006), [1985–1986 Transfer Binder] Fed. Sec. L. Rep. (CCH) ¶ 83,954 (SEC 1986).

10. Securities Exchange Act Release No. 16112 (1979). See Manges, *SEC Regulation of Issuer and Third-Party Tender Offers*, 8 Sec. Reg. L.J. 275 (1981).

11. Schedule 13E-3, 17 C.F.R. § 240.13e-100. *See Howing Co. v. Nationwide Corp.*, 826 F.2d 1470 (6th Cir. 1987), 927 F.2d 263 (6th Cir. 1991), 972 F.2d 700 (6th Cir. 1992).

12. *See, e.g.*, Note, *Rule 13e-3 and the Going-Private Dilemma: The SEC's Quest for a Substantive Fairness Doctrine*, 58 Wash. U.L.W. 883 (1980).

13. 472 U.S. 1 (1985).

than on the substantive fairness of the transaction. Because both §§ 13(e) and 14(e) were enacted as part of the Williams Act in 1968 (as an amendment to the Exchange Act) and contain in part similar language, the assertion that Rule 13e-3's disclosure of "fairness" provision is invalid may have an even stronger basis today. Nonetheless, an argument can be made that, in prescribing this requirement, the Commission has focused on its disclosure function rather than engaging principally in substantive regulation.[14] Note, moreover, that minority shareholders, provided they can show a material misrepresentation or nondisclosure along with the loss of an otherwise available state remedy in connection with the going private transaction, may avail themselves of the § 10(b) or § 14(a) right of action.[15]

§ 14.03 Proxy Contests

Under federal law, proxy contests principally are governed by § 14(a) of the Exchange Act and SEC rules prescribed thereunder. In this regard, the legal standards underlying a private right of action under § 14(a) are addressed in § 9.04. That discussion should be reviewed at this point.

Until relatively recently, it generally was thought that the tender offer had replaced the proxy battle as the means for procuring corporate control or effecting a change in corporate policies. "This situation was attributed to the difficulty of ousting an incumbent management (unless it was demonstrably incompetent and the insurgents had a large stock position), the significant amount of money and time consumed by a proxy fight, and the impossibility of recouping proxy fight costs if the insurgents failed to take control."[16] To a degree, however, the proxy fight has seen a partial renaissance. While this renaissance arguably may be more in response to market conditions than to regulatory developments, it also reflects changes in the regulatory context. Indeed, with the proliferation of state takeover statutes, SEC tender offer regulations, and court battles, the costs of pursuing a hostile tender offer can be exorbitant (*e.g.*, costs of acquiring a controlling interest, attorney and investment banker fees, and, depending upon market conditions, high interest rates).

Moreover, insurgents now are conducting proxy contests as a means to facilitate their hostile tender offers. See, for example, the Proxy Statement of Hilton Hotels Corporation and HLT Corporation at an Annual Meeting of Stockholders of ITT Corporation:

---

14. *See generally* Kofele-Kale, *The SEC's Going-Private Rules: Analysis and Developments*, 19 Sec. Reg. L.J. 139 (1991).

15. *See Virginia Bankshares, Inc. v. Sandberg*, 501 U.S. 1083 (1991); *Wilson v. Great American Industries, Inc.*, 979 F.2d 924 (2d Cir. 1992).

16. Brown, *Changes in Offeror Strategy in Response to New Laws and Regulations*, 25 Case W. Res. L. Rev. 843, 865–866 (1978). *See* Bainbridge, *Redirecting State Takeover Laws at Proxy Contests*, 1992 Wis. L. Rev. 1071.

This proxy statement (the "Proxy Statement") and the enclosed WHITE proxy card are being furnished to stockholders of ITT Corporation, a Nevada corporation (the "Company"), by Hilton Hotels Corporation, a Delaware corporation ("Hilton"), and HLT Corporation, a Delaware corporation and wholly owned subsidiary of Hilton ("HLT"), in connection with the solicitation of proxies from the Company's stockholders to be used at the 1997 Annual Meeting of Stockholders of the Company, including any adjournments or postponements thereof and any special meeting called in lieu thereof (the "Annual Meeting"), to take the following actions: (i) to elect up to 25 persons to be nominated by Hilton and HLT (the "Hilton Nominees") to the Board of Directors of the Company (the "Board"), who are expected, subject to their fiduciary duties, to take all actions as may be necessary to facilitate the [Tender] Offer (as defined herein) and the Proposed Hilton Merger (as defined herein); (ii) to approve a non-binding stockholder resolution urging the Board to arrange for the sale of the Company to Hilton, HLT or any bidder offering a higher price for the Company (the "Sale Resolution"); and (iii) to approve a stockholder resolution to repeal each and every provision of the Amended and Restated By-laws of the Company (the "Bylaws") adopted on or after July 23, 1996 and prior to the adoption of such resolution (the "Bylaws Resolution," and together with the Sale Resolution, the "Proposals").

GAF Corporation v. Heyman

United States Court of Appeals, Second Circuit

724 F.2d 727 (1983)

GEORGE C. PRATT, CIRCUIT JUDGE.

This is an expedited appeal from a judgment of the United States District Court for the Southern District of New York (Lloyd F. MacMahon, Judge), entered after a bitter proxy contest in which shareholders of plaintiff GAF Corporation voted decisively to replace the corporation's incumbent board of directors with an insurgent slate headed by defendant Samuel J. Heyman. The district court ruled that the insurgents violated § 14(a) of the Securities Exchange Act of 1934 . . . and Rule 14a-9(a) thereunder . . . by failing to disclose in their proxy materials any information concerning an action for breach of trust, brought by Heyman's sister against him and his mother a year before the 1983 campaign began, which GAF alleged cast doubt on Heyman's fitness to serve as a director. Although this family dispute among the Heymans did not involve GAF, the district court enjoined the entire insurgent slate from assuming the directorships to which they had been elected, set a new record date, and ordered a resolicitation of proxies and a new election. For the reasons below, we hold that non-disclosure of the Heyman family lawsuit was not a material omission in the context of this proxy contest. Accordingly, we reverse.

I. BACKGROUND

As will be apparent from the following recitation, this appeal arises out of a unique set of circumstances. Because our resolution of the central issue on appeal — the materiality of the Heyman family lawsuit — is tied so closely to the specific facts before us, we find it necessary to recount them in great detail.

A. The Parties

GAF is a Delaware corporation primarily engaged in the manufacture of specialty chemicals and building materials. Its stock is publicly traded on the New York Stock Exchange. As of March 9, 1983, the record date for the election of directors at the 1983 annual meeting, GAF had 45,000 shareholders, with 14,333,750 shares of common and 2,478,062 shares of convertible preferred stock outstanding. Roughly 40 percent of these shares were controlled by institutional investors.

Since its initial public offering in 1965, GAF's chairman of the board and chief executive officer has been Dr. Jesse Werner, a chemist by trade, who headed the slate of incumbent director-nominees seeking re-election in 1983. Management's remaining nine nominees had served on the GAF board for periods ranging from two to thirteen years. As a group, GAF's incumbent directors and officers controlled approximately 3.8 percent of the corporation's common stock.

Werner's counterpart in the insurgent camp was Samuel J. Heyman, a Connecticut businessman. During 1982 and 1983 Heyman organized, financed, and was the principal spokesman for "The GAF Shareholders' Committee for New Management" (the Committee). The Committee's slate of nominees included a number of businessmen and a former United States Senator, all of whom were handpicked by Heyman. As of the record date, Heyman, who owned no GAF stock prior to 1981, controlled approximately 4.72 percent of the corporation's common stock. Together, the insurgent slate controlled roughly 5.5 percent of all outstanding shares.

B. The Events of 1982: Threatened Contest, Settlement Agreement, and Litigation Fallout

Heyman first attempted to influence GAF's policies in January 1982, when he proposed that the corporation either be liquidated or buy back a significant percentage of its outstanding stock. Werner dismissed both alternatives as not "practically feasible".

In February and March, Heyman stepped up the pressure on management by preparing for a proxy contest at the 1982 annual meeting, scheduled for April. However, when Werner informed Heyman that GAF had received overtures from several corporations concerning a merger of the entire corporation or a sale of the building materials business, GAF and Heyman entered into a written settlement agreement under which Heyman agreed to forego any challenge at the 1982 annual meeting in exchange for management's commitment to pursue these transactions. GAF also agreed to reimburse Heyman for $250,000 in expenses he claimed to have incurred. On March 22, GAF announced in a press release, without disclosing the settlement that had been reached the night before, that it was entertaining proposals from three corporations regarding merger or sale transactions with a "view toward maximizing near-term benefits to [GAF] shareholders".

While the settlement agreement established a temporary truce, it ultimately created more problems than it resolved. Depending on which side is believed, GAF was either unwilling or unable to consummate any of the transactions contemplated by the agreement. On September 22, GAF formally renewed hostilities by suing Heyman in the District Court for the Southern District of New York claiming misrepresentation and breach of contract because Heyman had incurred less than $250,000 in expenses in connection with his threatened proxy contest. GAF sought to recover the shortfall.

On November 10, Heyman struck back in the same court with an individual and stockholders' derivative action against GAF and its board. His complaint alleged, among other things, that the board had made false representations concerning potential merger and sale negotiations in order to induce the Committee to withdraw its plan to wage a proxy contest in 1982, and continued to make such false representations in later progress reports to shareholders, with the objective of inducing shareholders to vote for management at the 1983 annual meeting. Both of these actions are pending.

C. The 1983 Campaign

Having been unable to influence the corporation's policies in 1982, Heyman decided to escalate his efforts in 1983. On January 27, he served a demand on GAF to inspect and copy a current list of shareholders under Del. Code Ann. tit. 8, § 220. When management refused, Heyman secured an order in the Delaware Chancery Court on February 16 requiring GAF to comply with his demand.

Before this order was issued, Heyman and his counsel met with Werner and counsel to the board in a final attempt to avoid what promised to be a costly and disruptive proxy war. At this meeting, Heyman reportedly offered to withdraw his challenge if Werner would resign. Not surprisingly, his offer was rejected, thus clearing the stage for the 1983 campaign.

The proxy contest was fiercely fought on several fronts. In addition to sending proxy materials directly to shareholders, both sides placed advertisements in the New York Times and the Wall Street Journal. The "total mix" of information available at the time of the election also included the many news stories that the closely watched contest had generated.

In the early stages of the contest, the insurgent Committee hammered away at two central themes. First, the Committee challenged [incumbent] management's 18-year record at GAF. Specifically, the Committee emphasized that:

(1) GAF common shares had lost more than 80 percent of their market value (adjusted for inflation);

(2) Dividends on GAF's common stock had recently been slashed by 75 percent to an all-time low;

(3) GAF had reported an average net income of less than $.22 per share annually, and the book value of its common stock had dropped from $14.97 per share to $4.58 per share;

(4) GAF had reported an aggregate operating loss of more than $46,000,000 in 1981 and 1982;

(5) Werner had pursued a program of random and haphazard acquisitions that cost the corporation hundreds of millions of dollars;

(6) Werner's record for executive turnover featured the termination of three successive GAF presidents in a two-year period; and

(7) Despite all of the foregoing, Werner had been "rewarded" with increasingly excessive compensation packages.

The Committee underscored these points by selectively quoting excerpts from the financial press that were sharply critical of GAF, in general, and Werner, in particular. For example, Forbes Magazine had described GAF as having "one of the worst corporate performance records in American industry." Similarly, Adweek had ranked Werner as one of the seven "most overpaid people in America."

The second theme in the platform unveiled by the Committee was its program to realize GAF's underlying values for its shareholders. The Committee advocated retention of GAF's building products division, at least until conditions in the housing market improved, and an immediate sale of the corporation's chemical business and classical radio station. After retirement of the corporation's long-term debt, the Committee's program envisioned a substantial distribution of the remaining cash proceeds to shareholders. Among the proxy materials circulated in support of this program were favorable opinion letters from the Committee's investment banker, Prudential-Bache, and its accounting firm, Arthur Andersen & Co.

Responding to the issues raised by the Committee, the incumbents defended their performance, criticized the Committee's program, and proposed an alternative program. With respect to their own financial record, they questioned the selected statistics, convenient years, and self-serving definitions relied on by the Committee. Further, the incumbents emphasized that the market price of GAF stock had soared recently.

As to the Committee's program, the incumbents initially opposed a sale of the chemical business and instead advocated disposition of the building products division. According to the incumbents, the Committee's plan to sell off the chemical division, retire the corporation's long-term debt, and distribute the remaining proceeds to shareholders was based on an unrealistic estimate of the market value of that division. They also argued that it would not be advisable to eliminate the reliable and highly profitable chemical business and become totally dependent on the cyclical building materials business. To buttress their position, the incumbents circulated an opinion letter from GAF's investment banker, Morgan Stanley & Co., which proclaimed that "the GAF Plan is superior".

While both sides' proxy materials focused primarily on these economic issues, the campaign was not without its share of personal attacks. For openers, each side repeatedly accused the other of bad faith in connection with the 1982 settlement. Beyond this, the Committee asserted that Robert Spitzer, one of GAF's outside directors, had testified under immunity in a 1979 federal prosecution that he had made illegal cash payoffs to a union official in return for labor concessions for Treadwell Corporation. The Committee also charged that Werner, a classical music enthusiast, had acquired GAF's unprofitable radio station to indulge his own personal hobby at the corporation's expense. The incumbents, on the other hand, went to great lengths to portray Heyman and the other members of the Committee as inexperienced opportunists who lacked the sound judgment needed to steward a public corporation. Perhaps a new low in corporate conflict was reached when, after meeting Heyman's children at a social event, Werner commented that "[t]hey looked as though they were rented for the evening."

During the last few weeks of the campaign, the substantive economic issues took on even greater importance when GAF announced a series of proposed transactions. On April 10, the corporation announced that the board had approved a leveraged buy-out of the building materials group by Southwestern General Corporation. This transaction, however, was "subject, among other things, to the preparation and execution of definitive agreements", with "no assurance that [it] will ultimately be consummated." Two days later, on April 12, GAF announced that it had entered into a back-up agreement under which Odyssey Partners would undertake to complete the buy-out of the building materials group if the deal with Southwestern General fell through.

Predictably, both of these deals were assailed by the insurgents. Then, unpredictably, on April 22, less than one week before the annual meeting, GAF announced that it had entered into a contract to sell the chemical business to Allied Corporation. The Committee promptly claimed that the plan it had espoused from the outset of the contest had been vindicated. At the same time, it cautioned shareholders that this latter deal could be jettisoned if the Werner management were re-elected. In fact, after the district court enjoined the insurgents from taking office, GAF did announce that the transactions with both Southwest General and Allied had been canceled.

The annual meeting on April 28 was just as chaotic as the last few weeks of the contest. In a transparent attempt to stave off defeat, the incumbent board refused to close the polls at the conclusion of the meeting. The Committee then obtained an order from the Delaware Chancery Court directing the Inspectors of Election to proceed with the tabulation of votes. The final tabulation confirmed that 58.6 percent of the shareholders favored the Committee over the incumbent board.

D. The Connecticut Action

1. The Complaint

On May 17, 1982, several months after the 1982 settlement between Heyman and GAF, Heyman's sister, Abigail, filed suit against him and his mother in the United

States District Court for the District of Connecticut. Abigail's 28-page complaint alleged that while acting in several fiduciary capacities, including partner, attorney-in-fact, and trustee, Heyman had denied Abigail information concerning her personal assets and converted some of those assets to his own use.

. . . .

The complaint sought an accounting, an order requiring disclosure of the information withheld, an order requiring a separation of assets, compensatory damages, punitive damages, and treble damages under a Connecticut statute applicable to theft.

2. Background of the Heyman Family Dispute

The Connecticut action arose out of what the special master appointed to supervise discovery in this case aptly described as "a very human family situation." When his father died in 1968, Heyman resigned his office as an Assistant United States Attorney in Connecticut in order to take charge of a successful family real estate business comprised of a series of partnerships, trusts, and closely held corporations. Sister Abigail, a professional photographer, had a stake in many of these ventures, but chose not to become actively involved. Instead, she granted Heyman a general power of attorney to conduct her financial affairs, similar to the power she had previously granted her father. It is undisputed that the family business, in general, and Abigail, in particular, have prospered in the fifteen years since Heyman assumed control.

The family relationship proceeded relatively smoothly until 1975, when Abigail, who had been divorced from her first husband, began living with a psychiatrist who was twenty years her senior and still married to his first wife. By this time, Heyman and his mother had begun to question Abigail's judgment, arguably with good cause. Just prior to her relationship with the psychiatrist, Abigail had become pregnant while unmarried, had an abortion performed, photographed her own abortion while the operation was in progress, published the photographs in a nationally circulated book, and discussed the matter in a televised interview. In addition, Abigail had suffered periods of severe depression and was receiving periodic psychiatric care.

With the onset of her relationship with the psychiatrist, whom she eventually married, Abigail began to demonstrate an interest in her financial affairs that she had never evidenced before. Heyman and his mother were convinced that Abigail was being manipulated by the psychiatrist, who they presumed to be interested in Abigail solely because of her wealth. Therefore, in 1976, they arranged to have Heyman transfer substantially all of Abigail's liquid assets, valued at approximately $850,000, along with a matching amount of his own assets, to an existing partnership between Heyman and Abigail (the Heyman Joint Venture). At the same time Heyman, acting as attorney-in-fact, signed Abigail's name to a new partnership agreement which in effect gave him exclusive control over these assets until 1990.

Over the next few years, Abigail made a number of requests for information concerning her financial affairs. After receiving what she apparently considered to be unsatisfactory responses from Heyman, Abigail revoked his power of attorney in September, 1981.

3. The Sealing Orders

On May 26, 1982, only nine days after Abigail's complaint was filed, and before any responsive pleading, the parties in the Connecticut action entered into a stipulation and order pursuant to which all proceedings were stayed pending settlement negotiations aimed at separating Abigail's financial interests from the family business. Significantly, the stipulation further provided for the sealing of the entire court file on this intra-family dispute.

. . . .

Heyman and his mother testified at their depositions in the instant action that they originally sought to seal the court file in May 1982 to maintain the confidentiality of a potentially embarrassing family dispute, not because Heyman was contemplating waging a proxy contest in 1983. However, Heyman also freely admitted that it was his ongoing struggle with GAF that led to the discovery provisions in the latter two stipulations.

4. GAF's Motion to Intervene

Despite the Heymans' extensive efforts to keep their lawsuit private, the appearance sheet in the court file was somehow not initially placed under seal. This document, which identified the parties and characterized the action as one for "breach of trust", was discovered by a team of private investigators hired by GAF. On March 11, 1983, in the midst of the proxy contest, GAF moved to intervene in the Connecticut action for the limited purpose of gaining access to the information contained in the court file. GAF's primary argument in its moving papers was that its shareholders had a right to discover whether any shares of GAF stock were involved in the action. It also argued that the shareholders were entitled to know whether Abigail's allegations impugned her brother's integrity.

At the same time that it filed the motion to intervene, GAF distributed the following press release to the news media and the Wall Street brokerage community:

> New York, March 13 — GAF Corporation announced today that it has moved to intervene in an action brought by Abigail Heyman, individually and on behalf of a minor, against parties including Samuel J. Heyman, individually and as a trustee. Abigail Heyman is the sister of Samuel J. Heyman.
>
> According to court records, the action is for breach of trust and is pending in the United States District Court for the District of Connecticut. Last May a writ of attachment for $10 million was obtained against Heyman in this suit which has since been released.
>
> The papers and proceedings, including the court docket and the complaint, have been sealed at the request of Heyman and the other parties.

Accordingly, the details of the complaint and related matters are not available to GAF, its shareholders, the press or the public at this time.

GAF, in seeking intervention in the suit, is not seeking any relief other than that the information in the suit be made available to the public and GAF shareholders. GAF's management believes that when a person such as Heyman asks stockholders of a public corporation to vote him into a position of trust in that corporation, all matters which may bear on his integrity and character should be made available to such stockholders.

Heyman's filings with the SEC show that certain trusts over which he has control own GAF stock. GAF is also seeking to ascertain whether any of such stock is the subject matter of, or could be affected by, the suit.

On March 31, Judge Daly denied GAF's motion to intervene. . . . GAF's motion for an expedited appeal from Judge Daly's ruling was denied by this court.

E. The Instant Action

1. GAF's Complaint

With its motion to intervene pending in the Connecticut action, on March 22, 1983 GAF filed its thirty-five page complaint in the instant action in the Southern District of New York. . . .

. . . .

2. GAF Seeks Discovery

In early April, less than four weeks before the 1983 annual meeting, GAF sought discovery in the instant action concerning the facts underlying the Connecticut action from the Heymans and their counsel. The Heymans, however, set aside their family differences and banded together in opposing these requests on the ground that the sealing orders precluded any such inquiry. To dispel any doubts about her sympathies in the proxy context, Abigail submitted an affidavit on April 12 declaring her wholehearted support for her brother.

Faced with this obstacle, GAF sought relief from the special master Judge Mac-Mahon had appointed to supervise discovery. After speaking with Judge Daly by telephone, the special master issued an order on April 21 upholding the Heymans' position. . . .

3. GAF Seeks Mandamus

GAF then petitioned this court for a writ of mandamus or prohibition permitting it to discover the facts underlying the Connecticut action. On April 27, the day prior to the annual meeting, an emergency panel of this court heard argument and issued an order granting the writ. "Assuming, without deciding, that Judge Daly could properly prevent disclosure of the documents and testimony he ordered sealed in the Connecticut action," the panel reasoned that "his sealing order could not prevent independent discovery of that information in a separate lawsuit." Thus, without disturbing the sealing orders themselves, the panel directed the special master and the district court to permit discovery of any documents that would have been discoverable if the Connecticut action had never been commenced.

4. Proceedings Before the District Judge

In the wake of this ruling, GAF's management, sensing it had lost the April 28 election, returned to the district court on May 2 and moved for a preliminary injunction to delay certification of the election results until the district court could determine whether resolicitation was required. In its moving papers, GAF resurrected the argument it had suggested in its motion to intervene, but apparently since abandoned, that the Connecticut action might be material insofar as it cast doubt on Heyman's integrity and fitness to serve as a director. . . .

5. Decision Below

. . . Given the exigencies of the case, the [district] court . . . deemed GAF's complaint amended to include what had now clearly become its central contention, that Heyman had failed to disclose material information regarding his fitness to serve as a director.

. . . .

On the basis of his conclusions, the district judge determined that the "drastic step" of resolicitation was the only appropriate remedy. He directed the defendants, in their resolicitation material, both to state that resolicitation had been ordered by the court and to accurately set forth the material allegations and facts pertaining to the Connecticut action. Finally, because over half of GAF's voting shares had changed hands in the three months since the original record date, the court established the date of its decision as the record date for the new election.

II. DISCUSSION

The general legal standards governing this appeal are not in dispute. The point of departure is § 14(a) of the Securities Exchange Act of 1934. . . .

A. Threshold Issues

. . . .

We . . . treat this appeal as one from a judgment entered following an accelerated trial on the merits based purely on documentary evidence including depositions. With the case in this posture, our scope of review is not limited by the clearly erroneous rule of Fed. R. Civ. P. 52(a), since the controlling issue of materiality turns on the application of a legal standard to the facts. . . .

B. The Materiality of the Connecticut Action

The positions of the parties regarding the central issue on appeal are fairly straightforward. Heyman contends that the Committee had no obligation to disclose in a GAF proxy fight either the contested, unproven, and unpursued allegations of a complaint filed in an unrelated intra-family dispute or the circumstances surrounding a family loan transaction not even mentioned in that complaint. In any event,

Heyman argues, GAF's dissemination of the "breach of trust" allegations in its March 13 press release cured these omissions, since the "total mix" of information available to GAF shareholders would not have been significantly altered by fuller disclosure. On the other hand, GAF argues that the fact that a candidate for a position as a corporate fiduciary is a defendant in a pending lawsuit, charging him with improper self-dealing and other fiduciary misconduct, is necessarily important to stockholders called upon to decide who should be entrusted with the stewardship of their collective investment.

In considering these competing arguments, we are guided not only by the principles outlined above, but also by SEC Regulation S-K. . . . Regulation S-K, together with more general provisions such as Rule 14a-9, "states the requirements applicable to the content of . . . proxy and information statements under § 14 of the Exchange Act". The regulation provides the following instructions regarding involvement in legal proceedings that must be disclosed:

(f) *Involvement in certain legal proceedings.* Describe any of the following events that occurred during the past five years and that are material to an evaluation of the ability or integrity of any director, person nominated to become a director or executive officer of the registrant:

(1) A petition under the Federal bankruptcy laws or any state insolvency law was filed by or against, or a receiver, fiscal agent or similar officer was appointed by a court for the business or property of such person, or any partnership in which he was a general partner at or within two years before the time of such filing, or any corporation or business association of which he was an executive officer at or within two years before the time of such filing;

(2) Such person was convicted in a criminal proceeding or is a named subject of a pending criminal proceeding (excluding traffic violations and other minor offenses);

(3) Such person was the subject of any order, judgment, or decree, not subsequently reversed, suspended or vacated, of any court of competent jurisdiction, permanently or temporarily enjoining him from, or otherwise limiting, the following activities:

(i) Acting as an investment adviser, underwriter, broker or dealer in securities, or as an affiliated person, director or employee of any investment company, bank, savings and loan association or insurance company, or engaging in or continuing any conduct or practice in connection with such activity;

(ii) Engaging in any type of business practice; or

(iii) Engaging in any activity in connection with the purchase or sale of any security or in connection with any violation of Federal or State securities laws;

(4) Such person was the subject of any order, judgment or decree, not subsequently reversed, suspended or vacated, of any Federal or State authority barring,

suspending or otherwise limiting for more than 60 days the right of such person to engage in any activity described in paragraph (f)(3)(i) of this Item, or to be associated with persons engaged in any such activity; or

(5) Such person was found by a court of competent jurisdiction in a civil action or by the Commission to have violated any Federal or State securities law, and the judgment in such civil action or finding by the Commission has not been subsequently reversed, suspended, or vacated.[17]

. . . .

Nothing in this detailed regulation, which has been relegated to a footnote in GAF's brief, required Heyman to make any disclosure about the unproven allegations in the Connecticut action, much less the disputed loan transaction. While this court and others have indicated that compliance with Schedule 14A does not necessarily guarantee that a proxy statement satisfies Rule 14a-9(a), . . . the regulation does provide us with the Commission's expert view of the types of involvement in legal proceedings that are most likely to be matters of concern to shareholders in a proxy contest. . . .

In our view, the regulation's emphasis on orders, judgments, decrees, and findings in civil proceedings, in stark contrast to its express coverage of all pending criminal proceedings, strongly suggests that regardless of how serious they may appear on their face, unadjudicated allegations in a pending civil action against a director-nominee should not automatically be deemed material. In a society as litigious as ours, where plaintiffs are permitted great latitude in their pleadings, a reasonable shareholder would not place much stock in the bald, untested allegations in a civil complaint not involving the subject corporation without first examining, among other relevant factors, the relationship between the parties, the nature of the allegations, the circumstances out of which they arose, and the extent to which the action has been pursued. Whether that information would be considered important in deciding how to vote would then depend on the issues involved in the proxy contest itself.

Applying the first part of this approach to the unique circumstances present here, all of the relevant factual indicia militate against a finding of materiality. First, the Connecticut action was "pending" only in a technical sense. The action was stayed on consent only nine days after it was commenced, before Heyman even filed a responsive pleading. No formal discovery had been conducted. . . .

Second, the Connecticut action did not in any way involve GAF. . . . Nor did Abigail's complaint allege any violations of the securities laws of the type referred to in Regulation

S-K. . . . While we do not mean to suggest that pending litigation against a director-nominee based on state law and involving a family or other non-public business can

---

[17]. [The SEC subsequently has amended this Item. As amended today, the Item still does not require disclosure of this pending lawsuit or the disputed loan transaction. See Item 401(f) of Regulation S-K; § 5.03[D] *supra*.]

never be material, actions of that nature are less likely to be matters of importance to public shareholders.

Third, the circumstances surrounding Abigail's allegations negate their materiality. All available evidence suggests that the action was nothing more than the outgrowth of an intra-family feud between Abigail and her new husband on one side and her mother and brother on the other. While Abigail's complaint did contain a myriad of allegations, both "serious" and petty, her apparent overriding objective was to separate her financial interests from the family business. Once her mother and brother agreed to pursue an amicable settlement, she in effect voluntarily withdrew the action. Furthermore, she subsequently swore that she supported her brother's slate in the proxy contest.

Thus, viewed in context, the three specific allegations in Abigail's complaint seized upon by GAF raise no serious question about Heyman's fitness to serve as a corporate director. Of even less significance is the $1,425,000 loan transaction, which was never specifically referred to in Abigail's complaint, but was the cornerstone of GAF's presentation below. While it may be true, as the district judge observed, that Abigail's general allegation as to diversion of assets was "broad enough to pertain to the loan" there is no basis for assuming that Abigail had any intention of asserting such a claim. Given that the "proxy rules simply do not require management to accuse itself of antisocial or illegal policies", . . . it would be fundamentally unfair to require Heyman to have anticipated and then disclosed the interpretation that GAF would place on the open-ended language of Abigail's complaint once the proxy contest was over. *See* Ferrara, Starr & Steinberg, *Disclosure of Information Bearing on Management Integrity and Competency*, 76 Nw. U. L. Rev. 555, 609 (1981).

Moreover, it is hardly surprising that Abigail's 28-page complaint never mentioned the loan transaction complained of by GAF. The loan was permitted by the elder Heyman's will and, as the district judge found, was "typical of many transactions engaged in by Heyman on behalf of the Heyman family entities" "except possibly in magnitude and duration". It would seem the "reasonable investor" would not have been influenced to change his proxy vote had the loan been disclosed.

The significance of the Connecticut action fades even further when its dormant allegations are compared with the issues that were raised in the proxy contest. Applying the literal language of Rule 14a-9(a), under which information omitted from a proxy statement is material if it is "necessary in order to make the statements therein not false or misleading", the district judge found that the Committee's proxy materials were defective because Heyman "presented himself to the shareholders as a man of considerable accomplishment and integrity" but "failed to hint at the serious allegations lodged against him or the transactions which are the basis of these claims." After reviewing the volumes of material that were generated during the proxy contest, however, we have found only a handful of excerpts that tend to support this view. For example, at the outset of the campaign, Heyman characterized himself and the Committee as "[h]aving all had extensive experience as responsible members of the corporate, business, and professional worlds". Similarly, after management pulled a complete reversal at the close of the contest and announced the proposed sale of the chemical business, the Committee inquired in a letter to shareholders, "Who can you rely upon to effectively distribute the proceeds?" But isolated excerpts of this nature cannot obscure the fact that the overwhelming weight of both sides' proxy literature and advertisements focused on fundamental economic issues of concern to shareholders: the record of management and the competing plans for realizing the asset values of GAF. Given the predominance of these economic issues, the district judge erred in holding that there was "a substantial likelihood" that a reasonable shareholder would have considered the Connecticut action "important in deciding how to vote." . . .

The court further erred by holding there was a "substantial likelihood" that disclosure of the action and its underlying facts "would have been viewed by the reasonable investor as having significantly altered the 'total mix' of information made available." . . . The fact that Heyman had been sued by his sister for "breach of trust" was disseminated by GAF more than six weeks before the annual meeting in its March 13 press release. The gist of the press release was also reported in the two Reuters news stories alluded to in GAF's complaint. Further, on the day of the election, a major story in the Wall Street Journal referred to GAF's attempt "to open the court papers in a suit brought against Mr. Heyman by his sister Abigail over family matters" as one of "a number of gambits that backfired or offended important stockholders."

GAF contends that "[n]o information whatever about the suit was ever included in direct communications to GAF shareholders." However, Heyman responds without contradiction "that GAF itself directly sent its press release to more than a dozen major institutions holding, or known to represent shareholders holding, a substantial number of GAF shares."

While there can be no doubt that the allegations and underlying facts of the Connecticut action were not "thoroughly aired," . . . we are convinced that this information "is of such dubious significance" that its disclosure may have "accomplish[ed] more harm than good". . . . In the "hurly-burly" of this contest, . . . particularly in its last few weeks when GAF announced deal after deal after deal, the shareholders had their hands full sorting out the proposed transactions and evaluating them in light of the combatants' competing programs. While GAF's incumbent management obviously would have preferred to shift attention away from these core economic issues, "bury[ing] the shareholders in an avalanche of trivial information", . . . would scarcely have served the interests of corporate democracy.

Moreover, the district court found that a reasonable person could conclude that Heyman had "acted with the best of motives, in good faith, in the best interests of Abigail, and for her benefit and protection." If resolicitation were required, Heyman would be free to characterize the facts underlying the Connecticut action in a similarly favorable fashion. In addition, he could state that Abigail, the supposed victim of his "breach of trust", supported his slate. It is therefore likely that the impact of GAF's press release would have been diminished rather than bolstered by any further disclosure.

Our conclusion that non-disclosure of the Connecticut action was not a material omission is reinforced by several additional factors. First, we consider it revealing that it was not until May 2, after the results of the election were apparent, that GAF asserted for the first time below that Heyman's failure to disclose the suit was material. GAF knew as early as March 13, when it issued its press release, that Abigail had sued Heyman for "breach of trust". Indeed, when it moved on March 11 to intervene in the Connecticut action, one of GAF's arguments was that the suit might implicate Heyman's integrity and fitness to serve as a director. Yet when it filed its complaint in this action on March 22, GAF advanced no such claim. Thus, there is a hollow ring to GAF's present argument that it was not until after this court issued the writ of mandamus that it could possibly have discovered the information necessary to support the theory upon which its whole case now rests.

Second, we cannot overlook that GAF is urging this court to hold Heyman to a stricter standard than GAF itself followed in deciding whether to disclose that a number of its incumbent directors had been defendants in various lawsuits alleging breach of fiduciary duty. Heyman claims, and GAF does not dispute, that (1) incumbent directors Sokol and Sommer were each alleged to have breached fiduciary duties as directors of American Cyanamid Company and Bristol-Meyers Company, respectively, and to have violated the securities laws, and that settlements in those actions resulted in tightening the control of the audit committee of each company; (2) incumbent director Berner was alleged to have breached fiduciary duties as president and chairman of the board of Curtiss-Wright Corporation by taking excessive compensation, and that settlement of the suits against him resulted in restricting his compensation and future rights to stock under Curtiss stock plans; (3) this court has previously determined that Berner committed a breach of trust and a violation of securities laws by unlawfully giving his brother-in-law confidential information which in turn was used to purchase stock at an unfair advantage; and (4) Berner and Werner were charged with breaching fiduciary duties *as directors of GAF*, by approving Werner's excessive compensation, and that settlement of this suit resulted in "measurable benefits to the Company."

At oral argument, GAF sought to distinguish these cases on the ground that they were all closed more than five years ago. But this at most establishes that GAF had complied with the "minimum" requirements of Schedule 14A. Applying to the incumbents the same sweeping standard that GAF would have us apply to Heyman, the integrity and fitness of these directors had been called into question to a sufficient extent to trigger a disclosure requirement under Rule 14a-9(a). If anything, the final decision or settlement agreement in a closed case involving management of a public corporation should be considered more important to voting stockholders than unadjudicated allegations in a pending family lawsuit.

This last point underscores the boundlessness of the disclosure requirement imposed by the district judge. Vast numbers of allegations arguably implicate a prospective director's "integrity and fitness". The ruling below, if left intact, would lead to a situation where proxy contestants, in order to minimize the risk of having an election set aside, would have to include in their solicitation materials descriptions, explanations, and denials regarding allegations in derivative actions, class actions, matrimonial disputes, and a host of other legal matters, all unrelated to the business of the subject corporation.

Furthermore, under the decision below, both sides in a proxy contest would have every incentive and legal right to pursue massive discovery to unearth facts which, it can later be claimed, amount to a breach of fiduciary duty that should have been alleged in a prior action against an opposing candidate. As this case graphically illustrates, the litigation ubiquitous in every proxy contest would thus become a forum for litigating, possibly relitigating, the issues in any pending or prior suit involving a director-nominee.

Finally, we think the district court was unduly influenced by what it perceived to be Heyman's bad faith in resisting GAF's efforts at discovery in the instant action. While we express no view on the wisdom of sealing the Connecticut action in the first place, the desire of the Heymans to keep their family dispute private is certainly understandable even in the absence of a proxy fight. This is not to say that the absence of an affirmative disclosure requirement is tantamount to a license to conceal. But the first three judicial officers who reviewed the sealing orders—Judge Daly, the special master, and Judge Knapp—all agreed with Heyman's interpretation that he could not properly discuss the sealed materials. That this court took a different view on the petition for mandamus does not mean, as the district court suggested, that Heyman was guilty of "suppression" or "obstruction".

III. CONCLUSION

The battle for control of GAF may not have been, as Heyman now claims, "a textbook case of corporate democracy". Nevertheless, it would be a perversion of the policies underlying § 14(a) and Rule 14a-9(a) to frustrate the will of a clear majority of GAF shareholders and require a new election under the circumstances present here. . . .

This was a proxy contest fought on the issues of GAF's financial performance and future corporate policy. Presented with a clear choice, the shareholders voted decisively in favor of the insurgent slate. Given this resounding mandate, it is inconceivable that fuller disclosure of the dormant Connecticut action would have had "a significant *propensity* to affect the voting process." . . .

The judgment of the district court is therefore reversed. The mandate shall issue forthwith.

Note

For an article critical of the foregoing decision, see Michaelson, *"Breach of Trust": The Duty to Disclose Pending Litigation in a Contest for Corporate Control*, 37 RUTGERS L. REV. 1 (1984).

As *GAF* illustrates, takeover bids, including proxy fights, can turn nasty, with name-calling and insulting assertions not being unusual. Consider the following example:

> [The insurgent] Holtzman disseminated a press release and accompanying cartoon. The cartoon depicts ONBANC's corporate board room. On the door, the name "ONBANCORP" has been altered to "OFFBANCORP." Several pigs dressed in business suits sit around the board-room table. One pig says "Mr. Chairman, I think we have a problem! Several shareholder proposals were passed with over five million votes. What should we do??" Another pig responds "Forget the Shareholders . . . This is *our* piggy bank!! Tell our lawyers to find a loophole to deny the vote." ONBANC views this cartoon as a false and prejudicial commentary on the conduct of its directors at the annual meeting.[18]

In view of the Second Circuit's decision in *GAF* (and your agreement or disagreement with the court's reasoning), should liability ensue under § 14(a) if the director, director-nominee, or executive officer failed to disclose that he/she was a defendant in pending civil litigation alleging that the subject party:

(1) engaged in "insider trading" while he/she was a director of a publicly held company?

(2) misappropriated funds from the family business, a privately held company?

(3) recklessly caused a catastrophic accident while driving under the influence of alcohol and/or an illegal substance (e.g., cocaine)?

With respect to a director's disclosure of "true purpose" or subjective revelation, consider the following.

Virginia Bankshares v. Sandberg
United States Supreme Court
501 U.S. 1083, 111 S. Ct. 2749, 115 L.Ed.2d 929 (1991)

[This case is contained in § 9.04[B].]

As briefly alluded to by the Second Circuit in *GAF*, § 14(a) of the Exchange Act and rules and regulations promulgated thereunder by the SEC regulate the solicitation of proxies by companies that have a security registered under § 12 of that Act.

---

18. *Onbancorp, Inc. v. Holtzman*, [1997–1998 Transfer Binder] Fed. Sec. L. Rep. (CCH) ¶ 99,545 (N.D.N.Y. 1997) (denying corporation's request for preliminary injunction).

SEC Proxy Rule Amendments on Shareholder Communications

Securities and Exchange Commission

Securities Exchange Act Release No. 31326 (October 16, 1992)

[This release is contained in § 9.04[C].]

Note

As the GAF proxy fight reveals, proxy contests are becoming an increasing part of the corporate landscape. This consequence may be due largely to the astronomical costs of pursuing a hostile tender offer (e.g., costs of acquiring a controlling interest, attorney and investment banker fees, and, depending upon market conditions, high interest rates), and the proliferation of complex federal and state takeover regulation (and resulting litigation). As seen by the proxy contest involving GAF, a number of these battles have had as the insurgents' principal objective the sale or liquidation of certain assets of the corporation, particularly where the company's stock was trading at what was viewed as an unreasonably low price. The proceeds from the sale of assets then may be passed onto the shareholders as a cash distribution. Also, as seen by the Hilton Hotels Corporation proxy statement earlier in this Section, a number of insurgents now are conducting proxy contests to facilitate their hostile tender offers.[19]

---

§ 14.04 Tender Offers

[A] What Is a Tender Offer?

Hanson Trust PLC v. SCM Corporation

United States Court of Appeals, Second Circuit

774 F.2d 47 (1985)

MANSFIELD, CIRCUIT JUDGE.

Hanson Trust PLC, HSCM Industries, Inc., and Hanson Holdings Netherlands B.V. (hereinafter sometimes referred to collectively as "Hanson") appeal from an order of the Southern District of New York, Shirley Wohl Kram, Judge, granting SCM

---

19. *See generally* R. Thomas & C. Dixon, Aranow & Einhorn on Proxy Contests for Corporate Control (1998); M. Waters, Proxy Regulation (1992); Bebchuck & Kahan, *A Framework for Analyzing Legal Policy Towards Proxy Contests*, 78 Calif. L. Rev. 1071 (1990); Fisch, *From Legitimacy to Logic: Reconsidering Proxy Regulation*, 46 Vand. L. Rev. 1129 (1993); Steinberg, *Fiduciary Duties and Disclosure Obligations in Proxy and Tender Contests for Corporate Control*, 30 Emory L.J. 169 (1981); Symposium on Proxy Reform, 17 J. Corp. L. No. 1 (1991); Thomas, *Judicial Review of Defensive Tactics in Proxy Contests: When Is Using a Rights Plan Right?*, 46 Vand. L. Rev. 503 (1997).

Corporation's motion for a preliminary injunction restraining them, their officers, agents, employees and any persons acting in concert with them, from acquiring any shares of SCM and from exercising any voting rights with respect to 3.1 million SCM shares acquired by them on September 11, 1985. The injunction was granted on the ground that Hanson's September 11 acquisition of the SCM stock through five private and one open market purchases amounted to a "tender offer" for more than 5% of SCM's outstanding shares, which violated § 14(d)(1) and (6) of the Williams Act, and (6) and rules promulgated by the Securities and Exchange Commission (SEC) thereunder. We reverse.

The setting is the familiar one of a fast-moving bidding contest for control of a large public corporation: first, a cash tender offer of $60 per share by Hanson, an outsider, addressed to SCM stockholders; next, a counterproposal by an "insider" group consisting of certain SCM managers and their "White Knight," Merrill Lynch Capital Markets (Merrill), for a "leveraged buyout" at a higher price ($70 per share); then an increase by Hanson of its cash offer to $72 per share, followed by a revised SCM-Merrill leveraged buyout offer of $74 per share with a "crown jewel" irrevocable lock-up option to Merrill designed to discourage Hanson from seeking control by providing that if any other party (in this case Hanson) should acquire more than one-third of SCM's outstanding shares (66 2/3% being needed under N.Y. Bus. L.- § 903(a)(2) to effectuate a merger) Merrill would have the right to buy SCM's two most profitable businesses (consumer foods and pigments) at prices characterized by some as "bargain basement." The final act in this scenario was the decision of Hanson, having been deterred by the SCM-Merrill option (colloquially described in the market as a "poison pill"), to terminate its cash tender offer and then to make private purchases, amounting to 25% of SCM's outstanding shares, leading SCM to seek and obtain the preliminary injunction from which this appeal is taken. . . .

. . . [Hanson's motive was that if it] could acquire slightly less than one-third of SCM's outstanding shares it would be able to block the $74 per share SCM-Merrill offer of a leveraged buyout. This might induce the latter to work out an agreement with Hanson, something Hanson had unsuccessfully sought on several occasions since its first cash tender offer.

. . . .

Within a period of two hours on the afternoon of September 11 Hanson made five privately-negotiated cash purchases of SCM stock and one open-market purchase, acquiring 3.1 million shares or 25% of SCM's outstanding stock. The price of SCM stock on the NYSE on September 11 ranged from a high of $73.50 per share to a low of $72.50 per share. Hanson's initial private purchase, 387,700 shares from Mutual Shares, was not solicited by Hanson but by a Mutual Shares official, Michael Price, who in a conversation with Robert Pirie of Rothschild, Inc., Hanson's financial advisor, on the morning of September 11 (before Hanson had decided to make any private cash purchases) had stated that he was interested in selling Mutual's Shares' SCM stock to Hanson. Once Hanson's decision to buy privately had been made, Pirie took Price up on his offer. The parties negotiated a sale at $73.50 per share after Pirie refused Price's asking prices, first of $75 per share and, later, of $74.50 per share. This transaction, but not the identity of the parties, was automatically reported pursuant to NYSE rules on the NYSE ticker at 3:11 P.M. and reported on the Dow Jones Broad Tape at 3:29 P.M.

Pirie then telephoned Ivan Boesky, an arbitrageur who had a few weeks earlier disclosed in a Schedule 13D statement filed with the SEC[20] that he owned approximately 12.7% of SCM's outstanding shares. Pirie negotiated a Hanson purchase of these shares at $73.50 per share after rejecting Boesky's initial demand of $74 per share. At the same time Rothschild purchased for Hanson's account 600,000 SCM shares in the open market at $73.50 per share. An attempt by Pirie next to negotiate the cash purchase of another large block of SCM stock (some 780,000 shares) from Slifka & Company fell through because of the latter's inability to make delivery of the shares on September 12.

Following the NYSE ticker and Broad Tape reports of the first two large anonymous transactions in SCM stock, some professional investors surmised that the buyer might be Hanson. Rothschild then received telephone calls from (1) Mr. Mulhearn of Jamie & Co. offering to sell between 200,000 and 350,000 shares at $73.50 per share, (2) David Gottesman, an arbitrageur at Oppenheimer & Co. offering 89,000 shares at $73.50, and (3) Boyd Jeffries of Jeffries & Co., offering approximately 700,000 to 800,000 shares at $74.00. Pirie purchased the three blocks for Hanson at $73.50 per share. The last of Hanson's cash purchases was completed by 4:35 P.M. on September 11, 1985.

In the early evening of September 11 SCM successfully applied to Judge Kram in the present lawsuit for a restraining order barring Hanson from acquiring more SCM stock for 24 hours. On September 12 and 13 the TRO was extended by consent pending the district court's decision on SCM's application for a preliminary injunction. Judge Kram held an evidentiary hearing on September 12–13, at which various witnesses testified, including Sir Gordon White, Hanson's United States Chairman, two Rothschild representatives (Pirie and Gerald Goldsmith) and stock market risk-arbitrage professionals (Robert Freeman of Goldman, Sachs & Co., Kenneth Miller of Merrill Lynch, and Daniel Burch of D. F. King & Co.). Sir Gordon White testified that on September 11, 1985, after learning of the $74 per share SCM-Merrill leveraged buyout tender offer with its "crown jewel" irrevocable "lock-up" option to Merrill, he instructed Pirie to terminate Hanson's $72 per share tender offer, and that only thereafter did he discuss the possibility of Hanson making market purchases of SCM stock. Pirie testified that the question of buying stock may have been discussed in the late forenoon of September 11 and that he had told White that he was

---

[20]. Section 13(d)(1) of the Securities Exchange Act requires any person or group acquiring beneficial ownership of more than 5% of the equity securities of certain issuers to file reports with the SEC. [See § 14.04[B].]

having Hanson's New York counsel look into whether such cash purchases were legally permissible.

SCM argued before Judge Kram (and argues here) that Hanson's cash purchases immediately following its termination of its $72 per share tender offer amounted to a *de facto* continuation of Hanson's tender offer, designed to avoid the strictures of § 14(d) of the Williams Act, and that unless a preliminary injunction issued SCM and its shareholders would be irreparably injured because Hanson would acquire enough shares to defeat the SCM-Merrill offer. Judge Kram found that the relevant underlying facts (which we have outlined) were not in dispute, and concluded that "[w]ithout deciding what test should ultimately be applied to determine whether Hanson's conduct constitutes a 'tender offer' within the meaning of the Williams Act . . . SCM has demonstrated a likelihood of success on the merits of its contention that Hanson has engaged in a tender offer which violates Section 14(d) of the Williams Act." The district court, characterizing Hanson's stock purchases as "a deliberate attempt to do an 'end run' around the requirements of the Williams Act," made no finding on the question of whether Hanson had decided to make the purchases of SCM before or after it dropped its tender offer but concluded that even if the decision had been made after it terminated its offer preliminary injunctive relief should issue. From this decision Hanson appeals.

DISCUSSION

. . . .

Since, as the district court correctly noted, the material relevant facts in the present case are not in dispute, this appeal turns on whether the district court erred as a matter of law in holding that when Hanson terminated its offer and immediately thereafter made private purchases of a substantial share of the target company's outstanding stock, the purchases became a "tender offer" within the meaning of § 14(d) of the Williams Act. Absent any express definition of "tender offer" in the Act, the answer requires a brief review of the background and purposes of § 14(d).

Congress adopted § 14(d) in 1968 "in response to the growing use of cash tender offers as a means of achieving corporate takeovers . . . which . . . removed a substantial number of corporate control contests from the reach of existing disclosure requirements of the federal securities laws." . . .

The typical tender offer, as described in the Congressional debates, hearings and reports on the Williams Act, consisted of a general, publicized bid by an individual or group to buy shares of a publicly-owned company, the shares of which were traded on a national securities exchange, at a price substantially above the current market price. . . . The offer was usually accompanied by newspaper and other publicity, a time limit for tender of shares in response to it, and a provision fixing a quantity limit on the total number of shares of the target company that would be purchased.

Prior to the Williams Act a tender offeror had no obligation to disclose any information to shareholders when making a bid. The Report of the Senate Committee on

Banking and Currency aptly described the situation: "by using a cash tender offer the person seeking control can operate in almost complete secrecy. At present, the law does not even require that he disclose his identity, the source of his funds, who his associates are, or what he intends to do if he gains control of the corporation." . . . The average shareholder, pressured by the fact that the tender offer would be available for only a short time and restricted to a limited number of shares, was forced "with severely limited information, [to] decide what course of action he should take." . . . "Without knowledge of who the bidder is and what he plans to do, the shareholder cannot reach an informed decision. He is forced to take a chance. For no matter what he does, he does it without adequate information to enable him to decide rationally what is the best possible course of action." . . .

The purpose of the Williams Act was, accordingly, to protect the shareholders from the dilemma by insuring "that public shareholders who are confronted by a cash tender offer for their stock will not be required to respond without adequate information." *Piper v. Chris-Craft Industries*, 430 U.S. 1, 35 (1977); *Rondeau v. Mosinee Paper Corp.*, 422 U.S. 49, 58 (1975).

Congress took "extreme care," . . . however, when protecting shareholders, to avoid "tipping the balance of regulation either in favor of management or in favor of the person making the takeover bid." . . . Indeed, the initial draft of the bill, proposed in 1965, had been designed to prevent "proud old companies [from being] reduced to corporate shells after white-collar pirates have seized control" . . . . Williams withdrew that draft following claims that it was too biased in favor of incumbent management. Tyson & August, *The Williams Act After RICO: Has the Balance Tipped in Favor of Incumbent Management?*, 33 Hastings L.J. 53, 61 (1983). In the end, Congress considered it crucial that the act be neutral and place " 'investors on an equal footing with the takeover bidder' . . . without favoring either the tender offeror or existing management." . . .

Congress finally settled upon a statute requiring a tender offer solicitor seeking beneficial ownership of more than 5% of the outstanding shares of any class of any equity security registered on a national securities exchange first to file with the SEC a statement containing certain information specified in § 13(d)(1) of the Act, as amplified by SEC rules and regulations. Congress' failure to define "tender offer" was deliberate. Aware of "the most infinite variety in the terms of most tender offers" and concerned that a rigid definition would be evaded, Congress left to the court and the SEC the flexibility to define the term. . . .

Although § 14(d)(1) clearly applies to "classic" tender offers of the type described above . . . courts soon recognized that in the case of privately negotiated transactions or solicitations for private purchases of stock many of the conditions leading to the enactment of § 14(d) . . . do not exist. The number or percentage of stockholders are usually far less than those involved in public offers. The solicitation involves less publicity than a public tender offer or none. The solicitees, who are frequently directors, officers or substantial stockholders of the target, are more apt to be sophisticated, inquiring or knowledgeable concerning the target's business, the solicitor's objectives, and the impact of the solicitation on the target's business prospects. In short, the solicitee in the private transaction is less likely to be pressured, confused, or ill-informed regarding the businesses and decisions at stake than solicitees who are the subjects of a public tender offer.

These differences between public and private securities transactions have led most courts to rule that private transactions or open market purchases do not qualify as a "tender offer" requiring the purchaser to meet the pre-filing strictures of § 14(d). . . . The borderline between public solicitations and privately negotiated stock purchases is not bright and it is frequently difficult to determine whether transactions falling close to the line or in a type of "no man's land" are "tender offers" or private deals. This had led some to advocate a broader interpretation of the term "tender offer" than that followed by us in *Kennecott Copper Corp. v. Curtiss-Wright Corp.*, 584 F.2d at 1207, and to adopt the eight-factor "test" of what is a tender offer, which was recommended by the SEC and applied by the district court in *Wellman v. Dickinson*, 475 F. Supp. 783, 823–24 (S.D.N.Y.), *aff'd on other grounds*, 682 F.2d 355 (2d Cir. 1982), *cert. denied*, 460 U.S. 1069 (1983), and by the Ninth Circuit in *SEC v. Carter Hawley Hale Stores, Inc.*, [760 F.2d 945 (9th Cir. 1985)]. The eight factors are:

(1) active and widespread solicitation of public shareholders for the shares of an issuer;

(2) solicitation made for a substantial percentage of the issuer's stock;

(3) offer to purchase made at a premium over the prevailing market price;

(4) terms of the offer are firm rather than negotiable;

(5) offer contingent on the tender of a fixed number of shares, often subject to a fixed maximum number to be purchased;

(6) offer open only for a limited period of time;

(7) offeree subjected to pressure to sell his stock;

(8) public announcements of a purchasing program concerning the target company precede or accompany rapid accumulation of large amounts of the target company's securities. . . .

Although many of the above-listed factors are relevant for purposes of determining whether a given solicitation amounts to a tender offer, the elevation of such a list to a mandatory "litmus test" appears to be both unwise and unnecessary. As even the advocates of the proposed text recognize, in any given case a solicitation may constitute a tender offer even though some of the eight factors are absent or, when many factors are present, the solicitation may nevertheless not amount to a tender offer because the missing factors outweigh those present.

We prefer to be guided by the principle followed by the Supreme Court in deciding what transactions fall within the private offering exemption provided by § [4(2)] [now § 4(a)(2)] of the Securities Act of 1933, and by ourselves in *Kennecott Copper* in determining whether the Williams Act applies to private transactions. That principle is simply to look to the statutory purpose. In *S.E.C. v. Ralston Purina Co.*, 346 U.S. 119 (1953), the Court stated, "the applicability of §4(1) [now §4(a)(2)], should turn on whether the particular class of persons affected need the protection of the Act. An offering to those who are shown to be able to fend for themselves is a transaction 'not involving any public offering.'" . . . Similarly, since the purpose of §14(d) is to protect the ill-informed solicitee, the question of whether a solicitation constitutes a "tender offer" within the meaning [of] §14(d) turns on whether, viewing the transaction in the light of the totality of circumstances, there appears to be a likelihood that unless the pre-acquisition filing strictures of that statute are followed there will be a substantial risk that solicitees will lack information needed to make a carefully considered appraisal of the proposal put before them.

Applying this standard, we are persuaded on the undisputed facts that Hanson's September 11 negotiation of five private purchases and one open market purchase of SCM shares, totaling 25% of SCM's outstanding stock, did not under the circumstances constitute a "tender offer" within the meaning of the Williams Act. Putting aside for the moment the events preceding the purchases, there can be little doubt that the privately negotiated purchases would not, standing alone, qualify as a tender offer, for the following reasons:

(1) In a market of 22,800 SCM shareholders the number of SCM sellers here involved, six in all, was minuscule compared with the numbers involved in public solicitations of the type against which the Act was directed.

(2) At least five of the sellers were highly sophisticated professionals, knowledgeable in the marketplace and well aware of the essential facts needed to exercise their professional skills and to appraise Hanson's offer, including its financial condition as well as that of SCM, the likelihood that the purchases might block the SCM-Merrill bid, and the risk that if Hanson acquired more than 33 1/3% of SCM's stock the SCM-Merrill lockup of the "crown jewel" might be triggered. . . .

(3) The sellers were not "pressured" to sell their shares by any conduct that the Williams Act was designed to alleviate, but by the forces of the marketplace. Indeed, in the case of Mutual Shares there was no initial solicitation by Hanson; the offer to sell was initiated by Mr. Price of Mutual Shares. Although each of the Hanson purchases was made for $73.50 per share, in most instances this price was the result of private negotiations after the sellers sought higher prices and in one case price protection, demands which were refused. The $73.50 price was not fixed in advance by Hanson. Moreover, the sellers remained free to accept the $74 per share tender off made by the SCM-Merrill group.

(4) There was no active or widespread advance publicity or public solicitation, which is one of the earmarks of a conventional tender offer. Arbitragers might conclude from ticker tape reports of two large anonymous transactions that

Hanson must be the buyer. However, liability for solicitation may not be predicated upon disclosures mandated by Stock Exchange Rules. . . .

(5) The price received by the six sellers, $73.50 per share, unlike that appearing in most tender offers, can scarcely be dignified with the label "premium." The stock market price on September 11 ranged from $72.50 to $73.50 per share. Although risk arbitragers sitting on large holdings might reap sizeable profits from sales to Hanson at $73.50, depending on their own purchase costs, they stood to gain even more if the SCM-Merrill offer of $74 should succeed, as it apparently would if they tendered their shares to it. . . .

(6) Unlike most tender offers, the purchases were not made contingent upon Hanson's acquiring a fixed minimum number or percentage of SCM's outstanding shares. Once an agreement with each individual seller was reached, Hanson was obligated to buy, regardless what total percentage of stock it might acquire. Indeed, it does not appear that Hanson had fixed in its mind a firm limit on the amount of SCM shares it was willing to buy.

(7) Unlike most tender offers, there was no general time limit within which Hanson would make purchases of SCM stock. Concededly, cash transactions are normally immediate but, assuming an inability on the part of a seller and Hanson to agree at once on a price, nothing prevented a resumption of negotiations by each of the parties except the arbitragers' speculation that once Hanson acquired 33 1/3% or an amount just short of that figure it would stop buying.

In short, the totality of circumstances that existed on September 11 did not evidence any likelihood that unless Hanson was required to comply with § 14(d)(1)'s pre-acquisition filing and waiting-period requirements there would be a substantial risk of ill-considered sales of SCM stock by ill-informed shareholders.

There remains the question whether Hanson's private purchases take on a different hue, requiring them to be treated as a "*de facto*" continuation of its earlier tender offer, when considered in the context of Hanson's earlier acknowledged tender offer, the competing offer of SCM-Merrill, and Hanson's termination of its tender offer. After reviewing all of the undisputed facts we conclude that the district court erred in so holding.

In the first place, we find no record support for the contention by SCM that Hanson's September 11 termination of its outstanding tender offer was false, fraudulent or ineffective. Hanson's termination notice was clear, unequivocal and straightforward. Directions were given, and presumably are being followed, to return all of the tendered shares to the SCM shareholders who tendered them. Hanson also filed with the SEC a statement pursuant to § 14(d)(1) of the Williams Act terminating its tender offer. As a result, at the time when Hanson made its September 11 private purchases of SCM stock it owned no SCM stock other than those shares revealed in its § 14(d) pre-acquisition report filed with the SEC on August 26, 1985.

The reason for Hanson's termination of its tender offer is not disputed; in view of SCM's grant of what Hanson conceived to be a "poison pill" lock-up option to Merrill, Hanson, if it acquired control of SCM, would have a company denuded as the result of its sale of its consumer food and pigment businesses to Merrill at what Hanson believed to be bargain prices. Thus, Hanson's termination of its tender offer was final; there was no tender offer to be "continued." Hanson was unlikely to "shoot itself in the foot" by triggering what it believed to be a "poison pill," and it could not acquire more than 49% of SCM's shares without violating the rules of the London Stock Exchange. Nor does the record support SCM's contention that Hanson had decided, before terminating its tender offer, to engage in cash purchases. . . .

Second, Hanson had expressly reserved the right in its August 26, 1985, pre-acquisition tender offer filing papers, whether or not tendered shares were purchased, "*thereafter* . . . to purchase additional Shares in the open market, in privately negotiated transactions, through another tender offer or otherwise." . . . Thus Hanson's privately negotiated purchases could hardly have taken the market by surprise. Indeed, professional arbitragers and market experts rapidly concluded that it was Hanson which was making the post-termination purchases.

Last, Hanson's prior disclosures of essential facts about itself and SCM in the pre-acquisition papers it filed on August 26, 1985, with the SEC pursuant to § 14(d)(1), are wholly inconsistent with the district court's characterization of Hanson's later private purchases as "a deliberate attempt to do an 'end run' around the requirements of the Williams Act." On the contrary, the record shows that Hanson had already filed with the SEC and made public substantially the same information as SCM contends that Hanson should have filed before making the cash purchases. The term "tender offer," although left somewhat flexible by Congress' decision not to define it, nevertheless remains a word of art. Section 14(d)(1) was never intended to apply to *every* acquisition of more than 5% of a public company's stock. If that were the case there would be no need for § 13(d)(1), which requires a person, *after* acquiring more than 5%, to furnish the issuer, stock exchange and the SEC with certain pertinent information. Yet the expansive definition of "tender offer" advocated by SCM, and to some extent by the SEC as amicus, would go far toward rendering § 13(d)(1) a dead letter. . . .

It may well be that Hanson's private acquisition of 25% of SCM's shares after termination of Hanson's tender offer was designed to block the SCM-Merrill leveraged buyout group from acquiring the 66 2/3% of SCM's stock needed to effectuate a merger. It may be speculated that such a blocking move might induce SCM to buy Hanson's 25% at a premium or lead to negotiations between the parties designed to resolve their differences. But we know of no provision in the federal securities laws or elsewhere that prohibits such tactics in "hardball" market battles of the type encountered here. . . . Thus the full disclosure purposes of the Williams Act as it now stands appear to have been fully satisfied by Hanson's furnishing to the public, both before and after termination of its tender offer, all of the essential relevant facts it was required by law to supply.

SCM further contends, and in this respect it is supported by the SEC as an amicus, that upon termination of a tender offer the solicitor should be subject to a waiting or cooling-off period (10 days is suggested) before it may purchase any of the target company's outstanding shares. However, neither the Act nor any SEC rule promulgated thereunder prohibits a former tender offeror from purchasing stock of a target through privately negotiated transactions immediately after a tender offer has been terminated. Indeed, it is significant that the SEC's formal proposal for the adoption of such a rule (Proposed Rule 14e-5) has never been implemented even though the SEC adopted a similar prohibition with respect to an *issuer's* making such purchases within 10 days after termination of a tender offer. *See* Rule 13e-4(f)(6). Thus, the existing law does not support the prohibition urged by SCM and the SEC. We believe it would be unwise for courts judicially to usurp what is a legislative or regulatory function by substituting our judgment for that of Congress or the SEC.

In recognition of Congress' desire in enacting the Williams Act to avoid favoring either existing corporate management or outsiders seeking control through tender offers . . . the role of the courts in construing and applying the Act must likewise be one of strict neutrality. . . . Although we should not hesitate to enforce the Act's disclosure provisions through appropriate relief, we must also guard against improvident or precipitous use of remedies that may have the effect of favoring one side or the other in a takeover battle when allegations of violation of the Act, often made in the heat of the contest, may not be substantiated. In this context the preliminary injunction, which is one of the most drastic tools in the arsenal of judicial remedies . . . must be used with great care, lest the forces of the free marketplace, which in the end should determine the merits of takeover disputes, are nullified.

In the present case we conclude that since the district court erred in ruling as a matter of law that SCM had demonstrated a likelihood of success on the merits, based on the theory that Hanson's post-tender offer private purchases of SCM constituted a *de facto* tender offer, it was an abuse of discretion to issue a preliminary injunction. . . .

The order of the district court is reversed, the preliminary injunction against Hanson is vacated, and the case is remanded for further proceedings in accordance with this opinion. The mandate shall issue forthwith.

Note

Does the Second Circuit's decision provide a means by which an acquiror can "sidestep" the Williams Act and SEC regulations thereunder? The WALL STREET JOURNAL evidently believes this to be the case. In an editorial dated October 7, 1985 and titled *A Happy Jig*, the JOURNAL applauded the *Hanson Trust* decision as signaling the emergence of a "new deregulated takeover market" in which acquirors would no longer "hav[e] to worry about the costs and delays of securities regulations," hence resulting in "more simplified takeovers—and more profits for shareholders." Do you agree with this assessment?[21]

In *Hanson Trust*, did the Second Circuit adequately take into account the purposes underlying the Williams Act? For example, although full disclosure certainly is an objective, it may be argued that another purpose is to ensure the evenhanded treatment of all shareholders, including the small unsophisticated stockholder. On the other hand, is the SEC culpable for declining to be more active in its rulemaking function in this context?

In 1983, the SEC established an Advisory Committee on Tender Offers. After conducting a series of meetings, the Advisory Committee issued its Report, consisting of 50 recommendations. Most pertinent for our purposes here, Recommendation 14 provides: "No person may acquire voting securities of an issuer, if, immediately following such acquisitions, such person would own more than 20 percent of the voting power of the outstanding voting securities of that issuer unless such purchases were made (i) from the issuer or (ii) pursuant to a tender offer. The Commission should retain broad exemptive power with respect to this provision."[22] What are the reasons underlying this recommendation? Does the recommendation make good policy? Presuming that the recommendation is sound, in what circumstances should the SEC exercise this proposed exemptive authority?

[B] Disclosure of Beneficial Ownership Interest

Section 13(d)(1) of the Exchange Act and Rule 13d-1 prescribed thereunder require any person or group of persons agreeing to act together who acquire beneficial ownership of more than five percent of a class of equity security registered under § 12 of the Act to disclose, within 10 days, specific information by filing a Schedule 13D with the SEC and by sending copies to the issuer and to each exchange on which the security is traded. Generally, "Schedule 13D requires disclosure of the identity of the issuer and the security, the identity, background, and citizenship of the reporting persons, the source and amount of funds used to acquire the securities, the purpose of the transaction, the reporting person's interest in the securities including trading history for the last 60 days, and any contracts, arrangements, understandings or relationships with respect to the securities to which the reporting person or group is a party."[23]

---

21. *See* Tyson, *The Williams Act After Hanson Trust v. SCM Corporation: Post-Tender Offer Purchases by the Tender Offeror*, 61 Tulane L. Rev. 1 (1986).

22. *See* Lowenstein, *Pruning Deadwood in Hostile Takeovers: A Proposal for Reform*, 83 Colum. L. Rev. 249, 317 (1983).

23. Bialkin, Attora & D'Alimonte, *Why, When and How to Conduct a Proxy Battle for Corporate Control*, in Proxy Contests and Battles for Corporate Control at 87, 117 (19181). *See CSX Corp. v. Children's Investment Fund Management (UK) LLP* 654 F.3d 276 (2d Cir. 2011); Block & Rudoff, *Schedule 14D Problems Associated with Large Accumulations of Stock*, 10 Sec. Reg. L.J. 3 (1982).

Importantly, the requirements of § 13(d) apply irrespective of whether the person (or group) acquiring five percent beneficial ownership intends to make a tender offer. The objective of the statute is to alert the securities markets of potential shifts in corporate control.[24] Although courts have declined to recognize a damages remedy under § 13(d),[25] a majority of courts (as discussed in Chapter 9 of the text—§ 9.02) have implied a private right of action for injunctive relief under §§ 13(d) and 14(d)-(e) on behalf of an issuer corporation.[26] The rationale is that, despite the Supreme Court's holding in *Piper v. Chris-Craft Industries* [430 U.S. 1 (1977)] that a defeated tender offeror does not have standing under § 14(e) to bring an action for damages, the target company frequently may be the only willing party with the resources to maintain an injunctive action against a prospective bidder. In situations where the bidder's potential conduct may harm the company and its shareholders, granting standing to the target corporation to seek injunctive relief is therefore a practical approach to protecting shareholders and the marketplace.[27]

The type of relief usually awarded for a § 13(d) violation has been: (1) to require the violating party to amend its previous disclosures and (2) to prohibit additional purchases until such corrective disclosure has been made. Some courts, however, have deemed such relief insufficient and have ordered disgorgement, disenfranchisement, divestiture, or rescission of shares acquired during the period that the misleading § 13(d) disclosures were disseminated in the marketplace. For example, in one key case, *SEC v. First City Financial Corporation, Ltd.*, 688 F. Supp. 705, 726–728 (D.D.C. 1988), *aff'd,* [1989–1990 Transfer Binder] Fed. Sec. L. Rep. (CCH) ¶ 94,801 (D.C. Cir. 1989), the district court reasoned:

> The Commission claims that defendants have profited from violations of section 13(d) by concealing their five percent position in Ashland and by continuing their purchases in a market where investors were wrongfully deprived of valuable information and thus could not value the stock accordingly. Defendants profited on the shares by approximately $2.7 million. The Commission requests the equitable remedy of disgorgement in addition to injunctive relief.

> Disgorgement as an equitable remedy is designed to compel defendants to "give up the amount by which [they] were unjustly enriched." . . . The principle is well established. . . .

> In this proceeding, defendants failed to file the Schedule 13D Statement by the March 14 deadline, and continued to acquire Ashland in a market where other participants were unaware of their five percent position and their

---

24. *See GAF Corp. v. Milstein*, 453 F.2d 709, 719 (2d Cir. 1971).

25. *See, e.g., Stromfeld v. Great Atlantic and Pacific Tea Co., Inc.*, 484 F. Supp. 1264 (S.D.N.Y. 1980).

26. *See, e.g., CSX Corporation v. Children's Investment Fund Management (UK) LLP*, 654 F.3d 276 (2d Cir. 2011); *Indiana National Corp. v. Rich*, 712 F.2d 1180 (7th Cir. 1983). *But see Polaroid Corp. v. Disney*, 862 F.2d 987 (3d Cir. 1988).

27. *See, e.g., Mobil Corp. v. Marathon Oil Co.*, 669 F.2d 366, 371 (6th Cir. 1981).

1120 · CORPORATE CONTROL ACQUISITIONS AND CONTESTS

future plans. Between March 14 and 25, defendants acquired 890,000 additional shares through [their broker] Greenberg at a cumulative cost of $42.7 million. When defendants' position was finally made public on March 25, the market responded immediately. The price increased by 4 3/4 (nearly 10 percent) on the first trade of the day, increasing by another five percent over the next several days. When the Belzbergs' threatened takeover was rejected, they resold their stock at a $15.5 million profit. That profit included the nearly $2.7 million, attributable to the 890,000 shares purchased in violation of section 13(d). The Commission requests that defendants disgorge the $2.7 million.

. . . .

The very purpose behind defendants' understanding with [their broker] Greenberg was to conceal their position in Ashland from the market place. By keeping its acquisitions secret, defendants were able to accumulate shares at artificially low prices. When they disclosed their holdings the price of stock escalated dramatically. The $51 price defendants received for their stock reflected the increase caused by the disclosure. The profits obtained from the buy-back arrangement were attributable to the violation and must be disgorged.

Although certain commentators applaud these tougher measures ordered by some courts, critics point out that § 13(d) actions frequently serve as a delaying tactic, providing target management with sufficient time to develop and implement a successful defensive strategy to fend off the hostile offeror.

A major problem with § 13(d) that has drawn attention is that a beneficial owner of more than five percent of a subject security need not disclose such ownership status until 10 days after attaining that status. As a result, such parties may acquire additional shares through privately negotiated transactions and open market purchases during that 10-day "window" period so long as the acquisitions do not constitute a "tender offer" and are in compliance with other applicable law. This loophole makes possible the accumulation of securities, representing a potential shift in corporate control, without adequate notification and disclosure of pertinent information to the marketplace. It has been proposed that Congress should close this loophole by either: (1) prohibiting additional accumulations above the five percent level unless there has been prior disclosure of the requisite information or (2) deeming acquisition of more than twenty (or some other) percent of an equity security, with certain exceptions, to constitute a tender offer, thereby triggering the disclosure and dissemination requirements of the Williams Act.[28]

---

28. *See, e.g.*, Advisory Comm. on Tender Offers, U.S. SEC, Report of Recommendations 21–22 (1983); Tender Offer Reform Act of 1987, H.R. 2172, 100th Cong., 1st Sess. (1987) (if enacted, would have prohibited, with certain exceptions, the acquisition of more than ten percent of a target's stock except by means of a tender offer).

Although the topic of antitrust is outside the scope of this text, certain provisions of the Hart-Scott-Rodino Antitrust Improvements Act of 1976 (HSR Act) impact on securities transactions. The HSR Act generally imposes upon certain tender offerors and their targets in specified transactions pre-acquisition notification and disclosure requirements. Pursuant thereto, information relevant to the transaction must be furnished to the Antitrust Division of the Department of Justice and the Federal Trade Commission.[29]

As a general rule, under the HSR Act, an acquiring entity that is of a certain size generally must file and follow that Act's preacquisition waiting period prior to purchasing a specified amount of the target corporation's voting securities. Hence, "notification under the [HSR] Act may be required at a time when the acquiring company owns a much lower percentage of the target's voting securities than it could purchase by the time a Schedule 13D is required to be filed."[30] Stated another way, "an accumulation of stock prior to making a hostile raid may trigger the obligation to file a Form [under the HSR Act], and thereby compel the raider to surface and disclose its intentions, even if it does not meet the five-percent reporting threshold for the filing of a Schedule 13D."[31]

[C] Constitutional Dimensions of State Takeover Statutes

In *Edgar v. MITE*, 457 U.S. 624 (1982), the Supreme Court, in an opinion written by Justice White, declared the Illinois Business Takeover Act unconstitutional on interstate commerce grounds, reasoning that the burdens imposed on interstate commerce by the Act were excessive in relation to the local interests served. Another portion of Justice White's opinion, not joined in by the majority of the Court, asserted that the Illinois Act was unconstitutional under the Supremacy Clause.

In the aftermath of the Supreme Court's decision in *MITE*, several state statutes, having provisions similar to the Illinois Act, were declared unconstitutional by the lower federal courts. Cognizant of the constitutional infirmities of their takeover statutes, several states responded by enacting "second generation" statutes that sought to pass constitutional scrutiny.[32]

---

29. *See generally*, S. AXINN ET AL., ACQUISITIONS UNDER THE HART-SCOTT-RODINO ANTITRUST IMPROVEMENTS ACT (3d ed 2008). Note that the threshold amounts to trigger the pre-acquisition notification and disclosure requirements of the Hart-Scott-Rodino Act are adjusted annually according to changes in the gross national product. For example, for 2013, the size of transaction threshold is $70.9 million.

30. Axinn, Fogg & Stoll, *Contests for Corporate Control Under the New Law of Preacquisition Notification,* 24 N.Y.L.S. L. REV. 857, 866–867 (1979).

31. M. LIPTON & E. STEINBERGER, TAKEOVERS AND FREEZEOUTS § 7.02[5] (2012).

32. *See* Romano, *The Political Economy of Takeover Statutes,* 73 VA. L. REV. 111 (1987).

The CTS Decision

In *CTS Corp. v. Dynamics Corp. of America*, 481 U.S. 69 (1987), the Supreme Court upheld one version of the second-generation statutes. There, the Court held that the Control Share Acquisitions Chapter of the Indiana Business Corporation Law does not violate the Constitution on either preemption or interstate commerce grounds. In brief, the Indiana statute, which applies to corporations chartered in Indiana and that have certain other connections with that state, focuses on the acquisition of "control shares" in such a corporation. Under the Act, a control share acquisition is one that, but for the operation of the Act, would raise the purchaser's voting power to or above any of three thresholds: (1) one-fifth and less than one-third, (2) one-third and less than a majority, or (3) above a majority. When a control share transaction occurs, the acquiring entity does not have voting rights with respect to those shares unless a majority of the disinterested shares[33] entitled to vote approves the transaction. Such vote must take place within 50 days if the acquiring entity so requests.

Even though the 50-day period of the Indiana statute exceeds the minimum 20-business-day period that a tender offer must remain open under the Williams Act, the Supreme Court stated that this extra delay was permissible. Only unreasonable delays, the Court asserted, are unconstitutional. Moreover, to preempt the Indiana Act, the Court thought, would bring into question the constitutionality of a wide variety of state corporate laws of hitherto unquestioned validity. Such statutes include permitting corporations to have cumulative voting and the staggering of director terms, which, like the Indiana statute, may delay or limit the exercise of control by a successful bidder. Hence, the Court concluded:

> In our view, the possibility that the Indiana Act will delay some tender offers is insufficient to require a conclusion that the Williams Act pre-empts the [Indiana] Act. The longstanding prevalence of state regulation in this area suggests that, if Congress had intended to preempt all State laws that delay the acquisition of voting control following a tender offer, it would have said so explicitly.[34]

Likewise, the *CTS* Court found that the Indiana statute does not offend the Commerce Clause. Upon examination, the Indiana Act neither discriminates against interstate commerce nor does it create an impermissible risk of inconsistent regulation by the various states. As a basis for its holding, the Court relied on the premise that a state's authority to regulate domestic corporations is a fundamental precept of corporate law. In its role as regulator of corporate governance, a state has an interest in facilitating stable relationships among the participants in its domestic corporations. Applying these principles, the Court stated:

---

33. "Interested shares" are those beneficially controlled by the entity acquiring the corporation, an officer or an inside director of the subject corporation.

34. 481 U.S. at 86.

The primary purpose of the [Indiana] Act is to protect the shareholders of Indiana corporations. It does this by affording shareholders, when a takeover offer is made, an opportunity to decide collectively whether the resulting change in voting control of the corporation, as they perceive it, would be desirable. A change of management may have important effects on the shareholders' interest; it is well within the State's role as overseer of corporate governance to offer this opportunity.[35]

The "Third-Generation" Statutes

After *CTS*, a number of different types of state "anti-takeover" statutes exist. These statutes, many of which have been upheld as constitutional,[36] play an integral role in the takeover process. Significantly, unlike the Illinois statute declared unconstitutional in *MITE*, these third-generation statutes do not directly impact an offeror making a tender offer for all shares outstanding. Nonetheless, aspects of these statutes may deter prospective offerors from engaging in takeover bids.

In addition to the control share acquisition type of statute upheld as constitutional in *CTS*, other types of statutes include:

"Fair Price" Statute—This type of statute reaches fundamental "second step" transactions, such as mergers or sales of substantially all assets, which frequently follow a hostile tender offer for a bare majority of the target's shares. The statute basically provides that such a transaction can be undertaken only if: (1) a majority of the disinterested shares of the subject corporation approve or (2) the same price is paid in the second-step transaction as was paid in the first-step tender offer. There are a number of variations to this type of statute.[37]

"Right of Redemption" Statute—With certain exceptions, this type of statute provides that once a person or group owns a specified percent (such as 20 percent) of a class of voting shares registered under the Exchange Act, that person or group is deemed to be a controlling shareholder. Attainment of that status requires such shareholder "to offer to purchase the remaining shares of all of the other shareholders at

---

35. *Id.* at 91. *See AMP, Inc. v. Allied Signal Corp.,* 168 F.3d 649 (3d Cir. 1999) (interpreting Pennsylvania control share acquisition statutes).

36. The Delaware statute has been upheld as constitutional. *See, e.g., BNS Inc. v. Koppers Co.,* 683 F. Supp. 458 (D. Del. 1988). *See generally,* Symposium, *Delaware Antitakeover Statute,* 65 Bus Law. No. 3 (2010). The Wisconsin Statute was constitutionally upheld in *Amanda Acquisition Corporation v. Universal Foods Corporation,* 877 F.2d 496 (7th Cir. 1989). *But see Rocket Acquisition Corp. v. Ventana Medical Systems, Inc.,* 2007 U.S. Dist. LEXIS 62361 (D. Ariz. 2007) (holding Arizona Anti-Takeover Act unconstitutional on basis that the statute Aconstitute[d] an impermissible risk of inconsistent regulation in violation of the Commerce Clause because of the statute's reach and application to foreign corporations").

37. *See generally* Scriggins & Clarke, *Takeovers and the 1983 Maryland Fair Price Legislation,* 43 MD. L. REV. 266 (1984).

a statutorily defined price reflecting the highest premium paid by [such shareholder] in accumulating target stock."[38]

"Classified Board" Statute—This statute (enacted, for example, in Massachusetts) requires all publicly held companies to have classified boards of directors, divided into three classes (being equal or nearly as equal in number as possible). Generally, each class is to serve staggered three-year terms. Removal of directors may be only for cause.[39]

"Other Constituency" or "Stakeholder" Statute—This type of statute, enacted in a majority of the states, authorizes a corporation's board of directors to consider non-shareholder interests, such as those of employees, customers, communities, and suppliers, when making business decisions. Whereas most states apply this type of statute to directors' conduct in general, some states limit its application to takeovers.[40]

"Disgorgement" Statute— Enacted in Pennsylvania, a target company or any of its shareholders suing derivatively may bring an action against a controlling person (or group) seeking disgorgement of any profits made upon the sale of such person's shares in the company if the sale is within 18 months after such person attained control status. Under the statute, control status is achieved when, for example, the person or group has voting power over at least 20 percent of the corporation's voting stock.[41]

"Business Combination Restriction" Statute—This type of statute, codified in such states as Delaware, New Jersey, New York, and Pennsylvania, generally provides that, with certain exceptions, if a person acquires a certain percentage of stock (e.g., 15 percent or more under the Delaware statute) without the approval of the board of directors of the subject corporation, that person becomes an interested shareholder and may not consummate a business combination (e.g., a merger) with the subject corporation for a substantial period of time (three years under the Delaware statute and five years under the New York statute). There are certain exceptions where the business combination restriction does not apply. One such exception under the Delaware statute is that the acquisition by a controlling shareholder of at least 85 percent of the voting stock[42] in a tender offer or other acquisition entitles the interested shareholder to engage in a merger without being subject to the three-year prohibition. Another exception occurs when the target's board of directors approves the

---

38. Bainbridge, *Redirecting State Takeover Laws at Proxy Contests*, 1992 Wis. L. Rev. 1071, 1099 (1992), *interpreting*, 15 Pa. Cons. Stat. Ann. §§ 2542–2546. *See generally* Newlin & Gilmer, *The Pennsylvania Shareholder Protection Act: A New State Approach to Deflecting Corporate Takeover Bids*, 40 Bus. Law. 111 (1984).

39. H.B. 5556, 1990 Mass. Adv. Legis. Serv. 5–6 (Law. Co-op).

40. Tyler, *Other Constituency Statutes*, 59 Mo. L. Rev. 373, 379–380 (1994) (citing state statutes). *See* Bainbridge, *Interpreting Nonshareholder Constituency Statutes*, 19 Pepp. L. Rev. 971 (1992); Committee on Corporate Laws, *Other Constituencies Statutes: Potential for Confusion*, 45 Bus. Law. 2253 (1990); Symposium, 21 Stetson L. Rev. No. 1 (1991).

41. *See* Bainbridge, *supra* note 38, at 1090–1096

42. Shares owned by the target's directors and officers are not counted when determining whether the interested shareholder attains 85 percent stock ownership. *See* 8 Del. Code Ann. § 203.

contemplated business combination before the time that the prospective acquiror becomes an interested shareholder.[43]

[D] Stakeholder Statutes

Emerging from the hostile takeover battles of the 1980s, stakeholder statutes have been enacted by over a majority of the states. The unifying principle of these statutes is that boards of directors may consider nonshareholder interests when making corporate decisions. Such "stakeholders" include, for example, the corporation's employees and the communities in which the entity conducts a significant amount of business.

[E] SEC Tender Offer Rules

The SEC has been active in the tender offer rulemaking setting. The rules are quite extensive, mandating, *inter alia*, that both the offeror and the subject (i.e., target) corporations file detailed disclosure schedules. For example, a Schedule TO must be filed with the SEC in issuer and third-party tender offers. Moreover, Rule 14d-9 requires the subject company to file with the Commission a Schedule 14D-9, which calls for the disclosure of specified information. The SEC "believes that the disclosure elicited by the Schedule will assist security holders in making their investment decisions and in evaluating the merits of a solicitation/recommendation."[44] Such information includes, if material, a description of any arrangement or other understanding and conflicts of interest between, among others, the offeror, the subject corporation, and their affiliates. Disclosure is also required in the Schedule of certain negotiations and transactions (e.g., merger negotiations) undertaken by the target company in response to the tender offer.[45] Moreover, in order to adhere to the disclosure requirements of Rule 14e-2, the subject company in the Schedule 14D-9 must

---

43. *See* 8 Del. Code Ann. § 203; N.Y. Bus. Corp. Law § 912(b). *See generally* Symposium, 63 Bus. Law. No. 3 (2010); Booth, *The Promise of State Takeover Statutes*, 86 Mich. L. Rev. 1635 (1988); Bradford, *Protecting Shareholders from Themselves? A Policy and Constitutional Review of a State Takeover Statute*, 67 Neb. L. Rev. 459 (1988); Brown, *Regulatory Intervention in the Market for Corporate Control*, 23 U.C. Davis L. Rev. 1 (1989); Butler & Ribstein, *State Anti-Takeover Statutes and the Commerce Clause*, 57 U. Cin. L. Rev. 611 (1988); Cox, *The Constitutional "Dynamics" of the Internal Affairs Rule — A Comment on CTS Corporation*, 13 J. Corp. L. 317 (1988); Hazen, *State Anti-Takeover Legislation: The Second and Third Generations*, 23 Wake Forest L. Rev. 77 (1988); Johnson & Millon, *Misreading the Williams Act*, 87 Mich. L. Rev. 1862 (1989); Palmiter, *The CTS Gambit: Stanching the Federalization of Corporate Law*, 69 Wash. U.L.Q. 445 (1991); Pinto, *The Constitution and the Market for Corporate Control: State Takeover Statutes After CTS Corp.*, 29 Wm. & Mary L. Rev. 699 (1988).

44. *See* Securities Exchange Act Release Nos. 16384 (1979), 42055 (1999).

45. Compare this disclosure requirement with the duty affirmatively to disclose merger and similar negotiations in other contexts, discussed in § 11.07. Rule 14d-9 allows target companies to solicit and make recommendations to their security holders to the same degree that offerors are permitted to do so, provided that any such communication is filed with the SEC on the date of first

advise shareholders of its position in regard to the tender offer and the reasons therefor.

The SEC's tender offer rules cover a number of other matters:

- Rule 14e-1 generally requires that tender offers remain open for at least 20 business days (although pursuant to an SEC staff no-action letter, certain tender offers for non-convertible debt securities may remain open for only five business days).

- Rule 14d-6(d) expressly requires an offeror to disclose promptly any material change in the information provided to shareholders.

- Rule 14e-8 prohibits a bidder from engaging in fraudulent or manipulative conduct when announcing a tender offer. For example, violation of Rule 14e-8 would occur if the supposed bidder had no intention or financial means to commence and complete the tender offer within a reasonable period.

- To reduce the previous regulatory imbalances between cash tender offers and stock exchange offers, the SEC elected to allow exchange offers to commence upon the filing of a registration statement. Nonetheless, the bidder cannot purchase any securities tendered in the exchange offer until the effectiveness of the registration statement and the timely disclosure of all material changes.

- Rule 14d-8 extends the proration period from the previous 10-calendar-day period to the entire period that the offer remains open (under Rule 14(e)(1) a tender offer must remain open, with certain exceptions, for at least 20 business days). Generally, Rule 14d-8 obligates a bidder in an oversubscribed partial tender offer "to take up and pay for" shares tendered on a pro rata basis "during the period such offer, request, or invitation remains open." The rule precipitated comment on the extent of the Commission's rulemaking authority and on the broader question of its effect on the balance between the bidder and target in two-tier offers, particularly where the pressure on shareholders to tender is accentuated by a price differential between the tender offer and the proposed subsequent merger.

- Rule 14d-11 allows bidders in third-party tender offers to have a subsequent offering period, lasting from three to 20 business days, as selected by the bidder, during which no withdrawal rights are permitted. If the bidder elects to have a subsequent offering period, the same consideration must be paid as was paid in the initial period.

- Other significant SEC actions in the tender offer context include the adoption of the "all holders" mandate under Rules 13e-4 and 14d-10.[46] The effect of these rules, in practical effect, is to prohibit discriminatory tender offers that passed

---

use and contains a legend advising security holders to read the Schedule 14D-9 disclosure document where it is provided. See Securities Exchange Act Release No. 42055 (1999).

46. 17 C.F.R. §§ 240.13e-4, 240.14d-10; Securities Exchange Act Release No. 23421 (1986).

muster in the Delaware Supreme Court's decision, *Unocal v. Mesa Petroleum Co.*, 493 A.2d 946 (Del. 1985). In *Unocal*, the Delaware high court, applying a modified version of the business judgment rule, upheld the target management's use of a discriminatory issuer tender offer, which excluded the hostile shareholder from participation. Under the SEC's "all holders" rule, by contrast, both issuer and third-party tender offers must be open to all shareholders and the best price paid to any tendering security holder must be paid to any other tendering security holder. Thus, the SEC's rule signifies that exclusionary tender offers for publicly held companies no longer remain a viable defensive strategy.

• Moreover, in 2006, the SEC adopted amendments to the best price rule to clarify that the rule's mandates extend only to the consideration offered and paid by the bidder to tendering shareholders. The amendments make clear that the best price rule does not encompass employment compensation, severance, or other types of employee benefit arrangements. Securities Exchange Act Release No. 54648 (2006). See Obi, *SEC Rule 14d-10(e)(2) Amendment: Is This the Optimal Solution to the Tender Offer "Best-Price Rule" Dilemma?*, 35 Sec. Reg. L. J. 355 (2007).

In adopting the 2006 amendments to the best price rule for both issuer and third-party tender offers, the Commission stated:

> We are adopting amendments to the language of the third-party and issuer tender offer best price rules to clarify that the provisions apply only with respect to the consideration offered and paid for securities tendered in a tender offer. We also are amending the third-party and issuer tender offer best price rules to provide that any consideration that is offered and paid accordingly to employment compensation, severance or other employee benefit arrangements entered into with security holders of the subject company that meet certain requirements will not be prohibited by the rules. Finally, we are amending the third-party and issuer tender offer best price rules to provide a safe harbor provision so that arrangements that are approved by certain independent directors of either the subject company's or the bidder's board of directors, as applicable, will not be prohibited by the rules. These amendments are intended to make it clear that the best price rule was not intended to capture employment compensation, severance or other employee benefit arrangements.

[F] Legitimacy of Defensive Tactics

[1] In General

To fend off hostile tender offers, target managements have employed a wide variety of defensive tactics. These maneuvers have included, for example, announcing an unprecedented dividend increase, issuing stock to a friendly third party, acquiring another corporation to raise antitrust obstacles, finding a "white knight" to make a competing offer, selling off profitable assets or divisions, adopting "poison pill" provisions, or making a tender offer for the original offeror. Indeed, the extent and nature of these antitakeover devices are seemingly unlimited due to the persistent ingenuity of expert counsel and investment bankers.

Definitions of a number of these defensive maneuvers and acquisition techniques follow:

> *Crown Jewel*— The "crown jewel" is the most prized asset of a corporation, i.e., that which makes it an attractive takeover target. A defensive tactic against a hostile tender offer may be to sell [or grant an option to purchase] that asset to another party, thereby removing the [key] asset that the unfriendly bidder was hoping to acquire and encouraging [it] to cease [its] offer without purchasing any shares of the subject company.

> *Golden Parachute*— A generous severance package that [compensates] certain key executives if control of [the subject] company changes.[47]

> *Lock-Up*—An arrangement, made in connection with the proposed acquisition of a publicly held business, that gives the proposed acquiror an advantage in acquiring the subject company over other potential acquirors. Lock-ups may take the form of: (a) a stock purchase agreement for [authorized but] unissued shares, (b) options to purchase [authorized but] unissued shares, (c) an option to buy certain assets (see "Crown Jewel"), (d) a merger agreement, (e) agreements providing for liquidated damages for failure to consummate an acquisition, (f) options and stock purchase agreements between the "white knight" and principal shareholders, and (g) other similar provisions.

> *Pac-Man Defense*— A tender offer by the subject company for the securities of the original bidder.[48]

> *Scorched Earth Defense*— Actions taken by the directors of the subject company to sell off the subject company's assets, or failing this, to destroy the character of the company to circumvent the bidder's tender offer.

> *Two-Tier Offer*— A two-step acquisition technique in which the first step (front end) is a cash tender offer and the second step (back end) is a merger in which remaining shareholders of the subject company typically receive securities of the bidder valued below the cash consideration offered in the first step tender offer. Despite the reduced consideration being offered in the merger, the merger is certain to be approved by the subject company's shareholders as the bidder, due to [its] acquisition of a controlling interest

---

47. *See* Johnson, *Government Regulation of Business: Golden Parachutes Revisited*, 23 Wake Forest L. Rev. 121 (1988); Riger, *On Golden Parachutes—Ripcords or Ripoffs? Some Comments on Special Termination Agreements*, 3 Pace L. Rev. 15 (1982); Ryan, *Corporate Directors and the "Social Costs" of Takeovers—Reflections on the Tin Parachute*, 64 Tulane L. Rev. 3 (1989).

48. *See* DeMott, *Pac-Man Tender Offers*, 1983 Duke L.J. 116.

in the subject company through the tender offer, will vote in favor of the merger.

Poison Pill— [An antitakeover provision whereby] certain securities [dividends or warrants] of the target company [are] convertible upon consummation of any [enumerated] transaction [or event] into the common stock [or other security] of the [target].[49]

Greenmail— The purchase of a substantial block of the subject company's securities by a [potentially] unfriendly suitor with the primary purpose of [inducing] the subject company to repurchase the block at a premium over the amount paid by the [potential] suitor.

Shark Repellants— Amendments to a potential [target] company's certificate of incorporation or by-laws that have been devised to discourage unsolicited approaches from unwanted bidders.[50]

White Knight— The party sought out by the subject company [in an attempt to fend off the unwanted bidder. Action taken by a white knight may include purchasing a large block of the target company's stock or making a competing tender offer].[51]

Problem

Bafco, Inc., a New York Stock Exchange listed company, makes a tender offer at a price of $53 per share for 51 percent of the issued and outstanding shares of Lilyck, Inc., which also is listed on the New York Stock Exchange. Before the announcement of the tender offer, Lilyck was trading on the Exchange at $38 per share. The Lilyck board of directors, upon receiving the advice of its counsel and investment banker, asserts that the price offered is inadequate, particularly in view of Lilyck's prospective increased growth in the long-term.

After being further advised by its counsel and investment banker, the Lilyck board takes a number of defensive measures, including: (1) granting key Lilyck management "golden parachutes," (2) adopting a "poison pill" provision to Lilyck's by-laws that, if triggered, would have the practical effect of forcing the liquidation of Lilyck; and (3) selling its oldest and most profitable division to an unrelated company, Jeibert, Inc., for a price Lilyck's investment banker deems to be "fair."

-----

49. *See, e.g.,* Chittur, *Wall Street's Teddy Bear: The "Poison Pill" As A Takeover Defense,* 11 J. Corp. L. 25 (1985); Dawson, Fence & Stone, *Poison Pill Defense Measures,* 42 Bus. Law. 423 (1987); Elofson, *Should Dead Hand Poison Pills Be Sent to an Early Grave?,* 25 Sec. Reg. L.J. 303 (1997); Lesser, *The "Poison Pill" Defense,* 22 Rev. Sec. & Comm. Reg. 11 (1989).

50. *See, e.g.,* Gilson, *The Case Against Shark Repellant Amendments: Structural Limitations of the Enabling Concept,* 34 Stan. L. Rev. 775 (1981); Hamermesh, *Corporate Democracy and Stockholder-Adopted By-Laws: Taking Back the Street?,* 73 Tulane L. Rev. 409 (1998); Johnson, *Anti-Takeover Actions and Defenses: Business Judgment or Breach of Duty?,* 28 Vill. L. Rev. 51 (1982).

51. Appendix 3 to Justice Arthur Goldberg's Separate Statement for the SEC Advisory Committee Report on Tender Offers (1983).

Bafco, in view of the actions taken by the Lilyck board, deems the offer unwise and decides to terminate its offer even though 35 percent of Lilyck shares thus far have been tendered. After Bafco's abandonment of the offer, Lilyck stock eventually decreases to $34 per share. Shareholders of Lilyck subsequently bring a $1.6 billion damages action against the directors of Lilyck, alleging violations of state corporate and federal securities law. Do the shareholders have a meritorious claim? Why or why not?

----

[2] *Federal Law*

With respect to the legitimacy of defensive tactics under federal law, the key issue is whether § 14(e), the antifraud provision of the Williams Act, regulates substantive conduct. In other words, is § 14(e)'s purpose solely that of ensuring adequate and fair disclosure or does the statute have a broader reach? In adhering to the former approach, the Supreme Court definitively resolved this issue in *Schreiber v. Burlington Northern, Inc.*, 472 U.S. 1 (1985). The statutory analysis and policy implications of that decision merit attention.

Prior to the Supreme Court's decision in *Schreiber*, commentators advocating a broader scope for § 14(e) relied on two grounds. As stated by one source:

> First, conduct by management that deprives shareholders of an opportunity to tender may be held to constitute "constructive fraud" within the meaning of section 14(e) of the Williams Act. Although the Supreme Court held in *Santa Fe Industries, Inc. v. Green* that "mere" breaches of fiduciary duty not amounting to "manipulation" or "deception" do not violate section 10(b) of the Exchange Act and rule 10b-5 promulgated thereunder, section 14(e) ought to be interpreted differently. Unlike section 10(b), section 14(e) by its own terms prohibits "fraudulent" acts or practices. This difference in statutory language and the legislative history of section 14(e) support giving it a broader reach than section 10(b). Second, defensive tactics, the practical effect of which is to prevent shareholders from tendering in response to a bid, may be viewed as "manipulative" under section 14(e). Under this rationale, target management may be found to have engaged in "manipulative" practices proscribed by section 14(e) when it undertakes maneuvers that artificially impede the operation of a fair market for the corporation's stock, such as granting options on valuable corporate assets to friendly third parties.[52]

----

52. Steinberg, *Some Thoughts on Regulation of Tender Offers*, 43 Md. L. Rev. 240, 252–253 (1984). See Junewicz, *The Appropriate Limits of Section 14(e) of the Securities Exchange Act of 1934*, 62 Tex. L. Rev. 1171 (1984); Levine, Lykos & Chafetz, *Application of the Federal Securities Laws to Defensive Tactics in Control Contests*, in Tender Offers: Developments and Commentaries at 193 (M. Steinberg ed., 1985); Loewenstein, *Section 14(e) of the Williams Act and the Rule 10b-5 Comparisons*, 71 Geo. L.J. 1311 (1983); Weiss, *Defensive Responses to Tender Offers and the Williams Act's Prohibition Against Manipulation*, 35 Vand. L. Rev. 1087 (1982).

Prior to *Schreiber*, a few courts held that certain defensive tactics engaged in by target management, even though fully disclosed, constituted "manipulation" under § 14(e). See *Mobil Corp. v. Marathon Oil Co.*, 669 F.2d 366 (6th Cir. 1981); *Data Probe Acquisition Corp. v. Datatab, Inc.*, 568 F. Supp. 1538 (S.D.N.Y. 1983), *rev'd*, 722 F.2d 9 (2d Cir. 1983). This argument has been foreclosed by the *Schreiber* decision.

Schreiber v. Burlington Northern, Inc.

United States Supreme Court

472 U.S. 1, 105 S. Ct. 2458, 86 L. Ed. 2d 1 (1985)

CHIEF JUSTICE BURGER delivered the opinion of the Court.

We granted certiorari to resolve a conflict in the Circuits over whether misrepresentation or nondisclosure is a necessary element of a violation of § 14(e) of the Securities Exchange Act of 1934.

I

On December 21, 1982, Burlington Northern, Inc., made a hostile tender offer for El Paso Gas Co. Through a wholly owned subsidiary, Burlington proposed to purchase 25.1 million El Paso shares at $24 per share. Burlington reserved the right to terminate the offer if any of several specified events occurred. El Paso management initially opposed the takeover, but its shareholders responded favorably, fully subscribing the offer by the December 30, 1982 deadline.

Burlington did not accept those tendered shares; instead, after negotiations with El Paso management, Burlington announced on January 10, 1983, the terms of a new and friendly takeover agreement. Pursuant to the new agreement, Burlington undertook, *inter alia*, to (1) rescind the December tender offer, (2) purchase 4,166,667 shares from El Paso at $24 per share, (3) substitute a new tender offer for only 21 million shares at $24 per share, (4) provide procedural protections against a squeeze-out merger of the remaining El Paso shareholders, and (5) recognize "golden parachute" contracts between El Paso and four of its senior officers. By February 8, more than 40 million shares were tendered in response to Burlington's January offer, and the takeover was completed.

The rescission of the first tender offer caused a diminished payment to those shareholders who had tendered during the first offer. The January offer was greatly oversubscribed and consequently those shareholders who retendered were subject to substantial proration. Petitioner Barbara Schreiber filed suit on behalf of herself and similarly situated shareholders, alleging that Burlington, El Paso, and members of El Paso's board violated § 14(e)'s prohibition of "fraudulent, deceptive or manipulative acts or practices . . . in connection with any tender offer." She claimed that Burlington's withdrawal of the December tender offer coupled with the substitution of the January tender offer was a "manipulative" distortion of the market for El Paso stock. Schreiber also alleged that Burlington violated § 14(e) by failing to disclose the "golden parachutes" offered to four of El Paso's managers. She claims that this non-disclosure was a deceptive act forbidden by § 14(e).

The District Court dismissed the suit for failure to state a claim. 568 F. Supp. 197 (Del. 1983). The District Court reasoned that the alleged manipulation did not involve a misrepresentation, and so did not violate § 14(e). The District Court relied on the fact that in cases involving alleged violations of § 10(b) of the Securities Exchange Act, this Court has required misrepresentation for there to be a "manipulative" violation of the section. . . .

The Court of Appeals affirmed. 731 F.2d 163 (1984). The Court of Appeals held that the acts alleged did not violate the Williams Act, because "§ 14(e) was not intended to create a federal cause of action for all harms suffered because of the proffering or the withdrawal of tender offers." . . . The Court of Appeals reasoned that § 14(e) was "enacted principally as a disclosure statute, designed to insure that fully-informed investors could intelligently decide how to respond to a tender offer." It concluded that the "arguable breach of contract" alleged by petitioner was not a "manipulative act" under § 14(e).

We granted certiorari to resolve the conflict . . . . We affirm.

II

A

We are asked in this case to interpret § 14(e) of the Securities Exchange Act. . . . The starting point is the language of the statute. . . .

Petitioner relies on a construction of the phrase, "fraudulent, deceptive or manipulative acts or practices." Petitioner reads the phrase "fraudulent, deceptive or manipulative acts or practices" to include acts which, although fully disclosed, "artificially" affect the price of the takeover target's stock. Petitioner's interpretation relies on the belief that § 14(e) is directed at purposes broader than providing full and true information to investors.

Petitioner's reading of the term "manipulative" conflicts with the normal meaning of the term. We have held in the context of an alleged violation of § 10(b) of the Securities Exchange Act:

Use of the word "manipulative" is especially significant. It is and was virtually a term of art when used in connection with the securities markets. It connotes intentional or willful conduct *designed to deceive or defraud* investors by controlling or artificially affecting the price of securities.

Ernst & Ernst v. Hochfelder, 425 U.S. 185, 199 (1976) (emphasis added).

Other cases interpreting the term reflect its use as a general term comprising a range of misleading practices:

The term refers generally to practices, such as wash sales, matched orders, or rigged prices, that are intended to mislead investors by artificially affecting market activity. . . . Section 10(b)'s general prohibition of practices deemed by the SEC to be "manipulative"—9 this technical sense of artificially affecting market activity in order to mislead investors—is fully consistent with the fundamental purpose of the 1934 Act "to substitute a philosophy of full disclosure for the philosophy of *caveat emptor.* . . ." . . . Indeed, nondisclosure is usually essential to the success of a manipulative scheme. . . . No doubt Congress meant to prohibit the full range of ingenious devices that might be used to manipulate securities prices. But we do not think it would have chosen this "term of art" if it had meant to bring within the scope of § 10(b) instances of corporate mismanagement such as this, in which the essence of the complaint is that shareholders were treated unfairly by a fiduciary.

Santa Fe Industries, Inc. v. Green, 430 U.S. 462, 476–477 (1977). The meaning the Court has given the term "manipulative" is consistent with the use of the term at common law, and with its traditional dictionary definition.

She argues, however, that the term manipulative takes on a meaning in § 14(e) that is different from the meaning it has in § 10(b). Petitioner claims that the use of the disjunctive "or" in § 14(e) implies that acts need not be deceptive or fraudulent to be manipulative. But Congress used the phrase "manipulative or deceptive" in § 10(b) as well, and we have interpreted "manipulative" in that context to require misrepresentation. Moreover, it is a " 'familiar principle of statutory construction that words grouped in a list should be given related meaning.' " . . . All three species of misconduct, *i.e.,* "fraudulent, deceptive or manipulative," listed by Congress are directed at failures to disclose. The use of the term "manipulative" provides emphasis and guidance to those who must determine which types of acts are reached by the statute; it does not suggest a deviation from the section's facial and primary concern with disclosure or Congressional concern with disclosure which is the core of the Act.

B

Our conclusion that "manipulative" acts under § 14(e) require misrepresentation or nondisclosure is buttressed by the purpose and legislative history of the provision. Section 14(e) was originally added to the Securities Exchange Act as part of the Williams Act. "The purpose of the Williams Act is to insure that public shareholders who are confronted by a cash tender offer for their stock will not be required to respond without adequate information." *Rondeau v. Mosinee Paper Corp.,* 422 U.S. 49, 58 (1975).

It is clear that Congress relied primarily on disclosure to implement the purpose of the Williams Act. Senator Williams, the Bill's Senate sponsor, stated in the debate:

> Today, the public shareholder in deciding whether to accept or reject a tender offer possesses limited information. No matter what he does, he acts without adequate knowledge to enable him to decide rationally what is the best course of action. This is precisely the dilemma which our securities laws are designed to prevent.

. . . .

The expressed legislative intent was to preserve a neutral setting in which the contenders could fully present their arguments. . . . To implement this objective, the Williams Act added §§ 13(d), 13(e), 14(d), 14(e), and 14(f) to the Securities Exchange Act. . . . [53]

Section 14(e) adds a "broad antifraud prohibition," . . . modeled on the antifraud provisions of § 10(b) of the Act and Rule 10b-5. . . . It supplements the more precise disclosure provisions found elsewhere in the Williams Act, while requiring disclosure more explicitly addressed to the tender offer context than that required by § 10(b).

While legislative history specifically concerning § 14(e) is sparse, the House and Senate Reports discuss the role of § 14(e). Describing § 14(e) as regulating "fraudulent transactions," and stating the thrust of the section:

> This provision would affirm the fact that persons engaged in making or opposing tender offers or otherwise seeking to influence the decision of investors or the outcome of the tender offer are under an obligation to make *full disclosure* of material information to those with whom they deal. . . .

Nowhere in the legislative history is there the slightest suggestion that § 14(e) serves any purpose other than disclosure, or that the term "manipulative" should be read as an invitation to the courts to oversee the substantive fairness of tender offers; the quality of any offer is a matter for the marketplace. To adopt the reading of the term "manipulative" urged by petitioner would not only be unwarranted in light of the legislative purpose but would be at odds with it. Inviting judges to read the term "manipulative" with their own sense of what constitutes "unfair" or "artificial" conduct would inject uncertainty into the tender offer process. An essential piece of information—whether the court would deem the fully disclosed actions of one side or the other to be "manipulative"—would not be available until after the tender offer had closed. This uncertainty would directly contradict the expressed Congressional desire to give investors full information.

Congress' consistent emphasis on disclosure persuades us that it intended takeover contests to be addressed to shareholders. In pursuit of this goal, Congress,

---

[53]. Section 13(d) requires those acquiring a certain threshold percentage of a company's stock to file reports disclosing such information as the purchaser's background and identity, the source of the funds to be used in making the purchase, the purpose of the purchase, and the extent of the purchaser's holdings in the target company. 15 U.S.C. § 78m(d). Section 13(e) imposes restrictions on certain repurchases of stock by corporate issuers. 15 U.S.C. § 78m(e). Section 14(d) imposes specific disclosure requirements on those making a tender offer. 15 U.S.C. § 78n(d)(1). Section 14(d) also imposes specific substantive requirements on those making a tender offer. These requirements include allowing shareholders to withdraw tendered shares at certain times during the bidding process, 15 U.S.C. § 78n(d)(5), the proration of share purchases when the number of shares tendered exceeds the number of shares sought, 15 U.S.C. § 78n(d)(6), and the payment of the same price to all those whose shares are purchased, 15 U.S.C. § 78n(d)(7). Section 14(f) imposes disclosure requirements when new corporate directors are chosen as the result of a tender offer.

consistent with the core mechanism of the Securities Exchange Act, created sweeping disclosure requirements and narrow substantive safeguards. The same Congress that placed such emphasis on shareholder choice would not at the same time have required judges to oversee tender offers for substantive fairness. It is even less likely that a Congress implementing that intention would express it only through the use of a single word placed in the middle of a provision otherwise devoted to disclosure.

C

We hold that the term "manipulative" as used in § 14(e) requires misrepresentation or nondisclosure. It connotes "conduct designed to deceive or defraud investors by controlling or artificially affecting the price of securities." . . . Without misrepresentation or nondisclosure, § 14(e) has not been violated.

Applying that definition to this case, we hold that the actions of respondents were not manipulative. The amended complaint fails to allege that the cancellation of the first tender offer was accompanied by any misrepresentation, nondisclosure or deception. . . .

Petitioner also alleges that El Paso management and Burlington entered into certain undisclosed and deceptive agreements during the making of the second tender offer. The substance of the allegations is that, in return for certain undisclosed benefits, El Paso managers agreed to support the second tender offer. But both courts noted that petitioner's complaint seeks redress only for injuries related to the cancellation of the first tender offer. Since the deceptive and misleading acts alleged by the petitioner all occurred with reference to the making of the second tender offer— when the injuries suffered by petitioner had already been sustained—these acts bear no possible causal relationship to petitioner's alleged injuries. The Court of Appeals dealt correctly with this claim.

. . . *Affirmed.*

Note

Do you agree with the approach taken by the Supreme Court in *Schreiber*? Why? Does it make good policy that the legitimacy of tactics employed by offerors and targets in mega-dollar tender offers for multinational companies should be assessed under the law of the target's state of incorporation (e.g., Delaware) rather than under federal law?

Even prior to *Schreiber*, although adopting certain substantive tender offer regulations (e.g., Rule 14d-8 extending the proration period to the entire period that the offer remains open—see § 14.04[E]), the focus of SEC attention was and continues to be centered on disclosure. For example, in addition to its specific tender offer rules, the Commission requires that the terms of "golden parachute" contracts be disclosed. With respect to disclosure of the material effects of anti-takeover proposals, the

Commission in *SEC v. Dorchester*, [1983–1984 Transfer Binder] Fed. Sec. L. Rep. (CCH) ¶ 99,613 (D.D.C. 1984), stated:

> The Commission again wishes to emphasize the need for adequate and accurate disclosure with respect to anti-takeover and other defensive measures ("anti-takeover measures"). Such measures are designed to deter contests for control or unfriendly takeovers, by making the subject company unattractive as a potential target and by making it more difficult to change a majority of the board of directors or to remove management. The anti-takeover measures also may help management to insulate a proposed corporate transaction, such as a merger or acquisition, from unwanted competition.
>
> Companies must disclose all the material effects of anti-takeover measures, including their impact on any proposed corporate transaction, whether hostile or friendly. It is also important that management's interest in the corporate transaction (including the existence of any actual or potential conflicts of interests) and the ultimate effect of the anti-takeover measures on shareholders be disclosed. Absent such disclosure, shareholders will be unable to make informed voting decisions on the matters being proposed. It is especially important, when management is considering or pursuing a leveraged buy-out with its attendant serious conflicts of interest, that full and fair disclosure of the impact of the anti-takeover measures on the proposed transaction be made.

---

[3] State Common Law

Paramount Communications, Inc. v. Time, Inc.

Delaware Supreme Court
571 A.2d 1140 (1990)

HORSEY, Justice:

Paramount Communications, Inc. ("Paramount") and two other groups of plaintiffs ("Shareholder Plaintiffs"), shareholders of Time Incorporated ("Time"), a Delaware corporation, separately filed suits in the Delaware Court of Chancery seeking a preliminary injunction to halt Time's tender offer for 51% of Warner Communication, Inc.'s ("Warner") outstanding shares at $70 cash per share. The court below consolidated the cases and, following the development of an extensive record, after discovery and an evidentiary hearing, denied plaintiffs' motion. In a 50-page unreported opinion and order entered July 14, 1989, the Chancellor refused to enjoin Time's consummation of its tender offer, concluding that the plaintiffs were unlikely to prevail on the merits. . . .

On the same day, plaintiffs filed in this Court an interlocutory appeal, which we accepted on an expedited basis. Pending the appeal, a stay of execution of Time's tender offer was entered .... Following briefing and oral argument ... we concluded that the decision below should be affirmed. We so held in a brief ruling from the bench and a separate Order entered on that date. The effect of our decision was to permit Time to proceed with its tender offer for Warner's outstanding shares. This is the written opinion articulating the reasons for our July 24 bench ruling.

The principal ground for reversal, asserted by all plaintiffs, is that Paramount's June 7, 1989 uninvited all-cash, all-shares, "fully negotiable" (though conditional) tender offer for Time triggered duties under *Unocal Corp. v. Mesa Petroleum Co.*, Del. Supr. 493 A.2d 946 (1985), and that Time's board of directors, in responding to Paramount's offer, breached those duties. . . .

Shareholder Plaintiffs also assert a claim based on *Revlon v. MacAndrews & Forbes Holdings, Inc.,* Del. Supr., 506 A.2d 173 (1986). They argue that the original Time-Warner merger agreement of March 4, 1989 resulted in a change of control which effectively put Time up for sale, thereby triggering *Revlon* duties. Those plaintiffs argue that Time's board breached its *Revlon* duties by failing in the face of the change of control, to maximize shareholder value in the immediate term.

Applying our standard of review, we affirm the Chancellor's ultimate finding and conclusion under *Unocal*. We find that Paramount's tender offer was reasonably perceived by Time's board to pose a threat to Time and that the Time board's "response" to that threat was, under the circumstances, reasonable and proportionate. Applying *Unocal*, we reject the argument that the only corporate threat posed by an all-shares, all-cash tender offer is the possibility of inadequate value.

We also find that Time's board did not by entering into its initial merger agreement with Warner come under a *Revlon* duty either to auction the company or to maximize short-term shareholder value, notwithstanding the unequal share exchange. Therefore, the Time board's original plan of merger with Warner was subject only to a business judgment rule analysis. *See Smith v. Van Gorkom*, Del. Supr. 488 A.2d 858, 873–74 (1985).

I

Time is a Delaware corporation with its principal offices in New York City. Time's traditional business is publication of magazines and books; however, Time also provides pay television programming through its Home Box Office, Inc. and Cinemax subsidiaries. In addition, Time owns and operates cable television franchises through its subsidiary, American Television and Communication Corporation. During the relevant time period, Time's board consisted of sixteen directors. Twelve of the directors were "outside," nonemployee directors. Four of the directors were also officers of the company. The outside directors included James F. Bere, chairman of the board and CEO of Borg-Warner Corporation (Time director since 1979); Clifford J. Grum, president and CEO of Temple-Inland, Inc. (Time director since 1980); Henry C. Goodwin, former chairman of Sonat, Inc. (Time director since 1978); Matina S. Horner, then president of Radcliffe College (Time director since 1975); David T. Kearns, chairman and CEO of Xerox Corporation (Time director since

1978); Donald S. Perkins, former chairman and CEO of Jewel Companies, Inc. (Time director since 1979); Michael D. Dingman, chairman and CEO of The Henley Group, Inc. (Time director since 1978); Edward S. Finkelstein, Chairman and CEO of Macy's Inc. (Time director since 1984); John R. Opel, former chairman and CEO of IBM Corporation (Time director since 1984); Arthur Temple, chairman of Temple-Inland, Inc. (Time director since 1983); Clifton R. Wharton, Jr., chairman and CEO of The Henley Group, Inc. (Time director since 1978); and Henry R. Luce III, president of The Henry Luce Foundation, Inc. (Time director since 1967). Mr. Luce, the son of the founder of Time, individually and in a representative capacity controlled 4.2% of the outstanding Time stock. The insider officer directors were J. Richard Munro, Time's chairman and CEO since 1980; N. J. Nicholas, Jr., president and chief operating officer of the company since 1986; Gerald M. Levin, vice chairman of the board; and Jason D. McManus, editor-in-chief of *Time* magazine and a board member since 1988.[54]

As early as 1983 and 1984, Time's executive board began considering expanding Time's operations into the entertainment industry. In 1987, Time established a special committee of executives to consider and propose corporate strategies for the 1990's. The consensus of the committee was that Time should move ahead in the area of ownership and creation of video programming. This expansion, as the Chancellor noted, was predicated upon two considerations: first, Time's desire to have greater control, in terms of quality and price, over the film products delivered by way of its cable network and franchises, and second, Time's concern over the increasing globalization of the world economy. Some of Time's outside directors, especially Luce and Temple, had opposed this move as a threat to the editorial integrity and journalistic focus of Time.[55] Despite this concern, the board saw the advantages of a vertically integrated video enterprise to complement Time's existing HBO and cable networks would enable it to compete on a global basis.

In late spring of 1987, a meeting took place between Steve Ross, CEO of Warner Brothers, and Nicholas of Time. Ross and Nicholas discussed the possibility of a joint venture between the two companies through the creation of a jointly-owned cable company. Time would contribute its cable system and HBO. Warner would contribute its cable system and provide access to Warner Brothers Studio. The resulting

---

[54]. Four directors, Arthur Temple, Henry C. Goodrich, Clifton R. Wharton, and Clifford J. Grum, have since resigned from Time's board. The Chancellor found, with the exception of Temple, their resignations to reflect more a willingness to step down than disagreement or dissension over the Time-Warner merger. Temple did not choose to continue to be associated with a corporation that was expanding into the entertainment field. Under the board of combined Time-Warner corporation, the number of Time directors, as well as Warner directors, was limited to twelve each.

[55]. The primary concern of Time's outside directors was the preservation of the "Time Culture." They believed that Time had become recognized in this country as an institution built upon a foundation of journalistic integrity. Time's management made a studious effort to refrain from involvement in Time's editorial policy. Several of Time's outside directors feared that a merger with an entertainment company would divert Time's focus from news journalism and threaten the Time Culture.

venture would be a larger, more efficient cable network, able to produce and distribute its own movies on a worldwide basis. Ultimately the parties abandoned this plan, determining that it was impractical for several reasons, chief among them being tax considerations.

On August 11, 1987, Gerald M. Levin, Time's vice chairman and chief strategist, wrote J. Richard Munro a confidential memorandum in which he strongly recommended a strategic consolidation with Warner. In June 1988, Nicholas and Munro sent to each outside director a copy of the "comprehensive long-term planning document" prepared by the committee of Time executives that had been examining strategies for the 1990's. The memo included reference to and a description of Warner as a potential acquisition candidate.

Thereafter, Munro and Nicholas held meetings with Time's outside directors to discuss, generally, long-term strategies for Time and, specifically, a combination with Warner. Nearly a year later, Time's board reached the point of serious discussion of the "nuts and bolts" of a consolidation with an entertainment company. On July 21, 1988, Time's board met, with all outside directors present. The meeting's purpose was to consider Time's expansion into the entertainment industry on a global scale. Management presented the board with a profile of various entertainment companies in addition to Warner, including Disney, 20th Century Fox, Universal, and Paramount.

Without any definitive decision on choice of a company, the board approved in principle a strategic plan for Time's expansion. The board gave management the "go-ahead" to continue discussions with Warner concerning the possibility of a merger. With the exception of Temple and Luce, most of the outside directors agreed that a merger involving expansion into the entertainment field promised great growth opportunity for Time. Temple and Luce remained unenthusiastic about Time's entry into the entertainment field.

The board's consensus was that a merger of Time and Warner was feasible, but only if: (1) a favorable stock-for-stock exchange could be negotiated; and (2) Time controlled the board of the resulting corporation and thereby preserved a management committed to Time's journalistic integrity. To accomplish these goals, the board stressed the importance of carefully defining in advance the corporate governance provisions that would control the resulting entity. Some board members expressed concern over whether such a business combination would place Time "*in play.*" The board discussed the wisdom of adopting further defensive measures to lessen such a possibility.[56]

Of a wide range of companies considered by Time's board as possible merger candidates, Warner Brothers, Paramount, Columbia, M.C.A., Fox, MGM, Disney, and

---

[56]. Time had in place a panoply of defensive devices, including a staggered board, a "poison pill" preferred stock rights plan triggered by an acquisition of 15 percent of the company, a fifty-day notice period for shareholder motions, and restrictions on shareholders' ability to call a meeting or act by consent.

Orion, the board, in July 1988, concluded that Warner was the superior candidate for a consolidation. Warner stood out on a number of counts. Warner had just acquired Lorimar and its film studios. Time-Warner could make movies and television shows for use on HBO. Warner had an international distribution system, which Time could use to sell films, videos, books and magazines. Warner was a giant in the music and recording business, an area into which Time wanted to expand. None of the other companies considered had the musical clout of Warner. Time and Warner's cable systems were compatible and could be easily integrated; none of the other companies considered presented such a compatible cable partner. Together, Time and Warner would control half of New York City's cable system; Warner had cable systems in Brooklyn and Queens; and Time controlled cable systems in Manhattan and Queens. Warner's publishing company would integrate well with Time's established publishing company. Time sells hardcover books and magazines, and Warner sells softcover books and comics.[57] Time-Warner could sell all of these publications and Warner's videos by using Time's direct mailing network and Warner's international distribution system. Time's network could be used to promote and merchandise Warner's movies.

In August 1988, Levin, Nicholas, and Munro, acting on instructions from Time's board, continued to explore a business combination with Warner. By letter dated August 4, 1988, management informed the outside directors of proposed corporate governance provisions to be discussed with Warner. The provisions incorporated the recommendations of several of Time's outside directors.

From the outset, Time's board favored an all-cash or cash and securities acquisition of Warner as the basis for consolidation. Bruce Wasserstein, Time's financial advisor, also favored an outright purchase of Warner. However, Steve Ross, Warner's CEO, was adamant that a business combination was only practicable on a stock-for-stock basis. Warner insisted on a stock swap in order to preserve its shareholders' equity in the resulting corporation. Time's officers, on the other hand, made it abundantly clear that Time would be the acquiring corporation and that Time would control the resulting board. Time refused to permit itself to be cast as the "acquired" company.

Eventually Time acquiesced in Warner's insistence on a stock-for-stock deal, but talks broke down over corporate governance issues. Time wanted Ross' position as a co-CEO to be temporary and wanted Ross to retire in five years. Ross, however, refused to set a time for his retirement and viewed Time's proposal as indicating a lack of confidence in his leadership. Warner considered it vital that their executives and creative staff not perceive Warner as selling out to Time. Time's request of a guarantee that Time would dominate the CEO succession was objected to as inconsistent with the concept of a Time-Warner merger "of equals." Negotiations ended when the

---

[57]. In contrast, Paramount's publishing endeavors were in the areas of professional volumes and text books. Time's board did not find Paramount's publishing as compatible as Warner's publishing efforts.

parties reached an impasse. Time's board refused to compromise on its position on corporate governance. Time, and particularly its outside directors, viewed the corporate governance provisions as critical for preserving the "Time Culture" through a pro-Time management at the top.

Throughout the fall of 1988 Time pursued its plan of expansion into the entertainment field. Time held informal discussions with several companies, including Paramount. Capital Cities/ABC approached Time to propose a merger. Talks terminated, however, when Capital Cities/ABC suggested that it was interested in purchasing Time or in controlling the resulting board. Time steadfastly maintained it was not placing itself up for sale.

Warner and Time resumed negotiations in January 1989. The catalyst for the resumption of talks was a private dinner between Steve Ross and Time outside director, Michael Dingman. Dingman was able to convince Ross that the transitional nature of the proposed co-CEO arrangement did not reflect a lack of confidence in Ross. Ross agreed that this course was best for the company and a meeting between Ross and Munro resulted. Ross agreed to retire in five years and let Nicholas succeed him. Negotiations resumed and many of the details of the original stock-for-stock exchange agreement remained intact. In addition, Time's senior management agreed to long-term contracts.

Time inside directors Levin and Nicholas met with Warner's financial advisors to decide upon a stock exchange ratio. Time's board had recognized the potential need to pay a premium in the stock ratio in exchange for dictating the governing arrangement of the new Time-Warner. Levin and outside director Finkelstein were the primary proponents of paying a premium to protect the "Time Culture." The board discussed premium rates of 10%, 15% and 20%. Wasserstein also suggested paying a premium for Warner due to Warner's rapid growth rate. The market exchange ratio of Time stock for Warner stock was .38 in favor of Warner. Warner's financial advisors informed the board that any exchange rate over .400 was a fair deal and any exchange rate over .450 was "one hell of a deal." The parties ultimately agreed upon an exchange rate favoring Warner of .465. On that basis, Warner stockholders would own slightly over 61% of the common stock of Time-Warner.

On March 3, 1989, Time's board, with all but one director in attendance, met and unanimously approved the stock-for-stock merger with Warner. Warner's board likewise approved the merger. The agreement called for Warner to be merged into a wholly-owned Time subsidiary with Warner becoming the surviving corporation. The common stock of Warner would then be converted into common stock of Time at the agreed upon ratio. Thereafter, the name of Time would be changed to Time-Warner, Inc.

The rules of the New York Stock Exchange required that Time's issuance of shares to effectuate the merger be approved by a vote of Time's stockholders. The Delaware General Corporation Law required approval of the merger by a majority of the Warner stockholders. The Chancellor concluded that the agreement was the product of "an arms-length negotiation between two parties seeking individual advantage through mutual action."

The resulting company would have a 24-member board, with 12 members representing each corporation. The company would have co-CEO's, at first Ross and Munro, then Ross and Nicholas, and finally, after Ross' retirement, by Nicholas alone. The board would create an editorial committee with a majority of members representing Time. A similar entertainment committee would be controlled by Warner board members. A two-thirds supermajority vote was required to alter CEO successions but an earlier proposal to have supermajority protection for the editorial committee was abandoned. Warner's board suggested raising the compensation levels for Time's senior management under the new corporation. Warner's management, as with most entertainment executives, received higher salaries than comparable executives in news journalism. Time's board, however, rejected Warner's proposal to equalize the salaries of the two management teams.

As its March 2, 1989 meeting, Time's board adopted several defensive tactics. Time entered an automatic share exchange agreement with Warner. Time would receive 17,292,747 shares of Warner's outstanding common stock (9.4%) and Warner would receive 7,080,016 shares of Time's outstanding common stock (11.1%). Either party could trigger the exchange. Time sought out and paid for "confidence" letters from various banks with which [it] did business. In these letters, the banks promised not to finance any third-party attempt to acquire Time. Time argues these agreements served only to preserve the confidential relationship between itself and the banks. The Chancellor found these agreements to be inconsequential and futile attempts to "dry up" money for a hostile takeover. Time also agreed to a "no-shop" clause, preventing Time from considering any other consolidation proposal, thus relinquishing its power to consider other proposals, regardless of their merits. Time did so at Warner's insistence. Warner did not want to be left "on the auction block" for an unfriendly suitor, if Time were to withdraw from the deal.

Time's board simultaneously established a special committee of outside directors, Finkelstein, Kearns, and Opel, to oversee the merger. The committee's assignment was to resolve any impediments that might arise in the course of working out the details of the merger and its consummation.

Time representatives lauded the lack of debt to the United States Senate and to the President of the United States. Public reaction to the announcement of the merger was positive. Time-Warner would be a media colossus with international scope. The board scheduled the stockholder vote for June 23; and a May 1 record date was set. On May 24, 1989, Time sent out extensive proxy statements to the stockholders regarding the approval vote on the merger. In the meantime, with the merger proceeding without impediment, the special committee had concluded, shortly after its creation, that it was not necessary either to retain independent consultants, legal or financial, or even to meet. Time's board was unanimously in favor of the proposed merger with Warner; and, by the end of May, the Time-Warner merger appeared to be an accomplished fact.

On June 7, 1989, these wishful assumptions were shattered by Paramount's surprising announcement of its all-cash offer to purchase all outstanding shares of Time for $175 per share. The following day, June 8, the trading price of Time's stock rose from $126 to $170 per share. Paramount's offer was said to be "fully negotiable."

Time found Paramount's "fully negotiable" offer to be in fact subject to at least three conditions. First, Time had to terminate its merger agreement and stock exchange agreement with Warner, and remove certain other of its defensive devices, including the redemption of Time's shareholder rights. Second, Paramount had to obtain the required cable franchise transfers from Time in a fashion acceptable to Paramount in its sole discretion. Finally, the offer depended upon a judicial determination that section 203 of the General [Corporation] Law of Delaware (The Delaware Anti-Takeover Statute) was inapplicable to any Time-Paramount merger. While Paramount's board had been privately advised that it could take months, perhaps over a year, to forge and consummate the deal, Paramount's board publicly proclaimed its ability to close the offer by July 5, 1989. Paramount executives later conceded that none of its directors believed that July 5th was a realistic date to close the transaction.

On June 8, 1989, Time formally responded to Paramount's offer. Time's chairman and CEO, J. Richard Munro, sent an aggressively worded letter to Paramount's CEO, Martin Davis. Munro's letter attacked Davis' personal integrity and called Paramount's offer "smoke and mirrors." Time's nonmanagement directors were not shown the letter before it was sent. However, at a board meeting that same day, all members endorsed management's response as well as the letter's content.

Over the following eight days, Time's board met three times to discuss Paramount's $175 offer. The board viewed Paramount's offer as inadequate and concluded that its proposed merger with Warner was the better course of action. Therefore, the board declined to open any negotiations with Paramount and held steady its course toward a merger with Warner.

In June, Time's board of directors met several times. During the course of their June meetings, Time's outside directors met frequently without management, officers or directors being present. At the request of the outside directors, corporate counsel was present during the board meetings and, from time to time, the management directors were asked to leave the board sessions. During the course of these meetings, Time's financial advisors informed the board that, on an auction basis, Time's per share value was materially higher than Warner's $175 per share offer. On this basis, the board concluded that Paramount's $175 offer was inadequate.

At these June meetings, certain Time directors expressed their concern that their stockholders would not comprehend the long-term benefits of the Warner merger. Large quantities of Time shares were held by institutional investors. The board feared that even though there appeared to be wide support for the Warner transaction,

Paramount's cash premium would be a tempting prospect to these investors. In mid-June, Time sought permission from the New York Stock Exchange to alter its rules and allow the Time-Warner merger to proceed without stockholder approval. Time did so at Warner's insistence. The New York Stock Exchange rejected Time's request on June 15; and on that day, the value of Time stock reached $182 per share.

The following day, June 16, Time's board met to take up Paramount's offer. The board's prevailing belief was that Paramount's bid presented a threat to Time's control of its own destiny and retention of the "Time Culture." Even after Time's financial advisors made another presentation of Paramount and its business attributes, Time's board maintained its position that a combination [with] Warner presented greater potential for Time. Warner presented Time with a much desired production capability and an established international marketing chain. Time's advisors presented the board with various options, including defensive measures. The board considered and rejected the idea of purchasing Paramount in a "Pac Man" defense.[58] The board considered other defenses as well, including a recapitalization, the acquisition of another company, and a material change in the present capitalization structure or dividend policy. The board determined to retain its same advisors even in light of the changed circumstances. The board rescinded its agreement to pay its advisors a bonus based on the consummation of the Time-Warner merger and agreed to pay a flat fee for any advice the advisors rendered. Finally, Time's board formally rejected Paramount's offer.

At the same meeting, Time's board decided to recast its consolidation with Warner into an outright cash and securities acquisition of Warner by Time; and Time so informed Warner. Time accordingly restructured its proposal to acquire Warner as follows: Time would make an immediate all-cash offer for 51% of Warner's outstanding stock at $70 per share. The remaining 49% would be purchased at some later date for a mixture of cash and securities worth $70 per share. To provide the funds required for its outright acquisition of Warner, Time would assume 7–10 billion dollars' worth of debt, thus eliminating one of the principal transaction-related benefits of the original merger agreement. Time also agreed to pay and amortize a $9 billion payment to Warner for the goodwill of the reputable and rapidly growing corporation.

Warner agreed but insisted on certain terms. Warner sought a control premium and guarantees that the governance provisions found in the original merger agreement would remain intact. Warner further sought agreements that Time would not employ its poison pill against Warner and that, unless enjoined, Time would be legally bound to complete the transaction. Time's board agreed to these last measures only at the insistence of Warner. For its part, Time was assured of its ability to extend its efforts into production arenas and international markets, all the while maintaining the Time identity and culture. The Chancellor found the initial Time-Warner

---

[58]. In a "Pac Man" defense, Time would launch a tender offer for the stock of Paramount, thus consuming its rival. *Moran v. Household Intern, Inc.*, Del. Supp., 500 A.2d 1346, 1350 n.6 (1985).

transaction to have been negotiated at arm's length and the restructured Time-Warner transaction to have resulted from Paramount's offer and its expected effect on a Time shareholder vote.

On June 23, 1989, Paramount raised its all-cash offer to buy Time's outstanding stock to $200 per share. Paramount still professed that all aspects of the offer were negotiable. Time's board met on June 26, 1989 and formally rejected Paramount's $200 per share second offer. The board reiterated its belief that, despite the $25 increase, the offer was still inadequate and that the Warner transaction offered a greater long-term value for the stockholders and, unlike Paramount, was not a threat to Time's survival and its "culture." Paramount then filed this action in the Court of Chancery.

II

The Shareholder Plaintiffs first assert a *Revlon* claim. They contend that the March 4 Time-Warner agreement effectively put Time up for sale, triggering *Revlon* duties, requiring Time's board to enhance short-term shareholder value and to treat all other interested acquirors on an equal basis. The Shareholder Plaintiffs base this argument on two facts: (i) the ultimate Time-Warner exchange ratio of .465 favoring Warner, resulting in Warner shareholders' receipt of 62% of the combined company; and (ii) the subjective intent of Time's directors as evidenced in their statements that the market might perceive the Time-Warner merger as putting Time up "for sale" and their adoption of various defensive measures.

The Shareholder Plaintiffs further contend that Time's directors, in structuring the original merger transaction to be "takeover-proof," triggered *Revlon* duties by foreclosing their shareholders from any prospect of obtaining a control premium. In short, plaintiffs argue that Time's board's decision to merge with Warner imposed a fiduciary duty to maximize immediate share value and not erect unreasonable barriers to further bids. Therefore, they argue, the Chancellor erred in finding: that Paramount's bid for Time did not place Time "for sale"; that Time's transaction with Warner did not result in any transfer of control; and that the combined Time-Warner was not so large as to preclude the possibility of the stockholders of Time-Warner receiving a future control premium.

Paramount asserts only a *Unocal* claim in which the shareholder plaintiffs join. Paramount contends that the Chancellor, in applying the first part of the *Unocal* test, erred in finding that Time's board had reasonable grounds to believe that Paramount posed both a legally cognizable threat to Time shareholders and a danger to Time's corporate policy and effectiveness. Paramount also contests the court's finding that Time's board made a reasonable and objective investigation of Paramount's offer so as to be informed before rejecting it. Paramount further claims that the court erred in applying *Unocal's* second part in finding Time's response to be "reasonable." Paramount points primarily to the preclusive effect of the revised agreement which denied Time shareholders the opportunity both to vote on the agreement and to respond to Paramount's tender offer. Paramount argues that the underlying motivation of Time's board in adopting these defensive measures was management's desire to perpetuate itself in office.

The Court of Chancery posed the pivotal question presented by this case to be: Under what circumstances must a board of directors abandon an in-place plan of corporate development in order to provide its shareholders with the option to elect and realize an immediate control premium? As applied to this case, the question becomes: Did Time's board, having developed a strategic plan of global expansion to be launched through a business combination with Warner, come under a fiduciary duty to jettison its plan and put the corporation's future in the hands of its shareholders?

While we affirm the result reached by the Chancellor, we think it unwise to place undue emphasis upon long-term versus short-term corporate strategy. Two key predicates underpin our analysis. First, Delaware law imposes on a board of directors the duty to manage the business and affairs of the corporation. 8 *Del. C.* § 141(a). This broad mandate includes a conferred authority to set a corporate course of action, including time frame, designed to enhance corporate profitability. [59] Thus, the question of "long-term" versus "short-term" values is largely irrelevant because directors, generally, are obliged to charter a course for a corporation which is in its best interests without regard to a fixed investment horizon. Second, absent a limited set of circumstances as defined under *Revlon*, a board of directors, while always required to act in an informed manner, is not under any *per se* duty to maximize shareholder value in the short term, even in the context of a takeover. In our view, the pivotal question presented by this case is: "Did Time, by entering into the proposed merger with Warner, put itself up for sale?" A resolution of that issue through application of *Revlon* has a significant bearing upon the resolution of the derivative *Unocal* issue.

A.

We first take up plaintiff's principal *Revlon* argument, summarized above. In rejecting this argument, the Chancellor found the original Time-Warner merger agreement not to constitute a "change of control" and concluded that the transaction did not trigger *Revlon* duties. The Chancellor's conclusion is premised on a finding that "[b]efore the merger agreement was signed, control of the corporation existed in a fluid aggregation of unaffiliated shareholders representing a voting majority—in other words, in the market." The Chancellor's findings of fact are supported by the record and his conclusion is correct as a matter of law. However, we premise our rejection of plaintiffs' *Revlon* claim on broader grounds, namely, the absence of any substantial evidence to conclude that Time's board, in negotiating with Warner, made the dissolution or breakup of the corporate entity inevitable, as was the case in *Revlon*.

---

[59]. In endorsing this finding, we tacitly accept the Chancellor's conclusion that it is not a breach of faith for directors to determine that the present stock market price of shares is not representative of true value or that there may indeed be several market values for any corporation's stock. We have so held in another context. *See Van Gorkom*, 488 A.2d at 876.

Under Delaware law there are, generally speaking and without excluding other possibilities, two circumstances which may implicate *Revlon* duties. The first, and clearer one, is when a corporation initiates an active bidding process seeking to sell itself or to effect a business reorganization involving a clear break-up of the company. However, *Revlon* duties may also be triggered where, in response to a bidder's offer, a target abandons its long-term strategy and seeks an alternative transaction also involving the breakup of the company. Thus, in *Revlon*, when the board responded to Pantry Pride's offer by contemplating a "bust-up" sale of assets in a leveraged acquisition, we imposed upon the board a duty to maximize immediate shareholder value and an obligation to auction the company fairly. If, however, the board's reaction to a hostile tender offer is found to constitute only a defensive response and not an abandonment of the corporation's continued existence, *Revlon* duties are not triggered, though *Unocal* duties attach.

The plaintiffs insist that even though the original Time-Warner agreement may not have worked "an objective change of control," the transaction made a "sale" of Time inevitable. Plaintiffs rely on the subjective intent of Time's board of directors and principally upon certain board members' expressions of concern that the Warner transaction *might* be viewed as effectively putting Time up for sale. Plaintiffs argue that the use of a lock-up agreement, a no-shop clause, and so-called "dry-up" agreements prevented shareholders from obtaining a control premium in the immediate future and thus violated *Revlon*.

We agree with the Chancellor that such evidence is entirely insufficient to invoke *Revlon* duties; and we decline to extend *Revlon's* application to corporate transactions simply because they might be construed as putting a corporation either "in play" or "up for sale." . . . The adoption of structural safety devices alone does not trigger *Revlon*.[60] Rather, as the Chancellor stated, such devices are properly subject to a *Unocal* analysis.

Finally, we do not find in Time's recasting of its merger agreement with Warner from a share exchange to a share purchase a basis to conclude that Time had either abandoned its strategic plan or made a sale of Time inevitable. The Chancellor found that although the merged Time-Warner company would be large (with a value approaching approximately $30 billion), recent takeover cases have proven that acquisition of the combined company might nonetheless be possible. . . . The legal consequence is that *Unocal* alone applies to determine whether the business judgment rule attaches to the revised agreement. . . .

---

[60]. Although the legality of the various safety devices adopted to protect the original agreement is not a central issue, there is substantial evidence to support each of the trial court's related conclusions. Thus, the court found that the concept of the Share Exchange Agreement predated any takeover threat by Paramount and had been adopted for a rational business purpose: to deter Time and Warner from being "put in play" by their March 4 Agreement. The court further found that Time had adopted the "no-shop" clause at Warner's insistence and for Warner's protection. Finally, although certain aspects of the "dry-up" agreements were suspect on their face, we concur in the Chancellor's view that in this case they were inconsequential.

B.

We turn now to plaintiffs' *Unocal* claim. We begin by noting, as did the Chancellor, that our decision does not require us to pass on the wisdom of the board's decision to enter into the original Time-Warner agreement. That is not a court's task. Our task is simply to review the record to determine whether there is sufficient evidence to support the Chancellor's conclusion that the initial Time-Warner agreement was the product of a proper exercise of business judgment.

We have purposely detailed the evidence of the Time board's deliberative approach, beginning in 1983–84, to expand itself. Time's decision in 1988 to combine with Warner was made only after what could be fairly characterized as an exhaustive appraisal of Time's future as a corporation. After concluding in 1983–84 that the corporation must expand to survive, and beyond journalism into entertainment, the board combed the field of available entertainment companies. By 1987 Time had focused upon Warner, by late July 1988 Time's board was convinced that Warner would provide the best "fit" for Time to achieve its strategic objectives. The record attests to the zealousness of Time's executives, fully supported by their directors, in seeing to the preservation of Time's "culture," i.e., its perceived editorial integrity in journalism. We find ample evidence in the record to support the Chancellor's conclusion that the Time board's decision to expand the business of the company through its March 3 merger with Warner was entitled to the protection of the business judgment rule.

The Chancellor reached a different conclusion in addressing the Time-Warner transaction as revised three months later. He found that the revised agreement was defense-motivated and designed to avoid the potentially disruptive effect that Paramount's offer would have had on consummation of the proposed merger were it put to a shareholder vote. Thus, the court declined to apply the traditional business judgment rule to the revised transaction and instead analyzed the Time board's June 16 decision under *Unocal*. The court ruled that *Unocal* applied to all director actions taken, following receipt of Paramount's hostile tender offer, that were reasonably determined to be defensive. Clearly that was a correct ruling and no party disputes that ruling.

In *Unocal*, we held that before the business judgment rule is applied to a board's adoption of a defensive measure, the burden will lie with the board to prove (a) reasonable grounds for believing that a danger to corporate policy and effectiveness existed; and (b) that the defensive measure adopted was reasonable in relation to the threat posed. Directors satisfy the first part of the *Unocal* test by demonstrating good faith and reasonable investigation. We have repeatedly stated that the refusal to entertain an offer may comport with a valid exercise of the board's business judgment. . . .

Unocal involved a two-tier, highly coercive tender offer. In such a case, the threat is obvious: shareholders may be compelled to tender to avoid being treated adversely in the second stage of the transaction. In subsequent cases, the Court of Chancery has suggested that an all-cash, all-shares offer, falling within a range of values that a shareholder might reasonably prefer, cannot constitute a legally recognized "threat" to shareholder interests sufficient to withstand a *Unocal* analysis. . . . In those cases, the Court of Chancery determined that whatever danger existed related only to the shareholders and only to price and not to the corporation.

From those decisions by our Court of Chancery, Paramount and the individual plaintiffs extrapolate a rule of law that an all-cash, all-shares offer with values reasonably in the range of acceptable price cannot pose any objective threat to a corporation or its shareholders. Thus, Paramount would have us hold that only if the value of Paramount's offer were determined to be clearly inferior to the value created by management's plan to merge with Warner could the offer be viewed—objectively—as a threat.

Implicit in the plaintiffs' argument is the view that a hostile tender offer can pose only two types of threats: the threat of coercion that results from a two-tier offer promising unequal treatment for nontendering shareholders; and the threat of inadequate value from an all-shares, all-cash offer at a price below what a target board in good faith deems to be the present value of its shares. Since Paramount's offer was all-cash, the only conceivable "threat," plaintiffs argue, was inadequate value. We disapprove of such a narrow and rigid construction of *Unocal*, for the reasons which follow.

Plaintiffs' position represents a fundamental misconception of our standard of review under *Unocal* principally because it would involve the court in substituting its judgment for what is a "better" deal for that of a corporation's board of directors. To the extent that the Court of Chancery has recently done so in certain of its opinions, we hereby reject such approach as not in keeping with a proper *Unocal* analysis. . . .

The usefulness of *Unocal* as an analytical tool is precisely its flexibility in the face of a variety of fact scenarios. *Unocal* is not intended as an abstract standard; neither is it a structured and mechanistic procedure of appraisal. Thus, we have said that directors may consider, when evaluating the threat posed by a takeover bid, the "inadequacy of the price offered, nature and timing of the offer, questions of illegality, the impact on contingencies other than shareholders, the risk of nonconsummation and the quality of securities being offered in the exchange." . . . The open-ended analysis mandated by *Unocal* is not intended to lead to a simple mathematical exercise: that is, of comparing the discounted value of Time-Warner's expected trading price at some future date with Paramount's offer and determining which is the higher. Indeed, in our view, precepts underlying the business judgment rule mitigate against a court's engaging in the process of attempting to appraise and evaluate the relative merits of a long-term versus a short-term investment goal for shareholders. To engage in such an exercise is a distortion of the *Unocal* process and, in particular, the application of the second part of *Unocal's* test, discussed below.

In this case, the Time board reasonably determined that inadequate value was not the only legally cognizable threat that Paramount's all-cash, all-shares offer could present. Time's board concluded that Paramount's eleventh hour offer posed other threats. One concern was that Time shareholders might elect to tender into Paramount's cash offer in ignorance or a mistaken belief of the strategic benefit which a business combination with Warner might produce. Moreover, Time viewed the conditions attached to Paramount's offer as introducing a degree of uncertainty that skewed a comparative analysis. Further, the timing of Paramount's offer to follow issuance of Time's proxy notice was viewed as arguably designed to upset, if not confuse, the Time stockholders' vote. Given this record evidence, we cannot conclude that the Time board's decision . . . that Paramount's offer posed a threat to corporate policy and effectiveness was lacking in good faith or dominated by motives of either entrenchment or self-interest.

Paramount also contends that the Time board had not duly investigated Paramount's offer. Therefore, Paramount argues, Time was unable to make an informed decision that the offer posed a threat to Time's corporate policy. Although the Chancellor did not address this issue directly, his findings of fact do detail Time's exploration of the available entertainment companies, including Paramount, before determining that Warner provided the best strategic "fit." In addition, the court found that Time's board rejected Paramount's offer because Paramount did not serve Time's objectives or meet Time's needs. Thus, the record does, in our judgment, demonstrate that Time's board was adequately informed of the potential benefits of a transaction with Paramount. We agree with the Chancellor that the Time board's lengthy pre-June investigation of potential merger candidates, including Paramount, mooted any obligation on Time's part to halt its merger process with Warner to reconsider Paramount. Time's board was under no obligation to negotiate with Paramount. Time's failure to negotiate cannot be fairly found to have been uninformed. The evidence supporting this finding is materially enhanced by the fact that twelve of Time's sixteen board members were outside independent directors. . . .

We turn to the second part of the *Unocal* analysis. The obvious requisite to determining the reasonableness of a defensive action is a clear identification of the nature of the threat. As the Chancellor correctly noted, this "requires an evaluation of the importance of the corporate objective threatened; alternative methods of protecting that objective; impacts of the 'defensive' action, and other relevant factors." . . . It is not until both parts of the *Unocal* inquiry have been satisfied that the business judgment rule attaches to defensive actions of a board of directors. As applied to the facts of this case, the question is whether the record evidence supports the Court of Chancery's conclusion that the restructuring of the Time-Warner transaction, including the adoption of several preclusive defensive measures, was a *reasonable response* in relation to a perceived threat.

Paramount argues that, assuming its tender offer posed a threat, Time's response was unreasonable in precluding Time's shareholders from accepting the tender offer or receiving a control premium in the immediately foreseeable future. Once again, the contention stems, we believe, from a fundamental misunderstanding of where the power of corporate governance lies. Delaware law confers the management of the corporate enterprise to the stockholders' duly elected board representatives. The fiduciary duty to manage a corporate enterprise includes the selection of a time frame for achievement of corporate goals. That duty may not be delegated to the stockholders. Directors are not obliged to abandon a deliberately conceived corporate plan for a short-term shareholder profit unless there is clearly no basis to sustain the corporate strategy. . . .

Although the Chancellor blurred somewhat the discrete analyses required under *Unocal*, he did conclude that Time's board reasonably perceived Paramount's offer to be a significant threat to the planned Time-Warner merger and that Time's response was not "overly broad." We have found that even in light of a valid threat, management actions that are coercive in nature or force upon shareholders a management-sponsored alternative to a hostile offer may be struck down as unreasonable and nonproportionate responses. . . .

Here, on the record facts, the Chancellor found that Time's responsive action to Paramount's tender offer was not aimed at "cramming down" on its shareholders a management-sponsored alternative, but rather had as its goal the carrying forward of a pre-existing transaction in an altered form. Thus, the response was reasonably related to the threat. The Chancellor noted that the revised agreement and its accompanying safety devices did not preclude Paramount from making an offer for the combined Time-Warner company or from changing the conditions of its offer so as not to make the offer dependent upon the nullification of the Time-Warner agreement. Thus, the response was proportionate. We affirm the Chancellor's rulings as clearly supported by the record. Finally, we note that although Time was required, as a result of Paramount's hostile offer, to incur a heavy debt to finance its acquisition of Warner, that fact alone does not render the board's decision unreasonable so long as the directors could reasonably perceive the debt load not to be so injurious to the corporation as to jeopardize its well-being.

Conclusion

Applying the test for grant or denial or preliminary injunctive relief, we find plaintiffs failed to establish a reasonable likelihood of ultimate success on the merits. Therefore, we affirm.

"Poison Pills" and Other Defensive Tactics

Subsequent Delaware cases continue to refine the parameters of the *Unocal* and *Revlon* standards. As the Delaware Supreme Court stated in *Unitrin, Inc. v. American General Corp.*, 651 A.2d 1361, 1368 (Del. 1995), "if the board of directors' response is not draconian (preclusive or coercive) and is within a 'range of reasonableness,' a court must not substitute its judgment for the board's." In a more recent decision, *Omnicare, Inc. v. NCS Healthcare, Inc.*, 818 A.2d 914 (Del. 2003), the Delaware Supreme Court (in a three to two decision) held that the defensive maneuvers at issue were coercive and were not within *Unocal's* range of reasonableness. The court stated:

> The defensive measures that protected the merger transaction are unenforceable not only because they are preclusive and coercive but, alternatively, they are unenforceable because they are invalid as they operate in this case. Given the specifically enforceable irrevocable voting agreements, the provision in the merger agreement requiring the board to submit the transaction for a stockholder vote and the omission of a fiduciary out clause in the merger agreement, completely prevented the board from discharging its fiduciary responsibilities to the minority stockholders when [the subsequent bidder] Omnicare presented its superior transaction. To the extent that a [merger] contract, or a provision thereof, purports to require a board to act or not act in such a fashion as to limit the exercise of fiduciary duties, it is invalid and unenforceable.

A number of Delaware decisions continue to view poison pills with significant deference. For example, in *Versata Enterprises, Inc. v. Selectica, Inc.,* 5 A.3d 586 (Del. 2010), the Delaware Supreme Court upheld a shareholder rights plan having a 4.99 percent trigger. The poison pill allegedly was adopted to protect the company's net operating losses (NOL) under the Internal Revenue Code.

In *Moore Corp. v. Wallace Computer Services, Inc.,* 907 F. Supp. 1545 (Del. 1995), a federal district court construing Delaware law supported use of the "just say no" defense. Applying the *Unocal* test, the court upheld a target corporation's board of director determination to retain its poison pill in the face of an all- cash all-share hostile tender offer at a 27 percent premium. Nonetheless, validation of a subject poison pill under Delaware law may be dependent on such "rights plan" being deemed reasonable and not draconian, preclusive or coercive. Moreover, judicial approval of a subject poison pill apparently is conditioned on the availability of the proxy mechanism to displace the incumbent board. As the court in *Moore* reasoned:

> [R]etention of the pill will have no discriminatory effect on shareholders, as is generally the result in any situation involving a coercive offer. . . . Second, and more important, retention of the pill will have no effect on the success of the proxy contest. . . . Here, the poison pill is triggered upon the acquisition of 20% of the shares of [the target] Wallace stock. Therefore, so long as Moore maintains a stock ownership percentage below that amount, it may safely wage its proxy contest free from the dramatic effect of the poison pill.

More recently, in *Air Products & Chemicals, Inc. v. Airgas,* 16 A. 3d 48 (Del. Ch. 2011), under the facts presented, the court upheld the target company board of directors' decision to maintain a poison pill having a 15 percent trigger when a *non-coercive* hostile takeover bid had been launched.

For other decisions focusing on poison pill provisions, including "dead hand" provisions (provisions that have the effect of maintaining incumbent directors in place even after an insurgent victory), compare *Quickturn Design Systems, Inc. v. Shapiro,* 721 A.2d 1281 (Del. 1998) (holding delayed redemption provision invalid under Delaware Corporation Code § 141(a)) and *Bank of New York v. Irving Bank Corp.,* 528 N.Y.S. 2d 482 (N.Y. Supr. Ct. 1988) (holding that dead hand provision contravened New York corporation law), with *Invacare Corp. v. Healthdyne Technologies, Inc.,* 968 F. Supp. 1578 (N.D. Ga. 1997) (interpreting Georgia law, upholding dead hand provision and stating that "the concept of continuing directors is an integral part of a takeover defense and is not contrary to public policy in Georgia") and *AMP, Inc. v. Allied Signal, Inc.,* 1998 U.S. Dist. Lexis 15671 (E.D. Pa. 1998) (upholding under Pennsylvania law validity of a "no-hand" poison pill).

In *Paramount Communications, Inc. v. QVC Network, Inc.,* 637 A.2d 34 (Del. 1993), the Delaware Supreme Court applied the *Revlon* standard in a change of control scenario. As evidenced by its decision in *Time,* however, *Revlon* duties do not arise in stock-for-stock mergers between widely held public corporations. In *Paramount Communications/QVC,* the court set forth the following with respect to a board's function in complying with its *Revlon* duties:

> In determining which alternative provides that best value for stockholders, a board of directors is not limited to considering only the amount of cash involved, and is not required to ignore totally its view of the future value of the strategic alliance. Instead, the directors should analyze the entire situation and evaluate in a disciplined manner the consideration being offered. Where stock or other non-cash consideration is involved, the board should try to quantify its value, if feasible, to achieve an objective comparison of the alternatives. In addition, the board may assess a variety of practical considerations relating to each alternative, including:

>> "[an offer's] fairness and feasibility; the proposed or actual financing for the offer, and the consequences of that financing; questions of illegality; the impact of both the bid and the potential acquisition on other constituencies, provided that it bears some reasonable relationship to general shareholder interests; the risk of non-consummation; the basic stockholder interests at stake; the bidder's identity, prior background and other business venture experiences; and the bidder's business plan for the corporation and their effects on stockholder interests."

Under Delaware law, what standard (e.g., business judgment rule, *Unocal,* or *Revlon*) applies with respect to the following actions taken by a board of directors after receiving the advice of the corporation's counsel and investment banker:

(1) The adoption of an anti-takeover amendment to the corporation's by-laws that, if implemented, would result in the liquidation of the company? The refusal to diffuse such a device in light of an all share, all cash offer at a substantial premium?

(2) Maneuvers employed to fend off a hostile acquiror in order to keep the company as an ongoing independent entity?

(3) The granting of lock-up provisions to a potential offeror where no other offeror is on the horizon?

(4) The granting of lock-up provisions to a white knight, the effect of which is to defeat a competing bid from a reputable offeror, where the white knight intends to operate the company as an ongoing concern with all its divisions intact?[61]

---

61. For commentary in assessing the validity of defensive tactics and related issues, *see, e.g.*, Bainbridge, *Exclusive Merger Agreements and Lock-Ups in Negotiated Corporate Acquisitions*, 75 Minn. L. Rev. 239 (1990); Bebchuk & Ferrell, *A New Approach to Takeover Law and Regulatory Competition*, 87 Va. L. Rev. 111 (2001); Bradford, *Stampeding Shareholders and Other Myths: Target Shareholders and Hostile Tender Offers*, 15 J. Corp. L. 417 (1990); de Fontenay, *Law Firm Selection and the Value of Transactional Lawyering*, 41 J. Corp. L. 393 (2015); Even et al., *How Low Can You Go? An Insiders' Perspective on Selectica v. Versata and NOL Poison Pills*, 39 Sec. Reg. L.J. 79 (2011); Gilson & Kraakman, *Delaware's Intermediate Standard for Defensive Tactics: Is There Substance to Proportionality Review?*, 44 Bus. Law. 247 (1989); Griffin, *The Costs and Benefits of Precommitment: An Appraisal of Omnicare v. NCS Healthcare*, 29 J. Corp. L. 569 (2004); Johnson & Millon, *Misreading the Williams Act*, 87 Mich. L. Rev. 1862 (1989); Johnson & Siegel, *Corporate Mergers: Redefining the Role of Target Directors*, 136 U. Pa. L. Rev. 315 (1987); Kerr, *Delaware Goes Shopping for a New Interpretation of the Revlon Standard: The Effect of the QVC Decision on Strategic Mergers*, 58 Alb. L. Rev. 609 (1995); Lipton, *Corporate Governance in the Age of Finance Corporatism*, 136 U. Pa. L. Rev. 1 (1987); Loewenstein, *Unocal Revisited: No Tiger in the Tank*, 27 J. Corp. L. 1 (2001); Steinberg, *Nightmare on Main Street: The Paramount Picture Horror Show*, 16 Del. J. Corp. L. 1 (1990); Taylor, *New and Unjustified Restrictions on Delaware Directors' Authority*, 21 Del. J. Corp. L. 837 (1996).

Chapter 15

Securities Law Enforcement

§ 15.01 Introductory Materials

Congress enacted the federal securities laws in light of a perceived need to protect investors and the integrity of the marketplace. To help ensure that the purposes of the federal securities laws are fulfilled, Congress vested the SEC with broad investigatory and enforcement powers. As part of its investigatory authority, the Commission may subpoena witnesses and records. Once the Commission obtains sufficient information to believe that a violation of the federal securities laws has occurred, it may bring an enforcement action either administratively or in a federal district court.

The overwhelming percentage of SEC enforcement actions are settled pursuant to the consent negotiation process where the defendant neither admits nor denies the Commission's allegations. Parties generally consent rather than litigate due to a number of factors. These include that the SEC may have a strong case, the financial costs involved in litigating with the Commission, avoidance of adverse publicity that would be generated by prolonged litigation, disruption of normal operations that would otherwise result due to management's attention being diverted, and fear of offensive collateral estoppel should the SEC emerge victorious. With respect to this last factor, there is the concern that an adverse decision in an SEC contested matter may result in the initiation of private damages actions in which the claimants seek to estop the defendants from relitigating issues resolved against them in the prior SEC action.[1]

SEC enforcement (as well as state "blue sky" securities enforcement) raises a multitude of issues. A number of the key topics are discussed in this Chapter.[2]

---

1. *See Parklane Hosiery Co., Inc. v. Shore*, 439 U.S. 322 (1979); authorities cited note 2 *infra*.

2. For more comprehensive coverage, *see, e.g.*, Symposium, *In Honor of Judge Stanley Sporkin*, 43 Sec. Reg. L. J. No. 1 (2015); Enforcement Manual Issued by the Securities and Exchange Commission Division of Enforcement (hereinafter SEC Enforcement Manual), available at, http://www .sec/divisions/enforce/enforcementmanual.pdf; American Bar Association, The Securities Enforcement Manual: Tactics and Strategies (Kirkpatrick & Lockhart, LLP (2d ed. 2007)); H. Friedman, Securities and Commodities Enforcement (2006); J. Long, M. Kaufman & J. Wunderlich, Blue Sky Law (2016); M. Steinberg & R. Ferrara, Securities Practice: Federal and State Enforcement (2d ed. 2001 & 2017 supp.).

[A] SEC Order Directing a Private Investigation

What does an SEC Order Directing a Private Investigation look like? The following is an illustration.

UNITED STATES OF AMERICA

BEFORE THE

SECURITIES AND EXCHANGE COMMISSION

In the Matter of XYZ Corporation:	ORDER DIRECTING A PRIVATE
File No.: _____	INVESTIGATION AND
	DESIGNATING OFFICERS
	TO TAKE TESTIMONY

I

The Commission's public files disclose that XYZ Corporation is a corporation with its principal executive offices in Sandusky, Ohio. Its common stock is registered with the Commission pursuant to Section 12(b) of the Securities Exchange Act of 1934 (the "Exchange Act") and is listed on the New York Stock Exchange (NYSE). XYZ Corporation has filed with the Commission registration statements and annual, quarterly and other periodic reports pursuant to Section 13 of the Exchange Act.

II

Members of the staff have reported information to the Commission tending to show that, during the period from on or about April 15, 2016, through the present:

A. XYZ Corporation, its present and former officers, directors, employees, affiliates and other persons or entities, directly and indirectly, in connection with the purchase or sale of securities, may have employed, or may be employing, devices, schemes or artifices to defraud, may have made, or may be making, untrue statements of material facts and may have omitted, or may be omitting, to state material facts necessary in order to make the statements made, in the light of the circumstances under which they were made, not misleading, and may have engaged, or may be engaging in transactions, acts, practices or courses of business which operate or have operated as a fraud and deceit upon other persons, including purchasers and sellers of such securities, concerning, among other things, the inventory, sales, payroll taxes, cash flow and the financial condition and performance of XYZ Corporation.

B. XYZ Corporation, its present and former officers, directors, employees, affiliates and other persons or entities, directly or indirectly, may have filed or caused to be filed with the Commission certain annual, quarterly and other reports and certifications in connection therewith pursuant to the Exchange Act which may have contained untrue statements of material facts or may have omitted information or material facts necessary in order to make the statements made, not misleading, and which may have failed to contain information required to be set forth therein concerning, among other things, the matters referred to in Paragraph II.A. above.

C. XYZ Corporation, its present and former officers, directors, employees, affiliates and other persons or entities, directly and indirectly, may have failed to or caused the failure to:

1. make and keep books, records, and accounts which, in reasonable detail, accurately and fairly reflect transactions and dispositions of the corporate funds of XYZ Corporation, and

2. devise and maintain a system of internal accounting controls sufficient to provide reasonable assurances that:

a. transactions are executed in accordance with management's general or specific authorization;

b. transactions are recorded as necessary to permit preparation of financial statements in conformity with generally accepted accounting principles or any other criteria applicable to such statements and to maintain accountability for assets;

c. access to assets is permitted only in accordance with management's general or specific authorization; and

d. the recorded accountability for assets is compared with the existing assets at reasonable intervals and appropriate action is taken with respect to any differences.

D. XYZ Corporation, its present and former officers, directors, employees, affiliates and other persons or entities, directly or indirectly, may have falsified, or caused the falsification of, books, records and accounts referred to in Subparagraphs II.C.1 and 2 above.

II

The Commission, having considered the foregoing, and deeming such acts and practices, if true, to be in possible violation of Section 17(a) of the Securities Act of 1933 and Sections 10(b), 13(a) and 13(b)(2)(A) and (B) of the Exchange Act of 1934 ("Exchange Act") and Rules 10b-5, 12b-20, 13a-1, 13a-13, 13a-14, 13b2-1, and 13b2-2 thereunder, and Sections 302 and 304 of the Sarbanes-Oxley Act finds it necessary and appropriate and hereby:

ORDERS, pursuant to Section 20(a) of the Securities Act and Section 21(a) of the Securities Exchange Act that a private investigation be conducted to determine whether any person, persons or entities have engaged, are engaging, or are about to engage in any of the aforesaid acts or practices, or in acts or practices of similar purport or object; and

FURTHER ORDERS, pursuant to Section 19(b) of the Securities Act and Section 21(b) of the Securities Exchange Act, that, for the purpose of such investigation, _____, _____, _____, _____, _____, and each of them, are hereby designated as officers of this Commission and each of them are empowered to administer oaths and affirmations, subpoena witnesses, compel their attendance, take evidence, and require the production of any books, papers, correspondence, memoranda or other records and materials deemed relevant or material to the investigation, and to perform all other duties in connection therewith as prescribed by law.

By the Commission

January 11, 2017   _____

                                                                    Secretary

                                 _____

[B] SEC Subpoena Order

The following is an illustration of an SEC Subpoena Duces Tecum.

SUBPOENA DUCES TECUM

UNITED STATES OF AMERICA

SECURITIES AND EXCHANGE COMMISSION

To _____

_____

*At the instance of*_____

you are hereby required to appear before _____

_____

_____

of the Securities and Exchange Commission, at _____

_____100 F. Street, Northeast _____

_____

In the City of Washington D.C. _____

on the 15th *day of* February, *2017, at 9:00 o'clock*

involving _____

_____

_____

And you are hereby required to bring with you and produce at said time and place the following books, papers, and documents:

_____

_____

_____

_____

_____

Fail not at your peril,

> *In testimony whereof, the seal of the*
> *Securities and Exchange Commission is*
> *affixed hereto, and the undersigned, a*
> *member of said Securities and Exchange*
> *Commission, or an officer designated*
> *by it, has hereunto set his hand at*
> *Washington D.C. on the 15 day of January, 2017*

_____

Staff Attorney (Officer)

[C] A Look at Blue Sky Enforcement

Blue sky enforcement mechanisms are fairly similar to those employed by the SEC. As former Dean Sargent points out, they comprise an important aspect of securities law enforcement:

> Blue sky enforcement actions are not only large in number, but varied in purpose and form. They may be used to combat both fraud and registration violations. They also may be used to discipline securities professionals carrying on business within the state. The action may take the shape of an informal investigation, a formal administrative proceeding, a civil suit by the administrator or a criminal prosecution. These actions frequently end in settlement, but they also may conclude with application of one or more of a variety of possible remedies, including denial, suspension, or revocation of a securities exemption or of a broker-dealer, agent, or investment adviser registration, an injunction, an appointment of a receiver, or a criminal conviction.[3]

§ 15.02 Collateral Estoppel Ramifications

As the following Supreme Court case aptly demonstrates, in determining whether to recommend settlement of an SEC enforcement action, counsel must assess the collateral estoppel ramifications. If the client elects to litigate (rather than settle) with

_____

3. Sargent, *Blue Sky Enforcement Actions — Some Practical Considerations*, 14 Sec. Reg. L.J. 343–344 (1987).

the SEC and loses, private claimants, fast on the trail of a Commission action, will seek to invoke offensively the doctrine of collateral estoppel.

Parklane Hosiery Co., Inc. v. Shore

United States Supreme Court

439 U.S. 322, 99 S. Ct. 645, 58 L. Ed. 2d 552 (1979)

MR. JUSTICE STEWART delivered the opinion of the Court.

This case presents the question whether a party who has had issues of fact adjudicated adversely to it in an equitable action may be collaterally estopped from relitigating the same issues before a jury in a subsequent legal action brought against it by a new party.

The respondent brought this stockholder's class action against the petitioners in a Federal District Court. The complaint alleged that the petitioners, Parklane Hosiery Co., Inc. (Parklane), and 13 of its officers, directors, and stockholders, had issued a materially false and misleading proxy statement in connection with a merger. The proxy statement, according to the complaint, had violated §§ 14(a), 10(b), and 20(a) of the Securities Exchange Act of 1934 as well as various rules and regulations promulgated by the Securities and Exchange Commission (SEC). The complaint sought damages, rescission of the merger, and recovery of costs.

Before this action came to trial, the SEC filed suit against the same defendants in the Federal District Court, alleging that the proxy statement that had been issued by Parklane was materially false and misleading in essentially the same respects as those that had been alleged in the respondent's complaint. Injunctive relief was requested. After a 4-day trial, the District Court found that the proxy statement was materially false and misleading in the respects alleged, and entered a declaratory judgment to that effect. *SEC v. Parklane Hosiery Co.*, 422 F. Supp. 477. The Court of Appeals for the Second Circuit affirmed this judgment. 558 F.2d 1083.

The respondent in the present case then moved for partial summary judgment against the petitioners, asserting that the petitioners were collaterally estopped from relitigating the issues that had been resolved against them in the action brought by the SEC.[4] The District Court denied the motion on the ground that such an application of collateral estoppel would deny the petitioners their Seventh Amendment right to a jury trial. The Court of Appeals for the Second Circuit reversed, holding that a party who

---

[4] A private plaintiff in an action under the proxy rules is not entitled to relief simply by demonstrating that the proxy solicitation was materially false and misleading. The plaintiff must also show that he was injured and prove damages. *Mills v. Electric Auto-Lite Co.,* 396 U.S. 375, 386–390. Since the SEC action was limited to a determination of whether the proxy statement contained materially false and misleading information, the respondent conceded that he would still have to prove these other elements of his prima facie case in the private action. The petitioners' right to a jury trial on those remaining issues is not contested.

has had issues of fact determined against him after a full and fair opportunity to litigate in a nonjury trial is collaterally estoppel from obtaining a subsequent jury trial of these same issues of fact. . . . Because of an intercircuit conflict, we granted certiorari.

I

The threshold question to be considered is whether, quite apart from the right to a jury trial under the Seventh Amendment, the petitioners can be precluded from relitigating facts resolved adversely to them in a prior equitable proceeding with another party under the general law of collateral estoppel. Specifically, we must determine whether a litigant who was not a party to a prior judgment may nevertheless use that judgment "offensively" to prevent a defendant from relitigating issues resolved in the earlier proceeding.[5]

A

Collateral estoppel, like the related doctrine of res judicata,[6] has the dual purpose of protecting litigants from the burden of relitigating an identical issue with the same party or his privy and of promoting judicial economy by preventing needless litigation. Until relatively recently, however, the scope of collateral estoppel was limited by the doctrine of mutuality of parties. Under this mutuality doctrine, neither party could use a prior judgment as an estoppel against the other unless both parties were bound by the judgment. Based on the premise that it is somehow unfair to allow a party to use a prior judgment when he himself would not be so bound, the mutuality requirement provided a party who had litigated and lost in a previous action an opportunity to relitigate identical issues with new parties.

By failing to recognize the obvious difference in position between a party who has never litigated an issue and one who has fully litigated and lost, the mutuality requirement was criticized almost from its inception. Recognizing the validity of this criticism, the Court in *Blonder-Tongue Laboratories, Inc. v. University of Illinois Foundation,* [402 U.S. 313] abandoned the mutuality requirement, at least in cases where a patentee seeks to relitigate the validity of a patent after a federal court in a previous lawsuit has already declared it invalid. . . .

B

The *Blonder-Tongue* case involved defensive use of collateral estoppel—a plaintiff was estopped from asserting a claim that the plaintiff had previously litigated and lost against another defendant. The present case, by contrast, involves offensive

---

[5] In this context, offensive use of collateral estoppel occurs when the plaintiff seeks to foreclose the defendant from litigating an issue the defendant has previously litigated unsuccessfully in an action with another party. Defensive use occurs when a defendant seeks to prevent a plaintiff from asserting a claim the plaintiff has previously litigated and lost against another defendant.

[6] Under the doctrine of res judicata, a judgment on the merits in a prior suit bars a second suit involving the same parties or their privies based on the same cause of action. Under the doctrine of collateral estoppel, on the other hand, the second action is upon a different cause of action and the judgment in the prior suit precludes relitigation of issues actually litigated and necessary to the outcome of the first action.

use of collateral estoppel—a plaintiff is seeking to estop a defendant from relitigating the issues which the defendant previously litigated and lost against another plaintiff. In both the offensive and defensive use situations, the party against whom estoppel is asserted has litigated and lost in an earlier action. Nevertheless, several reasons have been advanced why the two situations should be treated differently.

First, offensive use of collateral estoppel does not promote judicial economy in the same manner as defensive use does. Defensive use of collateral estoppel precludes a plaintiff from relitigating identical issues by merely "switching adversaries." Thus defensive collateral estoppel gives a plaintiff a strong incentive to join all potential defendants in the first action if possible. Offensive use of collateral estoppel, on the other hand, creates precisely the opposite incentive. Since a plaintiff will be able to rely on a previous judgment against a defendant but will not be bound by that judgment if the defendant wins, the plaintiff has every incentive to adopt a "wait and see" attitude, in the hope that the first action by another plaintiff will result in a favorable judgment. Thus offensive use of collateral estoppel will likely increase rather than decrease the total amount of litigation, since potential plaintiffs will have everything to gain and nothing to lose by not intervening in the first action.

A second argument against offensive use of collateral estoppel is that it may be unfair to a defendant. If a defendant in the first action is sued for small or nominal damages, he may have little incentive to defend vigorously, particularly if future suits are not foreseeable. . . . Allowing offensive collateral estoppel may also be unfair to a defendant if the judgment relied upon as a basis for the estoppel is itself inconsistent with one or more previous judgments in favor of the defendant. Still another situation where it might be unfair to apply offensive estoppel is where the second action affords the defendant procedural opportunities unavailable in the first action that could readily cause a different result.

C

We have concluded that the preferable approach for dealing with these problems in the federal courts is not to preclude the use of offensive collateral estoppel, but to grant trial courts broad discretion to determine when it should be applied. The general rule should be that in cases where a plaintiff could easily have joined in the earlier action or where, either for the reasons discussed above or for other reasons, the application of offensive estoppel would be unfair to a defendant, a trial judge should not allow the use of offensive collateral estoppel.

In the present case, however, none of the circumstances that might justify reluctance to allow the offensive use of collateral estoppel is present. The application of offensive collateral estoppel will not here reward a private plaintiff who could have joined in the previous action, since the respondent probably could not have joined in the injunctive action brought by the SEC even had he so desired. Similarly, there is no unfairness to the petitioners in applying offensive collateral estoppel in this case. First, in light of the serious allegations made in the SEC's complaint against the petitioners, as well as the foreseeability of subsequent private suits that typically follow a successful Government judgment, the petitioners had every incentive to litigate the SEC lawsuit fully and vigorously. Second, the judgment in the SEC action was not inconsistent with any previous decision. Finally, there will in the respondent's action be no procedural opportunities available to the petitioners that were unavailable in the first action of a kind that might be likely to cause a different result.

We conclude, therefore, that none of the considerations that would justify a refusal to allow the use of offensive collateral estoppel is present in this case. Since the petitioners received a "full and fair" opportunity to litigate their claims in the SEC action, the contemporary law of collateral estoppel leads inescapably to the conclusion that the petitioners are collaterally estopped from relitigating the question of whether the proxy statement was materially false and misleading.

II

The question that remains is whether, notwithstanding the law of collateral estoppel, the use of offensive collateral estoppel in this case would violate the petitioners' Seventh Amendment right to a jury trial.

. . . .

The law of collateral estoppel, like the law in other procedural areas defining the scope of the jury's function, has evolved since 1791. . . . [T]hese developments are not repugnant to the Seventh Amendment simply for the reason that they did not exist in 1791. Thus if, as we have held, the law of collateral estoppel forecloses the petitioners from relitigating the factual issues determined against them in the SEC action, nothing in the Seventh Amendment dictates a different result, even though because of lack of mutuality there would have been no collateral estoppel in 1791.

The judgment of the Court of Appeals is

Affirmed.

Note

In view of the Supreme Court's decision in *Parklane Hosiery*, consider the following:

> *Parklane Hosiery* may . . . vest the SEC with power to coerce non-culpable defendants into settling enforcement actions. Such defendants may fear the preclusive effects flowing from an unfavorable first judgment and the SEC may succeed in establishing securities violations where private litigants would fail. A defendant may rationally agree to the entry of a consent decree against him in the enforcement action, regardless of the merits of the action, in order to force private plaintiffs to prove independently the elements of their damage claim.[7]

---

7. Note, *Mutuality of Estoppel and the Seventh Amendment: The Effect of Parklane Hosiery,* 64 CORNELL L. REV. 1002, 1014–1015 (1979).

§ 15.03 Subpoena Enforcement

SEC investigations normally are nonpublic and may take the form of a preliminary inquiry or a formal investigation. Frequently, a substantial portion of the materials in the Commission's files is obtained in the informal stage through cooperation. However, if the SEC is unable to elicit the needed information informally, it must initiate a formal investigation and seek authorization from the courts to compel uncooperative sources to supply the desired information. An informal inquiry or investigation can be commenced by the SEC's enforcement division and does not involve the use of subpoenas. The formal investigation, on the other hand, requires Commission authorization and, when necessary, court enforcement as well.[8]

Pursuant to a formal order of investigation, which outlines the general scope of the Commission's inquiry, the SEC can issue subpoenas if it determines that the documents and witnesses ordered produced may be relevant. If the party to whom the subpoena is issued refuses to voluntarily produce the requested information, the Commission must petition a federal district court for an order that compels compliance with the subpoena.[9] Because the Commission's subpoena enforcement power is expansive and constitutes a necessary element of its investigations, the courts frequently order enforcement.

An SEC investigation serves to uncover facts that may reveal whether a violation of the securities laws has occurred. Because such an investigation by itself carries no formal sanctions, judicial intervention may be necessary to enforce compliance with an SEC subpoena. Accordingly, the courts possess the power to hold a party in contempt for noncompliance with subpoenas they have ordered enforced.[10] A party commits civil contempt by disobeying a court order after knowledge that the order has been issued.[11]

Hence, the SEC's use of its subpoena power is one of the Commission's most powerful investigatory tools. The broad scope of this power is evidenced by the following Supreme Court decision.

Securities and Exchange Commission v. Jerry T. O'Brien, Inc.

United States Supreme Court

467 U.S. 735, 104 S. Ct. 2720, 81 L. Ed. 2d 615 (1984)

JUSTICE MARSHALL delivered the opinion of the Court.

The Securities and Exchange Commission (SEC or Commission) has statutory authority to conduct nonpublic investigations into possible violations of the securities

---

8. *See* SEC Rules of Practice, 17 C.F.R. § 202.5; Securities Act Release No. 6345 (1981); SEC Enforcement Manual, *supra* note 2, at § 2.3.3.
9. *See, e.g.,* § 21(b) of the Exchange Act.
10. *See, e.g.,* § 21(c) of the Exchange Act.
11. See *Penfield Co. v. SEC*, 330 U.S. 585 (1947).

laws and, in the course thereof, to issue subpoenas to obtain relevant information. The question before us is whether the Commission must notify the "target" of such an investigation when it issues a subpoena to a third party.

I

This case represents one shard of a prolonged investigation by the SEC into the affairs of respondent Harry F. Magnuson and persons and firms with whom he has dealt. The investigation began in 1980, when the Commission's staff reported to the Commission that information in their possession tended to show that Magnuson and others had been trading in the stock of specified mining companies in a manner violative of the registration, reporting, and antifraud provisions of the Securities Act of 1933 and the Securities Exchange Act of 1934. In response, the Commission issued a Formal Order of Investigation authorizing employees of its Seattle Regional Office to initiate a "private investigation" into the transactions in question and, if necessary, to subpoena testimony and documents "deemed relevant or material to the inquiry."

Acting on that authority, members of the Commission staff subpoenaed financial records in the possession of respondent Jerry T. O'Brien, Inc. (O'Brien), a broker-dealer firm, and respondent Pennaluna & Co. (Pennaluna). O'Brien voluntarily complied, but Pennaluna refused to disgorge the requested materials. Soon thereafter, in response to several inquiries by O'Brien's counsel, a member of the SEC staff informed O'Brien that it was a "subject" of the investigation.

O'Brien, Pennaluna, and their respective owners promptly filed a suit in the District Court for the Eastern District of Washington, seeking to enjoin the Commission's investigation and to prevent Magnuson from complying with subpoenas that had been issued to him. Magnuson filed a cross-claim, also seeking to block portions of the investigation. O'Brien then filed motions seeking authority to depose the Commission's officers and to conduct expedited discovery into the Commission's files.

The District Court denied respondents' discovery motions and soon thereafter dismissed their claims for injunctive relief. The principal ground for the court's decision was that respondents would have a full opportunity to assert their objections to the basis and scope of the SEC's investigation if and when the Commission instituted a subpoena enforcement action. The court did, however, rule that the Commission's outstanding subpoenas met the requirements outlined in *United States v. Powell*, 379 U.S. 48 (1964), for determining whether an administrative summons is judicially enforceable. Specifically, the District Court held that the Commission had a legitimate purpose in issuing the subpoenas, that the requested information was relevant and was not already in the Commission's possession, and that the issuance of the subpoenas comported with pertinent procedural requirements.

Following the District Court's decision, the SEC issued several subpoenas to third parties. In response, Magnuson and O'Brien renewed their request to the District Court for injunctive relief. . . . For the first time, respondents expressly sought notice of the subpoenas issued by the Commission to third parties. Reasoning that respondents lacked standing to challenge voluntary compliance with subpoenas by third parties, and that, in any subsequent proceeding brought by the SEC, respondents could move to suppress evidence the Commission had obtained from third parties through abusive subpoenas, the District Court denied the requested relief.

A panel of the Court of Appeals for the Ninth Circuit affirmed the District Court's denial of injunctive relief with regard to the subpoenas directed at respondents themselves, agreeing with the lower court that respondents had an adequate remedy at law for challenging those subpoenas. 704 F.2d 1065, 1066–1067 (1983). However, the Court of Appeals reversed the District Court's denial of respondents' request for notice of subpoenas issued to third parties. In the Court of Appeals' view, "targets" of SEC investigations "have a right to be investigated consistently with the *Powell* standards." To enable targets to enforce this right, the court held that they must be notified of subpoenas issued to others.

The Court of Appeals denied the Commission's request for rehearing and rejected its suggestion for rehearing en banc. . . .

We granted certiorari because of the importance of the issue presented. . . . We now reverse.

II

Congress has vested the SEC with broad authority to conduct investigations into possible violations of the federal securities laws and to demand production of evidence relevant to such investigations. Subpoenas issued by the Commission are not self-enforcing . . . But the Commission is authorized to bring suit in federal court to compel compliance with its process.

No provision in the complex of statutes governing the SEC's investigative power expressly obliges the Commission to notify the "target" of an investigation when it issues a subpoena to a third party. If such an obligation is to be imposed on the Commission, therefore, it must be derived from one of three sources: a constitutional provision; an understanding on the part of Congress, inferable from the structure of the securities laws, regarding how the SEC should conduct its inquiries; or the general standards governing judicial enforcement of administrative subpoenas enunciated in *United States v. Powell,* 379 U.S. 48 (1964), and its progeny. Examination of these three potential bases for the Court of Appeals' ruling leaves us unpersuaded that the notice requirement fashioned by that court is warranted.

A

Our prior cases foreclose any constitutional argument respondents might make in defense of the judgment below. The opinion of the Court in *Hannah v. Larche,* 363 U.S. 420 (1960), leaves no doubt that neither the Due Process Clause of the Fifth Amendment nor the Confrontation Clause of the Sixth Amendment is offended when a federal administrative agency, without notifying a person under investigation, uses its subpoena power to gather evidence adverse to him. The Due Process Clause is not implicated under such circumstances because an administrative investigation adjudicates no legal rights, and the Confrontation Clause does not come into play until the initiation of criminal proceedings. These principles plainly cover an inquiry by the SEC into possible violations of the securities laws.

It is also settled that a person inculpated by materials sought by a subpoena issued to a third party cannot seek shelter in the Self-Incrimination Clause of the Fifth Amendment. The rationale of this doctrine is that the Constitution prescribes only *compelled* self-incrimination, and, whatever may be the pressures exerted upon the person to whom a subpoena is directed, the subpoena surely does not "compel" anyone else to be a witness against himself. If the "target" of an investigation by the SEC has no Fifth Amendment right to challenge enforcement of a subpoena directed at a third party, he clearly can assert no derivative right to notice when the Commission issues such a subpoena.

Finally, respondents cannot invoke the Fourth Amendment in support of the Court of Appeals' decision. It is established that, when a person communicates information to a third party even on the understanding that the communication is confidential, he cannot object if the third party conveys that information or records thereof to law enforcement authorities. Relying on that principle, the Court has held that a customer of a bank cannot challenge on Fourth Amendment grounds the admission into evidence in a criminal prosecution of financial records obtained by the Government from his bank pursuant to allegedly defective subpoenas, despite the fact that he was given no notice of the subpoenas. . . . These rulings disable respondents from arguing that notice of subpoenas issued to third parties is necessary to allow a target to prevent an unconstitutional search or seizure of his papers.

B

The language and structure of the statutes administered by the Commission afford respondents no greater aid. The provisions vesting the SEC with the power to issue and seek enforcement of subpoenas are expansive. For example, § 19(b) of the Securities Act of 1933 empowers the SEC to conduct investigations "which, in the opinion of the Commission, are necessary and proper for the enforcement" of the Act and to "require the production of any books, papers, or other documents which the Commission deems relevant or material to the inquiry." Similarly, §§ 21(a) and 21(b) of the Securities Exchange Act of 1934 authorize the Commission to "make such investigations as it deems necessary to determine whether any person has violated, is violating, or is about to violate any provision of this chapter [or] the rules or regulations thereunder" and to demand to see any papers "the Commission deems relevant or material to the inquiry."

More generally, both statutes vest the SEC with "power to make such rules and regulations as may be necessary or appropriate to implement [their] provisions. . . ." Relying on this authority, the SEC has promulgated a variety of rules governing its investigations, one of which provides that, "[u]nless otherwise ordered by the Commission, all formal investigative proceedings shall be non-public." In other words, the Commission has formally adopted the policy of not routinely informing anyone, including targets, of the existence and progress of its investigations. To our knowledge, Congress has never questioned this exercise by the Commission of its statutory power. And, in another context, we have held that rulemaking authority comparable to that enjoyed by the SEC is broad enough to empower an agency to "establish standards for determining whether to conduct an investigation publicly or in private."

It appears, in short, that Congress intended to vest the SEC with considerable discretion in determining when and how to investigate possible violations of the statutes administered by the Commission. We discern no evidence that Congress wished or expected that the Commission would adopt any particular procedures for notifying "targets" of investigations when it sought information from third parties.

The inference that the relief sought by respondents is not necessary to give effect to congressional intent is reinforced by the fact that, in one special context, Congress has imposed on the Commission an obligation to notify persons directly affected by its subpoenas. In 1978, in response to this Court's decision in *United States v. Miller,* [425 U.S. 435 (1976)] Congress enacted the Right to Financial Privacy Act, 92 Stat. 3697, 12 U.S.C. § 3401 *et seq.* That statute accords customers of banks and similar financial institutions certain rights to be notified of and to challenge in court administrative subpoenas of financial records in the possession of the banks. The most salient feature of the Act is the narrow scope of the entitlements it creates. Thus, it carefully limits the kinds of customers to whom it applies, §§ 3401(4), (5), and the types of records they may seek to protect, § 3401(2). A customer's ability to challenge a subpoena is cabined by strict procedural requirements. For example, he must assert his claim within a short period of time, § 3410(a), and cannot appeal an adverse determination until the Government has completed its investigation, § 3410(d). Perhaps most importantly, the statute is drafted in a fashion that minimizes the risk that customers' objections to subpoenas will delay or frustrate agency investigations. Thus, a court presented with such a challenge is required to rule upon it within seven days of the Government's response, § 3410(b), and the pertinent statutes of limitations are tolled while the claim is pending, § 3419. Since 1980, the SEC has been subject to the constraints of the Right to Financial Privacy Act. When it made the statute applicable to the SEC, however, Congress empowered the Commission in prescribed circumstances to seek *ex parte* orders authorizing it to delay notifying bank customers when it subpoenas information about them, thereby further curtailing the ability of persons under investigation to impede the agency's inquiries.

Considerable insight into the legislators' conception of the scope of the SEC's investigatory power can be gleaned from the foregoing developments. We know that Congress recently had occasion to consider the authority of the SEC and other agencies to issue and enforce administrative subpoenas without notifying the persons whose affairs may be exposed thereby. In response, Congress enacted a set of carefully tailored limitations on the agencies' power, designed "to strike a balance between customers' right of privacy and the need of law enforcement agencies to obtain financial records pursuant to legitimate investigations." The manner in which Congress dealt with this problem teaches us two things. First, it seems apparent that Congress assumed that the SEC was not and would not be subject to a general obligation to notify "targets" of its investigations whenever it issued administrative subpoenas. Second, the complexity and subtlety of the procedures embodied in the Right to Financial Privacy Act suggests that Congress would find troubling the crude and unqualified notification requirement ordered by the Court of Appeals.

C

The last of the three potential footings for the remedy sought by respondents is some other entitlement that would be effectuated thereby. Respondents seek to derive such an entitlement from a combination of our prior decisions. Distilled, their argument is as follows: A subpoena issued by the SEC must comport with the standards set forth in our decision in *United States v. Powell*, 379 U.S., at 57–58. . . .[12] Not only the recipient of an SEC subpoena, but also any person who would be affected by compliance therewith, has a substantive right, under *Powell*, to insist that those standards are met. A target of an SEC investigation may assert the foregoing right in two ways. First, the target may seek permissive intervention in an enforcement action brought by the Commission against the subpoena recipient. Second, if the recipient of the subpoena threatens voluntarily to turn over the requested information, the target "might restrain compliance" by the recipient, thereby forcing the Commission to institute an enforcement suit. A target can avail himself of these options only if he is aware of the existence of subpoenas directed at others. To ensure that ignorance does not prevent a target from asserting his rights, respondents conclude, the Commission must notify him when it issues a subpoena to a third party.

The holding of *Powell* was that the Commissioner of Internal Revenue need not demonstrate probable cause in order to secure judicial enforcement of a summons issued pursuant to § 7602 of the Internal Revenue Code. The Court then went on to sketch the requirements that the Commissioner would be obliged to satisfy:

> He must show that the investigation will be conducted pursuant to a legitimate purpose, that the inquiry may be relevant to that purpose, that the information sought is not already within the Commissioner's possession, and that the administrative steps required by the Code have been followed. . . . [A] court may not permit its process to be abused. Such an abuse would take place if the summons had been issued for an improper purpose, such as to harass the taxpayer or to put pressure on him to settle a collateral dispute, or for any other purpose reflecting on the good faith of the particular investigation.

There are several tenuous links in respondents' argument. Especially debatable are the proposition that a target has a substantive right to be investigated in a manner consistent with the *Powell* standards and the assertion that a target may obtain a restraining order preventing voluntary compliance by a third party with an

---

[12]. [This footnote has been moved to the text—ed.]

administrative subpoena. Certainly we have never before expressly so held. For the present, however, we may assume, *arguendo*, that a target enjoys each of the substantive and procedural rights identified by respondents. Nevertheless, we conclude that it would be inappropriate to elaborate upon those entitlements by mandating notification of targets whenever the Commission issues subpoenas.

Two considerations underlie our decision on this issue. First, administration of the notice requirement advocated by respondents would be highly burdensome for both the Commission and the courts. The most obvious difficulty would involve identification of the persons and organizations that should be considered "targets" of investigations. The SEC often undertakes investigations into suspicious securities transactions without any knowledge of which of the parties involved may have violated the law. To notify all potential wrongdoers in such a situation of the issuance of each subpoena would be virtually impossible. The Commission would thus be obliged to determine the point at which enough evidence had been assembled to focus suspicion on a manageable subset of the participants in the transaction, thereby lending them the status of "targets" and entitling them to notice of the outstanding subpoenas directed at others. The complexity of that task is apparent. Even in cases in which the Commission could identify with reasonable ease the principal targets of its inquiry, another problem would arise. In such circumstances, a person not considered a target by the Commission could contend that he deserved that status and therefore should be given notice of subpoenas issued to others. To assess a claim of this sort, a district court would be obliged to conduct some kind of hearing to determine the scope and thrust of the ongoing investigation. Implementation of this new remedy would drain the resources of the judiciary as well as the Commission.

Second, the imposition of a notice requirement on the SEC would substantially increase the ability of persons who have something to hide to impede legitimate investigations by the Commission. A target given notice of every subpoena issued to third parties would be able to discourage the recipients from complying, and then further delay disclosure of damaging information by seeking intervention in all enforcement actions brought by the Commission. More seriously, the understanding of the progress of an SEC inquiry that would flow from knowledge of which persons had received subpoenas would enable an unscrupulous target to destroy or alter documents, intimidate witnesses, or transfer securities or funds so that they could not be reached by the Government. Especially in the context of securities regulation, where speed in locating and halting violations of the law is so important, we would be loath to place such potent weapons in the hands of persons with a desire to keep the Commission at bay.

We acknowledge that our ruling may have the effect in practice of preventing some persons under investigation by the SEC from asserting objections to subpoenas issued by the Commission to third parties for improper reasons. However, to accept respondents' proposal "would unwarrantedly cast doubt upon and stultify the [Commission's] every investigatory move." Particularly in view of Congress' manifest disinclination to require the Commission to notify targets whenever it seeks information from others, we refuse so to curb the Commission's exercise of its statutory power.

III

Nothing in this opinion should be construed to imply that it would be improper for the SEC to inform a target that it has issued a subpoena to someone else. But, for the reasons indicated above, we decline to curtail the Commission's discretion to determine when such notice would be appropriate and when it would not. Accordingly, the judgment of the Court of Appeals is reversed, and the case is remanded for further proceedings consistent with this opinion.

It is so ordered.

Note

Responding to the Supreme Court's decision in *O'Brien*, Professor Maynard has opined:

> The SEC must be provided with the necessary tools to carry out its enforcement responsibilities under the federal securities laws, which were enacted for the protection of the investing public. But those powerful tools that have been given to the SEC to carry out its mandate, including the subpoena power and the power to impose significant sanctions on the target, are subject to potential abuse and may severely damage, without appropriate justification, the interests of the target of an investigation. In its *O'Brien* decision, the Supreme Court accepted the SEC's position that requiring notice to the target of third party subpoenas would impose an undue burden on the SEC's ability to carry out its enforcement responsibilities. What the Court failed to consider fully, however, are the legitimate concerns of a person who becomes the target of an SEC administrative investigation.[13]

There thus can be little question that SEC investigations can have severe collateral ramifications on the target's personal and business affairs. In view of these consequences and the potential for abuse, the courts have established a number of defenses and privileges which may be invoked by parties subject to an SEC investigation. Hence, although the Commission's subpoena power is tremendous, it is not absolute. In appropriate cases, the courts will deny the SEC's request for subpoena enforcement. *See, e.g., SEC v. Wheeling Pittsburgh Steel Corp.*, 648 F.2d 118 (3d Cir. 1981) (en banc). *See generally* Steinberg, *SEC Subpoena Enforcement Practice*, 11 J. Corp. L. 1 (1985).

---

13. Maynard, *SEC v. Jerry T. O'Brien, Inc.: Has the Supreme Court Overruled United States v. Powell?*, 18 Loy. L.A.L. Rev. 643, 645 (1985).

§ 15.04 Injunctions

[A] Standards for Imposition

As in any other type of case where permanent injunctive relief is sought, a defendant's violation of the federal securities laws is not by itself sufficient for the SEC to obtain an injunction. Rather, the test generally applied is whether there is a reasonable likelihood that the defendant, if not enjoined, will again engage in the violative conduct.[14] In identifying the relevant factors that demonstrate a reasonable likelihood of future violations, one appellate court pointed to "the degree of scienter involved, the sincerity of defendant's assurances against future violations, the isolated or recurrent nature of the infraction, defendant's recognition of the wrongful nature of his conduct, and the likelihood, because of defendant's professional occupation, that future violations might occur."[15] Other factors deemed relevant include the gravity of the offense committed,[16] the time elapsed between the violation and the court's decision,[17] whether the defendant, in good faith, relied on advice of counsel,[18] and the adverse effect an injunction would have on the defendant.[19]

The Supreme Court's decision in *Aaron v. SEC*[20] casts light on this issue. There, the Court held that the SEC must prove scienter in civil enforcement actions to enjoin violations of § 10(b) of the Exchange Act, Rule 10b-5 promulgated thereunder, and § 17(a)(1) of the Securities Act,[21] but need not prove scienter under § 17(a)(2) or § 17(a)(3).[22] The Court noted that under § 17(a)(2) and 17(a)(3), "the degree of intentional wrongdoing evident in a defendant's past conduct" is an important factor in determining whether the Commission has "establish[ed] a sufficient evidentiary predicate to show that such future violation may occur."[23] The presence or lack of scienter is "one of the aggravating or mitigating factors to be taken into account" in a court's exercise of its equitable jurisdiction.[24] In a concurring opinion, former Chief Justice Burger asserted that the SEC "will almost always" be required to show that the defendant's past conduct was more culpable than negligence. The Chief Justice concluded that "[a]n injunction is a drastic remedy, not a mild prophylactic, and should not be obtained against one acting in good faith."[25]

---

14. *See, e.g., SEC v. Advance Growth Capital Corp.*, 470 F.2d 40, 53 (7th Cir. 1972).

15. SEC *v. Universal Major Indus. Corp.*, 546 F.2d 1044, 1048 (2d Cir. 1976). *See SEC v. Cavanagh*, 155 F.3d 129 (2d Cir. 1998).

16. *See, e.g., SEC v. Manor Nursing Centers, Inc.*, 458 F.2d 1082, 1102 (2d Cir. 1972).

17. *See, e.g., SEC v. Monarch Fund*, 608 F.2d 938, 943 (2d Cir. 1979).

18. *See, e.g., SEC v. Lum's, Inc.*, 365 F. Supp. 1046, 1066 (S.D.N.Y. 1973).

19. *See, e.g., SEC v. Manor Nursing Centers, Inc.*, 458 F.2d 1082, 1102 (2d Cir. 1972).

20. 446 U.S. 680 (1980).

21. *Id.* at 687-696.

22. *Id.* at 696-700.

23. *Id.* at 701.

24. *Id.*

25. *Id.* at 703 (Burger, C.J., concurring).

It has been contended that the *Aaron* Court's language, even apart from the former Chief Justice's concurring opinion, could require the SEC to prove scienter in order to make a "proper showing" for obtaining injunctive relief under *any* section of the securities acts.[26] Indeed, more recently, the SEC has experienced greater difficulty in procuring injunctions.[27] Nonetheless, the absence of scienter may not preclude the granting of such relief where the applicable statutory provision requires only negligent culpability. For example, where a defendant has committed prior violations, where his/her carelessness has been egregious, where public investors have been severely injured, or where the defendant's occupation increases the probability of future violations, a court (considering the totality of the circumstances) may order injunctive relief.[28]

Importantly, under certain state securities law provisions, injunctions and even criminal convictions may be obtained without proof of scienter. As former Dean Sargent commented: "The current trend among the intermediate state appellate courts . . . seem[s] to be moving away from proof of guilty knowledge, mens rea, evil purpose, or even recklessness in criminal cases for securities fraud."[29]

[B] Implications of *Central Bank of Denver*

The Supreme Court's decision in *Central Bank of Denver* was believed by many authorities to preclude the SEC in certain situations from bringing an enforcement action premised on aider and abettor liability. However, unlike the *Hochfelder/Aaron* analogy addressed earlier, aiding and abetting a federal securities law violation statutorily gives rise to criminal liability exposure.[30] Under this rationale, the criminal aid-abet statute provided ample authority for the SEC to pursue aiders and abettors.[31]

Due to subsequent legislation (the PSLRA and the Dodd-Frank Act), it is now clear that the SEC has such aiding and abetting authority. This subject is addressed § 10.02 of the text. Significantly, the Dodd-Frank Act of 2010 also clarified that the requisite

---

26. *See* Huffman, *Aaron Restricts SEC Enforcement*, Legal Times, June 9, 1980, at 2.

27. *See, e.g., SEC v. Steadman*, 967 F.2d 1636 (D.C. Cir. 1992) (denying SEC's request for injunctive relief, court stated that "injunctive relief is reserved for willful lawbreakers or those whose operations are so persistently sloppy as to pose a continuing danger to the investing public"). Accord, *SEC v. Goble*, 682 F.3d 934 (11th Cir. 2012); *SEC v. M&A West, Inc.*, 538 F.3d 1043 (9th Cir. 2008); *SEC v. Happ*, 392 F.3d 12 (1st Cir. 2004). *See generally* Eisenberg, *Litigating with the SEC—A Reasonable Alternative to Settlement*, 21 Sec. Reg. L.J. 421 (1994).

28. *See SEC v. Washington County Utility District*, 676 F.2d 218 (6th Cir. 1982); *SEC v. Murphy*, 626 F.2d 633 (9th Cir. 1980). *See generally* Morrissey, *SEC Injunctions*, 68 Tenn. L. Rev. 427 (2001).

29. Sargent, *A Blue Sky State of Mind: The Meaning of "Willfully" in Blue Sky Criminal Cases*, 20 Sec. Reg. L.J. 96, 98 (1992).

30. 18 U.S.C. § 2(a).

31. *See* Bromberg, *Aiding and Abetting: Sudden Death and Possible Resurrection*, 24 Rev. Sec. & Comm. Reg. 133, 136 (1994).

mental culpability with respect to aiders and abettors is knowing or reckless conduct.[32]

Besides its aiding and abetting authority, the SEC has powerful enforcement weapons. For example, the Commission may bring an administrative cease and desist proceeding and procure money penalties and other relief against persons who are a "cause" of the alleged violation, thus encompassing those persons who "should have known" that their conduct "would contribute" to such violation. Hence, if the SEC elects to proceed administratively, the Commission should be able to spread the liability net as far. After all, establishing one as a "cause" of a violation should prove easier than proving aiding and abetting liability.

[C] Collateral Consequences

The primary purpose of injunctive relief under the federal securities laws is to deter future violative conduct, not to punish the violator. As Judge Friendly noted, however, an injunction can have severe collateral consequences.[33] For example, an injunction not only harms one's reputation but it also serves as the basis for contempt sanctions if the injunctive order subsequently is violated. Issuance of an SEC injunction can cause the suspension or revocation of a broker-dealer's registration, or constitute grounds for prohibiting any person from associating with a broker-dealer. Similarly, an injunction disqualifies the subject party from serving as a director, officer, or employee of a registered investment company. It can constitute a basis for barring an attorney, accountant, or other professional from practicing before the SEC. Additionally, a Regulation A as well as other exemptions from Securities Act registration may be unavailable to an enjoined issuer of securities. As a final example, the Commission frequently requires that an injunction be disclosed in certain filings, reports, statements, or other information sent to shareholders and investors.[34]

Largely because of these consequences, the courts have required the SEC "to go beyond the mere facts of past violations and demonstrate a realistic likelihood of recurrence."[35] Employing this standard, courts have concluded in a number of cases

----

32. *See* §9290 of the Dodd-Frank Act, amending §20(e) of the Securities Exchange Act; discussion §10.02 *supra*. For case law on this issue prior to the Dodd-Frank amendment, compare *Howard v. SEC,* 376 F.3d 1136 (D.C. Cir. 2004) (extreme recklessness standard applied), with *SEC v. KPMG LLP,* 412 F. Supp. 2d 349 (S.D.N.Y. 2006) (under circumstances at bar, requiring proof of actual knowledge).

33. *See SEC v. Commonwealth Chemical Securities, Inc.,* 574 F.2d 90, 99 (2d Cir. 1978). *See SEC v. Bartek,* [2012–2 Transfer Binder] Fed. Sec. L. Rep. (CCH) ¶ 96,963 [2012–2 Transfer Binder] Fed. Sec. L. Report (CCH) ¶ 96,963 (5th Cir. 2012) (holding permanent injunction to be punitive and therefore subject to §2462's five-year statute of limitations).

34. *See* Item 401(d) of Regulation S-K, 17 C.F.R. §229.401(d). *See generally* Andre, *The Collateral Consequences of SEC Injunctive Relief: Mild Prophylactic or Perpetual Hazard?,* 1981 U. ILL. L. REV. 625.

35. *SEC v. Commonwealth Chemical Securities, Inc.,* 574 F.2d 90, 100 (2d Cir. 1978).

that the SEC has not made a sufficient showing and have denied the Commission's request for injunctive relief.[36]

[D] Other Relief

Over the years, the SEC has sought, and successfully obtained, ancillary or other equitable relief against an enjoined party. In addition, the Commission today has a number of other judicial remedies, including: the levying of money penalties, an officer or director bar, establishment of a "Fair Fund" for the benefit of aggrieved investors, and executive forfeiture of payments and bonuses under certain circumstances.

Examples of equitable relief include disgorgement, appointment of a receiver, appointment of independent members to the board of directors, and appointment of a special counsel.[37] The basis for ordering such relief derives from the general equitable powers of the federal courts.[38] Indeed, even if a court refuses to grant the SEC's request for an injunction, it may nevertheless grant other equitable relief.[39] Any doubt as to the propriety of such relief has been resolved by the Sarbanes-Oxley Act (SOX). As amended by SOX, § 21(d) of the Securities Exchange Act, provides: "In any action or proceeding brought or instituted by the Commission under any provision of the securities laws, the Commission may seek, and any Federal court may grant, any equitable relief that may be appropriate or necessary for the benefit of investors."

[E] Modification or Dissolution of SEC Injunctions

In view of the collateral consequences imposed by SEC injunctions, subject parties may seek to have the particular injunction modified or dissolved. The traditional view, derived from the Supreme Court's decision in *United States v. Swift & Co.*,[40]

---

36. *See, e.g., SEC v. Happ*, 392 F.3d 12 (1st Cir. 2004); *SEC v. Caterinicchia*, 613 F.2d 102 (5th Cir. 1980).

37. *See, e.g., SEC v. Colello*, 139 F.3d 674 (9th Cir. 1998) (recouping proceeds from illegal conduct); *SEC v. Mayhew*, 121 F.3d 44 (2d Cir. 1997) (disgorgement).

38. *See SEC v. Wencke*, 622 F.2d 1363, 1369 (9th Cir. 1980). *See generally* Barnard, *Corporate Therapeutics at the Securities and Exchange Commission,* 2008 COLUM. BUS. L. REV. 793 (2008); Black, *Should the SEC Be a Collection Agency for Defrauded Investors?*, 63 BUS. LAW. 317 (2008); Cole, *The SEC's Corporate Cooperation Policy: A Duty to Correct or Update?*, 41 SEC. REG. L.J. 127 (2013); Hazen, *Administrative Enforcement: An Evaluation of the Securities and Exchange Commission's Use of Injunctions and Other Enforcement Methods*, 31 HASTINGS L.J. 444 (1979); Janvey, *An Overview of SEC Receiverships*, 38 SEC. REG. L.J. 89 (2010); McNew, *Money Penalties Against Publicly-Held Companies: A Proposal for Restraint*, 37 SEC. REG. L.J. 48 (2009); Velikonja, *Reporting Agency Performance: Behind the SEC's Enforcement Statistics*, 101 CORNELL L. REV. 901 (2010); Winship, *Fair Funds and the SEC's Compensation of Injured Investors*, 60 FLA. L. REV. 1103 (2008).

39. *See, e.g., SEC v. Commonwealth Chemical Securities, Inc.*, 574 F.2d 90, 102–103 (2d Cir. 1978). *See generally* Dent, *Ancillary Relief in Federal Securities Law: A Study in Federal Remedies*, 67 MINN. L. REV. 865 (1983); Siegel, *The Danger of Equitable Remedies*, 15 STAN. J. BUS. & FIN. 86 (2009).

40. 286 U.S. 106 (1932).

places a heavy burden upon the party seeking modification or dissolution. Writing at the time he was a federal appellate judge, former Justice Blackmun construed *Swift* as follows:

> (1) [T]hat, where modification and amendment of an existing decree is under consideration, there are "limits of inquiry" for the decree court and for the reviewing court; (2) that the inquiry is "whether the changes are so important that dangers, once substantial have become attenuated to a shadow"; (3) that the movants must be "suffering hardship so extreme and unexpected" as to be regarded as "victims of oppression"; and (4) that there must be "[n]othing less than a clear showing of grievous wrong evoked by new and unforeseen conditions." Phrased in other words, this means for us that modification is only cautiously to be granted; that some change is not enough; that the dangers which the decree was meant to foreclose must almost have disappeared; that hardship and oppression, extreme and unexpected, are significant; and that the movants' task is to provide close to an unanswerable case. To repeat: caution, substantial change, unforeseenness, oppressive hardship, and a clear showing are the requirements.[41]

Swift's stringent guidelines have been applied by numerous courts in a variety of contexts, including where modification or dissolution of an SEC injunction is sought.[42] A number of courts, however, have declined to follow *Swift's* rigorous requirements. These courts reason that subsequent Supreme Court decisions have departed from *Swift's* restrictive standards.[43] Hence, the Second Circuit, while noting that changes in fact or law provide the strongest reasons for modifying an injunction, held that modification or dissolution also is appropriate "where a better appreciation of the facts in light of experience indicate that the decree is not properly adapted to accomplishing its purposes."[44] Moreover, in view of the Supreme Court's decision in *Central Bank of Denver*, it remains to be seen the extent to which parties subject to SEC injunctions move to dissolve such injunctions on the basis of a change in the governing law. Thus far, such motions to dissolve have not occurred with frequency.

A significant decision departing from the *Swift* standards in the securities law area is *SEC v. Warren*.[45] Distinguishing *Swift*, the district court in *Warren* exercised its "inherent equitable power to weigh the severity of the alleged danger which the injunction was designed to eliminate against the continuing necessity for the injunction and the hardship brought by its prospective application."[46] Weighing

---

41. *Humble Oil & Refining Co. v. American Oil Co.*, 405 F.2d 803, 813 (8th Cir. 1969).
42. *See, e.g., SEC v. Advance Growth Capital Corp.*, 539 F.2d 649 (7th Cir. 1976).
43. *See Rufo v. Inmates of Suffolk County Jail*, 502 U.S. 367 (1992); *United States v. United Shoe Machinery Corp.*, 391 U.S. 244 (1968); *System Federation v. Wright*, 364 U.S. 642 (1961).
44. *King-Seeley Thermos Co. v. Aladdin Industries, Inc.*, 418 F.2d 31, 35 (2d Cir. 1979).
45. 76 F.R.D. 405 (W.D. Pa. 1977), *aff'd*, 583 F.2d 115 (3d Cir. 1978).
46. 76 F.R.D. at 408.

these factors, the court granted the motion to dissolve the injunction. On appeal, the Third Circuit affirmed on substantially the same reasoning.[47]

Another development in this area has been that, even where the SEC makes the necessary showing, some courts have hesitated to order an unconditional permanent injunction. The conditions that courts have attached to the imposition of an injunction include automatic dissolution after a fixed number of years, suspension after the defendant fulfills certain requirements, and permitting a petition for dissolution after a fixed period on a lesser showing than that required by *Swift*.[48] Although the SEC, at times, has agreed to certain of these limitations pursuant to the consent process, the Commission's position appears to be that upon making a proper showing, it is entitled as a matter of statutory right to the ordering of a permanent injunction.[49]

Hence, the continued viability of the stringent *Swift* standard is open to debate. Perhaps a better approach would be for courts faced with a motion to modify or dissolve an injunction to apply an ad hoc balancing test. This standard would consider such factors as (1) subsequent change of fact or law, (2) the extent of adverse, unforeseen collateral consequences, (3) whether the injunction has fulfilled its objectives, (4) whether the individual deterrent effect of the injunction has ceased, (5) the decree's effect on societal deterrence, (6) whether a government entity is a party to the litigation and the adverse effect that granting of the motion would have on the entity's resources, and (7) the extent and nature of the public or other countervailing interest involved.[50]

§ 15.05 SEC Administrative Enforcement Remedies

The SEC has several administrative enforcement remedies it may invoke when alleged violations of the federal securities laws have been committed. From a statistical perspective, the Commission is far more victorious in the administrative forum (litigating before administrative law judges) than in the federal courts. Perhaps, as a consequence of this "home court" advantage, the SEC brings a large percentage of its enforcement actions administratively. Defendants have responded by alleging that the SEC's improper use of the administrative forum is violative of the Appointments Clause and their right to Equal Protection under the Constitution. Thus far, the vast

---

47. 583 F.2d at 120–122.

48. *See, e.g.,* the district court's order as set forth in *SEC v. Blazon Corp.,* 608 F.2d 960 (9th Cir. 1979), the validity of which the Ninth Circuit did not resolve.

49. *See* Brief of the SEC at 10, *SEC v. Associated Minerals, Inc.,* Nos. 79-1449, 79-1450 (6th Cir. 1980); Morrissey, *SEC Injunctions,* 68 Tenn. L. Rev. 427 (2001). *See also* Sachs, *Harmonizing Civil and Criminal Enforcement of Federal Regulatory Statutes: The Case of the Securities Exchange Act of 1934,* 2001 U. ILL. L. REV. 1025 (2001).

50. For further discussion, *see* Steinberg, *SEC and Other Permanent Injunctions — Standards for Their Imposition, Modification, and Dissolution,* 66 CORNELL L. REV. 27, 71–73 (1980).

majority of courts have rejected the raising of these arguments as premature. *See, e.g., Tilton v. SEC,* 824 F.3d 276 (2d Cir. 2016) (holding that, with respect to pending SEC administrative processing, district court did not have subject matter jurisdiction over constitutional challenge under the Appointments Clause); *Jarkesy v. SEC,* 803 F.3d 9 (D.C. Cir. 2015) (holding that defendants must fully litigate administrative case prior to bringing a constitutional challenge in federal court); *Bebo v. SEC,* 799 F.3d 765 (7th Cir. 2015) (same). *But see Hill v. SEC,* 114 F. Supp. 3d 1297 (N.D. Ga. 2015) (preliminarily enjoining the SEC from conducting an administrative proceeding against the subject defendant), *rev'd,* 825 F.3d 1236 (11th Cir. 2016). Moreover, in a recent decision, the Tenth Circuit held that the SEC's administrative law judges are inferior officers who are not appointed in compliance with the Appointments Clause of the Constitution. *Bandimere v. SEC,* 2016 WL 7439007 (10th Cir. 2016). *See generally,* Jones, *The Fight Over Home Court: An Analysis of the SEC's Increased Use of Administrative Proceedings,* 68 SMU L. Rev. 507 (2015).

The following discussion highlights key SEC administrative enforcement remedies.

[A] Cease and Desist Orders

The SEC may seek an administrative cease and desist order as well as money penalties against *any* person based on *any* violation of the federal securities laws. A cease and desist order and money penalties also may be imposed against any person who is deemed a "cause" of the subject violation, signifying that such person knew or should have known that his/her conduct would contribute to the violation. Moreover, the order entered may require not only that the party cease and desist from the proscribed acts but that he/she effect compliance within prescribed time periods and pursuant to specified conditions.[51] Under this authority, the SEC has ordered subject parties to effect "undertakings" in a variety of factual settings.

Note that in order to obtain a cease and desist order, the SEC must prove a violation of the securities laws and provide a justifiable explanation why such sanction is appropriate.[52] A single isolated violation may not be sufficient.[53] With respect to the requisite culpability, negligence is sufficient for the entry of a cease and desist order if the underlying violation does not require scienter.[54] Where, however, the underlying violation requires proof of reckless or intentional misconduct, a showing of scienter may have to be made.[55]

---

51. *See* §8A of the Securities Act, §21C of the Exchange Act, §9(f) of the Investment Company Act, §203(k) of the Investment Advisors Act.

52. *See Geiger v. SEC,* 363 F.3d 481 (D.C. Cir. 2004) (also stating that the SEC may procure a cease and desist order on a lesser showing than that required for an injunction).

53. *See WHX Corp. v. SEC,* 362 F.3d 854 (D.C. Cir. 2004).

54. *See KPMG, LLP v. SEC,* 289 F.3d 109 (D.C. Cir. 2002).

55. *See Howard v. SEC,* 376 F.3d 1136 (D.C. Cir. 2004); § 15.06 herein. *See generally* Hansen, *The Securities and Exchange Commission's Use of Cease and Desist Powers,* 20 Sec. Reg. L.J. 339, 347–348 (1993) (asserting that SEC should be held to same showing in cease and desist proceeding as that

[B] Money Penalties

As set forth above, the SEC in administrative actions may levy money penalties against *any* person, provided that the Commission concludes that the penalty imposed is in the "public interest" and that the defendant engaged in the prohibited conduct (such as willfully violating the federal securities law, aiding and abetting, or failing reasonably to supervise another person under such party's control). In determining whether a money penalty and the extent to which such penalty is in the "public interest," Congress enumerated several factors that the Commission may consider.[56] Moreover, generally, the more severe the violation committed, the greater the money penalty that may be levied. Since 1990 (when this provision was enacted), the SEC frequently has levied money penalties in its administrative proceedings.[57]

[C] Refusal and Stop Orders

Section 8 of the Securities Act generally governs the time in which SEC-filed registration statements of securities offerings and amendments thereto become effective. Section 8(b) and § 8(d) respectively authorize the Commission to issue refusal orders and stop orders in connection with materially incomplete, inaccurate, or false and misleading registration statements. Furthermore, § 8(e) empowers the SEC to make an examination in any case in order to determine whether a stop order should be issued under § 8(d).[58]

[D] Summarily Suspending Trading in a Security

Summary suspensions of over-the-counter or exchange trading of a security are imposed by the SEC under § 12(k) of the Exchange Act. This sanction is not to exceed

---

required for an injunction). *See also, Precious Metals Assoc., Inc. v. CFTC*, 620 F.2d 900, 912 (1st Cir. 1980) (requiring Commodity Futures Trading Commission (CFTC) to show defendant's "proclivity to violate the law" to obtain cease and desist order).

56. Three tiers of money penalties exist with more severe penalties associated with each tier: tier (1)—technical violations, tier (2)—violations that encompass fraud, manipulation, or deliberate disregard of a regulatory mandate, tier (3)—violations that came within tier (2) above and that result (or pose the risk of resulting) in substantial losses. Moreover, in determining whether the penalty is in the "public interest," relevant factors include the severity of the defendant's conduct, the harm resulting from such conduct, the extent of unjust enrichment, whether the defendant is a repeat offender, the need to deter such conduct, and "such other matters as justice may require." *See* § 21B of the Exchange Act, '203(i) of the Investment Advisors Act, § 9(d) of the Investment Company Act.

57. When the Commission seeks a money penalty, a five-year statute of limitations evidently applies. *See 3M Corporation v. Browner*, 17 F.3d 1453 (D.C. Cir. 1994) (construing 28 U.S.C. § 2462). Note that the SEC can establish a "Fair Fund" for the benefit of aggrieved investors when disgorgement and/or a money penalty is/are ordered in an administrative enforcement action. *See also, Rockies Fund v. SEC,* 428 F 3d 1088 (D.C. Cir. 2005) (holding that ordering of third-tier money penalty by SEC without adequate explanation was arbitrary and capricious).

58. *See* McLucas, *Stop Order Proceedings Under the Securities Act of 1933: A Current Assessment*, 40 BUS. LAW. 515 (1985).

10 days. The Supreme Court in *SEC v. Sloan*[59] held that the Commission was not authorized to summarily suspend trading in a security for successive 10-day periods, unless such successive suspension was based on new circumstances. The Court thus required the SEC to provide notice and right to a hearing with regard to suspensions for extended periods.

[E] Broker-Dealer Disciplinary Sanctions

Broker-dealer (and associated persons) disciplinary sanctions may be imposed pursuant to several provisions contained in the Exchange Act. Persons or entities registered as broker-dealers, as well as any person "associated" with a broker-dealer, are vulnerable to SEC discipline under these provisions. After providing notice and opportunity for a hearing, broker-dealer sanctions may include outright revocation of registration (or denial of registration), suspension of registration, censure, or barring an associated person from associating with a broker-dealer (see § 15(b)(4) and § 15(b)(6) of the 1934 Act). Moreover, pursuant to § 15A, a broker-dealer or associated person, inter alia, can be barred from becoming a member (or becoming associated with a member) of a registered securities association (i.e., FINRA). Also, pursuant to § 19(h) of the Exchange Act, the SEC can suspend or revoke the registration or take other disciplinary action against a registered securities association as well as suspend or expel a member or person associated with a member of such association.[60]

Pursuant to the Dodd-Frank Act of 2010, the SEC now may impose collateral bars in its administrative enforcement proceedings. Accordingly, an associated person who violates the securities laws, may be subject to a bar from associating with any regulated entity, such as a broker-dealer or investment adviser.[61]

[F] Section 15(c)(4) Disciplinary Proceedings

Administrative proceedings involving certain defective Exchange Act reports filed with the SEC may be adjudicated pursuant to § 15(c)(4) of the 1934 Act. Section 15(c)(4) authorizes the Commission to order compliance with the provisions of § 12, 13, 14 or 15(d) of the Exchange Act and the rules or regulations thereunder. For example, if a § 12 or 15(d) registrant fails to comply with, in any material way, the continuous reporting requirements of § 13, such as the timely and accurate filing of annual and other periodic reports, the Commission may, after notice and opportunity for hearing, publish its findings and issue an order requiring compliance.

---

59. 436 U.S. 103 (1978).

60. *See* Mathews, *Litigation and Settlement of SEC Administrative Enforcement Proceedings*, 29 Cath. U.L. Rev. 215, 222–223 (1980). For SEC disciplinary proceedings against investment advisers, *see* § 203(e), (f) of the Investment Advisers Act, 15 U.S.C. § 80b-3(e), (f).

61. *See* § 925 of the Dodd-Frank Act, *amending*, §§ 15(b)(6)(A), 15B(c)(4)(C), 17A(c)(4)(C) of the Securities Exchange Act, § 203(f) of the Investment Advisers Act.

The order may be directed not only to the registrant but also to any person who "caused" such registrant's failure to comply.[62]

In 1984 Congress enacted the Insider Trading Sanctions Act (ITSA). The ITSA, *inter alia*, expanded § 15(c)(4) so as to enable the SEC to bring administrative actions to remedy violations of the proxy and tender offer provisions contained in § 14 of the Exchange Act. The Act also clarified that the Commission may proceed administratively against persons (such as officers, directors, and perhaps attorneys) who are a "cause" of a failure to comply with § 12, 13, 14 or 15(d).[63] Nonetheless, in view of legislation enacted in 1990 granting the SEC cease and desist power, § 15(c)(4) today is invoked on a far less frequent basis.[64]

[G] Section 21(a) Reports of Investigation

Section 21(a) of the Exchange Act allows the Commission, in its discretion, to "make such investigations as it deems necessary to determine whether any person has violated, is violating, or is about to violate any provision of this title," and "to publish information concerning any such violations." Moreover, pursuant to § 21(a), the SEC "may require or permit any person to file with it a statement in writing . . . as to all the facts and circumstances concerning the matter . . . investigated." Although a § 21(a) report is not actually an adjudicatory type of proceeding, it is used by the SEC as a substitute for administrative disciplinary or civil injunctive suits in marginal, nonegregious cases, at times having the effect of inducing subject parties to settle.

These settlements frequently enable the Commission to present its position regarding the conduct in question, thereby providing notice of the SEC's future enforcement posture on the issue. Moreover, through the § 21(a) report procedure, the Commission can avoid the usual requirement of having to find an actual violation while persuading subject parties to modify their conduct, or take, what the SEC views as, corrective steps. Hence, in these § 21(a) reports, the Commission criticizes policies and decisions made by subject parties, thus directing to all concerned the areas in which the Commission desires reform.[65]

Although the following SEC enforcement action occurred several decades ago, it serves as a striking example of the Commission's leverage to induce enhanced corporate governance and law compliance.

---

62. *See* McLucas & Romanowich, *SEC Enforcement Proceedings Under Section 15(c)(4) of the Securities Exchange Act of 1934*, 41 Bus. Law. 145 (1985).

63. *Id.*

64. *See In re Kern*, [1988–1989 Transfer Binder] Fed. Sec. L. Rep. (CCH) ¶ 84,342 (ALJ 1988), *aff'd solely as to discontinuation of proceedings*, [1991 Transfer Binder] Fed. Sec. L. Rep. (CCH) ¶ 84,815 (SEC 1991). *See generally Report of the ABA's Section of Business Law Task Force on SEC Section 15(c)(4) Proceedings,* 46 Bus. Law. 255 (1990).

65. For further discussion, *see* American Bar Association, *Report of the Task Force on Exchange Act Section 21(a) Written Statements,* 59 Bus. Law. 531 (2004).

In the Matter of Occidental Petroleum Corporation

Securities and Exchange Commission

[1980 Transfer Binder] Fed. Sec. L. Rep. (CCH) ¶ 82,622 (1980)

The Commission deems it appropriate in the public interest following an investigation by its Division of Enforcement that pursuant to Section 15(c)(4) of the Securities Exchange Act of 1934 (the "Exchange Act") proceedings be instituted with respect to Occidental Petroleum Corporation ("Oxy") to determine whether, during the period January 1, 1973 to the present, Oxy failed to make certain required disclosures in various filings submitted to the Commission pursuant to Section 13 of the Exchange Act and the Rules and Regulations promulgated thereunder.

Simultaneously with the institution of these proceedings, Oxy has submitted an Offer of Settlement for the purpose of disposing of the issues raised in these proceedings. Under the terms of its Offer of Settlement, incorporated herein by reference, Oxy, solely for the purpose of these proceedings, without trial or any adjudication, makes certain undertakings, and without admitting or denying any of the matters set forth herein, consents to the issuance of this Order of the Commission. In its Offer of Settlement to dispose of these proceedings, Oxy has made certain undertakings which are accepted by the Commission as detailed herein.

The Commission has determined that it is appropriate and in the public interest to accept the Offer of Settlement of Oxy and the undertakings contained in the Offer of Settlement, and, accordingly, issues this Order.

I

STATEMENT

A. INTRODUCTION

Oxy, a California corporation organized in 1920 with headquarters in Los Angeles, California, is engaged in exploring for and developing and producing natural resources, principally oil and gas outside of the United States and coal within the United States; marketing and transporting petroleum and petroleum products; and manufacturing and distributing chemicals of various types. Its securities are registered with the Commission pursuant to Section 12(b) of the Exchange Act and are traded on the New York Stock Exchange and other exchanges. Throughout all times relevant herein Oxy has filed annual and other periodic reports with the Commission pursuant to Section 13(a) of the Exchange Act and the Rules and Regulations promulgated thereunder. For the year ended December 31, 1979, Oxy reported net sales of approximately $9.55 billion and net income of approximately $561.7 million.

Oxy's oil and gas exploration and production operations are conducted throughout the world with the principal operations in Libya, the United Kingdom sector of the North Sea, Peru, Bolivia, the United States and Canada. For the year ended December 31, 1979, as reflected in Oxy's 1979 Annual Report on Form 10-K, all its oil and gas exploration and production operations, including the sale of its shares of oil production in these countries and additional crude oil purchased from Libya, accounted for approximately 42% of Oxy's total revenues, approximately 87% of its operating profit after Libyan taxes but before other income taxes and unallocated interest and corporate expenses, and approximately 39% of identifiable assets.

Oxy's chemical operations are conducted through Hooker Chemical Corporation ("Hooker"), a wholly-owned subsidiary, and its subsidiaries, including Hooker Chemicals & Plastics Corp., acquired by Oxy in 1968. Hooker, with over 18,400 employees, is a major producer of industrial chemicals, plastics, metal finishing chemicals and equipment, and agricultural chemicals and fertilizers. For the year ended December 31, 1979, as reflected in Oxy's 1979 Annual Report on Form 10-K, Oxy's chemical operations accounted for approximately 21% of Oxy's total revenues, approximately 7% of its operating profit and approximately 25% of identifiable assets.

As discussed below, various filings by Oxy with the Commission since January 1, 1975 did not contain certain required disclosures relating to: (1) Oxy's discharge of chemical or toxic wastes ("waste") into the environment; (2) the status of the proposed construction of a hydro-skimming refinery on Canvey Island; (3) the status of Oxy's negotiations with Libya concerning the financial arrangement pursuant to which Oxy operated in Libya; and (4) signed, undated letters of resignation which were submitted by certain nominees to Oxy's Board of Directors at the request of Dr. Armand Hammer, the Chairman of the Board.

B. ENVIRONMENTAL MATTERS

As a major chemical company with facilities throughout the United States, Oxy's wholly owned subsidiary, Hooker, is subject to compliance with various federal, state and local environmental protection laws and regulations restricting the discharge of pollutants in the environment. Such regulatory restraints have had and have a significant financial impact on Hooker with respect to increased expenditures attributable to compliance with environmental laws and actual or potential liabilities arising from its discharge of pollutants.

Set forth below is a description of the three areas of non-disclosure in Oxy's filings with the Commission with respect to matters regulating the discharge of waste into the environment, or otherwise relating to the protection of the environment, which the Commission, as a result of its investigation, believes should have been disclosed. Oxy did not disclose, in numerous instances, the required information concerning pending or contemplated administrative or judicial proceedings by governmental authorities arising under federal, state, or local law relating to the protection of the environment. In addition, as set forth below, Oxy did not make adequate disclosures in filings with the Commission concerning the effects that compliance with environmental regulations would have upon its capital expenditures and earnings. Finally, Oxy did not disclose certain potential material liabilities resulting from the leaching of wastes into the environment from various chemical disposal sites.

1. Disclosure of Environmental Proceedings Involving Oxy

In 1973, the Commission adopted amendments to its registration and reporting forms with respect to environmental matters which were designed to promote investor protection and at the same time promote the purposes of the National Environmental Policy Act of 1969. One such rule required reporting companies to disclose information relating to administrative or judicial proceedings arising under provisions relating to the protection of the environment and pending or known to be contemplated by governmental authorities.

Since at least 1974, Oxy has been the subject of numerous proceedings instituted by governmental authorities pursuant to federal, state or local governmental regulatory provisions and has frequently been involved in various types of proceedings relating to the environment. From April 1974 through December 1976, Oxy was involved in at least 90 legal proceedings with governmental units relating to the protection of the environment. Approximately three-quarters of these proceedings between 1974 and 1976 were administrative in nature and related to excessive emissions into the air, or the improper discharge of effluents into waterways, or violations of National Pollutant Discharge Elimination System ("NPDES") permits issued to various Oxy facilities. Corrective actions were undertaken by Oxy, and in most cases civil penalties ranging from $250 to $2500 per violation were imposed. Other proceedings between 1974 and 1976 involved administrative and criminal misdemeanor actions against Island Creek Coal Company, a wholly-owned subsidiary of Oxy, principally for the discharge of pollutants into streams in violation of West Virginia pollution control laws, all of which were terminated by settlement or, in the misdemeanor actions, by pleas of *nolo contendere*, resulting in the aggregate in fines or penalties of $19,736.00.

Prior to May 1977, Oxy did not disclose, as required, in any filing with the Commission the existence and nature of these 90 pending or contemplated proceedings relating to discharge of waste into the environment or otherwise relating to the protection of the environment.

Subsequent to Oxy's initial disclosures of the existence of proceedings in May 1977 in a Report on Form 10-Q for the period ending March 31, 1977, Oxy did not disclose on several occasions the existence of other contemplated legal proceedings relating to discharge of materials into the environment or otherwise relating to the protection of the environment. On other occasions, Oxy did not timely make certain required disclosures in filings with the Commission and the period of the nondisclosure was, in many cases, substantial.

. . . .

2. Disclosure of the effects of compliance upon Oxy's capital expenditures and earnings

As part of the Commission's 1973 amendments to its registration and reporting forms, the Commission required disclosure of "the material effects that compliance with federal, state and local provisions which have been enacted or adopted regulating the discharge of materials into the environment, or otherwise relating to the protection of the environment, may have upon the capital expenditures, earnings and competitive position of the registrant and its subsidiaries."

During the period from 1973 until 1977 . . . Oxy did not make required disclosure in filings with the Commission concerning the effects that compliance with provisions relating to the protection of the environment may have upon Oxy's capital expenditures and earnings.

Subsequent to May 1977, in various filings with the Commission, Oxy disclosed the amounts of capital expenditures relating to compliance with environmental regulations it had incurred for the current year and included estimates of environmentally related capital expenditures Oxy projected that it would incur in the succeeding two years. However, Oxy did not describe, or include within reported expenditures estimates of, the costs that it believed it would be required to incur in connection with possible remedial activities necessary to compensate for previous noncompliance with environmental regulations at certain Hooker facilities. . . .

3. Disclosure of Potential Liabilities Resulting From Disposal of Wastes

Significant property damage and personal injury has occurred near various waste disposal sites of Hooker. By at least 1977, the time varying with respect to specific sites . . . Hooker was exposed to material potential liabilities as a result of its ownership and use of these sites. Nevertheless, Oxy only disclosed in certain documents filed with the Commission including, for example, its Annual Report on form 10-K for the period ending December 31, 1977, that "[i]n light of the expansion of corporate liability in the environmental area in recent years, there can be no assurance that Occidental will not incur material liabilities in the future as a consequence of the impact of its operations upon the environment." Oxy did not specifically disclose the amount, or describe the nature or extent, of the potential liabilities of Hooker due to its discharge of substantial amounts of wastes, as set forth below. From the 1940s to the early 1970s, Hooker utilized essentially four sites in the Niagara Falls area of western New York State for the disposal of certain hazardous chemical wastes. . . . [T]he Niagara Falls disposal sites are the source of potential significant financial claims against Oxy. Claims have been made in presently existing lawsuits in excess of hundreds of millions of dollars as a result of the alleged leaching of wastes from dump sites and into the homes surrounding Love Canal and the waters of the Niagara River, which is a source of drinking water for the Niagara Falls area.

. . . .

C. OTHER DISCLOSURE MATTERS

Oxy failed in various filings with the Commission to disclose the full facts and circumstances surrounding the reasons for the halting of construction in 1975 of a proposed major hydroskimming refinery at Canvey Island, England and the risks and uncertainties concerning its investment there. Moreover, it did not disclose certain matters and risks related to Oxy's dispute with the Libyan government over the interpretation and implementation of the "fair remuneration" arrangements concerning certain operations in Libya. Finally, Oxy did not disclose that signed undated letters of resignation were submitted by certain nominees to Oxy's Board of Directors at the request of Dr. Armand Hammer.

. . . .

Signed, Undated Resignation Letters

During the period from approximately 1957 until the present, Dr. Armand Hammer for the most part recommended nominees for election to Oxy's Board of Directors.

Beginning at least as early as 1962, Hammer requested signed but undated letters from certain nominees to Oxy's Board of Directors in which each signator stated that he was tendering his resignation effective immediately ("undated resignation letters"). All of those persons who were requested to sign undated resignation letters did in fact sign the letters and returned them to Hammer who placed them in Oxy's personnel files where they remained.

During the period from 1962 through 1972, Hammer requested and received undated resignation letters from approximately ten persons who became directors of Oxy. With the exception of one director, who was a substantial shareholder of Oxy, the other persons who submitted the undated resignation letters were officers of the Company. None of the incumbent directors serving on Oxy's Board has signed such a letter, the last signatory director having left the Board in 1978.

During the period from approximately January 1, 1963 through 1978, Oxy filed with the Commission Annual Reports on Form 10-K, which did not disclose the existence of the undated resignation letters or the facts and circumstances surrounding the letters, including their purpose or the effects, if any, that such letters may have had.

II

CONCLUSIONS

The Commission finds that certain of Oxy's periodic reports filed with the Commission from 1973 through 1978 did not contain material disclosures as required by section 13 of the Exchange Act and the Rules and Regulations promulgated thereunder.

As discussed above, Oxy did not make certain required disclosures concerning pending or contemplated judicial and administrative proceedings as to which it was a party, and arising under federal, state and local provisions which regulate the discharge of materials into the environment. Further, Oxy did not adequately disclose the effect upon its business of compliance with federal, state and local laws relating to the protection of the environment. The total cost of compliance with environmental regulations includes not only those costs to bring facilities into full compliance with environmental regulations but also includes costs associated with past non-compliance with environmental regulations. Such costs may include fines, penalties and other amounts associated with plant shutdowns occasioned by environmental violations and cleanup and other costs to remedy past violations.

Moreover, as discussed above, since at least 1977, varying with respect to specific sites, Oxy has been confronted with significant potential liabilities for damages and injuries resulting from Oxy's environmentally related operations. Under the circumstances involved, the Commission believes Oxy should timely have disclosed these potential liabilities and reasonably ascertainable amounts of potential exposure and costs associated therewith and other facts in several of Oxy's filings with the Commission. During time periods discussed herein, Oxy did not have in place adequate company-wide methods or procedures which, when used to determine the nature and facts of the company's environmental compliance or to facilitate the development of compliance costs, would have assisted it in meeting its disclosure obligations.

. . . .

As indicated above, certain persons standing for election as directors of Oxy signed undated letters of resignation as directors of Oxy, which Oxy did not disclose in filings with the Commission. Full disclosure of the conditions under which persons stand for election to the Board of Directors of a corporation is important in order to enable shareholders and the investing public to understand the present circumstances under which a corporation is directed and the potential for changes in such direction in the future. Shareholders expect that the directors they elect will serve and function for the full elected term. Accordingly, any understandings or arrangements, whether oral or written, under which a director may not be able to do so, or pursuant to which the director's functions or term may be limited, should be fully disclosed.

III

OFFER OF SETTLEMENT

Oxy has submitted an Offer of Settlement to the Commission in which it undertakes that:

A. It will designate a director ("the director") satisfactory to the Commission, who shall:

i. Be responsible for preparing an environmental report (the "report") in which he shall:

a. Recommend procedures to the full Board of Directors to ensure that Oxy will be in a position to disclose, in accordance with the federal securities laws on a complete, timely and accurate basis, all required information relating to environmental matters.

b. Reasonably determine the potential costs which Oxy will be required to incur within the next three years to bring its facilities into compliance with present federal, state and local environmental requirements at its Hooker Chemical Corporation and Island Creek Coal Company domestic facilities.

c. Determine the maximum civil penalties that may be imposed on Oxy pursuant to relevant environmental provisions and identify the factors which may mitigate the risk that the maximum amount of such penalties are likely to be imposed.

d. Describe third party claims, proceedings or litigations regarding the impact of Oxy's operations on the environment and the amount sought thereunder based on alleged claims against the Company.

ii. Assure that any potential liabilities regarding the impact of Oxy's operations on the environment have been identified to the Board of Directors of Oxy and that appropriate disclosure has been made in filings with the Commission as required by the federal securities laws. In the event that the required disclosure concerning such potential liabilities has not been made in such filings, as of the date of the filing of the report with the Commission, pursuant to this Order, the director shall append to the report a list identifying such liabilities, not then the subject of litigation.

iii. Describe the relevant legal, interpretative and/or technological problems in those instances, if any, in which the director is unable to ascertain or determine the matters specified above.

B. The Commission may consult with the director and be provided access to documents received, used or generated in the preparation of the report described above in a manner and with such limitations as are satisfactory to the Commission and Oxy.

C. The director will utilize Oxy's newly elected senior environmental official ("the environmental officer") and an independent consulting firm ("independent consultant"), each of whom will be satisfactory to the Commission, to assist with the development of information for, and the preparation of, the report described above.

D. The environmental officer and the independent consultant, prior to completion and submission of the report as provided in Paragraph G below, can only be dismissed by the director or by a majority vote of the Board of Directors of Oxy upon the recommendation of the director.

E. Oxy will cooperate fully with the director by permitting him to review such documents and interview such employees of Oxy as he deems relevant to the preparation of the report. Furthermore, the director will have authority to retain experts whom he determines are reasonably necessary to complete the Report.

F. It will make appropriate disclosure of a change in its policy that neither Oxy nor any officer, director or employee of the company will request or receive any written or oral agreement, assurance or promise of any kind from any nominee to, or member of, Oxy's Board of Directors as it now is or may in the future be constituted, that such member would resign from the Board of Directors prior to the expiration of the term for which the director was nominated or elected by Oxy, in a filing with the Commission on Form 8-K in advance of requesting or receiving any such agreement, assurance or promise. This provision does not apply to a resignation initiated by a director or a resignation of a director sought or received in connection with the termination of his status as an officer of Oxy, provided that such resignation occurs within ninety (90) days of a request for or receipt of his agreement, assurance or promise to resign. In connection with this undertaking, Oxy has represented that no Oxy director, officer or employee has either sought or received any such agreement, assurance or promise from any current member of Oxy's Board of Directors.

G. Within 10 months of the date of the issuance of this Order, or such later date as the staff of the Commission and Oxy may agree, the director shall complete the report and submit it to the Board of Directors of Oxy.

H. Within 10 days of the submission of the report, to the Board of Directors, Oxy will transmit copies thereof to the Commission and, within 30 days of such submission, to file with the Commission on Form 8-K a description thereof and a summary of the principal conclusions and recommendations.

I. In connection with the recommendations of the director, the Board of Directors of Oxy will review them within 45 days of their receipt and adopt and implement such of the recommendations as it reasonably believes necessary or appropriate.

J. Within 60 days of the submission of the report to the Board of Directors, Oxy will file with the Commission on Form 8-K a description of the actions taken by the Board of Directors, if any, with respect to the recommendations of the director.

IV

ORDER

In view of the foregoing, the Commission deems it appropriate and in the public interest to accept the Offer of Settlement of Oxy and accordingly, IT IS HEREBY ORDERED that such proceedings be, and they hereby are instituted.

IT IS FURTHER ORDERED THAT Oxy:

1. Comply with the reporting requirements of the Exchange Act.

2. Amend its reports currently on file with the Commission by filing this Order on a Form 8-K within 30 days after the date of entry of this Order.

3. Include in its next quarterly report to shareholders a summary of the contents of this Order.

4. Upon Oxy becoming aware of non-compliance with its undertakings set forth herein, Oxy shall immediately notify the Commission of that fact and unless the Commission otherwise agrees, Oxy shall disclose such non-compliance in a Current Report on Form 8-K within 10 days.

5. Upon the entry of this Order, these proceedings are terminated, provided however, the Commission specifically reserves the right to reopen these

proceedings solely to enforce the Commission's Order or if Oxy fails to comply with its undertakings set forth in this Order. If these proceedings are reopened, the only issues in such proceedings shall be Oxy's failure to comply with its undertakings as set forth in this Order or its failure to comply with this Order.

By the Commission.

---

§ 15.06 Officer and Director Bars

The SEC may seek in federal court an order prohibiting a person from serving as an officer or director of a publicly held enterprise. Such an order may be conditional or unconditional; it may be of permanent duration or for a specified time period as directed by the court. The conditions for an officer or director bar are that the individual violated the antifraud provisions of § 17(a)(1) of the 1933 Act or § 10(b) of the 1934 Act (or any rule thereunder) and that such conduct demonstrates unfitness to serve in this fiduciary capacity.[66]

Even prior to Congress' enactment of an officer/director bar provision in 1990, the SEC occasionally procured such orders as a type of equitable relief. In one such case, the Second Circuit focused on proscribed conduct that occurred prior to the 1990 legislation. Granting broad equitable relief, the court ordered disgorgement of illicit profits, an officer/director bar, and a voting trust to sterilize the violators' controlling interests in publicly held entities.[67] Not surprisingly, the Commission has been inclined to invoke this remedy with greater vigor in view of the express statutory authority now provided by federal law.[68]

§ 15.07 Money Penalties

The SEC also may seek money penalties in judicial as well as administrative actions against *any* person for *any* violation of the securities laws or of an SEC cease and desist

---

66. *See* § 20(e) of the Securities Act, 15 U.S.C. § 77t(e); § 21(d)(2) of the Exchange Act, 15 U.S.C. § 78u(d)(2). Note that prior to the Sarbanes-Oxley Act, the standard was "substantial unfitness." Sarbanes-Oxley Act § 305, *amending,* § 20(e) of the Securities Act & 21(d)(2) of the Exchange Act.

67. *SEC v. Posner,* 16 F.3d 520 (2d Cir. 1994).

68. *See, e.g., SEC v. Softpoint, Inc.,* 958 F. Supp. 846 (S.D.N.Y. 1997); Callcott, *Patterns of SEC Enforcement Under the 1990 Remedies Act: Officer-And-Director Bars,* 21 Sec. Reg. L.J. 347, 360 (1994) (citing cases). *See also, SEC v. Patel,* 61 F.3d 137 (2d Cir. 1995) (order of permanent bar of corporate officer vacated and remanded for justifiable factual basis for such bar order). *See generally* Barnard, *Rule 10b-5 and the "Unfitness" Question,* 47 Ariz. L. Rev. 9 (2005); Barnard, *SEC Debarment of Officers and Directors After Sarbanes-Oxley,* 59 Bus. Law. 391 (2004).

order. With the proceeds of any such money penalty, the Commission may seek to establish a "Fair Fund" for the benefit of aggrieved investors (see §5.04[B][17][f] *supra*).

The penalty amount levied by the court is determined in view of the facts and circumstances and increases in amount according to the severity of the violation committed. Three tiers of possible money penalties are used, with the severity of the penalty depending on the egregiousness of the misconduct.[69]

In 2006, the Commission sought to clarify its policy with respect to the levying of money penalties against publicly held companies. As identified by the SEC, two key considerations are: the receipt (or absence) of a direct benefit to the corporation as a consequence of the illegality; and (2) whether the company's shareholders will be unfairly injured by the levying of a money penalty. Other factors, as enunciated by the Commission, include: "the need to deter the particular type of offense; the extent of the injury to innocent parties; whether complicity in the violation is widespread throughout the corporation; the level of intent on the part of the perpetrators; the degree of difficulty in detecting the particular type of offense; presence or lack of remedial steps by the corporation; and extent of cooperation with the Commission and other law enforcement."[70] Whether the SEC's pronouncement will result in greater predictability in this context awaits determination.

The SEC's release on the levying of money penalties against publicly held companies follows.

Statement of the Securities and Exchange Commission Concerning Financial Penalties

Release No. 2006-4 (2006)

The question of whether, and if so to what extent, to impose civil penalties against a corporation raises significant questions for our mission of investor protection. The authority to impose such penalties is relatively recent in the Commission's history, and the use of very large corporate penalties is more recent still. Recent cases have not produced a clear public view of when and how the Commission will use

---

69. *See* Hiler & Rose, *Analysis of Changes to the SEC's Enforcement Powers in the Dodd-Frank Act*, 42 Sec. Reg. & L. Rep. (BNA) 2354 (2010); Martin, Mirvis & Herlihy, *SEC Enforcement Powers and Remedies Are Greatly Expanded*, 19 Sec. Reg. L.J. 19 (1993). *See generally* Black, *Should the SEC Be a Collection Agency for Defrauded Investors?*, 63 Bus. Law. 317 (2008); Ferrara, Ferrigno, & Darland, *Hardball! The SEC's New Arsenal of Enforcement Weapons*, 47 Bus. Law. 33 (1991); Laby & Callcott, *Patterns of SEC Enforcement Under the 1990 Remedies Act: Civil Money Penalties*, 58 Alb. L. Rev. 5 (1994).

70. Statement of the Securities and Exchange Commission Concerning Financial Penalties, SEC Release No. 2006-4 (2006). *See* M. Steinberg & R. Ferrara *supra* note 2, at §6:8 (2013 supp.); McNew, *Money Penalties Against Publicly Held Companies: A Proposal for Restraint*, 37 Sec. Reg. L.J. 48 (2009).

corporate penalties, and within the Commission itself a variety of views have heretofore been expressed, but not reconciled.

The Commission believes it important to provide the maximum possible degree of clarity, consistency, and predictability in explaining the way that its corporate penalty authority will be exercised. To this end, we are issuing this statement describing with particularity the framework for our penalty determinations. . . .

In determining whether or not to impose penalties against the corporations in these cases, we carefully considered our statutory authority, and the legislative history surrounding that statutory authority.

In 1990, Congress passed the Securities Enforcement Remedies and Penny Stock Reform Act (the "Remedies Act"), which gave the Commission authority generally to seek civil money penalties in enforcement cases. The penalty provisions added by the Remedies Act expressly authorize the Commission to obtain money penalties from entities, including corporate issuers. These provisions also enhanced the Commission's authority to fine individuals. Today, we limit our discussion to penalties against corporations, although we view penalties against individual offenders as a critical component in punishing and deterring violative conduct.

The Remedies Act legislative history contains express references to penalty assessments against corporate issuers of securities. In its Report on the legislation, the Senate Committee on Banking, Housing, and Urban Affairs expressly noted both that the civil money penalty provisions would be applicable to corporate issuers, and that shareholders ultimately may bear the cost of penalties imposed on corporate issuers. According to the Report, such penalties should be assessed when the securities law violation that is the basis of the penalty has resulted in an improper benefit to the shareholders. It also cautioned that the Commission and courts should, in considering corporate issuer penalties, take into account whether the penalty would be paid by shareholders who had been the principal victims of the violation:

The Committee believes that the civil money penalty provisions should be applicable to corporate issuers, and the legislation permits penalties against issuers. However, because the costs of such penalties may be passed on to shareholders, the Committee intends that a penalty be sought when the violation results in an improper benefit to shareholders. In cases in which shareholders are the principal victims of the violations, the Committee expects that the SEC, when appropriate, will seek penalties from the individual offenders acting for a corporate issuer. Moreover, in deciding whether and to what extent to assess a penalty against the issuer, the court may properly take into account whether civil penalties assessed against corporate issuers will ultimately be paid by shareholders who were themselves victimized by the violations. The court also may consider the extent to which the passage of time has resulted in shareholder turnover.

As this discussion indicates, a key question for the Commission is whether the issuer's violation has provided an improper benefit to the shareholders, or conversely whether the violation has resulted in harm to the shareholders. Where shareholders have been victimized by the violative conduct, or by the resulting negative effect on the entity following its discovery, the Commission is expected to seek penalties from culpable individual offenders acting for a corporation. . . .

In addition to the benefit or harm to shareholders, the statute and its legislative history suggest several other factors that may be pertinent to the analysis of corporate issuer penalties. For example, the need for effective deterrence is discussed throughout the legislative history of the Remedies Act. The Senate Report also notes the importance of good compliance programs and observes that the availability of penalties may encourage development of such programs. The Senate Report also observes that penalties may serve to decrease the temptation to violate the law in areas where the perceived risk of detection of wrongdoing is small. Other factors discussed in the legislative history include whether there was fraudulent intent, harm to innocent third parties, and the possibility of unjust enrichment to the wrongdoer.

The Sarbanes-Oxley Act of 2002 changed the ultimate disposition of penalties. Section 308 of Sarbanes-Oxley (the Fair Funds provision) allows the Commission to take penalties paid by individuals and entities in enforcement actions and add them to disgorgement funds for the benefit of victims. Penalty moneys no longer always go to the Treasury. Under Fair Funds, penalty moneys instead can be used to compensate the victims for the losses they experienced from the wrongdoing. If the victims are shareholders of the corporation being penalized, they will still bear the cost of issuer penalty payments (which is the case with any penalty against a corporate entity). When penalty moneys are ultimately returned to all or some of the investors who were victims of the violation, the amounts returned are less the administrative costs of the distribution. While the legislative history of the Fair Funds provision is scant, there are two general points that can be discerned. First, the purpose of the provision is to provide an additional source of compensation to victims of securities law violations. Second, the provision applies to all penalties and makes no distinction between penalties against individuals or entities.

We have considered the legislative histories of both the Remedies Act and the Fair Funds provisions of the Sarbanes-Oxley Act in reaching the decisions we announce today.

We proceed from the fundamental principle that corporate penalties are an essential part of an aggressive and comprehensive program to enforce the federal securities laws, and that the availability of a corporate penalty, as one of a range of remedies, contributes to the Commission's ability to achieve an appropriate level of deterrence through its decision in a particular case.

With this principle in mind, our view of the appropriateness of a penalty on the corporation in a particular case, as distinct from the individuals who commit a securities law violation, turns principally on two considerations:

The presence or absence of a direct benefit to the corporation as a result of the violation. The fact that a corporation itself has received a direct and material benefit from the offense, for example through reduced expenses or increased revenues, weighs in support of the imposition of a corporate penalty. If the corporation is in any other way unjustly enriched, this similarly weighs in support of the imposition of a corporate penalty. Within this parameter, the strongest case for the imposition of a corporate penalty is one in which the shareholders of the corporation have received an improper benefit as a result of the violation; the weakest case is one in which the current shareholders of the corporation are the principal victims of the securities law violation. *The degree to which the penalty will recompense or further harm the injured shareholders.* Because the protection of innocent investors is a principal objective of the securities laws, the imposition of a penalty on the corporation itself carries with it the risk that shareholders who are innocent of the violation will nonetheless bear the burden of the penalty. In some cases, however, the penalty itself may be used as a source of funds to recompense the injury suffered by victims of the securities law violations. The presence of an opportunity to use the penalty as a meaningful source of compensation to injured shareholders is a factor in support of its imposition. The likelihood a corporate penalty will unfairly injure investors, the corporation, or third parties weighs against its use as a sanction.

In addition to these two principal considerations, there are several additional factors that are properly considered in determining whether to impose a penalty on the corporation. These are:

The need to deter the particular type of offense. The likelihood that a corporate penalty will serve as a strong deterrent to others similarly situated weighs in favor of the imposition of a corporate penalty. Conversely, the prevalence of unique circumstances that render the particular offense unlikely to be repeated in other contexts is a factor weighing against the need for a penalty on the corporation rather than on the responsible individuals.

The extent of the injury to innocent parties. The egregiousness of the harm done, the number of investors injured, and the extent of societal harm if the corporation's infliction of such injury on innocent parties goes unpunished, are significant determinants of the propriety of a corporate penalty.

Whether complicity in the violation is widespread throughout the corporation. The more pervasive the participation in the offense by responsible persons within the corporation, the more appropriate is the use of a corporate penalty. Conversely, within this parameter, isolated conduct by only a few individuals would tend not to support the imposition of a corporate penalty. Whether the corporation has replaced those persons responsible for the violation will also be considered in weighing this factor.

The level of intent on the part of the perpetrators. Within this parameter, the imposition of a corporate penalty is most appropriate in egregious circumstances, where the culpability and fraudulent intent of the perpetrators are manifest. A corporate penalty is less likely to be imposed if the violation is not the result of deliberate, intentionally fraudulent conduct.

The degree of difficulty in detecting the particular type of offense. Because offenses that are particularly difficult to detect call for an especially high level of deterrence, this factor weighs in support of the imposition of a corporate penalty.

Presence or lack of remedial steps by the corporation. Because the aim of the securities laws is to protect investors, the prevention of future harm, as well as the punishment of past offenses, is a high priority. The Commission's decisions in particular cases are intended to encourage the management of corporations accused of securities law violations to do everything within their power to take remedial steps, from the first moment that the violation is brought to their attention. Exemplary conduct by management in this respect weighs against the use of a corporate penalty; failure of management to take remedial steps is a factor supporting the imposition of a corporate penalty.

Extent of cooperation with Commission and other law enforcement. Effective compliance with the securities laws depends upon vigilant supervision, monitoring, and reporting of violations. When securities law violations are discovered, it is incumbent upon management to report them to the Commission and to other appropriate law enforcement authorities. The degree to which a corporation has self-reported an offense, or otherwise cooperated with the investigation and remediation of the offense, is a factor that the Commission will consider in determining the propriety of a corporate penalty.

This framework for the consideration of the propriety of corporate penalties is grounded in the Commission's statutory authority and supported by the legislative history underlying that authority. It is the Commission's intent that the elucidation of these principles will provide a high degree of transparency to our decisions in these and future cases, and will be of assistance to the Commission's professional staff, to corporate issuers and their counsel, and to the public.

. . . . .

---

§ 15.08 Sarbanes-Oxley Act and Dodd-Frank Act Enhanced Enforcement

As discussed in Chapters 5, 10, and elsewhere, the Sarbanes-Oxley Act (SOX) and Dodd-Frank Act provide the SEC with enhanced enforcement remedies. The following discussion highlights these key provisions:

- A court order may be obtained by the SEC freezing certain extraordinary payments made by a subject corporation to a corporate director, officer, employee, or other agent during a Commission investigation.

- The SEC may procure forfeiture of bonuses and disgorgement of profits by a chief executive officer and/or chief financial officer where a publicly held company must prepare an accounting restatement "as a result of misconduct." As held by a number of courts, this disgorgement remedy applies irrespective of whether the financial restatement was caused by a subject CEO's or CFO's personal misconduct.[71]

- An officer or director bar may be ordered based on the subject fiduciary being found liable for securities fraud and deemed "unfit" to serve in such capacity.

- Upon the levying of a civil money penalty, a "Fair Fund" for the benefit of aggrieved investors may be established to help offset their losses incurred as a result of the illegalities committed.

- The express authority of a federal court to award "any equitable relief that may be appropriate or necessary for the benefit of investors."

- In administrative cease and desist proceedings, the SEC may impose civil money penalties upon any violator. This money penalty may be levied based on violation of any provision of the securities acts, including where the defendant engages in negligent conduct. The amount of the penalty ordered is structured in three tiers, with more severe money penalties levied against those who engaged in fraud and whose conduct resulted in (or created a significant risk of) significant pecuniary harm.

- The SEC may pursue aiders and abettors not only for violations of the Securities Exchange Act and Investment Advisers Act, but now also under the Securities Act and the Investment Company Act. The requisite mental state for the imposition of aider and abettor liability is knowing or reckless misconduct.

- The SEC may invoke § 20(a) of the Securities Exchange Act to bring enforcement actions against "control persons." Prior to this clarification, the lower federal courts were divided regarding whether the SEC had this authority to use § 20(a) or whether the statute was solely applicable in private litigation.

- The Commission now may impose collateral bars in its administrative enforcement proceedings. An associated person who violates the securities laws is now subject to a bar from associating with any regulated entity, such as a broker-dealer or investment adviser. Prior to this clarification, there was uncertainty whether the Commission's bar authority was limited to the profession in which the violator engaged in the misconduct (such as whether a registered broker not only could be barred from associating with any broker-dealer firm but also from associating with any investment adviser firm).

- The clawback provision, enacted pursuant to the Sarbanes-Oxley Act of 2002 (SOX), is no longer limited to a subject reporting company's CEO and CFO. If an executive received unjust enrichment based on the company's inaccurate financial statements that have been restated, the company may recover such

---

71. *See, e.g., SEC v. Jensen*, 835 F.3d 1100 (9th Cir. 2016).

excessive incentive-based compensation from the executive without any show-ing of fault being necessary.

- The SEC has the authority to suspend or revoke the registration of a nationally recognized statistical rating agency (NRSRO) in regard to a specified class (or subclass) of securities if the NRSRO fails to establish and maintain sufficient resources for determining credit ratings in an acceptable manner.

- The SEC now has authority to award whistleblowers monetary awards of 10 to 30 percent where a money penalty off more than $1 million is levied if such whistleblower provided the SEC with "original information" (meaning infor-mation that is independent and not known by the Commission by any other means).

- The Supreme Court's restrictive decision in *Morrison v. National Australia Bank* (contained in § 8.13 herein) may be nullified in the U.S. government enforce-ment context. As now set forth, the SEC and the U.S. Department of Justice purportedly may bring government actions, even if the transactions did not occur in this country and did not harm U.S. citizens, if the "conduct and effects" test is met.

---

§ 15.09 SEC Settlements

SEC v. Citigroup Global Markets, Inc.

United States Court of Appeals, Second Circuit

752 F.3d 285 (2014)

Pooler, Circuit Judge:

The United States Securities and Exchange Commission ("S.E.C.") in conjunction with Citigroup Global Markets, Inc. ("Citigroup") appeals from the November 28, 2011 order of the United States District Court for the Southern District of New York (Rakoff, J.) refusing to approve a consent decree entered into by the parties and instead setting a trial date. Our Court stayed that order and referred the matter to a merits panel for consideration of the underlying questions. . . . We now hold that the dis-trict court abused its discretion by applying an incorrect legal standard in assessing the consent decree and setting a date for trial.

BACKGROUND

Complaint and Proposed Consent Judgment

In October 2011, the S.E.C. filed a complaint against Citigroup, alleging that Citi-group negligently misrepresented its role and economic interest in structuring and marketing a billion-dollar fund, known as the Class V Funding III ("the Fund"), and violated Sections 17(a)(2) and (3) of the Securities Act of 1933 (the "Act"). The complaint alleges that Citigroup "exercised significant influence" over the selection of $500 million worth of the Fund's assets, which were primarily collateralized by subprime securities tied to the already faltering U.S. housing market. Citigroup told Fund investors that the Fund's investment portfolio was chosen by an independent investment advisor, but, the S.E.C. alleged, Citigroup itself selected a substantial amount of negatively projected mortgage-backed assets in which Citigroup had taken a short position. By assuming a short position, Citigroup realized profits of roughly $160 million from the poor performance of its chosen assets, while Fund investors suffered millions of dollars in losses.

Shortly after filing of the complaint, the S.E.C. filed a proposed consent judgment. In the proposed consent judgment, Citigroup agreed to: (1) a permanent injunction barring Citigroup from violating Act Sections 17(a)(2) and (3); (2) disgorgement of $160 million, which the S.E.C. asserted were Citigroup's net profits gained as a result of the conduct alleged in the complaint; (3) prejudgment interest in the amount of $30 million; and (4) a civil penalty of $95 million. Citigroup also agreed not to seek an offset against any compensatory damages awarded in any related investor action. Citigroup consented to make internal changes, for a period of three years, to prevent similar acts from happening in the future. Absent from the consent decree was any admission of guilt or liability.

The S.E.C. also filed a parallel complaint against Citigroup employee Brian Stoker. . . . The Stoker complaint alleged that Stoker negligently violated Sections 17(a)(2) and (3) of the Act in connection with his role in structuring and marketing the collateralized debt obligations in the Fund.

Proceedings Before the District Court

The district court scheduled a hearing in the matter, and presented the S.E.C. and Citigroup with a list of questions to answer. The questions included:

- Why should the Court impose a judgment in a case in which the S.E.C. alleges a serious securities fraud but the defendant neither admits nor denies wrongdoing?

- Given the S.E.C.'s statutory mandate to ensure transparency in the financial marketplace, is there an overriding public interest in determining whether the S.E.C.'s charges are true? Is the interest even stronger when there is no parallel criminal case?

- How was the amount of the proposed judgment determined? In particular, what calculations went into the determination of the $95 million penalty? Why, for example, is the penalty in this case less than one-fifth of the $535 million penalty assessed in S.E.C. v. Goldman Sachs & Co.? What reason is there to believe this proposed penalty will have a meaningful deterrent effect?

- The proposed judgment imposes injunctive relief against future violations. What does the S.E.C. do to maintain compliance? How many contempt proceedings against large financial entities has the S.E.C. brought in the past decade as a result of violations of prior consent judgments?

- Why is the penalty in this case to be paid in large part by Citigroup and its share-holders rather than by the "culpable individual offenders acting for the corporation"? If the S.E.C. was for the most part unable to identify such alleged offenders, why was this?

- How can a securities fraud of this nature and magnitude be the result simply of negligence?

Both the S.E.C. and Citigroup submitted written responses to the district court's questions. On November 9, 2011, the district court conducted a hearing to explore the questions presented. A few weeks later, the district court issued a written opinion declining to approve the consent judgment. *S.E.C. v. Citigroup Global Markets Inc.*, 827 F.Supp.2d 328 (S.D.N.Y.2011) (*"Citigroup I"*). The district court stated that:

> before a court may employ its injunctive and contempt powers in support of an administrative settlement, it is required, even after giving substantial deference to the views of the administrative agency, to be satisfied that it is not being used as a tool to enforce an agreement that is unfair, unreasonable, inadequate, or in contravention of the public interest.

[The district court] found that the proposed consent decree:

> is neither fair, nor reasonable, nor adequate, nor in the public interest ... because it does not provide the Court with a sufficient evidentiary basis to know whether the requested relief is justified under any of these standards. Purely private parties can settle a case without ever agreeing on the facts, for all that is required is that a plaintiff dismiss his complaint. But when a public agency asks a court to become its partner in enforcement by imposing wide-ranging injunctive remedies on a defendant, enforced by the formidable judicial power of contempt, the court, and the public, need some knowledge of what the underlying facts are: for otherwise, the court becomes a mere handmaiden to a settlement privately negotiated on the basis of unknown facts, while the public is deprived of ever knowing the truth in a matter of obvious public importance.

The district court criticized the relief obtained by the S.E.C. in the consent decree, comparing it unfavorably with settlements entered in [two other enforcement actions] In [these two actions, namely,] *Bank of America* and *Goldman Sachs*, the district court noted, the parties stipulated to certain findings of facts. Without such an evidentiary basis in this case, the district court reasoned, "the Court is forced to conclude that a proposed Consent Judgment that asks the Court to impose substantial injunctive relief, enforced by the Court's own contempt power, on the basis of allegations unsupported by any proven or acknowledged facts whatsoever, is neither reasonable, nor fair, nor adequate, nor in the public interest."

Thus, the district court concluded:

> An application of judicial power that does not rest on facts is worse than mindless, it is inherently dangerous. The injunctive power of the judiciary

is not a free-roving remedy to be invoked at the whim of a regulatory agency, even with the consent of the regulated. If its deployment does not rest on facts — cold, hard, solid facts, established either by admissions or by trials — it serves no lawful or moral purpose and is simply an engine of oppression.

The district court refused to approve the consent judgment, and instead consolidated this case with the Stoker action and ordered the parties to be prepared to try both cases. . . .

. . . .

ANALYSIS

We review the district court's denial of a settlement agreement under an abuse of discretion standard. A district court abuses its discretion if it "(1) based its ruling on an erroneous view of the law," (2) made a "clearly erroneous assessment of the evidence," or (3) "rendered a decision that cannot be located within the range of permissible decisions."

The Scope of the Consent Decree

We quickly dispense with the argument that the district court abused its discretion by requiring Citigroup to admit liability as a condition for approving the consent decree. In both the briefing and at oral argument, the district court's pro bono counsel stated that the district court did not seek an admission of liability before approving the consent decree. With good reason — there is no basis in the law for the district court to require an admission of liability as a condition for approving a settlement between the parties. The decision to require an admission of liability before entering into a consent decree rests squarely with the S.E.C. As the district court did not condition its approval of the consent decree on an admission of liability, we need not address the issue further.

The Scope of Deference

We turn, then, to the far thornier question of what deference the district court owes an agency seeking a consent decree. Our Court recognizes a "strong federal policy favoring the approval and enforcement of consent decrees." "To be sure, when the district judge is presented with a proposed consent judgment, he is not merely a 'rubber stamp.'" The district court here found it was "required, even after giving substantial deference to the views of the administrative agency, to be satisfied that it is not being used as a tool to enforce an agreement that is unfair, unreasonable, inadequate, or in contravention of the public interest." . . . Other district courts in our Circuit view "[t]he role of the Court in reviewing and approving proposed consent judgments in S.E.C. enforcement actions [as] 'restricted to assessing whether the settlement is fair, reasonable and adequate within the limitations Congress has imposed on the S.E.C. to recover investor losses.'" . . .

The "fair, reasonable, adequate and in the public interest" standard invoked by the district court finds its origins in a variety of cases. Our Court previously held, in the context of assessing a plan for distributing the proceeds of a proposed disgorgement order, that "once the district court satisfies itself that the distribution of proceeds in a proposed S.E.C. disgorgement plan is fair and reasonable, its review is at an end." The Ninth Circuit—in circumstances similar to those presented here, a proposed consent decree aimed at settling an S.E.C. enforcement action—noted that "[u]nless a consent decree is unfair, inadequate, or unreasonable, it ought to be approved." *S.E.C. v. Randolph*, 736 F.2d 525, 529 (9th Cir. 1984).

Today we clarify that the proper standard for reviewing a proposed consent judgment involving an enforcement agency requires that the district court determine whether the proposed consent decree is fair and reasonable, with the additional requirement that the "public interest would not be disserved," in the event that the consent decree includes injunctive relief. Absent a substantial basis in the record for concluding that the proposed consent decree does not meet these requirements, the district court is required to enter the order.

We omit "adequacy" from the standard. Scrutinizing a proposed consent decree for "adequacy" appears borrowed from the review applied to class action settlements, and strikes us as particularly inapt in the context of a proposed S.E.C. consent decree. See Fed. R. Civ. P. 23(e)(2) ("If the proposal would bind the class members, the court may approve it only after a hearing and on a finding that it is fair, reasonable, and adequate."). The adequacy requirement makes perfect sense in the context of a class action settlement—a class action settlement typically precludes future claims, and a court is rightly concerned that the settlement achieved be adequate. By the same token, a consent decree does not pose the same concerns regarding adequacy—if there are potential plaintiffs with a private right of action, those plaintiffs are free to bring their own actions. If there is no private right of action, then the S.E.C. is the entity charged with representing the victims, and is politically liable if it fails to adequately perform its duties.

A court evaluating a proposed S.E.C. consent decree for fairness and reasonableness should, at a minimum, assess (1) the basic legality of the decree. . . . (2) whether the terms of the decree, including its enforcement mechanism, are clear. . . . (3) whether the consent decree reflects a resolution of the actual claims in the complaint; and (4) whether the consent decree is tainted by improper collusion or corruption of some kind. . . . Consent decrees vary, and depending on the decree a district court may need to make additional inquiry to ensure that the consent decree is fair and reasonable. The primary focus of the inquiry, however, should be on ensuring the consent decree is procedurally proper, using objective measures similar to the factors set out above, taking care not to infringe on the S.E.C.'s discretionary authority to settle on a particular set of terms.

It is an abuse of discretion to require, as the district court did here, that the S.E.C. establish the "truth" of the allegations against a settling party as a condition for approving the consent decrees. Trials are primarily about the truth. Consent decrees are primarily about pragmatism. "[C]onsent decrees are normally compromises in which the parties give up something they might have won in litigation and waive their rights to litigation." *United States v. ITT Continental Baking Co.*, 420 U.S. 223, 235 (1975). Thus, a consent decree "must be construed as . . . written, and not as it might have been written had the plaintiff established his factual claims and legal theories in litigation." . . . Consent decrees provide parties with a means to manage risk. "The numerous factors that affect a litigant's decision whether to compromise a case or litigate it to the end include the value of the particular proposed compromise, the perceived likelihood of obtaining a still better settlement, the prospects of coming out better, or worse, after a full trial, and the resources that would need to be expended in the attempt." These assessments are uniquely for the litigants to make. It is not within the district court's purview to demand "cold, hard, solid facts, established either by admissions or by trials," as to the truth of the allegations in the complaint as a condition for approving a consent decree.

As part of its review, the district court will necessarily establish that a factual basis exists for the proposed decree. In many cases, setting out the colorable claims, supported by factual averments by the S.E.C., neither admitted nor denied by the wrongdoer, will suffice to allow the district court to conduct its review. Other cases may require more of a showing, for example, if the district court's initial review of the record raises a suspicion that the consent decree was entered into as a result of improper collusion between the S.E.C. and the settling party. We need not, and do not, delineate the precise contours of the factual basis required to obtain approval for each consent decree that may pass before the court. It is enough to state that the district court here, with the benefit of copious submissions by the parties, likely had a sufficient record before it on which to determine if the proposed decree was fair and reasonable. On remand, if the district court finds it necessary, it may ask the S.E.C. and Citigroup to provide additional information sufficient to allay any concerns the district court may have regarding improper collusion between the parties.

As noted earlier, when a proposed consent decree contains injunctive relief, a district court must also consider the public interest in deciding whether to grant the injunction. *See eBay*, 547 U.S. at 391. . . . *eBay* makes clear that:

> a plaintiff seeking a permanent injunction must satisfy a four-factor test before a court may grant such relief. A plaintiff must demonstrate: (1) that it has suffered an irreparable injury; (2) that remedies available at law, such as monetary damages, are inadequate to compensate for that injury; (3) that, considering the balance of hardships between the plaintiff and defendant, a remedy in equity is warranted; and (4) that the public interest would not be disserved by a permanent injunction.

. . . "*eBay* strongly indicates that the traditional principles of equity it employed are the presumptive standard for injunctions in any context," be they preliminary or permanent. . . .

Our analysis focuses on the issue reached by the district court: that the district court must assure itself the "public interest would not be disserved" by the issuance of a permanent injunction.

. . .

The job of determining whether the proposed S.E.C. consent decree best serves the public interest, however, rests squarely with the S.E.C., and its decision merits significant deference:

> [F]ederal judges—who have no constituency—have a duty to respect legitimate policy choices made by those who do. The responsibilities for assessing the wisdom of such policy choices and resolving the struggle between competing views of the public interest are not judicial ones: "Our Constitution vests such responsibilities in the public branches."

. . . .

The district court correctly recognized that it was required to consider the public interest in deciding whether to grant the injunctive relief in the proposed injunction. However, the district court made no findings that the injunctive relief proposed in the consent decree would disserve the public interest, in part because it defined the public interest as "an overriding interest in knowing the truth." The district court's failure to make the proper inquiry constitutes legal error. On remand, the district court should consider whether the public interest would be disserved by entry of the consent decree. For example, a consent decree may disserve the public interest if it barred private litigants from pursuing their own claims independent of the relief obtained under the consent decree. What the district court may not do is find the public interest disserved based on its disagreement with the S.E.C.'s decisions on discretionary matters of policy, such as deciding to settle without requiring an admission of liability.

To the extent the district court withheld approval of the consent decree on the ground that it believed the S.E.C. failed to bring the proper charges against Citigroup, that constituted an abuse of discretion. In comparing the complaint filed by the S.E.C. against Citigroup with the complaint filed by the S.E.C. against Stoker, the district court noted that "[a]lthough this would appear to be tantamount to an allegation of knowing and fraudulent intent ('scienter,' in the lingo of securities law), the S.E.C., for reasons of its own, chose to charge Citigroup only with negligence, in violation of Sections 17(a)(2) and (3) of the Securities Act. . . ." The exclusive right to choose which charges to levy against a defendant rests with the S.E.C. . . . Nor can the district court reject a consent decree on the ground that it fails to provide collateral estoppel assistance to private litigants—that simply is not the job of the courts.

Finally, we note that to the extent that the S.E.C. does not wish to engage with the courts, it is free to eschew the involvement of the courts and employ its own arsenal of remedies instead. . . . The S.E.C. can also order the disgorgement of profits. . . . Admittedly, these remedies may not be on par with the relief afforded by a so-ordered consent decree and federal court injunctions. But if the S.E.C. prefers to call upon the power of the courts in ordering a consent decree and issuing an injunction, then the S.E.C. must be willing to assure the court that the settlement proposed is fair and reasonable. "Consent decrees are a hybrid in the sense that they are at once both contracts and orders; they are construed largely as contracts, but are enforced as orders." . . . For the courts to simply accept a proposed S.E.C. consent decree without any review would be a dereliction of the court's duty to ensure the orders it enters are proper.

CONCLUSION

For the reasons given above, we vacate the order of the district court and remand this case for further proceedings in accordance with this opinion. . . .

Lohier, Circuit Judge concurring:

I thank my panel colleagues for addressing many of my concerns in this case. In particular, today's majority opinion makes clear that district courts assessing a proposed consent decree should consider principally four factors: "(1) the basic legality of the decree; (2) whether the terms of the decree, including its enforcement mechanism, are clear; (3) whether the consent decree reflects a resolution of the actual claims in the complaint; and (4) whether the consent decree is tainted by improper collusion or corruption of some kind." . . . I write separately to make two more observations.

First, in my view, the "fair and reasonable" standard for assessing the appropriateness of monetary relief (as opposed to injunctive relief) involves a straightforward analysis of *only* the four factors identified by the majority and described above. If all four factors are satisfied, the perceived modesty of monetary penalties proposed in a consent decree is not a reason to reject the decree.

Second, I would be inclined to reverse on the factual record before us and direct the District Court to enter the consent decree. It does not appear that any additional facts are needed to determine that the proposed decree is "fair and reasonable" and does not disserve the public interest. Nor, to use the words of the majority opinion's holding, is there a "substantial basis . . . for concluding" that further development of the record will show that the proposed terms of this decree are not fair, reasonable, and in the public interest. Under the circumstances, though, it does no harm to vacate and remand to permit the very able and distinguished District Judge to make that determination in the first instance.

§ 15.10 Statutes of Limitations

As a general principle, with certain exceptions, a number of courts hold that there exists no applicable statute of limitations when the SEC seeks equitable relief.[72] Although some courts disagree,[73] this principle extends not only to Commission

---

72. *See, e.g., SEC v. Rind*, 991 F.2d 1486 (9th Cir. 1993). *But see SEC v. Bartek*, [2012–2 Transfer Binder Fed. Sec. L. Rep. (CCH) ¶ 96,963 (5th Cir. 2012) (holding SEC's request for permanent injunction and officer and director bar punitive and therefore subject to § 2462's five-year statute of limitations).

73. *See, e.g., SEC v. Graham*, 823 F.3d 1357 (11th Cir. 2016) (holding that SEC claims for declaratory relief and disgorgement subject to five-year statute of limitations as disgorgement is a "forfeiture" and declaratory relief is "punitive").

requests seeking injunctive relief but also possibly to other equitable remedies.[74] Nonetheless, the SEC's pursuit of stale claims certainly is relevant in a court's determination whether to grant the relief requested.[75] Moreover, when the SEC institutes an action for monetary penalties, a five-year statute of limitations applies. This five-year limitations period also extends to non-monetary disciplinary sanctions that are viewed as punitive rather than remedial.[76] The U.S. Supreme Court in 2017 determined that this five-year limitations period applies to SEC actions for disgorgement. *See Kokesh v. SEC*, 2017 WL 2407471 (2017).

In the following case, the Supreme Court addressed whether this five-year limitations period incorporates a discovery period — namely, whether the statute of limitations begins to run when the SEC discovered the fraud rather than at the time of the violation.

Gabelli v. SEC

United States Supreme Court

568 U.S. 442, 133 S. Ct. 1216, 185 L. Ed. 2d 297 (2013)

Chief Justice Roberts delivered the opinion of the Court.

The Investment Advisers Act makes it illegal for investment advisers to defraud their clients, and authorizes the Securities and Exchange Commission to seek civil penalties from advisers who do so. Under the general statute of limitations for civil penalty actions, the SEC has five years to seek such penalties. The question is whether the five-year clock begins to tick when the fraud is complete or when the fraud is discovered.

I

A

Under the Investment Advisers Act of 1940, it is unlawful for an investment adviser "to employ any device, scheme, or artifice to defraud any client or prospective client" or "to engage in any transaction, practice, or course of business which operates as a fraud or deceit upon any client or prospective client." The Securities and Exchange Commission is authorized to bring enforcement actions against investment advisers who violate the Act, or individuals who aid and abet such violations.

---

74. *See, e.g., SEC v. Kokesh*, 834 F.3d 1158 (10th Cir. 2016) (holding disgorgement not a "forfeiture" within § 2462's five-year statute of limitations) (cert. granted); *SEC v. Williams*, 886 F. Supp. 28 (D. Mass. 1995).

75. *See, e.g., SEC v. Rind*, 991 F.2d at 1492.

76. *See, e.g.,* 28 U.S.C. § 2462; *Johnson v. SEC*, 87 F.3d 484 (D.C. Cir. 1996) (under facts of case, SEC imposition of censure and six-month suspension deemed a "penalty," thereby invoking § 2462's five-year limitations period). *See generally* Brodsky & Eggers, *The Statute of Limitations in SEC Civil Enforcement Actions*, 23 Sec. Reg. L.J. 123 (1995); Gordon, *SEC Administrative Proceedings: Five-Year Statute of Limitations Period Held Applicable*, 24 Sec. Reg. L.J. 420 (1997).

As part of such enforcement actions, the SEC may seek civil penalties, in which case a five-year statute of limitations applies:

> "Except as otherwise provided by Act of Congress, an action, suit or proceeding for the enforcement of any civil fine, penalty, or forfeiture, pecuniary or otherwise, shall not be entertained unless commenced within five years from the date when the claim first accrued if, within the same period, the offender or the property is found within the United States in order that proper service may be made thereon." 28 U.S. C. § 2462.

This statute of limitations is not specific to the Investment Advisers Act, or even to securities law; it governs many penalty provisions throughout the U.S. Code. Its origins date back to at least 1839, and it took on its current form in 1948. . . .

B

Gabelli Funds, LLC, is an investment adviser to a mutual fund formerly known as Gabelli Global Growth Fund (GGGF). Petitioner Bruce Alpert is Gabelli Funds' chief operating officer, and petitioner Marc Gabelli used to be GGGF's portfolio manager.

In 2008, the SEC brought a civil enforcement action against Alpert and Gabelli. According to the complaint, from 1999 until 2002 Alpert and Gabelli allowed one GGGF investor — Headstart Advisers, Ltd. — to engage in "market timing" in the fund.

As this Court has explained, "[m]arket timing is a trading strategy that exploits time delay in mutual funds' daily valuation system." . . . Mutual funds are typically valued once a day, at the close of the New York Stock Exchange. Because funds often hold securities traded on different exchanges around the world, their reported valuation may be based on stale information. If a mutual fund's reported valuation is artificially low compared to its real value, market timers will buy that day and sell the next to realize quick profits. Market timing is not illegal but can harm long-term investors in a fund.

The SEC's complaint alleged that Alpert and Gabelli permitted Headstart to engage in market timing in exchange for Headstart's investment in a hedge fund run by Gabelli. According to the SEC, petitioners did not disclose Headstart's market timing or the *quid pro quo* agreement, and instead banned others from engaging in market timing and made statements indicating that the practice would not be tolerated. The complaint stated that during the relevant period, Headstart earned rates of return of up to 185%, while "the rate of return for long-term investors in GGGF was no more than negative 24.1 percent."

The SEC alleged that Alpert and Gabelli aided and abetted violations of §§ 80b-6(1) and (2), and it sought civil penalties under § 80b-9. Petitioners moved to dismiss, arguing in part that the claim for civil penalties was untimely. They invoked the five-year statute of limitations in § 2462, pointing out that the complaint alleged market timing up until August 2002 but was not filed until April 2008. The District

Court agreed and dismissed the SEC's civil penalty claim as time barred. [footnote—The SEC also sought injunctive relief and disgorgement, claims the District Court found timely on the ground that they were not subject to § 2462. Those issues are not before us.]

The Second Circuit reversed. It acknowledged that § 2462 required an action for civil penalties to be brought within five years "from the date when the claim first accrued," but accepted the SEC's argument that because the underlying violations sounded in fraud, the "discovery rule" applied to the statute of limitations. As explained by the Second Circuit, "[u]nder the discovery rule, the statute of limitations for a particular claim does not accrue until that claim is discovered, or could have been discovered with reasonable diligence, by the plaintiff." 653 F.3d 49, 59 (2011). The court concluded that while "this rule does not govern the accrual of most claims," it *does* govern the claims at issue here. As the court explained, "for claims that sound in fraud a discovery rule is read into the relevant statute of limitation." [footnote—The [Second Circuit] distinguished the discovery rule, which governs when a claim accrues, from doctrines that toll the running of an applicable limitations period when the defendant takes steps beyond the challenged conduct itself to conceal that conduct from the plaintiff. 653 F.3d, at 59–60. The SEC abandoned any reliance on such doctrines below, and they are not before us. . . .]

We granted certiorari.

II

A

This case centers around the meaning of 28 U.S.C. § 2462: "an action . . . for the enforcement of any civil fine, penalty, or forfeiture . . . shall not be entertained unless commenced within five years from the date when the claim first accrued." Petitioners argue that a claim based on fraud accrues—and the five-year clock begins to tick—when a defendant's allegedly fraudulent conduct occurs.

That is the most natural reading of the statute. "In common parlance a right accrues when it comes into existence. . . ." Thus the "standard rule" is that a claim accrues "when a plaintiff has a complete and present cause of action." . . . That rule has governed since the 1830s when the predecessor to § 2462 was enacted. . . . And that definition appears in dictionaries from the 19th century up until today. See, *e.g.,* 1 A. Burrill, A Law Dictionary and Glossary 17 (1850) ("an action *accrues* when the plaintiff has a right to commence it"); Black's Law Dictionary 23 (9th ed. 2009) (defining "accrue" as "[t]o come into existence as an enforceable claim or right").

This reading sets a fixed date when exposure to the specified Government enforcement efforts ends, advancing "the basic policies of all limitations provisions: repose, elimination of stale claims, and certainty about a plaintiff's opportunity for recovery and a defendant's potential liabilities." Statutes of limitations are intended to "promote justice by preventing surprises through the revival of claims that have been allowed to slumber until evidence has been lost, memories have faded, and witnesses have disappeared." . . . They provide "security and stability to human affairs." . . . We have deemed them "vital to the welfare of society," and concluded that "even wrongdoers are entitled to assume that their sins may be forgotten." . . .

B

Notwithstanding these considerations, the Government argues that the discovery rule should apply instead. Under this rule, accrual is delayed "until the plaintiff has 'discovered'" his cause of action. The doctrine arose in 18th-century fraud cases as an "exception" to the standard rule, based on the recognition that "something different was needed in the case of fraud, where a defendant's deceptive conduct may prevent a plaintiff from even *knowing* that he or she has been defrauded." This Court has held that "where a plaintiff has been injured by fraud and 'remains in ignorance of it without any fault or want of diligence or care on his part, the bar of the statute does not begin to run until the fraud is discovered.'" . . . And we have explained that "fraud is deemed to be discovered when, in the exercise of reasonable diligence, it could have been discovered." . . .

But we have never applied the discovery rule in this context, where the plaintiff is not a defrauded victim seeking recompense, but is instead the Government bringing an enforcement action for civil penalties. Despite the discovery rule's centuries-old roots, the Government cites no lower court case before 2008 employing a fraud-based discovery rule in a Government enforcement action for civil penalties. When pressed at oral argument, the Government conceded that it was aware of no such case. The Government was also unable to point to any example from the first 160 years after enactment of this statute of limitations where it had even asserted that the fraud discovery rule applied in such a context. . . .

Instead the Government relies heavily on *Exploration Co. v. United States*, 247 U.S. 435 (1918), in an attempt to show that the discovery rule should benefit the Government to the same extent as private parties. In that case, a company had fraudulently procured land from the United States, and the United States sued to undo the transaction. The company raised the statute of limitations as a defense, but this Court allowed the case to proceed, concluding that the rule "that statutes of limitations upon suits to set aside fraudulent transactions shall not begin to run until the discovery of the fraud" applied "in favor of the Government as well as a private individual." . . . But in *Exploration Co.*, the Government was itself a victim: it had been defrauded and was suing to recover its loss. The Government was not bringing an enforcement action for penalties. *Exploration Co.* cannot save the Government's case here.

There are good reasons why the fraud discovery rule has not been extended to Government enforcement actions for civil penalties. The discovery rule exists in part to preserve the claims of victims who do not know they are injured and who reasonably do not inquire as to any injury. Usually when a private party is injured, he is immediately aware of that injury and put on notice that his time to sue is running. But when the injury is self-concealing, private parties may be unaware that they have been harmed. Most of us do not live in a state of constant investigation; absent any reason to think we have been injured, we do not typically spend our days looking for evidence that we were lied to or defrauded. And the law does not require that we do so. Instead, courts have developed the discovery rule, providing that the statute of limitations in fraud cases should typically begin to run only when the injury is or reasonably could have been discovered.

The same conclusion does not follow for the Government in the context of enforcement actions for civil penalties. The SEC, for example, is not like an individual victim who relies on apparent injury to learn of a wrong. Rather, a central "mission" of the Commission is to "investigat[e] potential violations of the federal securities laws." SEC, Enforcement Manual 1 (2012). Unlike the private party who has no reason to suspect fraud, the SECs very purpose is to root it out, and it has many legal tools at hand to aid in that pursuit. It can demand that securities brokers and dealers submit detailed trading information. It can require investment advisers to turn over their comprehensive books and records at any time. And even without filing suit, it can subpoena any documents and witnesses it deems relevant or material to an investigation. . . .

The SEC is also authorized to pay monetary awards to whistleblowers, who provide information relating to violations of the securities laws. In addition, the SEC may offer "cooperation agreements" to violators to procure information about others in exchange for more lenient treatment. Charged with this mission and armed with these weapons, the SEC as enforcer is a far cry from the defrauded victim the discovery rule evolved to protect.

In a civil penalty action, the Government is not only a different kind of plaintiff, it seeks a different kind of relief. The discovery rule helps to ensure that the injured receive recompense. But this case involves penalties, which go beyond compensation, are intended to punish, and label defendants wrongdoers. . . .

Chief Justice Marshal used particularly forceful language in emphasizing the importance of time limits on penalty actions, stating that it "would be utterly repugnant to the genius of our laws" if actions for penalties could "be brought at any distance of time." *Adams v. Woods,* 2 Cranch 336, 342 (1805). Yet grafting the discovery rule onto § 2462 would raise similar concerns. It would leave defendants exposed to Government enforcement action not only for five years after their misdeeds, but for an additional uncertain period into the future. Repose would hinge on speculation about what the Government knew, when it knew it, and when it should have known it.

. . .

Determining when the Government, as opposed to an individual, knew or reasonably should have known of a fraud presents particular challenges for the courts. Agencies often have hundreds of employees, dozens of offices, and several levels of leadership. In such a case, when does "the Government" know of a violation? Who is the relevant actor? Different agencies often have overlapping responsibilities; is the knowledge of one attributed to all?

In determining what a plaintiff should have known, we ask what facts "a reasonably diligent plaintiff would have discovered." It is unclear whether and how courts should consider agency priorities and resource constraints in applying that test to Government enforcement actions. . . . And in the midst of any inquiry as to what it knew when, the Government can be expected to assert various privileges, such as law enforcement, attorney-client, work product, or deliberative process, further complicating judicial attempts to apply the discovery rule. . . .

To be sure, Congress has expressly required such inquiries in some statutes. But in many of those instances, the Government is itself an injured victim looking for recompense, not a prosecutor seeking penalties. Moreover, statutes applying a discovery rule in the context of Government suits often couple that rule with an absolute provision for repose, which a judicially imposed discovery rule would lack. *See, e.g.,* 21 U.S.C. § 335b(b)(3) (limiting certain Government civil penalty actions to "6 years after the date when facts material to the act are known or reasonably should have been known by the Secretary but in no event more than 10 years after the date the act took place"). And several statutes applying a discovery rule to the Government make some effort to identify the official whose knowledge is relevant. See 31 U.S.C. § 3731(b)(2) (relevant knowledge is that of "the official of the United States charged with responsibility to act in the circumstances").

Applying a discovery rule to Government penalty actions is far more challenging than applying the rule to suits by defrauded victims, and we have no mandate from Congress to undertake that challenge here.

. . . Given the lack of textual, historical, or equitable reasons to graft a discovery rule onto the statute of limitations of § 2462, we decline to do so.

The judgment of the United States Court of Appeals for the Second Circuit is reversed, and the case is remanded for further proceedings consistent with this opinion.

It is so ordered.

---

§ 15.11 Attorney-Client Privilege

[A] In General

In re: Kellogg Brown & Root, Inc.

United States Court of Appeals, District of Columbia Circuit

756 F.3d 754 (2014)

KAVANAUGH, *Circuit Judge*:

More than three decades ago, the Supreme Court held that the attorney-client privilege protects confidential employee communications made during a business's internal investigation led by company lawyers. *See Upjohn Co. v. United States*, 449

U.S. 383 (1981). In this case, the District Court denied the protection of the privilege to a company that had conducted just such an internal investigation. The District Court's decision has generated substantial uncertainty about the scope of the attorney-client privilege in the business setting. We conclude that the District Court's decision is irreconcilable with *Upjohn*. We therefore grant KBR's petition for a writ of mandamus and vacate the District Court's document production order.

I

Harry Barko worked for KBR, a defense contractor. In 2005, he filed a False Claims Act complaint against KBR and KBR-related corporate entities, whom we will collectively refer to as KBR. In essence, Barko alleged that KBR and certain subcontractors defrauded the U.S. Government by inflating costs and accepting kickbacks while administering military contracts in wartime Iraq. During discovery, Barko sought documents related to KBR's prior internal investigation into the alleged fraud. KBR had conducted that internal investigation pursuant to its Code of Business Conduct, which is overseen by the company's Law Department.

KBR argued that the internal investigation had been conducted for the purpose of obtaining legal advice and that the internal investigation documents therefore were protected by the attorney-client privilege. Barko responded that the internal investigation documents were unprivileged business records that he was entitled to discover. . . .

After reviewing the disputed documents *in camera*, the District Court determined that the attorney-client privilege protection did not apply because, among other reasons, KBR had not shown that "the communication would not have been made 'but for' the fact that legal advice was sought." . . . KBR's internal investigation, the court concluded, was "undertaken pursuant to regulatory law and corporate policy rather than for the purpose of obtaining legal advice." . . .

KBR vehemently opposed the ruling. The company asked the District Court to certify the privilege question to this Court for interlocutory appeal and to stay its order pending a petition for mandamus in this Court. The District Court denied those requests and ordered KBR to produce the disputed documents to Barko within a matter of days. . . . KBR promptly filed a petition for a writ of mandamus in this Court. A number of business organizations and trade associations also objected to the District Court's decision and filed an amicus brief in support of KBR. We stayed the District Court's document production order and held oral argument on the mandamus petition.

. . . .

II

We . . . consider whether the District Court's privilege ruling was legally erroneous. We conclude that it was.

Federal Rule of Evidence 501 provides that claims of privilege in federal courts are governed by the "common law—as interpreted by United States courts in the light of reason and experience." Fed. R. Evid. 501. The attorney-client privilege is the "oldest of the privileges for confidential communications known to the common law." *Upjohn Co. v. United States*, 449 U.S. 383, 389 (1981). As relevant here, the privilege applies to a confidential communication between attorney and client if that communication was made for the purpose of obtaining or providing legal advice to the client. . . .

In *Upjohn*, the Supreme Court held that the attorney-client privilege applies to corporations. The Court explained that the attorney-client privilege for business organizations was essential in light of "the vast and complicated array of regulatory legislation confronting the modern corporation," which required corporations to "constantly go to lawyers to find out how to obey the law, . . . particularly since compliance with the law in this area is hardly an instinctive matter." The Court stated, moreover, that the attorney-client privilege "exists to protect not only the giving of professional advice to those who can act on it but also the giving of information to the lawyer to enable him to give sound and informed advice." That is so, the Court said, because the "first step in the resolution of any legal problem is ascertaining the factual background and sifting through the facts with an eye to the legally relevant." In *Upjohn*, the communications were made by company employees to company attorneys during an attorney-led internal investigation that was undertaken to ensure the company's "compliance with the law." The Court ruled that the privilege applied to the internal investigation and covered the communications between company employees and company attorneys.

KBR's assertion of the privilege in this case is materially indistinguishable from Upjohn's assertion of the privilege in that case. As in *Upjohn*, KBR initiated an internal investigation to gather facts and ensure compliance with the law after being informed of potential misconduct. And as in *Upjohn*, *KBR's investigation was conducted under the auspices of KBR's in-house legal department, acting in its legal capacity.* [emphasis supplied] The same considerations that led the Court in *Upjohn* to uphold the corporation's privilege claims apply here.

The District Court in this case initially distinguished *Upjohn* on a variety of grounds. But none of those purported distinctions takes this case out from under *Upjohn*'s umbrella.

First, the District Court stated that in *Upjohn* the internal investigation began after in-house counsel conferred with outside counsel, whereas here the investigation was conducted in-house without consultation with outside lawyers. But *Upjohn* does not hold or imply that the involvement of outside counsel is a necessary predicate for the privilege to apply. On the contrary, the general rule, which this Court has adopted, is that a lawyer's status as in-house counsel "does not dilute the privilege." . . . As the [American Law Institute] Restatement's commentary points out, "Inside legal counsel to a corporation or similar organization . . . is fully empowered to engage in privileged communications." 1 Restatement [The Law Governing Lawyers] § 72, cmt. c, at 551.

Second, the District Court noted that in *Upjohn* the interviews were conducted by attorneys, whereas here many of the interviews in KBR's investigation were conducted by non-attorneys. But the investigation here was conducted at the direction of the attorneys in KBR's Law Department. And communications made by and to non-attorneys serving as agents of attorneys in internal investigations are routinely protected by the attorney-client privilege. . . . *Third*, the District Court pointed out that in *Upjohn* the interviewed employees were expressly informed that the purpose of the interview was to assist the company in obtaining legal advice, whereas here they were not. The District Court further stated that the confidentiality agreements signed by KBR employees did not mention that the purpose of KBR's investigation was to obtain legal advice. Yet nothing in *Upjohn* requires a company to use magic words to its employees in order to gain the benefit of the privilege for an internal investigation. And in any event, here, as in *Upjohn*, employees knew that the company's legal department was conducting an investigation of a sensitive nature and that the information they disclosed would be protected. KBR employees were also told not to discuss their interviews "without the specific advance authorization of KBR General Counsel." . . .

In short, none of those three distinctions of *Upjohn* holds water as a basis for denying KBR's privilege claim.

More broadly and more importantly, the District Court also distinguished *Upjohn* on the ground that KBR's internal investigation was undertaken to comply with Department of Defense regulations that require defense contractors such as KBR to maintain compliance programs and conduct internal investigations into allegations of potential wrongdoing. The District Court therefore concluded that the purpose of KBR's internal investigation was to comply with those regulatory requirements rather than to obtain or provide legal advice. In our view, the District Court's analysis rested on a false dichotomy. So long as obtaining or providing legal advice was one of the significant purposes of the internal investigation, the attorney-client privilege applies, even if there were also other purposes for the investigation and even if the investigation was mandated by regulation rather than simply an exercise of company discretion.

The District Court began its analysis by reciting the "primary purpose" test, which many courts (including this one) have used to resolve privilege disputes when attorney-client communications may have had both legal and business purposes. But in a key move, the District Court then said that the primary purpose of a communication is to obtain or provide legal advice only if the communication would not have been made "but for" the fact that legal advice was sought. In other words, if there was any other purpose behind the communication, the attorney-client privilege apparently does not apply. The District Court went on to conclude that KBR's internal investigation was "undertaken pursuant to regulatory law and corporate policy rather than for the purpose of obtaining legal advice." . . .

The District Court erred because it employed the wrong legal test. The but-for test articulated by the District Court is not appropriate for attorney-client privilege analysis. Under the District Court's approach, the attorney-client privilege apparently would not apply unless the sole purpose of the communication was to obtain or provide legal advice. That is not the law. We are aware of no Supreme Court or court of appeals decision that has adopted a test of this kind in this context. The District Court's novel approach to the attorney-client privilege would eliminate the attorney-client privilege for numerous communications that are made for both legal and business purposes and that heretofore have been covered by the attorney-client privilege. And the District Court's novel approach would eradicate the attorney-client privilege for internal investigations conducted by businesses that are required by law to maintain compliance programs, which is now the case in a significant swath of American industry. In turn, businesses would be less likely to disclose facts to their attorneys and to seek legal advice, which would "limit the valuable efforts of corporate counsel to ensure their client's compliance with the law." We reject the District Court's but-for test as inconsistent with the principle of *Upjohn* and longstanding attorney-client privilege law.

Given the evident confusion in some cases, we also think it important to underscore that the primary purpose test, sensibly and properly applied, cannot and does not draw a rigid distinction between a legal purpose on the one hand and a business purpose on the other. After all, trying to find *the* one primary purpose for a communication motivated by two sometimes overlapping purposes (one legal and one business, for example) can be an inherently impossible task. It is often not useful or even feasible to try to determine whether the purpose was A or B when the purpose was A and B. It is thus not correct for a court to presume that a communication can have only one primary purpose. It is likewise not correct for a court to try to find *the* one primary purpose in cases where a given communication plainly has multiple purposes. Rather, it is clearer, more precise, and more predictable to articulate the test as follows: Was obtaining or providing legal advice *a* primary purpose of the communication, meaning one of the significant purposes of the communication? As the Reporter's Note to the Restatement says, "In general, American decisions agree that the privilege applies if one of the significant purposes of a client in communicating with a lawyer is that of obtaining legal assistance." 1 Restatement § 72, Reporter's Note, at 554. We agree with and adopt that formulation—"one of the significant purposes"— as an accurate and appropriate description of the primary purpose test. Sensibly and properly applied, the test boils down to whether obtaining or providing legal advice was one of the significant purposes of the attorney-client communication.

In the context of an organization's internal investigation, if one of the significant purposes of the internal investigation was to obtain or provide legal advice, the privilege will apply. That is true regardless of whether an internal investigation was conducted pursuant to a company compliance program required by statute or regulation, or was otherwise conducted pursuant to company policy. . . .

In this case, there can be no serious dispute that one of the significant purposes of the KBR internal investigation was to obtain or provide legal advice. In denying KBR's privilege claim on the ground that the internal investigation was conducted in order to comply with regulatory requirements and corporate policy and not just to obtain or provide legal advice, the District Court applied the wrong legal test and clearly erred.

. . . .

In reaching our decision here, we stress, as the Supreme Court did in *Upjohn*, that the attorney-client privilege "only protects disclosure of communications; it does not protect disclosure of the underlying facts by those who communicated with the attorney." *Upjohn Co. v. United States*, 449 U.S. 383, 395 (1981). Barko was able to pursue the facts underlying KBR's investigation. But he was not entitled to KBR's own investigation files. As the *Upjohn* Court stated, quoting Justice Jackson, "Discovery was hardly intended to enable a learned profession to perform its functions . . . on wits borrowed from the adversary." *Id.* at 396 (quoting *Hickman v. Taylor*, 329 U.S. 495, 515 (1947) (Jackson, J., concurring)).

Although the attorney-client privilege covers only communications and not facts, we acknowledge that the privilege carries costs. The privilege means that potentially critical evidence may be withheld from the factfinder. Indeed, as the District Court here noted, that may be the end result in this case. But our legal system tolerates those costs because the privilege "is intended to encourage 'full and frank communication between attorneys and their clients and thereby promote broader public interests in the observance of law and the administration of justice.'"

We grant the petition for a writ of mandamus and vacate the District Court's . . . document production order . . . .

———————

Note

Undoubtedly, *Upjohn* and subsequent lower court decisions provide strong support for the sanctity of the attorney-corporate client relationship. In this regard, these decisions have proven to be particularly relevant to corporations conducting internal investigations undertaken on a voluntary basis. On the other hand, should the privilege apply where the special counsel has been appointed to conduct an internal investigation pursuant to ancillary relief granted by a federal court in an SEC enforcement action? What is special counsel's role in that setting? For example, is he/she (1) counsel for the corporation, (2) a legal auditor, or (3) an officer of the court? Compare *Handler v. SEC*, 610 F.2d 656 (9th Cir. 1979), and *In re LTV Securities Litigation*, 89 F.R.D. 595 (N.D. Tex. 1981) (attorney-client and work product privileges invoked with respect to special counsel appointed pursuant to an SEC consent decree), with, *SEC v. Canadian Javelin, Ltd.*, 451 F. Supp. 594, 596 (D.D.C. 1978), *vacated on other grounds*, [1979 Transfer Binder] Fed. Sec. L. Rep. (CCH) ¶ 96,742 (D.C. Cir. 1978) ("[T]he language of the . . . [consent] decree negates any notion of an attorney-client relationship between Javelin and special counsel and any notion of confidentiality with respect to communications made to special counsel . . . [whose] responsibilities were to [the district court] and to the American public"). *See* Gruenbaum & Oppenheimer, *Special Investigative Counsel: Conflicts and Roles*, 33 Rutgers L. Rev. 865 (1981).

Another interesting issue is the applicability of the attorney-corporate client privilege in shareholder derivative litigation. In the seminal case of *Garner v. Wolfinbarger*, 430 F.2d 1093 (5th Cir. 1970), the Fifth Circuit articulated a "good cause" exception to the attorney-corporate client privilege. The court reasoned:

> It is urged that disclosure is injurious to both the corporation and the attorney. Corporate management must manage. It has the duty to do so and requires the tools to do so. Part of the managerial task is to seek legal counsel when desirable, and, obviously management prefers that it confer with counsel without the risk of having the communications revealed at the instance of one or more dissatisfied stockholders. The managerial preference is a rational one, because it is difficult to envision the management of any sizeable corporation pleasing all of its stockholders all of the time, and management desires protection from those who might second-guess or even harass in matters purely of judgment.
>
> But in assessing management assertions of injury to the corporation it must be borne in mind that management does not manage for itself and that the beneficiaries of its actions are the stockholders. . . . [M]anagement judgment must stand on its merits, not behind an ironclad veil of secrecy which under all circumstances preserves it from being questioned by those for whom it is, at least in part, exercised.

430 F.2d. at 1101. Hence, the court held that the corporation's shareholders in a derivative action could obtain disclosure of otherwise privileged communications if they could establish "good cause." The Fifth Circuit set forth the following factors, although not all-inclusive, as relevant in this determination:

> [T]he number of shareholders and the percentage of stock they [the plaintiff-shareholders] represent; the bona fides of the shareholders; the nature of the shareholders' claim and whether it is obviously colorable; the apparent necessity or desirability of the shareholders having the information and the availability of it from other sources; whether, if the shareholders' claim is of wrongful action by the corporation, it is of action criminal, or illegal but not criminal, or of doubtful legality; whether the communication related to past or to prospective actions; whether the communication is of advice concerning the litigation itself; the extent to which the communication is identified versus the extent to which the shareholders are blindly fishing; the risk of revelation of trade secrets or other information in whose confidentiality the corporation has an interest for independent reasons.

430 F.2d. at 1104.

The *Garner* "good cause" exception to the attorney-client privilege has received judicial approbation. Indeed, some courts have extended its application. For example, in *Donovan v. Fitzsimmons*, 90 F.R.D. 583 (N.D. Ill. 1981), the court applied *Garner's* rationale to allow beneficiaries of a pension fund to overcome the attorney-client privilege asserted by the fund's trustees. Moreover, a number of courts have applied *Garner's* "good cause" exception in class actions. In this regard, however, the Ninth Circuit in *Weil v. Investment/Indicators Research & Management,* 647 F.2d 18, 23 (9th Cir. 1981), limited *Garner* to shareholder derivative actions, reasoning: "The *Garner* plaintiffs sought damages from [the] defendants on behalf of the corporation, whereas Weil seeks to recover damages from the corporation for herself and the members of her proposed class."[77]

[B] "Limited" Waiver Concept

Permian Corp. v. United States

United States Court of Appeals, District of Columbia Circuit

665 F.2d 1214 (1981)

MIKVA, CIRCUIT JUDGE.

This is an appeal from a permanent injunction barring the Securities and Exchange Commission ("SEC") from providing the United States Department of Energy with access to certain documents obtained from Occidental Petroleum Corporation and its subsidiary The Permian Corporation (denominated collectively as "Occidental"). The district court found that these documents were subject to the attorney-client and work product privileges, and that Occidental's arrangements for delivery of these documents to the SEC did not constitute a waiver of the privileges.

We conclude that the district court's finding of an agreement to preserve the work product privilege was not clearly erroneous. We also find, however, that Occidental waived the attorney-client privilege as to the documents by voluntarily disclosing them to the SEC. Accordingly, we affirm the district court's judgment in part, and we reverse and remand in part.

---

77. *See* O'Neal & Thompson, *Vulnerability of Professional-Client Privilege in Shareholder Litigation,* 31 Bus. Law. 1775 (1976). *See generally* M. Steinberg & R. Ferrara, Securities Practice: Federal and State Enforcement § 11.01 *et seq.* (2d ed. 2001 & 2017 supp.); Block & Barton, *Internal Corporate Investigations: Maintaining the Confidentiality of a Corporate Client's Communications with Investigative Counsel,* 35 Bus. Law. 5 (1979); Cole, *Revoking Our Privileges: Federal Law Enforcement's Multi-Front Assault on the Attorney-Client Privilege (And Why It Is Misguided),* 48 Vill. L. Rev. 469 (2003); Kenny & Mitchelson, *Corporate Benefits of Properly Conducted Internal Investigations,* 11 Ga. St. L. Rev. 657 (1995); Gergacz, *Attorney-Corporate Client Privilege,* 37 Bus. Law. 461 (1982); Schipani, *The Future of the Attorney-Client Privilege in Corporate Criminal Investigations,* 34 Del. J. Corp. L. 921 (2009); Mathews, *Internal Corporate Investigations,* 45 Ohio St. L.J. 655 (1984); Pitt & Morley, *Corporate Introspection in the Nineties: "To Thine Own Self Be True,"* 21 Sec. Reg. L.J. 148 (1993); Rosenfeld, *The Transformation of the Attorney-Client Privilege,* 33 Hastings L.J. 495 (1982); Schipani, *The Future of the Attorney-Client Privilege in Corporate Criminal Investigations,* 36 Del. J. Corp. L. 921 (2009); Sexton, *A Post-Upjohn Consideration of the Corporate Attorney-Client Privilege,* 57 N.Y.U. L. Rev. 443 (1982); Steinberg & Rogers, *The Joint Defense Doctrine in Federal Securities Litigation,* 18 Sec. Reg. L.J. 339 (1991).

I. THE FACTUAL CONTEXT

Most of the facts are undisputed. In 1978, Occidental proposed an exchange offer for shares of the Mead Corporation ("Mead"). Mead's management opposed the proposal, and initiated litigation in various courts. Occidental produced millions of documents in response to Mead discovery requests, but sought to preserve claims of privilege and confidentiality, at first by painstaking screening and later with the additional protection of a stipulation between Occidental and Mead providing that inadvertent production of a privileged document would not constitute a waiver of the privilege. Shortly thereafter, an order was entered in one of the federal district courts where the takeover litigation was proceeding, requiring both Mead and Occidental to give each other forty-eight hours' notice before submitting any potentially confidential document of the opponent to a state or federal regulatory agency, and requiring court permission for the submission if the opponent objected.

Meanwhile, Occidental was involved with the SEC, which was inquiring into the adequacy of Occidental's registration statement for the proposed exchange offer. Occidental was understandably concerned that the SEC approve the registration statement and permit it to become effective as soon as possible, so that the offer could be made. The SEC began an informal investigation of certain factual issues, including problems raised by counsel for Mead.

Occidental made available to the SEC some 1.2 million pages of documents. The sheer bulk of this response impaired its usefulness to the SEC, and SEC staff requested Occidental's permission "to secure the confidential Occidental information directly from Mead which had organized them around its adversarial issues and claims." The SEC made it clear that processing of the registration statement would be greatly facilitated by access to Occidental documents pre-sifted by Mead; without that access, considerable delay could result. The district court found that "[t]o avoid such delay Occidental's counsel negotiated with the SEC staff and Mead a procedure whereby the Commission would obtain confidential documents directly and expeditiously from Mead."

The nature of the resulting agreement was disputed in the district court. The record includes four letters from Occidental's counsel, three addressed to SEC staff and one addressed to counsel for Mead. The first two letters set forth a scheme for special handling of Occidental documents. Mead was permitted to deliver documents it had received in discovery to the SEC, but Mead was to inform Occidental within forty-eight hours of the identity of any documents delivered. All documents were to be stamped with a restrictive endorsement warning against disclosure by the SEC.[78] The SEC agreed not to

---

[78] The stamps read:

This Document constitutes a Trade Secret and/or Commercial or Financial Information which is Privileged and Confidential and may not be Released or Disclosed. Pursuant to procedures adopted by Occidental & the Securities & Exchange Commission, this Document may not be disclosed by the Commission to any third-party unless prior notice of such proposed disclosure has been given to Occidental.

deliver any of the Documents to any person other than a member of the Commission or the Staff or any other government agencies, offices or bodies or to the Congress for a reasonable period of time after notice to Occidental of the Staff's intention to deliver the Documents to such person.

. . . .

The other two letters, both from December 1978, suggest a less protective attitude towards the confidentiality of the documents. The district court found, however, that these letters formed part of a negotiation between Occidental and the SEC for a new arrangement that was never completed, and that they did not supersede the earlier agreement.

The letters evidencing Occidental's understandings with Mead and the SEC do not explicitly state that the SEC was forbidden to release confidential Occidental information to other government agencies. Counsel for Occidental stated, however, in an affidavit submitted to the district court, that "there was an oral understanding that Occidental would be advised as to governmental requests notwithstanding the letter," and that the terms of Occidental's agreement with the SEC "included [his] preclearance of the language of the stamped legends with the SEC staff." Occidental argued that this scheme was designed to permit assertion of claims of privilege whenever the SEC attempted to disclose Occidental data received from Mead to any third party. The district court found, "[f]rom all that has been submitted by the parties, including affidavits and declarations, . . . that this arrangement was an essential element of the discussions between the SEC staff and Occidental."

Mead submitted "somewhat fewer than 1,000 documents" to the SEC between October and December, 1978, when Occidental abandoned its proposed exchange offer. Among these were the thirty-six documents at issue in the present case, all written by Permian Corporation employees or Permian's outside counsel. Most of them relate to the legality of Permian's pricing practices for crude oil. The district court concluded that seven of these documents were protected in whole or in part by the attorney-client privilege, and that the other twenty-nine were privileged as attorney work product. The United States does not challenge the privileged character of the documents on appeal; it argues only that the privileges in question had been waived.

It appears that the thirty-six documents were all in the SEC's hands by December 8, 1978, and that Occidental was informed of this fact by December 11. In January 1979, the Department of Energy sought the documents from the SEC for use in an investigation of Permian's compliance with petroleum pricing regulations. Occidental promptly objected, and when the SEC reaffirmed its determination to release the documents to the Department of Energy in August 1979, Occidental commenced the present action.

II. DISCUSSION

We turn first to the twenty-nine documents that the district court found to be attorney work product. Appellants' only argument concerning these documents is that the district court's finding that Occidental had not waived the work product privilege was clearly erroneous. Appellants insist that the evidence demonstrates "that Occidental, although it may have preserved its privilege claims vis-a-vis non-governmental entities, clearly and intentionally waived its privilege claims vis-a-vis government agencies."

The documentary evidence available concerning Occidental's arrangements with the SEC is ambiguous. Occidental's September 22 letter to the SEC could be construed to permit release of Occidental data to other government agencies without notification to Occidental, and that letter is cited in the October 17 letter authorizing Mead to supply documents to the SEC. On the other hand, the October 17 letter also speaks more generally of stamps "in accordance with terms and conditions arranged between the [SEC] and Occidental," and the stamped legends refer broadly to disclosure by the SEC "to any third-party." These letters are not inconsistent with the existence of an oral agreement between Occidental and the SEC, worked out in October, by which the SEC agreed to limit confidential documents submitted by Mead to its own use, and to afford Occidental an opportunity to raise claims of privilege before disclosure to all third parties. Occidental's counsel asserted that such an agreement existed.

Appellants rely heavily on certain passages in Occidental's December letters to the SEC, but the district court found that these letters were part of a process of negotiation intended to lead to a modified agreement between the SEC and Occidental, a process that was never completed. Meanwhile, the court found "the former agreement of October, 1978 remained in effect." Again, the December letters are not inconsistent with this interpretation.

Appellants reject the district court's factual findings and ask this court to overturn them. By Fed. R. Civ. P. 52(a), this would require a conclusion that the district court's findings are "clearly erroneous." . . . We cannot say that appellants have met their burden in this case. The district court's reading of the December letters as groping for a new arrangement rather than restating existing understandings reflects a reasonable interpretation of their language in the factual context. The crucial October 17 letter is not inconsistent with Mr. Juceam's representations to the district court that there were further oral arrangements between himself and SEC staff. The SEC affidavits contradicting Mr. Juceam's account raise issues of credibility, and we are unable to say for certain that the district court resolved them erroneously. . . .

Our conclusion that the district court's finding of an agreement was not clearly erroneous applies not only to the work product privilege, but also to the attorney-client privilege. Nothing in the evidence suggests that the SEC or Occidental intended to treat these privileges differently. This finding, however, is not dispositive of the claim that Occidental's attorney-client privilege has been waived, because the legal significance of Occidental's arrangements for the question of waiver depends on the nature of the privilege asserted. This court has recently had occasion to contrast the strict standard of waiver in the attorney-client privilege context with the more liberal standard applicable to the work product privilege:

The attorney-client privilege exists to protect confidential communications, to assure the client that any statements he makes in seeking legal advice will be kept strictly confidential between him and his attorney; in effect, to protect the attorney-client relationship. Any voluntary disclosure by the holder of such a privilege is inconsistent with the confidential relationship and thus waives the privilege.

By contrast, the work product privilege does not exist to protect a confidential relationship, but rather to promote the adversary system by safeguarding the fruits of an attorney's trial preparations from the discovery attempts of the opponent. . . . A disclosure made in the pursuit of such trial preparation, and not inconsistent with maintaining secrecy against opponents, should be allowed without waiver of the privilege. We conclude, then, that while the mere showing of a voluntary disclosure to a third person will generally suffice to show waiver of the attorney-client privilege, it should not suffice in itself for waiver of the work product privilege.

United States v. AT&T, 642 F.2d 1285, 1299 (D.C. Cir. 1980).

In the present case, Occidental has destroyed the confidential status of the seven attorney-client communications by permitting their disclosure to the SEC staff. Whatever the truth may be concerning Occidental's arrangement to prevent release or disclosure of these documents to third parties by the SEC, there is no evidence in the record suggesting attempts to prevent their use by the SEC staff in the processing of Occidental's registration statement. Even after Occidental was specifically informed by Mead that the privileged documents had been submitted, Occidental did not request that they be returned unread. Occidental's eventual objections concerned only disclosure of the documents to the Department of Energy. Under these circumstances "it is clear that the mantle of confidentiality which once protected the documents has been so irretrievably breached that an effective waiver of the privilege has been accomplished."[79]

Occidental asks this court to create an exception to the traditional standard for waiver by adopting the "limited waiver" theory of *Diversified Industries, Inc. v. Meredith*, 572 F.2d 596 (8th Cir. 1977) (en banc). In that case, the Eighth Circuit stated:

We finally address the issue of whether Diversified waived its attorney-client privilege with respect to the privileged material by voluntarily

---

[79] Occidental's disclosures through Mead to the SEC were not inadvertent within the meaning of the doctrine recognized by some courts that preserves privilege claims when inadvertent disclosure is made despite diligent precautions in massive expedited discovery. *See, e.g., Transamerica Computer Co. v. IBM*, 573 F.2d 646 (9th Cir. 1978). . . . Occidental's initial delivery of these documents to Mead may have been inadvertent, but Occidental did not thereafter take necessary steps to preserve privilege claims as against the SEC before Mead's delivery of the documents. Nor did Occidental act to assert a privilege against the SEC when notified of the identity of the Mead submissions, though less than 1000 documents were involved.

surrendering it to the SEC pursuant to an agency subpoena. As Diversified disclosed these documents in a separate and nonpublic SEC investigation, we conclude that only a limited waiver of the privilege occurred. . . . To hold otherwise may have the effect of thwarting the developing procedure of corporations to employ independent outside counsel to investigate and advise them in order to protect stockholders, potential stockholders and customers.

. . . The Fourth Circuit has declined to apply *Diversified Industries* to grand jury proceedings following an SEC investigation, *In re Weiss*, 596 F.2d 1185 (4th Cir. 1979), and we find the "limited waiver" theory wholly unpersuasive.

First, we cannot see how the availability of a "limited waiver" would serve the interests underlying the common law privilege for confidential communications between attorney and client. As the Supreme Court has recently reiterated, "[t]he privilege recognizes that sound legal advice or advocacy serves public ends and that such advice or advocacy depends upon the lawyer being fully informed by the client"; the attorney's 'assistance can only be safely and readily availed of when free from the consequences or the apprehension of disclosure.'" The privilege depends on the assumption that full and frank communication will be fostered by the assurance of confidentiality, and the justification for granting the privilege "ceases when the client does not appear to have been desirous of secrecy." 8 J. Wigmore, *Evidence* § 2311, at 599 (McNaughton rev. 1961). The Eighth Circuit's "limited waiver" rule has little to do with this confidential link between the client and his legal advisor.[80] Voluntary cooperation with government investigations may be a laudable activity, but it is hard to understand how such conduct improves the attorney-client relationship. If the client feels the need to keep his communications with his attorney confidential, he is free to do so under the traditional rule by consistently asserting the privilege, even when the discovery request comes from a "friendly" agency.

Because the attorney-client privilege inhibits the truth-finding process, it has been narrowly construed, and courts have been vigilant to prevent litigants from converting the privilege into a tool for selective disclosure. . . . The client cannot be permitted to pick and choose among his opponents, waiving the privilege for some and resurrecting the claim of confidentiality to obstruct others, or to invoke the privilege as to communications whose confidentiality he has already compromised for his own benefit. In the present case, Occidental has been willing to sacrifice confidentiality in order to expedite approval of the exchange offer, and now asserts that the secrecy of the attorney-client relationship precludes disclosure of the same documents

---

[80] Unlike the Eighth Circuit, we cannot see how "the developing procedure of corporations to employ independent outside counsel to investigate and advise them" would be thwarted by telling a corporation that it cannot disclose the resulting reports to the SEC if it wishes to remain their confidentiality.

in other administrative litigation.[81] The attorney-client privilege is not designed for such tactical employment.

Finally, we reject the argument that some public policy imperative inherent in the SEC's regulatory program requires that the traditional waiver doctrine be overridden. Occidental insists that this court should respect the attempts that Occidental and the SEC made to "accommodate[] each other's interest — a mutual interest — in the integrity of the Commission's investigatory and registration processes." Important though the SEC's mission may be, we are aware of no congressional directive or judicially-recognized priority system that places a higher value on cooperation with the SEC than on cooperation with other regulatory agencies, including the Department of Energy. At least one district court has viewed the "limited waiver" doctrine as extending beyond SEC inquiries to Internal Revenue Service and grand jury investigations, see *In re Grand Jury Subpoena Dated July 13, 1979*, 478 F. Supp. 368 (E.D. Wis. 1979); we agree that the doctrine's rationale would dictate a wide scope of application for the "limited waiver." It is apparent that such a doctrine would enable litigants to pick and choose among regulatory agencies in disclosing and withholding communications of tarnished confidentiality for their own purposes. We believe that the attorney-client privilege should be available only at the traditional price: a litigant who wishes to assert confidentiality must maintain genuine confidentiality.

We therefore conclude that Occidental has waived any protection that the attorney-client privilege might once have afforded to any of the thirty-six documents in question. Regardless of Occidental's intent to preserve the privilege as against its adversary the Department of Energy, Occidental's disclosure of these documents to the SEC was incompatible with the continued survival of the privilege.

III. CONCLUSION

The district court found that twenty-nine of the thirty-six documents were subject to the work product privilege, and that this privilege had not been waived. The record does not compel such a conclusion, but the finding is not clearly erroneous and must be affirmed. The district court made no findings, however, concerning the privileged status of the other seven documents, except its finding that they were shielded by the attorney-client privilege which we hold Occidental has waived by its voluntary disclosure to the SEC. We therefore affirm the district court's judgment barring release of the twenty-nine work product documents, and remand for further

---

[81] It is true that Occidental's waiver of the privilege with respect to the SEC is implied from its conduct, not express, but both forms are equally binding. *In re Grand Jury Investigation of Ocean Transportation*, 604 F.2d at 675. We cannot agree with the district court's hint that "Occidental's decision to allow Mead to supply the documents to the SEC [was] less than wholly voluntary" because the SEC had indicated it would expedite processing of the registration statement. If Occidental's massive and amorphous response to the SEC's information requests necessitated lengthy review (and Occidental has not alleged insincerity or bad faith in the SEC's negotiation), then Occidental's acquiescence can only be attributed to its own preference for swifter approval of the registration statement at the risk of disclosure of confidential communications.

consideration of the remaining seven documents in proceedings not inconsistent with this opinion.

It is so ordered.

Note

As the federal appellate court observed in *Permian*, a number of courts (although constituting a minority view) have adopted the "limited" waiver rationale. Do you agree with the *Permian* court's reasoning for rejecting this concept? Consider the following:

> The *Permian* court did not consider either the equities of the limited waiver or the realities of corporate interaction with the government, to which the limited waiver is tailored. A more realistic disposition of the *Permian* case would have resulted had the court recognized that corporations and government agencies mutually benefit from an application of limited waiver. Voluntary corporate disclosures to government agencies, made under the assurance of a limited waiver, avoid unnecessary, time-consuming, and costly discovery and promote the efficient administration of justice. It should be evident that "voluntary disclosures to agencies should be encouraged rather than requiring that agency requests or subpoenas be fought to the hilt." . . . The limited waiver also encourages corporations to seek out and correct internal wrongdoing and thereby benefits government agencies by alleviating the investigatory burdens on those agencies.[82]

---

§ 15.12 Parallel Proceedings

Securities and Exchange Commission v. Dresser Industries, Inc.

United States Court of Appeals, District of Columbia Circuit

628 F.2d 1368 (1980) (En Banc)

J. SKELLY WRIGHT, CHIEF JUDGE.

Dresser Industries, Inc. (Dresser) appeals from a decision of the District Court requiring obedience to a *subpoena duces tecum* issued by the Securities and Exchange Commission (SEC) on April 21, 1978, and denying Dresser's motion to quash the subpoena. The subpoena was issued in connection with an SEC investigation into Dresser's use of corporate funds to make what are euphemistically called

---

82. Note, *Permian Corporation v. United States and the Attorney-Client Privilege for Corporations: Unjustified Severity on the Issue of Waiver*, 77 Nw. U. L. Rev. 223, 243 (1982).

"questionable foreign payments," and into the adequacy of Dresser's disclosures of such payments under the securities laws.

The principal issue facing this *en banc* court is whether Dresser is entitled to special protection against this SEC subpoena because of a parallel investigation into the same questionable foreign payments now being conducted by a federal grand jury under the guidance of the United States Department of Justice (Justice). Dresser argues principally that the SEC subpoena abuses the civil discovery process of the SEC for the purpose of criminal discovery and infringes the role of the grand jury in independently investigating allegations of criminal wrongdoing. On November 19, 1979 a panel of this court issued a decision affirming the District Court but, with Judge Robb dissenting, attaching a condition prohibiting the SEC from providing Justice with the information received from Dresser under this subpoena. Because of the importance of this issue to enforcement of the regulatory laws of the United States, this court voted to vacate the panel opinions and rehear the case *en banc*.

I. BACKGROUND

A. *Origin of the Investigations*

Illegal and questionable corporate payments surfaced as a major public problem in late 1973, when several major scandals implicated prominent American corporations in improper use of corporate funds to influence government officials in the United States and foreign countries. The exposure of these activities disrupted public faith in the integrity of our political system and eroded international trust in the legitimacy of American corporate operations abroad.[83] SEC investigation revealed that many corporate officials were falsifying financial records to shield questionable foreign and domestic payments from exposure to the public and even, in many cases, to corporate directors and accountants. Since the completeness and accuracy of corporate financial reporting is the cornerstone of federal regulation of the securities markets, such falsification became a matter of grave concern to the SEC.

Beginning in the spring of 1974 the SEC brought a series of injunctive actions against certain American corporations. It obtained consent decrees prohibiting future violations of the securities laws and establishing internal corporate procedures for investigation, disclosure, and prevention of illegal corporate payments. However, the problem of questionable foreign payments proved so widespread that the SEC devised a "Voluntary Disclosure Program" to encourage corporations to conduct

---

[83] The Senate Committee on Banking, Housing, and Urban Affairs reported in May 1977:
Recent investigations by the SEC have revealed corrupt foreign payments by over 300 U.S. companies involving hundreds of millions of dollars. These revelations have had severe adverse effects. Foreign governments friendly to the United States in Japan, Italy, and the Netherlands have come under intense pressure from their own people. The image of American democracy abroad has been tarnished. Confidence in the financial integrity of our corporations has been impaired. The efficient functioning of our capital markets has been hampered.
S. Rep. No. 114, 95th Cong., 1st Sess. 3 (1977).

investigations of their past conduct and make appropriate disclosures without direct SEC coercion. Participation in the Voluntary Disclosure Program would not insulate a corporation from an SEC enforcement action, but the Commission would be less likely to exercise its discretion to initiate enforcement actions against participants. The most important elements of the Voluntary Disclosure Program were (1) an independent committee of the corporation would conduct a thorough investigation into questionable foreign and domestic payments made by the corporation; (2) the committee would disclose the results of this investigation to the board of directors in full; (3) the corporation would disclose the substance of the report to the public and the SEC on Form 8-K; and (4) the corporation would issue a policy statement prohibiting future questionable and illegal payments and maintenance of false or incomplete records in connection with them. Except in "egregious cases" the SEC would not require that public disclosures include specific names, dates, and places. Rather, the disclosures might be "generic" in form. Thus companies participating in the Voluntary Disclosure Program would ordinarily be spared the consequences to their employees, property, and business that might result from public disclosure of specific instances of foreign bribery or kickbacks. However, companies participating in the Voluntary Disclosure Program had to agree to grant SEC requests for access to the final report and to the unexpurgated underlying documentations.

B. The Dresser Investigations

On January 27, 1976 an attorney and other representatives of Dresser met with members of the SEC staff to discuss a proposed filing. At the meeting Dresser agreed to conduct an internal inquiry into questionable foreign payments, in accordance with the terms of the Voluntary Disclosure Program. The next day Dresser submitted a Form 8-K describing, in generic terms, one questionable foreign payment. On November 11, 1976 Dresser filed a second Form 8-K reporting the results of the internal investigation. On February 10, 1977 the company supplemented this report with a third Form 8-K concerning a questionable payment not reported in the earlier reports. The reports concerned Dresser's foreign activities after November 1, 1973. All disclosures were in generic, not specific, terms.

As part of its general monitoring program the SEC staff requested access to the documents underlying Dresser's report. On July 15, 1977 Dresser refused to grant such access. The company argued that allowing the staff to make notes or copies might subject its documents to public disclosure through the Freedom of Information Act. Dresser stated that such disclosure could endanger certain of its employees working abroad. During the ensuing discussions with the staff Dresser attempted to impose conditions of confidentially upon any SEC examination of its documents, but the staff did not agree. Instead, it issued a recommendation to the Commission for a formal order of investigation in the Dresser case. This recommendation was predicated on the staff's conclusions that Dresser:

1. may have used corporate funds for non-corporate purposes;

2. may have made false and misleading statements concerning the existence of and circumstances surrounding material obligations of Dresser to certain foreign governments and to other entities; and

3. may have made false entries and caused false entries to be made upon the books and records of Dresser, and its affiliates and subsidiaries with respect to, among other things, payments to foreign government officials.

. . . . Moreover, the staff reported that Dresser's proxy soliciting materials, reports, and statements may have been misleading with respect to the potential risks involved in its conduct of business through questionable foreign payments, and may have included false statements in connection with such payments. Dresser vigorously opposed issuance of an order of investigation.

Meanwhile, the Department of Justice had established a task force on transnational payments to investigate possible criminal violations arising from illegal foreign payments. Two SEC attorneys participated in the task force. In the summer of 1977 the Justice task force requested access to SEC files on the approximately 400 companies, including Dresser, that had participated in the Voluntary Disclosure Program. Pursuant to Commission authorization the SEC staff transmitted all such files to the Justice task force in August 1977. After its preliminary investigation of the Form 8-K's submitted by Dresser under the Voluntary Disclosure Program, Justice presented Dresser's case to a grand jury in the District of Columbia on January 25, 1978.

. . . [T]he District of Columbia grand jury subpoenaed Dresser's documents on April 21, 1978. At roughly the same time the SEC issued a formal order of private investigation, authorizing the staff to subpoena the documents and to obtain other relevant evidence. Pursuant to that order the staff issued a subpoena duces tecum. . . . This subpoena covered substantially the same documents and materials subpoenaed by the grand jury, and more. Dresser did not respond to the subpoena.

. . . .

II. GENERAL PRINCIPLES

A. Parallel Investigations

The civil and regulatory laws of the United States frequently overlap with the criminal laws, creating the possibility of parallel civil and criminal proceedings, either successive or simultaneous. In the absence of substantial prejudice to the rights of the parties involved, such parallel proceedings are unobjectionable under our jurisprudence. As long ago as 1912 the Supreme Court recognized that under one statutory scheme—that of the Sherman Act—a transaction or course of conduct could give rise to both criminal proceedings and civil suits. *Standard Sanitary Manufacturing Co. v. United States,* 226 U.S. 20 (1912). The Court held that the government could initiate such proceedings either "simultaneously or successively," with discretion in the courts to prevent injury in particular cases. It explained:

The Sherman Act provides for a criminal proceeding to punish violations and suits in equity to restrain such violations, and the suits may be brought simultaneously or successively. The order of their bringing must depend upon the Government; the dependence of their trials cannot be fixed by a hard and fast rule or made imperatively to turn upon the character of the suit. Circumstances may determine and are for the consideration of the court. An imperative rule that the civil suit must await the trial of the criminal action might result in injustice or take from the statute a great deal of its power. . . .

The Supreme Court returned to this theme in *United States v. Kordel*, 397 U.S. 1 (1970). In that case the Food and Drug Administration (FDA) investigated a company and certain of its officers in connection with possible violations of the Federal Food, Drug, and Cosmetic Act, 21 U.S.C. § 301 *et seq.* Early in the investigation the FDA recommended and the United States Attorney filed an *in rem* action in federal district court seeking civil seizure of certain products. In connection with this suit the FDA filed extensive interrogatories with the company. Before the company had responded the FDA notified it that the agency was contemplating a criminal proceeding against it in connection with the same alleged violations of the statute. The company therefore moved to stay civil proceedings or, in the alternative, to extend the time for answering the interrogatories until after disposition of the criminal proceedings. [Subsequently criminal convictions were obtained.]

The officers [convicted] in *Kordel* argued that use of the civil discovery process to compel answers to interrogatories that could be used to build the government's case in a parallel criminal proceeding "reflected such unfairness and want of consideration for justice" as to require reversal. The Supreme Court did not agree. The Court noted that the government had not brought the civil action "solely to obtain evidence for its criminal prosecution," or without notice to the defendants that it contemplated a criminal action. Moreover, the defendant was not unrepresented by counsel and had no reason to fear "prejudice from adverse pretrial publicity or other unfair injury." Nor were there any other "special circumstances" suggesting that the parallel proceedings were unconstitutional or improper. In the absence of such "special circumstances" the Court recognized that prompt investigation of both civil and criminal claims can be necessary to the public interest.

. . .

The Constitution, therefore, does not ordinarily require a stay of civil proceedings pending the outcome of criminal proceedings. Nevertheless, a court may decide in its discretion to stay civil proceedings, postpone civil discovery, or impose protective orders and conditions "when the interests of justice seem[] to require such action, sometimes at the request of the prosecution, . . . sometimes at the request of the defense[.]" . . . The court must make such determinations in the light of the particular circumstances of the case.

Other than where there is specific evidence of agency bad faith or malicious governmental tactics, the strongest case for deferring civil proceedings until after completion of criminal proceedings is where a party under indictment for a serious offense is required to defend a civil or administrative action involving the same matter. The noncriminal proceeding, if not deferred, might undermine the party's Fifth Amendment privilege against self-incrimination, expand rights of criminal discovery beyond the limits of Federal Rule of Criminal Procedure 16(b), expose the basis of the defense to the prosecution in advance of criminal trial, or otherwise prejudice the case.[84] If delay of the noncriminal proceeding would not seriously injure the public interest, a court may be justified in deferring it. . . . In some such cases, however, the courts may adequately protect the government and the private party by merely deferring civil discovery or entering an appropriate protective order. The case at bar is a far weaker one for staying the administrative investigation. No indictment has been returned; no Fifth Amendment privilege is threatened; Rule 16(b) has not come into effect; and the SEC subpoena does not require Dresser to reveal the basis for its defense.

B. SEC Investigations

The case at bar concerns enforcement of the securities laws of the United States, especially the Securities Act of 1933 and the Securities Exchange Act of 1934. These statutes explicitly empower the SEC to investigate possible infractions of the securities laws with a view to both civil and criminal enforcement, and to transmit the fruits of its investigations to Justice in the event of potential criminal proceedings. The '34 Act provides in relevant part: "The Commission may, in its discretion, make such investigations as it deems necessary to determine whether any person has violated, is violating, or is about to violate any provision of this chapter[.]" Section 21(a) of the '34 Act. . . . This investigative authority includes the power to administer oaths and affirmations, subpoena witnesses, take evidence, and require production of any books, papers, correspondence, memoranda, or other records which the SEC deems relevant or material. If it determines that a person "is engaged or is about to engage in acts or practices constituting a violation" of the Act, the SEC may bring an action in federal district court to enjoin such acts or practices. Under the same subsection of the '34 Act the SEC may "transmit such evidence as may be available concerning such acts or practices . . . to the Attorney General, who may, in his discretion, institute the necessary criminal proceedings under this chapter." The '33 Act is to similar effect.

Effective enforcement of the securities laws requires that the SEC and Justice be able to investigate possible violations simultaneously. Dissemination of false or misleading information by companies to members of the investing public may distort the efficient workings of the securities markets and injure investors who rely on the accuracy and completeness of the company's public disclosures. If the SEC suspects that a company has violated the securities laws, it must be able to respond quickly: it must be able to obtain relevant information concerning the alleged violation and

---

[84] In some cases, the government seeks postponement of the noncriminal proceeding, to prevent the criminal defendant from broadening his rights of criminal discovery against the government.

to seek prompt judicial redress if necessary. Similarly, Justice must act quickly if it suspects that the laws have been broken. Grand jury investigations take time, as do criminal prosecutions. If Justice moves too slowly the statute of limitations may run, witnesses may die or move away, memories may fade, or enforcement resources may be diverted. The SEC cannot always wait for Justice to complete the criminal proceedings if it is to obtain the necessary prompt civil remedy; neither can Justice always await the conclusion of the civil proceeding without endangering its criminal case. Thus we should not block parallel investigations by these agencies in the absence of "special circumstances" in which the nature of the proceedings demonstrably prejudices substantial rights of the investigated party or of the government.

. . . .

IV. COOPERATION BETWEEN SEC AND JUSTICE

In its initial decision in this case, a panel of this court . . . affirmed the District Court and ordered enforcement of the SEC subpoena. Out of a concern that the SEC subpoena might somehow "subvert the limitations of criminal discovery," however, the panel, with one judge dissenting, modified the terms of the subpoena enforcement order. It required that "once the Justice Department initiates criminal proceedings by means of a grand jury, the SEC may not provide the Justice Department with the fruits of the Commission's civil discovery gathered after the decision to prosecute." We affirm the judgment of the District Court and reject the panel's modification.

First, we note that no party to this case had suggested or requested a modification such as that imposed by the panel majority, either in the District Court or in this court. In supplemental briefs submitted to the *en banc* court both the SEC and Justice vigorously oppose the modification, while Dresser's support for it is lukewarm at most. Dresser had argued that the SEC investigation is flatly prohibited. . . . The reactions of the parties, therefore, suggest that the panel's modification might serve more to impede securities law enforcement than to protect the interests of Dresser.

Second, we note that there is no support for the panel's modification in either the relevant statutes or legislative history. Both the '33 Act and the '34 Act—and other statutes related to securities law enforcement as well—expressly authorize the SEC to "transmit such evidence as may be available . . . to the Attorney General, who may, in his discretion, institute the necessary criminal proceedings under this subchapter." The statutes impose no limitation on when this transmittal may occur. The parties have not cited any portions of the legislative histories of these Acts relevant to this question, nor have we found any. But the SEC and Justice find considerable support for their interpretation in the legislative history of the Foreign Corrupt Practices Act of 1977.

The Foreign Corrupt Practices Act outlaws corporate bribery of foreign officials and inaccurate or misleading financial recordkeeping. In passing the statute Congress recognized the role of the SEC in combating such practices under the '33 and '34 Acts, and sought to "strengthen the Commission's ability to enforce compliance with the existing requirements of the securities laws[.]" Both the Senate and the House reports on the bill acknowledged the SEC's dual investigative role in preparing cases for civil and criminal enforcement actions. They also recognize the necessity of close cooperation between the SEC and Justice in preparing such cases. . . .

Although the legislative history of the Foreign Corrupt Practices Act is not directly probative of congressional intent governing the '33 and '34 Acts, these statements by the 95th Congress are nevertheless entitled to some weight. The remarks in the committee reports concerning the investigative practices of the SEC and Justice were not intended to change, but to reaffirm, past practice. This indicates that Congress understands and approves of the "close working relationship" between the agencies in their investigative capacities. Since such a "close working relationship" will govern the activities of the agencies in enforcing the laws against questionable foreign payments under the new statute, it would be impractical for us to attempt to screen the agencies from each other when they are investigating the same sort of offense under the former statutes.

Congress manifestly did not intend that the SEC be forbidden to share information with Justice at this stage of the investigation. Under the panel majority's theory of the case the SEC would be foreclosed from sharing the fruits of its investigation with Justice as soon as Justice begins its own investigation through a grand jury. Only by waiting until the close of the SEC proceeding before initiating its own grand jury investigation could Justice obtain access to the evidence procured by the SEC. In view of Congress' concern that the agencies share information "at the earliest stage of any investigation in order to insure that the evidence needed for a criminal prosecution does not become stale," and that the agencies avoid "a costly duplication of effort," it would be unreasonable to prevent a sharing of information at this point in the investigation.

Third, we note that there is little or no judicial precedent for the panel's modification. . . .

. . . .

Finally, we note that the panel's modification would serve no compelling purpose, and might interfere with enforcement of the securities laws by the SEC and Justice. . . .

. . . Thus this would be an inappropriate situation to impose a "prophylactic" rule against cooperation between the agencies. We believe the courts can prevent any injustice that may arise in the particular circumstances of parallel investigations in the future. We decline to adopt the position of the panel majority.

. . . .

Affirmed.

EDWARDS, CIRCUIT JUDGE, concurring.

I concur in the opinion of the court in this case. I wish to point out, however, that I do not read the court's opinion as expressing any view as to the proper outcome in a case of this sort *once an indictment has issued.* Once an indictment has issued, the policy interest expressed in *United States v. LaSalle National Bank*, 437 U.S. 298, 312 (1978), concerning the impermissibility of broadening the scope of criminal discovery through the summons authority of an agency, may come into play. I express no opinion as to whether or not the summons authority of a government agency may continue once an indictment has been issued or, if it may, whether protective conditions need be placed on the exercise of that power. These issues raise questions which are not presented here. The resolution of these questions, therefore, must await another day.

————————

Note

The *Dresser* decision fits within the general rule that parallel proceedings are prohibited or restricted only in "special circumstances." As the Fifth Circuit stated in *SEC v. First Financial Group of Texas, Inc.*, 659 F.2d 660, 666 (5th Cir. 1980): "There is no general federal constitutional, statutory, or common law rule barring the simultaneous prosecution of separate civil and criminal actions by different agencies against the same defendants involving the same transactions."

The *Dresser* court did not address whether the SEC may enforce an administrative subpoena in parallel proceedings after return of an indictment. The court and Judge Edwards in his concurrence, however, expressed concern over the potential for abuse in this context. What are these concerns? Should protective conditions be placed on the SEC's subpoena enforcement power after the grand jury has returned an indictment? What should be the scope of such a protective order?

Today, the potential adverse ramifications incurred from parallel proceedings no longer are confined to SEC-Department of Justice referral. As the *Permian* case contained in the preceding section aptly demonstrates, there is the distinct possibility that information transmitted to the SEC will be referred to other federal and state regulatory agencies. Moreover, pursuant to requests under the Freedom of Information Act, 5 U.S.C. §552, the Commission may release documents and other information to private litigants involving matters that previously were subject to SEC scrutiny. Hence, in today's expanding world of parallel proceedings, the adverse consequences that may flow from providing information to the SEC can be massive. *See generally* Pickholz, *The Expanding World of Parallel Proceedings*, 53 Temple L.Q. 1100 (1982); Steinberg & Brennan, *Parallel Proceedings*, 8 Corp. L. Rev. 335 (1985); Note, *Using Equitable Powers to Coordinate Parallel Civil and Criminal Actions*, 98 Harv. L. Rev. 1023 (1985).

In a more recent proceeding, *United States v. Stringer*, 408 F. Supp. 2d 1083, 1087–1088 (D. Ore. 2006), the district court dismissed the indictment. The court found that the Department of Justice's and the SEC's actions were so "grossly shocking and so outrageous as to violate the universal sense of justice." The court elaborated:

> The USAO [U.S. Attorney's Office] identified potential criminal liability and a few targets in the beginning of the investigation, and elected to

gather information through the SEC instead of conducting its own investigation. The government was concerned that the presence of a criminal investigation would halt the successful discovery by the SEC, witnesses would be less cooperative and more likely to invoke their constitutional rights, and that the rules of discovery would be invoked. . . . The government was aware that there was no parallel proceeding. . . . The strategy to conceal the criminal investigation from defendants was an abuse of the investigative process.

The Ninth Circuit reversed. *United States v. Stringer*, 521 F.3d 1189, 1196–1199 (9th Cir. 2008). The court reasoned:

District courts have occasionally suppressed evidence or dismissed indictments on due process grounds where the government made affirmative misrepresentations or conducted a civil investigation solely for purposes of advancing a criminal case. . . .

In this case, the district court concluded that the government should have told defendants of the criminal investigation and that it violated the standards laid down in *Kordel* when it failed to "advise defendants that it anticipated their criminal prosecution." It held that the government engaged in "trickery and deceit" . . .

In its appeal, the government argues that it had no legal duty to make any further disclosure of the existence of the pending criminal investigation. It points to the warnings in Form 1662 in which the government disclosed the possibility of criminal prosecution, and it stresses that it did not make any affirmative misrepresentations. . . .

The defendants argue that the district court properly held that the use of the evidence obtained by the SEC in a criminal prosecution would violate defendants' Fifth Amendment privilege against self-incrimination. The defendants were advised that the evidence could be used in a criminal investigation, but defendants did not invoke their Fifth Amendment privilege during the SEC investigation. The government on appeal correctly contends that defendants waived or forfeited their Fifth Amendment right against self-incrimination.

The privilege against self-incrimination protects an individual from being forced to provide information that might establish a direct link in a chain of evidence leading to his conviction. It may be waived if it is not affirmatively invoked. In *Minnesota v. Murphy* [465 U.S. 420 (1984)], the Supreme Court stressed that the privilege is lost if not affirmatively invoked, even if the defendant did not make a knowing and intelligent waiver. We have similarly stated that a "defendant's failure to invoke the privilege against self-incrimination waives a later claim of privilege." . . .

. . . .

The district court therefore erred in holding that defendants' waivers of the privilege were ineffective because they were not told of the U.S. Attorney's active involvement. The SEC Form 1662 used in this case alerts SEC investigative witnesses that the information can be used in a criminal proceeding. Defendants were on sufficient notice, and so were their attorneys. As one federal court has explained, all that was required was "sufficient notice . . . that any information could be used against [them] in a subsequent criminal proceeding." . . . That court emphasized that "SEC Form 1662 stated in no uncertain terms that the [g]overnment's request for information could be refused pursuant to the Fifth Amendment's protection against compelled self-incrimination." . . . We agree.

The SEC here went even further, warning each defendant at the beginning of each deposition that "the facts developed in this investigation might constitute violations of . . . criminal laws." Nonetheless, defendants proceeded to testify and failed to invoke their privilege against self-incrimination. Defendants have forfeited any claims that the use of their testimony against them in the criminal proceedings violates the privilege against self-incrimination.

The defendants next contend that the district court properly concluded that the government used the civil investigation solely to obtain evidence for a subsequent criminal prosecution, in violation of due process. The Supreme Court in *Kordel* made it clear that dual investigations must meet the requirements of the Fifth Amendment Due Process Clause. While holding that "[i]t would stultify the enforcement of federal law" to curtail the government's discretion to conduct dual investigations strategically, the Court suggested that a defendant may be entitled to a remedy where "the [g]overnment has brought a civil action solely to obtain evidence for its criminal prosecution." . . . In this case, the government argues that it did not violate defendants' due process rights because the civil investigation was not commenced solely to obtain evidence for a criminal prosecution.

It is significant to our analysis that the SEC began its civil investigation first and brought in the U.S. Attorney later. This tends to negate any likelihood that the government began the civil investigation in bad faith, as, for example, in order to obtain evidence for a criminal prosecution. . . . In *United States v. Unruh*, 855 F.2d 1363, 1374 (9th Cir. 1987), we held that a defendant was not entitled to dismissal of his indictment when the U.S. Department of the Treasury instituted its investigation before any indictment and in order to file its own civil complaint. . . .

A government official must not "affirmatively mislead" the subject of parallel civil and criminal investigations "into believing that the investigation is exclusively civil in nature and will not lead to criminal charges." . . . However, "we have consistently held that the failure of an IRS agent . . . to warn a taxpayer that an audit may have potential criminal ramifications does not render the search unreasonable." . . .

In this case, the SEC made no affirmative misrepresentations. The SEC did advise defendant of the possibility of criminal prosecution. The SEC engaged in no tricks to deceive defendants into believing that the investigation was exclusively civil in nature. The SEC's Form 1662 explicitly warned defendants that the civil investigation could lead to criminal charges against them: "Information you give may be used against you in any federal . . . civil or criminal proceeding brought by the Commission or any other agency." Defendants were represented by counsel, and the government provided counsel, so far as this record reflects, with accurate information. . . .

§ 15.13 International Enforcement

SEC Statement on International Enforcement Assistance (2012)

Enforcement cooperation is among the top priorities of the SEC's international program. Technological advances have facilitated the movement of capital across borders and increased investment opportunities for investors. However, these same advances also have enhanced the ability of those who prey on investors to transfer assets abroad or base their scams and fraudulent activities overseas in an effort to avoid detection and prosecution. As a consequence, securities regulators and other law enforcement and governmental agencies may find that reliance on domestic enforcement abilities is no longer sufficient to combat cross-border securities fraud. Strong international cooperation is vital to the quick, effective and appropriate resolution of international enforcement investigations.

SEC Framework for International Cooperation and Assistance

The SEC was among the first securities regulators to receive the legal authority to assist foreign counterparts in investigations of securities fraud. Today, the SEC can assist foreign securities authorities in their investigations using a variety of tools, including exercising the SEC's compulsory powers to obtain documents and testimony, subject to the governing rules.

Use of Compulsory Powers

Section 21(a)(2) of the Securities Exchange Act of 1934 authorizes the SEC to conduct investigations on behalf of foreign securities authorities (as defined by the Exchange Act) and compel the production of documents and testimony from any person and entity, irrespective of whether that person or entity is regulated by the SEC. . . .

Subject to certain considerations including a foreign securities authority's ability to provide reciprocal assistance, whether fulfillment of the request would prejudice the public interest, and appropriate assurances of confidentiality, the SEC may in its discretion:

- Assist a wide range of authorities that meet the broad statutory definition of "foreign securities authorities" as defined in Section 3(a)(50) of the Securities Exchange Act of 1934.

- Provide assistance regardless of whether the conduct in question constitutes a violation of US law.

Access to Information in the SEC's Files

The SEC has the ability to provide access to non-public information in its files with foreign persons. Section 24(c) of the Exchange Act and 17 C.F.R. §240.24c-1 (Rule 24c-1) thereunder provide that the Commission may, in its discretion and upon a showing that such information is needed, provide such non-public information in its possession to specified foreign persons. The authority requesting such non-public information must establish and maintain such safeguards as are necessary and appropriate to protect the confidentiality of files to which access is granted and information derived therefrom, and provide assurances of confidentiality to the Commission. . . .

. . . .

Mechanisms for Information Sharing in Securities Enforcement Matters

The SEC has approached enforcement-related information sharing on a multilateral, bilateral, and *ad hoc* basis. Multilateral and bilateral information sharing arrangements operate on the basis of memoranda of understanding (MOU) between securities authorities. Such MOUs delineate the terms of information-sharing between and among MOU signatories and create a framework for regular and predictable cooperation in securities law enforcement. Multilateral and bilateral MOUs detail the scope and terms of information-sharing among securities regulators.

In addition to multilateral, bilateral, and *ad hoc* understandings, the SEC also uses other mechanisms to facilitate information sharing, such as requests to foreign criminal authorities through mutual legal assistance treaties (MLATs) administered by the U.S. Department of Justice, [and] formal letters rogatory between a U.S. court and foreign judicial authorities.

In fiscal year 2011, the SEC made 772 requests to foreign authorities for enforcement assistance and responded to 492 requests from foreign authorities.

IOSCO Multilateral Memorandum of Understanding

In 2002, the *International Organization of Securities Commissions* (IOSCO) created a *Multilateral Memorandum of Understanding* (MMOU), the first global multilateral information-sharing arrangement among securities regulators. The SEC was among the first signatories to the MMOU. As of 2012, 80 securities and derivatives regulators had become signatories to the MMOU and 34 additional IOSCO members had expressed their commitment to become signatories. (IOSCO Members).

Pursuant to the MMOU, signatories agree, among other items, to provide certain critical information, to permit use of that information in civil or administrative proceedings, to onward share information with self-regulatory organizations and criminal authorities, and to keep such information confidential. In particular, the MMOU provides for the following:

- Sharing information and documents held in the regulators' files;
- Obtaining information and documents regarding transactions in bank and brokerage accounts, and the beneficial owners of such accounts;
- Taking or compelling a person's statements or, where permissible, a person's testimony.

The MMOU has significantly enhanced the SEC's enforcement program by increasing and expediting the SEC's ability to obtain information from a growing number of jurisdictions worldwide. Moreover, the MMOU has created incentives for jurisdictions that lack the legal ability to engage in effective information sharing to enact legislation that will enable them to do so.

. . . .

Bilateral Memoranda of Understanding

Before the establishment of the IOSCO MMOU, the SEC signed bilateral information sharing MOUs with the securities authorities of 20 different countries. Bilateral MOUs have proven crucial to investigations undertaken by the Commission's enforcement staff and, as such, the SEC considers these bilateral arrangements to be an excellent supplement to the information sharing mechanism of the IOSCO MMOU. In light of the IOSCO MMOU, the SEC staff now strongly recommends the negotiation of bilateral MOUs only if a foreign securities authority is empowered to provide assistance beyond that required by the IOSCO MMOU such as the ability to compel testimony or the gathering of Internet service provider, phone and other records other than bank, broker, and beneficial owner information on behalf of the requesting authority. . . .

Generally, the bilateral MOUs contain detailed provisions on use and confidentiality of information. The assistance available under the current MOUs varies in scope depending on the underlying statutory authority of the regulators that are party to the MOU.

Ad Hoc & Other Arrangements for Enforcement Cooperation

Although MOUs and the MMOU facilitate enforcement cooperation, such arrangements are not a prerequisite for the SEC to cooperate with foreign authorities regarding enforcement matters. The SEC also has cooperated on an *ad hoc* basis with foreign regulators with whom it has no bilateral MOU or who are not yet signatories to IOSCO MMOU. In the past, such *ad hoc* arrangements have included communiqués and joint statements that express a desire to develop greater enforcement cooperation capabilities. The SEC also has entered into undertakings for the exchange of information where existing law in the foreign jurisdiction prevents information sharing to the extent set for the in the IOSCO MMOU.

Chapter 16

The Role of Counsel

§ 16.01 Overview

Throughout the text, the role of securities counsel has received extensive coverage. Nonetheless, given the importance of this subject, a separate chapter is merited. To review the pertinent issues discussed herein, consider the following:

- Counsel's role in helping to ensure the client's compliance with the law in private and public offerings. In this regard, materials treating the "burden of proof file" (Chapter 3), Sarbanes-Oxley compliance (Chapter 5), and due diligence procedures (Chapter 7) are on point.

- Counsel's status as a "seller" under § 12 of the Securities Act as well as under the state securities laws. See Chapters 7, 9.

- Counsel's liability exposure as a primary violator, aider and abettor, control person, and under *respondeat superior* principles under federal and state law. See the cases contained in Chapters 9 and 10.

- Counsel's role in representing a client in an SEC investigation. See the materials in various sections of Chapter 15.

[A] Sarbanes-Oxley and the SEC's Response

Largely due to massive corporate debacles that wreaked havoc on investors and the integrity of the U.S. securities markets, Congress enacted the Sarbanes-Oxley Act of 2002 (Sarbanes-Oxley or SOX). Among its many significant provisions, Congress mandated that the Securities and Exchange Commission (SEC) promulgate a rule focusing on attorney "up the ladder" reporting with respect to a corporate client, when faced with a material violation of fiduciary duty, securities law, or similar violation by a subject corporate constituent (such as a director, officer or employee). Following Congress' directive, the SEC in 2003 adopted standards of professional conduct.

These standards as well as those proposed (but not adopted) have generated zealous responses from the practicing securities bar, corporate executives, and academicians. Much of the discussion has dealt with whether the SEC should require counsel to make a "noisy withdrawal" when faced with client fraud (or similar material violation). At this time, it is unlikely that the Commission will adopt such a provision.

The following discussion provides a succinct overview relating to attorney standards under the Sarbanes-Oxley Act and the SEC's promulgation of applicable standards thereunder. Under § 307 of SOX, Congress directed the SEC to adopt a rule:

> (1) requiring [a subject] attorney to report evidence of a material violation of securities law or breach of fiduciary duty or similar violation by the company or any agent thereof, to the chief legal counsel or the chief executive officer of the company (or the equivalent thereof); and

> (2) if the counsel or officer does not appropriately respond to the evidence (adopting, as necessary, appropriate remedial measures or sanctions with respect to the violation), requiring [such] attorney to report the evidence to the audit committee of the board of directors of the issuer or to another committee of the board of directors comprised solely of directors not employed directly or indirectly by the issuer, or to the board of directors.

Section 307 and the SEC's response resemble to some extent existing ethical standards as set forth by the American Bar Association, the American Law Institute, and the states. Responding to Congress' directive, the SEC adopted standards implementing "up the ladder" reporting.[1] In its 2003 rule adoption, however, the Commission declined to adopt the attorney "noisy withdrawal" provisions as proposed by the SEC in an earlier release. Under this proposal, if the corporate client refused to take appropriate corrective action after counsel dutifully went "up the ladder," counsel was obliged to make a "noisy withdrawal," notifying the SEC that such counsel disaffirmed documents that he or she had prepared during the course of the representation.[2]

The making of a noisy withdrawal, of course, sounds a siren that fraud or other grievous misconduct likely is afoot. Corporate fiduciaries and the securities bar (as well as such groups as the American Bar Association) reacted with alarm, asserting that such a noisy withdrawal mandate would drive a wedge between attorneys and corporate insiders. Afraid that counsel would "blow the whistle" (albeit by action rather than words), constituents of the business enterprise would be reluctant to seek legal advice on troubling subjects. Thus, the proposed provision, according to opponents, would be quite detrimental. Proponents favoring a noisy withdrawal provision, on the other hand, assert that counsel must have this leverage in order to better ensure that corrective action is taken, thereby protecting the corporate client, its shareholders, and creditors. Hence, faced with the reality that counsel must make a noisy withdrawal if appropriate steps are not undertaken, corporate insiders will be "persuaded" to act in compliance with the law.

---

1. *See* Securities Exchange Act Release No. 47276 (2003).

2. *See* Securities Exchange Act Release No. 46868 (2002) (setting forth proposed § 205.3(d)). As used in the proposed rule, "disaffirm" means:

> Disaffirm to the Commission, in writing, any opinion, document, affirmation, representation, characterization, or the like in a document filed with or submitted to the Commission, or incorporated into such a document, that the attorney has prepared or assisted in preparing and that the attorney reasonably believes is or may be materially false or misleading.

In light of the SEC's inaction on this subject during the past decade, it is unlikely that the Commission in the near future will adopt a noisy withdrawal provision or any of the proposed alternatives. One of these alternatives would require the affected company (rather than counsel) to notify the Commission of the attorney's withdrawal from representation on the basis that such counsel did not receive a suitable response to a report concerning a material violation. If the Commission had adopted this latter proposal, the rate of corporate adherence thereto may well have been problematic.

[B] State Ethical Rules

Today, at least 42 states permit or require an attorney to reveal a client's crime or fraud that threatens substantial financial loss. Pursuant to its 2003 amendments, the ABA Model Rules now permit such disclosure. Moreover, many states as well as ABA Model Rule 1.6 allow a lawyer under certain conditions to reveal client confidences in order to prevent, modify, or rectify substantial financial harm that "is reasonably certain to result or has resulted from the client's commission of a crime or fraud in furtherance of which the client has used the lawyer's services" (ABA Model Rule 1.6(b)(3). In this respect, the SEC standards adopted in 2003 generally are consistent with these state ethical standards.[3] They generally will have an impact only in states (such as California) that prohibit counsel's disclosure of client confidences and secrets in situations involving financial harm.

Also significant in this context is Model Rule 4.1(b). That rule provides: "In the course of representing a client a lawyer shall not knowingly ... fail to disclose a material fact when disclosure is necessary to avoid assisting a criminal or fraudulent act by a client, unless disclosure is prohibited by Rule 1.6."

Importantly, an attorney commits an ethical violation by counseling or assisting a client in conduct that the attorney knows is fraudulent. Moreover, depending on the circumstances, an attorney who discovers that a disclosure document that she drafted is materially false and is being relied upon by investors to their financial detriment should not simply withdraw from the representation. That alone may not be

---

3. *See* Section 205.3(d)(2) of the SECs Standards:

An attorney appearing and practicing before the Commission in the representation of an issuer may reveal to the Commission, without the issuer's consent, confidential information related to the representation to the extent the attorney reasonably believes necessary:

(i) To prevent the issuer from committing a material violation that is likely to cause substantial injury to the financial interest or property of the issuer or investors;

(ii) To prevent the issuer, in a Commission investigation or administrative proceeding from committing perjury, proscribed in 18 U.S.C. 1621; suborning perjury, proscribed in 18 U.S.C. 1622; or committing any act proscribed in 18 U.S.C. 1001 that is likely to perpetrate a fraud upon the Commission; or

(iii) To rectify the consequences of a material violation by the issuer that caused, or may cause, substantial injury to the financial interest or property of the issuer or investors in the furtherance of which the attorney's services were used.

sufficient. In such situations, counsel may have to disaffirm her work product, hence making a noisy withdrawal, in order to effectuate the withdrawal. As stated in an ABA Formal Opinion 92-366 (1992), "where the client avowedly intends to continue to use the lawyer's work product, this amounts to a *de facto* continuation of representation even if the lawyer has ceased to perform any additional work." Hence, "[t]he representation is not complete, any more than the fraud itself is completed."[4]

§ 16.02 Attorney Liability for Client Fraud

In the Lincoln Savings and Loan debacle, U.S. District Court Judge Stanley Sporkin, former SEC Director of the Division of Enforcement (and former General Counsel of the Central Intelligence Agency), asserted:

> Where were these professionals, a number of whom are now asserting their rights under the Fifth Amendment, when these clearly improper transactions were being consummated?

> Why didn't any of them speak up or disassociate themselves from the transactions?

> Where also were the outside accountants and attorneys when these transactions were effectuated?

> What is difficult to understand is that with all the professional talent involved (both accounting and legal) why at least one professional would not have blown the whistle to stop the overreaching that took place in this case.

Lincoln Savings and Loan Association v. Wall, 743 F. Supp. 901, 920 (D.D.C. 1990).

In the aftermath of Judge Sporkin's assertion, the Washington Post editorialized that "it is a charge to bar associations and accounting boards to consider this enormous failure of their professional standards to protect both clients and the public."[5] The financial fraud debacles of the last decade accentuate this point.

---

4. For further literature on attorney responsibility in this "new" era, *see, e.g.*, M. STEINBERG, LAWYERING AND ETHICS FOR THE BUSINESS ATTORNEY (4th ed. 2016); Symposium, 52 AM. U.L. REV. No. 3 (2003); Symposium, 8 STAN. J. LAW BUS. & FIN. No. 1 (2002); Symposium, 70 TENN. L. REV. No. 1 (2002); Symposium, 46 WASHBURN L.J. No. 1 (2006); Symposium, 3 WYOM. L. REV. No. 2 (2003); Cramton, *Enron and the Corporate Lawyer: A Primer on Legal and Ethical Issues*, 58 BUS. LAW. 143 (2002); Greenbaum, *The Attorneys Duty to Report Professional Misconduct: A Roadmap for Reform*, 16 GEO. J. LEG. ETH. 259 (2003); Nicholson, *A Hobsons Choice for Securities Lawyers in the Post-Enron Environment: Striking a Balance Between the Obligations of Client Loyalty and Market Gatekeeper*, 16 GEO. J. LEG. ETH. 91 (2002); Simon, *Whom (Or What) Does the Organizations Lawyer Represent?: An Anatomy of Intraclient Conflict*, 91 CALIF. L. REV. 57 (2003); Warren, *Revenue Recognition and Corporate Counsel*, 56 SMU L. REV. 885 (2003).

5. Editorial, *Judgment on Lincoln S & L*, WASH. POST, Aug. 8, 1990, at A26.

Problem

In the course of her duties as general outside counsel for Abso Property Investments, Inc. (API), a publicly held corporation whose stock is listed on the New York Stock Exchange, Melinda Jacobs has learned that API is the subject of heated litigation regarding one of its premier investment properties. While the lawsuit was filed a number of years ago, it is now reaching the trial phase. Thus far, API has not disclosed the suit and its potentially detrimental financial effects on the company in any of its SEC-filed documents. Damages sought by the plaintiffs exceed ten percent of API's annual revenues. A jury trial is scheduled to commence in three months.

(1) What are Jacobs' obligations as API's outside counsel in advising API with respect to disclosure?

(2) Assume that Jacobs approaches API's inside general counsel Harry Hairston about this issue. Hairston tells Jacobs, "Thank you for bringing this to our attention. It will be taken care of." Is this a satisfactory result? How should Jacobs proceed?

(3) Assume instead that when Jacobs approaches Hairston about the subject, she is told that there is already a committee in place to look into the issue of whether this is a material fact that should be disclosed, and that Hairston will get back to her when a decision is made. Is this a satisfactory result?

(4) What result if Hairston has the API board of directors appoint independent outside counsel to investigate the disclosure issue, and that counsel opines that the litigation is not material and therefore does not need to be reported?

(5) What should Jacobs do if she believes that, after talking to Hairston and "climbing the ladder" all the way to API's board of directors, API declines to provide adequate disclosure in its SEC documents as she concludes is required?

SEC Adopts Attorney Conduct Rule Under Sarbanes-Oxley Act
Securities and Exchange Commission
Press Release No. 2003-13 (January 23, 2003)

The Securities and Exchange Commission today adopted final rules to implement Section 307 of the Sarbanes-Oxley Act by setting "standards of professional conduct for attorneys appearing and practicing before the Commission in any way in the representation of issuers." In addition, the Commission approved an extension of the comment period on the "noisy withdrawal" provisions of the original proposed rule and publication for comment of an alternative proposal.

[In] 2002, the Commission voted to propose the standards of professional conduct. That proposal defined who is appearing and practicing before the Commission in the representation of an issuer. Attorneys were required to report evidence of a material violation "up-the-ladder" within an issuer. In addition, under certain circumstances, these provisions permitted or required attorneys to effect a so-called "noisy withdrawal"—that is, to withdraw from representing an issuer and notify the Commission that they have withdrawn for professional reasons.

The rules adopted by the Commission today will:

- require an attorney to report evidence of a material violation, determined according to an objective standard, "up-the-ladder" within the issuer to the chief legal counsel or the chief executive officer of the company or the equivalent;

- require an attorney, if the chief legal counsel or the chief executive officer of the company does not respond appropriately to the evidence, to report the evidence to the audit committee, another committee of independent directors, or the full board of directors;

- clarify that the rules cover attorneys providing legal services to an issuer who have an attorney-client relationship with the issuer, and who have notice that documents they are preparing or assisting in preparing will be filed with or submitted to the Commission;

- provide that foreign attorneys who are not admitted in the United States, and who do not advise clients regarding U.S. law, would not be covered by the rule, while foreign attorneys who provide legal advice regarding U.S. law would be covered to the extent they are appearing and practicing before the Commission, unless they provide such advice in consultation with U.S. counsel;

- allow an issuer to establish a "qualified legal compliance committee" (QLCC) as an alternative procedure for reporting evidence of a material violation. Such a QLCC would consist of at least one member of the issuer's audit committee, or an equivalent committee of independent directors, and two or more independent board members, and would have the responsibility, among other things, to recommend that an issuer implement an appropriate response to evidence of a material violation. One way in which an attorney could satisfy the rule's reporting obligation is by reporting evidence of a material violation to a QLCC;

- allow an attorney, without the consent of an issuer client, to reveal confidential information related to his or her representation to the extent the attorney reasonably believes necessary (1) to prevent the issuer from committing a material violation likely to cause substantial financial injury to the financial interests or property of the issuer or investors; (2) to prevent the issuer from committing an illegal act; or (3) to rectify the consequences of a material violation or illegal act in which the attorney's services have been used;

- state that the rules govern in the event the rules conflict with state law, but will not preempt the ability of a state to impose more rigorous obligations on attorneys that are not inconsistent with the rules; and

- affirmatively state that the rules do not create a private cause of action and that authority to enforce compliance with the rules is vested exclusively with the Commission.

In addition, the final rules modify the definition of the term "evidence of a material violation," which defines the trigger for an attorney's obligation to report up-the-ladder within an issuer. The revised definition confirms that the Commission intends an objective, rather than a subjective, triggering standard, involving credible evidence, based upon which it would be unreasonable, under the circumstances, for a prudent and competent attorney not to conclude that it is reasonably likely that a material violation has occurred, is ongoing or is about to occur.

The Commission voted to extend for 60 days the comment period on the "noisy withdrawal" and related provisions originally included in [the] proposed [standard]. Given the significance and complexity of the issues involved, including the implications of a reporting out requirement on the relationship between issuers and their counsel, the Commission decided to continue to seek comment and give thoughtful consideration to these issues.

The Commission also voted to propose an alternative to "noisy withdrawal" that would require attorney withdrawal, but would require an issuer, rather than an attorney, to publicly disclose the attorney's withdrawal or written notice that the attorney did not receive an appropriate response to a report of a material violation. Specifically, an issuer that has received notice of an attorney's withdrawal would be required to report the notice and the circumstances related thereto [to the SEC] within two days of receiving the attorney's notice. [At this point in time, the SEC has not adopted the proposed rule and appears unlikely to do so.]

––––––––––––

In the Matter of Carter and Johnson

Securities and Exchange Commission

[1981 Transfer Binder] Fed. Sec. L. Rep. (CCH) ¶ 82,847 (1981)

[In this Rule 2(e) (now Rule 102(e) proceeding), two prominent attorneys (Carter and Johnson who practiced with "Wall Street Firms") were charged with having violated the antifraud provisions of the securities laws as well as having violated standards of professional responsibility in connection with their representation of National Telephone Company. The Administrative Law Judge (ALJ) found that the attorneys had assisted National Telephone's management in concealing material facts concerning the company's financial condition and had failed to inform the company's board of directors concerning management's refusal to make adequate disclosures. The ALJ also held that the attorneys had engaged in improper professional conduct, thereby violating Rule 2(e).]

. . . .

For the reasons stated more fully below, we reverse the decision of the Administrative Law Judge with respect to both respondents. We have concluded that the record does not adequately support the Administrative Law Judge's findings of violative conduct by respondents. Moreover, we conclude that certain concepts of proper ethical and professional conduct were not sufficiently developed, at the time of the conduct here at issue, to permit a finding that either respondent breached applicable ethical or professional standards. In addition, we are today giving notice of an interpretation by the Commission of the term "unethical or improper professional conduct," as that term is used in Rule 2(e)(1)(ii). This interpretation will be applicable prospectively in cases of this kind.

The Purpose of Rule 2(e). The Commission promulgated Rule 2(e) pursuant to its general rule-making powers in order to protect the integrity of its processes. These powers were not exercised with a view to the creation of new administrative proceedings. . . . It is addressed to a different problem — professional misconduct — and its sanction is limited to that necessary to protect the investing public and the Commission from the future impact on its processes of professional misconduct.

Rule 2(e) represents a balancing of public benefits. It rests upon the recognition that the privilege of practicing before the Commission is a mechanism that generates great leverage — for good or evil — in the administration of the securities laws. A significant failure to perform properly the professional's role has implications extending beyond the particular transaction involved, for wrongdoing by a lawyer or an accountant raises the specter of a replication of that conduct with other clients.

Recognition of the public implications of the securities professional's role does not mean that the Commission has, by rule, imposed duties to the public on lawyers where such duties would not otherwise exist. Accountants, of course, issue audit reports that speak directly to the investing public and publicly represent that the code of conduct embodied in the statements of auditing standards promulgated by the AICPA has been followed. The duty of accountants to those who justifiably rely on those reports is well-recognized. But the traditional role of the lawyer as counselor is to advise his client, not the public, about the law. Rule 2(e) does not change the nature of that obligation. Nevertheless, if a lawyer violates ethical or professional standards, or becomes a conscious participant in violations of the securities laws, or performs his professional function without regard to the consequences, it will not do to say that because the lawyer's duty is to his client alone, this Commission must stand helplessly by while the lawyer carries his privilege of appearing and practicing before the Commission on to the next client.

[Note that Rule 102(e) has been codified in Section 4C of the Securities Exchange Act pursuant to Congress' enactment of the Sarbanes-Oxley Act of 2002.]

The Operation of Rule 2(e). The operation of subparagraphs (i) and (ii) of Rule 2(e) (1) responds to [relevant] policy considerations. . . . Subparagraph (i) provides for sanctions upon a finding that a respondent does "not . . . possess the requisite qualifications to represent others." The motivating concept is clear: the Commission's processes cannot function effectively without the existence of competent professionals who counsel and assist their clients in securities matters. The same focus is evident in subparagraph (ii), which provides for sanctions if a respondent is "lacking in character or integrity or [has] engaged in unethical or improper professional conduct."

The operation of subparagraph (iii) of the Rule reflects the same concerns. This provision provides for suspension or disbarment if the Commission finds, after notice of and opportunity for hearing, that a respondent has "willfully violated, or willfully aided and abetted the violation of any provision of the federal securities laws . . . or the rules and regulations thereunder." Not every violation of law, however, may be sufficient to justify invocation of the sanctions available under Rule 2(e). The violation must be of a character that threatens the integrity of the Commission's processes in the way that the activities of unqualified or unethical professionals do.

Against that background, we turn to an analysis of respondents' conduct. In our judgment, that conduct presents difficult questions under the applicable legal and professional standards.

. . . .

ETHICAL AND PROFESSIONAL RESPONSIBILITIES

A. The Findings of the Administrative Law Judge

The Administrative Law Judge found that both respondents "failed to carry out their professional responsibilities with respect to appropriate disclosure to all concerned, including stockholders, directors and the investing public . . . and thus knowingly engaged in unethical and improper professional conduct, as charged in the Order." In particular, he held that respondents' failure to advise National's board of directors of [executive officer] Hart's refusal to disclose adequately the company's perilous financial condition was itself a violation of ethical and professional standards referred to in Rule 2(e)(1)(ii).

Respondents argue that the Commission has never promulgated standards of professional conduct for lawyers and that the Commission's application in hindsight of new standards would be fundamentally unfair. Moreover, even if it is permissible for the Commission to apply—without specific adoption or notice—generally recognized professional standards, they argue that no such standards applicable to respondents' conduct existed in 1974–75, nor do they exist today.

We agree that, in general, elemental notions of fairness dictate that the Commission should not establish new rules of conduct and impose them retroactively upon professionals who acted at the time without reason to believe that their conduct was unethical or improper. At the same time, however, we perceive no unfairness whatsoever in holding those professionals who practice before us to generally recognized norms of professional conduct, whether or not such norms had previously been explicitly adopted or endorsed by the Commission. To do so upsets no justifiable expectations, since the professional is already subject to those norms.

The ethical and professional responsibilities of lawyers who become aware that their client is engaging in violations of the securities laws have not been so firmly and unambiguously established that we believe all practicing lawyers can be held to an awareness of generally recognized norms. We also recognize that the Commission has never articulated or endorsed any such standards. That being the case, we reverse the Administrative Law Judge's findings under subparagraph (ii) of Rule 2(e)(1) with respect to both respondents. Nevertheless, we believe that respondents' conduct raises serious questions about the obligations of securities lawyers, and the Commission is hereby giving notice of its interpretation of "unethical or improper professional conduct" as that term is used in Rule 2(e)(1)(ii). The Commission intends to issue a release soliciting comment from the public as to whether this interpretation should be expanded or modified.

B. Interpretive Background

Our concern focuses on the professional obligations of the lawyer who gives essentially correct disclosure advice to a client that does not follow that advice and as a result violates the federal securities laws. . . .

While precise standards have not yet emerged, it is fair to say that there exists considerable acceptance of the proposition that a lawyer must, in order to discharge his professional responsibilities, make all efforts within reason to persuade his client to avoid or terminate proposed illegal action. Such efforts could include, where appropriate, notification to the board of directors of a corporate client. . . .

We are mindful that, when a lawyer represents a corporate client, the client—and the entity to which he owes his allegiance—is the corporation itself and not management or any other individual connected with the corporation. Moreover, the lawyer should try to "insure that decisions of his client are made only after the client has been informed of relevant considerations." These unexceptionable principles take on a special coloration when a lawyer becomes aware that one or more specific members of a corporate client's management is deciding not to follow his disclosure advice, especially if he knows that those in control, such as the board of directors, may not have participated in or been aware of that decision. Moreover, it is well established that no lawyer, even in the most zealous pursuit of his client's interests, is privileged to assist his client in conduct the lawyer knows to be illegal. The application of these recognized principles to the special role of the securities lawyer giving disclosure advice, however, is not a simple task.

The securities lawyer who is an active participant in a company's ongoing disclosure program will ordinarily draft and revise disclosure documents, comment on them and file them with the Commission. He is often involved on an intimate, day-to-day basis in the judgments that determine what will be disclosed and what will be withheld from the public markets. When a lawyer serving in such a capacity concludes that his client's disclosures are not adequate to comply with the law, and so advises his client, he is "aware," in a literal sense, of a continuing violation of the securities laws. On the other hand, the lawyer is only an adviser, and the final judgment—and, indeed, responsibility—as to what course of conduct is to be taken must lie with the client. Moreover, disclosure issues often present difficult choices between multiple shades of gray, and while a lawyer's judgment may be to draw the disclosure obligation more broadly than his client, both parties recognize the degree of uncertainty involved.

The problems of professional conduct that arise in this relationship are well-illustrated by the facts of this case. In rejecting [the law firm of] Brown, Wood's advice to include the assumptions underlying its projections in its 1974 Annual Report, in declining to issue two draft stockholders letters offered by respondents and in ignoring the numerous more informal urgings by both respondents and [another attorney] to make disclosure, [National Telephone's executives] Hart and Lurie indicated that they were inclined to resist any public pronouncements that were at odds with the rapid growth which had been projected and reported for the company.

If the record ended there, we would be hesitant to suggest that any unprofessional conduct might be involved. [National Telephone's management—Hart and Lurie] were, in effect, pressing the company's lawyers hard for the minimum disclosure required by law. That fact alone is not an appropriate basis for a finding that a lawyer must resign or take some extraordinary action. Such a finding would inevitably drive a wedge between reporting companies and their outside lawyers; the more sophisticated members of management would soon realize that there is nothing to gain in consulting outside lawyers.

However, much more was involved in this case. In sending out a patently misleading letter to stockholders on December 23 in contravention of [the] express advice to clear all such disclosure with Brown, Wood, [and by engaging in a number of other troubling maneuvers,] the company's management erected a wall between National and its outside lawyers—a wall apparently designed to keep out good legal advice in conflict with management's improper disclosure plans.

Any ambiguity in the situation plainly evaporated in late April and early May of 1975 when Hart first asked [the attorney] Johnson for a legal opinion flatly contrary to the express disclosure advice Johnson had given Hart only five days earlier, and when Lurie soon thereafter prohibited the delivery of a copy of the company's April 1975 Form 8-K to Brown, Wood.

These actions reveal a conscious desire on the part of National's management no longer to look to Brown, Wood for independent disclosure advice, but rather to embrace the firm within Hart's fraud and use it as a shield to avoid the pressures exerted by the banks toward disclosure. Such a role is a perversion of the normal lawyer-client relationship, and no lawyer may claim that, in these circumstances, he need do no more than stubbornly continue to suggest disclosure when he knows his suggestions are falling on deaf ears.

C. "Unethical or Improper Professional Conduct"

The Commission is of the view that a lawyer engages in "unethical or improper professional conduct" under the following circumstances: When a lawyer with significant responsibilities in the effectuation of a company's compliance with the disclosure requirements of the federal securities laws becomes aware that his client is engaged in a substantial and continuing failure to satisfy those disclosure requirements, his continued participation violates professional standards unless he takes prompt steps to end the client's non-compliance. The Commission has determined that this interpretation will be applicable only to conduct occurring after the date of this opinion.

We do not imply that a lawyer is obliged, at the risk of being held to have violated Rule 2(e), to seek to correct every isolated disclosure action or inaction which he believes to be at variance with applicable disclosure standards, although there may be isolated disclosure failures that are so serious that their correction becomes a matter of primary professional concern. It is also clear, however, that a lawyer is not privileged to unthinkingly permit himself to be co-opted into an ongoing fraud and cast as a dupe or a shield for a wrong-doing client.

Initially, counseling accurate disclosure is sufficient, even if his advice is not accepted. But there comes a point at which a reasonable lawyer must conclude that his advice is not being followed, or even sought in good faith, and that his client is involved in a continuing course of violating the securities laws. At this critical juncture, the lawyer must take further, more affirmative steps in order to avoid the inference that he has been co-opted, willingly or unwillingly, into the scheme of non-disclosure.

The lawyer is in the best position to choose his next step. Resignation is one option, although we recognize that other considerations, including the protection of the client against foreseeable prejudice, must be taken into account in the case of withdrawal. A direct approach to the board of directors or one or more individual directors or officers may be appropriate; or he may choose to try to enlist the aid of other members of the firm's management. What is required, in short, is some prompt action[6] that leads to the conclusion that the lawyer is engaged in efforts to correct the underlying problem, rather than having capitulated to the desires of a strong-willed, but misguided client.

Some have argued that resignation is the only permissible course when a client chooses not to comply with disclosure advice. We do not agree. Premature resignation serves neither the end of an effective lawyer-client relationship nor, in most cases, the effective administration of the securities laws. The lawyer's continued interaction with his client will ordinarily hold the greatest promise of corrective action. So long as a lawyer is acting in good faith and exerting reasonable efforts to prevent violations of the law by his client, his professional obligations have been met. In general, the best result is that which promotes the continued, strong-minded and independent participation by the lawyer.

We recognize, however, that the "best result" is not always obtainable, and that there may occur situations where the lawyer must conclude that the misconduct is so extreme or irretrievable, or the involvement of his client's management and board

---

[6]. In those cases where resignation is not the only alternative, should a lawyer choose not to resign, we do not believe the action taken *must be successful* to avoid the inference that the lawyer had improperly participated in his client's fraud. Rather, the acceptability of the action must be considered in the light of all relevant surrounding circumstances. Similarly, what is "prompt" in any one case depends on the situation then facing the lawyer.

of directors in the misconduct is so thorough-going and pervasive that any action short of resignation would be futile. We would anticipate that cases where a lawyer has no choice but to resign would be rare and of an egregious nature.

[This case does not involve, nor do we here deal with, the additional question of when a lawyer, aware of his client's intention to commit fraud or an illegal act, has a professional duty to disclose that fact either publicly or to an affected third party. Our interpretation today does not require such action at any point. . . .] [7]

D. Conclusion

As noted above, because the Commission has never adopted or endorsed standards of professional conduct which would have applied to respondents' activities during the period here in question, and since generally accepted norms of professional conduct which existed outside the scope of Rule 2(e) did not, during the relevant time period, unambiguously cover the situation in which respondents found themselves in 1974–75, no finding of unethical or unprofessional conduct would be appropriate. That being the case, we reverse the findings of the Administrative Law Judge under Rule 2(e)(1)(ii). In future proceedings of this nature, however, the Commission will apply the interpretation of subparagraph (ii) of Rule 2(e)(1) set forth in this opinion.

An appropriate order will issue.

Securities and Exchange Commission v. Spiegel, Inc.

(U.S. Dist. Ct. N.D. Ill. 2003)

INDEPENDENT EXAMINER'S REPORT CONCERNING SPIEGEL, INC.

Stephen J. Crimmins, Independent Examiner

The Securities and Exchange Commission filed this civil action against Spiegel, Inc. on March 7, 2003. The SEC charged that Spiegel violated the federal securities laws by failing to file required periodic reports on Forms 10-K and 10-Q during 2002, and by failing to disclose advice from its auditor that Spiegel may not be able to continue as a "going concern." Upon commencement of this action, Spiegel consented to the entry of a partial final judgment of permanent injunction without admitting or denying the SEC's charges.

Spiegel likewise consented to this Court's appointment of the undersigned Independent Examiner to review Spiegel's financial records from January 1, 2000 to date, and to provide the Court and the parties with a written report (i) discussing Spiegel's financial condition and (ii) identifying any material accounting irregularities. The Court entered its order appointing the Independent Examiner on March 11, 2003. This report is respectfully submitted to the Court and served on the parties pursuant to that order as amended.

----

[7]. [This footnote has been moved to the text.]

Summary of Findings

Facing the need to improve poor sales performance in its retail subsidiaries, Spiegel embarked by 1999 on a program that one of its audit committee members later called "easy credit to pump up sales." Through various techniques involving both its retail subsidiaries and its captive credit card bank subsidiary, Spiegel tilted its portfolio of credit card customers decidedly in the direction of high-risk subprime borrowers. These were customers who often could not get credit elsewhere and who could be counted on to respond to the opportunity to buy merchandise with the easy credit Spiegel offered them.

At the time, the "new economy" was booming, and Spiegel was getting these risky credit card receivables off its own balance sheet by selling them to various off-balance-sheet special purpose entities through an asset-backed securitization program. This use of "easy credit to pump up sales" worked in the short term, and Spiegel reported to its directors that it had achieved a "return to profitability." This result also personally benefited certain Spiegel senior executives who were entitled to performance-based compensation.

But then the economy soured, and many of Spiegel's subprime customers stopped paying their credit card bills. Charge-offs of uncollectible credit card receivables climbed dramatically. With Spiegel's portfolio of credit card receivables suffering under this barrage of charge-offs, its asset-backed securitizations came dangerously close to hitting a performance "trigger" that would have sent Spiegel's securitizations spinning into a "rapid amortization" that would have destroyed Spiegel. Specifically to avoid this disaster, beginning in 2001, Spiegel manipulated at least one of the components used to calculate this securitization performance trigger, and in doing so, staved off a Spiegel bankruptcy for almost two years.

As Spiegel's financial condition worsened in late 2001, it breached all four loan covenants contained in its bank loan agreements. Spiegel tried desperately to renegotiate its financing with a consortium of 18 banks, but a myriad of problems frustrated this effort. As Spiegel was preparing to file its 2001 Form 10-K annual report due in March 2002, its auditor KPMG advised that it would have to give Spiegel a "going concern" opinion, based on Spiegel's inability to conclude its bank refinancing arrangements and other problems.

Spiegel decided not to file its Form 10-K with a going concern opinion. Soon afterwards, Nasdaq indicated that it would delist Spiegel. At the delisting hearing, Spiegel assured Nasdaq that it was only days away from concluding its refinancing arrangements, and that it would then be able to file its Form 10-K without a going concern opinion. After several days, Nasdaq advised Spiegel that it had a last chance to file its Form 10-K and that otherwise it would be immediately delisted.

Spiegel's Chicago-based management—supported by Spiegel's outside counsel Kirkland & Ellis and its outside auditors KPMG—strongly recommended that Spiegel file its Form 10-K in late May 2002. But the ultimate decision makers for Spiegel were in Germany. Spiegel was only 10% an American public company. About 90%

of its equity and all of its voting stock were in the hands of Michael Otto and his family [hereinafter Otto] in Hamburg, Germany. Indeed, Spiegel operated in effect as the American division of Otto's huge multinational retail empire, including 89 companies with over 79,000 employees in 21 countries around the globe.

On May 31, 2002 in Hamburg, Spiegel's executive or "board" committee (consisting of Michael Otto and an executive of his private company Otto Versand GmbH) and Spiegel's audit committee (consisting of one present and one former Otto Versand executive) rejected the views of Spiegel's management, Kirkland & Ellis and KPMG, and directed Spiegel not to file its already-late first-quarter 2002 Form 10-Q. As time went by, they likewise directed Spiegel not to file its remaining 2002 Forms 10-Q.

Spiegel's German decision-makers had been fully briefed on the array of serious problems Spiegel faced, including at a seven hour meeting with Spiegel's Chicago-based executives several weeks before. But they refused to allow Spiegel to file its reports with the SEC because they felt that a going concern opinion would cause Spiegel's suppliers to refuse to extend credit to Spiegel for the merchandise it purchased for resale. Such a result could lead Spiegel to bankruptcy. Likewise, Spiegel was concerned about the impact a going concern opinion would have on investors and employees.

It was only the prospect of an SEC Enforcement Division investigation that made Spiegel begin to belatedly file reports in February 2003 — after not having filed a single periodic report since November 2001 (its third-quarter 2001 Form 10-Q). This 15-month hiatus in periodic reporting left investors without the disclosures and other protections mandated by the federal securities laws. All investors could do during this period was to attempt to piece together several incomplete pieces of information from a few press releases and news stories.

This matter involves not simply a failure to make required SEC filings. Rather, it involves a failure to make disclosure of material information about Spiegel's financial condition that investors needed to make their investment decisions about Spiegel. The SEC has already charged Spiegel with fraud for failing to disclose its auditors' going concern position. But . . . investors likewise failed to get a variety of other material information about Spiegel's financial condition.

. . .

Ultimately, Spiegel was unable to dig itself out of this hole. Its financial condition just kept getting worse. On March 17, 2003, Spiegel filed a Chapter 11 bankruptcy case in the Southern District of New York — ten days after the SEC commenced the captioned action and six days after this Court appointed the Independent Examiner to conduct this investigation.

. . . .

Involvement of Spiegel's Professional Advisors

In the present case, the SEC charged Spiegel with fraud, and Spiegel consented (without admitting or denying liability) to a fraud injunction against the company.

When a fraud charge hits a public company, the question naturally arises whether its professional advisers could have done anything to prevent this "train wreck" that hurt the company and its shareholders, creditors and employees.

Spiegel's Legal Advisers. In evaluating the performance of Spiegel's lawyers, it is useful to consider rules recently adopted and other rules recently proposed by the SEC under Section 307 of the Sarbanes-Oxley Act, even though these SEC rules were not in effect at the time of the conduct here. Under [the] SEC rules, lawyers representing a public company must report "up the ladder"—as high as the board of directors, if necessary—if the lawyers "become aware" of "evidence" of a "material violation" of federal or state securities law or a material breach of fiduciary duty by the company (or its officer, director, employee or agent).

In addition, the SEC has proposed (but not yet adopted) so-called "noisy withdrawal" rules that would require lawyers to assess whether the company has made an "appropriate response within a reasonable time" to the matter the lawyer has reported up the ladder, and if not, whether "substantial injury" to financial interest or property of the issuer or investors has occurred or is likely. An outside attorney must then "withdraw forthwith from representing the issuer," and tell both the company and the SEC that the withdrawal was for "professional considerations." An inside attorney must cease participation in the matter. Both outside and inside attorneys must also disaffirm to the SEC any document the attorney assisted in preparing that "may be" materially false or misleading.

Robert Sorensen joined Spiegel as its general counsel at the end of June 2001. He brought in the firm of Kirkland & Ellis as principal outside counsel, in place of Rooks Pitts, to provide additional depth in corporate and securities matters. Rooks Pitts continued to represent Spiegel in securitization and other matters. As described above, by mid-May 2002, Kirkland & Ellis had plainly advised Spiegel that it was violating the law by not filing its Form 10-K, and that this illegal act could have serious consequences, including action by the SEC. Sorensen plainly concurred in this advice. The advice reached Spiegel's management, including its president Martin Zaepfel, who was also a member of Spiegel's board committee, which had the power to act for the full board. By the end of May, Zaepfel reported the advice to Michael Otto and Michael Cruesemann, the other two members of the board committee. Kirkland & Ellis also repeated this advice by phone to Spiegel's audit committee at the end of May. Plainly, Kirkland & Ellis and Sorensen reported "up the ladder" to Spiegel's audit committee and its board committee.

However, this was a case where reporting "up the ladder" was not enough. The advice from the lawyers here was rejected by Spiegel's audit and board committees, and the material information that should have reached investors was kept under wraps. White & Case became involved in Spiegel's affairs as counsel for Spiegel's "sole voting shareholder," Michael Otto and his corporate vehicles. Through its Hamburg partner Urs Aschenbrenner, White & Case "interpreted" for the Otto interests the advice received from Spiegel's U.S. legal advisors, and it clearly played a substantial role in helping Otto and the Spiegel board committee evaluate that advice. Aschenbrenner consulted with White & Case's New York office on Spiegel issues, and lawyers from the firm's New York office were substantively involved on various Spiegel matters—again as representatives of Spiegel's sole voting shareholder—during much of 2002.

Aschenbrenner began accompanying Cruesemann to meetings with Spiegel's lender banks in Spring 2002, and also attended Spiegel's delisting hearing before Nasdaq on May 17, 2002. On May 31, 2002, the day Spiegel's audit and board committees made the final decision not to file the Form 10-K, Aschenbrenner was invited to be present at the audit committee meeting, and the audit committee had Aschenbrenner phone Kirkland & Ellis on a speakerphone for the committee to get advice. Aschenbrenner was heard to challenge Kirkland and Ellis' advice on the need to file Spiegel's form 10-K and the consequences of non-filing. In the days following the May 31, 2002 meeting, it appears that neither Aschenbrenner nor his New York partners did anything to express their agreement with Kirkland & Ellis' advice.

Whatever the conclusion as to the lawyers' performance around the time of the May 31, 2002 audit and board committee meetings, the question naturally arises as to what the lawyers did to press Spiegel to make its required SEC filings through the balance of 2002—or otherwise to update, supplement or correct disclosures made in Spiegel's Forms 12b-25 and/or its press releases. There does not appear to be a record of either Kirkland and Ellis or White & Case advising Spiegel of the dire consequences of its continuing failure to file its Form 10-K and make full disclosure to investors after May 31, 2002.

After May 2002, it appears that Spiegel's German directors considered Kirkland & Ellis and Sorensen, along with the rest of Spiegel's U.S. management, to be "black painters"—meaning pessimists who were exaggerating the seriousness of the situation. Over the summer, Cruesemann suggested that Kirkland & Ellis, and perhaps Sorensen, be replaced. The effort to replace Kirkland & Ellis failed only when U.S. management pointed out the cost of bringing in a new firm to draft documentation for the refinancing and other pending matters.

At the same time, while ostensibly still only counsel for Spiegel's sole voting shareholder, White & Case assumed a prominent role in negotiating on Spiegel's behalf with its banks on the refinancing effort, with the OCC on FCNB issues, and with the insurer of the Spiegel securitizations. While still not technically retained as Spiegel's counsel, White & Case clearly enjoyed the confidence of Spiegel's sole voting shareholder, and an effort by White & Case to report "up the ladder" to Spiegel's audit and board committees that it shared the views of the "black painters" Kirkland & Ellis and Sorensen could have well caused Spiegel to comply with its obligations and avoid a fraud charge from the SEC.

As the months went by, Kirkland & Ellis continued to prepare and file Spiegel's Forms 12b-25 providing official notice of Spiegel's failure to file its remaining quarterly reports (Form 10-Q) for the balance of 2002. All of these recited that Spiegel was not filing its periodic reports because it was "not currently in compliance with its 2001 loan covenants and is currently working with its bank group to amend and replace its existing credit facilities," and thus "not in a position to issue financial statements . . . pending resolution of this issue." Of course, as Kirkland & Ellis knew, the real reason why Spiegel was not filing its periodic reports was that it did not want to disclose KPMG's going concern qualification and other material bad facts and circumstances threatening Spiegel's survival.

None of Spiegel's legal advisers withdrew — "noisily" or otherwise — from representing Spiegel. If the SEC's proposed withdrawal rule had then been in effect, the SEC would have been alerted to take action sooner, and investors would have received information they could have acted on to make informed investment decisions about Spiegel. In this case, the absence of a "noisy withdrawal" requirement allowed Spiegel to keep investors and the SEC in the dark.

. . . .

Note

Under the ethical rules, an attorney retained by a corporation (or other business enterprise) represents such enterprise acting through its duly authorized constituents (such as the board of directors or senior management). See Rule 1.13(a) of the American Bar Association's (ABA) Model Rules of Professional Conduct. Pursuant to Model Rule 1.13, if counsel for a corporation knows that an officer, employee, or another individual affiliated with that corporation is engaged in a violation of law that is likely to cause substantial injury to the corporation, then counsel shall use reasonable efforts to prevent the harm. The steps taken by counsel should be designed to minimize disruption and the risk of disclosing confidences. Such steps include (1) asking that the matter be reconsidered; (2) seeking a separate legal opinion concerning the matter for review by the appropriate authority in the enterprise; and (3) referring the issue to "higher authority in the organization, including if warranted by the circumstances, to the highest authority that can act on behalf of the organization as determined by applicable law." Provided that after referral to the board of directors or similar authority in the organization, the organization persists in the illegal conduct, counsel should resign from the representation. The Model Rules also permit counsel to reveal information outside the organization that counsel believes is necessary to prevent the client's commission of a fraudulent or criminal act that is likely to cause substantial financial harm.

[A] Duty to Disclose Client Fraud

As discussed earlier in this chapter, the vast majority of state ethical rules permit counsel to disclose client fraud that threatens substantial financial loss. With respect to § 10(b) liability, the courts have declined to impose liability upon lawyers as primary violators for their failure to disclose client fraud. The Seventh Circuit's statement in *Barker v. Henderson, Franklin, Starnes & Holt*, 797 F.2d 490, 496 (7th Cir. 1986), serves as a well-known example:

> The extent to which lawyers and accountants should reveal their client's wrongdoing—and to whom they should reveal—is a question of great moment. . . . We express no opinion on whether the [law firms] did what they should, whether there was malpractice under state law, or whether the rules of ethics (or other fiduciary doctrines) ought to require lawyers and accountants to blow the whistle in equivalent circumstances. We are satisfied, however, that an award of damages under the securities laws is not the way to blaze the trail toward improved ethical standards in the legal and accounting professions. Liability depends on an existing duty to disclose. The securities law therefore must lag behind changes in ethical and fiduciary standards. The plaintiffs have not pointed to any rule imposing on either [law firm] a duty to blow the whistle.

See Hays v. Page Perry, LLC, 26 F. Supp. 3d 1311 (N.D. Ga. 2014), *motion for reconsideration denied*, 2015 U.S. Dist. LEXIS 32381 (N.D. Ga. 2015) (dismissing malpractice suit against lawyer for not reporting client's illegalities to regulatory authorities and ruling that the attorney had no reporting-out obligation—no duty to "blow the whistle").

The Supreme Court's decision in *Janus Capital* (contained in § 10.03) likewise limits attorney liability exposure under § 10(b). Pursuant to Rule 10b-5(b), the Supreme Court ruled that a person must "make" a statement to incur primary liability under that provision. Hence, an attorney who declines to "blow the whistle" on his/her client does not "make" a statement. Likewise, absent active involvement in the client's misconduct, it is unlikely that a lawyer would be held liable for engaging in deception under Rule 10b-5(a) or (c) solely for refraining from disclosing his/her client's fraud.

[B] Attorney Malpractice and Negligent Misrepresentation

In addition to securities law liability, attorneys may be subject to liability to their clients and to third parties based on state common law concepts of negligence. Many states still require attorney client privity to state a malpractice action. *See, e.g., Pelham v. Griesheimer*, 92 Ill. 13, 440 N.E.2d 96, 99 (1982) ("The concept of [attorney-client] privity has long protected attorneys from malpractice claims by nonclients."); *Flaherty v. Weinberg*, 303 Md. 115, 492 A.2d 618, 620 (1985) ("[A]bsent fraud, collusion or privity of contract, an attorney is not liable to a third party for professional malpractice.").

Today, several courts permit certain allegedly injured third parties to sue an attorney based on negligence under a number of different theories. This expansion of liability under state law has affected securities counsel. For example, in *Vereins-Und Westbank A.G. v. Carter*, 691 F. Supp. 704, 709 (S.D.N.Y. 1988) (applying New York law), a non-client recipient of an opinion letter sued the attorney and his law firm for the negligent rendering of such opinion. The court denied the defendants' motion for summary judgment, reasoning that "liability for negligent misstatements to one not in contractual privity may attach where the statement is made for the principal purpose of having it relied upon by such person, and where its benefit to the party authorizing the statement stems precisely from such reliance by the third party."

An expansive approach holds that any reasonably foreseeable third party may bring suit against an attorney if the attorney's negligence proximately caused the loss. For example, in *Zendell v. Newport Oil Corp.*, 226 N.J. Super. 431, 544 A.2d 878 (1988), the court allowed purchasers of limited partnership interests to sue the law firm for its alleged negligence in the sale of securities in violation of the Securities Act's registration requirements. Even though the plaintiffs did not have an attorney-client or fiduciary relationship with the law firm, they were foreseeable third parties. Consequently, relying on the New Jersey Supreme Court's decision in *Rosenberg v. Adler*, 93 N.J. 324, 461 A.2d 138 (1983), it was held that the plaintiff-investors could maintain an action for negligent misrepresentation.

Another approach is that of the American Law Institute's (ALI) Restatement (Second) of Torts. Generally, under the Restatement's approach, attorneys may be held liable for negligent misrepresentation to their clients, to intended known beneficiaries, and to any unidentified person of an identified class of beneficiaries. Hence, the Restatement subjects attorneys to liability for negligence to unknown beneficiaries if such beneficiaries are members of a limited, identifiable class for whom the information was intended to be furnished. Broadly interpreted, the ALI Restatement may extend to investors who purchase securities in a limited or public offering.

The following case illustrates the liability consequences that may ensue when key information is not communicated to all of a law firm's attorneys who are working on a particular matter for a client.

Cromeans v. Morgan Keegan & Co., Inc.

69 F. Supp. 3d 934 (W.D. Mo. 2014)

Nanette K. Laughrey, District Judge.

The Court previously granted partial summary judgment in favor of Defendant Armstrong Teasdale, LLP on Plaintiff John Cromeans' claims for legal malpractice and negligent misrepresentation. Cromeans filed a motion to vacate the order which the Court denied. Upon further consideration, the Court grants the motion to vacate, in part. It finds that summary judgment should be granted on the malpractice claims, but should not be granted on Cromeans' negligent misrepresentation claim.

I. Discussion

A. Legal Malpractice

In granting summary judgment to Armstrong Teasdale on the legal malpractice claim, the Court recognized that an attorney-client relationship must ordinarily exist before a plaintiff can recover for legal malpractice against an attorney. But this element of a legal malpractice claim may be satisfied if a non-client plaintiff can show that the attorney performed services specifically intended by a client to benefit the plaintiff. . . . If specific intent is established, a six-factor balancing test is then used to determine, as a separate matter, the question of legal duty of attorneys to non-clients. Because Cromeans' evidentiary submissions failed to show that Morgan Keegan specifically intended Armstrong Teasdale's services to benefit the bond purchasers, the Court granted summary judgment to Armstrong Teasdale on the legal malpractice claim.

Therefore, the Court denies Cromeans' motion to vacate the grant of summary judgment in favor of Armstrong Teasdale on the legal malpractice claim.

B. Negligent Misrepresentation

Justifiable reliance is a necessary element of all negligent misrepresentation claims. In granting summary judgment to Armstrong Teasdale on Cromeans' negligent misrepresentation claim, the Court found that Cromeans could not prove reasonable reliance. Because Morgan Keegan did not hire Armstrong Teasdale to investigate the facts contained in the offering statement and Armstrong Teasdale disclaimed any responsibility for the accuracy of those facts, the Court concluded that justifiable reliance could not be shown. When making its decision, however, the Court overlooked evidence that Armstrong Teasdale made an affirmative misstatement of fact when it said "no facts have come to our attention which lead us to believe that the Official Statement contains" misrepresentations or omitted material facts.

In his motion to vacate, Cromeans cites evidence that Armstrong Teasdale had a contract with the Missouri Department of Economic Development (DED) to assist DED in attracting Chinese businesses to Missouri. When DED wanted a background check on a Chinese company, Mamtek, it contacted Armstrong Teasdale's agent, Mr. Li, to obtain whatever information he could about Mamtek. Mr. Li is a non-lawyer based in China, who was retained by Armstrong Teasdale to fulfill Armstrong Teasdale's contract with DED. Mr. Li made a phone call and did an internet search. In April 2010, Mr. Li reported to DED and to Maria Desloge, who was Armstrong Teasdale's Associate Director of the China Trade and Investment Office, that Mamtek's plant in Fujian Province, China, never started to manufacture, and that it could not because it did not meet the "zoning" requirements for that location. The offering statement, however, stated that the plant was operational.

Citing the [ALI] Restatement (Second) of Torts, § 552, Cromeans argues that Armstrong Teasdale is liable to the bond purchasers because Armstrong Teasdale knew [or should have known] that some statements in the offering statement were false. Section 552 provides, in relevant part:

> (1) One who, in the course of his business, profession or employment, or in any other transaction in which he has a pecuniary interest, supplies false information for the guidance of others in their business transactions, is subject to liability for pecuniary loss caused to them by their justifiable

reliance upon the information, if he fails to exercise reasonable care or competence in obtaining or communicating the information.

(2) Except as stated in Subsection (3), the liability stated in Subsection (1) is limited to loss suffered

> (a) by the person or one of a limited group of persons for whose benefit and guidance he intends to supply the information or knows that the recipient intends to supply it, and

> (b) through reliance upon it in a transaction that he intends the information to influence or knows that the recipient so intends or in a substantially similar transaction. . . .

The national trend is to recognize a cause of action by non-clients for negligent misrepresentations by professionals, including lawyers, if the requirements of § 552 of the Restatement are satisfied. . . .

Having concluded that Missouri will recognize Cromeans' negligent misrepresentation claim, the Court turns to the additional arguments made by Armstrong Teasdale as to why summary judgment should be granted on that claim. Armstrong Teasdale argues that Edward Li's information should not be attributable to it because Mr. Li was not an employee of Armstrong Teasdale. It also argues that Mr. Li's knowledge should not be imputed to the Armstrong Teasdale lawyer who actually prepared the offering statement because that lawyer did not have the information, and to impute the information to that lawyer would violate well-established principles of confidentiality.

Under Missouri law, a corporate entity "can obtain knowledge only through its agents and, under the well-established rules of agency, the knowledge of agents obtained in the course of their employment is imputed to the corporation." . . . Therefore, the fact that the lawyer making the false statement did not know it was false does not show that Armstrong Teasdale lacked knowledge of the false statement.

Armstrong Teasdale also suggests that Mr. Li's knowledge could not be shared within the firm because of professional rules of confidentiality, and therefore, his knowledge should not be imputed to the lawyer who prepared the offering statement that contained the false information. This argument is unpersuasive because the information Mr. Li gathered was publicly available. Information available to the public is not subject to non-disclosure rules. Further, Mr. Li is not an attorney and never provided legal services to DED. And he did provide the information to Maria Desloge, an Armstrong Teasdale employee.

In summary, there is evidence that Armstrong Teasdale, in the course of its professional duties, supplied information that it knew to be false to Morgan Keegan, knowing that Morgan Keegan intended to supply it to potential bond purchasers. Further, Cromeans arguably relied on that information and suffered loss as a result. This is sufficient to make a submissible claim for negligent misrepresentation under § 552. While Armstrong Teasdale disclaimed any responsibility for checking the accuracy of the facts, it could not with impunity include facts in the offering statement that it knew to be false, particularly in light of its affirmative statement that it knew of no facts contrary to the offering statement.

In view of the above, the order granting summary judgment to Armstrong Teasdale on the negligent misrepresentation claim was in error and is vacated.

[C] Duty to Supervise

In the Matter of Gutfreund, Strauss and Meriwether

U.S. Securities and Exchange Commission

[1992 Transfer Binder] Fed. Sec. L. Rep. (CCH) ¶ 85,067 (1992)

[This proceeding is contained in § 13.09[D].]

[D] Responding to Auditor Requests

A customary practice of auditors is to transmit audit inquiry letters to client corporations, which thereupon forward such requests to their counsel for assessment and response. Such a letter normally asks counsel to provide the auditor with certain information regarding the client's affairs. The information provided is employed by the auditor in opining on the corporation's annual financial reports. Among other items, the audit inquiry letter will seek information relating to contingent liabilities.

Such "loss contingency" requests may cause tension. On the one hand, there is counsel's desire to preserve the client's confidences and secrets, as well as the client's desire to avoid disclosure of unfavorable information. For example, disclosure of a contingent unasserted liability may amount to advertising a client's possibly illegal conduct—a particularly undesirable event for the corporation where a potential plaintiff is ignorant of the possible claim. In addition, disclosure of a client's confidences incurs risk of waiving both the attorney-client and work product privileges. On the other hand, the auditor has a legitimate need to obtain adequate information in order to fulfill its duties consistent with the policy supporting public confidence in published financial statements.

Competing against these considerations is the ever-present threat that an attorney's failure to disclose material facts may subject the attorney and client to liability exposure under the federal securities laws. In addition to potential liability for violation of the securities acts' antifraud provisions, SEC Rule 13b2-2's "lying to the auditor" rule may impose § 13(b)(2) liability on an officer or director of a registrant who, with the requisite intent, makes a materially false or misleading statement to an auditor. Such liability also extends to others (such as attorneys) who, with the requisite culpability, "provid[e] an auditor with an inaccurate or misleading legal analysis." Sarbanes-Oxley Act § 303(a).

In an effort to resolve these competing interests, the Financial Accounting Standards Board promulgated its Statement of Financial Accounting Standards No. 5 ("SFAS 5") (now known as Accounting Standards Codification (ASC) Topic 450— ASC 450-20) and the ABA adopted its Statement of Policy Regarding Lawyers' Responses To Auditors' Requests for Information. Pursuant to the truce arrived at through these pronouncements, the following applies with respect to "loss contingencies":

> When properly requested by the client, it is appropriate for the lawyer to furnish to the auditor information concerning the following matters if the lawyer has been engaged by the client to represent or advise the client professionally with respect thereto and he has devoted substantive attention to them in the form of legal representation or consultation:
>
>> (a) overtly threatened or pending litigation, whether or not specified by the client;
>>
>> (b) a contractually assumed obligation which the client has specifically identified and upon which the client has specifically requested, in the inquiry letter or a supplement thereto, [for] comment to the auditor;
>>
>> (c) an unasserted possible claim or assessment which the client has specifically identified and upon which the client has specifically requested, in the inquiry letter or a supplement thereto, [for] comment to the auditor.

According to the ABA Policy Statement, counsel normally should not express judgment as to the outcome of claims delineated unless it appears to counsel that an unfavorable outcome is either "probable" or "remote." With respect to *unasserted possible claims or assessments*, where a potential claimant has not manifested an awareness of the potential claim, disclosure is required only if the *client* concludes that "(i) it is probable that a claim will be asserted, (ii) there is a reasonable possibility, if the claim is in fact asserted, that the outcome will be unfavorable, and (iii) the liability resulting from such unfavorable outcome would be material to [the company's] financial condition."[8]

---

8. For further discussion on this subject, see American Bar Association, *Statement of Policy Regarding Lawyers' Responses to Auditors' Requests for Information*, 31 Bus. Law. 1709 (1976); Subcommittee on Audit Inquiry Responses, *Inquiry of a Client's Lawyer Concerning Litigation, Claims, and Assessments*, 45 Bus. Law. 2245 (1990); Bavinger & Sant, *Disclosure of Unasserted Claims Under GAAP and the Securities Laws: Inviting Liability*, 6 Insights No. 9, at 14 (Sept. 1992); Fuld, *Lawyers' Responses to Auditors—Some Practical Aspects*, 44 Bus. Law. 159 (1988); Hinsey, *Communications Among Attorneys, Management and Auditors*, 36 Bus. Law. 727 (1981); Hooker, *Lawyers' Responses to Audit Inquiries and the Attorney-Client Privilege*, 35 Bus. Law. 1021 (1980); Rigby, *The Attorney-Auditor Relationship: Responding to Audit Inquiries, the Disclosure of Loss Contingencies and the Work Product Privilege*, 35 Sec. Reg. L.J. 3 (2007); Winer & Seabolt, *Responding to Audit Inquiries in a Time of Heightened Peril*, 36 Sec. Reg. L. Rep. (BNA) 1902 (2004); Note, *Environmental Disclosures and SEC Reporting Requirements*, 17 Del. J. Corp. L. 483 (1992).

§ 16.03 Predecessor-Successor Communications

An important issue is the extent to which an attorney who resigns from a representation because of a client's fraud can inform the prospective successor lawyer of the facts and circumstances relating to the resignation. This issue surfaced in the saga that follows, *In re OPM Leasing Services, Inc.*

In re OPM Leasing Services, Inc.
United States Bankruptcy Court (S.D.N.Y. 1983)

REPORT OF THE TRUSTEE CONCERNING FRAUD

AND OTHER MISCONDUCT IN THE MANAGEMENT

OF THE AFFAIRS OF THE DEBTOR

James P. Hassett, Trustee of O.P.M. Leasing Services, Inc., submits this Report under section 1106(a)(4) of the Bankruptcy Code concerning fraud and other misconduct in the management of OPM's affairs.

. . . .

OPM: The Story in Brief

Mordecai Weissman founded his own leasing company in July 1970 at the age of twenty-three in hopes of prospering with a minimum investment of his own capital and effort. He called the new enterprise O.P.M. Leasing Services, Inc., a name whose mysterious initials often sparked curiosity as the company grew. Different explanations offered for the name wryly capture the different facets of the OPM debacle.

OPM's principals often told customers and others in the business and financial communities that "O.P.M." stood for "other people's machines." To the outside world that watched OPM grow into one of the nation's largest computer leasing companies, this explanation seemed to fit OPM's role as intermediary between computer manufacturers and computer users.

But the truth was that the initials stood for "other people's money." The name connoted the plan of Weissman and Myron S. Goodman, his brother-in-law and partner, to rely almost exclusively on funds advanced by others to run the business. But beyond that, the name reflected the pair's cynical, unscrupulous attitude toward financial and personal interests of other people. Seen from the inside, their business relied on corruption and deception from the start to create an illusion of success. Meanwhile OPM actually lost money at ever increasing rates. By the end Weissman and Goodman were able to continue operating only with other people's money they obtained by fraud of record proportions.

The fraud relied heavily on a factor identified in yet another explanation offered for the OPM initials—"other people's mistakes." Numerous financiers, businessmen, and professionals acted through ignorance, carelessness, poor judgment, or self-interest in ways that permitted the fraud to continue for years. This Report is not simply a story of the myth and reality of OPM; it is also a study of how outsiders who dealt with OPM allowed the fraud at OPM to occur.

. . . .

"Other People's Mistakes": The Outsiders

No less noteworthy than the remarkable saga of OPM from the inside is the combination of actions and inactions by various outsiders that permitted the fraud to occur and, in some instances, actively contributed to its success. Accountants, management consultants, lawyers, investment bankers, lessee representatives, bankers, and other businessmen all worked intimately with Goodman and Weissman in ways that exposed them to transactions used for the fraud. In the misguided belief that someone else was checking the bona fides of OPM's transactions or was acting to stop the fraud, all stood by while the fraud continued at an ever increasing pace.

. . . .

Lawyers

Lawyers played a critical role in the massive Rockwell lease fraud. Without their witting or unwitting assistance, the fraud simply could not have occurred.

The law firm of Singer Hutner Levine & Seeman (and its predecessor and successor firms) served as OPM's outside general counsel from 1971 to September 1980 and did not fully sever its relationship with OPM until December 1980. Singer Hutner closed all but seven of the fifty-four financings of fraudulent Rockwell leases.

Singer Hutner acquired OPM as a client in 1971 through Andrew B. Reinhard, the older brother of a close boyhood friend of Goodman. Reinhard was then a Singer Hutner associate and later became a partner. In 1972 Weissman and Goodman elected Reinhard the third director of OPM. As OPM's business expanded, Singer Hutner followed along, more than doubling in size to twenty-seven lawyers in 1980. By 1975 Singer Hutner participated in virtually every facet of OPM's business. Goodman likened the close relationship between OPM and Singer Hutner to a "bondage of the bookends."

From 1976 through 1980 Singer Hutner received legal fees of almost $7.9 million—sixty to seventy percent of its revenues—from OPM. Singer Hutner also received almost $2 million in reimbursement of expenses. While Singer Hutner lawyers, unlike Goodman, may not have regarded the firm as an adjunct to OPM, their prosperity was tied to OPM's success. The Trustee believes Singer Hutner was not sufficiently alert to the danger that its professional judgment might be impaired by its financial dependence on OPM.

One of the most difficult questions encountered during the Trustee's investigation was whether Reinhard knowingly participated in any of the fraudulent activities at OPM. Although the United States Attorney's Office determined not to seek a grand jury indictment against him, the decision not to prosecute is not dispositive.

The principal witness against Reinhard is Goodman. Goodman testified that, having previously told Reinhard about the early frauds at OPM, he informed Reinhard in early 1979 of his intention to finance three phantom Rockwell leases and successfully enlisted Reinhard's assistance in the fraud. Goodman says he told Reinhard that the financing was necessary to keep OPM in business because of a temporary cash shortage, that he would buy out the financings within several weeks, and that he would never engage in fraudulent financings again. According to Goodman, Reinhard resisted but eventually agreed to help. Goodman testified that Reinhard reluctantly assisted in several subsequent fraudulent financings.

Through his lawyers Reinhard denies he had any knowledge of fraud at OPM apart from information obtained by his firm in June and September 1980. On advice of counsel, Reinhard invoked his Fifth Amendment privilege and refused personally to respond to any questioning by the Trustee concerning the fraud.

Despite a number of internal inconsistencies and anomalies, Goodman's testimony has a ring of truth. Statements by other members of the OPM fraud team and Marvin Weissman tend to corroborate Goodman's testimony. On the other hand, Goodman is an acknowledged master liar and may have hoped implicating Reinhard would endear Goodman to the United States Attorney's Office. While the issue is by no means free from doubt, the Trustee believes there is substantial evidence that Goodman led Reinhard to become, however reluctantly, a knowing participant in the Rockwell fraud.

Apart from Reinhard's probable complicity in the fraud from the outset, Singer Hutner's conduct as OPM's counsel in closing fraudulent Rockwell financings cannot be justified. By early 1979 Singer Hutner had received indications that Goodman and Weissman were capable of serious illegality. Some lawyers were aware that Weissman and Goodman had engaged in lease fraud and commercial bribery, and the firm knew that Goodman had recently perpetrated a $5 million check kiting scheme. Singer Hutner also had knowledge of facts showing that OPM was suffering severe cash shortages that provided a motive for further fraud.

In the sixteen months between the first financing of phantom Rockwell leases in February 1979 and Goodman's first confession to Singer Hutner of serious wrongdoing in June 1980, numerous facts came to Singer Hutner's attention that should have raised suspicions about the bona fides of OPM-Rockwell leases. . . . With all these red flags, Singer Hutner should have exercised extreme caution in closing OPM-Rockwell lease financings. Instead, until June 1980 the firm closed these transactions on a business as usual basis.

On June 12, 1980, Goodman met with Joseph L. Hutner, a Singer Hutner partner, and confessed that he had engaged in past "wrongful transactions" in an amount exceeding $5 million. During a break in the meeting, Goodman somehow retrieved the letter . . . describing the details of the Rockwell fraud. Goodman refused to return the letter or provide additional details of his acknowledged wrongdoing, citing his desire for assurances that Singer Hutner would keep the information secret under the attorney-client privilege.

Singer Hutner promptly retained Joseph M. McLaughlin, then dean of Fordham Law School, and Henry Putzel, III, formerly an associate professor of professional responsibility at Fordham, to advise the firm on its ethical responsibilities in dealing with Goodman's disclosure. Whether or not Singer Hutner's conduct based on their advice was "ethical" (a legal question the Trustee does not address), it was woefully inadequate to prevent further fraud. After June 1980 Singer Hutner closed fifteen additional fraudulent Rockwell transactions totaling $70 million.

Singer Hutner kept Goodman's misdeeds secret and continued closing OPM transactions on the basis of certificates from Goodman attesting to the legitimacy of the transactions. The Trustee believes Singer Hutner was wrong in relying on Goodman's representations that the fraud had stopped and ignoring substantial evidence that it had not. . . . [O]n two occasions in June and July Singer Hutner lawyers noticed peculiarities in title documents used in fraudulent Rockwell lease financings that should have led them to seek to confirm their authenticity with third parties.

For months Goodman resisted pressure to make full disclosure of the fraud to Singer Hutner by a series of gambits including a threat to jump out of a window in OPM's ninth story offices if pressed further. In September 1980 Goodman finally came clean, or so he claimed. At a meeting with the Singer Hutner partners, Goodman described the mechanics of the Rockwell fraud and quantified it at $30 million—only about $100 million short of the truth. Notwithstanding Goodman's continued insistence that the fraud had stopped by June 1980, and Goodman's hysterical threat to "bring down this firm," on September 23 Singer Hutner voted to resign as OPM's counsel.

With Putzel's approval, Singer Hutner agreed to characterize its resignation misleadingly as a "mutual determination of our firm and [OPM] to terminate our relationship as general counsel." Singer Hutner also agreed to continue rendering legal services over a two and one-half month transition period to avoid unnecessary injury to OPM.

In late September or early October Goodman dropped the bombshell that the fraud had in fact continued throughout the summer of 1980. Despite this shocking acknowledgment by Goodman that he had continued to use Singer Hutner as an instrument of fraud even after his initial confession of wrongdoing, Putzel advised Singer Hutner that it could not ethically warn successor counsel of the danger that Goodman would use them to help finance additional fraudulent transactions.

After Singer Hutner's withdrawal, OPM's young in-house lawyers and the law firm of Kaye, Scholer, Fierman, Hays & Handler represented OPM in its lease transactions. Kept in the dark by Goodman and Singer Hutner about the real reasons for the departure of Singer Hutner, OPM's in-house staff unwittingly closed six fraudulent financings of Rockwell leases and Kaye Scholer unwittingly closed one.

Singer Hutner, of course, relies on the advice it received from McLaughlin and Putzel to justify its conduct during the summer and fall of 1980. While the Trustee does not attempt to resolve the question whether that advice was consistent with the legal profession's code of ethics, it is clear that McLaughlin and Putzel could have advised other courses, consistent with Singer Hutner's ethical responsibilities, that would have stopped the fraud. Although McLaughlin and Putzel in good faith considered their advice appropriate in the circumstances, the Trustee believes it was in fact the worst possible advice from the point of view of OPM, the third parties with whom it dealt, Singer Hutner's successor counsel, and Singer Hutner itself. Accordingly, McLaughlin and Putzel must shoulder significant responsibility for their client's conduct.

But Singer Hutner cannot properly shift all blame for its actions after Goodman's first confession of wrongdoing to McLaughlin and Putzel. While Singer Hutner relied on McLaughlin and Putzel for advice on its ethical obligations, McLaughlin and Putzel relied on the firm for the central factual predicate for their advice — whether the fraud was continuing. . . .

Viewed as a whole, the Trustee finds Singer Hutner's conduct nothing short of shocking, given the warnings it received before June 1980 and the remarkable events of the summer and early fall. Although Singer Hutner cites its ethical obligation not to injure its client unnecessarily, the most questionable aspects of Singer Hutner's conduct raise issues beyond professional ethics. Even after learning that Goodman had engaged in major wrongdoing, Singer Hutner continued to close OPM debt financings without obtaining prior disclosure of the nature of the wrongdoing and without independently verifying transaction facts. No rule of professional ethics can or should exempt lawyers from the general legal proscriptions against willful blindness to their clients' crimes or reckless participation in them.

. . . .

Note

As seen in *OPM*, predecessor counsel kept a closed-mouth approach, evidently for the purpose of preserving the former client's confidences and secrets. Unfortunately, this approach allows the former client to continue its fraudulent conduct, employing unwitting successor counsel as a resource to achieve its objectives.

An alternative response is as follows:

Former counsel should not stand idly by acquiescing in the former client's retention of successor counsel, thereby resulting in further injury to innocent victims. In such situations, predecessor counsel should send "red flags" to the inquiring attorney. For example, predecessor counsel may state: "I'm disinclined to explain why I resigned unless the former client gives me permission to tell you." If the client refuses to give such permission, this should signal to the inquiring attorney that the prospective engagement should be declined. In any event, and particularly if the representation is undertaken by successor counsel, such counsel should draft a memorandum documenting the results of such inquiry and the information obtained. Moreover, it would be prudent for predecessor counsel to document the contents of communications with prospective successor counsel.

Steinberg, *Attorney Liability for Client Fraud*, 1991 COLUM. BUS. L. REV. 1, 21–22 (1991). *See* Brown, *Counsel with a Fraudulent Client*, 17 REV. SEC. REG. 909 (1984); Comment, *The Client-Fraud Dilemma: A Need for Consensus*, 46 MD. L. REV. 436 (1987).

----

§ 16.04 Legal Opinions

Legal opinions play an important role for an attorney engaged in a transactional-type of practice. We earlier addressed legal opinions in the context of public offerings. Expertised statements that are contained in a registration statement include opinions issued by counsel, subjecting such counsel to § 11 liability exposure. See §§ 7.01, 7.03. Issuance of a fraudulent legal opinion also may subject counsel to § 10(b) liability as a primary violator. See §§ 8.01, 10.03. From a general securities practice perspective, consider the following:

> The form and substance of legal opinions in securities transactions should be carefully considered, and the "due diligence" requirements in securities law transactions should be carefully defined and understood by the opinion giver and the opinion recipient. Any required investigation of facts or law should be performed in a manner necessary both to discharge the professional responsibility of the attorney and to avoid creating any basis for potential liability. An attorney's legal opinion, is in essence, a reflection of his or her professionalism and expertise. Consequently, each attorney who prepares or reviews a legal opinion given in a securities transaction should exercise sound professional judgment and give careful and thoughtful attention to the language and meaning of the opinion, as well as to the factual investigation and legal research that are necessary to support the opinion. Additionally, because the client must ultimately bear the costs of any such legal opinion, the diligence and effort must be sensible and cost effective, and in the final analysis may, in many instances, be determined by agreement between the opinion giver and the opinion recipient.[9]

----

9. Rice & Steinberg, *Legal Opinions in Securities Transactions*, 16 J. CORP. L. 375, 377–378 (1991). *See generally* D. GLASER, S. FITZGIBBON & S. WEISE, LEGAL OPINIONS (3d ed. 2008 & supp.).

§ 16.05 Attorney-Client Privilege

In re: Kellogg Brown & Root, Inc.

United States Court of Appeals, District of Columbia Circuit

756 F.3d 754 (2014)

[This case is contained in § 15.11[A].]

---

§ 16.06 Conflicts of Interest

[A] Conflicts in SEC Proceedings

In the Matter of Blizzard and Abel

Securities and Exchange Commission

Investment Advisers Release No. 2032 (2002)

. . . .

We have an obligation to ensure that our administrative proceedings are conducted fairly in furtherance of the search for the truth and a just determination of the outcome. Even the appearance of a lack of integrity could undermine the public confidence in the administrative process upon which our authority ultimately depends. This concern cannot be addressed by the consent of [attorney] Small's clients to his representation of them. Rather, the issue is whether the Commission consents to the impact on its adjudicatory processes created by Small's multiple representation.

Here, a single attorney, Small, is representing respondent Abel, former respondent Berry, and several non-respondent clients in this matter. The Division, after negotiating a settlement with the former respondent and after interviewing Small's non-respondent clients, placed those clients of Small on the Division's witness list to testify against Abel at the hearing. Assuming these witnesses are called to testify, there are two possible outcomes: Either the witnesses will give testimony that is inconsistent with Abel's theory of defense, as the Division anticipates, or they will give testimony that is consistent with Abel's theory.

An attorney has a general duty to act in good faith, a duty that takes its shape from the larger object of preserving the integrity of the entire judicial process. As part of this duty, an attorney before any tribunal must advocate his client's position forcefully in order to advance the integrity of the proceeding. Here, however, Small's representation of Abel with respect to subject matters that are substantially related to his representation of the witness clients could result in divided loyalties that will prevent him from fulfilling his duty to act in good faith. This serious potential for prejudice to the integrity of the proceedings leads us to conclude, therefore, that Small may not represent any witness who may be called against Abel.

It does not alter our conclusion that an actual conflict has not yet been established. The "likelihood and dimensions of nascent conflicts of interest are notoriously hard to predict," especially in the case where an attorney represents multiple clients with respect to substantially-related matters. A "few bits of unforeseen testimony or a single previously unknown or unnoticed document may significantly shift the relationship" between multiple clients. We need not wait until an actual conflict taints the "adversarial presentation of evidence" where the nature of the multiple representation presents such a serious potential for conflict.

In reaching this conclusion, we are sensitive to the rights of individuals to be represented by the attorney of their choice. However, this is not an absolute right. Here, the right to counsel of one's choice is outweighed by the necessity of ensuring that our administrative proceeding is conducted with a scrupulous regard for the propriety and integrity of the process.

We are also aware that our decision will necessitate further delay in a matter that has already been the subject of lengthy delay. Indeed, Small accuses the Division of having moved to disqualify him "solely to harass and as a dilatory tactic." In that regard we find it difficult to understand why this issue was raised so late in the proceeding. The possibility that Small's representation of multiple clients might taint the proceeding was evident at least by the time Abel was charged as a respondent and the Division became aware that Small's other clients might be used to make its case against Abel. Leaving the matter so late in the process compounds the necessary delay and repetition of effort as new counsel prepares for representation of a new client or clients, which could have been avoided by addressing this matter earlier. While we are mindful of these unfortunate consequences, however, we nonetheless must maintain the integrity of the proceedings we are empowered to conduct.

Matter of Merrill Lynch, Pierce, Fenner & Smith, Inc.

Administrative Law Judge, Securities and Exchange Commission

[1973–1974 Transfer Binder] Fed. Sec. L. Rep. (CCH) ¶ 79,608

(ALJ 1973)

ULLMAN, ADMINISTRATIVE LAW JUDGE.

These proceedings were instituted by Commission order dated June 22, 1973 (Order) to determine whether respondents have violated certain provisions of the Securities Exchange Act of 1934 (Exchange Act) and of the Securities Act of 1933 (Securities Act), and if so, what remedial action is appropriate. The Order names as respondents Merrill Lynch, Pierce, Fenner and Smith (Merrill Lynch or Registrant), two men employed in its Research Division during the relevant period of approximately 21 months from March 1968 to November 1969, Philip E. Albrecht (Albrecht) and Willard Pierce (Pierce), and 47 persons then employed as registered representatives in Merrill Lynch offices throughout the nation.

. . . .

Merrill Lynch is charged with failure to supervise the persons subject to its supervision who committed the violations charged in the Order, and Albrecht, similarly, is charged with failure to supervise "a person who was subject to his supervision and who committed such violations." Merrill Lynch is charged with responsibility for all of the violations allegedly committed by each of the 49 other respondents.

The law firm Brown, Wood, Fuller, Caldwell and Ivey ("Brown Wood") filed answers on behalf of all respondents except one whose whereabouts apparently are unknown, . . . and one, . . . who is represented by the law firm Martin & Obermaier. The answers deny the violations alleged in the Order.

As a result of a letter dated August 20, 1973 from the Division [of Enforcement] to the undersigned, raising an issue of an alleged conflict of interest in Brown Wood's representation of Merrill Lynch, the employer, and some 47 registered representative employees or former employees, a pre-hearing conference for the purpose of hearing argument on that issue was held in New York City on September 26, 1973.

. . . .

The conclusion reached in this order is that if the decisions of the individual respondents to retain Brown Wood as their counsel are *informed* decisions, such representation may be continued. Accordingly, this order is being directed to each individual respondent to assure that he is substantially apprised of the arguments on both sides of the issue, and that his decision with regard to the selection of counsel, whether now reaffirmed or changed, is made with such knowledge. . . .

The basic contentions of the Division [of Enforcement] are that Brown Wood, having served for years as counsel to Merrill Lynch, and serving at present as its counsel in a host of legal proceedings including class actions deriving from the sale of Scientific shares, is unable to give to the defense of individual respondents its undivided loyalty and to defend their positions with the zeal required in an attorney-client relationship. Apart from the Division's contentions with regard to professional ethics inherent in requirements and proscriptions of the pertinent codes of ethics applicable to attorneys, it disputes the adequacy of representation by Brown Wood, and maintains that during the proceeding conflicts will arise which will make it impossible for Brown Wood to serve with equal diligence two masters, one of which is a substantial source of business for the firm. Without in any way questioning the integrity of the firm, the Division contends that Brown Wood has an indomitable desire to protect the Registrant, and that it is not sufficiently mindful of the needs of the individuals in anticipating their respective defenses. It seems to suggest, also, that the ability of a competent attorney to develop arguments in his client's favor cannot be minimized, and that the direction and emphasis of the attorney's thinking are important factors in developing such arguments and positions: that whole-hearted attention and zeal cannot be given to such effort when presented with divergent positions of two clients.

. . . .

Similarly, the Division contends that the exploration of the many charges during the hearing will be extensive and complex, and that differing approaches will be required for the defenses of individual respondents and for that of Merrill Lynch during the examination or cross-examination of witnesses and perhaps of individual respondents, whether account executives or research analysts. It also argues that because of the several pending class actions against Merrill Lynch arising out of the sale of Scientific, Brown Wood would be unable to fairly evaluate and recommend a settlement favorable to an individual respondent in the event Merrill Lynch believed that a settlement or settlements generally might compromise its own defense either in the instant proceedings or in other litigation.

The Division recognizes that a respondent in administrative proceedings normally has the right to be represented by counsel of his choice, and that an unfair denial of that right might constitute a denial of due process under the Constitution. It was pointed out and agreed at the oral argument, for example, that the Commission has no obligation to appoint counsel for a respondent who is unable to pay counsel fees. And in its reply brief the Division seems to concede that where it is not clear that a conflict of interest will occur between two or more clients of an attorney, the informed consent of the client or clients whose interests more likely would suffer in the event a conflict should develop can provide justification for the continuation of multiple representation, as here. This is the position reached in this order.

Brown Wood points out that it has represented each of the individual respondents during and prior to their respective depositions by the Division; that in each of the interviews the individual respondent was advised of Brown Wood's long-standing representation of Merrill Lynch, and was told that representation of the individual would be feasible "only if he was sure in his own mind that he had done nothing wrong"; that if a conflict of interest appeared to develop, Brown Wood would have to withdraw as his counsel and that, in turn, if a respondent felt that there was divergence of interest "he need only advise us and we would withdraw." Brown Wood points out that each individual respondent whom the firm represents has independently decided to retain it, that at the taking of depositions the Division advised each deposed witness of his right to choose other counsel; that in questionnaires sent by the Division to other registered representatives they were advised of their right to confer with and choose counsel other than Merrill Lynch's counsel; and that each registered representative chose to adhere to his original decision. . . .

Of course Brown Wood agrees with the caveat . . . that it must be continually alert for information which might indicate a conflict of interest; and that if such information is received it must apprise its client or clients thereof and reevaluate its position. This is a part of the risk taken by individual respondents who retain Brown Wood as counsel—that at some stage of the proceedings it is possible that new counsel, unfamiliar with the case, may have to be substituted.

The decision reached here also is consistent with the precept that a litigant's choice of counsel is an extremely important right which should not be denied him, absent considerations compelling a contrary conclusion: and it is consistent with a practical approach of permitting the clients to choose as their counsel, if they wish to do so on an informed basis, the attorneys who are most familiar with the case and with the potential vulnerability of those charged with the offenses. Apparently, it also may obviate problems that could arise with regard to some of the respondents—the matter of the cost of retaining counsel for their defense, even though reasonable efforts will be made to limit the introduction of evidence against individual respondents to particular sessions of the hearing.

... While the courts have stated that "The obligation to search out and disclose potential conflicts is placed on the attorney in order to put the client in a position to protect himself by retaining substitute counsel if he so desires," the client is not thereby freed from responsibility for his own informed decision. It is understood that the individual respondents are educated, experienced businessmen.

. . . .

[B] "Screening" Mechanisms

Rule 1.11 of the American Bar Association's Model Rules of Professional Conduct essentially adopts the propriety of the "screening" mechanism with respect to the former government attorney. As an initial point, Rule 1.11 disqualifies an individual attorney from representing a client in connection with a matter in which he/she participated "personally and substantially" as a public employee, unless the pertinent government agency consents in writing to such representation. Second, the rule vicariously disqualifies the law firm in which the former government attorney is employed unless "the disqualified lawyer is timely screened from any participation in the matter and is apportioned no part of the fee therefrom; and ... written notice is promptly given to the appropriate government agency to enable it to ascertain compliance with the provisions of this rule." Hence, if the above procedures are followed, the law firm with which the former government attorney is associated may undertake or continue representation in the matter.

Screening devices continue to be employed by law firms as a means to avert vicarious disqualification. The propriety of these mechanisms has received approbation by the Model Rules and the courts in the former government attorney context. An increasing number of courts also are accepting the use of such devices in attorney movement between *private* law firms. In this regard, the Sixth Circuit has opined:

> If the case reports are any indication, a motion to vicariously disqualify the law firm of an attorney who is himself disqualified as the result of his possession of the confidences of a former client, is becoming an increasingly popular litigation technique. Unquestionably, the ability to deny one's opponent the services of capable counsel, is a potent weapon. Confronted with such a motion, courts must be sensitive to the competing public policy

interests of preserving client confidences and of permitting a party to retain counsel of his choice.

Perhaps these motions have become more numerous simply because the changing nature of the manner in which legal services are delivered may present a greater number of potential conflicts. Certainly, the advent of law firms employing hundreds of lawyers engaging in a plethora of specialties contrasts starkly with the former preponderance of single practitioners and small firms engaging in only a few practice specialties. In addition, lawyers seem to be moving more freely from one association to another, and law firm mergers have become commonplace. At the same time that the potential for conflicts of interest has increased as the result of these phenomena, the availability of competent legal specialists has been concentrated under fewer roofs.

Consequently, these new realities must be at the core of the balancing of interests necessarily undertaken when courts consider motions for vicarious disqualification of counsel.

A reading of the cases would lead one to believe that the maintenance of confidentiality has been accorded paramount effect. And this is understandable, given the traditional concerns of the legal profession that client confidences be protected and that appearances of professional impropriety be avoided. In addition, courts have frequently pointed to the prohibition against other lawyers in a firm accepting or continuing employment when a member of the firm has been required by ethical considerations to decline or withdraw from that employment.

In our view, the Court of Appeals for the Seventh Circuit has taken the most realistic view of the methodology to be followed in resolving competing interests raised by such a disqualification motion. Where, as here, it has been demonstrated that disqualification will work a hardship, it is clear that the quarantined lawyer was privy to confidential information received from the former client now seeking disqualification of the lawyer's present firm, and there is a substantial relationship between the subject matter of the prior and present representations, then the district court must determine whether the presumption of shared confidences has been rebutted. Specifically, under the circumstances of this case as presented by the parties on appeal, it must be determined whether the confidence which [the disqualified attorney] acquired from the bank in the course of his prior representation and brought with him to [the law firm] have been passed on, or are likely to be passed on, to members of the firm. *Schiessle v. Stephens*, 717 F.2d 417, 421 (7th Cir. 1983). One method of rebutting the presumption is by demonstrating that specific institutional screening mechanisms have been implemented to effectively insulate against any flow of confidential information from the quarantined attorney to other members of his present firm. *LaSalle Nat'l Bank v. County of Lake*, 703 F.2d 252 (7th Cir. 1983). [As stated by the Seventh Circuit in *Schiessle*:]

> Such a determination can be based on objective and verifiable evidence presented to the trial court and must be made on a case-by-case basis. Factors appropriate for consideration by the trial court might include, but are not limited to, the size and structural divisions of the law firm involved, the likelihood of contact between the "infected" attorney and the specific attorneys responsible for the present representation, the existence of rules which prevent the "infected" attorney from access to relevant files or other information pertaining to the present litigation, or which prevent him from sharing in the fees derived from such litigation. [717 F.2d at 421]

Manning v. Waring, Cox, James, Sklar and Allen, 849 F.2d 222, 224–226 (6th Cir. 1988). See *In re County of Los Angeles*, 223 F.3d 990 (9th Cir. 2000).

Likewise, the ABA Model Rules of Professional Conduct today allow law firms, with certain requirements that must be met, to implement timely and effective screening mechanisms to avoid firm-wide disqualification where a personally disqualified lawyer moves from one law firm to another law firm. Allowing screening in this context represents the prevailing approach. Nonetheless, a number of states reject the use of screening to avert vicarious law firm disqualification.[10]

---

10. *See* M. Steinberg, Lawyering and Ethics for the Business Attorney 117–148 (4th ed. 2016).

Index

[References are to section numbers.]

A